M. PURBHOO

Using Sage 50 Accounting 2019

Canadian Edition

Covers both Sage 50 Premium Accounting® 2019 and Sage 50 Pro Accounting® 2019

Pearson

Pearson Canada Inc., 26 Prince Andrew Place, North York, Ontario M3C 2H4.

Credits

Ch 12 (p. 465) and App K (pp. A-169-A-171, A-174) screenshots from the Government of Canada, used with permission; Ch 13 (pp. 535, 536) screenshots from Bambora, used with permission; App K (p. 178 top) courtesy of SecureKey Concierge, used with permission; App K (p. A-178 bottom) screenshot from Scotiabank, used with permission.

Cover image: ©PureSolution/Shutterstock

978-0-13-566917-4

1 2019

Pearson

CONTENTS

PREFACE

Using Sage 50 Accounting 2019 provides full coverage of Sage 50 Accounting 2019 (Pro and Premium versions). The Student version (Release 2019.0) is also a Premium version program, so all users can learn the program with the same release used to create the data files, screens and keystrokes. Although we do not address the Quantum version of Sage 50, the book is also compatible with this version. We provide detailed instructions for downloading, installing and activating the Student version in Appendix A of this text.

As in last year's edition, the keystrokes and source documents, printed in colour with check boxes, are integrated throughout each chapter. All source documents are numbered.

No topics were added in this edition, but we created one new application: Kara's Kitchens (Inventory in Chapter 10).

But we maintained aspects of previous editions that have been well received:

- a diversity of companies and business situations, including non-profit, service and inventory businesses
- comprehensive and current tax coverage for different provinces, including GST, HST, PST and QST, and tax remittances
- a realistic approach
- easy-to-follow, step-by-step keystroke instructions and screen illustrations, updated for Version 2019
- current information that has been updated to reflect the business realities in 2019
- several company setup chapters increasing in complexity and a separate setup for payroll, all with keystroke instructions
- separate chapters for basic and advanced Accounts Receivable and Payable topics
- comprehensive company profiles and realistic source documents throughout the text to give you the "feel" of real companies

The Student DVD with Data Files for the text has the following resources:

- Pro and Premium version data files for all applications (except for the setup chapters: Chapters 7, 16 and 17)
- review questions and cases for each chapter (Appendix D)
- supplementary materials in Appendices E – M
- the interactive Accounting Cycle Tutorial, which introduces basic accounting terms and concepts

We continue to provide options for automatically installing data from the Student DVD: backup data files for Premium and Pro versions, and full Premium version data files for the source document applications in the text. Supplementary files are provided only as backup files. Of course, we still include detailed instructions on restoring backups. These alternatives have additional advantages: if computer speed and time permit, users can install the full data files; otherwise, the smaller backup files can be copied quickly, or backup files can be restored to your hard disk directly from the DVD one at a time. Premium version users can install both the full and backup sets of files. Backup files may be restored as often as needed without reinstalling.

The removable page-length bookmark attached to the back cover has a mini index and a ruler-marked edge to help you refer to specific lines on a page. This

NOTES

Sage 50 Accounting, Canadian Edition, was formerly named Sage Simply Accounting.

NOTES

Data and other files on the Student DVD are also available on the Web site for this text: <pearsoncanada.ca/text/purbhoo2019>.

Follow the instructions on the Web site to download the files to your hard drive.

bookmark should help to manage page-flipping, which is inevitable because most keystrokes for a transaction go beyond the page with the transaction.

As in the past, we work with module windows in the Enhanced view throughout the text, create user-specific customized shortcuts to access journals in other modules and use industry-specific terms for the different applications. Classic View margin notes like the following are included for users who prefer this approach:

CLASSIC VIEW
Notes for Classic view users

These notes describe how icons, keystrokes or terms in the Classic view are different from those in the Enhanced view.

The basic organization of the text is unchanged. Part One provides an overview and introduction to Sage 50 and sales taxes. Data applications that can be completed with both Pro and Premium versions are located in Part Two. We introduce the six ledgers of Sage 50 (General, Payables, Receivables, Payroll, Inventory and Division) in separate applications. Budgeting and bank transactions (deposits and account reconciliation) are covered in two more applications. Advanced Receivables and Payables features (orders and quotes, prepayments, tax remittances, credit card payments, transactions with foreign customers and suppliers and Internet links) are demonstrated in two more chapters. An online banking simulation (in Appendix I on the Student DVD) allows you to download a bank statement that integrates with data from the text. The required data files for all these chapters are set up in advance, and for each new type of transaction we provide detailed keystrokes and matching screens.

Four applications cover setting up a computerized accounting system using Sage 50. Again, detailed instructions with screen illustrations are given for each setup as you learn to design, convert and implement a complete accounting system.

- Chapter 4: set up a non-profit organization that uses only the General Ledger
- Chapter 7: set up an organization using the General, Payables and Receivables ledgers
- Chapter 9: add payroll to a data file that already has the General, Payables and Receivables ledgers
- Chapter 16: set up a comprehensive retail organization that uses the General, Payables, Receivables, Payroll and Inventory ledgers

In the final application in Part Two (Stratford Country Inn, Chapter 17), you set up a computerized accounting system on your own. All source documents in this chapter are realistic and descriptive.

Time & Billing and Departmental Accounting, advanced features available only in the Premium version, are covered in Part Three. Separate chapters and data files are prepared for these. All Part Three pages are edged with a blue stripe so that you can find them quickly.

For reference or further study, we include three appendices in Part Four of the text and 10 more on the Student DVD in PDF format — placing them on the DVD allows us to cover additional and advanced features of the program. The appendices on the Student DVD are available for you to read or print. These supplementary appendices are provided as reference material that should prove to be useful in any working environment.

USING THIS BOOK

The accounting applications in this text were prepared using Sage 50 Premium Accounting, Canadian Edition (Release 2019.0) and Sage 50 Pro Accounting, Canadian Edition software published by The Sage Group PLC. The Windows 10 operating system was used to create and test the screen images and keystrokes.

You must have a hard disk and DVD drive or a network system with Windows installed. If you do not have your own copy of the Sage 50 program, you can download the Student Premium software from the Sage Web site (refer to page xii and Appendix A). Network system users should work with the site administrator to ensure complete data access.

In addition, you should have a standard accounting text for reviewing accounting principles. The text provides some accounting principles and procedures, and the Review of Basic Accounting (Appendix M) and the Accounting Cycle Tutorial on the Student DVD also provide an introduction. However, these are not intended to replace the breadth and depth of most standard accounting texts. You should also consult the Help features of Sage 50 described in Chapter 1, because they also include information about accounting procedures.

The text is as simple and straightforward as we could make it, but familiarity with computers and some fundamentals of troubleshooting will make your progress through this text easier.

Student Resources

The Student DVD with Data Files

The Student DVD has an autorun feature that should open the Student DVD home page automatically when you insert the DVD into your DVD drive. From this home page you can choose to install data files, view the supplementary appendices (PDF format), run the Accounting Cycle Tutorial or browse the DVD. The Student DVD home page will remain open for you to make another selection until you close it.

NOTES
If you download the content from the Web site rather than get the files from the DVD, you will be downloading the entire DVD. Once the content is downloaded, clicking the Start.EXE file will open the DVD interface and you can follow the instructions presented in the text.

Complete instructions for installing and accessing the files on the Student DVD are provided in Chapter 1.

Separate data sets with separate installation programs will help you install the data set you need and make it easy for all users to follow the text. To choose the correct data set, you must know what version of Sage 50 you are using. You can get this information from the Welcome and Select Company window in the program (see page 8). SAGE 50 PRO ACCOUNTING or SAGE 50 PREMIUM ACCOUNTING appears in the Home window for all data files. You can open the Sample file to find this information. If you accepted the default installation settings, the program folder name in Program Files also matches the version. The Student version is a Premium version program, Release 2019.0.

NOTES
If you have the retail version of Sage 50, the program version will be on the program package or CD.

The Sage 50 desktop shortcut label also includes the version.

All installation programs create a data folder named SageData19 on drive C (Local Disk C: or [OS] C:). If you need to work with another location for your data, refer to page 6 in this text. You can install the data as often as you need to. We recommend renaming the previous folder to prevent overwriting all your previous files that may include data you want to keep. If you started by installing the backup files, you will not need to reinstall them because they remain unchanged.

You can restore backup files directly from the Student DVD to your hard disk. However, we recommend installing the backup files to your hard disk and keeping the original DVD safe for later use.

The following chart will help you install the data set you need from the Install Data screen:

FOR VERSION	**Pro Version 2019**
CLICK INSTALL BUTTON	Install Pro Version Backup Files
DATA SET (FOLDER ON DVD)	Pro_Backup_Version

FOR VERSIONS	**Student Version 2019** **Premium Version 2019** and **Quantum Version 2019**
CLICK INSTALL BUTTON	Install Premium Version Full Files
DATA SET (FOLDER ON DVD)	Premium_Full_Version_Data
	or
CLICK INSTALL BUTTON	Install Premium Version Backup Files
DATA SET (FOLDER ON DVD)	Premium_Backup_Version

If you are using Sage 50 Quantum Accounting, the Sage 50 Upgrade Company wizard will convert the Premium data files when you open them or restore them. Because the DVD files remain unchanged, you can install the same files later and use the Premium version. Before upgrading any data files, Sage offers the chance to create a pre-update backup of the data files.

Supplementary Data Files

In addition to the data files needed to work through the keystroke applications in the text, we provide supplementary files. Backup files are included for online bank reconciliation (Appendix I on the Student DVD) and importing accounting transactions from an Accountant's Copy (Chapter 12). These backup files will be located in the BANK and ACCOUNTANT folders in SageData19, respectively, when you install the data files. The ACCOUNTANT folder also has the journal entries that you import from a text file created by the accountant. The LOGOS folder includes company and inventory logos for the setup chapters and new inventory items.

Passwords

We have not added passwords to any data files to ensure maximum accessibility. However, if you are using the program in a multi-user or network environment that includes users and passwords, you will need to enter your user name and password before you can open the data files. Ask your instructor or site administrator for the user name and password that you should use. Refer to Chapter 16, page 688, and Appendix G on the Student DVD for instructions on working with passwords.

Working with Different Versions of Sage 50

Pro Version

NOTES

We used Windows 10 for all screenshots and keystrokes in this text and to create and test the data files. Fortunately, the screens and functionality of Sage 50 are the same for different versions of Windows. They differ only at the interface between Windows and Sage 50 – in the screens for browsing, opening and saving files. Sage 50 is also compatible with Windows 7 and Windows 8.

Although we have written this text primarily for the Premium version and show Premium version screens, you can use the Student DVD data files with the Pro, Premium and Quantum versions of Sage 50, Release 2019.0 or later, and with the Premium Student version (2019 only).

Therefore, we have tried to make version differences, such as differences in features, terminology and labels, as clear as possible. We use margin notes with a Pro version heading and icon to identify the differences:

PRO VERSION
Notes for Pro version users

These notes for Pro version users describe how screens, terms or keystrokes in the Pro version are different from those in the Premium version.

Student Version of Sage 50

The Student Premium version of Sage 50 must be downloaded from the Sage Web site (**sage.com/ca/about-us/education**). All copies of the 2019 Student version program have the same **serial number — 242P1U2-1000017**. Detailed instructions for downloading, installing, registering and activating your Student version of Sage 50 are provided in Appendix A. The installation procedure is the same for the regular retail CD version of the program. Only the activation process — also described in Appendix A — is different.

Students needing help with the program should work with their instructor. Additional help for students is available online from the student forum that you access from the following Web site: **sagecity.com/support_communities/sage_students**. For more information about accessing this site and posting your questions, refer to Appendix A in this text, pages A-10–A-12.

About the Student Version Program

The Student version is a fully functional Premium version that remains valid for 14 months after installation, but you cannot restore or open data files from previous versions with it. If you have already installed a Trial version, the date you installed it will count toward this 14-month limit. You can install only one version of Sage 50 Accounting 2019 on your computer. If you are using the Pro version or a Trial version and you want to install the Student Premium version, you must first completely uninstall the Pro or Trial version from the Control Panel in Windows (refer to Appendix A, page A–9). After you use a data set with the Student version for 14 months, you must use a regular retail licensed version of the program to access that data.

None of the data files were created with a Student or Trial version, so the data itself will not expire. If you have used the data with a Student version for 14 months, however, you may see a data expired message.

If you see a message that the program has expired when you try to install it or open a data set, and you have not yet used the program for 14 months, you should refer to page A–9 (Student Version Expired Error Message) and ask your instructor for assistance.

The differences between the Student version and the retail Premium version are very small, but we have identified them with margin notes as shown here:

STUDENT VERSION
Notes for Student version users

These notes describe how the Student version differs from the regular or retail Premium version.

Earlier Versions

If you try to access the data files with earlier versions of Sage 50 Accounting (2019.0 and earlier), Sage 50 displays an error message. In this case, you should download and install the Student version. Refer to Appendix A for information on downloading and installing the Student version.

Later Versions

Although the data files can be used with later versions of the software, you may see changes in screens, keystrokes and payroll tax amounts. Before you open a data file with a later version, the Sage 50 conversion wizard will update the data file to match the later version you are using. Always refer to the manuals and update notices for later versions. Once the file has been updated, you will no longer be able to use it with the earlier version or release, unless you reinstall the data files from the Student DVD.

For this reason, we recommend that you not install updates until you have finished working with the data files in the text. For the 2019 program, the option to modify your update settings, that is, to turn automatic updates off or on, is located on the Support Info screen (Home window, Help menu, About Sage 50). Automatic updates are not available for the Student version.

Quantum Version

This text can be used with Sage 50 Quantum Accounting. All the features covered in the text are available in the Quantum version, though you may see small variations in the screens. The Quantum version includes features that are not available in the Premium version — these advanced features are not covered in this text. If you are using the Quantum version, the Sage 50 data conversion wizard will convert the Premium data files when you open them or restore them. Because the DVD files remain unchanged, you can install and use the same files later with the Premium version.

Working Through the Applications

Keystroke Instruction Style

We have incorporated different paragraph styles for different kinds of statements in the text to help you identify the instructions that you must follow to complete the transactions correctly and see the screens that we present. These different styles are illustrated below:

Type `Foothills Hardware`

(Keystroke command line with text you type in a special font.)

Press enter or **press** the **Add button** to start the Add Account wizard.

(Keystroke command line – command word is in bold and the object of the command, what you press, is in colour. Commands are indented and spaced apart. Additional text or information for the line is shown in plain text.)

Or, you can click the Comment field to advance the cursor, or press tab repeatedly until the cursor is in the Comment field.

(Alternative keystroke sequence that you may want to use later. Paragraph is indented in block style and plain text style is used.)

Regular text is presented in normal paragraphs, like this one. **Key words** are shown in colour to make it easy to identify the topics. Names of icons, fields, text and tool buttons that you will see on-screen have all initial letters capitalized (for example, Adjust A Previously Posted Invoice tool or E-mail Confirmation Of Invoices And Quotes). Account names included in regular text paragraphs are italicized (for example, *Revenue from Sales* or *Cost of Goods Sold*).

✓ 1

Purchase Invoice #DS-642 **Dated May 1/21**

From Data Savers, $1 320 plus $198 HST for off-site data backup and restoration services for one year. Invoice total $1 518. Terms: net 30.

(Source document – with all text in colour – that you should enter using Sage 50. The ✓ in the check box indicates that keystroke instructions are provided. The number in colour in the lower part of the check box shows the source document number. All source documents are numbered in sequence.)

19

Cash Purchase Invoice #BC-6110 **Dated May 12/21**

From Bloomers, $1 280 plus $192 HST for batch of tree saplings to grow for future sales. Invoice total $1 472 paid in full by cheque #180.

(Source document – with all text in colour – that you should enter on your own using Sage 50. No keystroke instructions are provided – the upper part of the check box is empty and the lower part contains the source document number in colour.)

In addition to the different types of margin notes already described for the Pro and Student versions and the Classic view, the text includes regular margin Notes that contain additional important information for all users and Warning notes when extra attention is needed:

NOTES
Regular Notes

Regular Notes for all users providing additional general information.

WARNING!
Warning notes

Warning notes point out common errors or things to watch out for!
All users should read these notes carefully.

Order of Applications

Setup applications are introduced early in the text. Advanced users should have no difficulty working through the applications in the order given and may choose to skip some applications. However, at a minimum, we recommend working through all keystroke transactions (the ones with a ✓ in the check box beside them) so that you become familiar with all the journals before starting the more comprehensive applications.

There are alternative ways of using the text for introductory and advanced level courses. Students can complete the General, basic Payables, basic

Receivables, Payroll and Inventory transaction applications (Chapters 3, 5, 6, 8 and 10) in the introductory course and the remaining chapters later. Chapters 11 and 12 may be completed at any time after Chapter 6 because these chapters do not have payroll or inventory transactions. Chapters may also be completed in a different sequence, as outlined below and on the following page:

1. Read and work through the two Getting Started chapters in Part One.
2A. Complete the ledger applications in order: Binh's Bins (General), Groen Fields (basic Payables), Phoebe's Photo Studio (basic Receivables), Helena's Academy (Payroll), Kara's Kitchens (Inventory), Andersson Chiropractic Clinic and Maple Leaf Rags (advanced features of the first three ledgers) and Shady Corners* (Division or Project).
2B. (Premium version only) Complete the Part Three applications in any order: Ryder's Routes (Time & Billing) and Able & Associates (departmental accounting).
3. Complete Tesses Tresses (Chapter 15, account reconciliation and deposit slips) and Sound Inc. (Chapter 14, budgeting).
4. Complete the four setup applications in order: Love It Again (General), Air Care Services (three ledgers), Northern Lights (adding the Payroll ledger) and VeloCity (five ledgers).
5. Complete the Stratford Country Inn setup application with realistic source documents. Users may want to attempt this setup with the help of the setup wizards from the Setup menu in the Home window.
6. Complete the cash-basis accounting application in Appendix H at any time after Chapter 6.
7. Complete the setup for some of the other chapters based on the company information provided at the start of the chapter.
* Shady Corners (Division Ledger, Chapter 13) may be completed at any time after these chapters because it does not introduce keystrokes required for later applications. Later chapters may be completed before Shady Corners.

This order is shown graphically in the chart on the following page.

Organization within Chapters

All chapters are organized the same way. After stating the objectives of the chapter, a comprehensive company profile brings the business to life. This profile includes a description of the business's primary activities; its customers, suppliers, employees and inventory; historical financial data for all Sage 50 modules used by this company; and company-relevant accounting procedures.

Instructions for the chapter follow. The keystroke section comes next with detailed instructions for each new type of transaction (including reviewing and making corrections) or setting up the company files. For the setup chapters, the transactions follow the keystroke section. Otherwise, the keystrokes and transactions are presented together — the instructions for each new type of transaction follow the transaction.

Instructions and descriptions for reports for the module and features covered in a chapter appear at the end of the chapters.

Review questions and cases for all chapters can be found in Appendix D on the Student DVD.

AN ALTERNATIVE SEQUENCE FOR WORKING THROUGH THE APPLICATIONS

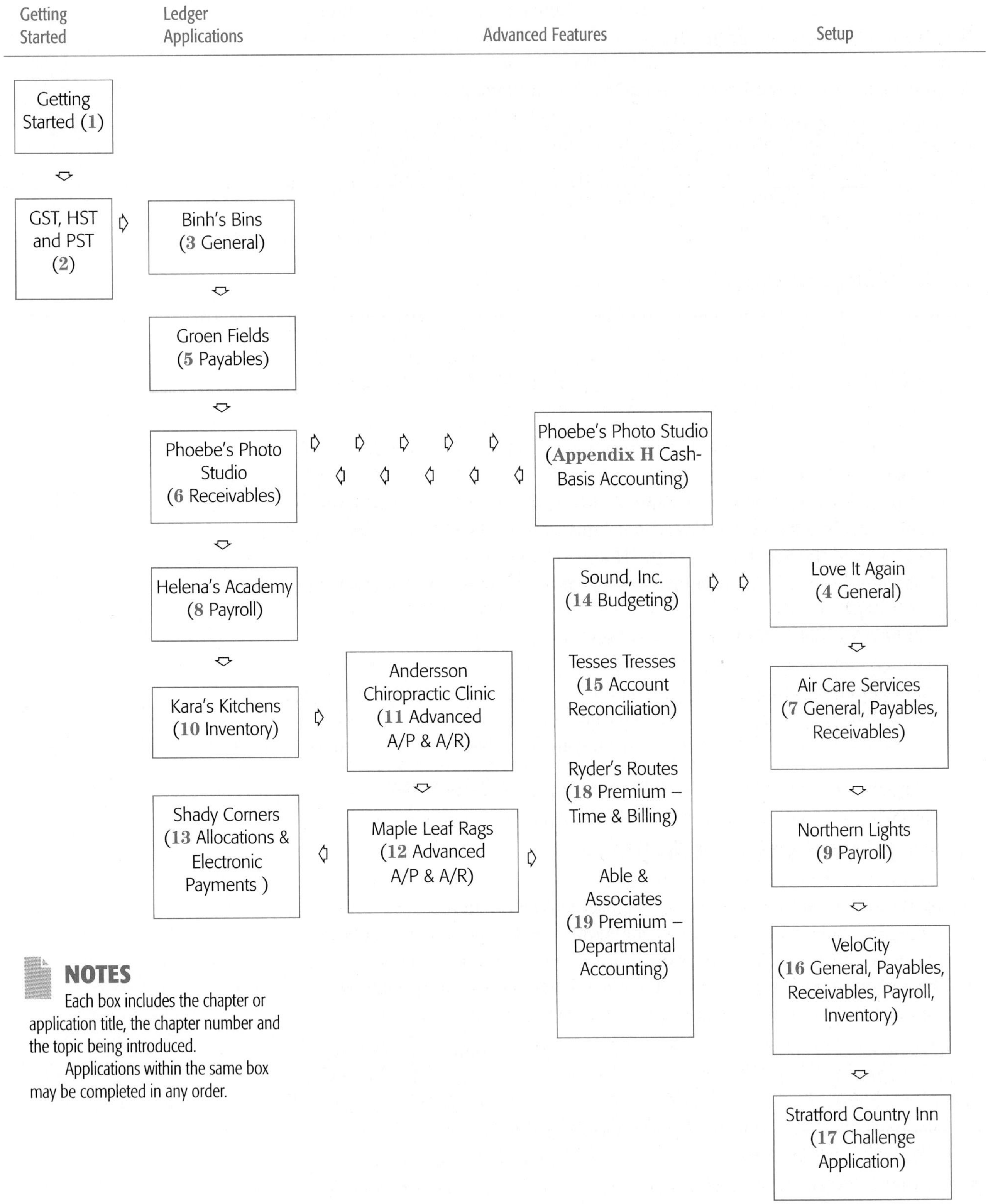

NOTES

Each box includes the chapter or application title, the chapter number and the topic being introduced.

Applications within the same box may be completed in any order.

Supplements

The Companion Web Site

A Companion Web site accompanies this text: **pearsoncanada.ca/text/purbhoo2019**. This site has all of the content from the Student DVD, which can be downloaded, along with an online banking simulation for VeloCity in Chapter 16, including the bank statement that you can download for reconciliation. Instructions for completing the simulation are in Appendix I on the Student DVD.

Instructor Supplements

- **Solutions** Solutions for all applications in the text are available as Sage 50 Premium Accounting backup files. These files have all the source document transactions in the text completed. The files must be restored with the Sage 50 program and all reports may be displayed or printed.
- **Additional Setup Files** Backup files for the setup chapters (Chapters 4, 7, 9, 16 and 17) are provided with setup completed and ready for entry of source documents. Two additional files are provided for Chapter 16 — for journal entries beginning in the second and third month of the applications. Files for bank reconciliation are also included: February bank reconciliation for Tesses Tresses; Case 8 in Appendix D for VeloCity; and Case 3 in Appendix D for Stratford Country Inn. Appendix D is on the Student DVD. These additional files are provided with the Solutions.
- **Instructor's Manual** The Instructor's Manual is a file in PDF format with information about all the instructor resource materials, teaching and testing suggestions and some troubleshooting tips.
- **Answers to Review Questions and Cases** includes answers to all the end-of-chapter questions and cases (Appendix D on the Student DVD). It is available as a PDF and a Microsoft Word document so that instructors may choose or modify individual answers.
- **Test Bank** Multiple-choice tests (with over 500 questions) organized by textbook chapter and several applied tests that require students to set up company files and enter source documents using Sage 50 are provided. The applied tests have alternate versions and may be completed as intermediate or end-of-course tests. All test files are provided in Microsoft Word format and may be modified by instructors. Solutions are included for all test items. For increased flexibility, the applied test solutions are Sage 50 backup files at two stages of completion: with the setup completed but history not finished and with all source transactions completed. The setup solution files may be given as separate tests (entering source transactions only) or they may be modified to create your own tests.
- **Source Documents** Source document files for all chapters are available. These PDF-formatted source document files do not include any keystrokes.

All instructor supplements except the source document files are available for download from a password-protected section of Pearson Canada's online catalogue **catalogue.pearsoned.ca**. Navigate to the catalogue page for this text to view a list of the supplements that are available. Contact your local sales representative for details and access.

ACKNOWLEDGMENTS

Every year at this stage, so near the end, and preparing the book for the publishing, I begin to think about thanking all who help to bring the project to fruition. Ultimately it is my responsibility to put all the pieces together, but many were involved in creating these pieces.

Some work quietly in the background in support positions. New artwork was professionally and carefully created by SPi Global. Carolyn Sebestyen assisted with technical advice and support and Alanna Ferguson ensured that corrected pages make it to reprint.

Keara Emmett, acquisitions editor, once again led the team. She negotiated the contracts with Sage and liaised with sales representatives and instructors whose questions provide important feedback. Other instrumental people at Pearson include Madhu Ranadive, Content Manager; Darcey Pepper, Marketing Manager; Pippa Kennard and Susan Johnson, who jointly fulfilled the role of Project Manager; Minjin Song, Permissions Project Manager; and Fiona Feng, Media Developer. Many of these people were new to the team this year, but all worked diligently to get the book done.

Leanne Rancourt, as developmental editor, copy editor and production editor, you reach out to all team members and coordinate everyone's efforts. I have come to depend on you and know that I can trust you in each of your roles. As in the past, I have enjoyed working with you. Maybe some day we will meet in person. Susan Bindernagel, who carefully proofread the entire manuscript, provided an independent look at the text. Mavis Gessner very carefully worked through the new material to make sure I did not miss anything, which is so easy to do when creating new material. Together, they continue to find ways to make this a better book.

Personnel at Sage provided access to the Sage resources needed to create this text and technical support — also essential components. And I appreciate the cooperation of Sage Payment Solutions and Bambora; by allowing access to these programs, they make it possible for the students to see how Sage 50 reaches further into the real world of business.

New project members always create special challenges, but we did it!

Without everyone's assistance, there could be no book. So, thank you. Now it's time to celebrate.

This book is dedicated to my children, who always inspire me, and to my friends, whom I rely on for stress-reducing diversions.

Mary Purbhoo

Part 1

Getting Started

CHAPTER ONE

Getting Started: Introduction to Sage 50

OBJECTIVES

After completing this chapter, you should be able to

- ***start*** the Sage 50 program
- ***open*** a working copy to access the data files for a business
- ***restore*** backup files to access data files for a business
- ***understand*** the help feature in Sage 50
- ***save*** your work
- ***back up*** your data files
- ***finish*** your session
- ***change*** default date format settings

GETTING STARTED

WARNING!
Sage 50 was formerly named Sage Simply Accounting.
You will be unable to open the data files with Sage 50 Accounting 2018 or earlier releases of Sage 50 Accounting.
The Student DVD with Data Files will be referred to as the Student DVD throughout the text.

NOTES
The instructions in this chapter for starting the program and copying files refer to Windows 10 procedures. If you are using a different version of Windows, please refer to Sage 50 and Windows Help and manuals for assistance with these procedures.
Sage 50 works best when you keep your Internet connection open.

Data Files and Abbreviations

The applications in this workbook were prepared using Windows 10 and the Sage 50 Premium Accounting and Sage 50 Pro Accounting (Release 2019.0) software packages produced by Sage. Formerly, this program was named Sage Simply Accounting. You will be unable to open the data files with any version or release of Sage 50 Accounting earlier than 2019, Release 0. Do not install updates for the Sage 50 program while working through this text. Later releases and versions of the software use later income tax tables and may have changes in screens or keystrokes. If you have a version other than Release 2019.0, you can download and install the Sage 50 Premium Accounting – Student Version program to work through the applications. Refer to Appendix A if you are installing the Student version.

The instructions in this workbook have been written for a stand-alone PC with a DVD drive and a hard drive with Windows correctly installed. Your printer(s) should be installed and accessible through the Windows program. Refer to the corresponding manuals for assistance with these procedures.

This workbook reflects the author's approach to working with Sage 50. There are alternative approaches to setting up company accounts and working with the software. Refer to Sage 50 and Windows Help for further details.

DATA APPLICATION FILE NAMES AND LOCATIONS (All folders and files are located in C:\SageData19\)

Company	Full File Installation	Backup File Installation	Chapter
Getting Started	START\START.SAI	START1.CAB	1
Binh's Bins	BINS\BINS.SAI	BINS1.CAB	3
Love It Again	TEMPLATE\SKELETON.SAI plus user setup	SKELETON1.CAB plus user setup	4
Groen Fields	FIELDS\FIELDS.SAI	FIELDS1.CAB	5
Phoebe's Photo Studio	PHOTO\PHOTO.SAI	PHOTO1.CAB	6
Air Care Services	user setup required	user setup required	7
Helena's Academy	HELENA\HELENA.SAI	HELENA1.CAB	8
Northern Lights	NORTHERN\NORTHERN.SAI plus user setup	NORTHERN1.CAB plus user setup	9
Kara's Kitchens	KITCHENS\KITCHENS.SAI	KITCHENS1.CAB	10
Andersson Chiropractic Clinic	ANDERSSON\ANDERSSON.SAI	ANDERSSON1.CAB	11
Maple Leaf Rags	MAPLE\MAPLE.SAI	MAPLE1.CAB	12
Shady Corners	SHADE\SHADE.SAI	SHADE1.CAB	13
Sound, Inc.	SOUND\SOUND.SAI	SOUND1.CAB	14
Tesses Tresses	TESS\TESS.SAI	TESS1.CAB	15
VeloCity	user setup required	user setup required	16
Stratford Country Inn	user setup required	user setup required	17
Ryder's Routes (Prem.)	RYDER\RYDER.SAI	RYDER1.CAB	18
Able & Associates Inc. (Prem.)	ABLE\ABLE.SAI	ABLE1.CAB	19
Phoebe's Photo Studio (Cash-Basis)	CASH\PHOTO-CASH.SAI	CASH1.CAB	Appendix H

The applications increase in complexity. Each one introduces new ledgers, setups or features as indicated in the following chart:

DATA APPLICATION	LEDGER USED						OTHER
	GL	AP	AR	PAY	INV	DIV	
Binh's Bins	*						
Love It Again	*						2
Groen Fields	*	*					
Phoebe's Photo Studio	*	*	*				3
Air Care Services	*	*	*				2, 3
Helena's Academy	*	*	*	*			
Northern Lights	*	*	*	*			2
Kara's Kitchens	*	*	*	*	*		3
Andersson Chiropractic Clinic	*	*	*				
Maple Leaf Rags	*	*	*				3, 4, 7
Shady Corners	*	*	*	*	*	*	3, 4, 7, 9
Sound, Inc.	*	*	*	*	*		3, 5, 7
Tesses Tresses	*	*	*		*		6
VeloCity	*	*	*	*	*		2, 3, 4, 7
Stratford Country Inn	*	*	*	*	*		1, 3, 7, 8
Ryder's Routes	*	*	*	*	*		PREMIUM 1
Able & Associates Inc.	*	*	*	*	*		PREMIUM 2
Phoebe's Photo Studios (Appendix H)	*	*	*				10

LEDGERS

GL = General Ledger
AP = Accounts Payable
AR = Accounts Receivable
PAY = Payroll
INV = Inventory
DIV = Division or Project Allocations

Other:
1 All realistic source documents (most chapters have some realistic source documents)
2 Setup application with keystrokes
3 Credit cards
4 Internet links
5 Budgeting
6 Account reconciliation
7 Foreign currency transactions
8 Setup application without keystrokes
9 Electronic payments
10 Cash-basis accounting

PREMIUM 1 Time & Billing; Build from Bill of Materials; Inventory locations (Premium version only)
PREMIUM 2 Departmental Accounting (Premium version only)

NOTES

Applications in Chapters 1 through 17 can be completed with both the Pro and the Premium versions. For the applications in Chapters 18 and 19 you must use the Premium version.

Data files for the applications in Chapters 4, 7, 9, 16 and 17 – the setup chapters – are not set up in advance. You must complete these setups on your own.

In addition to the data files, the Student DVD includes data files for cash-basis accounting in Appendix H (CASH folder or CASH1.CAB backup file), a backup file for Chapter 12 for importing entries from an accountant (ACCOUNTANT folder) and VELOBANK1.CAB (BANK folder), a backup file for online banking in Appendix I. Appendices H and I are on the Student DVD as PDF files.

The Sage 50 Program

Sage 50 is an integrated accounting program with many features that are suitable for small and medium-sized businesses. It includes several ledgers and journals that work together so that data entered in one part of the program will be linked to and available in other parts of the program. Ledgers are automatically updated from journal entries, and reports always include the most recent transactions and ledger changes. A business can use one or more accounting modules: General, Payables, Receivables, Payroll, Inventory, Project and, for the Premium and Quantum versions, Time & Billing. You need to set up only the features you use. Thus, if payroll is not used, there is no need to set up the Payroll module, and it can be hidden from view. A more complete description of the program and its features is presented in Chapter 16, pages 621–622.

Sage 50 Program Components

NOTES
For assistance with installing the Sage 50 program, refer to Appendix A.

NOTES
You can access the Sample Data file from the Sage 50 Welcome Select Company screen on page 8.

When you select the Typical Installation option, several components will be installed:

- **Sage 50 Program**: the program that you will need to perform the accounting transactions for your company.
- **Sample Data**: complete records for a sample company — Universal Construction.
- **Templates**: predefined charts of accounts and settings for a large number of business types.
- **Customizable Forms**: a variety of commonly used business forms.
- **Microsoft Office Documents**: a variety of Microsoft Office documents designed for integrated use with Sage 50.
- **Links** to online videos to help you learn how to use the program.
- **Microsoft Office 365 Integration**: a program link that connects your data with Microsoft Office if you have Sage and Microsoft subscriptions for this service.

The Student Data DVD

NOTES
Data and other files on the Student DVD are also available on the Web site for this text: <pearsoncanada.ca/text/purbhoo2019>.
Follow the instructions on the Web site to download the files to your hard drive.

Before you begin the applications, you must copy the data to your hard drive. The Student DVD has both full data files and Sage 50 backup files. The full data files are large and will take longer to install, so we provide only backup files for supplementary data files (refer to page xi) and for Pro users. Furthermore, you cannot work from CD or DVD files because they are read-only files. Keep the Student DVD in a safe place in case you need to start over from the original files. The following instructions will copy all the files to your hard drive and create the necessary folders.

Installing Your Data

NOTES
Sage 50 writes directly to your working data file as you enter transactions. Therefore, you cannot use read-only files as your working copy. All CD and DVD files are read-only files, so you cannot open the Sage 50 data files from the Student DVD.

WARNING!
Unless you have experience working with Windows folders, we recommend using the auto-install feature on the Student DVD to install your data set.

The Student DVD contains Pro and Premium versions of the data files and several supplementary files for the book. It also has programs that will automatically copy the data to a new SageData19 folder on your hard drive (drive C:). If you want to use a different location for your data files, proceed to page 6.

You must work with the correct version of the data set. If you are working with the Pro version, install the Pro data files — you cannot open Premium version files. If you are working with the Premium (or Student) version, install the Premium data files.

If you are using the **Pro version**, refer to the Pro Version margin notes throughout the text for the differences between the Pro and Premium versions for 2019.

Insert the **Student DVD** into your DVD drive. The home page appears:

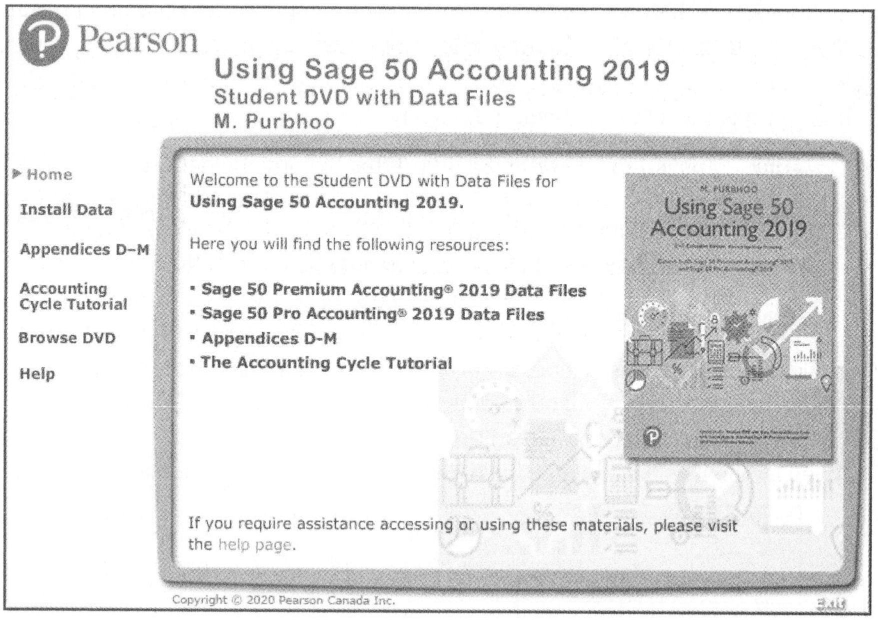

This page has your options for installing data files and viewing the additional resources and allows you to access these options from the left-hand side pane.

If the Student DVD home page does not open automatically when you insert the Student DVD,

Click the **Type Here To Search field** beside the **Windows Start icon** on your desktop task bar.

Type `d:\start.exe` (where D: is the drive letter for your DVD drive) — this file should be available on your DVD.

Click **D:\START.EXE** to open the installation options on the previous page.

Click **Install Data** to open your data installation options:

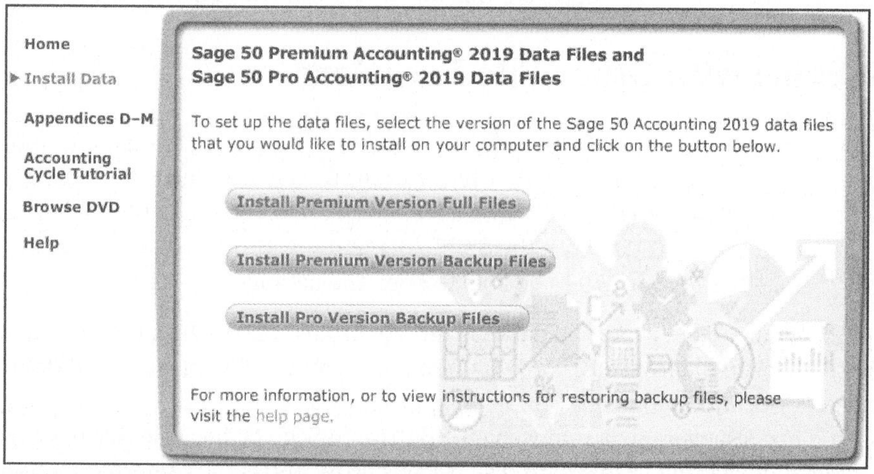

All data installation options will create the SageData19 folder on your hard drive in OS C: or Local Disk C: under This PC, and all files will be placed in this new folder.

The **Install Premium Version Full Files** option (~2 GBytes) will copy folders and files for each company data set in the primary keystroke chapters. In addition, you will have backup files for online banking and importing entries from an accountant. This installation requires substantially more time for copying the files.

The **Install Premium Version Backup Files** option (~60 MBytes) will install backup files for all the applications in the text except the setup chapters. When you restore

NOTES

If you are working with the Quantum version, you should install the Premium version files. Your program will automatically upgrade the files to the Quantum version when you open or restore them.

NOTES

If the Student DVD does not start automatically, open your Computer or Windows Explorer window. Right-click the DVD and click Explore. Double-click START.EXE to run the DVD.

Clicking Browse DVD on the DVD home page (in the left navigation pane) will open the DVD directory and list all the files on the Student DVD.

NOTES

Keystroke instructions that you must use have highlighted text in indented paragraphs, like the ones on this page starting with **Click**, **Type** and **Close**.

The command words are in **bold black** type and the object of the command is in **colour**.

Text you should type or key uses the `Courier font` after the command word **Type**.

Additional key words are also in **colour**.

NOTES

The Student DVD also has an appendix that reviews accounting principles and an interactive Accounting Cycle Tutorial that introduces basic accounting procedures for manual accounting.

NOTES

Windows 10 uses the name "This PC" for the computer, so this term will be used in this text. This name may be customized on your own computer, but we have not done so.

these with Sage 50, the default location will be the same as that for the Full File Installation option. If you are working on a slower computer, we recommend this option.

The **Install Pro Version Backup Files** option will install backup files for the applications for Pro users. Pro version files are provided only in backup format.

Instructions for restoring backup files begin on page 25.

Click **Install Pro Version Backup Files** to copy the data set for Pro 2019.

The Premium, Student Premium and Quantum versions use the same data files.

Click **Install Premium Version Full Files**, or

Click **Install Premium Version Backup Files**.

While the files are being copied, a black DOS window will open, scrolling through all the files being copied. This will take some time if you are installing the Premium Version Full Files, so please be patient. (Read the margin Notes.)

When all the files have been copied, you get a confirmation message:

Click **OK**. The data files are located in C:\SageData19. The DOS window closes.

You can also view the supplementary Appendix files on the DVD. You can save these PDF files to your hard drive or print them if you want.

Click **Appendices D-M** in the left navigation bar and then **click** the **file** you want.

Close the **PDF file** when you have finished viewing or printing it.

Click **Exit** to close the Student DVD window.

All the data files for the book are now located in the new SageData19 folder in drive C:. We will use the shorthand C: instead of This PC\C:, Local Disk C: or OS C:. We will open files and restore backups from this folder and use it as our working data folder.

NOTES
A black DOS Command screen will scroll through all the files as they are being copied to your hard drive. There are thousands of individual files in the full version data set, so this will take some time.

All data files will be copied to C:\SageData19\, the starting point we use throughout the text.

If you reinstall the files, you will be prompted to replace the older files. Your options are to replace all (type A), replace just this one file (type Y) or do not replace this one file (type N). Press enter after making your choice. Choosing All (typing A) will automatically replace all the files and you will not get this same prompt for each of the thousands of individual files.

If you installed the backup files initially, you can start again without reinstalling the files by restoring a backup.

Working with Other File Locations

You can copy the files to a different location by copying the data from the DVD just as you would copy other files to your hard drive. Choose the correct version of the data set (Pro or Premium) and be sure to copy the entire folder for each data set to include both the SAJ folder and the .SAI file. These must be kept together for Sage 50 to be able to open the data file.

You cannot open a Sage 50 data file directly from a CD or DVD, but you can restore a Sage 50 backup file from a CD or DVD. You must save the file on your hard drive before you can work with the data.

You can also work on a removable USB drive in Sage 50 because this is a rewritable medium, but working from a hard disk drive is faster and is the preferred method.

NOTES
Alternative instructions or commands that you may use are given in indented paragraphs without highlighting, like the paragraph beside this note beginning with "You can copy the files to."

Starting Sage 50

There are several ways to start the program. A Sage 50 shortcut icon was added to your desktop when you installed the program.

Double-click 

, the Sage 50 program shortcut on your desktop.

PRO VERSION
The desktop shortcut is labelled Sage 50 Pro Accounting Version 2019.

From this shortcut, you can pin the program to your Windows 10 Start page.

Right-click the **Sage 50 shortcut** to open a pop-up menu:

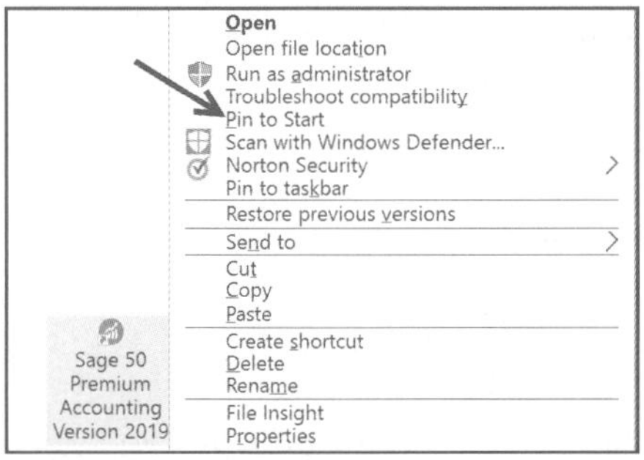

Click **Pin To Start**. You can now start Sage 50 from the Windows Start page (Tablet mode). A shortcut has been added here for the program:

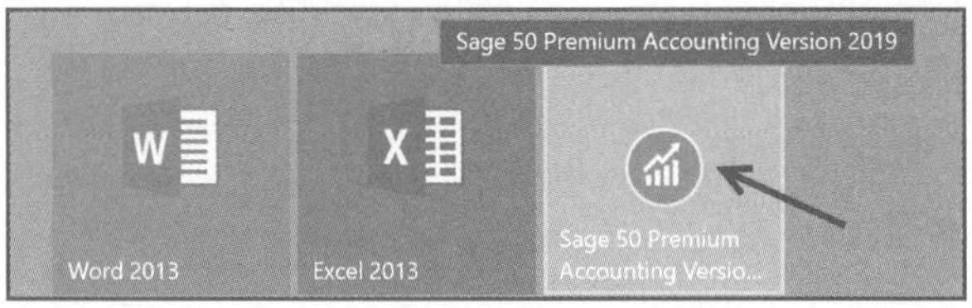

Click **Sage 50 Premium Accounting Version 2019**.

If you are not viewing your screen in Tablet mode, you will begin from (the Windows Start icon) in the task bar.

Click the **Start icon** to expand the Start menu. All your applications are in alphabetic order with their program icons. The shortcut you created earlier will be included in the tablet part of the screen.

Click the **Sage 50 Premium Accounting Version 2019** shortcut you added here to start the program:

You can also start the program from the Start menu that lists all programs or apps, beside the tablet portion on the desktop. Click the Expand icon above the first menu entry if necessary. Scroll down the list of programs or apps to Sage. Click Sage, and then click Sage 50 Premium Accounting Version 2019. Or,

Type `sage 50` in the Windows Cortana Search field:

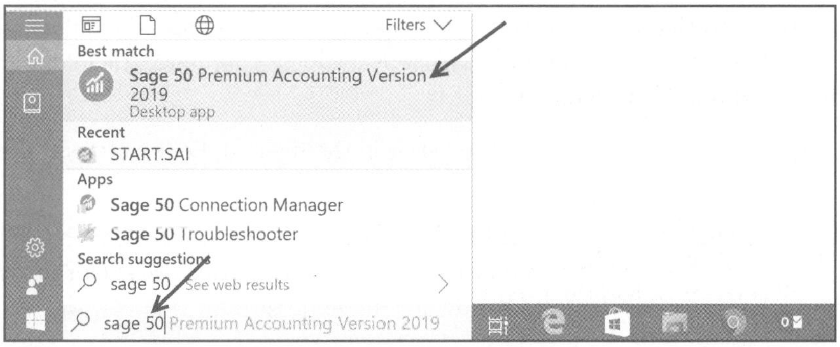

Click **Sage 50 Premium Accounting Version 2019** Desktop App to proceed.

NOTES
We intentionally use large arrow pointers in our screenshots.

NOTES
From this pop-up menu, you can also pin a shortcut to the desktop task bar and then click this shortcut to start the Sage 50 program.

PRO VERSION
The Start page shortcut is also labelled Sage 50 Pro Accounting Version 2019.

NOTES
Typing Sage in the Type Here To Search field will include your Sage 50 program in the list of search results. Then clicking the program name at this stage will start it.

PRO VERSION
You will click Sage and then click Sage 50 Pro Accounting Version 2019.
From the Search field, your Best Match entry will be Sage 50 Pro Accounting Version 2019.

NOTES
Data files you worked with recently may be listed ito the right of the search results.

NOTES

The Select Company window includes the version you are using. This window has Premium added to the program name.

The Select Company window option is located in the View menu (refer to Chapter 4, page 84).

WARNING!

You will be allowed to use the retail version of the program only for a limited time before entering the registration validation codes.

Remember to activate Payroll as well. Refer to Appendix A in this text. You must have a payroll ID code in order to use the Payroll features of the program.

You must register and activate the Student version before you can use it, but you will not need to activate payroll.

Refer to Appendix A for information about registering and activating your program.

NOTES

Your screens may look different if you have selected different viewing options, such as displaying the folders as icons, details or lists. The viewing options can be changed from the View icon drop-down menu.

WARNING!

Each application has many files containing different parts of the accounting information. All files must be contained in the same folder. If any file is missing, you will be unable to access the information. The auto-install procedure keeps the necessary files together.

NOTES

The path for the most recently used company file will be used initially. Therefore, we cannot be certain what your screen will have in the path field. Our instructions should direct you to the data files from any location.

We provide the complete path and extensions for files. These are folder options in Windows.

Sage 50 will open the registration screen the first time you use the program. Otherwise, you will open the Sage 50 Welcome and Select Company screen:

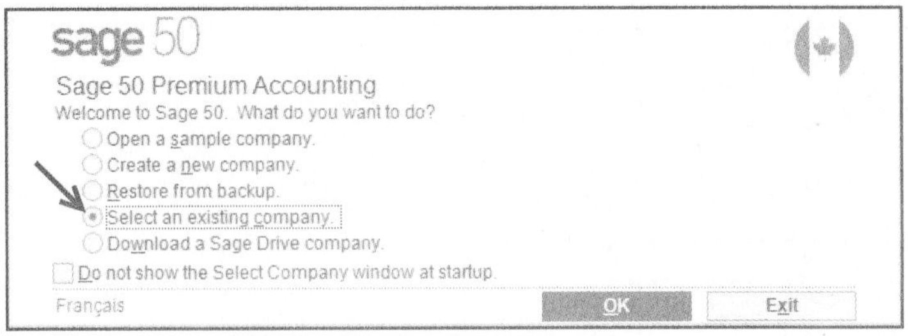

If you have not yet registered the program, refer to the boxed notes in Appendix A, pages A-3–A-4 in the text. Until you register and activate the program, you will be allowed to use the program only for a limited time. The Student version must be activated before you can use it. Refer to Appendix A, pages A-5–A-6 and A–9.

If you are restoring the Premium or the Pro version backup file, refer to page 25 for instructions.

Opening a Data File

The opening Sage 50 Welcome and Select Company screen gives you several options: working with the sample company files, creating new company files, restoring backup files or working with existing data files on your own computer or through a Sage Drive Internet connection. The next time, because we will have worked with the program before, the option to Open The Last Company You Worked On will be added with the name of the file you used (refer to page 26). If you choose this option when you use the same data set for several work sessions, you will bypass the Open Company windows (the next set of screens) and start with the Session Date screen on the next page.

If you are restoring backup files, refer to the instructions starting on page 25.

Click **Select An Existing Company**. **Click OK**.

The Sage 50 – Open Company window appears next. Our screen uses the Tiles view:

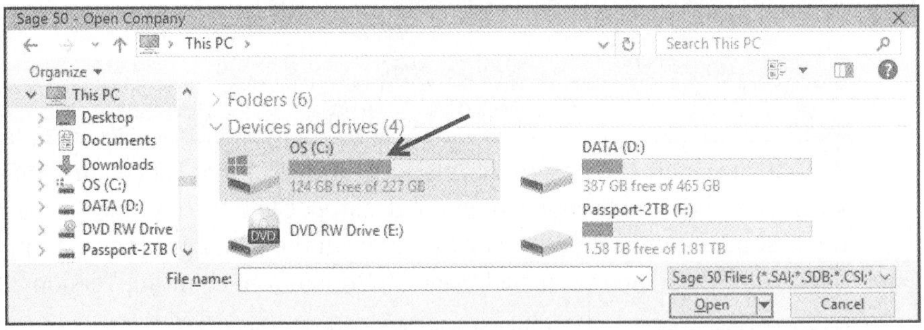

The initial path will be for the file you used most recently, and it will be selected for you to accept or to change. If this is the first time you are opening a data file, your path will be determined by your program and system settings. Therefore, the folder on your screen may be different from ours.

Click **This PC** in the left pane list or in the file path field on top to open the screen above.

Double-click **OS (C:)** or **Local Disk (C:)** or the name for the local hard drive C: on your computer to list the folders on this drive. Our next screen uses the Details view for the folders:

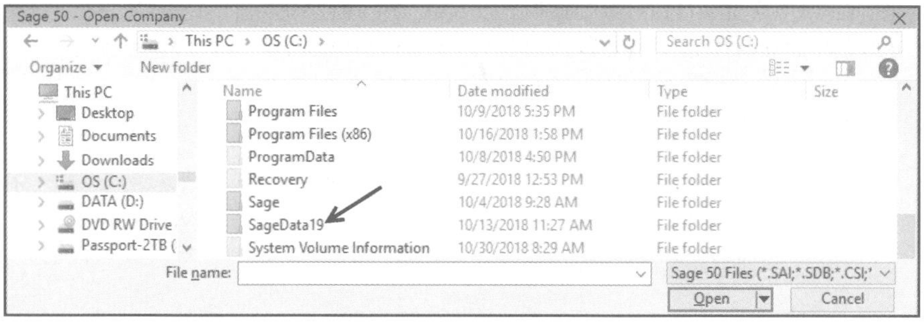

Click **SageData19**. (Click the SageData19 folder icon if your viewing mode is icons.) Then **click Open** for the files you installed from the Student DVD. We used the List view for folders in the next screen:

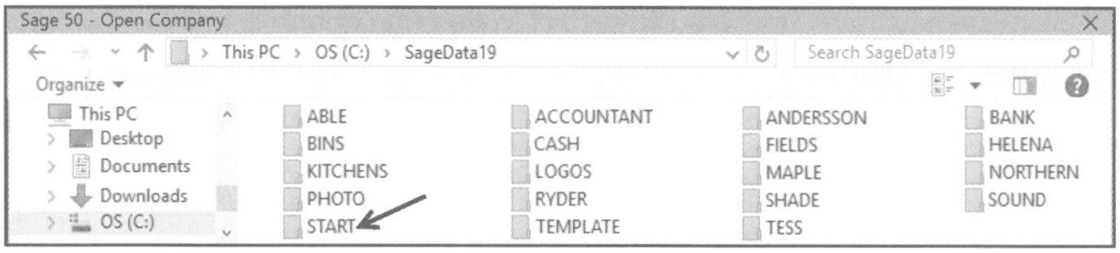

Click **START** (or its folder icon) and then **click Open**:

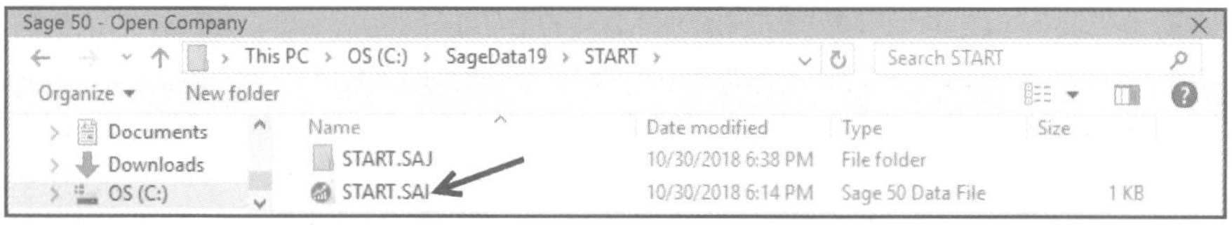

You can gain access to the company records only from the ***.SAI** file. Sage 50 recognizes this file extension as a Sage 50 format. The remaining data files for the company are in the SAJ folder. Both the .SAI file and the SAJ folder that are part of the data set must be located in the same folder. The complete data path [This PC>OS(C:)> SageData19>START] is added to the path field near the top of the screen. START is now the folder named in the Search field.

Click **START** (or the START icon), or click **START.SAI** (if you show file extensions) to select it and add it to the File Name field:

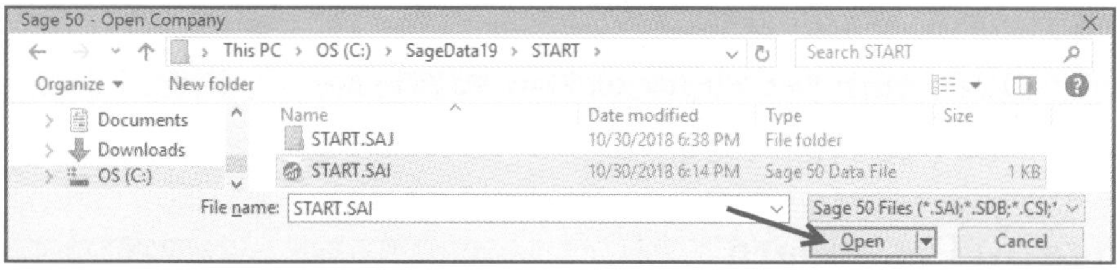

Click **Open** to open the session date screen:

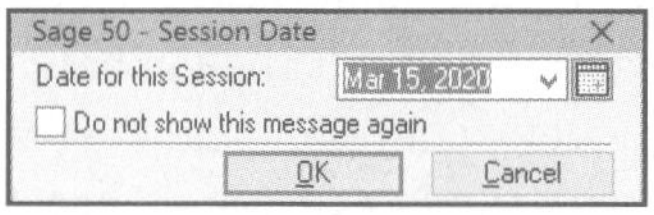

Click **OK** to accept the date and open the Home window. The session date is explained in Chapter 3.

NOTES

We use the default location for the data files from the automatic installation. If you installed the files to a different location, choose the drive and location for your setup.

PRO VERSION

You will have folders only for ACCOUNTANT, BANK and LOGOS. All data files are available as backup files. Refer to page 25 for instructions on restoring backup files.

NOTES

Showing the complete file path as we do is a Windows option. The open folder is named in the Search field.

WARNING!

If you are not showing file extensions, you will click START. Do not click the START.SAJ folder. The folder has a small folder icon beside the name. The .SAI file you need has a Sage 50 program icon beside the name.

NOTES

The session date is explained in Chapter 3, where you will also learn how to change the session date.

The session date drop-down list includes the current session date, the start and end of the fiscal period and the start of the next fiscal period. The list for any date field includes the dates commonly selected.

If passwords have been set up for the file, you will open the password entry screen before the session date window:

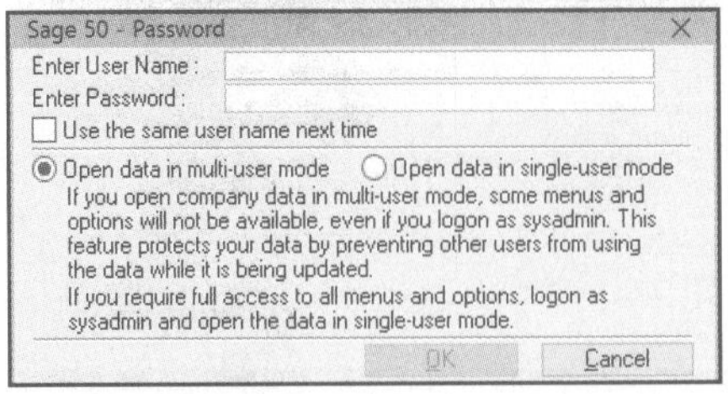

Ask your instructor or site administrator for the name and password to use. Enter your user name and password. Open the file in Single-User Mode. Click OK to open the session date screen. Refer to Chapter 16, page 686, and Appendix G on the Student DVD.

If you get a message that the data has been updated to a new file format, your program may be an earlier version than 2019, Release 0, and you will be unable to open the data file. You can install the 2019 Student version to work with this text (refer to Appendix A).

> **NOTES**
> We have not set passwords for any data files in this text, but your site administrator for the network may have done so. Refer to Appendix G for more information about passwords.

> **PRO VERSION**
> You may get an additional message about upgrading to the Premium version of Sage 50. Choose Do Not Show This Message Again.

> **PRO VERSION**
> The terms do not change. Customers and Vendors will replace Clients and Suppliers on the Getting Started screen.

The Sage 50 Getting Started Welcome screen opens:

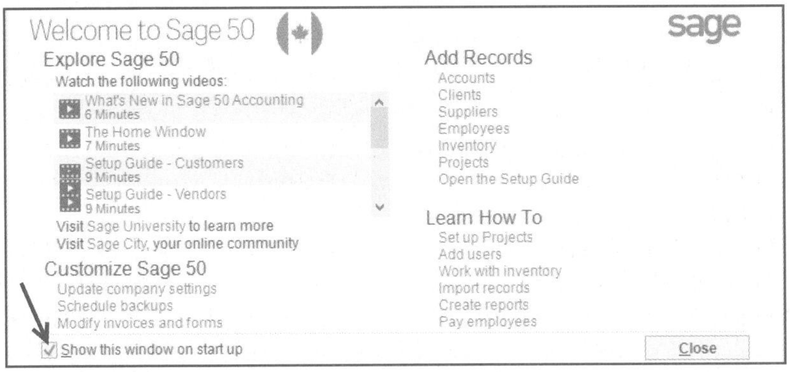

This screen outlines various options for getting assistance with the program when you have an Internet connection open. These include brief video tutorials and instructions for some basic steps you might need when setting up data files for a new company. You will start with this screen each time you open a data file in Sage 50, unless you have turned it off. After reading the options, you can close this screen now so that it will not appear each time you open this file. For other data files in this text, we have already turned off the selection.

> **NOTES**
> The contents of the Getting Started Guide will change to match the industry or business type of your company data set.

> **NOTES**
> You can open the Getting Started Guide at any time from the Home window View menu. Then click Show This Window On Start Up to add back the ✓ and have the window open each time you access this data file.

Click **Show This Window On Start Up** to remove the ✓.

Click **Close** to continue.

Sage 50 Dashboard

The main Sage 50 Dashboard Home window on page 11 should now be open.

The **title bar** is at the top of the Home window, and it contains the file name, START.SAI (or START); the Control Menu icon on the left-hand side; and the size buttons on the right-hand side. The **main menu bar** with the **Support** and **Search** functions on the right-hand side comes next. The Search field enables you to look up information in any journal or ledger, but support requires a service plan. This line is followed by the program name, Sage 50 Premium Accounting, and a **tool bar**. Tool buttons provide quick access to commonly used menu items. Different windows in the program have different buttons on the tool bar. Below the tool bar you will find the company name, Start Co., and the command to **Switch To Classic View** (refer to page 14).

> **PRO VERSION**
> The program name is Sage 50 Pro Accounting. Purchase replaces Supplier, and Create Sales Invoice replaces Create Client Invoice in the shortcuts pane.

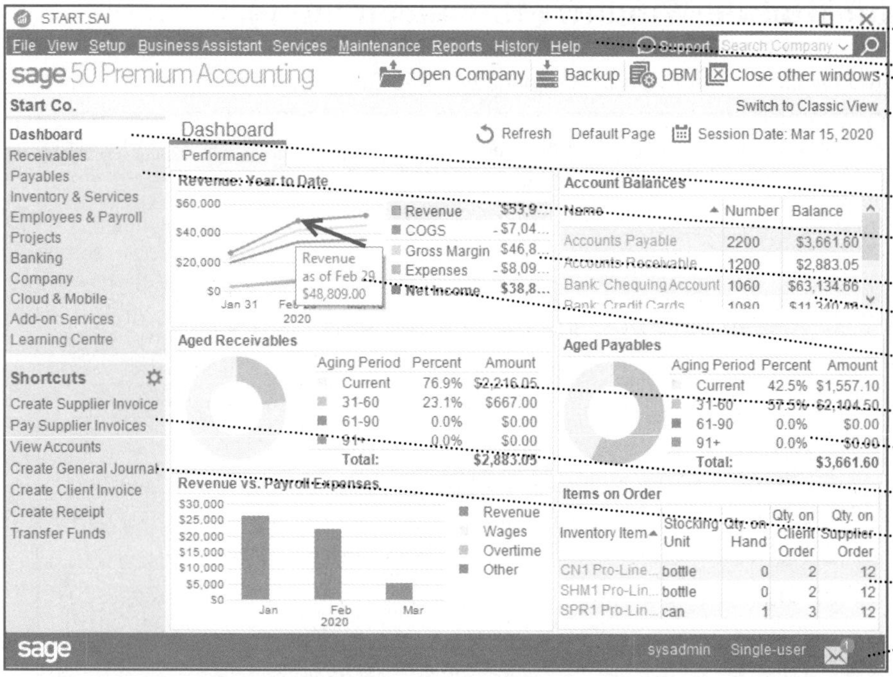

The **Modules pane** on the left-hand side of the window or navigation pane lists all the modules set up for this company. It also provides access to the Cloud & Mobile module for cloud backups and sharing company data with accountants or employees, or with the Office 365 programs. Through an Internet connection, the link to Add-on Services will provide more information about Sage 50 Payroll, cheque printing, Sage University and Sage 50 Direct Payments.

The Dashboard provides several key performance indicators in the various panes, including both graphic views and tables. Account balances for all bank, credit card, receivable and payable accounts indicate the cash position of the company. The first graph — for Revenue — has revenue, cost of goods sold and other expense information, providing both gross margin income and net income for the fiscal year to date. The Receivables and Payables graphs are pie charts with the totals divided among the different aging periods defined for the business. The proportion of the total that is overdue in each case is immediately apparent. The final two charts on the Dashboard report the relation between payroll expenses and total revenue and the items on order. This particular company has no employees, so the payroll expenses are zero.

Point to the **Revenue line** (the top line in the Revenue summary section) to access the amount details represented in this line.

Point to some **other segments** to expand the details for them.

For all graphs, details for part of a graph will appear in a bubble when you point to that part, as in the screen on this page with the detail for revenue as of February 29. Clicking any part of a graph will open the detailed Sage 50 report for that information.

Sage 50 reports are covered further in later chapters for each module.

Click **Cloud & Mobile** in the Modules pane on the left-hand side to access the data-sharing features of the program. These are subscription-based services offered by Sage.

Click **Add-on Services** in the Modules pane of the window to learn more about these features. Remember, you must be connected to the Internet to access the additional information from the Learn More links.

Click **Receivables** in the Modules pane.

NOTES

Sage Accounting, a small business online accounting program, was formerly named Sage One Accounting.

Sage 50 Module Window (Enhanced View)

The Receivables module window is usually the default Home window:

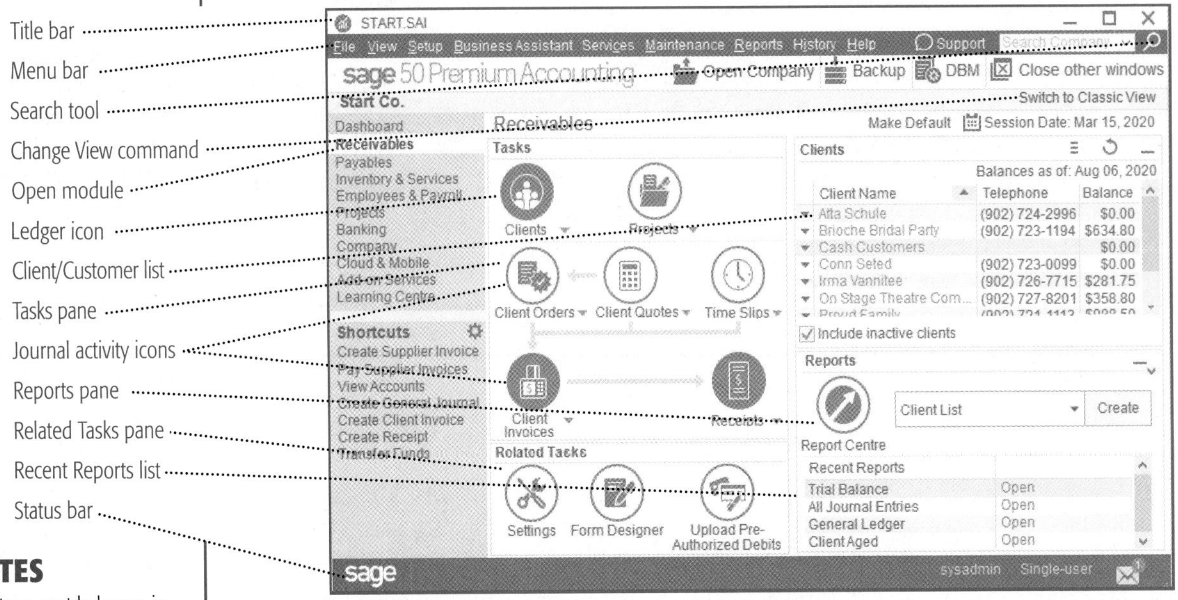

NOTES

Client account balances in the Client list are as of August 6. This date is later than the session date of March 15, indicating that there are postdated transactions.

PRO VERSION

Icon labels do not change. Customers will replace the Clients label for the ledger icon and list. Sales replaces Client for Invoices, Orders and Quotes. Purchase will replace Supplier in the shortcuts pane list.

You will not have an icon for Time Slips; Time & Billing is a Premium version feature.

NOTES

Appendix B has a complete chart of alternative terms used in Sage 50 for different types of industries.

PRO VERSION

Click the Sales Invoices shortcuts list arrow.

The module Home window is divided into several panes. The **Modules pane** lists all the modules available for this company data set. The open module — Receivables in this illustration — has a lighter background. The Receivables module is the default Home window for most of our chapters, but you can choose any module as the Home window. The contents of the Modules pane remains the same for all Home windows.

Below the list of modules, the **Shortcuts pane** allows one-click access to as many as 10 different tasks and activities that you set up or customize for each user.

The next column has all the icons you need to complete the activities for the module. The **upper Tasks pane** has the **ledger icons** for creating and modifying customer records from the Clients (Customers) window and Project records in the Projects window. The **lower Tasks pane** has the icons for **journal activities** or **transactions**. Activities for the module are represented by separate icons. Use these icons to enter the accounting transactions in this text. To access a function or activity, click the related icon to open the journal or ledger directly for that type of transaction.

In the Premium version, the icon labels change to suit the type of company. For the service company illustrated here, the ledger icon is labelled Clients.

Many ledger and journal icons have a **shortcuts drop-down list arrow**. Clicking an entry in an icon shortcuts list will access the activity directly and bypass the main task window. For example, you can begin adjusting an invoice to make a correction if an entry was posted in error, bypassing the first step of opening the journal.

Click the **shortcuts drop-down list arrow for Client Invoices** :

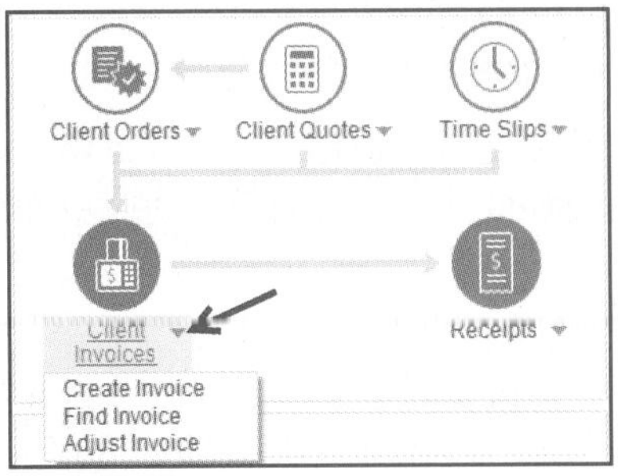

Click some **other shortcuts list arrows** for the different options.

Below the ledger and journal icons, you will find the **Related Tasks pane**. From the icons in this pane, you can perform other ledger-related activities, such as entering settings for the open ledger or creating customized forms.

The right-hand column also has three panes. The first has a **list of ledger accounts** for the selected module. For the Receivables module, the list has clients or customers with the phone number and outstanding balance. The Payables module window will have the list of suppliers or vendors. You can hide the phone and account balance details.

Below the list of customers or clients, the **Reports pane** allows direct access to all reports for the ledger from the **Reports drop-down list** and to the **Report Centre**, from which you can access all reports. Reports that you displayed most recently are listed in the **Recent Reports** section. Clicking a report in the Recent Reports list will open it with the report options you selected most recently.

The **status bar** appears last. In the Enhanced View, the status bar includes the user's name and user mode (single- or multi-user) and **messages** icon.

To work with another module, click the module you want in the Modules pane list.

NOTES

In all Home windows, the status bar explains the purpose of menu bar entries you point to. In other windows, the status bar describes the purpose of the icon or field that has the pointer. In the screenshot on this page, the General Journal window has Recalls A Saved Recurring Transaction in the status bar because the mouse is pointing to Recall in the pull-down menu.

Sage 50 on the Windows Desktop

Click **Make Default** between Receivables and Session Date in the module heading. (Click Receivables in the Modules pane list first if necessary.)

Now each time you open this data file, the Receivables module will be the starting point — **Default Page** has replaced Make Default.

Click **Create General Journal** in the Shortcuts pane list. This will open the General Journal with the Receivables Home window in the background.

Click the **Entry menu**. Our next screen has these settings with the desktop in the background:

NOTES

Many Sage 50 windows include a Home window tool  that brings the default Home window to the front without closing the other windows.

We used Windows 10 to illustrate this desktop. If you have a different version of Windows or use different Windows settings, your desktop may look different.

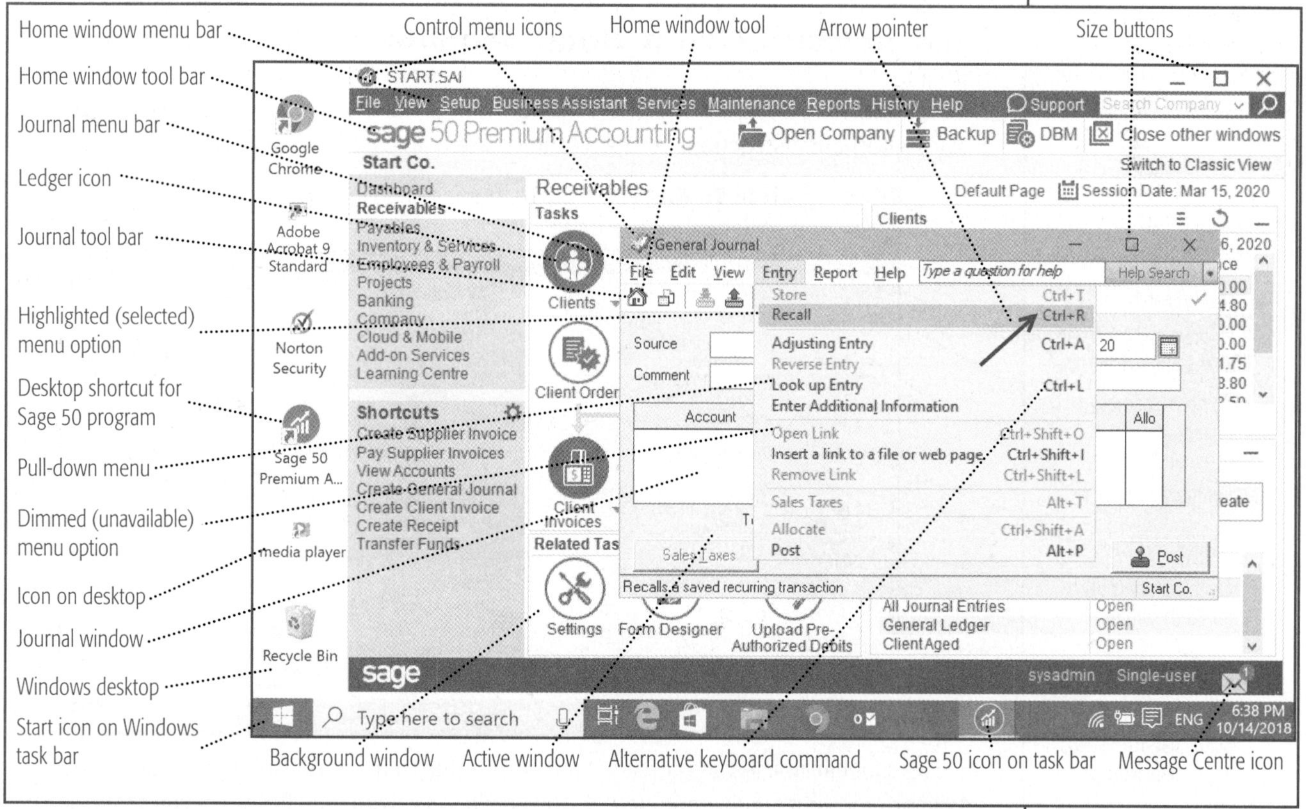

If you have messages from Sage for your account, the **Message Centre icon**  will have a number on it. Connect to the Internet and click this icon to access your messages.

NOTES

When you point to the Sage icon on the Windows task bar, two Sage 50 windows will pop up: the Home window and the journal window. Clicking the pop-up makes it the active window.

When you click or point to the Sage 50 icon on the Windows task bar, you see the two pop-ups for the windows you currently have open:

Click ☒ to close the Journal window and return to the Home window.

Click **Employees & Payroll** in the Modules pane.

This module now becomes the Home window, so its icons for ledger and journal activities are displayed. The ledger icon is now labelled Employees:

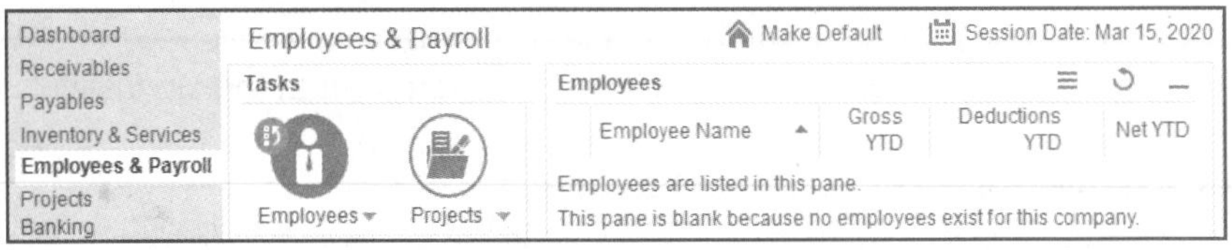

In this module, the **open history** symbol (a backward curved arrow) informs us that the Payroll Ledger is not set up — the history is not finished. When ledgers are not finished (in **history mode**), you can add and change historical data. When you create new company data files, all ledgers have this symbol.

Your Binh's Bins Home window (in Chapter 3) will be the Company Module with access only to the General Ledger and journals — Chart of Accounts and General Journal. Icons for unused features and ledgers that are not set up will be hidden.

Open and **close** some **other module windows** to access their task icons.

Sage 50 Classic View Home Window

Throughout this text, we will work from the Enhanced view Home window. However, we provide alternate instructions for using the Classic view in the Classic View margin notes.

Click **Switch To Classic View** to change the Home window:

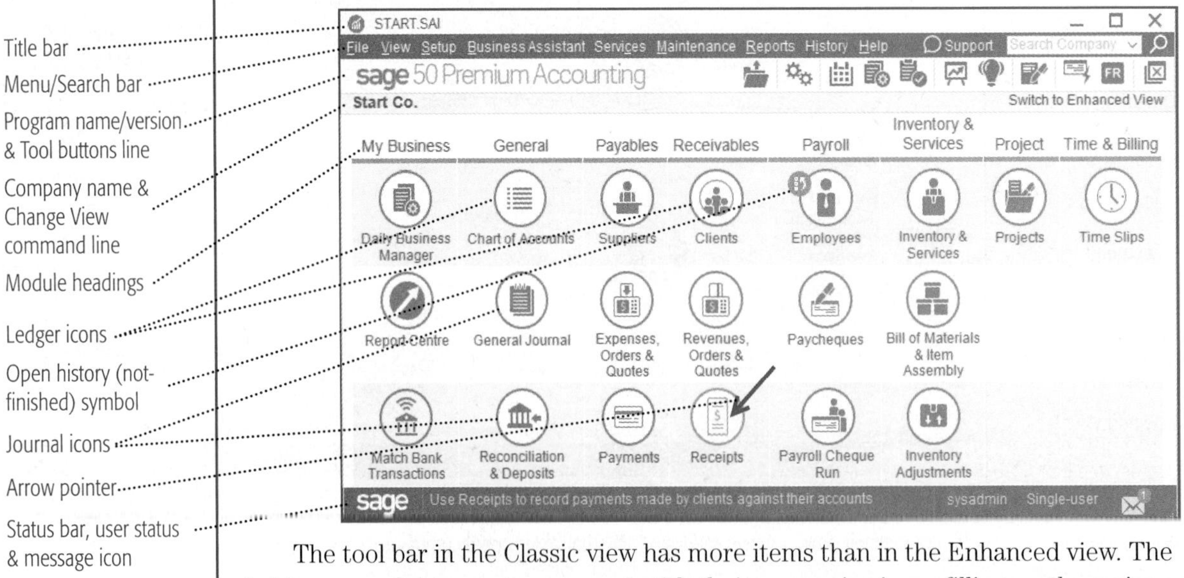

The tool bar in the Classic view has more items than in the Enhanced view. The **ledger** or module names come next with their respective icons filling up the major part of the window. The ledger icons in the top row are below the ledger or module name, and the **journal icons** are under their respective ledgers in the last two icon rows of the window. All journals and ledgers can be accessed from the icons in this single Classic view Home window. Below the journal icons we have the **status bar**. In this example, the status bar describes the purpose of the Receipts Journal because the pointer is on the Receipts icon.

The icons in the **My Business tab column** provide access to the Daily Business Manager (covered in Chapter 11), Report Centre and to bank account reconciliation from the Match Bank Transactions icon (covered in Appendix I on the Student DVD).

Hold the mouse pointer on a tool button to add a pop-up with the tool's name or function and its keyboard shortcut if there is one. Point to an icon to open its description or function in the status bar at the bottom of the window.

Click **Switch To Enhanced View** to change back to the Receivables window.

Sage 50 Help Features

Sage 50 provides program assistance in several different ways. You can display or print Help information on many topics. General accounting information, advice topics and Sage 50 software assistance are included.

The most immediate form of help comes from the **status bar** at the bottom of many program windows. It offers a one-line description of the icon or field that the mouse is pointing to. As you move the mouse around the screen, the status bar information changes accordingly. The message in the status bar is connected to the mouse position only. This may not be the same as the position of the cursor or insertion point, which is located wherever the mouse was when you last clicked the mouse button.

Many settings or options windows include a **Help button** that offers context-sensitive help for the procedure you are using.

STUDENT VERSION

Student version users may also obtain assistance by joining the student forum and posting questions online at <sagecity.com/support_communities/sage_students>.

Refer to Appendix A, page A–10, for more information about the student forum. Job opportunities are also posted on the student forum.

The Learning Centre

Start your **Internet connection**.

Click **Learning Centre** in the Modules pane:

NOTES

Access to the Learning Centre resources and tutorials requires an open Internet connection.

The Help menu may be used with or without Internet.

Through your Internet connection, the icons on this screen link to Sage University, the Online Knowledge Base, Videos and Tutorials and the Help menu for the topics named by the icon. The screen also has links to customer support and Sage City — the online community.

Click **Receivables** in the Modules pane to return to this Home window.

Sage 50 Advice

Sage 50 also includes **Advice** on a number of topics.

Choose the **Business Assistant menu**, then **click Business Advice** and **All Modules**:

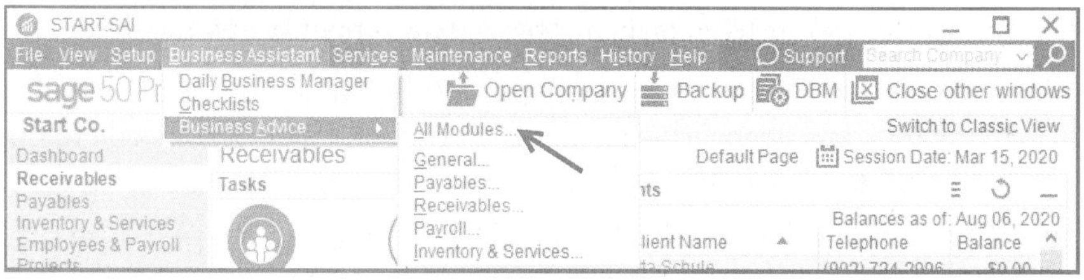

CLASSIC VIEW
In the Classic view, you can click the Advice tool .

PRO VERSION
Remember that the term Customers replaces Clients.

A list of topics opens:

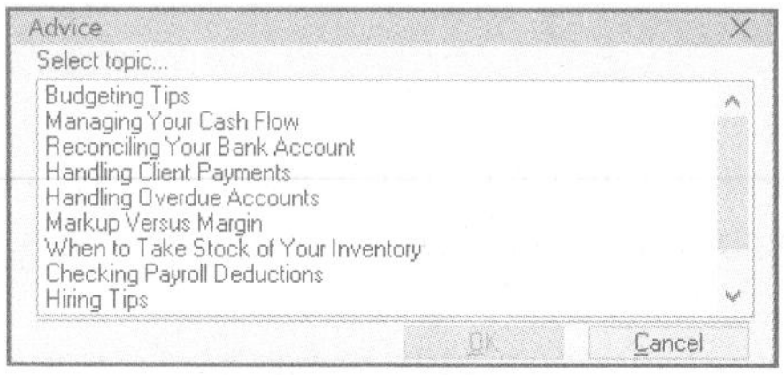

These topics provide general business information or accounting practices.

Click the **topic** you want and then **click OK**. **Close** the **advice report windows** when finished.

A final source of general assistance is available as **automatic advice**. Although this feature can be turned off from the Setup menu — User Preferences, View options, in the Home window (refer to pages 82–83) — if it is not needed, we strongly recommend leaving it on. When it is turned on, Sage 50 will provide important warning statements.

For example, for a customer who has exceeded the credit limit, the related Advisor warning will open:

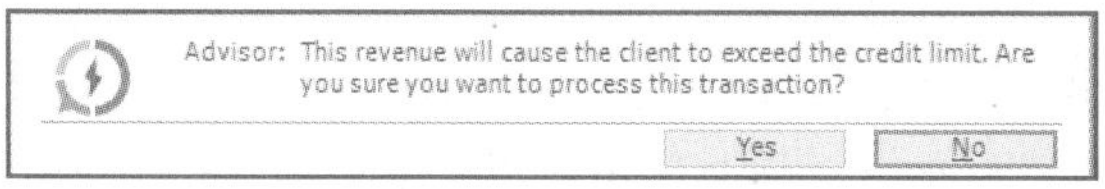

To proceed, you must make a decision in order to close the advice screen. In this case, you can click Yes to proceed with the sale or No to return to the invoice and make a change (perhaps by asking for a deposit).

NOTES
If you try to post a pay-later sale (client invoice) for any of the listed customers for $10 000, you will get the message about credit limits.

If you try to enter a sale to Irma Vanitee, you will get the message about the customer who pays late.

When you choose a customer with a history of making late payments (Irma Vanitee in this data file), the Advisor provides that information:

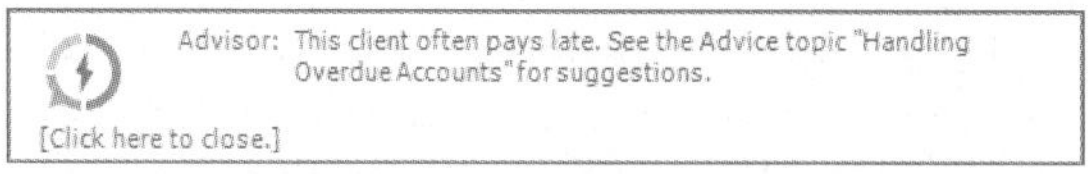

This message serves as a warning but does not allow you to make a decision before posting or prevent you from posting the transaction.

To close this message, click the Advisor icon as indicated [Click Here To Close].

The program also advises when year-end is approaching and it is time to complete year-end adjustments, when your chequing account is overdrawn or when inventory items reach the reorder point.

Sage 50 Messages

Sage 50 provides a number of different messages when you are working with the program. Some messages serve as warnings that you have made an error:

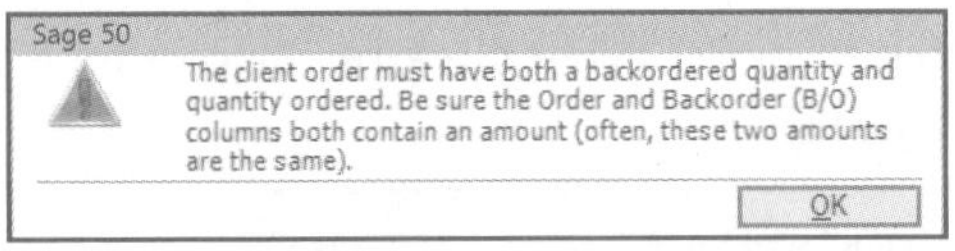

In this case, click OK to return to your previous screen and make the necessary corrections.

Sage 50 also asks you to confirm decisions that cannot be reversed:

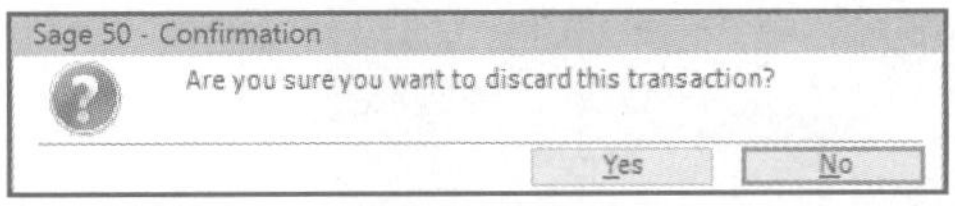

For these situations, click Yes to confirm your action or click No to return to the previous screen without making the change.

Finally, Sage 50 informs you when a requested action has been completed:

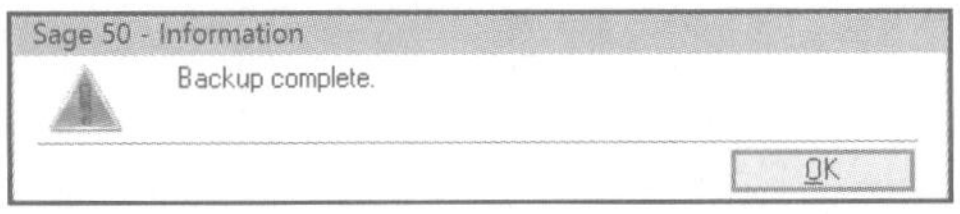

Click OK to continue — the completed step cannot be reversed.

The Help Menu

You can also use the program's built-in Help, with or without Internet access.

Click the **Help menu** in the Home window:

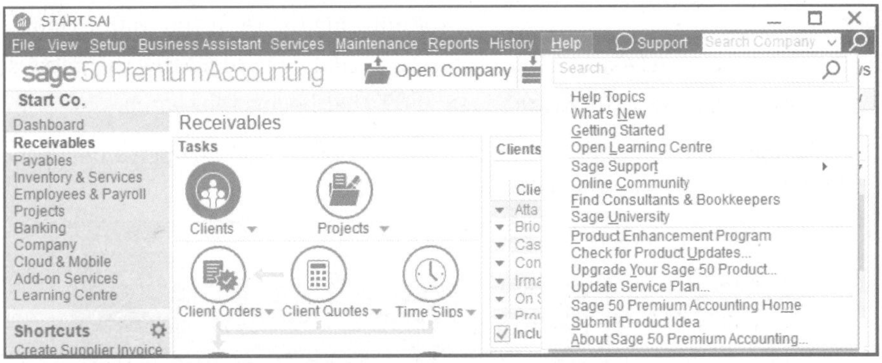

The Home window Help menu includes access to the online community for help, to the Learning Centre and its tutorials, and to product updates and support resources (access the knowledge base, chat with a Sage representative or find bookkeepers and consultants). These all require Internet access and the corresponding Sage service plan. In addition, without Internet access, you can get a description of new features and the Getting Started Guide and find the version number and serial number for your program (About Sage 50 Premium Accounting). The Support Info button on the About Sage 50 screen (from the Help menu) has your complete registration details. The option to **modify your update settings**, that is, to turn off or on automatic updates, is also located here.

If your Internet connection is active, you will have access to online help information. Much of the Help information is automatically installed with your Sage 50 program when you choose a typical installation and does not require an Internet connection.

The Help menu **Search field** has two parts: a text field for entering the term you want to look up and a Search icon that opens a starting Help information page.

Navigating Online Help

Start your **Internet connection**.

NOTES
The Search function in the Home window Menu bar begins a search for information within your data file, such as finding a record or transaction.

Choose the **Help menu** and **click Help Topics** or **click** the **Search icon** in the **Help menu Search field**:

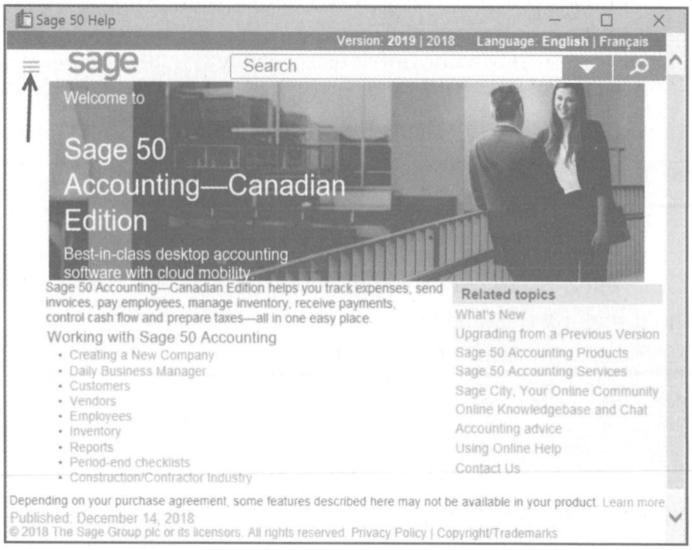

The initial Help window lists a number of general areas in Sage 50 for which you can get online information by clicking a topic. Information about these topics require an Internet connection.

The Web page header line has a **Contents** or **Index icon** beside Sage on the left.

The **Search field** on the right-hand side has three parts: a **text field** for entering the term you want to look up, an **arrow** that opens a list of subtopics and permits you to narrow the initial search area within Sage 50, and the **Search icon** that begins the search.

NOTES
The Contents or Index icon may be removed when you maximize your screen, make your screen wider or when you type in the Search text field. Instead you may see tab headings with drop-down lists.

Click the **Contents** or **Index icon** beside Sage to open a new pane with topics on the left-hand side of the window:

Click the **Search text field** and **type** `payments` **Press** *enter* or **click** the Search icon:

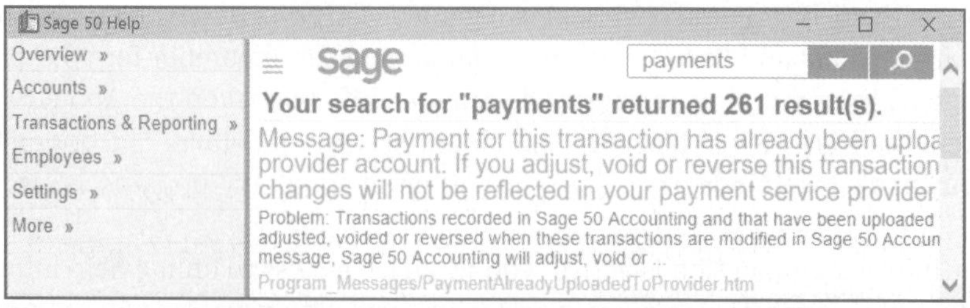

The information pane now has topics from the entire Sage 50 program that contain some information about payments — the term you entered. You can scroll through these entries to find the ones that are relevant, or you can narrow your search to reduce the number of results.

NOTES
Remember that Web pages are updated frequently, so your screens may be different from the ones we include. The screens included in this text were captured in April 2019.
Maximize the window or press *tab* to remove the menu list to read all the help information in these windows.

You can refine the list of search results. For example, you can look for payments that relate to clients (receipts) by clicking the arrow in the Search field and choosing Sales.

Major topics in the index pane are marked with a double arrow or as tab headings.

Clicking a topic with this double arrow beside it, or clicking the double arrow, will open a list of subtopics. If there are additional subtopics, they will also have a double arrow beside them.

Sometimes the contents list is replaced by tab headings with the same topics:

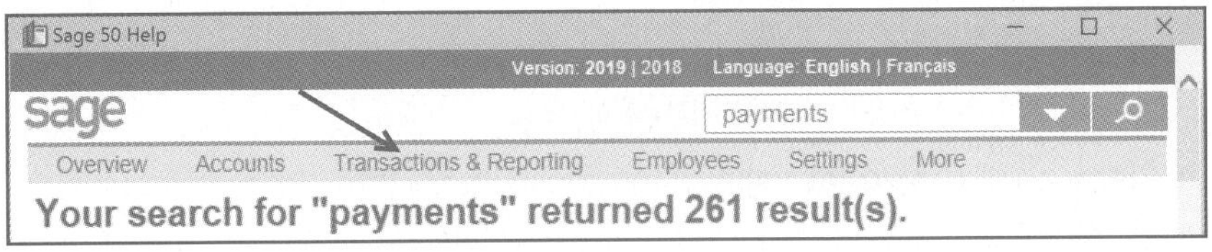

Click **Transactions & Reporting** in the Contents pane or its tab:

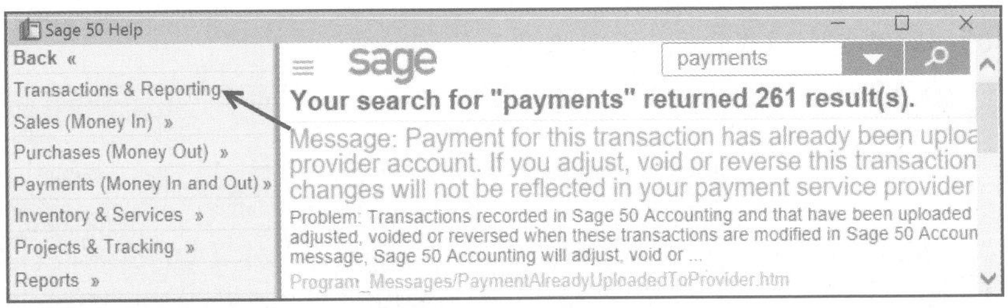

Information from your previous search will remain on-screen until you start a new search and select a final subtopic.

The contents or index pane now has a list of subtopics for the different types of transactions and reports. These entries still have a double arrow beside them, indicating that there are additional subtopics under each heading.

Click **Payments (Money In And Out)**, then **click** **Payments Window** and **Pay A Bill From A Vendor**:

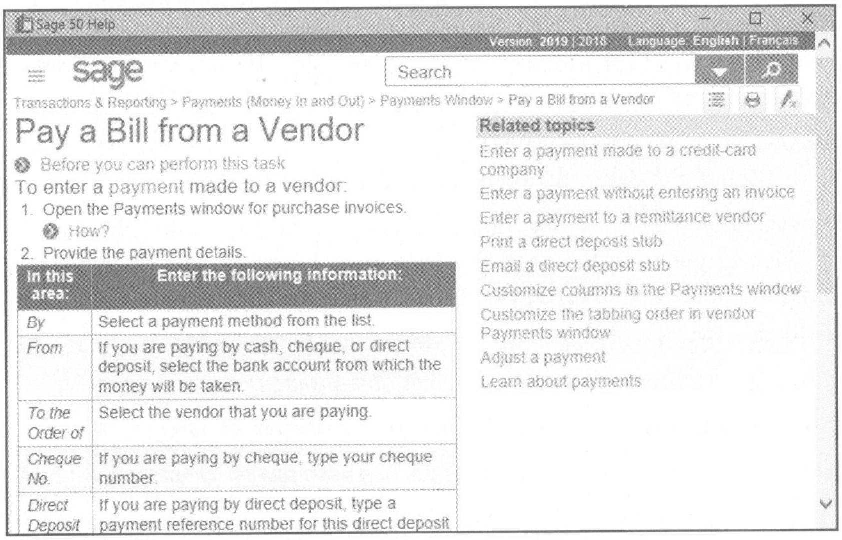

If your window has tabs, click the Payments (Money In And Out) in the drop-down menu from the Transactions & Reporting tab. Then click Payments Window and Pay A Bill From A Vendor in the list that opens next.

As soon as there are no further subtopics, the information pane will have details about the final topic you selected.

The Contents or Index pane has been removed. Instead, the path you followed is now at the top of the information pane:

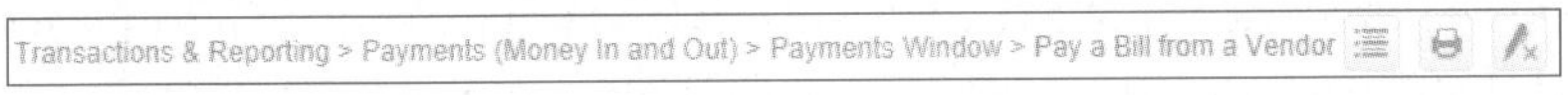

NOTES

Your window may include a list of related topics in the information pane. These offer a direct link to a topic with a single click.

NOTES
Pointing to a tool will open a pop-up label for the tool.

Three tools are located on the right-hand side of this path: Expand All topics (expand any topic in the information pane that has the **Expand icon**, the circled arrow like the ones beside Before You Can Perform This Task, or How), Print the details in the information pane and Remove Highlighting.

Clicking an Expand icon will provide additional information on the selected task, feature or question.

Click to close the **Help window**. The next section describes the same Help features without Internet access.

Close your **Internet connection** for the next group of instructions.

Navigating Help without Internet

Choose the **Help menu** and **click Help Topics**:

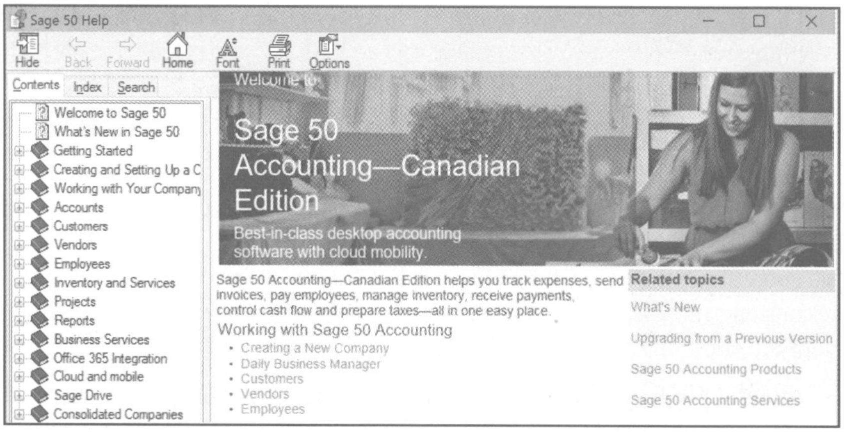

Without an Internet connection, the **Contents tab** is the starting point in the navigation pane on the left and the information pane is on the right, as before. The window includes a tool bar with a set of tool icons: Hide, Back, Forward, Home, Font, Print and Options with additional options in its drop-down menu.

The navigation pane has a list of topics. A **closed book icon** or beside a topic in the Contents tab navigation pane indicates that there are subtopics.

NOTES
If a topic has subtopics, it will have a book icon and you must choose a subtopic with the question icon to display the help information. If there are still multiple entries, there will be an additional book icon and you can choose from the list that Sage 50 offers at this stage.

A **question icon** beside a topic indicates that detailed help is available on that subject. Click a topic or its question icon to display information on that subject in the right-hand side information display pane of the Help window.

Click **Vendors** or click the closed book icon or beside Vendors in the Contents pane to open a list of subtopics.

The book icon beside Vendors has changed to an **open book icon** and the has changed to . The second list of topics has both **question icons** and book icons. Book icons indicate another level of subtopics. Clicking an open book title or an open book icon will close the book and hide the list of subtopics.

Click **Purchases** or **click** its closed book icon to view another list of subtopics.

Click **Paying Vendors (Payments)** or **click** its closed book icon to view another list of subtopics.

Click **Paying A Vendor** (with — a question icon — beside it):

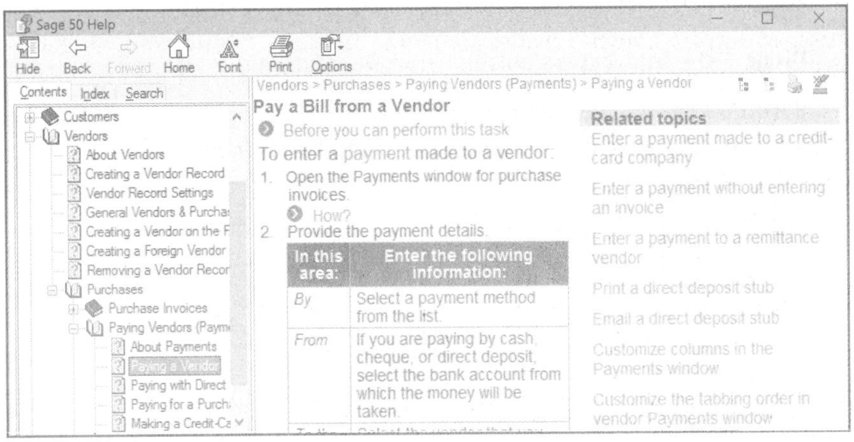

Because we have selected a specific topic with no more subtopics, the information pane display has changed. It now has the same set of steps obtained earlier from the Internet search for Pay A Bill From A Vendor.

As before, until you choose a different subtopic, the contents of the information pane do not change. Also as before, a header line shows the path and tools:

As in the information pane in the online search, clicking the Expand icon in the information pane will expand the list of topics related to this task or question. To expand all details, click the Expand All tool, the first tool in the header line.

Close the **Help window** to return to the Home window.

Click the **Help menu Search field** and **type** `payments`:

The Index tab screen opens with an alphabetic list of topics relating to the term you typed. The term we typed is entered in the Keyword field and the navigation pane now has an alphabetic list of topics relating to payments, the keyword entered.

Scroll down, click the term you want to look up and then click the Display button below the list to view the information on that subject. For example, choose Making To Vendors and click Display to display the information pane at the top of this page.

Click the **Search tab** in the Options pane:

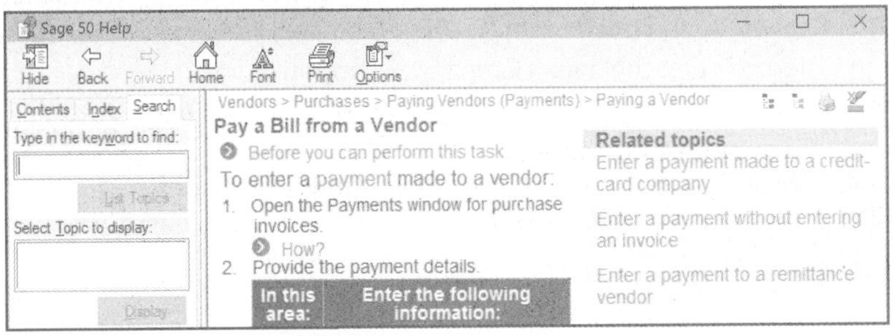

NOTES

The information pane in the Help window includes a list of related topics. Click one of these topics to open the information on that topic.

NOTES

You can also click the Index tab from any other Help window. Then type your term in the Keyword field and click Display. The information from your previous search will remain on display until you choose to display another topic.

NOTES

Without an Internet connection, clicking the Help Menu Help field Search icon opens the Search tab screen shown here.

Type `purchase orders` in the Keyword text field.

Click the **List Topics** button below the text field.

Scroll down the new list of topics related to Purchase Orders. **Click Enter A Purchase Order** and then **click Display**:

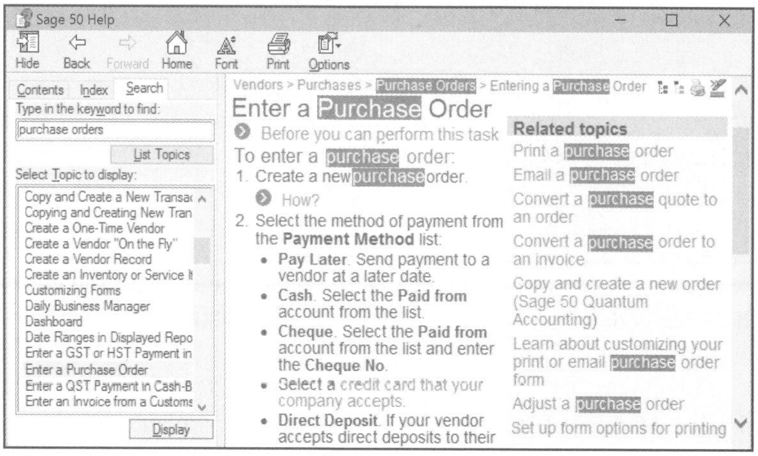

Because we have completed the request for a different search, the contents of the information pane now changes and displays the details we requested.

Search for **information** on other topics in the different option screens.

Close the **Help windows** when finished.

NOTES

Sage 50 allows you to enter earlier session dates but warns you first. If you have advanced the date incorrectly, you can reverse the decision as long as you have not advanced to a new fiscal year. Warnings are also given when you advance the date by more than one week or when you try to advance to a new fiscal period. These warnings should serve as signals that you may have made a mistake.

Date Formats and Settings

Before closing the program we will review date format settings. Date accuracy is very important because dates are used for discounts, payment terms and many reports.

Sage 50 has date format control settings within each file that are independent of the display date settings for Windows. When you enter dates using a series of two digits for month, day and year, it is important to know how these will be interpreted. For example, when you type 12-06-05, this date may be June 12, December 6 or June 5 and the year may be 2005, 1905, 1912 or 2012, depending on whether month, day or year comes first and whether your computer defaults to 1900 dates or is preset for 2000 dates.

Fortunately, Sage 50 allows you to enter and display dates as text. Thus, you can type June 5, 2012, in a date field. And if you want, you can display this date as Jun 05, 2012, even if you entered numbers in the date field. Sage 50 uses three letters to display the month when the text option is selected.

All date fields also have a **Calendar icon** that you can click to access a month-by-month calendar from which you can select a date. These two options will help you avoid making date errors from incorrect orders. To access the date settings,

CLASSIC VIEW

Right-click the Chart of Accounts icon and then click the Settings tool icon to open the General Settings window. Click Company.

Click the **Settings icon** in the Related Tasks pane, or **choose** the **Setup menu**, then **click Settings**. **Click Company** in the list of modules on the left to open the main Company Settings window.

NOTES

When you click the ⊞ beside Company, the list expands beneath the heading. You can click Date Format in either list to open the Date Format Settings window.

Company settings are described in detail in Chapters 4 and 7.

Each entry in the list opens the Settings screen for a different part of the program.

Click **Date Format** to open the Settings window for dates:

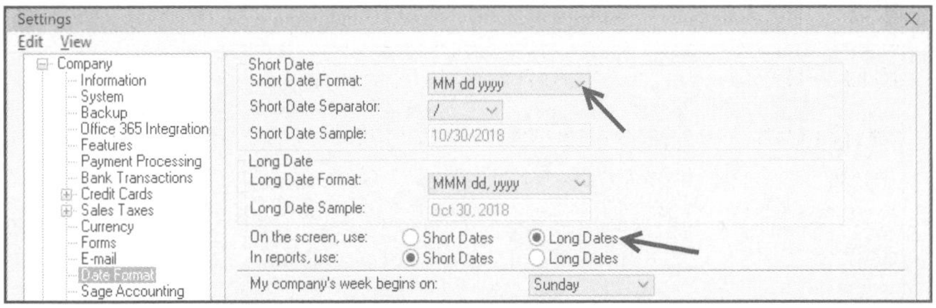

Each field has a drop-down list of format options. The **Short Date Format** uses two digits each for month and day. For the year, you can choose two or four digits. You can begin the date with month, day or year — the Short Date Format illustrates which comes first. The **Short Date Separator** character may be a slash, dash or period. This is the character that will appear on the screen regardless of how you enter the date. The sample illustrates the appearance for the current date (your computer system date) from your selections.

NOTES

Sage 50 displays only the first three letters of a month when you choose the long or text date format (entered as MMM in the selection list). Therefore, Oct is displayed for October, Jun will be displayed for June, and so on.

The **Long Date Format** displays the month as a three-letter text abbreviation. Either the month or the day can be first in the long date style. The sample has the current date with your selected format.

The next section allows you to select the short or long date styles for your screen and reports. You can select different date styles for your reports and screen displays.

We will use the long date format settings on screen for all files to avoid any confusion about dates when the numeric entry might be ambiguous. For reports you can use long or short date formats. For the files we provided in the data set, the month-day-year order is already selected for short and long formats.

To change the date format settings,

NOTES

Although most versions of Windows now default to the 2000s, showing a four-digit year will ensure that you know whether you are using 1900 or 2000 year dates.

A final date option allows you to indicate the normal first weekday for the business.

Click the **Short Date Format field list arrow** for the format options.

Click **dd MM yy** and observe the change in the sample.

Click **MM dd yyyy** again. Be sure that Month (MM) is the first part of the entry.

Click the **Long Date Format field list arrow** to view the format options.

Click **MMM dd, yyyy**.

Click **Long Dates** beside the option On The Screen, Use.

Click **OK** to save the settings.

Saving and Backing Up Your Work

Sage 50 saves your work automatically when you are working with the program. For example, when you post a journal entry or when you display or print reports, Sage 50 writes all the journal transactions to your file to compile the report you want. When you exit from the program properly, Sage 50 also saves all your work.

On a regular basis, you should also make a backup copy of your files. The Backup command is described in detail in Chapter 3.

Making Backups from the Data Management Icon

Close any other open **windows**. (**Click** the **Close Other Windows tool** .)

Click **Company** in the Modules pane.

PRO VERSION
The Pro version does not have the option to consolidate companies.

Click the **Data Management icon shortcuts list arrow**:

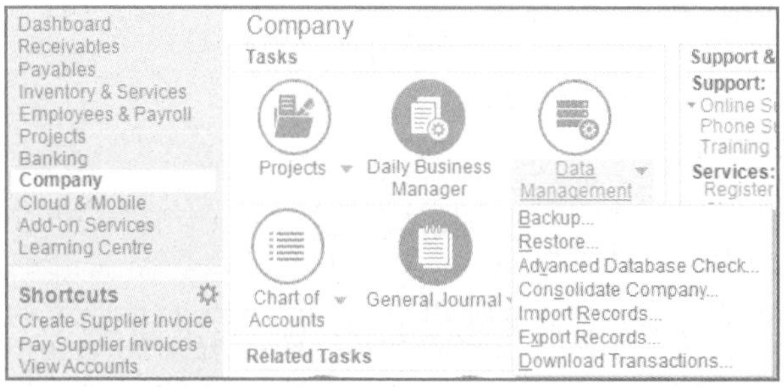

The Data Management icon in the Company window includes a shortcuts menu with options to back up and to restore a data file. It also has direct access to other functions, including exporting and importing records (covered in Appendix J on the Student DVD), checking your database for inconsistencies and fixing them if they are minor, and consolidating data from multiple companies.

Click the **Data Management icon** to start the Backup wizard, or **click Backup** on the icon's shortcuts list.

NOTES
Refer to page 50 for more information about the Backup wizard.

You can also start the backup procedure from any Home window.

Click the **Backup tool** or **choose** the **File menu** and **click Backup** to start the Backup wizard.

CLASSIC VIEW
The Classic View does not have a backup tool in the tool bar.

The wizard will create a separate backup folder inside your current working folder so that the backup will remain separate from your working copy.

Saving a Copy of Your Data File

While **Backup** creates compressed copies of the files that must be restored with the Restore command before you can use them, the next two options create new complete working copies of your data files that can be opened directly. Both save the file under a different file name so that you will have two working copies of the files — the original and the copy. You can create backups on a CD but not on a DVD with the Backup command.

Save As makes a copy, closes the original file and lets you continue to work with the new copy. Because the new file becomes your working file, you can use Save As to copy to any medium that you can also work from in Sage 50 — your hard drive or a removable memory stick or flash drive, but not a CD. **Save A Copy** makes a copy of the file and then allows you to continue working with the original file. You can use Save A Copy to save your files to a CD (but not to a DVD). You must copy the CD files back to your hard drive, and you may need to remove the read-only property before working with these files.

Because the data files are very large, we recommend using the Backup procedure described in Chapter 3 rather than Save As or Save A Copy for regular backups.

NOTES
You may want to use the Save A Copy or Save As command when you are unsure how a journal entry will be posted and you want to experiment with different methods of entering the same transactions.

NOTES
If you need to remove the read-only property, right-click the file name or icon in the Computer window and choose Properties from the pop-up menu. Click Read-Only to remove the ✓.

Choose the **File menu** and **click Save A Copy** to open the file name window.

You can save the copy in the same folder as the original by entering a different file name or, if you want to use the same name, you must use a different folder. We recommend using different folders.

Click a **different folder in the file path** to change folders.

Double-click a **folder** in the name and folders pane to open it.

To create a new folder inside the one that you have open,

Click **New Folder** (in the tool bar). **Click Browse Folders** first if necessary to reveal the New Folder option.

Type a **new name** to replace New Folder, the selected text.

Click the new **folder's icon** or **name** to select it. **Click Open**.

Double-click **NEW** in the File Name field (or **NEW.SAI** if you show file extensions).

Type the **new file name**. **Click Save**. You will return to your original file and you can continue working.

To save the file under a different name and work with the new file, use **Save As**.

Choose the **File menu** and **click Save As** to open the file name window.

The remaining steps are the same as Save A Copy. Change folders, create a new folder, rename the folder, open the new folder, type a file name for the copy and click Save. Remember to return to your original working copy before entering any transactions if you use the Save As command.

You can also back up all your data files at the same time by using Windows (in the Windows File Explorer or Computer windows) Copy and Paste commands. In this way, you can save the files to a different folder on your hard drive or a CD.

NOTES

You can also use the Windows Copy command to make CD copies of your data, but you must close the Sage 50 data file before you start to copy. Remember to copy the data folders when you copy from Windows to ensure that you keep all necessary files (the .SAI file and the SAJ folder) together.

You must use a DVD-writing program to copy your data files to a DVD.

You cannot open the data files from the CD or DVD. You must first copy them back to your hard drive and you may need to remove the read-only property.

Finishing a Session

Choose the **open window Control Menu icon** and **click Close** or **click**  to close the journal input form or display window you are working in.

Click the **Close Other Windows tool**  if you have several windows open. You will return to the main Home window.

Choose the **Sage 50 Control Menu icon**  and **click Close**, or **click**  or **choose** the **File menu** and **click Exit** to close the Home window. The backup prompt will open:

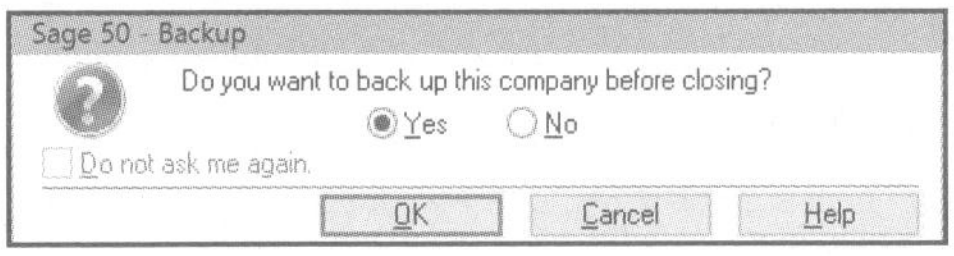

For this practice file, you do not need to create a separate backup file.

Click **No** to close the backup prompt. **Click OK**.

Your work will be saved again automatically when you complete this step. You should now be in the Windows desktop.

NOTES

All our data files are set up with the option to prompt you to back up the company data when you close the file.

Opening a Data File from a Backup

Double-click 

, the desktop program icon, or the **Sage 50 program** button on the Start window to open the Welcome and Select Company window.

NOTES

The first time you start the program, the option to Open The Last Company You Worked On will not be included. Refer to the Welcome and Select Company screen on page 8.

NOTES

You can start the Restore wizard from any open Sage 50 data file. From any Home window, choose the File menu and click Restore to start the Restore wizard.

Or, from the Company module window, start the wizard from the Data Management icon shortcuts list. Click the icon's list arrow and choose Restore (refer to page 24).

This is the same opening window as the one on page 8:

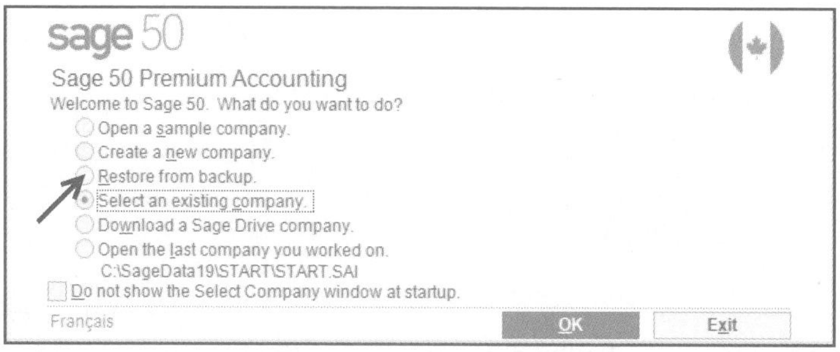

The opening window gives you several options: working with the sample company files, creating new company files, restoring backup files or working with existing data files. If you have worked with the program before, the option to **Open The Last Company You Worked On** appears with the name of the file you used most recently, as in our example. We need to restore a backup file.

If your working files are lost or damaged, you will also need to restore backup files.

You can also restore files from the Home window File menu of any data file, including the Sample Company file, or from the Company window Data Management shortcuts list.

Click **Restore From Backup**.

Click **OK** to start the Sage 50 Restore From Backup wizard:

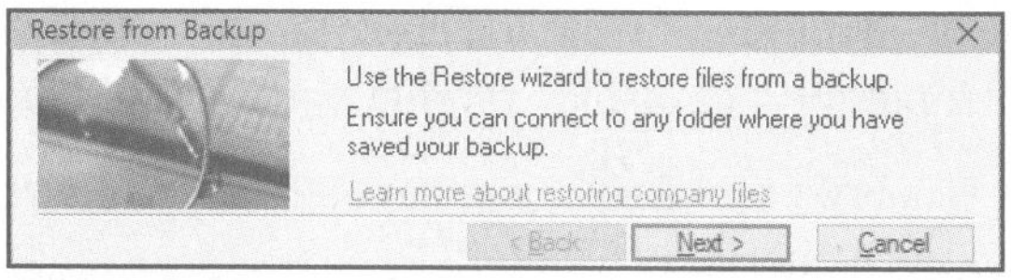

Click **Next** to begin:

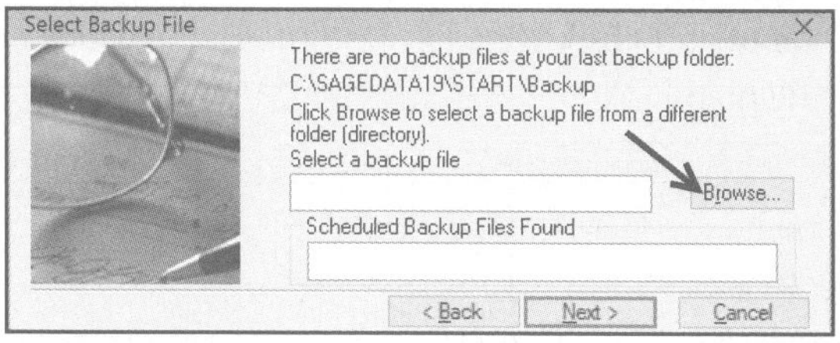

The first time you restore a backup, no default location or backup files are entered.

Click **Browse** to open the folder you worked in most recently.

The folder names in your Select field and Browse windows may be different from ours. Sage 50 uses a folder under Libraries\Documents as the default location for files, so you may have this as the selected folder initially. If you have opened another data file, the folder where that file is stored may be entered. To ensure consistency in file names and locations for our instructions, we always work with the folder we created when installing the data files, that is, C:\SageData19.

Click **This PC** in the path field at the top of the screen or in the left pane list of links, drives and folders. All your computer drives will be listed:

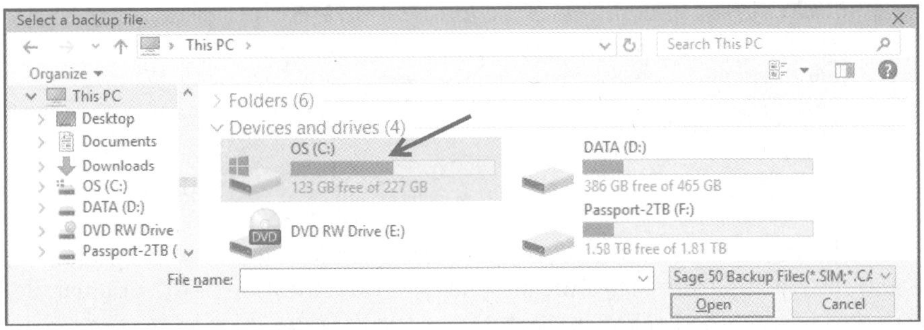

Double-click **OS(C:)** to list the files and folders in this drive:

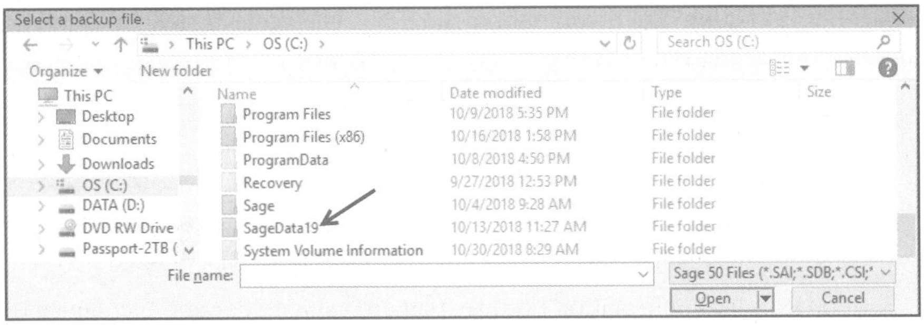

Click **SageData19** to select it, or click the SageData19 folder icon .

Click **Open** to list the files you copied from the Student DVD:

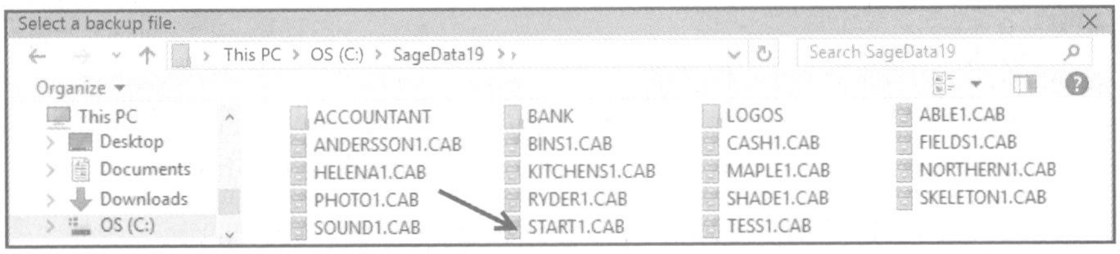

Only Sage 50 format backup files and folders are listed because we are working with the Restore Backup wizard.

Click **START1.CAB** to select it or click the START1.CAB icon  if you are in icon view. (Click **START1** if you are not showing file extensions.) START1 is added to the File Name field.

Click **Open**. You will return to the wizard with your backup files listed in the Select A Backup File text box and START1.CAB selected:

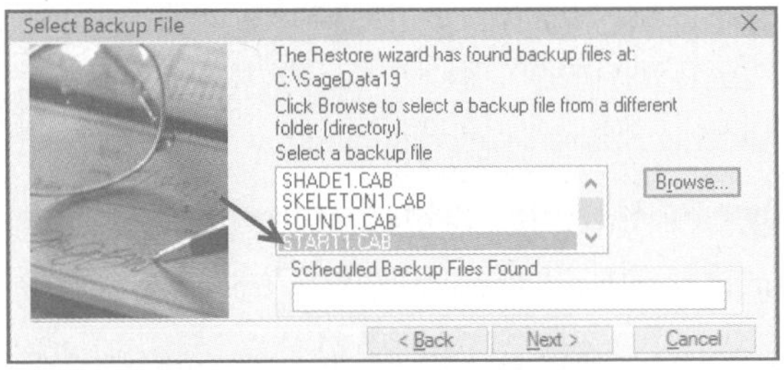

Click **Next** to continue. The screen will have the selections you have made:

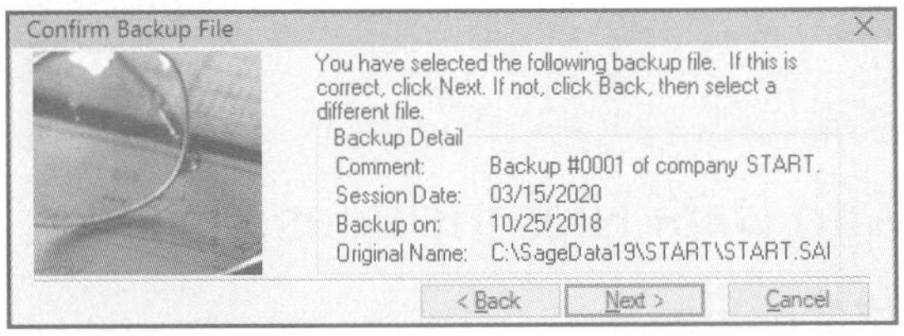

If the information is incorrect, click Back to return to the file selection screen.

NOTES

By default, Sage 50 assumes that backup files are in a Backup folder within the folder you recently used.

NOTES

Your screens may look different if you have selected different viewing options such as displaying the folders as lists or icons. The viewing options can be changed from the Views icon drop-down menu.

NOTES

We use the default location for the data files from the automatic installation. If you installed the files to a different location, choose the drive and folder for your setup.

PRO VERSION

The first backup file listed is ANDERSSON1.CAB – you will not have entries for ABLE and RYDER.

WARNING!

If you are not showing file extensions, click START1. The file name has a filing cabinet icon beside it (like the ones on this page).

NOTES

The dates on this screen may be entered with the day before the month – the format may be controlled by your Windows settings.

NOTES
The original name and location – the ones we used to create the initial backup file – will be the default ones used when you restore a backup. The default for the restored file will be C:\SageData19\START\START.SAI.

Click **Next** to continue if the information is correct:

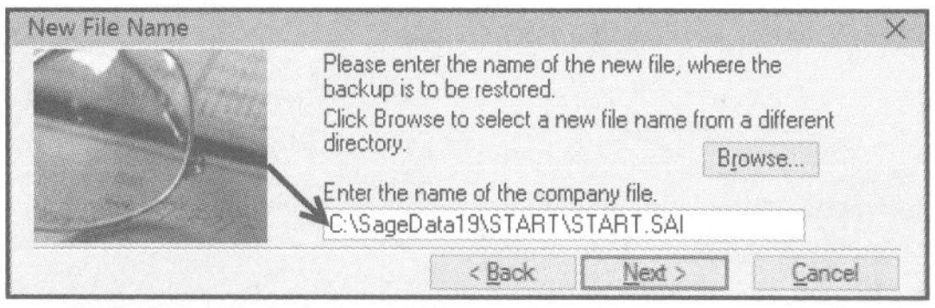

At this stage, you should enter the name of the file you are restoring. If you have created the backup from your own file, the name and location of the original file from which you created the backup are entered as the default.

We will create a new folder for each data set in this text. We will continue to work in the SageData19 folder. The default entry should be C:\SageData19\START\START. If a different name is entered,

Type `C:\SageData19\START\START`

Click **Next**.

You can choose a different location and file name by clicking Browse to access your folders. Enter the location and file name you want to use.

Sage 50 asks for confirmation because you are using folder and file names that are new. Sage 50 will create the new folders and files for you:

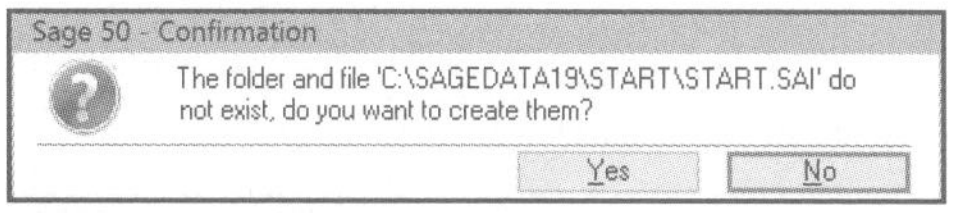

Click **Yes** to confirm and continue.

If you are replacing a file, you will be warned when you type the file name and location file. Click Yes if you are replacing a corrupt or unusable file.

Sage 50 now has all the data required to complete the restore process:

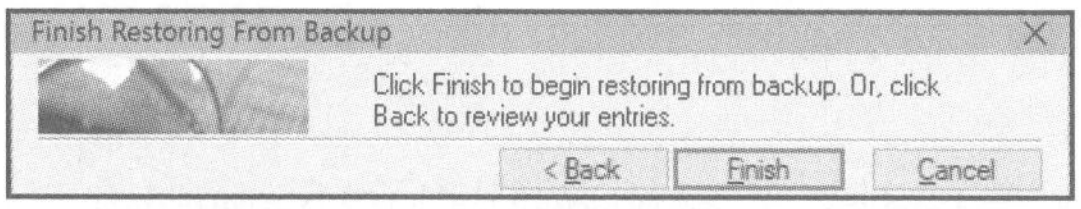

This is your last chance to change information by clicking Back.

Click **Finish** to begin restoring the file. The next screen prompts you to enter the session date:

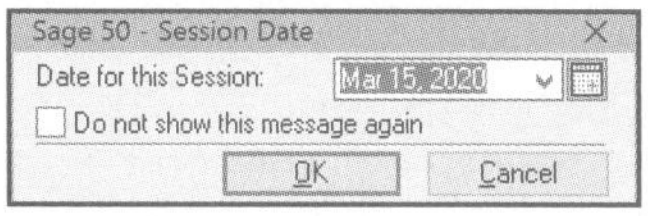

Click **OK** to open the Getting Started Welcome window on page 10.

Click **Show This Window On Start Up** to remove the ✓.

Click **Close** to continue to the Home window.

Continue with the instructions on page 10.

REVIEW

The Student DVD with Data Files includes Review Questions for this chapter.

CHAPTER TWO

GST, HST and PST

OBJECTIVES

After completing this chapter, you should be able to

- ***understand*** the terms relevant to the federal Goods and Services Tax
- ***understand*** the different methods of calculating the GST
- ***understand*** Harmonized Sales Tax in relation to GST
- ***understand*** how to file for GST or HST remittances or refunds
- ***understand*** other provincial sales taxes in relation to GST

GENERAL TAX INFORMATION

Definition of Goods and Services Tax: GST

NOTES

Quebec used to include GST in the price on which it calculated its Provincial Sales Tax (QST). Currently, no provinces use this approach. Provincial tax rates vary from province to province. See pages 32 and 34.

The Goods and Services Tax (GST) is levied by the federal government at the rate of 5 percent on most goods and services in Canada. Retailers pay the GST to their wholesalers and vendors but are allowed to deduct any GST they pay from the GST they collect from customers. Retailers remit the difference, GST owing, to the Receiver General for Canada or claim a refund with monthly or quarterly returns.

GST Registration Any business with annual sales exceeding $30 000 per year must register for GST collection and must collect GST on all applicable sales. Registration is optional for most smaller businesses. Businesses that are not registered for GST do not charge GST on sales to their customers, but they also cannot recover the GST they pay on business-related purchases.

NOTES

GST collected on sales is reduced by the GST on sales returns.

Collecting the GST The business must collect GST for those goods and services sold that are not zero rated or tax exempt. The business must remit GST at regular intervals, filing GST returns monthly, quarterly or annually and paying instalments, depending on annual income and GST owing.

Zero Rated Goods and Services Zero rated goods and services are those on which the tax rate is zero. These goods include basic groceries, prescribed medical devices, prescribed drugs, exported goods and services, agricultural products and fish products. A business selling only zero rated goods and services does not collect GST on sales, but it can still claim a refund for GST it pays for purchases.

NOTES
Unlike rent on personal residences, rent on business property is subject to GST.

NOTES
The input tax credit is reduced by the amount of GST for purchases returned.

NOTES
Purchases of goods and services on a reserve that are made by businesses or by individuals registered as Status Indians are also usually exempt from GST and HST.

NOTES
Visitors to Canada can request a refund for GST paid on goods purchased in Canada that they are taking home with them. They cannot claim a refund for goods and services they consumed in Canada, such as entertainment and dining.

Tax Exempt Goods and Services Tax exempt goods and services are those on which tax is not collected. These goods and services include health care, dental care, daycare services and rent on personal residences. Most educational and financial services are also included in this group. These businesses are not able to claim refunds for GST paid for business purchases related to selling tax exempt goods and services.

Paying the GST A business must pay GST for purchases made for business purposes, unless the goods or services purchased are zero rated or tax exempt. The business can use the GST paid as an input tax credit by subtracting the amount of GST paid from the amount of GST collected and remitting GST owing or claiming a refund. GST amounts paid on purchases for personal use do not qualify as input tax credits.

Bank and Financial Institution Services Most bank products and services are not taxable. Exceptions include safety deposit box rentals, custodial and safekeeping services, personalized cheques, self-administered registered savings plan fees, payroll services, rentals of night depository, rentals of credit card imprinters and reconciliation of cheques. Banks remit the full amount of GST they collect from customers. Because most bank services are not taxable, banks cannot claim input tax credits for GST they pay on business-related purchases.

GST on Imported and Exported Goods GST is not charged on exported goods. Customers in other countries who import goods from Canada do not pay GST. However, businesses in Canada must pay GST on the items they import or purchase from other countries. The GST is collected by the Canada Revenue Agency (CRA) when the goods enter Canada based on the purchase price (plus import duty) and current exchange rates. Businesses must pay this GST and other import duties before the goods are released to them.

Administering the GST

The federal government has approved different methods of administering the GST; the regular method is most commonly used.

The Regular Method

The regular method of administering the GST requires the business to keep track of GST paid for all goods and services purchased from vendors (less returns) and of GST collected for all goods and services sold to customers (less returns). It then deducts the GST paid from the GST collected and files for a refund or remits the balance owing to the Receiver General on a monthly or quarterly basis.

Accounting Examples Using the Regular Method (without PST)

SALES INVOICE Sold goods to customer for $200 plus $10 GST collected (5%). Invoice total, $210.

Date	Particulars	Debit	Credit
02/15	Accounts Receivable	210.00	
	GST Charged on Sales		10.00
	Revenue from Sales		200.00

PURCHASE INVOICE Purchased supplies from vendor for $300 plus $15 GST paid (5%). Invoice total, $315.

Date	Particulars	Debit	Credit
02/15	Supplies	300.00	
	GST Paid on Purchases	15.00	
	Accounts Payable		315.00

NOTES
GST Paid on Purchases is a contra-liability account because it normally has a debit balance while most liability accounts have a credit balance. Therefore, GST Paid on Purchases reduces the total GST liability to the Receiver General.

The GST owing is further reduced by any GST adjustments — for example, GST that applies to bad debts that are written off. If the debt is later recovered, the GST liability is also restored as an input tax credit adjustment.

Other Methods of Calculating GST

Certain small businesses may be eligible to use simpler methods of calculating their GST refunds and remittances that do not require them to keep a separate record for GST on each individual purchase or sale. The simplified accounting method, the streamlined accounting method and the quick method are examples of these alternatives.

NOTES

Under the quick method, the GST remittance or refund amount is based on a flat-rate percentage of total sales, including GST. The remittance rate varies for different types of businesses. GST paid on purchases of capital is an input tax credit to reduce the amount owing (or increase the refund).

These alternative methods of calculating GST are not used in the applications in this workbook.

Calculating GST Refunds or Remittances

The following example uses the regular method for a retailer who is filing quarterly:

Quarterly Total Sales (excluding GST)	$50 000.00	
Quarterly Total Qualifying Purchases	29 700.00	
5% GST Charged on Sales		$2 500.00
Less: 5% GST Paid on Purchases		
Cash Register (cost $1 000)	50.00	
Inventory (cost $25 000)	1 250.00	
Supplies (cost $500)	25.00	
Payroll Services (cost $200)	10.00	
Store Lease (cost $3 000)	150.00	
Total GST Paid		– 1 485.00
GST Remittance		$1 015.00

GST Remittances and Refunds

The business must file returns that summarize the amount of GST it has collected and the amount of GST it has paid. The CRA may require reports monthly, quarterly or yearly, depending on total sales. Yearly reports usually require quarterly instalments.

GST Collected on Sales	>	GST Paid on Purchases	=	GST Owing
GST Collected on Sales	<	GST Paid on Purchases	=	GST Refund

Accounting Examples for Remittances

Usually a business will make GST remittances because sales usually exceed expenses — the business operates at a profit. The following example shows how the GST accounts are cleared and a liability (*Accounts Payable*) is set up to remit GST owing to the Receiver General for Canada. In this case, the usual one, the Receiver General becomes a vendor for the business so that the liability can be entered and the payment made.

Date	Particulars	Debit	Credit
03/31	GST Charged on Sales	2 500.00	
	GST Paid on Purchases		1 485.00
	A/P - Receiver General		1 015.00
03/31	A/P - Receiver General	1 015.00	
	Chequing Bank Account		1 015.00

NOTES

The rules concerning the GST change periodically, as in the 2006 federal budget when the rate changed from 7 percent to 6 percent. In the 2007 budget, the rate was reduced again to 5 percent. Always refer to current guidelines.

Accounting Examples for Refunds

The example below shows how the GST accounts are cleared and a current asset account (*Accounts Receivable*) is set up for a GST refund from the Receiver General for Canada. In this case, the Receiver General owes money to the business; that is, it acts like a customer, so a customer record is set up to record and collect the refund.

Date	Particulars	Debit	Credit
03/31	GST Charged on Sales	1 500.00	
	A/R - Receiver General	500.00	
	GST Paid on Purchases		2 000.00
04/15	Chequing Bank Account	500.00	
	A/R - Receiver General		500.00

Harmonized Sales Tax: HST

Five provinces have adopted the Harmonized Sales Tax (HST) method of taxing goods and services: Prince Edward Island, Ontario, New Brunswick, Nova Scotia and Newfoundland and Labrador. When HST applies, the GST and provincial taxes are harmonized at a single rate. In all provinces, 5 percent of the HST rate is the federal portion, or GST, while the remainder is the provincial portion. Provincial retail sales tax rates vary from one province to another, so the HST rates also vary. In Ontario, the HST rate in 2019 is 13 percent (8 percent provincial); and in Nova Scotia, Prince Edward Island, New Brunswick and Newfoundland and Labrador, the rate is 15 percent (10 percent provincial). The HST replaces the separate GST and PST, and unlike those separate taxes, it is administered entirely at the federal level. This removes some administrative work both from the provincial Ministries of Finance and from the businesses that charge taxes to their customers. They have only one tax to calculate and remit.

NOTES

Prices shown to customers may have the HST included (tax-inclusive pricing), but they must show either the amount of HST included in the price or the HST rate. Most retailers show prices before taxes are included.

The full 13 or 15 percent Harmonized Sales Tax operates much like the basic GST: HST is applied at each level of sale and resale, and manufacturing; has the same business registration requirement of annual sales exceeding $30 000; is applied to the same base of goods and services; and is collected in the same way. HST returns and remittances are also calculated in the same way as GST returns and remittances. The business remits any excess of HST collected over HST paid for its business expenses, or claims a refund when HST paid exceeds the HST collected from customers.

The following example illustrates the application in Ontario where the HST rate is 13 percent:

Ontario business sold goods on account for $565, including $500 base price and HST at 13% ($65).

HST = (0.13 × 500) = $65
Total amount of invoice = $565

Date	Particulars	Debit	Credit
02/15	Accounts Receivable	565.00	
	HST Charged on Sales		65.00
	Revenue from Sales		500.00

A single remittance for the full 13 percent is made to the Receiver General; the provincial portion of the HST is not tracked or collected separately by the business.

The following examples show the journal entries for an HST remittance and an HST refund:

Remittance: A **New Brunswick** business calculates and pays HST owing
For Sales of $50 000 plus 15% HST; qualifying purchases of $30 000 plus 15% HST

Date	Particulars	Debit	Credit
03/31	HST Charged on Sales	7 500.00	
	A/P - Receiver General		3 000.00
	HST Paid on Purchases		4 500.00
04/15	A/P - Receiver General	3 000.00	
	Chequing Bank Account		3 000.00

Refund: A **New Brunswick** business qualifies and applies for an HST refund
For Sales of $30 000 plus 15% HST; qualifying purchases of $42 000 plus 15% HST

Date	Particulars	Debit	Credit
03/31	HST Charged on Sales	4 500.00	
	A/R - Receiver General	1 800.00	
	HST Paid on Purchases		6 300.00
04/15	Chequing Bank Account	1 800.00	
	A/R - Receiver General		1 800.00

NOTES
The quick method may also be used by small businesses registered for HST, and it operates in the same way as for GST alone.

Goods and Services Exempt for HST

Under the HST method, all items that are exempt for GST or are zero rated are also exempt or are zero rated for HST. In addition, each province has decided that some items will be exempt for HST and subject only to GST. For example, books and children's clothing (and hydroelectricity in Ontario) are exempt for HST but not for GST. For these goods, the customer pays only the 5 percent GST portion of the tax. At the retail level, for these special items a separate tax code for GST only is applied. When the business files its HST return, it will remit the HST collected plus the GST collected less the amounts of GST plus HST paid on qualifying business-related purchases on a single return.

The following example shows these calculations for a bookseller who also sells music CDs in Nova Scotia. HST at the rate of 15 percent (including a provincial portion of 10 percent) applies to the sale of CDs, while GST at the rate of 5 percent applies to the sale of books.

Quarterly Total Sales (excluding taxes)	$92 000	
Quarterly Total Qualifying Purchases (excluding taxes)	$52 000	
HST Charged on Sales (15% × 41 000)	$6 150	
GST Charged on Sales (5% × 51 000)	2 550	
Total GST/HST collected		$8 700
Less: GST Paid on Purchase of books for resale (5% × 21 000)	1 050	
HST Paid on other Purchases (15% × 31 000)	4 650	
Total HST Credits		–5 700
HST Remittance		$3 000

NOTES
Instead of applying different tax rates, retailers who sell PST-exempt goods may also charge the full HST rate but provide an immediate point-of-sale rebate to the customer for the provincial portion. They will then claim an adjustment for the rebate amount on their HST return to reduce the amount remitted.

The net effect of the two methods is the same for the customer and for the merchant.

GST and Provincial (Retail) Sales Taxes

NOTES

If a business purchases inventory for resale but later uses the inventory within the business instead, it must remit PST on this internal transaction. The business has become the final consumer of the products.

NOTES

Services may be exempt or taxable for PST. PST is usually charged on services such as repairs that are applied to goods that are themselves taxable for PST.

Insurance, such as for home and automobile, is one of the few services that is taxable for PST and not for GST.

The rules governing provincial sales taxes vary from province to province in terms of the tax rate, the goods and services that are taxed and whether Provincial Sales Tax (PST) is applied to the GST as well as to the base purchase price (that is, whether GST is taxable). In May 2019, no provinces charged PST on GST. The following examples assume that the item sold has both GST and PST applied.

Although GST is applied at each level of sale and resale (including the stages of manufacturing), PST is a retail sales tax and, therefore, is paid only by the final consumer of a product or service. Therefore, it is sometimes referred to as a Retail Sales Tax by the provincial governments, and the terms RST and PST are equivalent. Thus, a business purchasing inventory to sell to customers will not pay PST on these purchases. When the same business buys supplies or services for its use in conducting business, it must pay PST because it has become the final consumer of these goods or services.

PST is applied only on sales within a province, not on sales to customers in a different province or in a different country. HST and GST do apply to interprovincial sales. If the consumer's province applies HST, the consumer pays HST on purchases from other provinces. All consumers in Canada pay GST.

Alberta, the Northwest Territories, Yukon and Nunavut

Alberta, the Northwest Territories, Yukon and Nunavut do not have Provincial Sales Taxes. Customers in these regions pay only the 5 percent GST on their purchases. Thus, the examples provided earlier without PST illustrate the application of GST for these regions.

NOTES

In 2013, three provinces changed their provincial tax system. Prince Edward Island adopted the Harmonized Sales Tax to replace the separate GST and PST. Quebec changed its taxation method so that the provincial sales tax was not calculated on the base price plus GST (QST is no longer charged on GST). British Columbia stopped using HST and began applying separate GST and PST.

PST in Manitoba, Saskatchewan, British Columbia and Quebec

These four provinces apply PST to the base price of the sale, the amount without GST included. In Manitoba and British Columbia, the retail sales tax rate is 8 percent; in Saskatchewan, the rate is 6 percent; in Quebec, the rate is 9.975 percent. The following example illustrates the application in Manitoba.

Manitoba business sold goods on account for $500. GST charged is 5% and PST charged is 8%.

GST = (0.05 × 500) = $25
PST in Manitoba = (0.08 × 500) = $40
Total amount of invoice = $500 + $25 + $40 = $565

Date	Particulars	Debit	Credit
02/15	Accounts Receivable	565.00	
	GST Charged on Sales		25.00
	PST Payable		40.00
	Revenue from Sales		500.00

The full amount of PST collected on sales is remitted to the provincial Minister of Finance (less any applicable sales tax compensation).

Part 2

Applications

CHAPTER THREE

Binh's Bins

OBJECTIVES

After completing this chapter, you should be able to

- ***access*** the data files for the business
- ***open*** the General Journal
- ***enter*** transactions in the General Journal
- ***edit*** and ***review*** General Journal transactions
- ***post*** transactions
- ***create*** new General Ledger accounts
- ***adjust*** journal entries after posting
- ***display*** and ***print*** General Ledger and General Journal reports
- ***display*** and ***print*** comparative financial reports
- ***customize*** reports
- ***back up*** your data files
- ***advance*** the session date
- ***finish*** an accounting session

COMPANY INFORMATION

Company Profile

Binh's Bins is owned and operated by Binh Than in Red Deer, Alberta. Binh established his business shortly after settling in Canada with his family from Vietnam 10 years ago. Relying on his previous business experience and his observation that the Red Deer community was growing rapidly with both new construction and redevelopment, he started his dumpster business. He currently rents a large lot for storing his bins and trucks and shares office space with other small businesses to reduce his overhead costs. Starting alone, with one truck and a few different-sized dumpsters, he delivered dumpsters and dropped off the waste materials. He encouraged his customers to separate the waste products for more ethical disposal and to reduce costs. Now, with the two drivers he hired, he manages three trucks and many bins in various sizes. Binh still operates one of the trucks himself. A part-time assistant handles the scheduling and dispatching along with some bookkeeping duties, but payroll is managed by his local bank.

NOTES
Binh's Bins
672 Alleyway Drive
Red Deer, AB T4R 2T4
Tel 1: (403) 763-4127
Tel 2: (800) 455-4127
Fax: (403) 765-4842
Business No.: 743 647 398

Most of Binh's revenue comes from homes and businesses undergoing renovations. Some of these jobs are arranged by the owners, and some by their contractors.

Some of his customers have set up accounts with Binh's Bins, and he has accounts with his regular vendors and suppliers.

To convert his accounting records to Sage 50 in June, he has used the following:

- Chart of Accounts
- Trial Balance
- Accounting Procedures

CHART OF POSTABLE ACCOUNTS

BINH'S BINS

ASSETS
1080 Chequing Account
1200 A/R - Ontime Contracting
1220 A/R - Piper Creek Mall
1240 A/R - Redbird Brothers
1320 Prepaid Insurance
1340 Prepaid Rent
1360 Supplies
1520 Computers and Software
1540 Tools
1560 Dumpsters ▶
▶1580 Trucks

LIABILITIES
2100 A/P - Badlands Hardware
2120 A/P - Hoodoos Containers
2180 A/P - Red Deer Promotions
2650 GST Charged on Services
2670 GST Paid on Purchases

EQUITY
3100 Binh's Bins, Capital ▶
▶3150 Binh's Bins, Drawings
3600 Net Income

REVENUE
4100 Revenue from Dumpster Rentals
4150 Revenue from Subcontracting
4200 Interest Revenue ▶

▶EXPENSE
5020 Advertising & Promotion
5040 Bank Charges
5060 Insurance Expense
5080 Interest Expense
5100 Maintenance & Repairs
5110 Supplies Used
5120 Rental Expenses
5140 Phone/Internet Expenses
5150 Truck Expenses
5160 Wages Expenses

NOTES: The Chart of Accounts includes only postable accounts and the Net Income or Current Earnings account. Sage 50 uses the Net Income account for the Income Statement to calculate the difference between revenue and expenses before closing the books.

TRIAL BALANCE

BINH'S BINS

June 1, 2021		Debits	Credits
1080	Chequing Account	$ 64 360	
1200	A/R - Ontime Contracting	2 730	
1240	A/R - Redbird Brothers	5 880	
1320	Prepaid Insurance	7 000	
1340	Prepaid Rent	3 600	
1360	Supplies	580	
1520	Computers and Software	4 200	
1540	Tools	890	
1560	Dumpsters	53 180	
1580	Trucks	418 320	
2180	A/P - Red Deer Promotions		2 940
2650	GST Charged on Services		5 150
2670	GST Paid on Purchases	2 120	
3100	Binh's Bins, Capital		524 340
3150	Binh's Bins, Drawings	6 500	
4100	Revenue from Dumpster Rentals		75 000
4150	Revenue from Subcontracting		38 000
5020	Advertising & Promotion	2 730	
5040	Bank Charges	900	
5060	Insurance Expense	5 000	
5100	Maintenance & Repairs	3 680	
5110	Supplies Used	360	
5120	Rental Expenses	9 000	
5140	Phone/Internet Expenses	1 900	
5160	Wages Expenses	52 500	
		$645 430	$645 430

Accounting Procedures

GST

NOTES
Most bank and financial institution services used in this text are exempt from GST charges.
Alberta does not levy a provincial sales tax.

Binh's Bins has chosen the regular method for remittance of the Goods and Services Tax (GST). Binh records the GST collected from customers as a liability (credit) in the *GST Charged on Services* account. He records GST that he pays to vendors in the *GST Paid on Purchases* account as a decrease (debit) to his liability to the Canada Revenue Agency. His GST remittance or refund is calculated automatically in the *GST Owing (Refund)* subtotal. These accounts are included in the display or printout of the Balance Sheet. Binh's Bins files GST remittances or requests for refunds with the Receiver General for Canada on the last day of each fiscal quarter. (For details, please read Chapter 2 on the Goods and Services Tax.)

INSTRUCTIONS

NOTES
In these instructions, our starting point for opening the file is the Start file in Chapter 1 as the last company you worked on.
For detailed instructions on restoring data files, refer to Chapter 1, page 25.

1. **Open** or **restore** the **data for Binh's Bins**. Keystroke instructions begin below.
2. **Enter** the **source documents for June** in the General Journal in Sage 50 using the Chart of Accounts and Trial Balance for Binh's Bins. The procedures for entering each new type of transaction for this application are outlined step by step in the Keystrokes section with the source documents. These transactions have a ✓ in the completion check box beside the source document. The source documents are numbered — the number is placed below or in the lower part of the check box.
3. **Print** the **reports** on the following form after you have completed your entries. Information on reports begins on page 55.

REPORTS

Accounts
- ☐ Chart of Accounts
- ☐ Account List
- ☑ General Journal Entries: Jun 1 to Jun 30

Financials
- ☑ Comparative Balance Sheet dates: Jun 1 and Jun 30 with difference in percentage
- ☑ Trial Balance date: Jun 30
- ☑ Income Statement from Jan 1 to Jun 30
- ☑ General Ledger accounts: 1080 2650 3100 4100 from Jun 1 to Jun 30

KEYSTROKES

NOTES
To start from the backup file, click Restore From Backup on the Welcome Getting Started screen.
Click OK and click Next. Click Browse and locate the folder C:\SageData19 where you installed the data. Double-click SageData19. Click BINS1.CAB or BINS1 to select the file you need. Click Open. Click Next and confirm the details. Click Next.
Type C:\SageData19\BINS\BINS in the Name field if this is not the default entry. Click Next and click Yes to confirm the creation of the new folder and file.
Click Finish and wait for the session date to appear.

Opening Data Files

Double-click the **Sage 50 desktop shortcut** or the Sage 50 shortcut on the Windows Start page.

Click **Select An Existing Company** and **click OK**.

Locate the folder **C:\SageData19** where you installed the data.

Double-click the **SageData19 folder** to open it.

Double-click the **BINS folder** to open it.

Click **BINS** or **BINS.SAI** to select the file you need. **Click Open**.

Refer to Chapter 1, page 8, for detailed instructions on opening data files, or to page 25 if you are restoring a backup.

The next screen asks (prompts) you to enter the session date for this work session:

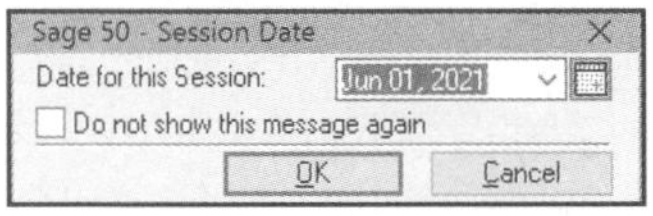

The date format on your screen is controlled by the Date Format Settings options in Sage 50, not by the format you use to enter the date. (Refer to page 22.)

The **session date** is the date of your work session — the date on which you are recording the accounting transactions on the computer. A business with a large number of transactions may record these transactions at the end of each day. One with fewer transactions may enter them once a week. In this workbook, transactions are entered once a week for most applications, so we update the session date one week at a time. The session date may or may not be the same as the date on which the transaction actually took place.

The session date for your first session is June 7, 2021. Since this is not the default on the screen, you must change the date. Every date field has a Calendar icon.

Click the **Calendar icon** to open the calendar:

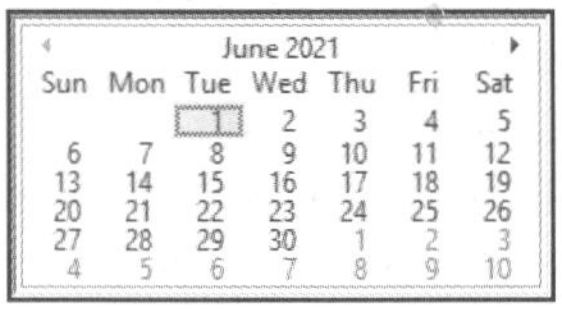

The calendar has the current session date highlighted with a blue background. The calendar for any date field also has the range of dates that will be accepted based on the settings chosen for the company files. The arrows allow you to move forward to a later month or back to a previous month. The calendar stops at the dates that indicate the range you may use. Click a date on the calendar to enter it or use one of the following alternative formats. For consistency, we use the same order of month, day and year throughout the text. Entering the year is optional in most date fields.

- use different characters to separate numbers: 06-07-21 or 06/07/21
- omit leading zeros or the year: 6/7/21 or 6-7
- leave spaces between numbers instead of separating characters: 06 07 21 or 6 7
- type lower or upper case text: june 7, 2021 or JUNE 7, 2021
- use three-letter abbreviations for the month: Jun 7 -21 or Jun 7 21
- use three-letter abbreviations for the month with the day first: 7 jun or 7Jun
- other non-alpha or non-numeric separating characters can also be used: 06&07 or 6*7
- in most date windows, you can omit the year

We will use a variety of date formats throughout this workbook, but we always use the text format for dates on-screen to minimize entering incorrect dates. Using the calendar to choose a date or using a text version to enter a date will prevent an incorrect date entry.

Click **7** on the June date calendar or

Type `jun 7` or `7jun`

Click **OK**.

NOTES
Many screens include a Cancel button. If you click Cancel, you will return to your previous screen without entering any changes.

NOTES
When you click the dimmed back arrow in the date calendar, nothing happens because the earliest date you can use for Binh's Bins is June 1.

NOTES
When you enter the date as text, the date is not ambiguous, so you can enter the day first. Similarly, you do not need to leave a space between the month and day because there is no ambiguity.

NOTES
Refer to Chapter 1, page 22, and Chapter 4, page 80, for instructions on changing date format settings.

NOTES
Keystrokes that you must follow have command statements like:

Type `jun 7` or
Click **OK**

Instruction lines are indented; command words are in **boldface**; text you type uses a special font (`Courier`); and things that you must click on or select are in **colour and bold**. This format makes it easy to find the instruction statements in the text.

PRO VERSION

The program name will be Sage 50 Pro Accounting. The status bar will not include the single-user status. The Pro version is a single-user program.

CLASSIC VIEW

The Classic view Home window includes an icon for the Reconciliation and Deposits Journal. In the Enhanced view, Banking is listed as a separate module and the Reconciliation and Deposits Journal is accessed from it.

NOTES

Remember that you can maximize the Home window. Refer to Chapter 1 for a more detailed description of the Home window.

NOTES

Although the Banking module is not used, it cannot be hidden if you want to use the General Journal.

NOTES

The Daily Business Manager is used in Chapter 11. The Learning Centre was introduced in Chapter 1. The Accountant's Copy is covered in Chapter 12.

The Company module Home window opens:

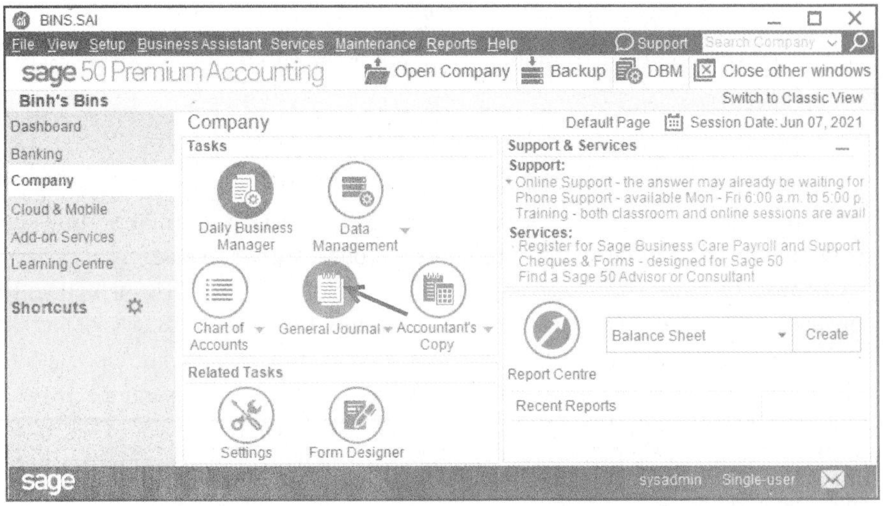

For Binh's Bins, the Company module is the default page. Only the General Ledger and Journal can be accessed for this file. When ledger icons are hidden, all main menu options related to those ledgers are also hidden or unavailable. (Click ☐ to maximize the window if necessary.) The Home window has the title bar on top with the file name, control menu icon and size buttons; the main menu bar comes next with the Chat With Support tool (Help menu) and Search function and tool (Edit menu) on the far right. The tool bar follows with the program name and tool buttons that permit quick access to commonly used menu items. The Home window tools (with their alternative pull-down menu locations) include Open Company and Backup (File menu), DBM — Daily Business Manager — (Business Assistant menu) and Close Other Windows (View menu).

The major part of the window is divided into three columns of panes or sections — the **Modules** and **Shortcuts** panes on the left; **Tasks** in the middle with Ledger and Journal icons and **Related Tasks**; and the **Support** and **Reports** panes on the right. Instead of ledgers in the upper Tasks pane, the Company window has access to the **Daily Business Manager** and **Data Management** tasks, such as backing up files, restoring files and checking for database errors. For the Company module, the upper right pane has access to support services for Sage 50. For other modules, this pane lists the ledger accounts. The session date and the change date Calendar icon are located above the Support pane.

Below these panes is the status bar with the user name (sysadmin) and status (Single-user) and message icon. In most windows, the status bar describes the purpose of the field or icon that has the pointer on it.

Entering General Journal Transactions

All transactions for Binh's Bins are entered from the General Journal icon in the Tasks pane:

Click the **General Journal icon** in the Tasks pane of the Company module Home window to open the General Journal.

The General Journal input form opens on your screen:

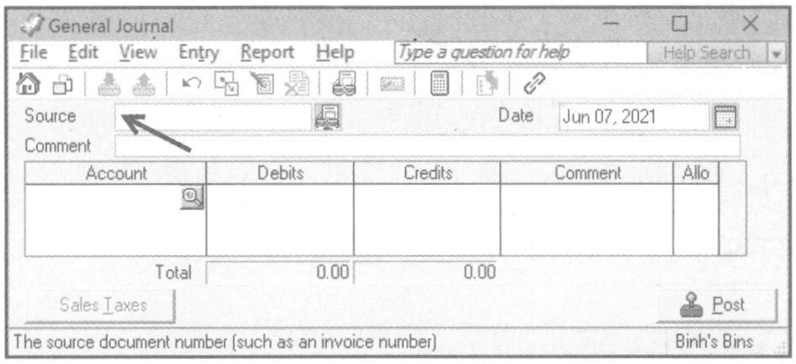

You are now ready to enter the first transaction in the General Journal input screen.

✓ 1

Purchase Invoice #BH-5621 **Dated June 2, 2021**

From Badlands Hardware, $155 plus $7.75 GST paid for paint and stencils to add logos to dumpsters. Purchase invoice total $162.75. Terms: net 20 days.

The cursor, a flashing vertical line, is blinking in the Source field, ready to receive information — up to 20 characters, including spaces. The Source field identifies the reference document from which you obtain the information for a transaction, in this case the invoice number. The status bar indicates the purpose of the Source field.

Type BH-5621

Press tab to advance to the Look Up Entry icon. **Press** tab again.

The cursor advances to the next field, the Date field. You should enter the transaction date here. The program enters the session date by default. It is highlighted, ready to be accepted or changed. Because the work was completed on June 2, 2021, the session date of June 7 is incorrect and must be changed.

Type 06-02

Press tab to move to the Calendar icon.

The text form of the date is displayed, even though we entered the date as numbers. The year is added to the date.

If you click the Calendar icon in the Date field now, the session date is on a white background with a frame around it. The current transaction date has a solid blue background.

Press tab again to accept the date and advance to the Comment field.

In the Comment field, you should enter a description of the transaction to make the permanent record more meaningful. You may enter up to 85 characters, including spaces.

Type Badlands Hardware **Press** tab.

The cursor moves forward to the first line of the Account field, creating a dotted box for the first account.

Sage 50 organizes accounts into financial statement sections or categories using the following boundaries for numbering:

- 1000–1999 Assets
- 2000–2999 Liabilities
- 3000–3999 Equity
- 4000–4999 Revenue
- 5000–5999 Expense

This system makes it easy to remember the first digit of an account. Double-clicking the Account field will display the list of accounts. If you type the first digit of an account

NOTES

The Refresh tool applies to multi-user use of the program, so it is dimmed for the single-user examples we have. This feature is not available in the Pro version.

NOTES

A check box with a ✓ indicates that keystroke instructions are provided for this source document.

The lower part of the check box contains the source document number (**1**).

NOTES

Use the bookmark attached to the back cover to mark the page with the source document.

WARNING!

Unless you change the date, the session date will become the posting date for the entry.

Remember that you can use any date format listed on page 39 and you may also omit the year.

NOTES

When you press tab after typing a date in the Date field, you will advance to the Calendar icon. You must press tab again to advance to the next input field. That is, you must press tab twice. If you choose a date from the calendar, pressing tab once will move the cursor to the next input field.

NOTES

Although Sage 50 allows you to use more than four digits for account numbers in the Premium version, we will use only four-digit numbers for the applications in Part Two of the text. This allows Pro and Premium version users to use the same account numbers.

number and then double-click or press (enter) while the cursor is flashing in any Account field, the program will advance the list to accounts beginning with that digit.

Click the **List icon**, or **double-click** the dotted box in the **Account column** to list the accounts.

The list of accounts appears on your journal screen:

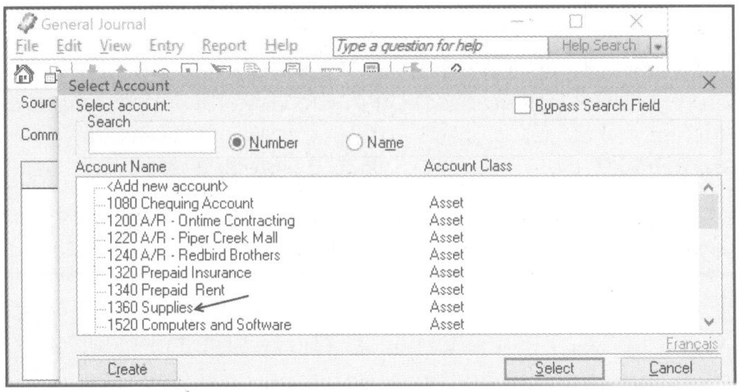

The beginning of the account list is displayed. The list includes only postable accounts — those that can be debited or credited in journal entries. The cursor is in the Search field. If you want to place the cursor in the account list directly from the Account field, you can choose the **Bypass Search Field** option. We will not select this option. Typing a number in the Search field selects the first account with that number. Following usual accounting practice, we enter the account to be debited first.

Click **1360 Supplies** to select this asset account.

Click the **Select button**. (A selected button has a darker frame or an inner dotted box.)

You can also double-click a selected account or press (enter) to add it directly to your journal entry form. Instead of using the selection list, you can find the number in the Chart of Accounts, type it in and press (tab).

Because the account number and name have been added to your input form, you can easily determine whether you have selected the correct account. If the screen does not display the entire account title, you can display the rest of the account title by clicking anywhere on the part that is showing, or you can maximize the journal window.

Your cursor is now positioned in the Debits field. The amount 0.00 is entered and selected, ready to be changed. All journals include a **Windows Calculator tool** that opens the calculator directly for easy calculation of amounts, if needed.

Click the Display The Windows Calculator tool to open the calculator. You can leave it open in the background for easy access.

Type amounts without dollar signs. You do not need to type decimals when you enter whole numbers. Sage 50 ignores any non-numeric characters that you type in an amount field.

Type `155`

Press (tab).

The cursor moves to the Comment field. You can add a comment for each account line in the journal. Account line comments are optional. You can add a comment for each line, for some lines or for none of the lines, but the extra details will be included in the journal report and will give you more information about the transaction.

Type `paint & stencils`

NOTES
Many fields that allow you to select an account or other information from a list have the Select or List icon to provide quick access to the list. Showing the List icon is an option that you select as a user preference setting.
Other fields have list arrows that provide a drop-down or pop-up list.

NOTES
If the cursor is in the Account field, you can also press (enter) to open the Select Account list.

NOTES
Command statements that are indented but do not have the boldfaced command words provide alternative keystrokes or optional instructions.
"You can also double-click..." is an example of an alternative command statement.

NOTES
You can also open the Windows Calculator from the View menu by clicking Show Calculator.

Press *tab*. Your input form is partially completed:

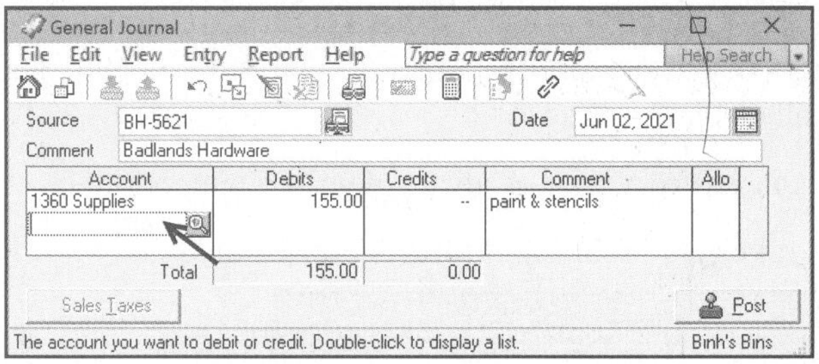

The cursor has advanced to the next line of the Account field, creating a dotted box and List icon for the next account for this transaction — the liability account *GST Paid on Purchases*. Remember, liability accounts start with 2. However, we will type 3 to include the end of the 2000-level accounts in the selection list.

Type 3

Click the **List icon** to advance your list to the 3000 accounts:

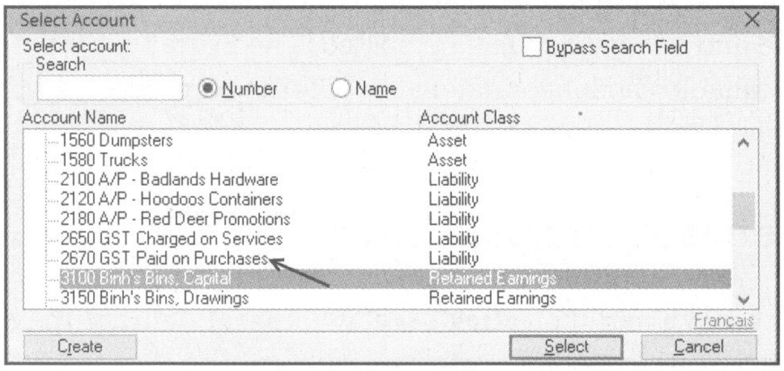

We have bypassed the Search field and selected the first account with the number we typed. This method quickly moves you to a later position in the list.

Click **2670 GST Paid on Purchases** from the displayed list to highlight it. If necessary, click a scroll arrow (▼ or ▲) to move through the account list to include *2670* in the display.

Press *enter*.

Again, the account number and name have been added to your transaction form. The cursor has advanced to the Credits field, which has 155.00 as the default amount because this amount will balance the entry. The amount is highlighted to indicate that you may edit it. This is a compound entry. You must change the amount to separate the GST, and you must delete the credit entry because the GST account is debited.

Press *del* to delete the credit entry.

Click the **Debits field** on the second journal line below 155.00 to move the cursor.

Type `7.75`

Press *tab* to advance to the optional Comment field.

Type `GST @ 5%`

Press *tab*. The cursor moves to the next line in the Account field.

Press *enter* to open the Select Account list. The cursor is in the Search field.

Type 2

The list advances to the 2000 accounts. The liability account *2100 A/P - Badlands Hardware*, the account we need, is selected because it is the first 2000-level account.

NOTES

If you know that the account you need is closer to the end of its numbered section, typing the next higher number takes you to the end of the section you want. For example, typing 3 advances to 3100 and includes 2670 in the display. In this way, your account is more likely to be included in the display. Typing 2 will open the list with 2100 at the end and you will have to scroll down to find 2670.

NOTES

Typing a negative number (adding a minus sign) in the Credits field will move the number to the Debits field. Typing a negative number in the Debits field will create a Credit entry.

Click **Select** to enter it and return to the journal.

The cursor advances to the Credits field again, where 162.75, the amount that will now balance the entry, is added. The amount is correct, so you can accept it. The total for the Credits column is still displayed as zero.

Press tab to update the totals and advance to the Comment field.

Type `terms: net 20` Your input form is now completed:

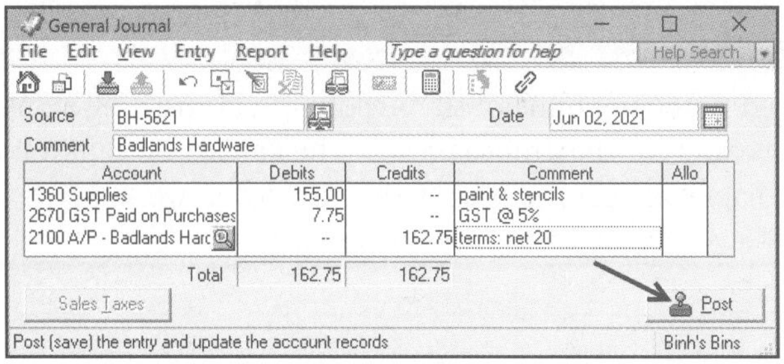

Until the debits and credits of a transaction are equal, you cannot post an entry. Once the entry is complete and balanced, it can be posted. The **Store** tool, for recurring entries, is also available (no longer dimmed). Before you proceed either to store or to post an entry, you should review the transaction.

> **NOTES**
> The Sales Taxes button will be covered in Chapter 5. Sales taxes are not set up for Binh's Bins, so the button remains dimmed.

> **NOTES**
> We will use the Store tool and the Sales Taxes button in the Groen Fields application (Chapter 5).

Reviewing the General Journal Entry

Choose the **Report menu** and then **click Display General Journal Entry**:

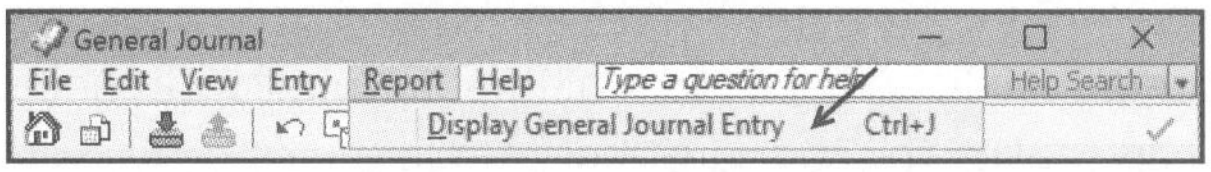

The journal entry that will be posted for the transaction is displayed:

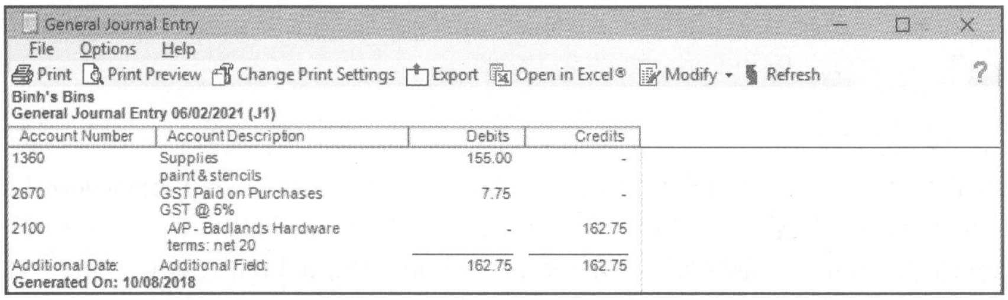

> **NOTES**
> Pressing ctrl + J will also display the journal entry in any journal. Refer to Appendix B for a list of Sage 50 keyboard shortcuts.

> **NOTES**
> If your display includes scroll arrows, you can use them to include more of your transaction.
> We use the short date format as the default for dates in reports, but we use the same order: month, day, year.

Click the **Maximize button** to change your display to full screen size if your transaction does not fit in your display window.

To return to your input form,

Click ☒ or **choose** the displayed entry's **Control Menu icon** and **click Close**.

> **NOTES**
> The Additional Date and Additional Field can be used to add more information to a journal entry. The Additional Information feature is available in all journals and will be introduced in Chapter 11.

> **NOTES**
> Refer to page 47 for assistance with correcting errors after posting.

CORRECTING THE GENERAL JOURNAL ENTRY BEFORE POSTING

Press tab to advance to the field that has the error. To move to a previous field, **press** shift and tab together (that is, while holding down shift, **press** tab). The field will be highlighted, ready for editing. **Type** the **correct information** and **press** tab to enter it.

You can also use the mouse to **point** to a field and **drag through** the **incorrect information** to highlight it. You can highlight a single number or letter or the entire field. **Type** the **correct information** and **press** tab to enter it.

continued...

CORRECTING THE GENERAL JOURNAL ENTRY BEFORE POSTING (CONTINUED)

To correct an account number, **click** the **incorrect account number** (or **name**) to select the field. **Press** enter to display the list of accounts. **Click** the **correct account**. **Click Select**. **Press** tab to advance the cursor and enter the correction.

Click an **incorrect amount** to highlight it. **Type** the **correct amount** and **press** tab.

You can insert a line or remove a line by clicking the line that will be moved down or removed. Then **choose** the **Edit menu** and **click Insert Line** or **Remove Line**.

To discard the entry and begin again, **click** [X] to close the journal or **click** the **Undo tool** to open a blank journal window. When Sage 50 asks whether you want to discard the entry, **click Yes** to confirm your decision.

Posting

Once you are sure that all the information is correct, you are ready to post the entry.

Click the **Post button** [Post] in the lower right-hand corner of the General Journal (the one that looks like a stamp) or **choose** the **Entry menu** and then **click Post**.

WARNING!
Don't post the transaction until you make sure that it is correct. Always review a transaction before posting it.

We have chosen the option to confirm when a transaction is posted successfully, so a confirmation message will open each time you post or record a transaction:

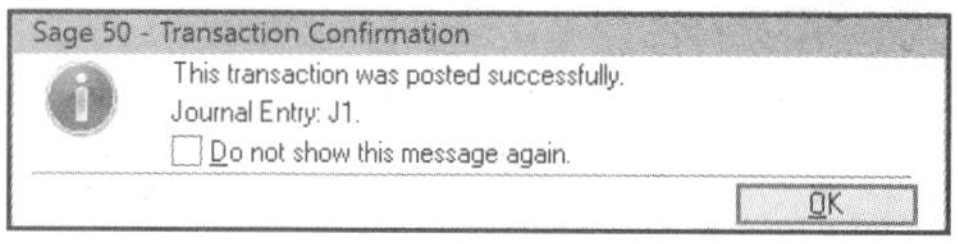

NOTES
This confirmation does not mean that you have entered the correct details, only that the entry could be posted – debits and credits were equal and data for required fields (Source and Date) were included.

Click **OK** to open a new blank General Journal input form.

You can now enter the next transaction for this session date.

Adding a New Account

The bank credit memo on June 3 requires an account that is not listed in your Chart of Accounts. Often a company will need to create new accounts as it expands or changes direction. These future needs are not always foreseen when the accounts are first set up. You must add the account *2250 Bank Loan* to enter the bank credit memo transaction.

NOTES
You can add new accounts from the Account field in any journal, from the Accounts window or any General Ledger window. The General Ledger and Accounts windows are introduced in Chapter 4.

✓ 2 **Bank Credit Memo #RDT-C4778** **Dated June 3, 2021**

From Red Deer Trust, $40 000 bank loan secured for purchase of additional large dumpster bins. Loan deposited into bank account. Create new Group account 2250 Bank Loan.

First, enter the Source for the memo.

Type RDT-C4778

Press tab **twice** to advance to the Date field. The date of the previous journal entry becomes the default date until you close the journal.

NOTES
When you close the journal and open it later, the session date becomes the default again.

Click the **Calendar icon** and then **click 3**.

Press tab to advance to the Comment field.

Type Red Deer Trust - new loan

Press tab and **double-click** the **Account field**.

Double-click **Chequing Account**.

Type 40000 (the amount of the loan) as the debit part of the transaction.

Press *tab* to advance to the Comment field for the account.

Type loan for extra bins

Press *tab* to advance to the Account field on the second journal line.

Click the **List icon** or **press** *enter* to open the Select Account list.

Click **Add New Account**, the first entry in the list, and **click Select** or **click** the **Create** button below the list of accounts.

This will begin the wizard for adding a General Ledger account:

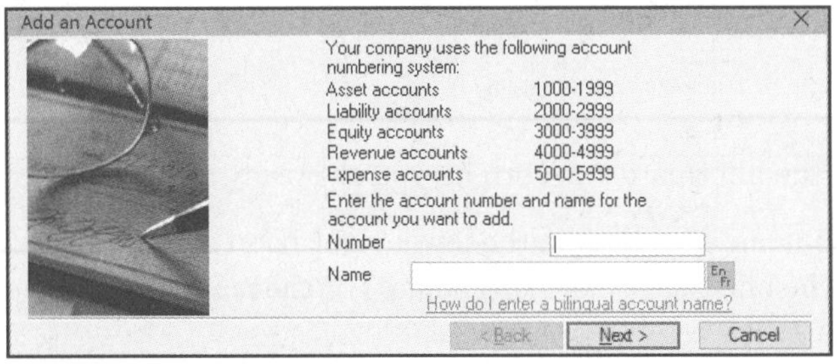

WARNING!
Enter account numbers carefully. You cannot change them after you post to the account in a journal entry.

The first screen prompts you for the account number and name. The cursor is in the Number field.

Type 2250 **Press** *tab*.

Type Bank Loan

Click **Next** or **press** *enter* to continue.

The next screen asks for the **GIFI code**. This is the four-digit account number assigned by the Canada Revenue Agency for this category of account to use in electronically filed business returns. GIFI codes are not used in this workbook. They are described in Appendix K.

NOTES
Next is selected, so you can press *enter* repeatedly to advance through the wizard screens that you do not need to change.

Click **Next** to skip this screen and continue.

The next screen asks whether this account is to be used as a **Heading** or **Total** in the financial statements. *Bank Loan* is an ordinary postable account that has a balance, so the default selection, No, is correct. A partial Balance Sheet illustrates account types.

Click **Next** to accept the default and continue.

The following screen deals with another aspect of the **account type**. Accounts may be **subtotalled** within their group of accounts. For example, if you have several bank accounts, you will want your Balance Sheet report to include the total cash deposited in all of them together. Different account types will be explained fully in the Love It Again application (Chapter 4), where you will set up the accounting records for a new company. For Binh's Bins, the two GST accounts are subtotalled.

Bank Loan is a Group account. It is not subtotalled with any other account, so the default selection, No, is correct.

WARNING!
Account types must be set correctly or you will get the error message that accounts are not in logical order when you try to display financial reports. If one of these messages opens, you can edit the account type. Refer to Chapter 4, page 89, for help with creating and editing accounts.

Click **Next** to continue.

The next wizard screen refers to the **account class**. Account classes are explained in Chapter 7. The default selection is the name of the section. Therefore, for account *2250*, Liability is the section and the default class. Generally, you can accept the default selection.

Click **Next** to continue.

Now you are being asked whether you want to **allocate** the balance of the account to different projects or divisions. Projects are not set up for Binh's Bins, so the default selection, set at No for Balance Sheet accounts, is correct.

Click **Next** to continue.

The next setting screen asks whether you want to include or **omit** this account **from financial statements** when it has a zero balance. Choosing Yes means that if the balance in this account is zero, the account will not be included in your financial statements. If you choose No, the account will be printed even if it has a balance of zero. Some accounts, such as *Chequing Account*, should always be printed in financial statements. In Chapter 4 we explain this setting. The default setting, to include accounts (not to omit), is never wrong.

Click **Next** to continue to the final screen with the selections you have made:

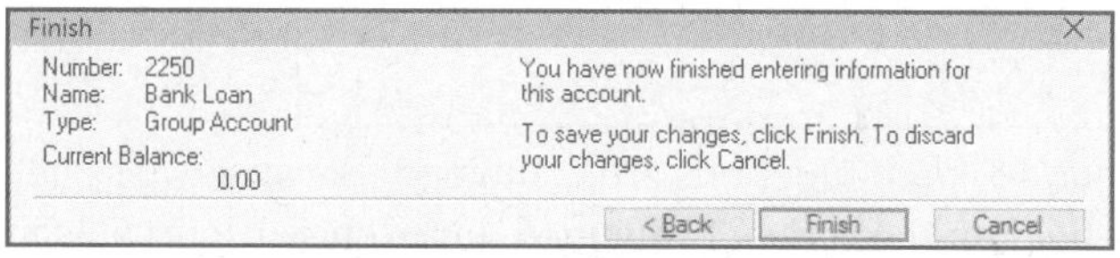
Finish
Number: 2250
Name: Bank Loan
Type: Group Account
Current Balance:
0.00
You have now finished entering information for this account.
To save your changes, click Finish. To discard your changes, click Cancel.
< Back
Finish
Cancel

Check your **work**. If you need to make corrections, **click Back** until you reach the screen with the error. **Make** the **correction** and **click Next** until you reach this final screen again.

When all the information is correct, you must save the new account information.

Click **Finish**.

You will return to the General Journal window with the new account added to the Account field. The cursor has not yet advanced, so you can change your account selection if you need to.

Click the **Credits field**. The balancing amount, $40 000, is added.

Press tab to accept the amount and advance to the Comment field.

Type `Red Deer Trust loan`

Display the **journal entry** to verify whether it is correct.

Close the **display**. **Make corrections** if you find errors.

Click **Post** Post to save the information. **Click OK** to confirm.

Enter the **next sale transaction** on your own.

3 **Purchase Invoice #HC-7655** **Dated June 3, 2021**

From Hoodoos Containers, $35 550 plus $1 777.50 GST to purchase additional dumpsters. Purchase invoice total $37 327.50. Terms: net 30 days.

Adjusting a Posted Entry

Sometimes after posting a journal entry you discover that it had an error. You can make corrections directly in the General Journal by adjusting the previously posted entry. Sage 50 allows you to make the correction by adjusting the entry without completing a reversing entry. The program creates the reversing and correcting journal entries when you post the correction so that the audit trail is complete. The purchase from Badlands Hardware on June 2 was posted with an incorrect amount. The General Journal should still be open.

NOTES
For Binh's Bins, the title for Projects is changed to Job Sites.

NOTES
Some reports have omitting accounts with zero balances as a report option.

NOTES
You can use the wizard in any Account field to create a new account at any time. You do not need to use the account after creating it when you return to the journal.

NOTES
3 A check box without a ✓ indicates that keystroke instructions are not provided for this source document.

The lower part of the check box contains the source document number (**3**).

✓ 4

Memo #1 **Dated June 4, 2021**

From Owner: The invoice from Badlands Hardware was entered incorrectly. The cost of the supplies was $170 plus $8.50 GST paid. The revised purchase invoice total is $178.50. Adjust the posted invoice to make the correction.

Click the **Adjust A Previously Posted Entry tool** in the tool bar, or

Choose the **Entry menu** and **click Adjusting Entry**.

The Search screen opens:

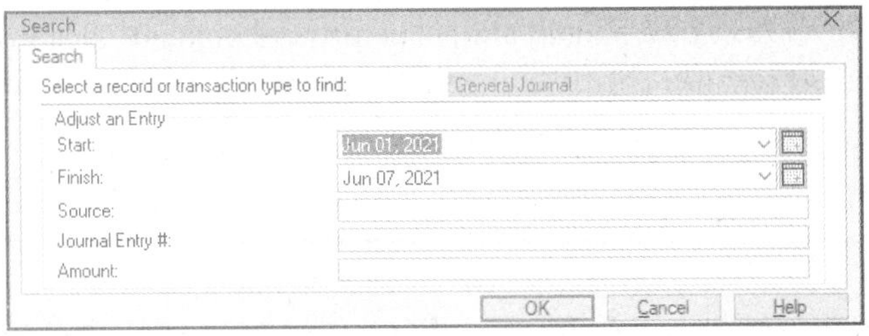

The Adjust An Entry and Search functions are combined. Because we selected the Adjust option, the Select field on the screen is dimmed, but General Journal is indicated as the search area. You can select a range of journal entry dates to search. The date we converted the data files to Sage 50 and the session date are the default start and finish dates for the list. If you know the source, journal entry number or amount, you can enter it in the Source, Journal Entry # or Amount field, respectively, and access the transaction entry directly by clicking OK. You must enter the exact source, journal entry number or amount for these searches (e.g., entering 162.75 in the Amount field).

We can accept the default dates because they include the transaction we need.

Click **OK** to list the journal entries:

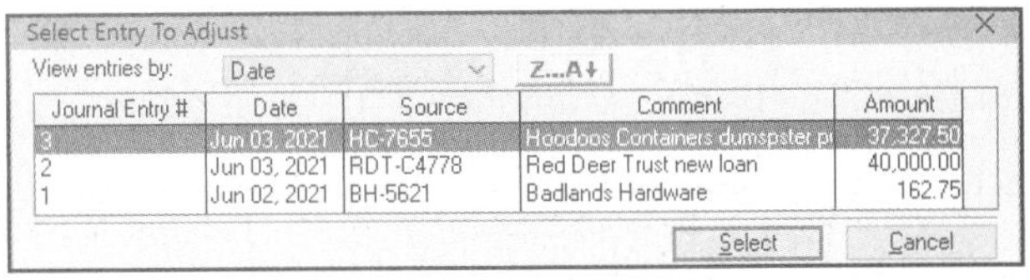

All journal entries are listed, with the most recent one at the top of the list (Z...A+ order for Date). You can choose the way the journal entries are sorted.

Click the **list arrow** beside the Date entry for **View Entries By**:

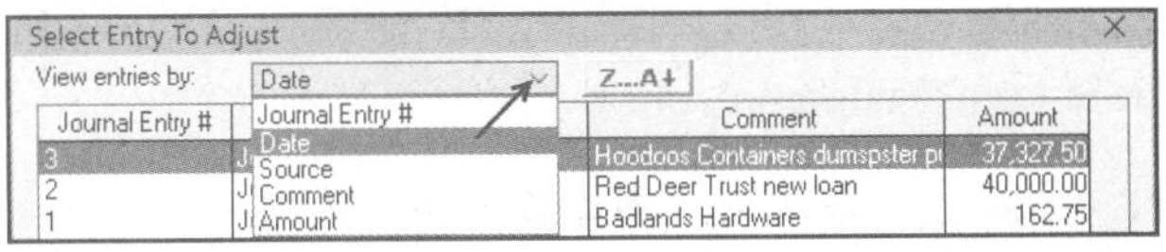

You can organize the list of entries by journal entry number, date, source number, comment or amount. The Z...A+ button lets you choose ascending or descending order.

Click **Journal Entry #**.

Click Z...A+ to reverse the order. The one we want is now first in the list and the button label has changed to A...Z+.

Click **Journal Entry #1, BH-5621** to select it.

Click **Select** or **double-click** to open the journal entry as it was posted:

NOTES

Pressing ctrl + A will also start the adjust entry process in any journal when the option is available.

NOTES

You should choose the order that makes it easiest to find your entry. That will depend on what information you entered and what you remember as well as how many entries you have.

NOTES

Although Journal Entry #1 is highlighted, the cursor is still on the A...Z+ button, so pressing enter does not open the journal because of the keystroke sequence we used.

You can also double-click anywhere on the line for an entry to open the transaction.

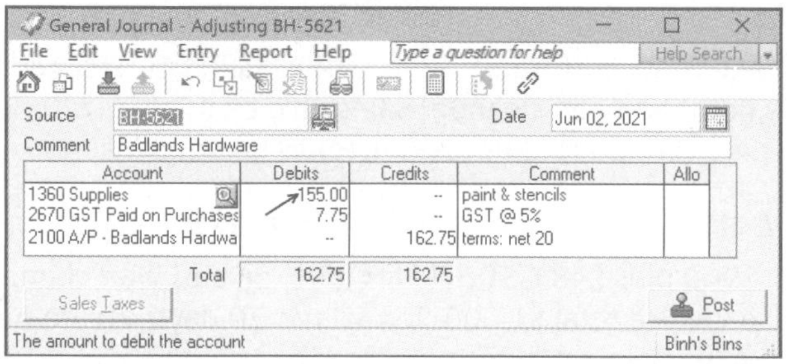

All fields may now be edited, just as if you had not yet posted the transaction. The title bar entry has changed to General Journal – Adjusting BH-5621.

Click **155.00**, the amount in the Debit column for *Supplies*, to select it for editing.

Type 170

Click **7.75** or **press** ↓ to select the Debit column amount for *GST Paid on Purchases*.

Type 8.5

Click **162.50**, the Credit column amount for *A/P - Badlands Hardware*.

Type 178.50 **Press** tab to update the totals with the correct amounts.

We will also modify the source to differentiate this correct entry from the original.

Click the **Source field** before the current entry (**before B**). **Type** (COR)

We will not change the date for this correction because the date affects the payment due date and the original date was correct.

Review the **entry** to display the correct transaction and **close** the **display**. **Make corrections** if necessary.

Click **Post** Post. **Click OK** to confirm the posting. The entry is J5. (J4 is the reversing entry created by the program.)

When you display the General Journal Report with Corrections selected (refer to page 63), the three entries for the purchase invoice — the original incorrect entry, a reversing adjusting entry created by the program (ADJBH-5621) and the correct entry (COR) BH-5621 — are included, providing a complete audit trail for the transaction and correction. Refer to the partial General Journal Report displayed on page 64.

NOTES
Usually clicking a number in a field will select the entire number. Sometimes, however, depending on exactly where you click, only part of the number is selected or an insertion point is added. Double-clicking will always select the entire number in the field so that you can edit it.

WARNING!
You can change the date for the final correct entry but not for the adjusting or reversing entry.
Dates should be changed only when they were incorrect because they affect the terms for sales and purchases.

REVERSING A GENERAL JOURNAL ENTRY AFTER POSTING

If you need to reverse an entry instead of making changes to it, **click** the **Reverse Entry tool** in the tool bar of the General Journal – Adjusting window, or **choose** the **Entry menu** and **click Reverse Entry**. You must confirm your decision before the action is taken. **Click Yes** to confirm and continue. Sage 50 does not delete the original entry. Instead it adds the reversing entry to the journal report for a complete audit trail. You can hide reversing entries in journal reports by not showing corrections.

Continue with the **journal entries** for the June 7 session date.

5 **Payment Cheque #488** **Dated June 5, 2021**
To Red Deer Promotions, $2 940 in payment of invoice #RDP-8668.

6 **Receipt #120** **Dated June 5, 2021**
From Redbird Brothers, cheque #98 for $5 880 in payment of invoice #BB-351.

NOTES
If you use Cheque #*xx* as the source for cheques, you can apply the report filter we describe in Appendix E.

NOTES
If you use BB-xx as the source for sales, you can apply the report filter we describe in Appendix E.

7

Sales Invoice #BB-363 **Dated June 6, 2021**

To Watershed Insurance (new customer), $6 400 plus $320 GST charged for dumpster rentals for flood damage cleanup. Sales invoice total $6 720. Terms: net 20 days. Create new Group account 1260 A/R - Watershed Insurance.

8

Purchase Invoice #SM-6111 **Dated June 6, 2021**

From Sylvan Motors, $960 plus $48 GST paid for lube, oil and filter changes for three trucks. Purchase invoice total $1 008. Terms: net 30 days. Create new Group account 2200 A/P - Sylvan Motors.

Advancing the Session Date and Backing Up Files

NOTES
We have set up the data files for Binh's Bins so that future-dated transactions are not allowed.

NOTES
Refer to page 24 for information on the Save As and Save A Copy commands.
A complete data set is about 100 Megabytes in size, while its backup file is around 4 Megabytes. The Save As and Save A Copy options require more disk storage space because the copy is not compressed.

When you have finished all the entries for the June 7 session date, the date for the next transaction is later than June 7. Therefore, you must advance the session date before you can continue. If you do not advance the date before posting the June 8 transaction, you will receive an error message.

Before advancing the date, however, close all open windows and then save and back up your work because you have already completed one week of transactions. Although Sage 50 saves automatically each time you post an entry or exit the program, it is important to know how to save and back up your work directly to a separate file and location or disk because your working files may become damaged and unusable.

Click ☒ or **choose** the **File menu** for the journal and **click Close** to close the General Journal.

To save a working copy of the file under a different file name, choose the File menu and click Save A Copy to continue working with the original file or Save As to open a new working copy of the file.

You are now ready to advance the session date to June 14.

Click the **Calendar icon** beside **Session Date: Jun 07, 2021** on the right-hand side of the Home window:

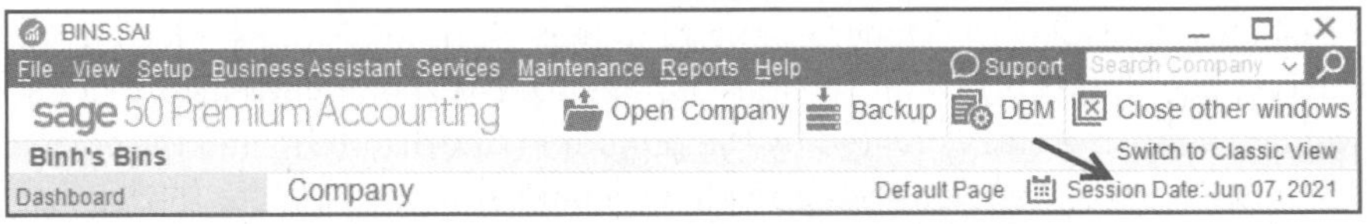

Or, **choose** the **Maintenance menu** and **click Change Session Date**:

WARNING!
You must close all windows before you can advance the session date or before you make a backup.
You can click the Home window Close Other Windows tool, ☒, or close each window separately. You also must be working in single-user mode to change the session date.

PRO VERSION
The Pro version does not include the option to Update Price Lists in the drop-down menu.

The Change Session Date window opens with the current session date highlighted:

Type 06-14-21 (or click the calendar icon and click 14).

Click **OK** to accept the new date.

A Sage 50 message advises you that you have not yet backed up your work:

The data files for this company have been prepared with the default warning to back up your work weekly. Since we also advance the session date by one week at a time, you will be reminded to back up each time you advance the session date.

Click **Yes** to proceed with the backup. The next screen asks for a file name for the backup:

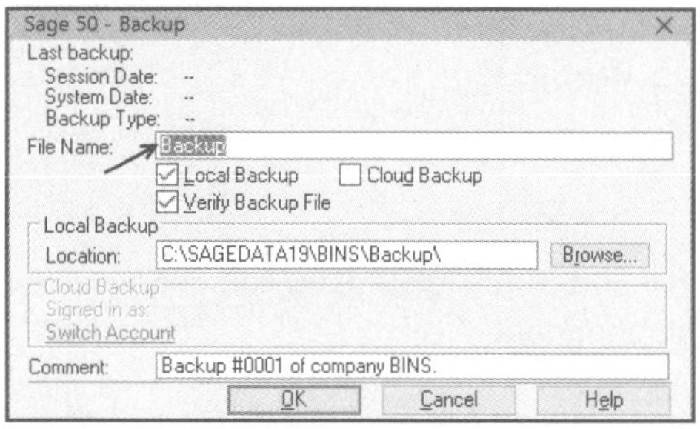

Sage 50 will create a file named Backup1 inside a new Backup subfolder of the folder that contains your working data files. You can edit the file name, location and comment. The name Backup is selected, so you can change the name.

Type BINS

If you want to change the location of the backup, click Browse, select a folder and file name and click OK.

Click **OK** to proceed.

When you name a new folder, an advisory message opens:

The program recognizes that the folder name is new and offers to create the folder. If you have typed the correct name and location,

Click **Yes** to accept the information and continue.

The backup file is different from the one you create by copying or using the Save A Copy or Save As command. The Save A Copy and Save As commands create a complete working copy of your data that you can access with the Sage 50 program directly. Backup creates a compressed file that must first be restored before you can use it to enter transactions. This backup file (BINS1.CAB) has 1 and the .CAB file extension added to the name.

After a brief interval, a message confirms that the backup is complete:

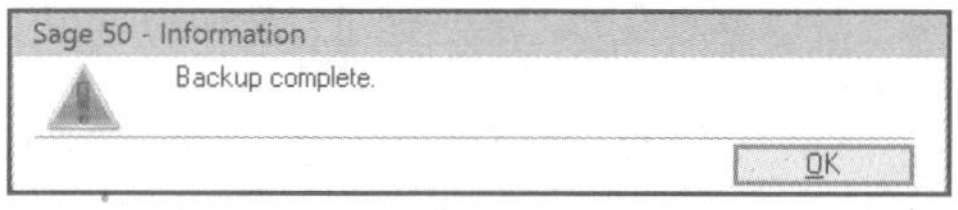

Click **OK** to proceed. You may now enter transactions for this session date.

If you have already created a backup for this data file, or when you change the session date again, you will be advised of the most recent backup date when you are prompted to back up again:

NOTES

You cannot create backups when working in multi-user mode.

With a paid subscription you can back up to the cloud instead of to your own computer, the default Local Backup option.

WARNING!

Be sure to back up each time you are prompted to do so or each time you advance the session date. If your files are damaged, your work will be lost unless you have a backup.

NOTES

For later backups, the backup message will have the previous backup file name and date. In this case the backup # will also be increased – refer to the example on page 52.

WARNING!

You cannot use the same name for the backup and data file if they are in the same folder. If you want to use the same name, you must use a different folder. By using the Backup folder, we can name the backup file BINS.

NOTES

If you do not show file extensions, the backup will be named BINS1.

NOTES

When you change the session date again, the prompt to back up the file will include the data file's session date and your computer's calendar date and time of the previous backup.

WARNING!

We recommend updating the backup name by adding a date or number to the name. For example, type BINS-2 for the next backup, then BINS-3 and so on. This will provide backups for different stages to return to if you later find errors.

Click **Yes** to continue.

Sage 50 will provide the same file name and location that you used for your most recent backup. The backup number in the Comment field will be updated.

Your backup information screens will have the system dates from your own computer:

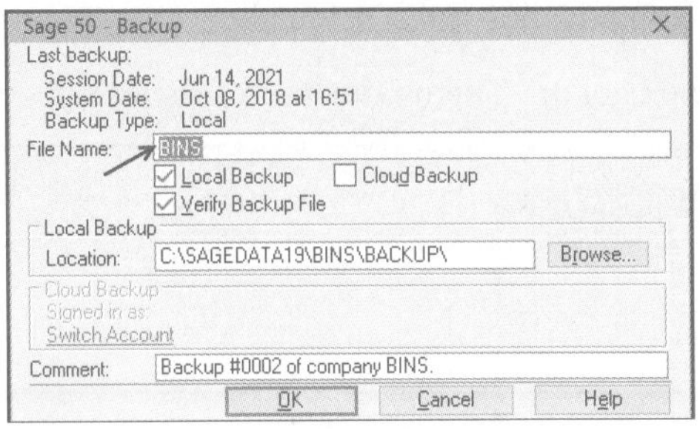

Click **OK**, or **make** the **changes** you want. Again, you can change the file name, its location or the comment.

Click **OK**.

If you use the same backup file name, you will be asked to replace the previous file:

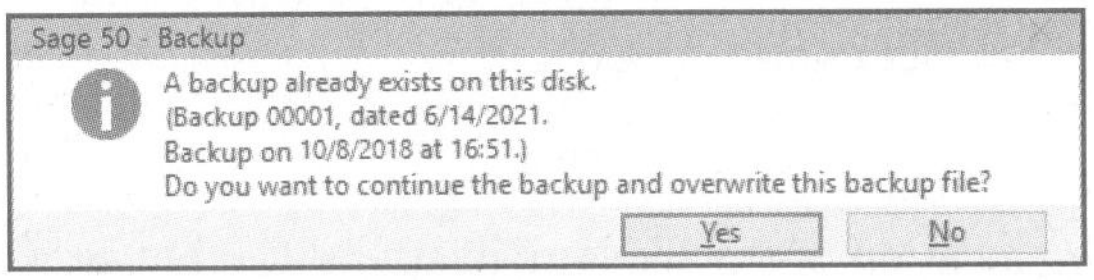

Clicking No will result in the message that the backup was unsuccessful. Then click OK to return to the Backup File Name screen.

Click Yes to continue with the replacement or click No to enter a different name.

Enter the **remaining transactions for June** and **advance** the **session date** as needed.

9 **Bank Debit Memo #RDT-D3691** **Dated June 8, 2021**

From Red Deer Trust, $129 for bank service charges.

10 **Purchase Invoice #WD-4499** **Dated June 10, 2021**

From Western Data , $840 plus $42 GST paid for new dispatch and scheduling software. Purchase invoice total $882. Terms: net 10 days. Create new Group account 2220 A/P - Western Data.

11 **Cheque #489 and Memo #2** **Dated June 11, 2021**

Binh paid his business telephone bill from his personal chequing account. He wrote cheque #489 for $361.20 to reimburse himself for this expense. The telephone bill was $344 plus $17.20 GST.

12 **Payment Cheque #490** **Dated June 11, 2021**

To Hoodoos Containers, $37 327.50 in full payment of account. Reference invoice #HC-7655.

13 **Receipt #121** **Dated June 12, 2021**

From Ontime Contracting, cheque #58821 for $2 730 in full payment of invoice #BB-338.

14 **Sales Invoice #BB-364** **Dated June 14, 2021**

To Piper Creek Mall, $3 800 plus $190 GST charged for dumpster rentals during renovations. Sales invoice total $3 990. Terms: net 30 days.

SESSION DATE – JUNE 21, 2021

☐ 15

To: Binh's Bins
672 Alleyway Drive
Red Deer, AB
T4R 2T4

Sylvan Motors
179 Towing Blvd.,
Red Deer, AB T4P 1S2
Tel: 403-775-6116

Date: June 15, 2021

No: SM-7941

Description of item	
Truck Repairs	1,900.00

GST # 65103 4274 RT0001 | **Terms:** net 30 days

Signature Binh Than

Subtotal	1,900.00
GST	95.00
Total	$1,995.00

☐ 16

Binh's Bins
672 Alleyway Drive
Red Deer AB T4R 2T4

RED DEER TRUST
399 Money Drive
Red Deer, AB T4S 3P1

No: 491

Date 2 0 2 1 0 6 1 8
Y Y Y Y M M D D

Pay One Hundred Seventy Eight dollars and 50 cents —— $ 178.50

TO THE ORDER OF
Badlands Hardware
449 Gadgets Way
Red Deer AB T4Y 5GO

PER Binh Than

⑈—⑆—— 40361 ⑆ 0491

Re: Pay (corrected) invoice BH-5621
$178.50

No: 491
June 18, 2021

☐ 17

Sales Invoice #BB-365 **Dated June 19, 2021**

To Sunnybrook Estates (new customer), $4 800 plus $240 GST charged for dumpster rentals during estate renovations. Sales invoice total $5 040. Terms: net 30 days. Create new Group account 1280 A/R - Sunnybrook Estates.

☐ 18

Payment Cheque #492 **Dated June 20, 2021**

To Western Data, $842 in payment of account. Reference invoice #WD-4499.

19 **Sales Invoice #BB-366** **Dated June 20, 2021**

To Ontime Contracting, $10 100 plus $505 GST charged for subcontracting fees for dumpster rentals and dumping charges. Sales invoice total $10 605. Terms: net 30 days.

20 **Receipt #122** **Dated June 21, 2021**

From Watershed Insurance, cheque #34497 for $6 720 in payment of invoice #BB-363.

SESSION DATE – JUNE 28, 2021

21 **Sales Invoice #BB-367** **Dated June 24, 2021**

To Watershed Insurance, $2 400 plus $120 GST charged for dumpster rentals for post-flood renovation contracts. Sales invoice total $2 520. Terms: net 30 days.

22 **Purchase Invoice #BP-2194** **Dated June 25, 2021**

From Beaver Ponds Paving, $4 040 plus $202 GST paid for resurfacing parking area to repair damage caused by equipment. Purchase invoice total $4 242. Terms: net 10 days. Create new Group account 2240 A/P - Beaver Ponds Paving.

23 **Cash Purchase Invoice #RDP-822** **Dated June 25, 2021**

From Red Deer Promotions, $900 plus $45 GST paid for Web site redesigns. Purchase invoice total $945. Terms: cash on receipt. Invoice paid in full with cheque #493.

24 **Cheque #494** **Dated June 28, 2021**

To Camp Liawannas, $2 290 for summer camp fees for daughter. Use Drawings account.

SESSION DATE – JUNE 30, 2021

25 **Memo #3** **Dated June 30, 2021**

From Owner: enter adjustments for prepaid insurance and rent expired:

Insurance for one month: $1 000

Rent for one month: $1 800

26

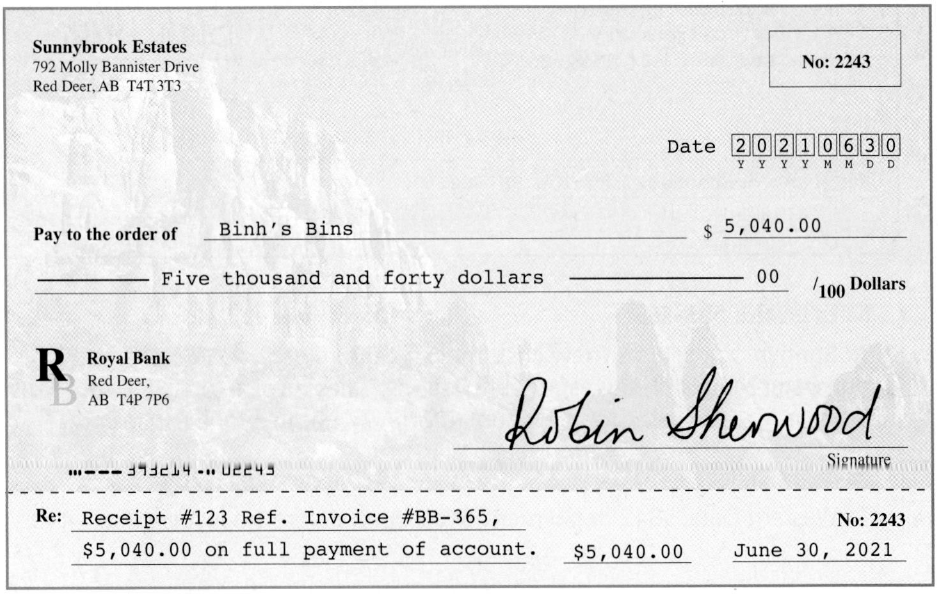
Sunnybrook Estates
792 Molly Bannister Drive
Red Deer, AB T4T 3T3

No: 2243

Date 20210630 (YYYYMMDD)

Pay to the order of Binh's Bins $ 5,040.00

Five thousand and forty dollars 00/100 Dollars

Royal Bank
Red Deer,
AB T4P 7P6

Robin Sherwood
Signature

⑈--- 393214 -⑈ 02243

Re: Receipt #123 Ref. Invoice #BB-365, $5,040.00 on full payment of account. $5,040.00 No: 2243 June 30, 2021

27

June 30, 2021

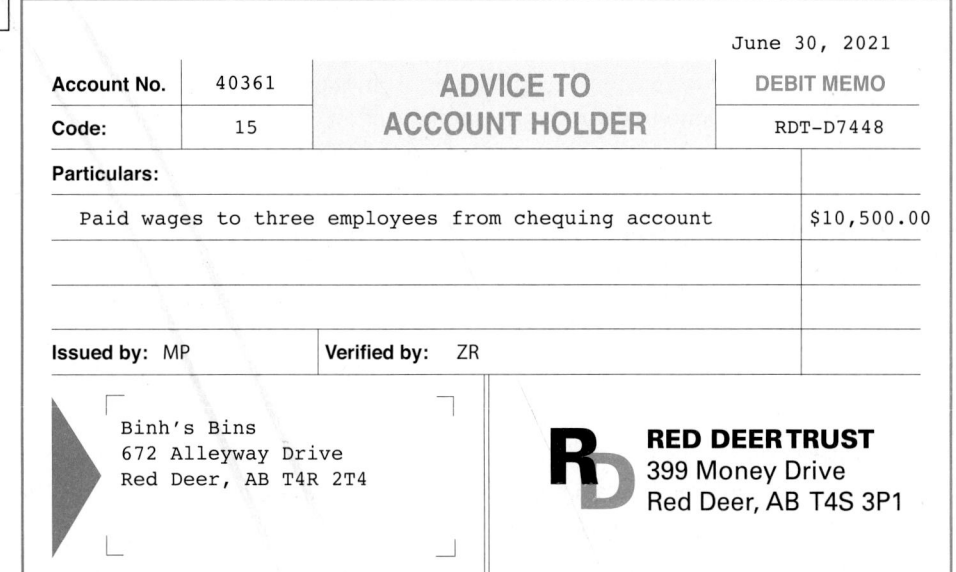

Account No.	40361	ADVICE TO ACCOUNT HOLDER	DEBIT MEMO
Code:	15		RDT-D7448

Particulars:

Paid wages to three employees from chequing account	$10,500.00

Issued by: MP **Verified by:** ZR

Binh's Bins
672 Alleyway Drive
Red Deer, AB T4R 2T4

RED DEER TRUST
399 Money Drive
Red Deer, AB T4S 3P1

28 **Memo #4** **Dated June 30, 2021**

Cheque #492 for $842 to Western Data was recorded with an incorrect amount. The cheque amount was $882. Adjust the entry to change the amount.

Displaying General Reports

A key advantage to using Sage 50 rather than a manual system is the ability to produce financial reports quickly for any date or time period. Sage 50 allows you to enter accounting data accurately so you can prepare the reports you need for reporting to government and investors and for business analysis.

Reports that are provided for a specific date, such as the Balance Sheet, can be produced for any date from the time the accounting records were converted to the computerized system up to the latest journal entry. Reports that summarize a financial period, such as the Income Statement, can be produced for any period between the beginning of the fiscal period and the latest journal entry.

Reports are available from multiple locations: the Accounts window, the Home window Reports menu, the Select A Report tool in the Classic view, and from the Reports list and the Report Centre in the Reports pane of the Home window.

The Reports Menu

From the Home window Reports menu, most General Ledger reports are located under the Financials submenu option:

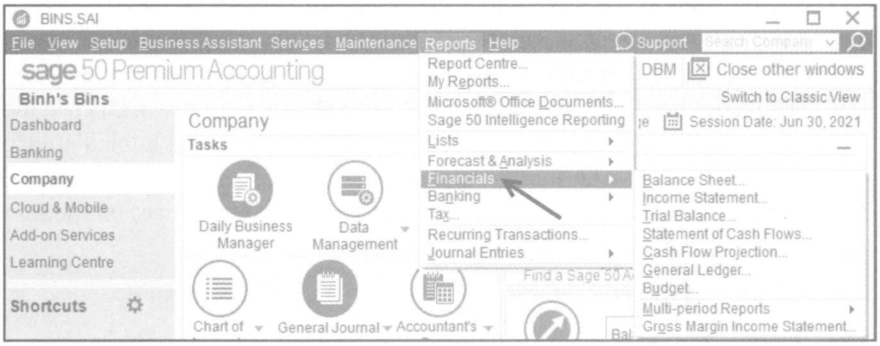

NOTES
Use the General Journal for the payroll transaction in this application.

NOTES
Report analysis is beyond the scope of this text.

NOTES
If you have data for more than one fiscal period, you can display and print reports for the previous fiscal periods.

NOTES
The Home window Reports menu has only the General Ledger reports because the other ledgers are hidden.

PRO VERSION
Sage 50 Intelligence, Forecast & Analysis, Multi-Period reports and Time & Billing reports are not available in the Pro version.

Accounts Window Reports Menu

Click the Chart of Accounts icon in the Home window (Classic view or Enhanced view) to open the Accounts window. All General Ledger reports will be available from the Reports menu in this window.

The Select A Report Tool in the Classic View

CLASSIC VIEW
Right-click a Classic view Home window icon to select it without opening the journal or ledger.

The **Select A Report tool** (on the Classic view Home window tool bar) provides a shortcut to displaying reports related directly to the ledger and journal icons. These include lists related to the ledgers such as the Chart of Accounts, supplier and employee lists, as well as all journal reports. The tool works in three different ways:

1. If a ledger or journal icon is selected but not open, the Modify Report window for that report is displayed immediately when you click the Select A Report tool. The label for the tool changes to name the report for a selected icon.
2. If no icon is highlighted, clicking the Select A Report tool produces the Select Report window that lists all journal reports and ledger lists. Click the list arrow and choose a report from this list. Click Select to display the report options window.
3. When the Accounts window is open, clicking the **Select A Report tool** opens the Select A Report window that lists all General Ledger reports. Click the list arrow , choose from this list and click Select to display the report or its options window. In other ledger windows, the reports list will include the reports related to that ledger.

NOTES
Financial, Account and Banking reports are all available from the Reports menu and Select A Report tool list in the Accounts window.

The Reports Pane and Report Centre

The Reports pane allows access to reports in three ways: from the Report Centre, from the list of recently viewed reports or from the drop-down list of reports for the module you have open. The Company module Reports list has Financial and Accounts reports:

PRO VERSION
Multi-Period reports are not available in the Pro version and are not in the list.

NOTES
Your pop-up list may point up or down when you click the report field, depending on the Sage 50 screen position on your desktop.

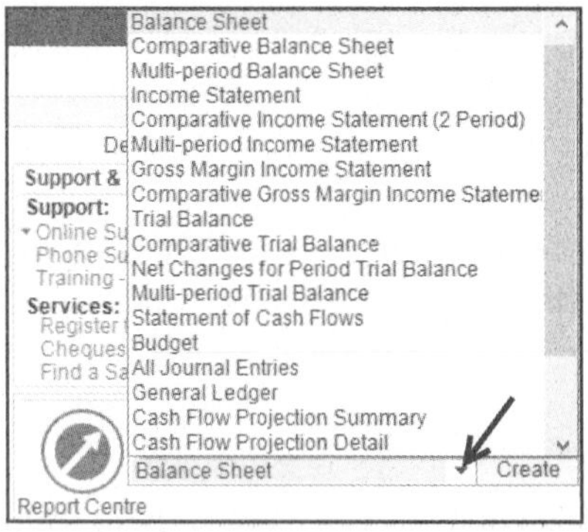

Clicking a report in this list will display it with the default report settings. Once you have displayed a report, it will be added to the **Recent Reports** pane list. Clicking the report in this list will display it with the settings you used most recently. If you have modified a report, using this list provides immediate access to your modified report.

We will work from the **Report Centre**. There are advantages to using the Report Centre: you can either display the report with the default settings immediately or display the Options windows. Furthermore, before opening the report, the purpose and a brief description of the report you want and a display of a sample report are on the same screen.

NOTES
The Recent Reports pane lists the last 10 reports you created with the settings you used for those reports.

Click the **Report Centre icon** in the Reports pane.

Click **Financials** in the Select A Report Type list:

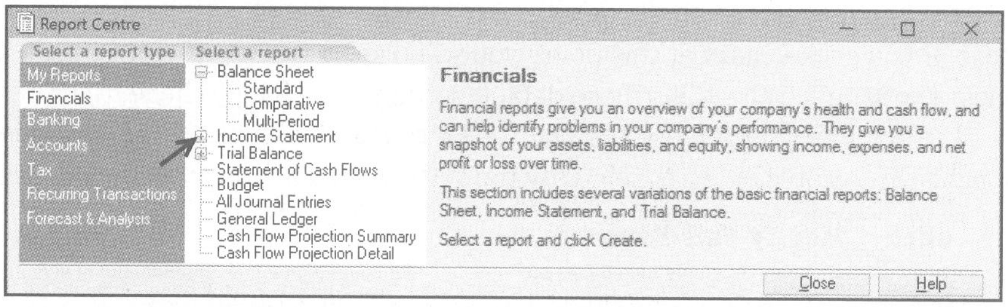

As from the Reports menu, reports for ledgers that are hidden are not available. Financial reports are selected when you start from the Company module Home window, and a list of the different financial reports is added. Several of the reports have a ⊞ beside them, indicating that there are different forms of the report. A brief explanation of Financial Reports appears.

Read the **description**.

Click the ⊞ beside each report type to expand the list.

Click **Balance Sheet** to display a general description of Balance Sheet reports:

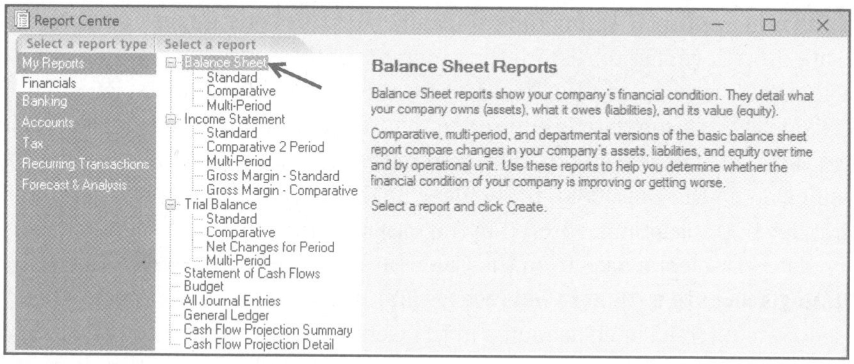

Because Balance Sheet is selected, the description now applies to that report. Standard (single-period) and Comparative (two-period) reports are available. When you have data for more than two months, you can also display Multi-Period Balance Sheets to compare periods ranging from 1 to 12 months.

Displaying the Balance Sheet

The Balance Sheet informs you of the financial position of the business on the date you select for the report. You can display the Balance Sheet at any time.

Click **Standard** below Balance Sheet:

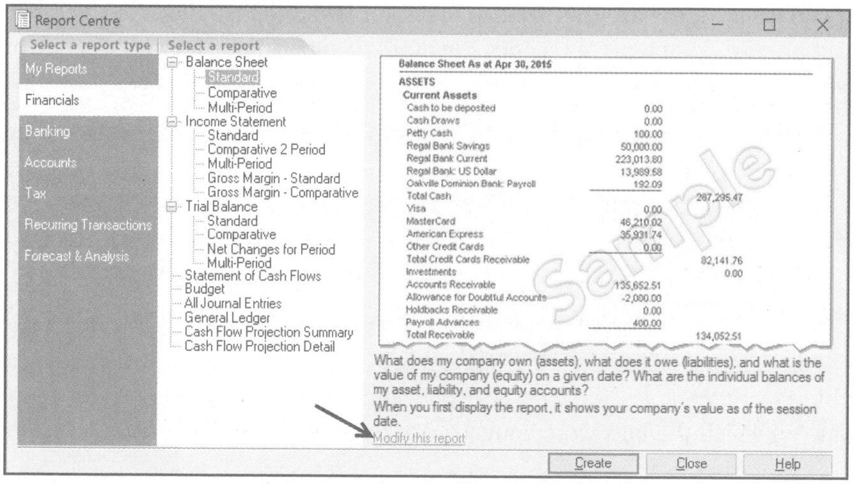

NOTES

When you open the Report Centre from a module window, the first report for that module is selected with the description for it. Balance Sheet – Standard and its description may be displayed initially from the Company module window. Clicking Financials will return you to the general description of financial reports and its list.

PRO VERSION

The Pro version does not have Forecast & Analysis reports or Multi-Period reports, so there are no entries for them.

The screen now has a sample of a standard Balance Sheet with its description and purpose. If you click **Create** at this point, you will display the report with the default settings. The sample report has these default settings. To change the settings or to display the defaults, you can use the **Modify This Report** option. We will use this approach so that you can learn to modify the settings to suit your specific needs.

Click **Modify This Report** to open the Balance Sheet options window:

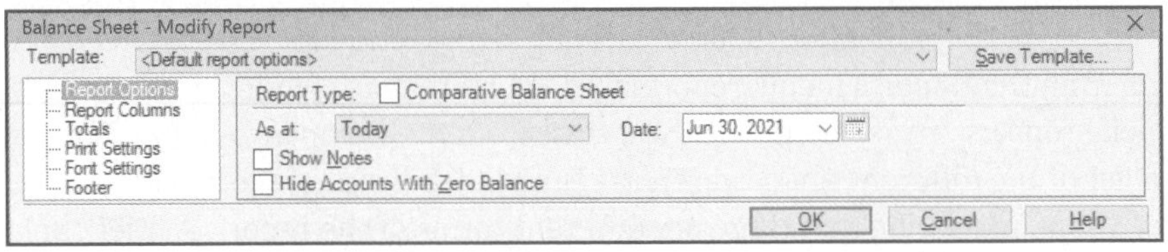

You can also choose the Reports menu, then choose Financials and click Balance Sheet. The report options window will open.

PRO VERSION
The Pro version does not have the option to Show Notes or the entries for Totals and Footer below Report Options.

Default Report Options is selected as the template the first time you access a report. The next time you open this window, the **Last Used Report Options** will be used as the template. This selection allows you to open the same report without re-entering dates and other options. At any time you can choose **Default Report Options** on the Template drop-down list to restore the program default settings.

The default is to use the session date for the report — Today is selected in the **As At** field. The session date is entered in the Date field to match the selection in the As At field. You can choose a standard time from the As At drop-down list, or you can enter a specific date in the Date field. In the **Date** field, you can select from a list that includes the first day of transactions entered in the program, the latest transaction date or the session date, or select a date from the Calendar icon to the right of the Date field.

NOTES
When you have postdated transactions, the latest transaction date will be later than the session date. Both dates will be on the drop-down list for the Date field.

Hiding accounts with zero balances is another option for the report. When you choose to omit zero balance accounts in the General Ledger (refer to page 93), you must select the option for each account individually, and the selection will apply to all reports that include this account. Here, you can choose the option selectively for different reports, and it will apply to all accounts in the report, overriding the ledger option.

Click the **As At field list arrow** to access the predefined date options:

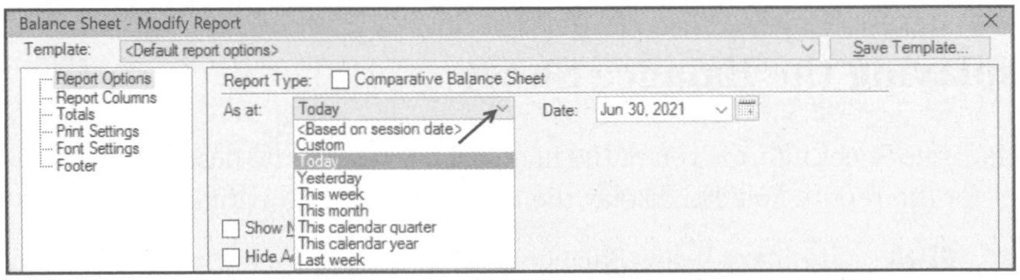

If you want to prepare the Balance Sheet for two different dates at the same time, you can use the Comparative Balance Sheet. Remember that this was also one of the options in the Report Centre window.

NOTES
Comparative statements are useful for financial analysis.

Click **Comparative Balance Sheet** to select this style of report and open the second date field:

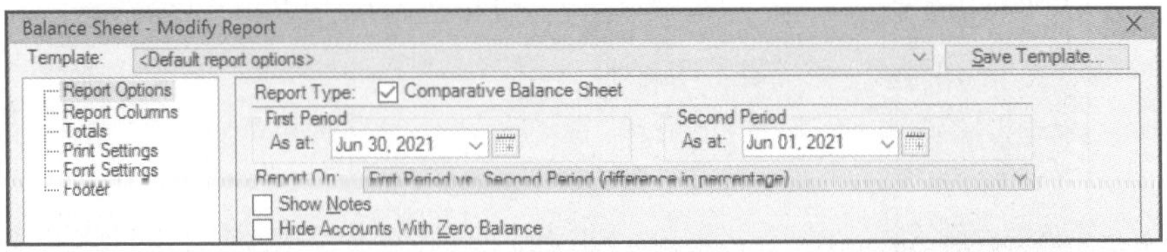

Your most recent session date is displayed in the first date field. The second date is the date on which the files were converted to Sage 50, the earliest transaction date.

Press tab to highlight the first date if you want to change it.

Click the **Calendar icon** to the right of the date (As At) field.

Choose a date from this calendar, select a date from the date field drop-down list or type the date you want using any accepted date format.

Press tab or **press** tab **twice** if you type the date.

Type the **second date** or choose from the date list or calendar.

Click the **Report On field** to display the report types in the drop-down list:

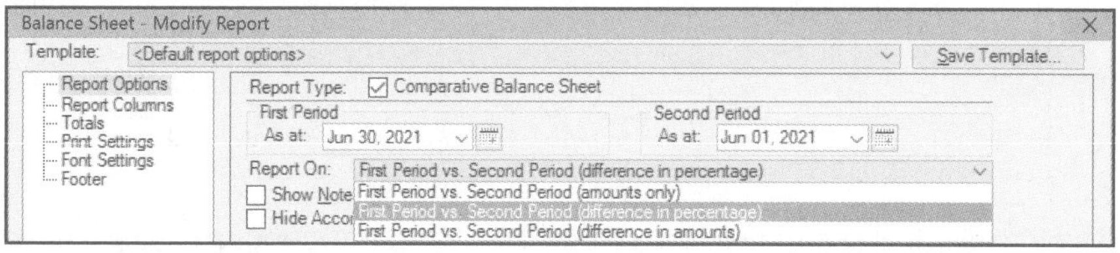

Choose **Amounts Only** if you want only the dollar balances for both dates. Choose **Difference In Percentage** if you want the dollar balances as well as the increase in percentage from the second, earlier period amount to the first, later period amount. Choose **Difference In Amounts** if you want the dollar balances together with the difference between them in dollars. The second, earlier period amount is subtracted from the first, later period amount to calculate the difference.

Click the report **contents** you want.

Click **OK** to display the Balance Sheet.

From any displayed report, you can change report options to create different reports.

Click the **Modify tool** and **choose Report Options** or **choose** the **Options menu** and **click Modify Report** to re-open the report options screen.

Click when you have finished to return to the Report Centre.

Displaying the Income Statement

The Income Statement is a summary of how much a business has earned in the interval you select for the statement. It includes all revenues, expenses and net income — the difference between revenues and expenses. You can view the Income Statement at any time from the Report Centre or the Reports menu. We will continue from the Report Centre. The Income Statement list should still be expanded with the options — to display a Standard (single-period), Comparative (two-period) or Multi-Period statement. If inventory costs are tracked, Gross Margin Statements that separate the cost of goods sold from other expenses can also be displayed when inventory is sold.

Click **Income Statement** and then **Standard** under Income Statement in the Select A Report list to display the report sample.

Click **Modify This Report** to open the report options window:

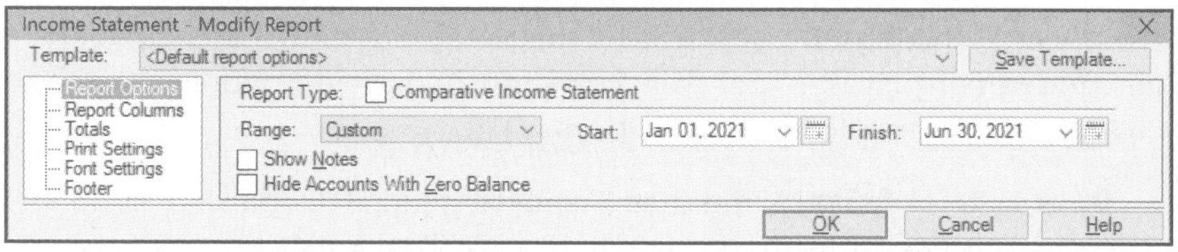

From the Home window, choose the Reports menu, then choose Financials and click Income Statement to open the Modify Report window.

NOTES

If you want a single Balance Sheet only, do not click Comparative Balance Sheet (the check box does not have a ✓ in it). Your most recent session date is displayed by default and highlighted. Choose from the calendar, choose from the date field list or type in the date you want. Click OK to display the Balance Sheet.

If you have accounting data for more than one fiscal period, you can display reports for the previous period as well as for the current period.

NOTES

The date list provided by the list arrow includes the earliest transaction date, the latest session date and the latest transaction date. The earliest transaction date and session date are frequent choices for the start and finish dates in reports.

NOTES

All reports include the option to modify them, so you can change your report options easily. Modifying reports is covered more extensively in Appendix E on the Student DVD.

PRO VERSION

The Pro version does not have the entries for Totals and Footer below Report Options or the option to Show Notes.

NOTES
The default report range is for the fiscal year up to the session date.

As with the Balance Sheet, you can hide accounts with zero balances. You can select the range of dates for the statement from the Range field list or from the Start and Finish field drop-down lists. You can also enter your own choices for the date range (Custom) by typing them in the Start and Finish fields or selecting other dates from the Calendar for those fields. The default range is the fiscal year to date.

Click the **Range field list arrow**:

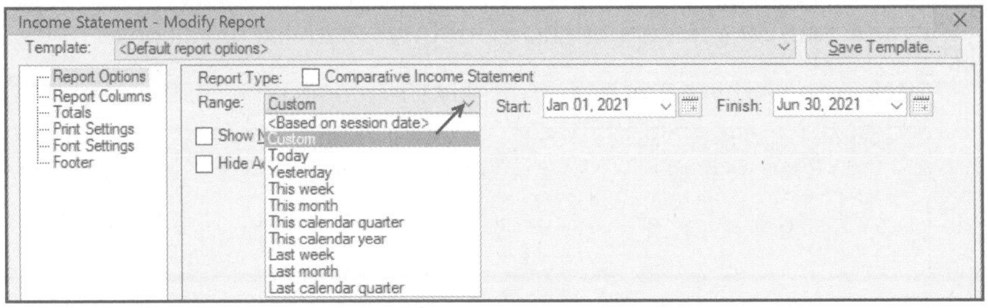

NOTES
If you have data for two fiscal periods, the dates for these two periods will be the defaults for comparative income statements.

The Income Statement also has a comparative report option, allowing comparisons between two different periods. You might want to compare the income for two months, quarters or years. For the comparative report, you have the same amount and difference options as the Balance Sheet.

Click **Comparative Income Statement** to select this option:

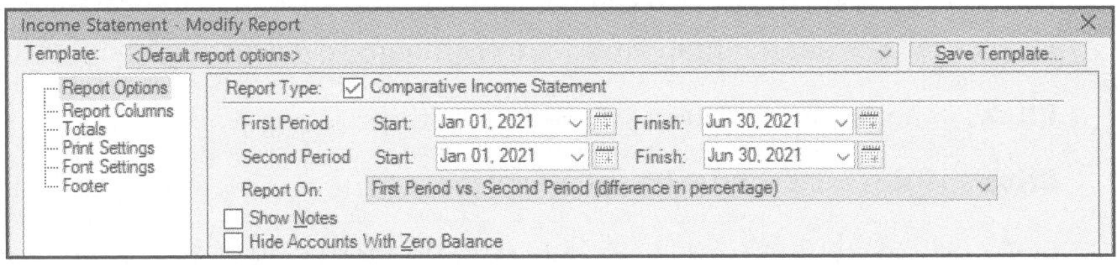

By default, the fiscal start date is provided as the start date for the first period and the second period, and the session date is the finish date for both periods when you select the comparative report.

NOTES
When other modules are used, the Home window Reports menu in the Premium version includes a Business Reports option with several analysis reports. One of these is a Comparative Income Statement – YTD To Last Year. The menu label for these reports changes to match the industry type.

You must enter beginning and ending dates for the period (or periods) you want your Income Statement to cover. Choose a date from the calendar, choose from the date field list or type in the dates.

Click the **Start date field** and **enter** the **date** on which your Income Statement period begins.

Press tab (**twice** if you type the date).

Enter the **date** that your Income Statement period ends.

Enter the **Start** and **Finish dates** for the second period and **choose** the report **content** for comparative reports.

Click **OK**. **Click** ☒ to close the display window when you have finished.

Displaying the Trial Balance

The Trial Balance has account balances for all postable accounts in debit and credit columns. You can display the Trial Balance at any time while working with the software and have the option to hide accounts with zero balances.

Click **Trial Balance** and then **Standard** under Trial Balance in the Select A Report list to display the sample Trial Balance.

Click **Modify This Report** to open the report options window:

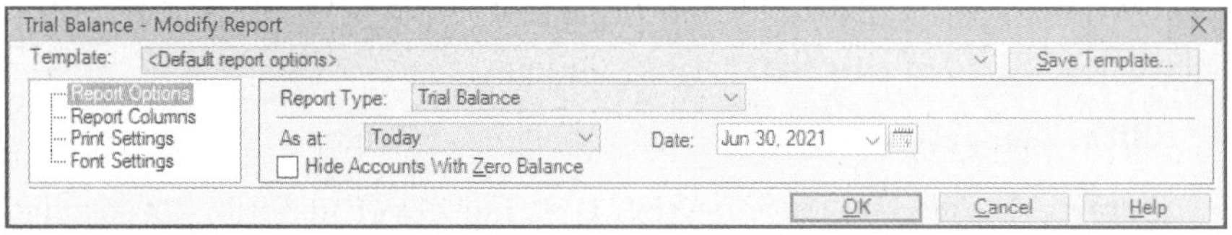

From the Home window choose the Reports menu, then choose Financials and click Trial Balance to open the report options window.

Click the **default date** and **enter** the **date** for which you want the Trial Balance or choose from the calendar.

Choose whether you want to **hide accounts with zero balances**.

The Trial Balance is also available in two other formats from the Report Type drop-down list:

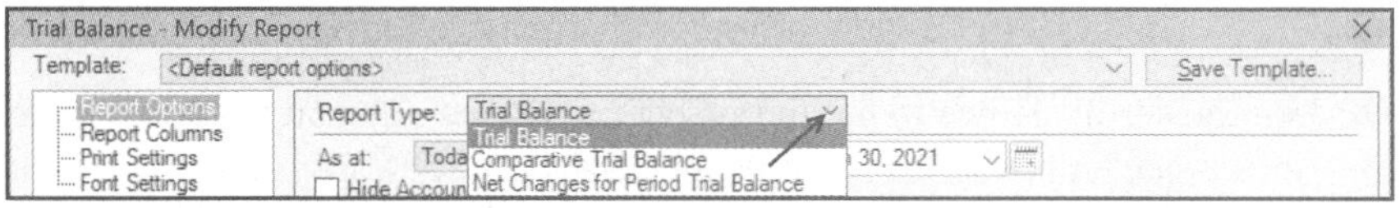

You can view a Comparative Report with the same options as the Balance Sheet, and a report that includes the Net Changes for the selected period — with the debit and credit amounts between the two dates that create the difference.

Click the comparative selection you want, enter the first and second dates and choose the report contents from the Report On list.

Click **OK** to display the Trial Balance.

Click ☒ to leave the display and return to the previous screen or window.

Displaying the General Ledger Report

The General Ledger Report lists all transactions and account balances for one or more accounts in the selected interval. You can display the General Ledger at any time.

Click **General Ledger** in the Select A Report list to display the sample report.

Click **Modify This Report** to open the report options window:

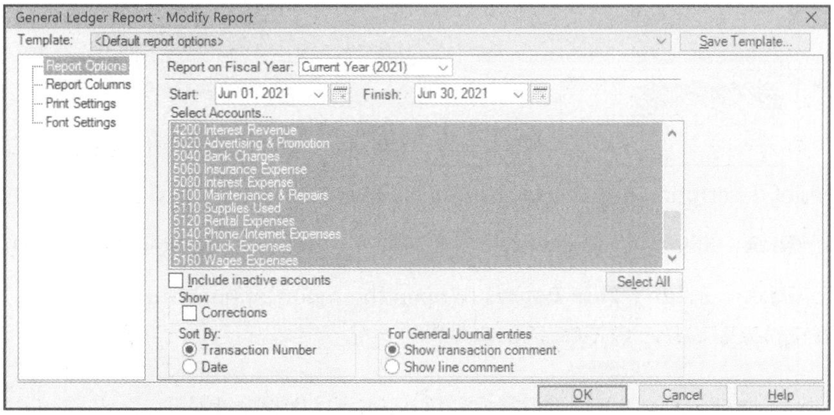

From the Home window choose the Reports menu, then choose Financials and click General Ledger to display the report options.

The General Ledger Report can be sorted in order of the transaction number (journal entry number) or the transaction date. The report includes account balances and transaction or account line comments. The earliest transaction and session dates are the default Start and Finish dates. All accounts are selected for the report initially. You

NOTES

When you do not show corrections, only the final correct entry is included in reports. In that case, sorting by date will place the adjusting entries in the correct chronological position.

can include or omit the corrections (adjusting and reversing entries) you made to journal entries with the **Show Corrections** option.

Click an **option** to select it or to change the default choices.

Enter the **starting date** for your General Ledger Report, choose a date from the calendar or choose a date from the Start field drop-down list.

Press *tab* (**twice** if you type the date).

Enter the **ending date** for your General Ledger Report.

The **Select All** option works like a toggle switch. When all accounts are selected, clicking Select All will remove all selections. With one or more accounts selected or with no selections, clicking Select All will include all accounts for the reports.

Click the **account**, or **press** and **hold** *ctrl* and **click** the **accounts** you want in order to include several individual accounts.

Use the scroll arrows to list more accounts if the one you want is not visible. Click Select All twice to clear all selections.

To select several accounts in a row, click the first one and then press and hold *shift* and click the last one you want to include in the list.

Choose the sorting method (date or journal entry) and the type of comment (transaction or account line) to include in your report.

Click **OK** to view the report.

Click ☒ to close the **display window** after viewing it.

CLASSIC VIEW
From the Home window, right-click the Chart of Accounts icon (Chart of Accounts) to select it. Click the Select A Report tool on the tool bar to open the report options.

Right-click an icon in the Home window (click the right mouse button) to select it without opening the ledger or journal. Clicking the left mouse button will open the journal or ledger.

Displaying the Chart of Accounts

The Chart of Accounts is a list of all accounts with the account number, name and account type and class.

Click **Accounts** in the Select A Report Type list (the list on the left) to expand the Select A Report list:

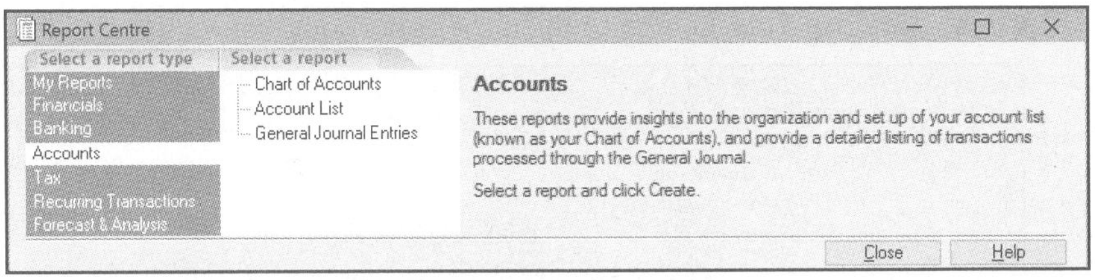

A brief description for the class of Accounts reports appears with the expanded list.

Click **Chart Of Accounts** in the Select A Report list to display the sample.

Click **Modify This Report** to open the report options window:

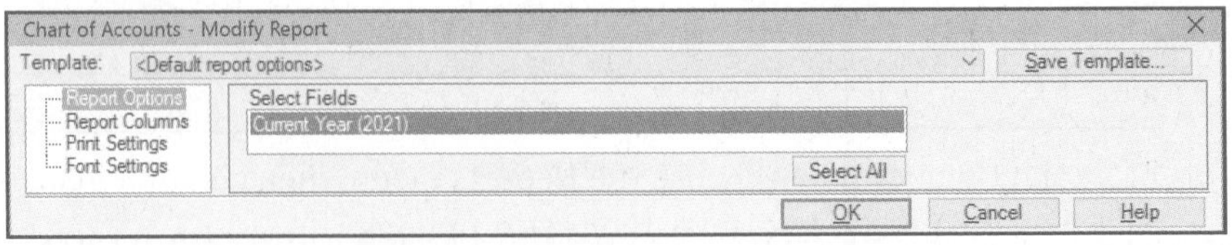

Or, choose the Reports menu, then choose Lists and click Chart Of Accounts to display report options.

Choose the **year** (in the Select Fields list).

NOTES
When you have data for more than one fiscal period, you can display the Chart of Accounts for any of these years. For Binh's Bins, only the Current Year is available.

The default report will include the account number, name, type and class.

Click **OK** to display the chart. **Close** the **display** when you have finished.

Displaying the Account List

If you want to display the Chart of Accounts with account balances or other selected details, you can use the Account List. For example, you could create an account list with only GIFI numbers or account balances as the additional information.

Click **Account List** in the Select A Report list to display the sample.

Click **Modify This Report** to open the report options window:

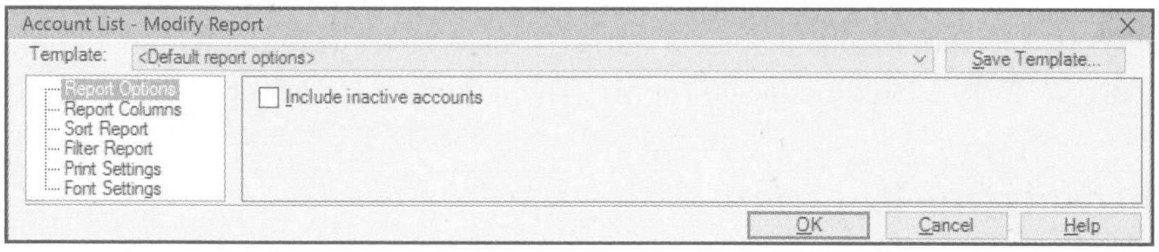

From the Home window, choose the Reports menu, then choose Lists and click Accounts to display the report options.

Click **OK** to view the report. The default report includes the account number and name, balance, account type and account class.

Click ☒ to close the **display window** after viewing it.

NOTES
You can select different details for the Account List Report by modifying the Report Columns. Refer to Appendix E on the Student DVD.

Displaying the General Journal

Click **General Journal Entries** in the Select A Report list to display the sample.

Click **Modify This Report** to open the report options window:

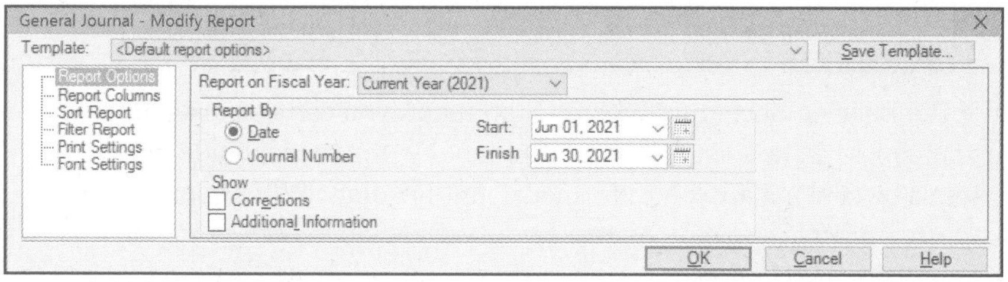

Or, choose the Reports menu, then choose Journal Entries and click General to display the report options.

Journal reports may omit correcting or adjusting entries or include them to provide a complete audit trail. You can select entries for the report either by the (posting) **Date** of the journal entries or by journal entry number. When you choose **Journal Number**, you must enter the first and last numbers for the entries you want to display. If you do not know the journal numbers, the date method is easier. Furthermore, your journal entry numbers might not match the ones we use if you have made any additional or correcting journal entries. Therefore, all reports in this workbook are requested by date — the default setting.

The earliest transaction and the latest session date are given by default for the period of the report.

Click **Corrections** to include the adjusting entries.

You can choose any dates for the Journal Report between the earliest transaction date and the last journal entry, including postdated entries if there are any.

CLASSIC VIEW
From the Home window, right-click the General Journal icon to select it. Click the Select A Report tool on the tool bar to open the report options.

PRO VERSION
The Pro version does not have the option to report on different fiscal years.

NOTES
Because we have only General Journal entries for Binh's Bins, this report will be the same as the one for All Journal Entries that you select from the Financials report list.

WARNING!
If you do not choose Show Corrections, the journal report will include only the latest corrected version of all entries. Showing the corrections will include the original incorrect entry, the reversing entry and the final correct one, thus providing a complete audit trail.

> **NOTES**
> From the Options menu in a displayed report, you can use the Find In This Report option to search for specific information. When you select the option, a Find field opens at the bottom of the report for you to enter the text you want to find. The Options menu also has a Find Next entry so you can continue searching for the next occurrence of the text.

> **NOTES**
> Sometimes, depending on who will need the report, you may want to omit the corrections.

> **NOTES**
> For example, you could create a Journal Report that displays only cheques by filtering on the Source field to match the word Cheque (or the entry you used for these transactions). We explain this in Appendix E on the Student DVD.

> **NOTES**
> You can easily rearrange columns by dragging a column heading to a new position, or change the width by dragging a column margin.

> **PRO VERSION**
> The option to show only totals or to collapse the amounts is not available in the Pro version.

> **NOTES**
> Clicking ⊞ beside a collapsed amount will expand the account display again.
> You can collapse all amounts at once by clicking Show Totals Only. Clicking Show All Accounts will expand the report and restore all individual amounts.

Accept June 1 and **June 30** as the dates for your Journal Report and **click OK**:

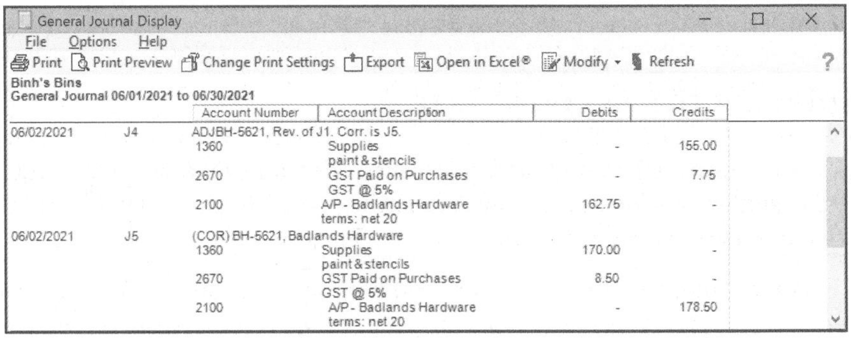

The reversing and the final corrected entry (J4 and J5) for Memo #1 on page 48 are included. J1 has the original incorrect entry. If corrections were not included, only J5, the final correct entry, would be in the report. The complete report provides the audit trail.

Customizing Reports

When we selected dates, comparative options or correcting journal entries, we were customizing reports. Modify Report windows also include customization options in the pane on the left. You can change the **columns** or fields in the report, sort reports and filter them. **Sorting** reports changes the order in which data are presented, while **filtering** reports selects the records to include according to the data fields used as selection criteria. Printing options may also be modified.

Reports already on display may also be modified. You can choose the elements you want to change from the **Modify tool** drop-down list:

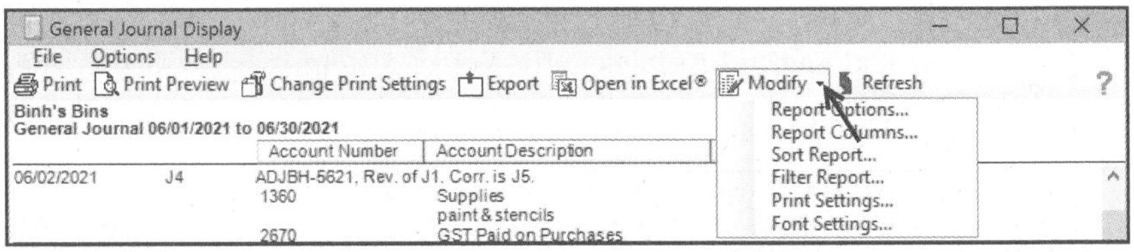

For the Balance Sheet and Income Statement, you can collapse individual amounts when you choose **Totals** as the element to modify. You may include only totals, or only some totals by clicking a ⊟ beside an account heading in the report:

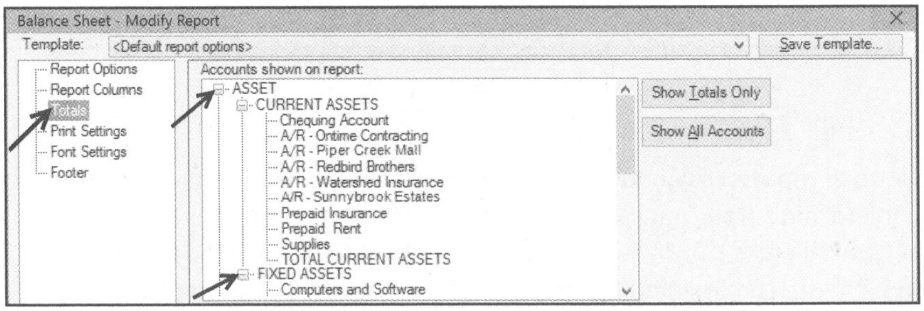

The ⊟ will change to a ⊞ when the amounts have been collapsed.

You can also modify columns directly in the display. For example, you can widen a column by dragging the header margin to the right or remove a column by dragging it to the left. Clicking a column head will sort the report by the contents of that column, if the report can be sorted. Report modifications are covered further in Appendix E.

Close the **displayed report** when finished.

Drill-Down Reports

Some reports can be accessed from other reports that you have opened or displayed. These are cross-referenced or drill-down reports.

Whenever the pointer changes to (a magnifying glass icon with a plus sign inside it), the additional reports can be displayed. When the other ledgers are used, detailed customer, vendor and employee reports are available from the General Ledger Report and from the General Journal.

NOTES
When you point to part of a report, the status bar informs you of the drill-down reports available.

Move the **mouse pointer** over various items in the first report. The type of second report available may change. The name of the second report will appear in the status bar.

Double-click while the magnifying glass icon is visible to display the second report immediately. The first report stays open in the background.

The General Ledger Report for a specific account can be accessed from the Balance Sheet, Income Statement, Trial Balance, Chart of Accounts or General Journal when you double-click an account number, name or balance amount. Journal transaction details and the General Ledger record for an account can be accessed from the General Ledger Report.

From any Journal Report, you can open the original transaction by double-clicking the Source or Comment.

While you have the additional drill-down report displayed, you may print it or drill down to other reports. (Refer to Printing General Reports below.)

Close the **second report** and then **close** the **first report** when you have finished viewing them. **Close** the **Report Centre**.

Printing General Reports

Display the **report** you want to print by following the instructions in the preceding pages on displaying reports.

WARNING!
Always check that the correct printer is selected before printing reports. The printer selection is saved with the data file and may be incorrect for your setup.

There are overall print settings for the company file. These are available from the Home window and from any open report. From the displayed report,

Click the **Change Print Settings tool** or **choose** the **File menu** and **click** **Reports & Forms**.

The Report & Form Options screen opens:

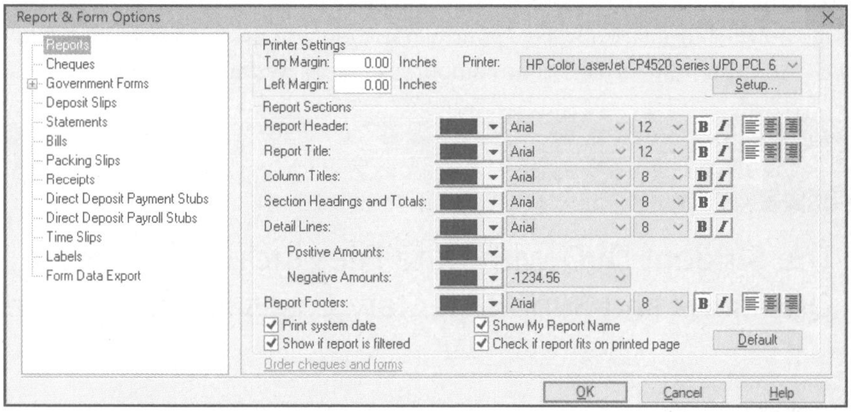

From the Home window, choose the Setup menu and click Reports & Forms.

PRO VERSION
Packing Slips and Time Slips will not appear on the list in the Pro version. The term Invoices replaces Bills.

NOTES
From the Setup or other option buttons, you can choose advanced settings for the report and printer.

NOTES
Refer to Appendix E for more detail on modifying Print Settings for individual reports.

These settings become the defaults for all company reports.

From this window, you can select a printer, set the margins and choose the default style for different parts of the report. You can also add the computer system date to the report and indicate whether the report is filtered. The **Default** button will restore the original program default settings for the report.

Choose your **printer** from the drop-down list in the Printer field.

Click **OK** to save your changes and return to the display or **click Cancel** if you do not want to save the changes you made.

If you want to change the appearance only for the displayed report, you should modify the displayed report. The Modify Report windows include Print Settings and Font Settings as elements that you can modify separately for each type of report.

Finishing a Session

Finish the last transaction you are working on for this session.

Click ☒ to close the transaction window (such as journal input or display) to return to the Home window.

You can click the Close Other Windows tool in the Home window if you have more than one open window. To restore the Home window,

Click the **Home window tool** in an open journal window. Or,

Click the **Sage 50 icon** on the desktop task bar and **click** the **Sage 50 Home window pop-up**.

Click the **Close Other Windows tool** in the Home window.

Click ☒ or **choose** the **File menu** and **click Exit** to close the program.

A message asks if you want to back up the data file first:

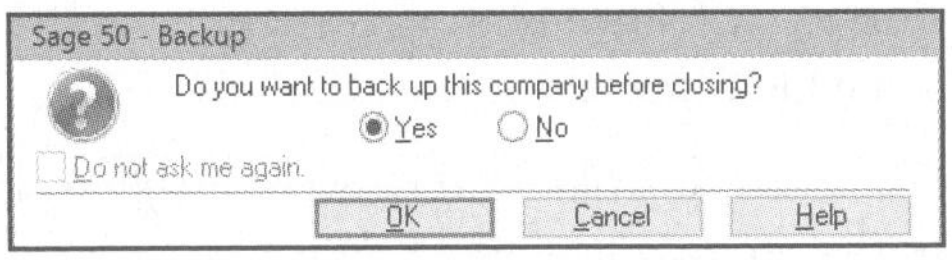

If you did not back up the file after the last set of transactions, you should do so now.

Click **OK** to start the backup procedure. Follow the instructions on pages 50–52 to complete the backup.

After the backup is complete, the file will close.

Sage 50 will automatically save your work when you finish your session and exit properly. You can now turn off your computer — or take a coffee break.

REVIEW

The Student DVD with Data Files includes Review Questions and Supplementary Cases for this chapter.

CHAPTER FOUR

It Again

OBJECTIVES

After completing this chapter, you should be able to

- ***plan*** and ***design*** an accounting system for a non-profit organization
- ***prepare*** a conversion procedure from manual records
- ***understand*** the objectives of a computerized accounting system
- ***create*** company files using the Skeleton starter file
- ***change*** the default home window
- ***set up*** the organization's accounts
- ***enter*** historical account information
- ***finish*** entering accounting history to prepare for transactions
- ***enter*** fiscal end adjusting transactions
- ***close*** the books and start a new fiscal period
- ***enter*** transactions for a previous fiscal period

COMPANY INFORMATION

Company Profile

NOTES
Love It Again
4-A Charity Drive
Toronto, ON M4G 2T2
Tel: (416) 885-8967
Fax: (647) 885-8967
Business No.: 127 362 648 RR0001

It Again is a store associated with a charitable organization that raises awareness of and supports research on heart disease in children, and encourages organ donations for heart transplants. Most of the store's merchandise is donated.

The store sells gently used children's clothing, toys, books, furniture and strollers. Used car seats and cribs are not accepted because of the high safety standards associated with these items. Special-occasion clothing is especially desirable because it is generally more costly to purchase and less worn. Repeat customers frequently donate gently used merchandise. Thus, in addition to the charitable aspect of the business, it promotes an ecologically friendly environment by preventing usable goods from entering landfill sites. The store also purchases discontinued items at reduced prices, such as out-of-print books, end-of-season clothing, floor models or slightly marked but otherwise undamaged goods. All items are priced to sell to encourage faster turnover and return customer visits.

NOTES
Because no cost is associated with donated items, they are not recorded as assets in the Chart of Accounts – separate records are kept for these items for inventory control.

Merchandise that is not sold within a short period of time is donated to local shelters that accommodate families or to organizations that support newly arrived immigrant and refugee families.

As a charity, the store makes every effort to minimize expenses. Overseen by a board of directors, the store pays only the salaried manager, Jeremy Fischer, who is assisted by a volunteer sales staff. These volunteers are often parents of children who have experienced heart-health issues.

Funds from the sale of items that were purchased are subject to HST at 13 percent (or GST at 5 percent for children's clothing and books). Donated items are not taxed on resale.

Volunteers handle all the day-to-day sales. The organization does incur some expenses: the manager's salary, rent, a computerized cash register to record all sales and donations, office supplies, promotional materials, telephones and so on.

The bank account has been set up for regular deposits and to write cheques for expenses. Some cash is also kept on hand at the store to make change for on-site sales and for incidental purchases. Most of the cash and cheques received are deposited immediately for security purposes, but for the sake of reducing the length of the exercise, monthly sales summaries and bank deposits are recorded.

Love It Again has decided to start using Sage 50 to keep the accounting records in August 2021, partway through its current fiscal year. The charity requires only General Ledger accounts. The following information is available to set up the accounts using the General Ledger:

- Chart of Accounts
- Income Statement
- Balance Sheet
- Trial Balance
- Accounting Procedures

CHART OF ACCOUNTS

LOVE IT AGAIN

ASSETS
1000 CURRENT ASSETS [H]
1020 Bank: Love It Again [A]
1100 Cash on Hand [A]
1150 Total Cash [S]
1190 Prepaid Expenses
1200 Purchased Clothing
1210 Purchased Books
1220 Other Purchased Items
1300 Office Supplies
1310 Other Supplies
1320 T-shirts
1390 TOTAL CURRENT ASSETS [T]

1500 FIXED ASSETS [H]
1510 Fax/Telephone
1520 Computers
1530 Store Furniture & Shelving
1590 TOTAL FIXED ASSETS [T] ▶

▶LIABILITIES
2000 CURRENT LIABILITIES [H]
2100 Bank Loan
2200 A/P - Kids Stuff
2300 A/P - Kids In Motion
2350 A/P - Wearable Designs
2400 A/P - Places For Us
2550 GST Charged on Sales [A]
2560 HST Charged on Sales [A]
2570 GST Paid on Purchases [A]
2580 HST Paid on Purchases [A]
2590 GST/HST Owing/Refund [S]
2690 TOTAL CURRENT LIABILITIES [T]

EQUITY
3000 EQUITY [H]
3560 Accumulated Surplus
3600 Net Income [X]
3690 TOTAL EQUITY [T] ▶

▶REVENUE
4000 REVENUE [H]
4020 Revenue: Donated Items
4040 Revenue: Purchased Clothing & Books
4080 Revenue: Other Purchases
4100 Revenue: Donations
4390 TOTAL REVENUE [T]

EXPENSE
5000 OPERATING EXPENSES [H]
5020 Rental Expense
5200 Supplies Used
5240 Postage Expense
5280 Maintenance Expenses
5300 Utilities Expenses
5320 Publicity & Promotion
5400 Wages - Manager
5420 Miscellaneous Expenses
5490 TOTAL OPERATING EXPENSES [T] ▶

▶5500 COST OF GOODS SOLD [H]
5510 Cost of Purchased Clothing & Books
5520 Cost of Other Purchases
5690 TOTAL COST OF GOODS SOLD [T]

NOTES: The Chart of Accounts is based on the current expenses and accounts. Account types are marked in brackets for subgroup Accounts [A], Subgroup totals [S], Headings [H], Totals [T] and Current Earnings [X]. All unmarked accounts are postable Group [G] accounts. The explanation of account types begins on page 86.

INCOME STATEMENT

LOVE IT AGAIN

For the Ten Months Ending July 31, 2021

Revenue		
4000	REVENUE	
4020	Revenue: Donated Items	$ 22 600.00
4040	Revenue: Purchased Clothing & Books	41 200.00
4080	Revenue: Other Purchases	33 400.00
4100	Revenue: Donations	9 800.00
4390	TOTAL REVENUE	$107 000.00
	TOTAL REVENUE	$107 000.00

Expense		
5000	OPERATING EXPENSES	
5020	Rental Expense	$18 000.00
5200	Supplies Used	320.00
5240	Postage Expense	1 850.00
5280	Maintenance Expenses	5 200.00
5300	Utilities Expenses	4 800.00
5320	Publicity & Promotion	1 230.00
5400	Wages - Manager	42 000.00
5490	TOTAL OPERATING EXPENSES	$73 400.00
	TOTAL EXPENSE	$73 400.00
	NET INCOME	$33 600.00

BALANCE SHEET

LOVE IT AGAIN

August 1, 2021

Assets			
1000	CURRENT ASSETS		
1020	Bank: Love It Again	$46 380.00	
1100	Cash on Hand	1 220.00	
1150	Total Cash		$47 600.00
1190	Prepaid Expenses		290.00
1200	Purchased Clothing		7 110.00
1210	Purchased Books		4 790.00
1220	Other Purchased Items		14 200.00
1300	Office Supplies		380.00
1310	Other Supplies		1 120.00
1320	T-shirts		360.00
1390	TOTAL CURRENT ASSETS		$75 850.00
1500	FIXED ASSETS		
1510	Fax/Telephone		390.00
1520	Computers		4 560.00
1530	Store Furniture & Shelving		8 600.00
1590	TOTAL FIXED ASSETS		$13 550.00
	TOTAL ASSETS		$89 400.00

Liabilities			
2000	CURRENT LIABILITIES		
2100	Bank Loan		$ 14 000.00
2200	A/P - Kids Stuff		904.00
2300	A/P - Kids In Motion		1 260.00
2350	A/P - Wearable Designs		339.00
2550	GST Charged on Sales	$2 060.00	
2560	HST Charged on Sales	4 342.00	
2570	GST Paid on Purchases	-605.00	
2580	HST Paid on Purchases	-4 795.00	
2590	GST/HST Owing/Refund		1 002.00
2690	TOTAL CURRENT LIABILITIES		$17 505.00
	TOTAL LIABILITIES		$17 505.00
Equity			
3000	EQUITY		
3560	Accumulated Surplus		$ 38 295.00
3600	Net Income		33 600.00
3690	TOTAL EQUITY		$ 71 895.00
	TOTAL EQUITY		$ 71 895.00
	LIABILITIES AND EQUITY		$89 400.00

TRIAL BALANCE

LOVE IT AGAIN

August 1, 2021	Debits	Credits
1020 Bank: Love It Again	$46 380.00	
1100 Cash on Hand	1 220.00	
1190 Prepaid Expenses	290.00	
1200 Purchased Clothing	7 110.00	
1210 Purchased Books	4 790.00	
1220 Other Purchased Items	14 200.00	
1300 Office Supplies	380.00	
1310 Other Supplies	1 120.00	
1320 T-shirts	360.00	
1510 Fax/Telephone	390.00	
1520 Computers	4 560.00	
1530 Store Furniture & Shelving	8 600.00	
2100 Bank Loan		$14 000.00
2200 A/P - Kids Stuff		904.00
2300 A/P - Kids In Motion		1 260.00
2350 A/P - Wearable Designs		339.00
2550 GST Charged on Sales		2 060.00
2560 HST Charged on Sales		4 342.00 ▶

August 1, 2021	Debits	Credits
▶ 2570 GST Paid on Purchases	$ 605.00	
2580 HST Paid on Purchases	4 795.00	
3560 Accumulated Surplus		$ 38 295.00
4020 Revenue: Donated Items		22 600.00
4040 Revenue: Purchased Clothing & Books		41 200.00
4080 Revenue: Other Purchases		33 400.00
4100 Revenue: Donations		9 800.00
5020 Rental Expense	18 000.00	
5200 Supplies Used	320.00	
5240 Postage Expense	1 850.00	
5280 Maintenance Expenses	5 200.00	
5300 Utilities Expenses	4 800.00	
5320 Publicity & Promotion	1 230.00	
5400 Wages - Manager	42 000.00	
	$168 200.00	$168 200.00

Accounting Procedures

HST

Registered charities have two options with respect to the GST and HST. Like regular for-profit businesses, they can register; charge taxes on sales, membership fees and so on; and claim taxes paid as input tax credits to reduce the liability to the Receiver General. The second option does not require collection of taxes but permits a Public Service Bodies' (PSB) rebate of taxes paid. Love It Again charges GST and HST because it sells merchandise. No taxes are charged on donated goods, but other sales are subject to regular tax charges. HST and GST paid toward operating expenses are deemed as input tax credits (ITCs). Other expenses, such as the cost of merchandise, are not ITCs.

Tax returns are prepared by debiting *GST* and *HST Charged on Sales* and crediting *GST* and *HST Paid on Purchases.* If a refund is due, it is entered as an *Accounts Receivable* debit entry that can be cleared when the rebate is received. After the remittance, the tax accounts will have residual balances that are cleared at year-end and recorded as income.

NOTES

HST does not apply to the sale of books or children's clothing – only GST applies to these sales. Therefore, Love It Again has both GST and HST accounts.

A charity must register for GST/HST to receive the PSB rebate. The federal portion of the rebate – 50 percent of the 5 percent GST paid (form GST66) – is separated from the provincial portion – 82 percent of the 8 percent PST paid (Ontario form RC7066SCH). (We have completed the rebate and net tax calculations for Love It Again. Refer to Case Five for Chapter 4 in Appendix D on the Student DVD.)

The provincial rebate percentage varies among provinces and for different types of non-profit organizations.

Bank Accounts

The proceeds from the sale of merchandise are entered into the *Cash on Hand* account. This account is also used for some small day-to-day purchases. Donation receipts are deposited directly to the *Bank: Love It Again* account. Cheques to suppliers for merchandise and operating and administrative expenses are also written from this bank account. Surplus cash — amounts not needed to make change for customers — is transferred regularly from *Cash on Hand* to *Bank: Love It Again.*

INSTRUCTIONS

1. **Set up** the **company accounts for Love It Again** in the General Ledger in Sage 50 using all the information provided in this application. Detailed keystroke instructions follow.
2. **Back up your work frequently** when working through this application to keep your backups updated.

   You may finish your session at any time while completing the setup. Simply open the Love It Again data file again, accept the session date and continue from where you left off.

   If you are using a different location for your data files, substitute the appropriate data path, including the drive and folder, for your data setup.
3. **Enter** the **source documents** that begin on page 98 in the General Journal in Sage 50 using the Chart of Accounts and other information provided.
4. **Print** the **following reports** after you have completed your entries — choose Previous Year (2021) as the reporting period:
   a. General Journal from July 1 to September 30
   b. Comparative Balance Sheet at September 30 and October 1 (amounts)
   c. Income Statement for the period October 1, 2020, to September 30, 2021

WARNING!
You must choose 2021 as the year for journal entries because there is no data for October 1, the default date for the Journal Report after you start the new fiscal year.

KEYSTROKES FOR SETUP

The following are the five key stages in preparing the Sage 50 program for use by a company:

1. creating company files
2. preparing the system
3. preparing the ledgers
4. printing reports to check your work
5. backing up your files and finishing the company history

The following keystroke instructions are written for a stand-alone PC with a hard drive. The keystroke instructions provided in this application demonstrate one approach to setting up company accounts. Always refer to the Sage 50 and Windows manuals and Help for further details.

NOTES
Using subsequent versions of Sage 50 may result in different screens and keystrokes from those described in this application.

NOTES
You must work in single-user mode to set up new company files. Access to most settings is restricted in multi-user mode.

Creating Company Files

The instructions we provide assume that you installed the Sage 50 data files on your hard disk in drive C: in the SageData19 folder.

Sage 50 provides both templates and starter files to make it easier to create files for a new company. These files contain different sets of accounts that match the needs of different kinds of businesses. By starting with one of these files, you eliminate the need to create all the accounts for your business from scratch.

There are many templates that work with the setup wizards to define not only accounts but also a number of settings for the different ledgers. The accounts and settings in these templates are suited to the type of business named by the files.

NOTES
The non-profit template has many more accounts, modules and features than are needed for Love It Again. This file, therefore, would require substantially more modification to make it match the company profile in this chapter.

NOTES

We want to illustrate different ways of creating company files. Therefore, the method of creating your company files from scratch is described in the Air Care Services setup application in Chapter 7.

Before 2016, the two Sage 50 starter files — Skeleton and Integration (Integration Plus) — could be updated to a later version of Sage 50. These files contain only a set of basic accounts. The Skeleton starter has only General Ledger accounts, whereas the Integration Plus starter is suitable for a variety of business types because it has the basic linked accounts for all the ledgers.

Both files are from an earlier version of the program (Simply Basic 2005) that cannot be updated with Sage 50 2019, so we created a Sage 50 Pro 2019.0 version copy of the Skeleton file to use with this text. We placed this file in the SageData19 folder with the other data files.

NOTES

The Student version program cannot open or update any data files from versions older than 2019 (Release 0).

The Skeleton starter files are best suited to the Chart of Accounts for Love It Again. These files contain only a few General Ledger accounts, headings and totals. They contain no linked accounts that link General Ledger accounts to the subsidiary ledgers. This is appropriate for Love It Again, which uses only the General Ledger.

You will have to customize any starter file to your particular company. Rarely are accounts and features identical for any two businesses.

The starter files are located in the TEMPLATE folder in the Sage 50 Premium Accounting Version 2019 folder — the folder containing your Sage 50 program.

We will open the SKELETON.SAI file from the SageData19\TEMPLATE folder.

Start the **Sage 50 program** to access the Select Company window.

Click **Select An Existing Company** to access the Open Company window:

NOTES

If you are using backup files, restore SageData19\SKELETON1.CAB or SKELETON1 to SageData19\AGAIN\AGAIN. Sage 50 will create the necessary new folder. Refer to page 25 for assistance with restoring backup files.

If you start from the backup file, you will not need to complete the additional step of saving the file after the Upgrade wizard has completed.

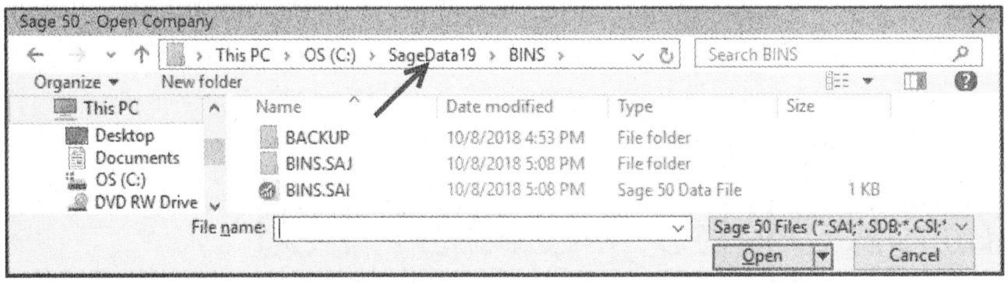

Click **SageData19** in the file path field to return to this folder and display all the folders you installed from the Student DVD.

Double-click **TEMPLATE** to open this folder.

Click **SKELETON** (or **SKELETON.SAI**) to select this data file. **Click Open** to view the Upgrade Company details:

PRO VERSION

The file will not be converted. You will begin with the Session Date screen on page 73 immediately, also skipping the selection of the type of company.

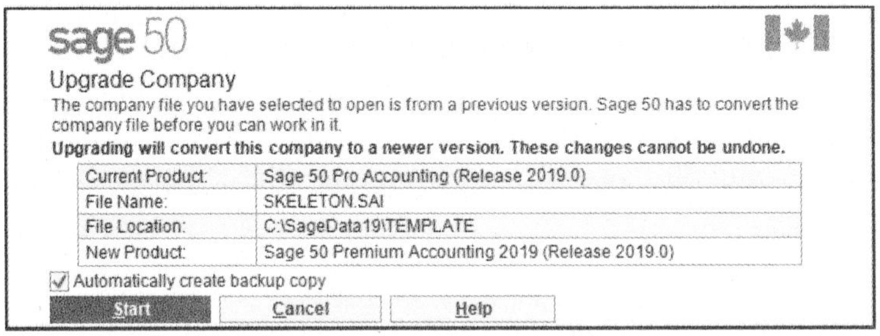

The Skeleton starter file must be converted to Premium Release 2019.0.

This screen has the name and location of the working file and the version changes that will be made if you proceed. File conversions cannot be reversed — once you convert a file you will be unable to open it in the earlier version, but you can back up the Skeleton file before proceeding.

NOTES

When you upgrade to a later release, you will be reminded about payroll tax changes because new releases of Sage 50 are tied to tax table changes that usually occur every six months.

Click **Start**.

You will now be asked to indicate the type of company you are working with. Different company types have different icon and journal labels in the Premium version.

Click the **list arrow beside Other**, the default entry, to list the types:

Click **Non-Profit** and then **click OK**.

The Session Date window opens with January 1, 2000, as the session date:

Click **OK** to accept the date for now. We will update it later.

The Getting Started Welcome screen and the Daily Business Manager will now open. One window may be open in the background behind the other.

Click to close the Daily Business Manager window. **Click Yes** to confirm.

Click **Show This Window On Startup** in the Getting Started window to remove the ✓, then **click** the **Close button** to close this window.

The Home window opens and all ledgers are available in the list of modules.

The Receivables ledger icon is labelled Supporters because we selected Non-Profit as the company type. For other types of companies, this icon may be labelled Customers or Clients. Projects are labelled Funds for non-profit companies.

The ledgers are not set up. An **open history** or **not-finished symbol** appears on Supporters, the ledger icon, indicating that you can enter historical data for the ledger. The other modules have the same symbol on ledger icons. Although you can make journal entries at this stage, you should first save this file under your company name, enter all the necessary company information and finish entering the history.

First we will copy the template files so we can use this original again if we need to.

NOTES

Clicking the Sage 50 icon on your Windows desktop task bar will let you know which Sage windows are open. Click the one you need to make it active and bring it to the front so that you can close it.

Click No if you are prompted to turn off the Daily Business Manager.

PRO VERSION

Sage 50 Pro Accounting is displayed as the program name.

The ledger icon labels are Customers and Projects. Sales Invoices replaces Statements and Sales replaces Supporter for the Quote and Order labels.

PRO VERSION

The open history symbol appears with the Customers icon.

Choose the **File menu** and **click Save As** so that we can work with the new copy:

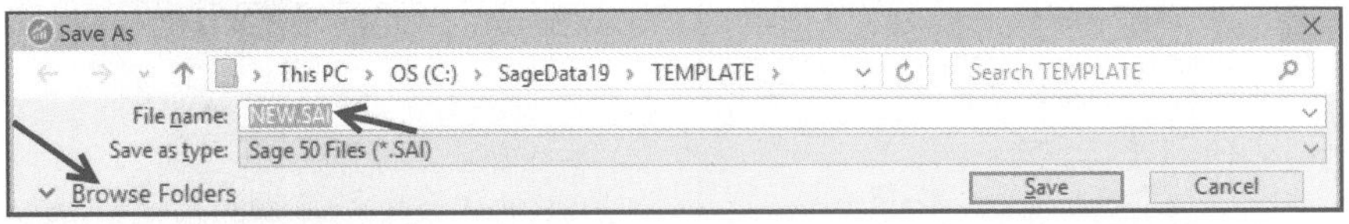

The Save As window opens. The path <C:\SageData19\TEMPLATE> indicates the location of the open SKELETON file. NEW.SAI (or NEW) is the default name for the new data file. We need to delete the name NEW and create a new data folder for Love It Again, but we want this under the SageData19 folder level.

NOTES
For consistency, we use upper case for the names of all files and folders, but you may choose to type the names in lower case. The screen display may sometimes be in upper case even though you entered a lower case name.

Click **SageData19** in the file path field. We need to return to the SageData19 folder where we will create the new data folder.

Delete **NEW** (or **NEW.SAI**) in the File Name field.

Click **Browse Folders** if necessary to expand the window and include the New Folder option:

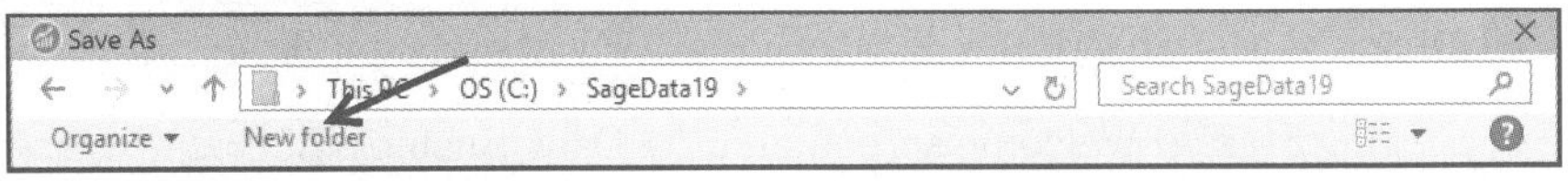

NOTES
When the Browse Folders option is selected, its label changes to Hide Folders and the arrow beside it changes direction.

Click **New Folder**. The name New Folder is selected as the folder name, so we can change it. **Type** AGAIN

Click the **AGAIN folder** and **click Open** or **double-click** the **AGAIN folder**:

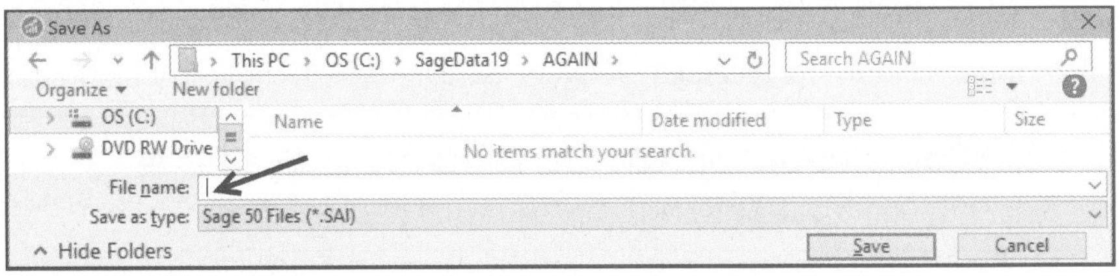

We can now enter the name for the new company file. NEW.SAI may be selected.

Click the **File Name field**. **Type** AGAIN and **click Save**.

Now the same Home window is open, but it has the file name AGAIN.SAI (or AGAIN) in the title bar:

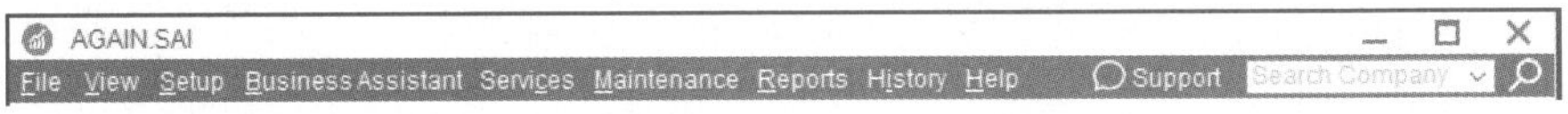

The Receivables module is the default for the Home window. We will change this default because Love It Again does not use this module.

Changing the Default Home Window

Love It Again uses only the General Ledger (Company module), so we will make this the Home window. The Receivables module has Default Page beside the name.

Click **Company** in the list of modules on the left to change the Home window.

Now we have the Chart of Accounts and the General Journal available. The message beside Company has changed to Make Default. Clicking this option for any module will select the displayed module as the default Home window.

Click **Make Default**. The Company heading now has Default Page beside it:

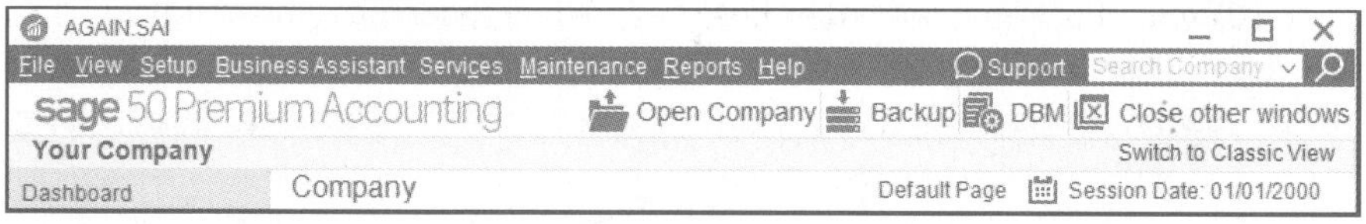

> **NOTES**
> The open history or not-finished symbol appears on the Chart of Accounts icon in the Company module window.

Preparing the System

Before entering financial records for a new company, you must prepare the system for operation. This involves changing the default settings to reflect the Love It Again company information, such as the company name and address, fiscal dates, screen display preferences and Chart of Accounts. Some initial defaults will not be suitable for Love It Again. You must also provide other information, such as the printer(s) that you will be using and the printing formats. This process of adding, deleting and modifying information is called customizing the system.

Changing Company Default Settings

Click the **Settings icon**  in the Related Tasks pane, or **choose** the **Setup menu** and **click Settings**:

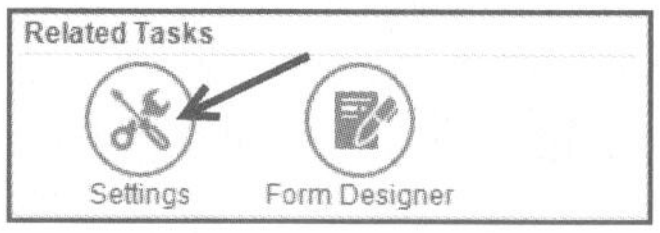

The Company Settings main menu window opens:

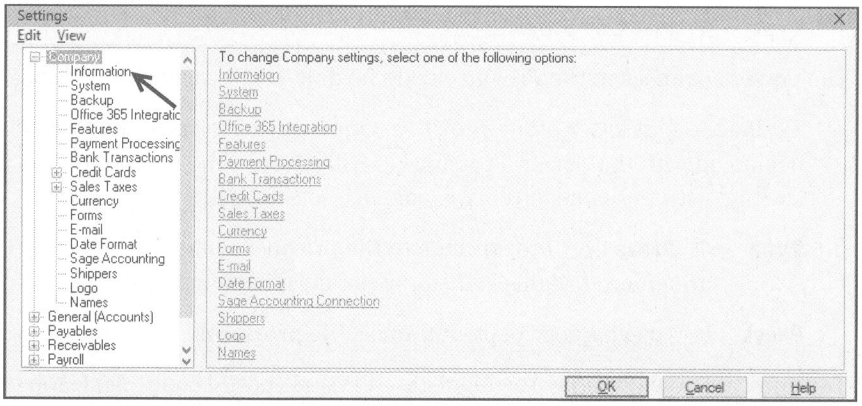

Most settings for a data file are entered from this central Settings screen. Most apply to features and modules not used by Love It Again. We will skip the screens that do not apply; they will be introduced in later chapters.

The modules are listed on the left. The remaining modules have a  beside them indicating they also have multiple settings. The larger right-hand pane begins with the same expanded list of entries for the selected module as the expanded list on the left. The open Company module has a  beside it.

Clicking a  beside an entry will expand the list and change the icon to . Clicking an entry in the list on the left without a  beside it or in the list on the right-hand side will open the options window for that entry.

Entering Company Information

Company settings apply to all modules of the company for all users of the data file.

> **NOTES**
> You cannot complete the setup in multi-user mode.

> **NOTES**
> The Sage 50 Setup menu includes a Setup Guide for modifying and creating ledger records. We will use this method to edit or modify the accounts.
> The Setup menu also has wizards for linked accounts, adding users and updating HST. Because none of these wizards modify all company settings, we cannot use them to complete the setup.

> **NOTES**
> If another module is open when you choose Settings, the settings for that ledger will open first. Click Company and then click Information to open the Information screen.

> **NOTES**
> Clicking the  beside a module name will collapse the expanded list.

Click **Information** (in either the left-hand side or right-hand side list) to open the Company information screen:

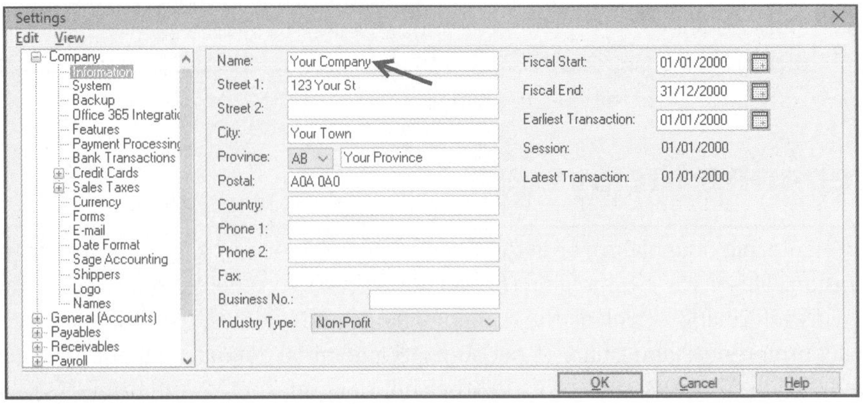

WARNING!
The initial date format for this file is day/month/year. This is evident from the Fiscal End date.

The Name field contains the information "Your Company" to let you know that this is where you should enter the name of your company.

Press *tab* or **drag through Your Company** to select this text.

Type `Love It Again` (add your own name). **Press** *tab*.

NOTES
You can personalize your files by adding your own name to the Name field (e.g., Love It Again – Sabeena) so that all reports printed will include your name for easy identification.

The cursor moves to the Street 1 field, the first address field. You can enter the address immediately because the current contents are already highlighted.

Type `4-A Charity Drive`

Press *tab* to advance to the second street address line (Street 2 field).

Press *tab* again to leave this field blank. The cursor advances to and highlights the contents of the City field.

Type `Toronto` **Press** *tab*.

The cursor advances to the Province code field. It, too, is ready for editing.

Typing the first letter of the province name will enter the first province beginning with that letter. Pressing ↓ will advance the list to the next province starting with the same letter. You can also select a code from the drop-down list.

NOTES
All provinces and territories in Canada have a two-letter abbreviation code.
Several province names begin with N. Typing N will enter NB for New Brunswick. Pressing the keyboard down arrow again will enter NL; pressing ↓ again will enter NS and so on.

Type `O` **Press** *tab* to advance to the province name field. ON and Ontario are entered as this is the only province beginning with "O."

Press *tab* again to accept Ontario as the province.

The cursor is now placed in the highlighted Postal (postal code) field. You do not have to type the capitals or spaces in postal codes.

Type `m4g2t2`

NOTES
All postal codes in Canada use the following pattern: Letter, Number, Letter, Number, Letter, Number. Any other sequence, as for other countries, will not be changed by the program, and you should enter the correct format.

The program automatically corrects the postal code format when you enter a Canadian postal code pattern.

In this case, all addresses will be in Canada, so we can leave the Country field blank. Now enter the telephone and fax numbers for the business. There is only one phone number, so the Phone 2 field will remain blank. You do not need to type brackets or hyphens for phone numbers. Sage 50 will correct the format when you enter a seven- or ten-digit phone number.

Click the **Phone 1 field**. The postal code format is corrected.

Type `4168858967`

Click the **Fax field**. The telephone number format is corrected.

Type 6478858967

Press tab to move to the Business No. field.

All companies must use a single Canada Revenue Agency business number that also serves as the HST registration number. All business numbers have an R*x* extension that indicates the business area for tax purposes.

Type 127362648 RR0001 **Press** tab.

There are a number of types of companies to choose from in the program. We selected the type when we upgraded the data file. You can select from the **Industry Type** list to change the type. Changing the company type will also change the icon labels.

Sage 50 will accept dates after January 1, 1900. You can store 100 years of accounting records.

The **Fiscal Start** field contains the date at which the current fiscal year begins. This date usually defines the beginning of the fiscal year for income tax purposes.

The **Fiscal End** is the date at which the company closes its books, usually one year after the fiscal start, and the end of the fiscal year used for income tax reporting purposes. For Love It Again, the fiscal end is two months after converting the files to Sage 50.

The **Earliest Transaction** date is the date on which the company converts its manual accounting records to the computerized system. Entries before this date are historical entries. The earliest transaction date must not be earlier than the fiscal start and not later than the fiscal end. The earliest transaction date will be the first session date when you are ready to enter journal transactions. Sage 50 automatically advances the earliest transaction date when you start a new fiscal year.

The **default date format** for this file is day-month-year. We will enter the fiscal dates in text form and then change the date format for the file. By entering text with four digits for the year initially, we will ensure that we enter the date correctly.

Press tab to advance to the Fiscal Start field.

Type oct 1 2020 **Press** tab **twice**.

Sage 50 entered 01/10/2020 as the fiscal start. The cursor is in the Fiscal End field.

Type sep 30 2021 **Press** tab **twice**.

Sage 50 has entered 30/09/2021 as the fiscal end. The cursor is now in the Earliest Transaction field.

Type aug 1 2021

The session date and the latest transaction date will change automatically as you complete journal entries and advance the session date from the Home window. When the **latest transaction date** is later than the session date, it indicates there are postdated journal transactions.

You cannot change the fiscal start or earliest transaction date after finishing the history and making journal entries. The company name, address and fiscal end date can be edited at any time. Return to any field with errors to correct mistakes.

You will need to save the fiscal dates before completing the next step.

Click **OK**.

PRO VERSION

You should select Non-Profit from the Industry Type drop-down list because you did not select it previously (there was no file conversion). Icon labels do not change when you select a different company type.

You can store seven years of company data.

NOTES

Companies may use a fiscal period shorter than one year for reporting purposes and close their books more frequently, but the most common period is one year.

NOTES

From the initial Fiscal End Date entry, 31/12/2000, you can tell that the date order is day-month-year. You cannot determine the order from the Start and Earliest Transaction dates.

NOTES

When we entered various dates, the program accepted dates between 1900 and 4000 without an error message. There appear to be no practical restrictions on the dates you can use.

WARNING!

Type the date as text to avoid number confusion, such as entering Jan 10 instead of Oct 1.

Type 2020 and 2021 (use four digits) for the year. If you type 20 and 21, Sage 50 will enter 1920 and 1921.

This file was updated from an earlier version, so it will revert to entering 1920 and 1921.

NOTES

When you view the Company Information again, the session and latest transaction dates will have been updated to match the new fiscal dates.

PRO VERSION
There is no warning about changing the industry type because the terminology does not change in the Pro version.

If you change the industry type from this Information screen, the following Sage 50 message requests confirmation before making the change:

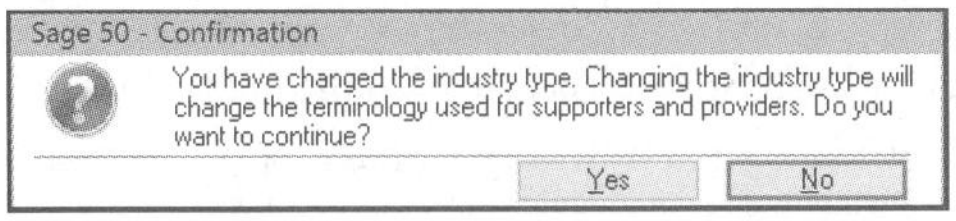

Click **Yes** to accept the changes.

WARNING!
You must save the new fiscal dates before changing the Do Not Allow Transactions Before date.

Setting System Defaults

Click the **Settings icon** Settings, or **choose** the **Setup menu** and **click Settings** to resume.

Click **System** in the list under Company to access the options:

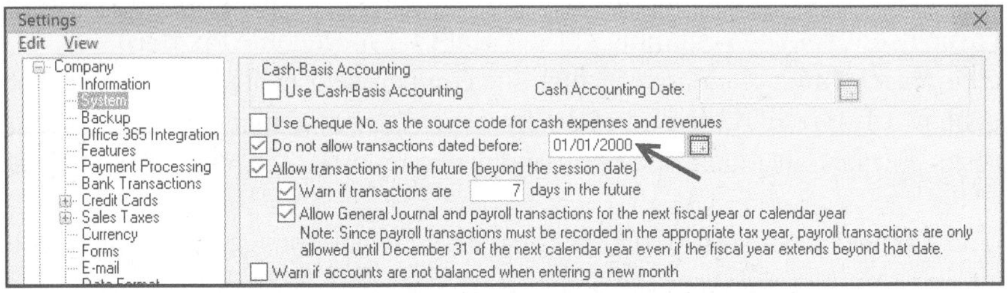

PRO VERSION
The option to enter transactions in a later fiscal or calendar year is not available.

NOTES
Refer to Appendix M on the Student DVD for more information on accrual- and cash-basis accounting. Refer to Appendix H on the Student DVD for an exercise with keystrokes that uses cash-basis accounting in Sage 50.

The Company System settings apply to all modules of the program.

This screen has several important settings. The first refers to whether the business is using **cash-basis accounting** instead of the default, **accrual-basis accounting**. The cash basis of accounting records revenues and expenses on the date the money is paid or received. In the accrual method, revenues and expenses are recorded on the transaction date (matching principle). To change to the cash-basis method, click the check box and enter the date on which the change is to take effect. This text uses the accrual basis. Do not change this setting.

PRO VERSION
The terms Purchases and Sales will replace Expenses and Revenues.

The next option relates to the use of the **Cheque Number As The Source Code For Cash Expenses And Revenues** in account reconciliation. Since Love It Again uses only the General Ledger, this option does not apply. When you are using the Payables and Receivables ledgers, you should turn on this option.

WARNING!
The date you enter for Do Not Allow Transactions Dated Before must not be earlier than the Earliest Transaction Date on the Company Information screen.

If the check box is not checked, you can leave the date field blank. You can also enter the date later.

If you did not save the new fiscal dates, you will get an error message when you enter Aug 1 2021 – the original fiscal year 2000 will restrict the date allowed.

The next option, **Do Not Allow Transactions Dated Before**, permits you to lock out transactions before the date you enter here to prevent posting incorrectly to an earlier date. Similarly, you should generally not **allow posting to future periods**, beyond the session date, unless you are entering a series of postdated transactions. You can add a warning for dates beyond a certain period as well. You can activate these features for specific transactions when needed by changing the settings so that you do not post with incorrect dates. We will restrict transactions before the earliest transaction date and not allow postdated transactions. Transactions before the earliest transaction date are not allowed after you finish the history.

Remember that the date format is still day-month-year.

Ensure that **Do Not Allow Transactions Dated Before** has a ✓.

Drag through the date **01/01/2000**.

Type `aug 1` (Sage 50 will add the year from the fiscal date information.)

Click **Allow Transactions In The Future** to remove the ✓ and not allow postdating.

NOTES
Refer to page 106 for details on allowing transactions in a previous year.

Since Sage 50 allows journal entries before the company setup details are completed, you can add a reminder **warning** as you continue to work with an incomplete and **unbalanced account history**. If you choose to post journal entries before completing the history, you should turn on the warning.

Setting Backup Options

Click **Backup** in the list under Company:

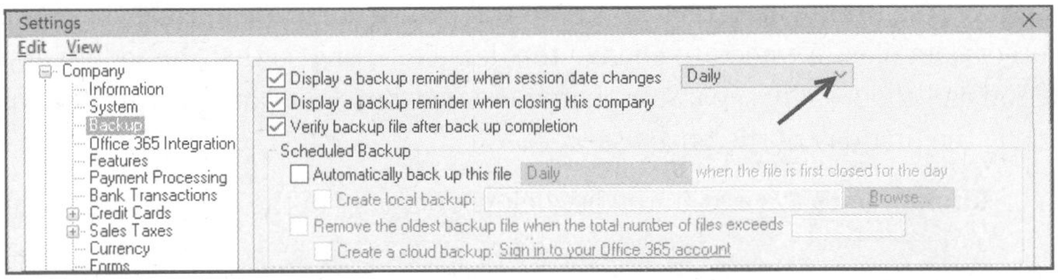

This screen has options for backing up company files. You can select the **frequency** with which you **back up** your data. Since we usually advance the session date weekly, we will choose Weekly as the backup frequency as well. The program prompts you to back up according to this entry.

Click the **Display A Backup Reminder field list arrow** and **choose Weekly**.

If you want a specific number of days as the interval between backups, choose Other and type the number in the Number Of Days field that opens.

The next option will provide a **reminder** to back up the file each time you close the company file. Leave the option selected because you should back up data files regularly.

You should **verify** the backup files regularly to ensure there are no errors that will prevent you from restoring the data later.

You can **schedule automatic backups** by choosing the frequency, the backup file location and the **number of old backup files** that should be saved.

Choosing Company Features

Sage 50 includes a number of features that are not used by Love It Again — they do not apply to the General Ledger. We can turn them off to reduce the complexity of the screens and setup.

Click **Features** in the list below Company in the left-hand side panel:

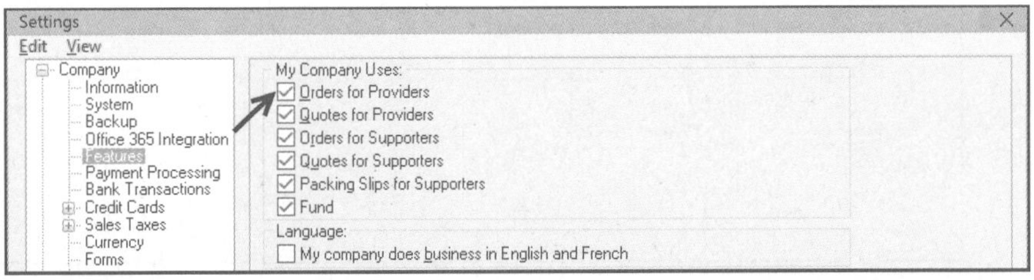

Orders, quotes and packing slips do not apply to General Ledger transactions. The final option refers to languages used. To create forms and add field names in both languages, you must choose the option to conduct business in English and French. The Settings option makes the language switch available for many name fields so you can enter names in both languages. The working language for the program is controlled from the View menu (refer to pages 84–85), not from the Features setting.

Click **each check box** or **feature** to change all settings. This will remove all checkmarks and add one to **My Company Does Business In English And French**, the final option.

Credit cards, sales taxes, currency, e-mail and form numbers, such as for invoices and quotes, do not apply to the General Journal transactions entered by Love It Again.

NOTES

Sage 50 forces the General Ledger to remain balanced, so this warning does not apply to Love It Again (refer to page 97).

PRO VERSION

Packing slips are not available in the Pro version. The terms Vendors, Customers and Project replace Providers, Supporters and Fund.

CLASSIC VIEW

The program's working language can be changed from the tool bar by clicking the Switch to French tool FR. The tool becomes Switch to English EN. Click this tool to change back to working in English.

Love It Again does not use Shippers or the additional Names fields in the General Ledger, so you can skip these screens as well.

Changing Date Formats

The date formats for the starter file are different from the formats we used for other files. To avoid entering incorrect dates, we will choose the same format that we used for our other data files. We need to change the default setting so that the month appears first. You can choose any separator character you want. You can also enter the day that is normally the first day of the business week.

Click **Date Format** in the list below Company in the left-hand side panel:

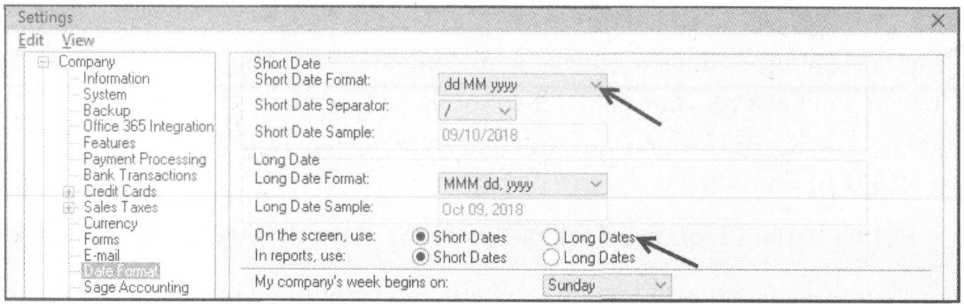

Choose **MM dd yyyy** from the Short Date Format drop-down list.

Choose another separator symbol from the Short Date Separator list, if you want.

On the screen we choose the long form for dates, that is, text style, to make them as clear as possible. You can choose long or short dates for reports.

Click **Long Dates** beside the option for On The Screen, Use.

Adding a Company Logo

Next we will add the company logo. This logo can be added to invoices or other company documents created in Sage 50.

Click **Logo**:

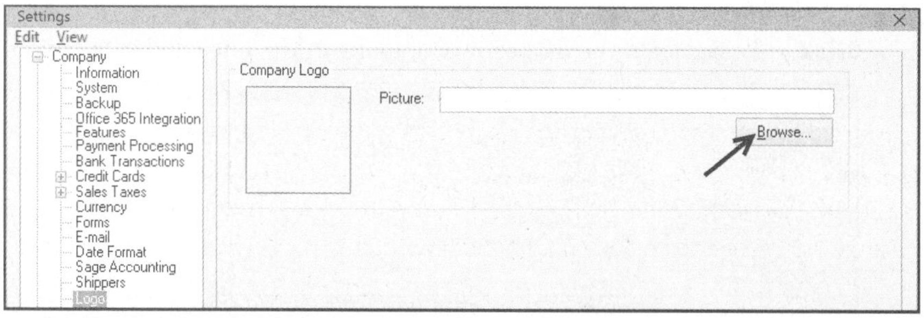

Click **Browse**. **Click This PC** (or Computer) in the left pane. **Double-click C:**. Then **double-click SageData19** and **LOGOS** to locate the folder with company logos.

Click **AGAIN.BMP** (or **AGAIN**) and **click Open** to return to the Logo Settings with the image and file name added:

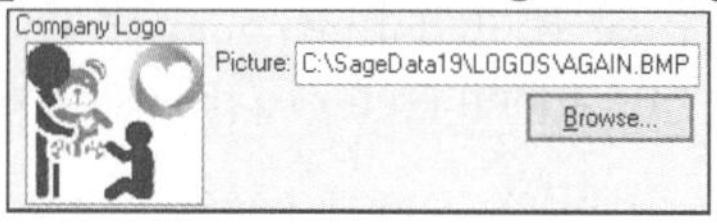

Setting General Defaults

To change the settings for the General Ledger for Love It Again,

Click **General (Accounts)** in the modules pane on the left:

NOTES

Some Company settings – Office 365 Integration, Payment Processing and Sage Accounting and Bank Transactions – link your Sage 50 data file with a subscription-based third-party application.

NOTES

The entry for Week Begins On is used for reports that have This Week To Date as an option for the date range.

NOTES

Company logo files are located in the SageData19\LOGOS folder. The default Browse starting point is the folder that contains your active data file.

You can also start by clicking in the Path field.

CLASSIC VIEW

From the Home window you can access the General Settings window by clicking the Settings tool and selecting Accounts. If the Chart of Accounts icon in the Home window is already selected, you will access the General Settings directly when you click the Settings tool.

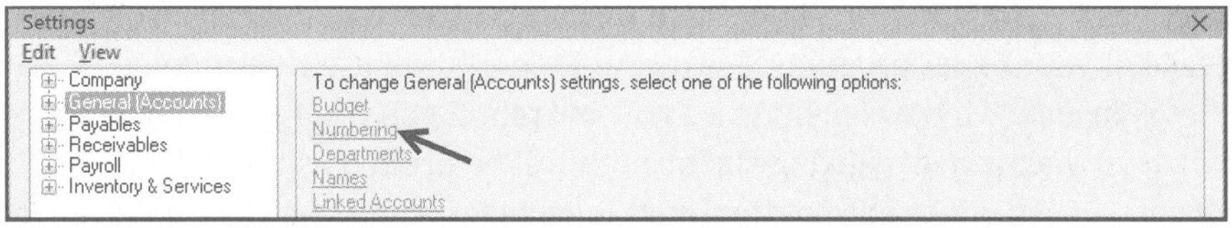

If you want Sage 50 to prepare budget reports, clicking **Budget** will open the Budget setup options and allow you to enter budget amounts for revenue and expense accounts and prepare budget reports. You can activate budgeting at any time.

Love It Again does not have different **Departments** to track expenses, so we do not need to turn on this option.

Click **Numbering**:

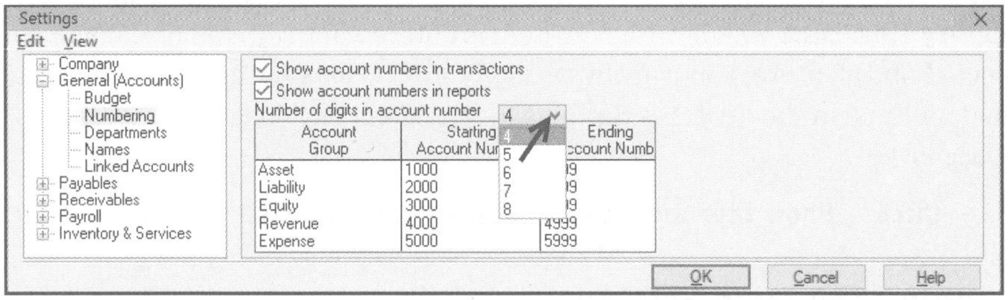

From the **Numbering** option, you can choose not to use account numbers in your reports and journal transactions when the account names are unique; that is, there is no duplication of names. We use account numbers in all the applications in this text.

You can also choose the **number of digits** for your account numbers. Each digit you add to create five- to eight-digit numbers will add an extra zero to the starting and ending number for the account group. For example, when you use six-digit numbers, the Asset accounts will range from 100 000 to 199 900, and the Liabilities accounts will range from 200 000 to 299 900. Using extra digits allows you to create more accounts.

For Love It Again, we use four-digit account numbers. You do not need to change the settings for the other ledgers — they are not used by Love It Again.

Click **OK** to save all the changes and return to the Home window. The session date is displayed with the new format — Aug 1, 2021.

Changing User Preference Settings

User preferences apply to individual users and indicate the way that person prefers to work with the data files. They do not affect the accounting processes. If you have multiple users who access the files, each user can set his or her own preferences.

All user preference settings can be changed at any time by clicking an option again.

Choose the **Setup menu**, then **click** **User Preferences**:

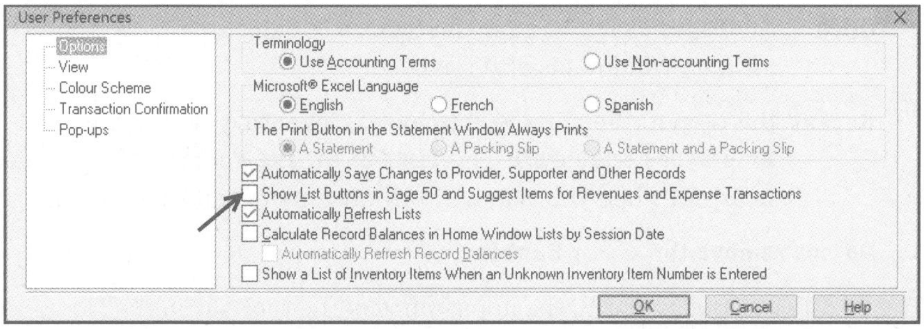

The first feature refers to the language used by the program. We use **accounting terms** throughout this workbook. If you choose non-accounting terms, the Payables Ledger will be named Vendors and Purchases in menus and so on. To follow the

NOTES

You can click the beside Company, as we did, to close the expanded Company list.

NOTES

The budgeting feature is explained in the Sound Inc. application, Chapter 14.

PRO VERSION

Departments are not available in the Pro version.

In the Pro version, you cannot change the number of digits for account numbers.

NOTES

When you do not use account numbers, Sage 50 will prevent you from entering duplicate account names.

NOTES

In Part Two of this text, we use four-digit account numbers so that account numbers will be the same for Pro or Premium users. We introduce Departments and five-digit account numbers in Part Three, Chapter 19, for Premium users.

NOTES

If you need to insert additional accounts, adding a digit to the account number creates room between adjacent account numbers.

PRO VERSION

The Automatically Refresh Lists option is not on the list because it refers to the multi-user options.

Because packing slips are not available in the Pro version, the option to choose between printing invoices or packing slips is also omitted.

NOTES

Appendix B lists equivalent accounting and non-accounting terms.

NOTES
The Excel language option will apply only if you have installed a non-English language version of the Excel program.

NOTES
The Refresh Lists option applies only to the multi-user version of Sage 50 Premium.

NOTES
Many account input fields, like the Account field that you saw in the General Journal in Chapter 3, have list buttons or icons. Other fields have list arrows that provide a drop-down or pop-up list to select from. Inventory and allocations are covered in Chapters 10 and 13, respectively.

PRO VERSION
There is no Time & Billing feature in the Pro version, so you will not need to hide it. The term Project replaces Fund.

CLASSIC VIEW
There are two lists: Modules and Icon Windows. Time & Billing is added to the Modules list. Banking is not included in the lists.

NOTES
When you hide modules and icon windows, all information about icon positions is removed. Sage 50 advises you of this when you display the records in the account windows by icon instead of by name. When you view a page, you can hide its icon window separately.

WARNING!
If you do not hide the remaining modules, you will be unable to complete the final setup step of finishing the history because essential information for those modules is missing.

WARNING!
Do not hide the Banking page. If you hide this page, you will be unable to access the General Journal.

instructions we provide, you should **Use Accounting Terms**. You can also choose the **language** of your **Excel** program — exported reports will use the language chosen here.

Some invoice windows include a **Print button**. If you print these invoices, you can set whether the invoice, packing slip or both will be printed as the default.

If you choose not to **automatically save changes** when you close a ledger record window, the program will prompt you to save changes when you close the ledger record and give you the option of always saving automatically. **Including the list selection button** in all account fields to select account numbers, vendors and so on is the option used in this text. The next feature allows the account **record balances** displayed in the Home windows (e.g., for customers) to be **calculated by session date** instead of by the latest transaction that may be earlier or later than the session date. The **refresh lists automatically** option applies when working in multi-user mode. You can select to show **inventory item lists** whenever a new item is entered in the item field. When you use the Project (Fund) feature, you can always **apply allocations** to the entire transaction. We turned off Fund in the Features Settings for this company (page 79), so this option has been removed.

Click **Show List Buttons In Sage 50 And Suggest Items....**

Changing the View Settings

Several important display or appearance options are controlled from the View option.

Click **View**:

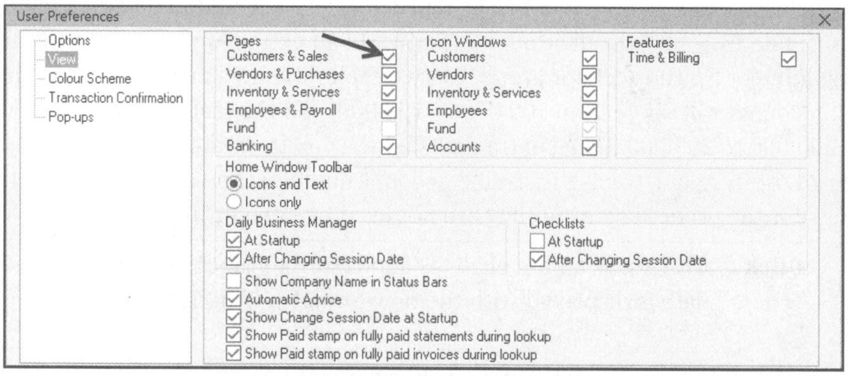

You can **hide**, that is, not display, the icons for **modules** or **pages** that you are not using. We must hide the modules that are not used before finishing the history. Fund is already deselected in the list of pages because we turned off the feature.

The **Icon Windows** check boxes allow you to hide the accounts icon window for the ledgers. Selecting the Chart of Accounts icon (or other ledger icon) with this option on will display the first ledger record instead of the Accounts window list of accounts. Icon windows can be hidden separately only if the module pages are not hidden.

Click the **Pages check box for Customers & Sales** to remove the ✓. The ✓ for Icon Windows is also removed.

Repeat this step for **Vendors & Purchases**, **Inventory & Services** and **Employees & Payroll**. The **Time & Billing Feature** ✓ is automatically removed when you remove both Customers and Employees.

Do not remove the ✓ for **Banking**.

The next two options refer to the appearance of the **tool bar** in the Home window. You can display the tools with text or as icons only. The Classic view Home window tool bar never includes text. In our data files, we include the text with the icons.

Sage 50 has reminders about upcoming activities such as payments that are due, discounts available and recurring entries. The **Checklists** and the **Daily Business Manager** can remind you of these activities each time you start the program, each time you advance the session date or both. Love It Again does not use these lists.

Click **At Startup** and **click After Changing Session Date** for **Daily Business Manager** to **remove** the ✓s.

If you clicked Yes to remove it when the Business Manager opened at startup, it will not have the ✓ now.

Click **After Changing Session Date** for **Checklists** to **remove** the ✓.

You can **Show Company Name In Status Bars** or omit this detail. We show the name.

Automatic Advice provides advisory messages automatically while you are entering transactions, as, for example, when customers exceed credit limits or the chequing account is overdrawn. Clicking removes the ✓ and the feature. Leave Advice turned on.

We also select to **show the session date** each time we start a work session. If your company has several users who log on frequently during a single day, bypassing this step would be efficient. In that case, the system administrator would update the session date for all users at the start of each business day.

Showing the **Paid Stamp** on invoices and payments is another option. If you hide the Vendors & Customers pages, these options will be dimmed because they no longer apply.

Click **Colour Scheme**. You can choose backgrounds from a variety of colours and patterns for the different journal windows.

NOTES

You can access Checklists and the Daily Business Manager at any time from the Business Assistant menu, even if the automatic display for them is turned off. You can turn on the automatic display again at any time from this User Preferences View settings screen.

Checklists are covered in Chapters 12 and 15; the Daily Business Manager is covered in Chapter 11.

NOTES

Remember that these are user preferences – each user can change these settings for personal preferences. User setup is described in Chapter 16 and Appendix G.

Confirming Posting of Transactions Settings

We will choose to have the program advise when transactions are successfully recorded.

Click **Transaction Confirmation**.

If a warning about losing icon position information opens (refer to margin Notes on page 82), click Yes to continue to the transaction confirmation window:

Click the **check box** beside Tell Me When A Transaction Is Posted Or Recorded Successfully to add a ✓ and turn on the confirmation.

Click **Pop-ups**:

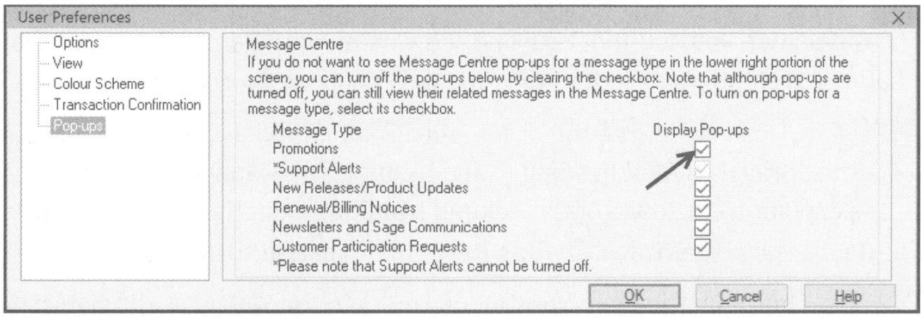

NOTES

We have turned off pop-ups for the data files we provided on the Student DVD.

Support Alerts is dimmed – you cannot turn off the display of these messages.

On this screen you control the types of messages Sage 50 will provide. Clicking a check box will remove a ✓ and prevent that type of message from appearing for this data file.

Click the **messages** that you do not want in order to remove the ✓s.

Click **OK** to save the settings and return to the updated Home window:

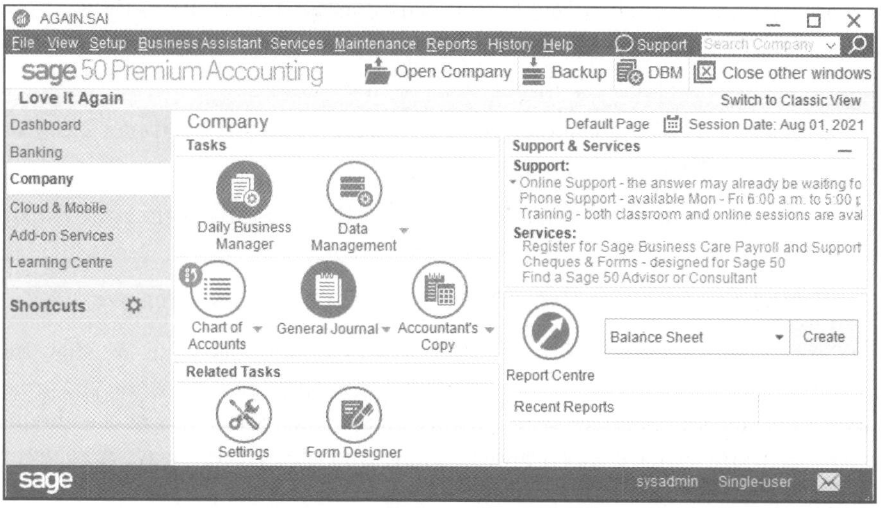

The unused modules (hidden pages) have been removed from the Modules pane list and the session date is displayed in the long date format we selected for the screen.

Changing View Menu Settings

Click the **View menu**:

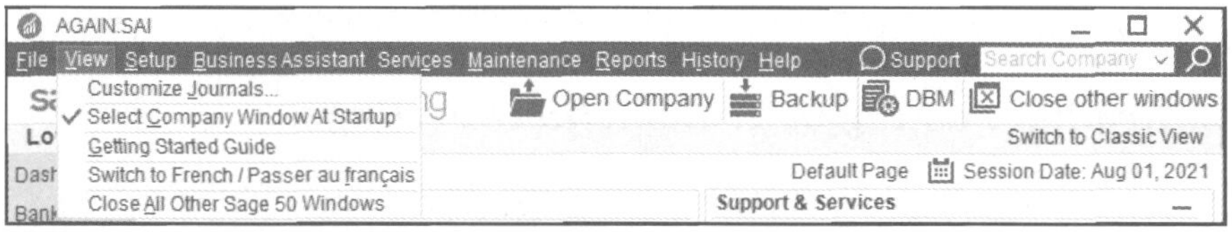

The View menu controls some appearance options for the program.

Each journal may be customized by hiding optional fields that are not used. You can also change the order in which journal fields are accessed from the *tab* key, that is, which field is next when you press *tab*. You can **customize all journals** from this menu or you can use the customize option within individual journals.

> To customize a journal, choose the View menu and click Customize Journals. Click the journal you want. Click Columns or Tabbing Order and click the columns or details you want to change. Hidden fields may be restored at any time by clicking their names again.
>
> Click OK to save the changes and return to the Home window.

The **Customize Journal** tool and View menu option in each journal provide the same options as the Home window View menu Customize Journals screen.

> You can also customize the order and size of journal columns. To change the order, drag a column heading to the location you want. To change the column size, point to the edge of the column heading; when the pointer changes to a double-headed arrow, drag the column margin to its new size.

The next choice on the main View menu refers to the **Welcome and Select Company window** that appears when you first start Sage 50. There are advantages to showing this window. If you regularly use the same data file, you can bypass the Open Company file window and open your data file with a single step by selecting Open The Last Company You Worked On. Similarly, you can restore a backup file from this window without first opening another data file. The View menu setting acts as a toggle switch, and you can change it at any time.

NOTES

We have not hidden fields in any journals used in the applications in this text, except by turning off features, so you can learn the full range of input options for each journal.

We provide instructions on how to customize journals in Chapter 6 and invoices in Appendix F on the Student DVD.

NOTES

If you have the Select Company window hidden or deselected, you will start from the Open Company window each time you start Sage 50. You can turn on the selection again from the Home window View menu in any open data file.

Sage 50 is a fully bilingual program. You can **switch the program language** (choose to work in French or in English) from the View menu with this toggle switch. When you are working in French, the View menu (now renamed *Vue*) option changes to *Passer A L'Anglais*/Switch To English.

You can also switch languages by clicking the Switch to French tool FR in the Classic view tool bar.

The final View menu option allows you to **close all other Sage 50 windows** in a single step, leaving only the Home window open. This menu choice is the same as the one provided by the Home window tool bar icon.

Changing the Printer Defaults

You may select a different printer for customized forms, or you may want to change the format of the printed reports.

The following instructions should assist you in making the selections you need.

Choose the **Setup menu** and **click Reports & Forms**:

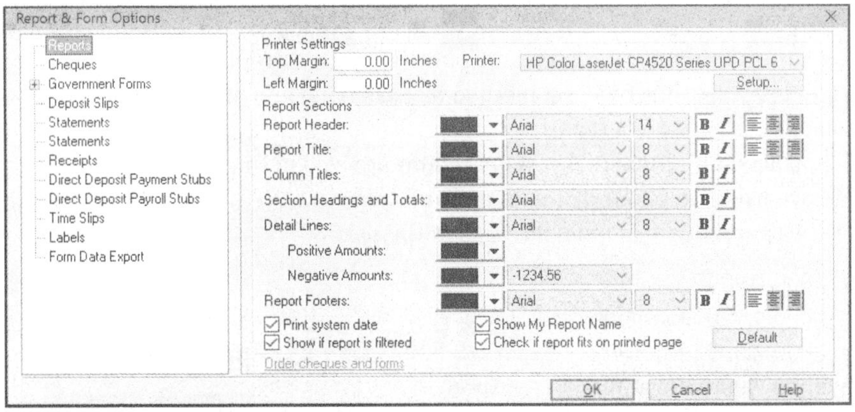

Printer selections are saved with each company file. If you use the file with another computer system or if you installed program updates, the selections may be incorrect. Sage 50 allows you to set up different printers and settings for reports, cheques, invoices, labels and so on. Many companies use different printers for their reports and preprinted forms and invoices. Even if you use one printer, you may want to adjust fonts, margins and form selections for each type of printed report or statement.

Choose the printer you will use for reports from the list provided by the arrow beside the field. All printers installed on your computer should be on the list. Change the page margins if necessary. For each part of the report, choose font, type size, colour and how to display positive and negative numbers by clicking the list arrows beside these fields. You can experiment to find the combination that will best fit the reports on the page. By default, reports include the computer system date and a message indicating whether filtering is applied.

To modify the printer setup for other outputs, click the relevant form in the list. You can modify printer setup information at any time by returning to this screen.

Additional printer settings may be available from the Setup button screen for print quality, paper source, paper size, two-sided printing, orientation and so on. The screens and options will vary from printer to printer.

Click **Cancel** to exit without making changes and return to the Home window, or click OK to leave each dialogue box and save the change.

CLASSIC VIEW

Click FR (the Switch to French tool) on the tool bar to change the program's working language to French.

The tool changes to EN. Click this tool to change back to working in English.

NOTES

The first entry for Statements refers to customer statements; the next entry refers to invoices.

PRO VERSION

The Time Slips entry is not included. The term Invoices replaces the second entry for Statements.

WARNING!

You should view the additional printer control screens, but you do not need to change them. The printer control screens will vary from one printer to another. Usually the default settings are correct. For that reason, we provide the printer instructions as optional command statements.

WARNING!

You need to choose a printer for reports and for each form listed. The default may be incorrect if you have changed your computer setup after installing the program. Printer settings may also be incorrect if you use a data file that was created on a different computer.

NOTES

Remember that you can end your session at any time and continue later from where you left off.

NOTES
Print the Chart of Accounts before you begin and compare it to the Chart of Accounts for Love It Again. Choose the Reports menu in the Home window, then choose Lists and click Chart of Accounts. Refer to page 62 for help with displaying the Chart of Accounts if necessary.

The Chart of Accounts from the Non-Profit template requires many more changes. To view its Chart of Accounts, you must create a new company using the Non-Profit Template.

NOTES
Account classes will be explained in Chapter 7 when you set up the files for Air Care Services. For now you can accept the default class settings.

Preparing the Ledgers

The third stage in setting up an accounting system involves preparing each ledger for operation. For Love It Again, this stage involves the following steps:

1. organizing all accounting reports and records (this step has been completed)
2. modifying some existing accounts (you will not need to delete any accounts)
3. creating new accounts
4. entering historical account balance information

Defining the Skeleton Starter Files

When you created the company files for Love It Again in stage one, Creating Company Files (page 71), some preset accounts were provided.

Print the **Chart of Accounts** for the current year to prepare for the next stage.

Accounts are organized by **section**: Asset, Liability, Equity, Revenue and Expense. The chart also has the **account type** — such as **H**eading (H), **S**ubgroup total (S), **T**otal (T), subgroup **A**ccount (A), **G**roup account (G) and Current Earnings (X) — and the account class. Account type is a method of classifying and organizing accounts within a section or subsection of a report.

Initial account numbers for each account are also in the Chart of Accounts.

We are using only four digits for account numbers, so the accounts in this chart follow the same sectional boundaries as in Chapter 3:

- 1000–1999 Assets
- 2000–2999 Liabilities
- 3000–3999 Equity
- 4000–4999 Revenue
- 5000–5999 Expense

The Format of Financial Statements

When setting up the complete Chart of Accounts for Love It Again, it is important to understand the composition and format of financial statements in Sage 50. The chart on the next page summarizes the application of the following rules in Sage 50.

The Balance Sheet is divided into three **sections**, each with **headings**: Asset, Liability and Equity. The Income Statement is divided into two sections with headings: Revenue and Expense.

Each section of the financial statements can be subdivided into groups. Assets can be divided into groups such as CURRENT ASSETS, INVENTORY ASSETS and PLANT AND EQUIPMENT. Liabilities can be divided into groups titled CURRENT LIABILITIES and LONG TERM DEBT. Equity, Revenue and Expense sections can also be divided. Groups may be further divided by creating subgroups.

Sage 50 requires that all accounts, including group headings, subgroup totals and group totals, be assigned numbers even if you do not use account numbers in transactions or reports. This is different from manual accounting, in which numbers are assigned only to postable accounts. Predefined section headings and section totals (e.g., ASSET, TOTAL ASSET and LIABILITY), however, are not assigned numbers by the program.

ORGANIZATION OF ACCOUNTS

BALANCE SHEET

Type	Number	Account Name	Amount	Amount
ASSET [section heading]				
H	**1000**	**CURRENT ASSETS**		
A	1020	Bank: Love It Again	xxx	
A	1100	Cash on Hand	xxx	
S	1150	Total Cash		xxx
G	1190	Prepaid Expenses		xxx
G	1200	Purchased Clothing		xxx
		–		
		–		
T	**1390**	**TOTAL CURRENT ASSETS**		**xxx**
H	**1500**	**FIXED ASSETS**		
G	1510	Fax/Telephone		xxx
G	1520	Computers		xxx
		–		
T	**1590**	**TOTAL FIXED ASSETS**		**xxx**
TOTAL ASSET [section total]				**xxx**
LIABILITY [section heading]				
H	**2000**	**CURRENT LIABILITIES**		
G	2100	Bank Loan		xxx
G	2200	A/P – Kids Stuff		xxx
		–		
T	**2690**	**TOTAL CURRENT LIABILITIES**		**xxx**
TOTAL LIABILITY [section total]				**xxx**
EQUITY [section heading]				
H	**3000**	**EQUITY**		
G	3560	Accumulated Surplus		xxx
X	3600	Net Income		xxx
		–		
T	**3690**	**TOTAL EQUITY**		**xxx**
TOTAL EQUITY [section total]				**xxx**
LIABILITIES & EQUITY				**xxx**

INCOME STATEMENT

Type	Number	Account Name	Amount	Amount
REVENUE [section heading]				
H	**4000**	**REVENUE**		
G	4020	Revenue: Donated Items		xxx
G	4040	Revenue: Purchased Clothing & Books		xxx
		–		
		–		
T	**4390**	**TOTAL REVENUE**		**xxx**
TOTAL REVENUE [section total]				**xxx**
EXPENSE [section heading]				
H	**5000**	**OPERATING EXPENSES**		
G	5020	Rental Expense		xxx
G	5200	Supplies Used		xxx
		–		
T	**5490**	**TOTAL OPERATING EXPENSES**		**xxx**
H	**5500**	**COST OF GOODS SOLD**		
G	5510	Cost of Purchased Clothing & Books		xxx
G	5520	Cost of Other Purchases		xxx
		–		
T	**5690**	**TOTAL COST OF GOODS SOLD**		**xxx**
TOTAL EXPENSE [section total]				**xxx**
NET INCOME				**xxx**

Type
H = Group **H**eading
T = Group **T**otal
G = Postable **G**roup Account
A = Postable Subgroup **A**ccount
S = Group **S**ubtotal
X = Current Earnings Account

Financial Statement Sections

These five rules apply to financial statement sections in Sage 50:

1. Each of the five financial statement sections has a **section heading** and a **section total**. You cannot change the titles for these headings and totals.
2. A **section total** is the total of the individual group totals within that section. The program will calculate section totals automatically and print them in the financial statement reports. The five section totals are
   - TOTAL ASSET
   - TOTAL LIABILITY
   - TOTAL EQUITY
   - TOTAL REVENUE
   - TOTAL EXPENSE
3. The Liability and Equity section totals are also automatically added together on the Balance Sheet. **LIABILITIES AND EQUITY** is the sum of TOTAL LIABILITY and TOTAL EQUITY.
4. Each section can have more than one group.

5. In the Income Statement, **NET INCOME**, the difference between TOTAL REVENUE and TOTAL EXPENSE, is automatically calculated and listed under TOTAL EXPENSE on the Income Statement.

Financial Statement Account Groups

Financial statement sections are further divided into user-defined account groups made up of different types of accounts. The following rules apply to account groups in Sage 50:

1. Each group must start with a **group Heading (H)**, which will be printed in boldface type. A heading is not considered a postable account, cannot be debited or credited through transaction entries and cannot have an amount assigned to it.
2. Groups contain one or more user-defined **postable accounts**. Postable accounts are those that can be debited or credited through journal transaction entries. Postable accounts may have an opening balance.
3. Postable accounts may be **subgroup Accounts (A)** or **Group accounts (G)**. Subgroup account balances appear in a separate column to the left of the Group account balances, which are in the right column.
4. Postable Subgroup accounts must be followed by a **Subgroup total (S)** account. A subgroup total is not a postable account and cannot be given an opening balance. The program automatically calculates a subgroup total by adding all preceding subgroup postable account balances that follow the last group, subgroup total or heading account. Subgroup total balances always appear in the right column with the Group accounts. For Love It Again, *GST Charged on Sales, HST Charged on Sales*, *GST Paid on Purchases* and *HST Paid on Purchases* are Subgroup accounts followed by the subgroup total *GST/HST Owing (Refund)*. The bank and cash accounts are also subtotalled.
5. Each group must end with a **group Total (T)**. All amounts in the right-hand column, for postable group and subgroup total accounts, are added together to form the group total. A group total is not a postable account. The program automatically calculates this total and prints it in boldface type.

   The chart on the previous page summarizes the application of these rules.

NOTES

Although omitting postable accounts in a group (between the Heading and Total) does not create an error message, it is not logical to have this account setup.

The Current Earnings (X) Account

There are two linked accounts for the General Ledger — **Retained Earnings** and **Current Earnings**, or Net Income. Both accounts are required and appear in the EQUITY section of the Balance Sheet. You do not need to change the links for these accounts.

The *Current Earnings* account is the only **Type X** account in the Chart of Accounts. This account is calculated as follows:

Current Earnings = Total Revenue - Total Expense

Current Earnings is not a postable account, but it appears with other Equity accounts in the Balance Sheet and on the Income Statement as Net Income. It cannot be removed, but its title and number can be modified (refer to the information on editing General Ledger accounts, page 89). *Current Earnings* is updated from any transactions that change revenue and expense account balances. At the end of the fiscal period when closing routines are performed, the balance of this account is added to *Retained Earnings* (or its renamed account) and then reset to zero.

For Love It Again, a charitable organization, the *Retained Earnings* account will be renamed *Accumulated Surplus*. *Current Earnings* will be renamed *Net Income*.

Preparing the General Ledger

As a first step, we must identify the changes needed in the Skeleton preset accounts to match the accounts needed for Love It Again. These changes are outlined below:

1. Some starter accounts provided by the program require no changes. For the following accounts, the account title, the initial account number and the account type are the same as those in the financial statements:

CURRENT ASSETS	1000	Type H
TOTAL CURRENT ASSETS	1390	Type T
CURRENT LIABILITIES	2000	Type H
TOTAL CURRENT LIABILITIES	2690	Type T
REVENUE	4000	Type H
TOTAL REVENUE	4390	Type T

NOTES
You will not need to delete any of the preset accounts for Love It Again.

NOTES
Remember that Type G accounts are Group accounts and Type A accounts are Subgroup accounts.

2. The following accounts have account titles or names that need to be changed. You must also change the account type for *Bank 1020* to Subgroup Account. The Account numbers are correct.

FROM (SKELETON ACCOUNTS)			**TO (LOVE IT AGAIN ACCOUNTS)**
Account Name	Number	Type	Account Name (Type)
Bank	1020	Type G	Bank: Love It Again (Type A)
Accounts Receivable	1200	Type G	Purchased Clothing
Accounts Payable	2200	Type G	A/P - Kids Stuff
EARNINGS	3000	Type H	EQUITY
Retained Earnings	3560	Type G	Accumulated Surplus
Current Earnings	3600	Type X	Net Income
TOTAL EARNINGS	3690	Type T	TOTAL EQUITY
General Revenue	4020	Type G	Revenue: Donated Items
EXPENSES	5000	Type H	OPERATING EXPENSES
General Expense	5020	Type G	Rental Expense

3. The following account requires changes in both the account name and the number:

FROM (SKELETON ACCOUNTS)			**TO (LOVE IT AGAIN ACCOUNTS)**	
Account Name	Number	Type	Account Name	Number
TOTAL EXPENSES	5390	Type T	TOTAL OPERATING EXPENSES	5490

Using the Setup Guide to Edit General Ledger Accounts

We will use the Setup Guide to modify the predefined accounts so that they match the ones used by Love It Again.

Click the **Setup menu** and **click Setup Guide**:

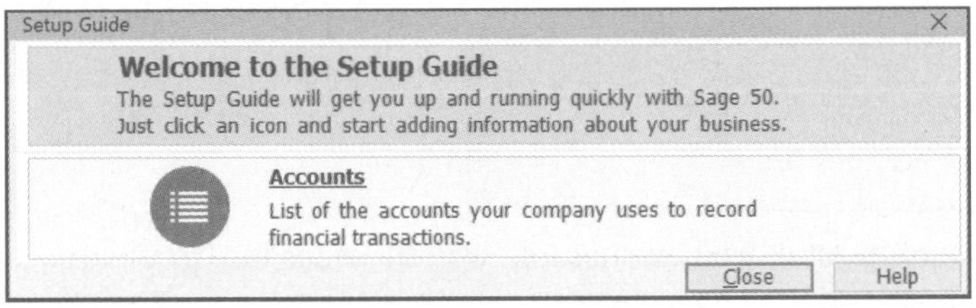

NOTES
When other modules are used, you can enter and modify records for them. We use the Guide to modify customer records in Chapter 6.

NOTES
The Opening Balance field for the Group Heading *CURRENT ASSETS* has – – entered instead of $0.00. This entry indicates that you cannot enter a balance for the account. Subgroup Totals will also have the option for an opening balance removed.

Click **Accounts**:

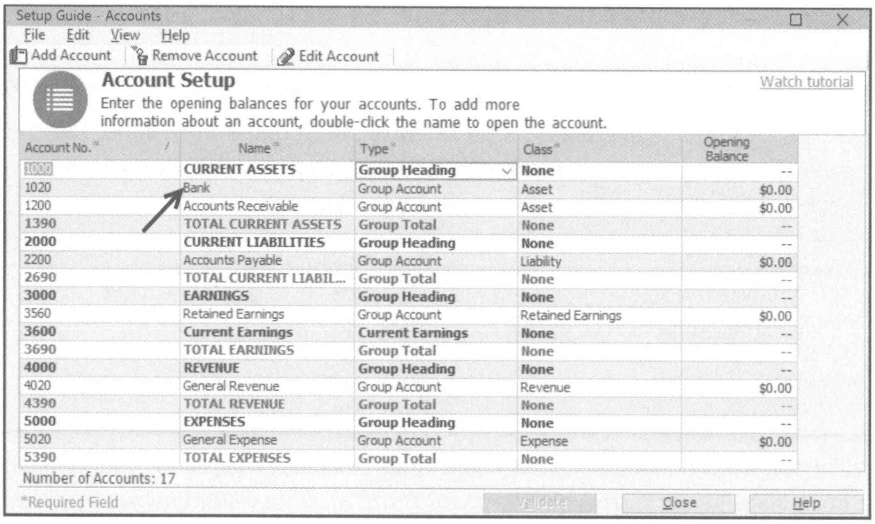

Account No.*	Name*	Type*	Class*	Opening Balance
1000	CURRENT ASSETS	Group Heading	None	--
1020	Bank	Group Account	Asset	$0.00
1200	Accounts Receivable	Group Account	Asset	$0.00
1390	TOTAL CURRENT ASSETS	Group Total	None	--
2000	CURRENT LIABILITIES	Group Heading	None	--
2200	Accounts Payable	Group Account	Liability	$0.00
2690	TOTAL CURRENT LIABIL...	Group Total	None	--
3000	EARNINGS	Group Heading	None	--
3560	Retained Earnings	Group Account	Retained Earnings	$0.00
3600	Current Earnings	Current Earnings	None	--
3690	TOTAL EARNINGS	Group Total	None	--
4000	REVENUE	Group Heading	None	--
4020	General Revenue	Group Account	Revenue	$0.00
4390	TOTAL REVENUE	Group Total	None	--
5000	EXPENSES	Group Heading	None	--
5020	General Expense	Group Account	Expense	$0.00
5390	TOTAL EXPENSES	Group Total	None	--

Compare this list and the Chart of Accounts you printed with the Love It Again Chart of Accounts, Balance Sheet and Income Statement provided in this application. Some accounts are the same, some account numbers match, but the names do not and some accounts you need are not yet in the program. You have to customize the accounts for Love It Again. The required changes are outlined on the preceding page.

The Guide allows us to edit a few details for all accounts from a single screen: the account number, name, type, class and opening account balance. We can also add and remove accounts from this screen.

NOTES
Do not double-click the account name – double-clicking will open the ledger record for the account (refer to page 93).

Click **Bank** in the Name field to highlight it for editing.

Type `Bank: Love It Again`

Click the **list arrow beside Group Account** in the Type field:

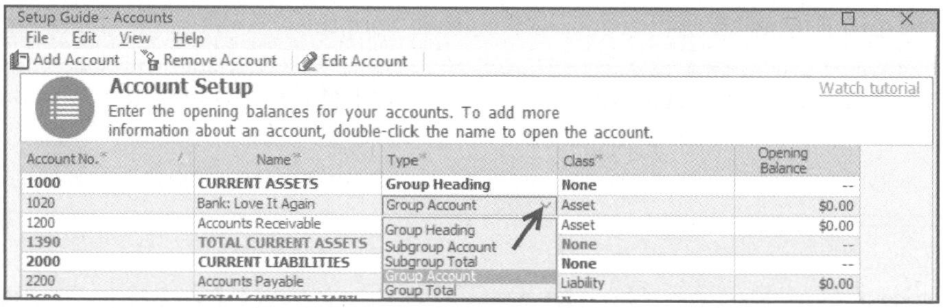

NOTES
You do not need to change the Type for any of the remaining predefined accounts.

Click **Subgroup Account**.

Make the **remaining account changes** on page 89 by clicking the appropriate field and typing the new information.

NOTES
Clicking Cancel will return you to the Guide so you can make corrections.

Click **Close**. Sage 50 advises that there is an error in the Chart of Accounts:

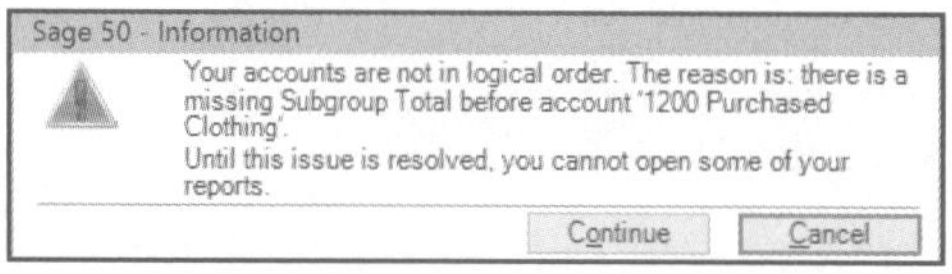

WARNING!
When the accounts are not in logical order, you cannot finish the history and you will be unbale to print financial reports.

Without the subgroup total, we have not followed the rules for Groups (page 88, rule 4). The accounts are not in logical order — a subtotal is missing. Periodically you can check the validity of accounts while you are editing or adding accounts (by clicking **Validate**) to determine whether you have made errors in your account type sequence that will prevent you from finishing the account history. When we add the subgroup account, *Cash on Hand*, and the subtotal, *Total Cash*, the accounts should be in logical order and the error will be corrected.

Click **Continue** to accept the error for now. **Click Close** to leave the Setup Guide.

Creating the Chart of Accounts: The Accounts Window

After modifying the predefined Skeleton accounts, the next step is to identify the accounts that you need to create or add to the preset accounts. Again, you should refer to the company Chart of Accounts on page 68 to complete this step.

The chart that follows has the accounts that you will need to create. The chart includes account names, account numbers, account types and the option to omit printing zero balances. It lists both postable (group and subgroup) and non-postable accounts (subgroup totals, group headings and group totals).

CHART OF ACCOUNTS TO BE CREATED

Account: *Number	*Name	Type	Omit
1100	Cash on Hand	[A]	No
1150	Total Cash	[S]	
1190	Prepaid Expenses		Optional
1210	Purchased Books		Optional
1220	Other Purchased Items		Optional
1300	Office Supplies		Optional
1310	Other Supplies		Optional
1320	T-shirts		Optional
1500	FIXED ASSETS	[H]	
1510	Fax/Telephone		Optional
1520	Computers		Optional
1530	Store Furniture & Shelving		Optional
1590	TOTAL FIXED ASSETS	[T]	
2100	Bank Loan		Optional
2300	A/P - Kids In Motion		Optional
2350	A/P - Wearable Designs		Optional
2400	A/P - Places For Us		Optional
2550	GST Charged on Sales	[A]	No
2560	HST Charged on Sales	[A]	No
2570	GST Paid on Purchases	[A]	No
2580	HST Paid on Purchases	[A]	No
2590	GST/HST Owing/Refund	[S]	
4040	Revenue: Purchased Clothing & Books		No
4080	Revenue: Other Purchases		No
4100	Revenue: Donations		No
5200	Supplies Used		Optional
5240	Postage Expense		Optional
5280	Maintenance Expenses		Optional
5300	Utilities Expenses		Optional
5320	Publicity & Promotion		Optional
5400	Wages - Manager		Optional
5420	Miscellaneous Expenses		Optional
5500	COST OF GOODS SOLD	[H]	
5510	Cost of Purchased Clothing & Books		Optional
5520	Cost of Other Purchases		Optional
5690	TOTAL COST OF GOODS SOLD	[T]	

Account Types: A = Subgroup Account S = Subgroup Total
G = Group Account H = Heading T = Group Total
* Account number and account name are required fields.

You are now ready to create the accounts in the Love It Again files.

From the Chart of Accounts icon  drop-down list, you can begin all ledger account record–related changes. You can also make many of these changes from the Setup Guide, but you will not have access to all ledger fields.

Click the **Chart of Accounts shortcuts list arrow**:

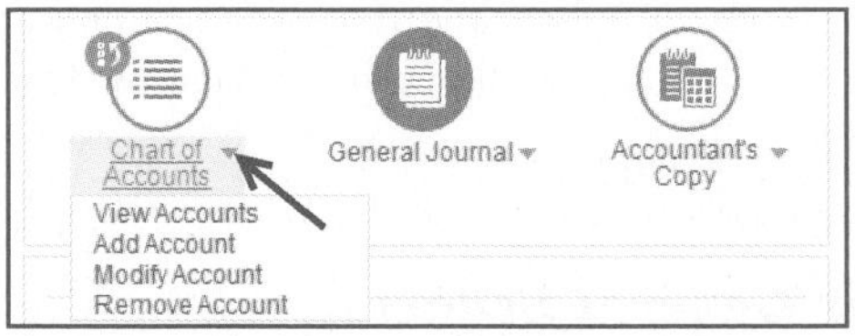

Click the **Chart of Accounts icon**  to open the Accounts window or **click View Accounts** from the Chart of Accounts shortcuts list.

Both methods will open the Accounts window.

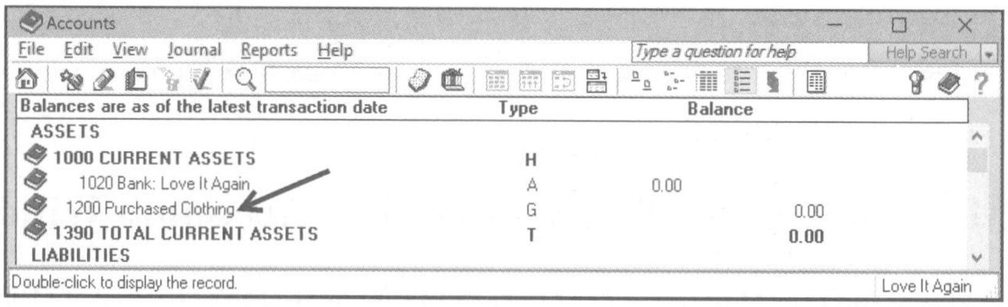

From this window, you can perform all ledger account–related activities. The tool buttons and menu options give access to the individual ledger records, and you can modify, delete, add records, display reports, access help and so on.

Click the Maximize button so that the Accounts window fills the screen. This will allow you to display more accounts and keep the Accounts window in view in the background while you are creating or editing accounts. To return the window to normal size, click the Restore button.

Several tools control the appearance of the Accounts window. The preset accounts should be displayed in the **Type** format. You can also display accounts in the Accounts window in the large or small **Icon** format with icons representing each account. In the Icon view, you can rearrange icons by dragging so that frequently used accounts appear at the top for easier access. New accounts are automatically added at the bottom of the screen, but they can be moved to the desired location.

Viewing accounts by **Name** will include the account numbers, names and balances in debit and credit columns. Accounts remain in numerical order as accounts are added.

For entering new accounts and editing a large number of existing accounts, it is easier to work with the accounts listed in numerical order. New accounts are inserted in their correct order, providing a better view of the progress during the setup phase. The addition of account type in the Type view is helpful for checking the logical order of accounts as they are created. You can change the Accounts window view at any time.

If you do not display the accounts by Type, you should change the viewing option.

Click the **Display By Type tool** or **choose** the **View menu** and **click Type**.

When others are using the same data file, you can click the **Refresh tool** to update your data file with changes that other users have made to accounts. In single-user mode, the tool is dimmed.

In the Accounts window, we can also check that the accounts are in proper sequence; that is, they follow the rules outlined on pages 86–88.

Click the **Check Validity Of Accounts tool** or **choose** the **File menu** and **click Check The Validity Of Accounts**:

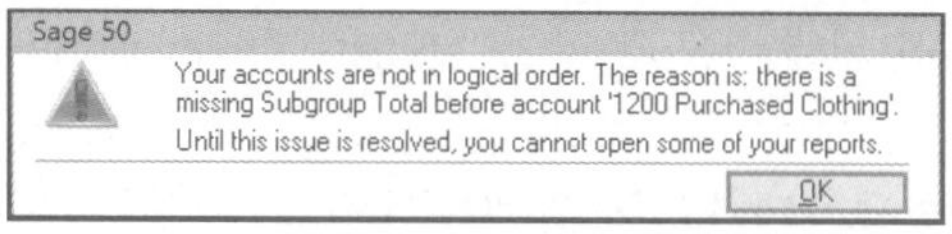

Sage 50 informs us that the accounts are not in logical order — the same information provided when we closed the Setup Guide or when we click the **Validate button**.

Click **OK** to return to the Accounts window.

Creating New Accounts in the General Ledger

You are now ready to enter the information for the first new account, *Cash on Hand*, using the chart on page 91 as your reference. The following keystrokes will enter the account name, number, type and option to include or omit zero balance accounts.

PRO VERSION
The Refresh tool is not on the tool bar.

NOTES
To edit an account from the Accounts window, double-click the account you want to change or click the account to select it and then either click the Edit tool or choose the File menu and click Open or press ctrl + O.

NOTES
Only one error is listed, the first one encountered in checking the Chart of Accounts for validity of account order. After you correct the first error, the second error will be listed, if there is one.

We are entering new accounts from the Accounts window, and it should still be open.

Click the **Create tool** on the Accounts window tool bar or **choose** the **File menu** and **click Create**.

You will open a new account window:

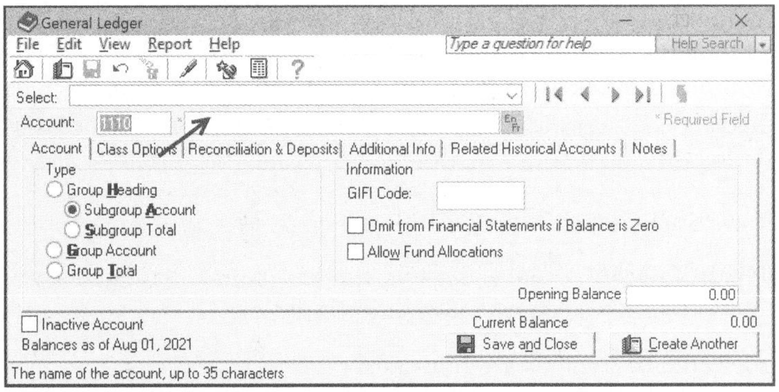

You can open this ledger record from the Setup Guide (refer to pages 94–95).

Or, you can press ctrl + N to open a new account ledger form from the Accounts window or from any account's General Ledger window.

The tabs that appear in the ledger depend on the account section as defined by the account number. If no number is entered initially, only the tabs that apply to all accounts appear. We will create the first account that was not in the Skeleton Chart of Accounts, *Cash on Hand*. The account type is selected as the most likely option for logical account order. The default account type depends on the account record you used most recently. For example, group total accounts are often followed by a Group account. The cursor is in the Account number field and the field is selected for editing. Sage 50 will not allow duplicate account numbers.

Two fields are required for accounts: the number and the name. An asterisk * appears beside a **required field** as long as it remains blank. Sage 50 may enter an account number and type that is the most likely next entry based on the previous selection. If an account number is entered as a default, the * will be removed. After the error message about logical order, account 1200 is selected in the Accounts window so that you can correct the error. Its preceding account is a Subgroup account, so another Subgroup account is expected. The account number will be selected for editing.

Sometimes, it may be appropriate to print an account with a zero balance, although zero balance accounts usually do not need to be printed. In Sage 50, you have the option to **omit accounts with zero balances** from financial statements. You may select this option in the General Ledger or in the options windows for financial reports.

The balances of bank accounts should always be displayed, so do not select Omit From Financial Statements If Balance Is Zero.

We are not using **GIFI** codes (Canada Revenue Agency's account numbering system for electronic report filing) or fund or project allocations, so we can leave these options unchanged. The **current balance** is displayed, but you cannot edit it. It is updated when you enter an opening balance and journal entries. The **opening balance** will be added later (refer to Entering Historical Account Balances on the following page). There is no additional account information. We are not using Account Reconciliation, so we can skip this tab screen. The Related Historical Accounts tab screen has the relationship between different account numbers that are used for the same account in multiple fiscal periods. They do not apply until you have data for more than two fiscal periods.

Type `1100` **Press** tab to advance to the Account name field.

Type `Cash on Hand`

PRO VERSION

pro The Pro version does not have the Refresh tool.

The Notes tab is also not available in the Pro version.

NOTES

The Account number field will be blank when you add a new account from the Setup Guide. Therefore, the ledger will not have all the tabs until you enter an account number.

NOTES

Depending on your previous step or cursor position, you may have a different initial account number and type.

NOTES

When no number is entered, only the Account, Class Options and Additional Information tabs are available. When you enter a 4000- or 5000-level account number, the Budget tab will be added. The Reconciliation & Deposits tab is included for all Balance Sheet accounts.

NOTES

Some reports have the option to hide zero balances for all the accounts in the report. If selected in a report, this option will override the ledger account selection of showing zero balances.

NOTES

GIFI codes and exporting GIFI reports are covered in Appendix K.

Information you enter on the Notes tab screen can be added to the financial statements (refer to the Modify Report screenshots on pages 58–60).

NOTES
Remember that if you do not use account numbers in transactions or reports, the account names must be unique.

NOTES
Account class (Class Options tab) is introduced in Chapter 7.

Click **Subgroup Account** to change the account type if necessary.

The bank and cash accounts together will be subtotalled.

Sage 50 enters an **Account Class** automatically (Class Options tab screen). For most accounts, the section heading is used (Assets, Liabilities, etc.). For Expense accounts, the default class is Cost of Goods Sold. This selection will not affect the financial statements for Love It Again, so you can accept the default selections for all accounts.

Check your work. **Make** any necessary **corrections** by clicking the incorrect field, selecting or dragging through the information if necessary and typing the correct information and pressing tab if necessary.

When the information has been entered correctly, save your work.

Click **Create Another** 

to save the new account and advance to another new account information window.

Both the number and name fields are now marked with an asterisk *.

Create the **remaining accounts** from page 91.

Subgroup totals, group headings and group totals — the non-postable accounts — will have the Balance fields removed when you choose these account types.

Click **Save And Close** 

to save the final account.

NOTES
You can end your session at any time by closing the General Ledger window. Then close the Accounts window to return to the Home window, or click the Close Other Windows tool in the Home window.

Display or **print** the **Chart of Accounts** to check the accuracy of your work.

If you find mistakes, edit the account information as described in the section on editing General Ledger accounts on page 89.

Entering Historical Account Balances

Before completing this step, we will create one more account to use as a test account for our Trial Balance. If you close the General Ledger before entering all the account balances, or if the total debits and credits are not equal, the program forces the Trial Balance to balance by adding the required debit or credit amount to another account.

This automatic adjustment may compensate for other errors in amounts, and you may be able to finish the history with errors in opening balances. You cannot change these balances after finishing the history. To detect this problem, we will create a test account and put all the adjustments into it. If all the balances are entered correctly, the test account will have a zero balance and we can remove the account.

WARNING!
Before you finish the history, the opening balance can be edited. The Current Balance has no data input field because you cannot edit it. Initially it is the same as the opening balance, but it changes when you add journal entries. Because you can enter journal transactions before finishing the history, this distinction is very important. The balance in the Accounts window is the current balance, which may not be the same as the opening balance.

After you finish the history, the Opening Balance field is removed.

Create the new Group account **1005 Test Account**.

You are now ready to enter the opening historical account balances for all postable (type G or A) accounts. The opening balances for Love It Again can be found in the Trial Balance on page 70. Accounts with zero balances are not included in the Trial Balance. You should skip these accounts when entering account balances.

You can enter opening balances from the Setup Guide or you can start from the Modify Account shortcut in the Chart of Accounts drop-down shortcuts list (refer to page 95). We will include both methods.

Entering Opening Account Balances from the Setup Guide

Click the **Setup menu** and **click Setup Guide**. **Click Accounts**:

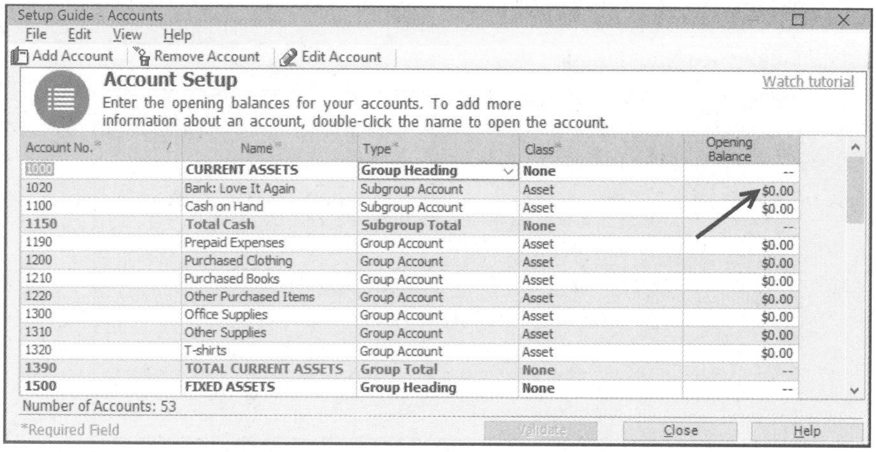

The Balance field is not available for Heading, Total and Subtotal accounts. The postable Group and Subgroup accounts initially have a zero balance.

Click **$0.00** in the Opening Balance field for *Bank: Love It Again*.

Type 46380 **Press** ⇩ to select the balance for the next account.

Enter the remaining account **balances** from the Trial Balance on page 70. Remember that *GST Paid on Purchases* and *HST Paid on Purchases* have a debit balance (add a minus sign).

WARNING!
Add a minus sign to the amounts for GST Paid on Purchases and HST Paid on Purchases to create debit entries for these accounts.

Double-click any account line to open the ledger record if you need to change other details for the account. (Refer to the screenshot on page 93.)

If you close the Setup Guide before entering all the account balances, or the Trial Balance is still unbalanced, you will be asked to correct the discrepancy:

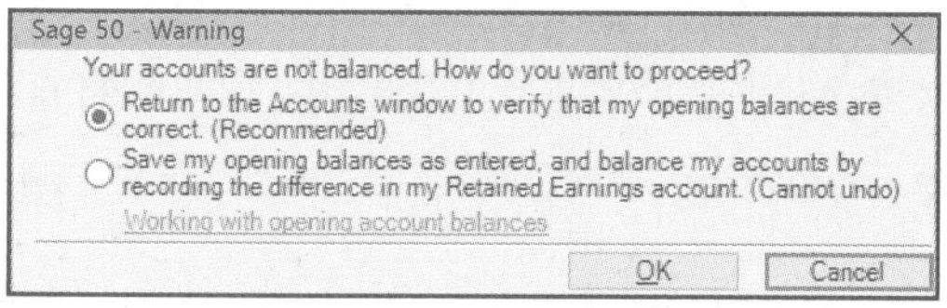

NOTES
You cannot use the Test Account to balance amounts in the Trial Balance from the Setup Guide. In this case, you should check that the Retained Earnings amount is correct.

You can either return to the Guide to make a correction or add the difference to the Retained Earnings account.

Make **your selection** and **click OK**. **Click Close** when finished to leave the Setup Guide.

Entering Opening Account Balances from the Search Window

Click the **Chart of Accounts shortcuts list arrow**.

Click **Modify Account**.

This Search window that opens is similar to the one in the General Journal that starts the Adjust Entry feature. Accounts is selected as the search field area:

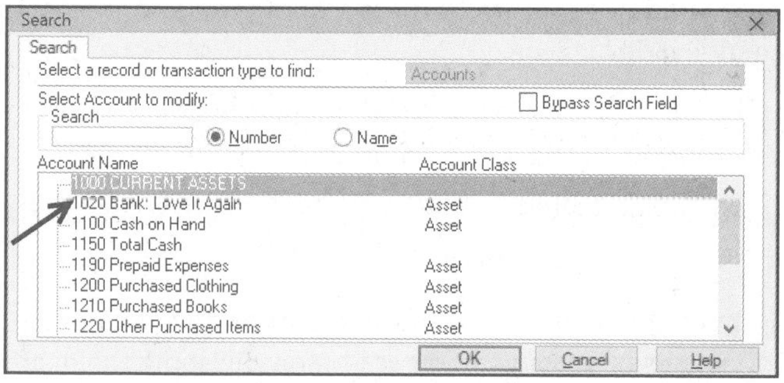

NOTES
You can advance to a later part of the account list by typing the first number in the Search field. You can also search by account name by choosing this option.

Double-click 1020 Bank: Love It Again.

The ledger window opens:

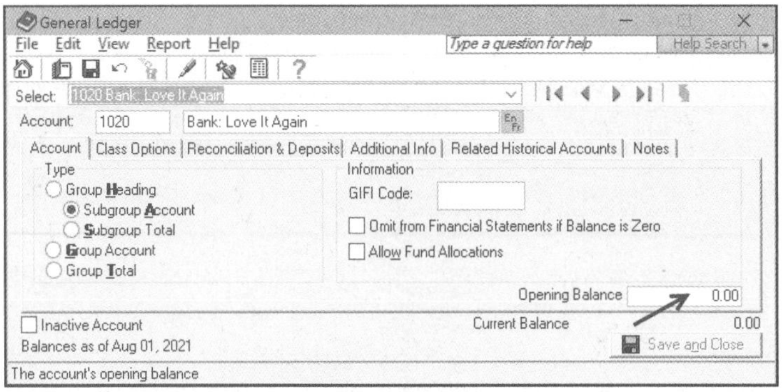

Click the **Opening Balance field** to highlight it.

Type 46380 **Press** (tab).

The Current Balance is updated, but you cannot change it directly. Sage 50 updates this balance automatically from journal entries.

To open a different ledger record, you can click the **Next Account tool** to open the ledger record for the next account in numerical sequence, or select an account from the **Select drop-down list**:

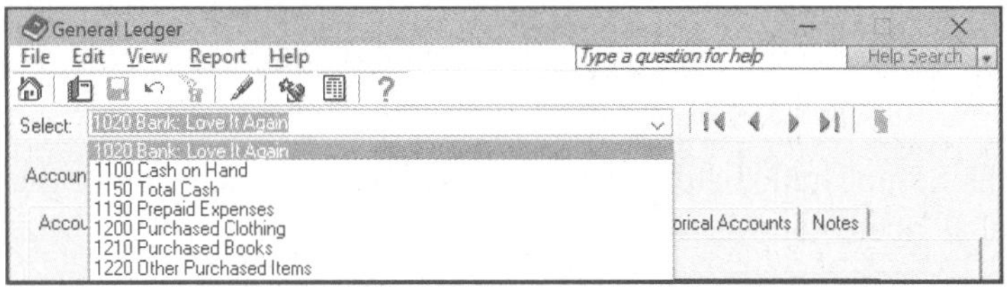

Enter the **balances** for the remaining accounts in the Trial Balance on page 70.

Remember that *GST Paid on Purchases* and *HST Paid on Purchases* have a debit balance (add a minus sign).

If you close the General Ledger window before entering all the account balances, or the Trial Balance is still unbalanced, you will be asked to correct the discrepancy:

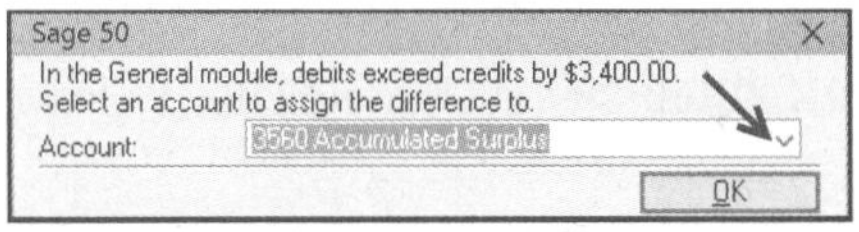

The message asks you to choose an account for the difference — an adjusting, balancing entry that will place the Trial Balance in balance. Choose *Test Account* from the drop-down list of accounts. Unlike the similar warning from the Guide, here you can choose any account from the drop-down list or accept the default. If this warning appears,

Choose **account 1005 Test Account** from the drop-down list. **Click OK**.

Close the **Ledger window** to return to the Accounts window after entering all the accounts and balances.

Display or **print** the **Chart of Accounts**, **Trial Balance**, **Balance Sheet** and **Income Statement** to check the accuracy of your work.

Choose the **Reports menu** in the Accounts window and **click Trial Balance** (or Balance Sheet or Income Statement).

Check all your **opening balances** carefully and **edit** any accounts with errors in **amounts**, **names** or **account numbers** before finishing the history.

WARNING!

Remember to enter the amounts for GST and HST Paid on Purchases with a minus sign to create a debit entry.

NOTES

As in the Setup Guide, the default account for the balancing entry is the Retained Earnings linked account – renamed Accumulated Surplus in our example. However, from the General Ledger, you can choose any postable account.

NOTES

When all account balances are correct and the Test Account has a zero balance, you can remove it. Open the Chart of Accounts window and click Test Account, or open its ledger record.

Or, click the account in the Setup Guide accounts window.

Click the Remove tool in either window and confirm that you want to remove the account by clicking Yes.

Close the **Accounts window** and any other open windows to return to the Home window.

Compare your reports with the information on pages 68–70 to be sure that all account numbers, names and balances are correct. The balance for *Test Account* should be zero. Make additional corrections if necessary.

WARNING!
If an account was used in journal entries, you can change account numbers only after two fiscal periods have passed without additional transactions.

Finishing the History

Making a Backup Copy

By having a backup copy of your files before finishing the history, you will be able to make changes easily, if you find an error, without having to repeat the entire setup from scratch. After the ledger history is finished, the program will not permit you to make certain changes, such as opening account balances and fiscal dates. You cannot change the account number for an account after making a journal entry to the account.

You should back up your unfinished open history files to a different folder so they can be easily identified (e.g., NF-AGAIN).

Choose the **File menu** and **click Backup**, or **click** the **Backup tool** .

Create a **backup copy** by following the instructions. Refer to page 50 and page 248 if you need help.

WARNING!
You can finish entering the history when the Trial Balance is in balance. Afterward, you cannot change opening balances, even if they are incorrect. You will need to make adjusting entries. Sage 50 always keeps the Trial Balance balanced. Therefore, checking for a zero balance in the Test Account can stop you from proceeding with incorrect account balances.

WARNING!
You cannot change the Fiscal Start date or the opening balance for an account after finishing the history.

Back up the not-finished Love It Again files before proceeding. Refer to Chapter 3 if you need further assistance.

Finishing the General Ledger History

You should be in the Home window.

Choose the **History menu** and **click Finish Entering History**.

A caution about making a backup first appears:

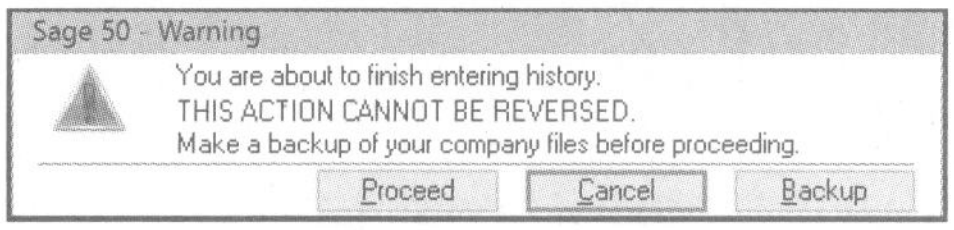

If you have not made a backup copy yet, click Backup and do so before proceeding. If you have made your backup copy, you should continue.

Click **Proceed**.

A different screen at this stage indicates that you have errors that must be corrected before you can continue:

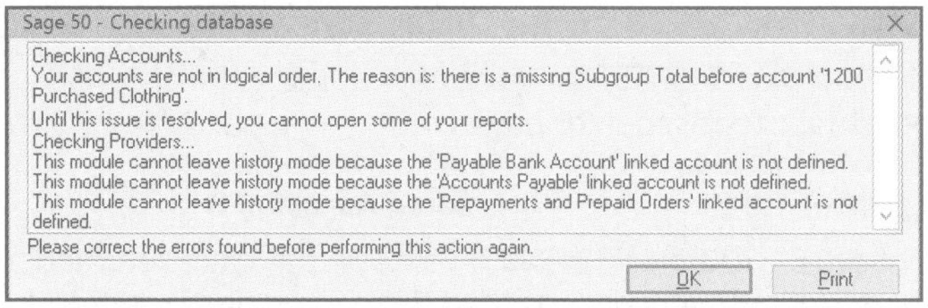

The message describes the mistakes you must correct. If your accounts are out of order, you cannot finish entering the history. If you did not hide the unused modules, you cannot finish entering the history because some essential linked accounts for these modules are not defined.

Read the error description carefully. Print the message for reference when you make corrections. Click OK to return to the Home window.

WARNING!
You must close all other windows before making a backup or before finishing the history.

WARNING!
You can verify that the file is correct before making a backup – choose the Finish History option. If the option to proceed is available, click Backup on this screen or click Cancel, make the backup and then finish the history.

NOTES
The first error on this screen states that accounts are not in logical order.

The remaining messages refer to missing linked accounts for modules that are not used but are also not hidden.

Make the necessary corrections. Remember to replace your previous unfinished history backup file. Then try again to finish the history.

The open or not-finished history symbol  has been removed from the Chart of Accounts icon. In the Setup Guide Accounts window, the Current Balance field has replaced the Opening Balance, but you cannot change these amounts.

You can now exit the program or continue by entering the source documents. Remember to advance the Session Date. Enter all transactions for Love It Again in the General Journal.

NOTES
If you unhide (view) the unused modules now, they will have the not-finished icon on the ledger icons. If you want to set them up later, you must first unhide or view them, as we do in Chapter 9.

SOURCE DOCUMENTS

SESSION DATE – AUGUST 7, 2021

1 **Cheque Purchase Invoice #PFU-4877** **Dated August 2/21**
From Places For Us, $1 800 plus $234 HST for monthly rent. Invoice total $2 034 paid by cheque #3421. Terms: payable on first day of each month.

NOTES
The HST rate in Ontario is 13 percent.

2 **Purchase Invoice #BC-10116** **Dated August 2/21**
From Bell Canada, $145 plus $18.85 HST for monthly telephone and Internet service. Invoice total $163.85. Terms: net 15. Create new Group account 2140 A/P - Bell Canada.

3 **Purchase Invoice #WD-2919** **Dated August 4/21**
From Wearable Designs, $210 plus $27.30 HST for new store uniform T-shirts for volunteer sales staff. Invoice total $237.30 due in 30 days.

NOTES
In most businesses, the Cash on Hand balance is usually small and is used only for paying small amounts. In this application, we are using the Cash on Hand account to record merchandise sales and to pay for any purchases that normally would require cash or credit card payments.

4 **Memo #1** **Dated August 4/21**
From Fischer: Give T-shirts to volunteer sales staff. Cost of T-shirts given out is $210. Reduce T-shirt asset account and charge the cost to Miscellaneous Expenses account.

5 **Cash Purchase Invoice #PI-2168** **Dated August 6/21**
From Picture It, $110 plus $14.30 HST for printing large poster to place in store window to solicit Halloween costumes and other donations. Invoice total $124.30 paid from Cash on Hand.

SESSION DATE – AUGUST 14, 2021

NOTES
Children's clothing and books are not subject to HST; GST at 5% only applies to sales and purchases of these items.

6 **Purchase Invoice #KS-9493** **Dated August 8/21**
From Kids Stuff, $900 plus $45 GST for children's clothing from store liquidation sale. Invoice total $945. Terms: net 20 days.

7 **Purchase Invoice #KIM-10990** **Dated August 8/21**
From Kids In Motion, $1 100 plus $143 HST for toys that were returned and strollers that were discontinued styles or slightly marked floor models. Invoice total $1 243. Terms: net 30 days.

8 **Cash Purchase Invoice #LT-4632** **Dated August 10/21**
From Loonie-Toonies, $150 plus $19.50 HST for holiday decorations for store. Invoice total $169.50. Paid from Cash on Hand. (Debit Other Supplies account.)

9

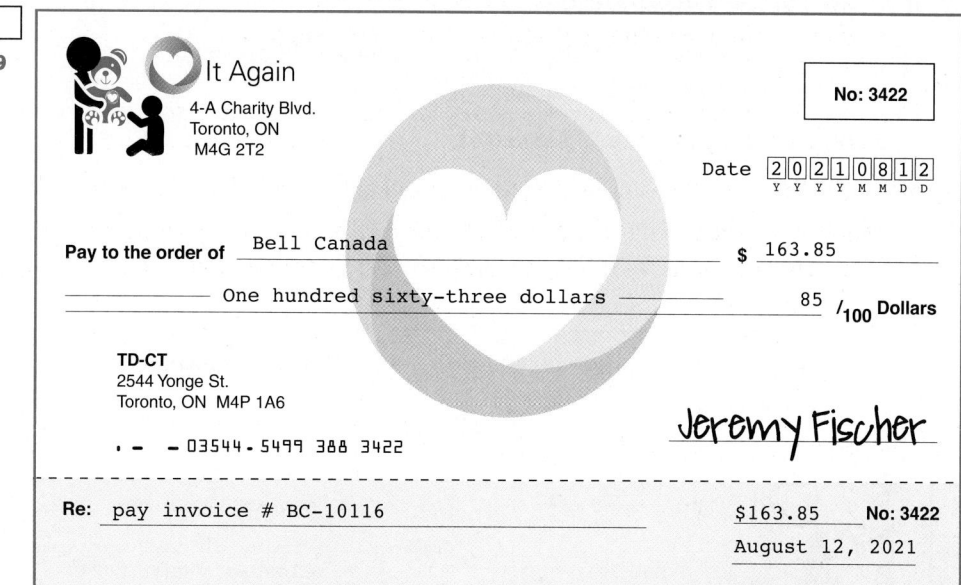

It Again
4-A Charity Blvd.
Toronto, ON
M4G 2T2

No: 3422

Date 2 0 2 1 0 8 1 2
Y Y Y Y M M D D

Pay to the order of Bell Canada $ 163.85

One hundred sixty-three dollars 85 /100 Dollars

TD-CT
2544 Yonge St.
Toronto, ON M4P 1A6

Jeremy Fischer

03544-5499 388 3422

Re: pay invoice # BC-10116 $163.85 No: 3422
August 12, 2021

SESSION DATE – AUGUST 21, 2021

10 **Funds Raised Form #FR-21-08** **Dated August 16/21**
Received $3 000 in donations to purchase new computer for store. Amount deposited to Bank: Love It Again.

11 **Purchase Invoice #DC-5306** **Dated August 17/21**
From Data Connections, $2 600 plus $338 HST for new computer with point-of-sale software. Invoice total $2 938. Terms: net 25 days. Create new account 2420 A/P - Data Connections.

12 **Cheque Purchase Invoice #P-44982** **Dated August 17/21**
From Pizzaz, $650 plus $84.50 HST to repair and repaint store sign – replace the word Love with heart logo. Invoice total $734.50 paid by cheque #3423.

SESSION DATE – AUGUST 28, 2021

13 **Cash Purchase Invoice #PH-9976** **Dated August 24/21**
From Pizza House, $320 plus $41.60 HST for pizza and soft drinks to show appreciation to volunteers. Invoice total $361.60. Paid from Cash on Hand.

14 **Payment Cheque #3424** **Dated August 26/21**
To Wearable Designs, $576.30 in payment of account. Reference invoice #WD-2919 and #WD-1813.

15 **Bank Debit Memo #HB-3881** **Dated August 28/21**
From Heartfelt Bank, $45.50 in bank charges for cheques and statement preparation. Create new Group account 5010 Bank Charges.

16 **Bank Debit Memo #HB-3996** **Dated August 28/21**
From Heartfelt Bank, $4 200 for payroll including all payroll expenses to pay store manager Jeremy Fischer wages for one month.

NOTES
Charge pizza purchase to Miscellaneous Expenses.

Advancing the Session Date

Sage 50 warns you as you approach the end of a fiscal period because important end-of-period adjusting entries are usually required.

Change the **session date** to **August 31**.

An Advisor message about preparing for year-end opens. Sage 50 displays this message about one month before the end of the fiscal period:

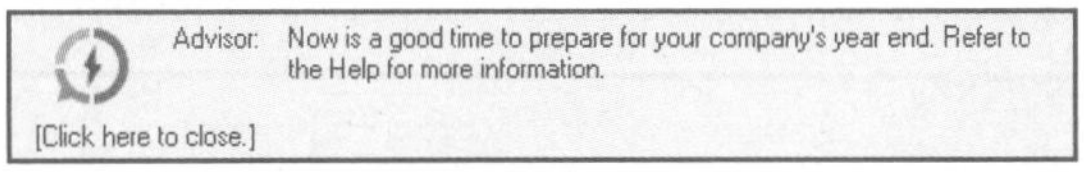
Advisor: Now is a good time to prepare for your company's year end. Refer to the Help for more information.
[Click here to close.]

Click to close the **Advisor**, **back up** your **data files** and **continue** with the **transactions** for August 31.

NOTES
No taxes are charged on sales of donated goods. Children's clothing and books are subject to 5% GST, while HST at 13% is charged on sales of other purchased items.

17

Love It Again
4-A Charity Blvd.
Toronto, ON
M4G 2T2

SALES SUMMARY FORM: FR-21-09
Date: August 31, 2021
Comment: Summary of cash receipts sales in August 2021

Description	Amount
Sales of donated items	$4 200.00
Sales of purchased clothing & books	4 300.00
Sales of other purchased items	8 680.00
GST on books and clothing sold	215.00
HST on sales of other purchased items	1 128.40
Received in cash by August 31, 2021	
Signature: Jeremy Fischer — **Total**	**$18 523.40**

18

Memo #2 **Dated August 31/21**
From Fischer: Deposited $18 200 from Cash on Hand (receipts from sales) to Bank: Love It Again.

19

Payment Cheque #3425 **Dated August 31/21**
To Kids Stuff, $1 849 in full payment of account. Reference invoices #KS-9493 and #KS-6279.

SESSION DATE – SEPTEMBER 15, 2021

When you change the session date to September 15, you will receive a date warning:

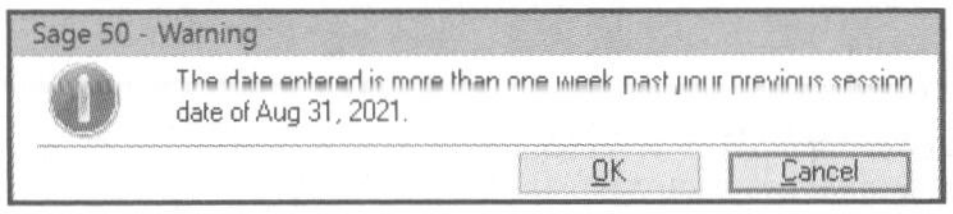
Sage 50 - Warning
The date entered is more than one week past your previous session date of Aug 31, 2021.
OK
Cancel

Normally a business would advance the session date by a shorter period, so the warning helps you avoid entering the wrong session date.

Click **OK** to confirm that you entered the date you intended.

20 **Cheque Purchase Invoice #PFU-9328** **Dated September 1/21**

From Places For Us, $1 800 plus $234 HST for monthly rent. Invoice total $2 034 paid by cheque #3426. Terms: payable on first day of each month.

21 **Purchase Invoice #BC-18588** **Dated September 2/21**

From Bell Canada, $145 plus $18.85 HST for monthly telephone and Internet service. Invoice total $163.85. Terms: net 15.

22 **Payment Cheque #3427** **Dated September 2/21**

To Kids In Motion, $2 503 in full payment of invoice #KIM-10990 and #KIM-8697.

23 **Payment Cheque #3428** **Dated September 12/21**

To Bell Canada, $163.85 in full payment of invoice #BC-18588.

24 **Funds Raised Form #FR-21-10** **Dated September 13/21**

Received $4 000 plus $520 HST for advertising on the charity's Web site. Total revenue received $4 520 deposited to Bank. Create new account: 4180 Revenue: Advertising.

SESSION DATE – SEPTEMBER 29, 2021

25 **Memo #3** **Dated September 19/21**

From Fischer: Presented Sunni Husein with $200 gift certificate for Volunteer Extraordinaire Award. Create new Group account 5430 Employee Gifts. Paid for gift certificate from Cash on Hand.

26 **Bank Debit Memo #HB-8310** **Dated September 20/21**

From Heartfelt Bank, $240 plus $31.20 HST for payroll services for one year. Total withdrawal from chequing account was $271.20. Create new expense account 5380 Payroll Services.

27 **Bank Debit Memo #HB-9778** **Dated September 28/21**

From Heartfelt Bank, $4 200 for payroll, including all payroll expenses, to pay store manager Jeremy Fischer wages for one month.

28 **Funds Received Form #FR-21-11** **Dated September 29/21**

Received $800 in donations. Amount deposited to Bank: Love It Again account.

29 **Cash Purchase Invoice #CP-2** **Dated September 29/21**

From Canada Post, $200 plus $26 HST for postage to mail donation receipts. Invoice total $226. Paid from Cash on Hand.

30 **Sales Summary Form #FR-21-12** **Dated September 29/21**

Summary of sales receipts during the month.

Revenue from donated items	$2 500
Revenue from purchased clothing & books	7 200
Revenue from other purchased items	8 000
GST @ 5%	360
HST @ 13%	1 040

Total $19 100 deposited to Cash on Hand.

NOTES

The year-end advisor may appear again when you advance the date to September 29.

The warning about the date being more than one week past the previous session date will be displayed again.

31 **Memo #4** **Dated September 29/21**

From Fischer: Deposited $18 500 from Cash on Hand (receipts from sales) to Bank: Love It Again.

32 **Bank Debit Memo #HB-10921** **Dated September 29/21**

From Heartfelt Bank, withdraw $14 200 from chequing account to repay loan for $14 000 plus $200 interest. Create new Group account 5100 Interest Expense.

33 **Bank Debit Memo #HB-10998** **Dated September 29/21**

From Heartfelt Bank, $45.50 in bank charges for cheques and statement preparation.

Adjusting Closing Entries

NOTES
Adjusting entries always involve an Income Statement and a Balance Sheet account. For example, you might debit Supplies Used (Income Statement account) and credit Supplies (asset account on the Balance Sheet), or debit Unearned Revenue and credit Customer Prepayments.

Two source document entries — adjustments for the remaining supplies — provide the details for these year-end adjustments for Love It Again. For other businesses, adjusting entries include depreciation entries, inventory adjustments, adjustments for prepaid expenses that have expired, accrued wages and so on. Most adjusting entries do not have an external source document that reminds you to complete them, and most of them are General Journal entries.

Change the **session date** to **September 30**.

If you had not advanced the session date on September 29, you would receive an Advisor message about preparing for year-end. This message is usually displayed on a date very close to the end of the fiscal period.

Close the **Advisor window** if necessary and **back up** your **data files**. **Continue** with the two adjusting entry **transactions**.

NOTES
Donated items are not included in these costs – no purchase cost is associated with them.

34

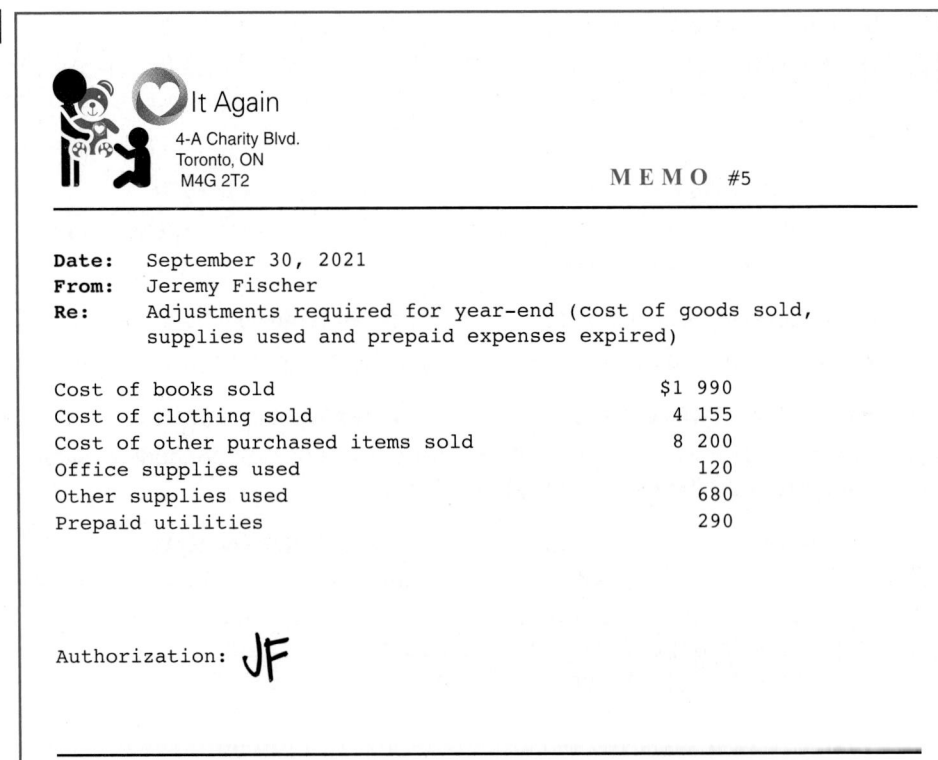

It Again
4-A Charity Blvd.
Toronto, ON
M4G 2T2

MEMO #5

Date: September 30, 2021
From: Jeremy Fischer
Re: Adjustments required for year-end (cost of goods sold, supplies used and prepaid expenses expired)

Cost of books sold	$1 990
Cost of clothing sold	4 155
Cost of other purchased items sold	8 200
Office supplies used	120
Other supplies used	680
Prepaid utilities	290

Authorization: JF

☐

35

It Again
4-A Charity Blvd.
Toronto, ON
M4G 2T2

MEMO #6

Date: September 30, 2021
From: Jeremy Fischer
Re: Final account adjustments required to clear outdated inventory of supplies and other goods (all items donated to family shelters)

Cost of purchased books donated	$ 570
Cost of purchased clothing donated	1 280
Cost of other purchases donated	1 990

Authorization: JF

KEYSTROKES FOR CLOSING

Starting a New Fiscal Period

Starting a new fiscal period is not a reversible step, so you should prepare a complete set of financial reports and make a backup of the data set as instructed in the next memo.

✓ 36 **Memo #7** **Dated September 30/21**

All accounts for the year are settled, so the books can be closed. Make a backup of the data files. Start a new fiscal period to close the books.

Print all the **financial reports** for Love It Again for September 30, 2021.

Back up your **data files** with a file name that indicates it is the year-end copy.

There are two methods for beginning a new fiscal year. The first is the method we have been using to change the session date.

Choose the **Maintenance menu** and **click Change Session Date** or **click** [Calendar icon], the Calendar icon beside Session Date.

The first date of the new fiscal period is always on the drop-down list of dates in the Session Date window. The program will not accept any dates later than October 1, 2021.

Type `October 1, 2021` or choose this date from the date field list or Calendar icon.

NOTES
You cannot start a new fiscal period in multi-user mode.

WARNING!
You should advance to the new fiscal period in two steps. First advance to the last day of the current fiscal period, and then advance to the first day of the new fiscal period. This control feature prevents you from advancing by mistake and losing important data or forgetting year-end adjusting entries.

WARNING!
Initially, from the last day of the fiscal period, you cannot advance the session date past October 1, the first day of the new fiscal period.

Click **OK**. Because this step is not reversible, Sage 50 provides a warning:

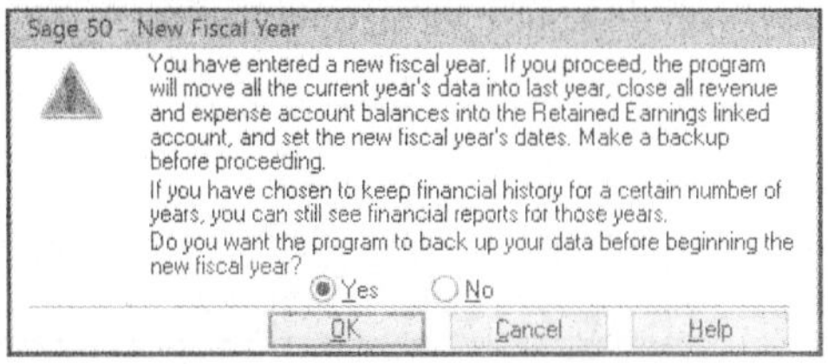

The expense and revenue amounts will be transferred to the capital account, but historical data will be saved in the data file.

Read the **warning** carefully.

The warning describes the changes about to take place in the data set. All revenue and expense accounts are reset to zero at the start of the new fiscal year. Their balances are closed out to the linked *Accumulated Surplus (Retained Earnings)* account, and the linked *Net Income (Current Earnings)* account is reset to zero to begin a new Income Statement. Previous-year entries are stored as data for the previous year. The program also updates the fiscal dates for the company by one year. The new fiscal end date becomes the final date allowed as a session date.

> **NOTES**
> If the history is not finished when you choose to start a new fiscal year, the program will ask if you have finished entering the history and give you a chance to do so. You must finish the history before you can start a new fiscal period.
> If you still have errors in your not-finished file, Sage 50 will list the errors that you must correct, as in the message on page 97, before you can finish the history and start a new fiscal period.

At this stage you can choose to back up the data files, continue with the date change or cancel the date change by clicking No.

Click **Cancel** to return to the Session Date window and then **click Cancel** again to close the Change Session Date screen. We will use the second menu option to change to a new fiscal year.

Choose the **Maintenance menu** and **click Start New Year**.

The next screen asks whether you want to start a new fiscal or calendar year:

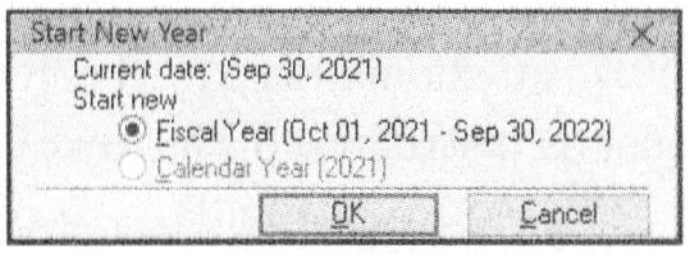

> **NOTES**
> The new calendar year entry, 2021 (that is, January 1, 2021), is earlier than the earliest date allowed in our data file (August 1, 2021), so the new Calendar Year option is dimmed. The start of the new fiscal year (October 1, 2021) also precedes the date for the next calendar year (January 1, 2022), so the New Fiscal Year option is selected.

The default will be the period that starts first. Start New Fiscal Year is correctly selected.

Click **OK** to continue.

A similar warning advises you to make a backup before proceeding:

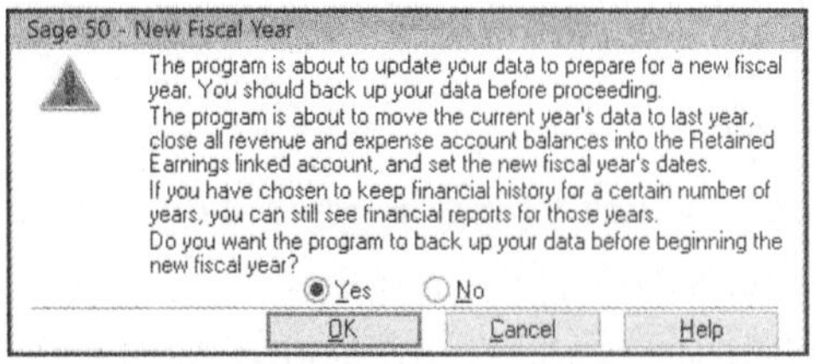

The default setting, again, is to make a backup before continuing. If you have not yet made a backup, do so now. If you do not want to begin a new year, you can click Cancel and the old dates will remain in effect.

Click **No** because you have already backed up your files.

Click **OK** to begin the new fiscal period.

The message confirms that the new year has been started:

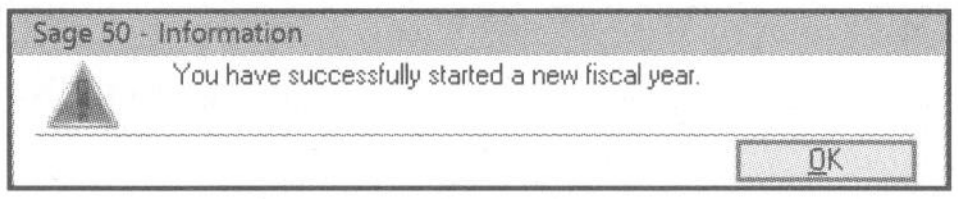

Click **OK** to close the message and display a warning about clearing data:

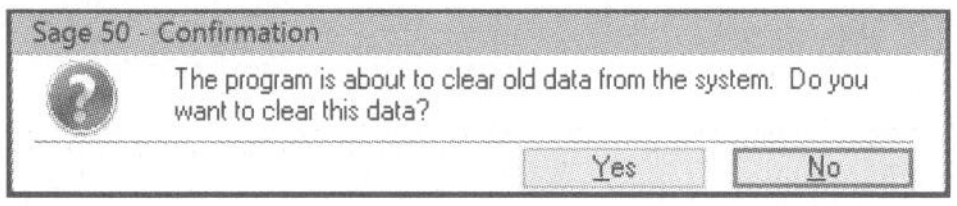

You have the option of retaining the old data or clearing it. Journal entries from the previous year are never cleared, and Income Statement and Balance Sheet details for the previous year are also retained.

Click **Yes** because Love It Again has no other data. If in doubt, choose No.

Another message now appears:

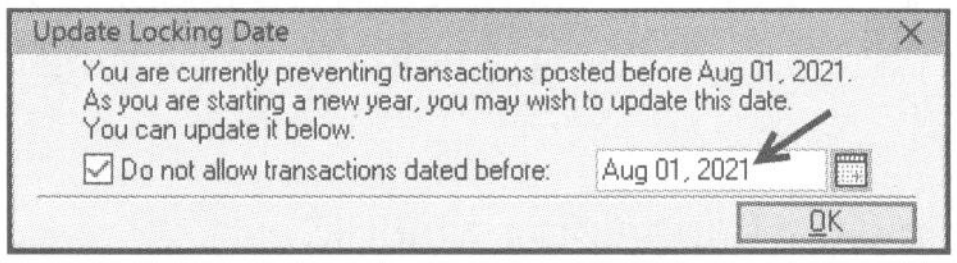

You must now change the earliest date for which you will allow transactions. We should not allow any transactions to the previous fiscal period so that the historical records cannot be altered in error.

Drag through **Aug 01, 2021**, the date entered.

Type 10/01

Click **OK** to continue. Close the message about payroll updates if it appears.

When you have more than one fiscal period, most financial reports offer comparisons with the previous year as an option. Journal reports and other reports are available for both periods — the Report On Fiscal Year field is available with Current Year and Previous Year options in a drop-down list.

Print the **Comparative Trial Balance** and **Balance Sheet** for September 30 and October 1.

Notice the changes in the capital accounts on the Balance Sheet. The *Net Income* balance for September 30 has been added to the *Accumulated Surplus* account to create the October 1 balance in the *Accumulated Surplus* account.

Print the **Comparative Income Statement for the previous year** (Oct. 1, 2020, to Sep. 30, 2021) and the **current fiscal year to date** (Oct. 1, 2021, to Oct. 1, 2021).

The Income Statement for the current year has no income or revenue. All accounts have a zero balance because you have not recorded any transactions for the new fiscal year.

The files are now ready for transactions in the new fiscal period. When you check the Company Information, the fiscal dates are updated and information about last year's dates has been added.

Choose the **Setup menu** and **click Settings**, or **click** the **Settings icon** .

NOTES

If you choose to clear old data, the program will clear the information you selected for the periods you entered in the Automatically Clear Data screen. Refer to Chapter 15, page 617.

We describe how to clear data from company files in Chapter 15.

WARNING!

If you have cleared paid invoices, these details will be unavailable for reports. Comparative Income Statements and Balance Sheets are always available for the two fiscal periods.

NOTES
After you start a new fiscal period, you cannot change the Fiscal Start date.

NOTES
The program assumes a fiscal year of one year, so the fiscal end will be advanced by 12 months.

Click **Company** if necessary and then **click** **Information**:

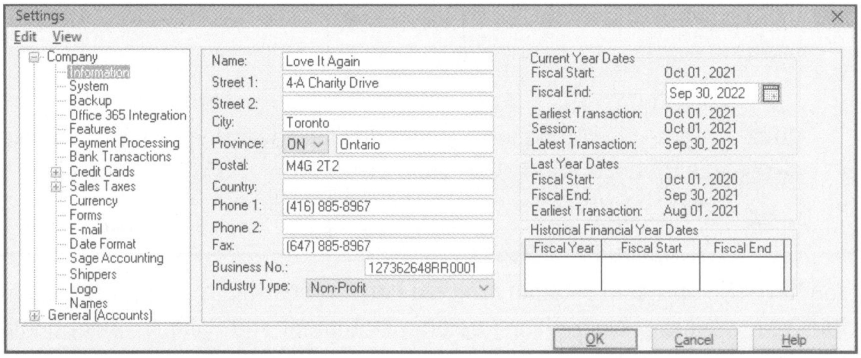

The new Fiscal Start is October 1, 2021, and the new Fiscal End is September 30, 2022. Sage 50 automatically updates the Fiscal End by 12 months, but you can edit the Fiscal End date if the fiscal period is shorter. In fact, this is the only date that you can edit after you have finished the history for a data file. The Earliest Transaction Date has also been updated to October 1, 2021. The dates for the previous fiscal period (Last Year Dates) are provided for reference.

Click **Cancel** to close the Company Information window.

NOTES
In Chapter 12, we show how to create a copy of your data for your accountant to update and how to import the transactions your accountant has completed for your company.

NOTES
Type the date in the Date field. You will be unable to select September 30 from the date field calendar.

Because the session date is Oct. 1, 2021, and we do not allow future-dated transactions, Oct. 1 is the only date allowed for journal entries until we advance the session date.

Entering Transactions for an Earlier Fiscal Period

Sometimes not all the information required is available before the books are closed for the fiscal period. However, it may be necessary to close the books (start a new fiscal period) so that transactions in the new year can be entered. The details of the adjusting entries can be calculated by an accountant who does not have the information until after a business has started entering transactions for a new year. Sage 50 allows you to post transactions to the previous year (but not to future fiscal periods) so that the financial statements for both the previous year and the current year will be correct.

✓ 37 **Memo #8** **Dated September 30/21**

After starting the new fiscal period, Fischer discovered a donation cheque #488129 for $500 that has not been recorded and should be added to the revenue for the previous fiscal period. He closed the books before making the entry. Read the margin Notes.

Open the **General Journal**. **Type** `Memo 8` in the Source field.

Click the **Date field** and **type** `Sep 30`

Enter the **remaining information** to complete the transaction.

Click the **Post button**. Sage 50 blocks the transaction:

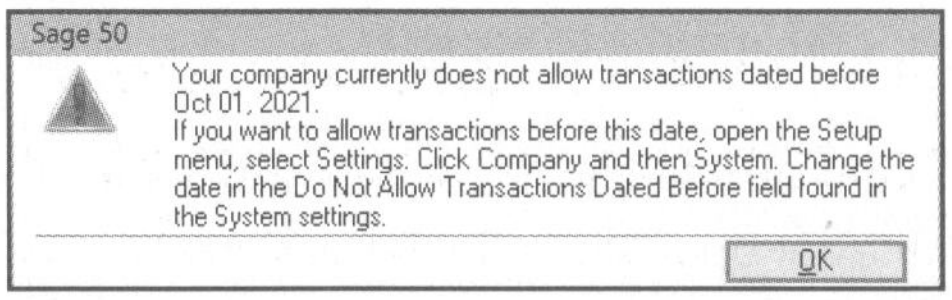

Before the program allows the entry, we must change the System Settings. We indicated that transactions earlier than Oct. 1, 2021, should not be allowed.

Click **OK** to close the message. **Close** the **journal** to discard the entry. **Click** **Yes** to confirm that you want to discard the entry.

Choose the **Setup menu** and **click** **Settings** or **click** the **Settings icon** .

Click **Company** if necessary and then **click System**.

This will access the Settings field we need:

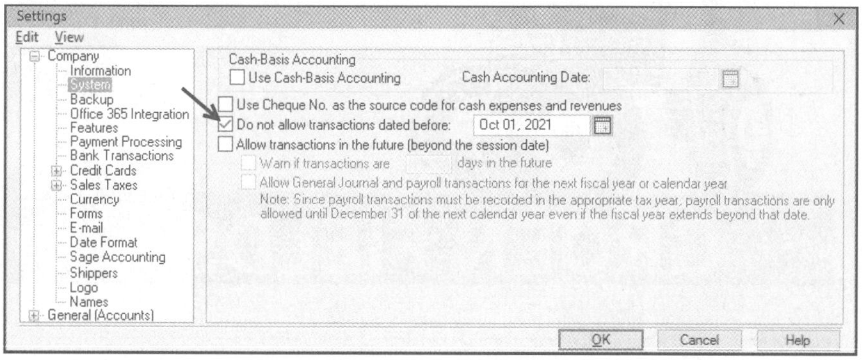

This is the same Settings screen we saw earlier, but now we must allow transactions in the previous period.

Click **Do Not Allow Transactions Dated Before** to **remove** the ✓.

Click **OK**.

Enter **Memo #8** again.

Review and then **post** it. This time you must confirm before the entry is posted:

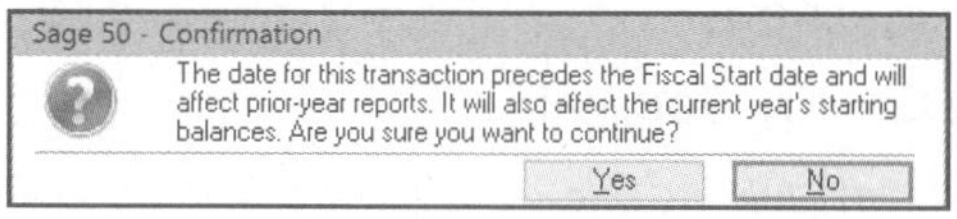

Because the transaction date is in a previous month or period, you are advised that prior period reports may be affected by the transaction. The warning gives you a chance to correct the date if it was incorrect. But we want to proceed. After completing the transaction, we will change the System Settings again to avoid mistakenly posting to the previous year.

NOTES

The warnings in Sage 50 make it difficult to post to the wrong year by mistake.

Click **Yes** to continue with posting.

Close the **General Journal**.

Click the **Settings icon**  or **choose** the **Setup menu**, then **choose Settings** and **click Company** and **System**.

Click **Do Not Allow Transactions Dated Before** to **add** the ✓.

Enter **Oct 1** as the date and **click OK**.

NOTES

To display and print reports after starting a new fiscal period, you must choose Previous Year (2021) to view the transactions for August and September.

REVIEW

The Student DVD with Data Files includes Review Questions and Supplementary Cases for this chapter.

CHAPTER FIVE

GROEN FIELDS

OBJECTIVES

After completing this chapter, you should be able to

- ***open*** the General and Payables journals
- ***enter*** supplier- or vendor-related purchase transactions
- ***enter*** supplier-related payment transactions
- ***enter*** partial payments to suppliers
- ***enter*** payments to suppliers with early payment discounts
- ***enter*** cash purchase transactions
- ***enter*** sales taxes in the General Journal
- ***create*** shortcuts in the Home window
- ***store*** recurring purchase transactions
- ***add*** new supplier accounts
- ***edit*** supplier accounts
- ***edit*** and ***review*** transactions in the journals
- ***recall***, ***use*** and ***edit*** stored purchase transactions
- ***adjust*** and ***reverse*** purchase invoices and payments after posting
- ***understand*** Payables Ledger linked accounts
- ***display*** and ***print*** payables transactions and reports

NOTES

Groen Fields
RR #2
Truro, NS B2N 5B1
Tel 1: (902) 454-6111
Tel 2: (800) 454-6000
Fax: (902) 454-6990
Business No.: 186 522 330 RT0001

COMPANY INFORMATION

Company Profile

Groen Fields, located outside of Truro, Nova Scotia, is owned by Arjen Groen and Ryan Field. (Arjen is a cousin of Julie and Jules Jardin, who own Shady Corners in Halifax. Groen is the Dutch name/translation and equivalent of the English name Green, and is often pronounced "green.") The nursery and tree farm supplies a number of garden centres in the area with annual bedding plants, perennials and ornamental trees. Most of the plants are grown from their own seed supplies, and the greenhouse allows Groen Fields to start the annual bedding plants in time for spring sales and garden planting. Trees and specialty plants are purchased when they are still small and then grown to the more mature sizes desired by customers. They also sell packaged seeds harvested from their own flowers.

Arjen Groen, together with his partner Ryan Field, manage the day-to-day activities of the business. Both specialized in horticulture at the Nova Scotia Agricultural College at Dalhousie University, where they met as undergraduates. Field continued his studies in Business Administration while Groen went on to complete a Master's degree in Agriculture. Most of the day-to-day farming work is carried out by their employees. One full-time manager looks after the greenhouse plants and lives in the main farmhouse during the winter. During the summer months, the manager shares the freshly painted three-bedroom bungalow with four co-op students from the Agricultural College. They prepare their own meals, but all other expenses are covered by the owners. The payroll is managed by the bank for a small fee.

Groen Fields has set up accounts with regular vendors or suppliers, such as the suppliers of seedlings, as well as the utility companies. Some suppliers offer discounts for early payment. Cleaning and maintenance of the office space in the large farmhouse and the bungalow are done professionally once a week by Spotless Company, and the owners have maintenance contracts for repairs of their farm equipment and delivery vehicles.

The nursery is classified as an agricultural business for tax purposes and charges HST on all sales and pays HST on most purchases. Some business-related purchases, however, are zero rated.

Field currently manages all the accounting records for the nursery and has just closed the books for the income tax year on April 30. Using the following information, Field has finished converting the manual records to Sage 50 for the new year beginning May 1, which is also the start of the planting season and Groen Fields' busiest month:

- Chart of Accounts
- Post-Closing Trial Balance
- Supplier Information
- Accounting Procedures

NOTES

HST, Harmonized Sales Tax, is charged instead of GST and PST in Nova Scotia. HST at 15 percent includes both GST at 5 percent and PST at 10 percent. Refer to the Accounting Procedures on page 111 and Chapter 2 for further details. For zero rated goods, the HST rate is 0.0 percent.

CHART OF POSTABLE ACCOUNTS

GROEN FIELDS

ASSETS

1080 Chequing Bank Account
1300 Seed Supplies
1310 Fertilizer
1320 Plant Care Supplies
1330 Office Supplies
1420 Annual Bedding Plants
1440 Perennial Plant Stock
1460 Tree Inventory
1480 Planters and Hangers
1510 Computer Software
1520 Computer Equipment
1540 Office Furniture
1560 Farming Equipment ▶
▶1570 Greenhouse
1580 Buildings & Property

LIABILITIES

2100 Bank Loan
2200 Accounts Payable
2650 HST Charged on Sales
2670 HST Paid on Purchases
2850 Mortgage Payable

EQUITY

3100 GF, Capital
3150 GF, Drawings
3600 Net Income ▶

▶REVENUE

4100 Revenue from Sales

EXPENSE

5020 Advertising and Promotion
5040 Bank Charges
5050 General Expense
5060 Cleaning Expenses
5070 Maintenance and Repairs
5080 Cost of Goods Sold
5090 Purchase Discounts
5100 Entertainment Expense
5110 Supplies Expense
5120 Hydro Expense ▶
▶5130 Data Management
5140 Interest Expense
5150 Soil Treatment Expenses
5160 Property Taxes
5190 Telephone and Internet
5220 Payroll Services
5240 Wages

NOTES: The Chart of Accounts includes only postable accounts and the Net Income or Current Earnings account. Sage 50 uses the Net Income account for the Income Statement to calculate the difference between revenue and expenses before closing the books.

POST-CLOSING TRIAL BALANCE

GROEN FIELDS

May 1, 2021		Debits	Credits
1080	Chequing Bank Account	$ 59 640.00	
1300	Seed Supplies	1 230.00	
1310	Fertilizer	780.00	
1320	Plant Care Supplies	2 145.00	
1330	Office Supplies	895.00	
1420	Annual Bedding Plants	5 890.00	
1440	Perennial Plant Stock	8 995.00	
1460	Tree Inventory	4 885.00	
1480	Planters and Hangers	2 255.00	
1500	Computer Software	5 295.00	
1520	Computer Equipment	8 310.00	
1540	Office Furniture	2 490.00	
1560	Farming Equipment	73 400.00	
1570	Greenhouse	120 500.00	
1580	Buildings & Property	625 800.00	
2100	Bank Loan		$120 000.00
2200	Accounts Payable		3 225.00
2650	HST Charged on Sales		4 555.00
2670	HST Paid on Purchases	2 465.00	
2850	Mortgage Payable		450 000.00
3100	GF, Capital		347 195.00
		$924 975.00	$924 975.00

SUPPLIER INFORMATION

GROEN FIELDS

Supplier Name (Contact)	Address	Phone No. Fax No.	E-mail Web Site	Terms Tax ID
Bloomers (C. D. Budd)	RR #3 Clyde River, NS B0W 1R0	Tel: (902) 544-6292 Fax: (902) 544-5217	budd@bloomers.com bloomers.com	2/10, n/30 385 345 863 RT0001
Crop Savers (Gen Nitro)	910 Main St. Greenfield, NS B0T 1E0	Tel 1: (902) 622-3188 Tel 2: (800) 622-2881	GN@cropsavers.com cropsavers.com	1/10, n/30 901 200 865 RT0001
Data Savers (N. T. Buggs)	4 Industrial Rd. Truro, NS B2C 8J6	Tel: (902) 721-5121 Fax: (902) 721-5522	ntbuggs@datasavers.com datasavers.com	net 30 567 321 443 RT0001
Dust Busters (Joan Waters)	60 Water St. Dartmouth, NS B2W 6R9	Tel 1: (902) 366-1551 Tel 2: (877) 366-1500	waters@dustbusters.com dustbusters.com	net 1 345 667 216 RT0001
Intertel (Les Chatter)	2 Communicate Rd. Truro, NS B2A 2K4	Tel: (902) 456-2355	chatter@intertel.ca intertel.ca	net 7
NS Gas (N. Bridge)	355 Pipeline Rd. Truro, NS B2A 5B1	Tel: (902) 454-8110	nbridge@naturalgas.com naturalgas.com	net 7
NS Hydro (N. Ergie)	83 Water St. Truro, NS B2W 6S9	Tel: (902) 455-5120	n.ergie@nshydro.ns.ca nshydro.ns.ca	net 7
Rural Property Repairs (Hy Drangea)	71 Ridge Way Currys Corner, NS B0N 1H0	Tel: (902) 499-3481 Fax: (902) 499-3482	hd@RPR.com RPR.com	1/20, n/30 124 653 775 RT0001
Spotless Company (Dee Tergent)	49 Scrub St. Truro, NS B2G 1V0	Tel: (902) 454-6611 Fax: (902) 454-3216	dtergent@spotless.com spotless.com	1/30, n/60 481 532 554 RT0001
Yardworks Inc. (J. Bigge)	20 Oceanview Dr. Sydney, NS B1P 2L2	Tel 1: (902) 777-2346 Tel 2: (888) 337-4599	jbigge@yardworks.com yardworks.com	net 10 288 411 754 RT0001

OUTSTANDING SUPPLIER INVOICES

GROEN FIELDS

Supplier Name	Terms	Date	Inv/Chq No.	Amount	Total
Crop Savers	1/10, n/30	Apr. 26/21	CS-1044	$ 800	$ 800
Data Savers	net 30	Apr. 6/21	DS-361	$1 200	$1 200
Rural Property Repairs	1/20, n/30	Apr. 25/21	RPR-1341	$1 725	
		Apr. 25/21	Chq #164	500	
			Balance owing		$1 225
			Grand Total		$3 225

Accounting Procedures

The Harmonized Sales Tax (Provincial Sales Tax and Goods and Services Tax)

In Nova Scotia, federal and provincial taxes are combined in the Harmonized Sales Tax, or HST, a single tax at the rate of 15 percent. The HST is applied to most goods and services. Groen Fields uses the regular method for calculating and remitting the HST. All items sold by the farm have HST added to them. At the end of each quarter, the HST liability to the Receiver General is reduced by any HST paid to suppliers on purchases. Some items, such as large farm equipment and fertilizer and seeds purchased in large quantities, are zero rated for HST purposes. Groen Fields' *HST Owing (Refund)* subgroup total account has the amount of HST that is to be remitted to the Receiver General for Canada on the last day of each quarter. (For details, please read Chapter 2 on the GST and HST.)

NOTES

For zero rated goods the HST rate is 0 percent. None of the sales are zero rated.

Most bank services and other financial institution services are exempt from HST charges. Bank payroll services are subject to HST charges.

Provincial sales tax is not levied as a separate tax in Nova Scotia. PST will be introduced in Chapter 6.

Open-Invoice Accounting for Payables

The open-invoice method of accounting for invoices allows a business to keep track of each individual invoice and partial payment made against the invoice. This is in contrast to methods that keep track only of the outstanding balance by combining all invoice balances owed to a supplier. Sage 50 uses the open-invoice method. Fully paid invoices can be cleared (removed) periodically; outstanding invoices cannot be cleared.

Discounts

When discounts for early payment are offered by suppliers, Groen Fields takes advantage of them by paying invoices before the discount period ends. When the payment terms are set up correctly for the supplier and invoice, and dates are entered correctly, discounts are calculated automatically by Sage 50 and credited to *Purchase Discounts*, a contra-expense account that has a credit balance and reduces overall expenses.

NOTES

Discounts for early payment may be calculated on pretax amounts or on the full invoice amounts. This choice is entered in the ledger settings for the vendor or supplier.

Purchase of Inventory Items and Cost of Goods Sold

Inventory items and supplies purchased are recorded in the appropriate inventory or supplies asset account. Periodically, these are counted to determine the value of items remaining and the cost price of inventory sold and supplies used. The manager then issues a memo to reduce the inventory or supplies asset account and to charge the cost price to the corresponding expense account. For example, at the end of each month the *Annual Bedding Plants* asset account (*1420*) is reduced (credited) and the *Cost of Goods Sold* expense account (*5080*) is increased (debited) by the cost price of the amount sold.

INSTRUCTIONS

1. **Enter** the **source documents for May** in Sage 50 using the Chart of Accounts, Trial Balance, Supplier Information and Accounting Procedures for Groen Fields. The procedures for entering each new type of transaction for this application are outlined step by step in the Keystrokes section with the source documents. These transactions are indicated with a ✓ in the upper part of the completion check box beside the source document. Source document numbers are included below the checkmark or in the lower part of the check box.

2. **Print** the **reports** indicated on the printing form below after you have completed your entries. Instructions for reports begin on page 146.

REPORTS

Accounts
- ☐ Chart of Accounts
- ☐ Account List
- ☐ General Journal Entries

Financials
- ☑ Comparative Balance Sheet dates: May 1 and May 31 with difference in percentage
- ☑ Income Statement from May 1 to May 31
- ☑ Trial Balance date: May 31
- ☐ All Journal Entries
- ☑ General Ledger accounts: 1420 4100 5080 from May 1 to May 31

Banking
- ☐ Cheque Log Report

Payables
- ☐ Supplier List
- ☑ Supplier Aged Detail for all suppliers May 31
- ☐ Aged Overdue Payables
- ☑ Purchases Journal Entries: May 1 to May 31
- ☑ Payments Journal Entries: May 1 to May 31

Mailing Labels
- ☐ Labels

KEYSTROKES

Opening Data Files

Open **SageData19\FIELDS\FIELDS** to access the data files for Groen Fields. Refer to page 8 if you need assistance with opening data files.

You are prompted to enter the session date, which is May 7, 2021, for the first group of transactions in this application.

Type `May 7 21`

Click **OK** to enter the first session date for this application.

The Payables module appears. This is the default page for Groen Fields.

NOTES
If you are working from backup files, restore SageData19\FIELDS1.CAB or FIELDS1 to SageData19\FIELDS\FIELDS. You should create the new folder. Refer to Chapter 1, page 25, if you need assistance with restoring files.

Accounting for Purchases

All supplier-related transactions can be entered from the Payables module window. Purchases from suppliers are entered in the Purchases Journal, which is accessed from the Purchase Invoices icon:

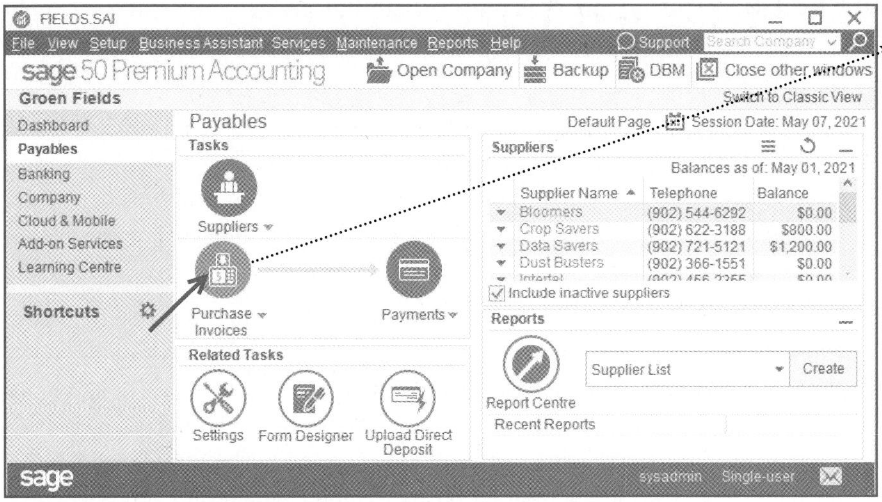

NOTES

Access to the Receivables, Payroll, Inventory and Division ledgers is hidden because these ledgers are not set up or ready to use.

PRO VERSION

Pro replaces Premium in the title bar. The term Vendors will replace Suppliers for all icon labels and fields.

The first transaction is a normal purchase invoice that will be paid later.

✓ 1

Purchase Invoice #DS-642 **Dated May 1/21**

From Data Savers, $1 320 plus $198 HST for off-site data backup and restoration services for one year. Invoice total $1 518. Terms: net 30.

Click the **Purchase Invoices icon** to open the Purchases Journal input form:

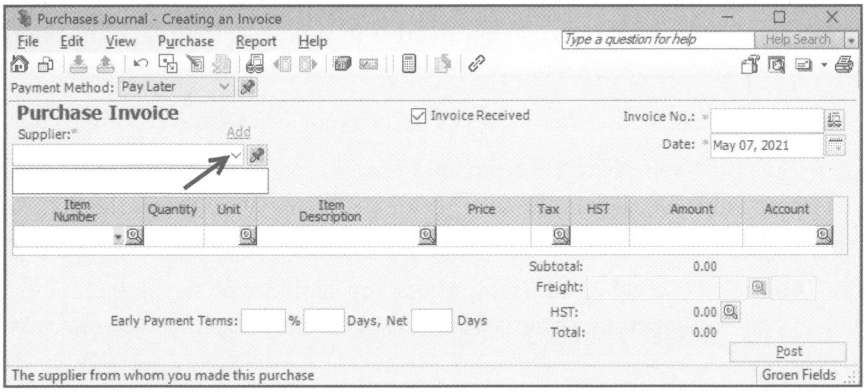

Move the mouse pointer across the various tool buttons and input fields. As you point to them, the labels and status bar messages change.

CLASSIC VIEW

In the Classic view Home window, click the Purchases icon to open the Purchases Journal.

PRO VERSION

The Refresh tool applies to multi-user mode and does not appear in the Pro version because this a single-user program.

Creating An Invoice is included in the title bar label and the option to Pay Later is correct because this is a credit purchase. Payment methods include cheque, cash, direct deposits and credit cards (when these are set up).

Most tool buttons should already be familiar. The Calculator tool button appears in the tool bar of the Purchases Journal and all other journal windows.

Several tool buttons have been added to the Purchases Journal window: Look Up An Invoice, Look Up Previous and Next Invoice, Track Shipments, Printer Settings, Print Preview, E-mail and Print. The Link tool opens a new screen with the option to add a link to this transaction, either to a file on your own computer or to a Web page.

Each tool will be discussed when used. The Projects or Divisions module is hidden, so there is no column for it in the journal.

Required fields are marked with * (an asterisk), as they are in other journals and ledgers.

NOTES

When the other features are not hidden, you will have a pull-down menu for Transaction types that includes quotes and purchase orders.

When payment is by cheque, a drop-down list of bank accounts is available. These topics are covered in later chapters.

WARNING!
You must click the list arrow to open the supplier list. Clicking the field will place an insertion point to prepare for typing a name.

Click the **Supplier** (or Vendor) **field list arrow** to expand the supplier list:

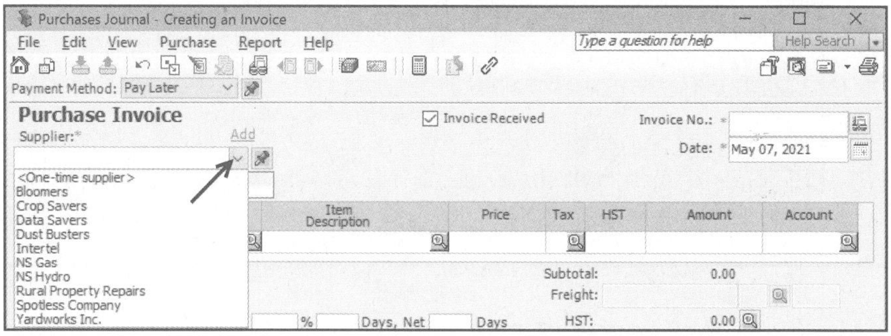

Whenever you have a downward pointing list arrow beside a field, you can make a selection from a drop-down list. Type the first letter of the supplier's name to advance to the names beginning with that letter. When you type in the Supplier field, the program fills in a name from the supplier list by trying to match the letters you type.

Click **Data Savers**, the supplier for this purchase, to select and enter it.

The supplier's name and address have been added to your input form, making it easy to check whether you have selected the correct supplier. Many other details have also been added by default from the supplier's record. The tax code and the account number usually stay the same for a supplier, so they are set up as defaults. The default payment method and payment terms for the supplier are also included. Any of these details can be edited if required. If you have made an error in your selection, click the Supplier field list arrow and start again. If you have selected correctly,

NOTES
If you use the same supplier or payment method for consecutive purchases, preselection can save data entry time. You can still select from the drop-down list. The pin will remain selected, so you can enter multiple purchases using the same payment method or from the same supplier as well.

Press *tab*. The cursor moves to the Same Next Time (pushpin) icon.

Click the **Same Next Time pushpin** (**Same**) tool to preselect this supplier for the next purchase. The tool is also beside the payment method selection. When selected, the pin is pushed in. Click it again to turn off the selection.

Click the **Invoice No. field**, where you should type the alphanumeric invoice number. In this way you will skip the Invoice Received check box.

Type `DS-642`

Press *tab* to select the Invoice Lookup icon.

Press *tab* again to advance to the Date field.

NOTES
The year is automatically added when you enter the month and day in the Date field of the Purchases Journal.

Enter the date the transaction took place, May 1, 2021. The session date appears by default, in long (text) format according to the settings for the company file. It is highlighted, ready to be accepted or changed. You need to change the date.

Type `may 1`

NOTES
Inventory is introduced in Chapter 10.
When orders and quotes are used, fields for these features will be added to the journal. (Refer to Chapter 11.)

Many of the invoice fields (Item Number, Quantity, Unit, Item Description and unit Price) pertain mainly to inventory items. Because we are not using the Inventory Ledger for this application, you can skip the inventory-related fields. Any information you type in these fields does not appear in the journal report. You can add a description in the Item Description field.

NOTES
When you are selling multiple quantities of an item, you can enter the quantity in the Quantity field and the unit price in the Price field. Sage 50 will then calculate the total amount.

Click the **Item Description field**.

Type `data backup service`

If necessary, you can change the tax code. To access the codes set up and available,

Click the **Tax field List icon** to open the list of tax codes for Groen Fields:

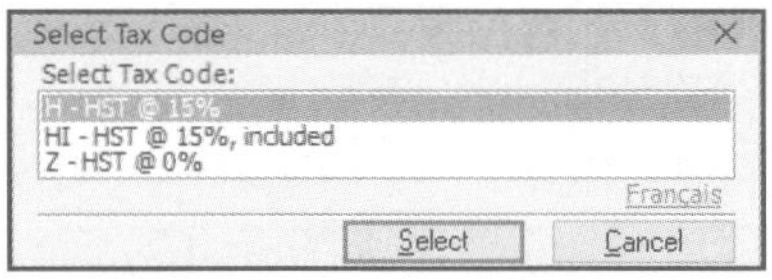

The selected tax code is H, that is, HST is charged on the purchase at 15 percent, and the tax is not included in the price. You can select a different code if needed, but in this case the tax code is correct.

Click **Cancel** so that the selection remains unchanged.

Click the **first line of the Amount field**, where you will enter the total amount for this purchase.

Type 1320

Press tab.

The cursor moves to the Account field. The Account field for this purchase refers to the debit part of the journal entry, normally the acquisition of an asset or the incurring of an expense. It could also be used to decrease a liability or to decrease equity if the purchase were made for the owner's personal use. When you work in the subsidiary Payables journal, Sage 50 will automatically credit your *Accounts Payable* **control account** in the General Ledger for the purchase. In fact, you cannot access *Accounts Payable* directly when the Payables Ledger is set up and linked. If you click the Account List icon, this account is not included.

In this example, the business has incurred an expense and the correct account, *Data Management,* the default for this supplier, is entered.

To select a different account, click the List icon for the Account field, double-click the Account field or press enter to open the Select Account screen. You can also add a new account from the Select Account screen.

Press tab to advance the cursor to the next invoice line. You can now enter additional purchases from this supplier if there are any.

Sage 50 uses the tax code to calculate and enter the tax amount automatically in the HST field when you enter the amount for the purchase.

Your screen has been updated with this information:

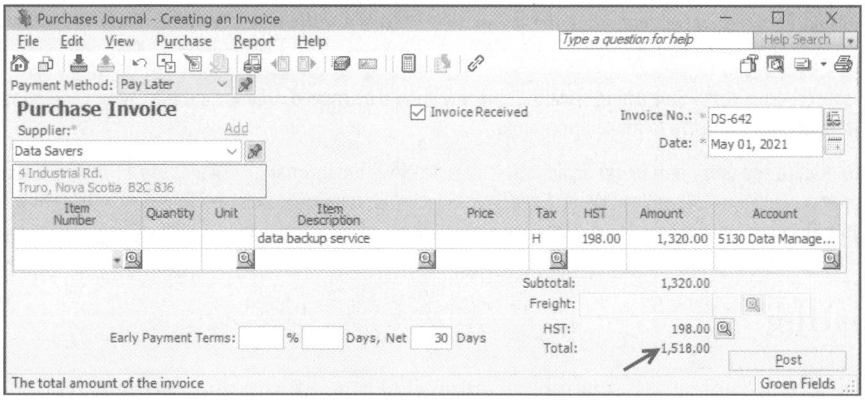

The payment terms have been set up as defaults for this supplier and are entered automatically. They can be edited if needed for specific purchases, but in this case they are correct. There is no discount, and full payment is due in 30 days. The **subtotal** (amount owing before taxes) and the **total** amounts are calculated and added automatically, so the entries for this transaction are complete and you are ready to review the transaction. By reviewing the journal entry, you can check for mistakes.

NOTES

For this application, the sales tax rate is set to 15 percent, the harmonized single tax rate for Nova Scotia. For provinces that have a separate or no provincial sales tax, the rate is 5 percent and tax codes will display as GST @ 5%.

Since the provincial and federal retail sales taxes are harmonized, there is no separate amount for PST. When PST is applicable and is set up in the defaults for the company, the program will calculate PST as well, based on the tax rates and codes entered for PST.

NOTES

Typing negative amounts will generate a credit entry with a debit for Accounts Payable. This is similar to entering a negative amount in the General Journal to switch debits to credits and vice versa.

NOTES

The account name may not fit in the account column if the column is very narrow. To change the width of a column, point to the heading column margin. When the pointer changes to a double-sided arrow, drag the margin line to the new location. Make a journal window wider by dragging the side frame. You can also maximize a journal window to occupy the entire screen.

> **NOTES**
> Pressing ctrl + J will also display the journal entry.

Reviewing the Purchases Journal Entry

Choose the **Report menu** and **click Display Purchases Journal Entry**:

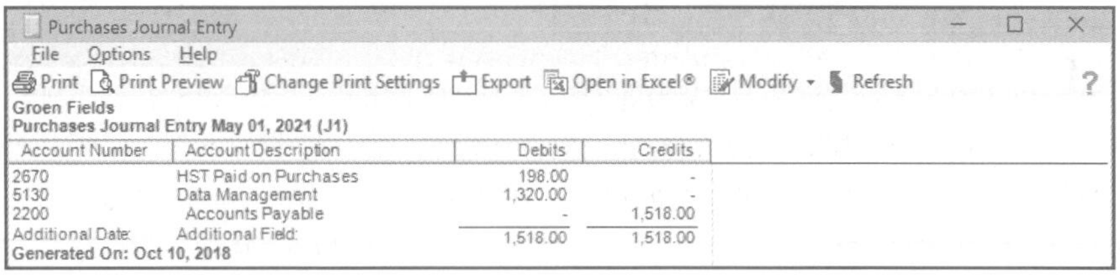

Purchases Journal Entry
File Options Help
Print | Print Preview | Change Print Settings | Export | Open in Excel® | Modify | Refresh
Groen Fields
Purchases Journal Entry May 01, 2021 (J1)

Account Number	Account Description	Debits	Credits
2670	HST Paid on Purchases	198.00	-
5130	Data Management	1,320.00	-
2200	Accounts Payable	-	1,518.00
Additional Date:	Additional Field:	1,518.00	1,518.00

Generated On: Oct 10, 2018

Sage 50 has automatically updated the *Accounts Payable* **control account** because the Payables and General ledgers are linked or fully integrated. Even though you did not enter account *2200*, Sage 50 uses it because it is defined as the linked account to which all "pay later" purchases should be credited. In fact, you cannot select *Accounts Payable* directly for posting when it is used as a linked account. *HST Paid on Purchases*, the linked tax account, is also automatically updated. Using the Purchases Journal instead of the General Journal to enter purchases is faster because you need to enter only half the journal entry. You should use this journal for purchases because the program credits the account of the selected supplier directly, prevents you from choosing an incorrect payables account and updates the total payables and tax amounts directly. The automatic selection of tax codes and accounts and calculation of tax amounts also makes the transaction simpler to enter and increases accuracy.

> **NOTES**
> Other linked accounts for the Payables Ledger include a bank account, a freight expense account and a purchase discounts account. Each linked account will be explained when it is used in this workbook.

> **NOTES**
> Using the Payables journals also makes it less likely to reverse debit and credit amounts in error.

Close the **display** to return to the Purchases Journal input screen.

> **NOTES**
> To correct a Purchases Journal entry after posting, refer to page 129 and Appendix C.

CORRECTING THE PURCHASES JOURNAL ENTRY BEFORE POSTING

Move to the field that has the error. **Press** tab to move forward through the fields or **press** shift and tab together to move back to a previous field. This will highlight the field information so you can change it. **Type** the **correct information** and **press** tab to enter it.

You can also use the mouse to **point** to a field and **drag through** the **incorrect information** to highlight it. **Type** the **correct information** and **press** tab to enter it.

If the supplier is incorrect, reselect from the supplier list by **clicking** the **Supplier field list arrow. Click** the name of the **correct supplier**. If the supplier terms or account are now incorrect, you should reverse the entry instead. Refer to page 141.

Click an **incorrect amount** to highlight it, **type** the **correct amount** and **press** tab to enter the change.

To select a different account, **click** the **Account List icon** to display the list of accounts. **Click** the **correct account** number to highlight it, then **click Select** and **press** tab to enter the change.

To insert a line or remove a line, **click** the **line** that should be moved. **Choose** the **Edit menu** and **click Insert Line** or **Remove Line** to make the change.

To discard the entry and begin again, **click** ☒ to close the journal or **click Undo** on the tool bar to open a blank journal window. When Sage 50 asks whether you want to discard the entry, **click Yes** to confirm your decision.

Posting

When you are certain that you have entered all the information correctly, you must post the transaction to save it.

> **NOTES**
> You can press alt + P to post the journal entry.

Click the **Post button** Post or **choose** the **Purchase menu** and **click Post** to save your transaction.

Click **OK** to confirm successful posting.

A new blank Purchases Journal form appears on the screen.

Storing a Recurring Journal Entry

The second transaction is the recurring purchase of soil treatment. Businesses often have transactions that are repeated regularly. For example, loan payments, bank charges and rent payments usually occur on the same day each month; supplies may be ordered daily or weekly; insurance payments may be less frequent but nonetheless regular. Groen Fields is invoiced weekly for the treatment service. By storing an entry and indicating the frequency, it can be recalled when it is needed without re-entering all the information.

✓ 2

Purchase Invoice #CS-1243 **Dated May 1/21**

From Crop Savers, $640 for soil testing and follow-up fertilizer treatment plus $96 HST. Invoice total $736. Terms: 1/10, n/30. Store as a weekly recurring entry.

The Purchases Journal should still be open with the correct date.

Choose **Crop Savers** from the supplier list. Or,

Click the **Supplier field** and **type** C

Click the **Invoice field**.

Type CS-1243

Enter a **description** for the purchase.

The tax code is correct; HST is charged on this service. The default payment terms and account are also correct.

Click the **Amount field**, **type** 640 and **press** tab to complete the transaction.

Choose the **Report menu** and **click** **Display Purchases Journal Entry** to review the entry.

Close the **display** and **make corrections** if necessary.

Click the **Store tool** on the tool bar or **choose** the **Purchase menu** and **click** **Store** to open the Store Recurring Transaction screen:

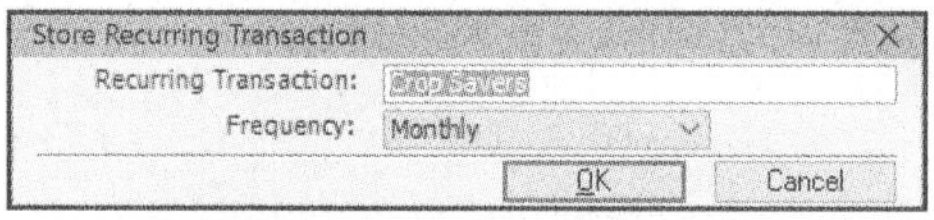

Sage 50 enters the supplier and Monthly as the default name and frequency for the entry. The cursor is in the name field. You can type another descriptive name to change it. Be sure to use one that you will recognize easily as belonging to this entry. The default frequency is incorrect since the invoices for soil treatments are received weekly.

Click **Monthly** to list the choices for the recurring frequency:

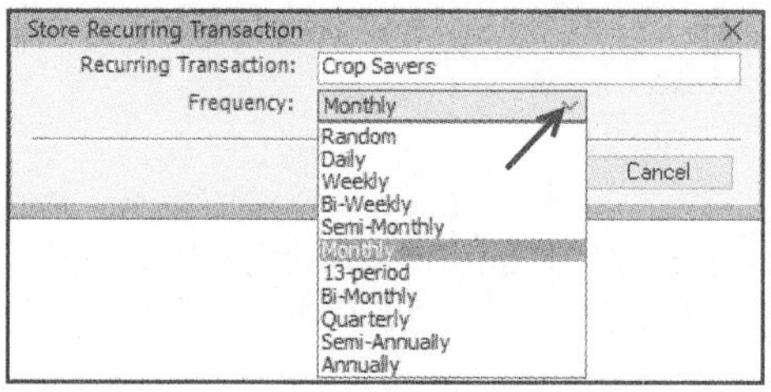

The frequency options are Random (for irregular purchases), Daily, Weekly, Bi-Weekly, Semi-Monthly, Monthly, 13-Period, Bi-Monthly, Quarterly, Semi-Annually and Annually.

Click **Weekly**.

NOTES

Typing the first letter of a supplier name in the Supplier field will add the first supplier name beginning with that letter. Because Crop Savers is the first supplier name starting with "C," it will be entered.

NOTES

The procedure for storing entries is the same for all journals when the option is available. Choose Store, assign a name to the entry, then choose a frequency and click OK to save it.

The shortcut for storing a transaction is ctrl + T.

NOTES

The recurring frequency options are Daily, Weekly (52 times per year), Bi-Weekly (26 times per year, or every two weeks), Semi-Monthly (24 times per year), Monthly (12 times per year), 13-Period (13 times per year, or every four weeks), Bi-Monthly (six times per year, or every two months), Quarterly (four times per year, or every three months), Semi-Annually (twice per year, or every six months), Annually (once per year) and Random (irregular intervals using the session date when the entry is recalled).

When you recall the stored entry, Sage 50 will advance the default journal date according to the frequency selected. The session date will be entered if the Random frequency is chosen.

Click **OK** to return to the Purchases Journal window.

The **Recall tool**  is now darkened and can be selected because you have stored a journal entry. The journal title bar label has also changed — to Using Recurring Crop Savers.

> **CORRECTING A STORED JOURNAL ENTRY**
>
> If you notice an error in the stored journal entry before posting, you must first **correct** the **journal entry** in the Purchases Journal window, then **click Store**. When asked to confirm that you want to overwrite or replace the previous version, **click Yes**.
>
> If you edit the journal entry after storing it and do not want to store the changed entry, Sage 50 will warn you that the entry has changed. **Click Yes** to proceed.

Posting

When you are sure that you have entered all the information correctly and you have stored the entry, you must post the transaction to save it.

Click the **Post button** [Post] or **choose** the **Purchase menu** and **click Post** to save your transaction. **Click OK** to confirm successful posting.

A new blank Purchases Journal form appears on the screen. The Recall tool is now available, so we can recall the purchase we stored. Our next transaction is a payment, however, not a purchase.

Close the **Purchases Journal window** to return to the Payables window.

The supplier balance amounts in the Home window have been updated for these two purchases.

Accounting for Payments

Payments are made from the Payments Journal icon in the Tasks pane:

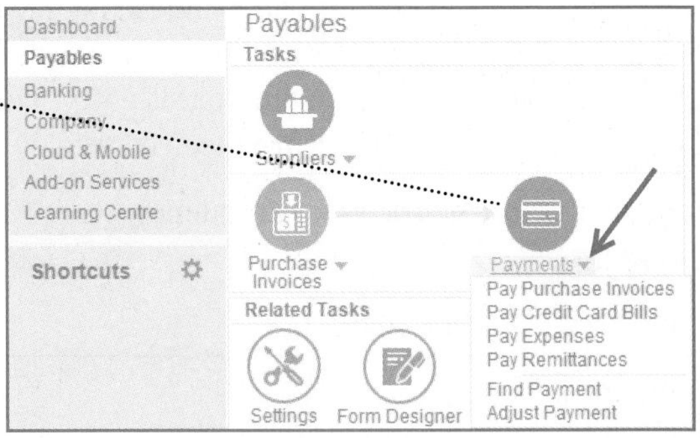

CLASSIC VIEW From the Classic view Home window, click the Payments icon  to open the Payments Journal. Pay Invoices will be selected as the default type of transaction.

PRO VERSION The term Vendors replaces Suppliers.

Click the **Payments icon list arrow** to list the shortcuts for different payment types.

When you click on one of these shortcuts, the journal will open with the correct type of payment transaction preselected.

Click **Pay Purchase Invoices** to open the Payments Journal:

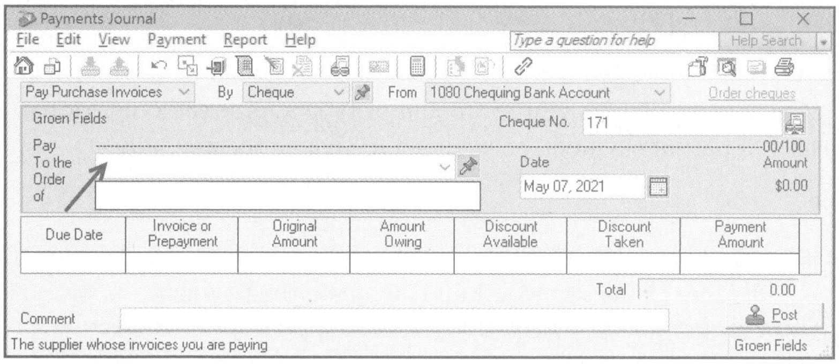

Pay Purchase Invoices is selected as the type of payment in the type of Pay transaction field because we made this selection in the Home window. Pay Invoices is also the default transaction type when you click the Payments icon. Cheque appears as the method of payment in the By field, and *1080 Chequing Bank Account* is the account the payment is made from. These defaults are correct for the first payment.

✓ 3 **Payment Cheque #171** **Dated May 2/21**

To Data Savers, $780 in partial payment of account. Reference invoice #DS-361.

Click the **To The Order Of** (Supplier) **field list arrow** to open the familiar list of suppliers displayed in alphabetic order.

Click **Data Savers** (or **type** D) to choose and enter the supplier to whom the payment is made.

The journal is updated with the outstanding invoices for the supplier:

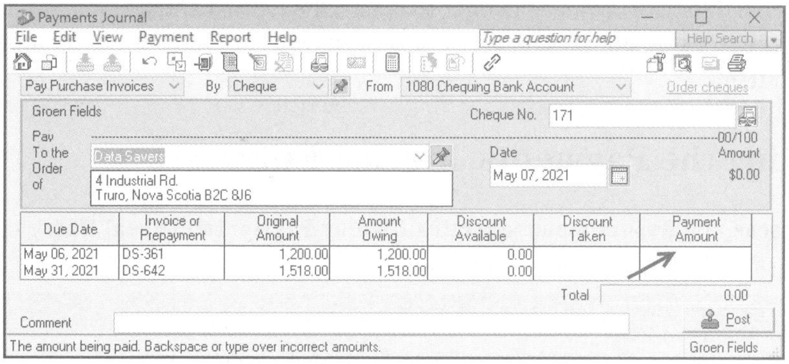

The addition of the supplier's name and address makes it easy to determine whether you have selected correctly. If you need to change the supplier, click the Supplier field list arrow to make a different selection from the supplier list. The cheque number is entered in the Number field. The next cheque number appears according to the settings for the company. It is correct, so you can accept it. Normally the cheque number should be correct. It can be edited, if necessary, for reversing or correcting entries.

The default session date is entered and is incorrect; you must change it.

Click the **Calendar icon** for the Date field.

Click **2** in the May section. **Press** (tab).

The year will be added correctly when you type the month and day in the Payments Journal Date field.

The cursor moves to the Due Date field for the first outstanding invoice. All outstanding invoices, including both the amount of the original invoice and the balance owing for the selected supplier, are listed on the screen.

Press (tab) to advance to the Discount Taken field. Since there is no discount, the field is blank and you can skip it.

PRO VERSION

The Refresh tools do not appear in the Pro version.

NOTES

The To The Order Of and payment method (By) fields have the Same tool that is in the Purchases Journal.

NOTES

When more than one bank account is set up, you can select the bank from the drop-down list beside From. In Chapter 11, you will use these upper fields to work with multiple bank accounts.

NOTES

You can type D in the Supplier field to enter Data Savers because this is the only supplier beginning with "D."

NOTES

When several invoices are paid to the same supplier or by the same method with separate cheques, you can click , the Same push pin tool, to keep the option selected after you post a payment.

NOTES

From the Pay drop-down list, you can select the other kinds of transactions for this journal, or you can choose the transaction type from the Payments icon shortcuts list in the Payables module window.

NOTES

Click (the Include Fully Paid Invoices tool) to display all paid and unpaid invoices for the selected supplier.

NOTES

The Lookup icon appears beside the cheque number and in the tool bar so you can look up previous payments.

Press tab again.

The amount outstanding for the selected invoice is highlighted as the payment amount. You can accept the highlighted amount or type another amount for partial payments. This is a partial payment, so we need to change the amount.

Type 780

Press tab to update the Total, advance the cursor to the Discount Taken field for the next invoice and complete the payment:

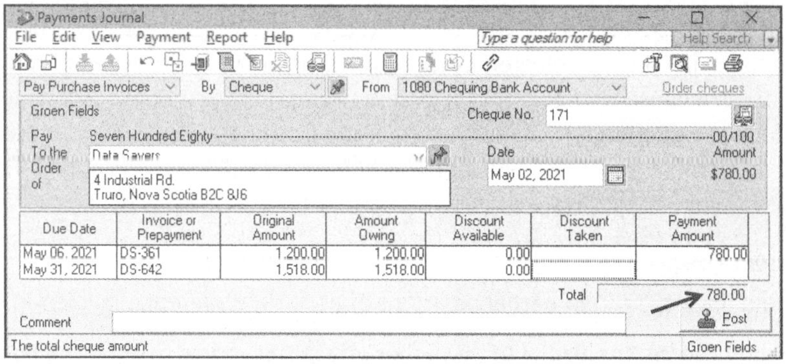

WARNING!
Neither the amount for the next invoice nor its discount should be highlighted since this invoice is not being paid. If its amount is highlighted or entered, you must delete it by pressing del and then tab to correct the total cheque amount (refer to page 131).

NOTES
The Print Preview tool allows you to review the cheque. The display will include the cheque to be printed, plus two copies of the related invoice and payment amount applied: one to submit and one for reference.

The upper cheque portion of the form is completed automatically. There is no field for account numbers in the Payments Journal — you need to enter only the amount of the payment on the appropriate invoice line.

As you pay invoices in the subsidiary Payments Journal, you do not enter any accounts, so you cannot make an incorrect selection. Sage 50 chooses the default linked accounts defined for the Payables Ledger to create the journal entry.

The entries for this transaction are complete, so you are ready to review and post your transaction.

NOTES
The direct link between the Payments and Purchases journals for each supplier provides a further reason for using the Purchases Journal for purchases. Outstanding amounts (and discounts) are calculated and displayed automatically, and ledger account balances and supplier records are updated automatically.

Furthermore, you cannot reverse debit and credit amounts in error.

Reviewing the Payments Journal Entry

Choose the **Report menu** and **click Display Payments Journal Entry** to display the transaction you have entered:

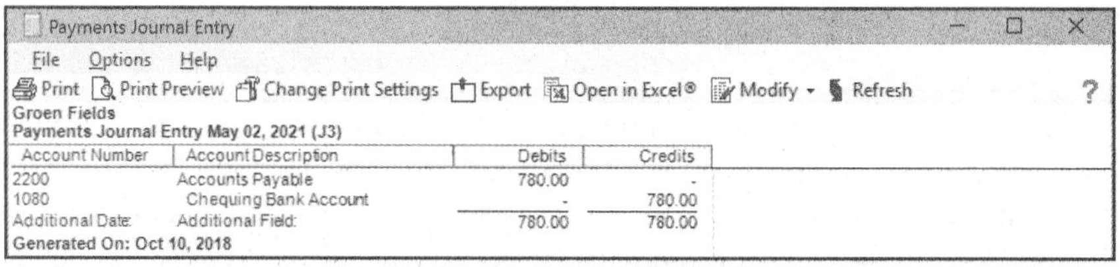

Sage 50 automatically creates a related journal entry when you complete a Payments Journal entry. The program updates *Accounts Payable* and *Chequing Bank Account* because the Payables and General ledgers are fully linked. *Chequing Bank Account* has been defined as the default Payables linked account to which payments are credited. The payment is also recorded to the supplier's account to reduce the balance owing.

Close the **display** to return to the Payments Journal input screen.

You can print the cheque, but you must do so before posting. However, you should preview it and verify that you have selected the correct printer and forms for printing cheques (refer to Chapter 4, page 85) and make corrections first, if necessary.

NOTES
When the batch printing option is selected in the settings for Forms, you can print cheques in batches after posting them. The Print Batches tool will be added to the tool bar. Batch printing is covered in Chapter 14.

To check printer settings, click the Change The Default Printer Settings tool in the journal.

Turn on the printer and click the Print tool.

CORRECTING THE PAYMENTS JOURNAL ENTRY BEFORE POSTING

Move to the field that has the error. **Press** *tab* to move forward through the fields or **press** *shift* and *tab* together to move back to a previous field. This will highlight the field information so you can change it. **Type** the **correct information** and **press** *tab* to enter it.

You can also use the mouse to **point** to a field and **drag through** the **incorrect information** to highlight it. **Type** the **correct information** and **press** *tab* to enter it.

If the supplier is incorrect, **click Undo** to undo the entry or **reselect** from the **Supplier** list by **clicking** the **Supplier list arrow. Click** the name of the **correct supplier**. You will be asked to confirm that you want to discard the current transaction. **Click Yes** to discard the incorrect supplier entry and display the outstanding invoices for the correct supplier. **Re-enter** the **payment** information for this supplier.

Make **corrections**. **Click** the **Print tool** if you want to print the cheque.

Posting

When you are certain that you have entered all the information correctly, you must post the transaction to save it.

Click the **Post button** (or **choose** the **Payment menu** and **click Post**) to save your transaction and then **click OK** to confirm.

Entering Cash Purchases

The property tax statement on May 2 is to be paid immediately on receipt of the assessment notice. Instead of recording the purchase and payment separately, you can record the payment with the purchase in the Payments Journal. This transaction also involves a company that is not listed as a supplier, so you must add Truro City Treasurer to the supplier list to record the transaction.

Suppliers can be added directly from the Payables Ledger or from the Supplier field in the Purchases Journal or the Payments Journal. We will add the new supplier from the Payments Journal. The Payments Journal should still be open.

✓ 4

Cash Purchase Invoice #Truro-2021 **Dated May 2/21**

From Truro City Treasurer (use Quick Add for the new supplier), $1 425 for semi-annual property taxes. Paid by cheque #172.

The date and the cheque number are correct. The date is unchanged from the previous Payments Journal transaction. The next available cheque number is entered by default, and the bank account is selected for the payment. Cheque numbers are updated in sequence for both invoice payment entries and cash purchases paid by cheque.

Click **Pay Purchase Invoices** to list the options for payment transactions:

Click **Make Other Payment** in the drop-down list.

If you have closed the Payments Journal, you can open the form for cash purchases from the Home window. Click the Payments icon list arrow and click **Pay Expenses** (refer to page 118). In this case, you must enter May 2 as the date.

NOTES

You can correct payment amounts after posting by clicking the Adjust Payment tool. Select the payment to adjust, just as you select a purchase invoice or General Journal entry for editing. Make the correction and post the revised payment.

To correct a payment after posting, refer to page 139 and to the section on NSF cheques on page 177.

CLASSIC VIEW

From the Classic view Home window, click the Payments icon to open the Payments Journal. Click Pay Purchase Invoices and then click Make Other Payment as the type of transaction.

> **WARNING!**
> If you have closed the Payments Journal, the session date will be entered and you must change it to May 2.

Journal input fields are added to the payment form:

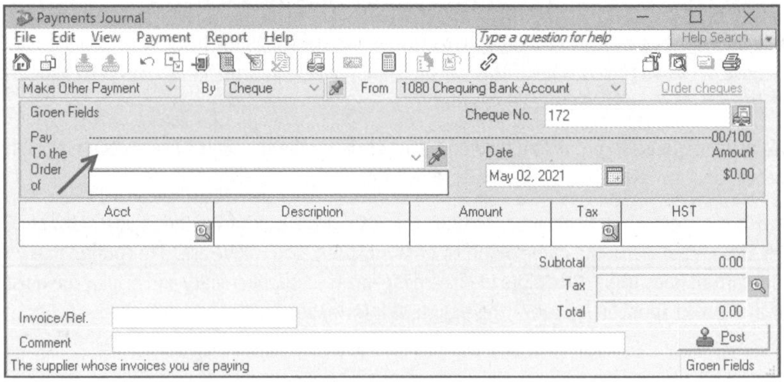

> **PRO VERSION**
> The term Vendor is used instead of Supplier in all journals.

Click the **To The Order Of (Supplier) field** to move the cursor.

Type `Truro City Treasurer` and then **press** *tab* to display the options for a new name:

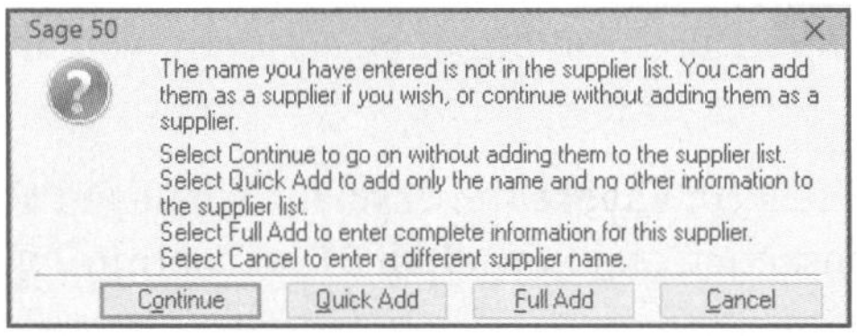

Sage 50
The name you have entered is not in the supplier list. You can add them as a supplier if you wish, or continue without adding them as a supplier.
Select Continue to go on without adding them to the supplier list.
Select Quick Add to add only the name and no other information to the supplier list.
Select Full Add to enter complete information for this supplier.
Select Cancel to enter a different supplier name.
Continue
Quick Add
Full Add
Cancel

> **NOTES**
> The Continue option will add the supplier's name to journal entries for purchase invoices entered in the Purchases Journal, but not for Other Payments entered in the Payments Journal.
> If you create a partial supplier record with Quick Add, you can add more supplier details later by editing the record.

The program recognizes that the name is new and gives you four options. **Continue** will add the name to the journal and the Journal Report and apply the default settings for the ledger. This option will not create a supplier record or include the name in the Supplier list. **Quick Add** will create a partial record with only the supplier's name and will apply the default settings for the ledger. **Full Add** will open a new ledger record for the supplier where you can add complete details. **Cancel** will return you to the journal. You can then type or choose another name if the one you typed was incorrect.

If you are making a cash purchase and you will not be making additional purchases from this supplier, you can choose **One-Time Supplier** from the Supplier list instead of adding the supplier. Then type the supplier's name and address in the text box area below the To The Order Of field. The default settings for the ledger will apply to the invoice, but you can change them if needed. The transaction will be included in the GST/HST report, but the supplier's name will not appear in supplier lists or in the journal reports.

We want to add a partial record for the new supplier.

Click **Quick Add** to return to the Payments Journal.

The supplier's name is added to the journal. Because an account is not set up for the supplier, you must enter the asset or expense account that is debited for the transaction.

> **NOTES**
> When you display the list of All Accounts and scroll down, Accounts Payable (account 2200) is not included.

Click the **Account field List icon** to open the Select Account list.

Click **Suggested Accounts** to modify the list:

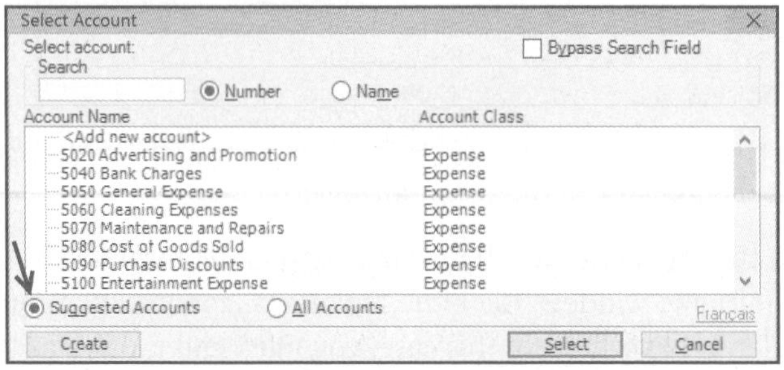

The list now has only the expense accounts, the ones used most often for purchases. This list is easier to work with because it is shorter. When you enter sales in the Sales Journal, the suggested accounts will list only revenue accounts.

Scroll down and **click 5160 Property Taxes**.

Click **Select** to add the account and advance to the Description field.

Type `semi-annual property taxes`

Press tab to advance to the Amount field.

Type `1425` **Press** tab.

Since no sales tax is charged on property taxes, the default entry of No Tax is correct.

Click the **Invoice/Ref. field**.

Type `Truro-2021` **Press** tab to advance to the Comment field.

The comment will become part of the journal record, so you should include it.

Type `Truro-2021, semi-annual property taxes`

The subtotal and total amounts are entered automatically on the Payments Journal screen — in this case they are the same because no taxes are added. Your payment form is completed and you are ready to review it:

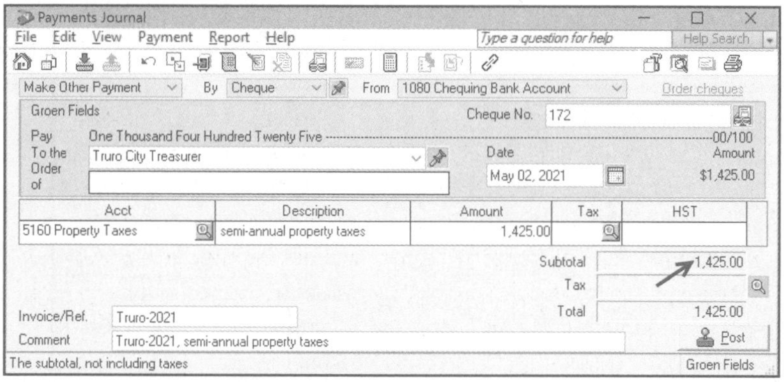

Choose the **Report menu** and **click Display Payments Journal Entry**:

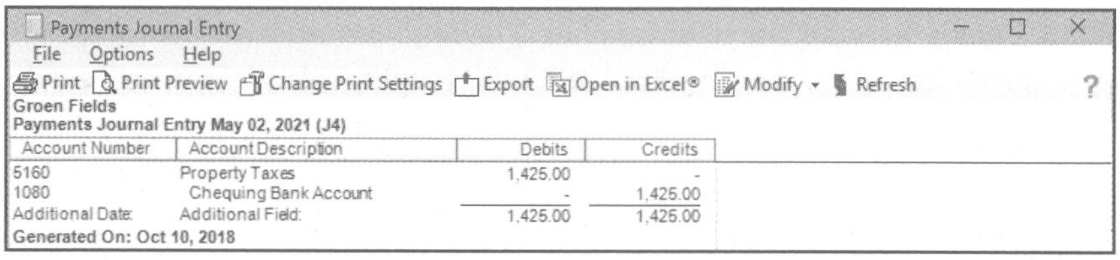

Payments Journal Entry
File Options Help
Print Print Preview Change Print Settings Export Open in Excel® Modify Refresh
Groen Fields
Payments Journal Entry May 02, 2021 (J4)
Account Number | Account Description | Debits | Credits
5160 Property Taxes 1,425.00 -
1080 Chequing Bank Account - 1,425.00
Additional Date: Additional Field: 1,425.00 1,425.00
Generated On: Oct 10, 2018

The program has automatically credited *Chequing Bank Account*, the Payables linked bank account, for the cash purchase instead of *Accounts Payable*.

Close the **display** when you have finished.

Make any **corrections** necessary. Double-click an incorrect entry and type the correct details.

Click the **Post button** Post to save the **entry** when you are certain that it is correct. **Click OK**.

Close the **Payments Journal** to return to the Home window.

Balance amounts in the Suppliers list pane have been updated — the amount owing to Data Savers has been reduced.

NOTES

You can use keyboard shortcuts to copy text. Drag through the text you want to copy to select it and press ctrl + C. Then click the field you want the text copied to and press ctrl + V.

NOTES

The Invoice/Ref. number is not added to the journal entry for Other Payment transactions, so we repeat it in the Comment field.

NOTES

If the purchase has taxes added, choose the tax code from the Tax field List icon selection list.

NOTES

You can preview this expense payment, just as you can preview invoice payment cheques. Two copies of the invoice details are added to the upper cheque portion.

NOTES
Entering cash purchases in the Payments Journal as an Other Payment or in the Purchases Journal is a personal preference.

Adding a New Supplier Record

Cash purchases and new suppliers may be recorded in the Payments Journal or the Purchases Journal. We will record the next cash purchase in the Purchases Journal after we add a full record for the supplier. You can create a new supplier record on the fly, as in the previous transaction, by choosing Full Add, or you can open the Payables Ledger for a new supplier record from the Add Supplier option in the Suppliers shortcuts list. For the next purchase, we will use the ledger option to enter a complete new record.

NOTES
BuyMore
✓ Terms: net 1
Expense account: 5020
Default payment method for invoices: Cheque
Tax code: H - HST @ 15%

✓ 5 **Memo #12** **Dated May 3/21**

Add a new record for BuyMore (contact B. S. Fullovit)
Located at 447 Slick St., Halifax, NS B3B 8J5
Tel: (902) 564-8907
E-mail: fullovit@buymore.ca

Click the **Suppliers icon shortcuts list arrow**:

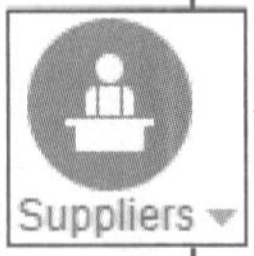

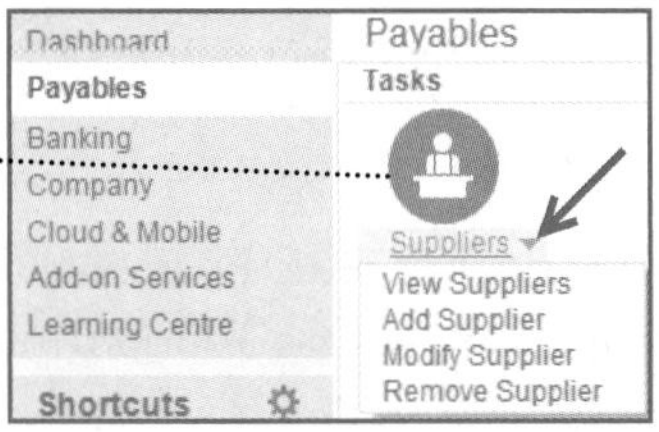

PRO VERSION
Click Add Vendor in the Vendors shortcuts list.

Click **Add Supplier** to open the Payables Ledger input form:

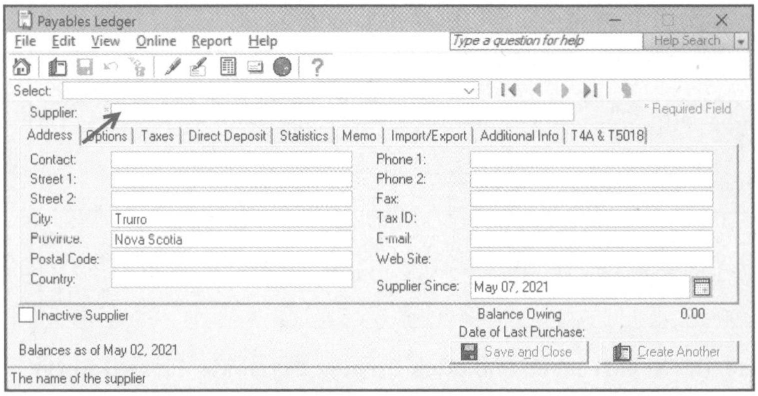

CLASSIC VIEW
From the Classic view Home window, click the Suppliers icon to open the Suppliers window. Then click the Create tool, or choose the File menu and click Create, or press ctrl + N. Close the Suppliers window after saving the new record.

PRO VERSION
The Pro version does not have the Refresh tool. The term Vendor replaces the term Supplier in all fields.

You are ready to enter the new supplier. The Supplier Address tab information screen appears first. Note that **required fields** have an * beside them as they do in the General Ledger. The supplier name is the only required field. Therefore, as soon as you begin to type in the Supplier field, the * is removed.

Type `BuyMore` **Press** tab.

The cursor advances to the Contact field, where you enter the name of Groen Fields' contact person at BuyMore. This field can also be used to enter a third address line if two street lines are insufficient. This field or any other may be left blank by pressing tab or clicking the next field for which you have information.

Type `B. S. Fullovit`

Press tab. The cursor moves to the Street 1 field.

Type `447 Slick St.`

NOTES
If you are missing any information for a supplier, you can leave the field blank and enter the details later by editing the record. Refer to page 138.
Although the extra fields are not required, entering the details in the ledger record will speed up journal entry when you choose the supplier.

The Street 2 field can be used for a second address line, if there is one.

By default, the program has entered the city, province and country from the Payables Ledger Address settings. We need to change the city.

Double-click **Truro** in the City field and **type** `Halifax`

Click the **Postal Code field** to move the cursor. The default entry for Province is correct.

When you enter a Canadian postal code, you do not need to use capital letters or leave a space within the postal code. The program makes these adjustments for you.

Type `b3b8j5` **Press** *tab*.

The format of the postal code has been corrected automatically. The cursor moves to the Country field. You can leave this field blank.

Press *tab*. The cursor moves to the Phone 1 field.

You do not need to insert dashes, spaces or brackets when you enter a telephone number. Telephone and fax numbers may be entered with or without the area code.

Type `9025648907` **Press** *tab*.

The format for the telephone number has also been corrected automatically. The cursor advances to the Phone 2 field for the supplier's second phone number. We do not have additional phone or fax numbers at this time. They can be added later when they are obtained. The Tax ID number refers to the business's federal tax or GST registration number. Adding e-mail and Web site information allows you to send purchase orders by e-mail and connect to the supplier's Web site directly from Sage 50. Type e-mail and Web addresses just as you enter them in your Internet program.

NOTES

The Tax ID must be a valid GST or HST registration number. Leave the field blank if you are unsure of the number or if you get an error message when you enter the number.

Click the **E-mail field**. **Type** `fullovit@buymore.ca`

The date in the Supplier Since field is the session date. You can enter a different date if this is appropriate. The Date Of Last Purchase is added automatically by the program based on the transactions you enter for the supplier.

Press *tab* **twice** to advance to the Supplier Since date field.

Type `May 3`

The last option concerns the supplier's status. You can make a supplier inactive and remove the name from the selection lists and reports. Suppliers that you will not use again can be made inactive.

NOTES

The Home window Suppliers pane and most reports have the option to include or omit inactive suppliers.

Click the **Options tab** to open the next supplier information screen:

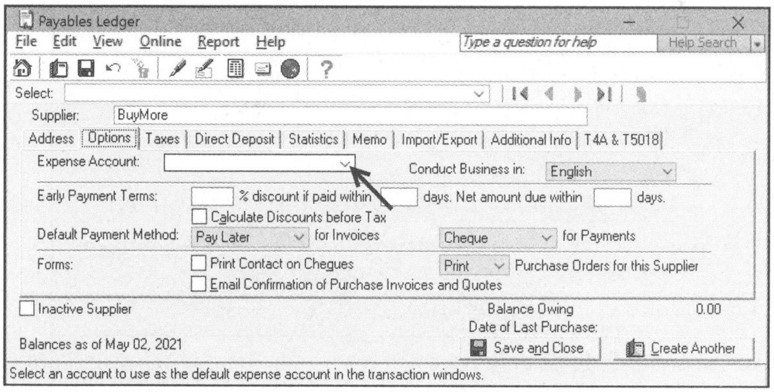

The Options screen has several important fields. In the first part of the Options screen, you can choose the default account and preferred language (English or French) for the supplier. Forms you send to that supplier will be in the selected language, although your own screens will not change. Although the default account field is named Expense Account — often an expense account is the default — you may select any postable account. If you usually buy the same kinds of goods from a supplier, entering a

NOTES
Any postable account – except the type X account for Current Earnings and Accounts Payable – can be used as the default expense account. This includes capital accounts, allowing you to set up the owner as a supplier and link the transactions to the Drawings account.

NOTES
If you need to create a new account for this supplier, type the new account number in the Expense Account field and press *tab*. Click Add to confirm that you want to create the account. The Add An Account wizard will open.

NOTES
Typing 0 (zero) in the Net Days field will leave the payment terms fields on the invoice blank. Therefore, we enter net 1 (one) when payment is due immediately.

default account saves time and prevents errors when completing journal entries. BuyMore provides promotional materials.

Click the **Expense Account list arrow** to list the accounts available.

Scroll down and **click 5020 Advertising and Promotion**.

In the **Early Payment Terms** section, you can enter the discount for early settlement of accounts and the term for full payment. Discounts may be calculated on the amount before taxes or on the full invoice (after-tax) amount. Three fields are used to enter the terms. The first has the discount rate as a percentage, and the second holds the number of days over which the discount remains valid. The final field has the number of days in which net payment is due. The source document states immediate payment is expected.

Click the **Net Due In ___ Days field** (Early Payment Terms section).

Type 1

For paying invoices and for Expenses (Other Payments), you can select the usual payment method for this supplier — the drop-down lists provide the options:

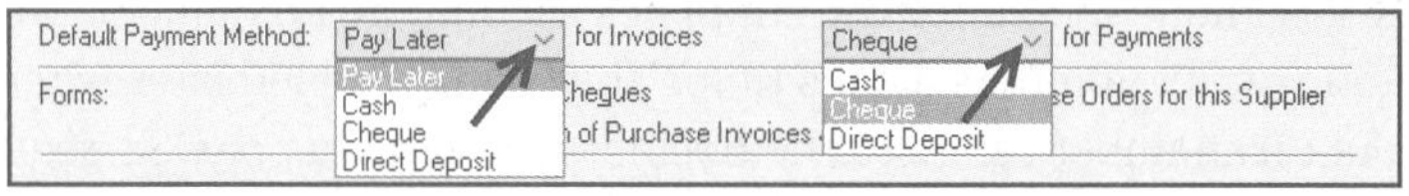

Pay Later and Cheque are the default selections, respectively. All invoices from BuyMore, however, are to be paid immediately, so the correct selection is Cheque.

Choose Cheque from the drop-down list for Invoices.

The remaining fields appear as check boxes. There are no discounts from this supplier. Leave the check box for Calculate Discounts Before Tax blank.

Selecting **Print Contact On Cheques** will add the name of the contact person to cheques. If the Contact field contains address information, check this box; otherwise, leave it unchecked — cheques are usually made payable to the business name.

The next option allows you to choose **Print or E-mail Purchase Orders For This Supplier** as the default setting, but you can change the selection for individual purchase orders if necessary. If you usually e-mail the orders, you should also check the **E-mail Confirmation Of Invoices And Quotes** option by clicking it.

The next input screen defines the tax options for this supplier.

WARNING!
The tax exempt option Yes should be selected only if all purchases from the supplier are tax exempt because this setting prevents taxes from being calculated on any purchases from the supplier.

Click the **Taxes tab** to open the screen:

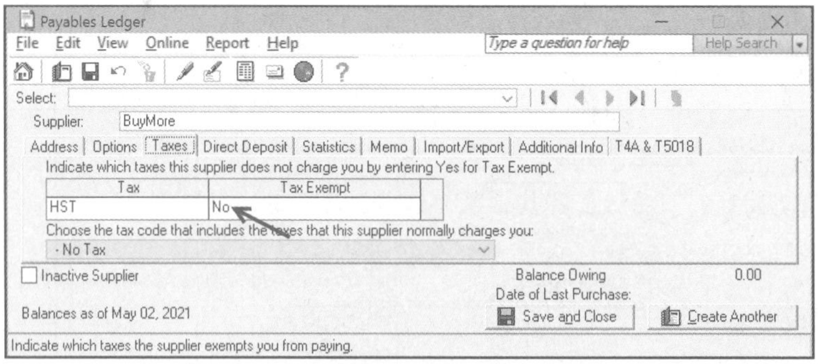

All the taxes Groen Fields usually pays are set up for the company and appear on the list. HST is the only applicable tax. The default option is to pay the tax — the option under Tax Exempt is set at No — that is, Groen Fields is not exempt from taxes on purchases from this supplier. Clicking No will change the tax exemption setting to Yes. This change would be appropriate for suppliers that do not provide goods or services, such as the Receiver General. Refer to Chapter 2 for further information about taxes.

To enter a default tax code for purchases from the supplier, we can choose a code from the drop-down list in the next field. The default setting, No Tax, is incorrect.

Click **No Tax** to open the list of the available codes:

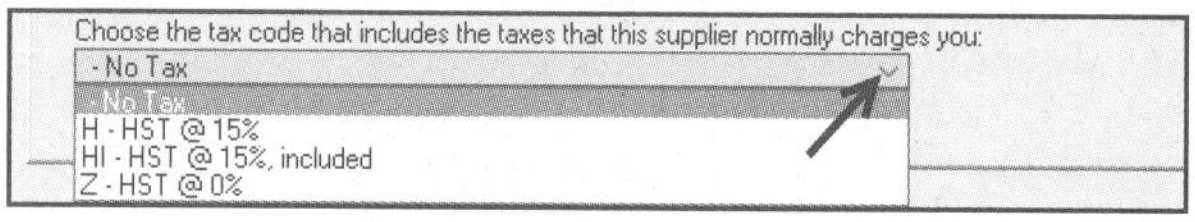

Four codes are defined for Groen Fields: **No Tax** and **Z** (zero rated – HST @ 0%) for suppliers from which purchases are exempt from tax; **H** for suppliers of normal taxable goods or services when HST is not included in the price; and **HI** for suppliers of taxable goods such as gasoline or liquor when the tax is included in the purchase price.

BuyMore charges HST but does not include it in the price.

Click **H - HST @ 15%.**

The remaining input screens will be introduced in later applications. The **Direct Deposit** tab screen holds the details for automatic payments from your bank account, the **Statistics** tab screen stores cumulative historical transactions, the **Memo** tab screen allows you to add messages to the Daily Business Manager and the **Import/Export** tab screen allows you to specify corresponding inventory item codes for your business and your suppliers. The **Additional Info** tab screen has customizable fields for other information. You can prepare **T4A** and **T5018 Slips** for suppliers and subcontractors (for contract and construction services) — this does not apply to Groen Fields.

Check your work carefully before saving the information because the options you select will affect the invoices directly.

CORRECTING A NEW SUPPLIER ACCOUNT

Move to the field that has the error by **pressing** tab to move forward through the fields or **pressing** shift and tab together to move back to a previous field. **Type** the **correct information.**

You can also highlight the incorrect information by dragging the cursor through it. You can now type the correct information.

After a field has been corrected, **press** tab to enter the correction.

To open a different tab screen, **click** the **tab** you want.

When you are certain that all the information is correct,

Click **Save And Close**  to save the supplier information and return to the Home window.

Entering Vendor Records from the Purchases Journal

Click the Purchase Invoices icon  to open the journal and click the Supplier field.

Type the new supplier's name in the Supplier field. Click the Add link (just above the Supplier field) to open a ledger record at the Address tab screen.

Or, press tab after typing the name. The program recognizes the name as new:

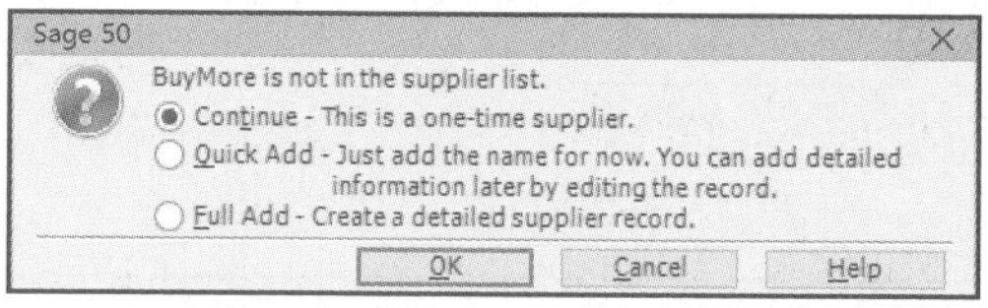

Full Add will open a Payables Ledger record at the Address tab screen with the supplier name entered as you typed it in the Supplier field. Add the remaining supplier details as described above. Click Save And Close to return to the invoice. The supplier's address, tax code and account are added to the invoice.

WARNING!

When the tax exempt settings are No, you can change the tax codes in the journals and the tax calculations will be correct. If the tax exempt settings are Yes, you can select a tax code in the journals, but no taxes will be calculated.

NOTES

The Daily Business Manager is covered in Chapter 11, and the Import/Export options are explained in Appendix J on the Student DVD. Direct deposits are covered in Chapter 13.

We use the Additional Info tab fields for the Payroll Ledger in Chapter 9.

CLASSIC VIEW

From the Classic view Home window, click the Purchases icon  to open the Purchases Journal.

NOTES

If you click the Add link before typing the name, add the name when the ledger record opens.

Entering Cash Purchases in the Purchases Journal

Open the **Purchases Journal**.

> **NOTES**
> Remember that we use the term "Cash Purchase" for purchases with payment by cheque.

✓ 6

Cash Purchase Invoice #BM-3492 **Dated May 3/21**

From BuyMore, $1 200 plus $180 HST for updating online sales catalogue. Terms: cash on receipt. Invoice total $1 380 paid in full by cheque #173.

Choose BuyMore from the Supplier drop-down list. **Press** tab.

We can now enter the transaction details, as we did for previous purchases. Cheque as the payment method is correct, because we added it in the ledger record.

To change methods, you can select from the Payment Method drop-down list:

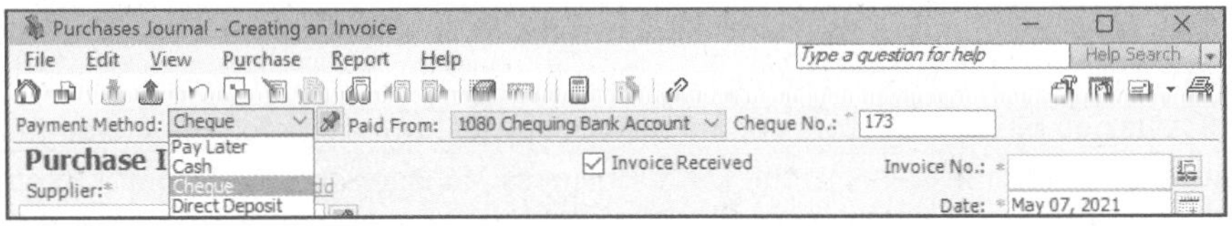

The payment options are the same as those in the Payments Journal for Other Payments, with the addition of Pay Later.

> **NOTES**
> The Net Days field is removed for the immediate payment, but discounts for early payment may still apply.

A Cheque No. field with the next cheque number has been added in the upper right-hand corner of the invoice form. The cheque number is updated automatically. The account number and payment terms are added from the supplier record information we entered. You need to add the invoice number, transaction date and amount.

Click the **Invoice No. field** and **type** `BM-3492`

Click the **Calendar icon** and **choose May 3**.

> **NOTES**
> Sometimes a business uses more than one bank account. If multiple accounts are set up, all bank accounts will be listed in the Paid From drop-down list. You can choose the appropriate bank account from the list for purchases by cheque and for payments. Credit cards, direct deposits and multiple bank accounts are used in later applications.

Click the **Amount field**.

Type `1200` **Press** tab. Add a description to complete the invoice:

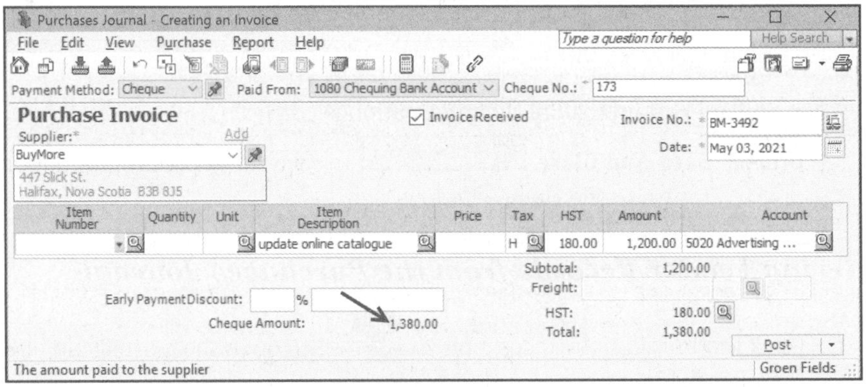

> **NOTES**
> You can preview this cash purchase, just as you can preview invoice payment cheques. Two copies of the invoice details are added to the upper cheque portion.

Choose the **Report menu** and **click Display Purchases Journal Entry** so you can review the journal entry before posting:

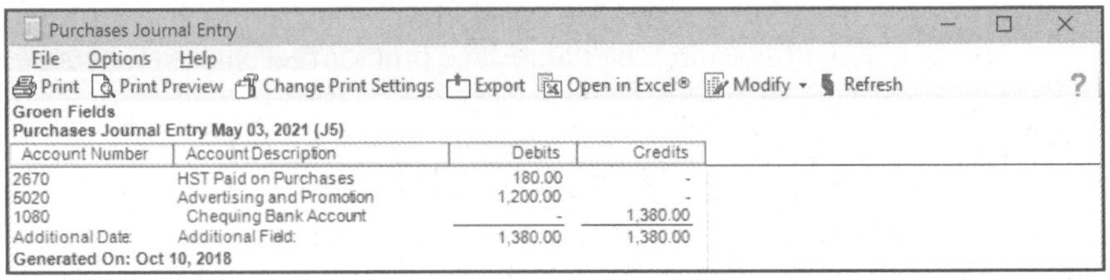

Account Number	Account Description	Debits	Credits
2670	HST Paid on Purchases	180.00	-
5020	Advertising and Promotion	1,200.00	-
1080	Chequing Bank Account	-	1,380.00
Additional Date:	Additional Field:	1,380.00	1,380.00

Generated On: Oct 10, 2018

This journal entry is like the one from the Payments Journal when we chose Make Other Payment, except for the addition of an HST amount. *Chequing Bank Account* is credited instead of *Accounts Payable*. The supplier record is updated for the transaction by including both an invoice and a payment for the same date. Because the journal entries are the same, the method you choose for entering cash purchases —

either in the Purchases Journal or as Other Payments in the Payments Journal — is a personal preference.

Close the **display**.

Check the **invoice** for errors and **make corrections**, just as you would for regular purchases. When the information is correct,

Click **Post** [Post] to save the transaction. **Click OK**.

Adjusting a Posted Invoice

In the same way that you can correct or adjust a previously posted entry in the General Journal, you can edit a Purchases Journal invoice after posting. Sage 50 will create the necessary reversing entry when you post the revised invoice.

✓ 7 **Memo #13** **Dated May 4/21**

From Owner: Adjust invoice #DS-642. The invoice from Data Savers included a one-time charge of $350 plus $52.50 HST to restore the system and recover data after data was compromised. The corrected invoice total is $1 920.50.

The Purchases Journal should still be open.

Click the **Adjust Invoice tool** or **choose** the **Purchase menu** and **click Adjust Invoice** to open the Search Purchase Invoices screen:

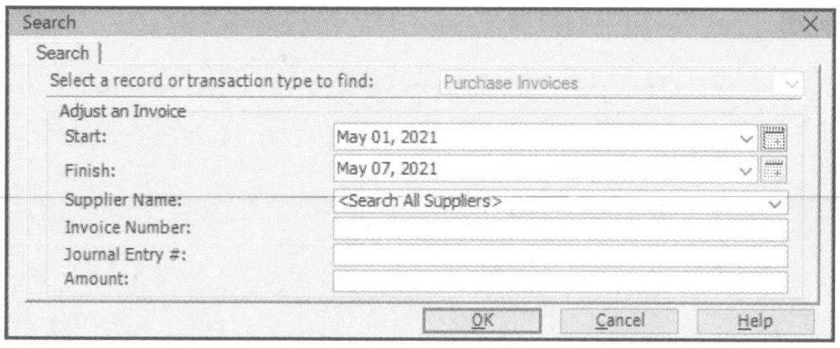

This is similar to the Search screen for the General Journal, with the additional option of searching by supplier name. The program enters default start and finish dates. You can edit these dates like any other date fields, or you can choose dates from the calendars. The default dates include all transactions for the journal, so we can accept them.

We will search all invoices by accepting the default to Search All Suppliers.

If you know the exact invoice number, journal entry number or amount, you can enter this in the corresponding field and click OK to select the invoice directly. These options all require entering the exact information; for example, typing 1518 in the Amount field.

Click **OK** to open the requested list of Purchases Journal invoices:

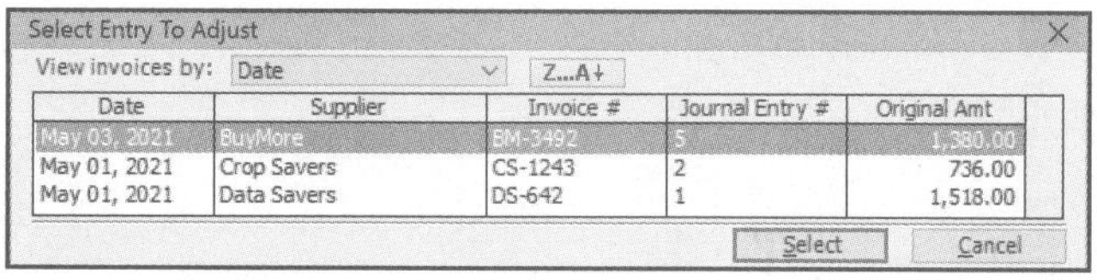

Invoices are ordered by date with the most recent one listed first and selected. The invoice we need is Journal Entry #1, DS-642. You can choose an order from the **View Invoices By** drop-down list: date, supplier, invoice number, journal entry number and amount are the options. Clicking the [Z...A] button will reverse the order of any list.

Click **DS-642**. (Click anywhere on the line to highlight the invoice.)

NOTES

The Post button now includes a list arrow with a drop-down list:

You can select Print & Post instead of Post as your default. With this selection, you will print the cheque automatically when you enter the invoice.

This option is available only for cash purchases because the printed invoices include cheques.

NOTES

You can also press ctrl + A to open the Adjust Invoice window from any journal. Refer to Appendix B for a list of keyboard shortcuts.

NOTES

From the Home window, you can choose Adjust Invoice from the Purchase Invoices drop-down shortcuts list to open the Search window.

NOTES

Searching by Invoice Number is the equivalent of searching by Source in the General Journal and requires entering an exact match.

NOTES

The cash purchases entered in the Payments Journal are not included in this list. You can adjust these transactions from the Payments Journal after choosing Make Other Payment, or from the Payments icon Adjust Payment shortcut (refer to page 131).

Click **Select** or **double-click** the **entry** to recall the selected transaction:

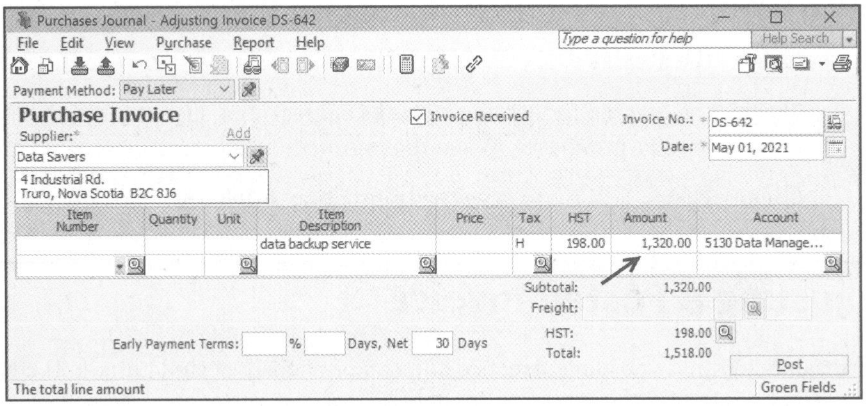

> **NOTES**
> The Post button for Pay Later invoices does not have a list arrow with the option to print.
> You can still print the invoice from the File menu Print option or from the Print tool.

> **NOTES**
> Adjusting Invoice DS-642 has replaced Creating An Invoice in the journal's title bar.

All fields are available for editing. We need to add the second service purchased.

Click **line 2** in the Amount field below 1320.

Type 350

Press *tab* to update the tax code and amount, totals and account.

Add an appropriate **description**.

You can add -R to the invoice number to complete the revised invoice:

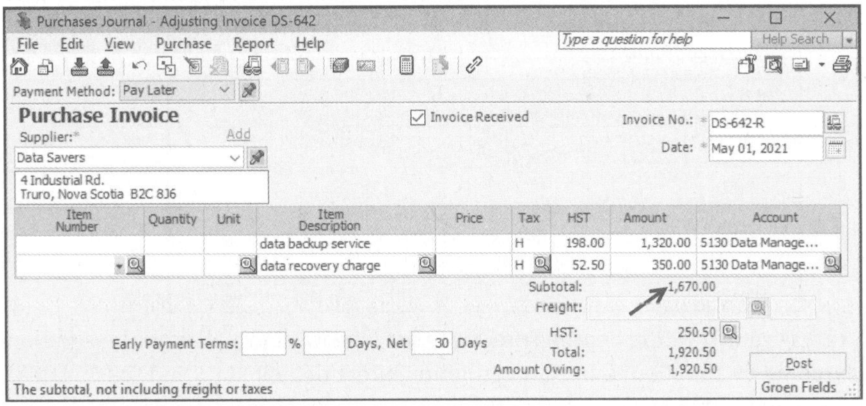

If you change the supplier, Sage 50 warns you and requires confirmation:

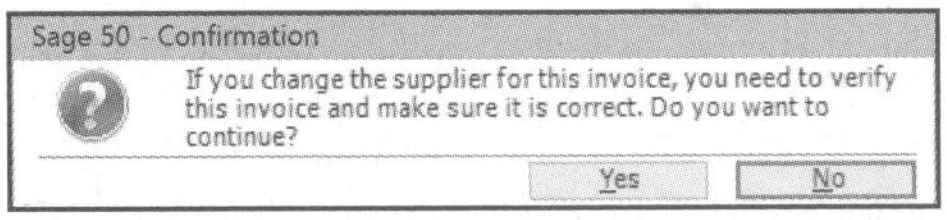

> **NOTES**
> If you change the supplier, the default settings for the previously selected supplier will still be used. Check your entry carefully before posting.
> If you need to change the supplier, you should reverse the original invoice and then enter it correctly. Refer to page 141.

Before posting the revised transaction, review it for accuracy.

Choose the **Report menu** and **click Display Purchases Journal Entry**:

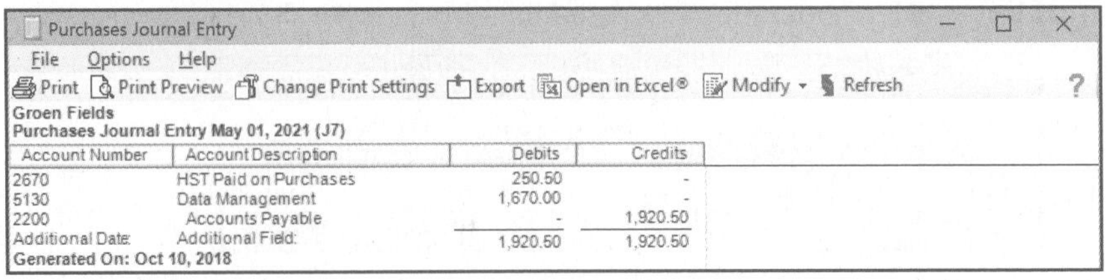

Although only one journal entry is displayed , three entries are posted — J1, the first one that was incorrect, J6, the second created by Sage 50 to reverse the incorrect entry, and J7, the final correct one that is displayed. All use the original posting date. The previous transaction we posted was entry J5 (refer to the screenshot on page 128).

> **NOTES**
> Dates should be changed only if they were incorrect. If you edit the date, the final correct entry will be posted with the revised date and will affect the payment terms. To include all three entries in the journal report, Corrections must be selected (refer to pages 149–150).

Close the **report display** when you have finished and **make** additional **corrections** if necessary.

Click the **Post button** Post, **click OK** and **close** the **Purchases Journal**.

CORRECTING CASH PURCHASES AND PAYMENTS FROM THE PAYMENTS JOURNAL

Purchases entered as Other Payments in the Payments Journal do not appear on the Search Purchase Invoices list from the Purchases Journal. You can, however, adjust these other payments from the Payments Journal as follows:

- **Click** the Home window **Payments icon** Payments **shortcuts list arrow**, and **click Adjust Payment**.
- **Select** your search parameters: the **date range**, **supplier**, **cheque number** and so on. **Click OK**.
- **Click** the **cheque/invoice** you want to adjust. All cheques used to pay invoices and for other payments will appear on this list.
- **Double-click** the **entry** or **click Select** to open the cheque.
- **Make** the **corrections**. **Review** your **entry** and **post** the revised transaction.
- If the **Payments Journal** is already open, **click Make Other Payment** from the transaction list if you want to adjust a cash purchase payment.
- **Click Pay Invoices** from the transaction list if you want to adjust a cheque used to pay invoices.
- **Click** the **Adjust Payment** or **Adjust Other Payment tool** or **choose** the **Payment menu** and **click Adjust Payment** or **Adjust Other Payment**.
- **Select** your search parameters. **Click OK** to open the list of cheques. Your list will include either invoice payment or other payment cheques, depending on the type of transaction you started from.
- **Make** the **corrections**. **Review** your **entry** and **post** the revised transaction.

Refer to page 139 for detailed instructions on correcting a payment cheque.

Entering Discounts for Early Payments

Entering discounts for early payments is very much like entering regular payments. The discounts are calculated and entered automatically when the invoices and dates are correct and the discount period has not expired.

> **NOTES**
> The confirmation message informs us that two journal entries were posted.

✓ 8 **Payment Cheque #174** **Dated May 4/21**

To Crop Savers, $792 in payment of account, including $8 discount for early payment. Reference invoice #CS-1044.

Click the **Payments icon** Payments to open the Payments Journal.

Choose **Crop Savers** from the list to display the outstanding invoices:

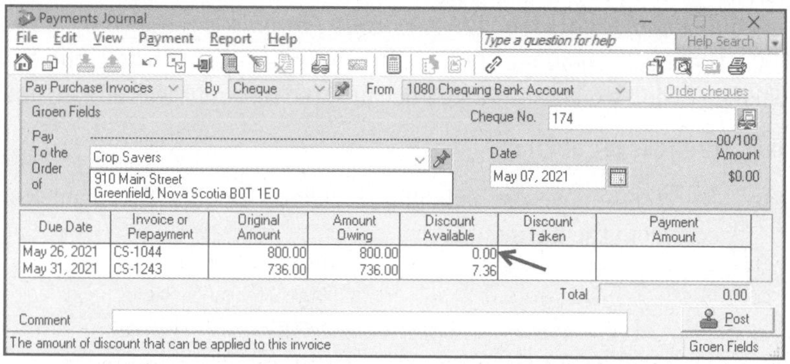

> **NOTES**
> The Payments Journal has the due date for the invoice, the net 30 date that is 30 days after the invoice date of April 26 for invoice #CS-1044.

Initially, no discount is available for invoice #CS-1044 because the session date is beyond the discount period — it is more than 10 days past the April 26 invoice date. The discount for the second invoice is available because the session date lies within the 10-day discount period.

Enter **May 4** as the date of the payment. **Press** (tab).

Discounts are now available for both invoices because the payment date falls within the 10-day discount period for them:

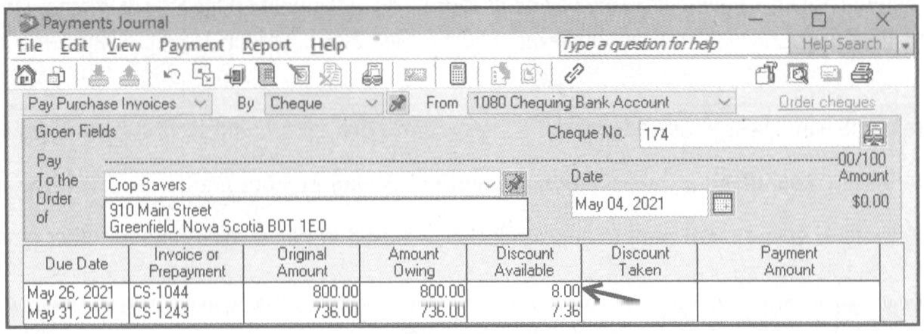

Press (tab) **twice** to advance to the Discount Taken field and enter the amount.

Press (tab) to advance to the Payment Amount field and accept the discount.

The discount has been subtracted from the invoice amount.

Press (tab) to accept the amount in the Payment Amount field and update the total and the cheque portion of the journal:

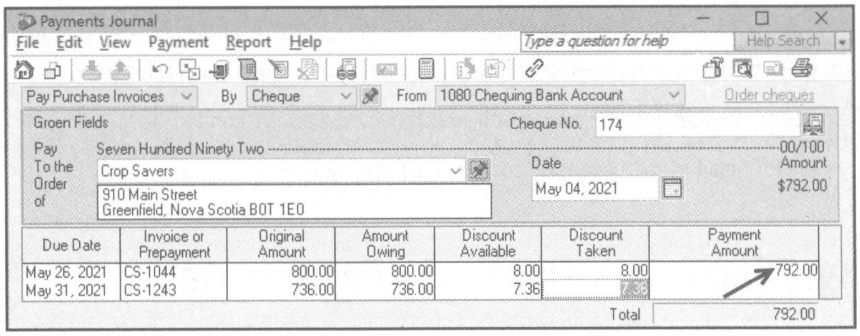

Press (ctrl) + **J** to display the payment as you have it entered so far:

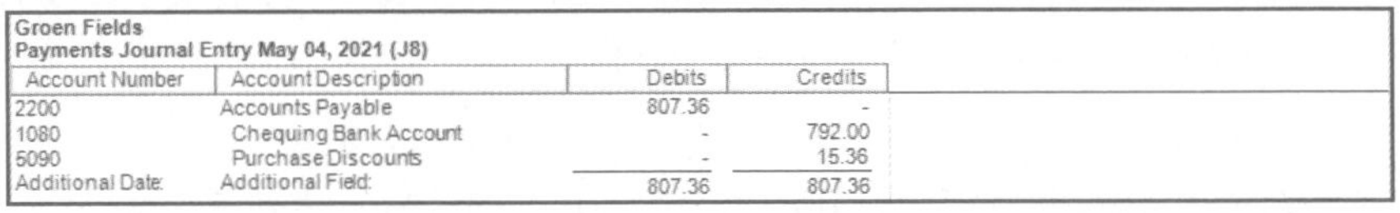

Groen Fields
Payments Journal Entry May 04, 2021 (J8)

Account Number	Account Description	Debits	Credits
2200	Accounts Payable	807.36	-
1080	Chequing Bank Account	-	792.00
5090	Purchase Discounts	-	15.36
Additional Date:	Additional Field:	807.36	807.36

WARNING!
If a second discount amount is displayed, you must delete it. It will be included in the journal entry even though the total payment and cheque amount appear correct. If you post at this stage, the discount will be accepted and included.

At this stage, a discount amount is entered for the second invoice, but this invoice is not being paid. Therefore, you must delete this discount entry to avoid adding it to the invoice.

If you do not delete this second discount, your entry will be posted with both discount amounts included — the total *Purchase Discounts* amount is $15.36 instead of $8.00. The cheque amount is correct, but *Accounts Payable* is reduced by $807.36 instead of $800, the invoice amount. If the next invoice is not paid within the discount period, its balance owing would be $728.64 because the discount was already taken.

Close the **journal display**.

WARNING!
Do not press (tab) after deleting the discount because this will add an amount paid for the second invoice. To be safe, you should click somewhere in the upper cheque portion of the form.

Press (del) to remove the highlighted second Discount Taken amount and complete the payment form:

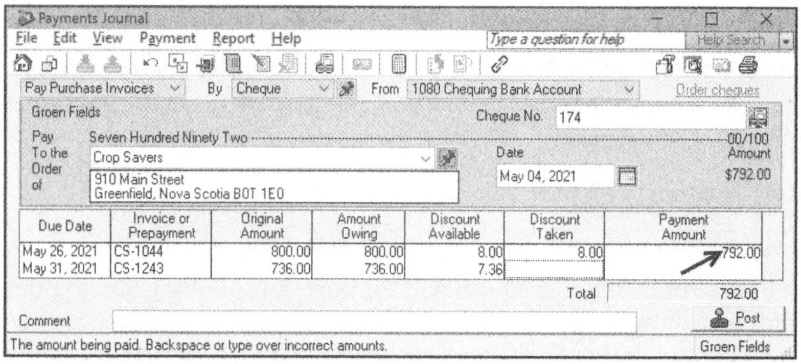

Choose the **Report menu** and **click Display Payments Journal Entry** to review the transaction before posting:

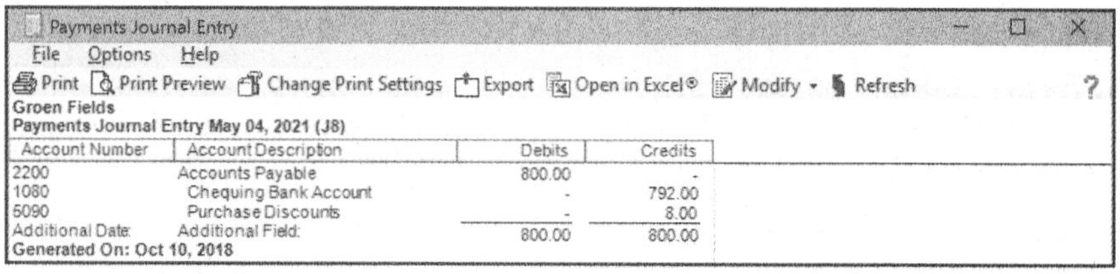
Payments Journal Entry
File Options Help
Print Print Preview Change Print Settings Export Open in Excel® Modify Refresh
Groen Fields
Payments Journal Entry May 04, 2021 (J8)

Account Number	Account Description	Debits	Credits
2200	Accounts Payable	800.00	-
1080	Chequing Bank Account	-	792.00
5090	Purchase Discounts	-	8.00
Additional Date:	Additional Field:	800.00	800.00

Generated On: Oct 10, 2018

In the related journal entry, the program has now updated the General Ledger *Accounts Payable* control account for the full, corrected amount of the invoice and reduced the balance owing to the supplier by the same amount. The amount taken from *Chequing Bank Account* is the actual amount of the payment, taking the single discount amount into consideration. The discount amount is automatically debited to the linked *Purchase Discounts* account. *Purchase Discounts* is a **contra-expense** account. It has a credit balance, so it reduces total expense and increases net income.

Close the **display** to return to the Payments Journal input screen and **correct** your **work** if necessary. (Refer to page 121 for assistance.)

Post the **transaction**. **Click OK**. **Close** the **Payments Journal**.

Using Continue to Enter New Suppliers

Sometimes you may want to include the name of a supplier in the journal record without creating a supplier record. In these situations, you can use the Continue feature. For the cheque to Anything on Paper, a cash purchase, we will use this approach.

✓ 9

Cash Purchase Invoice #AP-5899 **Dated May 7/21**

From Anything on Paper (choose Continue), $320 plus $48 HST to create and print packages for selling seeds (use Seed Supplies account). Invoice total $368 paid in full by cheque #175.

Click the **Purchase Invoices icon** 

to open the Purchases Journal.

Click the **Supplier field** and **type** `Anything on Paper`

Press *tab* to open the message about a new supplier name:

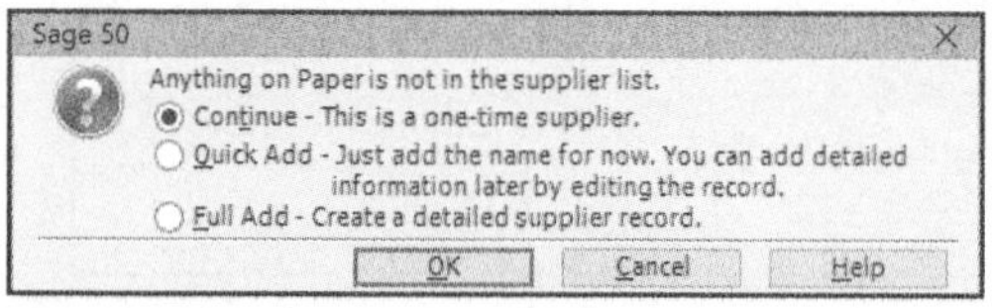

Click **OK** to return to the journal. (Continue was already selected.)

NOTES
If a second discount is not displayed, you can skip the step of deleting the discount amount, as on page 119.
When you point to the Amount field, the status bar message advises you how to enter or change the amounts.

NOTES
When you choose One-Time Supplier, you can type the supplier's name in the Address field. The supplier's name will not be included in journal reports.

NOTES
When you choose Continue for a new supplier in the Make Other Payment Journal, the name is not added to the journal entry.

NOTES
Pay Later is not an option when you choose Continue or One-Time Supplier. Only immediate payment is allowed – Cash and Cheque. Cash is the default.

NOTES
The total food bill from Better Foods was $190. Only 50 percent of entertainment expenses are eligible for tax deductions, so $95 was entered as the expense amount.

Press tab. Cash is the default payment method when you choose Continue.

Choose **Cheque** as the Payment Method and then **enter** the **remaining details** of the cash purchase as usual, including the tax code. **Review** and **post** the **transaction**.

Enter the next **two purchase transactions**.

10 **Cash Purchase Invoice #BF-100** **Dated May 7/21**

From Better Foods (choose Quick Add for the new supplier), $95 to purchase food for weekly appreciation barbecue for employees. Issue cheque #176. Charge to Entertainment Expense account and choose Cheque as the payment method. No tax is charged on basic groceries. Store this transaction as a weekly recurring entry.

11 **Purchase Invoice #SC-701** **Dated May 7/21**

From Spotless Company, $180 plus $27 HST for weekly cleaning of office. Purchase invoice total $207. Terms: 1/30, n/60. Store as a weekly recurring transaction.

Close the **Purchases Journal**.

CLASSIC VIEW
Users who are more familiar with Sage 50 may prefer to work from the Classic view. You can access all journals and ledgers from a single Classic view Home window, but you cannot add shortcuts.

Entering Sales Taxes in the General Journal

The sales summary on May 7 is entered in the General Journal because Groen Fields does not use the Receivables Ledger. When you set up and link sales tax accounts, you can add General Journal sales tax entries to the tax reports. A Sales Taxes button becomes available when you use one of these linked tax accounts in the General Journal. Groen Fields has two linked tax accounts, *HST Charged on Sales* and *HST Paid on Purchases*.

The General Journal is accessed from the Company module window that we used in the previous two chapters.

To open the Company module window, click Company in the Modules pane on the left-hand side of the Home window. Click the General Journal icon.

Instead, we will create a shortcut to open the General Journal.

Creating Shortcuts

Click the **Shortcuts icon** beside **Shortcuts** in the Shortcuts pane below the modules:

The Customize Shortcuts window opens:

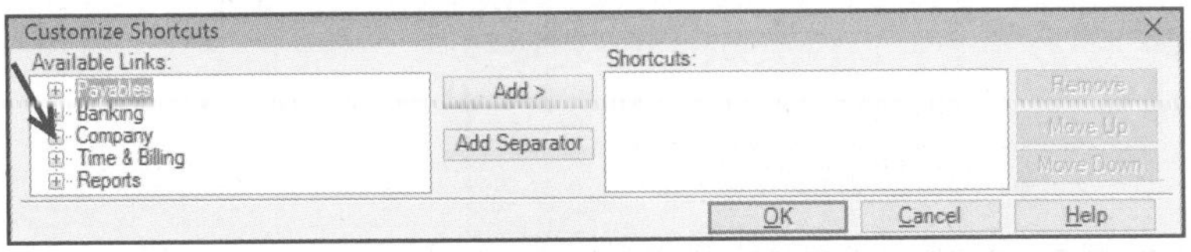

PRO VERSION
The entry for Time & Billing is not in the list of links.

Click the ⊞ beside **Company** to expand the list of Company tasks:

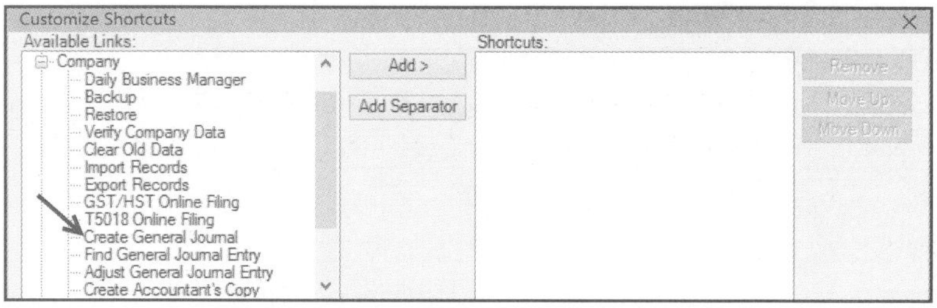

You can create up to 10 shortcuts for each user. The expanded list for each module has the items for which you can create shortcuts. Once you create a shortcut, you can click its name in the Shortcuts pane to access that journal or task directly.

Click **Create General Journal** in the list of Company tasks.

Click **Add >** to move this task to the Shortcuts box:

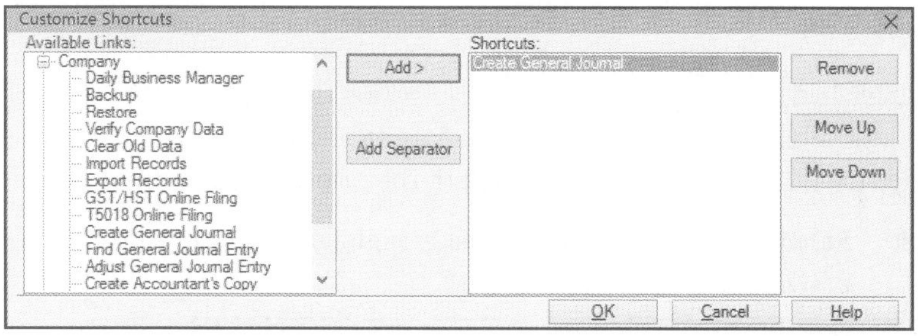

Click **OK** to return to the Home window. Create General Journal now appears in the Home window Shortcuts pane:

✓ 12

Cash Sales Summary #34 **Dated May 7/21**

From garden centres, $13 800 plus $2 070 HST for hardy spring annual bedding plants and hanger and planter arrangements. Total receipts $15 870 deposited in bank. Use the shortcut for the General Journal.

Click **Create General Journal** in the Shortcuts pane. The General Journal opens immediately. This shortcut will be available in the Home window for all modules.

Enter the **Source** and **Comment** for the sale. The session date is correct.

Choose **Chequing Bank Account** as the account to be debited and **type** 15870 as the amount. **Enter** an appropriate **Comment** for the account.

Choose **HST Charged on Sales** as the account. Advance to the credit column.

Type 2070 as the amount to be credited. **Press** tab to update the entry and continue:

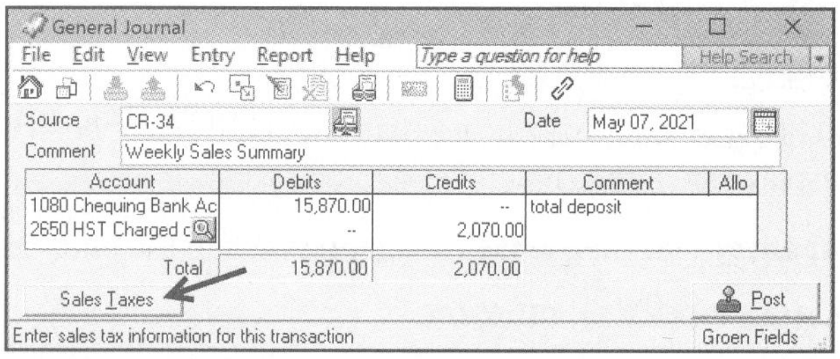

The **Sales Taxes** button became available as soon as you entered the tax amount.

NOTES
You can remove a shortcut if it is not needed. Just click the Shortcuts icon in the Home window. Click the shortcut in the Shortcuts pane. Then click Remove and OK.

NOTES
Use the General Journal for sales in this application. We will introduce the Sales Journal in Chapter 6.

NOTES
Follow the keystroke instructions for the General Journal from the Binh's Bins application starting on page 40.

NOTES

HST Charged on Sales is the linked tax account for sales. When you enter HST Paid on Purchases as the account, Purchase will be selected as the default transaction type because this account is linked to the Payables module.

Click the **Sales Taxes button** to open the tax detail screen:

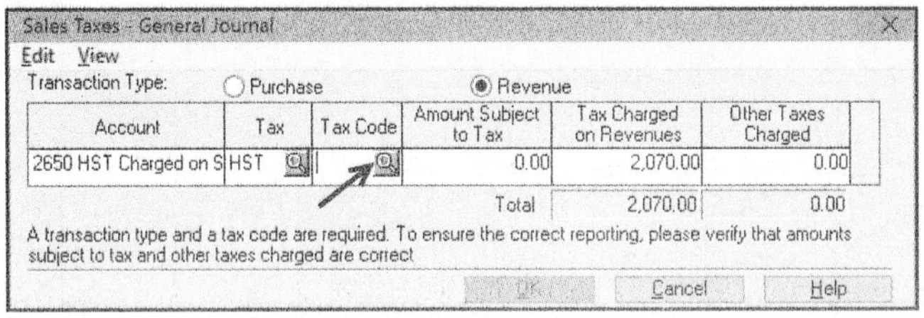

Because you entered *HST Charged on Sales* as the account, the transaction is recognized as a sale (Revenue). You can change the transaction type if it is not correct. The account and tax amount are already entered. We need to add the tax code.

Click the **List icon** in the Tax Code field to open the Tax Code list:

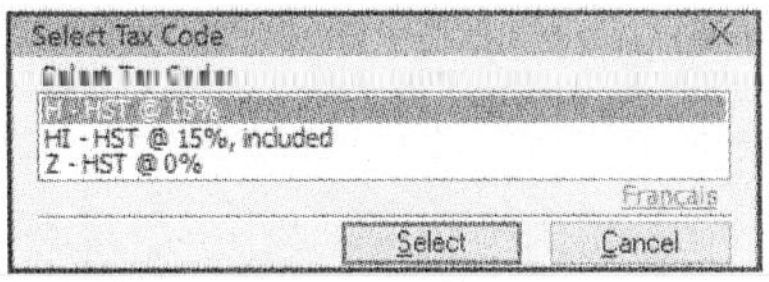

The same three tax codes that were in the Purchases and Payments journals are available. Sales have HST at 15 percent added to the price, so the correct code is H.

Click **Select** because code H is already highlighted. You will return to the tax detail screen:

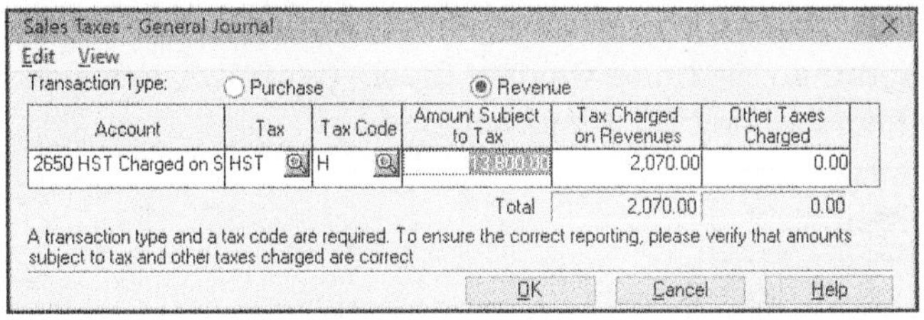

Because the tax amount was already entered, the sales amount — the Amount Subject To Tax — is calculated as soon as you select the tax code. The sales amount is correct, so we can continue. If the amount is not correct because there are other taxes included, you can edit the default amount and enter an amount for Other Taxes Charged.

Click **OK** to return to the journal.

Enter a **Comment** for the tax line and then add the final account line — **choose** account **4100**, accept the amount and **add** an appropriate **comment** to complete your journal entry:

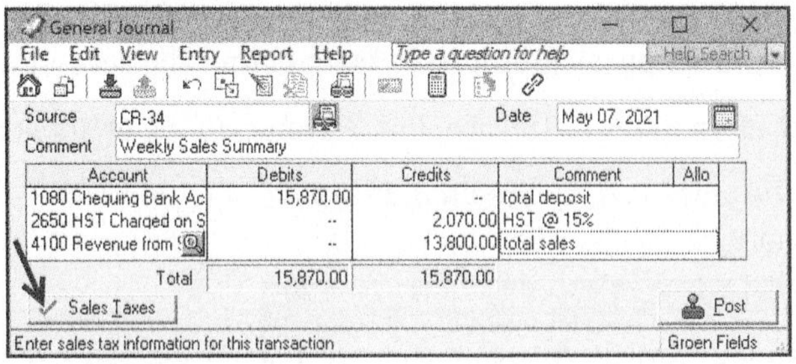

The Sales Taxes button has a ✓ on it to indicate that tax details have been added. Click the button again to display the details if you need to edit them.

Review the **journal entry** and then **close** the **display**. When the entry is correct,

Click the **Post button** Post. **Click OK**.

If you forgot to enter the tax codes for *HST Charged on Sales*, Sage 50 warns you and asks for confirmation that you do not want to add tax details:

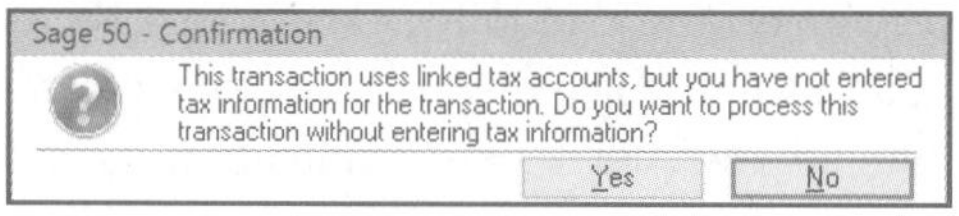

If you forgot to add the tax details, click No to cancel posting and open the Sales Taxes window. Add the missing details and then post the journal entry.

Close the **General Journal** to return to the Home window.

Advance the **session date** to **May 14**. **Back up** your **data file** when prompted.

Recalling a Stored Entry

The first journal entry for the May 14 session date is the recurring purchase from Crop Savers. Since we have stored this purchase, we do not need to re-enter all the information.

✓ 13

Purchase Invoice #CS-2100 **Dated May 8/21**

From Crop Savers, $640 for soil testing and follow-up fertilizer treatment plus $96 HST. Invoice total $736. Terms: 1/10, n/30. Recall stored entry.

Click the **Purchase Invoices icon** [Purchase Invoices] to open the Purchases Journal.

Click the **Recall tool** in the tool bar (or **choose** the **Purchase menu** and **click Recall**) to display the Recall Recurring Transaction dialogue box:

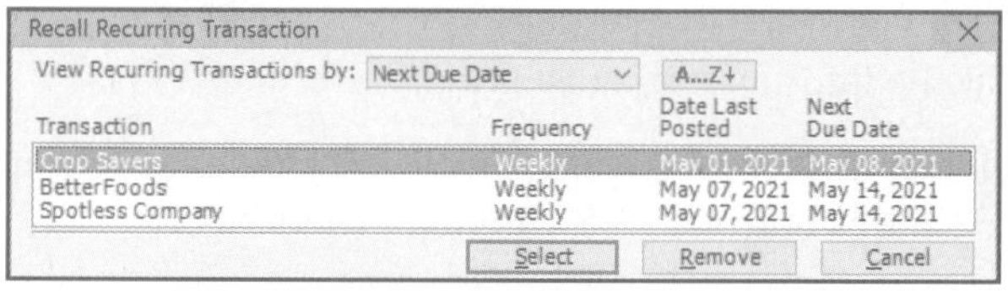

The stored entries are listed in order according to the next date that they will be repeated. If you want, you can display the stored entries in a different order.

Click the **View Recurring Transactions By list arrow** for your options:

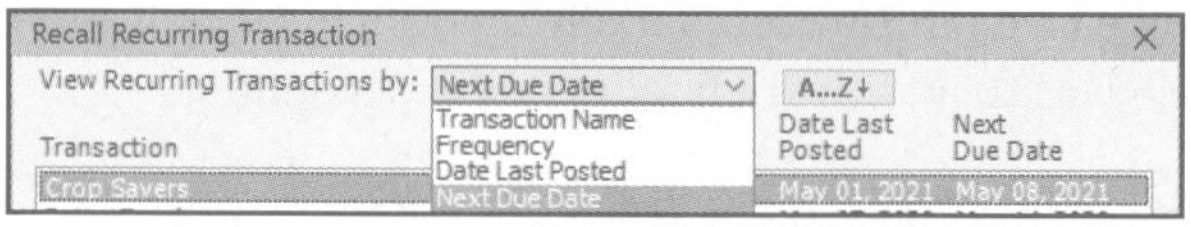

You can choose to view the stored entries in order by Transaction Name (which is the supplier's name if you did not change the default), Frequency (how often the transaction is repeated), the Date Last Posted or the Next Due Date. If you have a large number of stored entries it may be easier to find the one you need with a different order. You can also reverse the order for any of the order selections with the [A...Z] button. For our stored entries, the default selection, Next Due Date, placed the one we want first. Do not change the default.

From the Recall Stored Entry dialogue box you can remove an entry that is incorrect or no longer needed. Click an entry to select it. Click Remove and then click Yes to confirm that you want to delete the entry. (Refer to page 443.)

Crop Savers, the name of the entry we want to use, should be selected because it is the recurring entry that is due next.

Click **Crop Savers** if it is not already selected.

Click **Select** or **press** enter to return to the Purchases Journal.

NOTES

You can press ctrl + R to recall a stored entry.

The stored entry is displayed just as we entered it initially, except that the date has been advanced by one week, as needed, and the Invoice field is blank so we can enter a new invoice number. Remember that Sage 50 does not accept duplicate invoice numbers.

Click the **Invoice No. field** to move the cursor.

Type `CS-2100` to complete the entry. You should review it before posting.

Choose the **Report menu** and **click Display Purchases Journal Entry**.

Close the **display** when finished and **make** any necessary **corrections**.

Click the **Post button** Post. **Click OK** and then **close** the **journal**.

NOTES
Posting the recalled entry automatically updates the next due date based on the recurring frequency.

Editing Supplier Information

The Home window Suppliers pane has the option to hide or display account phone numbers and balances. There may be times when it is appropriate to hide these details for security purposes.

PRO VERSION
Remember that the term Vendors will replace the term Suppliers.

Click the **details** icon above the Suppliers list for the options:

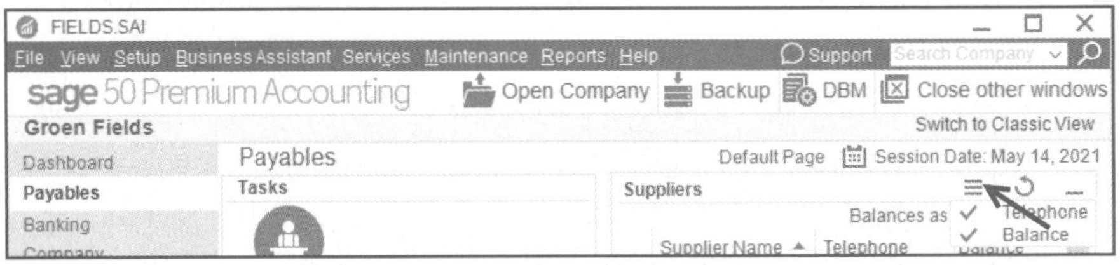

Checkmarks indicate that the information is displayed.

Click the details icon to **expand** the list and click the detail you want to hide. To restore a detail, click this button and the option to add the ✓.

Click **refresh** to update the supplier balance amounts.

Click **hide** to remove the entire **list**. Click **restore** to bring back the list.

NOTES
You can use the Refresh icon to update supplier balances when you choose not to refresh lists automatically (refer to pages 81–82).

Sometimes a supplier record must be revised after it is saved because the initial information has changed or because information initially unavailable is now known. We need to edit the record for NS Gas to add the default expense account.

✓ 14

Memo #14 **Dated May 8/21**

From Owner: Edit the supplier record for NS Gas to include a default expense account. Create a new Group account 5170 Heating Expense.

NOTES
You can open the Suppliers window by clicking the Suppliers icon in the Home window in either the Classic or the Enhanced view. From the Suppliers window, double-click the supplier you want to open the record at the Address tab screen.

Supplier records are accessed from the Suppliers icon shortcuts list, the Suppliers list pane or the Suppliers window. The list arrow beside the supplier in the Suppliers list pane has shortcuts for several tasks for the selected vendor. The journal or ledger will open with that supplier and task already selected. The drop-down shortcuts list with the Suppliers icon also has several options. Both lists provide access to supplier records:

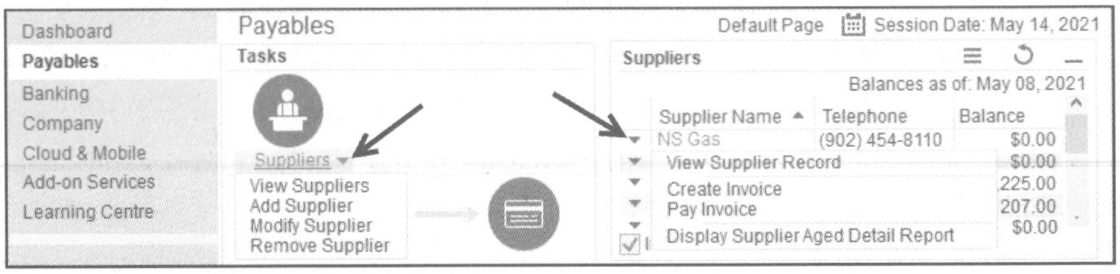

Click **NS Gas** in the Suppliers list (or click its list arrow and select View Supplier Record) to open the Address tab information screen. Or,

Click the **Suppliers icon shortcuts list arrow** and **click Modify Supplier** to open the Search Suppliers window:

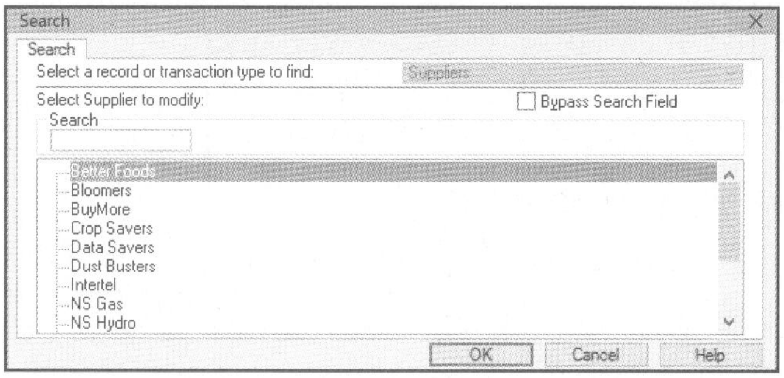

Each supplier on record is listed on the Search Suppliers selection window. Suppliers is entered as the search area.

Double-click **NS Gas** to open the Address tab information screen.

Click the **Options tab** to access the Expense Account field:

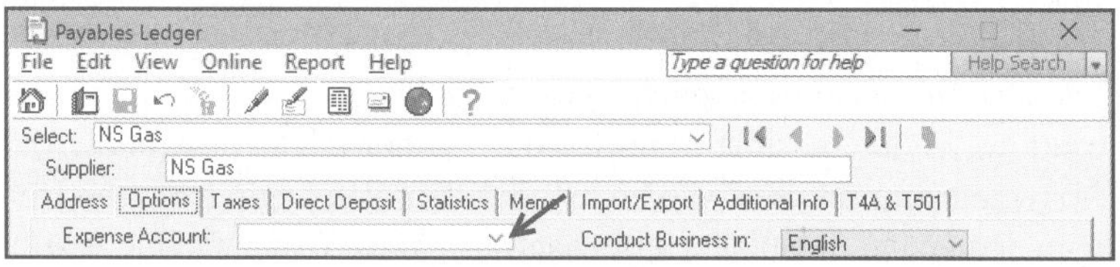

Click the **Expense Account field**.

You can choose an account from the list provided by the list arrow, type the account number or add a new account. We need to create an account.

Type 5170 **Press** *tab* and then **click Add** to start the Add An Account wizard. **Enter Heating Expense** as the account name and accept the remaining default settings. **Click Finish** to return to the ledger.

Click **Save And Close** [Save and Close] to close the Payables Ledger (supplier record) window and return to the Payables module window.

Click **Pay Expenses** from the Payments icon shortcuts list to open the Payments Journal, or **click** the **Purchase Invoices icon**.

Enter the **cash purchase from NS Gas**; the account will appear automatically.

15 **Cash Purchase Invoice #NSG-559932** **Dated May 8/21**

From NS Gas, $200 plus $30 HST for monthly supply of natural gas on equal billing method. Invoice total $230 paid in full by cheque #177. Because equal billing applies, store as a monthly recurring entry.

Adjusting a Posted Payment

Just as you can correct a purchase invoice after posting, you can correct a cheque that has been posted.

Choose **Pay Purchase Invoices** from the Payments transaction list in the Payments Journal. Open the Payments Journal first if necessary.

✓ 16 **Memo #15** **Dated May 9/21**

From Owner: Adjust cheque #171 to Data Savers. The numbers were transposed. The correct cheque amount was $870 in partial payment of invoice #DS-361.

PRO VERSION

Click the Vendors icon shortcuts list arrow and click Modify Vendor.

NOTES

Anything on Paper is not included in the list of suppliers. Because we chose Continue when we added the invoice for it on page 133, no record was created.

NOTES

Remember that although the field is named Expense Account, you can choose any postable account as the default for the supplier. You can also select a different account in the journal if necessary.

Click the **Adjust Payment tool** or **choose** the **Payment menu** and **click Adjust Payment** to open the Search screen for Adjust Payments:

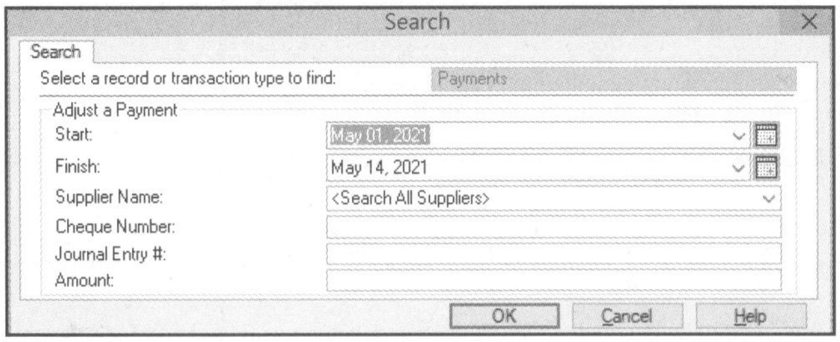

Again, the familiar Search window for the selected journal opens.

Click **OK** to list the cheques already posted for this date range:

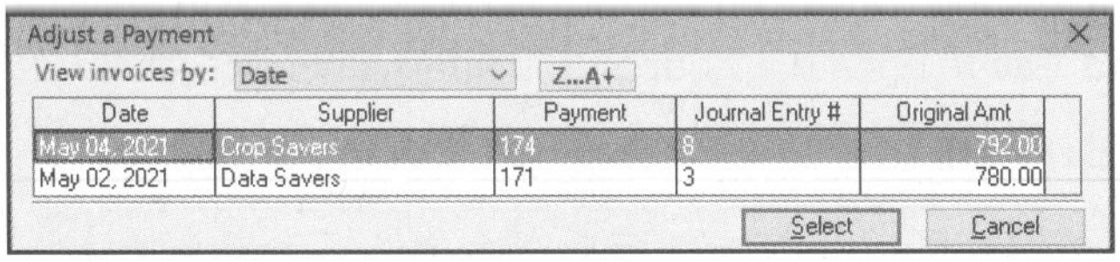

Only the two cheques used to pay invoices are listed because we started from the Pay Invoices window. When you start from the Make Other Payment window, only the cash purchase payment transactions will be listed. When you begin from the Home window Payments icon drop-down shortcuts list, both Make Other Payment and Pay Invoices transactions will be listed.

Double-click **Data Savers** to open the cheque we posted:

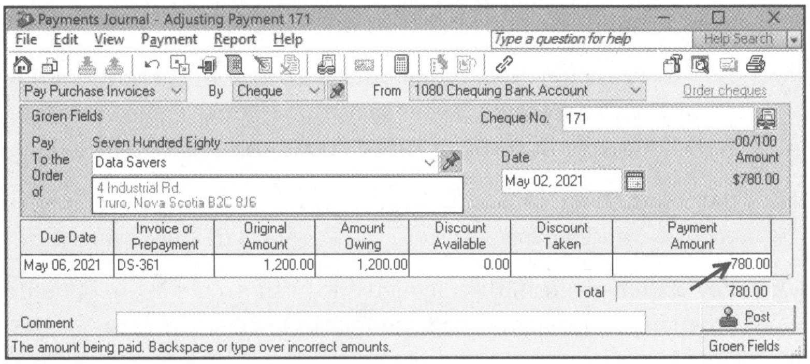

The cheque appears as it was completed. You can edit all the details (except the supplier).

Click **780.00** in the Payment Amount field.

Type `870`

Click the **Comment field**.

Type `previous chq amount incorrectly entered`

Check your **work** carefully. **Click Post** to save the changes:

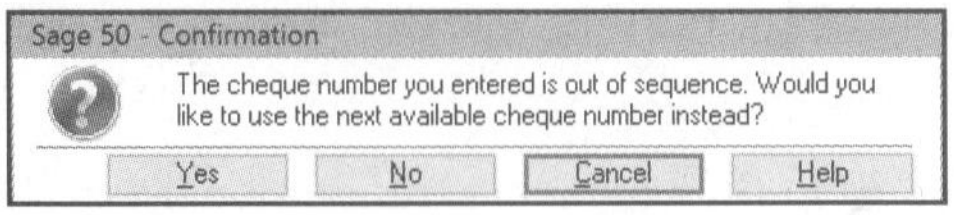

A message about the cheque number being out of sequence appears because we have already used this cheque number. The cheque number is correct, so we should continue without changing it.

Click **No** to accept the number and continue.

NOTES

Pressing ctrl + A will also open the Search window to begin the adjusting procedure.

NOTES

When you choose Adjust Payment from the Home window Payments icon shortcuts list, you will list all cheques – those used to pay invoices and those for other payments.

NOTES

Cash purchases entered in the Payments Journal are not included in this list. You can adjust these transactions from the Payments Journal after you select Make Other Payment (refer to page 131).

NOTES

If you cannot reprint the cheque using the same cheque number, you should click Yes to change the number.

Sage 50 will create the intermediate entry that reverses the original payment, and the original entry is also saved for a complete audit trail.

If you change a payment by selecting a different supplier, Sage 50 advises you that the original payment will be reversed and a new one created:

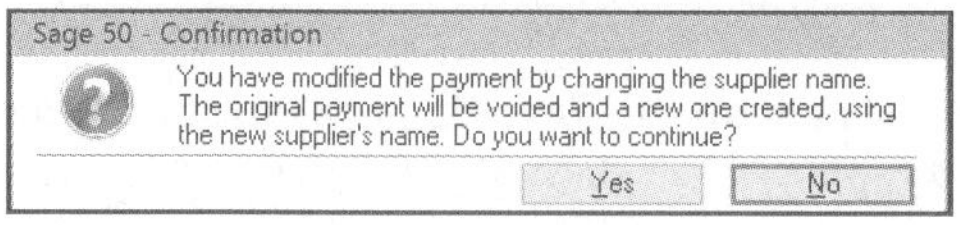

Click Yes to accept the changes or No to cancel the supplier change.

Enter the next group of three **transactions**.

17 **Cash Purchase Invoice #NSH-45321** **Dated May 9/21**

From NS Hydro, $240 plus $36 HST for one month of hydro service. Invoice total $276 paid in full by cheque #178.

18 **Payment Cheque #179** **Dated May 9/21**

To Crop Savers, $728.64 in payment of account, including $7.36 discount for early payment. Reference invoice #CS-1243.

19 **Cash Purchase Invoice #BC-6110** **Dated May 12/21**

From Bloomers, $1 280 plus $192 HST for batch of tree saplings to grow for future sales. Invoice total $1 472 paid in full by cheque #180.

NOTES

If you change the supplier for a cheque, Sage 50 will void (reverse) the cheque paid to the supplier named in the original transaction and create a new one for the revised supplier. You will be warned of this action so you can confirm the change or cancel it before it is made.

WARNING!

Remember to delete the discount taken amount for the second invoice for cheque #179.

Reversing a Posted Purchase Entry

The cash purchase entered for Bloomers selected an incorrect supplier. We will reverse this entry rather than adjust it because the default details such as account or payment terms may also be incorrect. These details do not change when you adjust the invoice by selecting a different supplier. Refer to the confirmation message on page 130.

Any journal that has an Adjust option also has the option to reverse an entry. You can also use the Lookup feature to begin.

The journal you used to enter the purchase should still be open, either the Payments Journal with Make Other Payment selected or the Purchases Journal. In each case, you can follow the steps below.

✓ 20 **Memo #16** **Dated May 12/21**

Cash Purchase Invoice #BC-6110 was entered for an incorrect supplier and account. The purchase was from Better Crop Tree Farms, a new supplier. Reverse the original entry.

Click the **Look Up Other Payment tool** in the Payments Journal with Make Other Payment selected, or the **Look Up An Invoice tool** in the Purchases Journal. Or,

Click the **Adjust Other Payment (Adjust An Invoice) tool** to open the Search screen.

Click **OK** to list the cheques (or purchases) already posted.

Double-click **Bloomers** to open this cash purchase. In the Purchases Journal, the entry has a Paid stamp on it. This is a User Preference View option (refer to page 82).

NOTES

Other payments in the Payments Journal do not include the Paid stamp.

NOTES

This screenshot was taken from the Lookup option for an Other Payment. When you start from the Adjusting option, Adjusting Other Payment 180 appears in the title bar.

The Purchases Journal title bar has Looking Up Invoice BC-6110 when you start from Lookup and Adjusting Invoice BC-6110 when you start from Adjust.

NOTES

The Receipts Journal display in Chapter 6, page 179, includes the two entries that result when you reverse a transaction.

NOTES

Better Crop Tree Farms
(contact Cedar Pines)
44 Grove Line, RR #4
Halifax, NS B3Y 1E1
Tel: (800) 566-7521
Web: BCTF.com
Terms: net 1
Payment method: Cheque
Expense account: 1460
Tax code: H - HST @ 15%

The Reverse tool in the tool bar is now available:

Click the **Reverse tool**, or **choose** the **Payment** (or **Purchase**) **menu** and **click Reverse Other Payment** (or **Invoice**).

Sage 50 warns you and requires confirmation:

Click **Yes** to confirm that you want to continue with reversing the entry.

Sage 50 will create the entry that reverses the original one automatically. Both the original and the reversing entry are included in the journal report when you choose Show Corrections. Sage 50 confirms that the entry was successfully reversed.

Click **OK**.

Enter the **purchase** for the correct supplier and date this time.

21 **Cash Purchase Invoice #BC-6110** **Dated May 12/21**

From Better Crop Tree Farms (use Full Add for the new supplier), $1 280 plus $192 HST for tree saplings. Invoice total $1 472 paid in full by cheque #181.

Changing a Stored Entry

The next entry is the purchase from Spotless Company. Going forward, Groen Fields will be invoiced on a monthly basis and at a different rate. Therefore, we need to update the stored entry. If a change is for a single purchase and will not be repeated, edit the entry after recalling it, but do not store the entry again.

✓ 22 **Purchase Invoice #SC-1219** **Dated May 14/21**

From Spotless Company, $1 200 plus $180 HST for one month of office cleaning as per new contract. Purchase invoice total $1 380. Terms: 1/30, n/60. Recall the stored transaction. Edit the amount and store the revised transaction as a monthly recurring entry.

Click the **Purchase Invoices** icon (Purchase Invoices) in the Payables window to open the journal.

Click the **Recall tool** on the tool bar, or **choose** the **Purchase menu** and **click Recall** to display the Recall Recurring Transaction dialogue box.

Double-click **Spotless Company**, the entry we want to use to display the purchase entry with the new date.

Click the **Invoice No. field** so you can add the invoice number.

Type SC-1219

Click **180.00**, the Amount, to highlight it so that you can edit it. Double-click if necessary to select the amount.

Type 1200

Press tab to enter the change.

Review the **journal entry** as usual to make sure that it is correct before proceeding.

Click the **Store button**, or **choose** the **Purchase menu** and **click Store**.

Choose **Monthly** as the new frequency and accept the name without change.

Click **OK**. Sage 50 now asks you to confirm your changes:

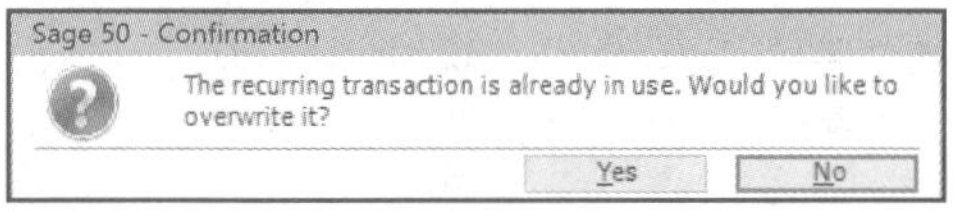
Sage 50 - Confirmation
The recurring transaction is already in use. Would you like to overwrite it?
Yes
No

Click **Yes** to confirm that you want to replace the previous stored version and return to the Purchases Journal.

Click the **Post button** Post to save the entry. **Click OK** and **close** the **Journal**.

Enter the **remaining journal transactions** for May.

23 **Cash Purchase Invoice #BF-101** **Dated May 14/21**

From Better Foods, $95 to purchase food for weekly barbecue for employees. Issue cheque #182. Recall stored entry.

NOTES

You can press ctrl + R to recall a stored entry.

24

DUST BUSTERS
WWW.DUSTBUSTERS.COM

60 Water St.
Dartmouth, NS B2W 6R9
Phone: (902) 366-1551 Toll free: (877) 366-15001

Invoice: DB-4857
Delivery Date: May 14, 2021
Sold to: Groen Fields
RR #2 Truro, NS
B2N 5B1
(902) 454-6111

Your Hydration Experts

Date	Description	Tax Code	Amount
May 14/21	Repairs to irrigation system	1	700.00
May 14/21	Install additional drip irrigation pipe	1	1 300.00
	Paid in full with cheque #183		

Thank you.

Signature Arjen Groen

Terms: Payment due on receipt of invoice.

Business No.: 345 667 216

HST	300.00
TOTAL	2 300.00

25 **Bank Debit Memo #AT-53186** **Dated May 14/21**

From Agri-Trust Credit Union, withdrawals from bank account for bi-weekly payroll:

Wages, including payroll taxes	$3 400.00
Payroll services	40.00
HST Paid on Purchases (payroll services)	6.00

NOTES

Use the General Journal for the payroll transaction in this application.

Remember to enter the sales tax code for the payroll services charge.

26 **Cash Sales Summary #35** **Dated May 14/21**

From garden centres, $16 400 plus $2 460 HST for early spring bedding plants and planter arrangements. Total receipts $18 860 deposited in bank.

SESSION DATE – MAY 21, 2021

27 **Purchase Invoice #CS-2987** **Dated May 15/21**

From Crop Savers, $640 for soil testing and follow-up fertilizer treatment plus $96 HST. Invoice total $736. Terms: 1/10, n/30. Recall stored entry.

28 **Cash Purchase Invoice #YI-345** **Dated May 16/21**

From Yardworks Inc., $26 000 for rototiller and tractor to prepare adjacent fields for business expansion. Invoice paid in full by cheque #184.

NOTES

Remember to select Cheque as the payment method for Yardworks Inc.

Large farm equipment purchased for business is zero rated for tax purposes.

29

INTERTEL

2 Communicate Rd.
Truro, NS
B2A 2K4

intertel.ca
chatter@intertel.ca

Account Inquiries: (902) 456-2355

Account Number
902 454-6111

Account Address
Groen Fields
RR #2 Truro, NS
B2N 5B1

Billing Date: May 17, 2021

ACCOUNT SUMMARY

Current Charges (April 13 - May 12)	
Business phone complete package	80.00
Mobile phone services	110.00
Internet service	55.00
	245.00
HST (93436 8697)	36.75
Total Current Charges	281.75
Previous Charges	
Amount of last bill	281.75
Payment Received April 19 – thank you	281.75
Adjustments	0.00
Balance Forward	0.00

Paid in full by cheque #185
Arjen Groen 05/17/21

Invoice: IT 557121	PLEASE PAY THIS AMOUNT UPON RECEIPT →	$281.75

30 **Cash Purchase Invoice #BF-102** **Dated May 17/21**

From Better Foods, $95 to purchase food for weekly barbecue for employees. Issue cheque #186. Recall stored entry. Edit the date and replace the stored entry.

31 **Cash Purchase Invoice #IFI-8250** **Dated May 18/21**

From Industrial Fuels Inc. (use Full Add for the new supplier), $1 260 including HST to fill diesel fuel tank on property. The diesel fuel supplies all farm vehicles. Issue cheque #187. Create new expense account, 5180 Fuel Expense.

NOTES

Industrial Fuels Inc.
Terms: net 1
Payment method: Cheque
Tax Code: HI
Expense Account: 5180 Fuel Expense

32 **Purchase Invoice #RPR-9257** **Dated May 18/21**

From Rural Property Repairs, $1 500 plus $225 HST to repair broken glass panes in greenhouse. Invoice total $1 725. Terms: 1/20, n/30.

33

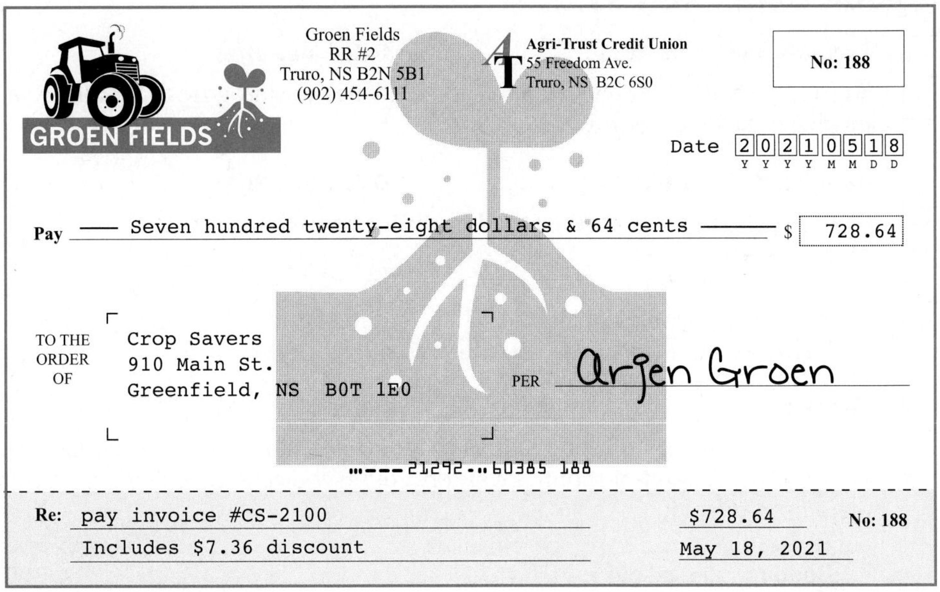

GROEN FIELDS

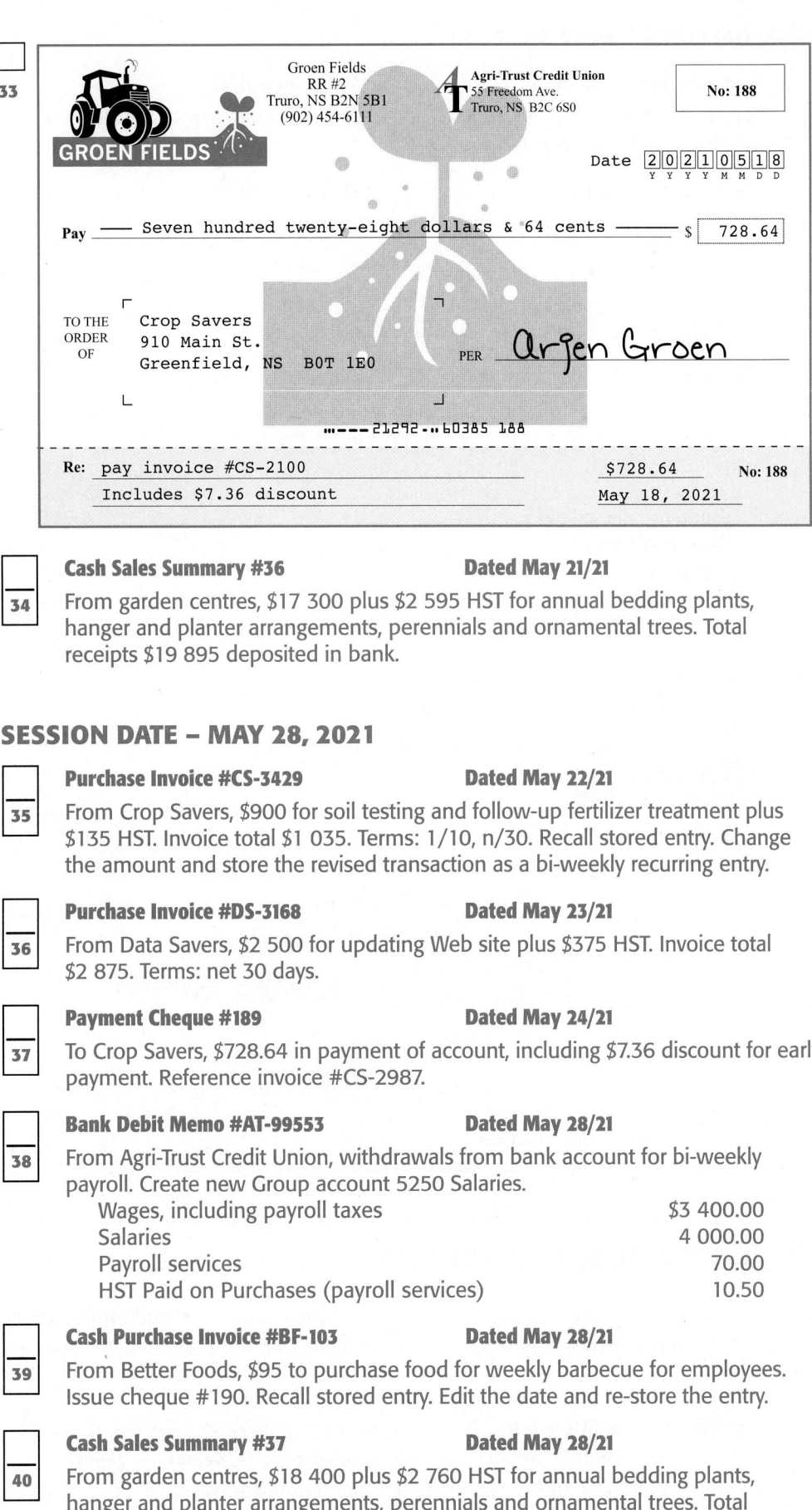

Groen Fields
RR #2
Truro, NS B2N 5B1
(902) 454-6111

Agri-Trust Credit Union
55 Freedom Ave.
Truro, NS B2C 6S0

No: 188

Date 2021 05 18 (YYYY MM DD)

Pay —— Seven hundred twenty-eight dollars & 64 cents —— $ 728.64

TO THE ORDER OF
Crop Savers
910 Main St.
Greenfield, NS B0T 1E0

PER Arjen Groen

⑈---21292-⑈60385 188

Re: pay invoice #CS-2100 — $728.64 — No: 188
Includes $7.36 discount — May 18, 2021

34 **Cash Sales Summary #36** **Dated May 21/21**

From garden centres, $17 300 plus $2 595 HST for annual bedding plants, hanger and planter arrangements, perennials and ornamental trees. Total receipts $19 895 deposited in bank.

SESSION DATE – MAY 28, 2021

35 **Purchase Invoice #CS-3429** **Dated May 22/21**

From Crop Savers, $900 for soil testing and follow-up fertilizer treatment plus $135 HST. Invoice total $1 035. Terms: 1/10, n/30. Recall stored entry. Change the amount and store the revised transaction as a bi-weekly recurring entry.

36 **Purchase Invoice #DS-3168** **Dated May 23/21**

From Data Savers, $2 500 for updating Web site plus $375 HST. Invoice total $2 875. Terms: net 30 days.

37 **Payment Cheque #189** **Dated May 24/21**

To Crop Savers, $728.64 in payment of account, including $7.36 discount for early payment. Reference invoice #CS-2987.

38 **Bank Debit Memo #AT-99553** **Dated May 28/21**

From Agri-Trust Credit Union, withdrawals from bank account for bi-weekly payroll. Create new Group account 5250 Salaries.

Wages, including payroll taxes	$3 400.00
Salaries	4 000.00
Payroll services	70.00
HST Paid on Purchases (payroll services)	10.50

39 **Cash Purchase Invoice #BF-103** **Dated May 28/21**

From Better Foods, $95 to purchase food for weekly barbecue for employees. Issue cheque #190. Recall stored entry. Edit the date and re-store the entry.

40 **Cash Sales Summary #37** **Dated May 28/21**

From garden centres, $18 400 plus $2 760 HST for annual bedding plants, hanger and planter arrangements, perennials and ornamental trees. Total receipts $21 160 deposited in bank.

NOTES

Remember to delete the discount taken amount for the second invoice.

NOTES

Remember to enter the sales tax code for the payroll services charge.

SESSION DATE – MAY 31, 2021

41

Purchase Invoice #B-8995 **Dated May 31/21**

From Bloomers, $600 plus $90 HST for seedlings to start growth for future sales. Invoice total $690. Terms: 2/10, n/30.

42

Bank Debit Memo #AT-100223 **Dated May 31/21**

From Agri-Trust Credit Union, withdrawals for bank charges and loan and mortgage payments:

Bank charges	$ 65
Mortgage payment (included $2 250 interest and $250 principal)	2 500
Loan payment (included $90 interest and $2 000 principal)	2 090

43

Memo #17 **Dated May 31/21**

From Owner: Make adjusting entries to reflect inventory sold and supplies used during May. The end-of-month inventory counts indicate the following amounts were used or sold:

Trees sold	$3 900
Bedding plants sold	4 800
Perennials sold	4 320
Planters sold	1 300
Seed inventory and supplies sold	900
Fertilizer used for soil treatment	520
Plant care supplies used	1 350

NOTES

Charge used inventory to Cost of Goods Sold, fertilizer to Soil Treatment Expenses and plant care supplies to Supplies Expense.

44

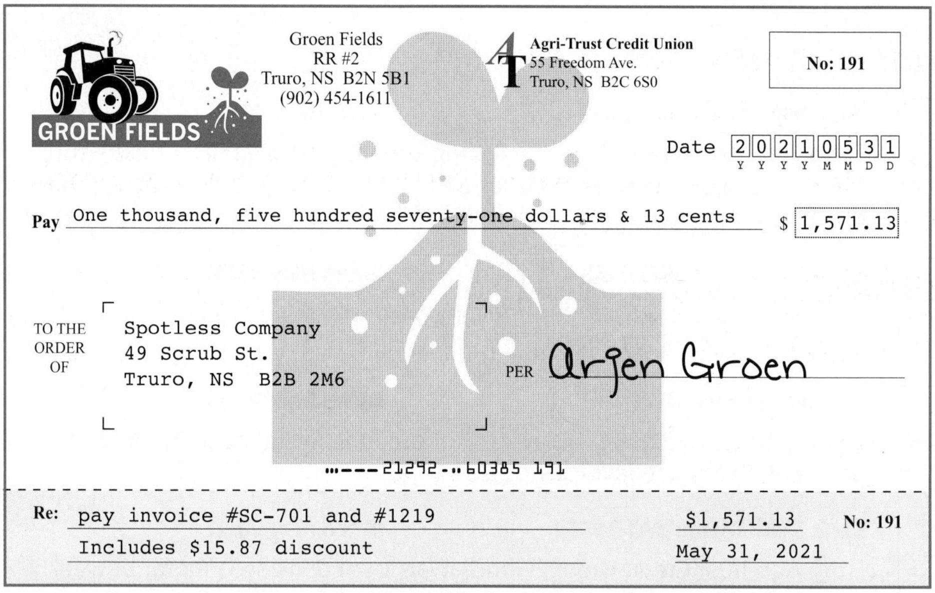
GROEN FIELDS

Groen Fields
RR #2
Truro, NS B2N 5B1
(902) 454-1611

Agri-Trust Credit Union
55 Freedom Ave.
Truro, NS B2C 6S0

No: 191

Date 20210531
Y Y Y Y M M D D

Pay One thousand, five hundred seventy-one dollars & 13 cents $ 1,571.13

TO THE ORDER OF
Spotless Company
49 Scrub St.
Truro, NS B2B 2M6

PER Arjen Groen

---21292--60385 191

Re: pay invoice #SC-701 and #1219
Includes $15.87 discount
$1,571.13
May 31, 2021
No: 191

Displaying Supplier Reports

Like General Ledger reports, supplier-related reports can be displayed and printed from multiple starting points: the Suppliers window, the Home window Reports menu and the Reports pane.

PRO VERSION

pro The term Vendor will replace Supplier in all report names and fields.

Click the Vendors Icon.

Click the **Suppliers icon** (Suppliers) to open the Suppliers window. The Reports menu in this window lists only supplier reports. **Select** the **report** you want from this list to open the report options window.

Choose the **Reports menu** in the Home window, then **choose Payables** and **click** the **report** you want for the report options.

Click the **Reports list arrow** in the Reports pane to list the supplier reports:

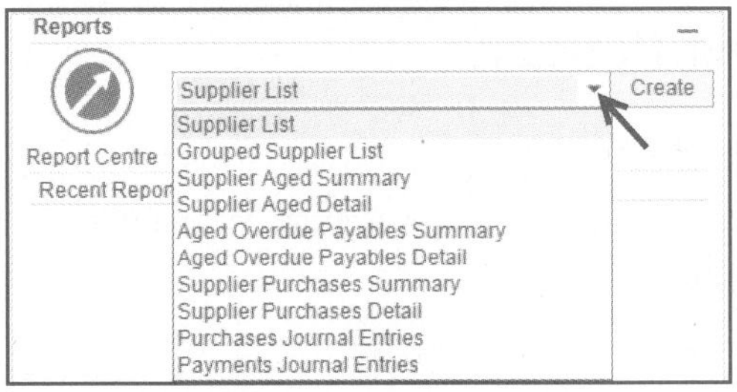

We will work from the Report Centre again so that we can include the report samples, descriptions and options.

Reporting from the Report Centre

Click the **Report Centre icon**  in the Home window.

Click **Payables** in the Select A Report Type list to open the list of available supplier reports:

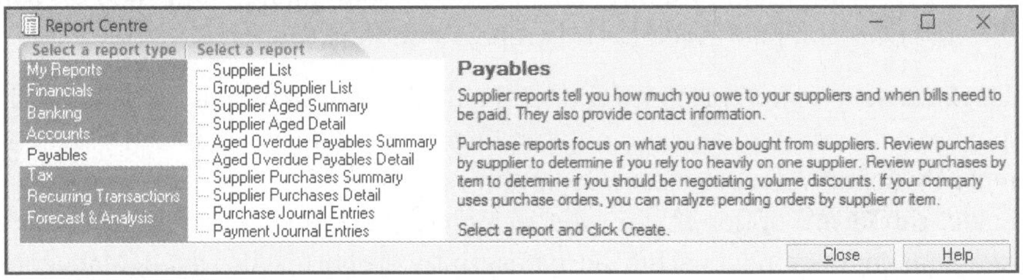

A general description of the Payables module reports with some suggestions of how the reports may assist with business decisions opens next.

Displaying Supplier Lists

Click **Supplier List** in the Select A Report list to open the sample report and description. **Click Modify This Report** for the report options:

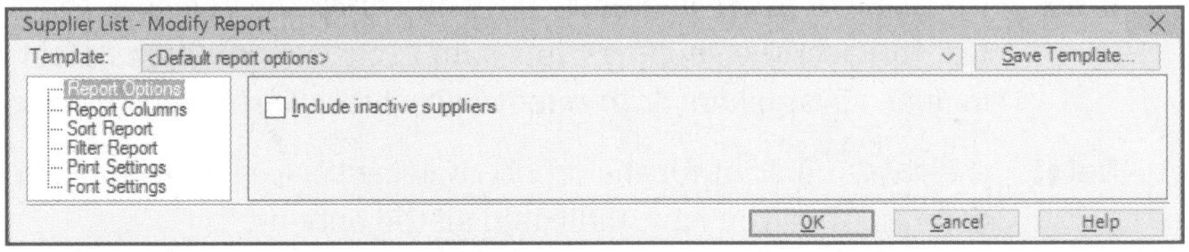

In any Home window, you can choose the Reports menu, then choose Lists and click Suppliers for the report options.

By default, the supplier address and balance owing are displayed. To include additional supplier details, you can choose the supplier record fields by customizing the Report Columns. You can include suppliers marked as inactive if you want.

Click **OK** to open the report.

Close the **display** when you have finished viewing the report.

You will return to the starting point for the report.

If you want to organize the list of suppliers, you can group them automatically by a number of criteria with the **Grouped Supplier List**. Organizing the list may be helpful for assigning suppliers to different staff for phone calls.

NOTES
The Supplier Purchases Report deals mainly with inventory. It will be introduced in a later application.

PRO VERSION
Grouped lists are not available.

NOTES
The Report Centre can also be accessed from the Reports menu.

CLASSIC VIEW
Click the Report Centre icon in the My Business column or open the Report Centre from the Reports menu.

PRO VERSION
Forecast & Analysis reports and Grouped Lists are not available in the Pro version.

CLASSIC VIEW
From the Home window, right-click the Suppliers icon . (Clicking the left mouse button will open the ledger.) The Select A Report tool label changes to the name of the report for the selected icon.

Click the Select A Report tool  on the tool bar.

PRO VERSION
Click Vendor List.

NOTES
You can drill down to the Supplier Aged Detail Report from the Supplier List.

Click Grouped Supplier List and then click Modify This Report. Click the Grouped By list arrow for your options. Close the display when you have finished viewing the report.

Displaying Supplier Aged Reports

NOTES
The Supplier Aged Summary and Detail reports are both available directly from the Report Centre.

PRO VERSION
pro Click Vendor Aged Summary.

You can display Supplier Aged reports at any time.

Click **Supplier Aged Summary** in the Select A Report list to open the sample report and description.

Click **Modify This Report** for the report options:

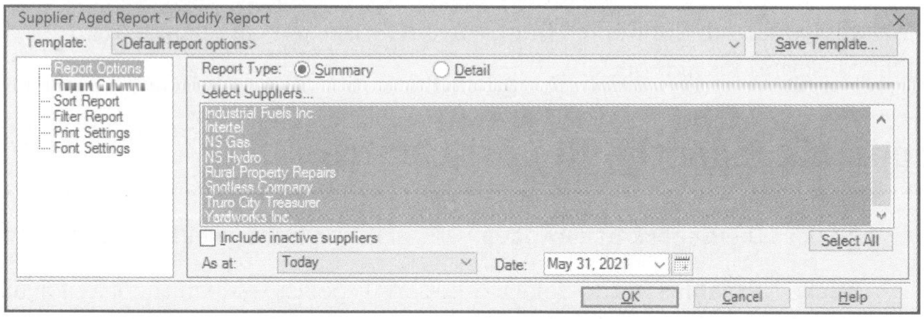

NOTES
If you chose either One-Time Supplier or Continue for Anything on Paper, it will not be included by name in the list of suppliers for reports. Suppliers for whom you used Quick Add will be included.

Or, from any Home window, choose the Reports menu, then choose Payables and click Supplier Aged for this report's options window.

NOTES
For the Detail Report, you can also choose the number of days worth of paid invoices to add to the report.

The **Summary** option provides the total balance owing to each supplier. It displays an alphabetic list of suppliers with outstanding total balances organized into aged columns. By default, the program selects this option.

NOTES
From the Supplier Aged Detail Report, you can drill down to look up invoices and supplier ledgers. From the Summary Report, you can drill down to the Detail Report.

Select the **Detail** option if you want to include individual outstanding invoices and payments made to suppliers. This more descriptive report is also aged. Management can use it to make payment decisions. With the Detail option, you can add supplier payment terms and contact information by clicking these options.

You can sort and filter the reports by supplier name or balance owing (or by aging period for the Summary Report). You can select or omit any columns to customize reports.

Click **Detail** to select the Detail Report.

Click the **name** or **press** and **hold** ctrl and **click** the **names** in the Suppliers List to select the suppliers you want in the report. **Click Select All** to include all suppliers or to remove all when all are selected.

Enter the **date** you want for the report or accept the session date given by default. After you have indicated all the options,

Click **OK** to open the report.

Close the **displayed report** when you have finished.

Displaying Aged Overdue Payables Reports

NOTES
You can drill down to look up invoices and to the Supplier Aged Report from the Aged Overdue Payables Report. From the Summary Report, you can drill down to the Detail Report.

You can display Aged Overdue Payables reports at any time.

Click **Aged Overdue Payables Summary** in the Select A Report list to open the sample report and description.

Click **Modify This Report** for the report options:

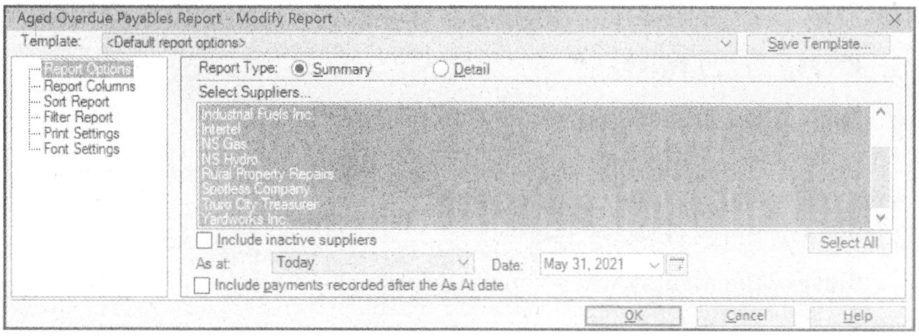

Or, from the Home window, choose the Reports menu, then choose Payables and click Aged Overdue Payables for the report options.

The Aged Overdue Payables Report includes the same information as the Supplier Aged Report, but it adds a column for the invoice amounts that are overdue. Supplier name and balance owing may be selected as the criteria for sorting and filtering. The **Summary Report** has totals for each supplier while the **Detail Report** includes details for each invoice and the option to add supplier contact information.

When you **Include Payments Recorded After The As At Date**, invoices for which you have remitted postdated cheques will be omitted from the report.

You can sort and filter the reports by supplier name or by the balance owing. You can select or omit any of the columns to customize the report.

NOTES
Postdated payments may be omitted because these invoices are deemed to be paid.

Choose **Summary** or **Detail**.

Press and **hold** ctrl and then **click** the **names** in the Suppliers List to select the suppliers that you want in the report. **Click Select All** to include all suppliers or to remove all when all are selected.

Enter the **date** you want for the report, or accept the session date given by default. After you have indicated all the options,

Click **OK** to open the report. One invoice from Rural Property Repairs and the balance on the first invoice from Data Savers are overdue.

Close the **displayed report** when you have finished.

Displaying the Purchases Journal Report

Click **Purchase Journal Entries** in the Select A Report list to open the sample report and description.

Click **Modify This Report** for the report options:

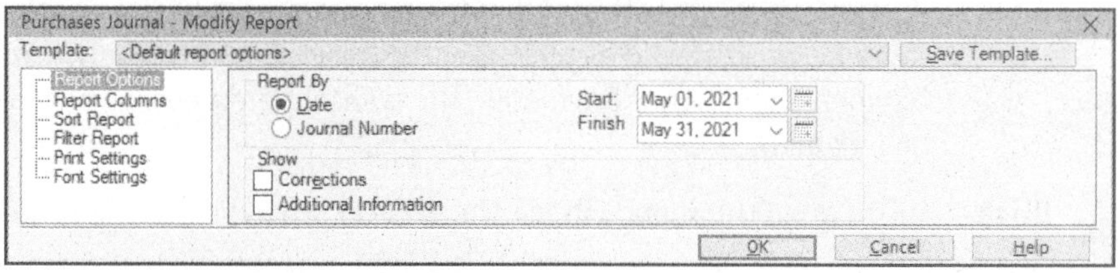

Or, choose the Reports menu, then choose Journal Entries and click Purchases.

Entries for the Purchases Journal can be selected by posting date or by journal entry number. By default, the Date option is selected, and the first transaction date and session date are the default dates for the report. All journal reports may be sorted and filtered by date, journal number, source or comment. You can choose the account name and number, and debits and credits columns to customize the report column settings. Correcting or adjusting entries may be included or omitted from the report.

CLASSIC VIEW
From the Home window, right-click the Purchases icon

to select it. Click the Select A Report tool

on the tool bar.

If no icons are selected in the Home window, Purchases and Payments Journal reports are available from the Select Report list when you click the Select A Report tool.

NOTES
The dates May 1 and May 31 are available from drop-down lists for both date fields.

NOTES
If you omit corrections, the journal reports will appear to be out of sequence because the journal entry numbers for the incorrect transactions and their reversing entries will be omitted from the report. Sorting the journal report by date and then by journal number will keep the related transactions together.

Type the **beginning date** for the transactions you want.

Press tab **twice**.

Type the **ending date** for your transaction period.

Click **Corrections** so that adjusting and reversing entries are included.

Click **OK** to open the report.

Close the **display** when you have finished.

Displaying the Payments Journal Report

CLASSIC VIEW
From the Home window, right-click the Payments icon to select it. Click the Select A Report tool on the tool bar.

Click **Payment Journal Entries** in the Select A Report list to open the sample report and description.

Click **Modify This Report** for the report options:

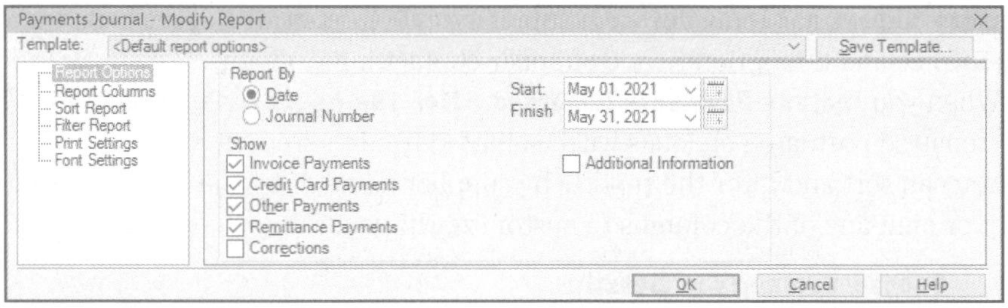

Or, choose the Reports menu, then choose Journal Entries and click Payments for the report options.

NOTES
You can drill down to the Supplier Aged Report and to the General Ledger Report from the Purchases Journal or the Payments Journal Report. You can also look up the original journal transaction.

For the Payments Journal, like other journal reports, you can select the transactions by posting date — the default setting — or by journal entry number. In addition, you can choose the type of payment for the report — invoice payments, credit card payments, other payments (cash purchases) and payroll remittance payments. All types are selected initially, and clicking any one will remove it from the report. Corrections or adjustments may be included or omitted. Clicking the options will change your selections.

Type the **beginning date** for the transactions you want.

Press tab **twice**.

Type the **ending date** for your transaction period.

Click **Corrections**.

NOTES
Including the types of transactions for which you have no entries does not result in an error message and will not change the report.
Payroll remittances are covered in Chapter 8. Credit card payments are covered in Chapter 12.

Click **Credit Card Payments** and **Remittance Payments** to remove the ✓s for them because we did not use these transaction types. Only Invoice Payments and Other Payments, the transaction types we entered, will be included.

Click **OK** to open the report. **Close** the **display** when you have finished.

Displaying All Journal Entries in a Single Report

To view the entries for all journals in a single report from a Home window, choose the Reports menu, then choose Journal Entries and click All.

From the Report Centre, click Financials in the Select A Report Type list and then click All Journal Entries in the Select A Report list. Click Display or choose Modify This Report if you want to change the default options.

Displaying Cheque Log Reports

If you regularly print cheques through Sage 50 from the Payables journals or the Payroll journals, you can display and print a summary of these printed cheques in the Cheque Log Report.

Click **Banking** in the Select A Report Type list to open the general description of banking reports and the list of available reports:

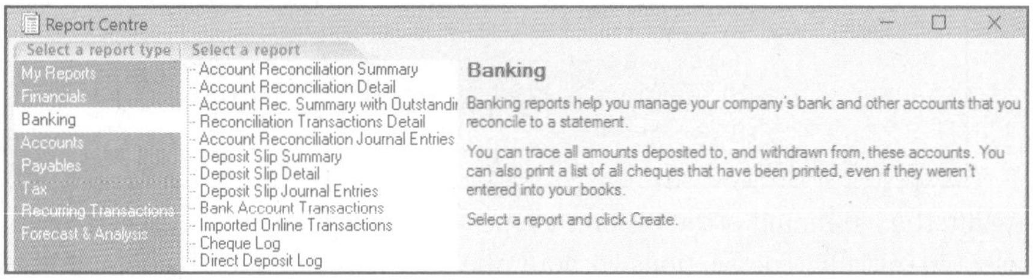

Click **Cheque Log** in the Select A Report list to open the sample report and description.

Click **Modify This Report** for the report options:

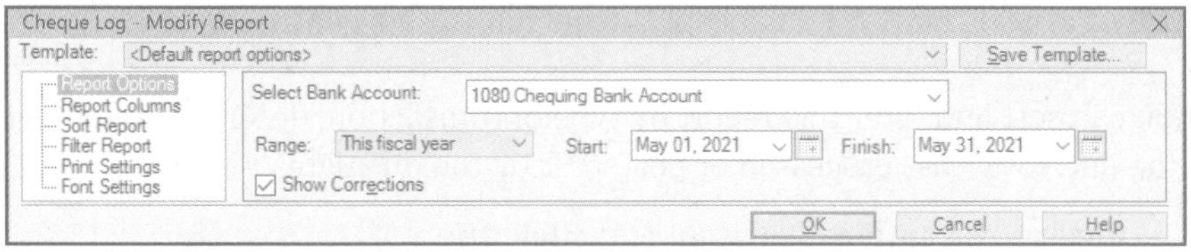

Or, from any Home window, choose the Reports menu, then choose Banking and click Cheque Log to open the report options window.

The report will have details for all cheques that you entered, including whether or not the journal entry was posted and the number of times the cheque was printed. If you do not print cheques through the program, these payments are listed with a 0 (zero) for the number of times printed. Corrections (adjusted and cancelled or reversed cheques) are included by default but can be omitted by clicking the default selection to Show Corrections. These cheques are identified as Reversed.

To customize the report, you can choose any of the column headings to sort or filter the report and you can choose to include or omit any of these columns.

Choose the **bank account** from the Select Bank Account drop-down list.

Enter the **Start** and **Finish dates** for the report.

Click **OK** to open the report.

Close the **display** when you have finished.

Recurring Transactions Report

If you have stored transactions, you can generate a report of these transactions.

Click **Recurring Transactions** in the Select A Report Type list to open the general description of the report type and the list of available reports:

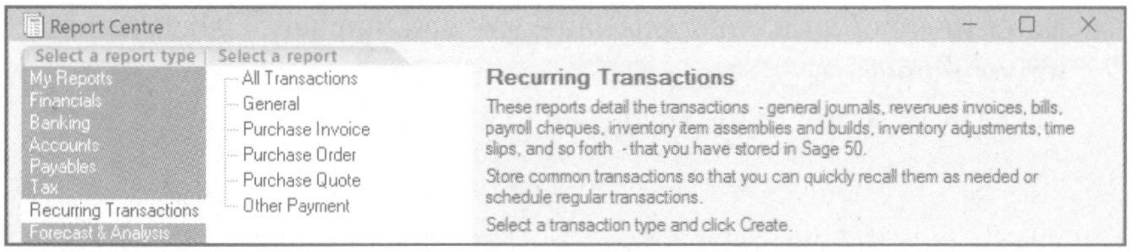

PRO VERSION
The Bank Account Transactions Report is not available in the Pro version.

NOTES
No drill-down reports are available from the Cheque Log Report, but you can sort or filter by any of the information in the report.

NOTES
Journals for hidden modules are not listed. When you use them and they allow recurring entries, they will be added to this list.

The list now includes the different types of transactions that can be stored.

Click **All Transactions** in the Select A Report list to open the sample report and description.

Click **Modify This Report** for the report options:

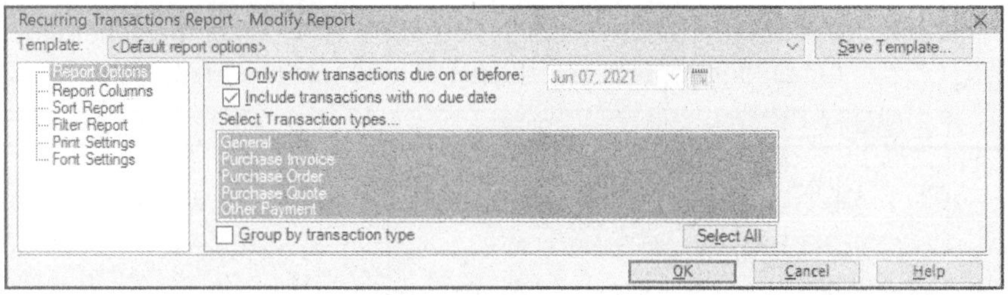

NOTES
When you choose Random as the frequency for recurring transactions, they do not include a due date.

Again, the list includes the different types of transactions that can be stored, and all are selected initially. Transactions without due dates are included by default but can be omitted by clicking the option to include them. You can restrict the report to include only those entries that are due within a specific time period by selecting **Only Show Transactions Due On Or Before** and entering a date. The default date for this option is one week past the session date, but you can enter any date you want. You can **Group** the report **By Transaction Type** or accept the default to show entries in order by the due date.

You can sort and filter this report by type of transaction, description, frequency, the date the entry was last processed or posted or by the due date.

Choose the **options** you want and **click OK**.

Double-click an **entry** in the report to recall it for the next due date.

Close the **Report Centre** when you have finished.

WARNING!
When you click the Print tool, printing will begin immediately with your current settings. Choosing Print from the File menu in the report will open the Print options screen and you can check and modify your printer selection and settings.

Printing Supplier Reports

Before printing supplier reports, make sure that you set the print options.

Display the **report** you want to print.

Click the **Change Print Settings tool** to open the Reports & Forms Settings screen. Check that you have the correct printer and form files selected for your report. **Close** the **Settings screen**.

Click the **Print tool** or **choose** the **File menu** and **click Print**.

WARNING!
You cannot display labels, so you should check the printer settings first.

Printing Mailing Labels

To print labels, you should first make sure that the print options have been set correctly and that your printer is turned on and has the correct labels paper. To set the program to use your printing labels,

Choose the Setup menu in the Home window and click Reports & Forms.
Click Labels in the list under Reports. Choose your printer.
Enter the appropriate margins, label size and number of labels across the page for your labels.
Click OK to return to the Home window.

Choose the **Reports menu** in the Home window, then **choose Mailing Labels** and **click Suppliers**:

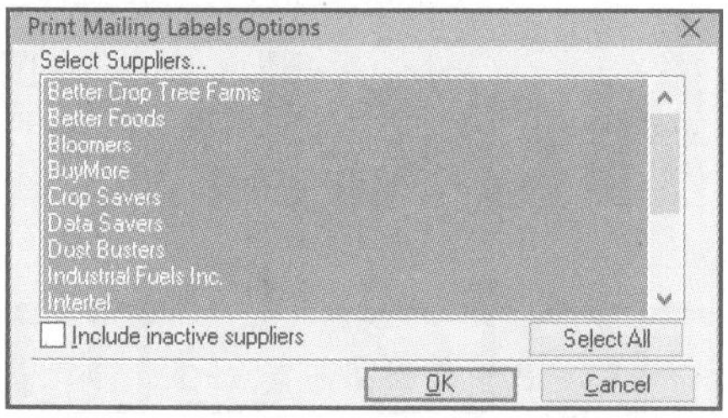

Press and **hold** ctrl and then **click** the **names** of the suppliers for whom you want labels, or **click Select All** to include all suppliers.

Click **OK** to print the labels. Printing will begin immediately.

Printing T4A and T5018 Slips

You can also print T4A and T5018 slips if you have suppliers with these options checked in the ledger records on the T4A & T5018 tab screen.

Choose the **Reports menu** in the Home window, then **choose Payables** and **click Print T4A Slips** or **Print T5018 Slips**. **Select** the **suppliers** you want for the report.

Close the **data file** to finish your Sage 50 session.

R E V I E W

The Student DVD with Data Files includes Review Questions and Supplementary Cases for this chapter.

PRO VERSION
Choose Mailing Labels and click Vendors.

NOTES
For practice, you can print the labels on plain paper.

NOTES
T5018 slips are compulsory for construction companies that pay subcontractors for construction services. The reports record the amounts paid and can be filed with the CRA electronically.

CHAPTER SIX

Phoebe's Photo Studio

OBJECTIVES

After completing this chapter, you should be able to

- ***enter*** transactions in the General, Payables and Receivables journals
- ***enter*** and ***post*** cash, credit card and account sale transactions
- ***enter*** and ***post*** customer payment transactions
- ***customize*** journals and ***preview*** invoices
- ***enter*** transactions including GST and PST
- ***store*** and ***recall*** recurring entries
- ***enter*** customer discounts and partial payments
- ***add*** and ***edit*** customer accounts
- ***reverse*** receipts to enter NSF cheques from customers
- ***edit*** and ***review*** customer-related transactions
- ***create*** shortcuts for General and Payables journal transactions
- ***display*** and ***print*** customer reports
- ***understand*** linked accounts for the Receivables Ledger

COMPANY INFORMATION

Company Profile

NOTES
Phoebe's Photo Studio
100 Light St., Suite 202
Winnipeg, MB R2T 7G4
Tel 1: (204) 649-3358
Tel 2: (888) 649-3358
Fax: (204) 642-4967
Business No.: 296 654 593

Phoebe's Photo Studio has its main portrait studio in Winnipeg, Manitoba. Here Phoebe Maniwake takes individual and family portraits and develops and prints the black-and-white photographs. She also has a summer residence outside of Riverton, Manitoba, on Lake Winnipeg that allows her easier access to the northern parts of the province as well as the Hecla / Grindstone Provincial Park where she composes her nature photographs for sale in galleries across Canada.

After completing an art program at the OCAD University, Maniwake opened her studio in Winnipeg, her home town, and has now had the studio for several years. In the summers she also accompanies Arctic cruises and other tours to photograph cruise passengers on location, as well as to take more of her own northern landscape photos. Revenue comes from these three sources: portraits (including students and weddings), photographing tour clients and art gallery sales. Sometimes she brings in a student for the summer as an assistant/apprentice to accompany her on her personal photo tours.

Most regular customers — families, galleries, cruise lines — have accounts with Phoebe's Photo Studio and receive a 2 percent discount if they pay within 10 days. They are asked to settle their accounts in 30 days, paying by cash or by cheque. PST and GST apply to all work completed by Phoebe's Photo Studio.

Accounts have been set up with a local photographic supplies store, a camera sales and repair store and some other regular suppliers.

After remitting all taxes before the end of June 2021, Maniwake converted the accounts for Phoebe's Photo Studio using the following information:

- Chart of Accounts
- Post-Closing Trial Balance
- Supplier Information
- Customer Information
- Accounting Procedures

CHART OF POSTABLE ACCOUNTS

PHOEBE'S PHOTO STUDIO

ASSETS
1080 Chequing Account
1100 Credit Card Bank Account
1200 Accounts Receivable
1300 Darkroom Supplies
1310 Photo Paper
1320 Framing Supplies
1340 Other Supplies
1440 Computers and Software
1460 Developing Equipment
1480 Camera Accessories
1500 Digital SLR Cameras ▶

▶1550 Van
1580 Studios

LIABILITIES
2100 Bank Loan
2200 Accounts Payable
2640 PST Payable
2650 GST Charged on Services
2670 GST Paid on Purchases
2850 Mortgage Payable

EQUITY
3560 P. Maniwake, Capital ▶

▶3600 Net Income

REVENUE
4100 Revenue from Tours
4140 Revenue from Portraits
4180 Sales Discounts

EXPENSE
5100 Advertising & Promotion
5120 Bank Charges & Card Fees
5130 Interest Expense
5140 Hydro Expense
5150 Framing Supplies Used ▶

▶5160 Photo Supplies Used
5170 Other Supplies Used
5190 Postage Expenses
5200 Purchase Discounts
5220 Telephone Expenses
5240 Travel Expenses
5260 Vehicle Expenses
5300 Wages
5310 Payroll Service Charges

NOTES: The Chart of Accounts includes only postable accounts and the Net Income or Current Earnings account.

POST-CLOSING TRIAL BALANCE

PHOEBE'S PHOTO STUDIO

June 30, 2021		Debits	Credits
1080	Chequing Account	$ 48 486	
1100	Credit Card Bank Account	2 900	
1200	Accounts Receivable	7 989	
1300	Darkroom Supplies	420	
1310	Photo Paper	2 620	
1320	Framing Supplies	1 380	
1340	Other Supplies	240	
1440	Computers and Software	14 900	
1460	Developing Equipment	5 600	
1480	Camera Accessories	6 320	
1500	Digital SLR Cameras	7 370	
1550	Van	21 900	
1580	Studios	320 000	
2100	Bank Loan		$ 10 000
2200	Accounts Payable		5 840
2850	Mortgage Payable		180 000
3560	P. Maniwake, Capital		244 285
		$440 125	$440 125

SUPPLIER INFORMATION

PHOEBE'S PHOTO STUDIO

Supplier Name (Contact)	Address	Phone No. Fax No.	E-mail Web Site	Terms Tax ID
Calm Air (Arie Fliegel)	50 Jett Ave. Winnipeg, Manitoba R2P 1S7	Tel: (800) 839-2256 Fax: (204) 476-5110	af@calmair.com calmair.com	1/15, n/30 566 478 913
Lumber Shed (C. Woods)	91 Walnut St. Winnipeg, Manitoba R3P 8V3	Tel: (204) 382-7845 Fax: (204) 383-2489	cwoods@lumbershed.com lumbershed.com	1/5, n/30 571 277 631
Manitoba Hydro (Mannie Ergs)	1 Watts Rd. Winnipeg, Manitoba R6G 2C1	Tel: (204) 435-2633	m.ergs@mnhydro.man.ca mnhydro.man.ca	net 1
Manitoba Telephone (Chata Lot)	11 Vocal Channel Winnipeg, Manitoba R3E 6R4	Tel: (204) 488-8532	manitobatel.ca	net 1
Riverton Garage (Karl Fixe)	6 Ford St. Riverton, Manitoba R0C 2R0	Tel: (204) 378-1297 Fax: (204) 378-6388	Karl@rivercars.com rivercars.com	net 30 344 566 872
Starlight Photo Solutions (Star Lightman)	300 Aurora St. Winnipeg, Manitoba R3P 4D5	Tel: (204) 577-1369 Fax: (204) 577-2229	star@sps.com sps.com	2/10, n/30 610 728 362
UPS Delivery (Yvette Panier)	8 Carrier Ave. Winnipeg, Manitoba R2C 6A1	Tel 1: (204) 698-2357 Tel 2: (800) 477-1UPS Fax: (204) 698-6102	ups.com	net 1 498 458 561
Web Exposure (B. Online)	72 Memorial Cres. Brandon, Manitoba R7A 3G5	Tel: (204) 469-8080 Fax: (204) 469-4987	online@webexposure.com webexposure.com	net 15 385 416 821

OUTSTANDING SUPPLIER INVOICES

PHOEBE'S PHOTO STUDIO

Supplier Name	Terms	Date	Invoice No.	Amount	Total
Calm Air	1/15, n/30	Jun. 26/21	CA-224	$3 900	$3 900
Lumber Shed	1/5, n/30	Jun. 21/21	LS-894	$1 050	$1 050
Riverton Garage	net 30	Jun. 16/21	RG-1904	$890	$890
			Grand Total		$5 840

CUSTOMER INFORMATION

PHOEBE'S PHOTO STUDIO

Customer Name (Contact)	Address	Phone No. Fax No.	E-mail Web Site	Terms Credit Limit
Borealis Delights (J. Franklin)	4 Lighter Way Winnipeg, Manitoba R4A 1E1	Tel 1: (204) 476-4669	franklin@borealis.com borealis.com	2/10, n/30 $15 000
Brandon Art Gallery (Art North)	49 Viewer St. Brandon, Manitoba R7B 2T5	Tel 1: (204) 823-5100 Tel 2: (204) 826-1297 Fax: (204) 826-2196	AN@bag.com bag.com	2/10, n/30 $10 000
Geraldine Reuben (G. Reuben)	4 Chapel Lane Winnipeg, Manitoba R4A 1E1	Tel: (204) 476-4669	GReuben@yahoo.com weddings.com/GR	2/10, n/30 $10 000
Kandinski Party (Sophia Kandinski)	77 Memory Lane Winnipeg, Manitoba R3G 5D2	Tel: (204) 326-7528 Fax: (204) 326-7436	skandinski@gmail.com kandinskis.com	2/10, n/30 $5 000

▶

Customer Name (Contact)	Address	Phone No. Fax No.	E-mail Web Site	Terms Credit Limit
Polar Discoveries (Robert Peary)	4 Exploration Ave. Churchill, Manitoba R0B 0E0	Tel: (204) 624-7900 Fax: (204) 624-7556	peary@polartours.com polartours.com	2/10, n/30 $15 000
Young'uns Preschool (Ella Little)	588 Totts Cres. Winnipeg, Manitoba R3P 4C2	Tel: (204) 369-4545 Fax: (204) 369-8765	ella@YPS.com YPS.com	2/10, n/30 $8 000

OUTSTANDING CUSTOMER INVOICES

PHOEBE'S PHOTO STUDIO

Customer Name	Terms	Date	Inv/Chq No.	Amount	Total
Geraldine Reuben	1/10, n/30	Jun. 25/21	PS-377	$2 260	
		Jun. 25/21	Chq #266	1 460	
		Jun. 27/21	PS-381	1 695	
			Balance owing		$2 495
Young'uns Preschool	1/10, n/30	Jun. 28/21	PS-383	$4 294	
		Jun. 30/21	PS-387	1 200	
			Balance owing		$5 494
			Grand Total		$7 989

Accounting Procedures

Open-Invoice Accounting for Receivables

The open-invoice method of accounting for invoices issued by a business allows the business to keep track of each individual invoice and of any partial payments made against it. In contrast, other methods keep track only of the outstanding balance by combining all invoice balances owed by a customer. Sage 50 uses the open-invoice method. Fully paid invoices can be removed (cleared) periodically.

NOTES

For a service business, the terms Revenues Journal and Client replace Sales Journal and Customer. These terms will be used interchangeably in this chapter.

Discounts for Early Payments

Phoebe's Photo Studio offers discounts to regular customers if they pay their accounts within 10 days. Full payment is expected in 30 days. Customers who pay by credit card do not receive discounts. No discounts are allowed on partial payments.

Some suppliers with whom Phoebe's Photo Studio has accounts set up also offer discounts for early payments.

NSF Cheques

If a cheque is deposited from an account that does not have enough money to cover it, the bank may return it to the depositor as NSF (non-sufficient funds). The NSF cheque from a customer requires a reversing entry in the Receipts Journal. Sage 50 can complete these reversals automatically (refer to Reversing a Receipt, page 177). In most companies, the accounting department notifies the customer who wrote the NSF cheque to explain that the debt remains unpaid. Many companies charge an additional fee to the customer to recover their bank charges for the NSF cheque. A separate sales invoice should be prepared for the additional charge. NSF cheques to suppliers are handled in the same way, through reversing entries in the Payments Journal.

Taxes (GST and PST)

Phoebe's Photo Studio is a service business using the regular method of calculating GST. GST, at the rate of 5 percent, charged and collected from customers will be recorded as a liability in *GST Charged on Services*. GST paid to suppliers will be recorded in *GST Paid on Purchases* as a decrease in tax liability. The balance owing, the difference between the GST charged and GST paid, or the request for a refund will be remitted to the Receiver General for Canada quarterly.

Phoebe's Photo Studio charges customers 8 percent PST on all sales and pays PST on some goods. The Studio is exempt from PST for purchases of items used in preparing photos, such as framing supplies, photo paper and developing chemicals because the customer pays PST on the products that use these components.

Cash and Credit Card Sales of Services

Cash and credit card transactions are a normal occurrence in most businesses. Sage 50 has payment options to handle these transactions. When you make the correct Payment Method or Paid By selection, the program will debit *Chequing Account* or *Credit Card Bank Account* instead of the *Accounts Receivable* control account (refer to Entering Cash Sales, page 170, and Entering Credit Card Sales, page 182).

INSTRUCTIONS

1. **Record entries for the source documents** in Sage 50 using all the information provided for Phoebe's Photo Studio. The procedures for entering each new type of transaction in this application are outlined step by step in the Keystrokes section with the source documents. These transactions are indicated with a ✓ in the upper part of the completion check box beside the source document. Source document numbers are included below the checkmark or in the lower part of the check box.
2. **Print** the **reports** indicated on the following printing form after you have finished making your entries. Instructions for reports begin on page 192.

REPORTS

Accounts
- ☐ Chart of Accounts
- ☐ Account List
- ☐ General Journal Entries

Financials
- ☑ Balance Sheet: July 31
- ☑ Income Statement from July 1 to July 31
- ☑ Trial Balance date: July 31
- ☑ All Journal Entries: July 1 to July 31
- ☑ General Ledger accounts: 1300 4100 4140 from July 1 to July 31
- ☐ Statement of Cash Flows
- ☑ Cash Flow Projection Detail Report for account 1080 for 30 days

Taxes
- ☑ GST Report July 31
- ☑ PST Report July 31

Banking
- ☐ Cheque Log Report

Payables
- ☐ Supplier List
- ☐ Supplier Aged
- ☐ Aged Overdue Payables
- ☐ Purchases Journal Entries
- ☐ Payments Journal Entries

Receivables
- ☐ Client List
- ☑ Client Aged Detail for all customers
- ☐ Aged Overdue Receivables
- ☑ Revenues Journal Entries: July 1 to July 31
- ☑ Receipts Journal Entries: July 1 to July 31
- ☐ Client Statements

Mailing Labels
- ☐ Labels

KEYSTROKES

Opening Data Files

Open the data file **SageData19\PHOTO\PHOTO** to access the data files for Phoebe's Photo Studio.

Type `July 8 2021` to enter the first session date.

Click **OK** to display a Sage 50 warning about the date:

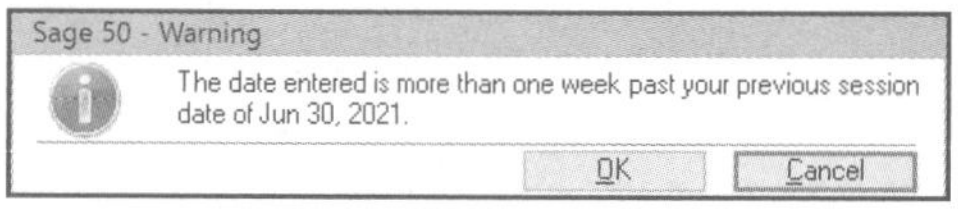

This warning appears whenever you advance the session date by more than one week, as we learned in Chapter 4. Normally a business would update its accounting records more frequently. If you have entered the correct date,

Click **OK** to accept the date entered and display the Home window.

The Payroll, Inventory and Project ledger names do not appear in the Modules pane list. These ledgers are hidden because they are not set up.

Accounting for Sales

Sales are entered in the Revenues Journal, accessed from the Client Invoices icon in the Receivables module Home window:

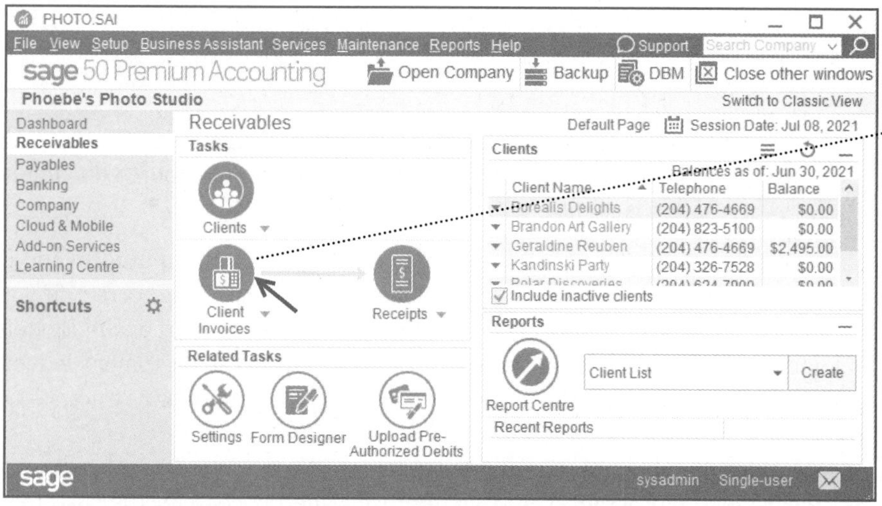

You can enter sales from the Client Invoices icon in the Receivables window. The Client Invoices label is used for service companies. For other company types, the label for this icon may be Sales, Invoices, Sales Invoices, Customer Invoices, Bills, Statements or Charges. The icon itself does not change.

Customer balances are given as of the date of the latest transaction.

✓ 1 **Sales Invoice #PS-391** **Dated July 1/21**

To Brandon Art Gallery, $4 200 plus $210 GST and $336 PST for sale of three framed original photographic prints. Invoice total $4 746. Terms: 2/10, n/30. Create new Group account 4120 Revenue from Gallery Sales. Customize the sales invoice by removing the columns not used by Phoebe's Photo Studio.

NOTES

If you are using backup files, restore SageData19\PHOTO1.CAB or PHOTO1 to SageData19\PHOTO\PHOTO. Refer to the instructions for restoring data files in Chapter 1, page 25, if you need assistance.

PRO VERSION

Icon labels are the same for all company types. Customers replaces Clients as the ledger icon label, and Sales replaces Client Invoices for the journal label.

Click the Sales Invoices icon

to open the Sales Journal. In the Pro version Classic view, this icon is labelled Sales.

WARNING!

Do not include PS- in the sales invoice number in the journal. The numeric portion will then be correctly updated by the program.

If you want to include PS- in the journal entries, you must update the invoice number manually for each invoice.

CLASSIC VIEW

Click the Revenues icon Revenues to open the Revenues Journal.

PRO VERSION

The term Sales Journal replaces Revenues Journal in the journal title bar, and Customer replaces Client in all fields.

The Time Slips and Refresh tools and the Order No. and Shipping Date fields do not appear in the Pro version.

WARNING!

You must click the list arrow to open the customer list. Clicking the Client field will place an insertion point to prepare for typing a name.

NOTES

The Client and Payment Method fields have the Same Next Time pushpin tool, the same tool used in the Purchases and Payments windows, and it serves the same purpose as in those journals.

NOTES

When you use the long date format, the parts of the date are entered as separate words. Double-clicking the date will select only one part of the date, either the month, the day or the year.

The year is added correctly in the Revenues Journal when you type the month and day.

Remember that you can always choose the date from the pop-up calendar in the Date field.

Click the **Client Invoices icon** to open the Revenues Journal input form:

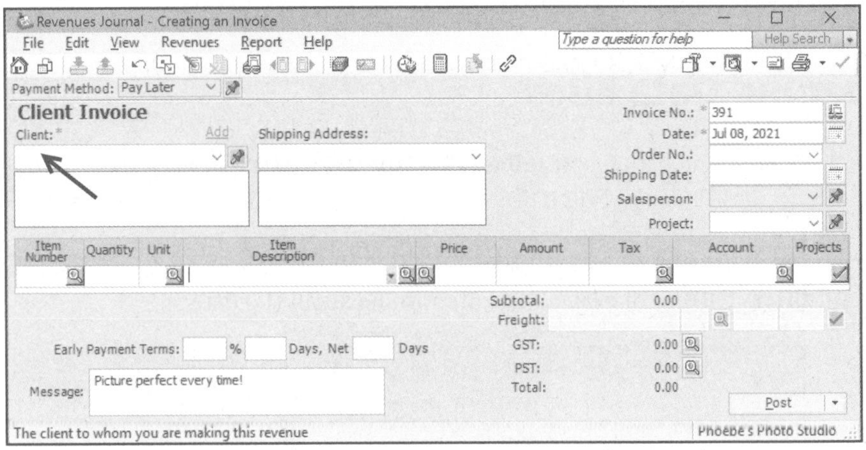

Most tool bar buttons in the Revenues Journal are familiar from other journals — Home window, Daily Business Manager, Store, Recall, Undo, Customize Journal, Calculator and Allocate. Print and E-mail buttons allow you to print or e-mail the invoice before posting to provide a customer or store copy of the sales invoice. You can also use tool buttons to preview an invoice, change print settings and look up, adjust or reverse a posted invoice. The tools for Additional Information, Track Shipments and Add Time Slip Activities will be explained when they are used.

Pay Later is the default payment option for the Revenues Journal.

Click the **Client field list arrow** to obtain the list of customers:

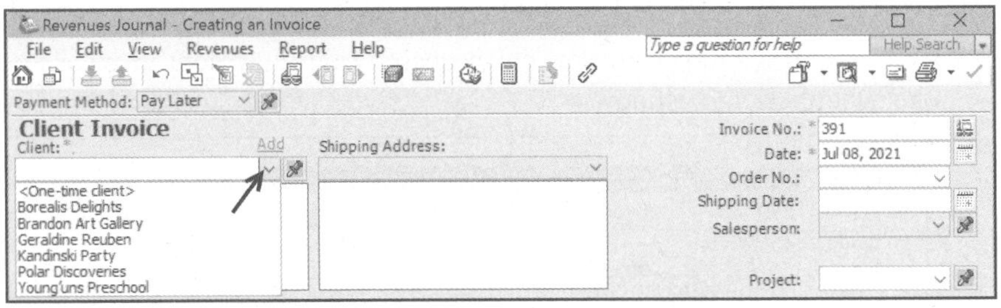

Click **Brandon Art Gallery**, the customer in the first source document, to select and enter it.

The customer's name and address have been added to your input form and Pay Later — the customer's default payment method for invoices — is correct. If you have made an error in your selection, click the client list arrow and start again. By default, the Client and the Shipping Address fields are completed from the customer's ledger record. You can edit the shipping address if necessary. If the information is correct, you can skip over the shipping information.

The invoice number, 391, the numeric portion, is entered and correct. It is updated automatically by the program. The payment terms and tax code for the customer have also been entered. The default revenue account for the Receivables module is entered as the default. We need to change it — and create a new account — for this customer.

The session date is the default transaction date, so you need to change it as well. Enter the date on which the transaction took place: July 1, 2021.

Click the **Date field Calendar icon**.

Click 1.

If you want, you can enter a quantity (three for the number of prints) and $1 400 as the price per unit in the Price field and let the program calculate the amount by multiplying the two together. You can use this method if you are selling more than one item that is not an inventory item.

Click the **Item Description field** on the first line. The Item Description field is used to enter a description or comment concerning the sale.

Type `three framed original photo prints`

Press tab. The cursor is now in the Price field.

The Price field refers to unit prices; it is not needed for this sale.

Press tab.

The cursor should now be positioned in the Amount field, where you will enter the amount for this invoice before taxes.

Type `4200` **Press** tab. This amount is entered as the invoice subtotal.

The cursor advances to the Tax field. The default tax code for the customer, GP, is entered from the customer record details in the data files and is correct. Customers pay both GST and PST on services. The invoice total has also been updated.

Press enter to list the tax code descriptions set up for Phoebe's Photo Studio:

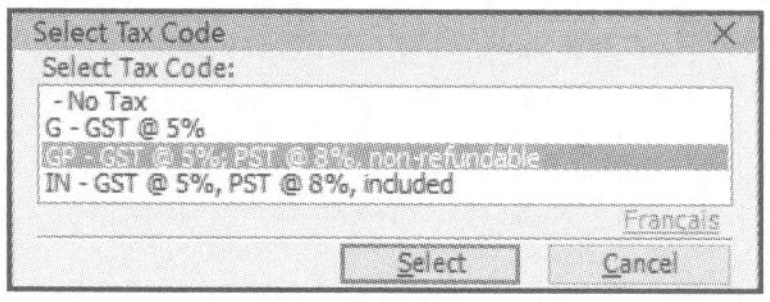

The tax code options are charge **No Tax** on the sale; code **G**, charge GST only; code **GP**, charge both GST and PST; and code **IN**, both GST and PST are charged and included in the price. PST is described as non-refundable.

You can select a different tax code from this list if the default is incorrect. Click the correct code and then click Select. You will return to the Revenues Journal with the cursor in the Account field.

Click **Cancel** to return to the journal.

Press tab to advance to the Account field.

The Account field in a sales invoice refers to the credit portion of the journal entry, usually a revenue account. Again, you cannot access *Accounts Receivable*, the linked account, directly. The software will automatically debit the *Accounts Receivable* control account in the General Ledger when you enter positive amounts.

You can set up a default revenue account for customers, just as you set up default expense accounts for suppliers. For Phoebe's Photo Studio customers, more than one revenue account applies. We have entered 4100 as the default account for the module, but it is not correct for this sale. In the Account field, you can choose an account from the list of accounts or create a new account, just as you can in any other account field. We need to create a new revenue account for this sale.

Type `4120` **Press** enter.

Press enter to open the Add An Account wizard (Add An Account is selected).

Press tab.

Type `Revenue from Gallery Sales` as the **account name** and **accept** the remaining **defaults**. **Click Finish** to return to the journal.

The new account number is added to the journal.

Press tab to advance the cursor to line 2 in the Item field, ready for additional sale items if necessary.

NOTES

You can also press tab repeatedly to move to any field you need.

NOTES

Entering a negative amount in the Amount field will generate a debit entry for the sale with a credit to Accounts Receivable.

This is similar to replacing credit amounts with debit amounts in the Purchases Journal when you type a negative number, and to switching between debits and credits in the General Journal by adding the minus sign to amounts.

NOTES

PST is usually charged on services applied to goods that are themselves taxable for PST.

NOTES

When you select a tax code from the selection list, the cursor advances to the next invoice field. When you choose Cancel, the cursor does not move to the next field.

NOTES

Accounts Receivable is not included in the Select Account list.

You can choose any postable account as the default revenue account for customers, just as you can use any account as the default expense account for suppliers.

NOTES

Because Add New Account is already selected, pressing enter will choose it.

The Message field can be used in two ways: you can set up a default comment for the business that appears on all invoices, or you can enter a comment at the time of the sale. You can add to or change a default comment if you want. The default comment is entered for Phoebe's Photo Studio.

The payment terms have been set up as defaults for customers as 2 percent discount in 10 days with net payment due in 30 days. You can change terms for individual customers or sales invoices.

NOTES
Payment terms can be modified for individual customers in the client ledger record. You can also edit the terms for individual sales in the Revenues Journal.

Click the **List icon beside the GST** or the **PST amount field** to provide the detailed summary of taxes included in the sale:

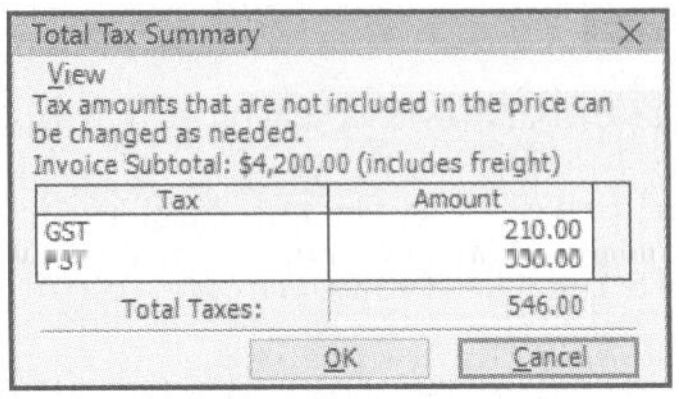

NOTES
If necessary, such as for rounding errors or to separate tax amounts that are combined, you can edit the tax amounts on the Tax Summary screen.

Close the **Tax Summary window** to return to the completed invoice:

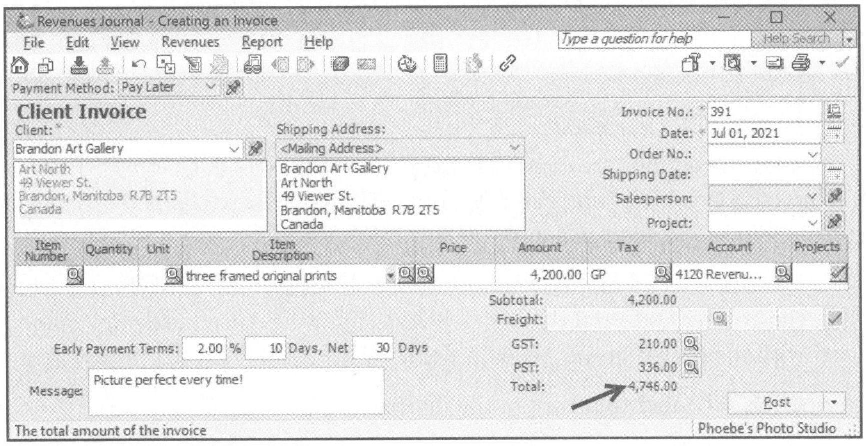

Before storing, printing or posting a Revenues Journal entry, review it carefully.

PRO VERSION
Choose the Report menu and click Display Sales Journal Entry.

Reviewing the Revenues Journal Entry

Choose the **Report menu** and **click Display Revenues Journal Entry** or **press** ctrl **+ J** to display the transaction:

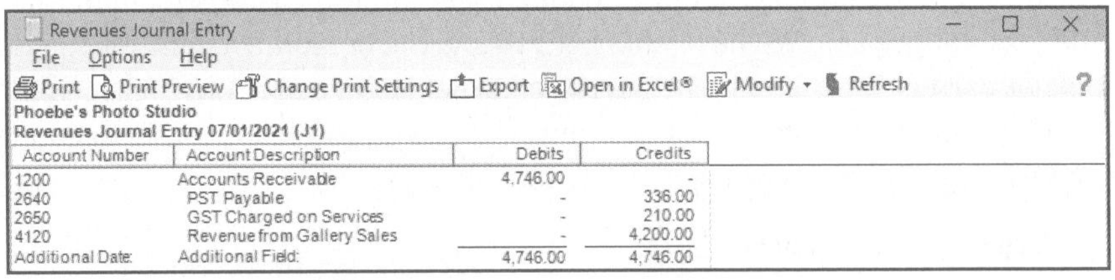

Review the **journal entry** to check for mistakes.

NOTES
Using the Revenues Journal for sales instead of the General Journal is recommended because the accounts, tax codes and payment terms can be set up automatically for the business or linked to individual customers. Preset linked accounts ensure that tax amounts are calculated and updated correctly. Outstanding amounts are directly connected with the correct customer and ledger records are updated. The total Accounts Receivable amount is also updated.

Furthermore, you are unlikely to reverse debit and credit amounts in error.

The display informs you that *Accounts Receivable*, the **control account**, has been updated automatically by Sage 50 because the Receivables and General ledgers are fully integrated. All credit sales are debited to *Accounts Receivable*, the default linked account for the Receivables Ledger. *GST Charged on Services* has also been updated correctly because of the tax code you entered and because *GST Charged on Services* was defined as the GST linked account for sales. Similarly, *PST Payable* is defined as the linked account for PST collected from customers, and it too is updated correctly because of the tax code. You did not need to enter any of these accounts or amounts directly in the Revenues Journal. The balance owing by this customer is also directly updated as a result of the linked *Accounts Receivable* account and journal entry.

Close the **display** to return to the Revenues Journal input screen.

CORRECTING THE REVENUES JOURNAL ENTRY BEFORE POSTING

Move to the field that has the error. **Press** tab to move forward through the fields or **press** shift and tab together to move back to a previous field. This will highlight the field information so you can change it. **Type** the **correct information** and **press** tab to enter it.

You can also use the mouse to **point** to a field and **drag through** the **incorrect information** to highlight it. **Type** the **correct information** and **press** tab to enter it.

If the customer is incorrect, **reselect** from the **Client** list by **clicking** the **Client list arrow**. **Click** the name of the **correct client**. Verify that the tax code, terms and default account are correct.

Click an **incorrect amount** or description to highlight it. Then **type** the **correct information** and **press** tab to enter the change.

To correct an account number or tax code, **click** the **Account List icon** to display the selection list. **Click** the **correct entry** to highlight it, then **click Select** and **press** tab to enter the change.

To insert a line or remove a line, **click** the **line** that you need to move. **Choose** the **Edit menu** and **click Insert Line** and **type** the new line or **click Remove Line** to delete a line.

To discard the entry and begin again, **click** [X] to close the journal or **click Undo** on the tool bar to open a blank journal window. When Sage 50 asks whether you want to discard the entry, **click Yes** to confirm your decision.

NOTES
Other Receivables Ledger linked accounts will be used and explained later. These are the Receivables bank account, Freight Revenue account and Sales Discount account.

NOTES
To correct Revenues Journal entries after posting, refer to page 184 and Appendix C.

Customizing the Sales Invoice

The sales invoice includes a number of fields/columns that we do not need. Before saving the invoice, we will customize it to remove the unnecessary columns.

Click the **Customize Journal tool** or **choose** the **View menu** and **click Customize Journal** to open the Settings options for Client Invoices:

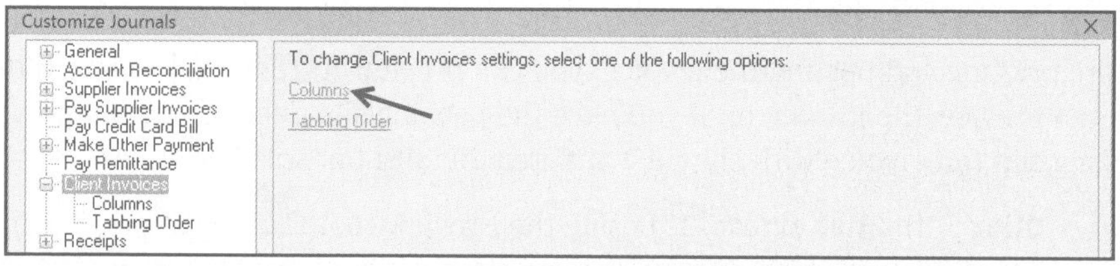

We can modify the selection of columns and the order in which the tab key advances you from one part of the invoice to another. For the Client Invoices (Sales Invoices), we will modify the column selections. For Receipts, we will modify the tabbing order.

Click **Columns** to open the column selection window:

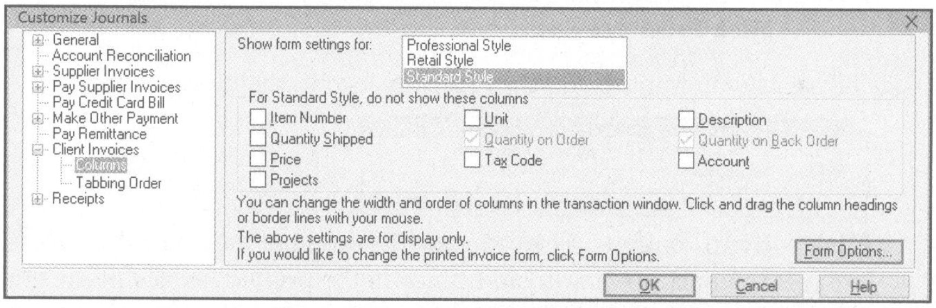

The Premium version has three predefined invoice styles for different business types. Each style displays a different set of columns. The Standard Style, the default, includes all columns. The Standard and Retail styles include columns for inventory and orders, while the Professional Style does not. The Tax Code, Account, Description and Projects columns are common to all styles.

NOTES
When Orders and Quotes are used (Company Settings, Features), they will be added to the list as forms you can customize. You can customize these forms differently from invoices in the Premium version.

PRO VERSION
Different invoice styles are not available in the Pro version. The Standard Style is the only one used, so there is no selection list. Form Options for printed invoices cannot be accessed from this window.

You cannot customize orders and quotes separately from invoices.

The term Purchase Invoices replaces Supplier Invoices, and Sales Invoices replaces Client Invoices.

WARNING!
These style selections do not change the on-screen invoice, so we started by modifying the Standard Style.
Screen columns can be modified by selecting an invoice style from the journal's View menu.

We can remove or hide most of the fields to match the Professional Style (refer to sidebar Warning). The columns we can remove are listed under the **For Standard Style, Do Not Show These Columns** heading. We can remove additional columns by clicking check boxes to add ✓s. The **Form Options** button accesses printer setup options for the forms. Modifying printed forms is covered in Appendix F on the Student DVD.

Click the **check boxes** for **Item Number**, **Quantity Shipped**, **Price**, **Unit** and **Projects**.

Click **OK** to return to the modified journal:

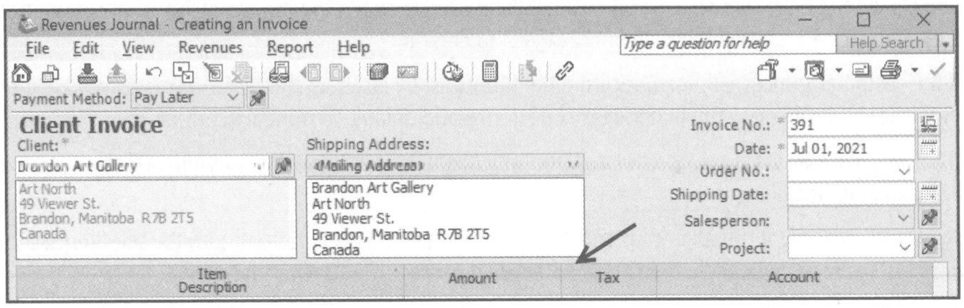

You can adjust the column spacing by dragging the column headings to change the size of columns and display all the information in all fields. We have resized the columns for this screenshot.

NOTES
You can customize journals by dragging the column headings to rearrange or remove columns or to change column size.

Point to the column heading margin. When the arrow changes to ⟷ (a double-headed arrow), drag the margin to its new location or size. Dragging the right column margin to the left until it overlaps the next column will remove that column. You can restore missing columns from the Customize Journal window.

Now when we press the *tab* key for the invoice details, the cursor will advance to the next field, and it will be one we use for the sale.

Previewing Invoices

Before printing and posting the invoice, you can preview it from the Preview tool. You can preview the invoice or, if you have the packing slip details, you can preview the packing slip (an invoice with shipping and item details, but without prices).

Click the **list arrow** beside the Preview tool to list preview options:

PRO VERSION
The Pro version does not have packing slips, so the Preview tool has no list arrow with options. The tool allows only previewing of invoices, and the File menu also has only this option.

Click **Print Preview For Invoice** or **choose** the **File menu** and **Invoices** and **click** **Print Preview**.

Sage 50 asks if you want to add the company logo to the invoice:

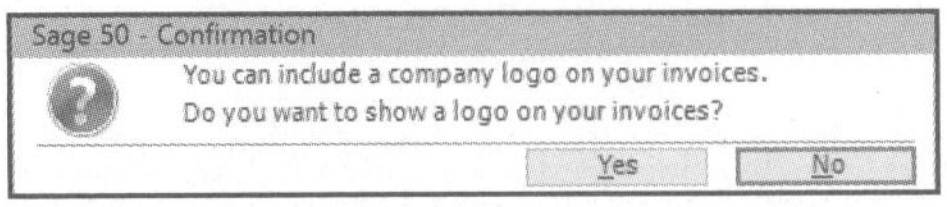

Click **No** to continue. The company file does not include a logo. We demonstrate how to add a logo to the printed invoice in Appendix F.

WARNING!
The file locations in the Printer and E-Mail Form must be correct for your setup or you will receive an error message. You can click Browse and locate the Forms folder inside the Sage 50 Premium Accounting Version 2019 folder. Choosing Invoice from the Description field list for Print and Email should provide the correct location automatically.

The form settings for the invoice must be correct. If your invoice form is not in the location indicated on the Report & Form Options page — when you have a customized form and its location has changed — Sage 50 provides an error message when you attempt to preview or print an invoice:

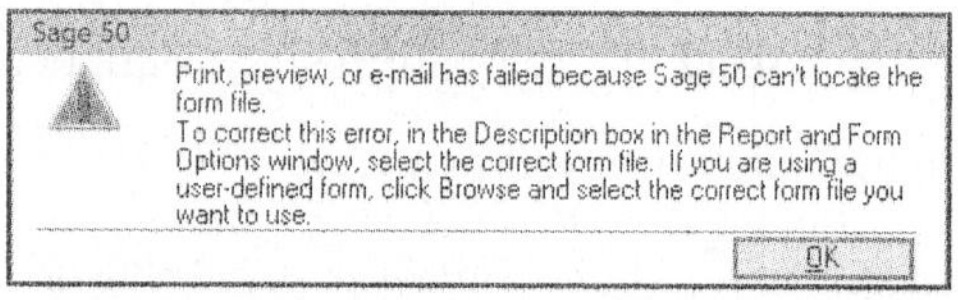

An incorrect form location provides a similar warning. Click OK if you see this message to open the Report & Form Options window:

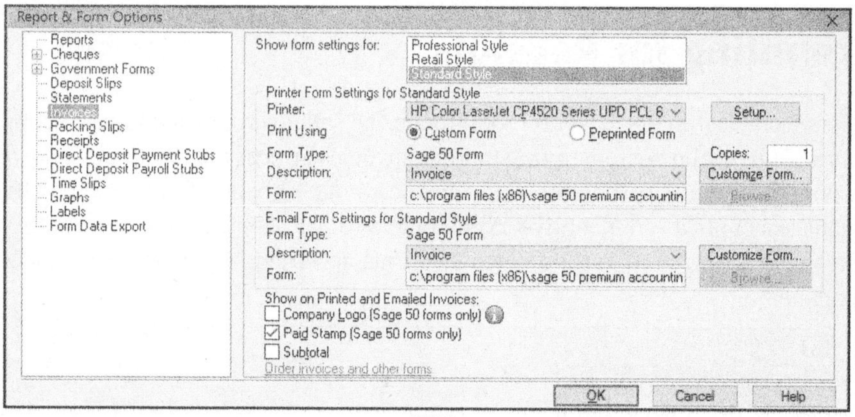

In the journal window, you can click [icon], the Change The Default Printer Settings tool, any time to open the Forms settings screen for customer invoices.

Choose Custom Form as the Print Using option and a valid file. Choosing Invoice in the Description field for Print and E-Mail Form settings will provide valid files. Click OK to return to the invoice. You should now be able to preview the invoice. Click the Print Preview For Invoice tool to display a copy of your invoice:

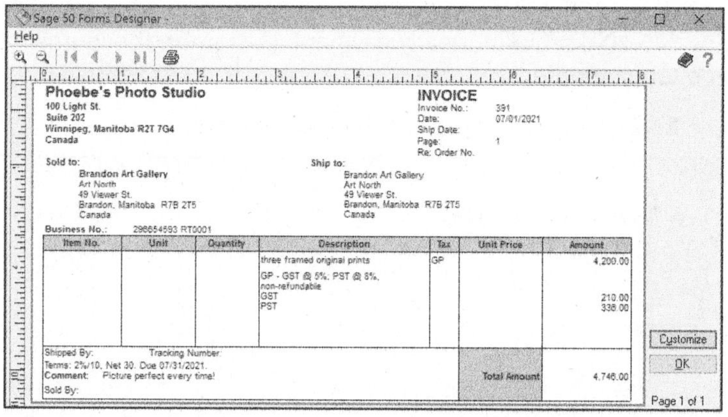

You can now print the invoice if you want by clicking the Print tool [icon] in the Preview window. Or, click OK, return to the Invoice, choose the File menu and click Print or click the Print tool in the journal window.

Posting

When you are certain that you have entered the transaction correctly, you must post it. The Revenues Journal Post button has a list arrow with two options:

If you regularly print invoices when you enter them, as for point-of-sale transactions, you can click Print & Post on this button (add a ✓). Print and Post becomes the default selection and the button label changes to reflect this choice: Print & Post

Previewing invoices is always recommended before printing. Because we do not want to print all invoices, we will accept the initial default setting to Post.

NOTES

A Sage 50 error message referring to the location of the default form in the Forms folder opens when the folder is missing or has moved.

NOTES

This screenshot has the form settings you need to preview the invoice. Choosing Custom Form as the Print Using selection and Invoice as the Description entry for both printed and e-mail copies should automatically provide the correct settings – if you have not customized the invoice.

NOTES

Customizing the journal does not change the printed invoice. Refer to Appendix F on the Student DVD to learn how to customize printed invoices and other forms.

You can start customizing the invoice from the Preview window by clicking the Customize button, or from the Report & Form Options window.

NOTES

Printing begins immediately when you start from the Print tool. If you need to check or change your printer settings, you should start printing from the File menu in the journal.

NOTES

If invoices are printed as a batch or when you are learning the program, you should use Post as the default selection.

Batch printing of invoices and other forms is covered in Chapter 14.

NOTES
You can also choose the Revenues menu and click Post or press *alt* + P to save your transaction.

Click the **Post button** Post. **Click OK** to confirm successful posting.

A new blank Revenues Journal form appears on the screen.

Close the **Revenues Journal** because the next transaction is a receipt. The balance for Brandon Art Gallery in the Clients pane list has been updated.

NOTES
A discount of 2 percent for paying within 10 days is comparable to an interest penalty of 36 percent per year – it costs the customer 2 percent to borrow the money for the extra 20 days.

Client balance amounts in the Clients list pane have been updated.

Accounting for Receipts

Receipts from customers are entered in much the same way as payments to suppliers. After you choose the customer, outstanding invoices appear automatically and you enter the payment amounts without entering any accounts. Phoebe's Photo Studio offers early payment discounts as an incentive to customers to pay their accounts promptly.

Receipts are entered in the Receipts Journal accessed from the Receipts icon in the Tasks pane:

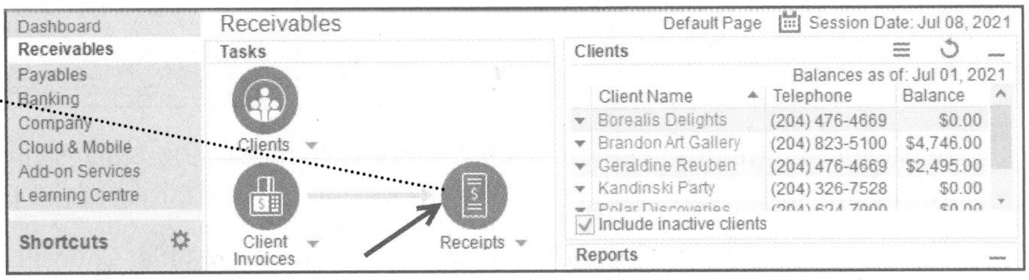

✓ 2

Receipt #41 **Dated July 2/21**

From Geraldine Reuben, cheque #302 for $1 754.80, including $754.80 in full payment of invoice #PS-377 and $1 000 in partial payment of invoice #PS-381, and allowing $45.20 discount for early payment. Customize the journal by changing the tabbing order.

CLASSIC VIEW
The Receipts icon is located below the Revenues icon. It has no shortcuts list arrow.

Click the **Receipts icon** to open the Receipts Journal:

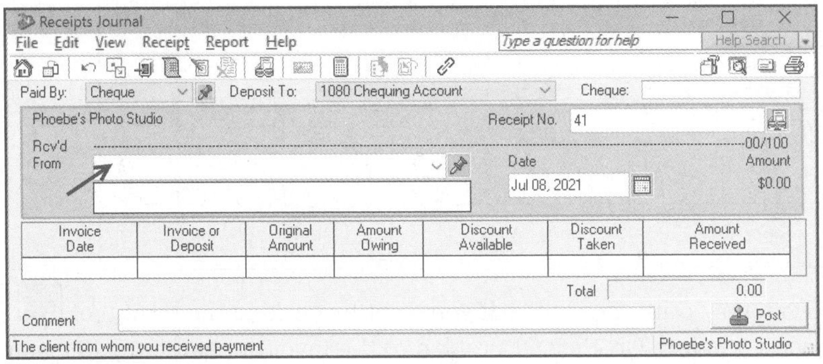

NOTES
Two refresh tools, [tool icon] and [tool icon], will refresh the journal with changes made by other users, such as the addition of new invoices. The list of outstanding invoices and the invoices themselves can be updated.

These tools are used when the option to refresh lists automatically is not selected – a User Preference setting (refer to pages 81–82).

PRO VERSION
The Refresh tools do not appear in the Pro version.

As with the Sales Invoice, you can customize the journal by removing fields and changing the tabbing order.

Click the **Customize Journal tool** [tool icon] or **choose** the **View menu** and **click Customize Journal**:

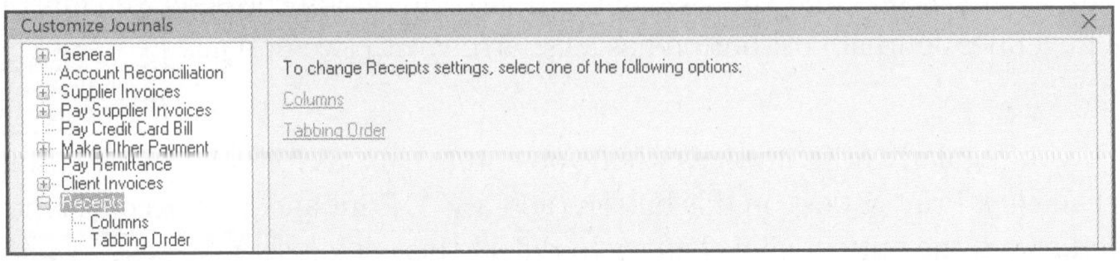

Click **Columns** to open the customization options for columns.

When they are not needed, you can remove the Invoice Date and the two Discount columns. Phoebe's Photo Studio offers discounts, so we must include these columns.

Click **Tabbing Order** in the list under Receipts to continue:

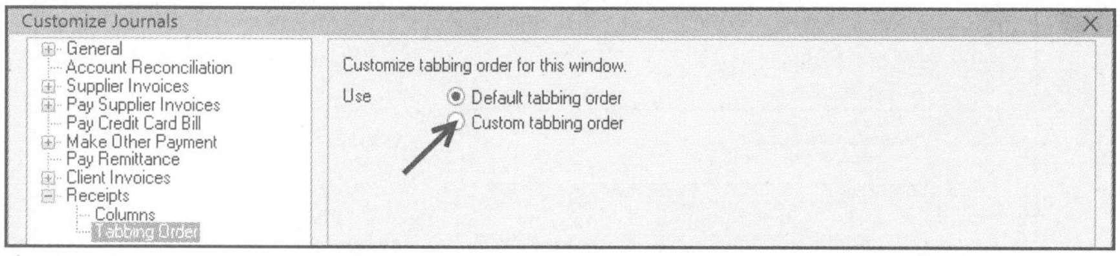

You can choose the default tabbing order or you can change the order.

Click **Custom Tabbing Order** to continue:

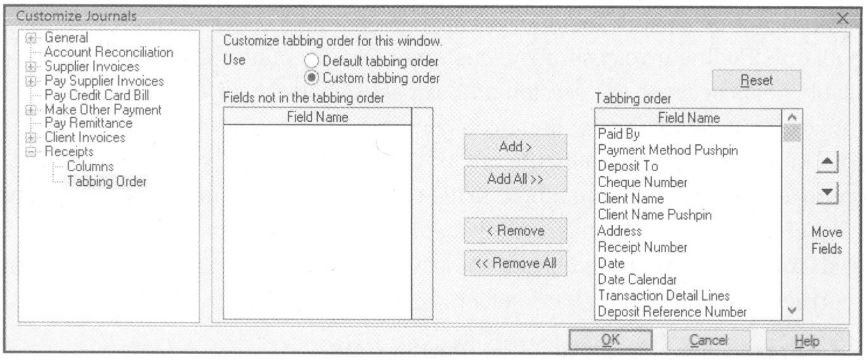

We will change the order so that after choosing the customer the cursor will move to the cheque number field in the upper right-hand corner. With the default order, the cursor reaches this field last, making it easy to forget to enter the number. The cheque number is not a required field, so the program does not warn you if you omit the number.

Cheque Number appears before Client Name. However, when you open the Receipts Journal, the cursor starts in the Client Name field, so the Cheque Number field is last. We want the second field to be the Cheque Number. The **Move Fields Up** and **Down arrows** beside the list are used to change the order.

Click **Cheque Number**.

Click the **Move Fields down button** beside the Tabbing Order list. This will place Cheque Number after the Client Name.

Click **Address** in the Tabbing Order column. **Click Remove** to skip all the address field lines when you press *tab*.

Removing fields from the tabbing order does not remove them from the journal, just from the tabbing sequence.

Click **OK** to return to the form. You can now enter the receipt.

Click the **From field list arrow** to display the Client list:

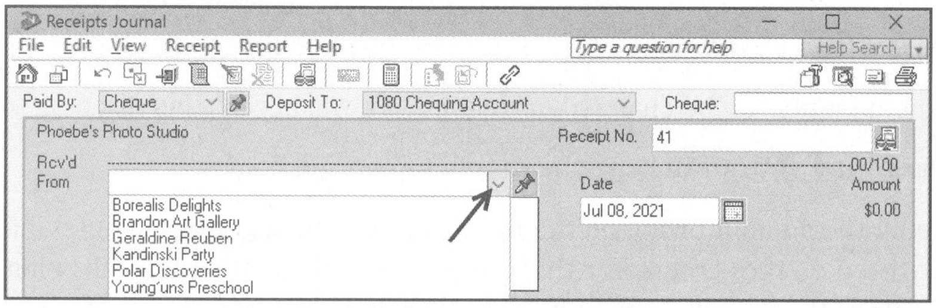

The From (Client) and Paid By fields have the Same Next Time tool also used in other journals.

PRO VERSION

In the Pro version, Customer replaces the term Client.

NOTES

You can customize the order further by making the Date field follow the Cheque Number and so on.

You can also choose to remove other fields that are not used, such as the Pushpins, Invoice Date and Original Amount. To access a skipped field after you remove it from the tabbing order, you can click the field.

Click **Geraldine Reuben** to choose this customer:

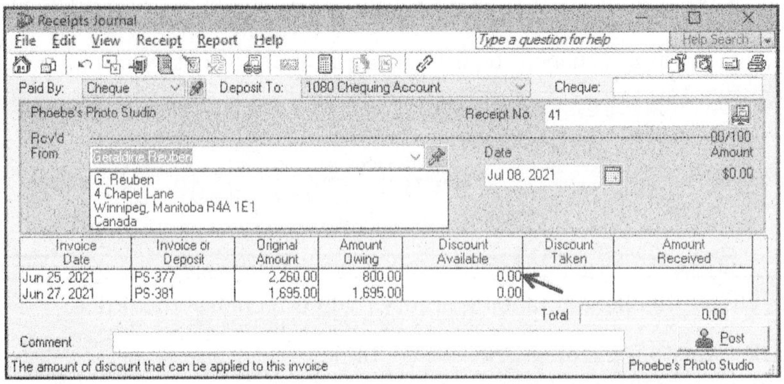

The customer's name and address have been added to your input form, together with all outstanding invoices for the customer. No discount is entered in the Discount Available fields because the session date is past the 10-day discount period.

As with payments to suppliers, you cannot enter account numbers in the Receipts Journal. You need to enter only the amount paid on the appropriate invoice line. The program automatically creates the journal entry using predefined linked accounts.

Phoebe's Photo Studio has a single bank account, so it is correctly selected in the **Deposit To** field. If you have chosen the wrong customer, display the list again and click the correct customer. If you have selected correctly,

NOTES
Sage 50 allows you to set up more than one bank account. When there is more than one bank account, choose the account from the Deposit To drop-down list.

Press (tab) to move to the **Cheque field**.

Type 302

The Receipt No. field records the receipt number, which increases automatically.

From the Lookup icon beside the Receipt No. field, you can look up previously posted receipts.

NOTES
You can use the Lookup button beside the Receipt No. field to review a receipt (refer to page 178).

We need to replace the session date with the date for this transaction.

NOTES
The year is added correctly in the Receipts Journal when you type the month and day.

Choose **July 2** from the Date field pop-up calendar. **Press** (tab) to move the cursor to the Invoice Date field. The discounts are now available:

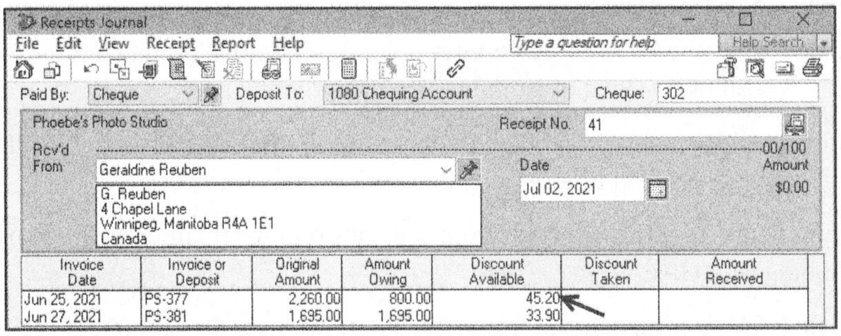

NOTES
For other company types, the Invoice Date column may be labelled Statement Date, Bill Date and so on.

The discount is 2 percent of the original amount, not the amount owing. Until the discount period has passed, the full discount remains available.

Press (tab) to advance to the Discount Taken field.

Discount amounts can be changed or deleted. We will accept this discount.

Press (tab) to advance to the Amount Received field.

NOTES
You can accept a highlighted amount or type an exact amount for a partial payment.

By default, the amount owing on the first invoice is highlighted. All outstanding invoices are listed on the screen. For this invoice, the full amount owing is being paid, so you can accept the default. Discounts are automatically subtracted from the amount owing.

Press (tab) to accept the discounted amount in the Amount Received field.

The cursor will advance to the Discount Taken field for the next invoice:

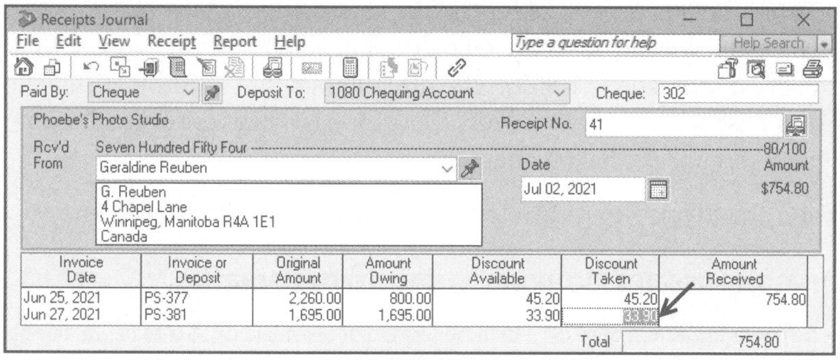

Because the payment for invoice PS-381 is only a partial payment, we need to remove the discount.

Press (del) to remove the discount for the second invoice.

Press (tab) to advance to the Amount Received field.

This time the full invoice amount is entered because the discount has been changed to zero. However, the full amount is not being paid, so we must edit the amount. To replace the highlighted default amount,

Type 1000

Press (tab) to enter the new amount and complete the invoice:

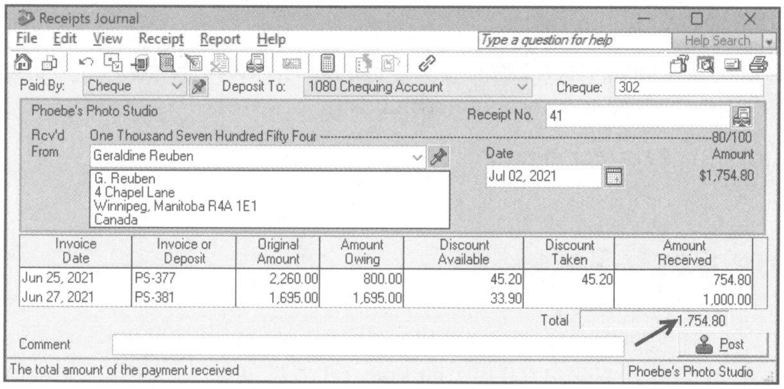

The upper cheque portion of the form has also been completed. In making Receipts Journal entries, you do not need to enter any accounts because Sage 50 chooses the linked bank and receivable accounts defined for the Receivables Ledger to create the journal entry.

You have made all the entries for this transaction, so you are ready to review before posting your transaction.

Reviewing the Receipts Journal Entry

Choose the **Report menu** and **click Display Receipts Journal Entry**:

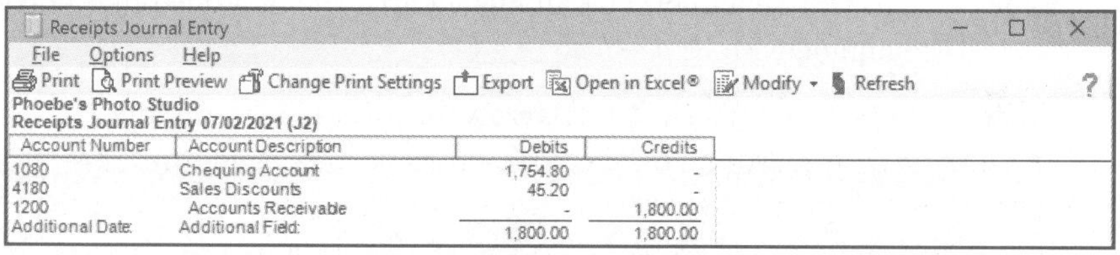

The related journal entry has been created for the Receipts Journal transaction. Sage 50 updates the General Ledger *Accounts Receivable* **control account** and *Chequing Account* because the Receivables and General ledgers are fully integrated.

WARNING!

When an invoice or discount amount is highlighted and it is not being included, press (del) to remove the amount from the total. Press (tab) to advance to the Amount Received field if you are entering a partial payment amount.

Refer to the screenshots for the Payment transaction on pages 132–133 for the error that results from not removing the second discount. Even though the cheque total appears correct on the screen, the posted entry will be incorrect.

NOTES

The direct link between sales and payments for a customer provides another reason for using the Receivables Ledger for sales entries instead of the General Ledger. In addition, discounts are calculated automatically when the dates are correct; you cannot select incorrect accounts, and total Accounts Receivable amounts are updated directly.

Furthermore, you are unlikely to reverse debit and credit amounts in error.

Phoebe's Photo Studio uses *Chequing Account* as its single default linked bank account for the Receivables Ledger as well as for the Payables Ledger. *Accounts Receivable* and the customer's balance owing are reduced by the full amount of the payment plus the amount of the discount taken ($1 800). The discount amount is automatically debited to the linked *Sales Discounts* account. *Sales Discounts* is a **contra-revenue account**. It has a debit balance and reduces total revenue.

Close the **display** to return to the Receipts Journal input screen.

CORRECTING THE RECEIPTS JOURNAL ENTRY BEFORE POSTING

Move to the field with the error. **Press** tab to move forward or shift and tab together to move back to a previous field. This will highlight the field contents. **Type** the **correct information** and **press** tab to enter it.

You can also use the mouse to **point** to a field and **drag through** the **incorrect information** to highlight it. **Type** the **correct information** and **press** tab to enter it.

If the customer is incorrect, **reselect** from the **Client** list by **clicking** the **Client list arrow**. **Click** the name of the correct **client**. To confirm that you want to discard the current transaction, **click Yes** to display the outstanding invoices for the correct customer. **Type** the **correct** receipt **information**.

You can also discard the entry and begin again. **Click** ☒ or **Undo** and then **click Yes** to confirm.

Posting

NOTES

You can print and preview receipts by clicking the Print or Preview icon, respectively. The preview includes the cheque and two copies of the invoice related to this payment, as well as the discount applied.

If you need to check or change your print settings, begin printing from the File menu in the journal.

When you are certain that you have entered all the information correctly, you must post the transaction to save it.

Click the **Post button** Post or **choose** the **Receipt menu** and **click Post** to save your transaction. **Click OK**.

Close the **Receipts Journal**.

Entering Cash Sales

For the next sale, the customer made an immediate payment by cheque. We use the term "cash sale" for all sales when immediate payment is made by cash or cheque.

This sale is to a customer that usually settles the account later, however, in this case they chose to pay by cheque and take the discount immediately.

✓ 3

Cash Sales Invoice #PS-392 **Dated July 3/21**

To Kandinski Party, $1 800 plus $90 GST and $144 PST for family portrait photo package before wedding. Terms: 2 percent discount ($40.68) with cash received on completion of work. Received cheque #569 for $1 993.32 in full payment.

PRO VERSION

Click the Sales Invoices icon Sales Invoices to open the Sales Journal.

Click the **Client Invoices icon** Client Invoices to open the Revenues Journal — the invoice number has been updated to 392.

Type K to choose and enter Kandinski Party, the first customer entry beginning with K.

NOTES

Kandinski's name is still highlighted after you type K, in case you need to choose a different name by typing other letters.

Pre-authorized debits (PAD) are covered in Chapter 13.

Click the **Payment Method list arrow** for the payment options:

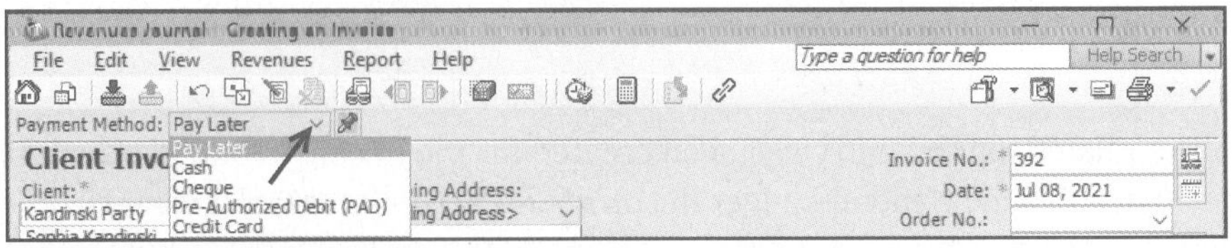

Pay Later, Cash, Cheque, Pre-Authorized Debit and Credit Card are the available payment methods. The customer's default payment method — Pay Later — is not correct for this invoice, and we can choose from the drop-down list.

Click **Cheque** as the method of payment to modify the invoice screen:

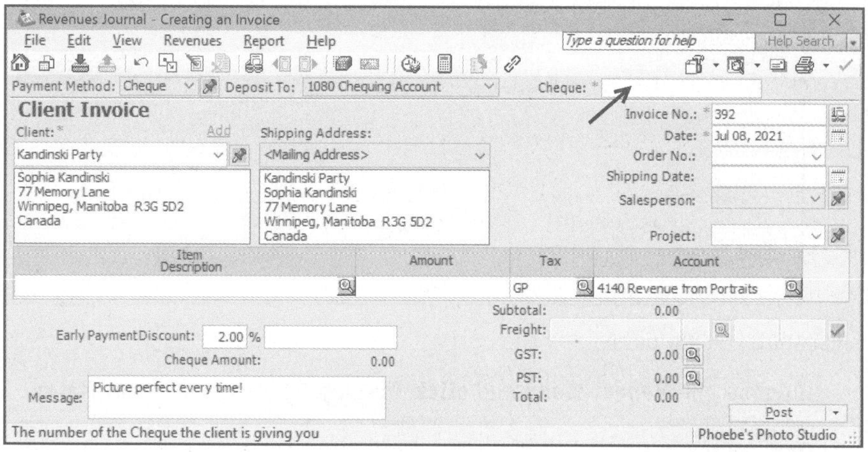

When you choose Cheque as the method of payment, a cheque number field is added in the upper right-hand corner of the invoice so that you can add the customer's cheque number. This is a required field in the Revenues Journal. The Deposit To bank account field is also added. In the payment terms section, the Net Days field has been removed and a Cheque Amount field has been added.

Press *tab* **repeatedly** to skip the Same tool and advance to the Cheque number field.

Type 569

Enter **July 3** in the Date field as the transaction date.

Enter a **description**. **Press** *tab* to advance to the Amount field.

Type 1800

Double-click the **Account field**.

The cheque amount below the terms has been updated to include the discount applied for the immediate payment, based on the customer's terms.

Click **Suggested Accounts** below the account list to modify the list:

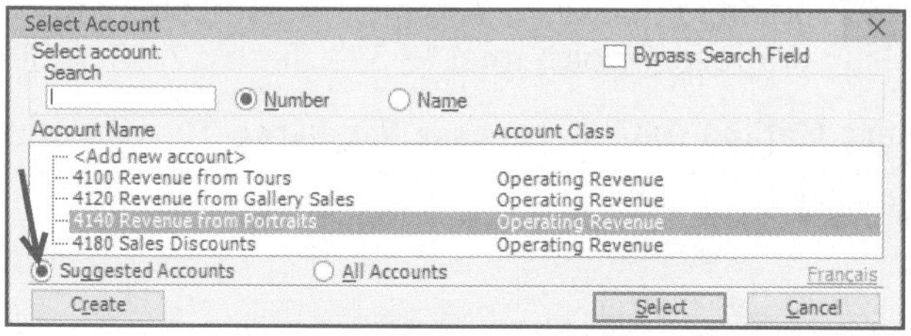

The list of suggested accounts now includes only revenue accounts because we are in the Revenues Journal. This shorter list makes it easier to select the correct account. For purchases, only expense accounts will be listed. You can switch back to the complete account list at any time by selecting **All Accounts**. When we close the journal, the Suggested Accounts button remains selected until we change the selection again.

In this case, however, the default account for the customer is correct and may still be selected.

Click **4140 Revenue from Portraits**. **Press** *enter*.

NOTES

When you choose Cash or Credit Card as the payment method, the Cheque No. field is not included. For Pre-Authorized Debits, the Cheque No. field becomes the PAD No. field.

NOTES

When you open the Purchases Journal, only the expense accounts will be listed. You will need to choose All Accounts to include asset accounts in the list.

Click the **Message field. Type** `Thank you` to complete the sales entry:

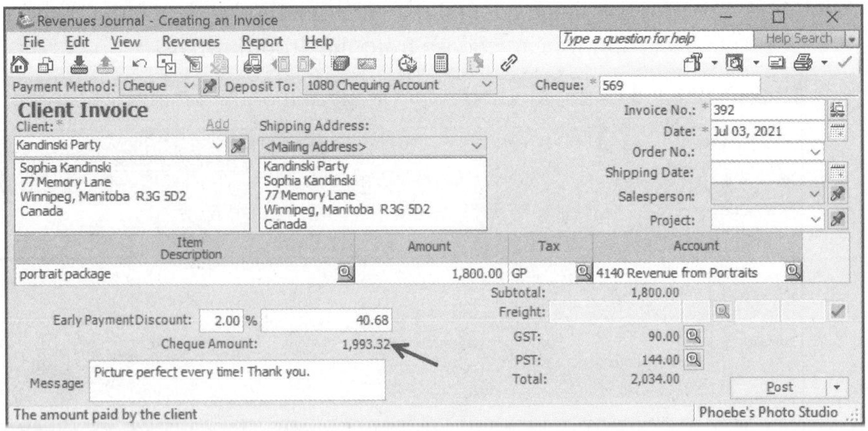

As usual, you should review the entry.

Choose the **Report menu** and **click Display Revenues Journal Entry**:

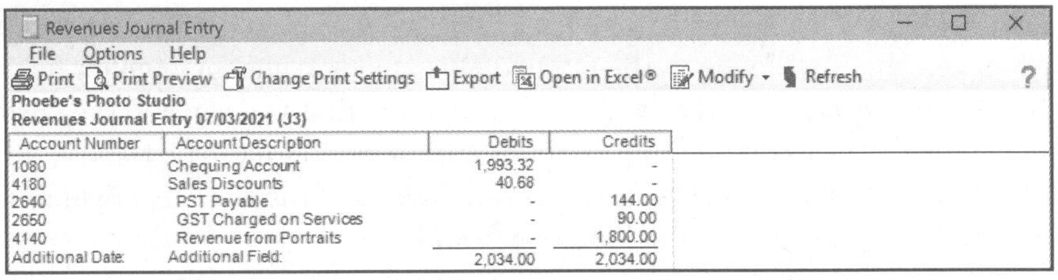

Chequing Account is debited automatically instead of *Accounts Receivable* because we selected Cheque as the method of payment.

Close the **display** when you have finished. **Make corrections** if necessary.

Click Post to save the entry. **Click OK**. Leave the journal open.

Adding a New Client

The next sale is to a new customer who should be added to your files. We will add the customer directly from the Revenues Journal.

NOTES
Marci Litman
✓ (contact Marci)
36 Runway Alley, Apt. 201
Oakbank, MB R0E 1J0
Tel: (204) 538-2436
Mobile: (204) 638-2436
E-mail: marci@hotmail.com
Web: marci.com
Terms: 2/10, n/30
Default invoice payment method: Pay Later
Revenue account: 4140
Tax code: GP
Credit limit: $3 000

✓ 4

Sales Invoice #PS-393 **Dated July 3/21**

To Marci Litman (use Full Add for the new customer), $2 100 plus $105 GST and $168 PST for modelling portfolio. Invoice total $2 373. Terms: 2/10, n/30.

Click the **Payment Method field** and **choose Pay Later**. The date is correct.

Click the **Client field**.

Type `Marci Litman`

Press *tab* to display the notice that you have typed a name that is not on the list. This notice provides the option to add a ledger record:

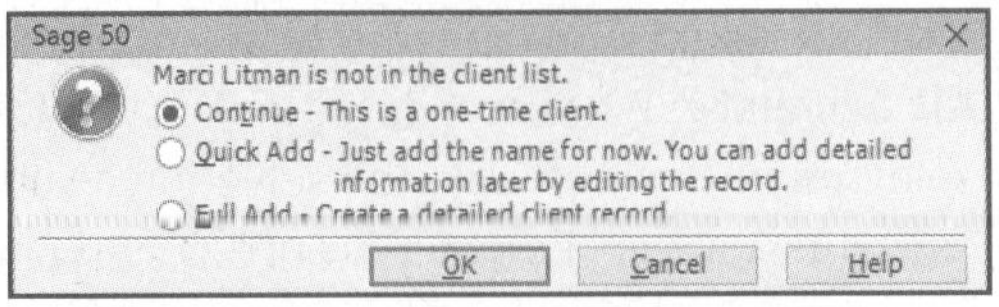

NOTES
Choosing Quick Add will return you to the journal with the name entered. A ledger record with the name and default settings is created.

The options are the same as for new suppliers. If you typed an incorrect name, click **Cancel** to return to the journal and start again. If you typed the name correctly, you can choose to add the customer's name only — **Quick Add** — or to add a full customer record with the **Full Add** option. If you need to change any defaults, you must choose Full Add. You can still skip customer fields that you do not need. The remaining option, **Continue**, will add the customer's name to the journal entry but will not create a ledger record for the customer or add the customer to the other Receivables Ledger reports.

Click **Full Add**.

Click **OK** to open the customer's Address information screen:

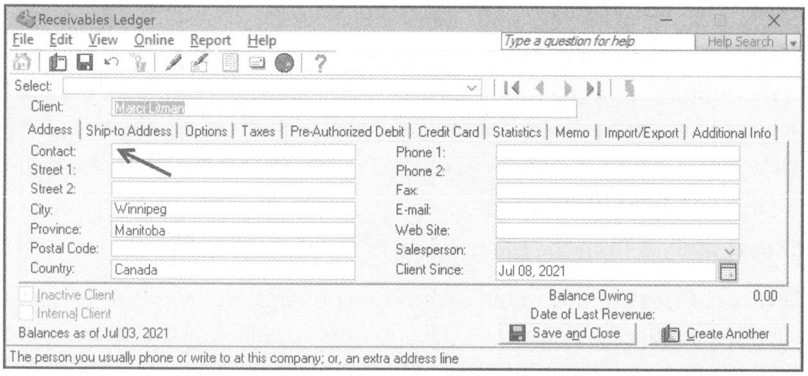

Clicking Add above the Client field in the journal opens this ledger form directly from the journal at the Address tab screen.

PRO VERSION
Remember that the term Customer replaces Client. The Internal Client option and the Refresh tool do not apply to the Pro version, so they will be omitted from the Pro version screens.

You are ready to enter your new customer. The Client field is completed with the new name highlighted for editing if necessary. The Client name is the only **required field** for new customer records. Because it is already entered, the asterisk * reminder symbol for required fields has been removed and the Save tool icon is available (not dimmed).

The field we need next is the Contact field. Enter the name of the individual Phoebe's Photo Studio normally deals with.

Click the **Contact field** or **press** *tab*.

Type `Marci`

Press *tab* to move the cursor to the Street 1 field.

Type `36 Runway Alley` **Press** *tab*.

Type `Apt. 201` **Press** *tab* to move to and select the City field.

The city, province and country in which Phoebe's Photo Studio is located have been entered by default from the Address Settings. The province is correct, but you must change the city.

Type `Oakbank`

Click the **Postal Code field**.

You do not need to use capital letters or to leave a space within Canadian postal codes. The program will make these adjustments automatically.

Type `r0e1j0`

Click the **Phone 1 field**. The postal code format is corrected automatically.

You do not need to add spaces, dashes or brackets for telephone numbers. Telephone and fax numbers may be entered with or without the area code.

Type `2045382436` **Press** *tab*. Enter the mobile number as Phone 2.

Type `2046382436` **Press** *tab* to move to the Fax field.

Press *tab* to skip the fax field and advance to the E-mail field.

The format for the telephone numbers has also been corrected automatically.

E-mail and Web addresses are typed exactly as you would type them in your regular Internet and e-mail programs. You can also add these details later when you actually want to use them. When you click the Web or E-mail tools, you will be prompted to enter the addresses if they are not part of the customer's record already.

Type `marci@hotmail.com` **Press** *tab*.

Type `marci.com`

When salespersons are set up, you can choose the name of the regular sales contact person for a customer from the drop-down list in the **Salesperson** field. Phoebe's Photo Studio does not have salespersons set up. Salespersons are covered in Chapter 9.

Litman is making her first purchase on July 3, but the session date is entered as the default date in the **Client Since** field.

Choose **July 3** from the Client Since field calendar icon.

PRO VERSION
The Pro version does not have an Internal Client option.

NOTES
Inactive clients may be included in or omitted from reports.

The **Internal Client** option applies when one department supplies services to another and charges for these services. The option is available when time and billing is used. If the customer no longer buys from the company, but you still want to keep the record on file, mark the customer as **Inactive**. The **Balance Owing** and **Date Of Last Sale** will be entered automatically by the program based on the customer's transactions.

Click the **Ship-To Address tab**.

Click the **Address Name list arrow** to list the predefined names:

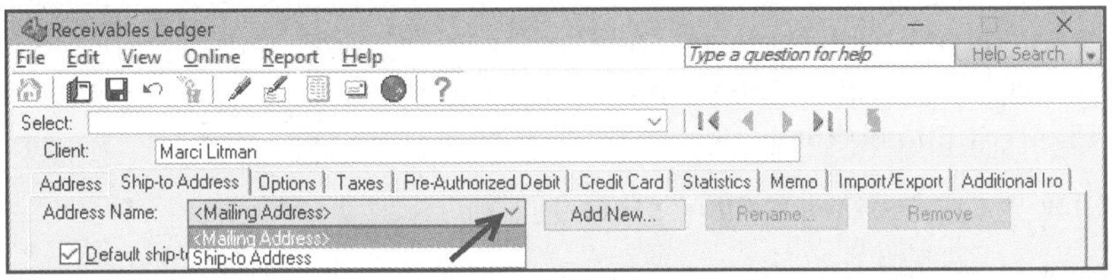

PRO VERSION
The Pro version allows only one additional address – the shipping address. You cannot edit the name of this second address. If the mailing address is different from the shipping address, click the Same As Mailing Address check box to remove the ✓ and then enter or edit the address fields.

You can enter multiple customer addresses and apply your own labels for these addresses. For example, you may have separate summer and winter addresses for residential customers or different store locations for wholesale customers. The billing address may be different from the location where a service is provided or products are delivered. The Shipping Address field in the journal has a list arrow for selecting one of the addresses you have defined. The mailing address is provided as the default ship-to address, as indicated by the ✓ for Default Ship-To Address and its entry in the Address Name field. The address information is dimmed because you cannot remove the mailing address on this screen. You can enter complete address and contact information for the shipping address, add new address labels and information for them, edit the labels and remove address names and labels that are not needed.

Click **Ship-To Address** (or another address name) in the drop-down list.

PRO VERSION
The Shipping Address fields are available immediately. You cannot remove these fields.

This will remove ✓ for the Default Ship-To Address and open the address fields for editing:

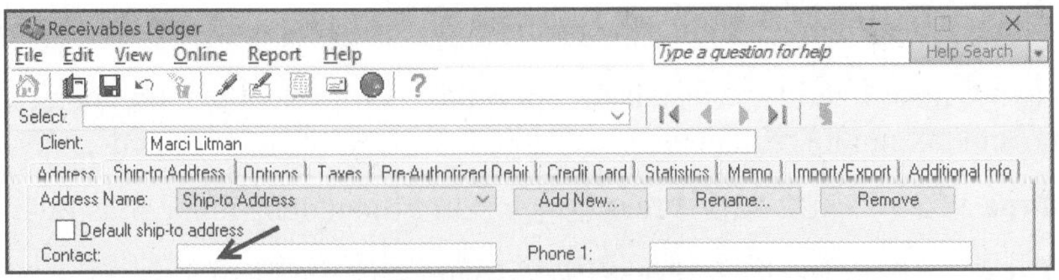

All the fields are now open for editing. You can make any address the Default Ship-To Address by clicking the check box when this label's information is displayed.

The shipping address is the same as the mailing address for this customer, so we can remove the ship-to address name for this customer.

Click **Remove** — Sage 50 requests confirmation:

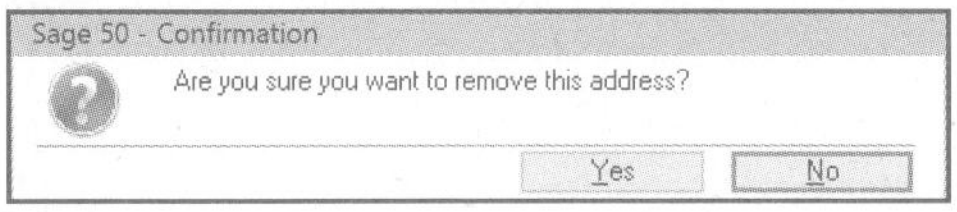

Click **Yes** to confirm the removal.

Click **Add New** to open the name field to add a new address:

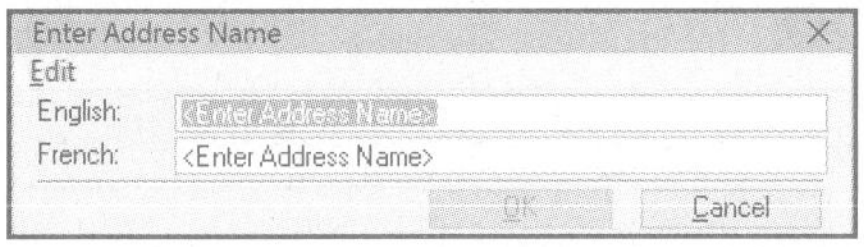

Type a new name and then click OK to include the new name in the Address Name field drop-down list. Then you can select it to add the address details.

NOTES
You can add back an address name that you removed by clicking Add New and re-entering its name.

NOTES
When you define a new address, it applies only to the customer whose record is open.

Click **Cancel** to return to the Ship-To Address tab screen.

Click the **Options tab**:

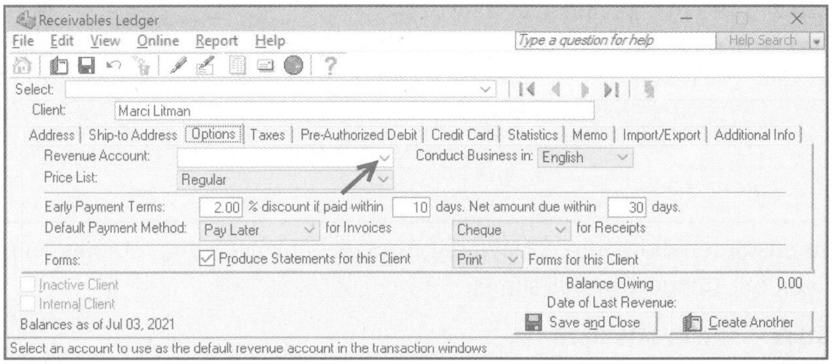

The first option is to add a default revenue account for the customer.

Click the **Revenue Account list arrow**.

Click **4140**.

NOTES
You can select any postable account as the default revenue account.
The customer's default account will appear in the journal and override the default linked revenue account.

The Options tab screen contains the details of the payment terms. The default terms are entered from the ledger settings. The **Price List** — Regular, Preferred or Web Price — refers to the prices customers pay for inventory items and will be introduced in Chapter 10. For Phoebe's Photo Studio, all customers pay Regular prices. You can select French or English as the customer's preferred **language for conducting business**. Sales invoices and other forms you prepare for customers will be printed in the language you select here. Your own program screens will not change.

The default company payment terms are correct for Marci Litman.

You can also choose the default payment methods the customer uses for invoices and for paying invoices (receipts) as you can for suppliers by selecting from the respective drop down lists:

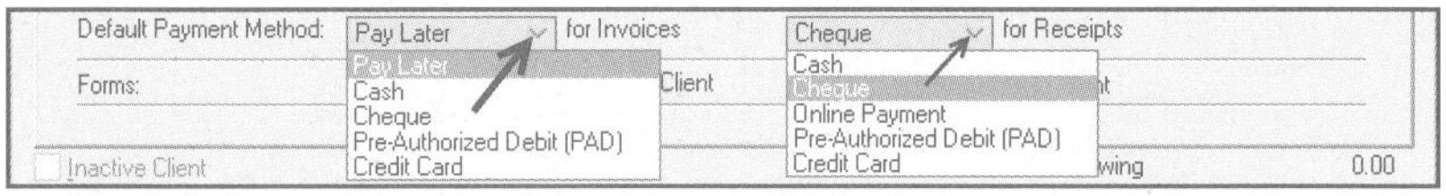

NOTES
If any customers make online payments to settle their accounts, you must enter the linked account to which the fees for this service are charged, as well as the Receivables account to which the payments are deposited.
Pre-authorized debits are covered in Chapter 13.

For Litman, the default selections, Pay Later and Cheque, are correct.

You can also **Produce Statements For This Client**, and you may print or e-mail invoices and quotes — selecting the option from the drop-down list. From the journal, you can change the print/e-mail selection. You should use the correct forms, but you can also print statements on ordinary printer paper.

You can change the Options tab settings at any time.

Click the **Taxes tab**:

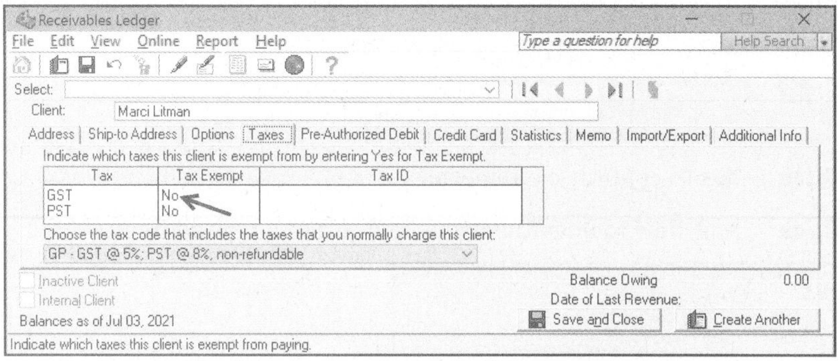

The customer is correctly described as **not Tax Exempt** for PST and GST, allowing accurate tax calculations for sales transactions to be included in tax reports. The default tax code taken from the ledger settings is also correct.

Click **GP - GST @ 5%; PST @ 8%, non-refundable** to list the codes available. Do not change the tax code for this customer.

Click the **Pre-Authorized Debit tab**:

If your customer allows direct payment from its bank account, you must enter the bank account information on this screen.

Click the **Credit Card tab**:

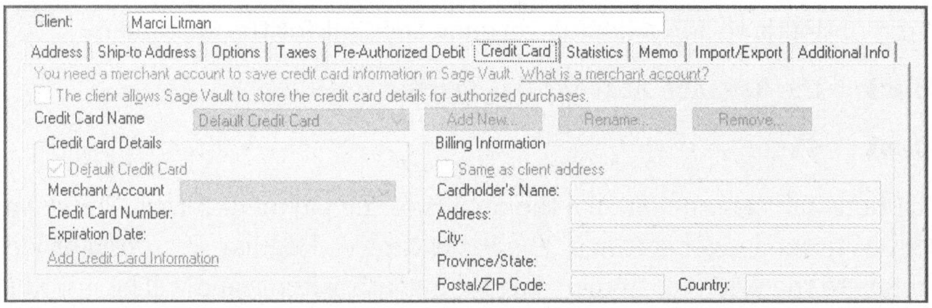

If you have a merchant credit card account and your customer allows automatic credit card payments, you must enter the information on this screen.

Click the **Statistics tab** to open the next screen we need:

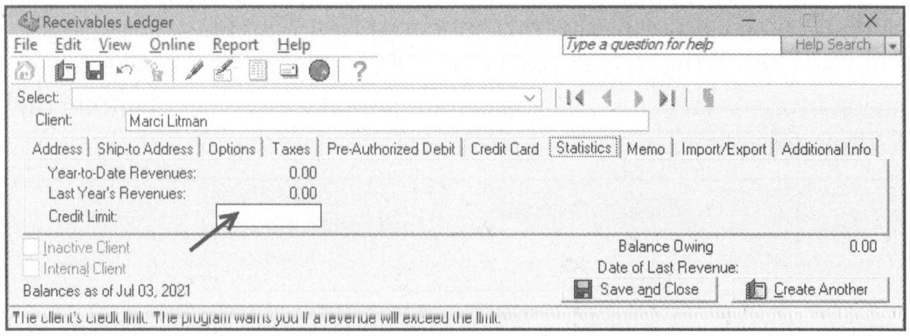

The Statistics screen has a summary of the sales to the customer for the current year and the previous year. These fields are updated from sales transactions.

WARNING!
Taxes will be added in the Revenues Journal only if you choose No as the Tax Exempt option in the customer's ledger record, even if you select the correct tax code in the journal.

NOTES
You must have a signed agreement from your customer allowing the pre-authorized debit. Then click the check box on this tab screen and enter the customer's banking details. Usually the customer provides a void cheque for the bank account details.

Pre-authorized debits are covered in Chapter 13.

NOTES
Credit card processing is not set up for Phoebe's Photo Studio, so all the fields are dimmed.

You must set up the data file for credit card processing and have a merchant account with Paya. You must also have a signed agreement from your customer allowing the pre-authorized credit card payments. Then click the check box on this tab screen and enter the customer's details. The credit card number is on a separate screen (Add Credit Card Information) that has a secured Internet connection to Sage Vault.

Credit card processing is covered in Chapter 13.

PRO VERSION
The term Sales replaces Revenues.

In the **Credit Limit** field, you can enter the customer's credit limit to help minimize bad debts. When a customer exceeds the credit limit, the program will provide a warning message before you can post the sale:

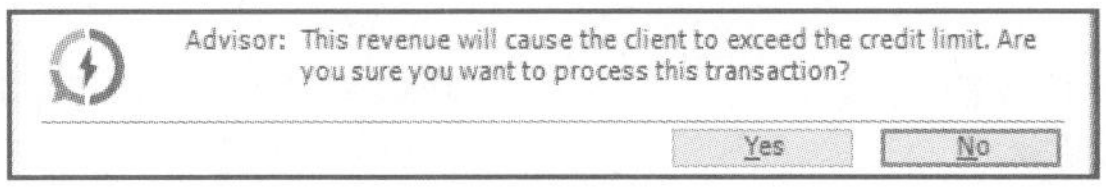

Advisor: This revenue will cause the client to exceed the credit limit. Are you sure you want to process this transaction?
Yes
No

You can click Yes to accept the over-the-limit sale, or No to return to the invoice and ask for a deposit to avoid exceeding the credit limit. Customers who have previously defaulted on making their payments can be placed on a cash-only basis by setting their credit limits to zero. Phoebe's Photo Studio is analyzing customer payment trends at present and will set Litman's limit at $3 000 on a trial basis.

Click the **Credit Limit field** to position the cursor and **type** 3000

> **NOTES**
> Sage 50 adds the total amount from the current sale to the balance owing to assess whether the customer has exceeded the credit limit.

> **NOTES**
> Customers should be notified of credit policy changes.

Saving a New Customer Account

The remaining tab screens are not required. They serve the same purpose as they do for suppliers. When you are certain that all the information is correct, you must save the newly created customer account and add it to the current list.

Click **Save And Close** [Save and Close] to save the new customer information.

You will return to the journal with the customer's default tax code, revenue account, terms and payment method. Any of these fields can be edited for an individual invoice.

Enter the **sale** (page 172) for Litman by following the procedures outlined earlier.

Review the **journal entry**. **Close** the **display** and **make corrections**.

Click [Post]. **Click OK** and then **close** the **Revenues Journal**.

Reversing a Receipt (NSF Cheques)

When a cheque is returned by the bank as NSF, you need to record the fact that the invoice is still outstanding. You can do this in the Receipts Journal by reversing the cheque.

✓ 5 **Bank Debit Memo #14321** **Dated July 4/21**

From Red River Credit Union, cheque #302 for $1 754.80 from Geraldine Reuben has been returned because of non-sufficient funds. Reverse the payment and notify the customer of the outstanding charges.

Click the **Receipts icon** [Receipts] **shortcuts list arrow**:

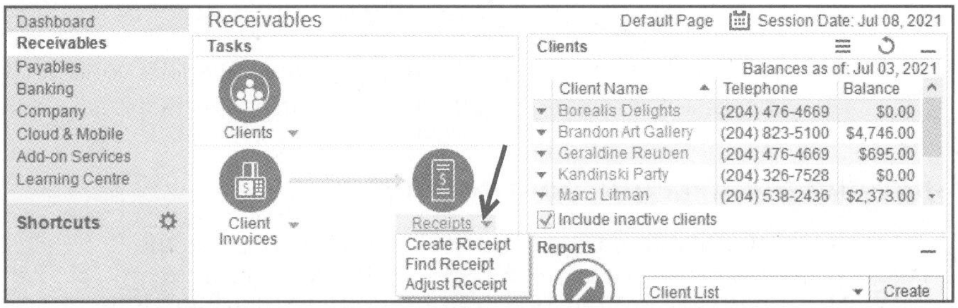

Click **Adjust Receipt** or **click** **Find Receipt**.

> **NOTES**
> The Home window Clients list pane has the balances as at July 3, the latest transaction date, and not at the session date. This selection is a user preference.

Or, with the Receipts Journal open,

Click the **Adjust Receipt tool**, **press** ctrl + **A**, or **choose** the **Receipt menu** and **click Adjust Receipt**.

Or, **click** the **Lookup tool**, **press** ctrl + **L**, or **choose** the **Receipt menu** and **click Look Up Receipt**.

The familiar Search screen opens with Receipts as the search area:

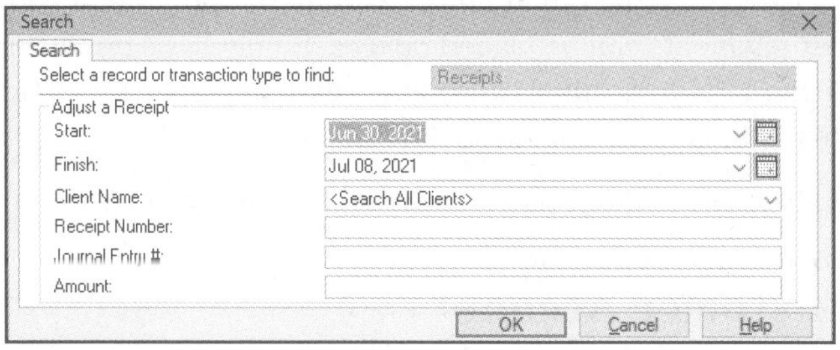

Click **OK** to list all the receipts we have entered:

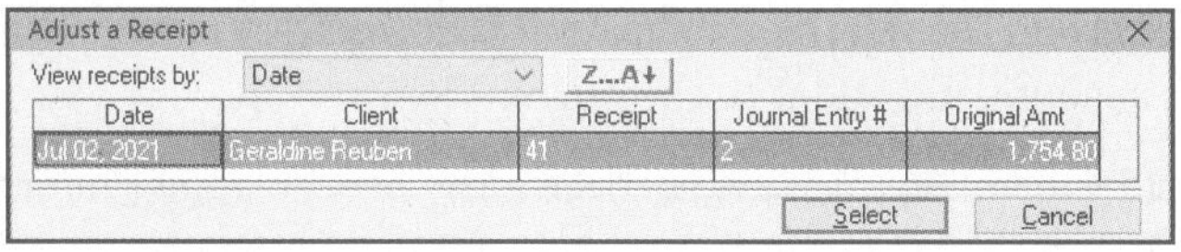

The single cheque we entered is selected — the one from Geraldine Reuben.

Press enter or **click Select** to open the cheque we entered:

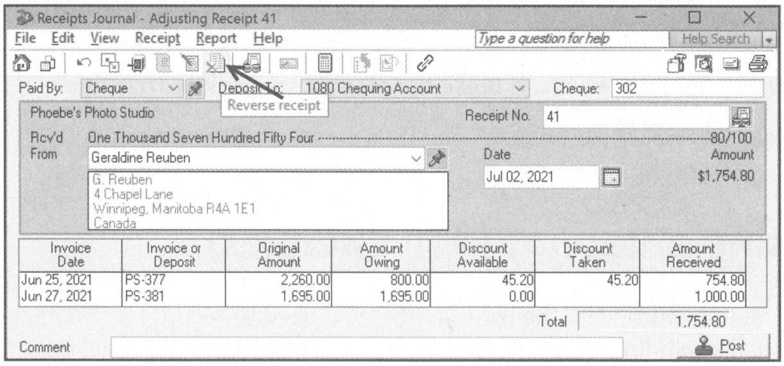

At this stage you can adjust the cheque by editing incorrectly entered information, just as you can edit a purchase invoice or payment cheque.

We need to reverse the cheque because it has been returned as NSF.

Click the **Reverse Receipt tool** or **choose** the **Receipt menu** and **click Reverse Receipt**. Sage 50 requires your confirmation to proceed:

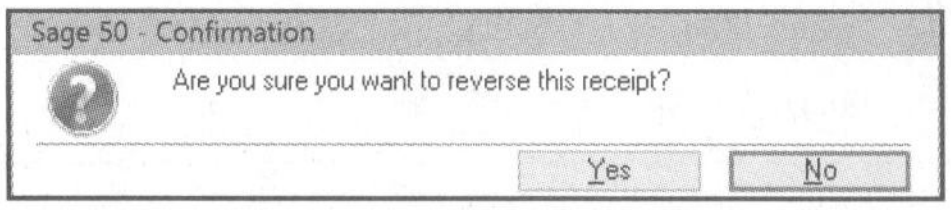

Click **Yes** to confirm the reversal. **Click OK** when Sage 50 confirms the successful reversal. A blank Receipts Journal form opens.

Displaying the Receipts Journal Report

We will review the Journal Report generated by reversing this receipt.

Click the **Home window tool** to return to the Home window.

Choose the **Reports menu**, then **choose Journal Entries** and **click Receipts** to open the report options window:

NOTES

The Lookup and Adjust tools both open the Search window. The Reverse tool and menu option are available from the journal windows provided by both.

From Lookup and Find Receipt, the search parameters will have Receipt Lookup as the heading and Select A Receipt in the window that lists the receipts.

NOTES

If you recorded a receipt incorrectly and do not need to reverse it, you can choose the Adjust Receipt tool to access the posted receipt and make the correction, just as you do for sales (page 184) or for payments (page 139).

NOTES

In Chapter 15, you will learn that you cannot reverse the receipt if the cheque is not deposited directly to the bank account when you enter the receipt (that is, the bank deposit is recorded later as a separate transaction). Instead, you must enter a negative receipt.

NOTES

If you started from the Lookup or Find Invoice option, the window title will be Receipt Lookup. Clicking the Adjust Receipt tool will open the fields for editing.

The first invoice line may or may not be highlighted or selected, depending on your starting point.

NOTES

If you change the customer when adjusting a receipt, the program will reverse the original receipt when you click Yes to confirm this action.

CLASSIC VIEW

From the Home window, right-click the Receipts icon. Click the Select A Report tool to open the Receipts Journal report options.

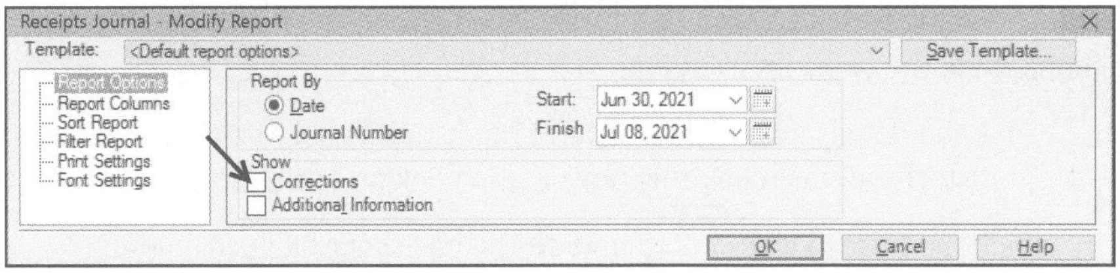

By default, corrections are not included in the report — we must include them in order to add adjusting and reversing entries. The remaining defaults are correct.

Click **Corrections** under the Show heading. **Click OK**:

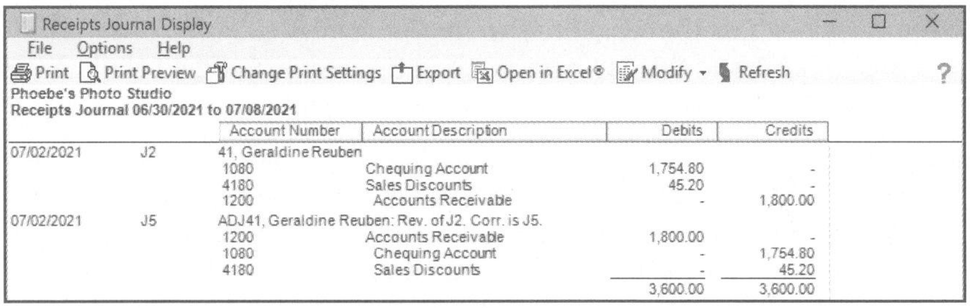

The report confirms that the two entries cancel each other — all amounts were reversed, including the discount. The original debits to *Chequing Account* and *Sales Discounts* were entered as credits in the reversing entry, and the credit to *Accounts Receivable* was changed to a debit. Sage 50 created the reversing entry automatically when we reversed the receipt, adding ADJ to the receipt number to link the two transactions.

When you adjust a receipt and post the corrected entry, Sage 50 will create the intermediate reversing entry automatically. Three entries result — the original incorrect one, the reversing entry and the final corrected version, just as they do when you make adjustments in the General, Purchases and Payments journals. By including Corrections in the Journal Reports, you can provide the complete audit trail.

Close the **display** when you have finished.

Restore the **Receipts Journal**.

Choose **Geraldine Reuben** from the Client list.

Both invoices have been fully restored. When the replacement payment is received, you can enter it in the usual way.

Close the **Receipts Journal** without entering a payment.

Editing Client Information

You can change customer information and you can change the way the Home window displays Clients pane details, just as you can modify the Suppliers pane.

Clicking the details icon at the top of the Clients pane lists the items that can be removed from this pane — the telephone number and balance owing:

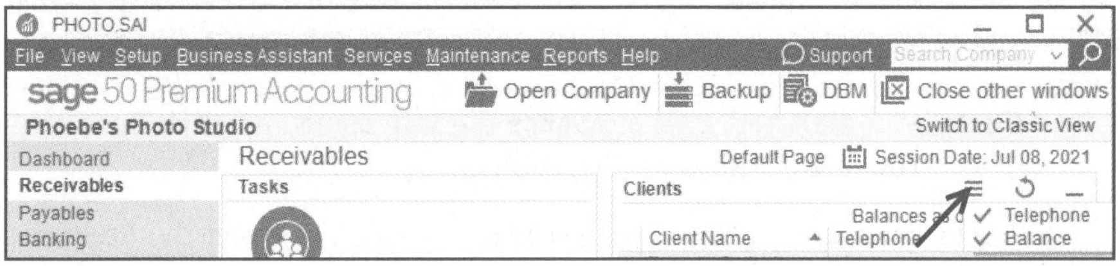

NOTES

You can also click the Report Centre icon. Then click Receivables, Receipts Journal Entries and Modify This Report to open the report options.

WARNING!

If you display the Journal Report from the Home window Reports pane list of reports, you will use the default settings, which do not show corrections. The message will state that there is no data to report because there are no other Receipts Journal entries.

NOTES

To restore the Receipts Journal, point to the Sage 50 icon or name on the Windows task bar. You should have pop-ups for both the Home window and the Receipts Journal. Click the Receipts Journal pop-up. (Refer to the screenshot on page 14.)

The ✓ indicates that information is displayed. When the computer is in a public area, you should hide the extra information.

Click the details icon to expand the list and click the detail you want to hide. To restore a detail, click this button and click an option to add the ✓.

Click the refresh icon to update the customer balance amounts.

Click the hide icon to remove the entire customer list and restore to bring back the list.

✓ 6

Memo #1 **Dated July 5/21**

From Owner: Edit the ledger record for Geraldine Reuben to change the payment terms to net 1 and the payment method to cheque. Certified cheques will be requested in the future. Set her credit limit to zero.

Edit the customer names as well — the last name should be first to keep the records in correct alphabetic order. Edit the records for Geraldine Reuben, Marci Litman and Borealis Delights. Change these customer names to Reuben, Geraldine; Litman, Marci; and Borealis Mysteries.

NOTES
From the Clients list pane shortcuts you can also enter transactions for the client or view that client's Aged Receivables Report.

PRO VERSION
pro
Click the Customers icon shortcuts list arrow.
Click the Customers icon to open the Customers window.

Most fields in the customer record can be changed at any time. Only the current balance owing, which is updated from sales and payment transactions, cannot be changed.

Click the **Clients icon shortcuts list arrow**:

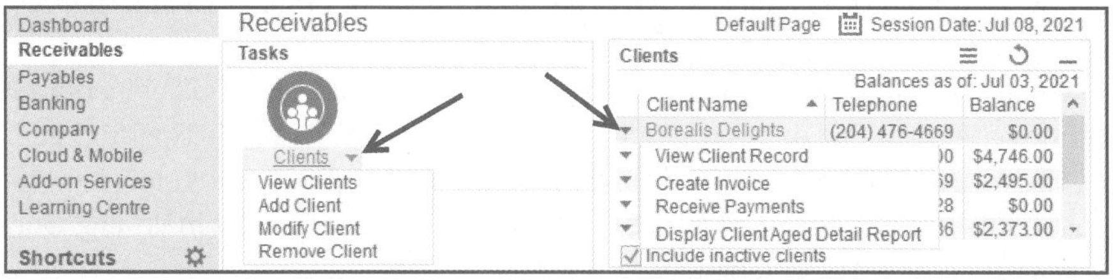

From the Clients shortcuts list, you can choose Modify Client. When the Search screen opens, you can select the customer.

You can click the customer's name in the right-hand Clients pane, or you can click the list arrow beside the customer's name and click View Client Record to open a record for a customer directly.

We will use yet another option — to work from the Clients window.

Click the **Clients icon** to open the Clients window:

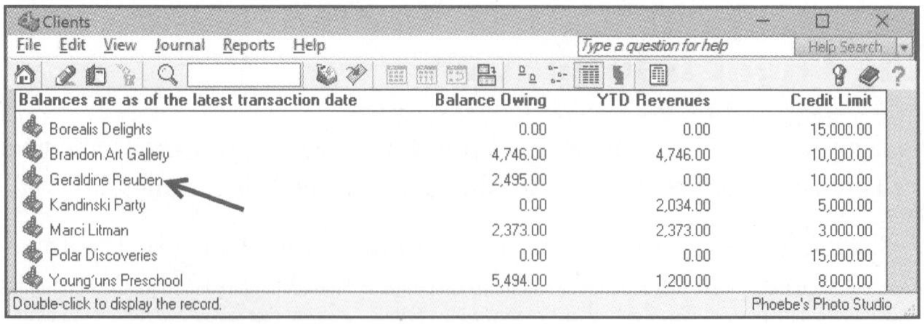
Clients
File Edit View Journal Reports Help
Type a question for help
Help Search
Balances are as of the latest transaction date
Balance Owing
YTD Revenues
Credit Limit
Borealis Delights 0.00 0.00 15,000.00
Brandon Art Gallery 4,746.00 4,746.00 10,000.00
Geraldine Reuben 2,495.00 0.00 10,000.00
Kandinski Party 0.00 2,034.00 5,000.00
Marci Litman 2,373.00 2,373.00 3,000.00
Polar Discoveries 0.00 0.00 15,000.00
Young'uns Preschool 5,494.00 1,200.00 8,000.00
Double-click to display the record.
Phoebe's Photo Studio

Click **Geraldine Reuben** to select her.

Click the **Edit tool** or **choose** the **File menu** and **click** **Open** or **double-click** **Geraldine Reuben**.

The Receivables Ledger record for Geraldine Reuben opens at the Address screen. First, we need to modify the Terms, which are located on the Options tab.

Click the **Options tab** to access the payment terms information:

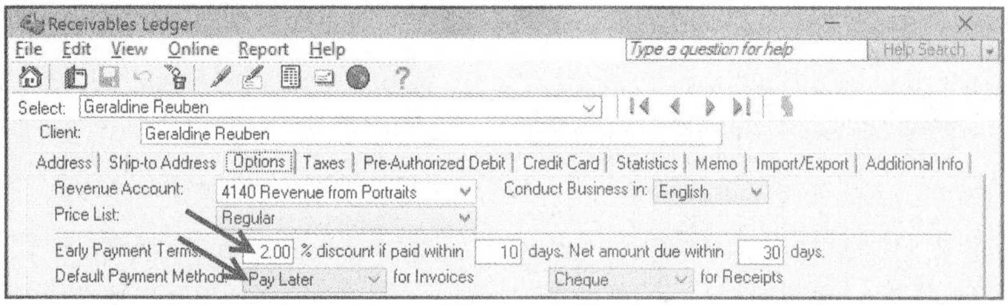

Click **2.00** in the % Discount field of the Early Payment Terms section.

Press del to remove the entry. **Press** tab to advance to the Days field.

Press del. **Press** tab to advance to the Net Days field. **Type** 1

Choose **Cheque** from the drop-down list as the Default Payment Method for Invoices and Receipts.

Click the **Statistics tab**:

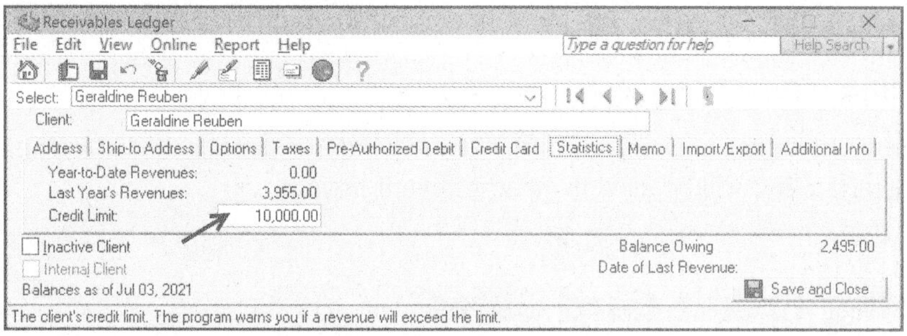

Click the **Credit Limit field** and **type** 0

To modify other customer records, click Next or Previous to move to a different record or choose the customer you need from the Select drop-down list. Your previous tab screen will remain selected.

Close the **Receivables Ledger** and **close** the **Clients window**.

NOTES
Typing zero (0) in the Net Days field will leave the field blank in the ledger and the journal.

Editing Records from the Setup Guide

Some customer information can be edited for all customers from a single location — the Setup Guide, just as we edited account information in Chapter 4.

Click the **Home window Setup menu** and **click** **Setup Guide**:

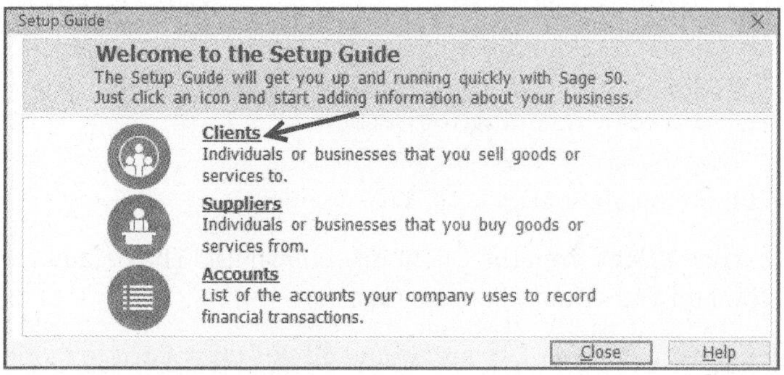

Information for clients, suppliers, accounts and employees (when the Payroll module is used) can be accessed from this guide.

PRO VERSION
You will click Customers in the Setup Guide window – the term Customers will replace the term Clients in all Setup Guide windows.

> **NOTES**
> The Setup Guide window includes the balance owing for each customer, but you cannot edit these amounts. Scroll to the right or make the window wider to add this column.

> **NOTES**
> Address tab details may also be modified for suppliers and employees in the Setup Guide.
> You must open the record to modify other record details – by double-clicking the name in the Setup Guide window, or from the Home window, as we described in the previous section.

> **NOTES**
> When you open the Setup Guide Client list again, the edited names will be in the correct alphabetic order.

Click **Clients**:

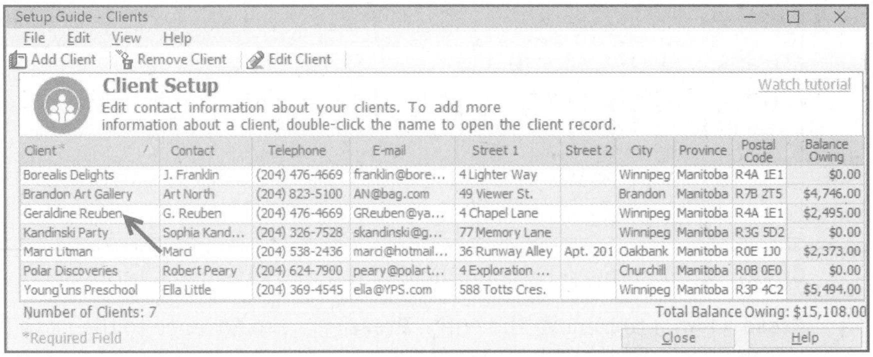

Client*	Contact	Telephone	E-mail	Street 1	Street 2	City	Province	Postal Code	Balance Owing
Borealis Delights	J. Franklin	(204) 476-4669	franklin@bore...	4 Lighter Way		Winnipeg	Manitoba	R4A 1E1	$0.00
Brandon Art Gallery	Art North	(204) 823-5100	AN@bag.com	49 Viewer St.		Brandon	Manitoba	R7B 2T5	$4,746.00
Geraldine Reuben	G. Reuben	(204) 476-4669	GReuben@ya...	4 Chapel Lane		Winnipeg	Manitoba	R4A 1E1	$2,495.00
Kandinski Party	Sophia Kand...	(204) 326-7528	skandinski@g...	77 Memory Lane		Winnipeg	Manitoba	R3G 5D2	$0.00
Marci Litman	Marci	(204) 538-2436	marci@hotmail...	36 Runway Alley	Apt. 201	Oakbank	Manitoba	R0E 1J0	$2,373.00
Polar Discoveries	Robert Peary	(204) 624-7900	peary@polart...	4 Exploration ...		Churchill	Manitoba	R0B 0E0	$0.00
Young'uns Preschool	Ella Little	(204) 369-4545	ella@YPS.com	588 Totts Cres.		Winnipeg	Manitoba	R3P 4C2	$5,494.00

Only information on the Address tab screens for the clients may be edited here. If you need to change other details, you can open the record by double-clicking a name.

Click **Geraldine Reuben** to highlight her name.

Type `Reuben, Geraldine`

Change the **names** for **Litman** and **Borealis Delights** in the same way.

Click **Close** and **click Close** again to return to the Home window.

The revised names now appear in the Home window Clients pane list in the correct alphabetic order and will be used in all other client listings.

Entering Credit Card Sales

> **NOTES**
> The transaction fee varies from one card company to another, as well as from one retail customer to another, and usually ranges from 2 to 4 percent. Stores that have a larger volume of credit card sales usually pay lower transaction fees.

Most businesses accept credit cards from customers in lieu of cash and cheques. Customers expect this convenience, and although businesses benefit by avoiding NSF cheques, they do incur a cost for this service. Credit card companies charge the business a transaction fee: a percentage of each sale is withheld by the card company.

Credit card sales are entered like other sales, by selecting the correct payment method and then entering the invoice details.

> **NOTES**
> When you recall the entry, you can edit amounts and, if necessary, the accounts. Refer to page 187.

✓ 7

Credit Card Sales Invoice #PS-394 **Dated July 5/21**

Sales Summary
To various one-time customers

Revenue from Passport Photos (new account)	$ 240.00
Revenue from Portraits	1 600.00
GST charged	92.00
PST charged	147.20
Total deposited to credit card bank account	$2 079.20

Create new Group account: 4160 Revenue from Passport Photos
Store the sale as a weekly recurring transaction.

> **PRO VERSION**
> pro Click the Sales Invoices icon  to open the Sales Journal. Then choose One-Time Customer.

> **NOTES**
> Close the message about credit card processing if it opens. Processing credit card payments is covered in Chapter 13.

Click the **Client Invoices icon** .

Choose **One-Time Client** from the Client drop-down list. The default Payment Method for One-Time Clients is Cash.

Click the **Payment Method list arrow** and **click Credit Card** to modify the invoice.

As for cash sales, the Net Days field for early payment discounts is removed and a Credit Card Amount field is added. There is no cheque number field for credit cards.

Type `Sales Summary` in the Address text box.

Enter **July 5** as the transaction date.

Click the **Item Description field** and **type** the **description** for the first sale item.

Press tab and **type** 240

Press tab **twice** and **type** 4160 as the account. **Press** tab to start the Add An Account wizard. **Enter** the **account name** and finish adding the account.

Enter the **second invoice line details** for the portrait revenue work. **Change** the **default account**. This step will complete the invoice:

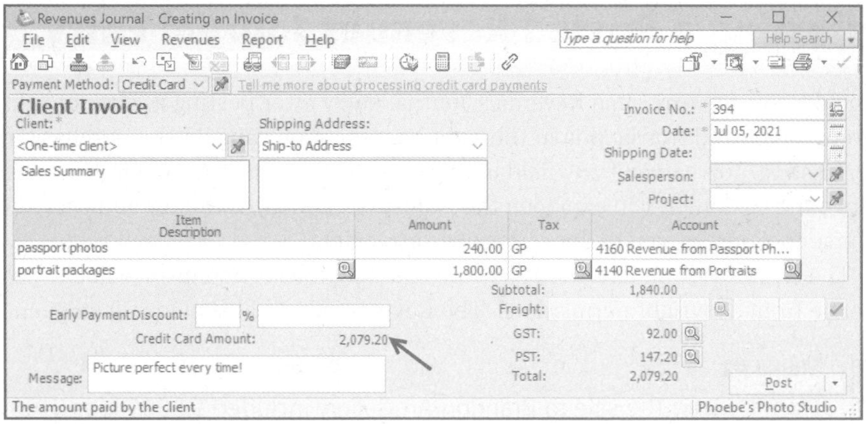

As usual, we will review the journal entry before posting.

Choose the **Report menu** and **click** **Display Revenues Journal Entry**:

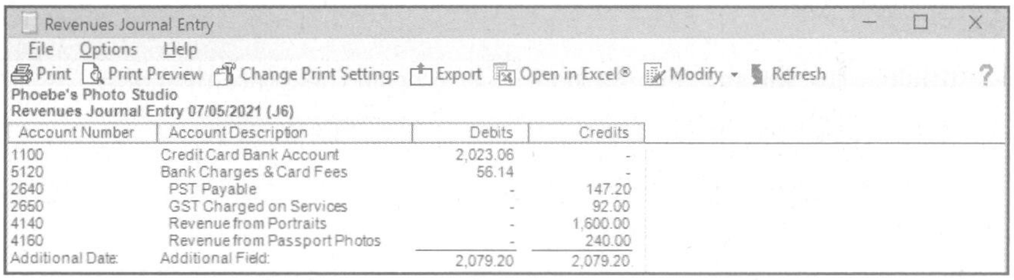

Account Number	Account Description	Debits	Credits
1100	Credit Card Bank Account	2,023.06	-
5120	Bank Charges & Card Fees	56.14	-
2640	PST Payable	-	147.20
2650	GST Charged on Services	-	92.00
4140	Revenue from Portraits	-	1,600.00
4160	Revenue from Passport Photos	-	240.00
Additional Date:	Additional Field:	2,079.20	2,079.20

This entry differs from the standard cash sale entry. Instead of *Chequing Account*, the linked *Credit Card Bank Account* is debited for the amount of the deposit, but this is less than the total amount of the sale. The client will pay $2 079.20 (the full invoice amount) to the credit card company but Phoebe's Photo Studio will receive $2 023.06. The deposit is reduced by the credit card company's transaction fee that is charged to the linked expense account *Bank Charges & Card Fees*. In this case, the credit card company withholds 2.7 percent of each transaction as the fee for using the card. This fee includes the cost to the credit card company for collecting from customers and assuming the risk of non-payment.

Close the **display** and **make corrections** to the invoice if necessary.

Before posting the transaction, we will store it so that we will not need to re-enter all the details the next time we enter the sales summary transaction.

Storing a Recurring Sales Entry

Completing and storing a recurring entry in the Revenues Journal is similar to storing a General or Purchases Journal entry.

Click the **Store tool**  or **choose** the **Sales menu** and **click** **Store**.

The familiar Store Recurring Transaction window appears with the customer name as the entry name and the default frequency, Monthly, selected. If you want, you can change the entry name to Sales Summary.

Click **Monthly** to display the frequency options. **Click Weekly** as the frequency.

Click **OK** to save the entry and return to the Revenues Journal. The Recall button will be available.

Click Post to save the journal entry. **Click OK**.

Adjusting a Posted Revenues Journal Entry

If you discover an error in a Revenues Journal entry after posting it, you can adjust or correct the posted transaction in the same way that you can adjust a purchase invoice after posting. You can edit any field in the invoice except the customer. If you need to change the customer, you can open the Adjust (or Lookup) window and click the Reverse tool, just as you do for purchases or receipts.

The entry for Brandon Art Gallery was missing the second invoice line to record the revenue from copyright permissions. The Revenues Journal should still be open.

✓ 8

Memo #2 **Dated July 5/21**

From Owner: The sale to Brandon Art Gallery included $2 000 plus $100 GST and $160 PST for copyright permissions to display artwork on the gallery Web site. The revised and correct invoice total is $7 006. Adjust the posted entry (reference invoice #PS-391). Create new Group revenue account: 4170 Revenue from Copyrights.

NOTES

Just as you can choose a specific supplier for purchase invoice adjustments, you can choose a specific customer and click OK to reduce the list of invoices to the selected customer. You can also enter an exact invoice number, journal entry number or amount, such as 391 for the invoice number, and click OK to access the invoice directly.

Click the **Adjust Invoice tool** to open the Search window:

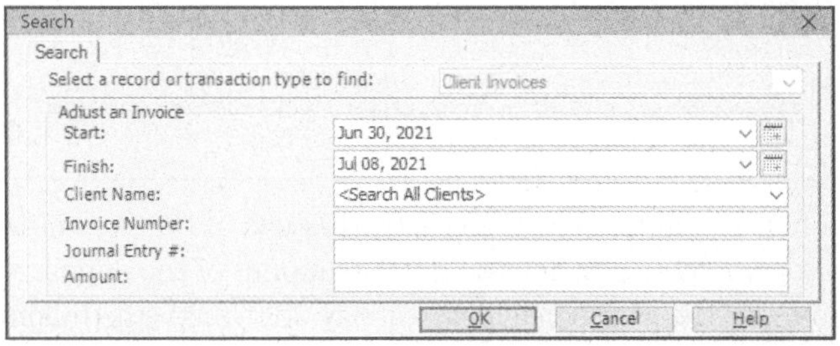

The default date and customer selections will include all invoices.

Click **OK** to open the Select Entry To Adjust screen:

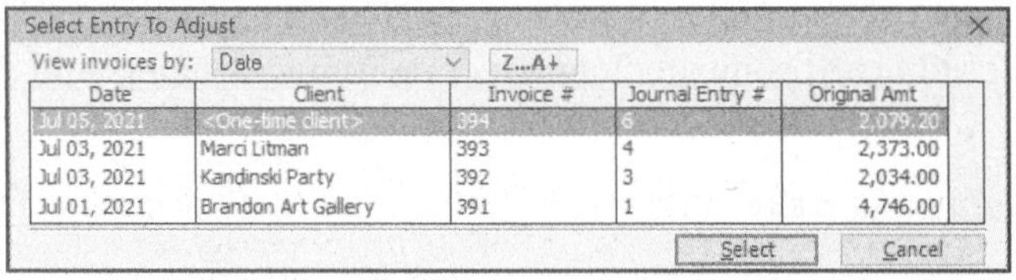

NOTES

If the invoice has already been paid, the program will ask if you want to create a credit note for the customer – a negative invoice. The default source for this invoice will be CN plus the original invoice number (e.g., CN-391), but you can enter a different reference number if you want.

This credit amount can be applied (paid) to other outstanding invoices for the customer.

We demonstrate credit notes in Chapter 10.

All Revenues Journal entries for the selected customers and within the selected date range are listed. You can **view** the list of transactions in order by date, the default selection, or by customer, invoice number, journal entry number or amount. Descending and ascending orders are available for each view from the Z...A **button**. To select by invoice, journal entry number or amount, you must enter the exact information.

Journal Entry #1 for Brandon Art Gallery is the one we need to edit.

Click **Brandon Art Gallery**.

To choose an invoice for adjusting, you can click on any part of the line for that invoice to highlight it then click Select, or you can double-click the entry to open the journal immediately.

Click **Select** to open the invoice. It is ready for editing:

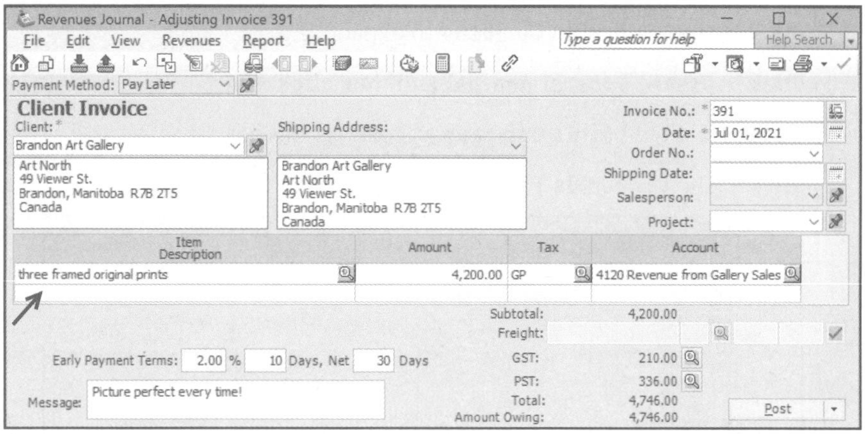

Click the **Item Description field** on the second line, below the first description.

Type `copyright permissions` **Press** *tab* to advance to the Amount field.

Type `2000` **Press** *tab*.

The default tax code and revenue account should be entered. You can select or change them if needed. Click the Tax field List icon to open the Tax Code screen and change the selection. We need to change the account.

Click the **Account field**. **Type** `4170`

Press *tab*. **Create** the **new revenue account** when prompted.

Click the **Message field** and **type** `Revised invoice`

As with other adjustments in other journals, this adjustment creates a reversing entry (J7) in addition to the corrected journal entry (J8). You will have all three transactions in the journal reports when you include corrections. You can preview the invoice to ensure that you made the changes correctly.

If you change the customer for an invoice, Sage 50 warns that the name will be changed, but the remaining information (terms, tax codes and so on) will not. If you need to change the customer for a posted invoice, you should reverse the original entry and then create a new invoice for the correct customer. This ensures that the correct customer's settings will apply to the sale.

Review the **entry**. **Close** the **display**. **Make corrections** if necessary.

Post the **transaction**. The transaction confirmation message tells you that two entries were posted for the adjustment. **Close** the **Revenues Journal**.

Adding Shortcuts for Other Transactions

Just as we added a shortcut for General Journal entries in Chapter 5, we can add shortcuts for the Payables journals and tasks we will use for Phoebe's Photo Studio. Refer to page 134 if you need help.

NOTES

You can change the invoice number if you want to make the audit trail clearer. For example, you can enter 391-R as the invoice number to identify it as a revised invoice.

If you change the date, only the corrected entry will have the revised date. Remember that changing the date will affect the discount period as well, so change the date only if it is incorrect.

NOTES

To reverse a sale, open the Adjusting Client Invoice (Sale) window and click the Reverse tool. Click Yes to confirm that you want to reverse the sale.

NOTES

Refer to page 164 and Appendix F on the Student DVD for more detail on previewing and printing invoices.

NOTES

When you close the journal, you may get a message about credit card processing. Click Do Not Show This Message Again to close the window. This message may appear when you post the entry or when you close the journal. Credit card processing is covered in Chapter 13.

PRO VERSION
Add shortcuts for Create General Journal, Create Purchase Invoice, Pay Purchase Invoices, Pay Expenses, View Vendors and View Accounts.

NOTES
Collapsing a list after finishing with it makes it easier to advance to the next ledger heading. Alternatively, you can scroll down the list.

✓ 9

Memo #3 **Dated July 5/21**

Create shortcuts for tasks and transactions in other modules.

Click the **Shortcuts tool** beside **Shortcuts** in the Shortcuts pane in the Home window.

Click the ⊞ **beside Company** to expand the list.

Click **Create General Journal** and then **click Add**.

Click the ⊟ **beside Company** to collapse this list.

Click the ⊞ **beside Payables** to expand this list:

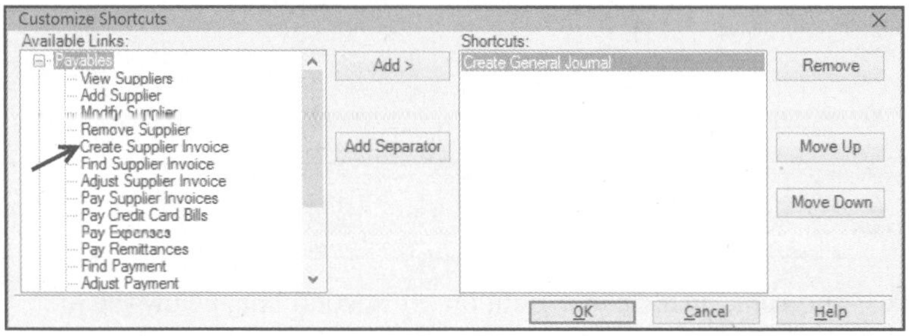

All transactions that are available from the Invoices, Payments and Suppliers drop-down lists can be added as Home window shortcuts. We will add shortcuts for the types of Payables transactions we use most frequently: creating and paying invoices and making other cash purchases (expenses). We will also add a shortcut to View Suppliers so that we can edit supplier records.

NOTES
You can add more shortcuts if you want. The maximum number is 10 for each user.
You must click Add for each shortcut you want.

Click **Create Supplier Invoice** and then **click Add**.

Click **Pay Supplier Invoices** and then **click Add**.

Click **Pay Expenses** and then **click Add**.

Click **View Suppliers** and then **click Add**.

Click the ⊞ **beside Banking** to expand the list.

NOTES
The View Accounts icon opens the Accounts window.

Click **View Accounts** and then **click Add**.

Click **OK** to return to the Home window with your shortcuts added:

These six tasks/windows are now available from any module Home window by clicking the shortcut.

Enter the **transactions** until the sales summary on July 12.

10

Payment Cheque #451 **Dated July 6/21**

To Calm Air, $3 861 in payment of account, including $39 discount for early payment. Reference invoice #CA-224.

NOTES
PST paid on purchases is included with the expense or asset part of the purchase because this tax is not refundable. Therefore, it is not recorded separately.

11

Purchase Invoice #RG-3160 **Dated July 6/21**

From Riverton Garage, $80 for gasoline for van, including taxes (use tax code IN). Terms: net 30.

12

Purchase Invoice #CA-392 **Dated July 6/21**

From Calm Air, $1 215 plus $60.75 GST. Invoice total $1 275.75 for return flight to Churchill. Terms: 1/15, n/30. Store as a bi-weekly recurring transaction.

13 **Sales Invoice #PS-395** **Dated July 7/21**

To Polar Discoveries, $2 270 plus $113.50 GST and $181.60 PST for tour customer photographs. Invoice total $2 565.10. Terms: 2/10, n/30.

14 **Payment Cheque #452** **Dated July 7/21**

To Lumber Shed, $1 050 in payment of account. Reference invoice #LS-894. The discount period has expired.

15 **Payment Cheque #453** **Dated July 7/21**

To Riverton Garage, $890 in payment of account. Reference invoice #RG-1904.

16 **Purchase Invoice #SPS-4668** **Dated July 8/21**

From Starlight Photo Solutions, $1 820 plus $91 GST for rolls of large photo paper for gallery prints. Invoice total $1 911. Terms: 2/10, n/30.

17 **Sales Invoice #PS-396** **Dated July 8/21**

To Calm Air (use Full Add for the new customer), $1 900 plus $95 GST and $152 PST for permission to use photographs on Web site. Invoice total $2 147. Terms: 2/10, n/30.

NOTES

Calm Air
(contact Arie Fliegel)
50 Jett Ave.
Winnipeg, MB R2P 1S7
Tel: (800) 839-2256
Fax: (204) 476-5110
E-mail: af@calmair.com
Web site: calmair.com
Revenue account: 4170
Terms: 2/10, n/30
Payment method: Pay later
Tax code: GP
Credit limit: $8 000

SESSION DATE – JULY 15, 2021

18 **Receipt #42** **Dated July 9/21**

From Litman, Marci, cheque #29 for $2 325.54, including $47.46 discount for early payment of invoice #PS-393.

19 **Sales Invoice #PS-397** **Dated July 9/21**

To Kandinski Party, $4 600 plus $230 GST and $368 PST for wedding photo package with DVD. Invoice total $5 198. Terms: 2/10, n/30. Create new Group revenue account: 4150 Revenue from Weddings. Allow the customer to exceed the credit limit.

20 **Receipt #43** **Dated July 10/21**

From Brandon Art Gallery, cheque #28874 for $6 865.88 in full payment of invoice #PS-391 with $140.12 discount for early payment.

21 **Receipt #44** **Dated July 11/21**

From Reuben, Geraldine, certified cheque #302 for $2 495 in full payment of account to replace NSF cheque. Reference invoices #PS-377 and #PS-381.

Recalling a Stored Sales Entry

The procedures for recalling and changing a stored entry are the same for all journals.

✓ 22 **Credit Card Sales Invoice #PS-398** **Dated July 12/21**

Sales Summary
To various one-time customers

Passport photos	$ 130.00
Portraits	1 200.00
GST charged	66.50
PST charged	106.40
Total deposited to credit card bank account	$1 502.90

Recall the stored transaction.

NOTES

Remember to change the amounts when you recall the sales summary.

NOTES

You can store the changed sales summary if you want. In this case, you should confirm that you are replacing the previous stored transaction.

Click the **Client Invoices** (Sales or Sales Invoices) **icon** [Client Invoices] to open the Revenues Journal.

Click the **Recall tool** or **choose** the **Revenues menu** and **click Recall** to display the Recall Recurring Transaction window.

Click the **transaction** you want to use. **Click Select** to display a copy of the entry previously posted.

Edit the **amounts** as needed.

The default date is entered according to the frequency selected. The payment method is still selected as Credit Card. The invoice number is updated automatically and the accounts and descriptions are correct, so the entry is complete.

Review the **entry** to be certain that it is correct. **Click** [Post] to save it.

When you make changes to a stored entry, Sage 50 warns that posting the entry may affect the next due date. This warning appears if you have made any changes to the entry before posting, although the message mentions only the date.

Click **Yes** to accept the change and post. **Click OK** to confirm posting.

Enter the **remaining transactions** for July.

NOTES
You must open the ledger record to make these changes for Litman.

23 **Bank Debit Memo #29321** **Dated July 15/21**

From Red River Credit Union, cheque #29 for $2 325.54 from Litman has been returned because of non-sufficient funds. Reverse the payment and notify the customer of the outstanding charges. Change the customer's terms to net 1 and set her credit limit to zero.

24 **Cash Purchase Invoice #UPS-6101** **Dated July 15/21**

From UPS Delivery, $380 for courier delivery of photographs to clients plus $19 GST. Invoice total $399. Issued cheque #454 in full payment.

25 **Purchase Invoice #CA-487** **Dated July 15/21**

From Calm Air, $1 215 plus $60.75 GST. Invoice total $1 275.75 for return flight to Churchill. Terms: 1/15, n/30. Recall the stored entry, edit the date and then store it as a weekly recurring transaction. Replace the previous stored transaction.

SESSION DATE – JULY 22, 2021

26 **Payment Cheque #455** **Dated July 17/21**

To Starlight Photo Solutions, $1 872.78 in payment of account, including $38.22 discount for early payment. Reference invoice #SPS-4668.

27 **Purchase Invoice #WE-56691** **Dated July 18/21**

From Web Exposure, $3 100 plus $155 GST and $248 PST for redesigning Web site with updated text and photos. Invoice total $3 503. Terms: net 15.

NOTES
Staples Business Depot
Expense account: 1340
Tax code: GP
Invoice payments by: Cheque
Leave the remaining fields blank.

28 **Cash Purchase Invoice #SBD-4821** **Dated July 19/21**

From Staples Business Depot (use Full Add for the new supplier), $60 plus $3.00 GST and $4.80 PST for stationery and office supplies. Invoice total $67.80. Paid by cheque #456.

29 **Payment Cheque #457** **Dated July 19/21**

To Calm Air, $1 262.99 in payment of account, including $12.76 discount for early payment. Reference invoice #CA-392.

30

Phoebe's Photo Studio
phoebephoto.com

100 Light St., Suite 202
Winnipeg, MB R2T 7G4
Phone: (204) 649-3358 Toll free: (888) 649-3358 Fax: (204) 642-4967

Invoice: PS-399
Date: July 19, 2021
Sold to: Borealis Mysteries
(J. Franklin)
4 Lighter Way
Winnipeg, MB R4A 1E1

Description	Tax Code	Amount
Photographs of tour customers	GP	1 140.00

bi-weekly recurring sale: [signature]

Picture perfect every time!

Payment Terms:	Customer Initials		
2/10, net 30		GST	57.00
		PST	91.20
GST #296 654 593	JF	TOTAL	1 288.20

31

Phoebe's Photo Studio
phoebestudio.com

100 Light St., Suite 202
Winnipeg, MB R2T 7G4
Phone: (204) 649-3358 Toll free: (888) 649-3358 Fax: (204) 642-4967

Invoice: PS-400
Date: July 19, 2021
Sold to: Sales Summary

Description	Tax Code	Amount
Passport photos	GP	180.00
Portrait packages	GP	1 400.00

Deposited to credit card bank account
July 19/21 [signature]

Picture perfect every time!

Payment Terms:	Customer Initials		
Credit Card		GST	79.00
		PST	126.40
Business No.: 296 654 593		TOTAL	1 785.40

NOTES
Remember to change the amounts when you recall the sales summary.

32 **Sales Invoice #PS-401** **Dated July 21/21**

To Polar Discoveries, $2 270 plus $113.50 GST and $181.60 PST for tour customer photographs. Invoice total $2 565.10. Terms: 2/10, n/30.

33 **Purchase Invoice #CA-598** **Dated July 22/21**

From Calm Air, $1 215 plus $60.75 GST. Invoice total $1 275.75 for return flight to Churchill. Terms: 1/15, n/30. Recall the stored entry.

34 **Purchase Invoice #RG-5619** **Dated July 22/21**

From Riverton Garage, $85 including taxes for gasoline. Terms: net 30.

35

Borealis Mysteries
4 Lighter Way
Winnipeg, MB R4A 1E1

No: 18963

Date 20210722
YYYYMMDD

Pay to the order of Phoebe's Photo Studio $ 1262.44

— One thousand two hundred sixty-two dollars ——— 44 /100 Dollars

RR Red River Credit Union
389 Prairie Blvd.
Winnipeg MB R2P 1B6

Signature

⑈---92999-⑆16883 18963

Re: pay invoice #PS-399 $1262.44 No: 18963
includes $25.76 discount (receipt #45) July 22, 2021

SESSION DATE – JULY 31, 2021

36 **Purchase Invoice #SPS-5936** **Dated July 25/21**

From Starlight Photo Solutions, $310 plus $15.50 GST for developing solutions and $420 plus $21 GST and $33.60 PST for camera repairs. Invoice total $800.10. Terms: 2/10, n/30. Create new Group expense account: 5180 Repair Expenses.

NOTES

Change the default account to 1300 for the developing solutions and apply tax code GP for the repair expenses.

37

Calm Air
50 Jett Ave.
Winnipeg, MB R2P 1S7
Tel: (800) 839-2256

RR **Red River Credit Union**
389 Prairie Blvd.
Winnipeg MN R2P 1B6

No: 2910

Date 20210726
YYYYMMDD

Pay — Two thousand one hundred forty-seven dollars — 00 $ 2,147.00

TO THE ORDER OF
Phoebe's Photo Studio
100 Light St. Suite 202
Winnipeg, MB R2T 7G4

PER

⑈---92999-⑆46771 2910

Re: pay invoice #PS-396 $2,147 No: 2910
(receipt #46) July 26, 2021

38

Payment Cheque #458 **Dated July 26/21**

To Starlight Photo Solutions, $400 in partial payment of account. No discount is allowed on the partial payment. Reference invoice #SPS-5936.

39

Cash Purchase Invoice #MT-421576 **Dated July 26/21**

From Manitoba Telephone, $290 plus $14.50 GST and $23.20 PST for telephone and Internet service. Invoice total $327.70. Paid by cheque #459.

40

Cash Purchase Invoice #MH-66832 **Dated July 26/21**

From Manitoba Hydro, $280 plus $14 GST for hydro for two studios. Invoice total $294. Paid by cheque #460.

41

Credit Card Sales Invoice #PS-402 **Dated July 26/21**

Sales Summary
To various one-time customers

Passport photos	$ 130.00
Portraits	1 200.00
GST charged	66.50
PST charged	106.40
Total deposited to credit card bank account	$1 502.90

Recall the stored transaction.

NOTES
Remember to change the amounts when you recall the sales summary.

42

Purchase Invoice #CA-622 **Dated July 29/21**

From Calm Air, $1 215 plus $60.75 GST. Invoice total $1 275.75 for return flight to Churchill. Terms: 1/15, n/30. Recall the stored entry.

43

Receipt #47 **Dated July 29/21**

From Polar Discoveries, cheque #43692 for $1 200 in partial payment of invoice #PS-395.

44

Sales Invoice #PS-403 **Dated July 30/21**

To Borealis Mysteries, $1 800 plus $90 GST and $144 PST for tour customer photographs. Invoice total $2 034. Terms: 2/10, n/30. Recall the stored entry and edit the date and amount. Store the revised entry.

45

Bank Credit Memo #55131 **Dated July 30/21**

From Red River Credit Union, $4 000 six-month loan at 7% interest for new dichroic enlarger approved and deposited to bank account.

46

Bank Debit Memo #61821 **Dated July 30/21**

From Red River Credit Union, pre-authorized monthly payroll for assistant.

Wages and payroll expenses	$3 000.00
Payroll services fee	30.00
GST paid on payroll service	1.50
Total withdrawal	$3 031.50

NOTES
Remember to enter the Sales Tax details for the payroll service fee.

47

Memo #4 **Dated July 31/21**

From Owner: Create new Group expense account for supplies used during the month: 5145 Darkroom Supplies Used. Enter adjustments for supplies used:

Framing supplies	$510
Photo paper & supplies	480
Darkroom supplies	290
Office & other supplies	140

48

Bank Debit Memo #62002 **Dated July 31/21**

From Red River Credit Union, pre-authorized withdrawals for service charges, mortgage and loan payments.

Bank charges, including NSF cheques	$ 135
Interest expense	1 120
Loan principal repayment	1 040
Mortgage principal repayment	420

Displaying Client/Customer Reports

PRO VERSION
Click the Customers icon  .

NOTES
Statements and labels are not available from the Reports pane or from the Report Centre. You can access these from the Reports menu in the Home window and the Clients window.

PRO VERSION
Remember that the terms Customer and Sales will replace Client and Revenues.

Client (or customer) reports can be accessed at any time from the Home or the Clients window, or from the Report Centre.

Click the Clients icon  to open the Clients window.

The Clients window Reports menu contains only client reports. Select the report you want from this list and follow the instructions below to choose report options. You can also obtain all client (customer) reports from the Home window **Reports menu**.

In the Receivables module Home window, the **Reports pane** includes all the customer reports in the drop-down list. Opening the reports from this list will display them immediately with the default settings. Clicking Client List expands the report list:

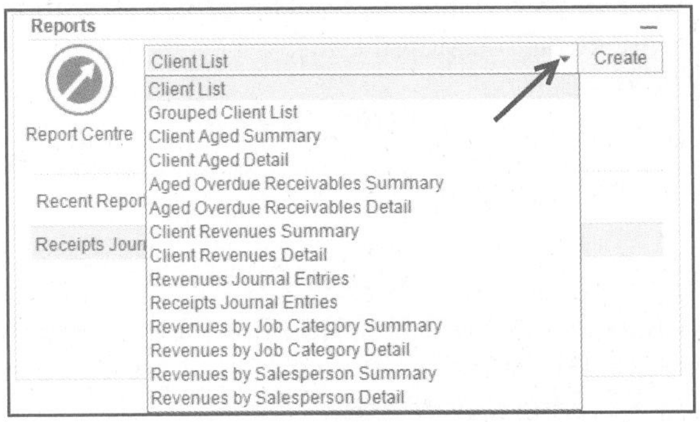

We will continue to work from the Report Centre so that we include the sample reports, descriptions and report options on the screen.

Click the **Report Centre icon**  in the Home window.

The Receivables reports are listed because we started from the Receivables window. The sample and description for Client List, the first report, are displayed:

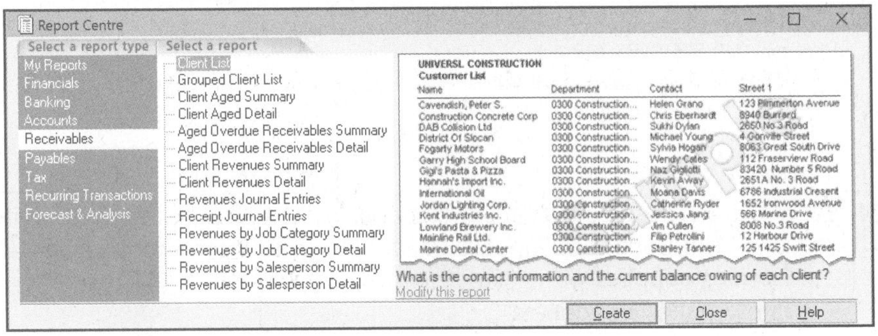

PRO VERSION
Grouped Client List and Forecast & Analysis reports are not available in the Pro version.

NOTES
Forecast & Analysis reports use data for multiple fiscal periods. They are covered briefly in Chapter 10.

NOTES
If another customer report is named in the Reports pane, its sample report will open when you click the Report Centre icon.

If you click Receivables in the Select A Report Type list, you will display the general description for Receivables reports.

Displaying Client/Customer Lists

Click **Client List** in the Select A Report list to open the sample report and its description.

Click **Modify This Report** to open the report options:

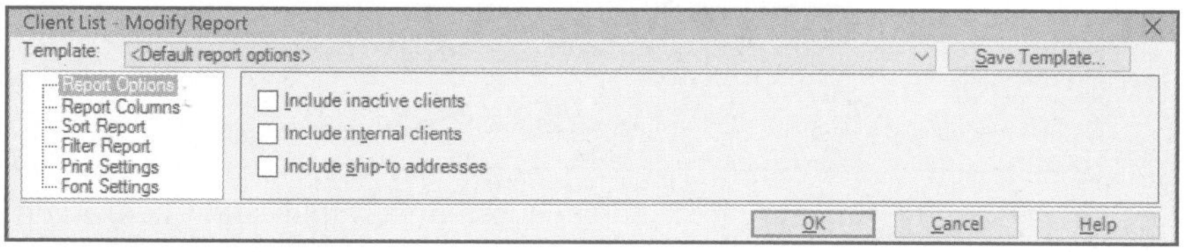

Or, choose the Reports menu, then choose Lists and Clients.

You can include or omit inactive and internal customers and shipping addresses. You can sort and filter Client Lists by any of the fields selected for the report. You can select customer record fields by customizing the Report Columns. You can also sort the columns directly in the report. For example, if you want to list customers in order according to the amount they owe, with the largest balance reported first, click the Balance column heading to sort the report by balance. Then click the heading again to reverse the order.

Click **OK**. **Close** the **display** when you have finished viewing it.

Displaying Grouped Client Lists

The Grouped Client List organizes clients by a specific criterion. You could use this list to prepare customer contact lists for salespersons in different regions.

Click **Grouped Client List** in the Select A Report list to open the sample report and its description.

Click **Modify This Report** to open the report options.

Click the **list arrow for the Group By field**:

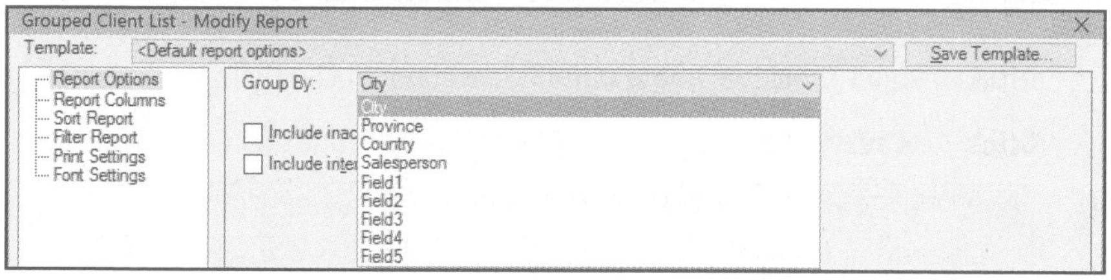

The criteria you can use to group the customers are displayed.

Choose the **grouping criterion** you want. **Click OK** to display the report.

Close the **display** when you have finished viewing it.

Displaying Client Aged Reports

Click **Client Aged Summary** in the Select A Report list to open the sample report and its description.

CLASSIC VIEW
From the Home window, right-click the Clients icon. Click the Select A Report tool.

NOTES
You can drill down to the Client Aged Report from the Client List.

PRO VERSION
The Pro version has only the option to Include Inactive Customers.

NOTES
Field1, Field2 and so on are extra fields you define for the company that appear on the Additional Information tab screens of customer records.

NOTES
You can drill down to look up invoices and to the Client Ledger from the Client Aged Detail Report. From the Summary Report you can drill down to the Detail Report.

Click **Modify This Report** to open the report options:

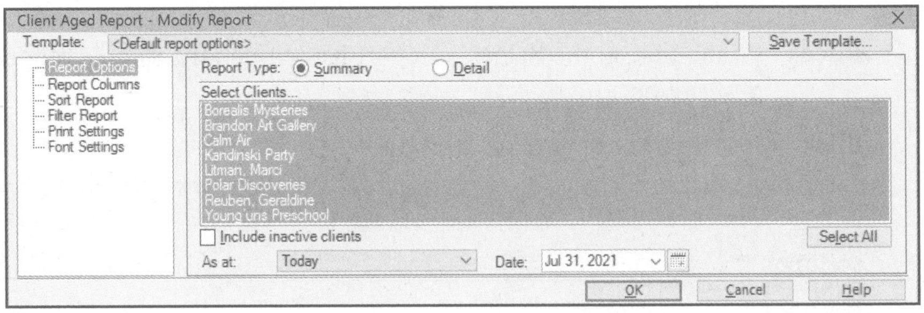

Or, choose the Reports menu, then choose Receivables and Client Aged.

New customers you entered using Quick Add will appear on the list of customers in the report options windows. Sales for one-time customers and customers for whom you chose the Continue option will not appear because these cash transactions did not create a ledger record or an entry for *Accounts Receivable*.

The **Summary** option will display an alphabetic list of the selected customers with outstanding total balances owing, organized into the aging periods columns set up for the company. The **Detail** option will include all the invoices and payments made by customers for the period you enter, up to 999 days. The current balance owing and unpaid invoices are always included. This more descriptive report is also aged and can be used to make credit decisions. You can add payment terms and contact information to the Detail Report. You can choose any columns in the report and sort and filter by name and balance owing to customize the Client Aged Report.

NOTES
The Client Aged and Aged Overdue Detail Reports are also available directly from the Select A Report list for Receivables in the Report Centre.

Click **Detail** to include details for individual transactions.

Enter the **date** for the report or accept the default session date.

Press and **hold** ctrl and **click** the **client names**. **Click Select All** to include all customers or remove them when they are all selected.

Click **OK** to open the report. **Close** the **displayed report** when finished.

Displaying Aged Overdue Receivables Reports

NOTES
You can drill down to look up invoices and to the Client Aged Report from the Aged Overdue Receivables Detail Report. From the Summary Report you can drill down to the Detail Report.

Click **Aged Overdue Receivables Summary** in the Select A Report list.

Click **Modify This Report** to open the report options:

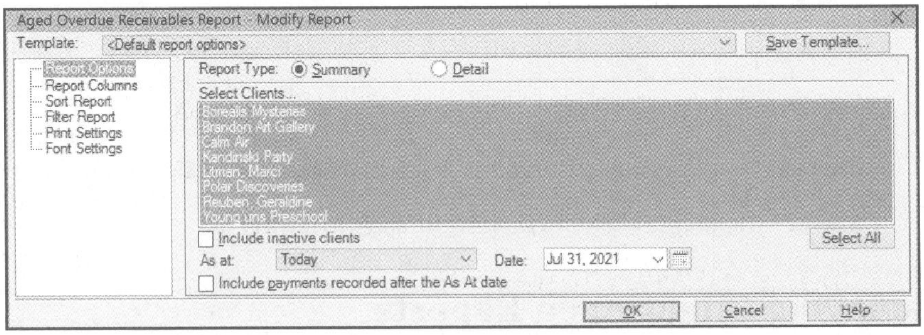

NOTES
You can use name and balance owing as the criteria for sorting and filtering the Aged Overdue Receivables reports and you can choose any of the columns in the report.

From the Home window, choose the Reports menu, then Receivables and then click Aged Overdue Receivables.

Enter the **date** for the report, or accept the default session date.

The **Summary** option will display an alphabetic list of the selected customers with outstanding total balances owing, organized into aging periods, with an additional column for the overdue amount. Individual invoices, due dates, payments, overdue amounts and the balance owing for the selected customers are added when you choose the **Detail** Report. Selecting **Include Payments Recorded After The As At Date** will add postdated receipts to the report and not count these clients as having overdue amounts.

Click **Detail** if you want to include invoice details and contact information.

Enter the **date** for the report, or accept the default session date.

Press and **hold** ctrl and **click** the appropriate **names** in the client list. **Click** **Select All** to include all customers or remove them all.

Click **OK** to open the report. **Close** the **displayed report** when finished.

NOTES
Invoices with postdated receipts are deemed to be paid, and can, therefore, be omitted from the report.

Displaying the Client Revenues Report

Click **Client Revenues Summary** in the Select A Report list to open the sample report and its description.

Click **Modify This Report** to open the report options:

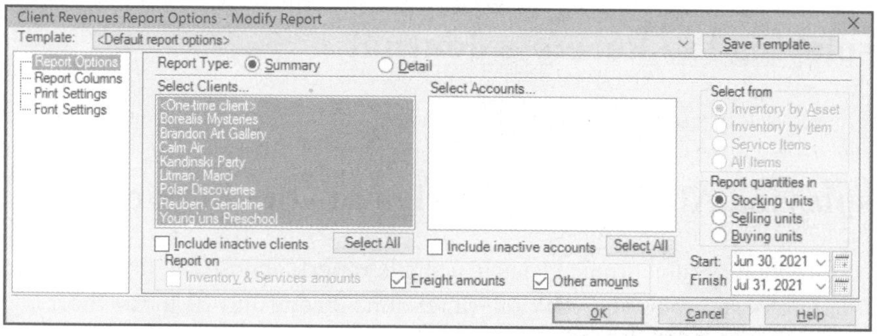

PRO VERSION
Click Customer Sales Summary to open this report.

NOTES
You can drill down to the Journal Report and the Client Aged Report and look up the invoice from the Client Sales Detail Report. From the Summary Report you can drill down to the Detail Report.

Or, choose the Reports menu and Receivables and click Client Revenues.

In this report, you can display the total number of transactions and the total sales for each customer (in the **Summary Report**) or the individual sales invoice amounts (in the **Detail Report**). The Detail Report also includes journal details (date, source, journal entry number and revenue amounts) for each transaction. Only the Other Amounts and Freight Amounts are available when the inventory module is not set up. When inventory items are set up, you can display the sales for these items as well. This report will be introduced again with inventory in Chapter 10. The earliest transaction and session date provide the default date range. You can select the customers to include.

Click **Detail** if you want to include the invoice details.

Press and **hold** ctrl and **click** the appropriate **names** in the customer list. **Click Select All** to include all customers or remove the entire selection.

Enter the **Start** and **Finish dates** for the report.

Click **OK** to open the report. **Close** the **displayed report** when finished.

NOTES
Each sales invoice line in the Detail Client Revenues Report is counted as one transaction for this report. For Brandon Art Gallery, four transactions are counted: the final two invoice lines, the original one we adjusted, and its reversing entry. This information becomes clear from the Detail version of the report.

Displaying the Revenues (Sales) Journal

Click **Revenues Journal Entries** in the Select A Report list. **Click** **Modify This Report** to open the report options:

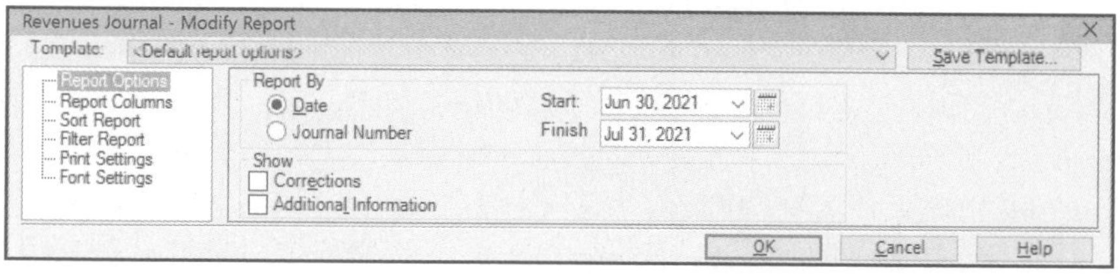

PRO VERSION
Click Sales Journal Entries to access the report.

CLASSIC VIEW
From the Home window, right-click the Revenues icon . Click the Select A Report tool . Revenues and Receipts Journal reports are also available from the Select A Report list when you click the Select A Report tool button if no icon is selected in the Home window.

NOTES
You can drill down to an invoice, to the Client Aged Report and to the General Ledger Report from the Revenues and the Receipts Journal reports. You can also look up the original journal transaction window.

From the Home window, choose the Reports menu, then choose Journal Entries and click Revenues (Sales) for the report options.

You can select Revenues Journal entries by posting date or by journal entry number. We use the default setting, By Date, for all reports in this workbook, so leave the selection unchanged. You can include **corrections** (adjusting and reversing entries) or omit them.

You can sort and filter journal reports by Date, Journal No., Source and Comment. You can choose account, description, debits and credits columns for the reports.

Enter the **beginning date** for the journal transactions you want. Or, choose a date from the list arrow selections.

Press *tab* **twice**. **Enter** the **ending date** for the transaction period.

Click **Corrections** to provide a complete audit trail.

Click **OK** to view the report. **Close** the **display** when you have finished.

Displaying the Receipts Journal

The Receipts Journal was covered earlier in this chapter. Refer to pages 178–179.

Displaying All Journal Entries in One Report

To include all journal entries in a single report, choose the Reports menu, then choose Journals and click All. Enter June 30 and July 31 in the Start and Finish date fields if these are not the default entries.

From the Report Centre, you can choose Financials and then All Journal Entries to include all transactions in a single report. Click Modify This Report to display the report options.

Displaying Tax Reports

The next three reports also include customer information. Because they are accessed from the Report Centre, they are included before the final customer reports that are accessed from the Home window Reports menu.

Tax reports provide the taxable purchases and sales with and without tax amounts included, the taxes paid or charged on each transaction and the totals.

Click **Tax** in the Select A Report Type list to open the list of tax reports:

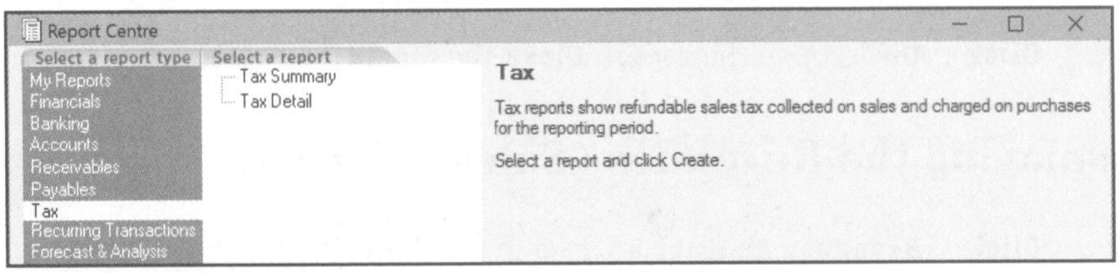

Click **Tax Summary** to display a sample report and description.

Click **Modify This Report** to display the Tax Report options window:

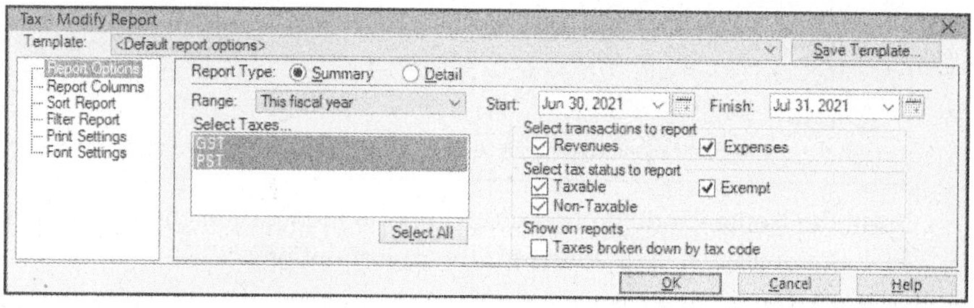

From the Home window, choose the Reports menu and click Tax to display the Tax Report options window.

All taxes that were defined for the company and included the option to report on them are listed in the **Select Taxes** field.

The earliest transaction and the session date are entered as the default date range for the report. You can include either transactions for revenues or expenses (sales or purchases) that include tax or for both. Both purchases and sales are reported by default for all taxes. In addition, the report can include taxable, exempt and non-taxable transactions. By default all are selected. You can also organize the report by **tax codes**.

The **Summary Report** has only the totals for each category selected while the **Detail Report** lists individual transactions for each category. You can include the total tax amounts for each tax code as well.

The reports include a column for **Other Taxes**. For the GST, this column has the PST related to the sale or purchase; for the PST, this column has the GST related to the sale or purchase.

PRO VERSION

The terms Sales and Purchases replace Revenues and Expenses.

NOTES

You can sort and filter tax reports by taxable amounts for purchases and sales including or excluding taxes, taxes paid/charged, other taxes paid/charged and total amounts including taxes.

No drill-down reports are available from tax reports.

Click **Detail** to select the more detailed level for the report.

Enter or **choose** the **dates** for which you want the report to start and finish.

Click a **tax name** in the Select Tax list to change the selection.

Click the **transactions** (Revenues or Expenses) to remove a ✓ or to add one if it is not there to include the transaction in the report.

Click a **transaction tax status** (Taxable, Exempt or Non-Taxable) to remove a ✓ or to add one if it is not there.

Click **Taxes Broken Down By Tax Code** to add this option to your report.

Once you have selected the options you want,

Click **OK** to view the report. **Close** the **display** when you have finished.

NOTES

Correcting (adjusting and reversing) entries are included automatically in tax reports. You cannot omit them.

Displaying Cash Flow Reports

Displaying the Statement of Cash Flows

Click **Financials** in the Select A Report Type list to open the list of reports:

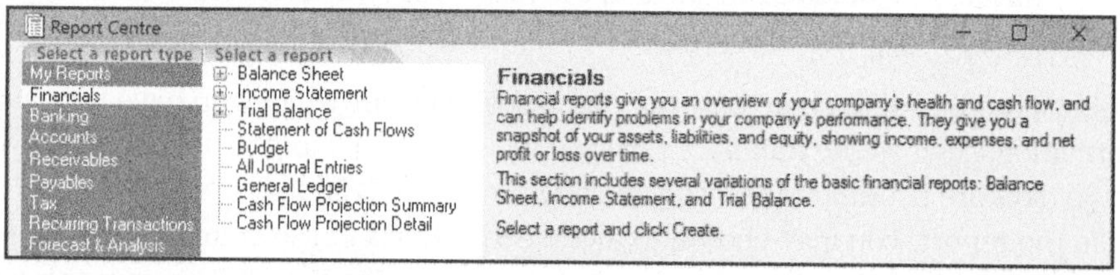

Click **Statement Of Cash Flows** to display a sample report and description.

NOTES

You cannot sort or filter the Statement of Cash Flows or the Cash Flow Projection Report, but you can choose report columns.

Click **Modify This Report** to display the Modify Report window:

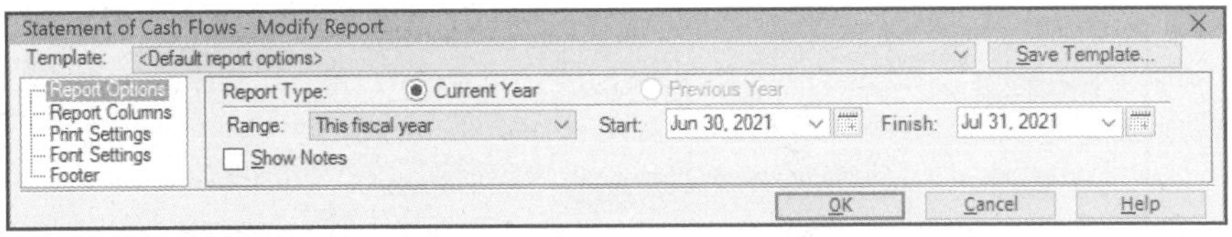

From the Home window, choose the Reports menu, then choose Financials and click Statement Of Cash Flows for the report options.

NOTES
You can drill down to the General Ledger from the Statement of Cash Flows.

The Statement of Cash Flows summarizes sources (income, investments, etc.) and uses (purchase of assets, etc.) of cash and changes in liabilities during the designated period. By organizing the transactions involving cash, net changes in cash positions, as well as changes in liabilities, the statement allows the owner to judge how efficiently cash is being used for the business. The owner can also judge whether potential problems will result from increases in liabilities or decreases in the collection of receivables.

Enter the **Start** and **Finish dates** for the report. The fiscal start and session dates are the defaults.

Click **OK** to view the report.

Close the **display** when you have finished.

Displaying Cash Flow Projection Reports

Cash Flow Projection reports predict the flow of cash in and out of an account — usually a bank account — over a specific future period based on current information.

Click **Cash Flow Projection Summary** to display a sample report and description. **Click Modify This Report** to display report options:

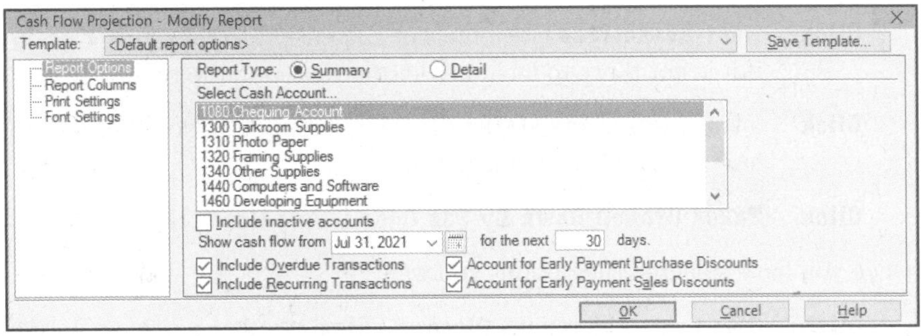

From the Home window, choose the Reports menu, then choose Financials and click Cash Flow Projection for the report options.

Click **1080 Chequing Account** or the account for which you want the report.

Click the **date field**. **Type** the **date** at which you want the projection to start.

Press *tab* **twice** to advance past the Calendar icon.

Enter the **number of days** in the future for which the report should project the cash flow.

NOTES
You might want to compare projection reports prepared with and without some of these extra details.

Usually, you will include only the number of days for which you have reasonable information, such as the number of days in which net payment is due. The session date and 30 days are useful periods, so you can accept the defaults.

In the report, you may choose to include **discounts** in the amounts you expect to receive or pay, and you may include **overdue transactions** or omit them if you expect them to remain unpaid. By default, all details are included. Clicking a detail that is already selected will remove it from the report. The Projection Report assumes overdue amounts will be paid and all other amounts will be paid on the invoice due date.

The report projects the account balance based on receivables and payables due and **recurring transactions** coming due within the time frame specified, if you include these. The **Summary Report** has the totals for the specified report period while the **Detail Report** includes, by date, the individual transactions that are expected.

Select the **additional categories** for which you want details.

Click **Detail** to include individual transactions.

Click **OK** to view the report.

Close the **display**. **Close** the **Report Centre** to return to the Home window.

Printing Client Reports

Display the **report** you want to print.

Click the **Change Print Settings tool** to check that you have the correct printer selected. **Click OK** to return to the report.

Click the **Print tool** or **choose** the **File menu** in the report window, and then **click Print**.

Close the **display** when you have finished.

Printing Client Statements

You can e-mail all customer statements or print them, or you can choose e-mail and print on a customer-by-customer basis according to the setting (preference) in the customer's ledger record Options tab screen (refer to page 175).

Set up your **printer** with the correct forms before you begin because statements are printed immediately when you click OK after selecting your options or previewing the statements.

Choose the **Reports menu** in the Home window, then **choose Receivables** and **click Client Statements**.

The customer list with statement options opens:

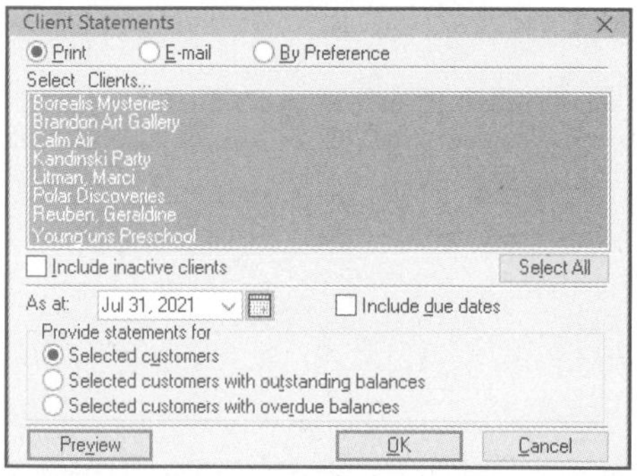

You can select some or all customers and create statements only for customers that have outstanding balances or only for customers with overdue amounts.

Press and **hold** ctrl and **click** the **clients** for whom you want to print statements, or **click Select All** to include all clients.

NOTES
Refer to Chapter 4, page 85, for details on setting up printers for different forms, reports and labels.

WARNING!
When you print from the Print tool, printing will start immediately. If you want to check your printer selection and settings, choose Print from the report's File menu.

NOTES
You can customize customer statements, but not mailing labels.

Customizing statements is similar to customizing invoices. Refer to Appendix F on the Student DVD for assistance with previewing and customizing forms.

NOTES
To preview statements, you must have the correct form settings. Before you start, choose the Setup menu and click Reports & Forms. Click Statements, and choose Custom Form and then choose Statements in the Description field for both printed and e-mailed forms.

Or, when you preview the statements and Sage 50 gives you an error message, click OK. The required Reports & Forms window will open. Enter the settings from the previous paragraph.

If you also want to customize the statements, choose User Defined Form in the Printed Form Description field. Click the Customize button to open the Form Designer. Save the new form when finished. Refer to Appendix F on the Student DVD.

Enter the **date** for the statements.

Click **Include Due Dates** if you want to add the payment due dates for invoices.

Click **Preview**. You should preview statements before printing them.

Click **OK** to close the preview and return to the options screen.

Click **OK** again to print the statements.

Printing Client Mailing Labels

You should turn on the printer, insert labels paper and set the program for printing labels before choosing the options for the labels, because printing begins immediately.

Choose the Setup menu in the Home window and click Reports & Forms. Click Labels. Enter the details for the labels. Click OK.

PRO VERSION
Choose Customers instead of Clients.
Your only options are to print mailing addresses or shipping addresses.

Choose the **Reports menu** in the Home window, then **choose Mailing Labels** and **click Clients** for the printing options:

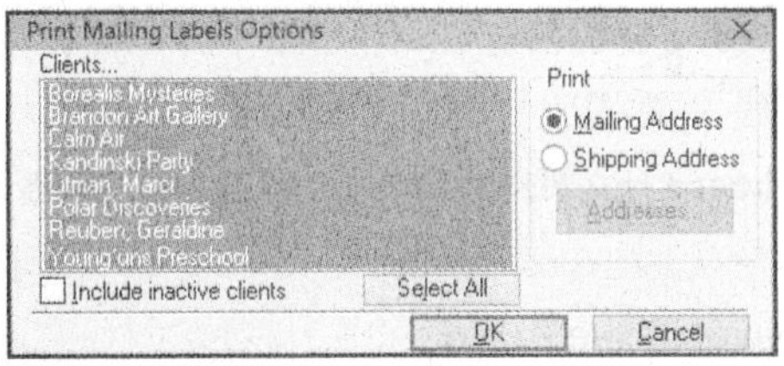

You can print labels for business mailing addresses, for shipping addresses or for any address list you created.

Press and **hold** ctrl and **click** the **clients** for whom you want to print the labels, or **click Select All** to include all customers. **Click OK**.

REVIEW

The Student DVD with Data Files includes Review Questions and Supplementary Cases for this chapter.

CHAPTER SEVEN

AirCare Services

OBJECTIVES

After completing this chapter, you should be able to

- ***plan*** and ***design*** an accounting system for a small business
- ***prepare*** procedures for converting from a manual system
- ***understand*** the objectives of a computerized system
- ***create*** company files
- ***create*** and ***understand*** linked accounts
- ***set up*** accounts in the General, Payables and Receivables ledgers
- ***enter*** historical information for suppliers and customers
- ***correct*** historical transactions after recording them
- ***set up*** credit cards for receipts and payments
- ***set up*** sales taxes and tax codes
- ***leave*** history in an unbalanced state
- ***finish*** entering history after entering journal transactions
- ***enter*** postdated transactions

COMPANY INFORMATION

Company Profile

NOTES
Air Care Services
100 Belair Avenue, Unit 25
Regina, SK S4T 4U2
Tel 1: (306) 456-1299
Tel 2: (888) 455-7194
Fax: (306) 456-3188
Business No.: 533 766 457

Air Care Services, located in sunny Regina, Saskatchewan, has been operating successfully for the past 15 years under the ownership and management of Simon Arturro. After his mechanical engineering education and several years' experience with heating installations, he became a certified installer of solar electrical panels. As more consumers are eager to rely less on fossil fuels as their source of power, the demand for solar energy is steadily increasing. Arturro has two assistants: a certified electrician and an assistant installer.

Revenue comes from four sources: installation of new units, repairs, service contracts and subcontracting. Most jobs are new installations, either for individual customers or subcontracts for building projects. Small and medium-sized home roof installation jobs are usually finished in two to four days. Repair work, outside of the service contracts, may include removing and replacing the panels when customers are replacing a roof. Arturro also offers annual service contracts that provide free labour for existing installations.

Some customers — homeowners, owners of office buildings and builders — have accounts with Air Care and receive a 1 percent discount if they pay within 10 days. They are asked to settle their accounts in 30 days, paying by cash or by cheque. PST and GST apply to all work completed by Air Care.

Accounts have been set up with a local hardware store, with suppliers of solar panels and inverters (units that convert the solar DC power to AC) and other regular suppliers.

After remitting all taxes before the end of March 2021, Arturro converted the accounts for Air Care using the following information:

- Business Information
- Chart of Accounts
- Income Statement
- Balance Sheet
- Trial Balance
- Supplier Information
- Customer Information
- Accounting Procedures

BUSINESS INFORMATION

AIR CARE SERVICES

COMPANY INFORMATION

Address: 100 Belair Avenue, Unit 25
Regina, Saskatchewan S4T 4U2
Telephone 1: (306) 456-1299
Telephone 2: (888) 455-7194
Fax: (306) 456-3188
Business No.: 533 766 457 RT0001
Fiscal Start: January 1, 2021
Fiscal End: June 30, 2021
Earliest Transaction: March 31, 2021
Company Type: Construction/Contractor

REPORTS & FORMS

Choose settings for your printer and forms

USER PREFERENCES

Options
Use Accounting Terms
Automatically Save Changes to Records
Show List Buttons
Calculate Record Balances in Home Window by Session Date

View Settings
Hide: Inventory & Services, Employees & Payroll, Job Sites, Time & Billing
Daily Business Manager: turn off
Checklists: turn off
Show Session Date at Startup

Transaction Confirmation: turned on

Pop-Ups: your preferences

COMPANY SETTINGS

System
Do not allow dates before March 31, 2021
Allow Future Transactions,
Warn If Transactions Are 7 Days In Future
Warn If Accounts Are Not Balanced

Backup
Backup Weekly; Display reminders
Turn off scheduled backup

Features
Do not use orders, quotes, packing slips & projects (job sites)
Use both French and English

Credit Card Information
Card Used: Visa
Payable Account: 2160
Expense Account: 5020

Card Accepted: Visa
Discount Fee: 2.9%
Expense Account: 5020
Asset Account: 1070

Card Accepted: MasterCard
Discount Fee: 2.7%
Expense Account: 5020
Asset Account: 1080

Sales Taxes
Taxes: GST; PST
Codes: G - GST @ 5%;
GP - GST @ 5%, PST @ 6%, non-refundable

Forms Settings (Next Number)
Sales Invoices No. 710
Receipts No. 200
Check for duplicates

Date Format
Short Date Format: MM dd yyyy
On The Screen Use Long Dates

Logo: SageData19\LOGOS\AIRCARE.BMP

GENERAL SETTINGS: No changes

PAYABLES SETTINGS

Address: Regina, Saskatchewan, Canada
Options
Aging Periods: 10, 30, 60 days
Discounts Before Tax: Yes

RECEIVABLES SETTINGS

Address: Regina, Saskatchewan, Canada
Options
Aging Periods: 10, 30, 60 days
Interest Charges: compound, 1.5% monthly rate, after 1 day
Statements: Include Invoices for 31 days
New Customer Tax Code: GP

Discounts
Payment Terms: 1/10, n/30 after tax
Discounts Before Tax: No
Line Discounts: No

Comments
Sales Invoice: Interest @ 1.5% per month charged on accounts over 30 days

BANK ACCOUNTS: NEXT CHEQUE NO.

Bank: Chequing 101

CHART OF ACCOUNTS

AIR CARE SERVICES

ASSETS
1000 CURRENT ASSETS [H]
1010 Test Balance Account
1060 Bank: Chequing [A]
1070 Bank: Visa [A]
1080 Bank: MasterCard [A]
1100 Net Bank [S]
1200 Accounts Receivable
1210 Prepaid Insurance
1300 Solar Panels
1310 Inverters
1320 Electrical Supplies
1340 Office Supplies
1390 TOTAL CURRENT ASSETS [T]

1400 SHOP & EQUIPMENT [H]
1440 Computer System
1460 Service Equipment
1480 Tools
1500 Van ▶
▶1550 Shop
1590 TOTAL SHOP & EQUIPMENT [T]

LIABILITIES
2000 CURRENT LIABILITIES [H]
2100 Bank Loan
2160 Credit Card Payable
2200 Accounts Payable
2640 PST Payable
2650 GST Charged on Sales [A]
2670 GST Paid on Purchases [A]
2750 GST Owing (Refund) [S]
2790 TOTAL CURRENT LIABILITIES [T]

2800 LONG TERM LIABILITIES [H]
2850 Mortgage Payable
2890 TOTAL LONG TERM LIABILITIES [T] ▶

▶**EQUITY**
3000 OWNER'S EQUITY [H]
3560 S. Arturro, Capital
3650 Net Income [X]
3690 UPDATED CAPITAL [T]

REVENUE
4000 GENERAL REVENUE [H]
4100 Installation Revenue
4140 Service Contract Revenue
4160 Subcontracting Revenue
4180 Sales Discounts
4200 Interest Revenue
4290 TOTAL REVENUE [T]

EXPENSE
5000 OPERATING EXPENSES [H]
5010 Bank Charges
5020 Credit Card Fees
5040 Purchase Discounts ▶
▶5060 Hydro Expense
5070 Maintenance Services
5110 Computer Supplies Used
5120 Office Supplies Used
5150 Solar Panels Used
5160 Inverters Used
5180 Insurance Expense
5190 Telephone Expense
5200 Loan Interest Expense
5210 Mortgage Interest Expense
5290 TOTAL OPERATING EXPENSES [T]

5300 PAYROLL EXPENSES [H]
5320 Wages
5340 Payroll Service Charges
5390 TOTAL PAYROLL EXPENSES [T]

NOTES: The Chart of Accounts includes all accounts. Account types are marked for all subgroup Accounts [A], Subgroup totals [S], Heading accounts [H], Total accounts [T] and the type X account. All other unmarked accounts are postable Group accounts.

INCOME STATEMENT

AIR CARE SERVICES

January 1 to March 31, 2021

Revenue		
4000	GENERAL REVENUE	
4100	Installation Revenue	$ 82 500
4140	Service Contract Revenue	9 900
4160	Subcontracting Revenue	21 000
4180	Sales Discounts	−800
4200	Interest Revenue	525
4290	TOTAL REVENUE	$113 125
TOTAL REVENUE		$113 125 ▶

▶ Expenses		
5000	OPERATING EXPENSES	
5010	Bank Charges	$ 225
5020	Credit Card Fees	590
5040	Purchase Discounts	−300
5060	Hydro Expense	750
5070	Maintenance Services	1 365
5110	Computer Supplies Used	1 200
5120	Office Supplies Used	1 150
5150	Solar Panels Used	36 000
5160	Inverters Used	16 000
5180	Insurance Expense	3 600
5190	Telephone Expense	400
5200	Loan Interest Expense	625
5210	Mortgage Interest Expense	2 400
5290	TOTAL OPERATING EXPENSES	$64 005
5300	PAYROLL EXPENSES [H]	
5320	Wages	12 000
5340	Payroll Service Charges	330
5390	TOTAL PAYROLL EXPENSES	$12 330
TOTAL EXPENSE		$76 335
NET INCOME (LOSS)		$36 790

BALANCE SHEET

AIR CARE SERVICES

March 31, 2021

Assets			
1000	CURRENT ASSETS		
1060	Bank: Chequing	$ 34 660	
1070	Bank: Visa	1 950	
1080	Bank: MasterCard	1 060	
1100	Net Bank		$ 37 670
1200	Accounts Receivable		24 200
1210	Prepaid Insurance		3 800
1300	Solar Panels		28 280
1310	Inverters		33 420
1320	Electrical Supplies		6 100
1340	Office Supplies		400
1390	TOTAL CURRENT ASSETS		$ 133 870
1400	OFFICE & EQUIPMENT		
1440	Computer System		10 500
1460	Service Equipment		10 000
1480	Tools		3 000
1500	Van		31 000
1550	Shop		110 000
1590	TOTAL SHOP & EQUIPMENT		$164 500
	TOTAL ASSETS		$298 370 ▶

▶ Liabilities			
2000	CURRENT LIABILITIES		
2100	Bank Loan		$ 25 000
2160	Credit Card Payable		1 010
2200	Accounts Payable		20 100
2640	PST Payable		1 530
2650	GST Charged on Sales	$1 530	
2670	GST Paid on Purchases	–840	
2750	GST Owing (Refund)		690
2790	TOTAL CURRENT LIABILITIES		$ 48 330
2800	LONG TERM LIABILITIES		
2850	Mortgage Payable		80 000
2890	TOTAL LONG TERM LIABILITIES		$ 80 000
	TOTAL LIABILITIES		$ 128 330
Equity			
3000	OWNER'S EQUITY		
3560	S. Arturro, Capital		$ 133 250
3650	Net Income		36 790
3690	UPDATED CAPITAL		$ 170 040
	TOTAL EQUITY		$ 170 040
	LIABILITIES AND EQUITY		$298 370

TRIAL BALANCE

AIR CARE SERVICES

March 31, 2021

		Debit	Credit
1060	Bank: Chequing	$ 34 660	
1070	Bank: Visa	1 950	
1080	Bank: MasterCard	1 060	
1200	Accounts Receivable	24 200	
1210	Prepaid Insurance	3 800	
1300	Solar Panels	28 280	
1310	Inverters	33 420	
1320	Electrical Supplies	6 100	
1340	Office Supplies	400	
1440	Computer System	10 500	
1460	Service Equipment	10 000	
1480	Tools	3 000	
1500	Van	31 000	
1550	Shop	110 000	
2100	Bank Loan		$ 25 000
2160	Credit Card Payable		1 010
2200	Accounts Payable		20 100
2640	PST Payable		1 530
2650	GST Charged on Sales		1 530
2670	GST Paid on Purchases	840	
2850	Mortgage Payable		80 000 ▶

		Debit	Credit
▶ 3560	S. Arturro, Capital		$133 250
4100	Installation Revenue		82 500
4140	Service Contract Revenue		9 900
4160	Subcontracting Revenue		21 000
4180	Sales Discounts	$ 800	
4200	Interest Revenue		525
5010	Bank Charges	225	
5020	Credit Card Fees	590	
5040	Purchase Discounts		300
5060	Hydro Expense	750	
5070	Maintenance Services	1 365	
5110	Computer Supplies Used	1 200	
5120	Office Supplies Used	1 150	
5150	Solar Panels Used	36 000	
5160	Inverters Used	16 000	
5180	Insurance Expense	3 600	
5190	Telephone Expense	400	
5200	Loan Interest Expense	625	
5210	Mortgage Interest Expense	2 400	
5320	Wages	12 000	
5340	Payroll Service Charges	330	
		$376 645	$376 645

SUPPLIER INFORMATION

AIR CARE SERVICES

Supplier Name (Contact)	Address	Phone No. Fax No.	E-mail Web Site Tax ID	Terms Account	YTD Purchases (Pre- & Post-Tax Payments) Tax Code
Beausejour Electrical Products (Janine Beausejour)	50 Shockley Rd., Unit 18 Regina, Saskatchewan S4F 2T2	Tel 1: (306) 476-5282 Tel 2: (306) 476-3997 Fax: (306) 476-5110	jb@beausejour.com beausejour.com 444 276 539 RT0001	1/10, n/30 (before tax) 1320	$2 100 ($2 000 & $2 100) G
Green Earth Products Inc. (Ezra Green)	2 Greening St. Regina, Saskatchewan S4F 9J9	Tel: (306) 475-6432 Fax: (306) 475-8600	egreen@greenearth.com greenearth.com 177 235 447 RT0001	1/10, n/30 (before tax) 1310	G
Killarney Solar Equipment (Kieper Warme)	91 Radiation St. Regina, Saskatchewan S4B 4F4	Tel: (306) 363-0210 Fax: (306) 363-2000	kw@heatexchange.com heatexchange.com 571 277 631 RT0001	1/5, n/30 (before tax) 1300	G
*Receiver General for Canada	Sudbury Tax Services Office PO Box 20004 Sudbury, Ontario P3A 6B4	Tel 1: (800) 561-7761 Tel 2: (800) 959-2221	cra-arc.gc.ca	net 1	($790 & $790) No tax
*Saskatchewan Energy Corp. (Kira Strong)	50 Watts Rd. Regina, Saskatchewan S4G 5K8	Tel 1: (306) 755-6000 Tel 2: (306) 755-3997 Fax: (306) 754-7201	accounts@seg.ca seg.ca 459 021 648 RT0001	net 10 5060	$840 ($800 & $840) G
*Saskatel (Sotto Voce)	4 Speakers Corners Regina, Saskatchewan S4L 4G2	Tel: (306) 361-3255	accounts@saskatel.ca saskatel.ca 492 304 597 RT0001	net 10 5190	$660 ($600 & $660) GP
Starbuck Advertising Agency (Pam Fletts)	300 Flyer St. Suite 800 Regina, Saskatchewan S4B 1C6	Tel: (306) 361-1727 Fax: (306) 361-8229	pfletts@saa.com saa.com 610 728 362 RT0001	net 10	$1 100 ($1 000 & $1 100) GP
Wheatfields Hardware (Nutley Bolter)	72 Hammer St. Regina, Saskatchewan S4P 1B8	Tel 1: (306) 369-0808 Tel 2: (306) 369-6222	nbolter@yahoo.com 385 416 821 RT0001	net 15 1480	$990 ($900 & $990) GP
Willow Garage (Axel Rodd)	699 Willow St. Regina, Saskatchewan S4P 1B3	Tel 1: (306) 368-6444 Tel 2: (306) 368-6000	axel@wefixcars.com wefixcars.com 129 732 012 RT0001	net 30	$440 ($400 & $440) GP

NOTES: *For Receiver General, Saskatchewan Energy Corp. and Saskatel, Cheque is the default payment method for invoices. For all other suppliers, Pay Later is the default.

OUTSTANDING SUPPLIER INVOICES

AIR CARE SERVICES

Supplier Name	Terms	Date	Inv/Chq No.	Amount	Tax	Total
Beausejour Electrical Products	1/10, n/30 (before tax)	Mar. 26/21	B-894	$10 000	$500	$10 500
		Mar. 26/21	Chq 94			4 500
	1/10, n/30 (before tax)	Mar. 28/21	B-921	2 000	100	2 100
			Balance owing			$ 8 100
Killarney Solar Equipment	1/5, n/30 (before tax)	Mar. 25/21	KS-1031	$20 000	1 000	$21 000
		Mar. 28/21	Chq 96			5 200
		Mar. 31/21	Chq 98			9 900
			Balance owing			$ 5 900
				Grand Total		$14 000

CUSTOMER INFORMATION

AIR CARE SERVICES

Customer Name (Contact)	Address	Phone No. Fax No.	E-mail Web Site	Terms Revenue Acct Tax Code	YTD Sales (Credit Limit) Customer Since
Grande Pointe Towers (Sophie Grande)	77 LaPointe Cr. White City Saskatchewan S0G 5B0	Tel: (306) 322-7500 Fax: (306) 322-7436	sgrande@GPTowers.com GPTowers.com	1/10, n/30 (after tax) 4100 GP	$11 000 ($20 000) Jan. 1/21
Midwest Funeral Home (N. Mourning)	8 Quiet St. Regina, Saskatchewan S4B 1E1	Tel: (306) 763-WAKE or (306) 763-9253 Fax: (306) 762-9301	nm@midwestfh.com midwestfh.com	1/10, n/30 (after tax) 4140 GP	($10 000) Aug. 1/19
Oak Bluff Banquet Hall (Ann Oakley)	4 Celebration Ave. Regina, Saskatchewan S4V 3H7	Tel: (306) 622-7391 Fax: (306) 622-7900	annie@OBBH.com OBBH.com	1/10, n/30 (after tax) 4160 GP	($20 000) Mar. 1/21
Passions Department Store (Mann E. Kinn)	44 Highlife Ave. Regina, Saskatchewan S4L 2K0	Tel: (306) 762-8662 Fax: (306) 763-9115	passions.com	1/10, n/30 (after tax) 4100 GP	$6 300 ($15 000) Jan. 1/16
Regina School Board (Ed Ducate)	49 Trainer St. Regina, Saskatchewan S4C 4B6	Tel 1: (306) 466-5000 Tel 2: (306) 466-1123 Fax: (306) 466-2000	edd@rdsb.ca rdsb.ca	1/10, n/30 (after tax) 4100 GP	$8 400 ($15 000) Mar. 1/21
Selkirk Community Centre (Elsa Peeples)	588 Populous St. Regina, Saskatchewan S4T 8N1	Tel: (306) 368-4575 Fax: (306) 368-2198	elsa@selkirk.com selkirk.com	1/10, n/30 (after tax) 4100 GP	($20 000) Jul. 1/18

NOTES: For all customers, Pay Later is the default payment method for invoices.

OUTSTANDING CUSTOMER INVOICES

AIR CARE SERVICES

Customer Name	Terms	Date	Inv/Chq No.	Amount	Total
Grande Pointe Towers	1/10, n/30 (after tax)	Mar. 24/21	699	$4 440	
		Mar. 28/21	Chq 4896	2 460	
	1/10, n/30 (after tax)	Mar. 28/21	703	2 220	
			Balance owing		$4 200
Regina School Board	1/10, n/30 (after tax)	Mar. 28/21	701	$22 200	
		Mar. 28/21	Chq 10367	2 200	
			Balance owing		$20 000
				Grand Total	$24 200

Accounting Procedures

Open-Invoice Accounting for Payables and Receivables

The open-invoice method of accounting for invoices allows the business to keep track of each individual invoice and any partial payments made against it. This method is in contrast to methods that keep track of only the outstanding balance by combining all invoice balances owed to a supplier or by a customer. Sage 50 uses the open-invoice method. When invoices are fully paid, they should be removed periodically after statements are received from the supplier or sent to the customers.

GST and PST

Air Care Services is a contractor business using the regular method of calculating GST. GST, at the rate of 5 percent, charged and collected from customers will be recorded as a liability in *GST Charged on Sales*. GST paid to suppliers will be recorded in *GST Paid on Purchases* as a decrease in tax liability. The balance owing, the difference between the GST charged and GST paid, or the request for a refund will be remitted to the Receiver General for Canada quarterly.

Air Care charges customers 6 percent PST on all sales and pays PST on some goods. Air Care is exempt from PST for purchases of items that are sold or used in the installation work because the customer pays PST on the sales using these products.

NOTES
Most bank services and other financial institution services are exempt from GST collection.
In 2018, Saskatchewan raised the PST rate from 5 percent to 6 percent.

Sales of Services

Accounts are set up for several customers. Other customers pay for their purchases immediately by cash, cheque or credit card. Separate bank accounts are set up for credit card deposits. You can enter transactions for cash and credit card customers by choosing One-Time Customer and typing the name of the customer in the Address field or by typing the customer's name in the Name field and choosing the Quick Add or Continue option.

For cash sales, the program will debit *Bank: Chequing* (or *Bank: Visa* or *MasterCard* for credit card payments) instead of the *Accounts Receivable* control account.

NOTES
The terms Invoice and Bill are interchangeable. The Premium version uses Bill for the construction/contracting business and the Pro version uses Sales Invoice.

Purchases

Most regular suppliers have given Air Care credit terms, including some discounts for early payment. Some purchases are accompanied by immediate payment, usually by cheque or credit card. Cheque payments are preferred because the cancelled cheques become part of the business records. Enter the cash transaction for purchases from new suppliers in the Payments Journal as an Other Payment or in the Purchases Journal. Choose the appropriate Payment Method; choose One-Time Supplier from the Supplier list and type the supplier's name in the Address field. You can also type the name in the Supplier field and choose Quick Add or Continue.

For cash purchases paid by cash or cheque, the program will credit *Bank: Chequing* instead of the *Accounts Payable* control account. For credit card purchases, *Credit Card Payable* is credited. All other accounts for this transaction will be appropriately debited and credited.

PRO VERSION
When we use the term Supplier for the Premium version, Pro version users should substitute the term Vendor.

Discounts

Air Care Services offers a 1 percent discount to account customers if they settle their accounts within 10 days. Full payment is requested within 30 days. These payment terms are set up as defaults. When the receipt is entered, if the discount is still available, the program will display the amount of the discount and the net amount owing automatically. Discounts are not allowed on partial payments or on cash purchases paid by cheque or credit card. All customer sales discounts are calculated on after-tax amounts.

Some suppliers also offer discounts, calculated on the amounts before taxes, for early settlement of accounts. Again, when the terms are entered for the supplier and full payment is made before the discount period expires, the program will display the pretax discount as available and automatically calculate a net balance owing. Payment terms vary from supplier to supplier.

INSTRUCTIONS

NOTES
Source documents begin on page 253 after the setup instructions.

1. **Set up** the **company accounts** using the Business Information, Chart of Accounts, Balance Sheet, Income Statement, Trial Balance and Supplier and Customer Information provided for March 31, 2021. Detailed instructions follow to assist you in setting up the company accounts.

   When you are ready to enter transactions (page 253), the Payables Ledger will be unbalanced. This is intentional to demonstrate working with an unfinished history and entering historical transactions after entering current transactions.

2. **Enter** the **transactions** beginning on page 253 in Sage 50 using the Chart of Accounts, Supplier Information, Customer Information and Accounting Procedures.

3. **Print** the **reports** checked on the printing form after completing your entries:

REPORTS

Accounts
- ☐ Chart of Accounts
- ☐ Account List
- ☐ General Journal Entries

Financials
- ✓ Comparative Balance Sheet: April 1 and May 1, difference in percentage
- ✓ Income Statement: January 1 to May 1
- ✓ Trial Balance: May 1
- ✓ All Journal Entries: April 1 to June 11
- ✓ General Ledger accounts: 1060 4100 4120 from April 1 to May 1

- ✓ Cash Flow Projection Detail Report for account 1060 for 30 days
- ☐ Statement of Cash Flows

Tax
- ✓ GST Report April 1 to May 1

Banking
- ☐ Cheque Log Report

Payables
- ☐ Supplier List
- ☐ Supplier Aged
- ✓ Aged Overdue Payables: May 1
- ☐ Expenses Journal Entries
- ☐ Payments Journal Entries

Receivables
- ☐ Customer List
- ☐ Customer Aged
- ✓ Aged Overdue Receivables: May 1
- ☐ Sales Journal Entries
- ☐ Receipts Journal Entries
- ☐ Customer Statements

Mailing Labels
- ☐ Labels

KEYSTROKES FOR SETUP

Creating Company Files

For Air Care Services, we will create the company files from scratch rather than use one of the starter files or templates. Once we create the files and define the defaults, we will add the accounts; define linked accounts for the General, Payables and Receivables ledgers; and create supplier and customer records.

Start the **Sage 50 program**.

You should open the familiar Sage 50, Welcome and Select Company window:

PRO VERSION
The program name is Sage 50 Pro Accounting.

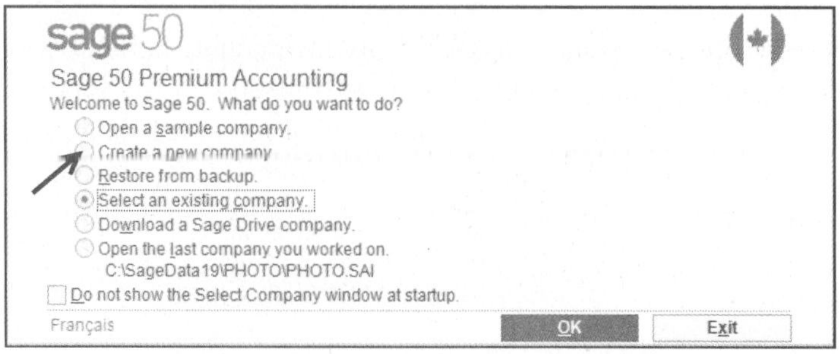

Click **Create A New Company**. **Click** **OK**.

You will start with the New Company Setup wizard introduction screen:

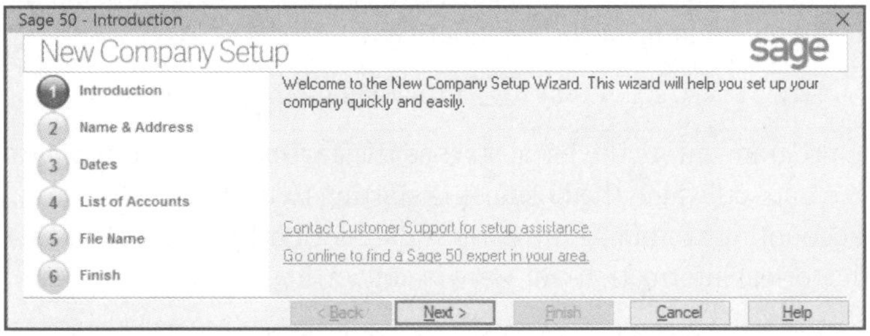

This screen introduces the Setup wizard and some support options.

Click **Next** to continue:

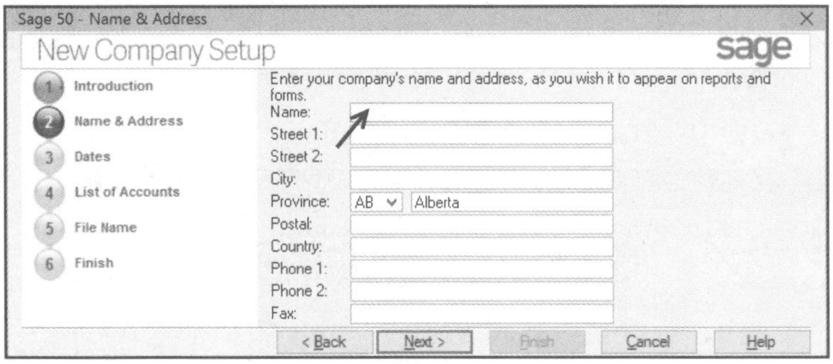

You must now enter company information for the business. The cursor is in the Name field. Alberta and its two-letter abbreviation — the first entry in the province list — are entered as defaults. Use the Business Information on page 202 to enter the company name and address details.

Type `Air Care Services` **Press** *tab* to enter the name.

Type `100 Belair Avenue` **Press** *tab* to enter the street address.

Type `Unit 25` **Press** *tab* to complete the address.

Type `Regina` **Press** *tab* and **Type** `S`

Click the **Postal Code field**. SK and Saskatchewan are entered automatically as this is the only province name beginning with S.

Type `s4t4u2` **Press** *tab* to enter the postal code.

Type `Canada` **Press** *tab*. **Type** `3064561299` **Press** *tab* to enter the phone number.

Type `8884557194` to enter the alternate number in the Phone 2 field. **Press** *tab* to advance to the Fax field. **Type** `3064563188`

Click **Next** to open the company fiscal dates screen:

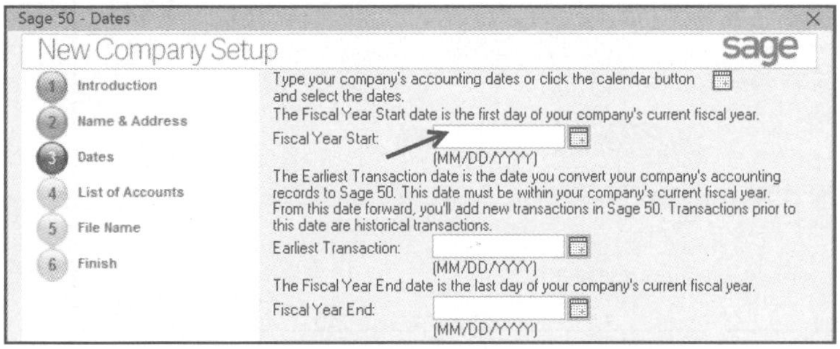

NOTES

Remember that you can personalize the data file by adding your own name to the company name.

WARNING!

We will set the date format with the Company settings. The initial date format for your new file is determined by your computer system settings, so your initial setting may be DD-MM-YYYY, MM-DD-YYYY or YYYY-MM-DD. The author's computer had MM-DD-YYYY as the setting, so this format is used initially for dates.

WARNING!
The Calendar icon starts with the current month for your computer system. It is easier to type in the dates than it is to scroll through several months to find the one you need.

Typing the date in text format ensures that you will enter it correctly. You should type a four-digit year the first time you enter a date in the year 2000 or later to be certain that the year will be 2021 and not 1921.

NOTES
To find out if you need to enter four digits for the year, try typing a date such as 26-5-18. This entry will also let you know if month or day comes first.

NOTES
The Earliest Transaction date is also the initial date before which you do not allow transactions.

NOTES
The list of accounts Sage 50 creates will include many accounts not required by Air Care.

PRO VERSION
Remember that icon labels are the same for all company types – Customer and Vendor are the terms used throughout the Receivables and Payables modules, respectively.

These company fiscal dates are like the ones you entered for Love It Again (Chapter 4) as part of the Company Information setup. The cursor is in the Fiscal Year Start field. This is the date on which the business begins its fiscal year. For Air Care Services, the fiscal start date is the beginning of the calendar year.

Type `jan 1 2021` **Press** *tab* to advance to the calendar.

Initially the program enters the fiscal start as the **earliest transaction date**. You need to enter the date on which the business is starting to use Sage 50 as its computerized accounting system — the earliest date for posting journal entries and the latest date for historical information. Air Care is converting its records on March 31.

Press *tab* to advance to the Earliest Transaction date field.

Type `mar 31 2021`

Press *tab* **twice** to advance to the Fiscal Year End field — the date Air Care Services ends its fiscal period. The end of the year is the default fiscal end date. Air Care Services' fiscal period is six months.

Type `jun 30 2021` **Click Next** to continue:

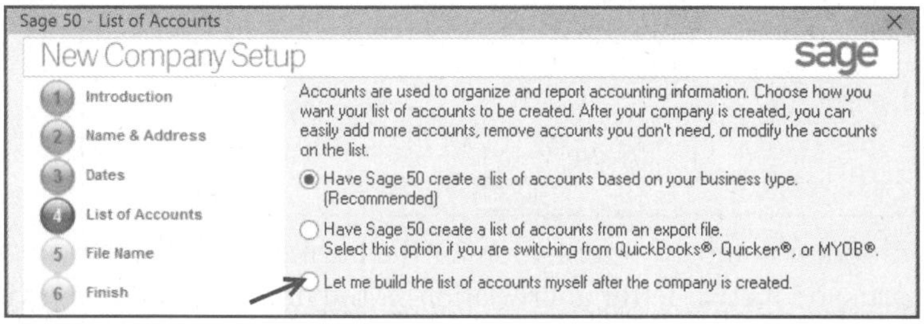

You can let Sage 50 create a set of accounts that are suitable for the business type you select, start from scratch to create the accounts or copy data exported from another program. The set of accounts created by the program will include many accounts not required for Air Care Services. Because our setup is relatively small and we want to demonstrate all the stages of the setup, we will create the accounts ourselves. This approach allows us to present all the options available for each stage.

Click **Let Me Build The List Of Accounts Myself After The Company Is Created**. **Click Next**:

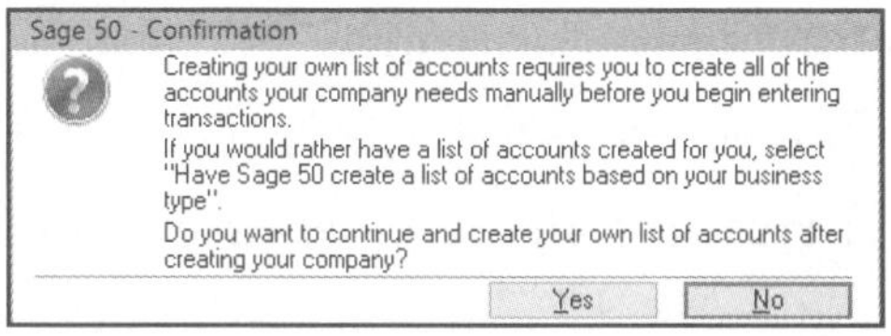

A message appears confirming your selection to create all the accounts on your own.

Click **Yes** to continue to the industry type selection list:

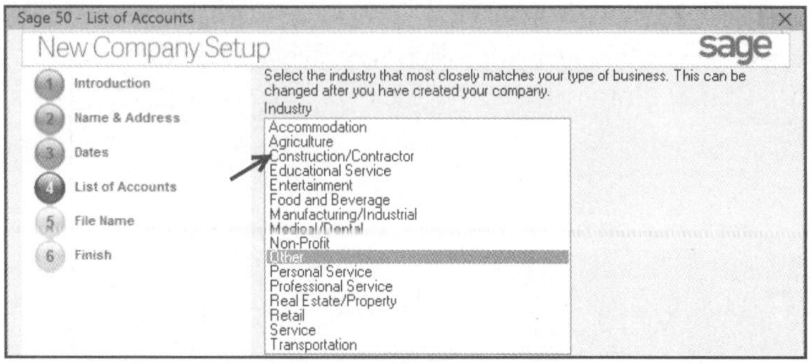

At this stage you should choose the type of business that best describes your company. This selection will determine some of the default settings and icon labels. Air Care Services is a construction/contractor business.

Click **Construction/Contractor** as the Industry type. **Click Next**:

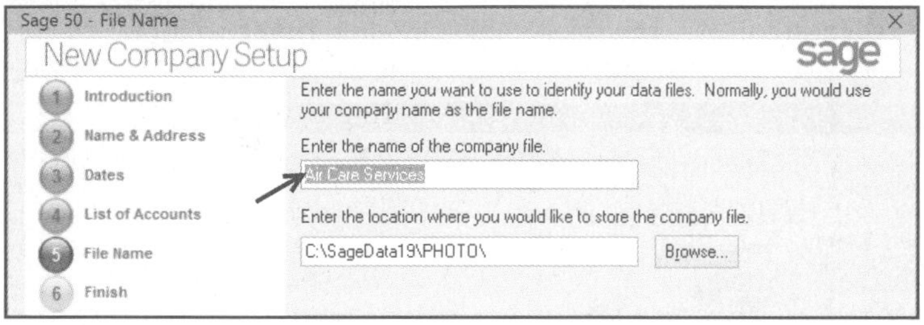

The File Name screen is now open and you must choose a file name and folder to store the new data set. The company name is entered as the default name for the data file, and it is selected.

Type AIRCARE **Press** *tab* to advance to the location field.

The last folder you used will be the default selection — that is, PHOTO, if you last worked with the Phoebe's Photo Studio data set. Change folders if necessary to access the one with your other data files. If you have already created the folder you want to use,

Click **Browse** to open the Browse For Folder screen to select a folder. Otherwise,

Drag through PHOTO in the folder name or the last folder in the location field.

Type AIRCARE to replace PHOTO or the last folder in the location field.

Click **Next** — Sage 50 requests confirmation:

Sage 50 asks if you want to create the new folder.

Click **Yes** to create the new folder and file:

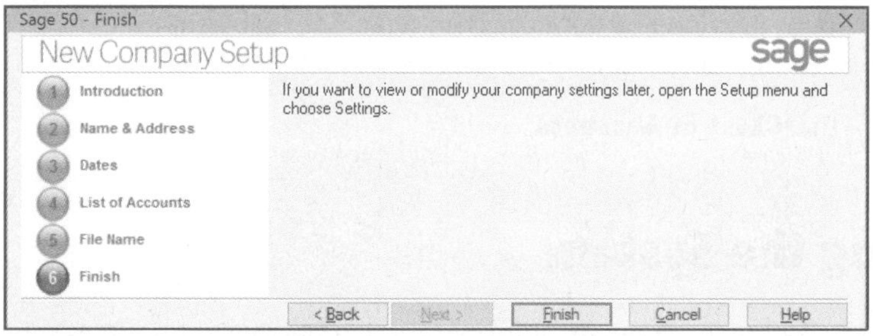

This screen reminds you that you can change this information from the Setup menu.

Click **Finish**. **Wait** for Sage 50 to finish creating the database for your new company files and open the final Setup screen:

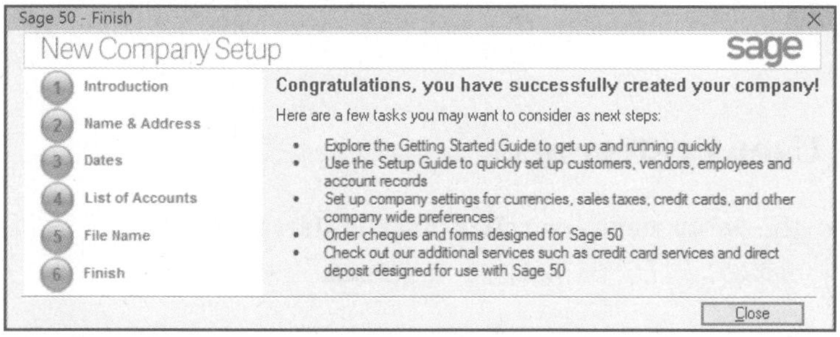

NOTES

Sage 50 will automatically add the correct file extension. You do not need to type it when you are creating a new data set.

You may type the new names in upper or lower case. For consistency we use upper case letters for names.

Click **Close** to complete the file creation stage. The Getting Started and Home window will be open.

Click **Show This Window On Startup** to remove the ✓ in the Getting Started Guide window so that it will not open each time you start the program.

Click **Close** to display the Receivables module Home window:

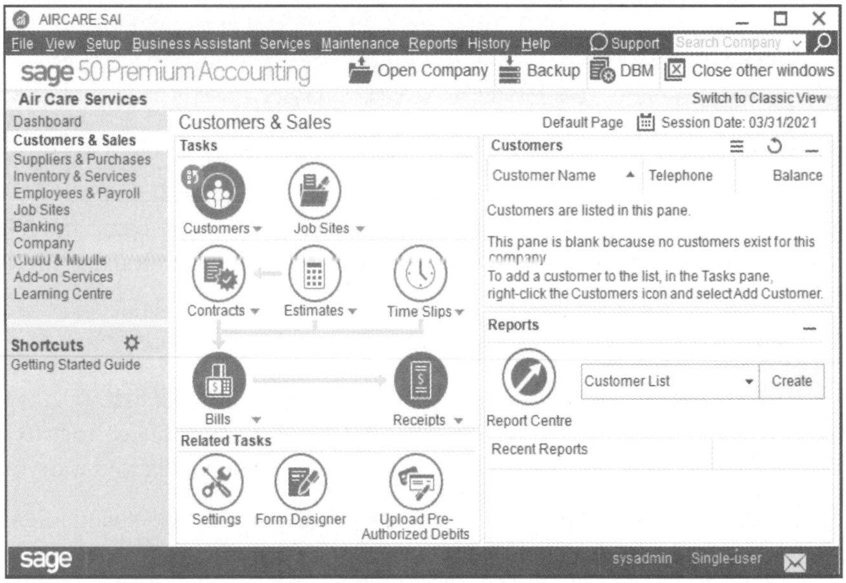

The Home window is now open with the name AIRCARE in the title bar. One shortcut, for the Getting Started Guide, is added by default. However, non-accounting terms are selected, so the module names are different from the ones in previous applications. Customers & Sales replaces Receivables, and Suppliers & Purchases replaces Payables. We will change these terms as part of the setup.

Because the ledgers are still open for entering historical information, , the open history symbol, is still on the Customers ledger icon. It is also added to the ledger icons in other module windows. No ledgers are hidden.

Display the **Chart of Accounts** for the Current Year.

The only account provided by default is the type X account, the General Ledger linked account, *Current Earnings*.

Close the **Chart of Accounts**.

Preparing the System

The next step is to enter the company information that customizes the files for Air Care Services. You begin by preparing the system and changing the defaults. Use the Business Information on page 202 to enter defaults for Air Care Services.

You should change the user preference and reports and forms defaults to suit your own work environment. The ones we provide will match the screens we provide.

Changing User Preferences

Choose the **Setup menu**, then **click** **User Preferences**.

NOTES
If you get a message about the payroll plan or any other Advisor messages, you can close them.
The Getting Started window may be hidden by the Home window initially. Click the Sage 50 icon in the task bar and then click the window you want to display.

NOTES
Your initial format for the session date will depend on your computer system date settings. You may have the day, month or year first, and the year may have two or four digits.

PRO VERSION
pro
Pro replaces Premium as the program name.
The Sales Invoices icon replaces Bills, and Job Sites are named Projects. You will not have icons for Estimates, Contracts or Time Slips.
In the Modules pane, the labels Vendors & Purchases and Projects are used.

NOTES
The list of equivalent accounting and non-accounting terms is provided in Appendix B.

NOTES
Update your backup copy frequently as you work through the setup. Until you change the backup settings (page 214), the file will be backed up automatically when you close the program.

NOTES
You may want to refer to the keystrokes in Chapter 4 to assist you in completing the setup and to the keystrokes in other chapters to assist you with the transactions for this application.

PRO VERSION
pro
The Automatically Refresh Lists option does not apply for the single-user Pro version.

If you are working in multi-user mode, decide whether you want to refresh lists automatically so that changes other users make affect your file immediately. The option to Show List Buttons is already selected.

Choose **Use Accounting Terms** so that your on-screen terms will match the ones used in this workbook.

Choose **Automatically Save Changes To Supplier, Customer And Other Records**.

Choose **Calculate Record Balances In The Home Window By Session Date**, instead of the default — balances based on the latest transactions.

Click **View**.

Click **Inventory & Services**, **Employees & Payroll** and **Time & Billing** to hide the unused modules and features. You can hide Job Sites if you want, but you do not need to.

Click **After Changing Session Date** for **Daily Business Manager** and **Checklists** to remove the two ✓s.

Choose **Show Change Session Date At Startup**.

Click **Transaction Confirmation**. **Confirm** that the **Confirmation Message Box** is checked to activate this option.

Click **Pop-ups**. Choose the messages you want to display and hide.

Click **OK** to save the preference changes and return to the Home window.

You will now have the familiar accounting term labels for the modules. At this stage the hidden modules have been removed from the Home window:

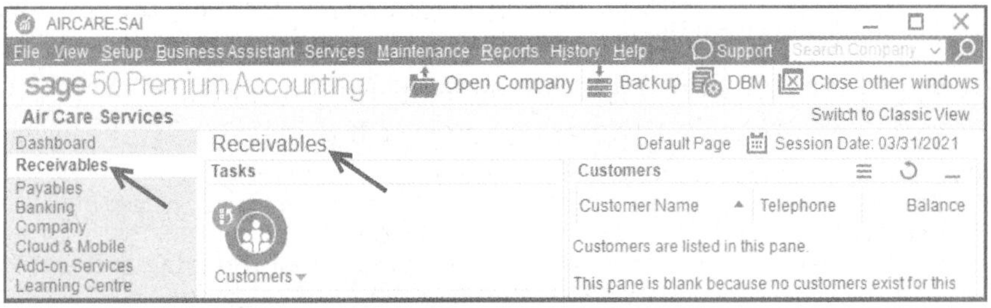

Changing Company Default Settings

Many of the next steps for setting up company defaults and entering General Ledger accounts can be completed directly from the Company module Home window. We will start from that point.

Click **Company** in the Modules list to change the Home window.

The company window is the same as the one we used for Binh's Bins and Love It Again. You can now open the Company Settings screen from the Settings icon, and you are able to create ledger accounts by clicking on the Chart of Accounts icon.

If you need help entering company settings, refer to page 75.

Changing Company Information

Click the **Settings icon** in the Related Tasks pane.

Click **Information** to display the Company Information screen.

NOTES

When you automatically save changes to records, you will not be prompted to save information each time you close a ledger after making a change.

When you display Home window record balances by the session date, they will not include postdated transactions. You can automatically refresh these amounts or refresh them yourself by clicking the Refresh tool.

PRO VERSION

The Time & Billing module is not available in Pro, so you do not need to hide it.

You will click Project instead of Job Site to hide this module.

NOTES

The option to show inventory lists does not apply to Air Care. You can remove this checkmark if you want.

NOTES

The session date is still set at the default format, based on your computer system settings. We will change this when we customize the Company Settings (Date Format options). We have hidden the Job Costs/Projects module.

WARNING!

You cannot complete many of the setup steps in multi-user mode.

CLASSIC VIEW

The Settings tool is available. Clicking it when a ledger icon is selected will display the settings for that ledger.

If you click the Settings tool when no ledger or journal icon is selected, you must select a ledger from the list.

From any Home window, you can also choose the Setup menu, then click Settings, Company and Information.

Most of the fields on this screen are already filled in based on the information we entered when we created the company files. You can edit the information if you made a mistake. We still need to add the business number.

Notice that the earliest transaction date appears as the session date on the Company Information screen. If there are any postdated transactions in the file, the Latest Transaction Date will be later than the session date.

You can return to the Company Information screen at any time to make changes. The program will set up defaults for the session date based on this information.

NOTES
The RT extension for the business number indicates the area of the business for reporting to the Canada Revenue Agency. For example, registered charity and payroll GST reports have different extensions than income tax.

Click the **Business Number field**.

Type 533 766 457 RT0001

Changing System Defaults

Click **System** in the list of company options on the left.

Most of the default System Settings are correct. Air Care uses the accrual basis of accounting, so Use Cash-Basis Accounting should remain unchecked. The option to Use Cheque No. as the source code can remain selected. This setting will include the cheque number in reports.

Initially, we will not allow any transactions before March 31, the earliest transaction date. We want to allow posting to future transactions but receive a warning if the dates are more than seven days in the future. Since you can enter transactions before completing the history, you should activate the warning about unbalanced accounts to prevent mistakes. The warning makes you aware of errors or omissions before you proceed too far with transactions.

NOTES
If you click the calendar for the prior transactions field, you cannot access any month before March. Entering a date prior to March 31 will generate an error with the advice that the date must be between March 31 (the earliest transaction date) and June 30 (the fiscal end date).

Click **Do Not Allow Transactions Dated Before** to add a ✓. **Press** tab.

Type 3-31-21 (This date entry is not ambiguous.)

Enter **7** as the number of days in the future before you are warned.

Click **Warn If Accounts Are Not Balanced When Entering A New Month**.

Changing the Backup Options

We will back up the files on a weekly basis and leave on the reminder to back up each time we close the data file.

NOTES
If you choose to back up your file automatically, leave the option checked and choose the backup frequency, the backup file location and the number of backup files you want to keep.

Click **Backup** in the list on the left. **Choose** **Weekly** as the frequency for Backup Reminders.

Click **Automatically Back Up This File** to remove the ✓.

Connected Services Settings

These features require subscribing to the Sage services and do not apply to Air Care.

If you have Office 365, you can modify your data file to integrate your Sage 50 customer and supplier data with your Microsoft Office file. The **Office 365 Integration** settings allow you to choose the Sage 50 data that connects with the Office program and to schedule the synchronization.

In **Payment Processing** settings, you choose EFT or Direct Payments as the method to receive payments, and you can choose to review the payments and create reports.

The **Bank Transactions** settings allow you to set up and connect to your bank accounts and to import bank statements.

Changing the Features Selections

Customizing the icons and features that appear can simplify journal entries.

Click **Features** in the list on the left.

Click **each feature** and the **language setting** to change the status.

This removes the unused features and makes bilingual data entry and forms available.

Since we need to choose linked accounts when we set up credit cards and sales taxes, we will create accounts before entering these settings. Since Air Care does not use other currencies, we can skip this setup screen.

PRO VERSION

Click My Company Does Business In English And French. The other features are already deselected.

Packing slips are not available in the Pro version.

Changing Forms Default Settings

Click **Forms** to display the Settings for Forms:

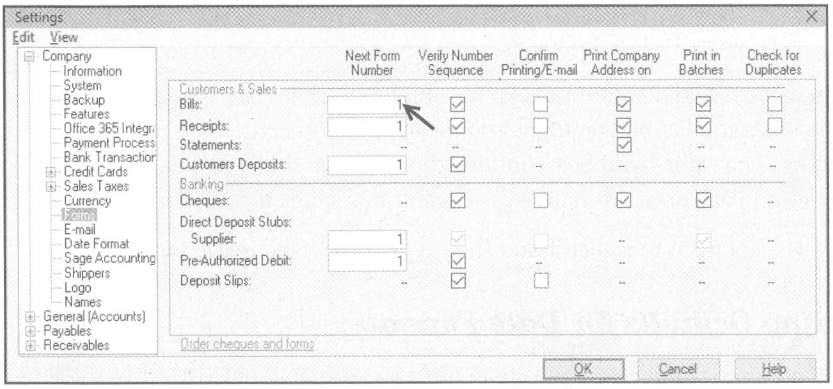

NOTES

Form Numbers are hidden for features in the modules that are not used. Employee Direct Deposit Stubs and Time Slips are also numbered when Payroll and Time Slips are used.

The Forms screen allows us to set up the automatic numbering sequences for business forms and to include warnings if the number you entered is a duplicate or out of sequence. You can set up the numbering sequence for all business forms that are generated internally or within the company.

We can skip the forms Air Care does not use — customer deposits, direct payments and pre-authorized debits. Cheque and bank deposit sequence numbers are added separately in the reports and forms settings for each bank account (refer to page 221).

Click the **Bills Next Form Number field**. **Type** 710

Click the **Receipts Next Form Number field**. **Type** 200

PRO VERSION

Click the invoices Next Form Number field. Invoice will replace the term Bill throughout the program.

The five column checklists on the Forms Settings screen allow you to **verify number sequences** and add reminders if you print bills or invoices, quotes, purchase orders and so forth. Verifying sequence numbers will warn you if you skip or duplicate a number and give you a chance to make a correction if necessary before posting. Choosing to **confirm** will set up the program to remind you to print or e-mail the form if you try to post before printing since posting removes the form from the screen. You should add confirmations if you print or e-mail these forms regularly.

The third column allows you to add the **company address** to various forms. If you use preprinted forms that already include the address, remove the checkmarks to avoid double printing this information. If you have generic blank forms, leave the checkmarks so that the address is included. The next column refers to **batch printing**. If you print in batches (for example, print all the invoices for the day at the end of each day) you should leave this option checked for the forms you use. The final column allows the program to check for **duplicate** bill and receipt numbers. We should check for these duplicates.

NOTES

The additional options in the columns also apply to cheques, deposit slips and pre-authorized debits, even though we do not have sequence numbers for cheques on the Forms Settings screen. These should be set correctly for your own setup.

NOTES

Batch printing is covered in Chapter 14.

Click the **check box for Bills** and the **check box for Receipts** in the Check For Duplicates column.

Click to add a ✓ to any check box and click again to remove a ✓.

Entering Default Comments for E-mail

The next step is to select your e-mail program and add default messages to e-mails. You can add the company phone and fax numbers to the message so that the customer or supplier can contact you more easily. Files you e-mail will be sent with PDF format attachments.

Click **E-mail** in the list of Company options to open the next Settings screen:

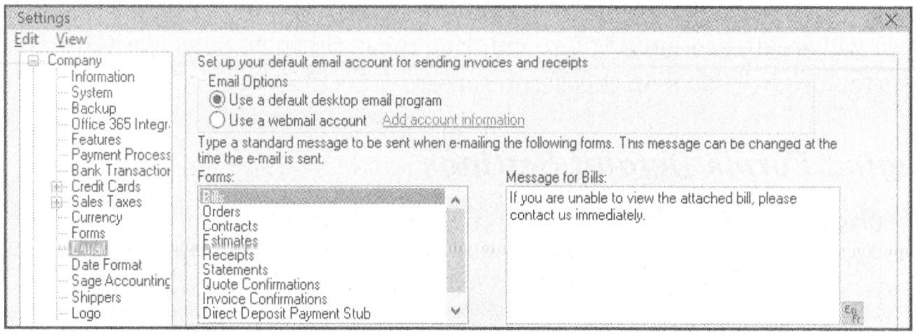

NOTES
E-mailing invoices and orders is covered in Chapter 12 and in Appendix J on the Student DVD.
If you choose from the Webmail Account drop-down list, you must enter your e-mail address. If you choose Other from this list, you will also need to add the SMTP server and port from your account settings.

You can use the default or select a webmail program from the drop-down list.

The left-hand list box contains the forms that you can e-mail to suppliers or customers. The right-hand box contains the message that will be added to the selected e-mail. You do not need to change the default messages for Air Care.

Click a form to select it and then type a message in the box beside it.

Entering Defaults for Date Formats

The default date formats use the short form on-screen. We want to use the long form so that the date will always be clear. Sunday is correct as the first day of the week.

WARNING!
Your date format settings should match the ones used in the text. The drop-down list allows you to select month, day or year to come first.
Select MM dd yyyy from the Short Date Format drop-down list.

Click **Date Format** in the list of Company options.

Choose **MM dd yyyy** from the Short Date Format drop-down list.

Click **Long Dates** beside On The Screen, Use to change the selection.

Adding a Company Logo

We will add the company logo next. The logo is located in the SageData19\LOGOS folder (or the folder you chose) where you installed the other data files.

Click **Logo** in the list on the left.

Click **Browse**. **Click This PC** (or **Computer**) in the left-hand pane. **Double-click C:**, **SageData19**, **LOGOS** and then **click AIRCARE**.

Click the **Open button** to add the image and file name:

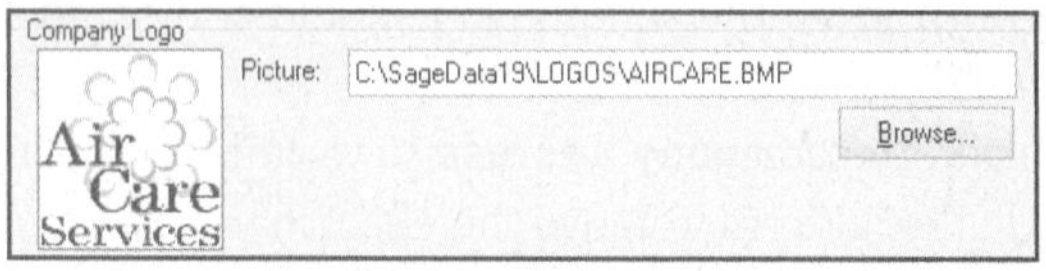

NOTES
The default folder should be the folder you are currently working in.
If you are showing file extensions, the picture file will be named AIRCARE.BMP.

Check the **information** you have just entered and **make** any necessary **corrections**, including corrections to the fiscal dates.

Click **OK** to save the new information and return to the Home window.

WARNING!
Verify that the Form locations for the forms are valid for your program setup. If they are not, you will get an error message when you try to close the Reports & Forms window. The default folder is Sage 50 Premium Accounting Version 2019\Forms.

Changing the Printer Defaults

Choose the **Setup menu** and **click Reports & Forms**.

The printer setting options for reports are given. Notice that the defaults include adding the computer system (calendar) date to reports and information about whether the report is filtered. You can check whether the report fits on the page to improve the appearance of your printed reports, and you can change Reports & Forms settings any time. When the settings are correct,

Click **OK** to save the new information, or **click Cancel** if you have not made any changes, and return to the Home window.

NOTES
Refer to Appendix E on the Student DVD for more information about printing options and customizing reports.

Preparing the Ledgers

Before entering the remaining settings, we should create the Chart of Accounts, because many of the settings require default or linked accounts.

The next stage in setting up an accounting system involves preparing each ledger, beginning with the General Ledger. This stage involves the following steps:

1. organizing all accounting reports and records (this step has been completed)
2. modifying the *Current Earnings* account
3. creating new accounts
4. setting up credit cards, taxes and other features
5. defining linked accounts for the ledgers
6. entering supplier and customer information
7. adding historical account balances, invoices and payments

NOTES
Although you can create new accounts as you need them in any Account field, creating them all at the beginning allows you to check them more easily for accuracy and type. In the same way, it is safer to add all the opening balances at once rather than one at a time to check that the Trial Balance is correct.

Preparing the General Ledger

Accounts are organized by section, including Assets, Liabilities, Equity, Revenue and Expense. **Account type** — such as **Heading** (H), **Subgroup total** (S), **Total** (T), **subgroup Account** (A), **Group account** (G) and **Current Earnings** (X) — is a method of classifying and organizing accounts within a section or subsection of a report.

The accounts follow the same pattern described previously:

- 1000–1999 Assets
- 2000–2999 Liabilities
- 3000–3999 Equity
- 4000–4999 Revenue
- 5000–5999 Expense

Use the Chart of Accounts, Income Statement and Balance Sheet on pages 203–204 to enter all the accounts you need to create. Remember to include all group headings, totals and subgroup totals in addition to the postable group and subgroup accounts.

NOTES
If necessary, refer to the Love It Again application, pages 86–88, for a review of the financial statement formats, the organization of accounts and the Current Earnings account.

NOTES
We are not using expanded account numbering so that the instructions will be the same for Premium and Pro version users in all chapters in Part Two.

Modifying Accounts in the General Ledger

The following keystrokes will modify the *Current Earnings* account in the General Ledger to match the account number defined in the Chart of Accounts.

In the Home window,

Click the **Chart Of Accounts icon** 

in the Accountants' Tasks pane to open the Accounts window.

The accounts should be displayed in Type view — in numerical order, with names, account types and balances. There is only one predefined account.

Double-click **3600 Current Earnings** to display its ledger record.

NOTES
If you prefer, you can use the Setup Guide for Accounts to modify and create the accounts. You can enter opening account balances from the Guide as well.

NOTES
If necessary, change the view by choosing the Accounts window View menu and clicking Type.

You can also open the ledger by clicking the account to select it. Then click the Edit tool button or choose the File menu and click Open.

Press tab to select the Account number field.

Type `3650` **Press** tab and **type** `Net Income`

The account types are dimmed because the *Current Earnings* account type must remain as type X. Only the account number and account name can be edited. You cannot enter a balance because the program automatically calculates the amount as the net difference between the total revenue and expense account balances for the fiscal period.

Click **Save And Close** Save and Close.

Close the Accounts window to return to the Home window unless you want to continue to the next step, which also involves working in the General Ledger.

NOTES
You can also close the ledger window directly to save the changes. If you did not choose to save changes automatically (page 213), you will be asked if you want to save the changes and if you want to always save changes without asking. Choose to save changes without asking.

Creating New Accounts in the General Ledger

We will enter account balances later as a separate step so that you can enter all balances in a single session. This may help you avoid leaving the data file with an incorrect Trial Balance.

NOTES
Refer to page 91 for assistance with creating new accounts from the Accounts window. If you prefer to use the Setup Guide, refer to page 89.

Open the **Accounts window** or any **account ledger window**, if necessary.

Click the **Create tool** in the Accounts window or **choose** the **File menu** and **click Create**.

NOTES
Pressing ctrl + N in the Accounts or General Ledger window or choosing Add Account from the Home window Chart of Accounts icon shortcuts list will also open a new ledger record form.

Enter **account information** for all accounts from the Chart of Accounts on page 203. Remember, you cannot use duplicate account numbers.

Type the **account number** and **press** tab.

Type the **account name** or title.

Click the **account Type** for the account.

If this is a postable account, indicate whether you want to omit the account from financial statements if its balance is zero. You do not need to change the default setting for Allow Project Allocations. The option will be checked when you enter 4000- and 5000-level accounts.

NOTES
The project allocation option will not apply until you choose to use projects. The default settings will then be appropriate – allocations are automatically allowed for revenue and expense accounts.

Skip the **Opening Balance field** for now. We will enter all account balances in the next stage.

When all the information is entered correctly, you must save your account.

Click **Create Another** Create Another to save the new account and advance to a new blank ledger account window.

WARNING!
Remember that Net Bank and GST Owing (Refund) are subgroup totals, following the subgroup bank and GST accounts, respectively.

Create the **remaining accounts** from the Chart of Accounts.

Click Save and Close to close the General Ledger account window after entering the last account.

Display or **print** your updated **Chart of Accounts** to check for account type errors as well as incorrect numbers and misspelled names. **Make corrections**.

Click the **Check The Validity Of Accounts tool** for descriptions of errors in account type. **Make** the **corrections** required.

Check the **validity** again and repeat the process until you receive the message that the accounts are in logical order.

Entering Opening Account Balances

The opening historical balances for Air Care Services can be found in the Trial Balance dated March 31, 2021, on page 204. Headings, totals and subgroup totals — the non-postable accounts — have no balances and the Balance field is removed.

> **NOTES**
> Refer to page 95 for assistance with entering opening account balances in the General Ledger window. If you prefer to use the Setup Guide, refer to page 94.

Use the *Test Balance Account* for any adjustments that would leave the Trial Balance in a forced balance position before you are finished or if one of the remaining balances is incorrect.

If you want to use the Retained Earnings linked account to enter these adjustments, do not enter opening balances until you have added the linked accounts for the General (Accounts) Ledger (pages 227–228). Using this approach, you should verify that this account has the correct opening balance.

> **NOTES**
> After entering all balances, the Test Balance Account should have a zero balance, and you can remove it.
> To remove the Test Balance Account, click its icon or name in the Accounts window and click the Remove tool, or choose the File menu and click Remove. Check that you have selected the right account. Click Yes to confirm that you want to remove the account.
> If the Test Balance Account balance is not zero, you cannot remove the account.

The Accounts window should be open.

Open the **General Ledger** account information window for the first account that has a balance, **1060 Bank: Chequing**.

Click the **Opening Balance field** to highlight its contents.

Type `34660`

Balances for accounts that decrease the total in a group or section (i.e., *GST Paid on Purchases*, *Sales Discounts* and *Purchase Discounts*) must be entered as negative numbers. The balances for these accounts have a (–) minus sign in the Balance Sheet or Income Statement. Balances for Drawings accounts would also be entered as negative amounts.

Correct the **information** if necessary by repeating the above steps.

Click the **Next button** in the Ledger window to advance to the next account ledger record.

Enter the **remaining account balances** in the Trial Balance by repeating the above procedures.

Close the **General Ledger window** to return to the Accounts window. You can check your work from the Trial Balance.

Choose the **Reports menu** in the Accounts window and **click Trial Balance** to display the Trial Balance. **Print** the **report** and **close** the **display**.

Correct the account **balances** if necessary. Open the ledger window, click the amount and type the correction.

Close the **Accounts window** if you want to finish your session.

Entering the Account Class: Bank Accounts

Before setting up the Payables and Receivables ledgers, we must change the account class for bank accounts and some other accounts. **Account class** is another way of organizing accounts into related groups. Each section may be divided into various classes. For example, assets may be subdivided into bank accounts, credit card accounts, receivables, inventory and so on. When you create a new account, the program assigns a default class (Asset, Liability, Equity, Operating Revenue or Cost of Goods Sold) according to the first digit of the account number. For most accounts, you can accept

> **NOTES**
> You can also change the account class in the Setup Guide for Accounts by selecting the correct class from the drop-down list in the Class column.
> The initial class for expense accounts is Expense when you create the account in the Guide.

this setting and the program will prompt you to change the class for special purpose accounts as needed. Bank accounts are not automatically reassigned by the program. You should also change the class for expense accounts by choosing either Expense or Operating Expense as the account class. Air Care does not sell merchandise and has no Cost of Goods Sold accounts.

Chequing bank accounts have additional information that must be entered in the ledger and therefore require that you change the class. You cannot select bank accounts for payments and receipts unless the **Bank** or **Cash class** is assigned. Bank class accounts must also be defined as such before you can select them as the default linked accounts for the Payables, Receivables and Payroll ledgers. The chequing account *Bank: Chequing* must be defined as a Bank class account.

NOTES
The available account classes vary for different account sections. For example, you cannot assign the Bank class to an expense account. You can assign the Bank class to liability accounts. This allows you to set up a line of credit as an account that you can choose to pay for purchases and update cheque numbers automatically. In Chapter 11, we define and use the Line of Credit liability account as a Bank class account.

Click the **Chart Of Accounts icon** Chart of Accounts if you closed the Accounts window.

Double-click **1060 Bank: Chequing** to open its ledger window.

Click the **Class Options tab** — the current class setting is Asset:

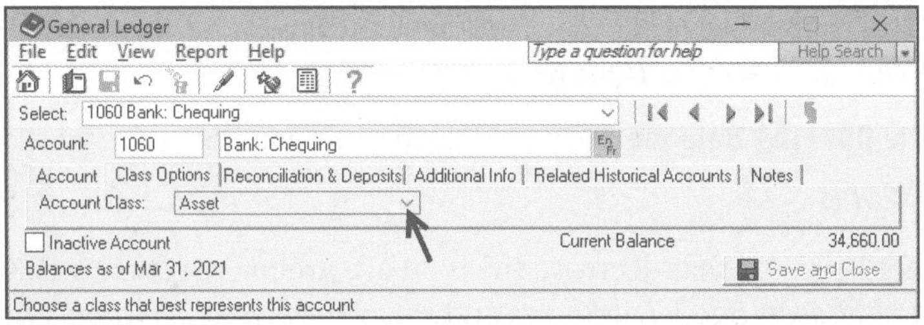

Click the **Account Class list arrow** to display the asset account class options.

Click **Bank** from the list to open the bank-related fields:

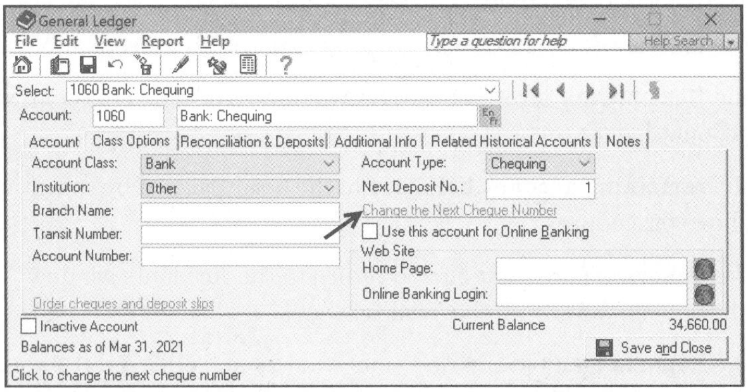

NOTES
Deposit slips are used in Chapter 15 together with account reconciliation. Online banking is introduced in Appendix I on the Student DVD.

This screen allows you to define the type of bank account, and Chequing, the default, is correct. You can also enter a starting number for the deposit slip sequence and identify the bank for online banking access. We are not using deposit slips in this exercise, so you can skip this field. When different currencies are used, the currency for the bank account is also identified on the Class Options tab screen.

Click **Change The Next Cheque Number** to open the cheque Form settings:

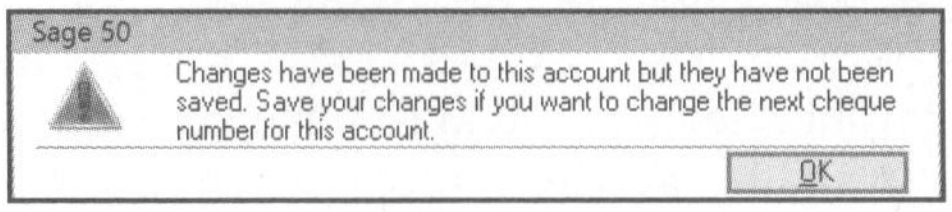

NOTES
Until you have saved the record or closed the ledger, the account class change has not been recorded. The cheque numbering fields for the account will not be available.

Before entering the cheque number, we need to save the account class change.

Click **OK** to return to the ledger window.

Click the **Save tool**, or **choose** the **File menu** and **click** **Save**.

Click **Change The Next Cheque Number** again to open the Form settings:

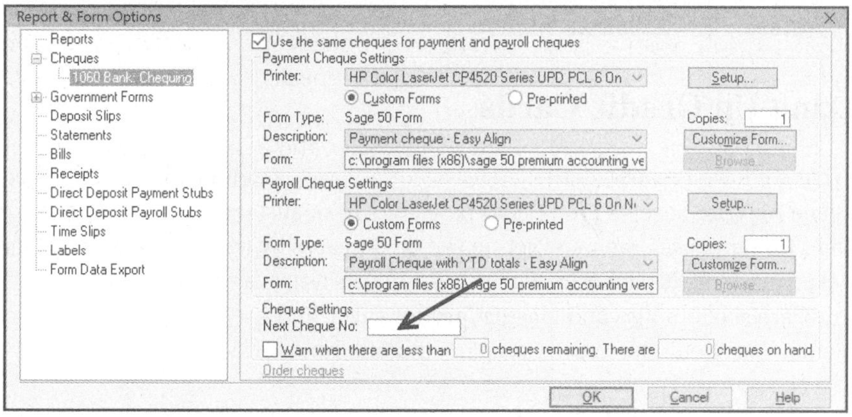

We need to enter only the cheque number.

Click the **Next Cheque No. field** near the bottom of the form. **Type** 101

Click **OK** to return to the account ledger window at the Class Options tab.

Defining the Class for Credit Card Accounts

Although credit card accounts are bank accounts, they are used as credit card linked accounts and are assigned the Credit Card class. Before setting up the cards with their linked accounts, we must change the account class for the accounts we need. We will change the linked asset accounts to the Credit Card Receivable class and the payable account to the Credit Card Payable class. If you also write cheques from or deposit customer cash or cheques to these accounts, you should use the Bank class so they will be available in the bank account fields in the journals and cheque numbers for them can be entered and updated automatically.

Click the **Next button** to advance to account *1070 Bank: Visa.*

Choose **Credit Card Receivable** from the Account Class list to change the class.

Click the **Next button** to open the ledger for *1080 Bank: MasterCard.*

Choose **Credit Card Receivable** from the Account Class list.

Click the **Select field list arrow** to open the list of accounts.

Click **2160 Credit Card Payable** to open this account ledger.

Choose **Credit Card Payable** from the Account Class list.

Defining the Class for Expense Accounts

Expense accounts are defined as Cost of Goods Sold by default when you create them from the General Ledger new account window. These account classes should be changed unless they refer to inventory cost accounts. When you create expense accounts from an Account field using the Add An Account wizard the default class is Operating Expense, and when you create accounts from the Setup Guide the default class is Expense, so you will not need to change these.

To create the Gross Margin Income Statement Report that applies when inventory is sold, you must correctly separate the Cost of Goods Sold accounts from other expenses.

Choose **account 5010** from the Select Account list to open the ledger.

Choose **Operating Expense** (or **Expense**) from the Account Class list.

Click the **Next button**. **Change** the **class** for all Group expense accounts.

WARNING!
To avoid an error message, the Form fields must contain valid file locations. The forms you need are in the Forms folder inside the Sage 50 Premium Accounting Version 2019 program folder.

NOTES
You do not need to change printer settings unless you are using different printers for different forms.

NOTES
The Class options available for 2160 – a liability account – are different from those for the asset accounts.

NOTES
You can assign the Payroll Expense class to the two payroll accounts.

Click **Save And Close** to close the Ledger window.

Close the **Accounts window** to return to the Home window.

Setting Up Credit Cards

Now that we have created all the ledger accounts, we can enter the remaining settings.

Since Air Care accepts credit card payments from customers and uses credit cards in payment for purchases, we must set up the credit cards by naming them and identifying the linked accounts for deposits, payments and fees associated with the cards.

Air Care accepts Visa and MasterCard for sales, and uses Visa for credit card payments. You should be in the Company module Home window.

Entering the Credit Cards

Click the **Settings icon** to open the Company Settings options list.

Click **Credit Cards** (**click Company** first if necessary):

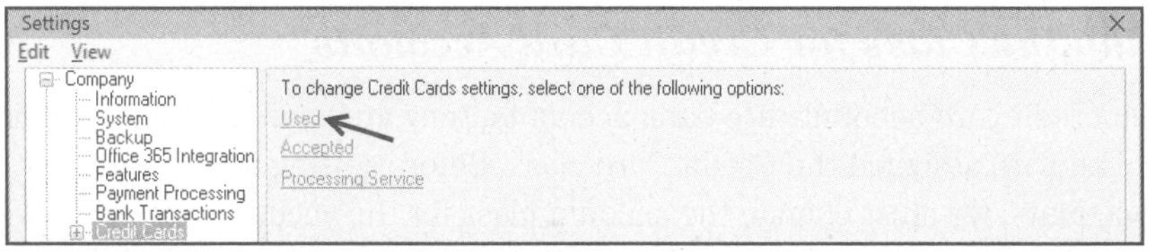

NOTES
You may get a message about credit card processing services, a fee-based service offered by Sage. Read and then close this message.
Information about this online service is also available from the Sales Journal when you choose a credit card for payment.

You can set up **Credit Cards Used** to make purchases from suppliers and **Credit Cards Accepted** to enter receipts from customers.

Click **Used** to open the screen for the cards that the business uses:

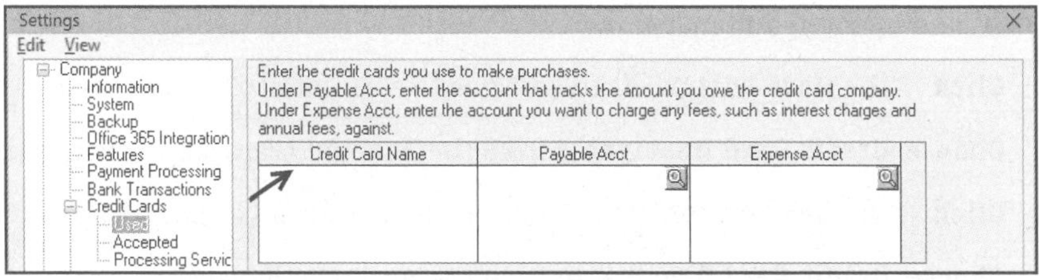

NOTES
The setup and use of credit card processing services are introduced in Chapter 13.

Each card named on this screen will appear in the Purchases and Payments journals in the Payment Method list. There is no discount fee associated with individual purchases, although there may be an annual or monthly fee attached to the card. Each card is listed on a separate line with its associated linked accounts.

Click the **Credit Card Name field** or **press** *tab*.

Type `Visa` **Press** *tab*.

The cursor moves to the **Payable Acct** field. This account is the liability account that records the balance owing to the card company.

Click the **Account List icon** to access the list of available accounts.

Click **2160**, the liability account for the card.

Click **Select** to add the account and move to the Expense Acct field.

WARNING!
You must choose a Bank, Cash or Credit Card Payable class account as the linked Payable account for credit cards used.

The **Expense Account** records any monthly or annual fees paid to the card company for the privilege of using the card and interest charges on cash advances or overdue amounts. Not all cards have user fees, but all cards charge interest on cash advances and balances not paid by the due date. These additional fees are added to this linked expense account for credit card payment transactions in the Payments Journal (refer to Chapter 12). Air Care uses one expense account for all credit card–related expenses.

Click the **Account List icon** to access the account list.

Double-click **5020**.

Cards accepted in payment from customers are set up in the same way as cards used.

Click **Accepted** in the Company list under Credit Cards.

If you did not change the account class correctly, Sage 50 provides a warning about incorrect account classes:

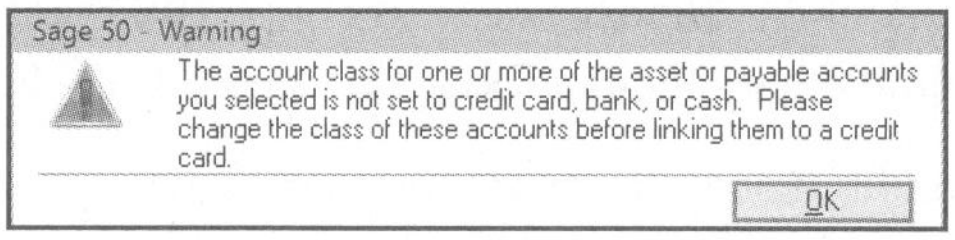
Sage 50 - Warning
The account class for one or more of the asset or payable accounts you selected is not set to credit card, bank, or cash. Please change the class of these accounts before linking them to a credit card.
OK

Click OK. Click Cancel to close the Credit Card Information window. Make the necessary account class changes and re-enter the credit card details.

The cards customers can use to make payments are entered on this screen:

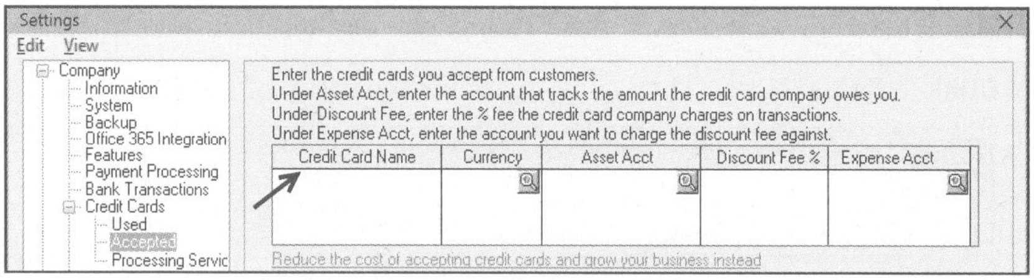

All the cards you name here will appear in the Payment Method list for Sales Invoices. Each card accepted should be listed on a separate line.

Click the **Credit Card Name field** or **press** *tab*.

Type `Visa` **Press** *tab*. The cursor advances to the **Currency** field.

Click the **List icon** for the options:

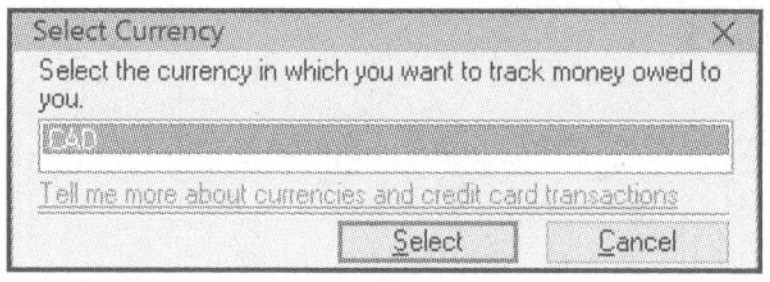
Select Currency
Select the currency in which you want to track money owed to you.
CAD
Tell me more about currencies and credit card transactions
Select
Cancel

You can choose the currency of this credit card. Air Care has only Canadian customers, so CAD is preselected. Credit cards in other currencies must be connected to Credit Card Receivable or Bank class accounts with those currencies.

Click **Select** or **press** *enter* to continue. **Press** *tab*.

The cursor is in the **Asset Acct** field, the linked account for deposits from the card company. Normally a bank account is set up for credit card deposits.

Click the **Account List icon** to display the accounts available for linking.

Click **1070 Bank: Visa** to choose the account.

Click **Select** to add the account and advance to the next field.

The cursor advances to the **Discount Fee %** field. The discount fee is the amount that the card company withholds as a merchant transaction fee for use of the card. This expense is withheld from the total invoice amount that the card company deposits to the business bank account for each sale. Fees vary from one credit card company to another and also for the type of business. For example, high-volume businesses pay a lower percentage than businesses with a smaller volume of sales.

NOTES

You can add a new account at this stage if necessary. Type the new account number and press *tab*. Click Add to start the Add An Account wizard. Remember to choose the correct account class – Credit Card Payable – (on the fifth wizard screen) when using the wizard. Additional screens related to bank account settings are added to the wizard when you select the correct account class. You do not need to enter information on these screens.

NOTES

Return to the section Defining the Class for Credit Card Accounts (page 221) if you need assistance with changing the account class.

PRO VERSION

The Currency option for credit cards is not available in the Pro version. You will advance to the Asset Account field after the Name.

WARNING!

You must choose either a Credit Card, Cash or Bank class account as the linked asset account for cards accepted. Although other accounts are included in the Select Account list, choosing them will give you a warning error message like the one on this page.

NOTES

Remember that if you use the Add An Account wizard to create the new bank accounts, you must indicate that the accounts are part of a subtotal (on the fourth wizard screen) and select Credit Card Receivable as the account class on the fifth wizard screen. You do not need to enter information on the additional bank-related screens.

NOTES

Debit cards may be set up as credit cards, with the discount fee entered as 0.0 percent.

If you do not know the discount fee or you have cards with different rates, leave the field blank and enter the charges when you reconcile the accounts.

Type 2.9 **Press** tab.

The cursor advances to the **Expense Acct** field. This is the linked account that will be debited automatically for the discount fee for a credit card sale. The expense amount or fee is the total invoice amount times the discount fee percentage.

Click the **Account List icon** to display the accounts available for linking.

Click **5020** to choose the account.

Click **Select** to add the account to the Card Information screen.

Enter **MasterCard** in the Name field. **Choose** Asset Account **1080**, **enter 2.7** in the Discount Fee % field and **choose** Expense Account **5020**.

You can enter information for additional credit cards the same way.

Setting Up Sales Taxes

Setting up sales taxes before entering supplier and customer records will allow us to choose default tax codes for customers and suppliers for automatic entry in journals.

Click **Sales Taxes**. The components for the setup of sales taxes are listed:

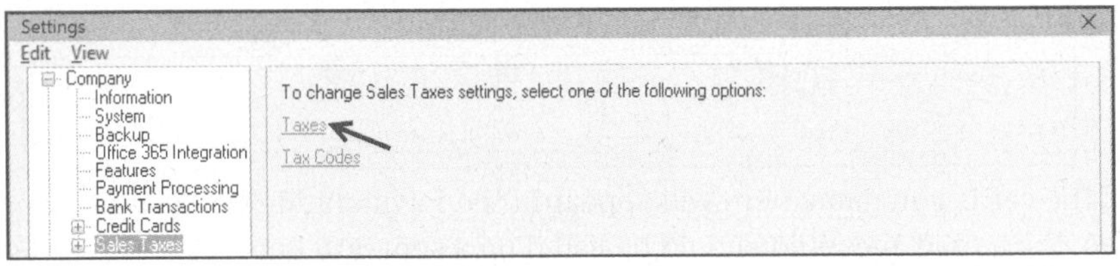

To set up sales taxes, we must identify the taxes that are charged and paid, and then define the codes that will be displayed in the journals.

Click **Taxes**:

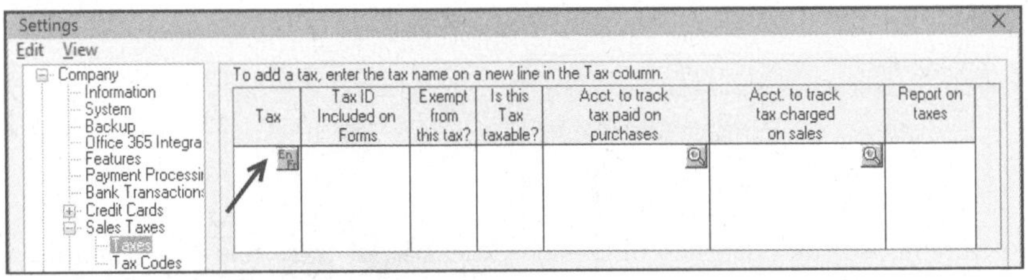

NOTES

Other taxes and tax codes can be added later if needed. The details for each tax and code can be modified if the tax legislation changes, as it has several times in the past.

Sage 50 has no preset tax information. You can customize the taxes to suit any business by entering the taxes applied and paid by a business and by creating the tax codes needed to account for the combinations of taxes. Taxes can be added later or edited if needed. Air Care has two taxes, GST and PST, and reports on both. Because PST is not refundable, PST paid is not tracked in a separate account.

Click the **Tax field** or **press** tab so you can enter the name of the tax.

Type GST and **press** tab to advance to the Tax ID field.

NOTES

PST registration is required for businesses that charge PST on sales and do not pay PST on purchases of merchandise that they sell to customers (only the final customer pays PST).

The tax number should be included on invoices, so you should enter it in this field. For GST, this is the business number. For PST, it is the provincial registration number that indicates the supplier is licensed to charge PST. GST numbers are normally included on forms because GST is refundable. PST numbers are not normally included on invoices.

Type 533 766 457 RT0001 **Press** tab.

The cursor moves to the **Exempt From This Tax?** column. Choose Yes only if your business — Air Care in this case — does not pay the tax. Air Care Services pays GST, so the default selection No is correct. The next field, **Is This Tax Taxable?** asks if another tax includes this tax in its base calculation. Currently no provinces apply this method of tax calculation. For Saskatchewan, where Air Care is located, the correct answer is No.

The next two fields define the linked accounts that **track the taxes paid** and the **taxes charged**. The taxes paid account records the total of the amounts entered in the GST field in the Purchases Journal whenever a purchase is made. Although you may choose an asset or a liability account, we use liability accounts because there is normally a balance owing to the Receiver General. If the tax is not refundable, such as PST paid, you should leave the account field for tracking taxes paid blank.

Click the **List icon for Acct. To Track Tax Paid On Purchases**.

Double-click **2670 GST Paid on Purchases**.

The cursor advances to the field for the Account To Track Tax Charged On Sales. This account records the total of the amounts entered in the GST field in the Sales Journal whenever a sale is made. You may use an asset or a liability account.

Choose **2650 GST Charged on Sales** from the List icon list of accounts.

The cursor advances to the **Report On Taxes** field. To generate tax reports from Sage 50, you should choose Yes. The Yes and No entries on the tax screens act as toggle switches. Clicking will change the entry from one to the other, and you can change these entries at any time.

Click **No** to change the default entry to Yes.

Press *tab* to advance to the next line and **type** PST

Click , the **List icon for Acct. To Track Tax Charged On Sales**.

Choose **2640 PST Charged on Sales**. **Press** *tab*.

Click **No** to change the default entry to Yes for reporting.

Click **Tax Codes**. The Tax Codes Settings screen opens:

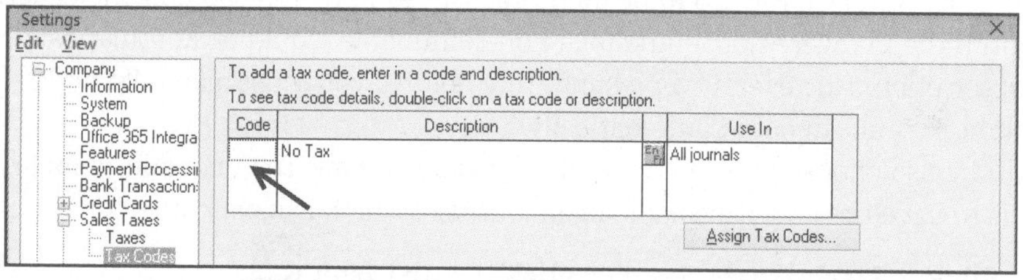

On this screen, you can create the tax codes required for all the different rates and combinations of taxes that apply to a business. No codes are entered initially, so the only entry is the blank code used when **No Tax** is applied. If you want to change or assign tax codes for all suppliers and customers, use the **Assign Tax Codes** feature.

Click the **Code column** below the blank on the first line.

Type G **Press** *tab* to move to the Description field.

Press *enter* or **double-click** to open the Tax Code Details screen:

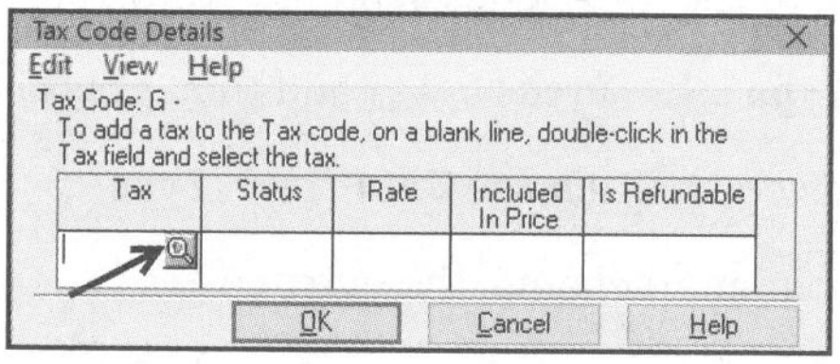

On this screen, you define how the tax is calculated and reported.

NOTES
Sales tax amounts entered in the General Journal are also tracked in these linked accounts.

NOTES
By using liability accounts for both taxes paid and taxes charged, we can display the subtotal (GST Owing) on the Balance Sheet. Normally a business owes GST because sales are larger than expenses.

NOTES
If you do not enter an account for the taxes charged, you must confirm that you will not be able to charge the tax on sales by clicking Yes.

NOTES
After creating all tax codes and all supplier and customer records, you can update all tax information from the Assign Tax Codes window. We use this approach in Chapter 16.

NOTES
If at any time the tax regulations change, you can return to this screen and change the settings. For example, BC replaced the HST with separate GST and PST, Prince Edward Island implemented the HST to replace the separate GST and PST, Nova Scotia changed the HST rate and Manitoba and Saskatchewan increased the PST rate. To make these changes in the data files, just edit the Rate in the Tax Code Details screen and the Description in the Tax Code screen. The description is not automatically updated when you change the tax rate. New tax codes may be needed as well.

NOTES
Charities eligible for a refund of 50 percent of the GST they pay can set up two taxes: one for the refundable portion and one for the non-refundable portion. Then create tax codes for the refundable tax at 2.4999 percent and for the non-refundable tax at 2.5001 percent. (The extra decimals will ensure that you avoid rounding errors resulting in overclaiming refunds.) For the non-refundable tax, you do not need to track taxes paid. They will then be added to the asset or expense portion of the entry, just like non-refundable PST.

Click the **Tax field List icon** to open the list of taxes entered:

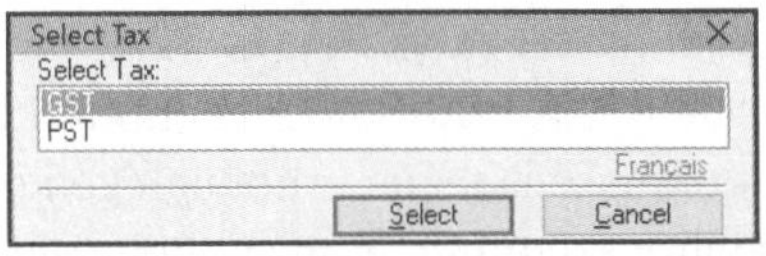

Both taxes we named are listed here. At this stage, you are asked to choose the taxes that should be applied (charged or paid) when this code is used in a journal entry.

Click **Select**, because GST is already selected, and return to the Details.

Defaults are entered for the remaining fields. The tax **Status** is Taxable, and this is correct — tax is calculated and charged. Other status options and their explanations can be viewed by clicking the List icon. The Non-Taxable Status is used when items are not taxed but their amounts are included in reports to the Receiver General. Similarly, the Exempt Status is used for items that are exempt from the tax but the amounts are included in the tax reports filed. For example, although food is zero rated (no tax is charged), suppliers may still claim a GST refund and must report their sales amounts.

The remaining fields are straightforward. **Rate** is the percentage rate for the tax. Taxes may be **included** in the sales and purchase prices or not included. If some suppliers include the tax and others do not, create two separate tax codes. And finally, is the tax **refundable** — that is, are the taxes paid on purchases refunded? GST is not included for any of Air Care's suppliers' or customers' prices and GST is refundable. Non-refundable taxes, like PST, for which you do not enter an account to track taxes paid on expenses, are automatically added to the asset or expense amount for the purchase.

Click the **Rate field**. **Type** 5

Click **No** in the Is Refundable column to change the entry to Yes.

Click **OK** to return to the Tax Codes screen for additional codes.

The description GST @ 5% appears beside the code G. You can edit the description if you want. If the tax were not refundable, non-refundable would be automatically added to the description. However, if you change any details, you must manually update the description. It is not updated automatically.

You can also choose in which journals you want to have the tax codes appear. The default is to have the codes available in all journals, which is usually the correct choice.

Click **All Journals** and then **click** the **List icon**:

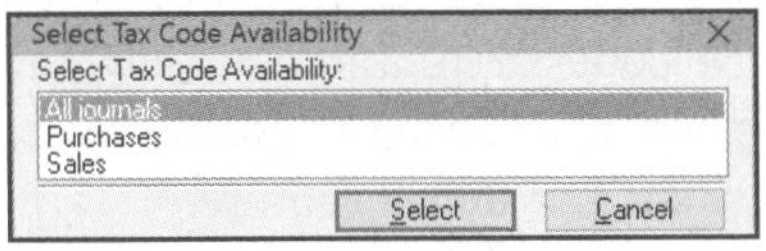

NOTES
Charities that do not charge GST but are eligible for GST refunds may choose to have tax codes available only in the Purchases Journal.

You can choose to have the tax codes available for all revenues, all expenses or all transactions (Purchases Journal, Sales Journal and General Journal). The default selection, All Journals, is correct for Air Care.

Click **Cancel** or **Select** to return to the Tax Codes screen.

Click the **Code field below G**. **Type** GP **Press** *tab* and then **press** *enter*.

Select **GST** as the first tax for this code. **Click** the **Rate field**. **Type** 5

Click **No** in the Is Refundable column to change the entry to Yes.

Press *tab*. **Select** or **type PST** as the second tax for this code.

Click the **Rate field**. **Type** 6 **Click OK** to return to the Settings screen. (PST is not refundable, so the default selection, No, is correct.)

Click the ⊟ **beside Company** to reduce the Settings list.

Linked Accounts

Linked accounts are accounts in the General Ledger that are affected by entries in journals for the other ledgers. We have seen some of these linked accounts at work in journal entries in previous chapters. For example, an entry to record a pay later sale in the Sales Journal will cause automatic changes in several General Ledger accounts. In the General Ledger, the *Accounts Receivable* [debit, +], *Revenue from Sales* [credit,+], *GST Charged on Services* [credit, +] and *PST Payable* [credit, +] accounts will all be affected by the sale. The type of change, debit or credit and increase [+] or decrease [–], is indicated in the brackets. The program must know which account numbers to use for posting journal entries in any of the journals. Often, you do not enter account numbers for linked accounts in the journals. It is this interconnection of accounts between ledgers that makes Sage 50 fully integrated.

Initially only *Current Earnings*, the General linked account for Current Earnings, is defined, so we must identify the remaining linked accounts for the General, Payables and Receivables ledgers. Air Care does not use the Payroll or Inventory ledgers, so you do not need to define linked accounts for them. Linked accounts are entered from the Settings screens for the ledgers, so we will enter them with other default ledger settings.

Changing Ledger Settings and Linked Accounts

Changing General Ledger Settings and Linked Accounts

Click **General (Accounts)** in the list on the left.

The General Ledger settings are correct for Air Care Services. The budget feature, departmental accounting and expanded account numbers are not used.

We need to add linked accounts.

Click **Linked Accounts** to display the General Linked Accounts window:

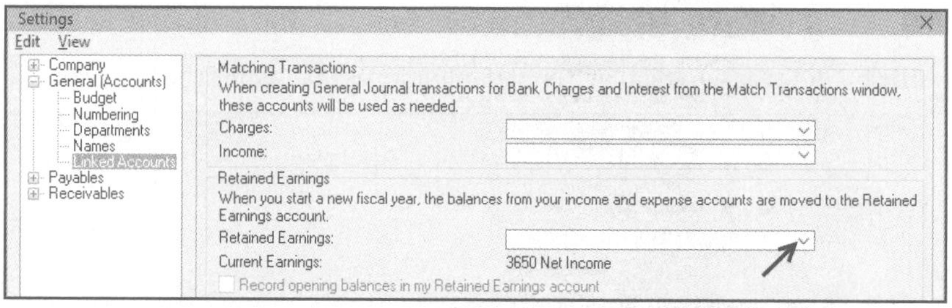

The first two linked accounts are used with the Match Bank Transactions feature and are not used by Air Care Services.

Click the **Retained Earnings field**.

The Retained Earnings account is the capital (equity) account to which expense and revenue accounts are closed at the end of the fiscal period. You must choose a capital (3000-range) account.

Click the **list arrow** beside the field. All postable capital accounts are listed.

Click **3560 S. Arturro, Capital**.

You can also type account numbers directly in the linked account fields. Then press *tab* to complete the entry and advance to the next field. If you type a new account number, you can create the new account.

WARNING!

You must define essential linked accounts before you can finish the history for a company and before you can enter sales and purchase transactions.

CLASSIC VIEW

The Settings tool can be used to enter linked accounts. Select (right-click) a journal icon and click the Settings tool to open the Linked Accounts window for that ledger. If no icon is selected, choose the journal name from the Select Setup list to display the linked accounts for the ledger. If a ledger icon is selected, clicking the Settings tool displays ledger settings.

PRO VERSION

Departmental Accounting and expanded Numbering (refer to page 81) are not included in the Pro version, so you will not have entries for them.

NOTES

Names are used to add labels for the additional fields in each ledger. Additional fields are named and used for the Payroll Ledger in Chapter 9 (refer to pages 321 and 338).

CLASSIC VIEW

In the Home window, right-click the General Journal icon General Journal. Click the Settings tool to open the General Linked Accounts screen.

Do not click (i.e., click the left mouse button) the journal icon because you want to select the icon without opening the journal. Right-clicking will select the icon.

WARNING!
Sage 50 will not allow you to remove accounts if they are being used as linked accounts. First, turn the linking function off by deleting the account in the Linked Accounts window. Then delete the account balance, save the changes and, finally, remove the account in the Accounts window. You cannot remove an account if it has a balance or if journal entries have been posted to it.

The Current Earnings account is predefined — the single type X account is always used. This linked setup cannot be changed, although you can modify the account number and account name.

The final option, to **Record Opening Balances In My Retained Earnings Account**, will automatically use the Retained Earnings linked account for amounts that will balance the Trial Balance when you close the ledger. With this option, Sage 50 will confirm the change to the linked account when you have a discrepancy:

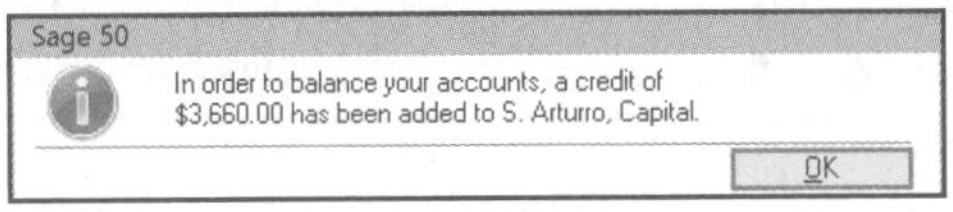

To use this option, you must define the Retained Earnings linked account before adding historical account opening balances. Click OK to confirm and to update the Retained Earnings opening balance.

We have already added the opening balances. You can choose the *Test Balance* account for a discrepancy, as we did in Chapter 4. The linked Retained Earnings account will still be the default selection:

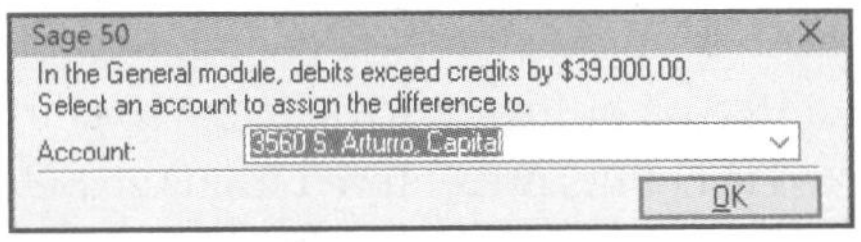

Choose the account you want from the drop-down list and click OK to confirm.

Payables Default Settings

NOTES
You can click the ⊟ beside entries for the other modules to collapse the Settings list.

Click **Payables** in the list on the left to expand the options list:

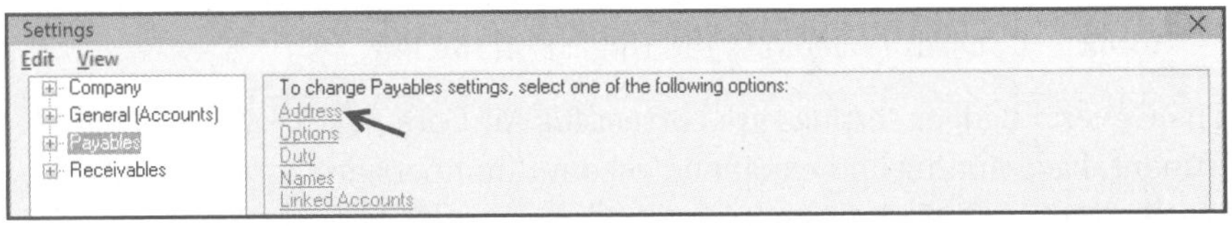

CLASSIC VIEW
In the Home window, right-click the Suppliers icon.

Click the Settings tool to open the Payables Ledger Settings screen.

The Payables Ledger has Address settings, general Options, settings for imports (Duty), Names for icons and additional ledger fields, and Linked Accounts. Air Care does not import items that have duty applied and does not use the additional fields.

Click **Address** to display the default address fields for the suppliers:

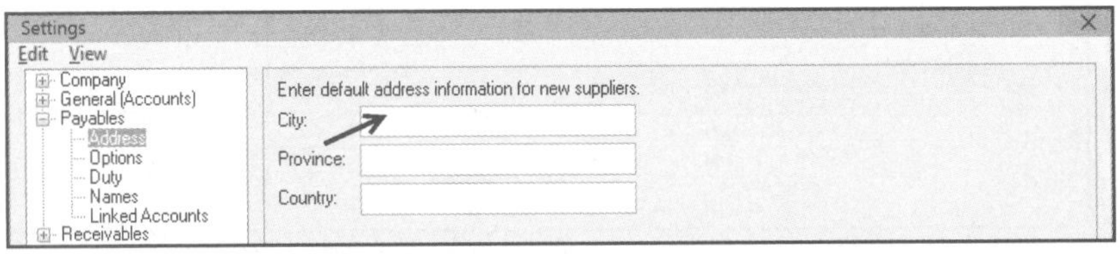

PRO VERSION
The term Vendor will replace Supplier on all Settings screens.

The information you enter here will be used in the ledger records as the defaults when you add suppliers. If most suppliers are in the same location, entering these locations here will save data entry time later. Most of the suppliers for Air Care are located in Regina, Saskatchewan.

NOTES
If all suppliers are in the same province but not in the same city, you can complete the Province field and leave the City field blank.

Click the **City field**.

Type `Regina` **Press** *tab* to advance to the Province field.

Type `Saskatchewan` **Press** *tab* to advance to the Country field.

Type `Canada`

Click **Options** to display the default settings for the Payables Ledger:

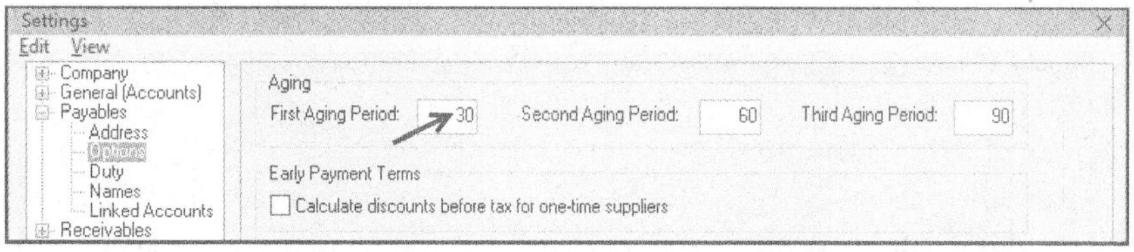

The option for the **aging** of accounts in the Payables Ledger is preset at 30, 60 and 90 days. We will change these options for Air Care to reflect the payment and discount terms most commonly used by Air Care's suppliers.

Press tab or **double-click 30** in the First Aging Period field.

Type 10 **Press** tab to advance to the Second Aging Period field.

Type 30 **Press** tab to advance to the Third Aging Period field.

Type 60

The second option determines how discounts are calculated. If the discount is taken only on pretax subtotals, the discount is calculated before taxes. If the discount is applied to the entire invoice amount, including taxes, the discount is not calculated before taxes. Air Care's suppliers calculate discounts before taxes, so you must change the setting.

Click **Calculate Discounts Before Tax For One-Time Suppliers**.

Changing Payables Terminology

Sage 50 has a set of default terms that it uses based on the type of company you define. These are the terms that changed for different company types in previous chapters. If you want, you can modify the default selections.

Click **Names** under Payables to display the Names and Terminology window:

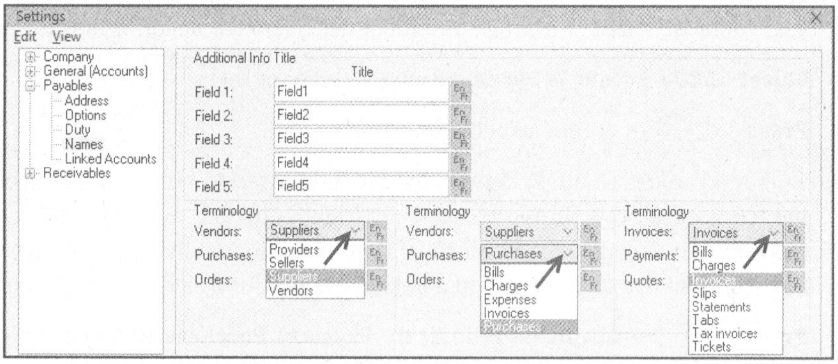

The Names window includes fields for five **Additional Information** names for the Payables Ledger. These will be used on the Additional Information tab screen for ledger records, and you have the option to include them in journal windows.

The second part of the screen has the terms used for icons and fields throughout the program. The names you can change — for Vendors, Purchases and Invoices — are available in their drop-down lists. You cannot modify the Payments label. The names you select will apply to icons, fields and reports.

If you want to use different names, click the field for the name you want to change and select a different name from the drop-down list.

Defining the Payables Linked Accounts

We will enter the Payables Ledger linked accounts next.

NOTES

Usually, clicking a number in a field will select the entire number. Sometimes, however, depending on exactly where you click, only part of the number is selected or an insertion point is added. Double-clicking will always select the entire number in the field so that you can edit it.

NOTES

The decision to calculate discounts before or after tax may also be affected by tax regulations.

NOTES

We will add discount terms to individual supplier records when we set up the Payables Ledger.

PRO VERSION

pro

The Names screen includes only the Additional Information fields. You cannot change the terminology in the Pro version.

CLASSIC VIEW

In the Home window, you can right-click the Purchases Journal or Payments Journal icon, Purchases or Payments. Click the Settings tool to open the Payables Linked Accounts screen.

Click **Linked Accounts** under Payables to display the Linked Accounts window:

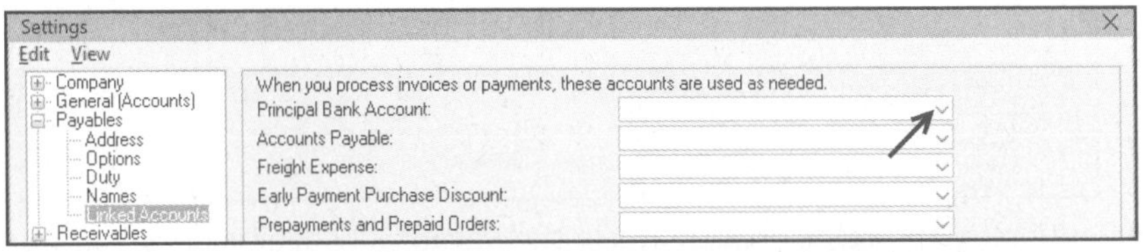

We need to identify the default General Ledger bank account used to make payments to suppliers. This is an essential linked account — it is required before you can finish the history for the company data file. Cash transactions in the Payments Journal will be posted to the bank account you select in the journal window. All Bank and Cash class accounts are available in the journals, and the **principal bank account** defined here will be selected as the default.

Clicking the drop-down list arrow for any linked account field will open the list of accounts available for linking. Only Bank class (or Cash) accounts may be used in the bank fields. That is why we needed to define the Bank class accounts first.

When additional currencies are used, fields will be available for linked bank accounts for those currencies as well. Because we have not set up foreign currencies, linked bank account fields for them are omitted. The chequing account is Air Care's principal bank account for supplier transactions.

Click the **Principal Bank Account field list arrow**. Only the single Bank class account is available for selection.

Click **1060 Bank: Chequing** and **press** tab.

NOTES

The total owed to all suppliers is the sum of the individual outstanding historical balances in the Supplier Ledger records.

The cursor advances to the **Accounts Payable** field. This control account is also required and is used to record the amounts owing to suppliers whenever a credit (Pay Later) Purchases Journal entry or invoice payment is completed. The balance in this account reflects the total owing to all suppliers, which must match the opening General Ledger balance for *Accounts Payable*. You must use a liability account in this field.

Select **2200 Accounts Payable** from the Account list.

Press tab to enter the account number.

The cursor advances to the **Freight Expense** field, used to record the delivery or freight charges associated with purchases. Only freight charged by the supplier should be entered using this account. Since Air Care's suppliers do not charge for delivery, you should leave this field blank. You can add a linked account for freight later if you need it.

Press tab to advance to the **Early Payment Purchase Discount** field. This account is used to record supplier discounts taken for early payments.

Choose **5040 Purchase Discounts** from the drop-down list.

Press tab to advance to the **Prepayments And Prepaid Orders** field.

NOTES

The linked account for prepayments is also a required linked account. Because we are not using the feature, we can enter Accounts Payable.

NOTES

Credit card and tax accounts are also linked accounts, and the accounts must be removed from the relevant Settings before you can remove the accounts.

Air Care's suppliers do not request prepayments at this time, but you cannot leave this field blank.

Choose **2200 Accounts Payable** from the drop-down list.

Check the linked accounts carefully. To **delete a linked account**, click it to highlight it and press del. You must complete this step of deleting the account from any linked accounts screen before you can remove the account in the General Ledger from the Accounts window.

To select a different account, highlight the one that is incorrect and type the correct number, or select an account from the drop-down list.

Receivables Default Settings

Click **Receivables** to display the Receivables Ledger choices:

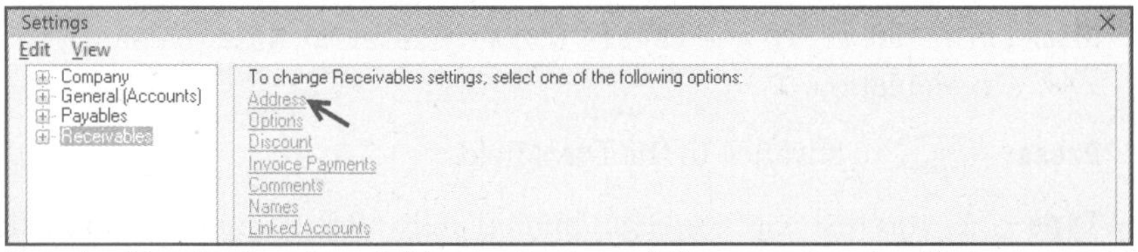

The Receivables Ledger has Address, Options, Discount, Invoice Payments and Comments settings, Names for icons and additional ledger fields, and Linked Accounts.

Click **Address** to display the default address fields for customers:

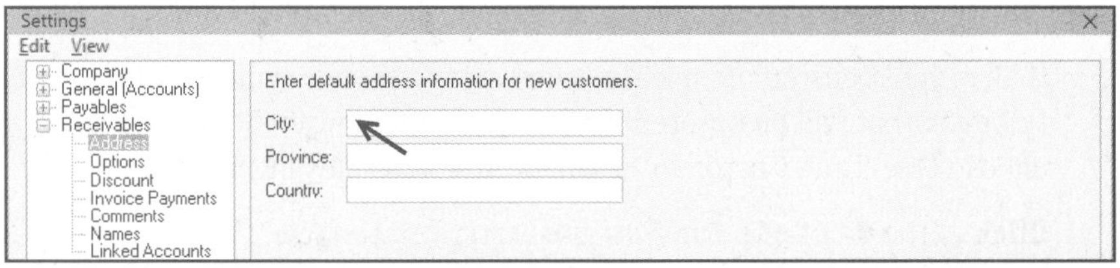

The information you enter here will be used in the ledger records as the defaults when you add customers. Most of Air Care's customers are located in Regina.

Click the **City field**. **Type** `Regina` **Press** *tab*.

Type `Saskatchewan` in the Province field.

Press *tab* to advance to the Country field. **Type** `Canada`

Click **Options** to display the default settings for the Receivables Ledger:

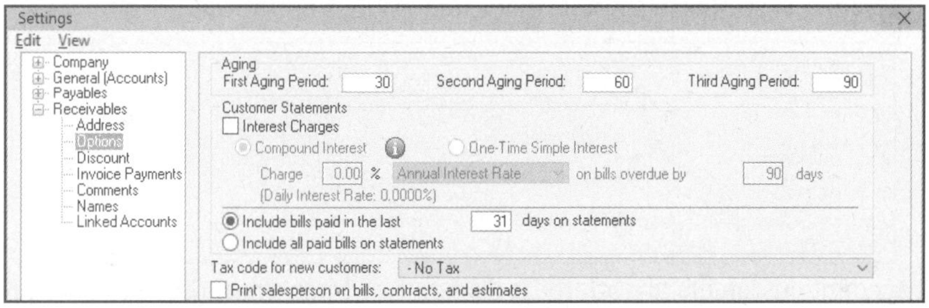

Air Care Services offers a 1 percent discount if customers pay within 10 days and expects full payment within 30 days. After 30 days, customers are charged 1.5 percent interest per month on the overdue accounts. Therefore, the **aging periods** 10, 30 and 60 days will be used, and we must change the default settings.

Press *tab*, or **double-click 30** in the First Aging Period field.

Type `10` **Press** *tab* to advance to the Second Aging Period field.

Type `30` **Press** *tab* to advance to the Third Aging Period field. **Type** `60`

Click **Interest Charges** to add a ✓ and select this feature.

Point to the **information button** to open a pop-up balloon with more information about how interest is calculated:

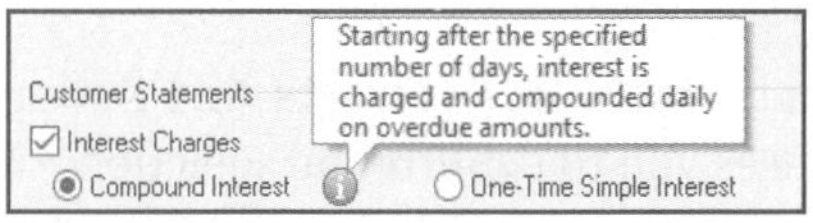

When interest is charged on overdue invoices, Sage 50 calculates interest amounts and prints them on the customer statements. However, the program does not create an invoice for the interest. You must create a separate entry for the interest amount.

The default selection, **Compound Interest**, is correct.

NOTES

You can click the ⊟ beside Payables to collapse the Settings list.

CLASSIC VIEW

In the Home window, you can right-click the Customers icon

. Click

(the Settings tool) to open the Receivables Ledger Settings screen.

NOTES

You can use customer statements to find the interest amount that you will enter on the invoice.

NOTES
The interest rate you enter may be an annual or monthly rate and may be compounded (interest charged on past due interest amounts) or not.

Press tab twice to select the contents of the Interest Charge rate field.

Type 1.5 **Press** tab to advance to the Annual Interest Rate entry.

Click the **list arrow** and **choose Monthly Interest Rate** to change the basis of calculation.

Press tab to advance to the Days field.

Type 1 Interest charges begin immediately after the net amount is due.

The next option relates to printing historical information on invoices. The maximum setting is 999 days. Air Care Services sends customer statements monthly, so the period should be 31 days. Invoices paid in the past 31 days will be included and you can include all paid bills. Unpaid invoices are always included. The default settings are correct.

If all or most customers use the same sales tax code, you can choose a **default tax code** that will be entered when you create new customers or when you choose One-Time Customer or Quick Add in a sales invoice.

Click the **Tax Code For New Customers list arrow**.

Click **GP - GST @ 5%; PST @ 6%** to use this as the default tax code.

When salespersons are set up, you can **print** the name of the **salesperson** on invoices, orders and quotes. Air Care does not have sales staff.

Entering Discount Settings

Next we must enter the payment terms for account customers.

Click **Discount** in the list under Receivables on the left:

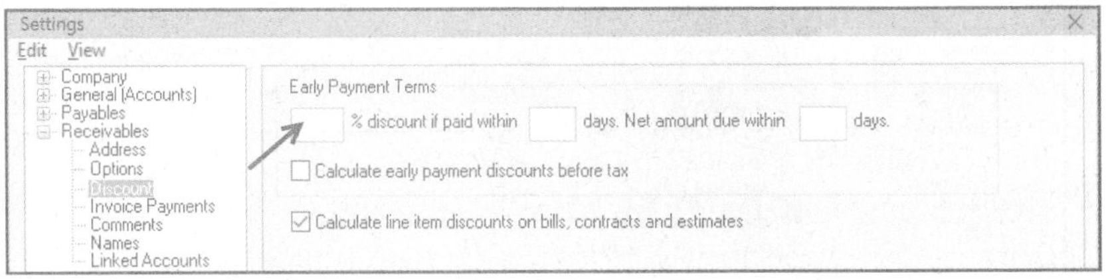

All account customers are offered a discount of 1 percent if they pay the full account balance in the first 10 days, and net payment is due in 30 days. All customer discounts are calculated on after-tax amounts, so the **Calculate Early Payment Discounts Before Tax** selection is correctly turned off.

Click the **% field** in the first Early Payment Terms field to advance the cursor.

Type 1.0 **Press** tab to advance to the Days field.

Type 10 **Press** tab to advance to the Net Days field and **type** 30

Sage 50 adds the payment terms you just entered as a default for all customers. Individual customer records or invoices can still be modified if needed.

Air Care does not use the remaining discount option — to apply discounts to individual lines on an invoice. A % Discount column will be added to the invoice form when you use this feature.

NOTES
We will use the line discount feature in Chapter 19.

PRO VERSION
Line discounts are not available in the Pro version, so you will skip this step and the confirmation message.

Click **Calculate Line Item Discounts On Bills, Contracts And Estimates** to remove the ✓. Sage 50 requires you to confirm the selection:

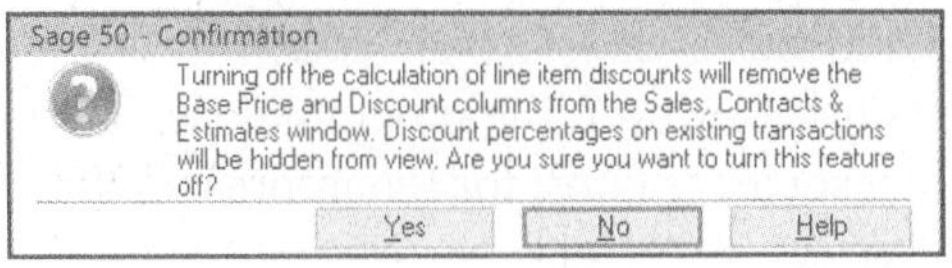

Click **Yes** to confirm the removal of line discounts.

If you later change the default customer payment terms, you will be asked whether you want to update all customer terms to match the new terms.

The **Invoice Payments** feature requires a service plan that includes online payments.

NOTES

The Invoice Payments settings allow you to set up the payment service you use to collect online payments from customers. For this, you need a service plan that includes online payments.

Entering Default Comments

Sage 50 allows you to add a default comment to the Message field on all customer forms. You can change the default message any time you want, and you can edit it for a particular form when you are completing the invoice, quote or order confirmation.

PRO VERSION

The field label Sales Invoices replaces Bills in the Pro version. Sales Orders and Sales Quotes will replace Contracts and Estimates.

NOTES

Contracts and Estimates are the terms used for Sales Orders and Sales Quotes for a construction or contractor business.

Click **Comments** under Receivables to open the screen for default comments:

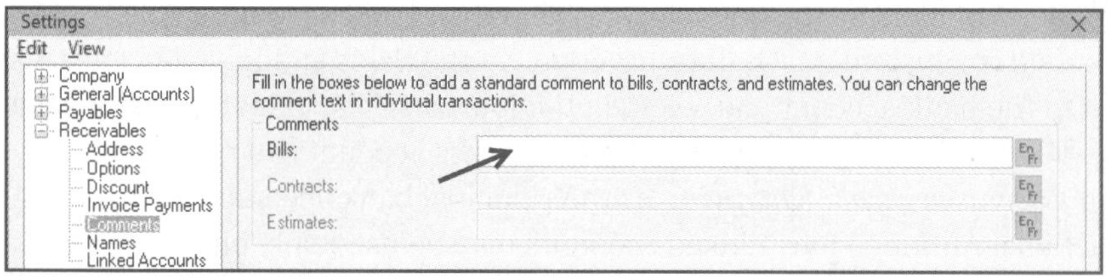

We want to add a comment that will appear on every customer invoice. The comment may include payment terms, company motto, notice of an upcoming sale or a warning about interest charges.

Click the **Bills (Invoices) field** to move the cursor.

Type `Interest @ 1.5% per month charged after 30 days.`

You can enter the same comment for all sales forms (invoices, orders and quotes), or you can add a unique comment for each. The comment fields for quotes and orders are dimmed because Air Care does not use these features.

Changing Receivables Terminology

The terms for the Receivables Ledger can also be customized.

Click **Names** under Receivables to display the Names and Terminology window:

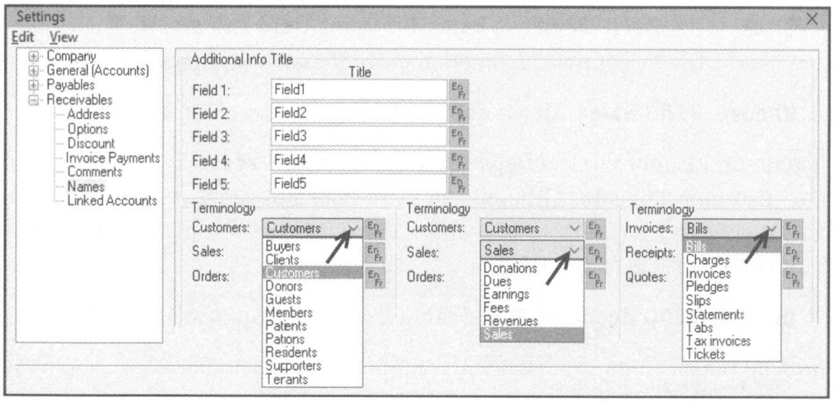

PRO VERSION

The Names screen includes only the Additional Information fields. You cannot change the terminology in the Pro version.

For Receivables, you can also name five additional fields to appear in ledger records and, if you choose, in journal windows.

The second part of the screen has the industry-specific terms used. The names you can change — for Customers, Sales and Bills (Invoices) — are available in the drop-down lists for each field. You cannot modify the Receipts label. The names you select will apply to icons, fields and reports.

If you want to use different names, click the field for the name you want and select a different name from the drop-down list.

CLASSIC VIEW
In the Home window, you can right-click the Sales Journal or Receipts Journal icon,  or . Click the Settings tool  to open the Receivables Linked Accounts screen.

NOTES
The linked accounts for Principal Bank, Accounts Receivable and Deposits are all essential linked accounts.

NOTES
Only the single Bank class account is available on the drop-down list.

When additional currencies are used, fields will be available for linked bank accounts for them as well. You can choose a separate linked account for each currency, or you can use the Canadian dollar account for more than one currency. Because we have not set up foreign currencies, their linked bank account fields are omitted.

WARNING!
You may prefer to leave the Default Revenue Account field blank. If you enter 4100 Installation Revenue as the default revenue account, you must remember to change the account for journal entries that require a different revenue account.

NOTES
If you accept online payments, you will need to enter the two linked accounts for them – one to record the receivables and one for related bank fees.

WARNING!
You must choose Yes to confirm the account class changes and continue. If you choose No, you will return to the Linked Accounts screen.

Defining the Receivables Linked Accounts

The Receivables Ledger linked accounts parallel those for the Payables Ledger.

Click **Linked Accounts** under Receivables:

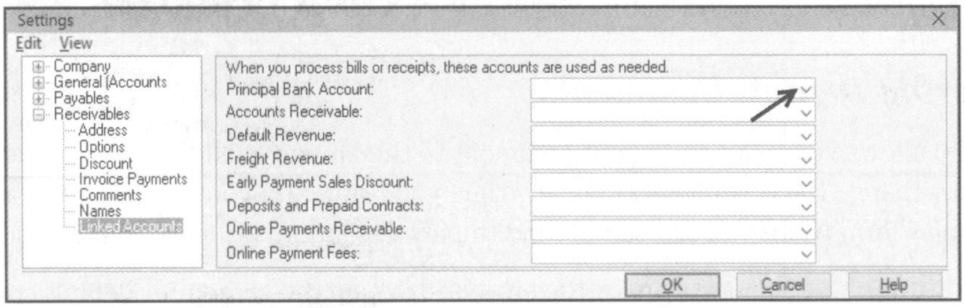

We need to identify the default General Ledger bank account used to receive payments from customers. Cash transactions in the Sales and Receipts journals will be posted to the bank account you select in the journals. The **principal bank account** will be the default account, but any Bank or Cash class account can be selected.

Air Care uses *Bank: Chequing* as the principal bank account for customer transactions. Although most linked accounts may be used only once, one bank account can be linked to the Payables, Receivables and Payroll ledgers.

Click the **Principal Bank Account field list arrow**.

Click **1060 Bank: Chequing** and **press** tab.

The cursor advances to the **Accounts Receivable** field. This control account records the amounts owed to Air Care by customers whenever a credit (Pay Later) Sales Journal invoice or receipt is entered. The General Ledger balance for *Accounts Receivable* reflects and must match the total owed by all customers (from the ledger records). You must use an asset account in this field.

Select **1200 Accounts Receivable** from the drop-down list. **Press** tab.

Click the **Default Revenue list arrow** and **choose 4100 Installation Revenue**.

Air Care does not charge for deliveries. Leave the Freight Revenue field blank.

Click the **Early Payment Sales Discount field list arrow**. This account records the discounts customers receive for early settlement of their accounts.

Choose **4180 Sales Discounts** from the drop-down list. **Press** tab.

The cursor advances to the **Deposits And Prepaid Orders** field. This account is linked to customer deposits. Although Air Care does not request customer deposits, this is an essential linked account, so we cannot leave this field blank. Because we do not use it, we can enter *Accounts Receivable*.

Choose **1200 Accounts Receivable** from the drop-down list.

The final two account are used with online payments and are not used by Air Care.

Click **OK** to open the program's message about class changes for account 3560:

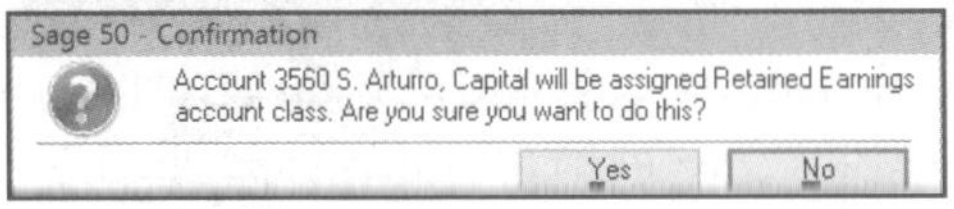

Many linked accounts must have a specific account class to be used as linked accounts. Normally, you can allow the program to assign and change the account class. The exceptions are the Credit Card and Bank class accounts, which you must define before you can choose them as linked bank accounts.

Click **Yes** to accept the change and save the linked account setting. Sage 50 displays a second confirmation message for account 2200:

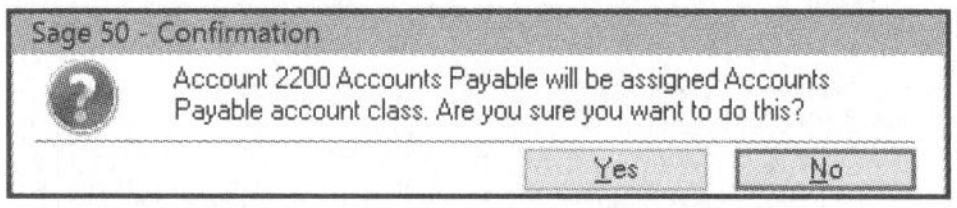

Click **Yes** to accept the class change and save the linked accounts. The final message about the account class change for account 1200 opens:

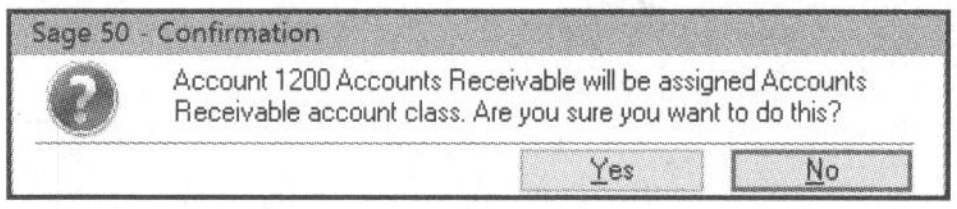

Click **Yes** to accept the change and return to the Home window.

This may be a good time to take a break.

Entering Suppliers in the Payables Ledger

Use the Supplier Information for Air Care Services on page 205 to enter supplier details and historical invoices. The following keystrokes will enter the information for Beausejour Electrical Products, the first supplier on Air Care Services' list.

You can enter new supplier records from the Setup Guide for Suppliers, but you can enter only some of the details on the Address tab screen. Because we need to add other details, we will work from the ledgers. You can open the ledger screen from the Payables module window Suppliers icon or from its shortcuts list. First we must open the Payables module window.

Click **Payables** in the Modules pane to open the window we need.

Click the **Suppliers shortcuts list arrow** and **choose View Suppliers**:

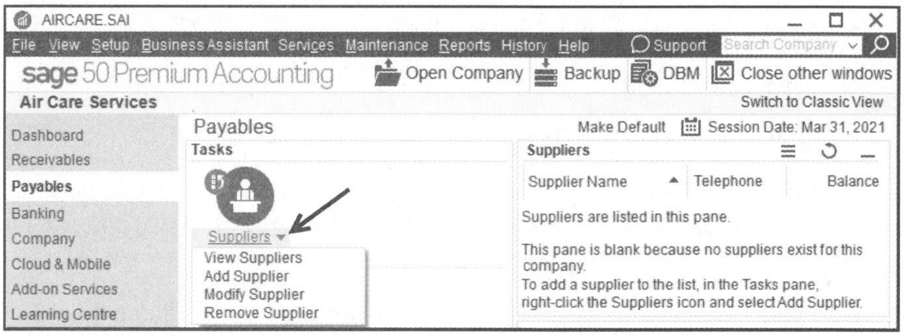

Or, **click** the **Suppliers icon**  in the Payables Home window:

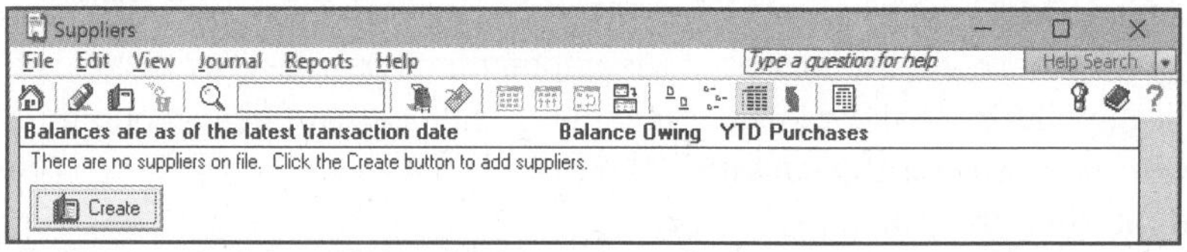

The Suppliers window is empty because no suppliers are on file. Once we add the supplier accounts, this window will contain a listing for each supplier that you can use to access the supplier's ledger record. The suppliers may be displayed in icon form or by name with balances and year-to-date amounts. The default is the listing by name.

Click the **Create button**  or the **Create tool**  in the Suppliers window.

WARNING!
The Retained Earnings, Accounts Payable and Accounts Receivable account classes must be assigned to their respective linked equity, payables and receivables accounts before you can proceed.

NOTES
If you click Add Supplier on the shortcuts list, you will open the New Supplier Ledger window immediately.

PRO VERSION
Click the Vendors icon to open the Vendors window. The term Vendor replaces Supplier in the Suppliers window and in all ledger windows.

NOTES
If you prefer to list the suppliers by icon in the Suppliers window, choose the View menu and click Icon or click the Display By Icon tool. New suppliers will be added at the end of the display, but you can drag icons to any position you want so that frequently used icons appear together at the top of the window.

If you display the suppliers by icon, you can restore the alphabetic order for the icons by choosing the View menu and clicking Re-sort Icons.

NOTES
Pressing ctrl + N in the Suppliers window or in a ledger record window will also open a new Supplier Ledger record form.

NOTES

If you choose to skip the Suppliers icon window from the Home window Setup menu (User Preferences, View), you will open this Payables Ledger (supplier) Address tab window immediately when you click the Suppliers icon.

Or, **choose** the **File menu** and **click Create**.

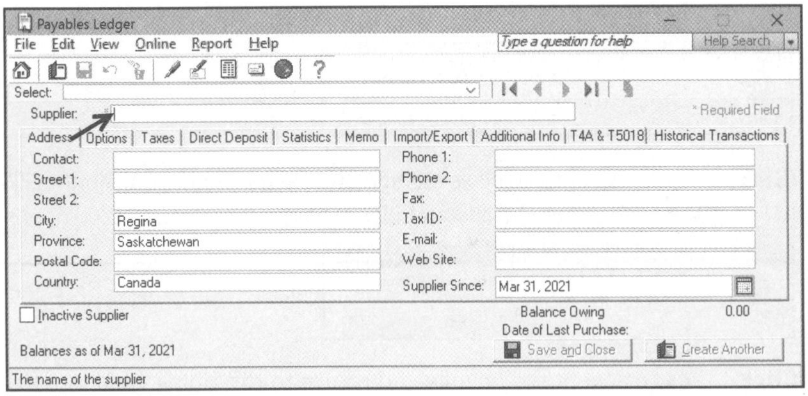

The supplier Address tab screen opens. Most of the supplier input screens should be familiar from entering records for new suppliers in previous chapters. The cursor is in the Supplier name field, the only required field for the record.

NOTES

As soon as you start typing the supplier name, the * and the * Required Field notations disappear. The Save And Close and Create Another buttons are also no longer dimmed.

Type `Beausejour Electrical Products` **Press** *tab*.

The cursor advances to the Contact field. Here you should enter the name of the person (or department) at Beausejour Electrical Products with whom Air Care Services will be dealing. This information enables a company to make professional and effective inquiries. For a small business, the owner's name may appear in this field.

NOTES

You may skip any of the Address tab fields, except the name, if the information is missing for the supplier. To move the cursor, just click the next field for which you have information. To edit any field, drag to highlight the contents and type the correct information.

Type `Janine Beausejour` **Press** *tab* to advance to the Street 1 field.

Type `50 Shockley Rd.` **Press** *tab* to move to the Street 2 field.

Type `Unit 18`

The program uses the Payables Address Settings as the defaults for the City, Province and Country fields. In this case, they are correct.

Click the **Postal Code field**

Type `s4f2t2`

Click the **Phone 1 field**

NOTES

Remember that the postal code sequence for Canada is letter, number, letter, number, letter and number.

The program corrects the format of the postal code. (Only Canadian postal codes are reformatted — those with the specific letter and number sequence.) You can enter phone and fax numbers with or without the area code.

Type `3064765282` **Press** *tab* to advance to the Phone 2 field.

Type `3064763997` **Press** *tab* to advance to the Fax field.

Type `3064765110` **Press** *tab* to advance to the Tax ID field.

The program corrects the format of the phone numbers. The Tax ID field allows you to enter the supplier's tax ID or business number. The next two fields contain the e-mail and Web site addresses for the supplier. Enter them just as you would type them in your e-mail and Internet programs.

Type `444 276 539 RT0001` **Press** *tab*.

Type `jb@beausejour.com` **Press** *tab*.

Type `beausejour.com` **Press** *tab*.

The cursor moves to the Supplier Since field. The program has entered the session date as the default, but we should change it to reflect the company's actual transaction history. All suppliers have been used by Air Care since January 1, 2016.

Type Jan 1 2016

The supplier's account balance appears at the bottom of the ledger. A supplier may be marked as **Inactive**, also at the bottom of the ledger, if there are currently no transactions. You have the option to include or omit inactive suppliers from reports. All Air Care's suppliers are active.

The remaining supplier details are entered from the other tab screens.

Click the **Options tab** to open the next screen:

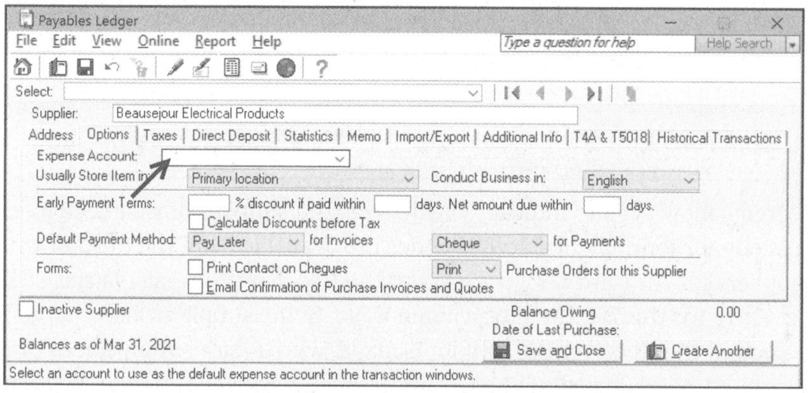

The supplier's name appears on each tab screen for reference. We want to enter the default expense account so that it will automatically appear in journal entries.

Click the **Expense Account list arrow**. All postable accounts are listed.

Click **1320 Electrical Supplies**.

When you use multiple currencies, they can also be linked to suppliers on the Options tab screen. The **Usually Store Item In** field refers to inventory locations. When multiple locations are used for storage, you can link the supplier to one of these locations. Air Care does not sell inventory and has only one location.

Regardless of the language you use to work in Sage 50, you can choose a language for the supplier so that all Sage 50 forms you send to this supplier will be in the language selected on the Options tab screen.

If the supplier offers a discount for early payment or has a term for the net amount, enter these details in this screen. The terms with Beausejour are 1/10, net 30.

Click the **% Discount field** (the first Early Payment Terms field).

Type 1 **Press** (tab) to advance to the If Paid In ___ Days field.

Type 10 **Press** (tab) to advance to the Net Due In ___ Days field.

Type 30

Click the **Calculate Discounts Before Tax check box** to select this option.

The default payment methods — Pay Later and Cheque — are correct. For **Receiver General**, **Saskatel** and **Saskatchewan Energy Corp.**, choose Cheque and Cheque.

Do not turn on the option to **Print Contact On Cheques** because the Contact field does not contain address information.

If you e-mail purchase orders to a supplier, choose this option from the drop-down list to replace the default option to print purchase orders. Click **E-mail Confirmation** if you e-mail purchase orders to be certain that the order is sent. Even if you choose Print as the default, you can still e-mail the order from the Purchases Journal.

If you subscribe to the service, all suppliers can be linked automatically to your contacts in Microsoft Outlook (Company Settings, Office 365 Integration.)

PRO VERSION

You will not have the Usually Store Item In Location field. There is no option to enter multiple locations.

NOTES

If you have not yet created the account you want to use as the default account, type the new account number in the Expense Account field and press (tab) to start the Add An Account wizard. Choose Add when asked if you want to create the account.

NOTES

Multiple inventory locations are used in Chapter 18.

NOTES

Remember that all supplier discounts are calculated on before-tax amounts.

NOTES

For suppliers who request payment on receipt, enter 1 in the Net Days field. When you enter zero in the Net Days field, the Terms fields remain blank and invoices will not be counted as overdue. Payment terms may be changed in the journal for individual invoices.

Select Cheque as the Payment Method for Invoices for the following suppliers:

Receiver General for Canada
Saskatchewan Energy Corp.
Saskatel

Click the **Taxes tab** to access the next input screen.

Click the **list arrow beside No Tax** to choose a default tax code:

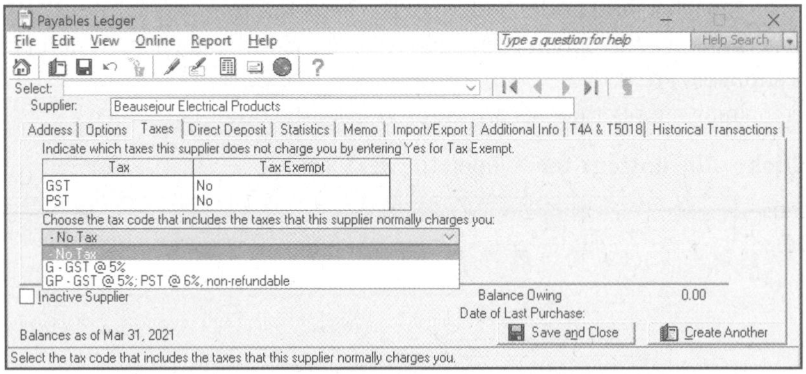

This screen allows you to indicate which taxes the supplier normally charges and the default tax code for journal entries. The codes are available from the drop-down list.

All suppliers for Air Care Services, except the Receiver General, charge GST, so the correct entry for the Tax Exempt column is No. Some suppliers also charge PST. Suppliers such as the Receiver General for Canada, who do not supply goods or services eligible for input tax credits, should have Yes in the Tax Exempt column. If you choose Yes, the tax will not be calculated in the Purchases Journal for that supplier, even if you choose a tax code that applies the tax.

Leave all **Tax Exempt** entry settings at **No** to make all tax codes available for purchases. Clicking No changes the entry to Yes.

Click **G - GST @ 5%** to select the code.

Click the **Direct Deposit tab** to open the next information screen:

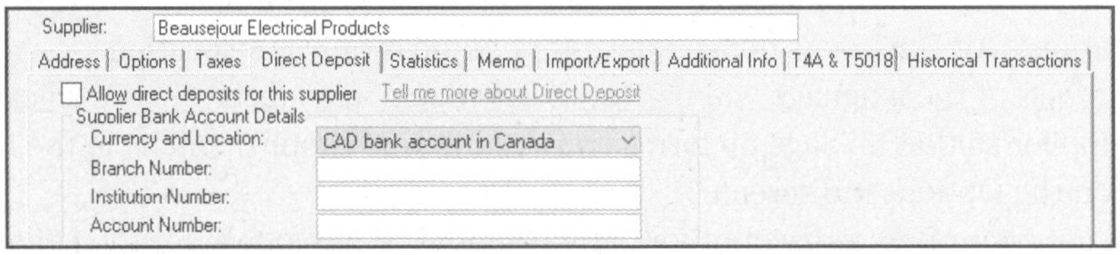

The Direct Deposit fields record your bank account details for automatic withdrawals you allow this supplier to make.

Click the **Statistics tab** to open the next information screen:

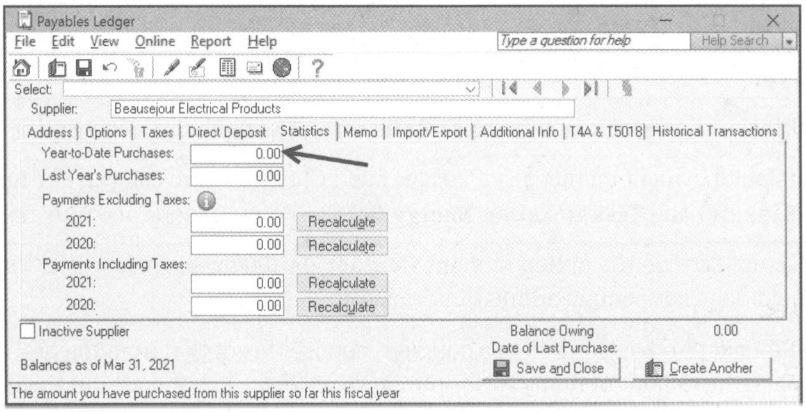

Point to the information button to learn about amounts without taxes:

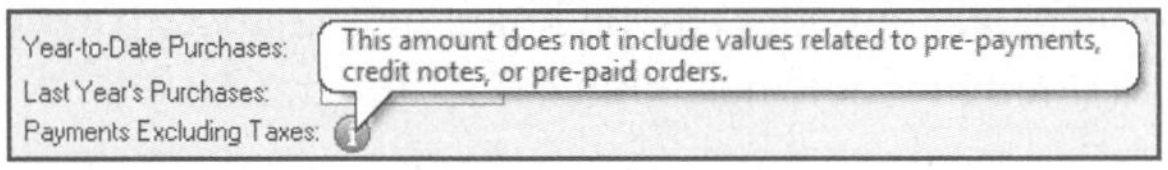

NOTES
When PST applies, businesses that sell inventory or other products do not pay PST on the products they purchase for sale or use to make the products they sell. Thus they are exempt from paying PST. If, however, the supplier provides other items that are subject to PST charges, you must choose No in the Exempt column for PST so that taxes can be calculated correctly for those items.

NOTES
Direct Deposit is covered in Chapter 13.

NOTES
When the supplier uses a foreign currency, the statistics summary information is presented for both currencies.

The amounts on the Statistics tab screen are continuously updated when you enter invoices and payment transactions.

The Statistics fields record the historical purchase and payment totals for two years and are updated automatically from journal entries. You can enter amounts with and without taxes.

Click the **Year-To-Date Purchases field**.

Type 2100

Click the **Payments Excluding Taxes for 2021 field**. **Type** 2000

Click the **Payments Including Taxes for 2021 field**. **Type** 2100

Click the **Memo tab** to advance to the next screen:

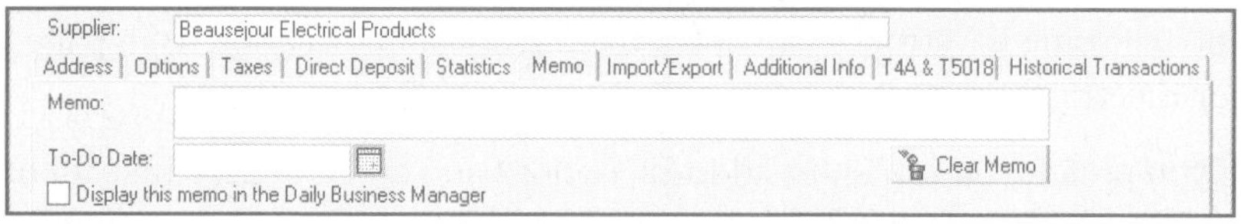

The Memo tab screen allows you to enter a message and date related to the supplier that may be added to the Daily Business Manager lists, the automatic reminder system.

Click the **Import/Export tab** to open the next information screen:

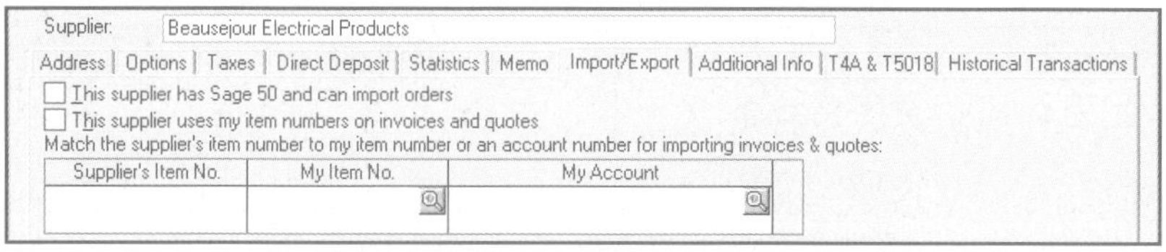

The Import/Export screen refers to orders and quotes. If the supplier also uses Sage 50, you can match the supplier's inventory item codes to your own for electronic transfers of information.

Click the **Additional Info tab**:

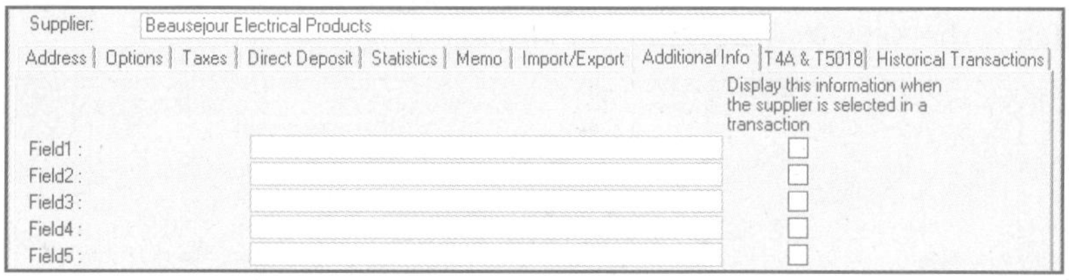

You can customize the records for any ledger by adding up to five fields. The customized names you added from the Names Settings option for the ledger will appear on this Additional Info screen. This additional information can be included in journal transaction windows and in Supplier List reports. Air Care Services does not use any additional fields.

Click the **T4A & T5018 tab**:

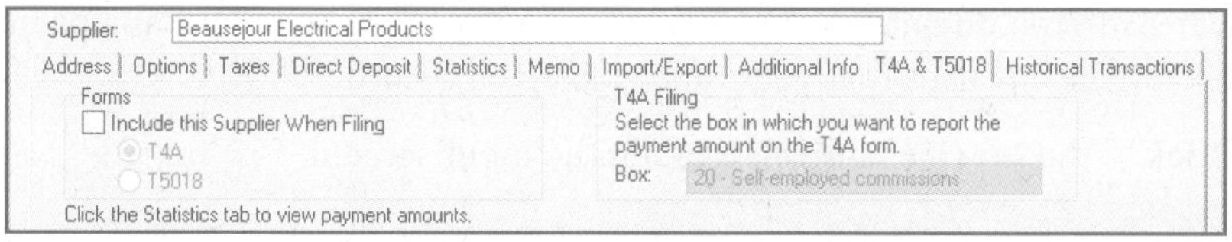

If the business pays subcontractors who require these forms for income tax purposes, enter the information here. Purchases from these suppliers will be used to prepare the forms. Air Care does not have subcontractors or contract employees, so we are now ready to enter the supplier's historical transactions.

Correct any **errors** by returning to the field with the mistake. **Highlight** the **errors** and **enter** the **correct information**.

NOTES

The message in the memo may be up to 255 characters in length.

The Daily Business Manager is used in Chapter 11.

The Import/Export feature is described in Appendix J on the Student DVD.

NOTES

When you and your supplier use the same item numbers, and you check this option, the matching part of the screen is no longer needed and is removed.

Importing orders is covered in Appendix J on the Student DVD.

NOTES

The field names on this tab screen are taken from the Names settings for the ledger (refer to page 229).

We will customize Payroll Ledger records by adding fields in Chapter 9.

NOTES

If you prepare T4A slips for the supplier, you can select the box on the form that is used for the amount paid.

WARNING!
Remember to click Calculate Discounts Before Tax for all suppliers who offer discounts.

If there are **no historical invoices**, proceed to the final step of saving the supplier record. Click Create Another [Create Another] and then click the Address tab to prepare for entering the next supplier.

For all suppliers, the date for **Supplier Since** is **January 1, 2016**.

Entering Historical Supplier Information

NOTES
If you have already created and saved the record, the Save Now option will be removed from the Historical Transactions tab screen. Instead, you will open the next screen asking you to choose Invoices or Payments.

You can enter all the historical invoices and payments for the fiscal year to date, but you must enter all outstanding invoices and partial payments toward them. Beausejour Electrical Products has outstanding invoices, so we must enter historical transaction details. The following keystrokes will enter the historical information from page 205 for Beausejour Electrical Products.

If you prefer, you can enter address, options and credit limit details for all suppliers before adding historical invoices and payments. Open a supplier ledger record by double-clicking the supplier's name in the Suppliers window. Then click the Historical Transactions tab to access the Invoices and Payments buttons.

WARNING!
Enter invoice details carefully. To correct a historical invoice amount, you must pay the invoice and clear the paid transactions (Maintenance menu); then reset the historical payments for the year to zero (Payables Ledger, Statistics tab screen) and re-enter the year-to-date amounts and the outstanding invoices. Refer to page 251.

Click the **Historical Transactions tab**:

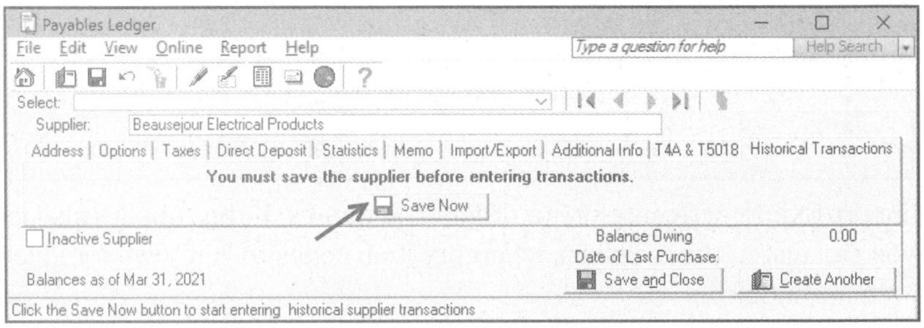

You must save or create the supplier record before adding historical invoices.

Click the **Save Now button** to modify the ledger screen:

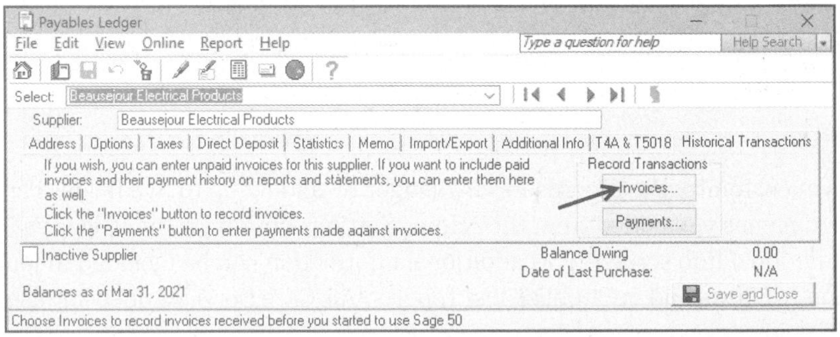

The Create Another button has been removed and the Save And Close button is dimmed again. The screen now has two new buttons: Invoices and Payments. You should select **Invoices** to record outstanding invoices and **Payments** to record any payments made against these invoices that you want to keep on record.

Click the **Invoices button** to open the input screen:

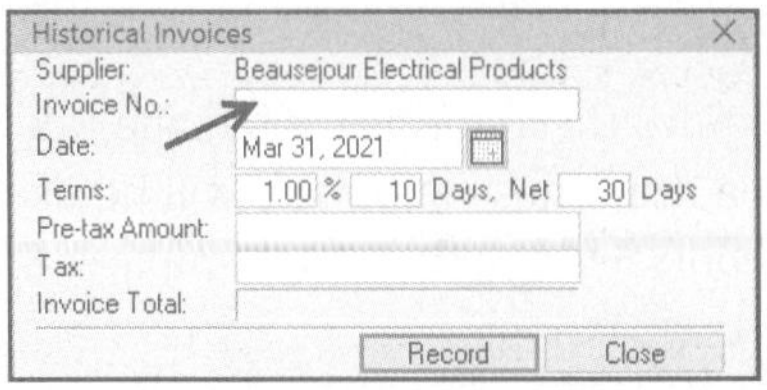

The cursor is in the Invoice No. field so you can enter the first invoice number.

Type B-894 **Press** tab to advance to the Date field.

Enter the invoice date to replace the default earliest transaction date. The invoice date must not be later than the earliest transaction date — the date allowed for the first journal transaction after the historical data in the setup.

Type 03-26-21

The Terms are entered from the Supplier record and are correct, although they can be edited if necessary. You should enter the amount for the first invoice. The amount is divided into pretax and tax amounts so that Sage 50 can correctly calculate the discount on the before-tax amount. When the option to calculate discounts before tax is not selected, a single amount field appears on the invoice for the full amount of the invoice with taxes included — as on page 246 for customers.

Click the **Pre-Tax Amount field** to advance the cursor.

Type 10000 **Press** tab to advance to the Tax amount field.

Type 500 **Press** tab to update the Invoice Total.

The total of all outstanding invoice and payment amounts must match the opening balance in the *Accounts Payable* control account in the General Ledger.

Correct any **errors**. **Press** tab to return to the field with the error and **highlight** the **error**. Then **enter** the **correct information**.

Be sure that all the information is entered correctly before you save your supplier invoice. If you save incorrect invoice information and you want to change it, refer to page 251 for assistance.

Click **Record** to save the invoice and to display a blank invoice for the supplier.

Enter **invoice B-921** (not the payment, Chq #94) for Beausejour Electrical Products by repeating the steps above. **Click Record**.

When you have recorded all outstanding invoices for a supplier,

Click **Close** to return to the ledger.

The two invoices have been added to the Balance Owing field at the bottom of the ledger screen. Now you can enter historical payment information for this supplier.

Click the **Payments button** to display the payments form:

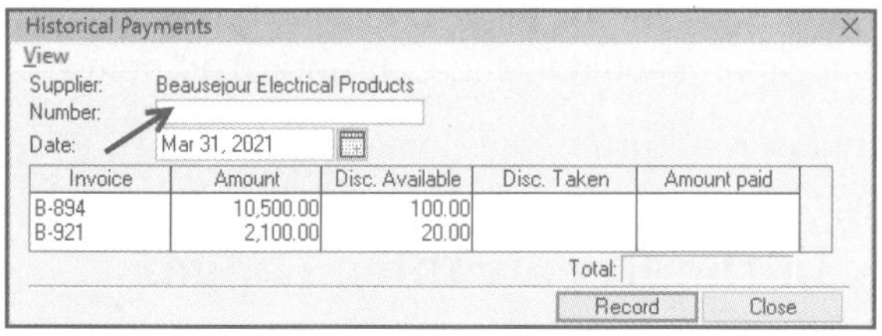

All outstanding invoices that you entered are displayed. Notice that the discount amounts are 1 percent of the pretax amounts. Entering historical payments is very much like entering current payments in the Payments Journal. You should make separate payment entries for each cheque.

Click the Number field if necessary to place the cursor in the cheque Number field.

Type 94 **Press** tab to advance to the Date field.

Enter the cheque date for the first payment toward invoice #B-894 to replace the default earliest transaction date.

Type 3-26

WARNING!
You must choose Record to save each invoice and payment and then Close the invoice form. If you close the input screen before selecting Record, the information is not saved.

NOTES
The View menu has the option to refresh the invoices from information added by other users. Because it applies only to the multi-user mode, it is not available in the Pro version.

NOTES
The discount amounts based on pretax amounts are $100 (1 percent of $10 000) and $20 (1 percent of $2 000).

NOTES
Clicking the Amount Paid field directly ensures the discount amount is not entered.

WARNING!
When an amount appears in the Disc. Taken field, you must delete it before recording a partial payment. Otherwise, the balance owing to the supplier will be incorrect. The total owing to vendors will not match the Accounts Payable General Ledger balance and you will be unable to finish the history.

Click the **Amount Paid column** on the line for Invoice #B-894.

Because the full amount is not being paid, the discount does not apply. The full amount of the discount will remain available until the 10 days have passed. If the balance is paid within that time, the full discount will be taken.

The full invoice amount, displayed as the default, is highlighted so you can edit it.

Type 4500 **Press** tab. **Press** del to delete the Disc. Taken amount.

Check the **information** carefully and **make corrections** before you proceed.

Click **Record** to save the information and display another payment form for this supplier in case there are additional payments to record.

The amount owing for invoice #B-894 has been updated to include the payment you entered, but the full discount amount remains available.

Repeat these procedures to enter any other payments to this supplier.

When you have recorded all payments for the outstanding invoices,

Click **Close** to return to the supplier information form.

On the Statistics tab screen, the invoices and payment you entered have been included to increase the totals for 2021.

Click the **Create tool** or **press** ctrl + **N** to enter the next supplier.

Click the **Address tab** to prepare for entering the next supplier record.

NOTES
If you display suppliers by icon, you can restore the alphabetic order for icons by choosing the View menu and then Re-sort Icons.

Sage 50 has created a Supplier icon and listing for Beausejour Electrical Products in the Suppliers window. The default view for suppliers is to list them alphabetically by name with the balance owing and year-to-date purchases. The Create button has been removed, although the Create tool is still available.

NOTES
Even though the historical invoices and payments were entered correctly, you will have an outstanding historical difference. This is addressed on page 251.

Enter the **remaining suppliers** and historical transactions on page 205.

Click **Save And Close** Save and Close to close the Supplier Ledger after entering the last supplier record (it has no historical transactions).

Display or **print** your **Supplier List** to check the address details from the Reports menu in the Suppliers window.

Display or **print** a **Supplier Aged Detail Report**. Include terms and historical differences. Your report should include a historical difference.

Close the **Suppliers window** to return to the Home window.

Entering Customers in the Receivables Ledger

NOTES
You can use the Setup Guide for Customers to add the new records, but you are limited to entering some of the details on the Address tab screen. You must open the ledger to enter additional information.

Use the Customer Information chart for Air Care Services on page 206 to complete this step. The following keystrokes will enter the information for Grande Pointe Towers, the first customer on the list for Air Care Services. You should open the Receivables window.

Click **Receivables** in the Modules pane list to open the window we need.

Click the **Customers icon** Customers to display the Customers window. The Customers window is empty because there are no customers on file yet.

Click the **Create button** Create or **tool** in the Customers window, or **choose** the **File menu** and **click Create**.

You will open the Receivables Ledger new customer Address tab screen:

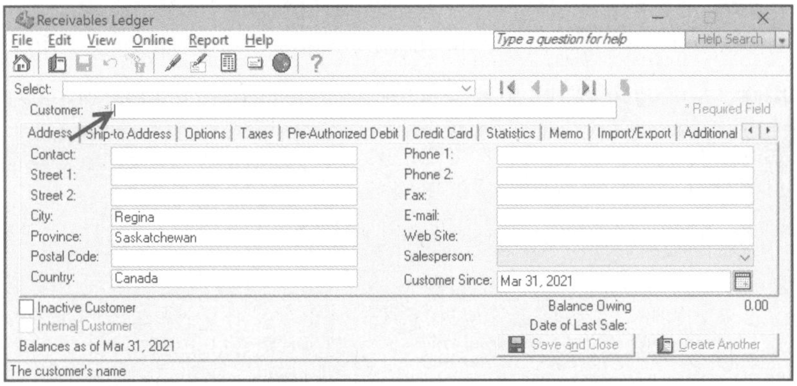

The customer information screen opens at the Address tab screen. The cursor is in the Customer field, the only required field. The default Province and Country entered from the module's Address settings are correct, but we need to change the city name.

Type `Grande Pointe Towers` **Press** *tab*.

You may skip any address tab fields if information is missing. Just click the next field for which you have information to move the cursor.

Air Care's primary contact about a sale should be entered in the Contact field.

Type `Sophie Grande` **Press** *tab* to advance to the Street 1 field.

Type `77 LaPointe Cr.` **Press** *tab* to move to the Street 2 field.

Press *tab* to advance to the City field. We need to replace the default entry.

Type `White City`

Click the **Postal Code field**. **Type** `s0g5b0`

Click the **Phone 1 field**. The postal code format is corrected.

Type `3067227500` **Press** *tab*. The format is corrected automatically.

Click the **Fax field**.

Type `3063227436` **Press** *tab* to advance to the E-mail field.

Type `sgrande@GPTowers.com` **Press** *tab*.

Type `GPTowers.com` to enter the Web site.

Press *tab* **twice** to move to the Customer Since date field.

Type `Jan 1 21`

The current balance is included at the bottom of the Ledger window. Like suppliers and accounts, customers may be marked as inactive and omitted from reports if they have not bought merchandise or services for some time.

Click the **Ship-To Address tab**:

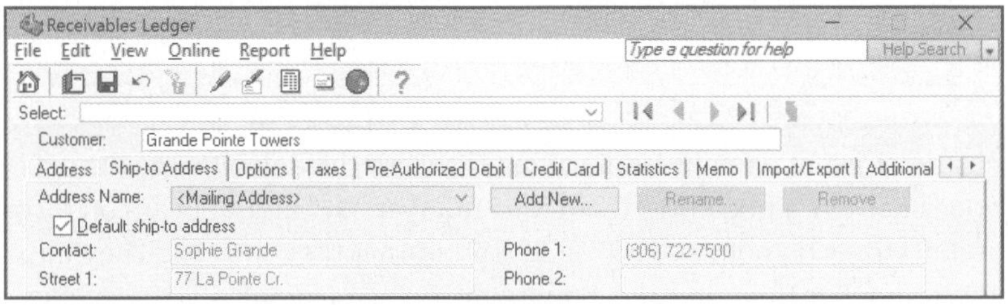

NOTES

If you choose not to view the Customers icon window from the Home window Setup menu (User Preferences, View), you will open this Receivables Ledger window immediately when you click the Customers icon.

PRO VERSION

The Pro version does not have the option to define Internal Customers.

NOTES

As soon as you start typing the customer's name, the * and the * Required Field notations disappear. The Save And Close and Create Another buttons also became available.

NOTES

Remember that the postal code sequence for Canada is letter, number, letter, number, letter and number.

NOTES

The Internal Customers option works with the Time & Billing feature and is used to identify other departments within the company that use your services. The time and cost for these internal services can be tracked. Time and billing is covered in Chapter 18.

Customers will be added to your Microsoft Outlook contacts if you have Office 365 and subscribe to the service.

PRO VERSION

The Pro version does not allow multiple addresses. Only one mailing and one shipping address can be entered. Click Same As Mailing Address to remove the ✓ if you need to change the mailing address.

NOTES
As soon as you choose another address in the Address Name field, the address fields will open. Refer to Chapter 6 for more information on shipping addresses.

The Ship-To Address screen allows you to enter multiple addresses for customers who want merchandise to be shipped to different addresses. You can apply labels to each address. The default setting is to use the mailing address as the shipping address.

Click the **Options tab** to access the customer's payment and invoice options:

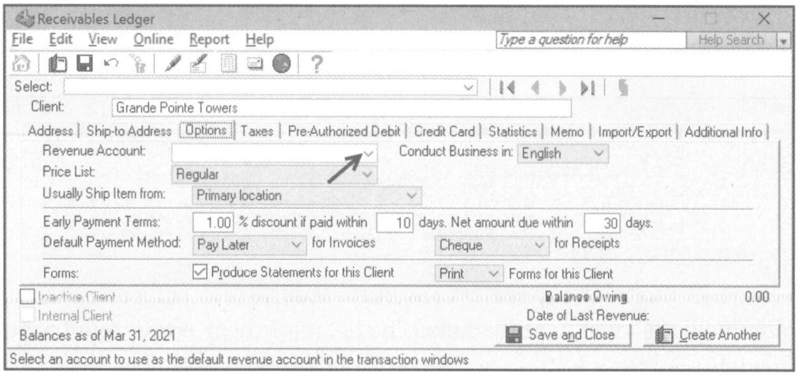

NOTES
The option to calculate discounts before or after tax is selected for the Receivables Ledger as a whole (refer to page 232). You cannot change the setting for individual customers.

PRO VERSION
You will not have the options for inventory location (Usually Ship Item From) or Internal Customer.

Most of the options are taken from the settings for the Receivables Ledger, and all the default settings are correct. You can select English or French as the customer's language — all forms you send to the customer will be prepared in the selected language. The **Price List** field applies to inventory and services prices that can be set at different rates for different customers. Air Care supplies customized services and does not use the Inventory module. The payment terms are entered automatically from the Receivables Settings and the default payment methods are also correct. Terms can be edited if necessary for individual customers and invoices in the Sales Journal. Air Care charges interest on overdue accounts, so we need to be able to **produce statements**.

When a business sells inventory from more than one location, you can link a customer to one of these locations with the entry in the **Usually Ship Item From** location field. Air Care has only one location. The customer's currency is also defined on the Options tab screen when a business uses more than one currency.

NOTES
Multiple inventory locations are used in Chapter 18.

You need to add only a default revenue account for the customer. Although there are three revenue accounts that apply to customers, most customers use Air Care's installation services, so we can choose this as the default. Remember that you can choose a different account in the Sales Journal for any invoice. You may prefer to omit the default revenue account to avoid using an incorrect revenue account for sales.

NOTES
If you do not add a default revenue account for a customer, the default linked revenue account for the ledger (page 234) will be entered in the journal.

Click the **Revenue Account field list arrow**.

Click **4100 Installation Revenue**.

Click the **Taxes tab**:

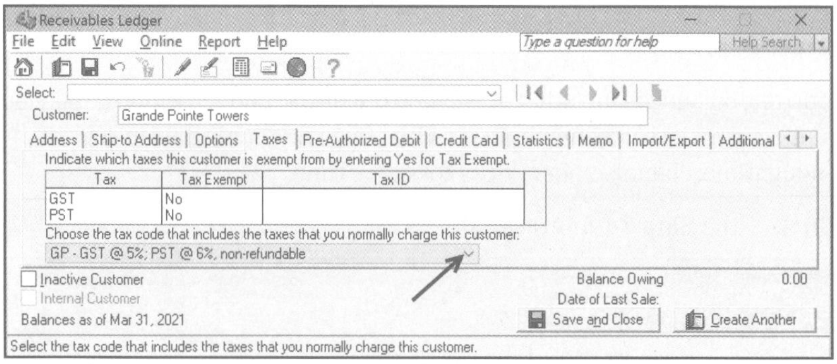

NOTES
The PST Tax ID number identifies retailers that can collect PST from their customers and are exempted from paying the tax on purchases of the items they sell.

NOTES
You can change the default tax code for individual customers if necessary by choosing a different code from the Tax Code list. You can also change the code for individual invoices or amounts on the invoice.

The customer is not exempt from paying taxes, so the defaults are correct. If the customer does not pay a tax, enter the tax ID number so that it appears on invoices. For example, retail stores do not pay PST on inventory that they will sell. They must register and have a tax number to permit the exemption. Some customers are also exempt from

GST payments. Taxes will be calculated only if the customer is marked as not tax exempt. The default tax code, GP - GST @ 5%, PST @ 6%, non-refundable, should be entered.

The **Pre-Authorized Debit** and **Credit Card** screens hold the customer's bank and credit card information when you are authorized to make automatic withdrawals.

NOTES
Pre-authorized debit and automatic credit card charges are covered in Chapter 13. These tab screens are also illustrated in Chapter 6, page 176.

Click the **Statistics tab** to view the next set of customer details:

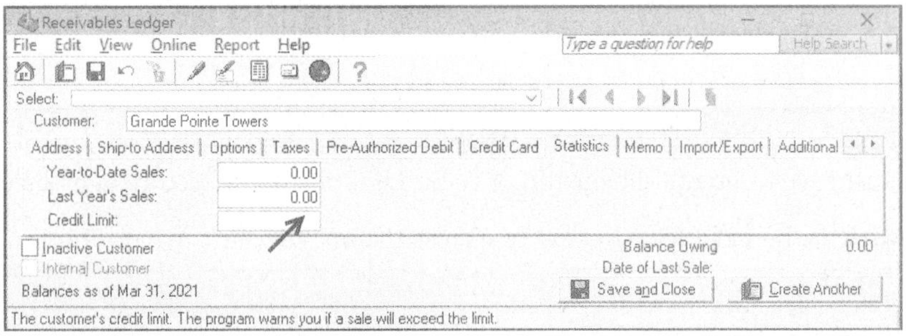

Balances will be included automatically once you provide the outstanding invoice information. **Year-To-Date Sales** are updated from journal entries, but you can add a historical balance as well. When you have two years of data, there will be an amount for last year's sales too. Records for foreign customers will have sales summary amounts and balances in both currencies.

The **Credit Limit** is the amount that the customer can purchase on account before payments are required. If the customer goes beyond this credit limit, the program will issue a warning when you attempt to post the invoice. You can accept the sale or revise it.

Click the **Year-To-Date Sales field**.

Type 11000 **Press** tab **twice** to advance to the Credit Limit field.

Type 20000

The **Memo tab** screen for customers is just like the Memo tab screen for suppliers. It allows you to enter messages related to the customer. If you enter a reminder date, the program can display the message in the Daily Business Manager on the date you provide. If the customer also uses Sage 50, you can match the customer's inventory codes to your own on the **Import/Export tab** screen to allow for electronic data transfers. The **Additional Info tab** screen allows you to enter details for the custom-defined fields you created for customers, similar to the Additional Info tab fields for suppliers.

NOTES
The Daily Business Manager is covered in Chapter 11.
The Additional Information field labels are defined on the Receivables Names Settings screen (refer to page 233).

Correct errors by returning to the field with the error. **Click** the appropriate **tab**, **highlight** the **error** and **enter** the **correct information**. You can correct address and options details any time.

If there are no historical invoices, proceed to the final step of saving the customer record (page 248). Click Create Another [Create Another] and then click the Address tab to prepare for entering the next customer. Sage 50 has created a listing for the customer in the Customers window.

Entering Historical Customer Information

As for suppliers, you can enter all historical invoices and payments for the year to date, but you must enter outstanding invoice amounts. The following keystrokes will enter historical information for Grande Pointe Towers from page 206.

Click the **right scroll arrow** ▶ on the tab heading line to access the tab for Historical Transactions.

NOTES
If you have already saved (created) the record, the Save Now option on the Historical Transactions tab screen will be removed. Instead, you will open the next screen asking you to choose Bills or Payments.

Click the **Historical Transactions tab**:

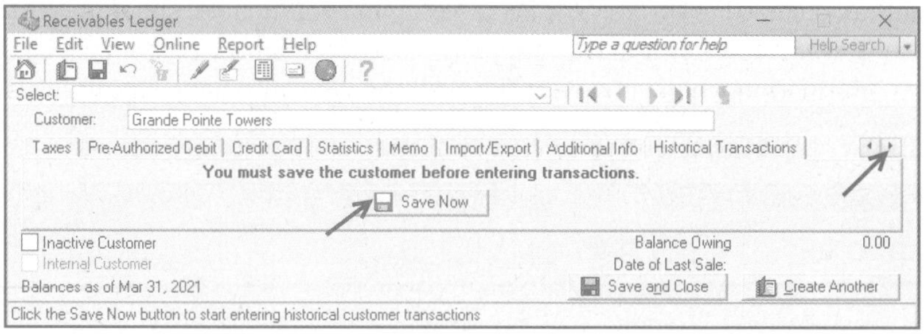

You must save or create the customer record before adding historical invoices.

Click the **Save Now button** to access the invoice and payment buttons:

PRO VERSION
pro Invoices replaces Bills on the Historical Transactions tab screen and the Historical Bills screen below.

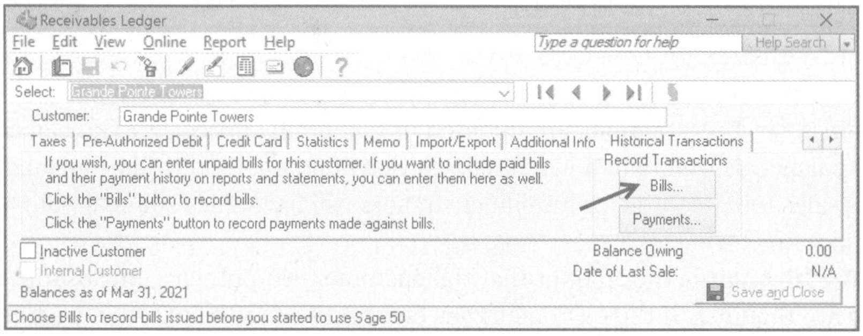

Again, the Create Another button has been removed and the Save And Close button is dimmed because you have already saved the record.

> If you prefer, you can enter address, options and credit limit details for all customers before adding historical bills and payments. Open a customer ledger record by double-clicking the customer's name in the Customers window. Then click the Historical Transactions tab to access the Bills and Payments buttons.

Just as in the Payables Ledger, you enter invoices and payments separately. You can use the Payments option to record any payments against previous invoices that you want to keep on record. The totals of all outstanding invoices, after payments, must match the opening balance in the *Accounts Receivable* control account in the General Ledger.

WARNING!
Enter invoice details carefully. To correct a historical invoice amount, you must pay the invoice and then clear paid transactions (Maintenance menu); then re-enter the outstanding invoices. Refer to page 251.

Click the **Bills button** to display the input form:

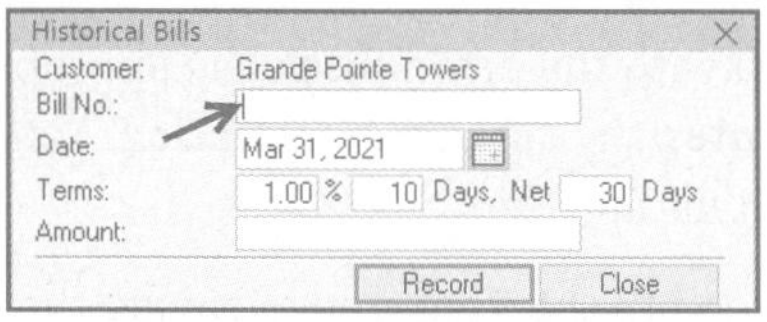

There is a single Amount field because customer discounts are calculated on after-tax amounts. When discounts are calculated before tax, there is an additional input field so that the sale and the tax amounts can be entered separately, as we saw in the Payables Historical Invoices screen. The earliest transaction date is the default invoice date. The cursor is in the Bill No. field so you can enter the first invoice number.

Type 699 **Press** *tab* to advance to the Date field.

Type mar 24

Because the payment terms are correctly entered, we can skip them. Discounts are calculated after taxes, so only the single after-tax amount is needed.

NOTES
This invoice amount will be added to the Year-To-Date Sales amount on the Statistics tab screen.

Click the **Amount field**. **Type** 4440

Correct errors by returning to the field with the error, **highlighting** the **error** and **entering** the **correct information**.

Check the **information** carefully before saving the invoice.

Incorrect invoices can be changed only by paying the outstanding invoices, clearing paid transactions (Home window, Maintenance menu, Clear Data, Clear Paid Transactions, Clear Paid Customer Transactions) and then re-entering the statistics and invoices (refer to page 251).

Click **Record** to save the invoice and to display a new blank invoice form for this customer.

Repeat these **procedures** to record the second invoice for this customer.

Click **Close** to return to the Historical Transactions window after entering all invoices for a customer.

WARNING!
You must click Record for each invoice you enter to save it. Clicking Close will discard the entry.

The program has added the customer's balance to the ledger window. You are now ready to record the payment made by Grande Pointe Towers against the first invoice.

Click the **Payments button** to display the customer Historical Payments form:

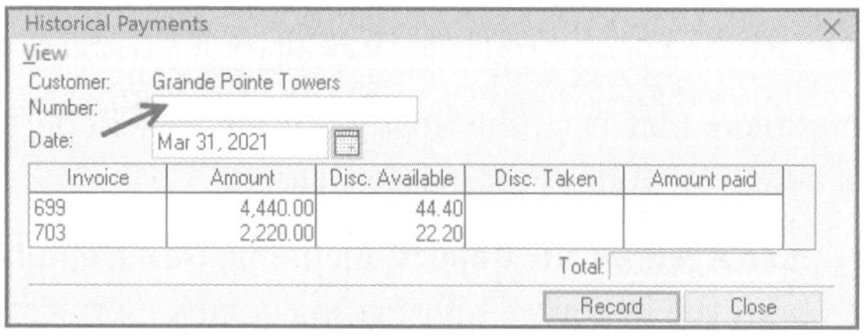

All outstanding invoices that you entered are displayed. Entering historical customer payments is much like entering current receipts in the Receipts Journal. As for supplier historical payments, the earliest transaction date, March 31, is the default. This date is less than 10 days after the invoice dates, so the discounts are still available. The first discount amount — $44.40— is 1 percent of the total after-tax invoice amount.

Click the Number field to place the cursor in the customer cheque number field if necessary.

Type `4896` **Press** *tab* to advance to the Date field.

Type `03-28`

Discounts can be taken only when the full payment is made before the due date, so we must skip the Discount fields. The full discount remains available until the discount period has ended.

Click the **Amount Paid column** on the line for invoice #699.

The full invoice amount is displayed as the default and highlighted so you can edit it.

Type `2460` **Press** *tab*. **Press** *del* to remove the second discount amount.

WARNING!
If an amount appears in the Disc. Taken field, delete it before recording a partial payment. If you do not, you cannot finish the history because the ledgers will not be balanced.

Check your **information** carefully before you proceed and **make corrections** if necessary.

Click **Record** to save the information and to display another payment form for this customer in case there are additional payments to record.

The full discount remains available after the payment — its amount is not reduced, although the balance owing has been reduced.

Repeat these steps to enter other payments by this customer if there are any.

When you have recorded all outstanding payments by a customer,

Click **Close** to return to the customer information form.

In the ledger, the balance owing has been updated to $4 200 to include the payment entry just completed.

Click the **Address tab** to prepare for entering the next customer.

Click the **Create tool** to open another new customer input screen.

Saving a Customer Record without Historical Information

When all the information is entered correctly, you must save the customer information. If you have not added historical information,

Click **Create Another** [Create Another] to save the information and advance to the next new customer input screen.

Click the **Address tab** to prepare for entering the next customer.

Repeat these **procedures** to enter the remaining customers and historical transactions on page 206. After entering the last customer,

Click **Save And Close** [Save and Close] to close the Customer Ledger window.

Display or **print** the **Customer List** from the Customers window Reports menu to check the accuracy of your address information.

Display or **print** a **Customer Aged Detail Report**, including terms and historical differences, to check the historical information. Your report should have no historical differences for customers.

Close the **Customers icon window** to return to the Home window.

WARNING!
Make a backup copy before proceeding. If you finish entering the history and discover an incorrect amount, you can correct the error without re-entering all the information.

Preparing for Journal Entries

The last stage in setting up the accounting system involves closing the historical entries. This step indicates that all historical data have been entered and cannot be changed. You can proceed with journalizing before you finish the history, but you must finish the history before beginning a new fiscal period. Finishing the history involves changing the status of each ledger from an open to a finished history state. In the open history state the ledgers are not integrated, so you can add or change historical information in one ledger without affecting any other ledger. It is easier to correct mistakes.

WARNING!
You cannot use Save As with CDs or DVDs in Sage 50. You can use Backup and Save A Copy to make CD backups.

Refer to page 23 for more information on backup methods and storage media.

NOTES
If you have made previous backups, your backup sequence number and file name will be different from ours.

Cloud backup requires a subscription to the service.

Making a Backup of the Company Files

To make a backup of the not-finished files, you can use Save A Copy from the File menu or use the Backup command. Both methods allow you to keep working in your original working data file.

Choose the **File menu** and **click Backup** or **click** the **Backup tool**:

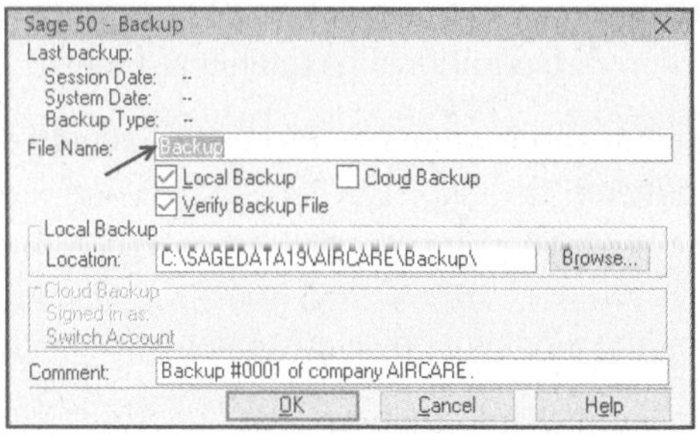

On this backup screen, you should enter the name and location of the new backup.

Click **Browse**:

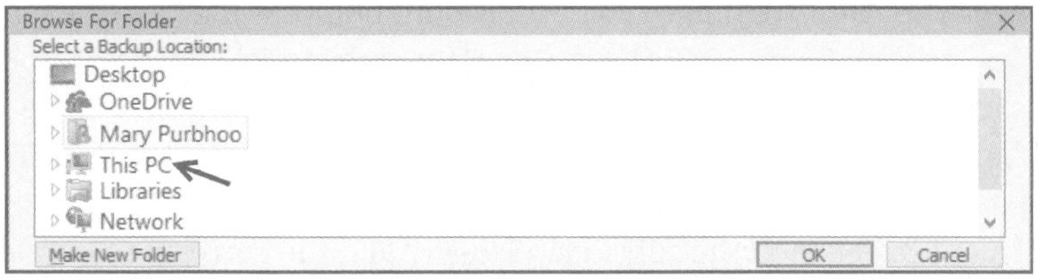

Click **This PC** or **Computer** and **C:**. **Scroll down** and **click SageData19** to locate and select the SageData19 folder with your other data files.

Click the **Make New Folder button** and **type** `NF-AIR` to replace New Folder — the selected name. **Click OK** to return to the Backup screen.

Double-click **Backup** in the File Name field. **Type** `NF-AIRCARE`

Click **OK** to begin backing up the data file.

The "NF" designates files as not finished (the history is still open) to distinguish them from the ones you will work with to enter journal transactions. Continue by following the backup instructions on-screen. You can use another name and location for your backup if you want. This will create a backup copy of the files for Air Care Services.

Click **OK** when the backup is complete.

NOTES
Substitute the appropriate drive and folders for the location of your files.

Working with Unfinished History

Sage 50 allows you to enter current journal transactions before the history is finished and balanced. In this way, you can keep the journal records current and enter the historical details later when there is time available to do so, or the setup may be completed later by a different individual.

There are, however, a number of elements that you must complete before you can make journal entries. You must define the essential linked accounts before you can use the journals, so you must create General Ledger accounts for them. You must enter historical customer and supplier invoices before you can enter payments for them, and invoices must have the correct payment terms and dates. Automatic payroll tax calculations are also unavailable until the history is finished.

You do not need to enter General Ledger opening account balances. These balances may be added later in the Opening Balance field on the Account tab screen. The General Ledger also has the current balance, which changes as you post new journal entries. However, without the opening balances, the current balance is not correct and you cannot generate accurate reports. The Trial Balance will include only amounts from the journal entries, making it more difficult to trace the correct historical amounts.

Some errors may be corrected at any time. For example, after entering journal transactions and after finishing the history, you can correct account, supplier and customer names and address details, but you cannot change historical amounts because their dates precede the earliest transaction date.

From a control point of view, it is preferable to enter all historical information first so that you do not confuse the historical and current data or work with accounts that are not correct in some way. You cannot change account numbers after the accounts are used in journal entries, so some corrections will be difficult to make later. After you start journalizing, the balances for *Accounts Receivable* and *Accounts Payable* reflect all the entries made to date. There may be mistakes in current journal entries as well as in the history, making it more difficult to find the historical errors later.

There are a number of checks that you can perform to increase the accuracy of your work. You should compare your reports carefully with the financial reports for your

WARNING!
Read this section carefully before proceeding.

NOTES
You can create new accounts "on the fly" while making journal entries by using the Add An Account wizard. You will also be prompted to add the essential linked accounts when you try to open the journals. Some linked accounts, such as Sales Discounts, are not essential and you can access the journals without them. However, a journal entry that includes a discount cannot be posted without the linked account, so there are some accounts that you must create before you can use the journals.

WARNING!
Make sure that the Test Account balance is zero. An error in this amount will not prevent you from finishing the history.

company — the charts given at the beginning of this application — and make corrections. Pay particular attention to correct account numbers and historical invoices. Printing Supplier and Customer Aged Detail reports with historical differences and payment terms can reveal errors in invoices or payments. The Accounts window has an option to check the validity of accounts from the File menu or the tool button. The Home window Maintenance menu has an option to **check data integrity** that looks for differences in balances between the subsidiary ledgers and the corresponding General Ledger control accounts. All these checks help point to mistakes that should be corrected before proceeding.

NOTES

From the Supplier Aged Detail Report with historical difference, you would also learn that the supplier history was not correct.

NOTES

Notice that the unused, hidden ledgers are balanced. If you view these ledgers and finish the history, you will be unable to add historical information for them later.

If you finish the history when the unused ledgers are hidden, they remain in the unfinished state and you can add historical information later. (Refer to Chapter 9.)

Choose the **Maintenance menu** and **click Check Data Integrity**:

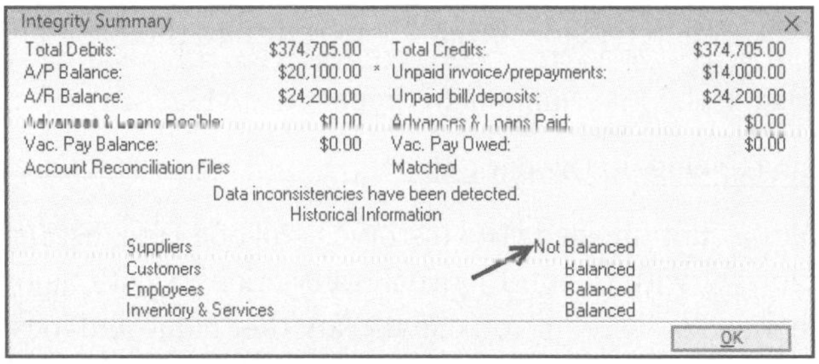

Click **OK** to return to the Home window.

Both the data integrity check and the error summary (on this page) that opens when we attempt to finish the history inform us that the supplier history is not correct — the A/P Balance does not match the Unpaid Invoices amount. This error will prevent us from finishing the history. (Remember that this imbalance was intentional; the Accounts Payable discrepancy amount at this stage is $6 100.)

Choose the **History menu** and **click Finish Entering History**:

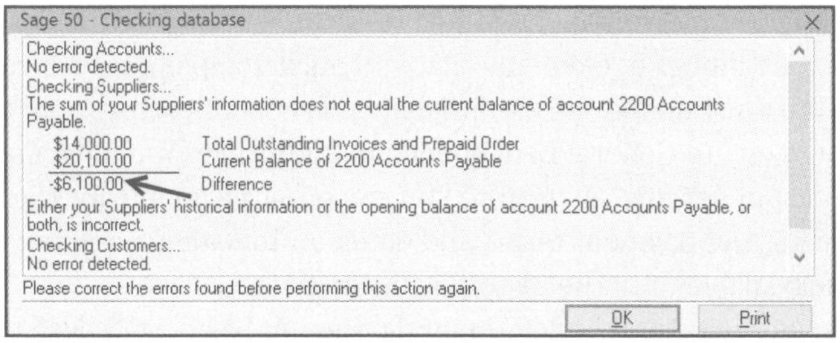

When all your essential linked accounts are defined and all historical amounts balance, you will be warned that this step cannot be reversed, as in Chapter 4, page 97. Otherwise, Sage 50 warns about errors that prevent you from finishing the history. For example, the accounts may be out of order if a subgroup total is missing after a set of subgroup accounts, or the Receivables Ledger balances may not equal the *Accounts Receivable* control account balance. If you have omitted an essential linked account, that information will also be included on this screen.

In this case, we learn that the Suppliers or Accounts Payable history is not balanced, the same information we had in the data integrity check. Because we know that the Trial Balance is correct, we may be missing a historical Payables Ledger invoice.

Click **Print** to print the message for reference to help you correct mistakes.

Click **OK** to return to the Home window.

We can proceed with entering the source documents. When the missing invoice surfaces, we can enter it and finish the history. You can proceed with journal entries until you start the next fiscal period. At that point, you must finish the history.

Correcting Historical Invoices

In reviewing all the records for the year to date, Air Care discovered part of the discrepancy between the Accounts Payable balance and the Supplier Ledger balances. Invoice #B-921 from Beausejour Electrical Products was incorrectly entered. The correct amount was $4 000 plus $200 tax, and the amount for cheque #94 was $3 800. We will correct these errors before making journal entries. The first step is to pay the invoices already entered. You must pay the invoices before you can clear them. You also cannot use the same invoice numbers if you have not cleared the incorrect entries.

Click **Payables** in the Home window Modules pane list.

Click **Beausejour Electrical Products** in the Suppliers list pane to open the ledger.

Click the **Historical Transactions tab**.

Click **Payments** to open the Historical Payments form:

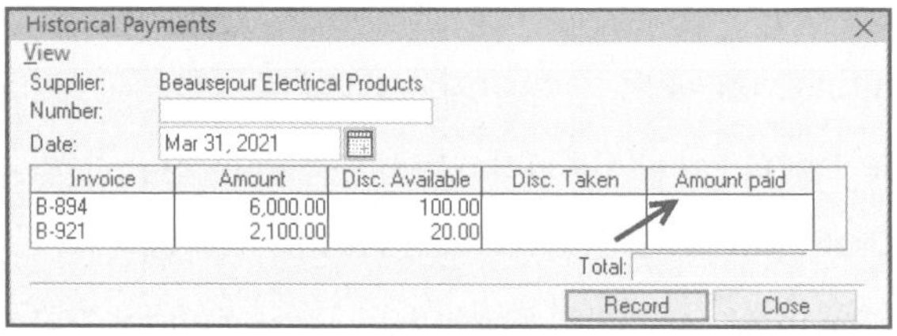

Type 95 in the Number field.

Type 3-28 in the Date field.

Click the **Amount Paid column for Invoice B-894** to enter the full amount owing and avoid including the discount amount.

Click the **Amount Paid column for Invoice B-921** and **press** *tab* to enter the amount and update the total.

Click **Record** and then **click Close**.

Click the **Statistics tab**. The year-to-date amounts have been updated.

Delete the **year-to-date** expense and payment **amounts** to restore the balance amounts to zero. **Close** the **Supplier Ledger record**.

> **WARNING!**
> Be certain that the Discount Taken amounts are not selected and included in the amounts paid.

Next we must clear the paid transactions for Beausejour. This step will remove invoices and payments from the records, allow us to reuse the invoice numbers and provide accurate reports. Unless you clear the paid invoices, you cannot use the same invoice number again.

Choose the **Maintenance menu** and then **choose Clear Data** and **Clear Paid Transactions**. **Click Clear Paid Supplier Transactions**:

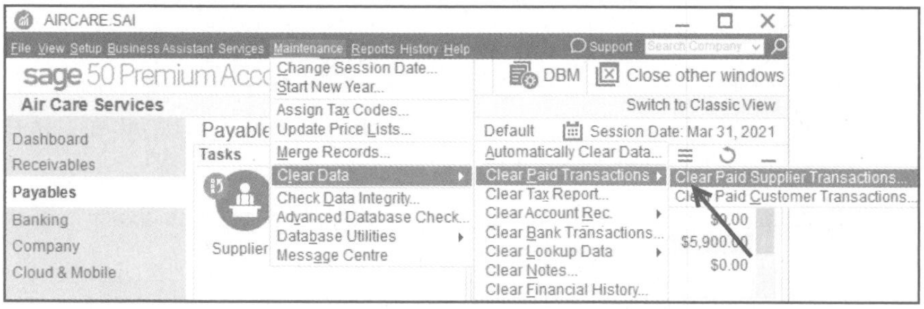

> **PRO VERSION**
> Choose Clear Paid Vendor Transactions.
> The Maintenance menu does not include the option to update price lists.

> **NOTES**
> If you do not clear the transactions, they will be stored for the supplier and will be included in the Aged Detail Report. By clearing them, you can also use the original invoice and cheque numbers. Duplicate numbers are not allowed, but if they are cleared the numbers are not stored.

> **NOTES**
> You must pay and clear all invoices for the supplier and then re-enter all invoices. Otherwise, the errors will be included in the aged reports and the historical amounts on the Statistics tab screen will be incorrect.

You will open the list of suppliers:

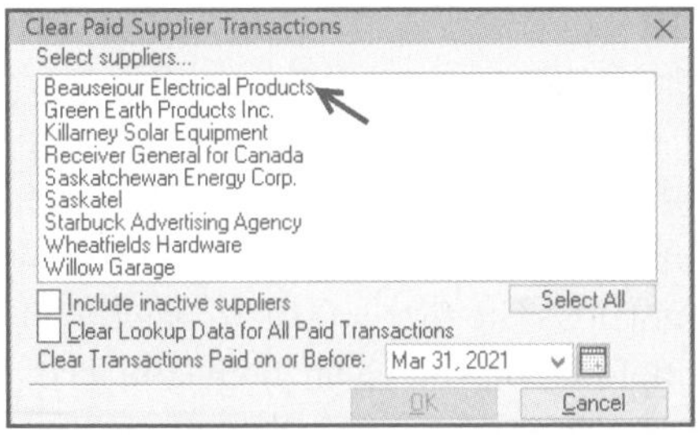

Click **Beausejour Electrical Products** to select the supplier.

Accept the **default date** and the other **settings** and **click OK**:

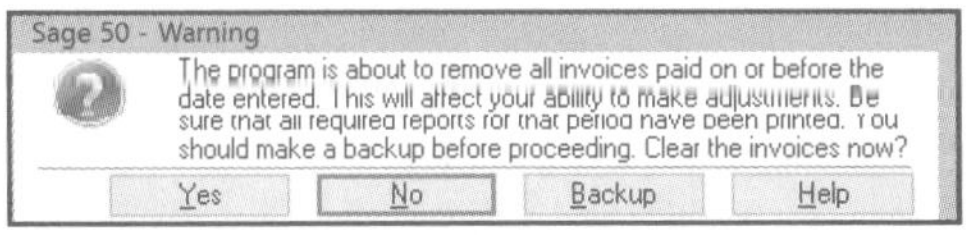

Sage 50 warns that cleared invoices cannot be adjusted or included in reports.

Click **Yes** to confirm that you want to clear the data.

Click **Beausejour Electrical Products** in the Home window Suppliers list pane.

Click the **Statistics tab**. **Enter $2 100** as the YTD Purchases.

Enter **$2 000** as the Payments for 2021 Excluding Taxes and **$2 100** as the Payments Including Taxes.

Click the **Historical Transactions tab**.

Enter the **correct invoices** and **payments** in the following chart:

Supplier Name	Terms	Date	Inv/Chq No.	Amount	Tax	Total
Beausejour Electrical Products	1/10, n/30 (before tax)	Mar. 26/21	B-894	$10 000	$500	$10 500
		Mar. 26/21	Chq 94			3 800
	1/10, n/30 (before tax)	Mar. 28/21	B-921	4 000	200	4 200
			Balance owing			$ 10 900

Close the **Supplier Ledger record**.

Advance the **session date** to **April 7** to prepare for the journal entries.

> **NOTES**
> Sage 50 will provide this same reminder when you advance the session date to May 1. The Accounts Payable discrepancy has been reduced to $3 300.

When we change the session date to April 7, Sage 50 reminds us of the imbalance because we are entering a new month and we turned on the warning (page 214):

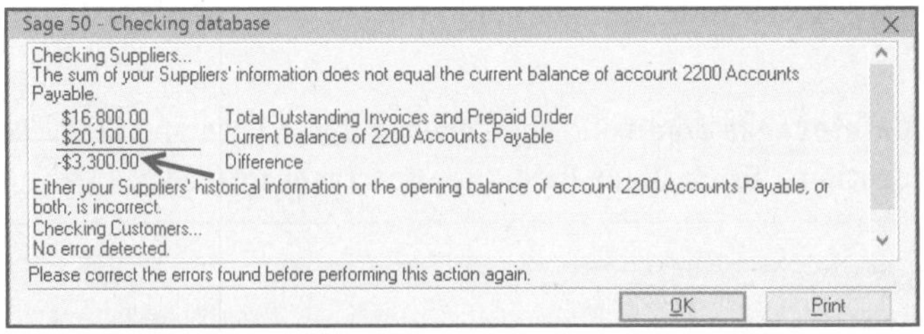

Click **OK**. There are still invoices outstanding. They will be entered in the May 1 memo (Memo #8).

Back up your **file** again. You can now exit the program or continue by entering the transactions that follow.

SOURCE DOCUMENTS

SESSION DATE – APRIL 7, 2021

1 **Memo #1** **Dated April 1/21**
Create shortcuts for General Journal entries, purchase invoices, pay expenses (other payments) and pay invoices, the journals used in this chapter.

2 **Sales Invoice #710** **Dated April 1/21**
To Selkirk Community Centre, $1 800 plus $90 GST and $108 PST for removing and reapplying solar panels for roof replacement. Invoice total $1 998. Terms: 1/10, n/30. Create new Group account 4120 Repairs Revenue.

3 **Receipt #200** **Dated April 2/21**
From Grande Pointe Towers, cheque #5033 for $2 435.60, including $1 935.60 in full payment of invoice #699 and $500 in partial payment of invoice #703, and allowing $44.40 discount for early payment. Customize the journal by changing the tabbing order so that the cheque number follows the customer number.

4 **Purchase Invoice #WH-42001** **Dated April 3/21**
From Wheatfields Hardware, $1 500 plus $75 GST and $90 PST for new ladders and other tools. Invoice total $1 665. Terms: net 15.

5 **Payment Cheque #101** **Dated April 4/21**
To Beausejour Electrical Products, $10 760 in payment of account, including $140 discount for early payment. Reference invoices #B-894 and #B-921.

6 **Payment Cheque #102** **Dated April 4/21**
To Killarney Solar Equipment, $5 900 in payment of invoice #KS-1031.

7 **Sales Invoice #711** **Dated April 5/21**
To Selkirk Community Centre, $18 000 plus $900 GST and $1 080 PST for installing additional solar panels. Invoice total $19 980. Terms: 1/10, n/30.

8 **Memo #2** **Dated April 6/21**
Create new tax code IN using taxes GST at the rate of 5% and PST at the rate of 6%. GST is included and refundable; PST is included and not refundable. The description is not included, so you must add it.

9 **Memo #3** **Dated April 6/21**
Edit the supplier record for Willow Garage. Change the default tax code to IN and create 5240 Vehicle Expenses, a new Group expense account as the default expense account for the supplier.

10 **Purchase Invoice #W-1993** **Dated April 6/21**
From Willow Garage, $120 including taxes (tax code IN) for gasoline for van. Store the transaction as a bi-weekly recurring entry. Terms: net 30.

11 **Receipt #201** **Dated April 7/21**
From Regina School Board, cheque #12488 for $19 778 including $222 discount for early payment. Reference invoice #701.

12 **Sales Invoice #712** **Dated April 7/21**
To Hazel Estates (use Full Add for the new customer), $1 200 plus $60 GST and $72 PST for a one-year service contract. Invoice total $1 332. Terms: 1/10, n/30.

WARNING!
Be sure to select the correct revenue account for sales. You may need to change the default selection.

NOTES
You can also add shortcuts for View Suppliers and View Accounts (Banking module). Refer to pages 134 and 185 if you need assistance with creating shortcuts.

WARNING!
A screen with the Opening Balance field will be added when you create new accounts because the history is not finished. Leave this field blank.

NOTES
You can customize the sales invoice by removing the columns that are not used by Air Care Services – Item Number, Quantity, Unit, Price and Job Sites – and the purchase invoice by removing the columns that are not used by Air Care Services – Item Number, Quantity, Unit, Price and Job Sites.

NOTES
Allow Selkirk Community Centre to exceed the credit limit.

NOTES
Add the description GST@5% included; PST@6% included, non-refundable. By omitting some spaces in the description, you will be able to enter all the text.

NOTES
Hazel Estates
(contact Joelle Beausoleil)
488 Sunshine St., Ste 1200
Moose Jaw, SK S4G 5H3
Tel 1: (306) 367-7711
Tel 2: (877) 367-9770
Fax: (306) 369-2791
E-mail: JB@hazelestates.com
Web: hazelestates.com
Terms: 1/10, n/30
Payment method: Pay later
Revenue account: 4140
Tax code: GP
Credit limit: $10 000

13

Visa Sales Invoice #713 **Dated April 7/21**

Sales Summary
To various one-time customers

Repairs revenue	$3 600
Service contract revenue	2 800
GST charged	320
PST charged	384
Total deposited to Visa bank account	$7 104

SESSION DATE – APRIL 14, 2021

14

Bank Debit Memo #14321 **Dated April 8/21**

From Flatlands Credit Union, cheque #5033 for $2 435.60 from Grande Pointe Towers has been returned because of non-sufficient funds. Reverse the payment and notify the customer of the outstanding charges.

15

Memo #4 **Dated April 8/21**

From Owner: Change the payment terms for Grande Pointe Towers to net 1. Certified cheques will be requested in the future. Set the credit limit to zero.

16

Memo #5 **Dated April 8/21**

From Owner: The work done for Hazel Estates included $1 600 plus $80 GST and $96 PST for replacement of damaged microinverters. The revised and correct invoice total is $3 108. Adjust invoice #712 to add the extra amount.

17

MasterCard Sales Invoice #714 **Dated April 9/21**

To Vinod Residence (use Full Add for the new customer), $600 plus $30 GST and $36 PST for repairs. Invoice total $666 paid in full by MasterCard.

NOTES
Vinod Residence
(contact Viran Vinod)
56 House St.
Regina, SK S4P 8K1
Tel: (306) 761-8114
E-mail: v.vinod@interlog.com
Terms: net 1
Payment: By MasterCard
Revenue account: 4120
Tax code: GP
Credit limit: $2 000

18

Receipt #202 **Dated April 10/21**

From Selkirk Community Centre, cheque #533 for $7 978.02, including $1 978.02 in full payment of invoice #710 with $19.98 discount for early payment, and $6 000 in partial payment of invoice #711.

19

Purchase Invoice #GE-2579 **Dated April 10/21**

From Green Earth Products Inc., $14 000 plus $700 GST for microinverters. Invoice total $14 700. Terms: 1/10, n/30. Store as a bi-weekly recurring entry.

20

Cash Purchase Invoice #WI-6913 **Dated April 11/21**

From Westrock Insurance (use Quick Add), $185 per month for a one-year car insurance policy with $2 000 000 liability coverage and $4 000 deductible. Terms: first month payable in advance on acceptance of quote followed by monthly instalments at the end of each month. Pay first month's premium of $185 in advance. Issue cheque #103. Store as a recurring monthly transaction.

NOTES
Use Full Add for the new supplier if you want to add the default expense account (Insurance Expense). GST is not charged on insurance, so you must delete the tax code.

21

Memo #6 **Dated April 11/21**

Recall the stored entry for car insurance from Westrock Insurance to enter a postdated payment for next month's premium of $185. Issue cheque #104 postdated for May 11. After posting, recall the entry again and make a postdated payment for the premium due June 11 with cheque #105.

NOTES
Add B and C to the original purchase invoice numbers for the postdated payment entries.

22

Payment Cheque #106 **Dated April 14/21**

To Green Earth Products Inc., $14 560 in payment of account, including $140 discount for early payment. Reference invoice #GE-2579.

NOTES
If you used the Payments Journal for the cash purchases, remember to reset the date for the invoice payment.

23 **Receipt #203** **Dated April 14/21**

From Selkirk Community Centre, cheque #586 for $13 780.20 in payment of account, including $199.80 discount for early payment. Reference invoice #711.

SESSION DATE – APRIL 21, 2021

24 **Bank Debit Memo #35589** **Dated April 15/21**

From Flatlands Credit Union, cheque #12488 for $19 778 from Regina School Board has been returned because of non-sufficient funds. Reverse the payment and notify the customer of the outstanding charges.

25 **Cash Purchase Invoice #SAA-1098** **Dated April 15/21**

From Starbuck Advertising Agency, $1 100 plus $55 GST and $66 PST for flyers on clean energy alternatives. Create new Group expense account: 5230 Promotion Expenses. Invoice total $1 221. Paid by cheque #107.

26 **Receipt #204** **Dated April 15/21**

From Hazel Estates, cheque #230 for $3 076.92 in full payment of account, including $31.08 discount for early payment. Reference adjusted invoice #712.

27 **Cash Purchase Invoice #FX-3467** **Dated April 16/21**

From FedEx (use Quick Add for the new supplier), $460 for special delivery of solar panels plus $23 GST. Invoice total $483. Issued cheque #108 in full payment. Create new Group account 5220 Delivery Expenses.

NOTES

Change the tax code to G for the purchase from FedEx.

28 **Payment Cheque #109** **Dated April 16/21**

To Wheatfields Hardware, $1 665 in payment of account. Reference invoice #WH-42001.

29

AirCare Services
aircare.com clean energy for a better future
100 Belair Ave., Unit 25
Regina, SK S4T 4U2
Phone: (306) 456-1299 Toll free: (888) 455-7194 Fax: (306) 456-3188

Invoice: 715
Date: April 19, 2021
Sold to: Oak Bluff Banquet Hall
(Ann Oakley)
4 Celebration Ave.
Regina, SK S4V 3H7

Description	Tax Code	Amount
Installation of additional solar panels	GP	20 000.00
Adjustments to older solar panels	GP	2 000.00

Authorization to exceed credit limit: Simon Arturo

Interest at 1.5% charged on accounts over 30 days.	Payment Terms: 1/10, net 30	Customer Initials	GST	1 100.00
			PST	1 320.00
	GST #533 766 457	AO	TOTAL	24 420.00

NOTES

You will need to edit the default account for Oak Bluff Banquet Hall.

30

Cash Purchase Invoice #SEC-44371 **Dated April 19/21**

From Saskatchewan Energy Corp., $200 plus $10 GST for two months of hydro service. Invoice total $210. Paid by cheque #110.

31

Cash Purchase Invoice #SKT-36128 **Dated April 19/21**

From Saskatel, $330 plus $16.50 GST and $19.80 PST for telephone, cellular and Internet service. Invoice total $366.30. Paid by cheque #111.

32

AirCare Services

aircare.com clean energy for a better future

100 Belair Ave., Unit 25
Regina, SK S4T 4U2
Phone: (306) 456-1299 Toll free: (888) 455-7194 Fax: (306) 456-3188

Invoice: 716
Date: April 20, 2021
Sold to: Sales Summary

Description	Tax Code	Amount
Installation upgrades	GP	6 000.00
Service contracts	GP	900.00

Deposited to Visa bank account
April 20/21 *Simon Cantonna*

Thank you.	Payment Terms: Visa Credit Card	Customer Initials	GST	345.00
			PST	414.00
	Business No.: 533 766 457		TOTAL	7 659.00

SESSION DATE – APRIL 30, 2021

33

Purchase Invoice #W-3468 **Dated April 22/21**

From Willow Garage, $120 including taxes (use tax code IN) for gasoline for van. Terms: net 30. Recall stored entry and edit the date.

34

Purchase Invoice #GE-4906 **Dated April 24/21**

From Green Earth Products Inc., $14 000 plus $700 GST for microinverters. Invoice total $14 700. Terms: 1/10, n/30. Recall stored entry.

35

Purchase Invoice #KE-1679 **Dated April 25/21**

From Killarney Solar Equipment, $30 000 plus $1 500 GST for solar panels. Invoice total $31 500. Terms: 1/5, n/30.

36

Sales Invoice #717 **Dated April 25/21**

To Grande Pointe Towers, $24 000 for new subcontracting job, plus $1 200 GST and $1 440 PST. Invoice total $26 640. Terms: net 1. Grande Pointe Towers has provided a certified cheque in full payment of their account.

NOTES

Close the Advisor message for Grande Pointe Towers about the customer often paying late.

37

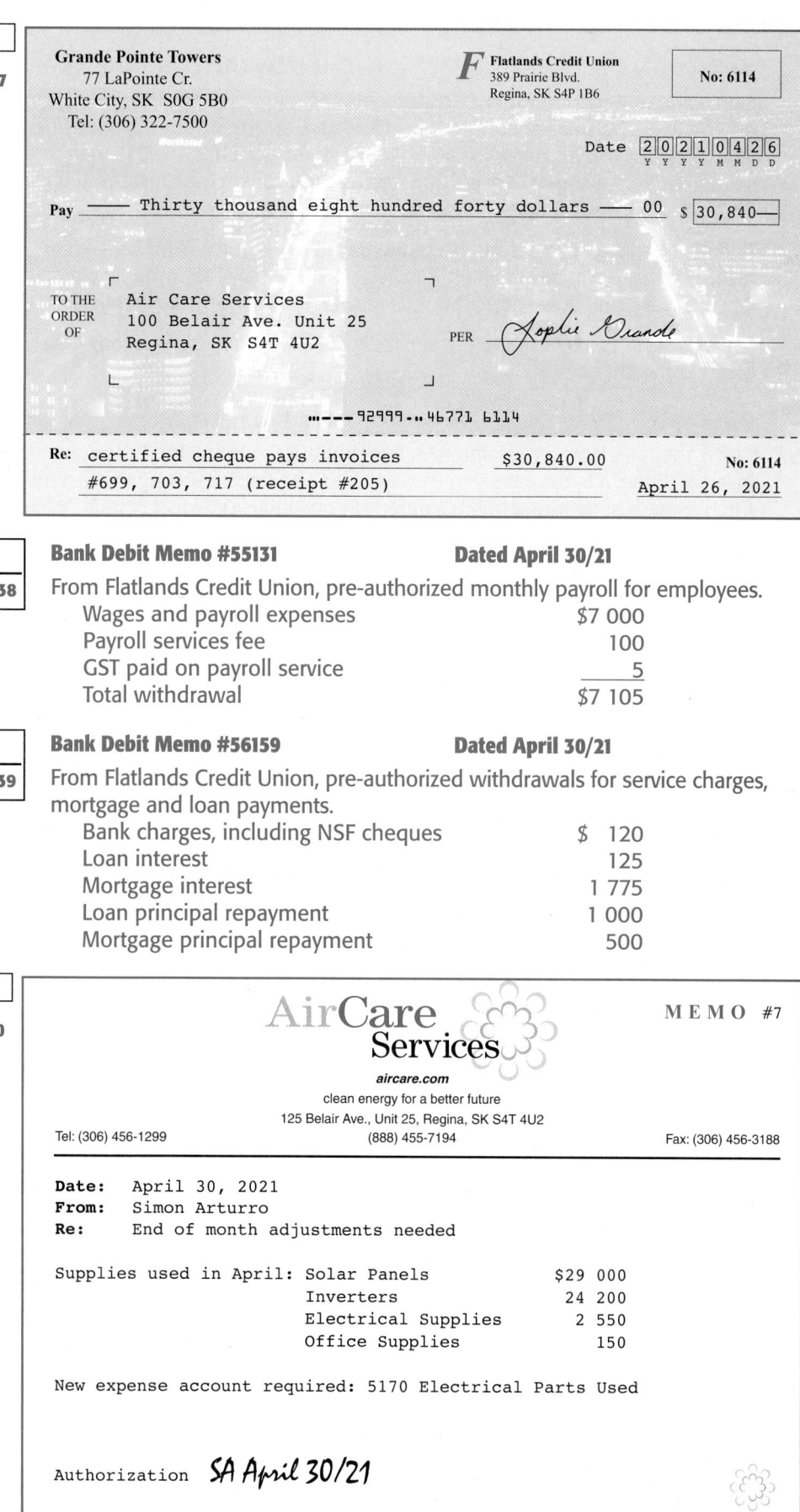

Grande Pointe Towers
77 LaPointe Cr.
White City, SK S0G 5B0
Tel: (306) 322-7500

Flatlands Credit Union
389 Prairie Blvd.
Regina, SK S4P 1B6

No: 6114

Date 2 0 2 1 0 4 2 6
Y Y Y Y M M D D

Pay —— Thirty thousand eight hundred forty dollars —— 00 $ 30,840——

TO THE ORDER OF
Air Care Services
100 Belair Ave. Unit 25
Regina, SK S4T 4U2

PER *Sophie Grande*

⑈---92999-⑆46771 6114

Re: certified cheque pays invoices #699, 703, 717 (receipt #205) — $30,840.00 — No: 6114 — April 26, 2021

38

Bank Debit Memo #55131 **Dated April 30/21**

From Flatlands Credit Union, pre-authorized monthly payroll for employees.

Wages and payroll expenses	$7 000
Payroll services fee	100
GST paid on payroll service	5
Total withdrawal	$7 105

39

Bank Debit Memo #56159 **Dated April 30/21**

From Flatlands Credit Union, pre-authorized withdrawals for service charges, mortgage and loan payments.

Bank charges, including NSF cheques	$ 120
Loan interest	125
Mortgage interest	1 775
Loan principal repayment	1 000
Mortgage principal repayment	500

40

AirCare Services

MEMO #7

aircare.com
clean energy for a better future
125 Belair Ave., Unit 25, Regina, SK S4T 4U2
(888) 455-7194

Tel: (306) 456-1299 Fax: (306) 456-3188

Date: April 30, 2021
From: Simon Arturro
Re: End of month adjustments needed

Supplies used in April:		
	Solar Panels	$29 000
	Inverters	24 200
	Electrical Supplies	2 550
	Office Supplies	150

New expense account required: 5170 Electrical Parts Used

Authorization *SA April 30/21*

NOTES

When you enter May 1 as the session date, Sage 50 reminds you that the Payables Ledger history is not balanced. There is still a difference of $3 300 – refer to page 252.

WARNING!

You must enter these outstanding invoices as historical invoices and the payments as current payments or you will be unable to finish the history.

NOTES

Refer to page 240 if you need help with adding historical invoices.

SESSION DATE – MAY 1, 2021

41

Memo #8 **Dated May 1/21**

From Owner: Received monthly statements showing missing historical information. The statement from Wheatfields Hardware included an overdue amount of $1 100 from invoice #WH-20001 dated March 24, 2021. The statement from Starbuck Advertising Agency included an overdue amount of $2 200 from invoice #SAA-987 dated March 14, 2021.

Add the historical invoices for these two transactions in the Supplier Ledger records as historical transactions. You can open the Payables module window or use the View Suppliers shortcut to access the records for these suppliers.

Pay these two invoices in the Payments Journal as current transactions dated May 1 using cheques #112 and #113.

42

Memo #9 **Dated May 1/21**

Check the data integrity (Maintenance menu) after entering the historical invoices. Make a backup copy of the data files and finish entering the history. Choose the History menu in the Home window and click Finish Entering History.

43

Memo #10 **Dated May 1/21**

From Owner: Print or preview customer statements. One invoice for Regina School Board is overdue. Complete sales invoice #718 for Regina School Board for $29.39, the interest charges on the overdue amount. Terms: net 15 days. Use the No Tax code for the interest charges and choose Interest Revenue as the account. Remember to remove the early payment discount.

REVIEW

The Student DVD with Data Files includes Review Questions and Supplementary Cases for this chapter.

CHAPTER EIGHT

HELENA'S ACADEMY

OBJECTIVES

After completing this chapter, you should be able to

- ***open*** the Payroll Journal
- ***enter*** employee-related payroll transactions
- ***understand*** automatic payroll deductions
- ***understand*** Payroll Ledger linked accounts
- ***edit*** and ***review*** payroll transactions
- ***adjust*** Payroll Journal invoices after posting
- ***enter*** employee benefits and entitlements
- ***complete*** payroll runs for a group of employees
- ***release*** vacation pay to employees
- ***remit*** payroll taxes
- ***enter*** payroll transactions in a future year
- ***display*** and ***print*** payroll reports
- ***prepare*** Record of Employment and T4 slips

COMPANY INFORMATION

Company Profile

NOTES
Helena's Academy
250 Satchel Lane
Edmonton, AB T7F 3B2
Tel: (780) 633-8201
Fax: (780) 633-8396
Business No.: 189 245 053

Helena's Academy was opened in Edmonton, Alberta, in 2002 by Helena Teutor as a small private junior elementary school. The school has maintained its small size in order to offer individualized programming with high academic standards for students with artistic interests and abilities. Helena works as principal and also teaches the upper grades. Two other teachers handle the kindergarten and junior primary grades. Although all teachers have a background in fine arts and are trained music teachers, an additional half-time art and music specialist rotates among all the classes. A full-time office administrator, caretaker and classroom assistant make up the rest of the staff. The classroom assistant also runs the after-school program.

Parents pay tuition fees in two instalments, one before the start of the school year in August and the second at the end of December. They pay additional fees to participate in the after-school programs. Three teachers offer private half-hour weekly music lessons that parents also pay for separately each month.

All classes are split-grade classes, an arrangement required by the small school enrolment, but desired because of the opportunities for students to help each other. Older students in each class, even in kindergarten, are expected to help their younger classmates. All parents are also required to volunteer in the classroom and library, and the kindergarten parents provide the healthy daily snacks for the kindergarten classes. The volunteer expectations are viewed favourably by the families at the school because they enable parents to understand and reinforce the learning philosophy of the school.

The school closes for the month of July each year, but all teachers and staff return to work in August to plan their programs for the coming year. The caretaker uses this month before students return to catch up on repairs and maintenance.

Individual client accounts are not set up for this exercise, and tuition fees for the first semester have been paid. Fees for the after-school program and private lessons are paid on the first of each month. No taxes are charged on any of the school's fees, and as an educational institution providing only tax-exempt services, the Academy is not eligible for GST refunds on the taxes it pays. The school has accounts set up with a few regular suppliers, and some of these offer discounts.

On October 1, 2021, Helena's Academy converted its accounts using the following information:

- Chart of Accounts
- Trial Balance
- Supplier Information
- Client Information
- Employee Profiles and Information Sheet
- Accounting Procedures

CHART OF POSTABLE ACCOUNTS

HELENA'S ACADEMY

ASSETS
1080 Bank: Chequing Account
1090 Bank: Savings Account
1100 Investments: Restricted Use Funds
1200 Fees Receivable
1240 Advances & Loans Receivable
1260 Prepaid Taxes
1280 Office Supplies
1300 Art Supplies
1320 Library Material
1340 Textbooks
1520 Classroom Computers
1540 Office Equipment
1560 Furniture
1580 Vehicle
1620 School Premises ▶

▶LIABILITIES
2100 Bank Loan
2200 Accounts Payable
2300 Vacation Payable
2310 EI Payable
2320 CPP Payable
2330 Income Tax Payable
2400 RRSP Payable
2410 Family Support Payable
2430 Medical Payable - Employee
2440 Medical Payable - Employer
2460 WCB Payable
2920 Mortgage Payable

EQUITY
3560 Academy, Invested Capital
3580 Retained Surplus
3600 Net Income ▶

▶REVENUE
4020 Revenue from School Fees
4040 Revenue from Lessons
4060 Revenue from Programs
4100 Revenue from Interest

EXPENSE
5020 Purchase Discounts
5040 Bank Charges
5060 Hydro Expenses
5080 Insurance Expense
5100 Office Supplies Used
5110 Textbook Expenses
5120 Art Supplies Used
5140 Interest Expense
5180 Promotional Expenses
5190 Property Taxes
5200 Telephone Expenses ▶

▶5210 Vehicle Expenses
5250 Wages: Teaching Staff
5260 Wages: Support Staff
5280 Wages: Music Lessons
5310 EI Expense
5320 CPP Expense
5330 WCB Expense
5380 Tuition Fees Expense
5400 Medical Premium Expense

NOTES: The Chart of Accounts includes only postable accounts and Net Income.

TRIAL BALANCE

HELENA'S ACADEMY

October 1, 2021

		Debits	Credits
1080	Bank: Chequing Account	$ 220 010.00	
1090	Bank: Savings Account	160 000.00	
1100	Investments: Restricted Use Funds	540 000.00	
1260	Prepaid Taxes	2 700.00	
1280	Office Supplies	4 100.00	
1300	Art Supplies	3 850.00	
1320	Library Material	14 500.00	
1340	Textbooks	5 300.00	
1520	Classroom Computers	6 800.00	
1540	Office Equipment	4 900.00	
1560	Furniture	16 000.00	
1580	Vehicle	23 000.00	
1620	School Premises	640 000.00	
2100	Bank Loan		$ 65 000.00
2200	Accounts Payable		1 880.00
2300	Vacation Payable		3 841.68
2310	EI Payable		1 241.00
2320	CPP Payable		2 979.66
2330	Income Tax Payable		5 453.81
2400	RRSP Payable		300.00
2410	Family Support Payable		1 000.00
2430	Medical Payable - Employee		484.00
2440	Medical Payable - Employer		484.00
2460	WCB Payable		392.30
2920	Mortgage Payable		420 000.00 ▶
▶ 3560	Academy, Invested Capital		$ 685 000.00
3580	Retained Surplus		57 665.79
4020	Revenue from School Fees		480 000.00
4040	Revenue from Lessons		500.00
4060	Revenue from Programs		3 000.00
4100	Revenue from Interest		2 150.00
5040	Bank Charges	$ 66.00	
5060	Hydro Expenses	1 220.00	
5080	Insurance Expense	3 680.00	
5100	Office Supplies Used	240.00	
5110	Textbook Expenses	800.00	
5120	Art Supplies Used	280.00	
5140	Interest Expense	4 600.00	
5180	Promotional Expenses	2 800.00	
5190	Property Taxes	1 800.00	
5200	Telephone Expenses	350.00	
5210	Vehicle Expenses	600.00	
5250	Wages: Teaching Staff	35 956.40	
5260	Wages: Support Staff	29 370.48	
5280	Wages: Music Lessons	1 680.00	
5310	EI Expense	1 443.02	
5320	CPP Expense	2 979.66	
5330	WCB Expense	762.68	
5380	Tuition Fees Expense	660.00	
5400	Medical Premium Expense	924.00	
		$1 731 372.24	$1 731 372.24

SUPPLIER INFORMATION

HELENA'S ACADEMY

Supplier Name (Contact)	Address	Phone No. Fax No.	E-mail Web Site	Terms Tax ID
Alberta Workers' Compensation Board	55 Payout Cr. Edmonton, AB T5J 2S5	Tel: (780) 498-3999 Fax: (780) 498-7999	wcb.ab.ca	net 1
Aspen Life Financial (A.M. Weller)	280 Wellness Blvd. Edmonton, AB T6G 2B7	Tel: (780) 327-7164 Fax: (780) 327-8109	aspenlife.com	net 1
Energy Supply Services (N.U. Cleer)	690 Service Ave. Edmonton, AB T6T 4G4	Tel: (780) 456-3293 Fax: (780) 456-1229	nucleer@ess.ca ess.ca	net 1
Loomis Art Supplies (Dee Ziner)	64 Canvas St. Edmonton, AB T5Z 2S4	Tel: (780) 462-1706 Fax: (780) 452-1700	dz@loomis.com loomis.com	1/10, n/30 186 519 187
Maintenance Enforcement Program (Al I. Mony)	43 Brownlee St. Edmonton, AB T5J 3W7	Tel: (780) 422-5555 Fax: (780) 401-7575	alberta.mep@gov.ab.ca justice.gov.ab.ca/mep	net 1
Receiver General for Canada	56 Heron Rd. Ottawa, Ontario K3A 6B4	Tel 1: (800) 561-7761 Tel 2: (800) 959-2221	cra-arc.gc.ca	net 1
Rocky Mountain Trust (Rocky)	59 High St. Edmonton, AB T4P 1M3	Tel: (780) 388-1825 Fax: (780) 388-2663	rockymtntrust.ca	net 1
Telus Alberta (Toks Lotts)	499 Cellular Rd. Edmonton, AB T8F 2B5	Tel: (780) 348-5999	telus.com	net 1

OUTSTANDING SUPPLIER INVOICES

HELENA'S ACADEMY

Supplier Name	Terms	Date	Invoice No.	Amount	Total
Loomis Art Supplies	1/10, n/30	Sep. 29/21	LA-438	$1 880	$1 880

CLIENT INFORMATION

HELENA'S ACADEMY

Client Name	Address
Parents of Students	Edmonton

(individual client records are not set up for this application)

EMPLOYEE INFORMATION SHEET

HELENA'S ACADEMY

	Helena Teutor	Marina Booker	Lars Teicher	Arte Tiste	Neela Nerture	Morty Filer	Jerome Handie
Position	Principal	Teacher	Teacher	Specialist	Assistant	Office Admin	Caretaker
Social Insurance No.	699 344 578	277 639 118	403 401 599	513 288 191	129 495 768	374 588 127	813 402 302
Address	21 Socratic Blvd. Edmonton, AB T5H 2L2	49 Dewey Pl. Edmonton, AB T6K 4K2	15 Practicum St. Edmonton, AB T5B 4C1	2 Creative Way Edmonton, AB T6H 1X3	93 Formula Cr. Edmonton, AB T5E 2L2	10 Basics Lane Edmonton, AB T5A 4K2	4 Repairal Cr. Edmonton, AB T5B 4C1
Telephone	(780) 466-7736	(780) 436-9015	(780) 463-4870	(780) 429-5656	(780) 488-8554	(780) 440-3301	(780) 461-1328
Date of Birth (mm-dd-yy)	7-28-78	9-14-90	10-5-90	7-18-88	5-19-86	4-3-83	3-3-80
Federal (Alberta) Tax Exemption – TD1							
Basic Personal	$12 609 (19 369)	$12 609 (19 369)	$12 609 (19 369)	$12 609 (19 369)	$12 609 (19 369)	$12 609 (19 369)	$12 609 (19 369)
Other Indexed	–	$14 839 (19 369)	–	$19 749 (30 581)	$12 609 (19 369)	$12 609 (19 369)	–
Other Non-indexed	–	$3 640 (4 544)	–	–	–	$6 140 (7 948)	–
Total Exemptions	$12 609 (19 369)	$31 088 (43 282)	$12 609 (19 369)	$32 358 (49 950)	$25 218 (38 738)	$31 358 (46 686)	$12 609 (19 369)
Employee Earnings							
Regular Wage Rate	–	–	–	$40.00	$26.00	$28.00	$28.00
Overtime Wage Rate	–	–	–	–	$39.00	$42.00	$42.00
Regular Salary	$5 500	$4 600	$4 200	–	–	–	–
Pay Period	monthly	monthly	monthly	semi-monthly	semi-monthly	semi-monthly	semi-monthly
Hours per Period	160	160	160	44	82.5	82.5	82.5
Lessons (#/Period)	–	$30.00 (16)	$30.00 (12)	$30.00 (22)	–	–	–
Vacation	4 weeks	4 weeks	4 weeks	6% retained	6% retained	6% retained	6% retained
Vacation Pay Owed	–	–	–	$2 179.20	$533.52	$564.48	$564.48
WCB Rate	0.89	0.89	0.89	0.89	1.15	0.89	2.44
Employee Deductions							
Medical	$44.00	$88.00	$44.00	$44.00	$44.00	$44.00	$22.00
RRSP	$100.00	$50.00	$50.00	–	$25.00	–	$25.00
Family Support	–	–	$500.00	–	–	–	$250.00
Additional Tax				$200.00			
EI, CPP & Income Tax Calculations are built into Sage 50.							
Direct Deposit	No	Yes	Yes	No	Yes	No	Yes

NOTES: Medical premiums are deducted every pay period. The amounts are adjusted for the monthly rates.

Employee Profiles and TD1 Information

Employee Benefits and Entitlements All employees are entitled to 10 days per year as sick leave. If the days are not needed, employees can carry these days forward to a new year, to a maximum of 90 days. Currently, all employees have some unused sick leave days accrued from previous years. Most employees take their vacations in July when the school is closed, with salaried employees receiving their regular salary and the full-time hourly workers receiving the retained vacation pay at the end of June with their regular paycheque. Vacation pay cannot be accumulated or carried forward beyond the fiscal year. Tiste is the exception; he has not yet collected any vacation pay this year.

In keeping with the educational goals, the Academy encourages all employees to continue their education by paying part of their tuition fees for college or university programs. Booker and Filer are currently taking courses and receiving the tuition fee benefit. A second benefit applies to all employees — the Academy pays 50 percent of the medical premiums for an extended health care insurance plan. Both benefits are taxable income for the employee and expenses for Helena's Academy.

NOTES
In January 2009, the province of Alberta eliminated the provincial medical plan premiums. Private health care plans usually cover the costs of services not included in the provincial plan, such as prescription drugs, dental care or semi-private hospital rooms.

Music Lessons Booker, Teicher and Tiste give private music lessons at lunchtime and after school. Parents pay the school $35 per half-hour lesson and the school pays the teachers. These fees are set up on a "piece rate" basis at $30 per lesson for teachers and added to each paycheque.

Employer Expenses In addition to the expenses for the tuition fees and medical premium benefits, Helena's Academy pays the compulsory CPP, EI and WCB.

Helena Teutor As the principal and founder of the school, Teutor frequently speaks to parent groups in order to promote the school. She also teaches the senior class of grades 4, 5 and 6 students and hires new staff when needed. She is married and has no children. Since her husband is also fully employed, she uses the single federal and provincial tax claim and medical premium amounts. At the end of each month, she receives her salary of $5 500 per month by cheque. She makes monthly contributions to her RRSP plan as well.

Marina Booker is the regular teacher for the primary class of grade 1, 2 and 3 students. She supplements her monthly salary of $4 600 with income from private music lessons offered through the school. For each half-hour lesson taught in the previous month, she earns $30. Booker is married with one child and claims the basic, spousal and child amounts for income tax purposes. She also has a claim for her RRSP contributions and her tuition fees of $3 640 for a four-month university course and the $226 per month provincial education deduction for the part-time course. She pays medical premiums at the family rate. Her pay is deposited directly to her bank account every month.

NOTES
The Academy pays Booker's tuition fees at the rate of $140 per pay period until the full amount is paid.
The federal child claim is allowed only for infirm children.

Lars Teicher teaches the two junior and senior kindergarten classes. He too supplements his monthly salary of $4 200 with income from private music lessons at $30 per lesson. Teicher is separated from his wife and is required to make family support payments. For this, $500 is deducted from each paycheque. As a single employee, he claims only the basic federal and provincial amounts for income tax purposes, but he does have an additional deduction for his RRSP contributions. He also pays the single rate toward the provincial medical plan. He too has his paycheque deposited directly to his bank account.

Arte Tiste is the half-time art teacher who works four hours in the school every afternoon, dividing his time among the three classes but concentrating on the senior class. He spends the mornings painting in his home art studio. Although he is single, he can claim the spousal equivalent plus caregiver amounts because he looks after his infirm brother. These claims significantly reduce the income tax he pays on his wages of

$40 per hour. He provides art lessons after school at the per-lesson rate of $30. His medical premium is deducted from his semi-monthly paycheque at the family rate to cover himself and his brother. His 6 percent vacation pay is retained. Instead of receiving his vacation pay in June like the other hourly workers, Tiste takes his vacation pay sometime in the fall to pay for his December travels. Because Tiste has additional income from the sale of his paintings, he has elected to pay additional federal taxes in each pay period instead of making extra quarterly tax remittances on this extra income. Tiste is paid by cheque twice each month.

NOTES
Because full-time hourly employees are paid twice a month, the hours worked in the pay period vary. The number of regular hours may be either 75 (10 days) or 82.5 hours (11 days), based on working 7.5 hours per day. Occasionally a half-month period has 12 working days for a total of 90 regular hours.

Neela Nerture works full-time in the school as a classroom assistant and also runs the after-school program for children who require daycare. She divides her time among the three classes as needed by the teachers and program schedules. Nerture is married and fully supports her child and her husband while he is finishing his studies. Therefore, she pays the family medical premiums and has the basic and spousal claim amounts for income taxes. She is paid twice a month at the hourly rate of $26 per hour. When she works more than 7.5 hours in a day, she earns $39 per hour for the extra time. Overtime is often required for extended daycare and can be charged back to the parents. This extra charge encourages parents to pick up their children on time. On top of her pay, she earns 6 percent vacation pay that is retained until the end of June. Nerture has her paycheques deposited directly to her bank account.

NOTES
Nerture's child is not eligible for the federal claim amount.

Morty Filer runs the school office, handling the routine phone calls to and from parents, arranging lessons, scheduling parent volunteers, collecting fees and doing the bookkeeping. For these duties he earns $28 per hour for the first 7.5 hours each day in each half-month pay period and is paid by cheque. For additional hours, he earns $42 per hour. The 6 percent vacation pay he earns on his regular and overtime wages is retained until the end of June. Filer supports his wife and claims both the basic and spousal federal and provincial amounts for tax purposes. His medical premium is at the family rate. He has an additional claim for his university tuition of $6 140 and the $226 per month provincial education deduction for the eight-month school year.

NOTES
The Academy pays Filer's tuition at the rate of $145 per pay period until the full amount is paid.

Jerome Handie is the caretaker for the school and grounds. He works year-round, except for his vacation time in July, cleaning the school's rooms and providing general maintenance. During August, he paints the classrooms and steam-cleans all carpets. From each semi-monthly paycheque that is deposited to his bank account, $250 is withheld to support his ex-wife and two children. He claims only the basic federal and provincial amounts for tax purposes and the single medical premium. He also makes contributions to his RRSP program with regular payroll deductions. His hourly pay rate is $28 for the first 7.5 hours per day and $42 per hour for any additional time. His vacation pay is calculated and retained at the rate of 6 percent.

Accounting Procedures

Taxes: GST and PST

NOTES
The sales tax amounts are included with the asset or expense portion of the purchase.

As an educational institution that offers only tax-exempt services, Helena's Academy is not eligible for any refunds on the GST it pays for products and services. Therefore, no sales taxes are set up in this application — taxes are not tracked — and the prices in the source documents include all taxes. Provincial sales tax is not charged in Alberta.

Discounts

NOTES
For an educational service company, the Customers icon is labelled Clients, Sales Invoices are labelled as Statements and Sales or Revenues are renamed Fees.

For suppliers who offer discounts on after-tax purchase amounts, these terms are set up in the supplier records so that Sage 50 will automatically calculate the discount when full payment is made within the discount period. No discounts are offered on school fees.

Direct Payroll Deposits

The Academy allows employees to have their regular pay deposited directly to their bank accounts or to be paid by cheque. Four employees have selected direct payroll deposits.

Payroll Remittances

Some suppliers are identified as payroll authorities with the following remittances: EI, CPP and income tax are remitted to the Receiver General for Canada; medical premiums are remitted to Aspen Life Financial; Workers' Compensation Board (WCB) premiums are remitted to Alberta Workers' Compensation Board; RRSP contributions are remitted to Rocky Mountain Trust; family support payments are remitted to the Maintenance Enforcement Program. All payments are remitted monthly for the pay period ending the previous month.

Tuition fees are reimbursed directly to the employee on their regular payroll cheques.

PRO VERSION
In the Pro version, Customer replaces the term Client, Vendor replaces the term Supplier, Sales Invoices replaces the icon label Statements and Sales Journal replaces the term Fees Journal.

INSTRUCTIONS

1. **Enter** the **transactions** in Sage 50 using the Chart of Accounts and Supplier, Client and Employee Information. The procedures for entering new transactions for this application are outlined step by step in the Keystrokes section with the source documents.
2. **Print** the **reports** marked on the following printing form after you have finished making your entries:

REPORTS

Accounts
- ☐ Chart of Accounts
- ☐ Account List
- ☐ General Journal Entries

Financials
- ☑ Balance Sheet: Dec. 31
- ☑ Income Statement: Aug. 1 to Dec. 31
- ☑ Trial Balance date: Dec. 31
- ☑ All Journal Entries: Oct. 1 to Dec. 31
- ☑ General Ledger accounts: Oct. 1 to Dec. 31 5250 5260 5280
- ☐ Statement of Cash Flows
- ☑ Cash Flow Projection Detail Report: for 1080 for next 30 days

Banking
- ☐ Cheque Log Report

Payables
- ☐ Supplier List
- ☐ Supplier Aged
- ☐ Aged Overdue Payables
- ☐ Purchases Journal Entries
- ☐ Payments Journal Entries

Receivables
- ☐ Client List
- ☐ Client Aged
- ☐ Aged Overdue Receivables
- ☐ Fees Journal Entries
- ☐ Receipts Journal Entries
- ☐ Client Statements

Employees & Payroll
- ☐ Employee List
- ☑ Summary for all employees
- ☐ Deductions & Expenses
- ☑ Remittances Summary Report: for all payroll authorities Dec. 31
- ☑ Payroll Journal Entries: Oct. 1, 2021, to Jan. 15, 2022
- ☑ T4 Slip for Tiste
- ☑ Record of Employment for Tiste
- ☑ Year End Review (PIER) for all employees

Mailing Labels
- ☐ Labels

KEYSTROKES

Open **SageData19\HELENA\HELENA.SAI** for Helena's Academy. **Enter** **October 15** as the session date.

The Employees & Payroll module window opens. This is the default Home window for Helena's Academy.

NOTES
If you are using the backup files, restore HELENA1.CAB or HELENA1 to SageData19\HELENA\HELENA.

PRO VERSION
The shortcuts will be named Create Sales Invoices and Pay Purchase Invoices.

Create **shortcuts** for **Create General Journal** (Company), **Create Statement** (Receivables) and **Pay Expenses** or **Create Purchase Invoice** and **Pay Invoices** (Payables).

If you choose not to create shortcuts, you can change modules each time you need to access a journal in a different module.

NOTES
The option to confirm successful posting of transactions is turned on, so you should click OK each time this message appears.

Enter the **cash sale** and the **cash purchase** and **payment transactions**.

Transaction confirmation is turned on, so you should click OK after posting each transaction. We will not repeat this instruction.

1 **Cash Sales Invoice #1036** **Dated Oct. 1/21**

To parents of students, $3 200 total monthly fees for after-school programs and $2 130 total monthly fees for individual music lessons. Deposited $5 330 to chequing account. You can customize the journal by removing the columns not needed, including the Tax Code column.

NOTES
Global Liability Inc.
Terms: net 1
Expense account: 5080
Payment method: Cheque

2 **Cash Purchase Invoice #GL-38827** **Dated Oct. 2/21**

From Global Liability Inc. (use Full Add for new supplier), $1 800 for monthly premium on a one-year insurance policy for school and staff. Paid by cheque #211. Store as a recurring monthly entry.

3 **Payment Cheque #212** **Dated Oct. 5/21**

To Loomis Art Supplies, $1 861.20 in payment of account, including $18.80 discount for early payment. Reference invoice #LA-438.

NOTES
Remember that you must have a valid and active Payroll ID code from Sage to use the payroll features if you are not using the Student version.

Choose the Services menu in the Home window and click Payroll And Support for more information.

Entering Payroll Transactions

Payroll transactions may be entered in the Payroll Journal or in the Payroll Run Journal. We will provide instructions for both methods. If you are preparing paycheques for more than one employee, the Payroll Run Journal is usually faster.

Individual paycheques are entered in the Payroll Journal that you open from the Paycheques icon:

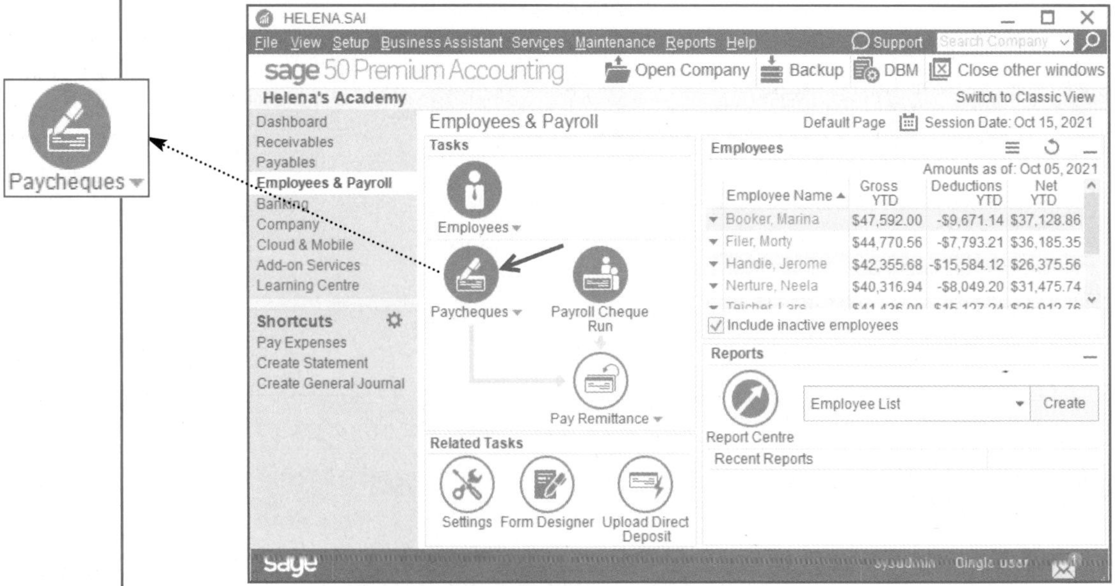

Click the **Paycheques icon** to open and display the Payroll Journal:

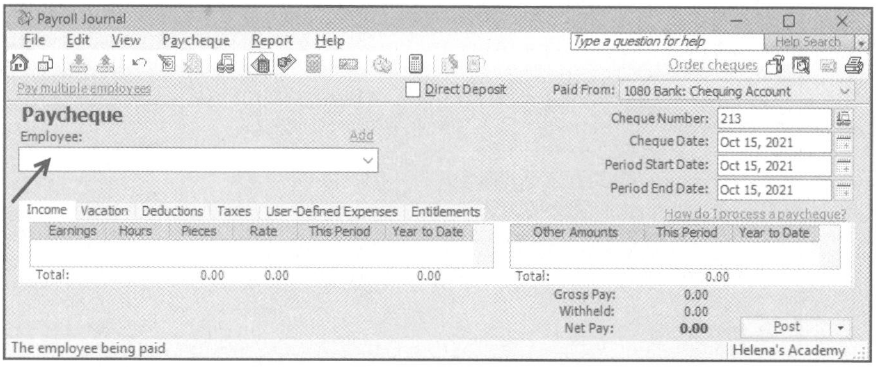

The Calculate Taxes Automatically, Enter Taxes Manually and Recalculate Taxes tools apply specifically to the Payroll Journal. Automatic calculation is selected.

The Time Slips tool is dimmed — it is used to add information from time slips for the employee and will be covered in Chapter 18. The remaining tools — Home window, Daily Business Manager, Store, Recall, Undo, Adjust Paycheque, Reverse Paycheque, Look Up Paycheque, Enter Additional Information, Windows Calculator and Refresh — serve the same purpose as they do in other journals. You can also change report form options, and preview and e-mail the paycheque before printing. Adjust, Reverse and Look Up Paycheque are the Payroll equivalent of these tools in other Journals.

Four hourly paid employees are paid on the first payroll date. Filer is first.

✓ 4

Employee Time Summary Sheet #19 **Dated Oct. 15/21**

For the pay period from October 1 to October 15, 2021

Name of Employee	Regular Hours	Overtime Hours	Lessons	Tuition	Advance (Repaid)	Loan (Repaid)	Sick Days	Direct Deposit
Filer, Morty	82.5	4	–	$145	$200	–	–	No
Handie, Jerome	82.5	2	–	–	–	–	1	Yes
Nerture, Neela	82.5	–	–	–	–	–	–	Yes
Tiste, Arte	44.0	–	24	–	–	–	–	No

a. Using Employee Time Summary Sheet #19 and the Employee Information Sheet, complete payroll for hourly paid employees. Handie has taken one sick day.
b. Issue $200 advance to Morty Filer and recover $50 from each of the following four paycheques.
c. Issue cheques #213 and #214 and Direct Deposit (DD) slips #55 and #56.

The cursor is in the Employee field.

Click the **Employee field list arrow** to open the employee list:

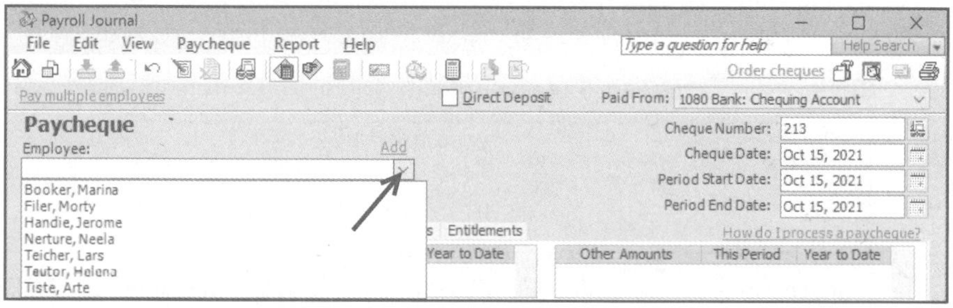

Click **Filer, Morty** to select this employee and add his name to the form. If you have not chosen correctly, return to the employee list and select again.

PRO VERSION

The Refresh and Time Slips tools are not included in the Pro version.

NOTES

The Payroll Journal has a link below the tool bar to switch to the Payroll Run Journal to Pay Multiple Employees. The Payroll Run Journal is introduced on page 285.

NOTES

The pay period for hourly paid employees included 11 days and 7.5 hours per day.

NOTES

Use the bookmark attached to the back cover to mark the page with the source document.

NOTES

You can add new employees from the Payroll Journal. Type the new name in the Name field. Press *tab* and click Add. Or, click the Add link above the Employee field. You will open the Employee Ledger window. There is no Quick Add option for employees because additional details are required for income tax purposes.

NOTES
Year To Date amounts in payroll are always based on the calendar year, not on the fiscal year as in other modules.

Press `tab` to add the payroll details for the selected employee:

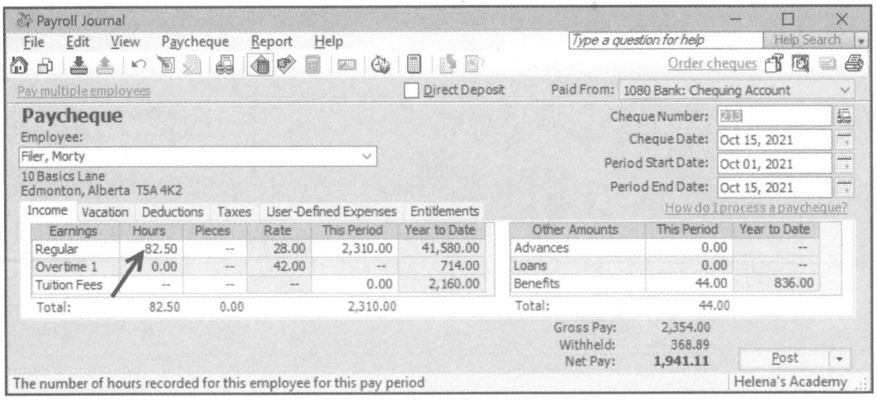

Most of the payroll form is completed automatically based on the ledger details for the employee. The cursor is now in the Cheque Number field. The employee's address has been added. The cheque number, 213, should be correct based on automatic numbering. If the number is incorrect, you can change it.

NOTES
Helena's Academy uses a single chequing account for Payables and Payroll cheques, so there is a single sequence of cheque numbers.

There are three date fields. In the **Cheque Date** field, you should enter the date of payment. The session date, October 15, has been entered by default, and it is correct. The **Period Start Date** field and the **Period End Date** field refer to the first and last day of the pay period for the employee. The Period End Date may be later or earlier than the cheque date. In this case, the session date is also the same as the pay period ending date, so you can accept the default date again.

NOTES
The period end date is usually earlier than the cheque date for hourly paid employees, who must complete the hours and have this summary submitted to the payroll department before a cheque is prepared.

The period start date is based on the number of pay periods per year for the employee and will be updated accordingly for the next paycheque.

The Payroll Journal has several tabs. The **Income** tab screen has all the sources of income for the employee divided into two categories: Earnings and Other Amounts. **Earnings** include the regular income sources such as Regular and Overtime wages for the hourly paid employees and tuition fees repaid. Employee records are set up so that only their own sources of income appear on the form. The **Other Amounts** pane has all the other sources of income, including payroll advances, loans and taxable benefits. Year-to-date amounts based on the calendar year are added for all fields.

NOTES
You can define 20 different sources of income in addition to the predefined ones.

If sales commissions are paid to employees, they must be calculated separately and added manually.

The **Regular Hours** field contains the number of hours an employee has worked for the regular pay rate during the pay period. You can edit the default entry. The **Overtime** field contains the number of overtime hours an employee has worked during the pay period. No default number of overtime hours is entered because the time varies. If there are different overtime rates, you can set up a second overtime field and rate or create additional incomes. For example, employees may be paid more for overtime work on Sundays or holidays than in the evenings.

The **Gross Pay** amount (the pay rate times hours worked plus other income and earnings amounts) is calculated and added to the bottom portion of the journal window. The total amount **Withheld** for taxes and other deductions and the **Net Pay** also appear at the bottom of the journal.

For salaried employees, the **Salary** field will replace the Regular and Overtime fields and salary amounts are entered automatically from the employee record.

Click the **Taxes tab**. Tax amounts are calculated automatically:

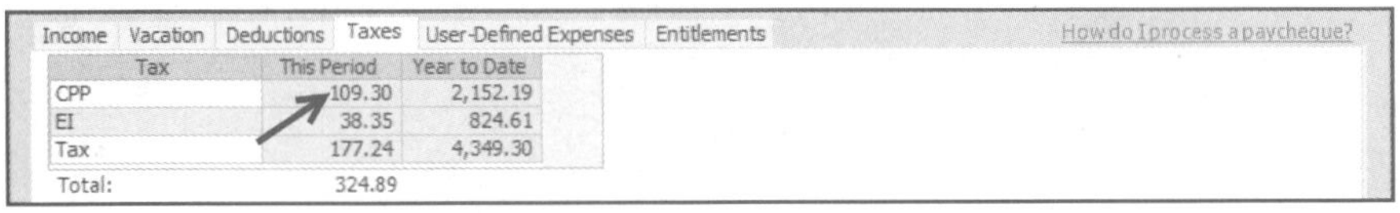

Because we have chosen to let the program complete the tax calculations, the Tax fields are not available for editing. If you need to edit the tax amounts, clicking the **Enter Taxes Manually tool** will open the Tax fields so you can edit amounts.

Click the **Income tab** to continue with the payroll entry. This pay period included eleven 7.5 hour days, so the number of regular hours is correct.

Click the **Overtime 1 Hours field**.

Type 4 **Press** tab to advance to the **Tuition Fees This Period** field.

The Gross Pay is updated to include the overtime pay. Vacation pay and all year-to-date amounts are also updated continually as you add information.

If amounts are not updated, click the **Calculate Taxes Automatically tool** on the tool bar. The option to enter taxes manually may be selected, an option that allows you to edit tax amounts but will not update these amounts automatically.

Helena's Academy pays a portion of eligible tuition fees, and the amount refunded to employees — a taxable benefit — is entered in this income field. Because the amount is paid directly to the employee, and it is taxable, it is set up as an income amount. Filer is currently receiving $145 per pay period as the refund for his tuition until the entire amount has been repaid.

Type 145 **Press** tab to add the tuition fees amount to gross pay.

The cursor now highlights the amount for Advances in the Other Amounts pane. An advance of $200 for Morty Filer has been approved by management for a personal emergency, so we need to enter this amount. The **Advances This Period** field is used to enter amounts advanced to an employee in addition to his or her normal pay from wages or salary. An advance offered to an employee is displayed as a positive amount. An advance recovered is indicated as a negative amount in this same field. Advanced amounts are taxable in the period received. Advance amounts owing will appear in the Year To Date column for Advances.

The **Benefits** field under Other Amounts is used to enter the total amount of taxable benefits a business offers to its employees, such as health insurance or dental plans when the payments are made to a third party. Half of Filer's medical premium is paid by Helena's Academy. Benefit amounts are included in the gross income to arrive at the amount of income tax and then subtracted again to determine the net pay amount.

Click the **Advances This Period field** if necessary.

Type 200 **Press** tab.

Click the **Vacation tab**:

Income | Vacation | Deductions | Taxes | User-Defined Expenses | Entitlements — How do I process a paycheque?

Type	This Period Hours	This Period Amount	Year to Date Hours	Year to Date Amount
Balance Forward (as of Jan 01, 2021)	--	--	--	--
Vacation Earned	--	160.68	--	2,559.72
Vacation Paid *	0.00	0.00	--	1,834.56
Vacation Owed	--	--	--	725.16

* These hours are recorded as EI Insurable Hours

The **Vacation tab screen** has the employee amounts for this period based on the income and the year-to-date amounts. Sage 50 automatically calculates an amount in the **Vacation Earned This Period Amount** field and displays it as a default. Filer's default amount, calculated at the vacation pay rate of 6 percent, will be retained by the business — accrued in the *Vacation Payable* account — until he takes a vacation in July or leaves the employ of the Academy. Therefore, the Vacation Paid amount on this cheque is zero. (Refer to the Employee Information Sheet on page 262 for each employee's vacation pay rate.) The Vacation Paid amount in the Year To Date column has the amount of vacation pay paid to the employee already this calendar year.

The total accumulated vacation pay owing (withheld since vacation pay was last paid and including this pay) is entered in the Year To Date amount field for the Vacation Owed. This amount will appear in the **Vacation Paid This Period** field as a default when you turn off the option to retain vacation in the Employee Ledger (refer to page 278).

NOTES

To verify that tax amounts have changed, click the Taxes tab. Click the Income tab again to continue with the payroll entry, and click the Tuition Fees This Period field to position the cursor.

NOTES

The tuition fee benefit could also be set up in the Employee Ledger so that it is added automatically. When the entire amount has been paid, you would remove it from the ledger. Instead, we will enter the amount in the journal.

NOTES

By dividing the tuition fee benefit among several pay periods, the income tax burden will also be spread out over several paycheques.

NOTES

Advances not repaid before the end of the year are converted to payroll loans automatically by Sage 50. Preferred interest rate amounts are taxable benefits.

NOTES

Benefits are not paid in cash to the employee. They are added to gross pay to determine income tax and then subtracted again to determine the net pay.

Deleting the amount and then re-entering it will provide the changes in gross pay and amounts withheld that demonstrate the tax implications of benefits.

Premiums paid to private health care providers are not usually taxable benefits for employees, but we want to show the tax effect of benefits.

NOTES

Salaried employees receive their regular paycheques during vacations instead of vacation pay. They receive vacation days as an entitlement.

NOTES

If the amount of a deduction or user-defined expense is incorrect, and it is not a one-time change, you should edit the Employee Ledger record. The next time you open the Payroll Journal for the employee, the edited amount will be entered.

Click the **Deductions tab**:

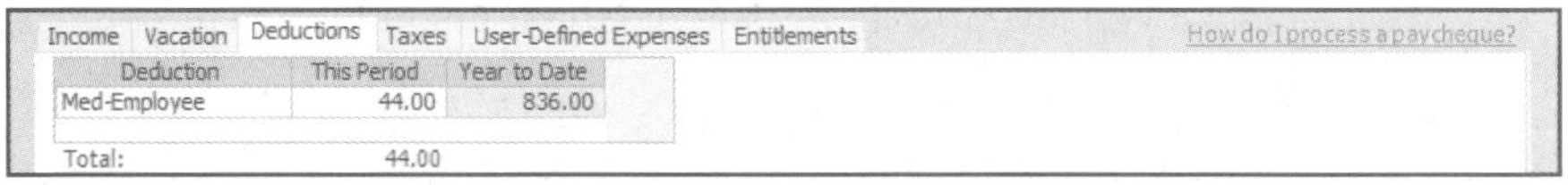

The **Deductions tab screen** has the employee medical deduction entered automatically from the amounts stored in the ledger record. For other employees, the RRSP contributions and/or family support payments also appear on this screen. These amounts can be edited in the journal if necessary.

NOTES

If the User-Defined Expenses amount is omitted from the record, it can be entered in the Payroll Journal as needed.

Click the **User-Defined Expenses tab**:

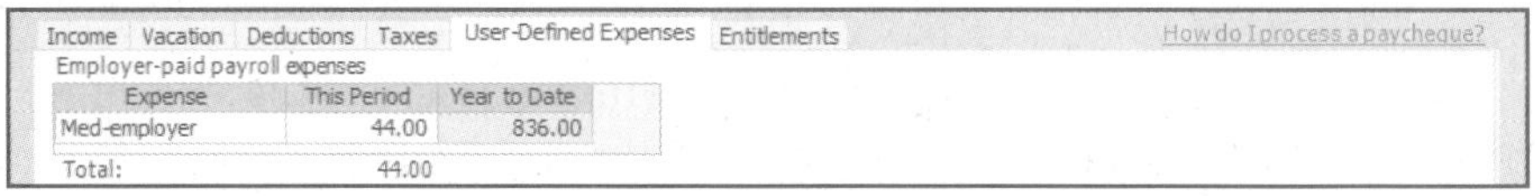

The employer contribution to medical premiums (an employer expense) is also set up as an automatic entry that appears on the User-Defined Expenses tab screen.

We will use the Entitlements tab screen for Handie's payroll entry.

NOTES

The Post button has a list arrow that provides the option to select Print & Post as the default setting. With this selection, you will automatically print the paycheque when you post the entry.

Click the **Income tab** to continue:

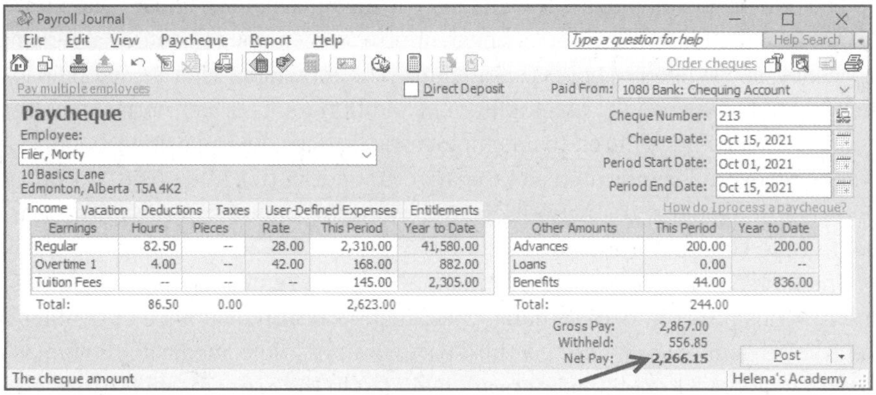

You have now entered all the information for Filer, so you should review the completed transaction before posting.

Reviewing the Payroll Journal Transaction

Choose the **Report menu** and **click Display Payroll Journal Entry**. The transaction you have just completed opens:

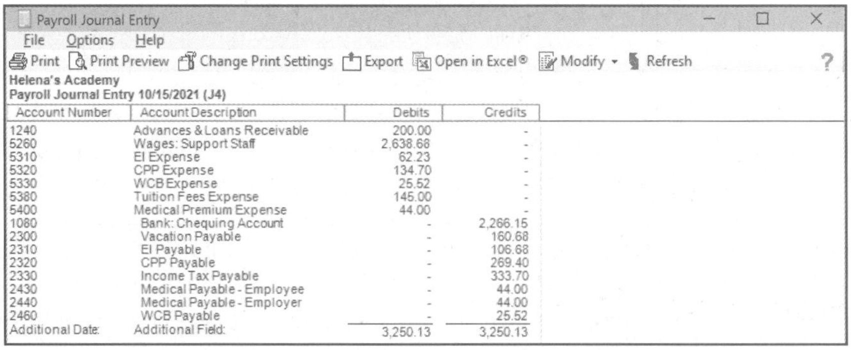

Payroll Journal Entry
File Options Help
Print Print Preview Change Print Settings Export Open in Excel® Modify Refresh
Helena's Academy
Payroll Journal Entry 10/15/2021 (J4)

Account Number	Account Description	Debits	Credits
1240	Advances & Loans Receivable	200.00	-
5260	Wages: Support Staff	2,638.68	-
5310	EI Expense	62.23	-
5320	CPP Expense	134.70	-
5330	WCB Expense	25.52	-
5380	Tuition Fees Expense	145.00	-
5400	Medical Premium Expense	44.00	-
1080	Bank: Chequing Account	-	2,266.15
2300	Vacation Payable	-	160.68
2310	EI Payable	-	106.68
2320	CPP Payable	-	269.40
2330	Income Tax Payable	-	333.70
2430	Medical Payable - Employee	-	44.00
2440	Medical Payable - Employer	-	44.00
2460	WCB Payable	-	25.52
Additional Date:	Additional Field:	3,250.13	3,250.13

NOTES

If you are using a version of the Sage 50 program later than Release 2019.0, your tax amounts and total amount withheld may be different from ours because different tax tables are used. Your Gross Pay and Vacation amounts should always be the same as ours.

The tax tables for Release 2019.0 cover the period from Jan. 1, 2018, to Dec. 31, 2018, as indicated in the confirmation note on page 272. The rates in later tax tables may be different.

All accounts in the journal entry have been defined as linked accounts for the Payroll Ledger, so you do not enter any account numbers directly. All the relevant wage expense accounts have been debited. The hourly wages and tuition fee benefit are tracked in separate wage expense accounts. The expense for vacation pay is added to the wages expense account. In addition, all the wage-related liability accounts and *Bank:*

Chequing Account have been updated automatically because the Payroll Ledger is linked to the General Ledger. Vacation pay owed or retained is tracked in the *Vacation Payable* liability account.

Sage 50 uses the Canada Revenue Agency tax formulas to calculate the deduction amounts for CPP, EI and income tax. These formulas are updated every six months. The remaining deductions are determined from Employee Ledger entries that can be modified for individual employees.

Payroll expense accounts reflect the employer's share of payroll tax obligations. The liabilities reflect the amounts that the owner must remit to the appropriate agencies and include both the employer's share of these tax liabilities and the employee's share (deductions withheld). For example, CPP contributions by the employee are matched by the employer. Therefore, the *CPP Expense* (employer's share) is one-half of the *CPP Payable* amount (employee plus employer's share). WCB is paid entirely by the employer, so the expense amount is the same as the liability amount. Medical contributions by employer and employee are equal, but they are represented in different accounts — the employer's share is included in expense and payable accounts, *Medical Premium Expense* and *Medical Payable - Employer*, while the employee's share appears only in the payable account, *Medical Payable - Employee*. For EI, the employer's share (*EI Expense*) is 1.4 times the employee's share. The tuition benefit is tracked separately as a debit to *Tuition Fees Expense*.

NOTES

Both the employer's and the employee's share of the medical premiums are payable to Aspen Life Financial.

The province of Alberta has eliminated the personal medical premiums for the provincial health plan.

Close the **display** to return to the Payroll Journal input screen.

CORRECTING THE PAYROLL JOURNAL ENTRY BEFORE POSTING

Move the cursor to the field that contains the error. If you need to change screens to access the field you want, **click** the appropriate **tab**. **Press** tab to move forward through the fields or **press** shift and tab together to move back to a previous field. This will highlight the field information so that you can change it. **Type** the **correct information** and **press** tab to enter it.

You can use the mouse to **point** to a field and **drag through** the **incorrect information** to highlight it. You can highlight a single number or letter or the entire field. **Type** the **correct information** and **press** tab to enter it.

Click an **incorrect amount** to highlight it. **Type** the **correct amount** and **press** tab.

You can discard the entry by **clicking** or **Undo** or by returning to the Employee list and **clicking** a **different employee** name. **Click** the name of the **correct employee** and **press** tab. When prompted, confirm that you want to discard the incorrect entry. **Click Yes**, and start again.

NOTES

Correcting Payroll Journal entries after posting is covered on page 275.

You can preview the paycheque before printing it. You can also modify the reports and forms settings from the journal. Tool buttons are included for both these functions. You must have selected Custom Forms in the Reports and Forms settings screen to preview the cheque. The default form locations (file name references) should be correct (refer to margin Notes). However, they may refer to incorrect file locations because these settings are saved with the data file that was created with different default settings.

NOTES

If you get an error message about the form location when you preview the cheque, click OK. The Reports & Forms window should open immediately. Or, in the Journal, click the Change The Default Printer Settings tool to access the form settings. Choose Custom Forms. In the Description fields, choose the generic forms Payment Cheque for payments and Payroll Cheque With YTD Totals for paycheques. These selections should automatically enter the forms you need in the Forms folder in the Sage 50 Premium Accounting Version 2019 folder. Click OK.

You should now be able to preview the payment.

Click the **Print Preview tool** (read the margin Notes). Sage 50 requests a confirmation because of the effect of advances on tax calculations:

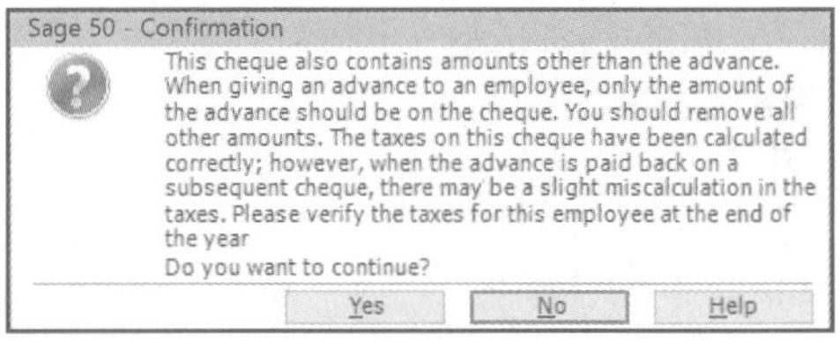

The warning advises that payroll advances are usually issued in a separate cheque to allow for correct payroll tax calculation. Advances are taxable amounts; advances repaid

> **NOTES**
> A real business should work only with the current payroll tax tables. Sage provides regular payroll updates when you sign up for the payroll service. We cannot change the source dates in the text after publishing, and using fixed dates and program (tax table) versions ensures that you can obtain the same results we do.
> You cannot update payroll tax tables in the Student version.

> **NOTES**
> Payroll Journal entries may be stored as recurring entries before posting. Follow the same steps as you do for recurring sales or purchases.

later will reduce the tax for that period. We included the advanced amount with the cheque to familiarize you with Sage 50 warning messages.

Click **Yes** to continue. You must confirm that your dates do not match the payroll formula dates:

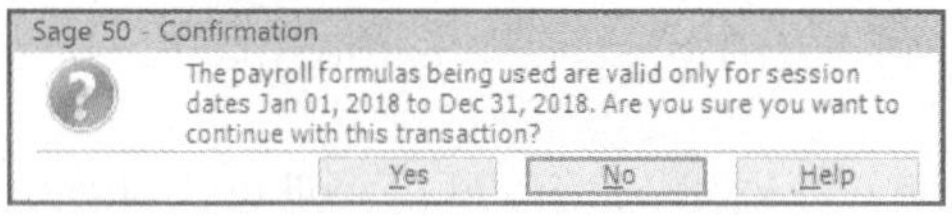

The caution is displayed whenever the dates of the transaction are different from the dates of the tax tables in your Sage 50 program.

Click **Yes** to continue to the preview. At this point, you have not yet posted the transaction, so you can still make changes if needed.

The preview includes the cheque and cheque stub with payroll summary details for the current period and the year to date.

Click **OK** to close the preview when finished to return to the journal.

Posting

When all the information in your journal entry is correct,

Click **Post** [Post ▾]. The Post button list arrow provides the option to print and post, which may be selected as the default setting.

A blank Payroll Journal input screen opens.

Entering Payroll Entitlements

> **NOTES**
> Refer to the Employee Time Summary Sheet on page 267 for Handie's payroll details.
> Uploading direct deposits is covered in Chapter 13.

Choose **Handie, Jerome** from the Employee list. **Press** (tab):

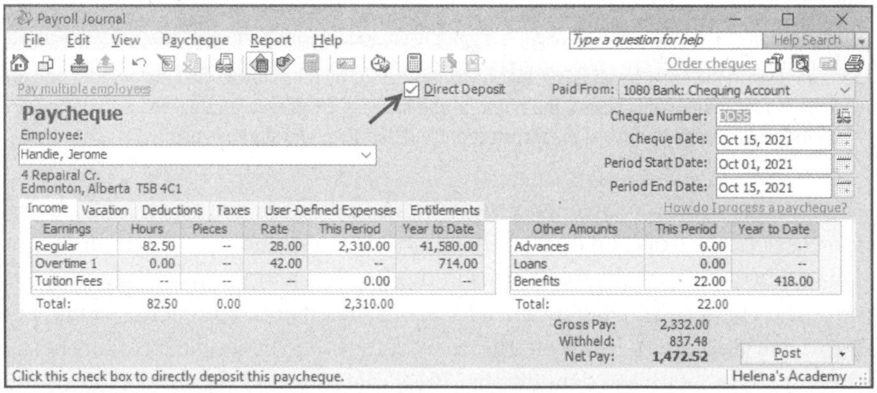

Handie's payroll details are added to the form. Instead of a cheque number, the entry DD55 appears on the form because the check box for **Direct Deposit** is selected. Handie has chosen to have his pay deposited directly to his bank account. The bank account deposit details are added to the employee's ledger record.

Handie has overtime hours for this pay period.

Click the **Hours field** beside Overtime 1. **Type** 2

Click the **Deductions tab** to open these fields.

Handie has two deductions in addition to the medical premium: one for his RRSP contribution and one for his family support payment.

Jerome Handie has taken a sick leave day during the pay period. We add this information on the Entitlements tab screen.

Click the **Entitlements tab** to open these fields:

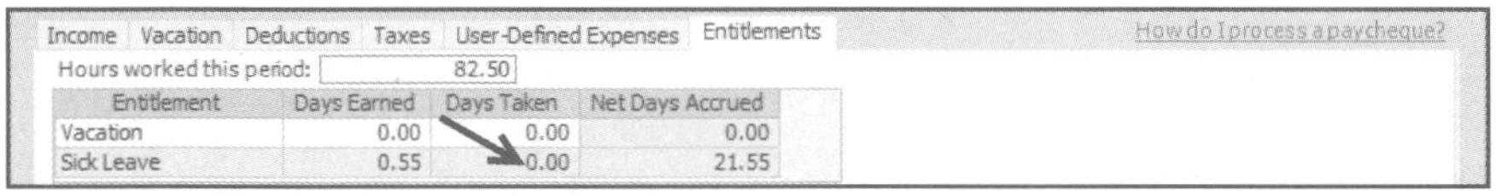

Two entitlements are defined for Helena's Academy: vacation days (only for salaried employees) and sick leave days for all full-time employees. The amounts entered in the Days Earned fields are the number of days earned only for this pay period — one half-month. Sick leave is accrued at the rate of 5 percent per hour worked. The total number of days accrued from prior work periods is recorded and updated in the ledger record and on the employee's cheque stub. If the number of days taken exceeds the number of days accrued, you will be asked if you want to allow a negative balance.

The entry 82.5 in the Hours Worked This Period field is based on 11 days, the default we entered as a setting in the employee's ledger record. If the number of hours is different for a single pay period, you can change the number of hours.

Handie has taken one day of sick leave in this pay period.

Click the **Days Taken column beside Sick Leave**.

Type 1 **Press** tab to update the Net Days Accrued:

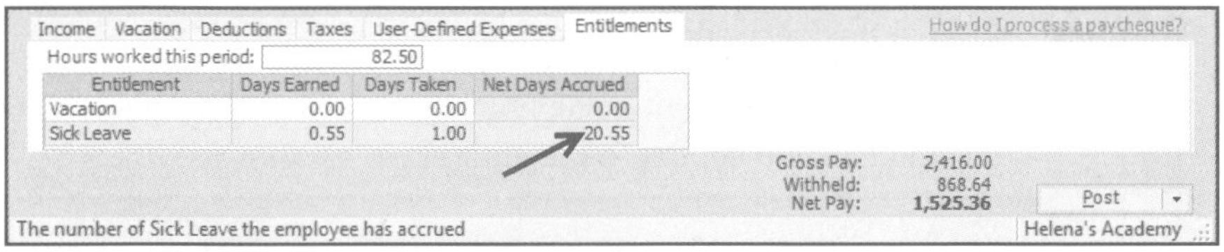

Entitlements do not affect gross pay, net pay or taxes, so you can review the entry.

Choose the **Report menu** and **click Display Payroll Journal Entry**:

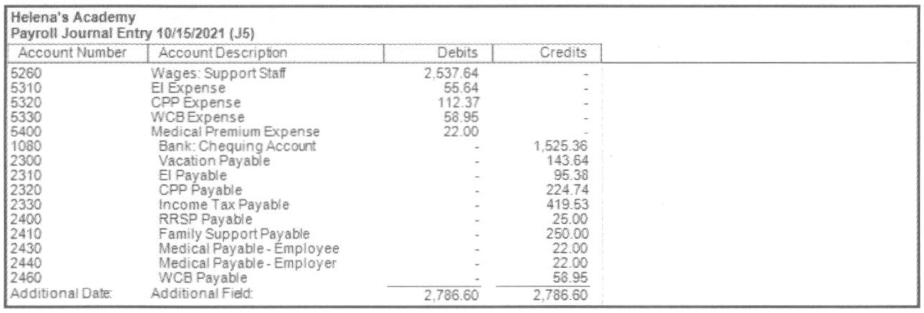

Helena's Academy
Payroll Journal Entry 10/15/2021 (J5)

Account Number	Account Description	Debits	Credits
5260	Wages: Support Staff	2,537.64	-
5310	EI Expense	55.64	-
5320	CPP Expense	112.37	-
5330	WCB Expense	58.95	-
5400	Medical Premium Expense	22.00	-
1080	Bank: Chequing Account	-	1,525.36
2300	Vacation Payable	-	143.64
2310	EI Payable	-	95.38
2320	CPP Payable	-	224.74
2330	Income Tax Payable	-	419.53
2400	RRSP Payable	-	25.00
2410	Family Support Payable	-	250.00
2430	Medical Payable - Employee	-	22.00
2440	Medical Payable - Employer	-	22.00
2460	WCB Payable	-	58.95
Additional Date:	Additional Field:	2,786.60	2,786.60

This entry is similar to the previous one, with the additional payable entries for RRSP and family support. Entitlements taken do not appear in the payroll journal entry, but the days accrued are recorded on the cheque stub and in the employee's ledger record.

Close the **journal entry display** to return to the journal.

Make **corrections** to the journal entry if necessary.

Click Post to save your work.

Click **Yes** to bypass the warning about payroll dates. **Click** the **Income tab**.

Select **Nerture, Neela** for the next payroll transaction. **Press** tab.

All the default entries are correct for Nerture. No changes are required.

Click Post. **Click Yes** to bypass the warning about payroll dates.

Select **Tiste, Arte** for the next payroll transaction.

NOTES

For every 20 days of work, the employee is entitled to one day of sick leave (the rate is 5 percent).

For some entitlements, employers may require the employee to work a minimum number of months before taking any time off.

The total number of days accrued appears in the journal and is also printed on the cheque stub.

NOTES

To preview a direct deposit stub, click the Preview tool. The deposit stub has the message "non-negotiable" added.

If you get an error message about missing forms, click OK. The Reports & Forms window should open immediately. Or, in the Journal, click the Change The Default Printer Settings tool to access the form settings. Choose Custom Forms. In the Description fields, choose the generic form Direct Deposit Payroll Stubs as the description. These selections should automatically enter the files you need in the Forms folder in the Sage 50 Premium Accounting Version 2019 folder. Click OK.

You should now be able to preview the payment.

Press tab to add his default payroll amounts:

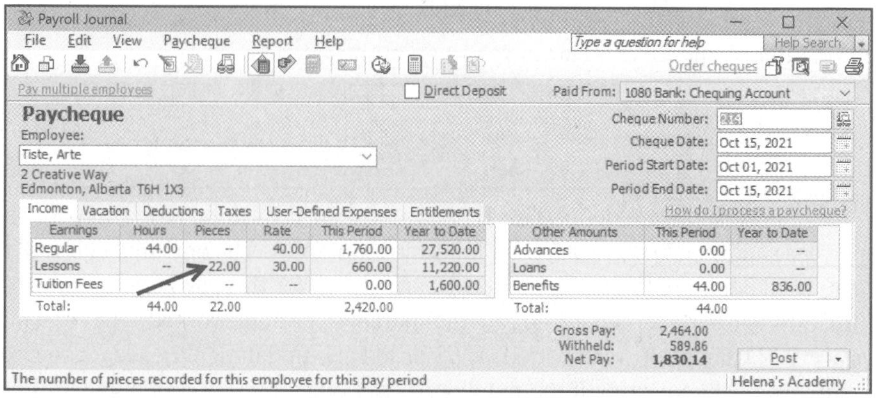

Tiste has 44 entered as the regular number of hours per period. Because this half month has 11 days and he works 4 hours per day, the default entry is correct. Tiste does not receive overtime pay.

Lesson rates and a default number of lessons per period are also entered in each teacher's ledger record. Sage 50 calculates the total dollar amount by multiplying the per lesson piece rate times the number of lessons. You can define a different rate for each employee. Tiste has given 24 individual lessons in the past two weeks, so we need to change the default entry from 22 to 24.

NOTES
If different rates are paid for different kinds of work, you can define additional piece rate fields.

Click **22.0** in the Pieces field for Lessons.

Type 24 **Press** tab to enter the number of Lessons for This Period, update all amounts and complete the entry:

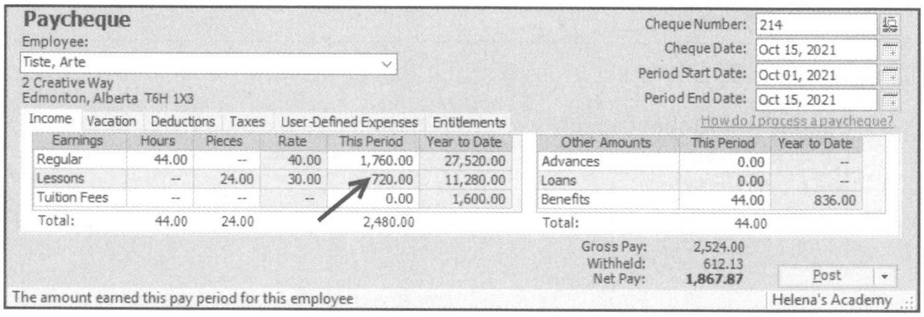

Press ctrl + **J** to open the journal entry display:

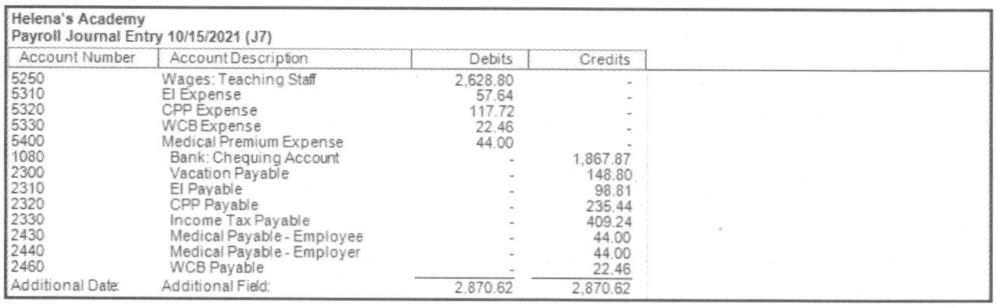

Helena's Academy
Payroll Journal Entry 10/15/2021 (J7)

Account Number	Account Description	Debits	Credits
5250	Wages: Teaching Staff	2,628.80	-
5310	EI Expense	57.64	-
5320	CPP Expense	117.72	-
5330	WCB Expense	22.46	-
5400	Medical Premium Expense	44.00	-
1080	Bank: Chequing Account	-	1,867.87
2300	Vacation Payable	-	148.80
2310	EI Payable	-	98.81
2320	CPP Payable	-	235.44
2330	Income Tax Payable	-	409.24
2430	Medical Payable - Employee	-	44.00
2440	Medical Payable - Employer	-	44.00
2460	WCB Payable	-	22.46
Additional Date:	Additional Field:	2,870.62	2,870.62

NOTES
Tiste has $200 in additional federal taxes deducted from each paycheque. This amount is not separated from other income tax amounts in the journal or in the report. It is combined with regular income tax as a single entry for Income Tax Payable.

Again, we have a similar journal entry. For each employee, you can choose one account for all sources of income, or you can choose the separate default linked accounts for each income. For Tiste, a teacher, we have linked all his incomes to *Wages: Teaching Staff* rather than to the *Wages: Support Staff* account used for other hourly employees. Therefore, his wages for lessons are included with the expense for teaching wages. For salaried teachers, lesson wages are linked to a separate expense account.

Close the **display** when finished and **make corrections** if necessary.

Post the **entry** and **click Yes** to bypass the warning about payroll formulas.

Close the **Payroll Journal window** to return to the Home window.

Advance the **session date** to October 31 and **back up** your **data file**.

Adjusting Payroll Entries

The memo on October 17 explains the need for a paycheque correction.

✓ 5 **Memo #1** **Dated Oct. 17/21**

From Manager: Morty Filer returned his paycheque for adjustment. He worked 6 hours of overtime during the week but was paid for only 4 hours. He has also taken one day of sick leave that was not recorded. Adjust his paycheque and re-issue cheque #213 to make the correction.

Sage 50 does not require reversing and correcting entries for these situations. Instead, you can complete a paycheque adjustment in the Payroll Journal, as you do in the other journals. You can access the Adjust Paycheque screen in different ways.

Click the **Paycheques icon shortcuts list arrow** and **click Adjust Paycheque**. Or,

Click the **Paycheques icon** 

. **Click** the **Adjust Paycheque tool**  or **choose** the **Paycheque menu** and **click Adjust Paycheque**.

These methods will open the familiar Search window:

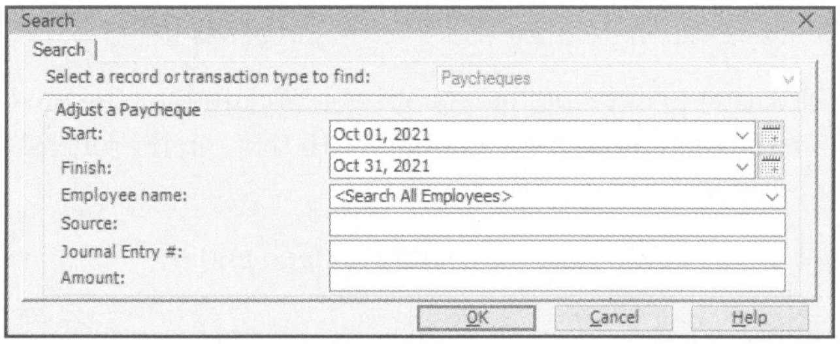

Paycheques is selected as the search area because of our starting point.

You can select beginning and ending dates to create the list. You can also enter the source (cheque or direct deposit number), journal entry number or amount and click OK to access the paycheque immediately.

The default dates are the earliest transaction date and the session date for the data file. We can accept the default dates to have all payroll transactions listed.

Click **OK** to access the list of posted payroll entries:

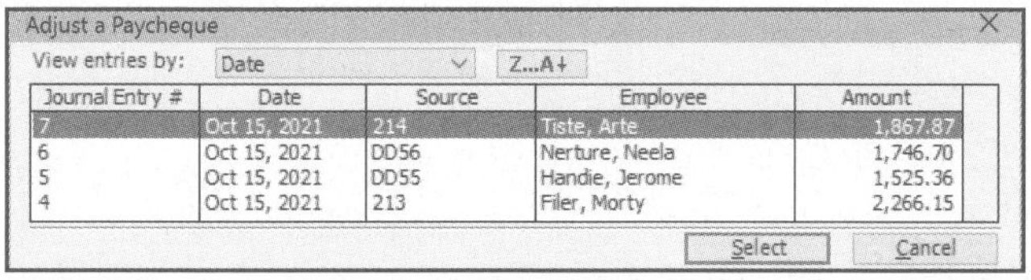

Adjust a Paycheque
View entries by: Date
Z...A+
Journal Entry # | Date | Source | Employee | Amount
7 | Oct 15, 2021 | 214 | Tiste, Arte | 1,867.87
6 | Oct 15, 2021 | DD56 | Nerture, Neela | 1,746.70
5 | Oct 15, 2021 | DD55 | Handie, Jerome | 1,525.36
4 | Oct 15, 2021 | 213 | Filer, Morty | 2,266.15
Select
Cancel

Click **Journal Entry #4 Filer, Morty** to select Filer's journal entry.

Click **Select** to display the entry that was posted.

First, Sage 50 reminds you about recalculating taxes:

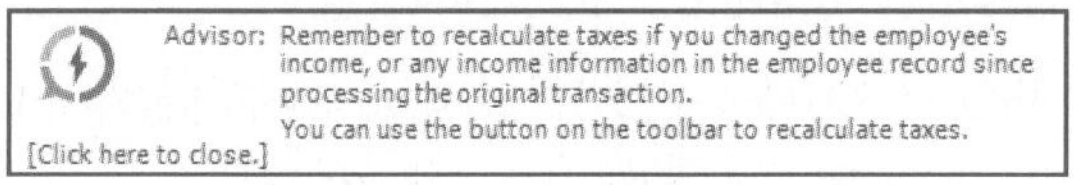

NOTES
You can look up Payroll Journal entries the same way you can look up transactions in other journals.

NOTES
In the Payroll Journal, pressing ctrl + A also opens the Adjust entry search screen, as it does in the other journals.

NOTES
Your journal entry numbers may be different if you have made other correcting or adjusting entries.

Sage 50 advises you that tax recalculation will not be automatic if you change any amount on the payroll entry. The Recalculate Taxes button is no longer dimmed.

Click the **Advisor icon** to close the warning and display the journal:

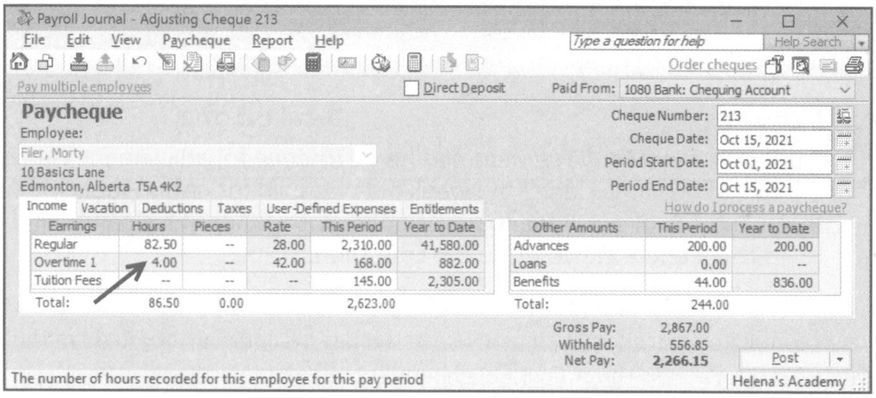

This is a duplicate of the payroll entry. All fields can be edited except the employee name. If you change the date for the new cheque to October 17, the reversing entry will retain the original posting date. Normally you would prepare a new cheque. However, Filer has returned the cheque, so we can use the same number. We need to change the number of overtime hours.

> **NOTES**
> Dates should be changed only if they are incorrect.

> **NOTES**
> If you need to change the employee or cancel a paycheque for other reasons, you can reverse the payroll transaction. Refer to page 277.

Click **4.00** in the **Hours column for Overtime 1** to select the current entry.

Type 6 **Press** *tab* to enter the change and update the gross pay.

Click the **Entitlements tab**.

Type 1 in the Days Taken field for Sick Leave and **press** *tab*.

The Vacation Pay and Withheld amounts have not been updated for the new amount of gross pay. Compare your Vacation tab screen amounts with those in the journal screen display on page 269.

> **NOTES**
> Until you recalculate the taxes, the total amount withheld from gross pay is still $556.85 and the Vacation Earned Amount for the period is still $160.68.

Click the **Taxes tab**. Tax amounts have not changed and they can be edited:

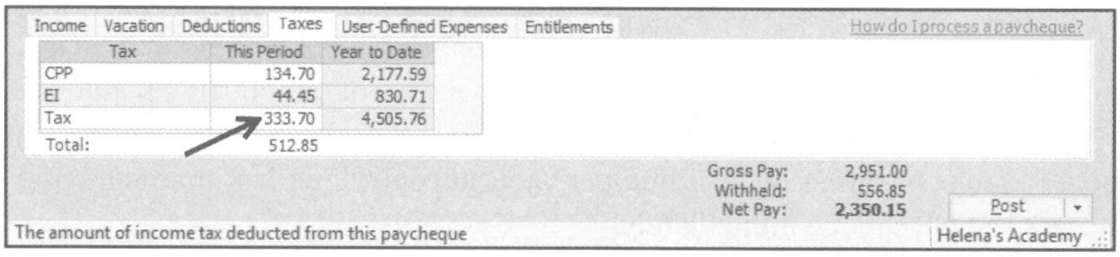

> **WARNING!**
> Do not confuse the Recalculate Taxes tool with the Windows Calculator tool. The Calculator tool is the last one on the left-hand side of the tool bar before the Refresh tools.

Click the **Recalculate Taxes button** on the Payroll Journal tool bar or **choose** the **Paycheque menu** and **click Recalculate Taxes**:

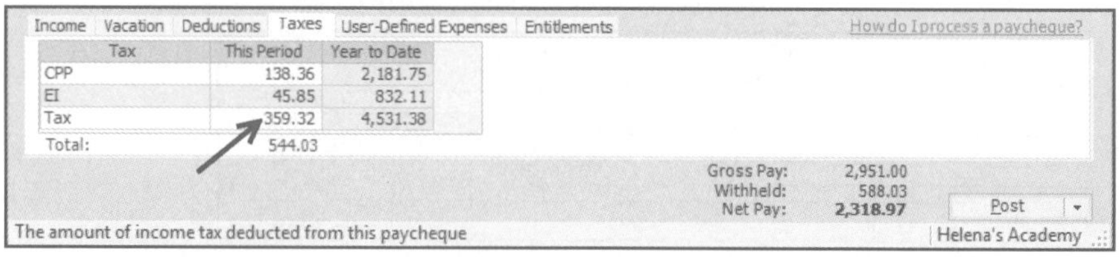

All the tax deduction and vacation pay amounts are updated for the extra hours.

Click the **Vacation tab** to verify that the Vacation amount has increased from $160.68 to $165.72.

Review the Payroll Journal **entry**. **Close** the **display** when you have finished.

Make **corrections** if necessary. **Click** Post to save the adjustment.

> **NOTES**
> The adjusted entry you display is J9. The reversing entry in the background is J8.

Sage 50 displays a warning when you do not recalculate the taxes:

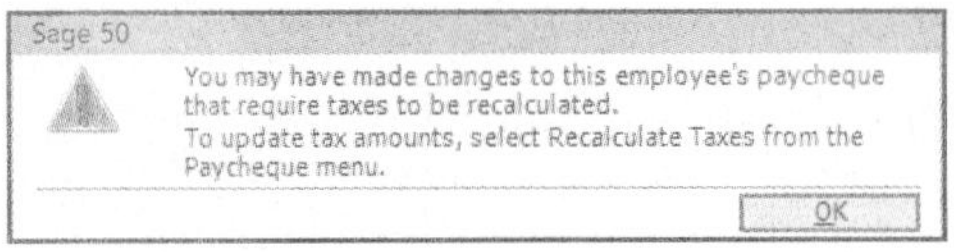

Sage 50 displays another warning when you do not change the cheque number:

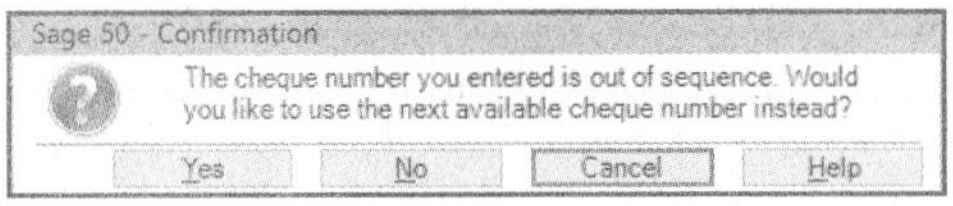

Read the question in the warning carefully. To change the cheque number to the next number in the automatic sequence, click Yes. In this case, you can use the duplicate cheque number because Filer returned the original cheque.

Click No to continue. **Click** OK to confirm posting the two journal entries.

Close the **Payroll Journal** to return to the Home window.

When you display the Payroll Journal and include corrections, you will have three journal entries for Filer: the original entry (J4), the reversing adjusting entry (J8) and the final correct entry (J9).

All three journal entries are posted with the original date, unless you changed it.

Reversing a Paycheque

You should reverse an entry to correct it when you have selected the wrong employee or if you need to delete it. The Reverse tool performs this in a single step.

Open the Payroll Journal.

Click the Adjust Paycheque tool or press ctrl + A.

Define your search parameters and click OK to access the list of posted entries.

Double-click the entry you want to reverse to open the journal entry.

Click the Reverse Paycheque tool or choose the Paycheque menu and click Reverse Paycheque.

Click Yes to confirm that the entry will be reversed.

Sage 50 saves both the original and the reversing entry. When you show corrections for journal reports, you have a complete audit trail.

Releasing Vacation Pay

Tiste needs to receive his retained vacation amount to pay for his booked vacation.

✓ 6

Memo #2 **Dated Oct. 17/21**

Tiste has booked his vacation and will receive his retained vacation pay to pay for the holiday. Release the accrued retained vacation pay for Arte Tiste and issue cheque #215.

Before releasing the vacation pay, we will view the setting in the employee ledger that controls whether vacation pay is retained or released with each paycheque. There are several ways to open the employee record.

From the Home window, you can access the employee record from the Employees icon shortcuts list or from the Employees pane. The Employees pane also has a drop-down list for creating an employee paycheque or report. (Refer to page 278.)

NOTES

The program provides a warning about the cheque sequence because we selected to verify number sequences in the Forms Settings window (refer to page 215).

NOTES

The procedure for reversing a transaction is the same in all journals when the option is available.

You can also click the Lookup tool to view a payroll transaction and then click the Reverse tool.

CLASSIC VIEW

Click the Employees icon to open the Employees window. Then double-click the entry for Tiste to open his record. Or, click Tiste to select the employee and then click the Edit tool or choose the File menu and click Open to open his ledger record.

NOTES

From the Employees pane shortcuts list arrow you can complete other tasks directly for the selected employee – create a paycheque or display the Detail Report.

You can hide the year-to-date details for employees from the Employees list pane, just as you can hide details for vendors and customers.

Click the details icon for the list of details you can hide. Refer to page 286.

NOTES

In the Employees window, if Tiste is selected, you can click the Payroll Journal icon or choose the Journal menu and click Payroll Journal to access the journal with Tiste already selected.

NOTES

If the Use column has a ✓, the item will appear in the journal for this employee. There is no ✓ for Overtime 1, so Overtime does not appear in the journal's Earnings column for Tiste (refer to the Payroll Journal screen for Tiste on page 274).

The Income tab screen also has the option to record all wage expenses in a single account. This option was selected for Tiste.

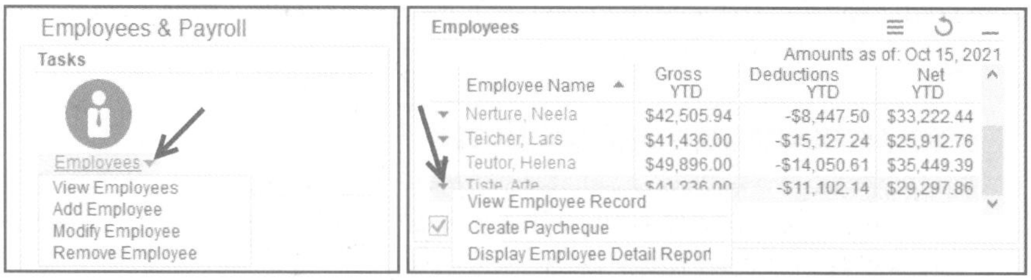

The **Modify Employees** shortcut opens the Search window and you can choose from the list of employees.

The **Employees icon**  or the **View Employees** shortcut will open the Employees window:

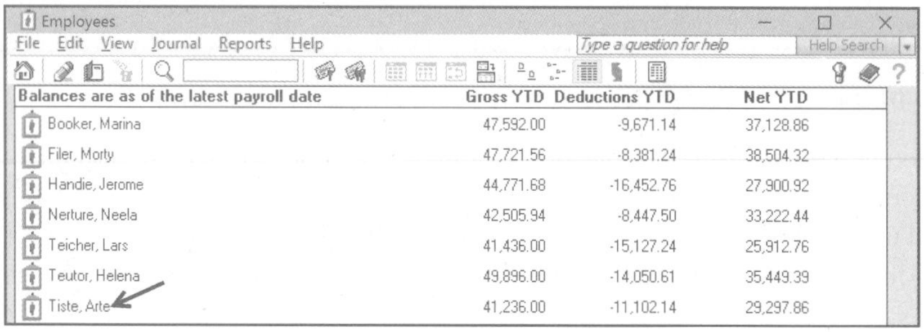

Double-click **Tiste** to view his ledger record. Or, in the Home window Employees pane,

Click **Tiste** or **click** the **shortcuts list arrow** beside his name and **choose** **View Employee Record**. The record opens with the Personal tab screen.

Click the **Income tab** to access the vacation pay settings:

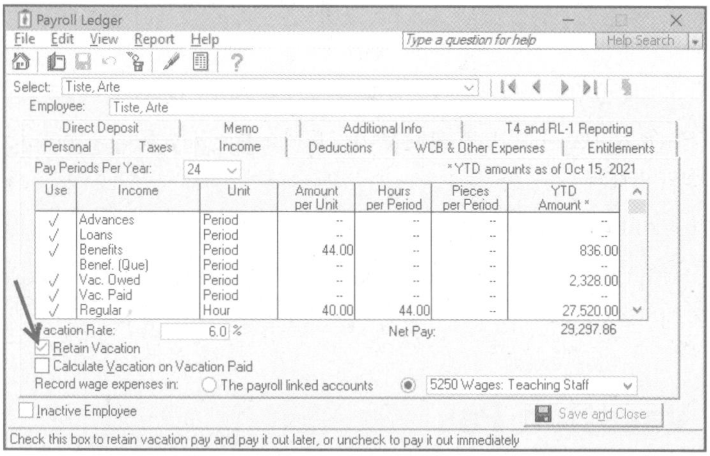

The checkmark for **Retain Vacation** indicates that vacation pay for Tiste is withheld. It can be released when Tiste receives his retained pay. If the vacation pay is paid out with each paycheque, the Retain Vacation checkbox should not be marked.

We do not need to make any changes to the ledger — we can pay out his retained vacation pay directly from the journal.

Close the **Ledger window** to return to your starting point. Close the Employees window if it is open.

Click the **Paycheques icon** .

Choose **Tiste** from the employee list and **press** tab to continue. **Click** the **Vacation tab**:

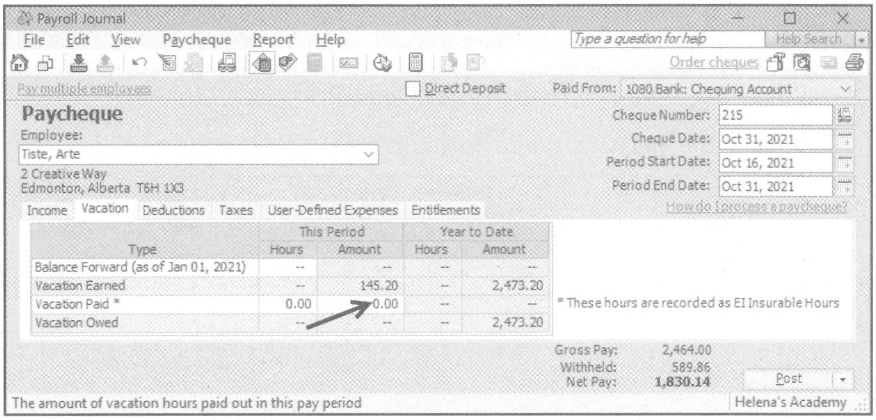

This is a normal journal entry with default amounts and retained vacation pay. Tiste has already received his paycheque so, in this case, vacation pay should be issued as a separate cheque. To do this, we must remove all the regular amounts. No regular hours should be included, and benefits and optional deductions do not apply to vacation pay.

Click the **Income tab**:

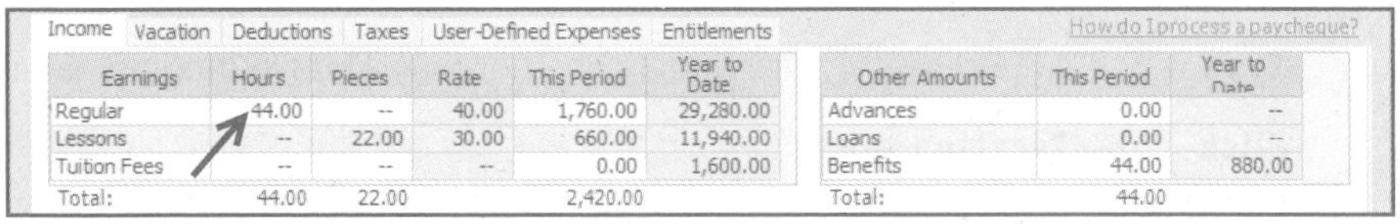
Income Vacation Deductions Taxes User-Defined Expenses Entitlements
How do I process a paycheque?
Earnings Hours Pieces Rate This Period Year to Date
Regular 44.00 -- 40.00 1,760.00 29,280.00
Lessons -- 22.00 30.00 660.00 11,940.00
Tuition Fees -- -- -- 0.00 1,600.00
Total: 44.00 22.00 2,420.00
Other Amounts This Period Year to Date
Advances 0.00 --
Loans 0.00 --
Benefits 44.00 880.00
Total: 44.00

Click **44.00** in the Regular Hours field. (Double-click if the entire amount is not selected.)

Press *del*. **Press** *tab* to select the entry for number of lessons (Pieces).

Press *del* to remove the entry and **press** *tab* to update the amounts again.

Click **44.00** in the Benefits This Period field. **Press** *del*.

Press *tab*. The Vacation tab screen opens — the vacation earned amount is now zero, but we still need to delete other amounts.

Tiste's medical premium amount should also be deleted before recording the entry. This is a one-time change, and it should be made directly in the journal.

Click the **Deductions tab** to open this screen:

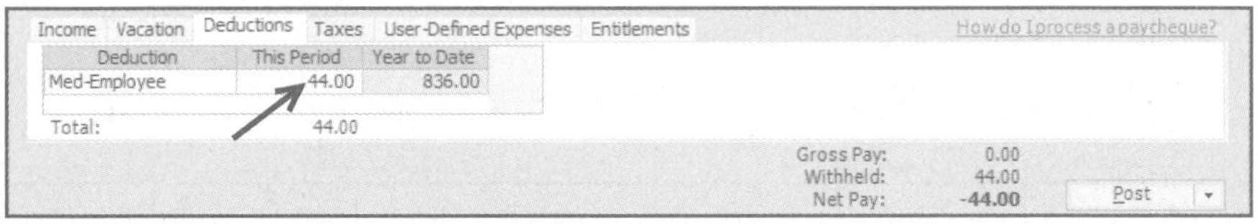

Click **44** in the Med-Employee This Period field and **press** *del*.

Click the **User-Defined Expenses tab**:

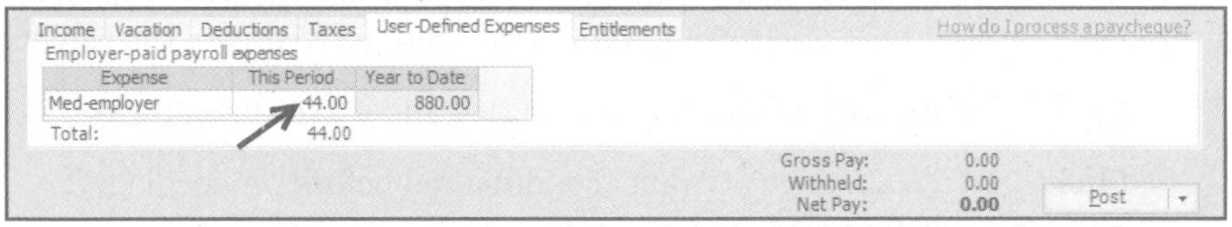

Click **44** in the Med-employer This Period field and **press** *del*. **Press** *tab*:

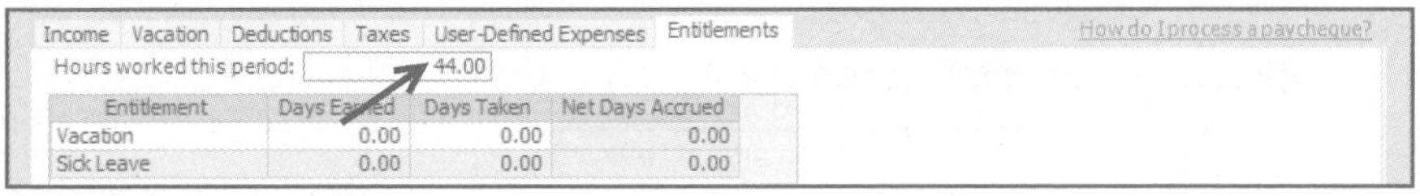

NOTES

The Vacation Earned Amount ($145.20) is the vacation pay on the wages for this pay period and is included in the Vacation Owed Amount.

When you remove the regular hours and number of lessons, the earned amount is reduced to zero and the vacation pay owed is also reduced by $145.20.

Employers should always check whether provincial regulations require them to add Insurable Hours for vacation paid.

NOTES

Although the benefit, deduction and user-defined expense amounts do not change the vacation pay amount, they should not be charged to the employee or the employer. The amounts for this period were already included on the original paycheque for regular hours.

> **NOTES**
> Tiste, a part-time employee, does not receive entitlements – his entries for days earned are blank. For other employees, delete the number of hours in the Entitlements tab screen because entitlements are not earned on vacation pay. This step will remove the entries for Days Earned.

The journal is updated and the Entitlements tab screen opens. For employees with entitlements, you must reduce the Days Earned amounts to zero:

Click **44.00** in the Hours Worked field. **Press** *del* to remove the entry.

Click the **Vacation tab** to open this screen:

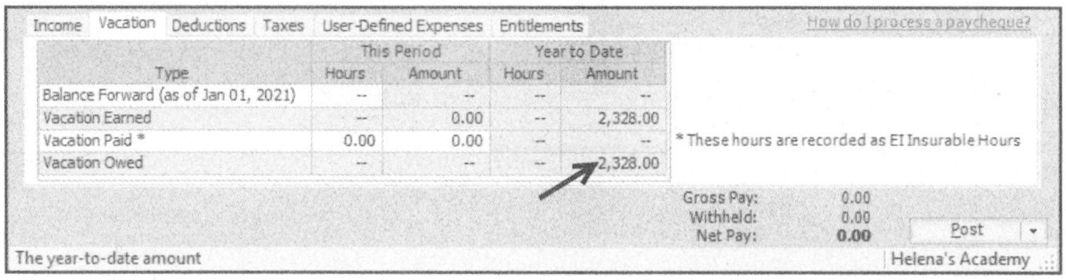

Type	This Period Hours	This Period Amount	Year to Date Hours	Year to Date Amount
Balance Forward (as of Jan 01, 2021)	--	--	--	--
Vacation Earned	--	0.00	--	2,328.00
Vacation Paid *	0.00	0.00	--	--
Vacation Owed	--	--	--	2,328.00

The Amount This Period entry has been removed. The Gross Pay, Withheld and Net Pay amounts are all reduced to zero.

The vacation pay amount that has accrued since the last time it was paid out is the Vacation Owed Amount, $2 328. This is the amount that will be paid now by entering it in the Vacation Paid Amount field.

Click **0.00** in the Vacation Paid Amount This Period field.

Type 2328 **Press** *tab* to update the net pay. The Deductions tab opens.

Click the **Vacation tab**:

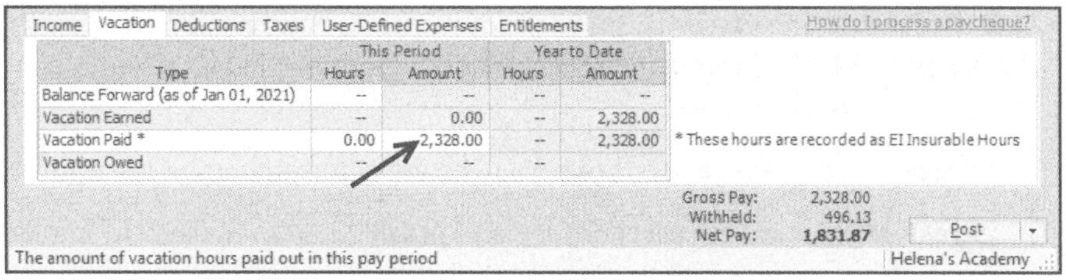

Type	This Period Hours	This Period Amount	Year to Date Hours	Year to Date Amount
Balance Forward (as of Jan 01, 2021)	--	--	--	--
Vacation Earned	--	0.00	--	2,328.00
Vacation Paid *	0.00	2,328.00	--	2,328.00
Vacation Owed	--	--	--	

The Gross Pay amount now matches the vacation paid amount and taxes have been updated. We still need to change the dates for the paycheque.

Enter **Oct 17** as the cheque date and **Oct 15** as the Period Start and End date.

Choose the **Report menu** and **click** **Display Payroll Journal Entry**:

> **NOTES**
> The additional tax amount is included for this payment. To remove it, you would need to choose Enter Taxes Manually after making all the other changes. Then edit the income tax amount by subtracting $200, the additional tax amount withheld. Or, you can make a one-time change to the entry in the employee's ledger record. Remember to change it back after completing the vacation pay entry.

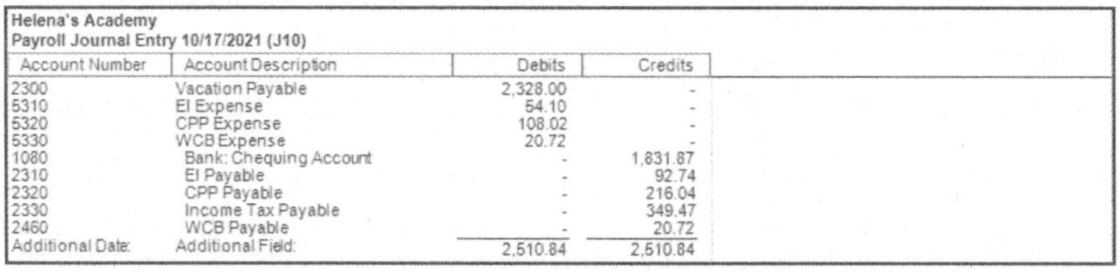

Helena's Academy
Payroll Journal Entry 10/17/2021 (J10)

Account Number	Account Description	Debits	Credits
2300	Vacation Payable	2,328.00	-
5310	EI Expense	54.10	-
5320	CPP Expense	108.02	-
5330	WCB Expense	20.72	-
1080	Bank: Chequing Account	-	1,831.87
2310	EI Payable	-	92.74
2320	CPP Payable	-	216.04
2330	Income Tax Payable	-	349.47
2460	WCB Payable	-	20.72
Additional Date:	Additional Field:	2,510.84	2,510.84

The released vacation pay is entered as a debit (decrease) to *Vacation Payable*. Payroll taxes are charged on the vacation pay, as they are on other wages, because taxes were not paid on the retained vacation pay. The employer's expense for vacation pay, a debit to the linked wages expense account, was recognized when the original paycheque was prepared. At that time *Vacation Payable* was credited to create the liability.

Close the **display** to return to the journal and **make corrections** if necessary.

Click Post. Sage 50 wants confirmation before proceeding:

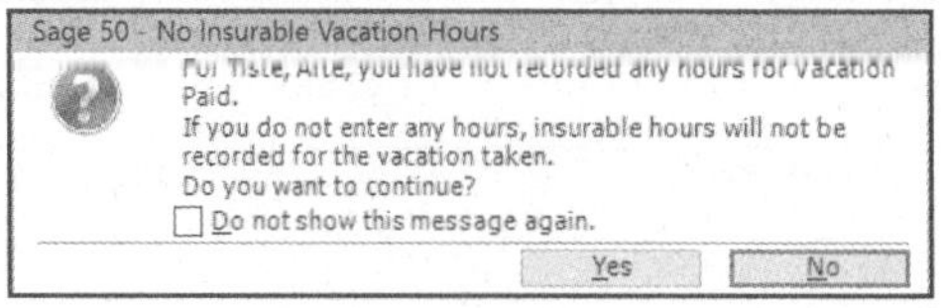

If the employee is taking regular time off for vacation, you should enter the number of hours in the Hours field beside Vacation Paid.

Click **Yes** to continue and then **click Yes** again to bypass the payroll dates warning. **Close** the **Payroll Journal**.

Making Payroll Tax Remittances

Sage 50 tracks payroll liabilities and remittances when the suppliers are linked to payroll taxes. Helena's Academy has five suppliers for whom remittances are due.

✓ 7

Memo #3 **Dated Oct. 17/21**

Make payroll remittances for the pay period ending October 1.
Receiver General for Canada: EI, CPP and income tax
Aspen Life Financial: Medical premiums from employee and employer
Alberta Workers' Compensation Board: WCB
Rocky Mountain Trust: RRSP
Maintenance Enforcement Program: Family support payments
Issue cheques #216 to #220.

Taxes are remitted from the Payments Journal. You can open this journal from the Payables module Payments Journal or its Home window shortcuts list, or from the Employees & Payroll module.

We will demonstrate the access from the Payroll window first.

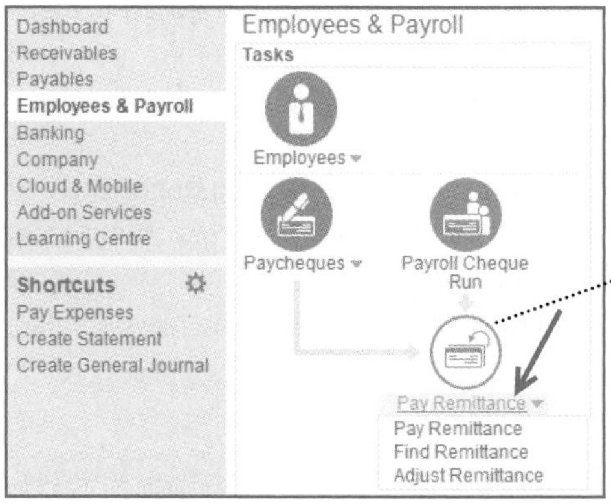

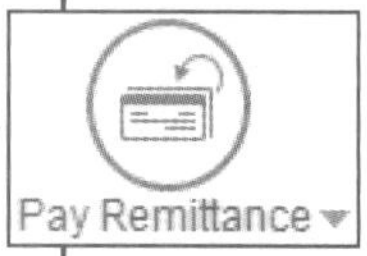

Click the **Pay Remittance icon** to open the Payments Journal form we need.

Click the **To The Order Of list arrow** for the remittance suppliers set up:

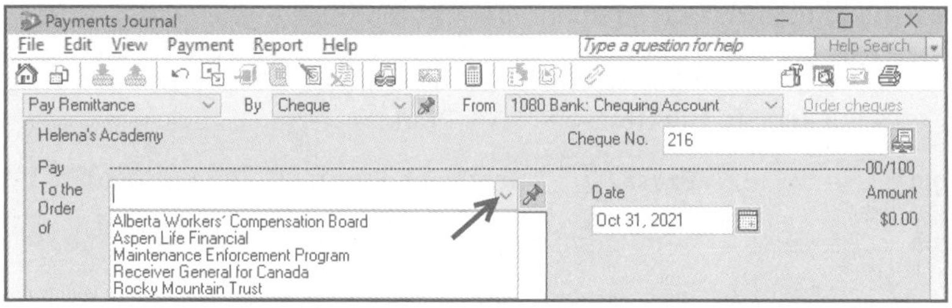

The five suppliers who collect payroll deductions and taxes are listed. The first remittance will be to the Receiver General for EI, CPP and income tax.

Click **Receiver General for Canada** to select the supplier.

NOTES

The Pay Remittance shortcuts list includes the options to Find and Adjust remittances. Other Payments Journal options are not on the list.

CLASSIC VIEW

Click the Payments icon  to open the Payments Journal. Then select Pay Remittance from the Pay transaction list to open the journal form we need (refer to page 285).

The Payments Journal is updated with the taxes collected for this supplier:

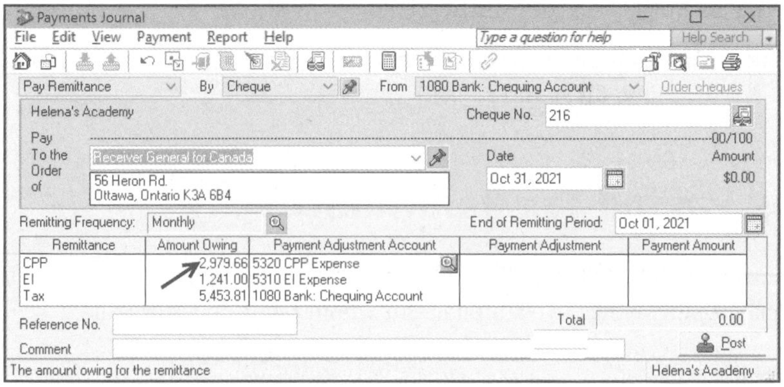

Three taxes are remitted to the Receiver General for Canada. The balances are the amounts in the General Ledger linked accounts as at the remittance period end date, October 1. For Helena's Academy, taxes were not remitted immediately before the files were converted to Sage 50 and the payroll tax liability accounts had outstanding balances. These balances match the amounts in the Trial Balance for October 1 on page 261. The remitting period and the next payment due date are entered as Payroll Ledger settings.

The Remittance Journal has two date fields: one for the date of the cheque and a second below the cheque section for the payroll period covered by the remittance. The session date is the default cheque date. The **End Of Remitting Period date** is entered as a Payroll setting. When you change the End Of Remitting Period date, the amounts will be updated to the General Ledger amounts at that date. Remittances are usually due one month after the pay period they cover, so we are paying the taxes that were withheld to the end of September. The period end date is updated according to the frequency of payment entered as a Payroll Remittance setting.

The **Payment Adjustment** field should be used for any tax expenses that are not already included in the payable account balances. Separate linked accounts may be used for these adjustments. A positive entry will increase the tax expense and the total amount submitted. Negative adjustment amounts will decrease the tax expense amount and the total amount submitted.

The full amount is being paid for each tax.

Click the **Payment Amount column for CPP** to enter the amount owing as the payment amount.

Press ↓ to enter the payment amount for EI.

Press ↓ to enter the payment amount for Tax.

Press *tab* to accept the final payment, update the cheque amount and advance to the Reference No. field.

Type `Memo 3A` **Press** *tab* to advance to the Comment field.

Type `Payroll tax remittance for September`

NOTES

Accept the default amounts in your data file, unless you know that you have made an error in the paycheque. In that case, you should correct the paycheque first.

NOTES

In Chapter 9, we explain how to enter the Payroll Ledger settings for remittances.

NOTES

Because the earliest date allowed is October 1, we cannot enter September 30 as the date for the end of the remitting period. The amounts for October 1 are the same as the amounts for September 30.

If any employees were paid on October 1, you must enter September 30 as the pay period ending date. In this case, September 30 would also be the earliest transaction date.

NOTES

The Reference No. is added for the Remittance Journal report, so you do not need to repeat it in the Comment as we did for Other Payment entries in this journal.

Enter **Oct 17** as the cheque Date to complete the form:

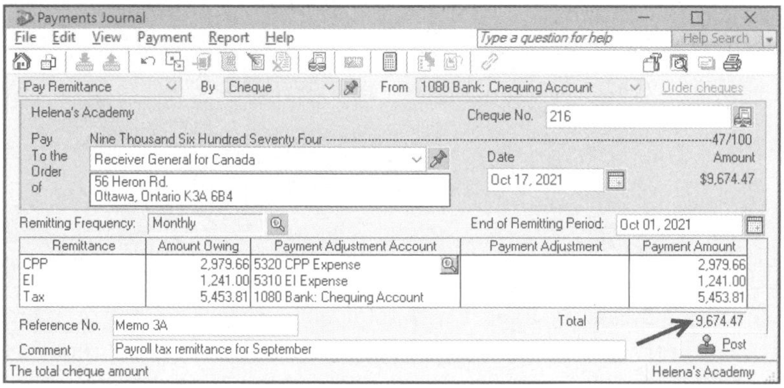

We can now review the journal entry.

Choose the **Report menu** and **click Display Payments Journal Entry**:

Helena's Academy
Payments Journal Entry

		Account Number	Account Description	Debits	Credits
10/01/2021	(J11)	Memo 3A, Receiver General for Canada : Payroll tax remittance for September			
		2310	EI Payable	1,241.00	-
		2320	CPP Payable	2,979.66	-
		2330	Income Tax Payable	5,453.81	-
		2200	Accounts Payable	-	9,674.47
10/17/2021	(J12)	216, Receiver General for Canada : Payroll tax remittance for September			
		2200	Accounts Payable	9,674.47	-
		1080	Bank: Chequing Account	-	9,674.47
Additional Date:	Additional Field:			19,348.94	19,348.94

The remittance creates two journal entries. The three payroll liability accounts have been debited to reduce the liability, and *Accounts Payable* is credited with October 1 as the effective date to reflect the liability to the Canada Revenue Agency. If you had entered adjustments, those amounts would be debited (for positive adjustments) to the corresponding linked account. The second entry recognizes the payment on the cheque date, October 17 — it clears the *Accounts Payable* liability with a credit entry to the Bank account.

Close the **display** when finished.

CORRECTING THE PAYROLL REMITTANCE

Move the cursor to the field that contains the error. **Double-click** or **drag through** the **incorrect information** to highlight it. **Type** the **correct information** and **press** *tab* to enter it. **Enter** a different **remittance end period date**, if this is appropriate, to enter the amounts owing for that date.

You can discard the entry by **clicking** ☒ or **Undo** ↶ or by returning to the Supplier list and **clicking** a **different supplier** name. **Click** the name of the **correct remittance supplier** and **press** *tab*. When prompted, confirm that you want to discard the incorrect entry. **Click Yes** and start again.

You can adjust a remittance **after posting** as you can other payments. **Choose Adjust Remittance** from the Pay Remittances icon shortcuts list. Or, open the Pay Remittance journal and **click** the **Adjust Remittance tool** or **choose** the **Payment menu** and **choose Adjust Remittance. Enter** the search **criteria** you want to determine the list of payments. Only remittances appear on this list. **Select** the **remittance** that requires correction and **make** the **changes** you need. **Post** the revised correction after reviewing it.

From the journal's Report menu you can also display the Remittance Report, the same report that you get from the Home window Reports menu or Report Centre. If you display this report before posting the payment, the payment amounts will still be zero. First, we must make corrections and post the payment.

Make **corrections** if necessary and then **post** the **payment**.

NOTES

Amounts entered in the Payment Adjustment field affect the balances in the linked adjustment accounts and not the liability account balances. For Helena's Academy, we are using the related expense account for adjustments to the employer's liability amounts and the Bank account for adjustments to employee deductions.

You must identify a linked account if you enter a payment adjustment.

NOTES

You can adjust and reverse remittance payments just as you can other payments when the Remittance Payment Journal is open, but not when another type of payment transaction is selected.

From the Payments icon shortcuts list in the Payables window, the option to Find Payment will include all payment entries, including remittances. Select the remittance to view the transaction you want and then click the Adjust or Reverse tool from the lookup window.

Choose the **Report menu** and **click Display Remittance Report**:

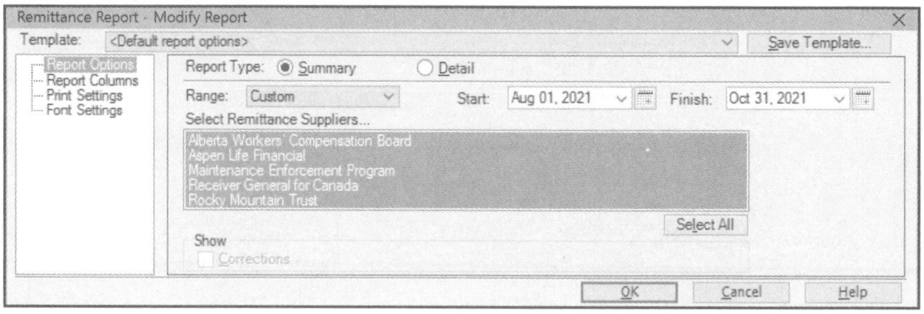

You can display a **Summary Report** with total amounts for each tax or a **Detail Report** with a line entry for each tax for each payroll transaction in the report period. You can prepare the report for one or more payroll authorities, and you can choose a remittance period for the report. We can accept the default dates — we want the report for October. Only one remittance was posted, so we will view the Summary Report for the Receiver General to display the remittance we just completed.

> **NOTES**
> The Amount column entries in the report reflect only the amounts from Payroll Journal entries for the four paycheques on October 15 and Tiste's vacation pay. They do not include the opening balance forward amounts.
> The note reminds us that the report accounts only for transactions completed with the Pay Remittance feature.

Click **Receiver General For Canada** and then **click OK** to open the report:

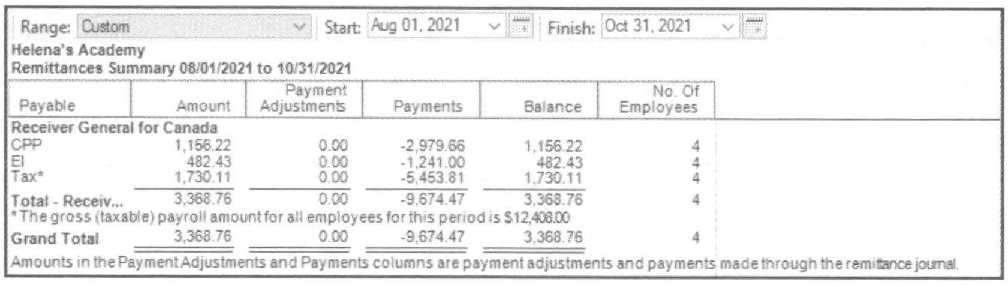

Range: Custom Start: Aug 01, 2021 Finish: Oct 31, 2021

Helena's Academy
Remittances Summary 08/01/2021 to 10/31/2021

Payable	Amount	Payment Adjustments	Payments	Balance	No. Of Employees
Receiver General for Canada					
CPP	1,156.22	0.00	-2,979.66	1,156.22	4
EI	482.43	0.00	-1,241.00	482.43	4
Tax*	1,730.11	0.00	-5,453.81	1,730.11	4
Total - Receiv...	3,368.76	0.00	-9,674.47	3,368.76	4
*The gross (taxable) payroll amount for all employees for this period is $12,408.00					
Grand Total	3,368.76	0.00	-9,674.47	3,368.76	4

Amounts in the Payment Adjustments and Payments columns are payment adjustments and payments made through the remittance journal.

The report includes the total of Payroll Journal entry amounts for all tax, adjustments, payments and final balances. The new balances are the total amounts for the October paycheques for the four employees and the vacation pay for Tiste.

> **NOTES**
> When you choose Receiver General for Canada again as the supplier, the remitting period date has been advanced by one month and the current account balances are displayed.

> **NOTES**
> The Medical liability has two entries, one for the employee's share and one for the employer's share.

Close the **report** when finished to return to the Payments Journal.

Choose **Aspen Life Financial** as the supplier for the next remittance.

Pay the **two Medical premium amounts**. The dates October 1 and October 17 should be correct from the previous remittance.

Enter **Memo 3B** in the Reference field and **enter** an appropriate **comment**.

Review and then **post** the **payment**.

Choose **Alberta Workers' Compensation Board** as the supplier.

Pay the **WCB amount**.

Enter **Memo 3C** in the Reference field and **enter** an appropriate **comment**.

Review and then **post** the **payment**.

Choose **Rocky Mountain Trust** as the supplier for the next remittance.

Pay the **RRSP contributions** withheld.

Enter **Memo 3D** in the Reference field and **enter** an appropriate **comment**.

Review and then **post** the **payment**.

Choose **Maintenance Enforcement Program** as the supplier.

Pay the **Family Support payments** withheld.

Enter **Memo 3E** in the Reference field and **enter** an appropriate **comment**.

Review and then **post** the **payment**. **Close** the **Payments Journal**.

Entering Remittances from the Payables Module Window

Click Payables in the Modules pane list to open the Payables Home window. Click the Payments icon shortcuts list arrow:

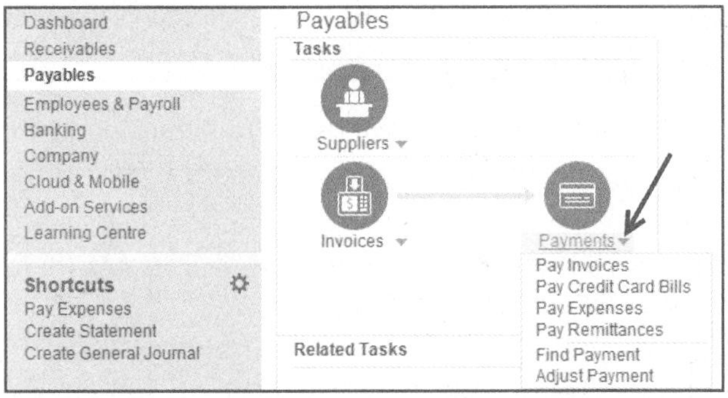

The shortcuts include Pay Remittances. Click Pay Remittances to modify the Payments Journal.

You can also click the Payments icon  to open the Payments Journal. Once the journal is open, click Pay Invoices to access the payment types:

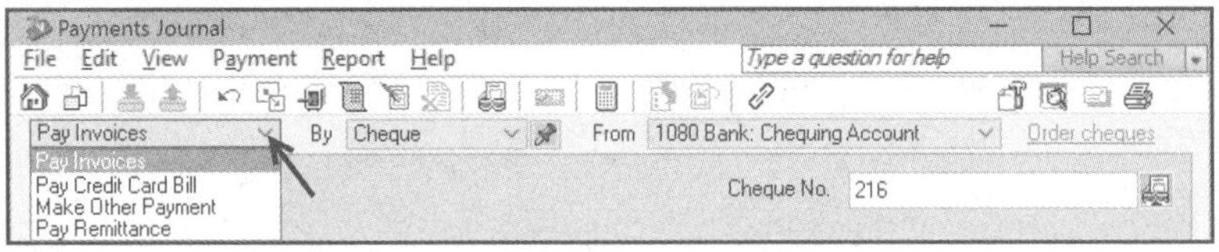

Click Pay Remittance to modify the Payments Journal. Choose the remittance supplier and continue with the remittance entry as outlined above.

Enter the **next two cash purchase transactions** and then close the journal.

8 **Cash Purchase Invoice #ESS-4689** **Dated Oct. 17/21**

From Energy Supply Services, $810 including taxes for heat and hydro on equal monthly billing plan. Store as a recurring monthly entry. Paid by cheque #221.

9 **Cash Purchase #TA-113368** **Dated Oct. 20/21**

From Telus Alberta, $220 including all taxes for one month of telephone services. Invoice total paid in full with cheque #222.

Completing a Payroll Cheque Run

When several employees are paid at the same time, you can complete a payroll cheque run to prepare all the cheques and journal entries in a single transaction.

Click **Employees & Payroll** in the Modules list to return to the default page.

The Payroll Run Journal is used to pay multiple employees:

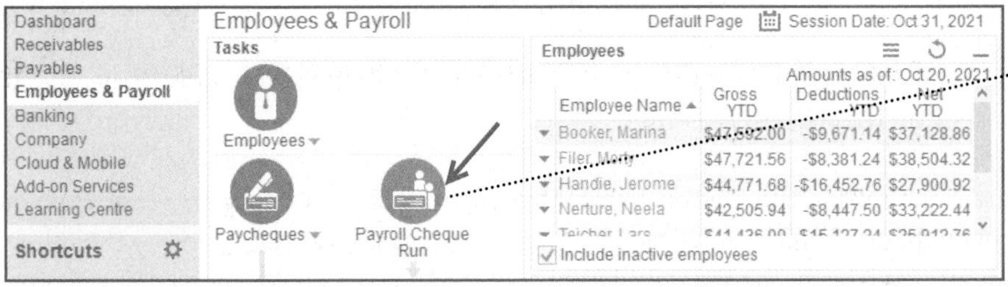

All the amounts in the Home window Employees list have been updated.

PRO VERSION
Remember that you will see Vendors as the icon label instead of Suppliers. Pay Purchase Invoices replaces Pay Invoices in the shortcuts drop-down list.

NOTES
The Payroll Cheque Run icon does not have a shortcuts list.

Employee list balances are at the latest transaction date, October 20.

NOTES

You can update the amounts in the Employees pane by clicking the Refresh tool above the list.

PRO VERSION

pro The Refresh and Reset tools apply to multi-user operation of the program. They do not apply or appear in the single-user Pro version. The Time Slips tool also does not appear in the Pro version.

NOTES

The Payroll Run Journal has a link below the tool bar to switch to the Payroll Journal if you want to Pay One Employee.

You must use the Payroll Journal to edit tax amounts or previous payroll entries.

NOTES

You cannot adjust or reverse paycheques from the Payroll Run Journal – Adjust and Reverse entry tools are not included in the tool bar. However, paycheques prepared here can be adjusted in the Payroll Journal. Refer to page 295.

Taxes cannot be changed in the Payroll Run Journal – the Manually Calculate Taxes tool is omitted from the tool bar.

The Store and Recall tools are also missing.

As you can for suppliers and customers, you can hide the year-to-date details for employees from the Employees pane details list tool:

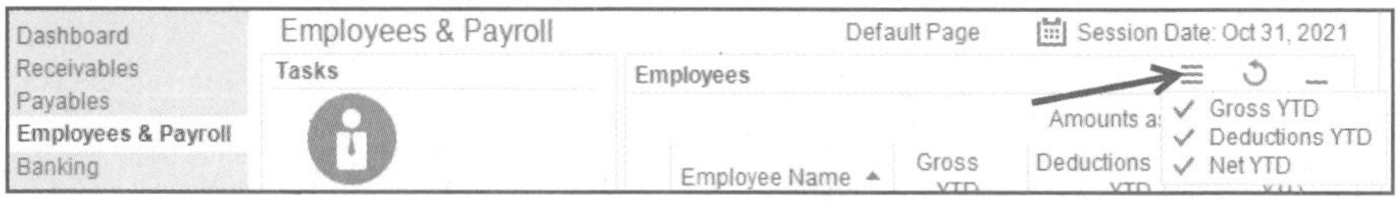

Click the **Payroll Cheque Run icon** to open the Payroll Run Journal:

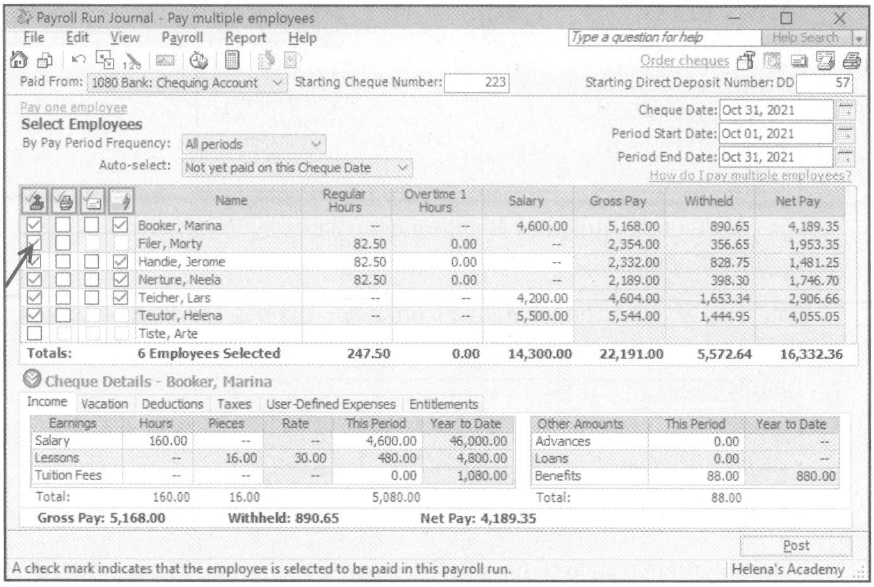

From this screen you can pay all employees, and you can enter or edit any details that you can enter or edit in the Payroll Journal. Employees are listed in alphabetic order, and checkmarks indicate who will be paid in this payroll run. If there is no checkmark in the **Post column**, you will not create a paycheque for that employee.

The **Renumber icon** is used to update cheque and deposit numbers. The Pay Period Start and Pay Period End dates match the longest pay period for the selected employees.

The form also includes deposit information in the **Direct Deposit column**. A ✓ in this column indicates that the pay will be deposited to the employee's bank account. Both the next Cheque and Direct Deposit Numbers are on the form.

For direct deposit employees, you can check the **E-mail column** if you e-mail the cheque stubs to them. This check box is dimmed for employees paid by cheque.

By adding ✓s to the **Print column**, you can print cheques and deposit stubs directly from the summary.

The upper journal pane lists all active employees, with summary information for each. You can **edit** three details directly in the **summary pane** without opening the cheque details — the number of regular and overtime hours for hourly paid employees and salary amounts for salaried employees. This offers a quick way to complete simple payroll runs.

You cannot change the Gross Pay, Net Pay or Withheld amounts. Sage 50 calculates these from the details you enter.

The lower pane has the cheque details for the selected employee with tabs that mirror the tabs in the Payroll Journal. Because Booker is selected, her cheque details are provided initially. To change details that are not in the summary pane — the other details that are available in the Payroll Journal — you can access fields by selecting an employee and the appropriate tab screen.

In the summary on the following page, all employees are to be paid on October 31.

✓ 10

Employee Time Summary Sheet #20 **Dated Oct. 31/21**

For the pay periods from October 16 to October 31 and October 1 to October 31, 2021

Name of Employee	Regular Hours	Overtime Hours	Lessons	Tuition	Advance (Repaid)	Loan (Repaid)	Sick Days	Direct Deposit
Filer, Morty	75.0	2	–	$145.00	($50)	–	1	No
Handie, Jerome	75.0	2	–	–	–	–	–	Yes
Nerture, Neela	75.0	–	–	–	–	–	–	Yes
Tiste, Arte	40.0	–	24	–	–	$100	–	No
Booker, Marina	160	–	16	$140.00	–	–	1	Yes
Teicher, Lars	160	–	12	–	–	–	–	Yes
Teutor, Helena	160	–	–	–	–	–	–	No

a. Using Employee Time Summary Sheet #20 and the Employee Information Sheet, complete payroll for all employees.
b. Recover $50 advanced to Morty Filer.
c. Issue $100 loan to Tiste and recover $25 from each of the next four paycheques.
d. Issue cheques #223, #224 and #225 and DD slips #57, #58, #59 and #60.

NOTES

The October 31 paycheque included 10 days for hourly paid employees – 75 regular hours.

Enter 75 as the regular and entitlement hours for Filer, Handie and Nerture and 40 as the regular hours for Tiste.

The program selects all employees for inclusion if their pay cycle has ended because All Periods is entered as the **By Pay Period Frequency**. You can select any single pay frequency from the list or all of them. If you select 24 periods, only the four hourly employees will be marked with a ✓.

Initially, all employees have a ✓ in the **Post column** except Tiste. From the Auto-Select options you can decide how to select the employees to be paid. Because the initial selection is **Not Yet Paid On This Cheque Date**, Tiste is excluded — he received his vacation pay after October 15.

Click the **Auto-Select list arrow**:

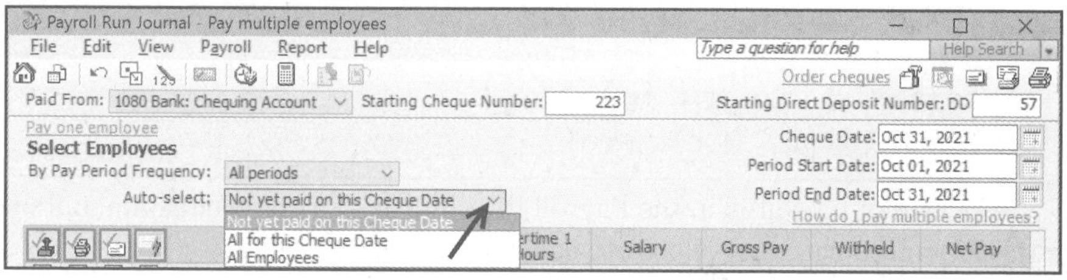

You can select all employees, all employees who should be paid on this date or all employees not yet paid for this cheque date.

Click **All For This Cheque Date**. Tiste is now marked for payment, too.

The cheque date, pay period end date and initial cheque and deposit numbers can all be edited if necessary.

You can remove an employee from the payroll run by clicking the ✓ in the Post column to remove it. You can change the direct deposit status for an employee by clicking the ✓ in the Direct Deposit column to remove it. A cheque will then be created instead.

NOTES

You cannot change from payment by cheque to direct deposit unless the Direct Deposit option is selected in the ledger record for the employee and you have entered the necessary bank details (refer to page 337).

Click **Filer** to select this employee with his income details on the screen:

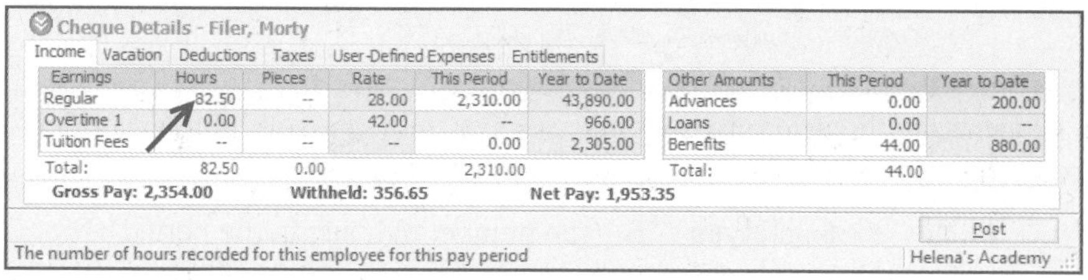

NOTES

Clicking the employee name will open the details for that employee directly. Then you can change to any other tab screen to select other details for that employee if you want.

This screen is just like Filer's Income tab screen in the Payroll Journal on page 268, and we can enter or edit all amounts in the same way as in that journal. For Filer, we need to change the number of regular hours and add the overtime hours, the tuition fee amount and the advances repayment. All these details are entered in the Income tab screen.

Click **82.5** in the **Regular Hours** field. **Type** 75 **Press** (tab). **Type** 2 to add the Overtime 1 Hours.

Press (tab) to select the Tuition Fees amount. **Type** 145 **Press** (tab).

By default, –200.00, the entire amount owing, is entered as the Advances Amount for This Period. Filer is repaying $50 each pay period, so we must change the amount.

WARNING!
Remember to enter a negative number for advances that are repaid.

Type -50 **Click** the **Vacation tab**:

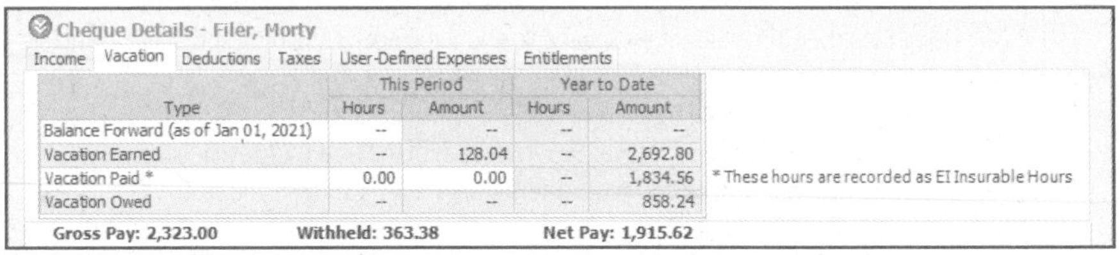

Cheque Details - Filer, Morty

Income | Vacation | Deductions | Taxes | User-Defined Expenses | Entitlements

Type	This Period Hours	This Period Amount	Year to Date Hours	Year to Date Amount
Balance Forward (as of Jan 01, 2021)	--	--	--	--
Vacation Earned	--	128.04	--	2,692.80
Vacation Paid *	0.00	0.00	--	1,834.56
Vacation Owed	--	--	--	858.24

* These hours are recorded as EI Insurable Hours

Gross Pay: 2,323.00 Withheld: 363.38 Net Pay: 1,915.62

Vacation amounts are calculated and updated automatically.

NOTES
Vacation may be paid in the same way as in the Payroll Journal. Enter the Vacation Owed Amount in the Vacation Paid Amount field.

Click the **Deductions tab**:

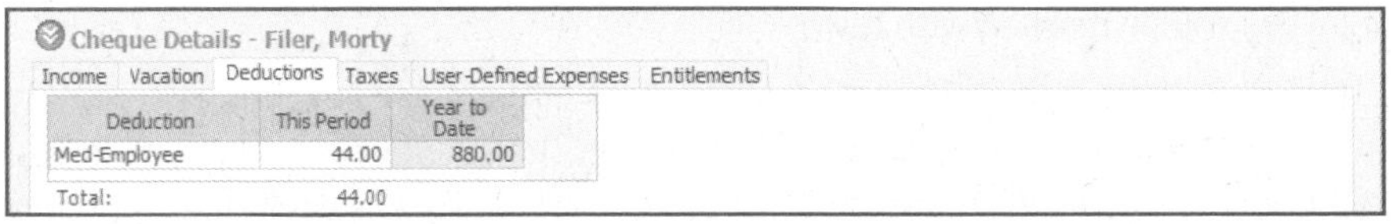

Cheque Details - Filer, Morty

Income | Vacation | Deductions | Taxes | User-Defined Expenses | Entitlements

Deduction	This Period	Year to Date
Med-Employee	44.00	880.00
Total:	44.00	

The deduction amounts are correct, but they are available for editing.

Click the **Taxes tab**:

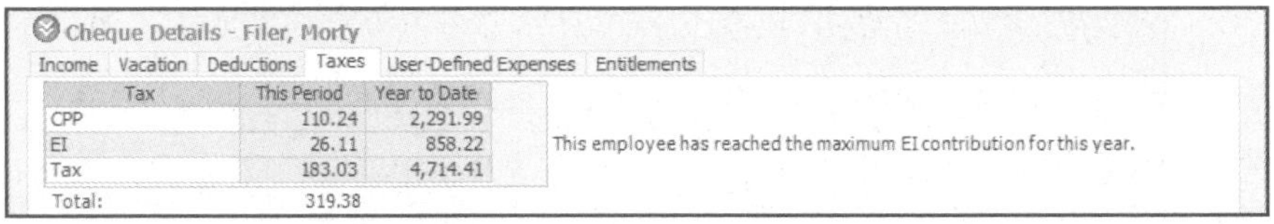

Cheque Details - Filer, Morty

Income | Vacation | Deductions | Taxes | User-Defined Expenses | Entitlements

Tax	This Period	Year to Date
CPP	110.24	2,291.99
EI	26.11	858.22
Tax	183.03	4,714.41
Total:	319.38	

This employee has reached the maximum EI contribution for this year.

Taxes cannot be edited in the Payroll Run Journal. To change tax amounts you must use the Payroll Journal and choose to calculate taxes manually.

Click the **User-Defined Expenses tab**:

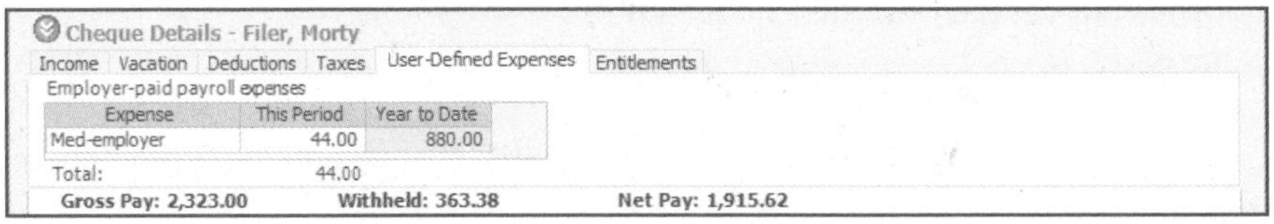

Cheque Details - Filer, Morty

Income | Vacation | Deductions | Taxes | User-Defined Expenses | Entitlements

Employer-paid payroll expenses

Expense	This Period	Year to Date
Med-employer	44.00	880.00
Total:	44.00	

Gross Pay: 2,323.00 Withheld: 363.38 Net Pay: 1,915.62

The employer's expense for the medical premium is included here and can be edited if required. Entitlements can also be edited — for Filer, we need to change the number of hours worked on the Entitlements screen and enter the sick leave day he took.

Click the **Entitlements tab**:

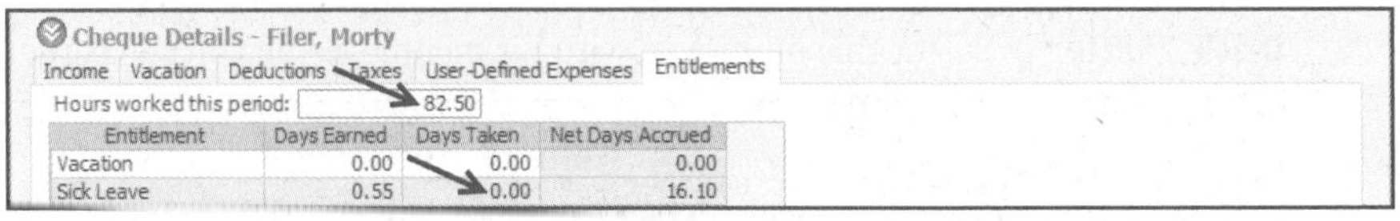

Cheque Details - Filer, Morty

Income | Vacation | Deductions | Taxes | User-Defined Expenses | Entitlements

Hours worked this period: 82.50

Entitlement	Days Earned	Days Taken	Net Days Accrued
Vacation	0.00	0.00	0.00
Sick Leave	0.55	0.00	16.10

Once again, the fields are the same as those in the Payroll Journal Entitlements tab screen (refer to page 273).

NOTES
Remember that the entry for Days Earned reflects only the amount earned for this pay period based on the number of hours worked in this pay period.

Click **82.5** and **type** 75 (the number of hours in the period).

Click **0.00** in the Days Taken field for Sick Leave. **Type** 1

Click **Handie** to select him and prepare for entering his additional details.

As soon as you select another employee, you will open a warning about partial repayments of advances:

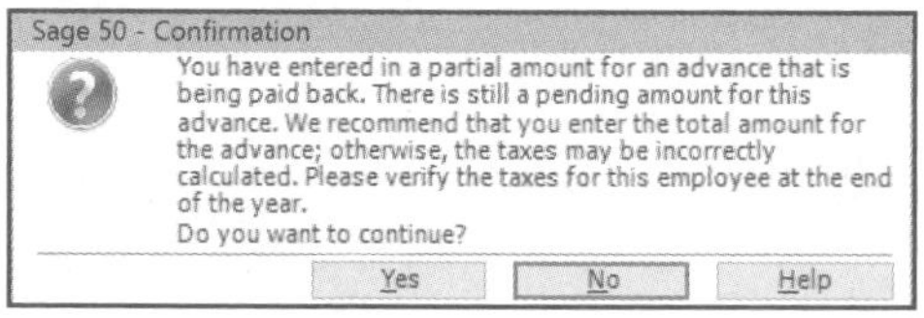

The warning advises that the entire amount of an advance should be repaid at one time to facilitate the correct calculation of taxes.

Click **Yes** to continue. The Entitlements tab screen details open for Handie.

We need to update the number of regular and overtime hours for Handie. We can change this in the upper summary pane. Handie is already selected.

Press tab to highlight his Regular Hours in the summary pane. **Type** 75

Press tab to select the Overtime 1 Hours entry for Handie.

Type 2 to enter the Overtime hours. **Press** tab to update all amounts.

Type 75 as the number of hours worked in the Entitlements tab screen.

Nerture's pay requires only a change in the number of hours.

Click **Nerture** in the summary pane. **Press** tab and **type** 75

Type 75 as the number of hours worked in the Entitlements tab screen

For Tiste, we need change the number of hours, increase the number of lessons and add the loan. We can access all these fields in the Cheque Details pane.

Click **Tiste**. **Click** the **Income tab** to open the Cheque Details pane.

Click **44.00** in the Regular Hours field. **Type** 40

Click **22.00** in the Pieces column for Lessons. **Type** 24

Click **0.00 beside Loans** in the column for This Period.

Type 100 **Press** tab to update all amounts.

Click **Booker** to prepare for entering the additional details for her.

Loans do not generate the warning that advances do.

The Income tab should still be open. The screenshot on page 286 has the income details for Booker.

Booker is a salaried employee who also teaches music lessons after school. The default entry from the ledger record is correct. Her regular salary is also entered as a default, but both amounts can be edited if necessary in the Cheque Details pane. The salary amount can be edited in the summary pane as well.

We need to add her tuition fees benefit and enter one day of sick leave.

Click **0.00** in the column for Tuition Fees This Period.

Type 140 **Press** tab to update all amounts.

Click the **Entitlements tab**. **Click** the **Days Taken field beside Sick Leave**.

Type 1 **Press** tab to update the form, reducing the number of Net Days Accrued to 18.07.

NOTES

Each time you enter a partial repayment for an advance, Sage 50 will provide this warning. Click Yes.

Taxes for partial repayments of advances may not add up to the same amount as those for the total advance because different tax brackets may apply.

We chose the partial repayment method to include the various warning and confirmation messages in Sage 50.

NOTES

You do not need to change the entitlement hours for Tiste. They do not apply because Tiste does not receive these entitlements.

No changes are required for Teicher or Teutor's salaried paycheques, so the transaction is complete and ready to review:

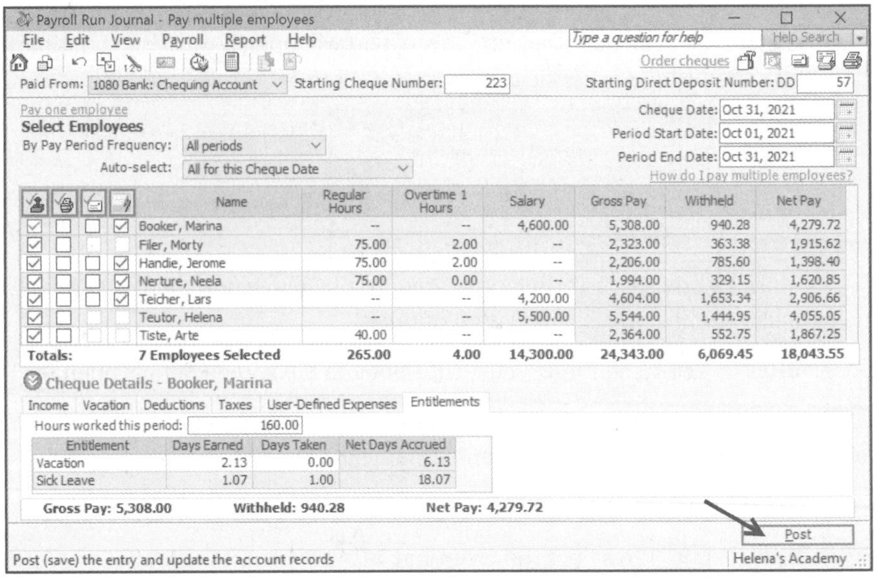

Choose the **Report menu** and **click Display Payroll Journal Entry** to review the seven journal entries, one for each employee in the payroll run.

Close the **display** when finished.

You can print paycheques from the Payroll Run Journal, but you cannot preview them. You can modify the reports and forms settings from the journal tool button.

Turn on your **printer**.

Choose the **Report menu** and **click Print Payroll Cheque Run Summary** to provide a printed record of the payroll run transactions paid by cheque or **click Print Direct Deposit Stub Summary** to provide a printed record of the payroll run transactions paid by direct deposit. You cannot display these summaries.

Click **Post** [Post] to save the transaction. **Click Yes** to bypass the warning about payroll formula dates.

Before posting, Sage 50 warns about pay period dates — some employees are paid monthly and some bi-monthly. Therefore the pay period is not correct for all employees:

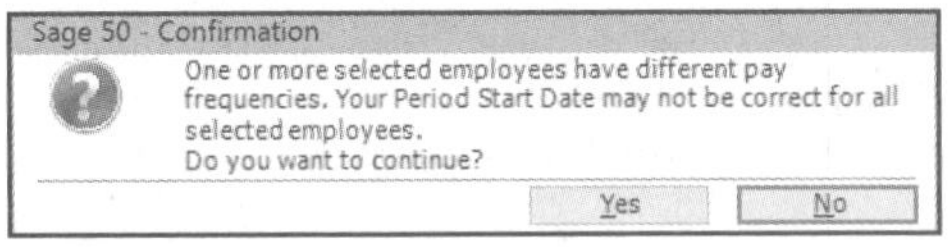

Click **Yes** to continue.

Employees should be selected **By Pay Period Frequency** from the drop-down list and paid in separate payroll cheque runs:

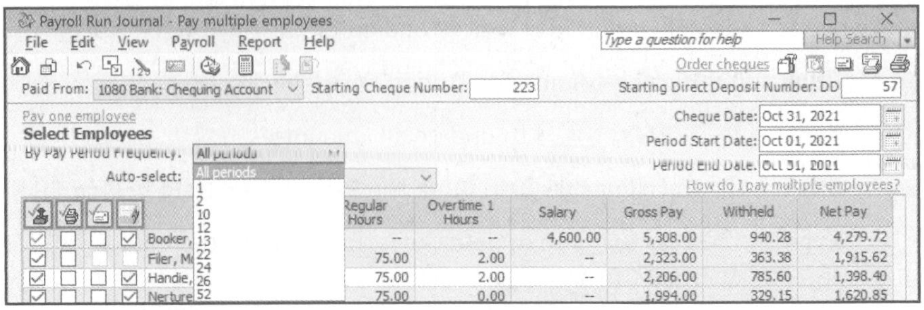

NOTES

To print from the Payroll Run Journal, click the Print check box in the second column beside the employee's name. Then click the Print tool, press ctrl + P or choose the File menu and click Print Payroll Cheques.

To print direct deposit stubs, choose the File menu and click Print Direct Deposit Stubs.

Or, you can use the respective tool buttons.

You will print the requested forms for all employees selected for printing.

The Post button in the Payroll Run Journal does not include the Print & Post option that is available in the Payroll Journal.

This time, we will accept and post the single transaction.

The confirmation message advises that seven journal entries were posted. The Payroll Run Journal remains open with the direct deposit and cheque numbers updated after the payroll run cheques and direct deposits. All employees are still selected with pay amounts because of the Auto-Select entry.

Choose **Not Yet Paid On This Cheque Date** from the Auto-Select list and update the form:

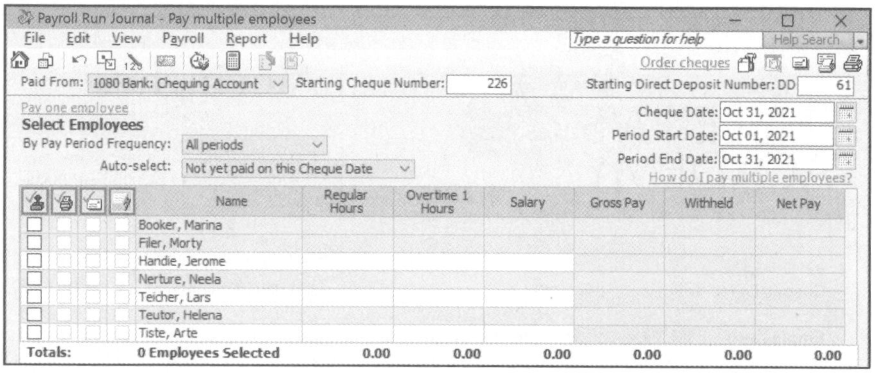

Now, no employees are selected because they have all been paid. There are no ✓s in the Post column. The Starting Cheque and Direct Deposit numbers have been updated.

Close the **Journal** to return to the Home window.

Enter the following **source documents** for October 31 and November 15.

11

Bank Debit Memo #277581 **Dated Oct. 31/21**

From Scholar Heights Bank, $4 255 was withdrawn from chequing account for the following pre-authorized transactions:

Bank charges	$ 55
Interest on bank loan	320
Reduction of principal on bank loan	880
Interest on mortgage	2 500
Reduction of principal on mortgage	500

Store as a recurring monthly entry.

12

Bank Credit Memo #467116 **Dated Oct. 31/21**

From Scholar Heights Bank, $1 800 interest on investments and bank account was deposited to chequing account. Store as a recurring monthly entry.

13

Memo #4 **Dated Oct. 31/21**

Complete end-of-month adjusting entries for the following:

Office supplies used	$180
Art supplies used	735
Textbooks damaged	795
Prepaid property taxes	900

You can store this as a recurring monthly entry if you want.

SESSION DATE – NOVEMBER 15, 2021

14

Cash Sales Invoice #1037 **Dated Nov. 1/21**

To parents of students, $3 200 total monthly fees for after-school programs, and $2 280 total monthly fees for individual music lessons. Deposited $5 480 to chequing account.

15 **Cash Purchase Invoice #GL-38827-B** **Dated Nov. 2/21**

To Global Liability Inc., $1 800 for monthly insurance premium as stated on policy #GL-38827. Paid by cheque #226. Recall stored entry.

16 **Cash Purchase Invoice #ES-1446** **Dated Nov. 15/21**

From Engine Services (use Quick Add), $440 including taxes for gasoline, tire repairs, oil change and lubrication on vehicle. Invoice total paid in full with cheque #227.

17

NOTES

This pay period included 11 days at 7.5 hours each for hourly employees, so the default entries of 82.5 hours and 44 for Tiste are correct.

NOTES

Type −50 in the Advances This Period field for Filer and −25 in the Loans This Period field for Tiste to recover these amounts.

The warning about the partial repayment of Filer's advance amount will open again.

HELENA'S ACADEMY

Aim higher!

Employee Time Summary Sheet
Business No.: 189 245 053 RP 0001

#21
Cheque Date: November 15, 2021

First day of pay period: November 1, 2021
Last day of pay period: November 15, 2021

Employee	M. Filer	J. Handie	N. Nerture	A. Tiste	H. Teutor	M. Booker	L. Teicher
SIN	374 588 127	813 402 302	129 495 768	513 288 191	699 344 578	277 639 118	403 401 599
Nov 1-5	37.5	39.5	37.5	20			
Nov 8-12	37.5	39.5	37.5	20			
Nov 15	7.5	7.5	7.5	4			

Reg. hrs	82.5	82.5	82.5	44			
Overtime	--	4	--	--			
Lessons	--	--	--	22			
Tuition	145.00	--	--	--			
Loan	--	--	--	-25.00			
Advance	-50.00	--	--	--			
Sick leave	--	--	1	--			
Chq/DD #	Chq 228	DD61	DD62	Chq 229			

Payroll Prepared by: Morty Filer Nov 15/21

When you first open the Payroll Run Journal for the November 15 pay period, the four hourly paid employees will be selected:

Pay one employee
Select Employees
By Pay Period Frequency: All periods
Auto-select: Not yet paid on this Cheque Date

Cheque Date: Nov 15, 2021
Period Start Date: Nov 01, 2021
Period End Date: Nov 15, 2021
How do I pay multiple employees?

				Name	Regular Hours	Overtime 1 Hours	Salary	Gross Pay	Withheld	Net Pay
☐				Booker, Marina						
☑	☐			Filer, Morty	82.50	0.00	--	2,354.00	330.54	1,979.46
☑	☐	☐	☑	Handie, Jerome	82.50	0.00	--	2,332.00	799.13	1,510.87
☑	☐	☐	☑	Nerture, Neela	82.50	0.00	--	2,189.00	398.30	1,746.70
☐				Teicher, Lars						
☐				Teutor, Helena						
☑	☐			Tiste, Arte	44.00	--	--	2,464.00	576.57	1,843.43
Totals:				**4 Employees Selected**	**291.50**	**0.00**	**0.00**	**9,339.00**	**2,104.54**	**7,080.46**

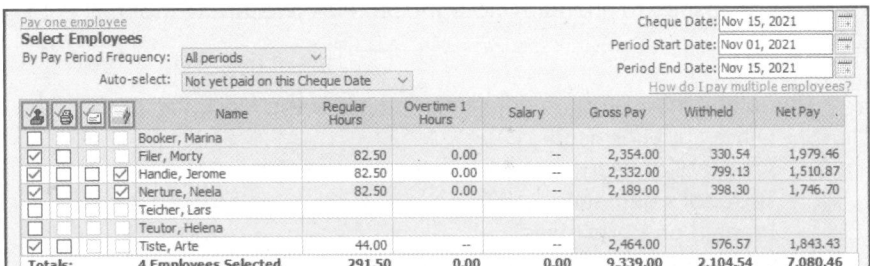

The salaried employees are not due to be paid until November 30 and are not selected.

Complete the **November 15 payroll run** for the four employees.

Advance the **session date** to **November 30**; **make** a **backup**. **Continue** entering **transactions** up to the payroll adjustment for December 17.

18 **Cash Purchase Invoice #ESS-5568** **Dated Nov. 17/21**

From Energy Supply Services, $810 including taxes for heat and hydro on equal monthly billing plan. Recall the stored entry. Paid by cheque #230.

19

Memo #5 **Dated Nov. 17/21**

Make payroll remittances for the pay period ending October 31.

- Receiver General for Canada: CPP, EI and income tax
- Aspen Life Financial: Medical premiums from employee and employer
- Alberta Workers' Compensation Board: WCB
- Rocky Mountain Trust: RRSP
- Maintenance Enforcement Program: Family support payments

Issue cheques #231 to #235. (Read margin Notes and Warning.)

20

Cash Purchase #TA-193245 **Dated Nov. 20/21**

From Telus Alberta, $245 including all taxes for one month of telephone services. Invoice total paid in full with cheque #236.

21

HELENA'S ACADEMY

Aim higher!

Employee Time Summary Sheet
Business No.: 189 245 053 RP 0001

#22
Cheque Date: November 30, 2021

*First day of pay period: November 1, 2021
**First day of pay period: November 16, 2021
Last day of pay period: November 30, 2021

Employee SIN	M. Filer 374 588 127	J. Handie 813 402 302	N. Nerture 129 495 768	A. Tiste 513 288 191	H. Teutor 699 344 578	M. Booker 277 639 118	L. Teicher 403 401 599
Nov 1-5	pd	pd	pd	pd	→	→	→
Nov 8-12	pd	pd	pd	pd	→	→	→
Nov 15-19	30.0	30.0	32.5	16	→	→	→
Nov 22-26	37.5	39.5	39.5	20	→	→	→
Nov 29-30	15.0	15.0	17.0	8	→	→	→
Reg. hrs	82.5	82.5	82.5	44	160	160	160
Overtime	--	2	6	--	--	--	--
Lessons	--	--	--	22	--	16	12
Tuition	145.00	--	--	--	--	140.00	--
Advance	-50.00	--	--	--	--	--	--
Loan	--	--	--	-25.00	--	--	--
Sick leave	--	--	1	--	--	--	--
Chq/DD #	Chq 237	DD63	DD64	Chq 238	Chq 239	DD65	DD66

Payroll Prepared by: Morty Filer Nov 30/21
*Monthly pay cycle **Bi-monthly pay cycle

22

Bank Debit Memo #422344 **Dated Nov. 30/21**

From Scholar Heights Bank, $4 255 was withdrawn from chequing account for the following pre-authorized transactions. Recall the stored entry.

Bank charges	$ 55
Interest on bank loan	320
Reduction of principal on bank loan	880
Interest on mortgage	2 500
Reduction of principal on mortgage	500

23

Memo #6 **Dated Nov. 30/21**

Complete end-of-month adjusting entries for the following:

Office supplies used	$175
Art supplies used	620
Textbooks damaged	505
Prepaid property taxes	900

WARNING!

If any employees were paid on November 1, you must enter October 31 as the end of the remitting period.

NOTES

The default date entry for the End Of Remitting Period is November 1, one month past the previous October 1 remittance. If you enter October 31 instead, a message opens about the date preceding the current period, which may affect prior period earnings (because October 31 is in the previous month). You can click Yes to confirm that this is correct or you can accept November 1 as the remittance period ending date.

NOTES

Type –50 in the Advances This Period field for Filer and –25 in the Loans This Period field for Tiste to recover these amounts.

The November 30 pay period includes 11 days for hourly paid employees.

Select 24 as the Pay Period Frequency to complete the paycheque run for the four hourly employees. Post this entry and then select 12 as the Frequency to complete the paycheque run for the remaining three salaried employees. By this method, the starting dates will be adjusted correctly and Sage will not display the warning about different pay frequencies.

NOTES

Remember that when you store adjusting entries, you must edit the source and amounts when you recall the transaction.

24 **Bank Credit Memo #64567** **Dated Nov. 30/21**

From Scholar Heights Bank, $1 800 interest on investments and bank account was deposited to chequing account. Recall the stored entry.

SESSION DATE – DECEMBER 15, 2021

> **NOTES**
> The CRA usually posts the new TD1 claim amounts on its Web site at the beginning of December for the following year, but payroll tax tables may be revised every six months. Sage includes updated tax rates in the regular updates that an active business requires. The December program update also includes a wizard for updating TD1 amounts.

When you approach the end of a calendar year, the year-end advisor message opens, similar to the year-end advisor messages we saw earlier.

The message includes information about renewing the payroll plan (to ensure tax rates in your program are up to date) and preparing for tax updates:

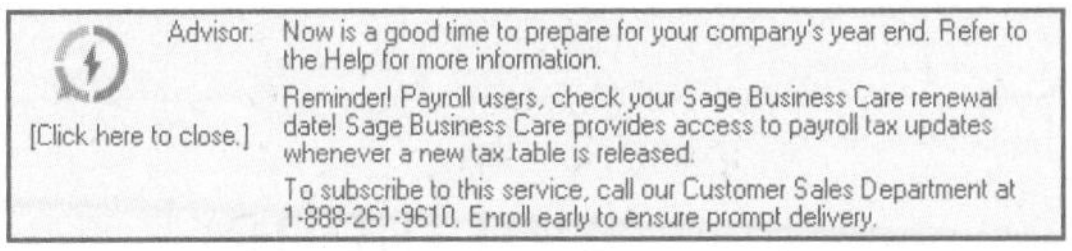

Advisor:
[Click here to close.]
Now is a good time to prepare for your company's year end. Refer to the Help for more information.
Reminder! Payroll users, check your Sage Business Care renewal date! Sage Business Care provides access to payroll tax updates whenever a new tax table is released.
To subscribe to this service, call our Customer Sales Department at 1-888-261-9610. Enroll early to ensure prompt delivery.

Read and then **close** the **Advisor message**. An active business should install program updates when they are available to keep its TD1 and payroll tax rates up to date.

25 **Cash Sales Invoice #1038** **Dated Dec. 1/21**

To parents of students, $2 400 total monthly fees for after-school programs, and $1 580 total monthly fees for individual music lessons. Deposited $3 980 to chequing account.

26 **Cash Purchase Invoice #GL-38827-C** **Dated Dec. 2/21**

To Global Liability Inc., $1 800 for monthly insurance premium as stated on policy #GL-38827. Paid by cheque #240. Recall the stored entry.

> **NOTES**
> Type –50 in the Advances This Period field for Filer and –25 in the Loans This Period for Tiste to recover these amounts.
> The December 15 pay period includes 11 days for hourly paid employees.

27

HELENA'S ACADEMY

Aim higher!

Employee Time Summary Sheet
Business No.: 189 245 053 RP 0001

#23
Cheque Date: December 15, 2021

First day of pay period: December 1, 2021
Last day of pay period: December 15, 2021

Employee	M. Filer	J. Handie	N. Nerture	A. Tiste	H. Teutor	M. Booker	L. Teicher
SIN	374 588 127	813 402 302	129 495 768	513 288 191	699 344 578	277 639 118	403 401 599
Dec 1-3	22.5	23.5	23.5	12			
Dec 6-10	37.5	38.5	40.5	20			
Dec 13-15	22.5	22.5	23.5	12			

Reg. hrs	82.5	82.5	82.5	44			
Overtime	--	2	5	--			
Lessons	--	--	--	22			
Tuition	145.00	--	--	--			
Loan	--	--	--	-25.00			
Advance	-50.00	--	--	--			
Sick leave	--	--	--	--			
Chq/DD #	Chq 241	DD67	DD68	Chq 242			

Payroll Prepared by: Morty Filer Dec 15/21

> **NOTES**
> Sage 50 no longer gives the warning about advances for Filer because the full balance is being repaid.

SESSION DATE – DECEMBER 31, 2021

28 **Memo #7** **Dated Dec. 17/21**

Make payroll remittances for the pay period ending November 30.
- Receiver General for Canada: CPP, EI and income tax
- Aspen Life Financial: Medical premiums from employee and employer
- Alberta Workers' Compensation Board: WCB
- Rocky Mountain Trust: RRSP
- Maintenance Enforcement Program: Family support payments

Issue cheques #243 to #247.

Adjusting a Payroll Cheque Run Entry

We can adjust a Payroll Run Journal entry from the Payroll Journal, just as we edited the transaction for Filer. Tiste has handed in his resignation and should repay the remainder of his loan. As described in Memo #8, Tiste should also receive his final vacation pay.

✓ 29

HELENA'S ACADEMY

Aim higher!

MEMO #8

From the desk of Morty Filer
Dated: Dec. 17, 2021

RE: Payroll Adjustment required for Arte Tiste and vacation pay

Adjust the Dec. 15 paycheque for Tiste —
Tiste is leaving the Academy and should receive his total accrued vacation pay.
In addition, he should have the full loan amount recovered from his paycheque.
The original cheque #242 has been voided. Issue cheque #248 and increase the loan recovered to $50.
Include the vacation pay owing to him in the revised paycheque.

Paycheque (cheque #248) released *Dec 17/21 Morty Filer*

Click the **Paycheques icon**.

Click the **Adjust Paycheque tool** or **press** ctrl + **A**.

Click **OK** to access the list of posted payroll entries. All the entries from both payroll journals are included.

Double-click the **Dec. 15 entry for Tiste**.

Click the **Advisor icon** to close the warning about recalculating taxes.

The paycheque we entered for Tiste opens:

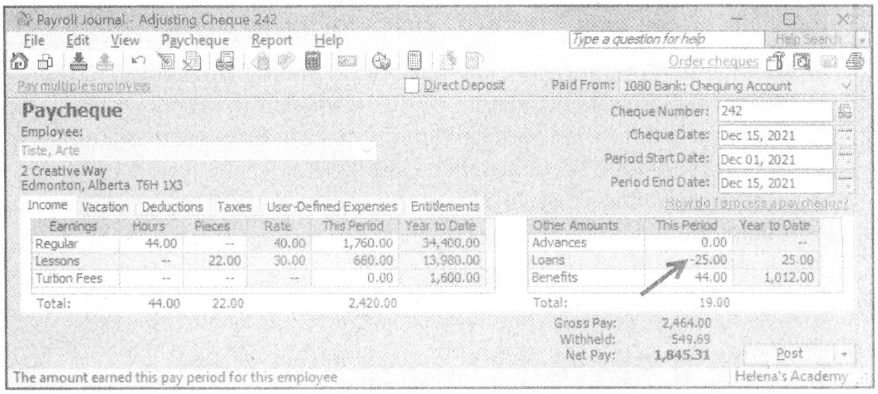

Click **-25** in the **This Period field for Loans** to select the current entry.

Type `-50` **Press** `tab` to enter the change and update the gross pay. The Year To Date amount for Loans is reduced to zero.

Click the **Vacation tab**.

Amounts are entered in the Vacation Earned and Vacation Owed fields:

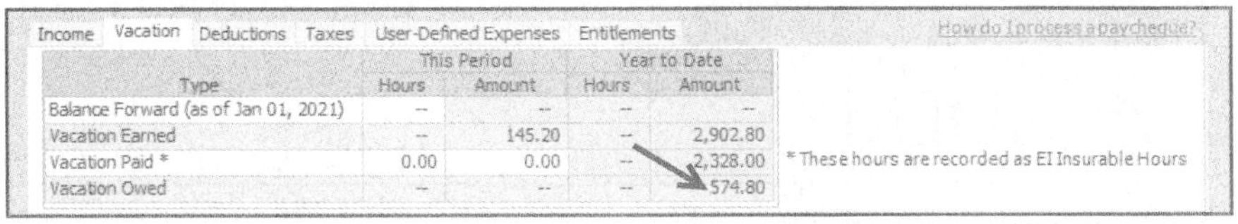

The vacation owed amount, $574.80, includes the amount for this paycheque (Vacation Earned) and amounts withheld since vacation was last paid.

Click the **Vacation Paid Amount field** and **type** `574.80`

Press `tab` and **click** the **Vacation tab** again.

Click the **Recalculate Taxes tool** on the Payroll Journal tool bar or **choose** the **Paycheque menu** and **click Recalculate Taxes**:

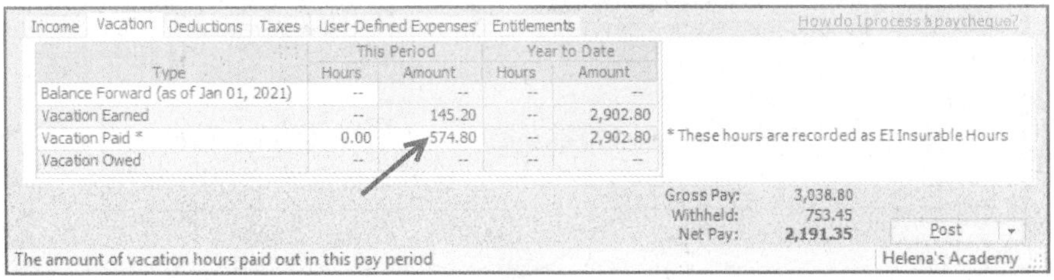

Review the Payroll Journal **entry**. **Close** the **display** when you have finished. **Make corrections** if necessary.

Click `Post` to save the adjustment.

Click **Yes** to bypass the message about hours and **click Yes** again to **accept** the next cheque number (#248).

Close the **Payroll Journal**. **Enter** the **next group of transactions**.

30

Cash Purchase Invoice #ESS-7889 **Dated Dec. 17/21**

From Energy Supply Services, $810 including taxes for heat and hydro on equal monthly billing plan. Recall the stored entry. Paid by cheque #249.

31

Cash Purchase #TA-266778 **Dated Dec. 20/21**

From Telus Alberta, $215 including all taxes for one month of telephone services. Invoice total paid in full with cheque #250.

32

Employee Time Summary Sheet #24 **Dated Dec. 31/21**

For the pay periods December 16 to December 31 and December 1 to December 31, 2021

Name of Employee	Regular Hours	Overtime Hours	Lessons	Tuition	Advance (Repaid)	Loan (Repaid)	Sick Days	Direct Deposit
Filer, Morty	90.0	–	–	$145.00	–	–	–	No
Handie, Jerome	90.0	4	–	–	–	–	–	Yes
Nerture, Neela	90.0	–	–	–	–	–	1	Yes
Booker, Marina	160	–	10	$140.00	–	–	–	Yes
Teicher, Lars	160	–	8	–		$200	–	Yes
Teutor, Helena	160	–	–	–	–	–	–	No

a. Using Employee Time Summary Sheet #24 and the Employee Information Sheet, complete payroll for all employees. Hourly paid employees are paid for their regular hours during the Christmas holiday break.

b. Issue $200 loan to Teicher and recover $50 from each of the next four paycheques.

c. Issue cheques #251 and #252 and DD slips #69, #70, #71 and #72.

33

Bank Credit Memo #69886 **Dated Dec. 31/21**

From Scholar Heights Bank, $1 800 interest on investments and bank account was deposited to chequing account. Recall the stored entry.

34

Bank Debit Memo #532281 **Dated Dec. 31/21**

From Scholar Heights Bank, $4 265 was withdrawn from chequing account for the following pre-authorized transactions. Recall the stored entry and edit the bank charges amount. Store the revised entry.

Bank charges	$ 65
Interest on bank loan	320
Reduction of principal on bank loan	880
Interest on mortgage	2 500
Reduction of principal on mortgage	500

35

Memo #9 **Dated Dec. 31/21**

Complete end-of-month adjusting entries for the following:

Office supplies used	$230
Art supplies used	650
Textbooks damaged	550
Prepaid property taxes	900

36

Cash Sales Invoice #1039 **Dated Dec. 31/21**

Received $300 000 payment for school fees for the next semester. Total cash deposited to bank account.

Entering Paycheques in a Future Year

Sometimes you will need to prepare payroll transactions in advance, such as when the payroll preparation date falls during a holiday period. When that date also falls in a future calendar year, you need to separate the year-to-date amounts for the two years for income tax reporting purposes. Sage 50 allows you to enter payroll entries for a later year and tracks these amounts separately. Current year reports are not affected.

NOTES

Holidays are counted as regular days worked, so the pay period for hourly paid employees is 12 days. Change the number of regular and entitlement hours to 90 for the hourly employees.

Remember to remove Tiste from the list of employees paid in this pay period.

Select 24 as the Pay Period Frequency to complete the paycheque run for the hourly employees. Post this entry and then select 12 as the Frequency to complete the paycheque run for the remaining three salaried employees.

NOTES

Enter the fees payment as revenue.

PRO VERSION

This feature is not available in the Pro version. Instead, you can start a new calendar year (refer to page 309). Then complete the payroll run.

PRO VERSION
To complete this payroll entry in the Pro version, you must first start the new calendar year (advance the session date to January 1, 2022).

NOTES
The option to post transactions to the next fiscal or calendar year applies only to Payroll and General Journal entries.

WARNING!
You must add the year for these pay dates. If you do not, January 2021 will be the default entries and these dates are not allowed – they are earlier than October 1, 2021, the Earliest Transaction Date allowed in the Company Settings (refer to the screenshot on this page).

NOTES
This pay cycle includes 75 hours, 10 days at 7.5 hours per day.

✓ 37

Employee Time Summary Sheet #25 — Dated Jan. 15/22

For the pay period January 1 to January 15, 2022

Name of Employee	Regular Hours	Overtime Hours	Lessons	Tuition	Advance (Repaid)	Loan (Repaid)	Sick Days	Direct Deposit
Filer, Morty	75.0	–	–	$145	–	–	–	No
Handie, Jerome	75.0	–	–	–	–	–	–	Yes
Nerture, Neela	75.0	–	–	–	–	–	–	Yes

a. Using Employee Time Summary Sheet #25 and the Employee Information Sheet, complete payroll for hourly paid employees. (If required, adjustments for overtime hours worked will be made on the following paycheque.)
b. Issue cheque #253 and Direct Deposit (DD) slips #73 and #74.

Permission to complete these entries is controlled from the Company Settings:

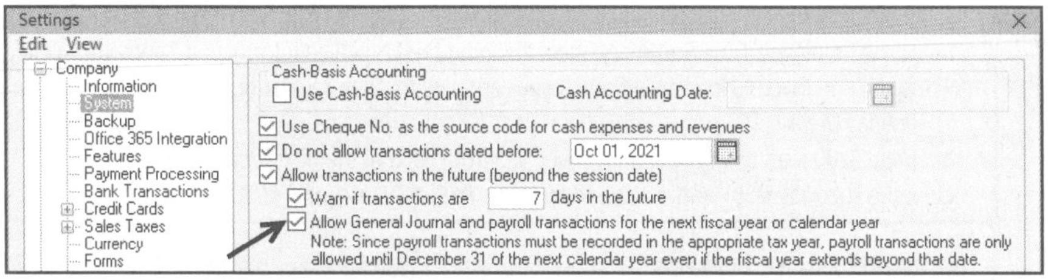

Because the beginning of term is a very busy period, Filer may not have time to complete the first payroll entry in January. He can create these cheques in December.

Open the **Payroll Run Journal**. **Enter Jan 1, 2022** as the **Period Start Date**, and **Jan 15, 2022** as the **Period End** and **Cheque Dates**. The journal is revised:

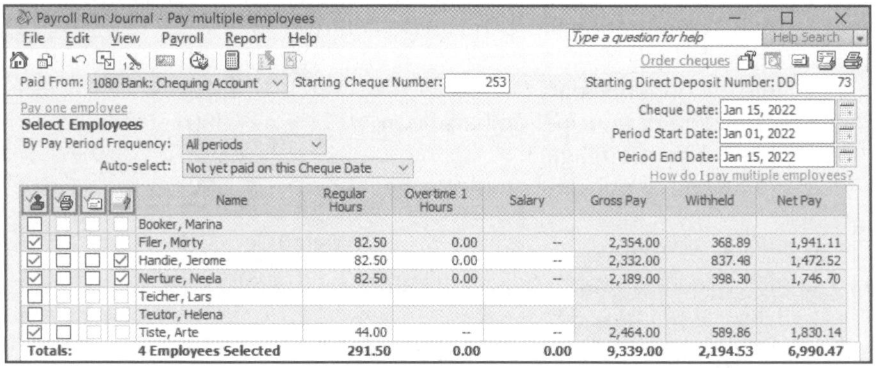

All hourly paid employees are selected. Tiste should not be paid — he has resigned.

Click the **Post column** for **Tiste** so that he will not be paid in January.

Click **Filer's name** and **type** 145 as his tuition amount for this period.

Enter 75 as the number of Regular and Entitlement hours for all employees to complete the entry.

Review your **entry** and **make corrections** if needed.

Click **Post** for another confirmation warning:

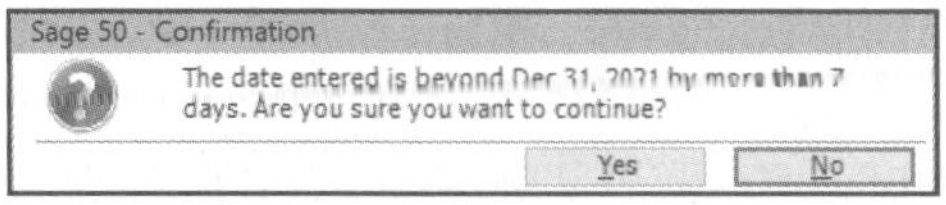

Our Company System Settings allow future dates but warn if these are more than seven days in the future (refer to the screenshot above).

Click **Yes** to continue.

The next message warns about using a date in a future calendar year:

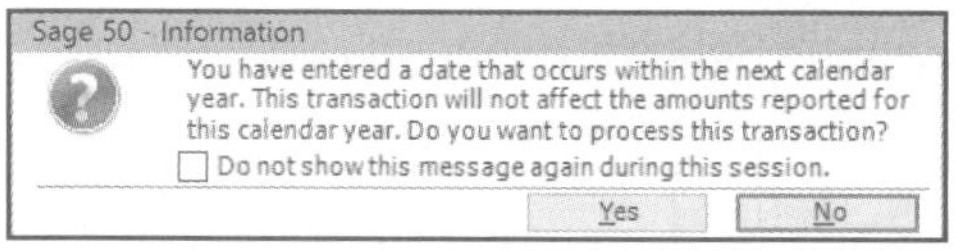

Read the message carefully — it advises that prior year amounts (those for 2021) will not be affected by this entry.

Click **Yes** to continue and save the payroll entry. **Close** the **journal**.

Terminating an Employee

When an employee leaves the company, his or her ledger record should be updated with the date of termination and the reason for leaving. Then a record of employment can be issued that indicates the number of hours worked and the total income. This form is used to determine eligibility for Employment Insurance.

Tiste will be leaving work to care for his brother, so he has received his last paycheque and we should modify his record. We will work from the Employees window so that we can also print reports.

NOTES
From the Report Centre, you can print only the reports that you can display. For reports that are only printed, you must start from the Employees window or from the Reports menu.

✓ 38 **Memo #10** **Dated Dec. 31/21**

Prepare a Record of Employment and T4 slip for Tiste.

Click the **Employees icon** 

to open the Employees window.

Double-click **Tiste, Arte** to open his ledger record at the Personal tab screen:

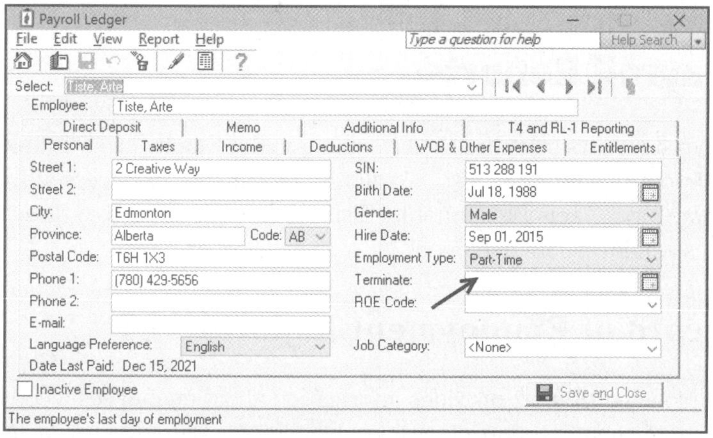

We need to enter the Terminate date and the ROE (Record of Employment) Code.

NOTES
You can also open the ledger record for Tiste by clicking his name in the Home window Employees pane list. Then, you can view reports from the Home window Reports menu.

Click the **Terminate field**. **Type** `12 15`

Click the **ROE Code list arrow** to access the codes available:

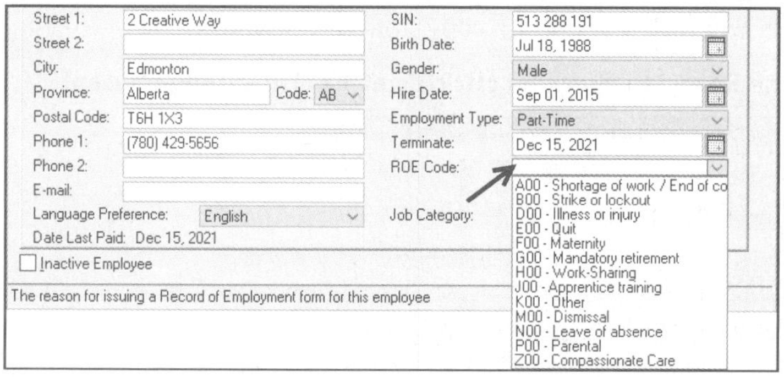

PRO VERSION
You need to add the year (2021) to the termination date because you have started a new year.

Click **Z00 - Compassionate Care.**

Click the **Save tool** to open the following confirmation message:

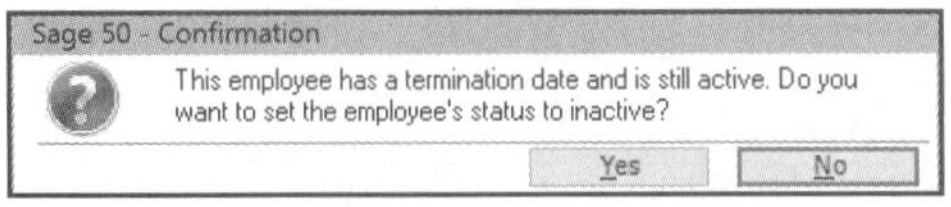

NOTES
Data for the inactive employees can still be included in any reports by choosing to include inactive employees.

Normally, employee status is changed to inactive when they have left the company so the employee's name will not appear in employee lists for journals or reports.

Click **Yes** to change Tiste's status to inactive.

Click the **T4 and RL-1 Reporting tab**:

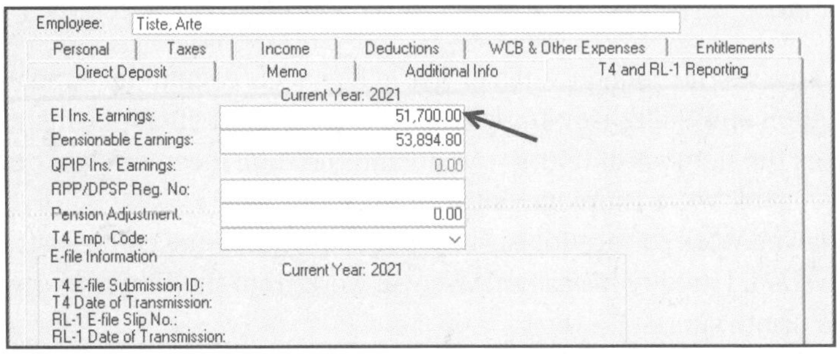

The year-to-date insurable earnings amount is tracked in the Employee Ledger on the T4 and RL-1 Reporting tab screen. This amount is needed for the ROE report.

Close the **ledger record.**

We will now be able to print a Record of Employment for Tiste. We will print this report from the Employees window.

Printing Payroll Reports

You can access payroll reports from the Reports menu in the Employees window and from the Home window. In addition, most payroll reports can also be accessed from the Report Centre. Some payroll reports cannot be displayed; they are printed directly.

The Employees window should be open.

NOTES
You cannot access the Record of Employment from the Report Centre.
Submitting ROE reports to Service Canada electronically from Sage 50 is covered in Appendix K.
Service Canada is the branch of the federal government that deals with Employment Insurance and pensions.

Printing Record of Employment Reports

The Record of Employment Report provides information about employees who have terminated their employment to determine their eligibility for Employment Insurance benefits. The report includes the length of employment, earnings, total number of hours worked and the reason (code) for termination. You can print the report only for employees who have been terminated, and you must have the correct preprinted forms.

Reports are remitted directly to Service Canada. Employees may view their ROE on the Service Canada Web site or request a copy from the employer.

Choose the **Reports menu**, and **click** **Print Record Of Employment**:

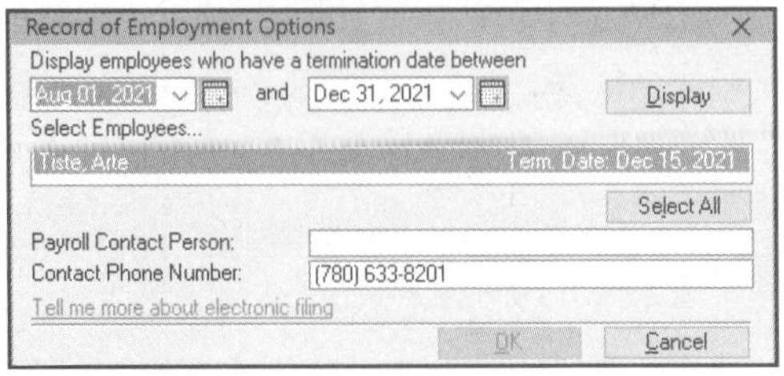

NOTES
The Record Of Employment Options screen includes a link to information about electronic filing. To use the link, you must be connected to the Internet.

From the Home window, choose the Reports menu, then choose Payroll and click Print Record Of Employment.

Tiste is the only employee listed in this option window because he is the only one with a termination date, and he is already selected. The date range includes the fiscal year to date. If you have data for a different time period, you can change these dates and then click Display to update the list of employees. For this report, you need to provide the name and telephone number to contact about the company payroll.

If there are more employees with termination dates, you can click Select All to create reports for all the listed employees.

Click the **Payroll Contact Person field**. **Type** `Morty Filer`

Click **OK** to continue:

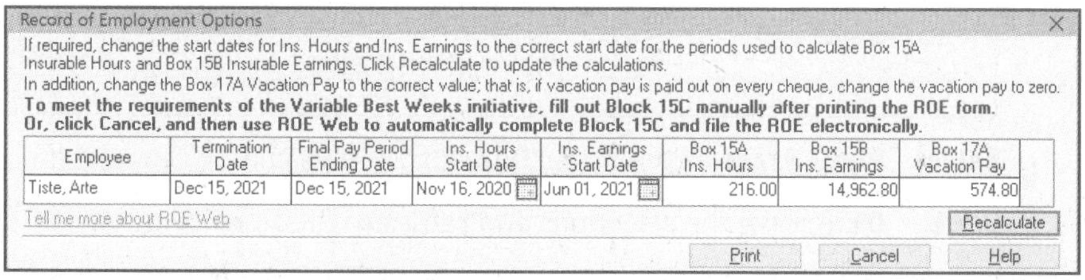

You now have the summary details for the selected employee. They include only the amounts entered in the payroll journals; they do not include the year-to-date opening balance amounts. You can edit the fields in this window. If you have payroll data for a longer period, you can enter those dates and recalculate the amounts. However, only the three months of payroll data we entered in Sage 50 are tracked in this form, so we must update the details.

According to the ledger record (page 300), Tiste has $51 700 in EI insurable earnings this year (the maximum amount for 2018). He has also worked additional hours before October. His total number of hours is 1 040 (52 weeks x 20 hours per week). And finally, he has received all his vacation pay, so this amount should be changed to zero. You can also edit the start dates for EI insurable hours and earnings.

Enter **Jan 1** in the Ins. Hours Start Date field and also in the Ins. Earnings Start Date field.

Click **216.00** in the Box 15A Ins. Hours field.

Type `1040`

Press *tab* to select the Ins. Earnings amount.

Type `51700`

Press *tab* to select the Vacation Pay amount.

Press *del*. Check your entries.

Click **Print**. Sage 50 provides an additional warning:

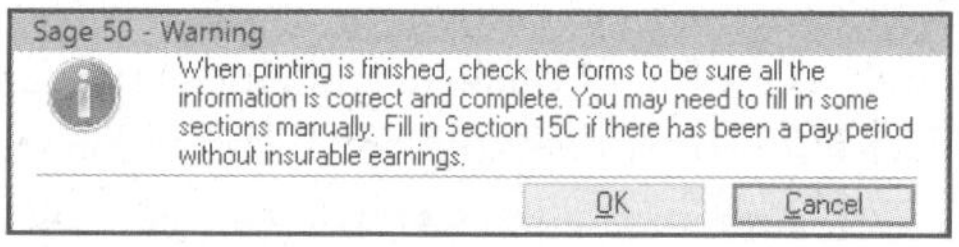

You may need to add missing details on the form manually if the final printed form is not complete.

Click **OK** to begin printing. **Close** the **Employees window**.

NOTES

You cannot view the employee's ledger record while the Record of Employment report or its options window is open.

NOTES

Because our tax tables apply to 2018, the 2018 maximum amounts for EI Insurable Earnings and Pensionable Earnings will apply. These are $51 700 and $55 900, respectively.

Once an employee earns the maximum amounts, no further pay amounts are added and no further EI or CPP (respectively) will be deducted.

PRO VERSION

pro

You need to add the year 2021 to the termination date because you have started a new year.

NOTES

For practice, you can print the ROE on plain paper, but you will not have any labels for the details on the report.

NOTES

When you submit the forms electronically, you have a chance to review and edit all the details before submitting.

Printing T4s

Before printing T4s, you should check your printer and forms selections.

Choose the **Setup menu**, then **choose Reports & Forms** and **click Government Forms** and **click Federal Payroll** to display the options:

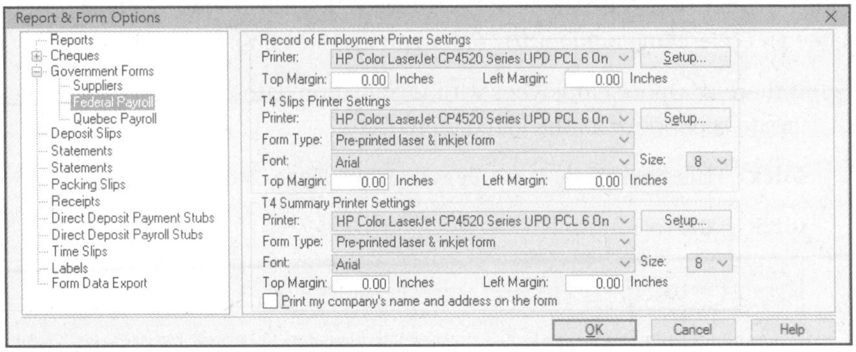

Select **Plain Paper** as the Form Type for T4 Slips and T4 Summary.

Click **OK** to save the selections and return to the Home window.

T4 slips and Relevé 1 slips are also not available for display, but they can be printed. Relevé 1 slips are used only in Quebec, and the Print Relevé 1 Slips Report Options screen will list only employees for whom Quebec is the province of taxation. Relevé 1 options are similar to those for T4 slips. You can print T4 slips, which are compulsory for employees filing income tax returns, using either the tax statement forms from the Canada Revenue Agency (CRA) or plain paper. You should retain payroll information for employees who leave during the year so that you can prepare T4 slips to mail to them.

Choose the **Reports menu**, then **choose Payroll** and **click Print T4 Slips And Summary** (or Print Relevé 1 Slips) to display the options:

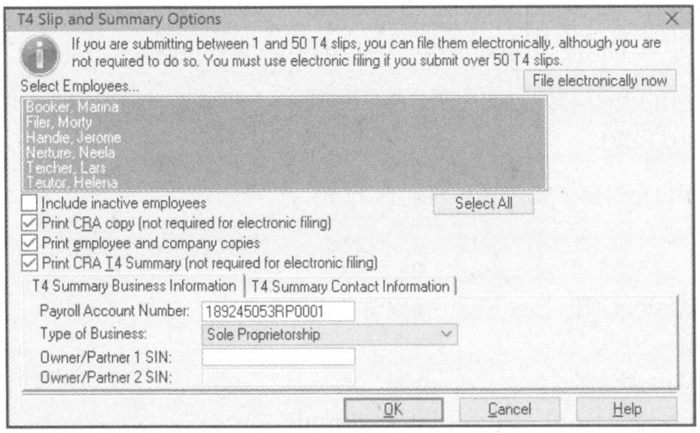

You need to select employees in order to prepare their T4 slips. Inactive employees are not listed by default. You can print copies of the T4s for the employees and the company and for the Canada Revenue Agency (CRA). You can also print the summary for the CRA. All are selected as the default.

To submit the report, you must include the type of business, business payroll account number (the business number with an RP code extension), the social insurance numbers (SIN) of the owners/partners, the name of the person who can be contacted about the form and the phone number and position of that individual. The payroll account number should be entered from the Company Settings Information window.

Click **Include Inactive Employees** to add Tiste to the list.

Click **Tiste, Arte**.

NOTES
When you select plain paper to print T4s, all the required labels are added.

NOTES
You cannot access T4 Slips from the Report Centre.
Submitting T4s electronically to the Canada Revenue Agency is covered in Appendix K.

NOTES
You can also print the T4 Slips and Summaries from the Employees window. Choose the Reports menu and click Print T4 Slips And Summary to open the options window.

PRO VERSION
pro You need to select the year (2021) because you have started a new year.

NOTES
If you file T4 reports electronically, you do not need to print copies for the Canada Revenue Agency.

NOTES
The payroll account number and the social insurance number (SIN) must be valid numbers and you cannot leave these fields blank.

Press and hold *ctrl* and click the names of the employees for whom you want the report printed, or click Select All to prepare T4s for all employees.

Select the **Type Of Business**. **Click** the **Type** that applies: sole proprietorship, partnership, private corporation or other.

Enter **189245053RP0001** (without spaces) in the Payroll Account Number field if it is not entered automatically.

Enter the **social insurance number** of the owners or partners. You can enter Teutor's social insurance number (from page 262) as the owner's SIN.

NOTES
The RP extension indicates that this is a Payroll account number.
Teutor's social insurance number is 699 344 578.

On the second tab screen, you must enter the contact details for the person completing the forms.

Click the **T4 Summary Contact Information tab** to open the contact fields:

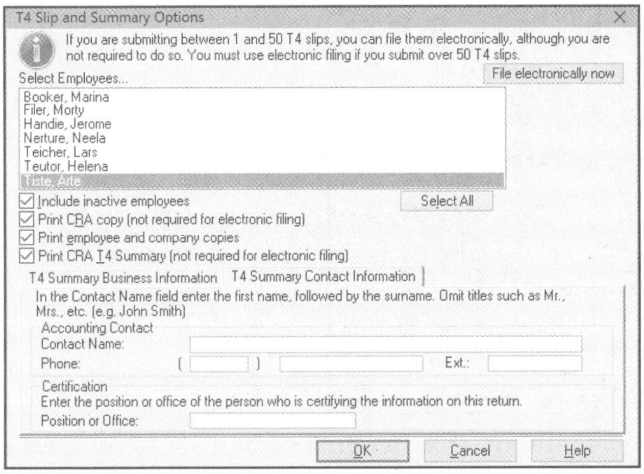

NOTES
The T4 Options screen includes a link for filing T4 slips electronically.

All the details on this form are required and you must enter both a first and last name. You can use Morty Filer's name with the school phone number (refer to page 259), and enter Office Manager as his position.

NOTES
Morty Filer is the office manager. His work phone number is (780) 633-8201.

Enter the **contact details** for the person completing the forms: name, phone number and position in the company.

Click **OK** to open the warning:

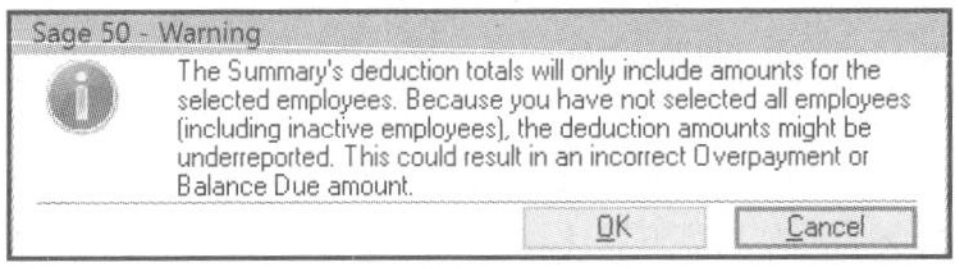

The warning appears when you do not select all employees because the remittance amounts apply to all employees. Thus, reported amounts for employer contributions may be incorrect.

Click **OK** to open the T4 Box Options screen:

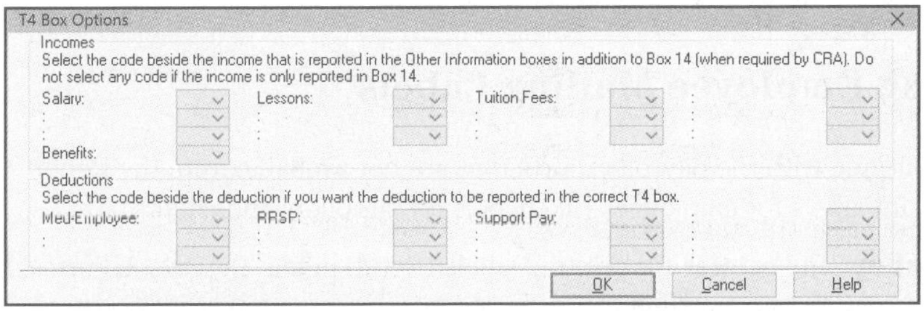

NOTES
The printed T4 slips will also include descriptions of the purpose of each box on the form. This information is used by the employee to complete his or her income tax return and can serve as a guide for employers preparing the T4s.

Each box on the T4 slip is numbered and can be designated for a specific deduction or income. You can choose a form box number for these amounts if they are related to income tax and should be included on the T4s. Each item has a list of box numbers that you can select. Income and tax items that are standard for T4s are not listed because their boxes are already assigned. If you do not change the box selections, the income amounts on this screen are all combined and the deductions listed are not reported. You can check with the CRA to learn what each box number is used for. The **Help** button also provides information about the numbers that should be used for different types of income and deductions.

Choose appropriate **box numbers** for the items that should appear on the T4.

Click **OK** to begin printing.

After the T4s are printed, the T4 Summary report is displayed:

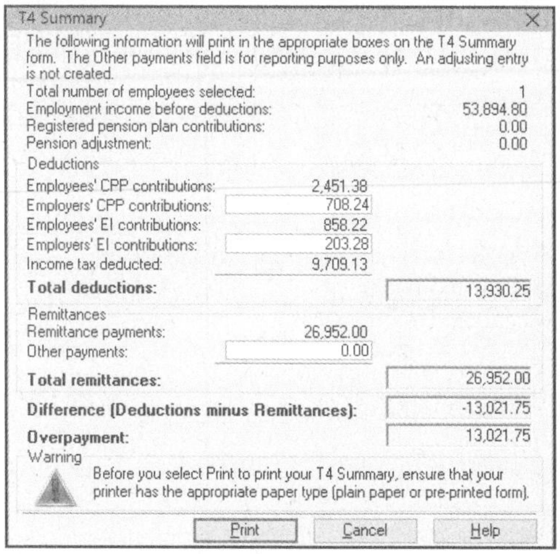

The contribution amounts are only those for Tiste because he was the only employee selected. Remittance amounts are those for all employees for three months. Employer contribution amounts are those related to this employee for three months while employee amounts are the year-to-date totals for the individual. When you do not set up the program at the start of the calendar year, the employer contribution and remittance year-to-date totals are not included in the payroll history. You should edit the amounts.

Click **Print** to continue when the amounts are correct.

After printing, you should have a summary of the items printed:

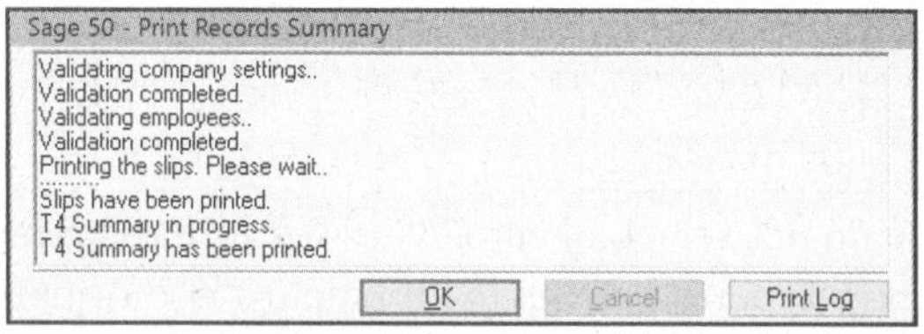

Click **Print Log** to print this summary or **click OK** to close the summary.

Close the **Employees window**.

Printing Employee Mailing Labels

We will continue with the payroll reports that are not available from the Report Centre. You can print labels for employees (like labels for suppliers and clients).

Set up the **printer** for printing labels (Setup menu, Reports & Forms, Labels) before starting.

Choose the **Reports menu**, then **choose Mailing Labels** and **click Employees**.

NOTES

Total income includes vacation pay paid and benefits.

Employee year-to-date historical amounts are entered in the ledger record when you set up the Payroll module, and they are included in the T4 Summary. However, year-to-date employer amounts are not included as part of the setup, so these amounts may be incomplete.

If you entered all payroll transactions for the year, the amounts on the summary should be correct.

You can edit the employer payment amounts for CPP and EI.

NOTES

Remember to check that you have selected the correct printer for your setup. When you click Print or Print Log, printing will start immediately and you cannot change the selected printer.

NOTES

You cannot display mailing labels.

You can include or omit inactive employees.

You will display the list of employee names:

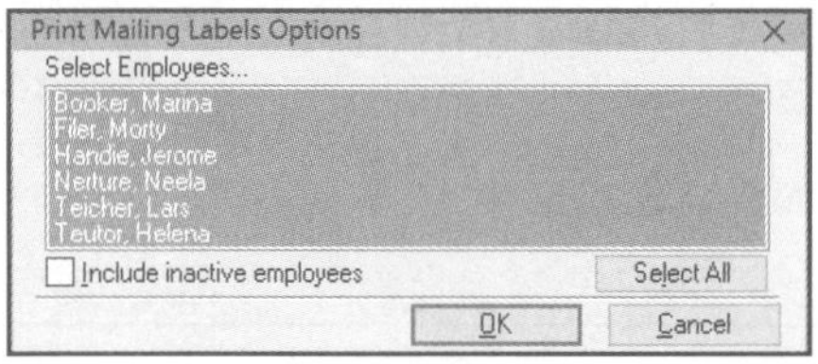

Press and **hold** ctrl and **click** the **employees' names** you want to print labels for, or **click Select All** to include all employees. **Click OK** to start printing.

To print other reports, **display** the **report** you want to print as instructed below. **Choose** the **File menu** from the report window and **click Print**. **Choose** your **printer**. **Click OK**. **Close** the **display** when finished.

Displaying Payroll Reports

Most payroll reports can be accessed from the Employees window Reports menu, the Home window Reports menu, the Reports drop-down list in the Reports pane or the Report Centre.

In the Reports pane, click the list arrow in the Reports field to open the list of reports:

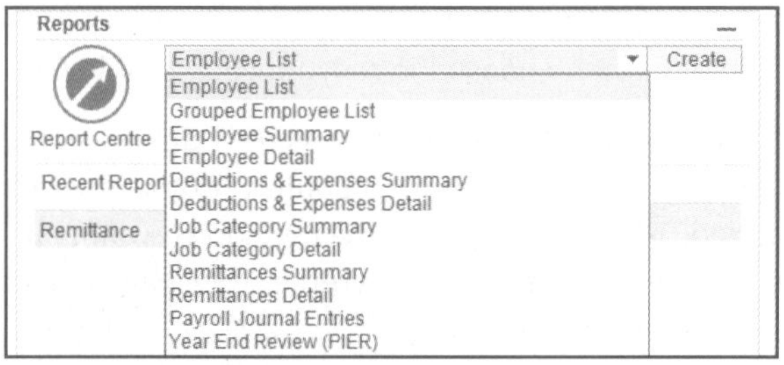

As usual, we will work from the Report Centre to include sample reports and the report description and purpose.

Click the **Report Centre icon** in the Reports pane.

Click **Employees & Payroll** in the Select A Report Type list for the general description of payroll reports:

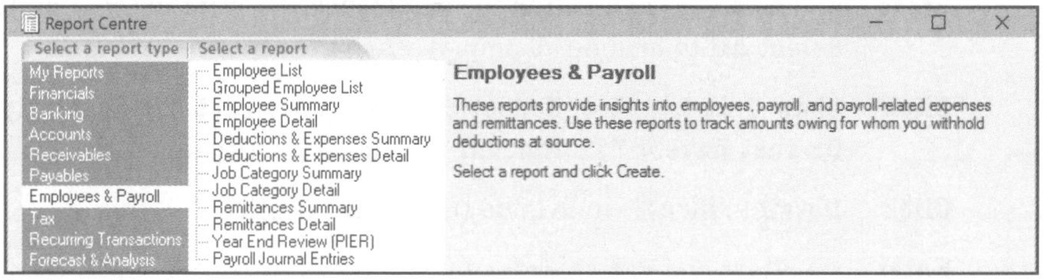

Displaying Employee Lists

Lists of employees are available, just like lists for other ledgers. The report will display a list of all current employees, together with data for all the details you choose. The default report has the address, phone number and date of hire.

Click **Employee List** in the Select A Report list.

NOTES
You can also print the labels from the Employees window. Choose the Reports menu and click Employee Labels to open the options window.

PRO VERSION
The Pro version does not have Grouped Lists.

NOTES
The Job Category Report will be covered in Chapter 9.

NOTES
The Grouped Employee List allows you to sort the employees into categories according to a number of criteria, such as the city they live in or the additional fields you create for the ledger.

PRO VERSION
The Pro version does not have Forecast & Analysis reports or Grouped Lists.

CLASSIC VIEW
From the Home window, right-click the Employees icon. Click the Select A Report tool, to open the Modify Report window for Employee Lists.

NOTES

You can drill down to the Employee Detail Report from the Employee List.

You can sort and filter the list by the fields available for the Employee List.

To access Employee Lists from the Home window, choose the Reports menu, then choose Lists and click Employees for the report options.

Click **Modify This Report** for the report options:

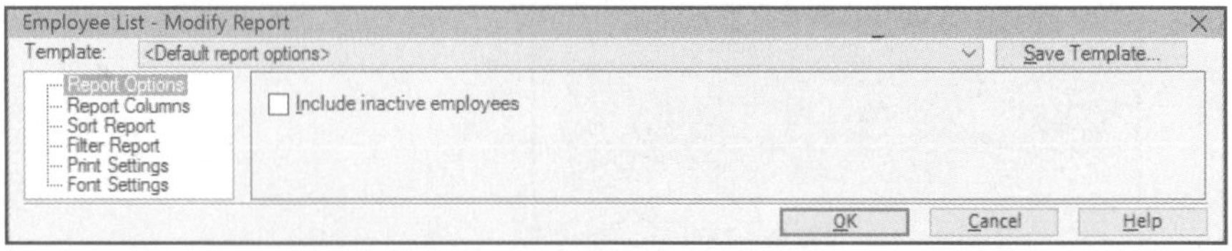

To select employee fields, you can customize the Report Columns. Choose Custom Report Column Settings and select the ones you want.

Close the **display** when you have finished.

Displaying Employee Reports

Click **Employee Summary** in the Select A Report list.

Click **Modify This Report** for the report options:

PRO VERSION

The Pro version Modify Report screen will have 2021 dates included because a new calendar year was started for the January 15 paycheques. Select 2021.

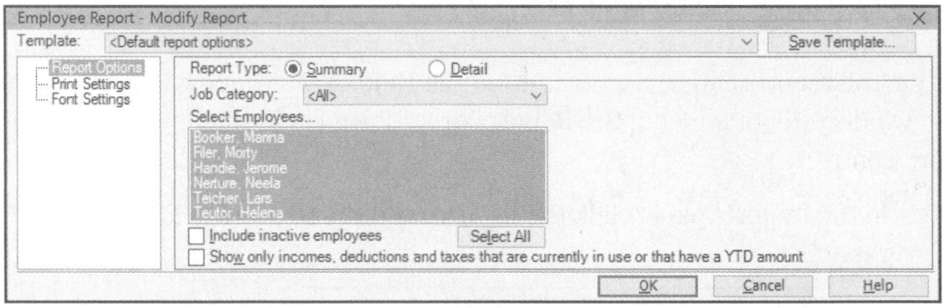

Or, choose the Reports menu, then choose Payroll and click Employee.

NOTES

The Summary Report also has the tax claim amounts and rates of pay for each employee.

NOTES

Sorting, filtering and column selection are not available for the Employee Summary Report.

You can drill down to the Detail Report from the Summary Report. From the Detail Report you can look up the Payroll Journal entry and open the Employee Ledger.

The **Summary Report** has accumulated totals for the selected employees for all incomes, deductions and payments, including historical amounts prior to the first Sage 50 entry; it is updated each pay period. You cannot change the date of the Summary Report.

You can include or omit inactive employees from the report. You can also omit details that have no amounts or have not been used.

If you use job categories, you can prepare a report for a specific category by choosing it from the drop-down list of categories.

You cannot customize the Employee Summary Report. You can use the **Detail Report** to include individual amounts for each paycheque. To prepare a report for specific deductions or payments, you can customize the column selection for the Detail Report.

Click **Include Inactive Employees** if you want to report on them as well.

Press and **hold** *ctrl* and **click** the **employees** you want in the report, or **click** **Select All** to include all employees in the report.

Click **Show Only Incomes, Deductions And Taxes That Are Currently In Use Or That Have A YTD Amount** to omit fields with no entries.

Click **Detail** to include individual transaction details.

Enter the **Start** and **Finish dates** for the Detail Report.

Click **Report Columns** in the left-hand pane. **Click Custom Report Column Settings**:

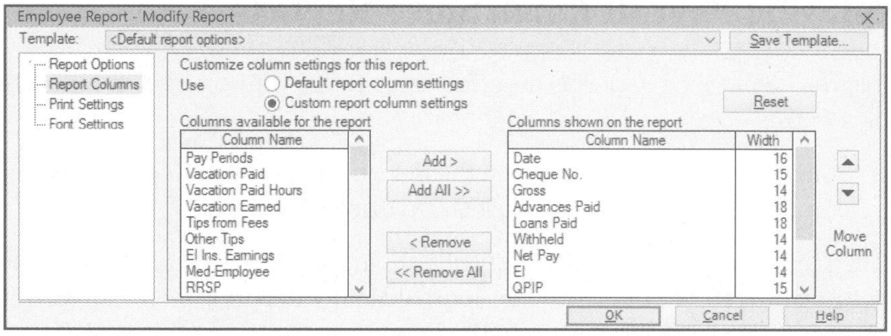

The right-hand side of this window has the information that is included by default, and the left side has the details that you can add to the report. The amount for each detail you choose will be listed for each payroll period in the selected date range for the selected employees, together with the totals for the period selected. The calendar year provides the default dates for the Detail Report.

Select the **columns** you want to include or remove.

Click **OK** to open the report.

Close the **display** when you have finished.

Displaying Deductions and Expenses Reports

NOTES
From the Summary Deductions and Expenses Report you can drill down to the Detail Report. From the Detail Report you can drill down to the Employee Detail Report and look up the paycheque.

Click **Deductions & Expenses Summary** in the Select A Report list.

Click **Modify This Report** for the report options:

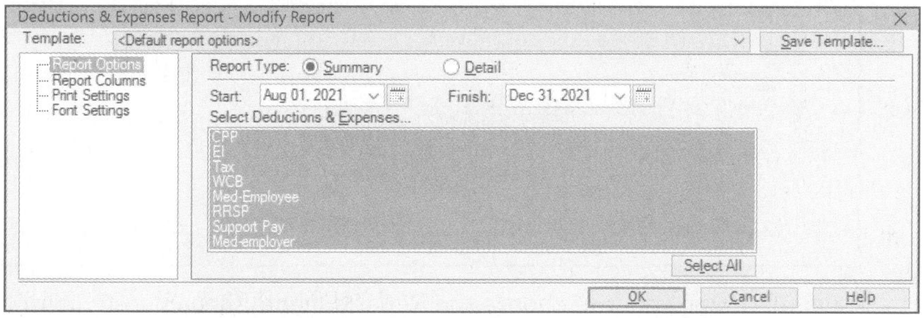

From the Home window, choose the Reports menu, then choose Payroll and click Deductions & Expenses.

This report provides details for all payable amounts resulting from deductions and expenses. Only amounts entered in the payroll journals in Sage 50 will be included in this report. Prior historical balance amounts for the year to date from the employee records will not be included. The **Summary Report** has the total amounts and the number of employees to whom the deduction or expense applied for each payroll item in the selected date range. The **Detail Report** includes individual entries for each selected item, with the date, cheque or deposit number, employee, job category, amount, period totals and number of employees.

You can customize the report by selecting the columns you want to include.

Select the details you want in the report and the date range for the report. The earliest transaction and session dates are the default selections.

Press and **hold** *ctrl* and **click** the **deductions** and **expenses** you want in the report, or **click** **Select All** to include all details in the report.

Enter the **Start** and **Finish dates** for the report.

Click **OK** to open the report. **Close** the **display** when you have finished.

NOTES
From the Remittance Summary Report, you can drill down to the Detail Report. From the Detail Report, you can drill down to the Supplier Ledger, the Employee Detail Report, the journal entry and look up the entry in the Payroll Journal.

Displaying Payroll Remittance Reports

The Payroll Remittance Report is described on page 284. To access this report from the Report Centre,

Click Remittances Summary in the Select A Report list. Click Modify This Report for the report options and click OK to display the report.

The Payroll Remittance Journal Entries are included with the Payments Journal Entries Report (refer to the Payments Journal Modify Report screen on page 150). To access this journal report from the Report Centre,

Click Payables in the Select A Report Type list. Click Payment Journal Entries and Modify This Report for the options. Remittance Payments should have a ✓ in the check box as the default selection. Click OK to display the report.

NOTES
You cannot sort or filter the PIER report.
You can modify this report by selecting the report columns, removing any of the default information or adding the amounts for expected EI and CPP deductions and the number of paycheques and pay periods.

Displaying Year End Review (PIER) Reports

The PIER (Pensionable and Insurable Earnings Review) report provides the total amounts contributed for the year to date for EI and CPP. Based on the Insurable Earnings amount for each employee (also in the report), the program determines whether the employee has contributed the correct amounts and displays the amount of under- or overcontributions.

Click **Year End Review (PIER)** in the Select A Report list.

Click **Modify This Report** for the report options:

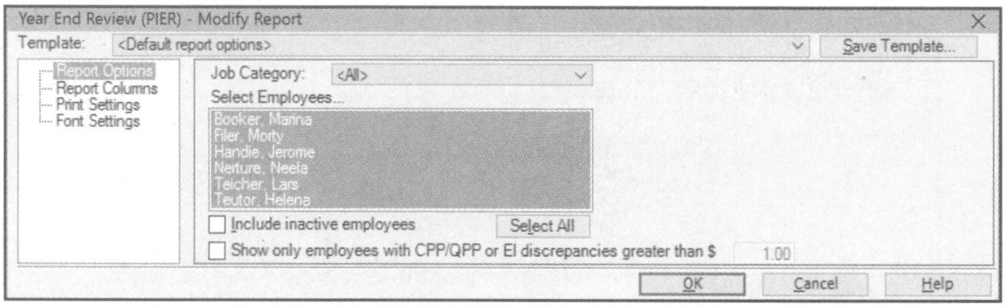

NOTES
The PIER report for Helena's Academy informs us that three employees have undercontributed to CPP and two employees have overcontributed to EI.
After starting a new year, you can choose the year for the PIER report.

From the Home window, choose the Reports menu, then choose Payroll and click Year End Review (PIER) to display the report options.

You can define the minimum discrepancy that should be included and then prepare the report only for those employees who have a discrepancy of this amount or more. The default amount is $1.00.

Click **Include Inactive Employees** to add these employees to the list.

Click the **name** of the employee you want the report for, **press** and **hold** ctrl and **click additional names** or **click Select All** to include all employees in the report.

Click **OK** to display the report. **Close** the **display** when you have finished.

CLASSIC VIEW
From the Home window, right-click either the Paycheques or the Payroll Cheque Run icon,

or

Then click the Select A Report tool  to open the Modify Report window for the Payroll Journal Report.

Displaying the Payroll Journal

The Payroll Journal Report includes all transactions from the Payroll Journal and the Payroll Run Journal.

Click **Payroll Journal Entries** in the Select A Report list.

Click **Modify This Report** for the report options:

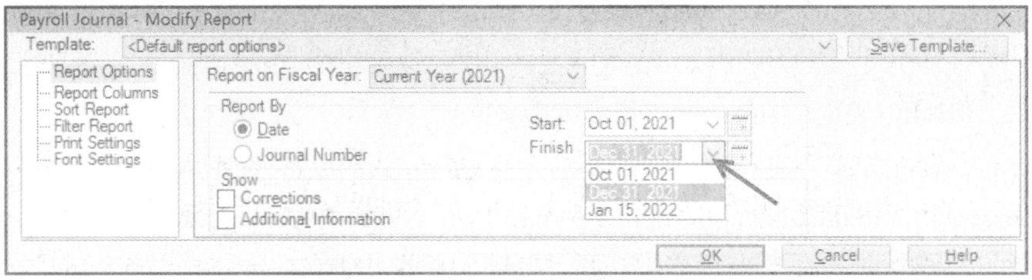

Or, choose the Reports menu, then choose Journal Entries and click Payroll to display the Options window.

The usual sort and filter journal options are available for the Payroll Journal Report, and the Date option we use for selecting transactions is the default. Your earliest transaction and session dates appear as the default Start and Finish dates.

Type the **beginning** and **ending dates** for the report.

Click **Corrections** to include the original and reversing entries for the paycheques you adjusted or reversed.

Click **OK**. **Close** the **display** when you have finished.

NOTES

January 15, 2022, the latest transaction date, will be included in the drop-down lists in the date fields.

NOTES

You can drill down to the Employee Detail Report and the General Ledger Report from the Payroll Journal.

Displaying All Journal Entries

Remember that you can include the journal entries for all journals in a single report.

From the Report Centre, choose the Financials list of reports and then click All Journal Entries to open the report options window.

From the Home window, choose the Reports menu, then choose Journal Entries and click All to open the report options window.

Click Corrections to include the reversed and adjusted entries.

Starting a New Calendar Year

When you are ready to advance to the next session date at the end of December, you must start a new year.

Close **all other windows** except the Home window. You can click  (the Close Other Windows tool).

Choose the **Maintenance menu** and **click** **Start New Year**:

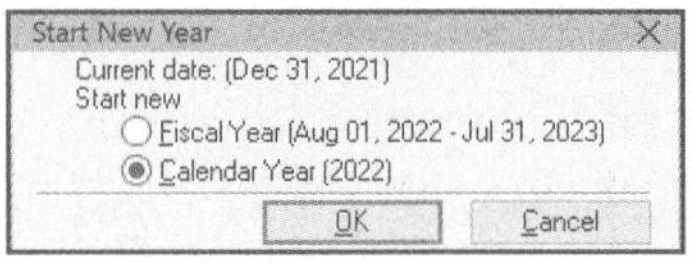

Because the fiscal period ends July 31, 2022, the new calendar year comes first and this will be the default option.

Click **OK** to continue to the next information screen:

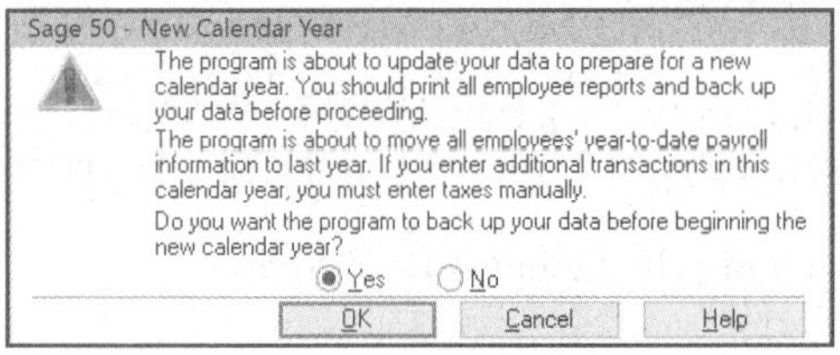

This message advises you about the changes that Sage 50 will make when you start the new year. Because this step is not reversible, you should have an end-of-year backup. This is the default selection.

Click **OK** to proceed with the backup.

After the backup has been completed, Sage 50 will provide the confirmation message that the date has been changed and the reminder to update TD1 amounts:

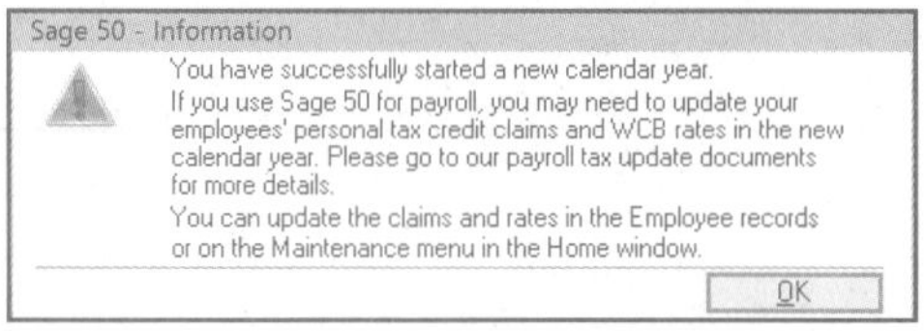

Click **OK** to proceed to the locking date screen:

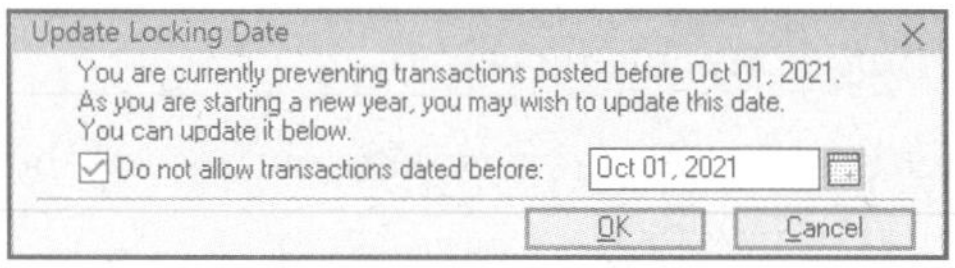

Enter **Jan 1 2022** as the new date on this screen.

Click **OK** to return to the Home window.

Click the **Refresh tool** above the Employees list pane to update the amounts to include the latest transaction entries:

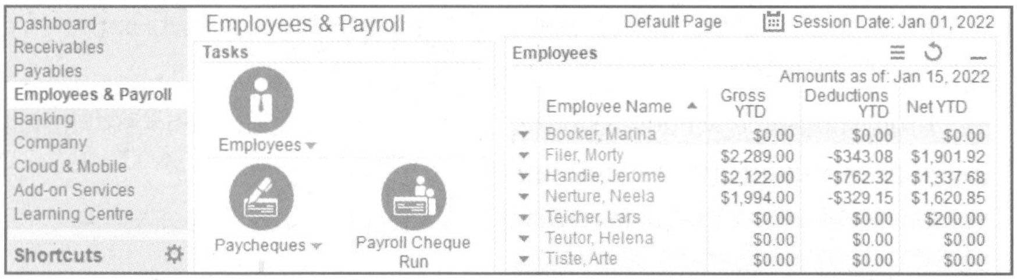

The new year-to-date amounts are the balances as at January 15 for the hourly paid employees. Teicher's loan amount, carried forward from his December 31 paycheque, is also included.

If you have not entered any payroll transactions yet when you start the new calendar year, the amounts in the Employees list pane will be zero except for Teicher's loan amount.

NOTES
Showing balances as at the session date, which is January 1 (a User Preference Options setting), will also lead to zero amounts in the Employees list pane.

REVIEW

The Student DVD with Data Files includes Review Questions and Supplementary Cases for this chapter.

CHAPTER NINE

NORTHERN Lights

OBJECTIVES

After completing this chapter, you should be able to

- ***add*** the Payroll Ledger to a company data file
- ***enter*** Payroll Ledger settings
- ***enter*** Payroll Ledger linked accounts
- ***create*** Employee Ledger records
- ***enter*** employee historical information
- ***set up*** payroll remittances with remittance suppliers
- ***set up*** taxes for income, benefits and deductions
- ***create*** job categories
- ***assign*** employees to job categories
- ***enter*** salespersons on invoices
- ***display*** and ***print*** job category and salesperson reports

COMPANY INFORMATION

Company Profile

NOTES
Northern Lights
25 Snowy Court
Whitehorse, YT Y1A 2B2
Tel: (867) 873-8201
Fax: (867) 873-8396
Business No.: 324 732 916

Northern Lights, owned by M. Promtou, opened with its first play in Whitehorse, Yukon, in 1999. Now Northern Lights, a theatre with a seating capacity of 350, regularly runs two plays each month, five nights a week. Afternoons are used for rehearsals. Two actors, a director, a box office and a stand concession employee, an usher and a sound and light engineer make up the full-time staff. For plays requiring more players, actors are hired from an agency as needed, and the director and owner also step into roles occasionally. The actors volunteer one morning each week to run drama workshops in schools. The owner is involved primarily in promoting the theatre, and usually the theatre is nearly filled.

Northern Lights has established favourable account terms with regular suppliers, including some discounts for early payment. All discounts are calculated on after-tax amounts. Most tickets are sold to season's subscribers and individual customers. A few organizations — tour companies that offer a theatre night as part of the tour package, charities using theatre nights as a fundraiser, local book groups

PRO VERSION
The term Vendor will replace Supplier. Purchases replaces the term Expenses in the program for journals and reports.

and a community theatre school— regularly buy blocks of tickets. Discount terms for these account customers also encourage timely payment of accounts.

Tickets, food and beverages sold by Northern Lights are subject to 5 percent GST. Northern Lights pays the 5 percent GST on all purchases except food.

On May 31, 2021, Promtou closed his books so he could begin using the payroll feature in Sage 50. The following information summarizes his data:

- Chart of Accounts
- Post-Closing Trial Balance
- Supplier Information
- Customer Information
- Employee Profiles and Information Sheet
- Accounting Procedures

CHART OF POSTABLE ACCOUNTS

NORTHERN LIGHTS

ASSETS
1080 Bank: Chequing
1100 Bank: Credit Card
1200 Accounts Receivable
1240 Loans Receivable
1260 Prepaid Insurance
1280 Office Supplies
1300 Cleaning Supplies
1320 Food & Beverage Inventory
1520 Computer System
1540 Concession Appliances
1560 Van
1580 Sound & Light Equipment
1600 Theatre Seats & Furnishings
1620 Theatre Building
1620 Theatre Property ▶

▶LIABILITIES
2100 Bank Loan
2200 Accounts Payable
2250 Accrued Wages
2300 Vacation Payable
2310 EI Payable
2320 CPP Payable
2330 Income Tax Payable
2400 EHC Payable - Employee
2410 VRSP Payable
2420 Tuition Fees Payable
2440 EHC Payable - Employer
2450 Players' Guild Payable
2460 WCB Payable
2650 GST Charged on Services
2670 GST Paid on Purchases
2920 Mortgage Payable ▶

▶EQUITY
3560 M. Promtou, Capital
3600 Current Earnings

REVENUE
4020 Revenue: Ticket Sales
4040 Revenue: Concession Sales
4060 Revenue: Movies
4140 Sales Discounts

EXPENSE
5010 Purchase Discounts
5020 Advertising Expenses
5040 Bank Charges
5050 Credit Card Fees
5060 Hydro Expenses
5080 Insurance Expense ▶

▶5100 Cleaning Supplies Used
5140 Food & Beverages Sold
5160 Telephone Expenses
5180 Maintenance and Repairs
5200 Van Expenses
5410 Salaries: Performance Staff
5420 Wages: Support Staff
5430 Vacation Earned
5440 Commissions
5450 Sales Bonuses
5510 EI Expense
5520 CPP Expense
5530 WCB Expense
5560 Travel Allowances
5570 Tuition Fees Expense
5580 EHC Premium Expense

NOTES: The Chart of Accounts includes only postable accounts and Current Earnings.

POST-CLOSING TRIAL BALANCE

NORTHERN LIGHTS

June 1, 2021

		Debits	Credits
1080	Bank: Chequing	$ 53 040.30	
1100	Bank: Credit Card	5 525.00	
1200	Accounts Receivable	12 600.00	
1240	Loans Receivable	350.00	
1260	Prepaid Insurance	2 200.00	
1280	Office Supplies	1 240.00	
1300	Cleaning Supplies	780.00	
1320	Food & Beverage Inventory	2 000.00	
1520	Computer System	7 200.00	
1540	Concession Appliances	4 950.00	
1560	Van	24 800.00	
1580	Sound & Light Equipment	160 000.00	
1600	Theatre Seats & Furnishings	140 000.00	
1600	Theatre Building	250 000.00	
1620	Theatre Property	120 000.00	
2100	Bank Loan		$45 000.00 ▶
▶ 2200	Accounts Payable		$ 9 960.00
2250	Accrued Wages		1 150.00
2300	Vacation Payable		4 143.16
2310	EI Payable		1 227.23
2320	CPP Payable		2 625.00
2330	Income Tax Payable		3 661.61
2400	EHC Payable - Employee		948.48
2410	VRSP Payable		250.00
2420	Tuition Fees Payable	$ 4 000.00	
2440	EHC Payable - Employer		948.48
2450	Players' Guild Payable		90.59
2460	WCB Payable		541.72
2650	GST Charged on Services		8 860.00
2670	GST Paid on Purchases	3 250.00	
2920	Mortgage Payable		260 000.00
3560	M. Promtou, Capital		452 529.03
		$791 935.30	$791 935.30

SUPPLIER INFORMATION

NORTHERN LIGHTS

Supplier Name (Contact)	Address	Phone No. Fax No.	E-mail Web Site	Terms Tax ID
Class Acts (Tempe Handler)	78 Extra St. Whitehorse, YT Y1A 3V2	Tel: (867) 667-3601 Fax: (867) 667-1577	tempe@classacts.com classacts.com	1/10, n/30 (after tax) 366 455 285 RT0001
Manulife Financial (M.T. Handed)	7 Fiscal Way Whitehorse, YT Y1A 2K4	Tel: (867) 993-3488 Fax: (867) 993-8109	manulife.com	net 1
Midnight Sun Bakery (D. Lishus)	43 Danish Ave. Whitehorse, YT Y1A 2S6	Tel: (867) 633-3929 Fax: (867) 633-3935	lishus@midnightsun.ca midnightsun.ca	1/10, n/30 (after tax) 445 668 718 RT0001
Otto's Autos (Otto Sparks)	64 Mechanic St. Whitehorse, YT Y1A 2S4	Tel: (867) 689-7106 Fax: (867) 689-7188	sparks@ottos.com ottos.com	net 1 672 910 189 RT0001
Receiver General for Canada		Tel: (800) 561-7761	cra-arc.gc.ca	net 1
Stage Stagers (A. Carpenter)	244 Woods Rd. Whitehorse, YT Y1A 4A1	Tel: (867) 666-8877 Fax: (867) 666-9100		2/15, n/30 (after tax) 458 459 765 RT0001
Thirst Quenchers (Thurston Wade)	555 Water St. Whitehorse, YT Y1A 1N6	Tel: (867) 634-1618 Fax: (867) 634-5127	tw@tq.com tq.com	net 30 129 554 374 RT0001
YT Energy (Sol R. Heater)	33 Windmill Rd. Whitehorse, YT Y1A 3C3	Tel: (867) 841-1298	srh@yteg.ca yteg.ca	net 10
Yukon Telephone (Kommue Nicate)	91 Cellular Way Whitehorse, YT Y1A 8B5	Tel: (867) 665-2355	yttel.ca	net 10
Yukon Workers' Compensation Board (I.T. Herts)	55 Accidental Cr. Whitehorse, YT Y1A 3X6	Tel: (867) 668-7199	ytwcb.com	net 1

OUTSTANDING SUPPLIER INVOICES

NORTHERN LIGHTS

Supplier Name	Terms	Date	Invoice No.	Amount	Total
Stage Stagers	2/15, n/30	May 27/21	SS-4011	$6 510	$6 510
Thirst Quenchers	net 30	May 3/21	TQ-644	$3 450	$3 450
				Grand Total	$9 960

CUSTOMER INFORMATION

NORTHERN LIGHTS

Customer Name (Contact)	Address	Phone No. Fax No.	E-mail Web Site	Terms Credit Limit
Literati Borealis (Lotta Reads)	3 Volumis Cr. Whitehorse, YT Y1A 5D3	Tel 1: (867) 668-2563	lreads@literati.com literati.com	1/15, n/30 (after tax) $7 000
Polar Discoveries (Robert Peary)	4 Exploration Ave. Churchill, MN R5P 4C2	Tel: (204) 369 4545 Fax: (866) 369-4545	rp@polardiscoveries.com polardiscoveries.com	1/15, n/30 (after tax) $15 000
SAD (Seasonal Affective Disorder) Foundation	56 Sliepers Rd. Whitehorse, YT Y1A 6F3	Tel 1: (867) 664-7155 Tel 2: (800) 664-9175	SAD.com/yt	1/15, n/30 (after tax) $10 000
Subscribers				net 1
Whitehorse Little Theatre (B. Little)	5 Performance Ct. Whitehorse, YT Y1A 2W2	Tel: (867) 536-7188 Fax: (867) 536-7528	little@wlt.com wlt.com	1/15, n/30 (after tax) $10 000

OUTSTANDING CUSTOMER INVOICES

NORTHERN LIGHTS

Customer Name	Terms	Date	Invoice No.	Amount	Total
Literati Borealis	1/15, n/30	May 28/21	344	$4 200	$4 200
Polar Discoveries	1/15, n/30	May 30/21	348	$8 400	$8 400
				Grand Total	$12 600

EMPLOYEE INFORMATION SHEET

NORTHERN LIGHTS

	Taika Tikett	Kay Kabanza	Ayla Usher	Bev Ridges	Jiane Apsimak	Francine Player	Pawluk Staige
Gender	Male	Female	Female	Female	Female	Female	Male
Position	Box Office Staff	Engineer	Usher	Concession Staff	Director	Actor	Actor
	Support	Support	Support	Support	Performance	Performance	Performance
	Full Time	Full Time	Full Time	Full Time	Full Time	Full Time	Full Time
Social Insurance No.	218 738 631	638 912 634	931 771 620	552 846 826	422 946 541	726 911 134	822 546 859
Address	29 Stubbs Rd.	2 Aural Rd.	63 Walker Blvd.	34 Stratford Ln.	410 Revue Ave.	11 Asides Cres.	122 Spotlight Ct.
	Whitehorse, YT	Whitehorse, YT	Whitehorse, YT	Whitehorse, YT	Whitehorse, YT	Whitehorse, YT	Whitehorse, YT
	Y1A 4K2	Y1A 6D2	Y1A 5M8	Y1A 4C1	Y1A 1X3	Y1A 2L2	Y1A 8B3
Telephone	(867) 689-7595	(867) 356-7995	(867) 668-2291	(867) 634-8138	(867) 536-6353	(867) 667-6291	(867) 456-2238
Date of Birth (mm-dd-yy)	8-10-89	8-8-79	3-31-93	11-3-91	5-21-81	7-31-83	11-3-86
Date of Hire (mm-dd-yy)	11-6-19	2-7-14	12-4-18	4-6-14	1-1-12	8-5-17	6-6-12
Federal (YT) Tax Exemption – TD1							
Basic Personal	$12 609 (12 609)	$12 609 (12 609)	$12 609 (12 609)	$12 609 (12 609)	$12 609 (12 609)	$12 609 (12 609)	$12 609 (12 609)
Other Indexed	$12 609 (12 609)	$28 165 (28 165)	–	–	$12 609 (12 609)	–	$12 609 (12 609)
Non-Indexed	$1 935 (1 935)	–	$11 260 (11 260)	–	–	–	–
Total Exemptions	$27 153 (27 153)	$40 774 (40 774)	$23 869 (23 869)	$12 609 (12 609)	$25 218 (25 218)	$12 609 (12 609)	$25 218 (25 218)
Additional Fed Taxes	$50	$100	–	–	–	–	–
Employee Taxes							
Historical Income Tax	$1 120.30	$3 610.30	$571.74	$1 919.40	$3 628.10	$3 517.20	$2 626.80
Historical EI	$308.91	$468.10	$162.24	$271.64	$492.80	$408.90	$408.90
Historical CPP	$685.03	$1 106.50	$352.13	$555.99	$1 145.60	$915.60	$926.70
Deduct EI; EI Rate	Yes; 1.4	Yes; 1.4	Yes; 1.4	Yes; 1.4	Yes; 1.4	Yes; 1.4	Yes; 1.4
Deduct CPP, Tax	Yes	Yes	Yes	Yes	Yes	Yes	Yes
Employee Income							
Pay Periods	26 (bi-weekly)	26 (bi-weekly)	26 (bi-weekly)	26 (bi-weekly)	12 (monthly)	12 (monthly)	12 (monthly)
Vacation Rate	6% retained	8% retained	6% retained	6% retained	0% (3 weeks)	0% (3 weeks)	0% (3 weeks)
Record Wage Exp in	Linked Accts	Linked Accts	Linked Accts	Linked Accts	Linked Accts	Linked Accts	Linked Accts
Loans: Hist Amt	$100.00	$150.00	$100.00	(use) ✓	(use) ✓	(use) ✓	(use) ✓
Benefits per Period	$41.54	$41.54	$20.77	$20.77	$90.00	$45.00	$90.00
Benefits: Hist Amt	$1 015.40	$415.40	$1 807.70	$207.70	$450.00	$225.00	$450.00
Vacation Pay Owed	$939.00	$1 992.00	$345.28	$866.88	–	–	–
Vacation Paid	$610.00	$458.00	–	–	–	–	–
Regular Wage Rate	$18.00	$30.00	$16.00	$16.00	(do not use)	(do not use)	(do not use)
(Hours per Period)	(80 hours)	(80 hours)	(80 hours)	(80 hours)	–	–	–
Reg. Wages: Hist Amt	$14 400.00	$24 000.00	$8 320.00	$13 440.00	–	–	–
Overtime 1 Rate	$27.00	$45.00	$24.00	$24.00	(do not use)	(do not use)	(do not use)
Overtime 1: Hist Amt	$810.00	$900.00	$312.00	$504.00	–	–	–
No. Sold/Number	$0.10	(do not use)	(do not use)	$0.10	(do not use)	(do not use)	(do not use)
No. Sold: Hist Amt	$440.00	–	–	$504.00	–	–	

▶

EMPLOYEE INFORMATION SHEET CONTINUED

	Taika Tikett	Kay Kabanza	Ayla Usher	Bev Ridges	Jiane Apsimak	Francine Player	Pawluk Staige
Employee Income Continued							
Salary	(do not use)	(do not use)	(do not use)	(do not use)	$4 900.00	$4 350.00	$4 350.00
(Hours per Period)	–	–	–	–	(160 hours)	(160 hours)	(160 hours)
Salary: Hist Amt	–	–	–	–	$24 500.00	$21 750.00	$21 750.00
Commission	(do not use)	(do not use)	(do not use)	(do not use)	1% ticket sales	(do not use)	(do not use)
Commission: Hist Amt	–	–	–	–	$1 650.00	–	–
Travel Allow	–	–	–	–	–	$50.00	$50.00
Travel Allow: Hist Amt	–	–	–	–	–	$250.00	$250.00
Employee Deductions							
VRSP	$100.00	$150.00	(use) ✓	(use) ✓	$300.00	$400.00	$200.00
VRSP: Hist Amt	$1 000.00	$1 500.00	–	–	$1 500.00	$2 000.00	$1 000.00
EHC-Employee	$41.54	$41.54	$20.77	$20.77	$90.00	$45.00	$90.00
EHC-Employee Hist Amt	$415.40	$415.40	$207.70	$207.70	$450.00	$225.00	$450.00
Players' Guild Fees	(do not use)	(do not use)	(do not use)	(do not use)	(do not use)	1.01%	1.01%
Guild Fees: Hist Amt	–	–	–	–	–	$221.95	$224.20
WCB and Other Expenses							
WCB Rate	1.55	3.38	1.75	1.55	1.55	1.55	1.55
Tuition Fee	$60.00	–	$160.00	–	–	–	–
Tuition Fee: Hist Amt	$600.00	–	$1 600.00	–	–	–	–
EHC-Employer	$41.54	$41.54	$20.77	$20.77	$90.00	$45.00	$90.00
EHC-Employer: Hist Amt	$415.40	$415.40	$207.70	$207.70	$450.00	$225.00	$450.00
Entitlements: Rate, Maximum Days, Clear? (Historical Amount)							
Vacation: Rate, Max	–	–	–	–	8%, 25 days	8%, 25 days	8%, 25 days
Clear? (Days Accrued)	–	–	–	–	No (20 days)	No (10 days)	No (25 days)
Sick Leave: Rate, Max	5%, 20 days	5%, 20 days	5%, 20 days	5%, 20 days	5%, 20 days	5%, 20 days	5%, 20 days
Clear? (Days Accrued)	No (16 days)	No (14 days)	No (10 days)	No (18 days)	No (16 days)	No (16 days)	No (18 days)
Personal Days: Rate, Max	2.5%, 10 days	2.5%, 10 days	2.5%, 10 days	2.5%, 10 days	2.5%, 10 days	2.5%, 10 days	2.5%, 10 days
Clear? (Days Accrued)	No (4 days)	No (6 days)	No (8 days)	No (3 days)	No (6 days)	No (4 days)	No (6 days)
Direct Deposit							
Yes/No	Yes	Yes	No	No	Yes	No	Yes
Branch No., Institution No.	06722, 180	49921, 300	–	–	30099, 103	–	12084, 285
Account No.	4556221	2883912	–	–	2009123	–	2399012
Percent	100%	100%	–	–	100%	–	100%
Additional Information							
Emergency Contact	Kierin Tikett	Marie Kabanza	Alex Usher	Petra Blackstone	Dene Uniak	Sima Player	Marina Staige
Contact Number	(867) 689-1892	(867) 356-1469	(867) 668-4573	(867) 634-6353	(867) 536-2197	(867) 667-7995	(867) 456-5602
T4 and RL-1 Reporting							
EI Insurable Earnings	$16 260.00	$25 358.00	$8 632.00	$14 448.00	$26 150.00	$21 750.00	$21 750.00
Pensionable Earnings	$17 275.40	$25 773.40	$10 439.70	$14 655.70	$26 600.00	$21 975.00	$22 200.00
Withheld	$3 529.64	$7 100.30	$1 293.81	$2 954.73	$7 216.50	$7 288.65	$5 636.60
Net Pay	$12 830.36	$18 407.70	$7 438.19	$11 493.27	$18 933.50	$14 711.35	$16 363.40

NOTES: Travel Allowances are reimbursement income.
Medical (EHC) premiums are deducted every pay period. The amounts are adjusted for the monthly rates.
EI, CPP and income tax are calculated automatically by the program.
Vacation pay at the rate of 6 percent is approximately equal to three weeks' vacation and 8 percent is equal to approximately four weeks.

Employee Profiles and TD1 Information

Employee Benefits and Entitlements All employees work full time and are entitled to 10 days per year as sick leave and five days' leave for personal reasons. If the days are not needed, employees can carry these days forward to a new year, to a maximum of 20 and 10 days, respectively. Currently, all employees have some unused sick leave and personal leave days accrued from the previous year. Salaried employees are allowed to carry forward two of their three weeks' vacation entitlement. That is, they are allowed to accumulate a maximum of 25 unused vacation days at any one time. Northern Lights also set up a voluntary retirement savings program (VRSP) with Manulife that allows employees to deduct from their paycheques to pay directly to their plans.

To encourage personal development, Northern Lights pays 50 percent of the tuition fees for any employee enrolled in college or university programs. Currently, Usher and Tikett are receiving the tuition fee benefit. This taxable benefit is considered an expense for Northern Lights. A second benefit applies to all employees — Northern Lights pays 50 percent of the premiums for an extended health care plan (EHC).

NOTES
Taxable benefits are not paid in cash to the employee. However, they are added to gross pay to determine income tax and then subtracted again to determine the net pay.

Sales Bonuses Northern Lights records the number of tickets and beverages sold in excess of a base number each week and pays Tikett and Ridges, respectively, a piece rate bonus of 10 cents per unit; this bonus is added to each paycheque.

Employer Expenses Northern Lights currently has two employer payroll expenses beyond the compulsory CPP, EI and WCB: 50 percent of the employees' EHC premiums and 50 percent of eligible tuition fees. In addition, Player and Staige receive a travel allowance as compensation for using their cars to volunteer at community schools.

Jiane Apsimak is the artistic and managing director of the theatre and oversees the production of each play, schedules work, hires new staff and discusses problems with the owner, who does not participate in the day-to-day affairs of the business. She is married and has no children. Since her husband is not employed, she uses the basic and spousal federal and provincial tax claim amounts and pays the family health care premium. At the end of each month, her salary of $4 900 per month plus a commission of 1 percent of revenue from ticket sales, net of taxes, is deposited to her account. She is recorded as salesperson for all these sales for the purpose of calculating her commission. She makes monthly contributions to her VRSP as well. In lieu of vacation pay, she is entitled to take three weeks of paid vacation each year.

Kay Kabanza is the sound and lighting engineer controlling all the electronic equipment. She has several years of experience with Northern Lights. Her regular pay of $30 per hour is supplemented by overtime wages at the rate of $45 per hour when she works more than 40 hours per week. In addition, she receives vacation pay at the rate of 8 percent of her total wages, but this amount is retained until she chooses to take a vacation. She has already received some of the vacation pay owing to her this year. She is married and fully supports her husband and an infirm and dependent sister, so she claims the spousal, disability and infirm caregiver amounts for income tax purposes. She also pays EHC premiums at the family rate and deducts $150 per pay as VRSP contributions. To offset the tax from additional income, she chooses to have an additional $100 in taxes withheld each pay period. She has received a loan of $150, which she will repay over the next three pay periods. Her bi-weekly pay is deposited directly to her bank account.

NOTES
The spousal claim amount is not allowed for the same person for whom the infirm caregiver amount is claimed. Kabanza has the disability amount transferred from her sister.

Ayla Usher the usher, earns $16 per hour, $24 per hour overtime when she works more than 80 hours in two weeks. She worked part time while a full-time student and is now a full-time employee while studying part time. Thus her $11 260 tuition fee is added to the basic federal and provincial claim amounts for income tax purposes. She is also entitled to the tuition benefit — 50 percent of her tuition is paid by Northern Lights at the rate of

$160 per pay. Usher's bi-weekly pay by cheque is supplemented by 6 percent vacation pay, which is retained, and she pays single EHC premiums.

Bev Ridges handles all concession sales. Ridges is single, so she claims the basic TD1 amount and pays the single EHC premium from her wages of $16 per hour and $24 for overtime hours. Her bi-weekly pay, paid by cheque, includes a piece rate bonus of $0.10 per beverage over a base amount. The 6 percent vacation pay is retained.

Taika Tikett manages the box office and telephone sales. He is married with no dependants, so he pays family EHC premiums and has the basic and spousal TD1 claim amounts. Because he studies business part time at the local community college, he has additional federal and provincial claims for his tuition of $1 935. From his bi-weekly deposited pay, he contributes $100 to a VRSP program. His pay is $18 per hour and $27 for overtime hours with 6 percent vacation pay; he also has a piece rate bonus added of $0.10 per ticket above a base number sold. Northern Lights pays half of his tuition. This taxable benefit, entered on Tikett's paycheque at the rate of $60 per paycheque, has already been paid for five months, and Tikett has also taken some vacation time with pay.

Francine Player is one of two actors with Northern Lights. Because she is single, Player claims the basic single TD1 amount and pays the single EHC premium. Player earns a base salary of $4 350 per month by cheque, contributes $400 of this to her VRSP and can take three weeks of vacation yearly. One morning per week she teaches and performs at community schools and is reimbursed for her travel expenses.

Pawluk Staige is the second actor with Northern Lights. As a single parent who supports one child, he pays the family EHC premium. For income tax purposes, he claims the spousal amount. At the end of each month, Staige has his monthly salary of $4 350 deposited to his bank account. He also contributes $200 from his pay to his VRSP program with regular payroll deductions. As a salaried employee, he is entitled to take three weeks of paid vacation per year. Like Player, Staige volunteers in community schools teaching acting and improvisation and is reimbursed for his travel costs.

Accounting Procedures

Taxes: GST and PST

GST at the rate of 5 percent applies to sales and purchases in Yukon. All sales and all purchases — other than food and some beverages — have GST applied. Northern Lights uses the regular method for remitting the GST. It records the GST collected from customers as a liability in *GST Charged on Services*. GST paid to suppliers is recorded in *GST Paid on Purchases* as a decrease in the liability to the Canada Revenue Agency. The GST refund or remittance is calculated automatically in the *GST Owing (Refund)* subgroup total account. Northern Lights files for a refund or remits the balance owing to the Receiver General for Canada by the last day of the month for the previous quarter.

Tax codes are set up in the defaults for the company so that Sage 50 can automatically calculate the tax when it applies.

NOTES

PST is not applied in Yukon. Purchases of food and some beverages are zero rated.

Discounts

All account customers are offered a discount of 1 percent on the after-tax amount of the sale if they pay their accounts in full within 15 days. Full payment is requested in 30 days. Discount terms are set up as the default in the customer records. Some suppliers also offer discounts on after-tax purchase amounts. These discount terms are set up in the supplier records so that Sage 50 will automatically calculate the discount when full payment is made within the discount period.

Direct Payroll Deposits

Promtou allows employees to have their regular pay deposited directly to their bank accounts or to be paid by cheque. Four employees have selected direct payroll deposits.

Payroll Remittances

Four suppliers are identified as payroll authorities with the following remittances: EI, CPP and income tax are remitted to the Receiver General for Canada; EHC and VRSP premiums are remitted to Manulife; Workers' Compensation Board premiums are remitted to the Yukon Workers' Compensation Board; and Players' Guild fees are paid to the Canadian Actors' Guild.

INSTRUCTIONS

1. **Set up** the **Payroll Ledger** using the employee information, employee profiles and TD1 information. Detailed keystroke instructions for setting up payroll follow.
2. **Enter** the **transactions** in Sage 50 using the Chart of Accounts and Supplier, Customer and Employee Information. The first source document is on page 343.
3. **Print** the following **reports** after you have finished making your entries:

REPORTS

Accounts
- ☐ Chart of Accounts
- ☐ Account List
- ☐ General Journal Entries

Financials
- ☑ Comparative Balance Sheet: June 1 and June 30 with difference in percentage
- ☑ Income Statement: June 1 to June 30
- ☑ Trial Balance date: June 30
- ☑ All Journal Entries: June 1 to June 30
- ☑ General Ledger accounts: June 1 to June 30: 4020 5410 5420
- ☐ Statement of Cash Flows
- ☑ Cash Flow Projection Detail Report: for 1080 for next 30 days

Tax
- ☐ GST Report

Banking
- ☐ Cheque Log Report

Payables
- ☐ Supplier List
- ☐ Supplier Aged
- ☐ Aged Overdue Payables
- ☐ Expenses Journal Entries
- ☐ Payments Journal Entries

Receivables
- ☐ Customer List
- ☐ Customer Aged
- ☐ Aged Overdue Receivables
- ☐ Sales Journal Entries
- ☐ Receipts Journal Entries
- ☑ Sales by Salesperson June 1 to June 30
- ☐ Sales by Job Category
- ☐ Customer Statements

Employees & Payroll
- ☐ Employee List
- ☑ Summary for all employees
- ☐ Deductions & Expense
- ☐ Job Category
- ☐ Remittances
- ☑ Payroll Journal Entries: June 1 to June 30
- ☐ T4 Slips
- ☐ Record of Employment
- ☐ Year End Review (PIER)

Mailing Labels
- ☐ Labels

NOTES

Remember that you must have a valid and active Payroll ID code from Sage in order to use the payroll features for non-Student versions of the program.

Choose the Services menu and click Payroll And Support for more information.

PAYROLL SETUP KEYSTROKES

Adding the Payroll Module

Open **SageData19\NORTHERN\NORTHERN** to access the data file for **Northern Lights**. **Accept** June 1 as the **session date**.

The Payroll module is hidden because it was not used. Before we can set it up, we need to unhide it. We will then work from this module to enter settings and employees.

Choose the **Setup menu** and **click User Preferences** to open the Options screen.

Click **View** to access the screen we need:

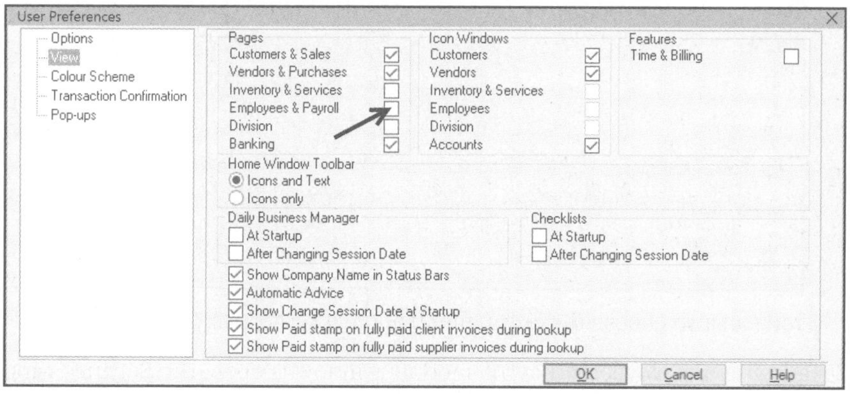

Click the **Pages check box for Employees & Payroll** to add ✓s for Pages and Icon Windows.

Click **OK** to save the settings and return to the Home window.

Click **Employees & Payroll** in the Modules pane list:

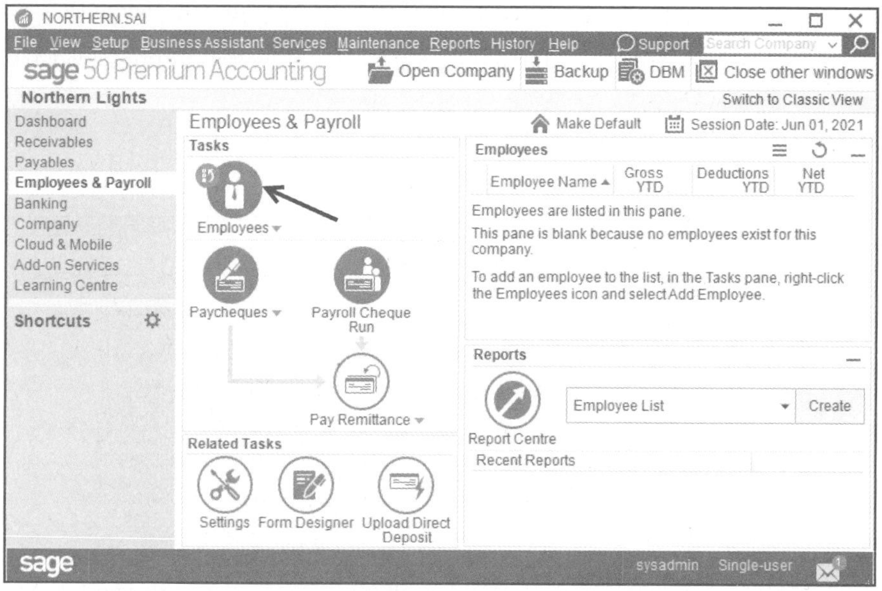

All Payroll module icons have been added. The open or not-finished history symbol  on the Employees icon indicates that the module history is open or unfinished. If you try to finish the Payroll history now, Sage 50 will generate an error message about several missing linked accounts.

From the Employees & Payroll window we can enter ledger settings and records.

Setting Up the Payroll Ledger

Before you can enter Payroll Journal transactions, you must set up the payroll module. This involves the same steps as setting up other ledgers:

1. Change the settings for the ledger.
2. Create Employee Ledger records.
3. Add historical employee data.
4. Back up the data file and finish the history.

NOTES

If you are using the backup installation set or the Pro version, restore SageData19\NORTH1.CAB or NORTH1 to SageData19\NORTHERN\NORTHERN to open the data file for Northern Lights.

CLASSIC VIEW

The User Preferences View screen has two columns: one for Modules that includes Time & Billing and one for the Icon Windows. The module name is Payroll.

PRO VERSION

The Pro version does not have the Time & Billing feature, and Project replaces Division as the module label.

NOTES

Clicking the Pages check box will add the ✓s for viewing both the Module and Icon Windows. Then you can remove the ✓ for the Icon Window if you want.

NOTES

You can make Employees & Payroll your default home page while you are completing the payroll setup. When you close the file and re-open it, you will open this page to continue the setup.

NOTES

If you open the Payroll Journal now, you will display the message that essential linked accounts are missing. Clicking OK will then open the Linked Accounts Settings screen. The history for all other modules is finished and they are ready to use.

CLASSIC VIEW

From the Home window, right-click the Employees icon. Then click the Settings tool. You can also click the Settings tool and select Employees from the drop-down list.

NOTES

In any module window, click the Settings icon and then click Payroll to open the Payroll Settings screen.

Changing Payroll Ledger Settings

Click the **Settings icon** to open the Payroll Settings screen:

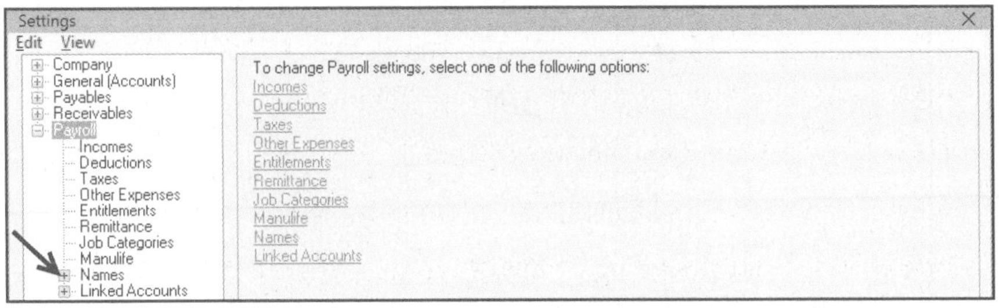

You can also choose the Setup menu and click Settings. Click Payroll if necessary.

Because the Employees & Payroll module window is open, the Settings window opens with the Payroll Settings list. For payroll, we need to define the types of income paid to employees; the payroll deductions; payroll taxes; employee entitlements; remittances; job categories; names for income, deductions and additional fields; and linked accounts for all these functions. We will begin by entering names and deleting the ones we do not need. The reduced list will be easier to work with.

Click the ⊞ **beside Names** and the ⊞ **beside Linked Accounts**.

This will expand the list, making the links to all the Payroll settings available.

Changing Payroll Names

NOTES

By modifying the names first, only the ones we need to set up will appear on later screens.

Click **Income & Deductions** under the Names subheading:

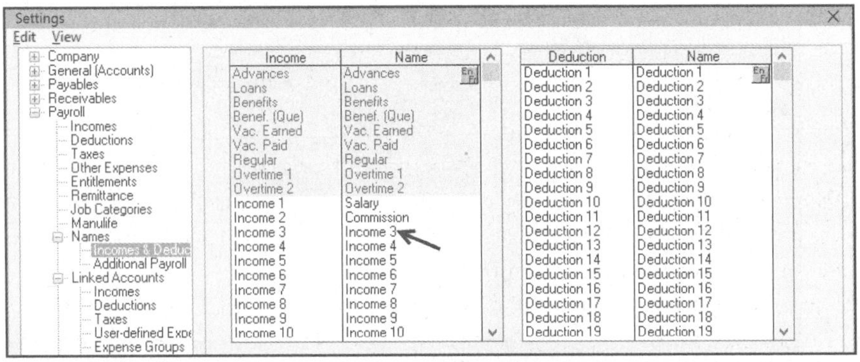

PRO VERSION

The Expense Groups entry under Linked Accounts is not included in the Pro version.

NOTES

You can enter names for any of these fields later if you need to add more incomes or deductions.

The first screen we need to modify has all the names for incomes and deductions used. Many of the standard income types are mandatory and cannot be changed. These fields are on a shaded background. Some of the other default names are also correct, so you do not need to redefine them. You can leave Income 1 and Income 2, labelled "Salary" and "Commission," unchanged because Northern Lights has salaried employees and pays a sales commission to Apsimak. There is allowance for 20 different kinds of income in addition to the compulsory ones and 20 different payroll deductions. Each income and deduction label may have up to 12 characters, including spaces.

Northern Lights uses an additional income field for the piece rate bonus that is based on the number of tickets or beverages sold. The travel allowance for Player and Staige is also set up as an income. The remaining income fields are not used.

Northern Lights also has three payroll deductions at this time: VRSP, the Registered Retirement Savings Plan; the employee share of extended health care plan premiums (EHC-Employee); and the actors' guild fees. The remaining deductions are not used.

NOTES

Northern Lights does not use Expense Groups (under Linked Accounts).

Click **Income 3 in the Name column** to highlight the contents.

Type `No. Sold` **Press** *tab* to advance to the Income 4 field.

Click the **En/Fr language icon** to open the extra fields if you want to enter labels or names in both French and English.

Type `Travel Allow` **Press** tab to advance to the Income 5 field.

Press del. **Press** tab to advance to the Income 6 field.

Press del. **Press** tab to advance to the Income 7 field.

Press del to remove the entry. **Press** tab to select the next field.

Delete the **remaining Income names** until they are all removed.

Press tab after deleting Income 20 to select Deduction 1 in the Name column. **Press** tab again if you are in the Deduction column.

Type `VRSP` **Press** tab to advance to the second deduction Name field.

Type `EHC-Employee` **Press** tab to highlight the next field.

Type `Guild Fees` **Press** tab to highlight the next field.

Delete the **remaining deductions** because Northern Lights does not use them.

Click **Additional Payroll** under the Names subheading:

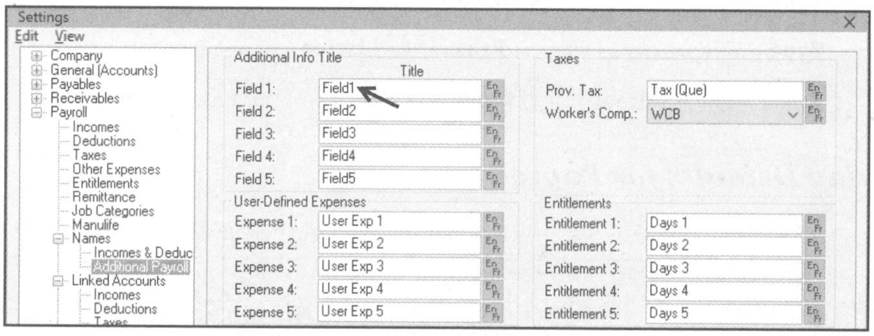

The Prov. Tax field is used for additional payroll taxes applied by the province. You can change the tax name. Since we will not enter linked accounts for provincial payroll taxes, the program will automatically skip the related payroll fields. WCB (Workers' Compensation Board) is entered as the name for Workers' Compensation because we selected Yukon as the business province.

We can also name the additional ledger fields, the additional payroll expenses for Northern Lights and the entitlements for employees. Northern Lights pays 50 percent of the employees' health care plan medical premiums and eligible tuition fees and a travel allowance to Player and Staige. It provides sick leave and personal leave days for all employees, as well as vacation days for salaried employees as entitlements. First, we will name the additional ledger fields. These fields will store the name and phone number of each employee's emergency contact.

Double-click **Field1** or **press** tab.

Type `Emergency Contact`

Press tab **twice** to skip the language label icon and highlight the next field.

Type `Contact Number`

Press tab **twice**. **Press** del to delete the name for Field3.

Delete the **names** for Field4 and Field5.

Benefits and expenses can be handled in different ways. The medical premium payment is a taxable benefit for employees. It is also entered as a user-defined expense because the premiums are paid to a third party rather than to the employee. Tuition, the

NOTES

We are setting up travel allowances as income – it will be added to the paycheque as non-taxable income. When it is paid separately to the employees, it is set up as a user-defined expense.

NOTES

If clicking does not highlight the field contents, drag through an entry to select it. Double-clicking will open the English/French names screen.

WARNING!

If you later change the province in the Company Information screen, the WCB name entered for Worker's Comp. will not change automatically. You must enter the correction manually by choosing from the drop-down list.

NOTES

The Worker's Comp. drop-down list has several other employer expenses that may apply to all employees. The list includes HST, which may be applied to some contract or free-lance employees.

You may use up to 20 characters to name the additional fields and 12 characters for user-defined expenses.

NOTES

When you are not using both French and English (Company Settings, Features options) you will press tab once after each entry.

other taxable benefit and user-defined expense, is also paid to a third party — the educational institution. Benefits paid directly to the employee on the payroll cheque should be set up as income. Reimbursements for expenses may be entered as non-taxable income or as user-defined expenses. Because we repay the expenses on the payroll cheque, we define them as reimbursements — an income type that is not taxable — and link them to an expense account. If we entered them as user-defined expenses, we would create both a linked payable and expense account and issue a separate payment to the employee.

> **NOTES**
> For Northern Lights, we use the generic Benefits field to enter all employee benefits.

> **NOTES**
> You can use up to 12 characters, including spaces, for user-defined expense and entitlement names – that is why we omitted the space for the Personal Days entitlement name.

Drag through **User Exp 1**, the Expense 1 field, to highlight the contents.

Type `Tuition Fees` **Press** (tab) **twice**.

Type `EHC-Employer` **Press** (tab) **twice**.

Press (del). **Press** (tab) **twice** to select Expense 4. **Press** (del).

Press (tab) **twice** to select Expense 5. **Press** (del).

Drag through **Days 1**, the Entitlement 1 field, to highlight the contents.

Type `Vacation` **Press** (tab) **twice** to select the next entitlement name.

Type `Sick Leave` **Press** (tab) **twice**.

Type `PersonalDays` **Press** (tab) **twice**.

Press (del). **Press** (tab) **twice** to select the final name. **Press** (del).

Setting Defaults for Payroll

> **NOTES**
> The incomes with shaded background are defined by the program and cannot be changed – System is entered in the Type column.

Click **Incomes** under the Payroll heading to display the income setup:

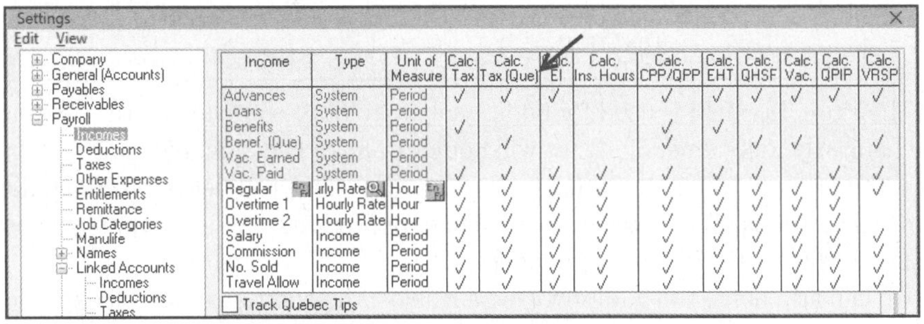

At this stage, we will change the tax settings for Incomes and Deductions.

We will first modify this screen by hiding the columns that do not apply to Yukon so that only the columns we need are on-screen at the same time.

> **NOTES**
> When you close and re-open the Payroll Settings screen, the hidden and resized columns will be restored – the column changes you made are not saved.
> QHSF is the provincial health services plan for Quebec.
> QPIP (Quebec Parental Insurance Plan) provides parental leave benefits to EI insurable employees. Both employers and employees pay into the plan.
> EHT (Employer Health Tax) applies only in Ontario.

Point to the **right-hand column heading margin for Calc. Tax (Que.)** until the pointer changes to a two-sided arrow ✥.

Drag the **margin to the left** until the column is hidden.

Point to the **right-hand column heading margin for Calc. EHT** until the pointer changes to a two-sided arrow. **Drag** the **margin to the left**.

Remove the **columns for Calc. QHSF** and **Calc. QPIP** in the same way.

> **NOTES**
> VRSP refers to voluntary registered pension plans that the company sets up for employees. They are managed by Manulife for Sage.

Only the income names you did not delete (pages 320–321) appear on this screen. For each type of income you must indicate what taxes are applied and whether vacation pay is calculated on the income. Most of the information is correct. Regular and overtime hours are paid on an hourly basis, while salary and commissions are paid at designated income amounts per period. All taxes apply to these types of income in Yukon, so these default settings are correct. Vacation pay, however, is paid only to the hourly paid employees, so some checkmarks should be removed. In addition, we should designate the type of income for No. Sold and Travel Allow, the incomes we added, and the taxes that apply. Choosing the type of income will change the defaults that are applied, so we make this change first.

Click **No. Sold** to place the cursor on the correct line.

Press *tab* to move to the Type column. A List icon is added.

Click the **List icon** to access the list of income types we can select:

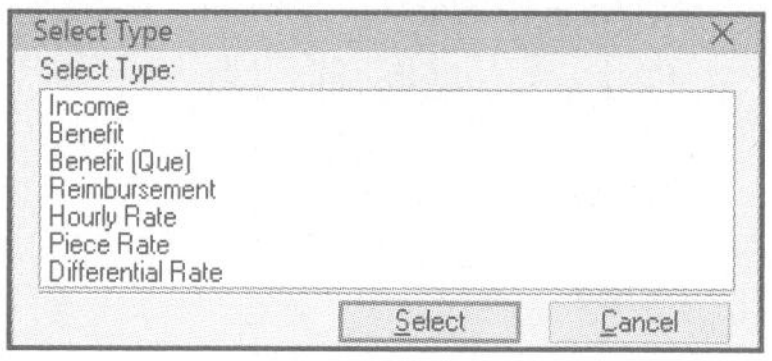

By default, all new income entries are assigned to the **Income** type. This assignment is correct for Salary. Taxable benefits paid to a third party should be classified as **Benefits** (read the Warning note). The benefit amount is added to income to determine taxes and then subtracted again to calculate the net pay amount. Taxable benefits paid directly to the employee instead of a third party should also be classified as Income. If a benefit is added to net pay, it should be classified as Income. Tuition is not paid to the employee, so it is a benefit.

Reimbursements are not taxable — the employee is being repaid for company-related expenditures. The **Piece Rate** type calculates pay based on the number of units. **Differential Rates** apply to different hourly rates paid at different times and are not used by Northern Lights.

Click **Piece Rate** to select this type for No. Sold.

Click **Select** to add the Type to the Settings screen. **Press** *tab*.

The cursor advances to the Unit of Measure field and the entry has changed to Item. The amount paid to employees is based on the number of tickets or beverages sold.

Type `Number`

The checkmark for Insurable Hours was removed as soon as we changed the type.

Click **Travel Allow** and **press** *tab*.

Click the **List icon** and **click Reimbursement**.

All checkmarks are removed because this type of income is not taxable.

We need to modify one more Insurable Hours setting. The number of hours worked determines eligibility for Employment Insurance benefits. Regular, overtime and salary paid hours are included but commissions are not — no time can be reasonably attached to commissions, so they are not counted. The checkmark for it should be removed. The ✓ for No. Sold was automatically removed when we changed the income type.

Click **Commission** to select this income line.

Press *tab* **repeatedly** until the cursor is in the **Calc. Ins. Hours field**.

Click to remove the ✓, or **press** the **space bar**.

We also need to modify the entries for vacation pay. In Yukon, vacation pay is calculated on all performance-based wages. This includes the regular wages, overtime wages and piece rate pay. We need to remove the remaining ✓s. Salaried workers receive paid time off rather than a percentage of their wages as vacation pay. We do not need to remove the ✓ for Overtime 2. If it is used later, vacation pay will be calculated on it as well. The settings for VRSP are correct — all incomes are included in gross pay, except overtime, and are selected by default.

WARNING!

If you choose Benefit from this Select Type list of income categories, the expense amount for it will not be reported in the journal entry – as if it happens behind the scenes – and requires a separate journal entry to make the payment to the employee.

NOTES

An alternative approach for tuition fees is to set them up as a taxable income (on which vacation pay is not calculated) and add the amount to the employee's paycheque. You would use this method when the employee pays the tuition and is repaid (as in Helena's Academy, Chapter 8, and VeloCity, Chapter 16). Tuition is not a reimbursement type of income because it is taxable – you cannot change tax settings when you choose Reimbursement.

NOTES

Vacation pay is calculated on all wages. This calculation includes the piece rate pay – number of tickets or beverages – because it is a performance-based wage or income. Vacation pay is not applied to benefits.

The regulations governing vacation pay are set provincially.

Click **Salary** in the Income column.

Press *tab* **repeatedly** to get to the **Calc. Vac. column**.

Click to remove the ✓, or **press** the **space bar**.

Press ⇩ to place the cursor in the **Calc. Vac. field for Commission**.

Click to remove the ✓, or **press** the **space bar** and complete the Settings:

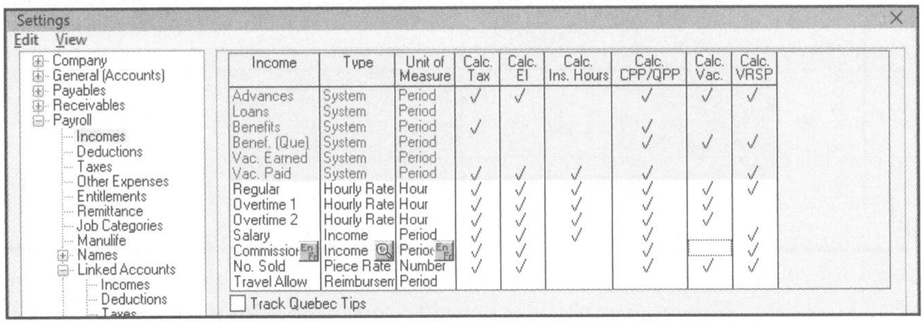

Click **Deductions** under the Payroll heading:

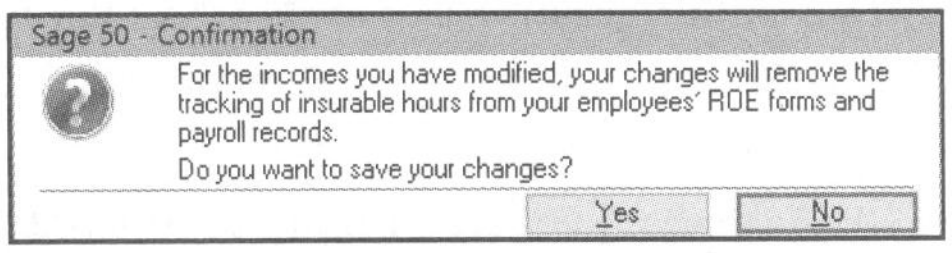

You are warned that the changes will affect the insurable earnings amounts reported on the Record of Employment. The changes are correct, so you should continue.

Click **Yes** to continue to the Deductions settings:

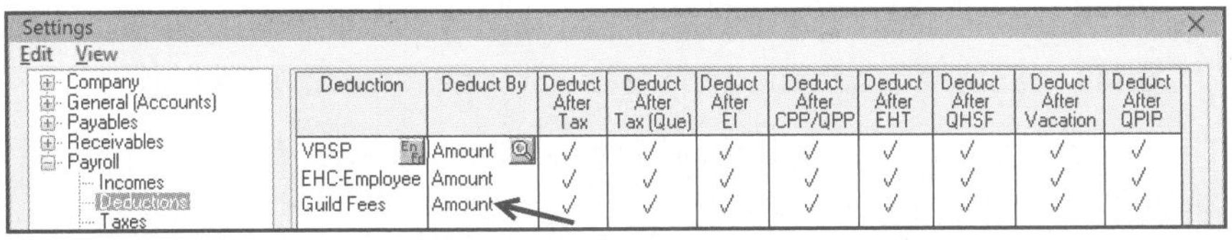

Only the deduction names you entered earlier appear on this screen. You can calculate deductions as a percentage of the gross pay or enter a fixed amount. The default is to deduct by amount. This is the correct selection for EHC-Employee and VRSP. Guild fees are deducted as a percentage.

Click **Guild Fees**. **Press** *tab* to select Amount. **Click** the **List icon** for the Deduct By field:

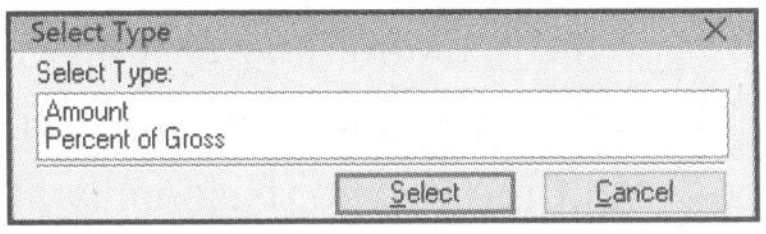

Click **Percentage of Gross** and then **click** **Select**.

All deductions are set by default to be calculated after all taxes (Deduct After Tax is checked). For EHC-Employee and Guild Fees, this is correct — they are subtracted from income after all payroll taxes have been deducted. However, VRSP contributions qualify as tax deductions and will be subtracted from gross income before income tax is calculated, but not before EI, CPP and so on, so you must change only this setting.

Click the **Deduct After Tax column** for VRSP to remove only the one ✓ and change the setting to before tax.

The remaining settings are correct. VRSP is deducted after the other payroll taxes and vacation pay because these deductions are based on gross wages.

Click **Taxes** under the Payroll heading:

NOTES

Vacation pay is also paid for statutory holidays. Northern Lights pays workers their regular pay for these days, as if they had worked. For occasional workers, this pay may be calculated as a percentage of wages.

In Quebec, vacation pay is also paid on benefits.

NOTES

Although checkmarks will remain for the columns we hid, the fields for them will be skipped in ledger screens and journals because we will not enter linked accounts for them.

The program will not allow you to add checkmarks for overtime hours in the Calculate VRSP column. Refer to the lower pop-up message in the second screenshot on page 326.

NOTES

You can modify the Deductions screen as you modified the Income Settings screen so that only the columns you need are on-screen. You can remove the Deduct After Tax (Que.), EHT, QHSF and QPIP columns.

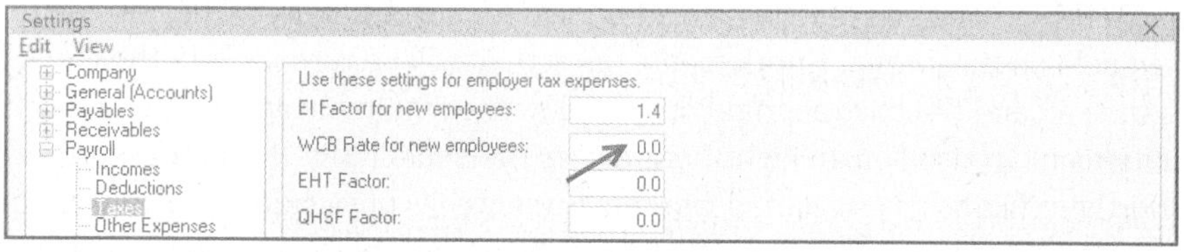

This next group of fields refers to the rate at which employer tax obligations are calculated. The factor for Employment Insurance (**EI Factor**) is correct at 1.4 — the employer's contribution is set at 1.4 times the employee's contribution. In the next field, you can set the employer's rate for **WCB** (Workers' Compensation Board) premiums. On this screen, you can enter the rate that applies to most Northern Lights employees. We will modify the rates for Kabanza and Usher in their ledger records.

The next field, **EHT Factor**, is the percentage of payroll costs that the employer contributes to the provincial health plan in Ontario. The rate is based on the total payroll costs per year. It does not apply to employees in other provinces.

The **QHSF Factor** (Quebec Health Services Fund) applies to payroll in Quebec, so we do not need to enter it. QHSF is similar to EHT.

Click the **WCB Rate field**.

Type 1.55

The Quebec tax fields will not be available for employees because we will not enter linked accounts for them. They do not apply to employees in Yukon.

Click **Other Expenses** under the Payroll heading:

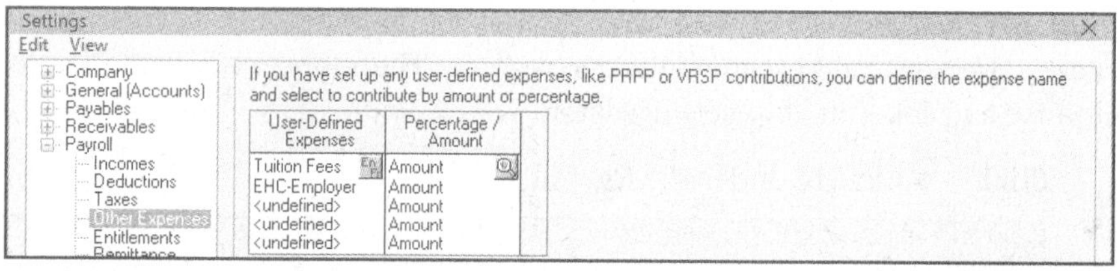

The default settings for employer expenses are correct — both expenses are calculated by amount.

Click **Entitlements** under the Payroll heading:

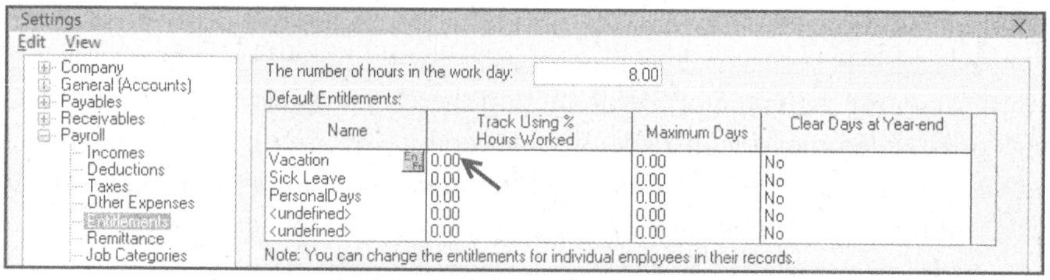

On this screen you can enter the rules for entitlements that apply to all or most employees. When we enter the rules here, they will be added to each employee's record. You can change entitlement amounts for individual employees in their ledger records.

Entitlements may be given directly or may be linked to the number of hours worked. For example, usually employees are not entitled to take vacation time or sick leave until they have worked for a certain period of time. You can use the **Track Using % Hours Worked** to determine how quickly vacation or sick days accumulate. For example, one day per month equals about 5 percent of hours worked. Thus, you would enter 5 percent if the employee is entitled to 12 days of leave per year. You can also indicate the **Maximum** number of **Days** per year that an employee can take or accumulate. And finally, you must indicate whether the unused days are **cleared at the end of a year** or can be carried forward. If the days earned but not used at the end of a year are carried forward, then the Maximum will still place a limit on the number of days available. When the maximum

NOTES

The WCB rate is based on the injury history and risk factors for the job and for the industry. Kabanza and Usher have different rates than the others because their jobs are in different rate classes.

If WCB does not apply, you can select a different expense name from the drop-down list on the Additional Payroll Names Settings screen and then enter rates for this expense.

NOTES

EHT applies to payroll in Ontario. The factor or rate ranges from 0.98 to 1.95 depending on the total payroll amount.

QHSF is used for Sound Inc. in Chapter 14.

NOTES

Northern Lights does not contribute to the VRSP, so this is not entered as a user-defined expense.

NOTES

You can also apply entitlements as a fixed amount per year by omitting the tracking percentage, entering a maximum and then entering the balance for the employee in the ledger.

NOTES

The number of hours per working day is set at 8 by default, but you can change this. For Helena's Academy, we changed it to 7.5. You can also change the entry for individual employees in their ledger records.

number of days has been reached, no additional days will accrue — the entry in the Days Earned field on the journal Entitlements tab screen will be zero — until the employee takes time off and the days accrued drops below the maximum again. The number of days of entitlement is based on an eight-hour day as the default, but this can be changed.

Northern Lights gives salaried workers three weeks of vacation (tracked at 8 percent) and allows a maximum of 25 days. Sick leave at 10 days per year is earned at the rate of 5 percent to a maximum of 20 days. Personal leave days (5 days per year) accrue at the rate of 2.5 percent to a maximum of 10 days. None are cleared at year-end.

Northern Lights allows two weeks of vacation time and sick leave and one week of personal days to be carried over to the following year.

NOTES

Three weeks' vacation is equivalent to about 6 percent when paid as a percentage of wages. When tracked as a percentage of hours worked, 8 percent will yield about four weeks of time off.

Click the **Track Using % Hours Worked field for Vacation**.

Type 8 **Press** tab to advance to the Maximum Days field.

Type 25 **Press** tab.

Click the **Track Using % Hours Worked field for Sick Leave**.

Type 5 **Press** tab to advance to the Maximum Days field.

Type 20 **Press** tab.

Click the **Track Using % Hours Worked field for PersonalDays**.

Type 2.5 **Press** tab to advance to the Maximum Days field.

Type 10 **Press** tab.

Until we identify linked accounts we cannot set up Remittances. To set up Job Categories, we must first create employee records. Therefore, we will add Payroll Remittance and Job Category settings later.

Click **Manulife** under the Payroll heading:

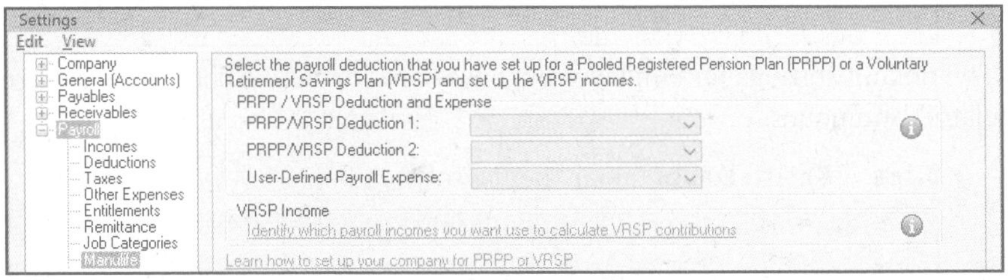

Here we enter the name of the deduction that is set up for the voluntary retirement savings plan. No employer contribution is added by Northern Lights, so there is no user-defined expense associated with the plan. Pointing to the information buttons  provides additional information about entering the required information:

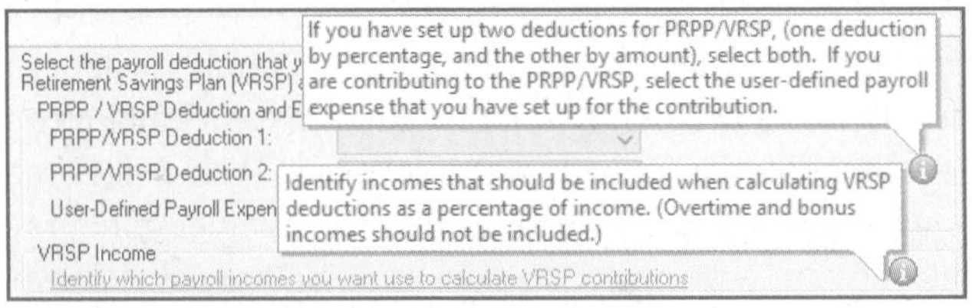

NOTES

Clicking the first underlined link (Identify Which...) will open the Income Settings screen on page 322.

Clicking the Learn How... link opens Help information with more information about these plans.

CLASSIC VIEW

You can access the Payroll Ledger linked accounts by right-clicking the Paycheques or the Payroll Cheque Run icon,

or

.

Then click the Settings tool . You can also click the Settings tool and select Payroll from the drop-down list. Or, choose the Setup menu, then click Settings, Payroll, Linked Accounts and Income.

If no Home window icon is selected, you can use the Settings tool pop-up list, choose Payroll and click Select.

Click the **list arrow for PRPP/VRSP Deduction 1**. The three deduction names we entered earlier are listed.

Click **VRSP**.

Identifying the Payroll Linked Accounts

There are many linked accounts for payroll because each type of income, tax, deduction and expense that is used must be linked to a General Ledger account. You do not need to create any of these accounts; they are already in the Chart of Accounts. The following **linked accounts** are used by Northern Lights for the Payroll Ledger:

PAYROLL LINKED ACCOUNTS

Income

Principal Bank	1080	Bank: Chequing			
Vacation Owed	2300	Vacation Payable	Advances & Loans	1240	Loans Receivable
Vac. Earned	5430	Vacation Earned	Salary	5410	Salaries: Performance Staff
Regular	5420	Wages: Support Staff	Commission	5440	Commissions
Overtime 1	5420	Wages: Support Staff	No. Sold	5450	Sales Bonuses
Travel Allow	5560	Travel Allowances	Overtime 2: Not used		

Deductions	**Deduction Payable Account**	**Payment Adjustment**
VRSP:	2410 VRSP Payable	2410 VRSP Payable
EHC-Employee:	2400 EHC Payable - Employee	2400 EHC Payable - Employee
Guild Fees:	2450 Players' Guild Payable	2450 Players' Guild Payable

Taxes

Payables			**Expenses**	**Payment Adjustment**
EI	2310	EI Payable	5510 EI Expense	5510 EI Expense
CPP	2320	CPP Payable	5520 CPP Expense	5520 CPP Expense
Tax	2330	Income Tax Payable		1080 Bank: Chequing
WCB	2460	WCB Payable	5530 WCB Expense	5530 WCB Expense

EHT, Tax (Que.), QPP, QHSF, QPIP: Not used

User-Defined Expenses

Payables			**Expenses and Payment Adjustments**
Tuition Fees	2420	Tuition Fees Payable	5570 Tuition Fees Expense
EHC-Employer	2440	EHC Payable - Employer	5580 EHC Premium Expense

Click **Incomes** under the Linked Accounts subheading:

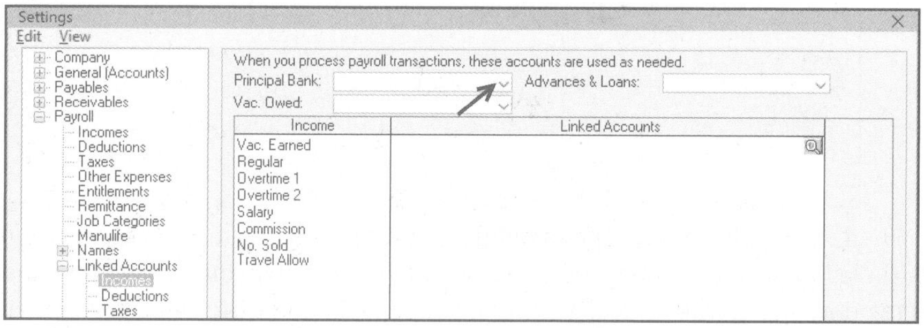

The linked accounts for all types of income appear together on this first screen. You must identify a wage account for each type of employee payment used by the company, even if the same account is used for all of them. Once the Payroll bank account is identified as the same one used for Payables, the program will apply a single sequence of cheque numbers for all cheques prepared from the Payables and Payroll journals.

Accounts you can use for more than one link will be available in the drop-down list. Otherwise, once an account is selected as a linked account, it is removed from the list.

To enter accounts, you can **type** the **account number** or **select** the **account** from the drop-down list and **press** *tab* to advance to the next linked account field.

Choose **1080 Bank: Chequing** for the Principal Bank field.

Choose **2300 Vacation Payable** for the Vacation Owed field.

Choose **1240 Loans Receivable** for the Advances & Loans field.

Choose **5430 Vacation Earned** for Vac. Earned.

Choose **5420 Wages: Support Staff** for Regular and Overtime 1. Do not enter an account for Overtime 2.

NOTES
You can also access the Payroll Linked Accounts screens from the Setup menu (and from the Payroll Journal at this stage). Choose Settings and click Payroll and Linked Accounts or open the journal and click OK in response to the warning about missing essential linked accounts.

NOTES
All the accounts you will need for this stage are already in the Chart of Accounts.

However, you can add accounts from the Linked Accounts windows. Type a new number, press *enter* and choose to add the account.

NOTES
The deleted income and deduction names do not appear on the screens for linked accounts. Deleting the unused names also simplifies the data entry for linked accounts.

NOTES
Only the single bank class account is available on the Principal Bank drop-down selection list.

WARNING!
Do not enter linked accounts for Overtime 2 and other unused incomes. In this way, the program will skip these fields in the employee records.

Choose **5410 Salaries: Performance Staff** for Salary.

Choose **5440 Commissions** for Commission.

Choose **5450 Sales Bonuses** for No. Sold.

Choose **5560 Travel Allowances** for Travel Allow.

Click **Deductions** under Linked Accounts for the next set of accounts:

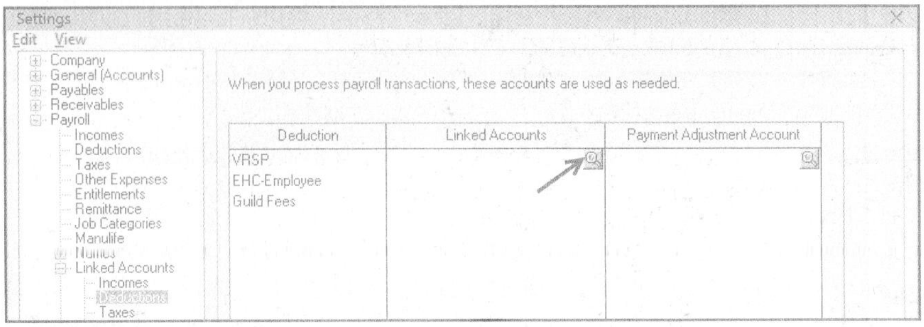

The names here are the ones you entered in the Names: Incomes & Deductions screen. If you deleted a name, it will not appear here.

Enter the **Deductions** and **Payment Adjustment linked accounts** for **VRSP**, **EHC-Employee** and **Guild Fees** from the chart on page 327.

Click **Taxes** under Linked Accounts to access the next set of linked accounts:

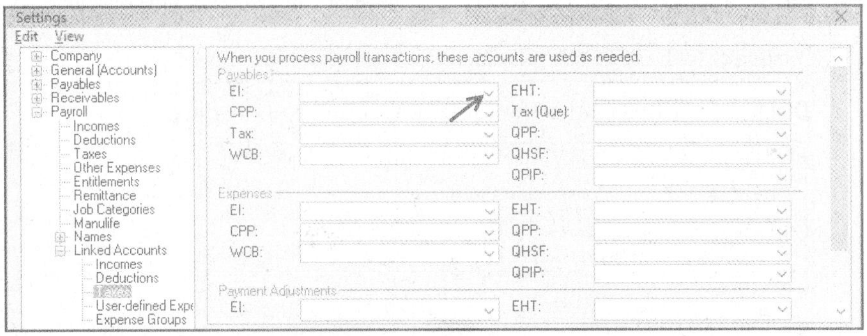

NOTES
Payment Adjustment accounts are not essential. You may omit them until you need to use them for a remittance. If you enter an adjustment amount, Sage 50 will prompt you to enter the linked account. At that stage, you can choose an account or create a new one.

When the employer pays the tax, linked payable and expense accounts are needed. Only the employee pays the income tax, so only the payable linked account is needed. This tax does not create an employer expense. For EI and CPP, employee contributions are added to those of the employer to calculate the total amount payable.

WARNING!
Do not enter linked accounts for the unused taxes. In this way, the program will skip these fields in the employee records.

Enter the **linked Payables accounts** for **EI**, **CPP**, **Tax** and **WCB** in the **Payables** section. **Enter** the **linked accounts** for **EI**, **CPP** and **WCB** in the **Expenses** section and for the related **Payment Adjustments** accounts from the chart on page 327.

Click **User-Defined Expenses** under the Linked Accounts subheading to open the screen for the final Payroll accounts:

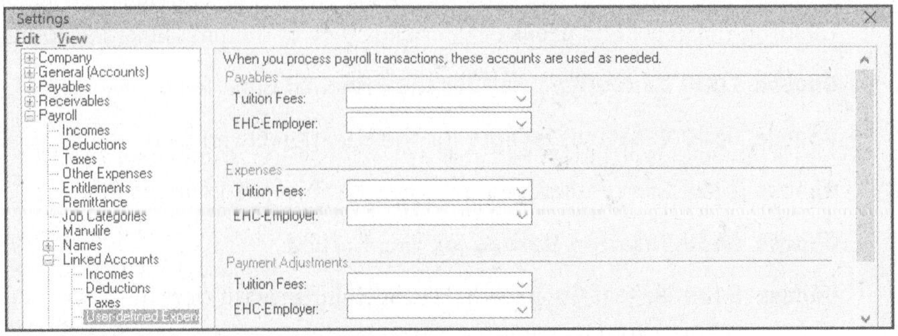

Enter the **linked Payable accounts**, the **linked Expenses accounts** and the **linked Payment Adjustments accounts** for **Tuition Fees** and **EHC-Employer**. Refer to the chart on page 327.

Check the **linked** payroll **accounts** against the chart on page 327 before proceeding. Click each heading under Linked Accounts to open the different screens.

Changing Payroll Form Settings

Before closing the Settings screens, we still need to enter the form number to set up the automatic numbering of direct deposit slips. This number is entered with the other automatic numbering sequences as part of the Company Settings.

Click **Company** and then **click** **Forms** to open the number setup screen:

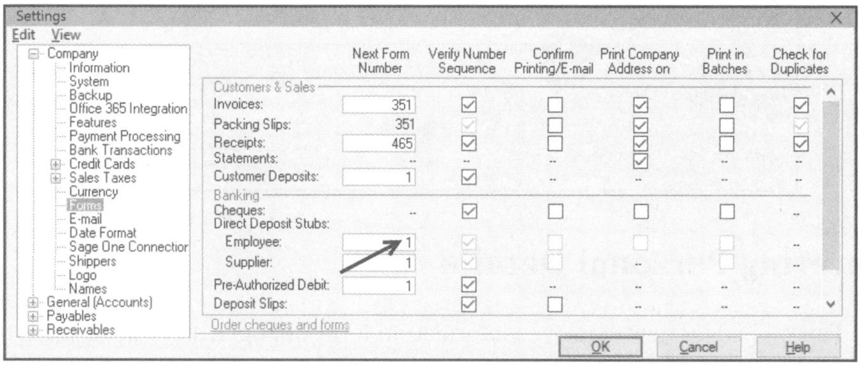

Click the **Direct Deposit Stubs Next Form Number field** for **Employees**.

Type 242

Click **OK** to save the Settings changes:

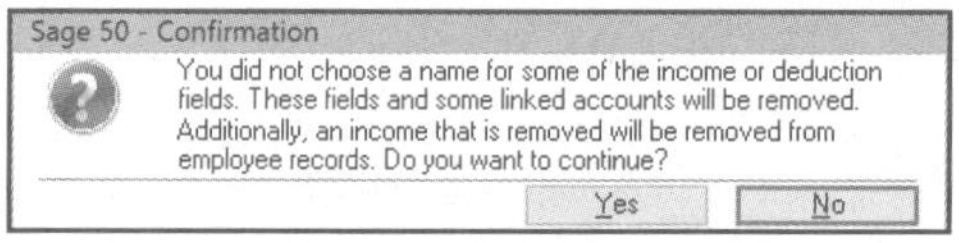

Because we deleted some income and deduction names, we are being warned that any accounts linked to these deleted fields will also be removed. We can proceed.

Click **Yes** to open a second confirmation message:

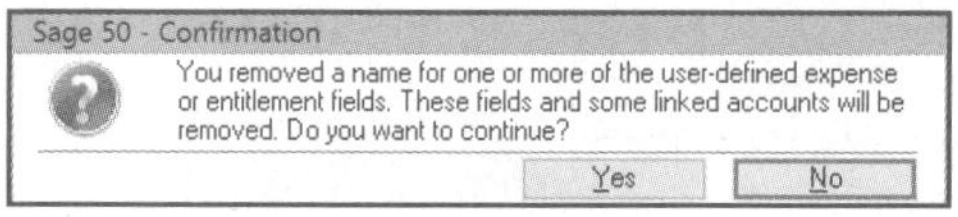

Again, we are warned because of the other field names we deleted.

Click **Yes** to continue and return to the Payroll Home window.

Entering Employee Ledger Records

Use the Northern Lights Employee Information Sheet and Employee Profiles on pages 314–317 to create the employee records and add historical information.

We will enter the information for Northern Lights employee Taika Tikett.

Click the **Employees icon** 

in the Home window.

PRO VERSION

The entry for Packing Slips is not included.

NOTES

You are still unable to finish the Payroll history (History menu). Although we have entered linked accounts, the ledger is unbalanced because the Loans Receivable and Vacation Payable ledger account balances do not match these amounts in the employee records. These are the control accounts for the Payroll Ledger.

The Data Integrity Check will indicate that historical information for employees is not balanced.

The Employees icon window is blank because no employees are on file at this stage.

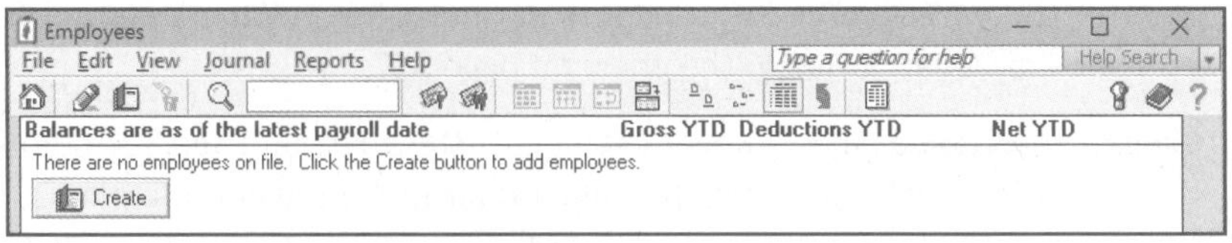

Click the **Create button** Create or **choose** the **File menu** and **click Create**.

Or, to bypass the Employees window and open the Payroll Ledger employee window,

Click the **Employees icon shortcuts list** and **choose Add Employee**:

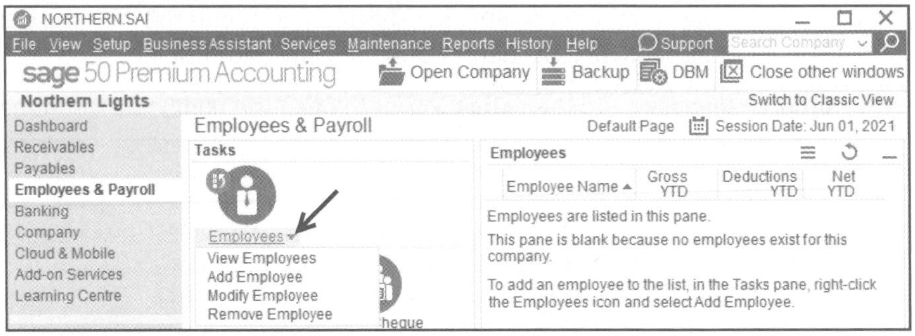

Entering Personal Details

The Payroll Ledger new employee information form will open so you can begin to enter the employee record. There are many required fields in the Employee Ledger records because this information links to government income tax tables and rules.

The opening Personal information page holds the personal details for the employee:

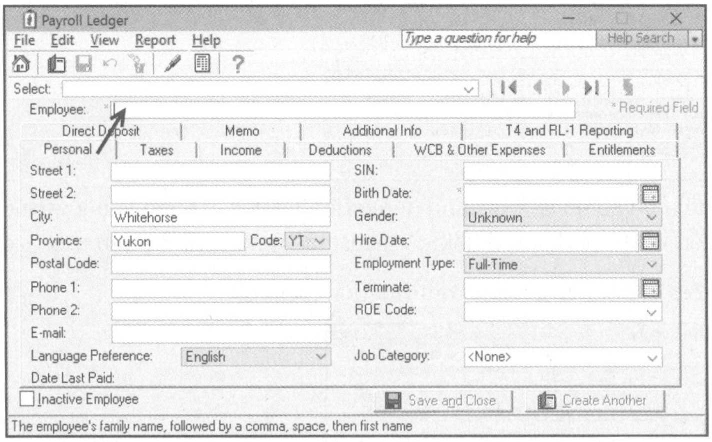

The Payroll Ledger has a large number of tabs for the different kinds of payroll information and many required fields — those marked with an asterisk *. The default city, province and province code for the business are entered and are correct. The cursor is in the Employee field. If you enter the surname first, employee lists will be in correct alphabetic order. You can change the Address tab screen information at any time.

Type `Tikett, Taika` **Press** *tab*.

The cursor advances to the Street 1 field.

Type `29 Stubbs Rd.`

Click the **Postal Code field**.

Type `y1a4k2` **Press** *tab*.

NOTES

If you hide the Employees icon window (Setup menu, User Preferences, View screen), the Payroll Ledger window opens immediately when you click the Employees icon.

You will also skip the Employees window if you use the Add Employee shortcut.

NOTES

The Set Field Names tool in the ledger window will open the Payroll Settings Additional Names screen where we added emergency contact field names.

NOTES

As in other ledgers, required fields that you cannot leave blank are marked with an asterisk *.

On the Personal tab screen, the employee name and the date of birth are essential. All other fields on this screen can be completed later.

The program corrects the postal code format and advances the cursor to the Phone 1 field.

Type 8676897595 **Press** *tab* to correct the phone number format.

The default **Language Preference** is correctly set as English.

Click the **Social Insurance Number (SIN) field**. You must use a valid SIN.

Type 218738631 **Press** *tab* to advance to the Birth Date field.

Enter the month, day and year using any accepted date format.

Type 8-10-89 **Press** *tab* **twice** to advance to the Gender field.

Choose **Male** from the drop-down list. **Press** *tab*.

The cursor moves to the Hire Date field, which should contain the date when the employee began working for Northern Lights.

Type 11 6 19 **Press** *tab*. **Full-Time** as the employment type is correct.

The next two fields will be used when the employee leaves the job — the date of termination and the reason for leaving that you can select from the drop-down list. The final option designates employees as active or inactive. All employees at Northern Lights are active, so the default selection is correct.

Job Categories are used to identify salespersons who can be linked to specific sales so that their sales revenue is tracked and used to calculate commissions. The employee's Job Category can be selected here from the drop-down list if categories are already set up, or you can place employees in categories later from the Payroll Settings screen. We will create categories later and assign employees to them at that stage.

When you use Sage 50 to pay employees, the Date Last Paid will be entered automatically by the program.

The remaining details for the employee are entered on the other tab screens.

Entering Tax Information

Click the **Taxes tab** to advance to the next set of employee details:

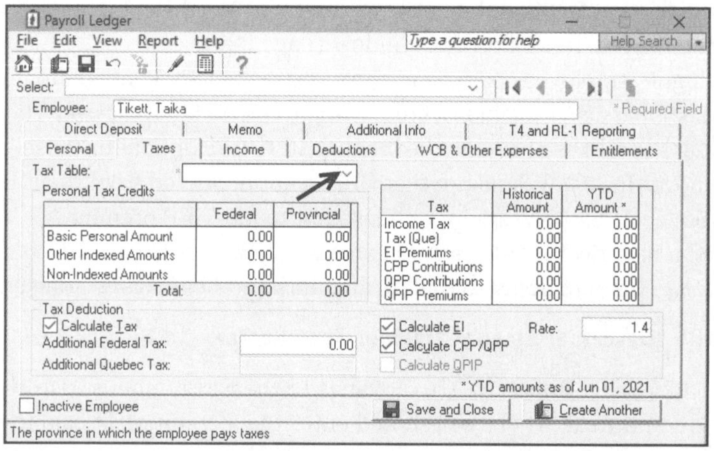

This screen allows you to enter income tax–related information. **Personal Tax Credits** are divided between **federal** and **provincial** and then again among the **basic** amount, the total of all other amounts that are **indexed** and the total of amounts that are **non-indexed**. Provincial personal income taxes are not linked to the rates for federal income taxes, so separate claim amounts are needed. Sage 50 will enter the total claim amount. The total is used to calculate income taxes for each paycheque. Historical tax amounts for the year to date are also entered on this screen.

NOTES
The program will allow you to omit the social insurance number, but you must enter the employee's date of birth. The SIN can be added later and is required for the Record of Employment. The date of birth is required because it determines whether CPP deductions are mandatory.

NOTES
The termination date and reason for leaving a job will determine the employee's eligibility to collect Employment Insurance. Refer to page 299.

NOTES
You should drag the column margins so that all amounts and headings are on-screen. The YTD column may be hidden initially, and you cannot maximize ledger windows.

NOTES
The Tax Table (Province) is the only required field on this screen. Taxes will be based on the minimum basic claim amounts if no claim amounts are entered. Tax Table is a required field because different provinces and territories have different basic claim amounts and income tax rates.

Click the **Tax Table list arrow**. A list of provinces and territories appears on the screen. This is a required field.

Click **Yukon**, the territory of taxation for Northern Lights for income tax purposes.

Press tab to advance to the Basic Personal Amount label.

Press tab again for the Federal amounts field, which holds the basic claim amount.

Type 12609 **Press** tab to advance to the field for the Provincial Basic Personal Amount.

Type 12609 **Press** tab to advance to the field for Other Federal Indexed Amounts.

Type 12609 **Press** tab to advance to the field for Other Provincial Indexed Amounts.

Type 12609 **Press** tab to advance to the Federal Non-Indexed Amounts.

Type 1935 **Press** tab to advance to the Provincial Non-Indexed Amounts.

Type 1935

Usher is the only other employee who has non-indexed amounts.

Press tab to update the totals. **Click** the **Additional Federal Tax** field.

When an employee has chosen to have additional federal income tax deducted from each paycheque, enter the amount of the deduction in the **Additional Federal Tax** field. Employees might make this choice if they receive regular additional income from which no tax is deducted. By making this choice, they avoid paying a large amount of tax at the end of the year and possible interest penalties.

Type 50

For **Kabanza** enter **100** in the Additional Federal Tax field.

If an employee is insurable by EI, you must leave the box for **Deduct EI** checked. The default EI contribution factor, 1.4, for all employees at Northern Lights is correct. We entered it in the Payroll Taxes Settings window (page 325).

All Northern Lights employees pay income tax and make CPP contributions, so these check boxes should also remain selected. Employees under 18 or over 70 years of age do not contribute to CPP, so clicking the **Deduct CPP/QPP** option for these employees (to remove the ✓) will ensure that CPP is not deducted from their paycheques. Employees over 65 years may choose not to pay CPP premiums.

We will enter the historical year-to-date tax amounts next (for five months of pay). You should drag the column margins so that all amounts and headings are on-screen.

Click the **Historical Amount field** for **Income Tax**

Type 1120.30 **Press** tab to advance to the EI Premiums Historical Amount field, where you should enter the amount of EI paid to date.

Type 308.91 **Press** tab to move to the CPP Contributions Historical Amount field.

Type 685.03

NOTES
When you subscribe to the payroll services plan, you can update the tax claim amounts with the aid of a tax wizard. Only the indexed amounts will be updated.

NOTES
Deduction amounts for tuition are not subject to indexing. For provinces that allow a claim for months of study, this amount is also not subject to indexing.

NOTES
All employees between 18 and 65 must pay CPP premiums if they are employed. They may collect CPP as early as 60 years, with a reduction for taking the pension early, or after 65 with increased payouts for the delay in collecting.

If an employee does not pay a tax, click the Calculate Taxes check box for it.

WARNING!
Enter employee historical payroll details carefully. You will be unable to edit these fields after finishing the history.

These historical details are needed because there are yearly maximum amounts for CPP and EI contributions. Totals for optional deductions are retained in the employee record. They must also be correct because they are used to create T4s for tax reporting.

NOTES
The program skips the Quebec tax fields because no linked account was entered for the extra provincial tax.

Entering Income Amounts

We defined all the types of income for Northern Lights when we set up Names (refer to page 320). All the details you need to complete the Income tab chart are on pages 314–315. The following list summarizes the types of income used by each employee. Not all will be used on all paycheques.

- Loans and Benefits: all employees (read margin Notes)
- Vac. Owed and Vac. Paid: all hourly paid employees (read margin Notes)
- Regular: four hourly paid employees — Tikett, Kabanza, Usher, Ridges
- Overtime 1: four hourly paid employees — Tikett, Kabanza, Usher, Ridges
- No. Sold: two hourly paid employees — Tikett, Ridges
- Salary: three salaried employees — Apsimak, Player, Staige
- Travel Allow: two actors — Player, Staige
- Commission: Apsimak

Click the **Income tab** to open the next screen of employee details:

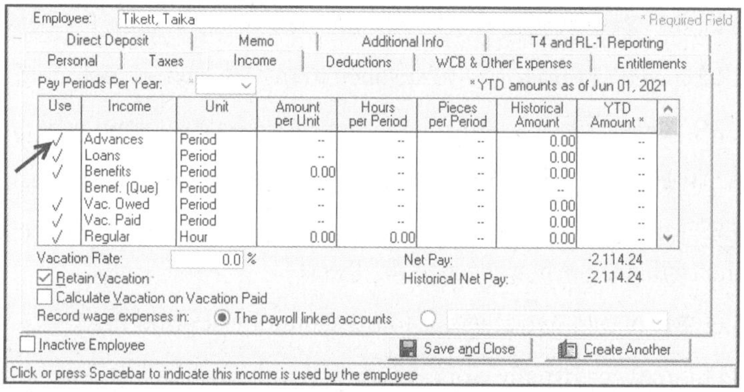

On the Income chart you can indicate the types of income that each employee receives (the **Use** column), the usual rate of pay for that type of income (**Amount Per Unit**), the usual number of hours worked (**Hours Per Period**), the usual number of units for a piece rate pay base (**Pieces Per Period**) and the amounts received this calendar year before entering the first paycheque in Sage 50 (**Historical Amount**). The **Year-To-Date (YTD) Amount** is added automatically by the program based on the historical amounts you enter and the paycheques entered in the program.

Checkmarks must be entered in the Use column to make the fields available in the Payroll journals, even if they will not be used on all paycheques.

We need to add the historical loans, benefits and vacation amounts for Tikett. Tikett has $100 in loans not yet repaid, and he has not received all the vacation pay earned last year. The total of the advances/loans and vacation owed amounts for all employees must match the opening General Ledger balances for the corresponding linked accounts.

Two employees have received some of their vacation pay this year. We enter that amount in the **Vac. Paid Historical Amount** field. Vacation pay not yet received is entered in the **Vac. Owed Historical Amount** field. Any loans paid to the employees and not yet repaid are recorded in the **Loans Historical Amount** field. There is no record of loan amounts recovered.

Pay Periods Per Year refers to the number of times the employee is paid, or the pay cycle. This is a required field. Tikett is paid every two weeks, 26 times per year.

NOTES

The incomes that are used by an employee are marked with a ✓ in the chart on pages 314–315 or have an amount in the employee's column.

NOTES

Checkmarks are added by default for all incomes, deductions and expenses that have linked accounts entered for them.

The checkmarks for Advances, Loans, Benefits, Vacation Owed and Vacation Paid cannot be removed.

NOTES

Because advances are taxable, Northern Lights issues short-term loans to employees instead.

NOTES

If calculating vacation on vacation paid is required by legislation, you should click the check box for this option.

WARNING!

The totals for all employees for advances and loans paid and vacation pay owing must match the corresponding General Ledger linked account balances before you can finish entering the history. These are the two control accounts for the Payroll Ledger.

NOTES

The negative amount for Net Pay at this stage is the sum of the year-to-date tax amounts.

Click the **list arrow** beside the field for **Pay Periods Per Year**:

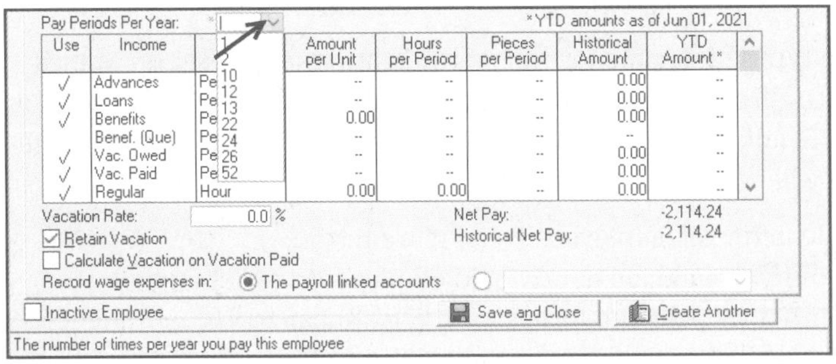

NOTES
Employees may be paid yearly (1), semi-annually (2), monthly for 10 months (10), monthly (12), every four weeks (13), every two weeks for a 10-month year (22), twice a month (24), every two weeks (26) or weekly (52).

Click **26**.

Click the **Historical Amount column beside Loans** to move the cursor.

Type `100` **Press** *tab* to move to the Benefits Amount Per Unit column.

NOTES
The Benefits Amount Per Unit for Tikett and Usher includes only the medical premium. The historical amount includes the medical benefit and tuition fees already paid.

The medical premiums paid by the employer are employee benefits.

Type `41.54` **Press** *tab* to move to the Historical Amount for Benefits.

Type `1015.40` **Press** *tab* to advance to the Vac. Owed Historical Amount.

Type `939` **Press** *tab* to advance to the Historical Vac. Paid Amount.

Type `610` **Press** *tab* again to advance to the **Use column for Regular**.

Press *tab* to advance to the Amount Per Unit field where we need to enter the regular hourly wage rate for Tikett.

NOTES
The Net Pay and Historical Net Pay are continually updated as you add income and deduction amounts. Benefits do not change the Net Pay amount because they are not paid to the employee.

WARNING!
Do not click the Use column beside Regular for hourly paid employees as that will remove the checkmark.

Type `18` **Press** *tab* to advance to the Hours Per Period field.

Bi-weekly paid employees usually work 80 hours per period. Salaried workers normally work 160 hours each month. You can change the number of hours and the rate in the Payroll journals.

Type `80` **Press** *tab* to advance to the Historical Amount field.

Historical income and deduction amounts for the year to date are necessary so that taxes and deductions can be calculated correctly and T4 statements will be accurate.

NOTES
When an amount varies from one pay period to another, you should leave its Amount Per Unit field blank in the ledger and enter the amount in the journal.

Type `14400` **Press** *tab*.

This amount is entered automatically in the YTD column and the cursor advances to the Use column for Overtime 1.

Press *tab* so you can enter the overtime hourly rate.

Type `27`

Press *tab* **twice** to advance to the Historical Amount field. There is no regular number of overtime hours.

NOTES
No linked account was entered for Overtime 2, so no checkmark appears beside it.

Type `810` **Press** *tab* to advance to the Overtime 2 Use column.

Some income types do not apply to Tikett, so they should not be checked. The next income that applies is No. Sold, the piece rate method of pay. We need to enter the rate or amount per unit (number) and the historical amount. There is no fixed number of pieces per period.

If no linked account is entered for an income, the Use column will be blank, as for Overtime 2.

NOTES
Pressing the space bar when you are in the Use column will also add a ✓ or remove one if it is there.

Pressing ⇩ will move you to the next line in the same column.

Click the **Use column beside Salary** to remove the ✓.

Click the **Use column beside Commission** to remove the ✓.

Click the **Use column beside Travel Allow** to remove the ✓.

Click **No. Sold** in the Income column to select the line. Do not click the Use column. **Press** tab.

Type 0.10 to enter the amount received for each set. **Press** tab **twice**.

Type 440 to enter the historical amount.

For **Player** and **Staige**, click the Use column for Regular, Overtime 1, Commission and No. Sold to remove the ✓s. Enter the monthly **Salary** (Amount Per Unit) and press tab. Enter **160** as the number of hours worked in the pay period for them. Press tab and enter the historical amount. You cannot remove the ✓s for Vac. Owed and Vac. Paid, even if they are not used. Enter the amount per unit and the year-to-date amounts for **Travel Allow**.

For **Apsimak**, remove the ✓s for the Regular, Overtime 1 and No. Sold, and enter the **Salary** per period, the number of hours and the year-to-date amounts. Leave **Commission** checked and enter **1650** as the historical amount. There is no regular amount for each pay period.

Retaining Vacation pay is normal for full-time hourly paid employees. Part-time and casual workers often receive their vacation pay with each paycheque because their work schedule is irregular. You will turn the option to retain vacation off for these employees — their vacation pay will then be added to each paycheque. If the employee is salaried and does not receive vacation pay, the option should also be turned off. For employees who receive vacation pay, leave the option to Retain Vacation checked and type the vacation pay rate in the % field.

Double-click the **% field beside Vacation Rate**.

Type 6

For **Apsimak**, **Player** and **Staige**, click Retain Vacation to remove the ✓.

Employee wages may be linked to their separate **Payroll Linked Accounts** or they can all be linked to the single expense account that you select from the drop-down list. Wage income expenses for all Northern Lights employees are linked to the default accounts entered on pages 327–328, so the default selection is correct.

Entering Payroll Deduction Amounts

The next step is to enter current and historical details for deductions, just as we did for income. You must indicate which deductions apply to the employee (Use column), the amount or percentage normally deducted and the historical amount — the amount deducted to date this year.

Click the **Deductions tab** to open the screen for payroll deductions:

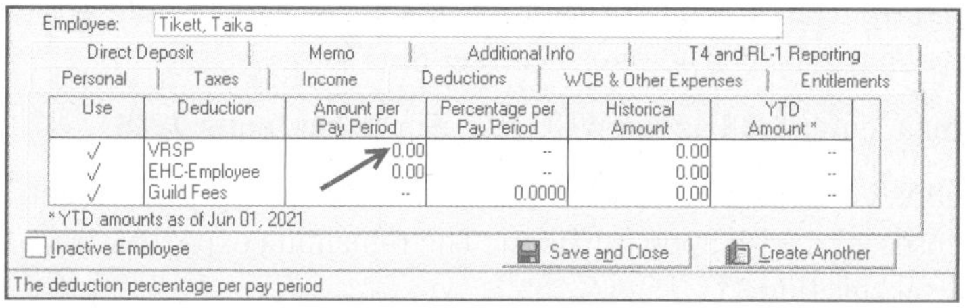

All deductions are selected in the Use column (a ✓ is entered).

By entering deduction amounts or percentages here, they will be included automatically on the Payroll Journal input forms. Otherwise, you must enter them

NOTES

Remember that commissions must be calculated manually and entered in the Payroll journals. The Commission field in the Payroll Ledger allows only a fixed amount, not a percentage of sales, as the entry.

NOTES

When you select a specific account, all wage expenses for that employee will be linked to the same account – the one you identify in this field. If you want to use different accounts for different wage expenses, you must use the linked accounts.

For Tiste, in Chapter 8, we linked a single account to all his wages.

NOTES

For one-time changes, you can edit deduction amounts in the Payroll journals on the Deductions tab screen.

NOTES

If the employee's ledger record Use column does not have a ✓, that field will be removed from the Payroll Journal for the employee.

manually in the journal for each pay period. Not all employees make VRSP contributions at this time, but they may do so later, so we will leave this field available. When you enter the amounts or percentages here, the deductions are automatically added in the journal, but changes can still be made in the journals. You should make permanent changes by editing the Employee Ledger record. Tikett has VRSP contributions withheld from his pay.

When deductions are made as a percentage, as for Guild Fees, the Percentage Per Pay Period field is available.

Click **VRSP** in the Deduction column to select the line. **Press** tab.

The cursor advances to the Amount Per Period field. You should enter the amount that is withheld in each pay period.

Type 100 **Press** tab to advance to the Historical Amount field.

Type 1000 **Press** tab to update the YTD Amount.

Press tab to advance to the Use column for EHC-Employee.

Press tab to advance to the Amount Per Pay Period field.

Type 41.54 **Press** tab to advance to the Historical Amount field.

Type 415.40 **Press** tab to update the YTD Amount.

Click the **Use column for Guild Fees** to remove the ✓.

For **Player** and **Staige**, enter the percentage per period and year-to-date amounts for **Guild Fees**. The remaining deductions are not used by Northern Lights. The names were deleted, so they do not appear on our chart or in the ledger.

NOTES
The program skips the Amount Per Pay Period field when the deduction is set up to be calculated by percentage. When it is set up to be deducted by amount, the program will skip the Percentage Per Pay Period field.

Entering WCB and Other Expenses

In other provinces, the tab label will be changed to match the name used for WCB in that province. Ontario uses the name WSIB — Workplace Safety and Insurance Board — instead of WCB, so the tab label will be WSIB & Other Expenses.

Click the **WCB & Other Expenses tab**:

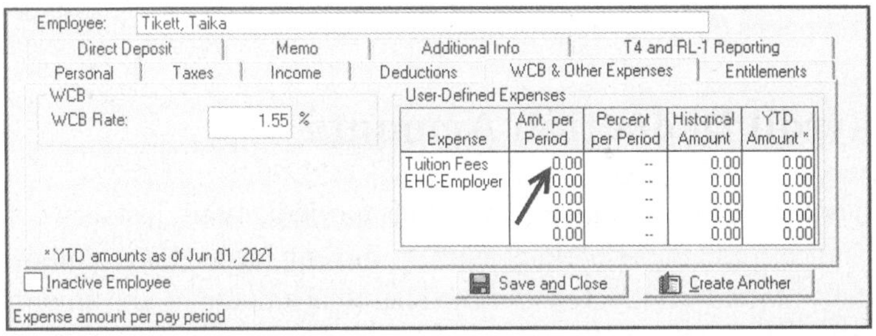

The user-defined expenses we created in the Additional Payroll Names screen (page 321) and the default WCB rate (page 325) are entered on this screen. The default WCB rate is entered from our setup information, but you can enter a different rate for an individual employee in this field. The rate is correct for Tikett.

For **Kabanza**, enter **3.38** as the WCB rate. For **Usher**, enter **1.75**.

Other user-defined expenses are also added on this screen. Northern Lights has two user-defined expenses, and both apply to Tikett. The remaining expenses are not used by Northern Lights at this time.

Click the **Tuition Fees Amt. Per Period**. Enter the amount that the employer contributes in each pay period.

Type 60 **Press** tab to advance to the Historical Amount field.

NOTES
You should drag the column margins so that all amounts and headings are on-screen. The YTD column may be hidden initially.

NOTES
Kabanza and Usher have different WCB rates because their jobs are in a different rate class.

NOTES
The employer expense for tuition benefit is set up to be entered automatically. The benefit amount will be added in the Payroll Journal.

Type 600

Click the **EHC-Employer Amt. Per Period**. **Type** 41.54

Press *tab* to advance to the Historical Amount field. **Type** 415.40

For **Usher**, enter **160** as the Tuition Fees Amt. Per Period and **1600** as the Historical Amount.

Entering Entitlements

Click the **Entitlements tab**:

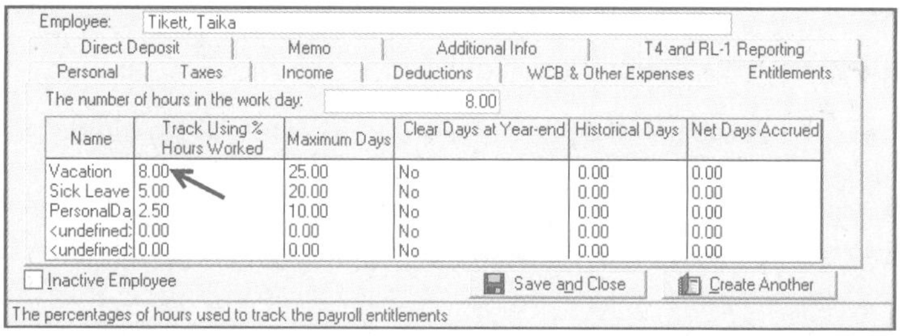

We entered the default rates and amounts for entitlements as Payroll Settings (pages 325–326), but they can be modified in the ledger records for individual employees.

We must also enter the historical information for entitlements. The number of **Historical Days** will include any days carried forward from previous periods. The number of days accrued cannot be greater than the maximum number of days defined for the entitlement for an employee. The number of **Net Days Accrued**, the amount unused and available for carrying forward, is updated automatically from the historical information and current Payroll Journal entries.

You cannot enter information directly in the Net Days Accrued field.

Tikett receives vacation pay instead of paid time off, so the vacation entitlements details should be removed. The defaults for sick leave and personal days are correct.

Click the **Track Using % Hours Worked field for Vacation**.

Press *del* to remove the entry 8.00.

Press *tab* to advance to the Maximum Days field. **Press** *del*.

Click the **Historical Days field for Sick Leave**. **Type** 16

Press ↓ to advance to the Historical Days field for PersonalDays. The number of days is added to the Net Days Accrued.

Type 4 **Press** *tab* to add the amount to the Net Days Accrued field.

For Apsimak, Player and Staige, the default entries for tracking and maximum days are correct, but you must enter the Historical Days for each entitlement.

Entering Direct Deposit Information

Four employees have elected to have their entire paycheques deposited directly to their bank accounts. On this screen, we need to enter the bank account details. For each employee who has selected the Direct Deposit option, you must turn on the selection in the **Direct Deposit Paycheques For This Employee** check box. Then you must add the five-digit Transit or **Branch Number**, the three-digit Bank or **Institution Number**, the bank **Account Number** and finally the amount that is deposited, or the percentage of the cheque. Refer to the bank account deposit details on page 315.

NOTES

You should drag the column margins so you can include all the columns and amounts on-screen.

NOTES

If employees take days before the sufficient number of hours worked have been accrued, the program will warn you. Then you can allow the entry for entitlements or not. This permission is similar to allowing customers to exceed their credit limits.

NOTES

Third parties, such as Bambora, provide the service of transferring the payroll deposits to the employees' bank accounts.

Direct deposits are covered in Chapter 13.

NOTES
All banks in Canada are assigned a three-digit bank or institution number, and each branch has a unique five-digit transit number. You must enter the correct number of digits for these.
Account numbers may vary from five to twelve digits.

NOTES
The paycheque deposit may be split among more than one bank account by entering different percentages for the accounts, but the total must add to 100%. Or, you can enter amounts instead for each account.
To delete bank account details, click the employee's Direct Deposit tab. Click Active in the Status column to change the entry to Inactive and then delete the bank information. Click the check box for Direct Deposit Paycheques to remove the ✓.
For individual paycheques, you can click the Direct Deposit check box in the journal to remove the ✓ and pay the employee by cheque.

NOTES
The Daily Business Manager is covered in Chapter 11.

NOTES
Additional information for other ledgers may also be displayed or hidden in journal transactions.
In the Manulife section, you can indicate the plan type (pooled – PRPP – or Voluntary – VRSP) and enter the employee's Manulife plan number.

WARNING!
The Contact Number field is not predefined as a telephone number, so the format will not be corrected automatically by the program.

Click the **Direct Deposit tab**:

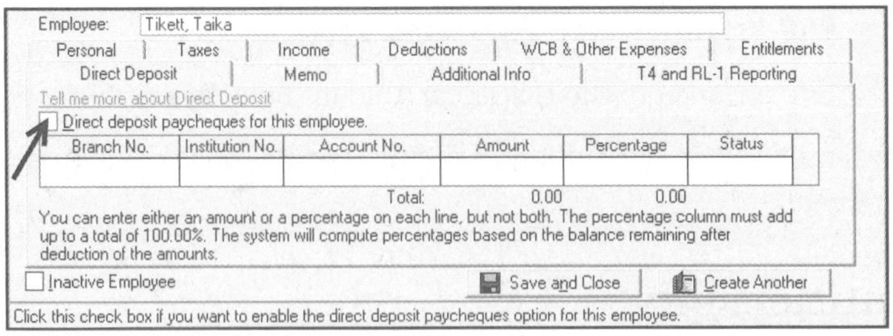

Click the **Direct Deposit Paycheques For This Employee check box** to add a ✓.

Click the **Branch No. field**.

Type 06722 **Press** tab to advance to the Institution No. field.

Type 180 **Press** tab to advance to the Account No. field.

Type 4556221 **Press** tab **twice** to advance to the Percentage field.

Type 100

Click the **Memo tab**:

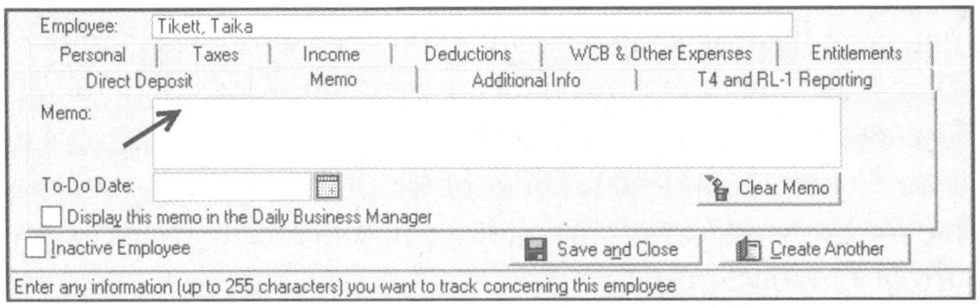

The Memo tab will not be used at this time. You could enter a note with a reminder date to appear in the Daily Business Manager; for example, a reminder to issue vacation paycheques on a specific date, to recover advances and loans or to celebrate a birthday.

Entering Additional Information

Northern Lights enters emergency contacts for each employee.

Click the **Additional Info tab** to access the additional fields:

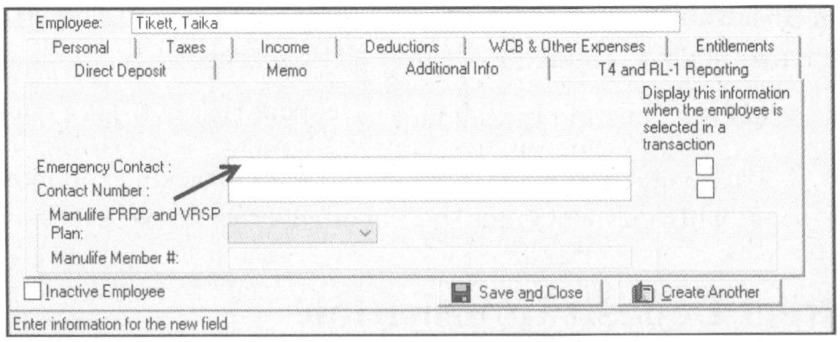

You can indicate whether you want to display any of the additional information when the employee is selected in a transaction. We do not need to display the contact information in the Payroll Journal. Enter the contact information from page 315.

Click the **Emergency Contact field**.

Type Kierin Tikett **Press** tab **twice**.

Type (867) 689-1892 to enter the contact's phone number.

Entering T4 and RL-1 Reporting Amounts

The final information screen allows you to enter the year-to-date EI insurable and pensionable earnings. By adding the historical amounts, the T4 slips prepared for income taxes at the end of the year and the Record of Employment termination reports will also be correct. Refer to the T4 historical information on page 315.

Click the **T4 and RL-1 Reporting tab** to open the final screen:

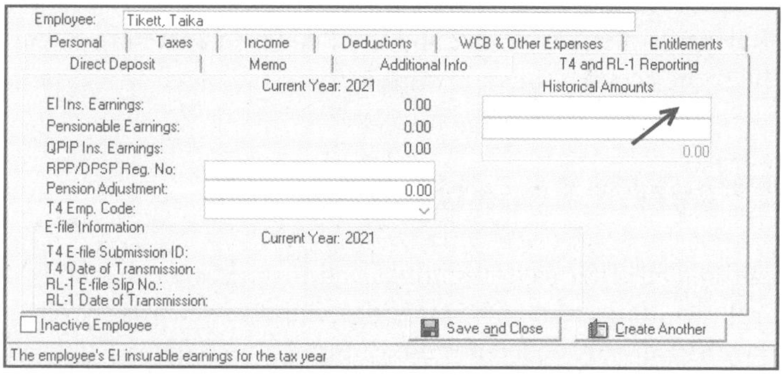

In the **Historical Amounts field for EI Ins. Earnings**, you should enter the total earned income received to date that is EI insurable. The program will update this total every time you make payroll entries until the maximum salary on which EI is calculated has been reached. At that time, no further EI premiums will be deducted.

Pensionable Earnings — the total of all income plus benefits — are also tracked by the program. This amount determines the total income that is eligible for the Canada Pension Plan. Again, when the maximum is reached, no additional CPP is deducted. The **Pension Adjustment** amount is used when the employee has a workplace pension program that will affect the allowable contributions for personal registered pension plans and will be linked with the Canada Pension Plan. Workplace pension income is reduced when the employee also has income from the Canada Pension Plan. Since Northern Lights has no company pension plan, the Pension Adjustment amount is zero and no pension plan registration number is needed.

The T4 Employee Code applies to a small number of job types that have special income tax rules.

Double-click the **Historical Amounts field for EI Ins. Earnings**.

Type 16260

Double-click the **Historical Amounts field for Pensionable Earnings**.

Type 17275.40

Correct any employee information **errors** by returning to the field with the error. **Highlight** the **error** and **enter** the **correct information**. **Click each tab** in turn so that you can check all the information.

When all the information is entered correctly, you must save the employee record.

Click **Create Another** [Create Another]. Changes are saved automatically.

A new blank employee information form opens.

Click the **Personal tab** so that you can enter address information.

Repeat these procedures to **enter** other employee **records** using the information on pages 314–317.

Click [Save and Close] after entering the last record to save it and close the Payroll Ledger.

NOTES

The EI Insurable amount is the total of gross wages, including overtime wages and vacation pay. If EI is calculated on the income, the income is added to EI Insurable Earnings.

For pensionable earnings, benefits are added to EI insurable amounts.

NOTES

The T4 Employee Code is required only for the types of employment in the drop-down list for the field. No employees with Northern Lights are in these positions.

WARNING!

Do not finish the history until you have printed your reports to check all the historical setup information and made a backup.

When you close the Employee Ledger after entering the last hourly employee, or after all employees, you may get the message that the payroll history is balanced, asking if you want to finish the history now. Choose No.

NOTES

If you started from the Add Employee shortcut, you will return directly to the Payroll Home window.

Do not finish the **history** yet!

The Payroll Ledger is now balanced — the General Ledger amounts for *Advances & Loans Receivable* and *Vacation Payable* match the total of these historical amounts for all employees. Therefore, it is possible to finish the history now. However, other amounts that are not verified may be incorrect and you will be unable to change them after finishing the history.

Close the **Employees window** to return to the Home window.

Display or **print** the **Employee List** and the **Employee Summary Report** to check the accuracy of your work.

Setting Up Payroll Remittances

NOTES
Remember that if you are not using the Student version you must have a valid and current payroll service plan with Sage to ensure the payroll tax tables you use are current and that tax amounts will be correctly calculated.

Because we have entered all other payroll settings and records, we can modify the final settings — for payroll remittances and job categories. Supplier records are also required for this step, but they had already been entered. Entering remittance settings involves these steps: linking the suppliers who receive payroll remittance amounts to the taxes or deductions they receive and entering payment frequency and next remittance dates.

Linking Remittances to Suppliers

The chart below identifies remittance suppliers, the liability linked to each supplier, the remitting period frequency and the ending payroll date for the next remittance period.

NOTES
We will not add a remittance supplier for tuition because it may be paid to different institutions.

PRO VERSION
Remember that the term Vendors is used instead of Suppliers.

PAYROLL SUPPLIERS

Supplier	Payroll Liability	Remitting Frequency	Next Remittance Period End Date
Receiver General for Canada	EI	Monthly	June 30, 2021
	CPP	Monthly	June 30, 2021
	Tax	Monthly	June 30, 2021
Manulife Financial	EHC-Employee	Monthly	June 30, 2021
	EHC-Employer	Monthly	June 30, 2021
Yukon Workers' Compensation Board	WCB	Monthly	June 30, 2021
Manulife Financial	VRSP	Monthly	June 30, 2021

Click the **Settings icon**  to open the Payroll Settings screen.

Click **Payroll** and then **click** **Remittance** to open the screen we need:

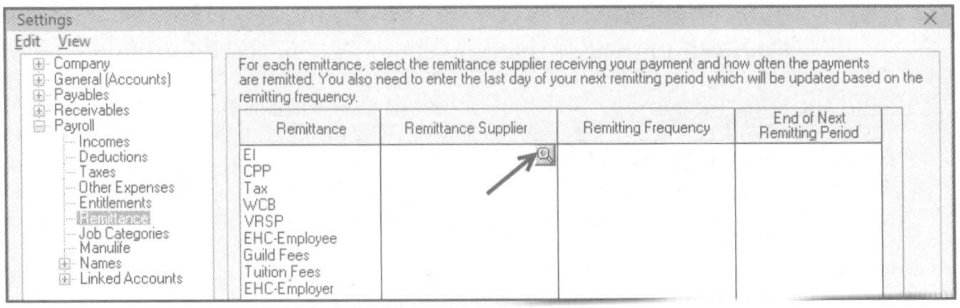

All the payroll items that are linked to liability (remittance) accounts are listed: taxes, deductions and user-defined expenses. For each liability, we can select a supplier and payment frequency from lists and then enter the date of the last pay period covered by the next remittance payment.

Click the **List icon** in the Remittance Supplier column on the line for EI. The selection list opens with all suppliers included:

Click **Receiver General for Canada**.

Click **Select** or **press** *enter* to return to the Remittance Settings screen.

The cursor advances to the Remittance Frequency field for EI. The frequency for all remittances is Monthly. The next remittance for all liabilities will be made on June 30.

Click the **List icon** in the Remitting Frequency field. **Double-click** **Monthly**. **Press** *tab* to advance to the End Of Next Remitting Period field.

Type `6 30` **Press** *tab*.

Enter the remaining **suppliers**, **frequencies** and **dates** from page 340.

NOTES

You can also double-click the supplier's name to add it to the Settings screen.

If you type the first few letters of the name and then press *tab*, the Select Supplier list will have the supplier you need selected. Press *enter* to add the name to the Settings screen.

When you choose Receiver General for CPP and Income Tax, the frequency and date will be entered automatically from the one for EI. When you choose Manulife for EHC-Employee and EHC-Employer, the entries from VRSP will be added automatically. You can change these if they should be different.

Entering Job Categories

Job categories can be used to identify salespersons and to organize reports.

Click **Job Categories**:

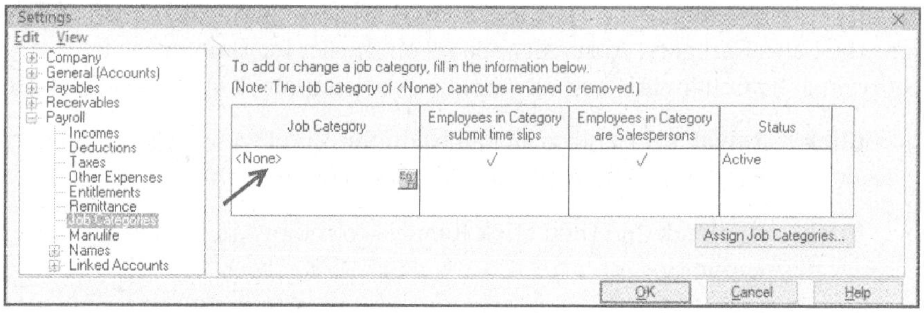

PRO VERSION

The column for Submit Time Slips is not available in the Pro version. It applies to Time & Billing, a Premium feature.

On the Job Categories screen, you enter the names of the categories and indicate whether the employees in each category submit time slips and whether they are salespersons. Categories may be active or inactive. We need a new category called Sales.

If you do not create categories, all employees can be selected in the Sales Journal and can submit time slips. Employees in the category <None> are salespersons, allowing them to be selected in the journal when no categories are set up or assigned.

Click the **Job Category field below <None>**.

Type `Sales` **Press** *tab* to add checkmarks to the next two columns and set the status to Active.

Click the **Job Category field below Sales**.

Type `Other` **Press** *tab* to add the checkmarks.

The Other category does not apply to sales or time slips, so we need to change the settings. Employees in the Other category should not appear in the Salesperson field on sales invoices. We will remove the ✓s for them.

Click the ✓ in the column Employees In Category Submit Time Slips.

Click the ✓ in the column Employees In Category Are Salespersons.

Click **Sales** in the Job Category list.

Click **Assign Job Categories** to change the screen:

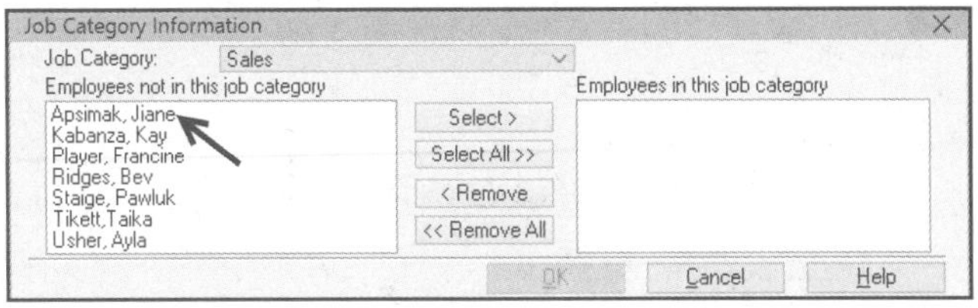

The screen is updated with employee names. Initially all are Employees Not In This Job Category.

You can add employee names to the category by choosing an employee and clicking **Select** or by choosing **Select All**. Once employees are in a category (the column on the right), you can remove them by selecting an employee and clicking **Remove** or clicking **Remove All** to move all names at the same time. Apsimak is the only person responsible for soliciting ticket sales from subscribers and groups.

Click **Apsimak** and then **click Select** to place her in the Sales category.

Click the **Job Category drop-down list**:

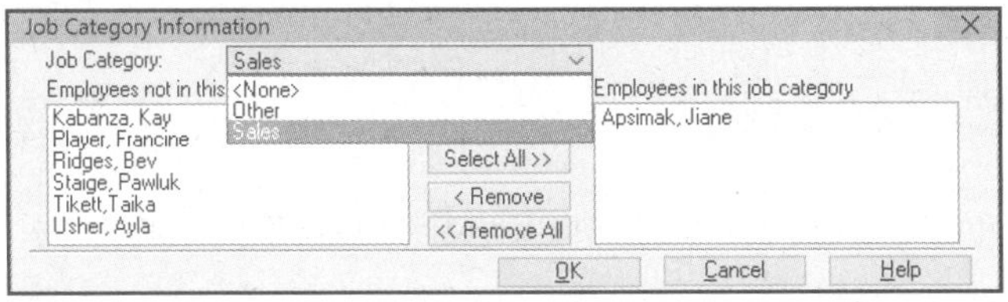

NOTES
<None> is one of the category list choices.
Employees may be in more than one job category.

Click **Other**.

For the Sales Category, Apsimak appears on the list for Employees In This Job Category. For the Other category, all employees are initially Not In This Job Category.

Click **Select All** to place all names on the Employees In This Job Category list. Now we need to remove Apsimak's name from this list.

Click **Apsimak** and then **click Remove** to remove her name from the Other category.

Click **OK** to save the information and return to the Settings screen. **Click OK** to save the settings and close the Settings screen.

WARNING!
If the payroll history is not finished, you must calculate and enter taxes manually. You will also be unable to use the Payroll Run Journal.

Finishing Payroll History

Once the setup is complete, we can back up the data file and finish the payroll history. Like the other modules, you can use the Payroll journals before finishing the history. However, the automatic payroll calculation feature will be turned off and you cannot use the Payroll Run Journal. Therefore, we should finish the history first. We can also check the data integrity as we did for Air Care to check if there are any data inconsistencies that we need to correct.

NOTES
These two payroll control accounts are like Accounts Payable and Accounts Receivable in that the total of all employee historical amounts must match the account balances in the General Ledger records.

Choose the **Maintenance menu** and **click Check Data Integrity**.

Two control accounts are used for the Payroll Ledger — *Advances & Loans Receivable* and *Vacation Payable*. The General Ledger account balance for these must equal the total advances and loans paid and the total vacation owed to all employees. The Historical Information entry for **Employees** should be **Balanced**.

Click **OK** to close the Data Integrity window.

Compare your amounts with the ones on pages 314–315, and if corrections are necessary, modify the Employee Ledger records.

Once we finish the history we cannot change any historical amounts. Therefore, we should prepare a backup first.

Back up the **data file**. Refer to page 248 if necessary.

Choose the **History menu** and **click Enter Historical Information** and **Payroll**:

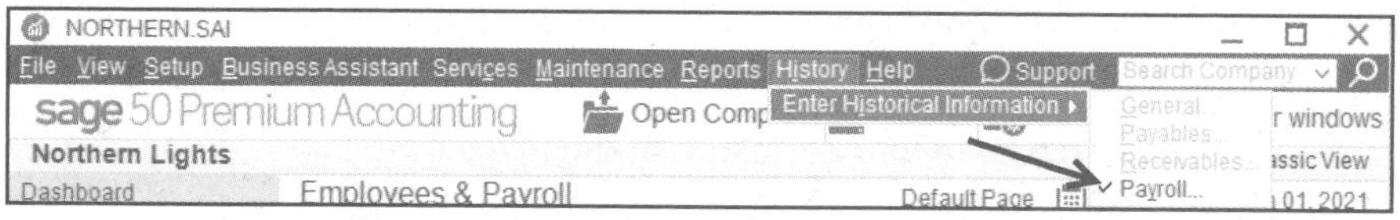

When we added the Payroll module, the History menu became available again, but only for this module — the other modules are dimmed and have the ✓ removed because the history for them is finished. When you finish the Payroll history, the Home window has all modules in the finished history state — the not-finished icon will be removed from the Employees icon and the History menu will be removed from the Home window. You are now ready to enter transactions.

Click **Proceed** in response to the Sage 50 warning about finishing the history.

Adding Salespersons to Sales Invoices

The first transaction adds the salesperson to an invoice, applying the job category we set up to track sales for commissions.

When employees receive sales commissions, you can add the salesperson's name to the sales invoice. You can then use the Sales By Salesperson Report to determine the sales revenue amount for calculating the commission. After creating job categories, we indicated for each category whether its employees were salespersons and then identified the employees in the category.

Advance the session date to **June 7**.

Click **Receivables** in the Modules pane list and **make** this your **default page** again if you made Employees & Payroll your default Home page.

✓ 1

Cash Sales Invoice #351 **Dated June 1/21**

From Subscribers, $64 000 plus $3 200 GST for advanced ticket sales. Sales total amount $67 200 deposited to chequing account. Enter Apsimak as the salesperson. Store as a monthly recurring transaction.

NOTES

Enter Apsimak as the salesperson for all ticket sales, either in the journal or by adding her to the customer records (as explained on pages 344–345).

Click the **Sales Invoices icon** to open the Sales Journal.

Choose **Subscribers** as the customer. Cash is selected as the payment method.

Enter **June 1, 2021** as the invoice date.

Enter a **description** for the sale.

Enter **64000** as the invoice amount.

PRO VERSION
pro The Order No. and Shipping Date fields are not included. The label Projects replaces Divisions.

Click the **Salesperson list arrow** to open the list of salespersons:

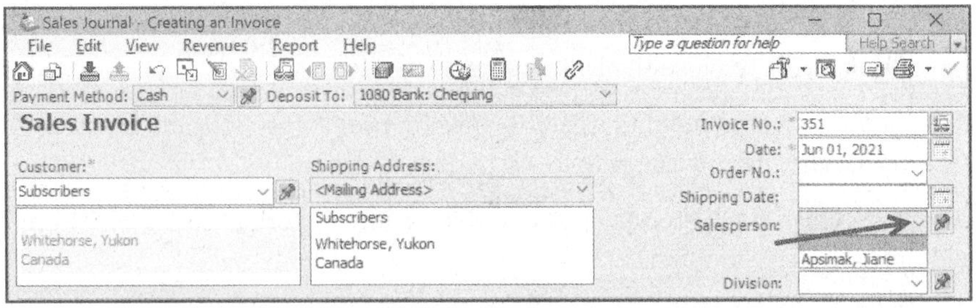

Apsimak is the only employee responsible for sales at Northern Lights, so she is the only employee we placed in the Sales job category. Therefore, Apsimak is also the only name listed. All other employees are in the second category labelled "Other," which does not have any salespersons.

NOTES
The Use The Same Salesperson pin icon is the same as the Use The Same Customer Next Time tool, and it works the same way.
If Job Categories are not set up, all employees are on the Salesperson field drop-down list. By default, they are in the category <None>, and employees in this category are salespersons (refer to the screenshot on page 341).

Click **Apsimak** to add her name to the invoice.

Click the **Use The Same Salesperson pin icon** .

This will lock in the salesperson's name on the invoice 

in the Salesperson field until we close the journal.

The pin has changed  — it now looks like it has been pushed in.

If you leave the journal open in the background, the salesperson remains selected. If you close the journal, you must reselect the salesperson for each invoice. You must close the journal before advancing the session date.

Review the **journal display**. The salesperson is not added to the journal report.

Close the **display** when finished.

Check your **work** and **make corrections** if necessary.

Store the **transaction** to recur **monthly**. Apsimak will be entered as the salesperson in the stored transaction.

Post the **invoice** and **minimize** (or close) the **Sales Journal**.

Adding Salespersons to Customer Records

Because Apsimak is the only salesperson, we can add her name to all customer records. By changing the ledger records, Apsimak will be entered in the Sales Journal automatically for these customers. For new customers, you can create a full, but incomplete, record and add the salesperson, or you can add the name in the journal.

NOTES
You can still select a different salesperson in the journal if the default selection is incorrect for an individual sale.

Click **Subscribers** in the Customers pane list to open the ledger. **Click** the **Salesperson field list arrow**:

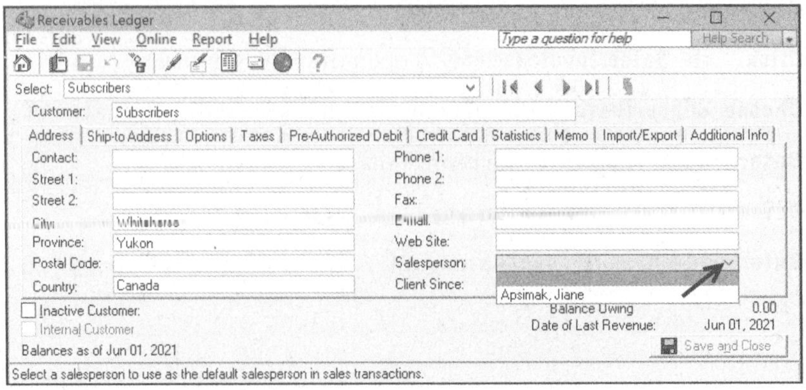

Click **Apsimak** to add her name. **Click** the **Next Record tool** or the **Previous Record tool** to open another record.

Choose **Apsimak** for all the remaining customers. **Click** **Save And Close** to return to the Home window.

When you open the sales journal and choose any customer on record, Apsimak will be entered automatically in the Salesperson field.

Continue with the **transactions** for June.

2 **Memo #20** **Dated June 1/21**
Add shortcuts for entries in other journals.

3 **Memo #21** **Dated June 2/21**
Complete an adjusting entry to reverse the year-end accrued wages entry for $1 150. (Debit 2250 Accrued Wages and credit 5420 Wages: Support Staff.)

4 **Cash Purchase Invoice #OA-2378** **Dated June 2/21**
From Otto's Autos, $420 plus $21 GST for maintenance service and repairs to delivery truck. Invoice total $441. Paid by cheque #841. Change the default tax code to G for this transaction.

5 **Payment Cheque #842** **Dated June 2/21**
To Thirst Quenchers, $3 450 in payment of account. Reference invoice #TQ-644.

6 **Purchase Invoice #TQ-845** **Dated June 3/21**
From Thirst Quenchers, $580 plus $29 GST for taxable beverages and $310 for tax exempt beverages. Invoice total $919. Terms: net 30. Store as a bi-weekly recurring entry.

7 **Purchase Invoice #MSB-12990** **Dated June 5/21**
From Midnight Sun Bakery, $1 150 for tax exempt freshly baked goods delivered daily and invoiced weekly. Terms: 1/10, n/30. Store as a weekly recurring entry.

8 **Purchase Invoice #SS-4556** **Dated June 5/21**
From Stage Stagers, $680 plus $34 GST for costumes and wigs. Invoice total $714. Terms: 2/15, n/30. Create a new Group asset account: 1340 Costumes.

9 **Sales Invoice #352** **Dated June 5/21**
To Literati Borealis, $1 200 plus $60 GST for group ticket sales. Invoice total $1 260. Terms: 1/15, n/30. Enter Apsimak as the salesperson. Store as a recurring bi-weekly transaction.

10 **Receipt #465** **Dated June 6/21**
From Literati Borealis, cheque #612 for $4 158 in payment of account, including $42 discount for early payment. Reference invoice #344.

11 **Cash Purchase Invoice #GN-2991** **Dated June 6/21**
From Grey Eyes Narwal (use Quick Add), $6 500 plus $325 GST for copyright permission to perform his play. Invoice total $6 825 paid in full with cheque #843. Create a new Group expense account: 5120 Copyright Expenses.

12 **Cash Purchase Invoice #YTE-78522** **Dated June 7/21**
From YT Energy, $600 plus $30 GST for one month of hydro services. Invoice total $630 due within 10 days to avoid interest penalty. Paid in full with cheque #844.

NOTES
You will need shortcuts for Create General Journal (Company), Create Supplier Invoice and Pay Supplier Invoices (Payables), View Employees, Payroll Cheque Run and Create Paycheque (Employees & Payroll).
You can Pay Remittances and Make Other Payments from the Pay Supplier Invoices transaction drop-down list. You can adjust paycheques from the Payroll Journal.

PRO VERSION
pro Purchase will replace Supplier for the shortcut labels.

NOTES
Enter the purchase from Thirst Quenchers on two separate invoice lines so that you can apply the correct tax codes.

WARNING!
Remember not to include the discount for the second invoice in payments and receipts.

NOTES

Before you can add the Remittance supplier, you must save the other Deduction settings (name and linked account). You can create the new account in the Deductions Linked Accounts screen.

Refer to page 320 if you need help with adding deduction names, pages 327–328 for entering linked accounts, page 340 for setting up payroll remittances and page 335 for entering employee deductions.

The deduction is by amount and after all taxes. You will need to save the name and linked account before you can add the remittance supplier (click OK and then open the Payroll Remittance Settings).

SESSION DATE – JUNE 14, 2021

13

NORTHERN Lights

Memo #22
From Owner's Desk

Dated June 9/21

Apsimak received her income tax assessment and must pay additional taxes for the previous year. She has Canada Revenue Agency approval to pay at the rate of $100 per month for the rest of the year.

Modify the Payroll Settings to add Tax Arrears as Deduction 4 (Names, Deductions) with the linked payable account (2470 Tax Arrears Payable).

Add the Receiver General as the Remittance supplier linked to this deduction with monthly remittances starting June 30.

Add the $100 deduction to Apsimak's ledger record (Deductions Tab).

M. Promtou

14 **Payment Cheque #845** **Dated June 9/21**

To Stage Stagers, $6 379.80 in payment of account, including $130.20 discount for early payment. Reference invoice #SS-4011.

15 **Receipt #466** **Dated June 10/21**

From Polar Discoveries, cheque #3774 for $8 316 in payment of account, including $84 discount for early payment. Reference invoice #348.

16 **Sales Invoice #353** **Dated June 11/21**

To Whitehorse Little Theatre, $3 200 plus $160 GST for group ticket sales. Invoice total $3 360. Terms: 1/15, n/30. Enter Apsimak as the salesperson. Store as a recurring bi-weekly transaction.

17 **Purchase Invoice #MSB-13428** **Dated June 12/21**

From Midnight Sun Bakery, $1 150 for tax exempt freshly baked goods delivered daily and invoiced weekly. Terms: 1/10, n/30. Recall stored transaction.

18 **Sales Invoice #354** **Dated June 12/21**

To SAD Foundation, $6 000 plus $300 GST for theatre fundraising event. Invoice total $6 300. Terms: 1/15, n/30. Enter Apsimak as the salesperson.

19 **Sales Invoice #355** **Dated June 13/21**

To Polar Discoveries, $4 000 plus $200 GST for group ticket sales. Invoice total $4 200. Terms: 1/15, n/30. Enter Apsimak as the salesperson. Store as a recurring bi-weekly transaction.

20 **Payment Cheque #846** **Dated June 13/21**

To Midnight Sun Bakery, $1 138.50 in payment of account, including $11.50 discount for early payment. Reference invoice #MSB-12990.

21 **Cash Purchase #YTT-11229** **Dated June 14/21**

From Yukon Telephone, $360 plus $18 GST for one month of telephone services. Invoice total $378. Paid in full with cheque #847.

22

Northern Lights Theatre
Employee Time Summary Sheet #16

NORTHERN Lights

Pay period start: June 1, 2021
Pay period end: June 14, 2021

Cheque Date: June 14, 2021

Employee SIN	A. Usher 931 771 620	B. Ridges 552 846 826	T. Tikett 218 738 631	K. Kabanza 638 912 634	F. Player 726 911 134	P. Staige 822 546 859	J. Apsimak 422 946 541
Week 1	40	42	40	40			
Week 2	40	40	40	42			
Regular hrs	80	80	80	80			
Overtime hrs	–	2	–	2			
Number sold	–	940	990	–			
Benefits	180.77	20.77	101.54	41.54			
Loan	-50.00	200.00*	-50.00	-50.00			
Sick leave days	–	1	–	–			
Personal days	1	–	–	–			
Chq/DD #	Chq 849	Chq 848	DD243	DD242			

* new loan to be repaid at $50 per paycheque

Completed by: Tikett 6/14/21

SESSION DATE – JUNE 21, 2021

23 **Memo #23** **Dated June 15/21**

Ridges returned her paycheque because the entry for overtime hours was not correct. Adjust her paycheque to add 4 hours of overtime, for a total of 6 overtime hours. Post this entry with cheque #850 (use the next cheque number when prompted).

24 **Purchase Invoice #TQ-1285** **Dated June 17/21**

From Thirst Quenchers, $580 plus $29 GST for taxable beverages and $310 for tax exempt beverages. Invoice total $919. Terms: net 30. Recall stored entry.

25 **Purchase Invoice #SS-8256** **Dated June 18/21**

From Stage Stagers, $5 050 plus $252.50 GST for building stage set. Invoice total $5 302.50. Terms: 2/15, n/30. Create a new Group expense account: 5250 Set Building Expenses.

26 **Sales Invoice #356** **Dated June 19/21**

To Literati Borealis, $1 200 plus $60 GST for group ticket sales. Invoice total $1 260. Terms: 1/15, n/30. Enter Apsimak as the salesperson. Recall stored entry.

27 **Purchase Invoice #MSB-14102** **Dated June 19/21**

From Midnight Sun Bakery, $1 150 for tax exempt freshly baked goods delivered daily and invoiced weekly. Terms: 1/10, n/30. Recall stored entry.

28 **Payment Cheque #851** **Dated June 19/21**

To Stage Stagers, cheque #851 for $5 896.17 in payment of invoices #SS-4556 and SS-8256 and including $120.33 discount for early payment.

NOTES

You can use the Payroll or the Payroll Run Journal to complete the payroll transactions. For the Payroll Run Journal, select 26 as the pay period frequency.

WARNING!

Remember to edit the benefit amount for Usher so that the tuition amount is included – type 180.77 in the Benefits This Period field. For Tikett, enter 101.54 as the benefit amount.

Or, you can edit their ledger records by entering these amounts as the Amount Per Period for Benefits.

Type –50 in the Loans This Period field for Usher, Tikett and Kabanza and 200 as the loan amount for Ridges.

NOTES

Remember to click the Recalculate Taxes tool after changing the overtime hours.

NOTES

Apsimak will be entered as the salesperson in the stored transaction.

NOTES
Employee income is entered on the Income tab screen. Refer to page 333.

29

NORTHERN Lights

Memo #24
From Owner's Desk

Dated June 20/21
Tikett will receive an increase in his hourly wage because he will have more responsiblity for administration for Northern Lights. He is taking over some of the tasks formerly completed by Apsimak. Modify Tikett's ledger record. Beginning with his next paycheque, his new wage rate will be $20 per regular hour and $30 for each hour of overtime work.

M. Promtou

30 **Receipt #467** **Dated June 20/21**
From Polar Discoveries, cheque #5120 for $4 158 in payment of account, including $42 discount for early payment. Reference invoice #355.

31 **Receipt #468** **Dated June 20/21**
From Literati Borealis, cheque #2692 for $1 247.40 in payment of account, including $12.60 discount for early payment. Reference invoice #352.

32 **Receipt #469** **Dated June 20/21**
From SAD Foundation, cheque #4439 for $3 237 in partial payment of account. Reference invoice #354.

33 **Cash Purchase Invoice #BE-6998** **Dated June 21/21**
From Blackfoot Equipment (use Quick Add), $540 plus $27 GST to repair sound equipment. Invoice total $567 paid by cheque #852.

SESSION DATE – JUNE 30, 2021

34 **Payment Cheque #853** **Dated June 22/21**
To Midnight Sun Bakery, cheque #853 for $1 138.50 in payment of invoice #MSB-13428, including $11.50 discount for early payment.

35 **Sales Invoice #357** **Dated June 25/21**
To Whitehorse Little Theatre, $3 200 plus $160 GST for group ticket sales. Invoice total $3 360. Terms: 1/15, n/30. Enter Apsimak as the salesperson. Recall stored transaction.

36 **Purchase Invoice #MSB-15029** **Dated June 26/21**
From Midnight Sun Bakery, $1 150 for tax exempt freshly baked goods delivered daily and invoiced weekly. Terms: 1/10, n/30. Recall stored transaction.

37 **Memo #25** **Dated June 26/21**

From Manager: Receipt #469 from SAD Foundation for $3 237 was entered incorrectly. On June 20, cheque #4439 for $6 237 was received from SAD Foundation in full payment of invoice #354, including $63 for early payment. Adjust or reverse the original receipt and enter the correct receipt amount.

38 **Sales Invoice #358** **Dated June 27/21**

To Polar Discoveries, $4 000 plus $200 GST for group ticket sales. Invoice total $4 200. Terms: 1/15, n/30. Enter Apsimak as the salesperson. Recall stored transaction.

39 **Bank Debit Memo #532281** **Dated June 28/21**

From NorthWest Bank, $2 085 was withdrawn from the chequing account for the following pre-authorized transactions:

Bank charges	$ 85
Interest on bank loan	120
Reduction of principal on bank loan	880
Interest on mortgage	750
Reduction of principal on mortgage	250

Create new Group account: 5110 Interest Expense

40

NORTHERN Lights

Northern Lights Theatre
Employee Time Summary Sheet #17

Cheque Date: June 28, 2021

Pay period start: June 15, 2021
Pay period end: June 28, 2021

Employee	A. Usher	B. Ridges	T. Tikett	K. Kabanza	F. Player	P. Staige	J. Apsimak
SIN	931 771 620	552 846 826	218 738 631	638 912 634	726 911 134	822 546 859	422 946 541
Week 1	42	42	40	40			
Week 1	40	42	42	40			
Regular hrs	80	80	80	80			
Overtime hrs	2	4	2	–			
Number sold	–	940	998	–			
Benefits	180.77	20.77	101.54	41.54			
Loan	-50.00	-50.00	-50.00	-50.00			
Sick leave days	–	–	–	1			
Personal days	–	1	–	–			
Chq/DD #	Chq 855	Chq 854	DD245	DD244			

* personal day to enroll in university course

Completed by: Tikett 6/28/21

41 **Visa Sales Invoice #359** **Dated June 30/21**

To one-time customers, $6 000 plus $300 GST for single ticket purchases during June. Invoice total $6 300 paid by Visa and deposited to Bank: Credit Card. Enter Apsimak as the salesperson.

42 **Cash Sales Invoice #360** **Dated June 30/21**

To one-time customers, $8 600 plus $430 GST for concession sales and $9 600 plus $480 GST for movie ticket sales during June. Sales total $19 110 deposited to chequing account.

NOTES

If you use the Adjust Receipt tool to correct the receipt, Sage 50 will automatically make the reversing entry. Delete the original Payment Amount. You will need to enter the amount of discount taken manually. It may be easier to reverse the receipt (refer to page 177) and then enter the customer's payment correctly.

When you reverse the receipt, the new receipt number will be updated to 470.

NOTES

Type –50 in the Loans This Period field for Usher, Ridges, Tikett and Kabanza to recover the loans.

Type 180.77 in the Benefits This Period field for Usher and 101.54 for Tikett unless you edited the ledger records.

WARNING!

Do not enter Apsimak as the salesperson for the non-ticket sales, and be sure to choose the correct revenue account.

43

Memo #26 **Dated June 30/21**

Complete an adjusting entry for one month of prepaid insurance expired. The one-year insurance policy was purchased on December 31, 2020, for $2 400.

44

Cash Purchase Invoice #BL-38455 **Dated June 30/21**

From Bright Lights (use Quick Add), $2 100 plus $105 GST for repairs to lighting system. Invoice total $2 205 paid in full with cheque #856.

45

Memo #27 **Dated June 30/21**

Pay Apsimak, Player and Staige their monthly salary. Issue cheque #857 and deposit slips #246 and #247. Jiane Apsimak earned a sales commission of $818 for the month of June and took five days' vacation.

NOTES

The travel allowance for Player and Staige is set up in their ledger record so that the amount is included automatically as a non-taxable income.

Use the Vacation Days Taken field on the Entitlements tab screen to enter the vacation days.

46

Memo #28 **Dated June 30/21**

Complete month-end adjusting entries for supplies used in June. Create a new Group expense account: 5130 Office Supplies Used.

Food inventory sold	$3 680
Beverage inventory sold	2 050
Cleaning supplies used	220
Office supplies used	120

47

Memo #29 **Dated June 30/21**

Bev Ridges is taking one week of vacation time. Release her retained vacation pay and issue cheque #858. Enter 40 as the number of hours for the vacation paid because this will replace her regular work days during this week.

NOTES

Refer to page 277 if you need help preparing the vacation paycheque.

Displaying Salesperson Reports

Click the **Report Centre icon** in the Home window.

Click **Receivables** to open the list of customer reports. Two additional reports are available when we add salespersons to journal entries.

✓ 48

Memo #30 **Dated June 30/21**

Adjust the paycheque for Apsimak. She has returned her deposit pay stub because her earned commission was incorrect. Use the Sales By Salesperson Report to verify that the correct amount was $928, not $818. Prepare direct deposit #248 to replace the incorrect payment.

NOTES

Use the next available direct deposit number for the adjusted paycheque.

Displaying the Sales by Salesperson Report

Click **Sales By Salesperson Summary** in the Select A Report list.

Click **Modify This Report** to open the report options:

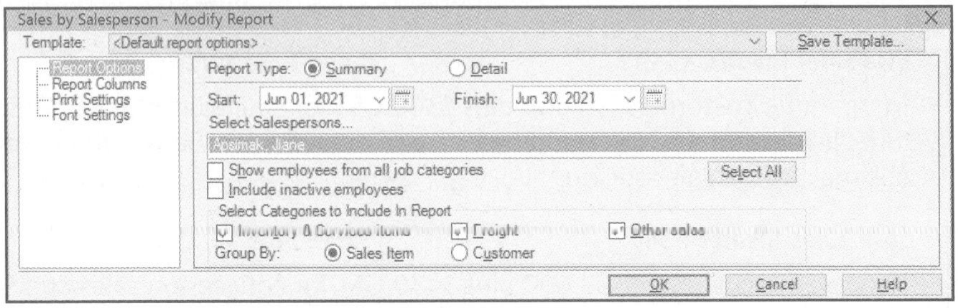

Or, you can choose the Reports menu, then choose Receivables and click Sales By Salesperson to open the report options screen.

Apsimak is the only employee designated as a salesperson, so only her name appears on the list, and she is already selected. You have the option to include all employees, but we do not need them all — we want Apsimak's June sales data. The default dates for Start and Finish cover the period we want. You can group the sales information by customer or by sales item. You can also include information for freight and other non-inventory sales. For Northern Lights, we need to include only the Other Sales because inventory and freight do not apply. You can prepare this report as a **Detail Report** with a line item for each sale, or as a **Summary Report** with totals only for each item or customer.

You can exclude amounts that do not apply. Click Freight and Inventory & Services Items to remove the ✓s.

Click **OK** to open the report. The total sales revenue for May was $92 800, so Apsimak's commission amount (1 percent) should be changed to $928.

Close the displayed **report**.

Adjust the **payroll entry** to increase the commission amount. Remember to **recalculate taxes**. **Post** the revised **entry**.

NOTES

You can also access the Sales by Salesperson Report from the Reports menu under Services Reports. The Services Reports entry will be renamed to match the industry type for other companies. Thus, this report may be named Business Reports, Retail Reports, Construction Reports and so on in the Reports menu.

Displaying the Sales by Job Category Report

This next report is similar except that it combines the information for all employees in each category. Because we have only one person in the Sales category, reporting by this category should give us the same information as the Sales By Salesperson Report.

Open the **Report Centre**.

Click **Sales By Job Category Summary** in the Select A Report list.

Click **Modify This Report** to open the report options:

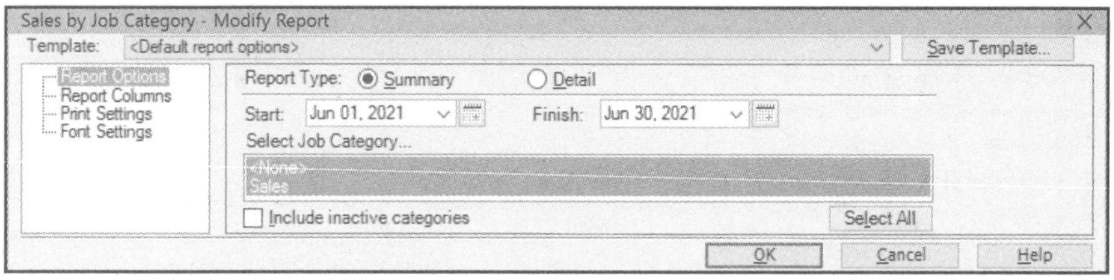

Or, you can choose the Reports menu, then choose Receivables and click Sales By Job Categories to open the report options screen.

Again the default dates give us the report for the month we need. Categories that do not have salespersons in them are not included in this report. You can create a **Detail Report** with a listing for each individual invoice or a **Summary Report** that provides the total for each selected category.

Click **Sales** to select only this category. **Click OK** to display the total sales for all persons in the Sales category.

Close the **report** when finished. **Close** the **Report Centre**.

NOTES

Because employees in the <None> category are salespersons, this category is included in the report options.

NOTES

For both the Sales by Salesperson and Job Category reports, you can drill down to the Detail Report from the Summary Report. From the Detail Report you can drill down to look up the sales invoices.

NOTES

Create a new supplier record for Canadian Actors' Guild.

Tax Code: No tax

Terms: net 1.

You cannot add the remittance supplier when the journal is open.

Refer to page 340 for help with adding a remittance supplier.

WARNING!

When you choose Receiver General for the second remittance (Tax Arrears), you must reset the End Of Remitting Period date to June 30. The date automatically advances after the tax remittance. When prompted, save the new remittance period dates.

Repeat this procedure for VRSP, the second remittance to Manulife.

Enter the **remittances for June 30** to complete the application.

49

Memo #31 **Dated June 30/21**

Create a new supplier record: Canadian Actors' Guild. Link this supplier as the remittance supplier for employee Guild Fees deductions.
Using the payroll remittance option, remit the following payroll taxes for the pay period ending June 30, including the balance owing from May:

To Receiver General: EI , CPP and Income Tax
To Receiver General: Tax Arrears
To Manulife Financial: EHC - Employee and EHC - Employer
To Manulife Financial: VRSP
To Yukon Workers' Compensation Board: WCB
To Canadian Actors' Guild: Guild Fees

Issue cheques #859 through #864 in payment.

REVIEW

The Student DVD with Data Files includes Review Questions and Supplementary Cases for this chapter.

CHAPTER TEN

OBJECTIVES

After completing this chapter, you should be able to

- ***enter*** inventory-related purchase transactions
- ***enter*** inventory-related sale transactions of goods and services
- ***make*** inventory adjustments
- ***assemble*** new inventory items from other inventory
- ***enter*** returns on sales and purchases
- ***create*** credit notes
- ***enter*** sales to preferred customers
- ***enter*** freight on purchases
- ***understand*** the integration of the Inventory Ledger with the Payables, Receivables and General ledgers
- ***create*** new inventory items
- ***display*** and ***print*** inventory reports

COMPANY INFORMATION

Company Profile

NOTES
Kara's Kitchens
354 Thunderbird Ave.
Brandon, MB R3T 3B7
Tel 1: (204) 642-2665
(204)-642-COOK
Tel 2: (800) 642-2665
Fax: (204) 642-9100
Business No.: 245 138 128

Kara's Kitchens, in Brandon, Manitoba, sells a small selection of luxury large kitchen appliances. Kara Cutter, the owner, opened her business a few years ago after retiring from her career as a professional chef, gaining business experience with another store and completing some business courses. Cutter has two employees to assist with the sales to customers — private homeowners, cooking schools and developers. Cutter teaches the basic cooking classes — with university students as the target audience — and the gourmet classes.

Several of the appliance suppliers offer discounts to the store for early payment. Accounts are also set up for other supplies and services that are provided locally. Installation, delivery and equipment maintenance are contracted out. The store uses a credit card for some purchases.

All account customers are given discounts for early payment, and some preferred customers receive additional discounts. Customers who pay by cash, debit or credit card do not receive any discounts and pay for delivery.

NOTES
RST, Retail Sales Tax, is the name of the provincial sales tax in Manitoba.

All items and services sold by the store are set up as inventory so that sales can be monitored. GST is charged on all sales and services. RST (Retail Sales Tax) is charged on sales of inventory items, but not on books or on the services — the cooking classes. The store pays GST and RST on all taxable purchases, but inventory purchased for resale in the store is exempt from RST.

Cutter used the following information to convert the accounting records to Sage 50 on August 1, 2021:

- Chart of Accounts
- Post-Closing Trial Balance
- Supplier Information
- Customer Information
- Employee Information
- Inventory Information
- Accounting Procedures

CHART OF POSTABLE ACCOUNTS

KARA'S KITCHENS

ASSETS

Current Assets
1060 Bank Account: Chequing
1080 Bank Account: MasterCard
1090 Bank Account: Visa
1100 Investments
1200 Accounts Receivable
1260 Office Supplies
1280 Prepaid Insurance

Inventory Assets
1520 Ranges and Cooktops
1540 Refrigerators
1550 Dishwashers
1560 Books

Centre & Equipment
1640 Computer Equipment
1670 Furniture & Fixtures
1680 Classroom Equipment
1700 Retail Premises
1730 Company Vehicle ▶

▶LIABILITIES

Current Liabilities
2100 Bank Loan
2200 Accounts Payable
2250 Credit Card Payable
2310 EI Payable
2320 CPP Payable
2330 Income Tax Payable
2410 Group Insurance - Employer
2420 Group Insurance - Employee
2460 WCB Payable
2640 RST Payable
2650 GST Charged on Sales
2670 GST Paid on Purchases

Long Term Liabilities
2820 Mortgage Payable

EQUITY
3560 Share Capital
3600 Current Earnings ▶

▶REVENUE

General Revenue
4020 Revenue from Sales
4040 Revenue from Services
4060 Sales Discounts
4150 Interest Revenue
4200 Freight Revenue

EXPENSE

Operating Expenses
5010 Advertising and Promotion
5020 Bank Charges
5030 Credit Card Fees
5035 Promotional Package Services
5040 Damaged Inventory
5060 Cost of Goods Sold
5065 Cost of Services
5080 Freight Expense
5090 Purchase Discounts
5100 Purchases Returns ▶

▶5130 Depreciation
5190 Delivery Expense
5200 Hydro Expense
5210 Insurance Expense
5220 Interest Expenses
5240 Maintenance of Premises
5250 Equipment Maintenance & Installation
5260 Supplies Used
5280 Telephone Expenses
5285 Vehicle Expenses

Payroll Expenses
5300 Salaries
5310 Commissions
5330 EI Expense
5340 CPP Expense
5350 WCB Expense
5370 Gp Insurance Expense

POST-CLOSING TRIAL BALANCE

KARA'S KITCHENS

August 1, 2021		Debits	Credits
1060	Bank Account: Chequing	$ 137 920.00	
1080	Bank Account: MasterCard	8 570.00	
1090	Bank Account: Visa	7 320.00	
1100	Investments	230 000.00	
1200	Accounts Receivable	30 510.00	
1260	Office Supplies	625.00	
1280	Prepaid Insurance	3 300.00	
1520	Ranges and Cooktops	220 680.00	
1540	Refrigerators	123 750.00	
1550	Dishwashers	21 390.00	
1560	Books	3 000.00	
1640	Computer Equipment	7 350.00	
1670	Furniture & Fixtures	20 500.00	
1680	Classroom Equipment	23 000.00	
1700	Retail Premises	250 000.00	
1730	Company Vehicle	36 000.00	▶
▶ 2100	Bank Loan		$ 80 000.00
2200	Accounts Payable		33 600.00
2250	Credit Card Payable		280.00
2310	EI Payable		704.00
2320	CPP Payable		1 601.00
2330	Income Tax Payable		3 533.00
2410	Group Insurance - Employer		680.00
2420	Group Insurance - Employee		680.00
2460	WCB Payable		412.00
2640	RST Payable		3 600.00
2650	GST Charged on Sales		5 100.00
2670	GST Paid on Purchases	$ 2 150.00	
2820	Mortgage Payable		180 000.00
3560	Share Capital		815 875.00
		$1 126 065.00	$1 126 065.00

SUPPLIER INFORMATION

KARA'S KITCHENS

Supplier Name (Contact)	Address	Phone No. Fax No.	E-mail Web Site	Terms Tax ID
A-Plus Kitchens (Bonnie Baker)	7 Onondaga Dr. Vancouver, BC V4G 4S5	Tel: (604) 588-3846 Fax: (604) 588-7126	bbaker@Aplus.com Aplus.com	2/10, n/30 (before tax) 466 254 109 RT0001
Chillers Inc. (Olive Lamb)	1500 Icicle Rd. Red Deer, MB R6S 1T4	Tel 1: (204) 597-4756 Tel 2: (888) 597-4756	o.lamb@chillers.com chillers.com	2/10, n/30 (before tax) 344 566 799 RT0001
Cook's Kitchens (Pepper Cook)	43 Breadalpane Ave. Hamilton, ON L8H 5J5	Tel: (905) 529-7235 Fax: (905) 529-2995	p.cook@cookskitchens.ca cookskitchens.ca	2/5, n/20 (before tax) 244 573 655 RT0001
Grand Life Insurance			net 1	
Keep Cold Appliances (Jack Frost)	39 Winter St. Brandon, MB R4M 3K9	Tel: (204) 777-8133 Fax: (204) 777-8109	frost@keepcold.com keepcold.com	1/15, n/30 (before tax) 274 309 483 RT0001
Manitoba Bell (Annie Heard)	82 Wireless Alley Brandon, MB R3B 5R9	Tel: (204) 781-2355	heard@bell.ca bell.ca	net 7
Manitoba Energy (Manny Watts)	91 NacNab St. Brandon, MB R3R 2L9	Tel: (204) 463-2664	watts@mbenergy.ca mbenergy.ca	net 7
Receiver General for Canada		Tel: (800) 561-7761	cra-arc.gc.ca	net 1
Riverview Sunoco (Mick Annick)	101 Niska Dr. Brandon, MB R3R 2H3	Tel: (204) 622-6181	mick@goodforcars.com goodforcars.com	net 20
Workers' Compensation Board				net 1

OUTSTANDING SUPPLIER INVOICES

Supplier Name	Terms	Date	Inv/Chq No.	Amount	Tax	Total
Keep Cold Appliances	1/15, n/30 (before tax)	July 20/21	KC-618	$32 000	$1 600	$33 600

CUSTOMER INFORMATION

KARA'S KITCHENS

Customer Name (Contact)	Address	Phone No. Fax No.	E-mail Web Site	Terms Credit Limit
*Botelli Developments (Gina Botelli)	30 Cherry St. Brandon, MB R3A 1C7	Tel: (204) 699-2911 Fax: (204) 697-2735	gina@botelli.com botelli.com	2/10, n/30 $40 000
*Brandon Culinary Arts (Basil Marjoram)	3000 Richmond St. Brandon, MB R3A 6A9	Tel: (204) 529-3000 Fax: (204) 529-3477	marjoram@BCU.ca BCU.ca	2/10, n/30 $30 000
*Cloves Fine Dining (Honey Cinnamon)	1 First Ave. Brandon, MB R4B 0J9	Tel 1: (204) 622-9250 Tel 2: (204) 622-9238 Fax: (204) 622-9729	hc@cloves.ca cloves.ca	2/10, n/30 $40 000
Lavender Estates (Daisy Harris)	9 Lavender Ct. Brandon, MB R3B 3J6	Tel: (204) 782-7300 Fax: (204) 782-8190	harris@lavender.com lavender.com	1/10, n/30 $25 000
Marigold Inn (Arianna Appleby)	29 Marigold Ct. Brandon, MB R4A 2M2	Tel: (204) 762-8664	arianna@marigold.inn.com marigold.inn.com	1/10, n/30 $25 000
The Potts Corporation (Francine Potts)	6 Orchard Grove Brandon, MB R3A 3B8	Tel: (204) 787-1226	fpotts@the.potts.com the.potts.com	1/10, n/30 $50 000

NOTES: The * indicates preferred price list customers. A record is also set up for Credit Card Customers.

OUTSTANDING CUSTOMER INVOICES

Customer Name	Terms	Date	Inv/Chq No.	Amount	Total
Brandon Culinary Arts	2/10, n/30 (after tax)	July 29/21	2463	$13 560	$13 560
Marigold Inn	2/10, n/30 (after tax)	July 25/21	2459	$16 950	$16 950
				Grand Total	$30 510

EMPLOYEE INFORMATION SHEET

KARA'S KITCHENS

Employee	Ginger House	Pat A. Kaik
Address	2 Cherry Ave. Brandon, MB R3B 2V7	300 Croissant Cres. Brandon, MB R4G 4K8
Telephone	(204) 426-1817	(204) 688-5778
Social Insurance No.	532 548 625	488 655 333
Date of Birth (mm-dd-yy)	09/21/78	05/24/84
Federal (Manitoba) Tax Exemption - TD1		
Basic Personal	$12 609 (9 626)	$12 609 (9 626)
Tuition/Education	$6 000 (6 720)	
Total	$18 609 (16 346)	$12 609 (9 626)
Employee Earnings		
Salary (Hours per Period)	$4 200.00 (160 Hours)	$4 200.00 (160 Hours)
Commission	0.5% of sales (less returns)	0.5% of sales (less returns)
Employee Deductions		
Group Insurance	$170	$170
EI, CPP & Income Tax	Calculations are built into Sage 50.	

Employee Profiles and TD1 Information

Pat A. Kaik and **Ginger House** both handle sales in the store and demonstrate the features of the appliances for customers. Kaik also assists with the accounting. Both are salaried employees who receive their $4 200 monthly pay by cheque and contribute $170 each period to a group insurance plan. This amount is matched by the employer — a benefit for the employees. Kaik and House are single and self-supporting with no dependants, so they have the basic claim amounts for income tax. House also has tuition and education amounts for courses she completed this year. Instead of vacation pay, they take three weeks of vacation with regular pay each year. Neither has received any payroll advances or loans.

Both employees are listed as salespersons. They receive a sales commission of 0.5 percent of their net sales (sales less returns) with each paycheque. Their names are entered as salespersons on invoices so that the commissions can be tracked for the Sales by Salesperson Report.

INVENTORY INFORMATION

KARA'S KITCHENS

Code	Description	Min Stock	Prices Reg	(Pref)	Unit	Qty on Hand	Total (Cost)	Taxes
Ranges and Cooktops: Total asset value $220 680 (Linked Accounts: Asset 1520, Revenue 4020, COGS 5060)								
R010	Range: 5 burner, smooth surface, convection	5	$2 950	(2 630)	each	10	$20 650	GP
R020	Range: smooth surface, convection, 2 ovens	5	3 540	(3 300)	each	10	24 730	GP
R030	Range: smooth surface, induction	5	4 250	(3 900)	each	10	29 500	GP
R040	Range: smooth surface, slide-in	5	4 240	(3 900)	each	10	29 500	GP
R050	Range: smooth surface, slide-in, 2 ovens	4	5 290	(4 800)	each	10	36 600	GP
R060	Wall oven: convection, single oven	3	4 300	(3 950)	each	5	15 000	GP
R070	Wall oven: convection, double oven	5	5 300	(4 910)	each	5	18 000	GP
R080	Cooktop: smooth surface, 5 burner	4	3 150	(2 950)	each	5	10 500	GP
R090	Cooktop: smooth surface, induction	3	4 380	(3 940)	each	5	15 500	GP
R100	Gas Range: 5 burner w/grill, 2 ovens	5	5 290	(4 880)	each	4	14 600	GP
R110	Gas Cooktop: 5 burner w/grill	4	4 380	(4 100)	each	2	6 100	GP
Books Total asset value $3 000 (Linked Accounts: Asset 1560, Revenue 4020, COGS 5060)								
Book1	Basic Cooking: w/online subscription	10	60	(50)	book	50	1 250	G (RST Exempt)
Book2	Gourmet Cooking: w/online subscription	10	80	(70)	book	50	1 750	G (RST Exempt)
Refrigerators: Total asset value $123 750 (Linked Accounts: Asset 1540, Revenue 4020, COGS 5060)								
F010	Refrigerator: Fr. door, drawer freezer, 28 cu ft	5	3 100	(2 880)	each	6	13 020	GP
F020	Refrigerator: Fr. door, shelf freezer, 28 cu ft	5	3 600	(3 320)	each	6	15 120	GP
F030	Refrigerator: Fr. door, drawer freezer, 32 cu ft	5	3 850	(3 640)	each	6	16 050	GP
F040	Refrigerator: Fr. door, shelf freezer, 32 cu ft	5	5 100	(4 860)	each	6	21 300	GP
F050	Refrigerator: Fr. door, shelf freezer, 36 cu ft	5	6 900	(6 500)	each	6	28 860	GP
F060	Refrigerator: Fr. door, built-in, 36 cu ft	3	8 400	(7 900)	each	5	29 400	GP
Dishwashers Total asset value $21 390 (Linked Accounts: Asset 1550, Revenue 4020, COGS 5060)								
D010	Dishwasher: 3 rack, fixed	10	2 200	(1 980)	each	6	9 000	GP
D020	Dishwasher: 3 rack, flexible tines & racks	10	2 950	(2 700)	each	6	12 390	GP
Classes (Linked Accounts: Revenue 4040, COGS 5065)								
C010	Cooking 101: Basic Recipes		350	(290)	session			G (RST Exempt)
C020	Gourmet Cooking: Introductory		450	(410)	session			G (RST Exempt)
C030	Gourmet Cooking: Advanced		550	(490)	session			G (RST Exempt)

NOTES: Buying units, selling units and stocking units are the same for all items. Inventory is not oversold.

Accounting Procedures

The Goods and Services Tax (GST): Remittances

Kara's Kitchens uses the regular method for remittance of the Goods and Services Tax. GST collected is recorded as a liability in *GST Charged on Sales*. GST paid, recorded in *GST Paid on Purchases*, decreases the liability. The store files its return with the Canada Revenue Agency (CRA) quarterly, either requesting a refund or remitting the balance owing.

Retail (Provincial) Sales Tax (RST)

Retail Sales Tax of 8 percent is applied to all cash and credit sales of goods in Manitoba. Customers do not pay RST on books or on the cooking classes provided by Kara's Kitchens. RST on goods is remitted quarterly to the Minister of Finance.

NOTES

RST is not usually charged on services, but it is charged on services applied to items that have RST applied, such as repairs or assembly.

Books and children's clothing are normally exempt from RST.

RST at the rate of 8 percent is also paid on purchases that are not inventory items for resale. Because RST paid is not refundable, it is charged to the asset or expense account associated with the purchase, not to a separate account.

Sales Invoices

Kara's Kitchens allows customers to pay on account or by cash, cheque or credit card. The keystrokes for cash and credit card inventory transactions are similar to those for account sales, except for the method of payment. The program will automatically debit the appropriate bank account instead of *Accounts Receivable*.

Source documents for cash and credit card sales are presented as summaries to avoid a large number of small revenue transactions. A record for Credit Card Sales is set up to track these sales, with Visa as the default invoice payment method.

You can print and e-mail sales invoices through the program. Before posting the Sales Journal transaction, preview the invoice. Then click the Print button or the E-mail button.

Credit Card Sales and Purchases

Kara's Kitchens has set up its accounts for credit card sales and purchases.

Freight Expenses and Charges

When a business purchases inventory items, the cost of any freight that cannot be directly allocated to a specific item must be charged to *Freight Expense*. This amount is regarded as an expense rather than a charge to an inventory asset account. Freight or delivery charges to customers are allocated to *Freight Revenue*.

Discounts

To encourage customers to settle their accounts early, Kara's Kitchens offers its regular account customers a 1 percent discount on after-tax amounts if they pay their accounts within 10 days. Discounts are calculated automatically when the payment terms are set up and the customer is eligible for the discount. There are no discounts on credit card sales.

In addition, some customers have preferred price list status that entitles them to reduced prices. Regular and preferred prices are set up in the Inventory Ledger, so the prices are entered automatically. For preferred customers, the discount rate is increased to 2 percent if payment is made within 10 days. Net payment is due in 30 days for all customers.

Promotional Packages

Each August, Kara's Kitchens offers promotional packages that include a variety of appliances, one book and one session of basic cooking classes. These packages incur additional costs for the cooking classes.

Returns

Returned goods are a normal part of retail businesses. Kara's Kitchens provides full refunds on unused or damaged items returned within 14 days. Returned items are debited to the contra-revenue account *Sales Returns* so that the returns can be tracked. Refer to page 382.

Returns on purchases also occur regularly. Refer to page 384.

INSTRUCTIONS

1. **Record entries** for the source documents in Sage 50 using the Chart of Accounts, Trial Balance, and Supplier, Customer, Employee and Inventory Information provided. The procedures for entering each new type of transaction are outlined step by step in the Keystrokes section with the source documents.
2. **Print** the **reports** indicated on the following printing forms after finishing your entries. Instructions for inventory reports begin on page 391.

REPORTS

Accounts
- [ ] Chart of Accounts
- [ ] Account List
- [ ] General Journal Entries

Financial
- [x] Balance Sheet date: Aug. 31
- [x] Income Statement: Aug. 1 to Aug. 31
- [x] Trial Balance date: Aug. 31
- [x] All Journal Entries: Aug. 1 to Aug. 31
- [x] General Ledger accounts: 1520 1540 1550 4020 4040 from Aug. 1 to Aug. 31
- [ ] Statement of Cash Flows
- [ ] Cash Flow Projection Detail Report
- [x] Gross Margin Income Statement: Aug. 1 to Aug. 31

Tax
- [ ] Report on

Banking
- [ ] Cheque Log Report

Payables
- [ ] Supplier List
- [ ] Supplier Aged
- [ ] Aged Overdue Payables
- [ ] Purchases Journal Entries
- [ ] Payments Journal Entries
- [ ] Supplier Purchases

Receivables
- [ ] Customer List
- [ ] Customer Aged
- [ ] Aged Overdue Receivables
- [ ] Sales Journal Entries
- [ ] Receipts Journal Entries
- [ ] Customer Sales
- [x] Sales by Salesperson: Aug. 1 to Aug. 31
- [ ] Customer Statements

Payroll & Employees
- [ ] Employee List
- [x] Summary: All employees
- [ ] Deductions & Expenses
- [ ] Remittances
- [ ] Payroll Journal Entries
- [ ] T4 Slips
- [ ] Record of Employment
- [ ] Year End Review (PIER)

Inventory & Services
- [ ] Inventory & Services List
- [x] Summary
- [ ] Quantity
- [ ] Inventory Statistics
- [x] Sales Summary for all Services: from Aug. 1 to Aug. 31
- [x] Transaction Summary for R040 Range: smooth surface, slide-in: Aug. 1 to Aug. 31
- [ ] Price Lists
- [x] Item Assembly Journal Entries: Aug. 1 to Aug. 31
- [x] Adjustments Journal Entries: Aug. 1 to Aug. 31

Mailing Labels
- [ ] Labels

Forecast & Analysis
- [ ] Forecast
- [ ] Customer Analysis
- [ ] Product Analysis
- [x] Sales Analysis Report: Aug. 1 to Aug. 31

KEYSTROKES

Accounting for Inventory Sales

Open **SageData19\KITCHENS\KITCHENS** to access the data files for Kara's Kitchens.

Type 8 7 21 or **choose Aug. 7** from the calendar and **click OK**.

This will enter the session date August 7, 2021. The familiar Receivables module window appears. Inventory & Services has been added to the Modules pane list. Inventory sales are entered in the Sales Journal.

NOTES

If you are working from backups, restore the backup file SageData19\KITCHENS1.CAB or KITCHENS1 to SageData19\KITCHENS\KITCHENS.

Refer to the instructions in Chapter 1, page 25, if you need assistance with restoring files from backups.

> **NOTES**
> We have selected Retail as the type of industry for Kara's Kitchens because it sells inventory items. The Division (Project) module and fields are hidden.

> **NOTES**
> Use the bookmark attached to the back cover to mark the page with the source document.

> **CLASSIC VIEW**
> Click the Sales icon to open the Sales Journal.

> **PRO VERSION**
> The invoice does not include Order No. or Shipping Date fields.

> **NOTES**
> Remember that you can customize the columns and tabbing order. Refer to pages 163 and 166.

The first transaction involves the sale of inventory items. Many of the steps are identical to those you used for sales in previous applications. You will be using the inventory database and all the Sales Invoice fields to complete this transaction.

✓ 1

Sales Invoice #2470 — **Dated August 1, 2021**

Sold by Kaik to Lavender Estates

1	D020	Dishwasher: 3 rack, flexible tines & racks	$2 950	each
1	F060	Refrigerator: Fr. door, built-in, 36 cu ft	8 400	each
2	R030	Range: smooth surface, induction	4 250	each
1	Book2	Gourmet Cooking: w/online subscription	80	/book
2	C020	Gourmet Cooking: Introductory	450	/session
		Delivery (tax code G)	200	
		GST	5%	
		RST	8%	

Terms: 1/10, n/30.

Click the **Sales Invoices icon** to open the familiar Sales Journal:

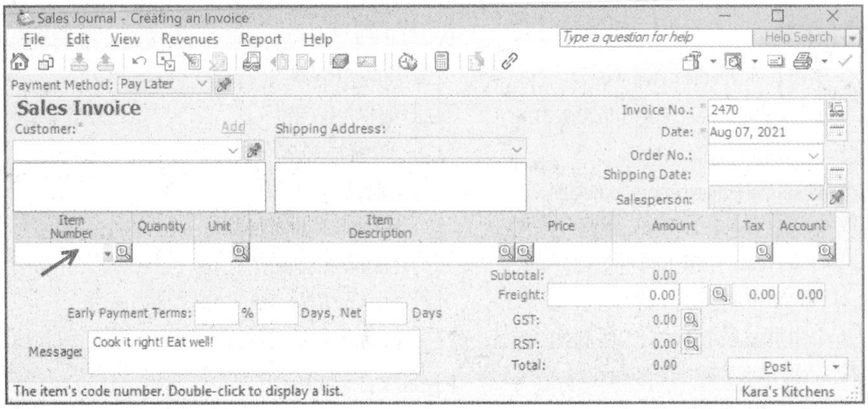

The Sales Journal looks the same as in earlier data files, except for the Sales Journal we customized for Phoebe's Photo Studio in Chapter 6. All the invoice fields are used when we sell inventory. Pay Later is the journal's default payment method.

Click the **Customer field list arrow** to display the list of customers.

Click **Lavender Estates** to enter the customer's name and address.

The Shipping Address, Invoice number, payment method, payment terms and tax code defaults are all correct. If necessary, you can edit them. The Order No. is not used for invoices.

Click the **Date field Calendar icon** to advance the cursor. The default session date is incorrect.

Click **1** on the August calendar.

Click the **Salesperson field** and **choose Kaik** as the salesperson.

One line is used for each inventory item or service sold by the business. A separate line would also be used for non-inventory sales and to enter returns or allowances.

Click the **Item Number field List icon**, or **click** the **field** and **press** *enter* or **double-click** to access the inventory list:

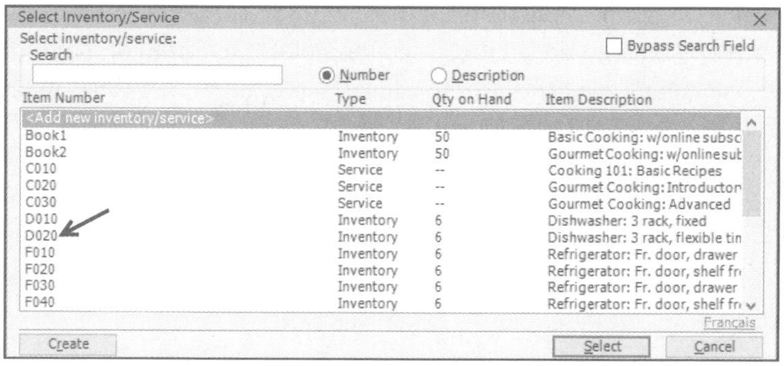

You can add new inventory items from the Select Inventory/Service screen, just as you can add accounts from the Select Account screen. Items are listed in order by number or code, and, for inventory items, available quantities are included for reference.

The cursor is in the Search field. We will bypass the Search field so that future references to this list will place the cursor in the list rather than in the Search field.

Click **Bypass Search Field** so that the next time the cursor will start in the item list.

Click in the list and type the first letter of a code if you want to advance the list to the codes beginning with that letter.

Click **D020 Dishwasher: 3 rack, flexible tines & racks** from the list.

Click **Select** to add the inventory item to your form. If you have made an incorrect selection, return to the Item Number field and reselect from the inventory list.

You can also type the code number in the Item Number field and press *tab*, but you must match the case of the code number in the ledger.

The cursor moves to the Quantity field. The program adds information in each field automatically, based on the inventory record information. All the information except quantity and amount is added by default as soon as you enter the inventory item number. If you select a preferred customer, the default price is the preferred customer price instead of the regular selling price (refer to the screens on page 382).

You should enter the number of units of this item sold in the Quantity field.

Type 1 **Press** *tab*.

If your company settings do not allow inventory levels to go below zero, the program prevents you from continuing when you enter a quantity greater than the available stock, more than 6 in this case, with this warning:

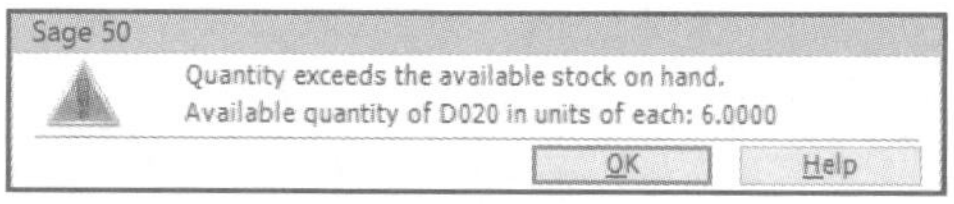

Click OK to return to the journal so you can reduce the quantity.

Since the remaining default information is correct, you do not need to change it. The default tax code — GP — is the code entered for the customer because the customer pays both GST at 5 percent and RST at 8 percent. Services have been set up in the Inventory Ledger so that by default RST is not applied.

The program automatically calculates an amount based on the selling price per unit. This figure appears in the Amount field.

The default revenue account for the item is entered, but it can be accepted or changed. You would change the account for returns and allowances or exceptional entries. Accept the default revenue account for this sale.

NOTES

No quantities for services are in the list because they are not held in stock.

NOTES

If you want to search for items by description, type a letter in the Item Description field – the list will have all items that include the letter you typed and it will be sorted alphabetically by description.

To have all items sorted by description instead of by item number, click the List icon in the Description field.

The option to sort items by number or description in the Inventory Settings (page 662) applies only to lists in the Adjustments and Item Assembly journals. Both sorting methods are available for sales and purchases.

NOTES

Inventory codes are case sensitive – you must type D020 in the journal (match the upper case D in the item code) to enter the item directly in the journal. To use the list of items, you can type a lower case letter to advance to a later part of the list.

NOTES

Inventory items can be oversold, but you must change the Inventory Ledger settings to allow the quantity on hand to go below zero. This setting is used in Chapter 13 and the setup for it is explained in Chapter 16.

NOTES

If your company settings allow, you may want to oversell the items so that the customer can purchase backordered inventory stock.

NOTES
If you have entered a default revenue account for the customer that is different from the one for the item, the account for the item replaces the customer's revenue account.

NOTES
If you type the entire code in lower case letters (or upper case letters), the Item field drop-down list will include the single item. You can click it and press *tab* to advance to the Quantity field.

NOTES
If you want to type in the item codes instead of using the selection list for each item, turn on Caps Lock for your keyboard. This will speed up your data entry and ensure that you are using the correct case. Type the item code and then press *tab* to advance to the Quantity column.

NOTES
The quantity for D020 has not yet been reduced because the sale has not been completed.

WARNING!
The cursor does not advance to the Quantity field when you select from the drop-down lists, so if you type the quantity before pressing *tab*, you will enter an incorrect code.

NOTES
The inventory list is also available when you type in the Item Description field, but it is sorted by description instead of by item number.

You can select another tax code from the Tax Code list if necessary. You can also edit the price to change the selling price for a particular item or customer. To change the account, click the Account field List icon, press *enter* or double-click in the Account field to obtain a list of accounts.

Press *tab* **repeatedly** to advance to the next invoice line and update the first line because all the default record information is correct.

Or, you can click the Item Number field on the second line — the next blank invoice line.

Type f

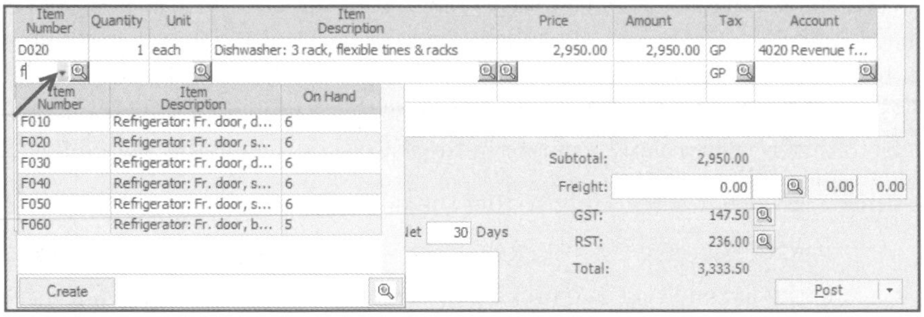

The Item Number field now provides a drop-down item list. Click to select an item from this list. When you type the first letter or number of the code (in this case, the letter f) the drop-down list has the items starting with F. Eight items can be displayed at one time, but you can scroll down to access more items. You can also create a new inventory item from this drop-down list.

Click **F060** and **press** *tab* to advance to the Quantity field. **Type** 1

Enter the **remaining sale items** using the steps above.

As you complete each line and advance to the next, the totals and tax amounts at the bottom of the form are updated to include the last item entered. A new invoice line opens automatically. When you press *tab* after entering the quantity (2) for item R030, Sage 50 automatically enters the amount as the quantity multiplied by the unit price.

GP — the customer's tax code — is entered as the tax code for the books and service items, but only GST is added to the invoice total — the RST amount does not increase when you add these items. We will confirm this when we review the journal entry.

To include more invoice lines on your screen, drag the lower frame of the Sales Journal window down or maximize the window.

At this stage, before adding delivery (freight) charges, the inventory portion of the invoice is complete:

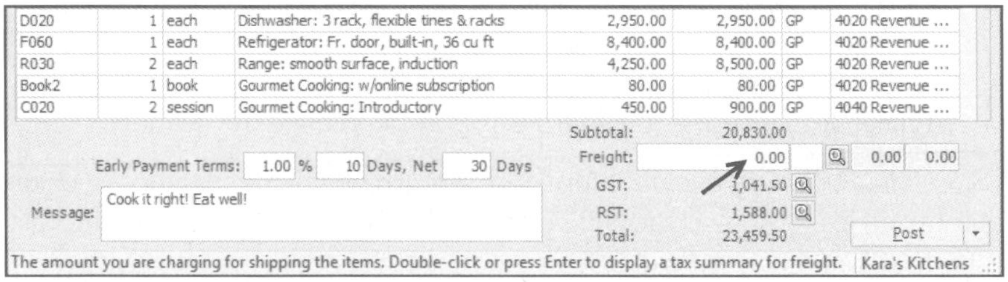

D020 1 each Dishwasher: 3 rack, flexible tines & racks 2,950.00 2,950.00 GP 4020 Revenue ...
F060 1 each Refrigerator: Fr. door, built-in, 36 cu ft 8,400.00 8,400.00 GP 4020 Revenue ...
R030 2 each Range: smooth surface, induction 4,250.00 8,500.00 GP 4020 Revenue ...
Book2 1 book Gourmet Cooking: w/online subscription 80.00 80.00 GP 4020 Revenue ...
C020 2 session Gourmet Cooking: Introductory 450.00 900.00 GP 4040 Revenue ...
Subtotal: 20,830.00
Early Payment Terms: 1.00 % 10 Days, Net 30 Days
Freight: 0.00 0.00 0.00
GST: 1,041.50
Message: Cook it right! Eat well!
RST: 1,588.00
Total: 23,459.50
Post
The amount you are charging for shipping the items. Double-click or press Enter to display a tax summary for freight.
Kara's Kitchens

Click the **first Freight field**, the amount field, below the Subtotal.

Type 200 **Press** *tab*.

The customer's tax code, GP, is entered as the default, so you must change it. Freight is not automatically connected with a tax code.

Type G or **press** enter to open the familiar list of tax codes. **Click G** and then **click Select**.

Press tab to complete the journal entry:

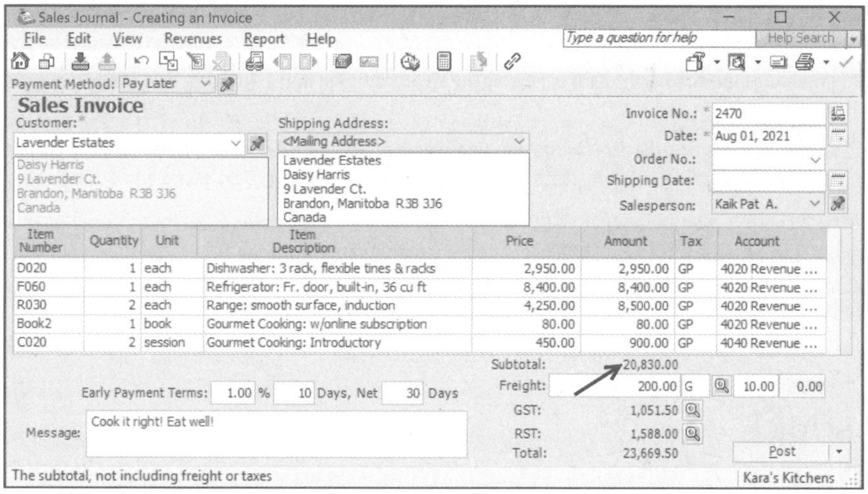

You should review the journal entry before posting it.

Reviewing the Inventory Sales Journal Transaction

Choose the **Report menu** and **click Display Sales Journal Entry**:

Kara's Kitchens
Sales Journal Entry 08/01/2021 (J1)

Account Number	Account Description	Debits	Credits
1200	Accounts Receivable	23,669.50	-
5060	Cost of Goods Sold	13,880.00	-
1520	Ranges and Cooktops	-	5,900.00
1540	Refrigerators	-	5,880.00
1550	Dishwashers	-	2,065.00
1560	Books	-	35.00
2640	RST Payable	-	1,588.00
2650	GST Charged on Sales	-	1,051.50
4020	Revenue from Sales	-	19,930.00
4040	Revenue from Services	-	900.00
4200	Freight Revenue	-	200.00
Additional Date:	Additional Field:	37,549.50	37,549.50

RST and GST tax amounts are separated. RST is not charged on the sale of books or cooking classes — 8% × $19 850 = $1 588 — while GST is charged on sales and services plus freight — 5% × $21 030 = $1 051.50. Both taxes are calculated correctly because of the tax codes and exemptions assigned in the Inventory Ledger records. Books and classes are marked as exempt for RST.

All relevant accounts have been updated automatically because the Inventory and Receivables ledgers are linked to the General Ledger. Therefore, the linked asset, revenue and expense accounts defined for each inventory item have been debited or credited as required. In addition, the linked accounts we saw earlier are used — *RST Payable*, *GST Charged on Sales* and *Accounts Receivable*. The inventory database and customer record are also updated. Linked inventory accounts are available only for inventory-related transactions — they are not available on account selection lists in journal account fields.

Kara's Kitchens uses the average cost method to determine the cost of goods sold. If the stock for an inventory item was purchased at different times and prices, the average of these prices would be used as the cost of goods sold.

Close the **display** to return to the journal input screen.

NOTES

Pressing ctrl + J will also open the journal display.

WARNING!

You should always check that the taxes are correct. If you are unsure, you can change the tax code for the books and service items to G. This extra step is required in Chapters 16, 17 and 18.

NOTES

Kara's Kitchens uses a single cost of goods sold account for all inventory items.

In the Premium version you can choose the first-in, first-out (FIFO) method of costing. By choosing the average cost method, we are able to show the same screens for Pro and Premium version users.

NOTES
For corrections of other, non-inventory invoice details, refer to page 163.

WARNING!
If you adjust a posted invoice to correct for selecting the wrong customer, the customer options, such as payment terms, price list or tax codes, are not updated and may be incorrect. For these errors, you should reverse the entry.

CORRECTING THE INVENTORY SALES ENTRY

To **correct** an **item** on the inventory line, **click** the **incorrect field** to move the cursor and highlight the field contents. **Press** *enter* to display the list of inventory items, tax codes or accounts. **Click** the **correct selection** to highlight it, then **click Select**, or for the remaining fields, **type** the **correct information**. **Press** *tab* to enter the change.

If you **change** the **inventory** item, **re-enter** the **quantity sold** in the Quantity field. **Press** *tab* to update the totals.

To **insert** a **line**, **click** the **line below** the one you want to add. **Choose** the **Edit menu** and **click Insert Line**. To **remove** a **line**, **click** the **line** you want to delete; **choose** the **Edit menu** and **click Remove Line**.

To correct errors after posting, **click** the **Adjust Invoice tool** in the Sales Journal or **choose** the **Sales menu** and **click Adjust Invoice**. Or **choose Adjust Invoice** from the **Sales Invoices icon drop-down shortcuts list** in the Home window. Refer to page 184.

If this is a recurring inventory sale, you can store it just like other sales.

Posting

When all the information in your journal entry is correct, you must post the transaction.

Click Post to save the transaction. **Click OK**.

Close the **Sales Journal** to exit to the Home window.

Create **shortcuts** as described in the following memo.

NOTES
Transaction confirmation is turned on, so you should click OK when you post or record each transaction. We will not continue the reminder for this step.

NOTES
You can also add shortcuts for Pay Expenses and View Accounts if you want.

2

Memo #1 **Dated August 1, 2021**

Create shortcuts for transactions in other modules (Create Purchase Invoice, Pay Purchase Invoices, Create General Journal and Payroll Cheque Run).

Accounting for Inventory Purchases

The third transaction involves the purchase of inventory items. Inventory purchases are entered in the Purchases Journal, and many of the steps are the same as those for other credit purchases. Now the inventory database will provide the additional information.

✓ 3

Purchase Invoice #KC-884 **Dated August 2, 2021**

From Keep Cold Appliances

4	F010	Refrigerator: Fr. door, drawer freezer, 28 cu ft	$ 9 000.00
4	F020	Refrigerator: Fr. door, shelf freezer, 28 cu ft	10 080.00
	Freight		200.00
	GST		964.00
	Total		$20 244.00

Terms: 1/15, n/30.

Click **Create Purchase Invoice** in the Shortcuts pane to display the familiar Purchases Journal input form window:

CLASSIC VIEW
Click the Purchases icon to open the journal.

NOTES
If you did not create shortcuts, click the Payables entry in the Modules pane list to open the Payables window. Then click the Purchase Invoices icon to open the journal.

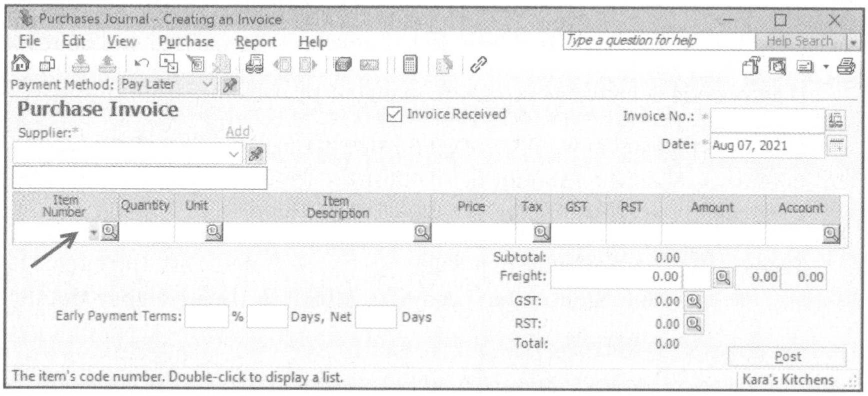

Click the **Supplier field list arrow** to display the list of suppliers.

Click **Keep Cold Appliances** from the list to add it to your input form.

Pay Later, the default payment method for this supplier, is correctly entered.

Check your selection. If you chose an incorrect supplier, select again from the supplier list. If you selected correctly, proceed by entering the invoice number.

Click the **Invoice No. field**.

Type KC-884 **Press** *tab* **twice**.

The cursor advances to the Date field, where you should enter the invoice date.

Type Aug 2

Click the **Item Number field**.

Press *enter* or **click** the **List icon** to open the list of inventory items.

You can add new inventory from the Select Inventory/Service window here as well.

Scroll down and **click** **F010 Refrigerator: Fr. door, drawer freezer, 28 cu ft** from the list to highlight it.

Press *enter*. If you have made an incorrect selection, return to the Item Number field and select again.

You can also **type** f to open a partial list, as you did in the Sales Journal. The first items (up to eight) beginning with F will be included. You can scroll down to access more items if there are more. Press *tab* to move to the Quantity field.

The cursor advances to the Quantity field. The Item Description field should now have the name of the item, Refrigerator: Fr. door, drawer freezer, 28 cu ft: F010. The default price is the most recent purchase price. Now enter the quantity for this item.

Type 4 **Press** *tab*.

The cursor advances to the Unit field. The Unit and Description are correct based on Inventory Ledger records.

The Price field records the most recent unit price paid for the purchase of the inventory items. This amount should not include any GST paid that can be used as an input tax credit. The price has changed since the previous purchase, so it is now incorrect. We will update the price by changing the total amount.

Click **8,680.00**, the Amount entered as the default.

Type 9000 **Press** *tab* to update the unit Price to $2 250.

PRO VERSION

pro The term Vendor will replace Supplier.

NOTES

If you want to search for items by description, you can type the first letter in the Item Description field to provide a list of all items that include the letter you typed. The list will be sorted alphabetically by description.

NOTES

Remember that you can customize the tabbing order and you can change a column width by dragging a margin heading.

NOTES

The next time you purchase this item, the new price, $2 250, will be entered as the default.

NOTES
RST is not paid on items that are purchased for resale because the store is not the final customer.

The correct tax code — code G — is entered by default from the supplier record. Kara's Kitchens pays only GST on purchases of inventory items that will be resold.

If a tax code is incorrect, you can change it by selecting from the Tax Code list.

When purchasing new inventory, no price is recorded. You should enter the quantity and, in the Amount field, enter the total purchase amount. Press *tab* to advance the cursor. Sage 50 will calculate the price per unit.

Press *tab* **repeatedly** to advance to the next line, with the cursor blinking in the Item Number field again, or **click** the **Item Number field** below the first entry.

The cursor skips the RST amount field because the supplier tax code does not include RST. The Account field was also skipped because you cannot change the entry for inventory purchases. The account number is dimmed and the Account field is not available for inventory purchases. The Asset account for the inventory purchase is defined in the Inventory Ledger as the linked account for purchases and sales. To change the account in the journal, you must edit the Inventory Ledger record. The default account for the supplier does not apply to the inventory purchase.

Enter the **second item** from the source document, using the same steps that you used to record the first item. The default price and amount are correct.

The inventory details of the invoice are completed and you are ready to enter the freight charge:

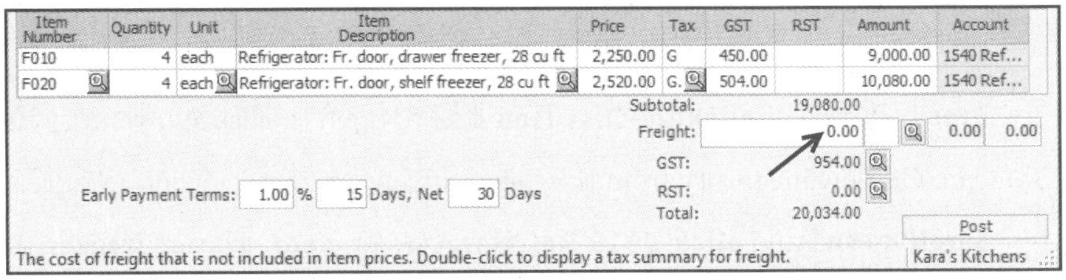

The Freight fields are used to enter any freight charges that cannot be allocated to the purchase of a specific item and to enter the taxes paid on the freight charges. There are four Freight fields: the base amount of the freight charge, tax code, GST amount and, finally, the RST amount. Because GST is paid on freight you must enter a tax code if the supplier charges freight.

Click the **first Freight field**, the amount field, below the Subtotal.

Type 200 **Press** *tab*.

NOTES
RST is not charged on freight in Manitoba when it is applied to an RST-exempt purchase. The correct tax code for freight is code G – GST @ 5%.

The tax code for the supplier, code G, should be entered by default, and it is correct.

If the tax code for freight is not entered automatically, press *enter* to open the familiar list of tax codes. Click G and then click Select.

You do not need to enter amounts for the taxes on freight; they are calculated as soon as you enter the amount of freight charged and the tax code.

Sage 50 calculates the amount of GST (and RST if it is paid) and updates all the totals.

Your input form is now complete:

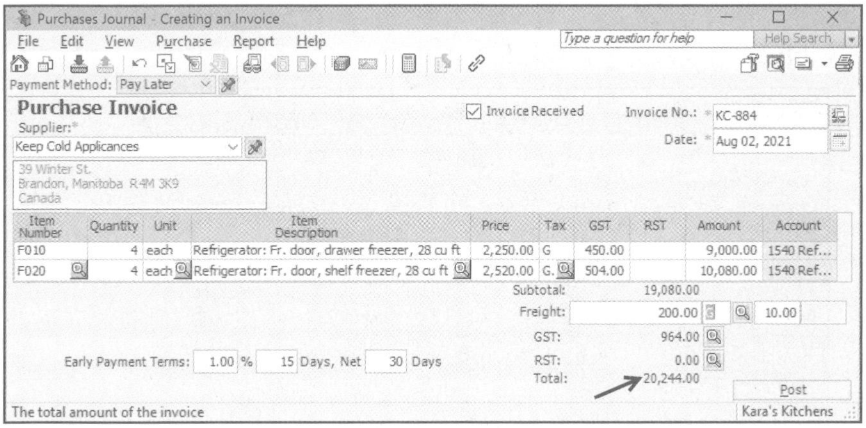

The Subtotal includes all items purchased but does not include freight or taxes.

Reviewing the Inventory Purchase Transaction

As usual, we will review the journal entry before posting it.

Choose the **Report menu** and **click Display Purchases Journal Entry**:

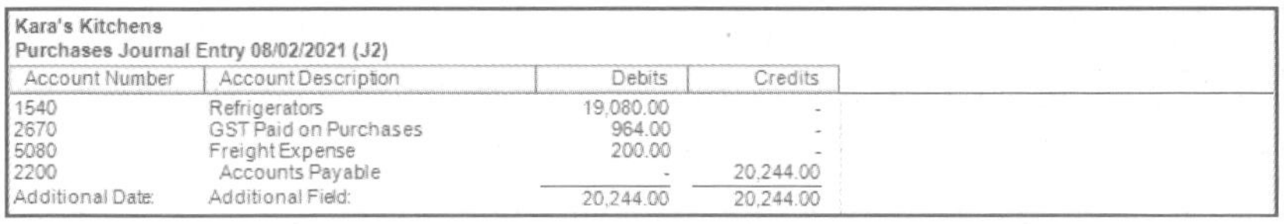
Kara's Kitchens
Purchases Journal Entry 08/02/2021 (J2)

Account Number	Account Description	Debits	Credits
1540	Refrigerators	19,080.00	-
2670	GST Paid on Purchases	964.00	-
5080	Freight Expense	200.00	-
2200	Accounts Payable	-	20,244.00
Additional Date:	Additional Field:	20,244.00	20,244.00

The program has automatically updated all accounts relevant to this transaction. The appropriate inventory asset account (*Refrigerators*), *Accounts Payable, GST Paid on Purchases* and *Freight Expense* have been updated as required because the ledgers are linked — the inventory purchase uses only predefined linked accounts. The inventory database and the supplier record are also updated.

Close the **display** to return to the Purchases Journal input screen.

CORRECTING THE INVENTORY PURCHASES JOURNAL ENTRY

If the inventory item is incorrect, **reselect** from the **inventory** list by **pressing** enter while in this field. **Click Select** to add the item to your form. **Type** the **quantity** purchased and **press** tab to update the totals.

Account numbers cannot be changed for inventory items on the purchase invoice. They must be edited in the Inventory Ledger.

To **insert** a new **line**, if you have forgotten a complete line of the invoice, **click** the **line** that should come after the line you forgot. **Choose** the **Edit menu** and **click Insert Line** to add a blank invoice line to your form. To **remove** a complete **line**, **click** the **line** you want to delete, **choose** the **Edit menu** and **click Remove Line**.

For assistance with correcting other invoice details, refer to page 116.

To correct an inventory purchase after posting, use the **Adjust Invoice tool** or **choose** the **Purchase Menu** and **click Adjust Invoice**. Refer to page 129. If you selected the wrong supplier, you should reverse the purchase transaction (refer to page 141).

Posting

When all the information in your journal entry is correct, you must post the transaction.

Click Post. **Close** the **Purchases Journal**.

NOTES

Pressing ctrl + J will also open the journal display.

NOTES

If this is a recurring purchase, you can store it, just like other recurring purchases.

WARNING!

If you adjust a posted invoice to correct for selecting the wrong supplier, the supplier options, such as payment terms and tax codes, are not updated and may be incorrect. For these errors, you should reverse the entry.

The Inventory Module

Click **Inventory & Services** in the Modules pane list:

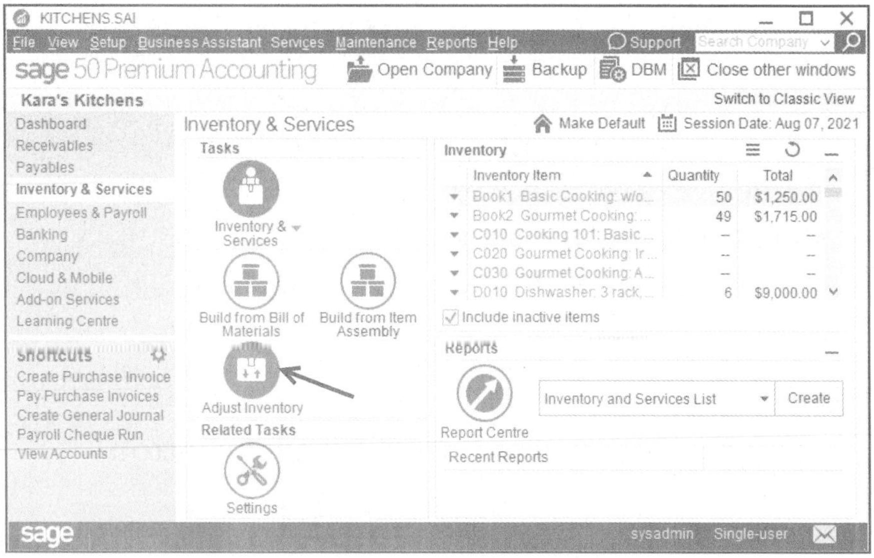

The Inventory module has icons for the ledger records, journal entries and settings. Records are listed in the Inventory Item list pane as they are for other modules so you can access them directly, and all quantities have been updated for the recent sale and purchase. The Reports pane includes all inventory reports in the Reports list.

PRO VERSION
The Inventory module in the Pro version does not include the Build From Bill Of Materials icon.
You will have journal icons only for Build From Item Assembly and Adjust Inventory.

NOTES
You can hide the Quantity and Total inventory details in the Inventory list pane just as you can hide customer and supplier details. For services, these fields are blank.
Click the details icon to open the list of details you can hide. Click a detail to remove it.
Click the refresh icon to update inventory details.
Click the hide icon to remove the entire list.
Click the restore icon to bring back the hidden list.

Making Inventory Adjustments

Sometimes inventory is lost, stolen or damaged and adjusting entries are required to reflect the expenses. These inventory adjustments are made in the Inventory Adjustments Journal in the Inventory & Services window. This journal is also used to record lost inventory that is recovered and inventory that is used by the business instead of being sold to customers.

✓ 4 **Memo #2** **Dated August 2, 2021**
From Owner: Adjust inventory records for Books, item Book2. Four (4) books incurred water damage and are unsalable. Charge losses to Damaged Inventory.

CLASSIC VIEW
Click the Inventory Adjustments icon.

Click the **Adjust Inventory icon** to open the blank Adjustments Journal:

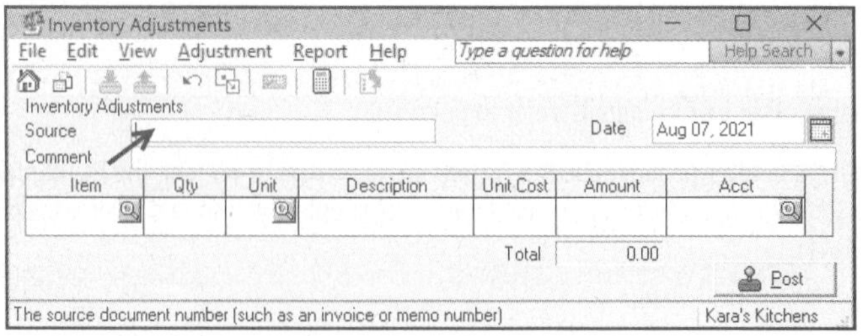

The cursor is in the Source field. The source for an adjustment will normally be a memo from a manager or owner.

Type Memo 2 **Press** *tab*.

The cursor is in the Date field, with the session date entered and highlighted.

PRO VERSION
The Pro version does not include the Refresh tool.

Type `08-02` **Press** *tab* **twice** to place the cursor in the Comment field to add a brief explanation for this transaction.

Type `Water damage to books` **Press** *tab*. The cursor advances to the Item field.

Press *enter* or **click** the **Search tool** to display the familiar inventory list.

The quantities on this list have also been updated to include the previous sale and purchase. Services are not included in the list because they have no quantities in stock and cannot be lost or damaged.

Double-click Book2 Gourmet Cooking to select and add it to the form.

The item description, Gourmet Cooking: w/online subscription, the unit, unit cost and account have been added automatically. The cursor advances to the Quantity (Qty) field. You need to indicate that the inventory has been reduced because of the damaged item. You do this by typing a **negative** number in the field. Remember always to enter a negative quantity when there is an inventory loss. If lost inventory is recovered later, enter the adjustment with a positive quantity.

Type `-4` **Press** *tab*.

The cursor advances to the Unit field. The rest of the journal line is completed automatically. In the Amount field, a negative amount, reflecting the inventory loss, automatically appears as a default based on the average cost. In the Account field, *Damaged Inventory*, the default linked account for inventory losses, appears for this entry. This is the correct account.

> If you need to choose another account, press *enter* to display the list of accounts and select the account as usual. You can also edit the unit cost or amount if you know that the price of the unit was different from the default price, the average of all inventory in stock. You can store and recall Adjustments Journal entries just as you do entries in other journals, but you cannot look up or adjust them after posting.

Your entry is complete and you are ready to review it:

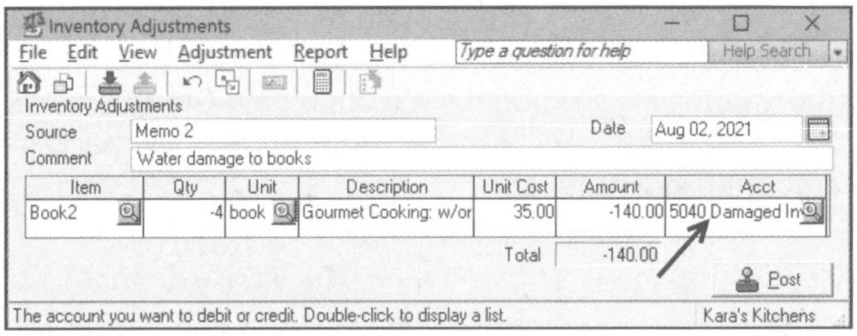

Reviewing the Adjustments Journal Entry

Choose the **Report menu** and **click Display Inventory Adjustments Journal Entry** to display the transaction you have entered:

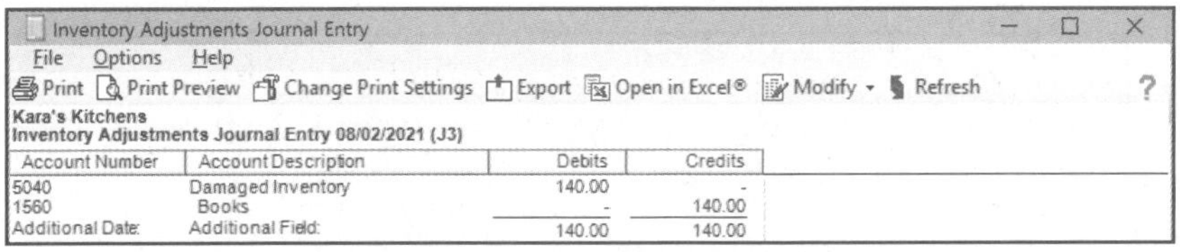
Inventory Adjustments Journal Entry
File Options Help
Print Print Preview Change Print Settings Export Open in Excel® Modify Refresh
Kara's Kitchens
Inventory Adjustments Journal Entry 08/02/2021 (J3)

Account Number	Account Description	Debits	Credits
5040	Damaged Inventory	140.00	-
1560	Books	-	140.00
Additional Date:	Additional Field:	140.00	140.00

Sage 50 has automatically updated the relevant accounts for this transaction. The appropriate inventory asset defined for this inventory item, *Books*, and the inventory

NOTES
Stores that sell inventory frequently use some of their inventory stock in the store. Use the Adjustments Journal to record these transfers by choosing the appropriate asset or expense account to replace the default inventory adjustments linked account for inventory losses. Enter negative quantities because the inventory stock is reduced. Because the store has become the final customer – it has bought the items from itself – it is responsible for reporting the purchase and paying RST on the cost price of these internal sales.

NOTES
Pressing *ctrl* + J will also open the journal display.

NOTES
The second Inventory Ledger linked account is used for item assembly costs in the Item Assembly Journal. Item assembly is introduced in the next transaction.

database have been reduced to reflect the loss at the average cost price. *Damaged Inventory*, the Inventory linked expense account that was defined for inventory losses or adjustments, has been debited or increased.

Close the **display** to return to the Adjustments Journal input screen.

CORRECTING THE ADJUSTMENTS JOURNAL ENTRY

Move to the field that has the error. **Press** tab to move forward or **press** shift and tab together to move back to a previous field. This will highlight the field information so you can change it. **Type** the **correct information** and **press** tab to enter it.

You can also use the mouse to **point** to a field and **drag** through the **incorrect information** to highlight it. **Type** the **correct information** and **press** tab to enter it.

If the inventory item is incorrect, **reselect** from the **inventory** list by **pressing** enter while in this field. **Click Select** to add it to the form. **Type** the **quantity** and **press** tab. After changing any information on an inventory item line, **press** tab to update the totals.

You can insert and remove lines by selecting these options from the Edit menu.

To start over, **click** or **Undo** (or **choose** the **Edit menu** and **click Undo Entry**). **Click Yes** when asked to confirm that you want to discard the transaction.

WARNING!
You cannot adjust or look up an inventory adjustment after posting, so check the entry carefully before posting.

Posting

When all the information in your journal entry is correct, you must save the transaction.

Click the **Post button** Post.

Close the **Adjustments Journal** to return to the Inventory window. The next keystroke transaction creates new inventory items.

Adding a New Inventory Item

Before assembling the promotional packages, we will create the necessary new inventory items. Memo #3 has the inventory item details.

✓ 5

Memo #3 **Dated August 2, 2021**

Create new inventory items for promotions. Create a new Group asset account, 1570 Promotional Offers, to use as a linked account for the new packages. The linked Variance account is not required.

Number	Description	Unit	Min Level	Regular Price	Preferred Price	Linked Accounts Asset	Revenue	COGS	Tax	Picture
BTS1	Kitchen Package: w/microwave	pkg	1	$8 300	(7 900)	1570	4020	5060	GP	BTS1
BTS2	Kitchen Package: w/minifridge	pkg	1	$10 200	(9 500)	1570	4020	5060	GP	BTS2
R120	Microwave: 1.1 cu ft	each	5	$180	(160)	1520	4020	5060	GP	
F070	Refrigerator: mini, 8 cu ft	each	5	$320	(290)	1540	4020	5060	GP	

Inventory items can be added from any inventory item field in a journal, from the Inventory & Services icon (that opens the Inventory & Services window) or from the icon's Add Inventory & Service shortcut:

Click the **Inventory & Services icon** to open the Inventory & Services window:

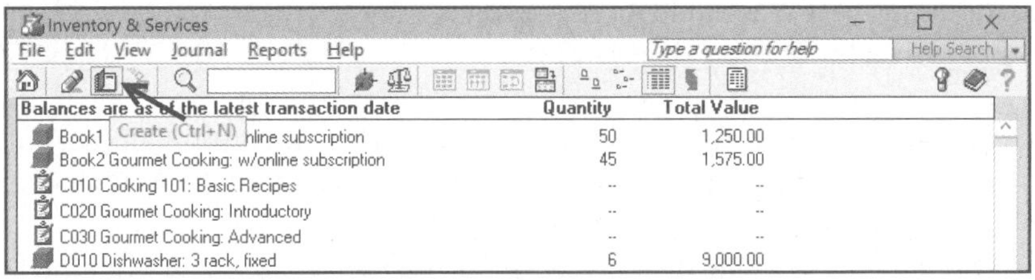

This window is like the Accounts, Suppliers, Customers and Employees windows in other modules, and it lists all inventory items and services. If you choose the Add Inventory shortcut, you will open a new ledger record directly and skip this Inventory & Services window.

Click the **Create tool**, **choose** the **File menu** and **click Create** or **press** *ctrl* + **N.**

Each of these methods opens the Inventory & Services Ledger:

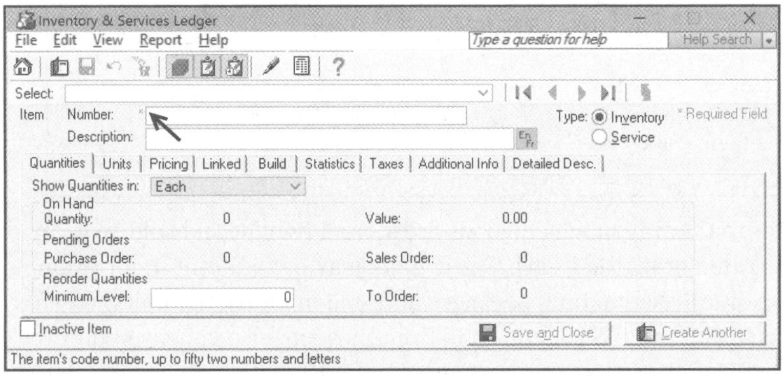

The Inventory & Services Ledger record has many of the tools that are available in other ledgers, including the Refresh tool. The **Show** tool icons allow you to limit the Select field list to inventory items, services or activities (for time and billing). If all three tools are selected, the list includes all three kinds of items. All Show tools are selected for Kara's Kitchens, so all records will be included in the Select list.

You can enter both inventory and service items in the Inventory Ledger. You can designate a service as an activity with time and billing information attached. Activities are available for the time and billing features and for selection as internal services — services that are provided by one department to another within the company and can be tracked as expenses. The Time & Billing function will be covered in Chapter 18.

The packages are inventory, so as a result the type selection is correct and the fields we need are included. The Quantities tab information is displayed because it is the first tab screen. As usual, **required fields** are marked with an asterisk *.

The setup option we selected for inventory sorts the items by code or number. Therefore, the Item Number field is the first item field. When you choose to sort by description, the longer Description field will come first. (Refer to Chapter 16, page 662.)

From the source document information, you must enter the item code and description. The first Item field contains the code or number of the inventory item — the only required field on this screen; the second Item field contains the description or item name.

Click the **Item Number field**.

Type `BTS1` **Press** *tab* to advance to the Item Description field.

Type `Kitchen Package: w/microwave`

Click the **Minimum Level field** in the Reorder Quantities section.

NOTES

You can add inventory items from any journal inventory field when the selection list is available, that is, in the Sales, Purchases, Adjustments and Item Assembly journals. Click the List icon in the Item field to open the selection list. Click Add New Inventory/Service and press *enter* or click the Create button to open the Inventory Ledger window. (Refer to the screenshot on page 361.)

PRO VERSION

The Pro version does not have the Build tab. It applies to the Build From Bill Of Materials option in the Bill Of Materials & Item Assembly Journal. This feature is not available in the Pro version.

NOTES

As in other ledgers and journals, the Refresh tool applies when you work in multi-user mode. Clicking the tool will update the record with changes made by other users who are accessing the data file at the same time.

PRO VERSION

The Time & Billing function is not available in the Pro version. The Pro version has only two Show tools – one for inventory items and one for service items. The Refresh tool is also not on the Pro version Select item line.

NOTES

When you print inventory reports, items that have fallen below the minimum level will be flagged.

Here you must enter the stock level at which you want to reorder the item in question, or in this case, assemble more packages.

Type 1

The Quantity On Hand, Value, and Order fields are updated from journal entries. Before the Inventory Ledger history is finished, you can add this information as historical data.

The entry for Units (**Show Quantities In**) on this screen is taken from the Units tab screen.

NOTES

When you use different units for selling, buying and stocking, you can choose one of these units from the list in the Show Quantities In field.

Click the **Units tab**:

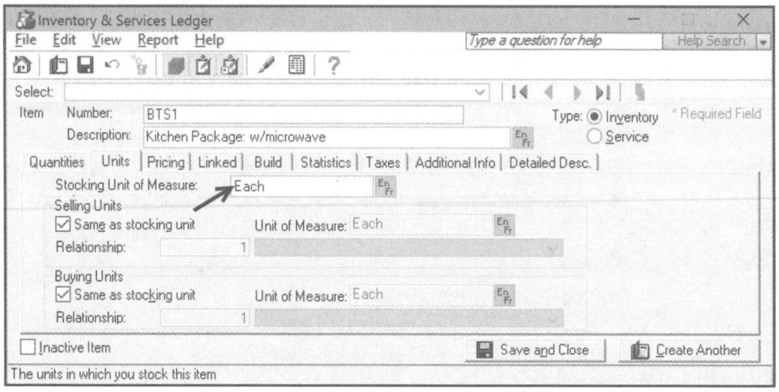

Units refer to the way in which goods are stored, bought and sold (e.g., by the dozen, by the tonne or by the item). These units may be different if, for example, merchandise is purchased in bulk packages and sold in individual units. When a store buys or stocks inventory in different units from those it sells, you also enter the relationship between the sets of units, for example, 12 units per carton.

Kara's Kitchens measures all units the same way, so only one entry is needed.

Double-click **Each** in the Stocking Unit Of Measure field. **Type** pkg

Click the **Pricing tab**:

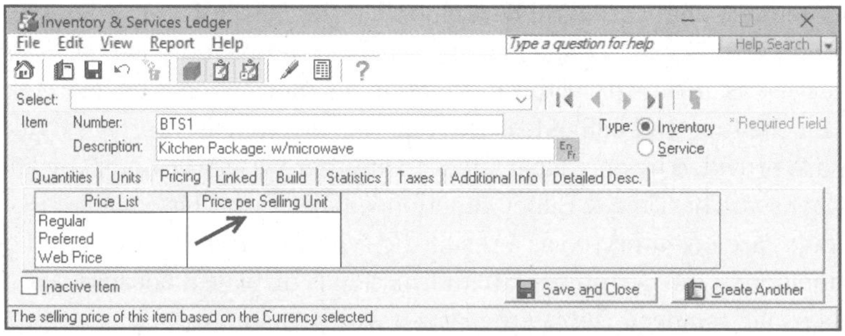

NOTES

You can select the price list in the Sales Journal from the Price field select list icon. By adding it to the customer's record, the correct price is selected automatically in the journal.

NOTES

The Premium version allows you to create additional price lists. The Pro version does not include this feature. When you create additional price lists (Inventory Ledger Settings), they will be added to this screen, and you can enter prices for them.

A business may have different price lists. Each item may be assigned a regular price, a selling price for preferred customers and a Web price. Kara's Kitchens has three customers with preferred customer status, marked with the asterisk * in the Customer Information list on page 355. Regular, preferred and Web selling prices can also be entered in foreign currencies when other currencies are used.

Click the **Price Per Selling Unit column** beside Regular.

Type 8300

Press *tab* to advance to the Price Per Selling Unit field for preferred prices.

The regular price is entered as the default Preferred and Web Price.

Type 7900 to replace the default preferred price entry.

Click the **Linked tab** to access the linked accounts for the inventory item:

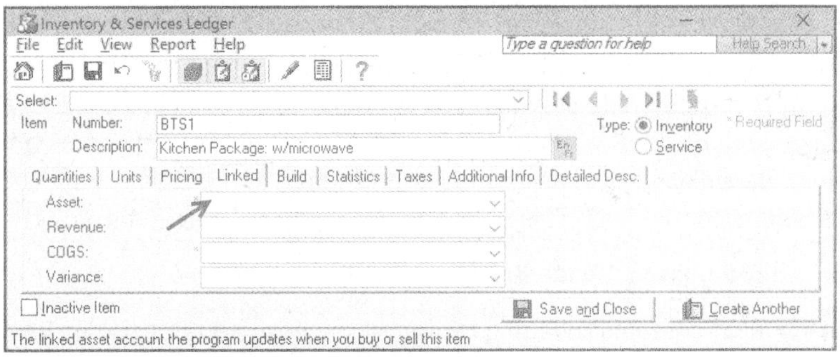

> **NOTES**
> For other ledgers, the linked accounts are defined for the entire ledger. For example, there is only one Accounts Receivable account.
> These linked asset accounts serve as the control accounts for the Inventory Ledger – the total value of all items linked to one asset account must equal the asset account's General Ledger balance.

There are two sets of linked accounts for inventory: those that apply to the entire ledger — the default accounts for inventory adjustments and item assembly costs — and those that apply to specific inventory items. The ones in the ledger are item specific and are used as the default accounts whenever inventory items are sold or purchased. By defining linked accounts for each item in the Inventory Ledger, each inventory item can be related to separate asset, revenue, expense and variance accounts. Two of these four **linked accounts** are **required**: the linked asset account and COGS (Cost of Goods Sold). You cannot choose or change the asset account in the Purchases Journal, and it is not available on the account selection list in any journal. You also cannot change or select the Asset or Cost of Goods Sold account for Sales. Sage 50 automatically enters them in the background — there are no fields for them on-screen.

In the **Asset** field, you must enter the linked asset account affected by purchases and sales of this item. A list of accounts is available from the drop-down list arrow in the Asset field. Only asset accounts are available in the list for the Asset field. Because the account we need does not exist yet, we cannot choose it from the account list for the field. We can create it here.

> **NOTES**
> When you type the account name in the field at the same time and then press *tab*, the wizard will add both the number and the name for the account. Some account fields with list arrows allow you to enter both the number and name for new accounts; those with List icons do not.

Click the **Asset field**.

Type `1570 Promotional Offers` **Press** *tab*.

The next screen allows you to create the new account:

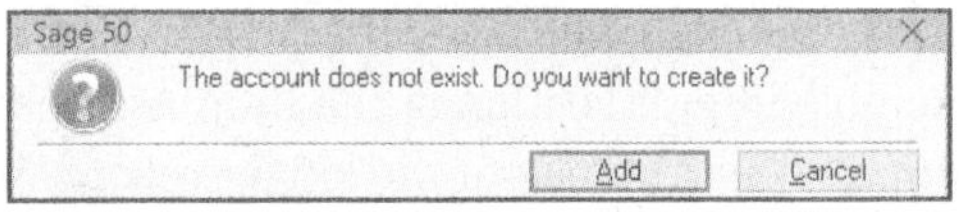

Click **Add** to proceed to the Add An Account wizard. **Click Next** to continue.

Accept the **remaining** account **settings** and **finish** creating the account.

After you click Finish, you will generate another message advising you of an account class change for the linked account:

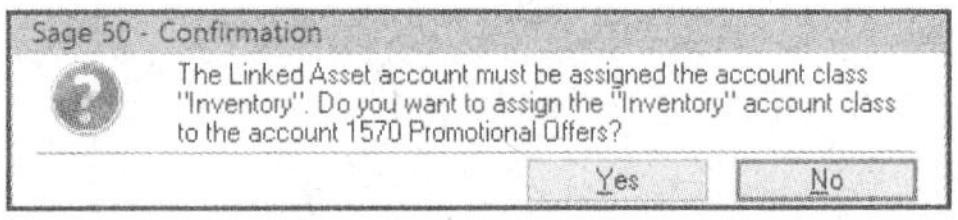

> **NOTES**
> If necessary, you can create new linked revenue and expense accounts in the same way you created the new asset account.

Click **Yes** to accept the change. Clicking No will return you to the Linked Accounts screen so you can select a different account.

In the **Revenue** field, you must enter the linked revenue account that will be credited when this inventory item is sold. You can type the account number or select from the list. Only revenue accounts are available for the Revenue field.

Click the **Revenue field list arrow** to list the revenue accounts available.

Click **4020 Revenue from Sales** to enter it on your form.

> **NOTES**
> The linked revenue account is not a required account – you can choose an account in the Sales Journal when you sell inventory. This allows you to use a different account in the journal, such as for returns. The linked asset and COGS accounts are required. You do not enter them when entering inventory sales or purchases – the program adds them automatically.

WARNING!
Check the linked account numbers carefully. If they are incorrect, corresponding journal entries will be posted incorrectly. If you discover the error when you are reviewing the journal entry, you should delete the journal entry line and then edit the Inventory Ledger record before posting.

Click the **COGS field list arrow** (Cost of Goods Sold expense) to list the expense accounts available.

In the **COGS** field, you must enter the linked expense account that will be debited when this inventory item is sold. Only expense accounts are available for the COGS field and the Variance field. Kara's Kitchens uses the single *Cost of Goods Sold* account for all inventory items. The linked COGS account is also required and must be assigned the Cost of Goods Sold account class. This class has already been assigned from other items.

Click **5060 Cost of Goods Sold** from the list.

NOTES
Variance accounts are used in the Shady Corners application in Chapter 13.

The **Variance** field contains the linked variance expense account used when the inventory sold is on order, before the goods are in stock. At the time of the sale, *Cost of Goods Sold* is debited for the average cost of the inventory on hand, or based on previous purchases. When the goods are received, the actual purchase price may be different from this historical average cost. The price difference is charged to the variance account. Kara's Kitchens does not allow inventory to be oversold, so you can leave the Variance account field blank.

PRO VERSION
Click the Statistics tab at this stage.
The Pro version does not have a Build tab because this screen applies to Build From Bill Of Materials, a function not available in the Pro version.

Click the **Build tab**:

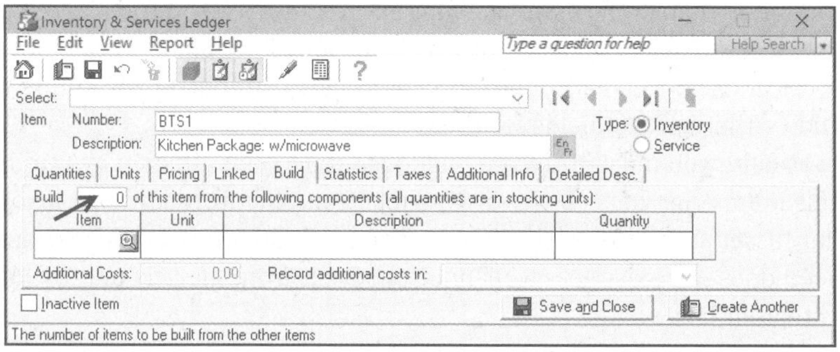

NOTES
You can define multiple levels of building – one item may be made from other items that in turn are made from multiple inventory items.

On the Build tab screen, you enter the inventory components needed to make the item. You identify the number of items you are building and the component items required to build this number. This process is similar to the one found in the Components section of the Item Assembly Journal (refer to page 377). When it is time to build the item (in the Bill Of Materials & Item Assembly Journal), you indicate how many items you are building — the Assembled Items section of the Item Assembly — and the rest of the details are taken from the Build screen of the ledger record. We will use the Build feature in Chapter 18.

Click the **Statistics tab**:

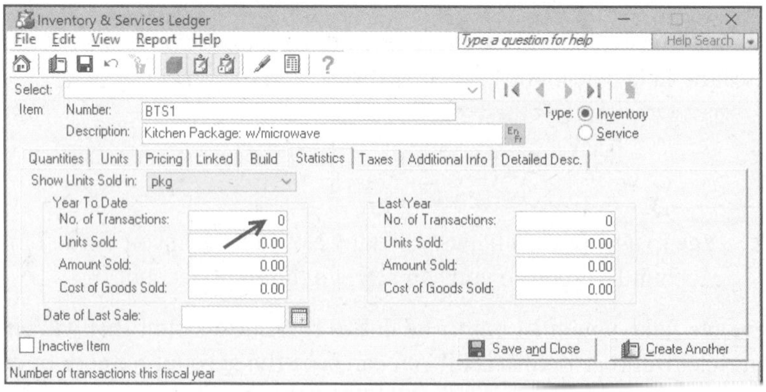

NOTES
You can enter the historical date using any of the usual date formats, with or without the year.

This screen applies to historical data. Since this is a new inventory item, there are no previous sales, and you should leave all entries at zero. The **Date Of Last Sale** is the most recent date that this item was sold. The **Year To Date** section refers to historical information for the current fiscal period, and the **Last Year** fields apply to the previous year. Inventory Statistics are added to inventory tracking reports.

The **No.** (number) **Of Transactions** refers to the total number of times the item was sold. For example, if one customer bought the item on three separate dates, there would be three transactions. If four customers bought the item on one day, there would be four transactions. If one customer bought four of the same item at one time, there would be one transaction. The **Units Sold** counts the total number of items that were sold on all occasions to all customers in the relevant period. The **Amount Sold** field holds the total sale price of all items sold in the period, and the **Cost Of Goods Sold** field records the total purchase price of all items sold.

If you have historical data for the item, you can add it. Sage 50 continually updates the Statistics tab fields from journal entries.

Click the **Taxes tab**:

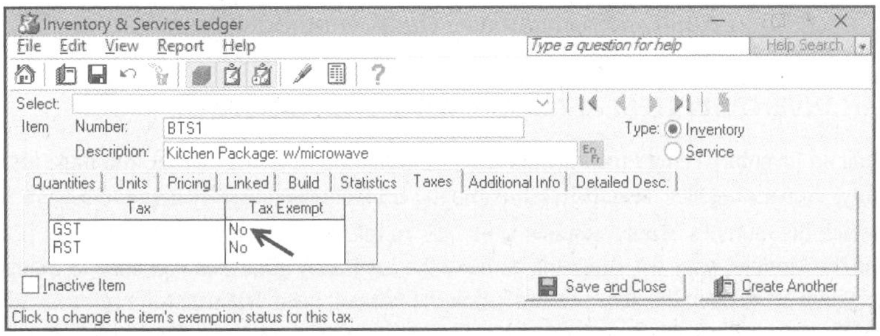

NOTES
The tax exemption in the ledger record will ensure that a tax is not applied. Books and service items were marked as tax exempt for RST on this screen so that RST does not apply to their sales. The default tax code in the journal is taken from the customer's ledger record.

All taxes set up for the company will appear on this screen. RST and GST may be charged or omitted by default. Because most goods have these taxes applied to the sale, the default is to charge them — No is entered in the Tax Exempt column. The **Tax Exempt** entry is a toggle switch. Clicking the current entry changes it. The default settings are correct — both taxes are charged. Books and services provided by Kara's Kitchens were designated as tax exempt for RST.

When inventory items are imported and duty is charged, you enter the duty rate on this screen as well.

The **Additional Info** tab allows for custom-defined information fields relating to the item, just like the Additional Info tab in other ledgers. It is not used by Kara's Kitchens.

Click the **Detailed Desc. tab**:

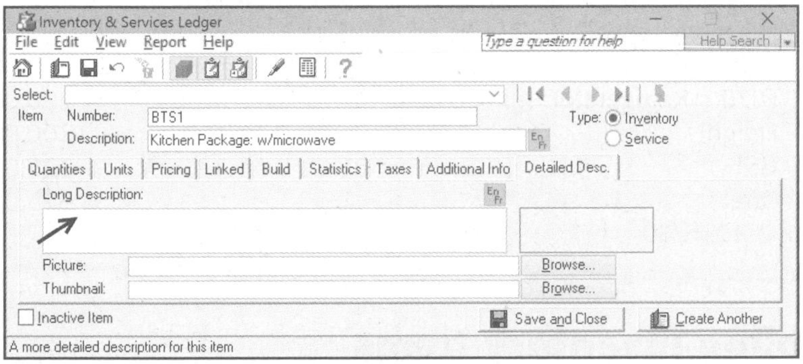

NOTES
You could enter the list of components in the Description field if this is an item that is built from other items.

NOTES
The image files BTS1.BMP and BTS2.BMP (or BTS1 and BTS2) were copied to the SageData19\LOGOS folder when you installed your other data files.

On this screen you can enter a detailed description of the inventory item and the name of a file and location where an image of the item is stored. The bitmap (.BMP) file for this item was copied to the SageData19\LOGOS folder with your other data files.

Click **Browse** beside the Picture field to open the file location window.

Locate and **open** the **SageData19 folder**. **Double-click** **C:**, **SageData19** and **LOGOS** to open this folder. **Double-click** **BTS1** (or **BTS1.BMP**).

NOTES
Because we do not know your initial default location, we continue to use C:\SageData19 as the location for all the files for this text. This allows us to give clear file path instructions.

The image and file name have been added:

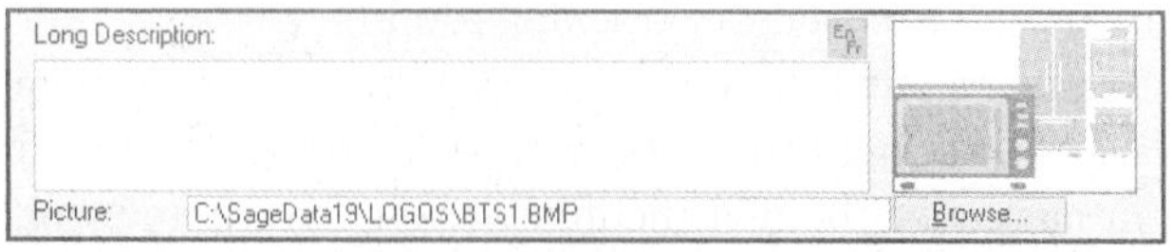

When all the information is correct, you must save your information.

CORRECTING THE INVENTORY ITEM BEFORE CREATING THE RECORD

Correct the information if necessary by **clicking** the field that contains the **error**. **Click** the appropriate **tab** to change information screens if necessary. **Highlight** the **error** and **type** the **correct information**. **Press** tab to enter the correction.

Click **Create Another** [Create Another] to save the new record. The ledger remains open so you can add the second new item.

EDITING AN INVENTORY ITEM AFTER CREATING THE RECORD

You cannot edit an Inventory Ledger record while you are using the item in a journal. You must first **delete** the **journal line containing the item**. (**Click** the **journal line**, **choose** the **Edit menu** and **click Remove Line**.) Then **click** the journal's **Home window tool** to return to the Home window. **Click Inventory & Services** in the Modules pane list. **Click** the name of the **inventory item** that you need to change in the Inventory pane Item list to open the item's record. **Click** the **tab** you need. **Highlight** the **information** that is incorrect, and then **type** the **correct information**. **Close** the **Ledger window**. **Click** the **Home window journal icon you need** (or the task bar icon/button for the journal) to return to the journal.

Click the **Quantities tab**.

Enter all the details for the remaining three new items from page 370.

Click [Save and Close] to save the new record. Both items are added to your ledger list of inventory items.

Close the **Inventory & Services window** to return to the Home window.

Enter the following **purchase** for two new items and then **close** the **journal**.

NOTES

Because these are new items, there is no historical cost. Enter the total cost for each item in the corresponding Amount field.

6

Purchase Invoice #APK-2106 **Dated August 2, 2021**

From A-Plus Kitchens

20	R120	Microwave: 1.1 cu ft	$2 200.00
20	F070	Refrigerator: mini, 8 cu ft	4 200.00
		Freight	100.00
		GST	325.00
		Total	$6 825.00

Terms: 2/10, n/30.

Assembling Inventory Items

Inventory item assembly can be used to build new inventory from other inventory items, to create package offers of two or more regular items for sale at a special price or to reserve inventory for a special project or contract. Kara's Kitchens' new inventory items, the promotional packages, are offered at reduced prices, and the cost is the sum of the original component costs. Kara's Kitchens uses the inventory Bill Of Materials & Item Assembly Journal to create the promotional packages. The journal can be used to build from Item Assembly or from the Bill Of Materials.

The journal's two methods can be started from separate Home window icons. We will use the Item Assembly approach:

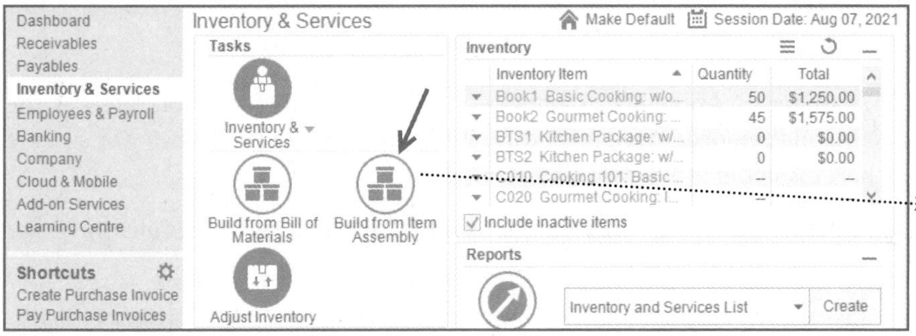

Click the **Build From Item Assembly icon** to open the Journal:

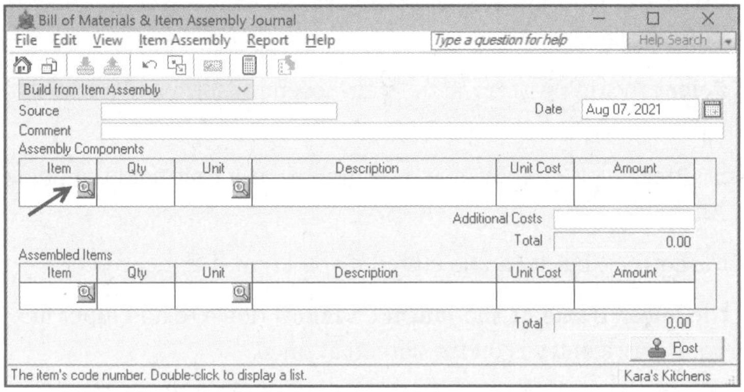

There are two ways to assemble items in the Premium version of Sage 50: Item Assembly or Build From Bill Of Materials as defined in the ledger on the Build tab screen (refer to page 374). When you build items from the bill of materials, the journal has only the assembled items part — the components information is drawn from the ledger record. The bill of materials method will be covered in Chapter 18. We will use the item assembly method now. You can access both methods from the Build drop-down list in the journal:

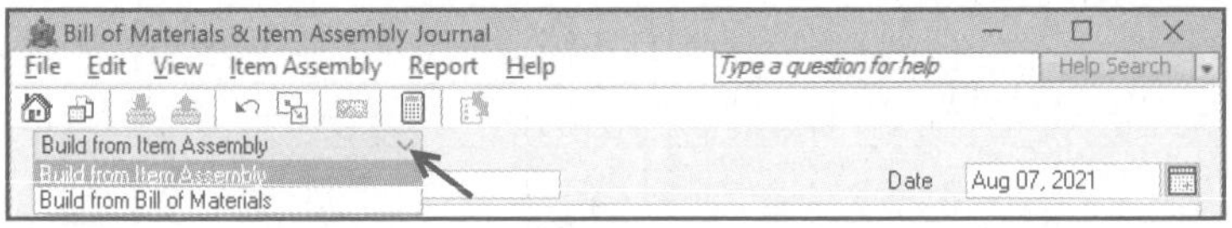

We are using the item assembly method, so you do not need to modify the journal.

✓ 7

Item Assembly #IA-01 **Dated August 3, 2021**

Create five (5) back-to-school promotional Kitchen Packages with microwave. Transfer 5 of each component item as follows:

5	R010	Range: 5 burner, smooth surface, convection	$2 065	each
5	F010	Refrigerator: Fr. door, drawer freezer, 28 cu ft	2 202	each
5	D010	Dishwasher: 3 rack, fixed	1 500	each
5	R120	Microwave: 1.1 cu ft	110	each
5	Book1	Basic Cooking: w/online subscription	25	each

Additional Costs (for Basic Cooking classes) 1 250 /session

Assembled Items

5	BTS1	Kitchen Package: w/microwave	$6 152	/pkg

Click the **Source field**, where you should enter the reference or form number.

Type IA-01 **Press** tab to advance to the Date field. Enter the date of the transfer.

PRO VERSION
In the Pro version, only the Item Assembly approach is available.

CLASSIC VIEW
Click the Bill Of Materials & Item Assembly icon

to open the journal. Click Build From Item Assembly if necessary.

NOTES
We will use the term Item Assembly Journal to refer to the Bill Of Materials & Item Assembly Journal.

PRO VERSION
The drop-down list is not available. The cursor will be in the Source field.

CLASSIC VIEW
Click Build From Item Assembly in the Build drop-down list if necessary to open the journal form we need.

Type 08-03 **Press** tab **twice** to advance to the Comment field.

Type Create promotional microwave packages

Press tab to advance to the first line in the Item field.

You are in the **Assembly Components** section. This first section refers to the items that are being removed from inventory, the "from" part of the transfer or assembly. Together, these items will form the promotional package.

Press enter or **click** the **List icon** to display the familiar inventory selection list.

If needed, you can add new inventory items from the Select Inventory list in the Item Assembly Journal. Services are not on this list because they cannot be assembled.

Click **R010 Range: 5 burner, smooth surface, convection** to select the first item needed.

Click **Select** to add the item to the item assembly form and advance to the Quantity (Qty) field. You must enter the quantity.

Type 5 **Press** tab to advance the cursor to the Unit field to update the Amount.

The unit cost is correct, but it can be edited if you know it is incorrect.

Drag the **lower frame of the journal window** down to add input lines so that your entire entry is on the screen at once.

Click the **next line** in the Item column.

Select the next **inventory item** to be included, **enter** the **quantity** and then continue to **enter** the **remaining components** for the package.

At this stage, the Assembly Components portion is complete:

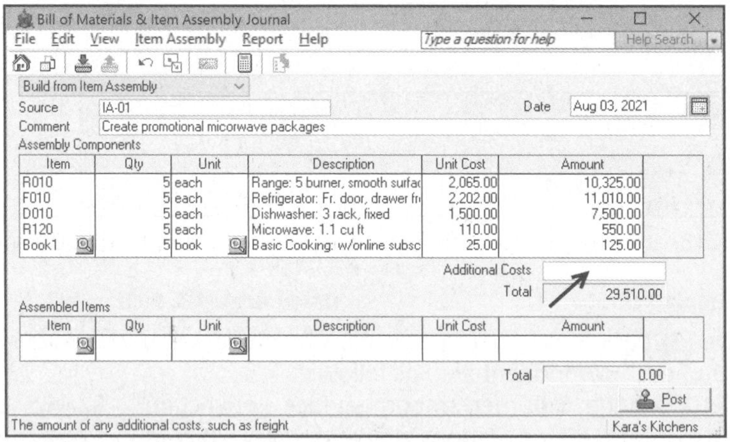

The middle part of the item assembly form contains two fields: Additional Costs and Total. **Additional costs** may come from shipping or packaging involved with assembling, moving or transferring the inventory. Services involved in the package may also be entered as additional costs. The extra costs for all items transferred should be entered into the Additional Costs field. The **Total** is calculated automatically by Sage 50 to include the individual costs of all items transferred — the assembly components — plus any additional costs. Kara's Kitchens has additional costs of $1 250 ($250 per package) for the basic cooking classes.

Click the **Additional Costs field**.

Type 1250 **Press** tab to update the total.

NOTES

The unit cost may be different when the cost of transferred items is lower than the default because older stock is being transferred and it was purchased at a lower price. If you change the unit cost, press tab to update the amount.

NOTES

Services have no quantities or purchase costs, so you cannot choose them for item assemblies. Therefore, we enter them as Additional Costs.

The cursor advances to the first line in the Item column of the **Assembled Items** section. This section refers to the new or reserved inventory, the item being assembled or the "to" part of the transfer.

Press enter or **click** the **List icon** to display the familiar inventory selection list.

Click **BTS1 Kitchen Package: w/microwave** to select the item we created.

Click **Select** or **press** enter to add the item to the item assembly form and advance to the Quantity (Qty) field.

Type 5

The Unit Cost and Amount fields are blank because the cost of the new item is still unknown. The unit cost of assembled items is the total cost of all assembly components, plus additional costs, divided by the quantity or number of units assembled. When a single type of item is assembled and the quantity is greater than one, it is simpler to enter the quantity and amount (the Total in the assembly components portion in the top half of the form) and let the program calculate the unit cost. You can also enter the individual item cost in the Unit Cost field and allow the program to calculate the Amount (Qty × Unit Cost). We will enter the total from the upper portion of the journal.

Click the **Amount field**.

Type 30760 **Press** tab to enter the cost and update the unit cost and total.

The unit cost, $6 152, has been added, and the totals in the two parts of the assembly form should now be the same. If they are not, you will be unable to post the entry.

Your item assembly form is now complete:

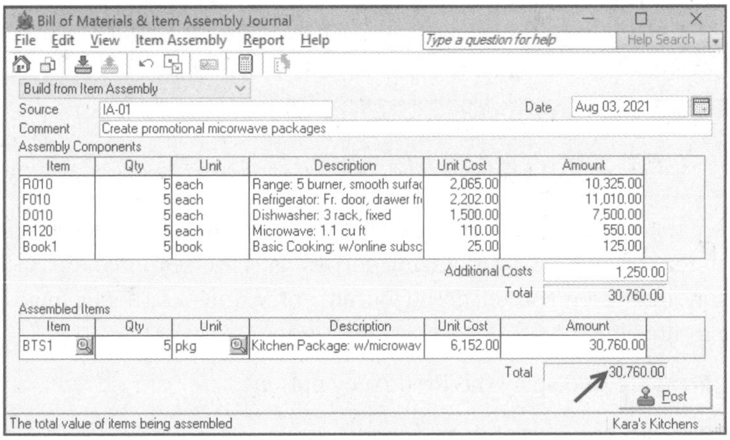

Bill of Materials & Item Assembly Journal

File Edit View Item Assembly Report Help

Build from Item Assembly

Source IA-01 Date Aug 03, 2021

Comment Create promotional micorwave packages

Assembly Components

Item	Qty	Unit	Description	Unit Cost	Amount
R010	5	each	Range: 5 burner, smooth surfa	2,065.00	10,325.00
F010	5	each	Refrigerator: Fr. door, drawer fr	2,202.00	11,010.00
D010	5	each	Dishwasher: 3 rack, fixed	1,500.00	7,500.00
R120	5	each	Microwave: 1.1 cu ft	110.00	550.00
Book1	5	book	Basic Cooking: w/online subsc	25.00	125.00

Additional Costs 1,250.00

Total 30,760.00

Assembled Items

Item	Qty	Unit	Description	Unit Cost	Amount
BTS1	5	pkg	Kitchen Package: w/microwav	6,152.00	30,760.00

Total 30,760.00

Post

The total value of items being assembled Kara's Kitchens

Reviewing the Item Assembly Journal Entry

Choose the **Report menu**, then **click Display Bill Of Materials & Item Assembly Journal Entry** to display the transaction you have entered:

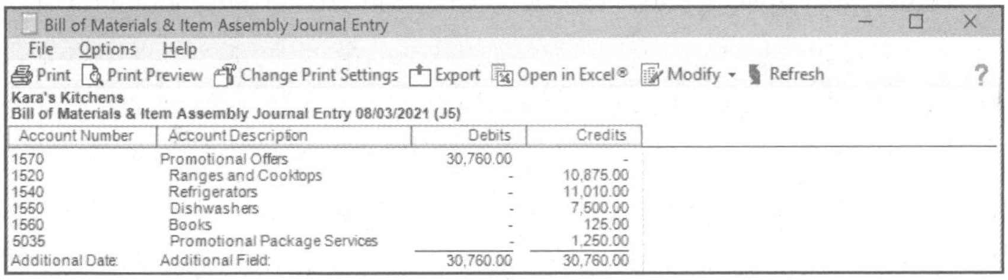

Bill of Materials & Item Assembly Journal Entry

File Options Help

Print Print Preview Change Print Settings Export Open in Excel® Modify Refresh

Kara's Kitchens

Bill of Materials & Item Assembly Journal Entry 08/03/2021 (J5)

Account Number	Account Description	Debits	Credits
1570	Promotional Offers	30,760.00	-
1520	Ranges and Cooktops	-	10,875.00
1540	Refrigerators	-	11,010.00
1550	Dishwashers	-	7,500.00
1560	Books	-	125.00
5035	Promotional Package Services	-	1,250.00
Additional Date:	Additional Field:	30,760.00	30,760.00

NOTES
You could also add the new inventory items, the packages, and the new asset account, 1570 Promotional Offers, directly from the journal while creating the new item.

NOTES
Because the two totals must be the same, entering the total cost and allowing the program to determine the unit cost ensures this balance.

Of course, this method will work only when you are assembling one item at a time.

PRO VERSION
In the Pro version, you will choose the Report menu and then click Display Item Assembly Journal Entry to place the transaction on-screen.

NOTES
Pressing ctrl + J will also open the journal display.

Sage 50 has moved the inventory items from their original asset accounts (credit entries to *Ranges, Refrigerators, Dishwashers* and *Books*) to the newly created inventory account (debit entry to *Promotional Offers*). The quantities for all items involved have been updated in inventory selection lists and quantity reports. The necessary items are taken out of their regular individual item inventory account and transferred to the new account. Thus the quantities of the original items are reduced because they have been transferred to the new item. Additional Costs are assigned to *Promotional Package Services*, the linked account defined for these costs. This is a contra-expense account — the credit entry for the expense account is added (debit amount) to the inventory value of the assembled inventory asset.

Close the **display** to return to the Item Assembly Journal input screen.

CORRECTING THE ITEM ASSEMBLY JOURNAL ENTRY

Move to the field that has the error. **Press** tab to move forward through the fields or **press** shift and tab together to move back to a previous field. This will highlight the field information so you can change it. **Type** the **correct information** and **press** tab to enter it. You must advance the cursor to the next field to enter a change.

You can also use the mouse to **point** to a field and **drag** through the **incorrect information** to highlight it. **Type** the **correct information** and **press** tab to enter it.

If an inventory item is incorrect, **press** enter while the cursor is in the Item field to **display** the appropriate **list**. **Double-click** the **correct inventory item**. **Re-enter** the **quantity** and **press** tab to update the totals.

WARNING!

When you recall an Item Assembly transaction, the unit costs and amounts for assembly components may be different from the original entry. The average cost may have changed since you posted the entry if you purchased new components at different prices. The new average cost price will be displayed. The quantities will be correct.

Correcting entries may also change the average unit cost.

Because the item assembly is a complex transaction, it is very easy to make a mistake, so check your work carefully. You may also want to store the original entry. If you discover later that you have made an error, you can recall the entry and add a minus sign to each quantity and to the Additional Costs amount to create a reversing entry.

But first you should make corrections.

Click the **Store button** to display the familiar Store Recurring Transaction screen:

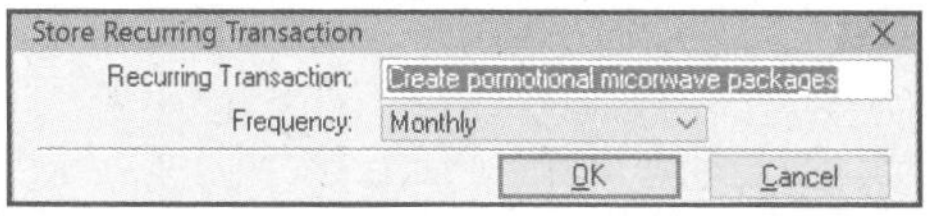

Because this is not a regular recurring transaction, we will use the **Random** frequency. Choosing the Random frequency for recurring entries uses the session date as the default transaction date when you recall the journal entry. You can then change the transaction date as needed.

Click **Monthly** to display the Frequency options.

Click **Random** to select this frequency.

Click **OK** to save the entry and return to the Item Assembly Journal — the Recall button is now active.

Posting

Click the **Post button** Post when you are certain that all the information is correct.

Enter the next **assembly transaction**.

8 **Item Assembly #IA-02** **Dated August 3, 2021**

Create five (5) back-to-school promotional Kitchen Packages with minifridge.
Transfer 5 of each component item as follows:

5	R030	Range: smooth surface, induction	$2 950	each
5	F030	Refrigerator: Fr. door, drawer freezer, 32 cu ft	2 675	each
5	D020	Dishwasher: 3 rack, flexible tines & racks	2 065	each
5	F070	Refrigerator: mini, 8 cu ft	210	each
5	Book1	Basic Cooking: w/online subscription	25	each
Additional Costs (for Basic Cooking classes)			1 250	/session

Assembled Items

5	BTS2	Kitchen Package: w/minifridge	$8 175	/pkg

Store the assembly as a recurring transaction with random frequency.

NOTES
Do not forget to save the item assembly as a recurring transaction with Random as the frequency.

When you post the second assembly entry, you will open a low inventory message:

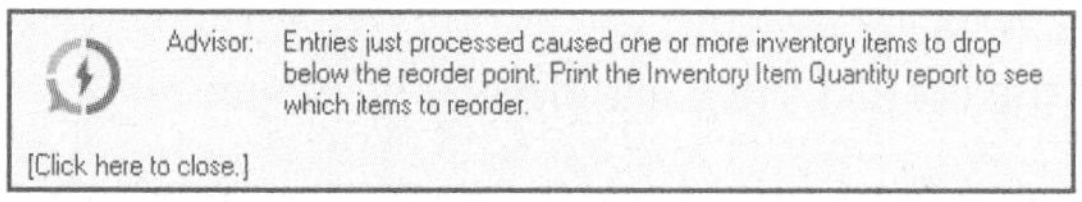
Advisor: Entries just processed caused one or more inventory items to drop below the reorder point. Print the Inventory Item Quantity report to see which items to reorder.
[Click here to close.]

Read the **Advisor message** about low inventory and then **click** to close it.

Close the **Journal** to return to the Inventory & Services module window.

Click **Receivables** in the Modules pane list to restore this window.

Add **shortcuts** for **Item Assembly** and **Inventory Adjustments** from the Inventory & Services list in the Customize Shortcuts window.

Selling to Preferred Customers

Sage 50 allows you to record multiple inventory prices and to identify customers by the prices they will pay (preferred, regular, Web or a user-defined price). Sales for each group of customers are entered the same way since the program automatically enters the correct price depending on the customer selected and the price option in their ledger record.

✓ 9 **Sales Invoice #2471** **Dated August 3, 2021**

Sold by House to Cloves Fine Dining (preferred customer)

3	R100	Gas Range: 5 burner w/grill, 2 ovens	$4 880	each
2	R110	Gas Cooktop: 5 burner w/grill	4 100	each
		Delivery (tax code G)	200	
		GST	5%	
		RST	8%	

Terms: 2/10, n/30.

Cloves Fine Dining is a preferred customer — Preferred is entered as the Price List on the customer's Options tab screen.

Click Cloves Fine Dining in the Customers pane to open the ledger record. Click the Options tab. Preferred is entered in the Price List field. Close the ledger record.

Click the **Sales Invoices icon** 

to open the Sales Journal.

Pay Later is the correct selection for this sale to Cloves Fine Dining. The Invoice number is also correct by default.

Choose **Cloves Fine Dining** from the Customer list.

Type `Aug 3` in the Date field and **choose** **House** as the salesperson.

NOTES
The price for each price list you have, including the ones you created, will be on this list, so you can select the price for individual sales or items.

PRO VERSION
pro The Pro version does not have the option to create additional user-defined price lists.

NOTES
Remember to change the tax code for freight (delivery) to G.

Type r in the **Item Number field**. Scroll down and **click R100 Gas Range: 5 burner w/grill, 2 ovens** to add it. **Press** tab to advance to the Quantity field.

Type 3 **Press** tab to add the first item at the preferred customer price of $4 880 instead of $5 290, the regular price.

Click the **Price field List icon** to open the Select Price list:

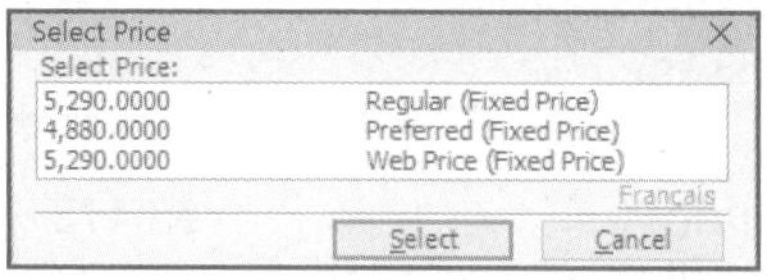

You can also select the item price you need from this screen.

Click the price you want and then click Select to use it in the journal.

Click **Cancel** because the correct price has already been entered.

Enter the **second item and freight** for this customer to complete the entry:

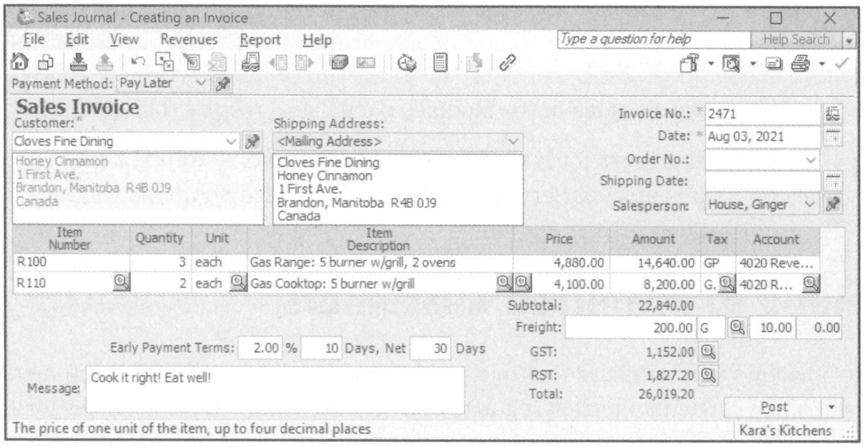

Choose the **Report menu** and **click Display Sales Journal Entry** to review:

Kara's Kitchens
Sales Journal Entry 08/03/2021 (J7)

Account Number	Account Description	Debits	Credits
1200	Accounts Receivable	26,019.20	-
5060	Cost of Goods Sold	17,050.00	-
1520	Ranges and Cooktops	-	17,050.00
2640	RST Payable	-	1,827.20
2650	GST Charged on Sales	-	1,152.00
4020	Revenue from Sales	-	22,840.00
4200	Freight Revenue	-	200.00
Additional Date:	Additional Field:	43,069.20	43,069.20

This entry looks the same as a regular non-discounted sale. Revenue is reduced because of the change in selling price, but this change is not recorded as a discount.

Close the **display** when finished. **Make corrections**. **Post** the **entry**. **Click Yes** to allow the customer to exceed the credit limit.

Entering Sales Returns

Customers may return purchases for many different reasons. For example, the size, colour or quality may have been other than expected. Stores have different policies with respect to accepting and refunding returns. Most stores place reasonable time limits on the period in which they will give refunds. Some stores offer credit only, and some charge a handling fee on goods returned. Kara's Kitchens will provide full refunds for purchases within two weeks of the sale if the items have not been used or are damaged. Sales returns are entered in the Sales Journal and are similar to sales, but the quantity is entered with a minus sign — a negative quantity is sold. Different accounts may be used.

✓ 10

Sales Return #2470-R **Dated August 3, 2021**

Returned from August1 sale to Kaik by Lavender Estates:

−1	R030	Range: smooth surface, induction	4 250 each
	GST		5%
	RST		8%

Terms: 1/10, net 30. Create new Subgroup revenue account: 4050 Sales Returns.

The return must use the same customer and payment method as the original sale. Pay Later is correctly selected. The Sales Journal should still be open.

Choose **Lavender Estates** from the Customer list.

You should use a different invoice number so that the return can be differentiated from a normal sale.

Click the **Invoice No. field** and **type** 2470-R

Enter **Aug. 1** in the Date field to match the date of the original sale.

Enter **Kaik** as the salesperson.

Click the **Item Number field** and **type** r to open the inventory list.

Click **R030 Range: smooth surface, induction** to enter it and **press** (tab) to move the cursor to the Quantity field.

This adds the first item returned by the customer at the regular price.

Type −1 **Press** (tab).

A positive amount appears in the Price field and a negative amount is added to the Amount field — a positive price times the negative quantity. The tax amounts are also negative.

We should change the default account so that returns can be tracked separately.

Click the **Account field List icon** and **type** 4050

Press (tab) and **add Sales Returns**, the new account. Do not forget to change the account type to **Subgroup** (the account balance is included in a Subtotal).

Enter additional items returned, if there are any, in the same way.

Your journal entry is complete:

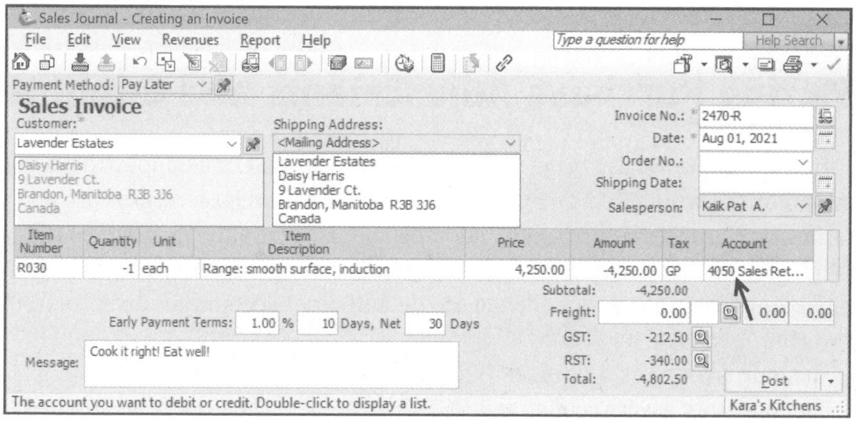

NOTES
Using the same terms for the return as for the sale will prorate the discount for the amount of the return. For this situation, you also need to enter the same dates for both transactions. In this way, we enter the return as if we are adjusting the original sale.

NOTES
Most stores have separate forms for returns with their own number sequences.

NOTES
The salesperson should be entered for sales returns because commissions are calculated on total sales less returns.

WARNING!
If you do not change the account type to Subgroup, your accounts will not be in logical order and you will be unable to generate reports. In this case, you must edit the account type.

NOTES
In the Comment field, you could add the reason for the return.

Choose the **Report menu** and **click Display Sales Journal Entry** to review it:

Kara's Kitchens
Sales Journal Entry 08/01/2021 (J8)

Account Number	Account Description	Debits	Credits
1520	Ranges and Cooktops	2,950.00	-
2640	RST Payable	340.00	-
2650	GST Charged on Sales	212.50	-
4050	Sales Returns	4,250.00	-
1200	Accounts Receivable	-	4,802.50
5060	Cost of Goods Sold	-	2,950.00
Additional Date:	Additional Field:	7,752.50	7,752.50

The entry is the reversal of a regular sale. The inventory asset account has been debited because inventory is added back. *Sales Returns* — a contra-revenue account — is debited, reducing revenue, and *Accounts Receivable* is credited to reduce the balance owing in the customer's account — money is effectively being returned to the customer. Similarly, *RST Payable* and *GST Charged on Sales* are debited because the tax liabilities have decreased, and finally the expense account *Cost of Goods Sold* is credited because this expense has been reversed.

For credit card sales, the return entry will also reverse credit card fees expenses.

Close the **display** when finished. **Make corrections** if necessary.

Post the **entry**. **Close** the **Sales Journal**.

NOTES

If we adjusted the original sale, we would have a single entry in the Receipts Journal for the reduced adjusted amount. The net result should be the same. However, we would be unable to choose a separate account for the return.

If the customer pays within the discount period, both the original sale amount and the amount of the return will have the discount applied.

In the Receipts Journal for this customer, a negative amount has been entered for the return:

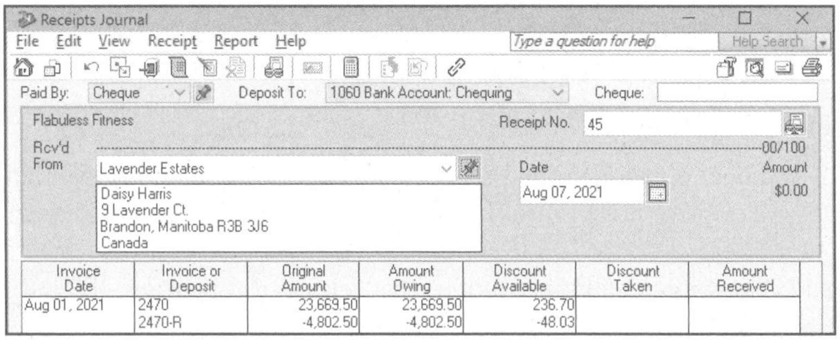

NOTES

The negative invoice we created for the return has no invoice date. Therefore it would also have no due date. Discounts, however, will apply and expire according to the date of the original invoice.

When the customer makes the final payment, accept the Amount Received field for the return to subtract the amount of the return from the original invoice.

Enter the **payment to Keep Cold Appliances**.

11 **Payment Cheque #461** **Dated August 3, 2021**

To Keep Cold Appliances, $53,331.20 in payment account including $512.80 discount for early payment. Reference invoices #KC-618 and #KC-884.

Entering Purchase Adjustments and Credit Notes

Returns on purchases also occur for a variety of reasons. For example, the goods may be damaged or the wrong items may have been shipped. Purchase returns are entered in the same way as sales returns — by adding a minus sign to the quantity so that all the amounts become negative. The supplier and payment method must be the same as the original purchase. You cannot change the default asset account for inventory purchases or returns.

The journal entry is a reversed purchase entry.

The inventory asset account and *GST Paid on Purchases* will be credited to decrease the inventory and restore the tax liability. *Accounts Payable* will be debited to reduce the amount owing to the supplier. Freight charges, when entered as a negative amount, will also be reversed.

Adjustments for purchases of inventory are made in the same way as other purchase adjustments. However, differences occur when the invoice has already been paid.

✓ 12

Adjust Purchase Invoice #KC-884-R **Dated August 4, 2021**

From Keep Cold Appliances, Credit Note			
3	F010	Refrigerator: Fr. door, drawer freezer, 28 cu ft	$ 6 750.00
3	F020	Refrigerator: Fr. door, shelf freezer, 28 cu ft	7 560.00
		Freight	200.00
		GST Paid	725.50
Total Invoice			$15 235.50
Total Credit amount			$4 815.70
Terms: net 30 days.			

Open the **Purchases Journal**. **Click** the **Adjust Invoice tool** and **select** invoice **KC-884** from **Keep Cold Appliances**.

Type `KC-884-R` as the invoice number.

Click **4**, the Quantity for F010 and **type** 3

Click **4**, the Quantity for F020 and **type** 3

Change the **payment terms** to **net 30** to complete the entry:

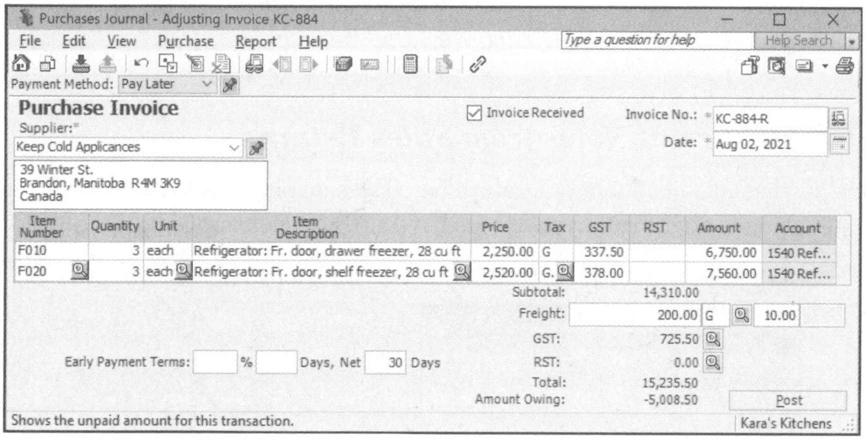

The amount owing appears as a negative amount on the invoice, but unlike the sales return, all other amounts are still positive.

Review the **journal entry** — it looks like a normal purchase entry.

Close the **display**. **Make corrections** if needed.

Click **Post**.

NOTES
Changing the payment terms for this transaction does not affect the credit note amount.

Creating Automatic Credit Notes from Returns

When you reverse or adjust an invoice after an account has been paid, and the original purchase was a "pay later" transaction, as in this example, Sage 50 can automatically create a credit note for the adjustment or reversing entry.

First, you may see a confirmation that payments have already been applied:

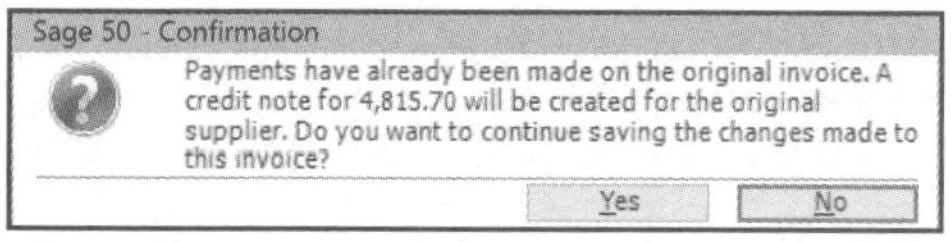

Click Yes to continue if you see this message. (Sometimes this message opens and closes quickly and the next message is displayed directly.)

NOTES
The amount owing in the journal is different from the credit note amount by the amount of the discount on the original payment.
Refer to the Notes on the following page.

NOTES

The credit note amount is calculated as follows:

$20 244 was the amount on the original invoice;

$15 235 is the amount on the adjusted invoice;

$5 008.50 is the difference between the invoice amounts.

The calculation of the credit amount is complicated by the discount ($192.80) that was already taken. The discount taken should be prorated to reduce the credit. The preferred method of entering this transaction is as a return. If the same terms are applied to the returned items, the credit amount will also be reduced by the discount and it will be correctly adjusted.

NOTES

The return creates three journal entries: the reversal of the original purchase invoice, the reversal or cancellation of the discount and the final correct purchase entry. The net result in the journal's Amount Owing column is a credit balance of $4 815.70, not $5 008.50, the amount in the Purchases Journal.

NOTES

The credit note does not have a due date in the Payments Journal.

An additional message about the credit note will open (read the margin Notes):

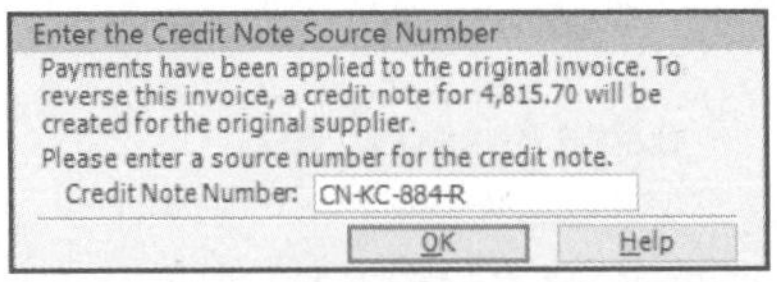

You can accept or change the default note number — the original invoice number preceded by CN that designates this as a credit note.

Click **OK** to continue.

In the Payments Journal, the credit note is entered as an invoice with a negative amount that you can accept to reduce the amount you pay for future purchases. The paid invoice is entered with the adjusted amount when you include fully paid invoices:

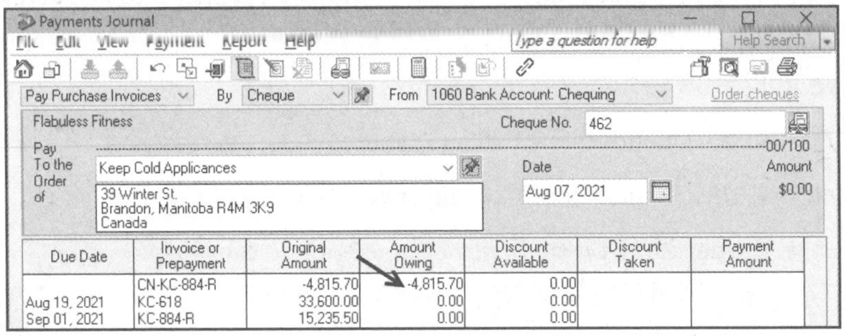

Automatic Credit Notes from Sales Returns

When posting an adjustment or a return for a sales invoice that has been paid, you may first get a notice advising that payments have already been applied to the invoice.

Click Yes to confirm. Instead, the credit note may open immediately:

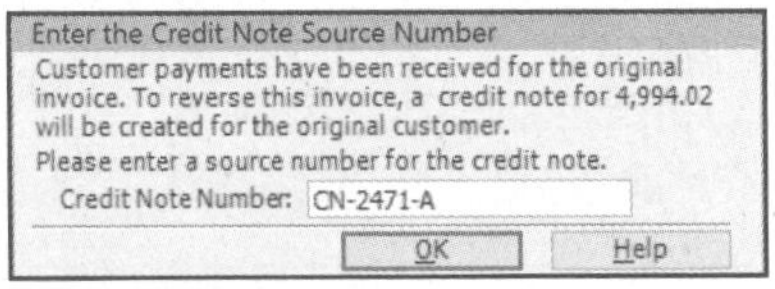

You can accept the default note number — the original invoice number preceded by CN that designates this as a credit note. Click OK to confirm the entry. The credit note for the customer is a negative invoice — in the Receipts Journal for the customer, it appears as a negative amount that you can accept with the next customer payment to reduce the amount owing by the customer.

Enter the **remaining transactions** for August.

13 **Receipt #45** **Dated August 4, 2021**

From Marigold Inn, cheque #4782 for $16 780.50 in payment of account including $169.50 discount for early payment. Reference invoice #2459.

14 **Receipt #46** **Dated August 6, 2021**

From Brandon Culinary Arts, cheque #14701 for $13 288.80 in payment of account including $271.20 discount for early payment. Reference invoice #2463.

15

To:
Customer: **Kara's Kitchens**
Address: 354 Thunderbird Ave.
Brandon, MB R3T 3B7
Reg # 245138128 RT0001

A-Plus Kitchens
7 Onandaga Dr., Vancouver, BC V4G 4S5
Tel: (604) 588-3846 Fax: (604) 588-7126
Aplus.com

Invoice #: APK-2182
GST # 466 254 109 RT0001

Aug. 6, 2021

qty	code	item	total
5	D010	Dishwasher: 3 rack, fixed @1,500	7 500.00
5	D020	Dishwasher: 3 rack, flexible tines & racks @2,100	10,500.00
4	R100	Gas Range: 5 burner w/grill, 2 ovens @3,700	14,800.00
4	R110	Gas Cooktop: 5 burner w/grill @3,100	12,400.00
		Freight	400.00
		GST	2,280.00
		Invoice Total	47,880.00

Terms: 2/10, n/30 *BB*

NOTES
Edit the purchase prices as required.

16

INVOICE # 2472
Kara's Kitchens
354 Thunderbird Ave.
Brandon, MB R3T 3B7
#245138128 RT0001

Sold to: Botelli Developments
Address: 30 Cherry St.
Brandon, MB R3A 1C7
ATTN: Gina Botelli

Salesperson: Kaik

Date: Aug. 7/21

QTY	CODE	DESCRIPTION	PRICE/UNIT	TAX CODE	TOTAL
4	D010	Dishwasher: 3 rack, fixed	1,980	GP	7,920.00
4	D020	Dishwasher: 3 rack, flexible tines & racks	2,700	GP	10,800.00
8	R040	Range: smooth surface, slide-in	3,900	GP	31,200.00
4	F040	Refrigerator: Fr. door, shelf freezer, 32 cu ft	4,860	GP	19,440.00
4	F060	Refrigerator: Fr. door, built-in, 36 cu ft	7,900	GP	31,600.00

Preferred Customer, Free Delivery for large volume purchase PAK

Allow customer, to exceed credit limit KC

Terms: 2/10, n/30	**GST** 5%	5,048.00
	RST 8%	8,076.80
	Invoice Total	**114,084.80**

Tel 1: (204) 642-2665 or (800) 448-2665 Fax: (204) 642-9100
karaskitchens.com
cook it right, eat well

NOTES
Remember to change the tax code for delivery (freight).

SESSION DATE – AUGUST 14, 2021

17

Memo #4 **Dated August 9, 2021**

Create new inventory item:

Number	Description	Unit	Min Level	Regular Price	Preferred Price	Linked Accounts Asset	Revenue	COGS
F080	Refrigerator: Fr. door, no freezer, 36 cu ft	each	2	$3 200	(2 900)	1540	4020	5060

18

Purchase Invoice #CI-6891 **Dated August 9, 2021**

From Chillers Inc.

5	F030	Refrigerator: Fr. door, drawer freezer, 32 cu ft	$13 375.00
5	F040	Refrigerator: Fr. door, shelf freezer, 32 cu ft	19 000.00
3	F060	Refrigerator: Fr. door, built-in, 36 cu ft	17 640.00
3	F080	Refrigerator: Fr. door: no freezer, 36 cu ft	6 000.00
	Freight		200.00
	GST		2 810.75
	Total		$59 025.75

Terms: 2/10, n/30.

NOTES

F080 is a new inventory item, so there is no historical cost and the Amount field is blank. You will need to enter an amount.

19

Memo #5 **Dated August 9, 2021**

Edit the selling price for item F040 Refrigerator: Fr. door, shelf freezer, 32 cu ft to reflect the increase in the purchase price. The new regular and Web price will be $5 300 and the preferred price will be $4 900.

20

NOTES

Remember to change the tax code for delivery (freight).

KARA'S KITCHENS

INVOICE # 2473
Kara's Kitchens
354 Thunderbird Ave.
Brandon, MB R3T 3B7
#245138128 RT0001

Sold to: Marigold Inn
Address: 29 Marigold Ct.
Brandon, MB R4A 2M2
ATTN: Arianna Appleby

Salesperson: House

Date: Aug. 14/21

QTY	CODE	DESCRIPTION	PRICE/UNIT	TAX CODE	TOTAL
1	R100	Gas Range: 5 burner w/grill, 2 ovens	5,290	GP	5,290.00
2	R110	Gas Range: 5 burner w/grill	4,380	GP	8,760.00
		Delivery		G	200.00

Terms: 1/10, n/30	**GST** 5%	712.50
	RST 8%	1,124.00
	Invoice Total	**16,086.50**

Tel 1: (204) 642-2665 or (800) 448-2665 Fax: (204) 642-9100
karaskitchens.com
cook it right, eat well

21

Receipt #47 **Dated August 14, 2021**

From Botelli Developments, cheque #36991 for $111 803.10 in payment of account including $2 281.70 discount for early payment. Reference invoice #2472.

22 **Cash Purchase Invoice #BDS-9033** **Dated August 14, 2021**

From Brandon Daily Spectator (use Quick Add for new vendor), $1 200 plus $60 GST and $96 RST for ads to run for 12 weeks. Purchase invoice total $1 356 paid in full by cheque #462. Create new Group account: 1290 Prepaid Advertising.

SESSION DATE – AUGUST 21, 2021

23 **Purchase Invoice #CA-4134** **Dated August 17, 2021**

From Cook's Kitchens

10	R010	Range: 5 burner, smooth surface, convection	$20 650.00
5	D010	Dishwasher: 3 rack, fixed	7 500.00
5	D020	Dishwasher: 3 rack, flexible tines & racks	10 500.00
	Freight		200.00
	GST		1 942.50
	Total		$40 792.50

Terms: 2/5, n/20.

24 **Receipt #48** **Dated August 17, 2021**

From Cloves Fine Dining, cheque #19664 for $10 000 in partial payment of invoice #2471.

25 **Cash Purchase Invoice #MB-59113** **Dated August 19, 2021**

From Manitoba Bell, $240 plus $12.00 GST and $19.20 RST for phone service. Purchase invoice total $271.20 paid by cheque #463 in full payment.

26 **Payment Cheque #464** **Dated August 19, 2021**

To Chillers Inc., $57 901.45 in full payment of account of invoice #CI-6891 including $1 124.30 discount for early payment.

27 **Cash Purchase Invoice #ME-34910** **Dated August 20, 2021**

From Manitoba Energy, $210 plus $10.50 GST paid for hydro service. Purchase invoice total $220.50 paid by cheque #465.

28 **Payment Cheque #466** **Dated August 20, 2021**

To A-Plus Kitchens, $26 825, including $6 825 in full payment of account of invoice #APK-2106 and $20 000 in partial payment of invoice #APK-2182.

SESSION DATE – AUGUST 31, 2021

29 **Sales Invoice #2474** **Dated August 23, 2021**

Sold by House to Brandon Culinary Arts

2	R070	Wall oven: convection, double oven	$4 910 each
2	R080	Cooktop: smooth surface, 5 burner	2 950 each
1	F050	Refrigerator: Fr. door, shelf freezer, 36 cu ft	6 500 each
	Delivery (tax code G)		200
	GST		5%
	RST		8%

Terms: 2/10, n/30.

30 **Purchase Invoice #RS-7533** **Dated August 25, 2021**

From Riverview Sunoco, $520 plus $26 GST and $41.60 RST for vehicle repairs and gasoline for company vehicle. Purchase invoice total $587.60. Terms: net 20.

WARNING!

You will need to add the tax code and the account for the new supplier in the journal.

Alternatively, you can use Full Add and enter these details in the supplier's record.

31

Bank Debit Memo #91431 **Dated August 28, 2021**

From Red River Credit Union, authorized withdrawals were made from the chequing account on our behalf for the following:

Bank service charges	$ 65
Mortgage interest payment	1 880
Mortgage principal reduction	220
Bank loan interest payment	420
Bank loan principal reduction	480

NOTES
Choose Credit Card Customers for the Visa and MasterCard sales summaries.

32

MasterCard Sales Invoice #2475 **Dated August 30, 2021**

Sold by Kaik to Credit Card Sales (sales summary)

10	Book1	Basic Cooking: w/online subscription	$ 60 /book	$ 600
10	Book2	Gourmet Cooking: w/online subscription	80 /book	800
1	BTS1	Kitchen w/microwave	8 300 /pkg	8 300
5	R120	Microwave: 1.1 cu ft	180 each	900
5	F070	Refrigerator: mini, 8 cu ft	320 each	1 600
10	C010	Cooking 101: Basic Recipes	350 /session	3 500
5	C020	Gourmet Cooking: Introductory	450 /session	2 250
5	C030	Gourmet Cooking: Advanced	550 /session	2 750
	GST		5%	1 035
	RST		8%	864
	Total paid by MasterCard			$22 599

NOTES
When you close the Sales Journal after posting the second credit card sale, you may see a message about credit card processing. Choose Do Not Show Me Again and then close the message.

WARNING!
Remember to change the payment method for the MasterCard sales summary and to change the tax code for delivery.

33

KARA'S KITCHENS

INVOICE # 2476
Kara's Kitchens
354 Thunderbird Ave.
Brandon, MB R3T 3B7
245138128 RT0001

Sold to: Visa Sales Summary
Address: Credit Card Customers

Salesperson: House

Date: Aug. 30/21

QTY	CODE	DESCRIPTION	PRICE/UNIT	TAX CODE	TOTAL
5	Book1	Basic Cooking: w/Online Subscription	60	G	300.00
5	Book2	Gourmet Cooking: w/Online Subscription	80	G	400.00
3	BTS1	Kitchen Package: w/microwave	8,300	GP	24,900.00
3	BTS2	Kitchen Package: w/minifridge	10,200	GP	30,600.00
3	D010	Dishwasher: 3 rack fixed	2,200	GP	6,600.00
10	C010	Cooking 101: Basic Recipes	350	G	3,500.00
10	C020	Gourmet Cooking Classes: Introductory	450	G	4,500.00
4	C030	Gourmet Cooking Classes: Advanced	550	G	2,200.00
		Delivery		G	200.00

Direct deposit to Visa account GH

Terms: Visa

GST 5%	3,660.00
RST 8%	4,968.00
Total	**81,828.00**

Tel 1: (204) 642-2665 or (800) 448-2665 Fax: (204) 642-9100
karaskitchens.com
cook it right, eat well

NOTES
Use the Sales by Salesperson Summary Report (by Sales Item) to find the net sales for each employee. Do not include freight or other sales in the report.

The report by customer does not allow you to omit freight and other amounts.

34

Memo #6 **Dated August 31, 2021**

Prepare the payroll for the two salaried employees, House and Kaik. Add 0.5 percent of revenue from sales and services for August as a commission to their salaries. Issue payroll cheques #467 and #468.

Displaying Inventory Reports

Most inventory reports can be displayed from the Reports menu in the Inventory & Services window, from the Home window Reports menu, from the Inventory & Services module window Reports pane drop-down list and from the Report Centre. We will access the reports from the Report Centre.

Click the **Report Centre icon** in any window.

Click **Inventory & Services** to open the list of inventory reports:

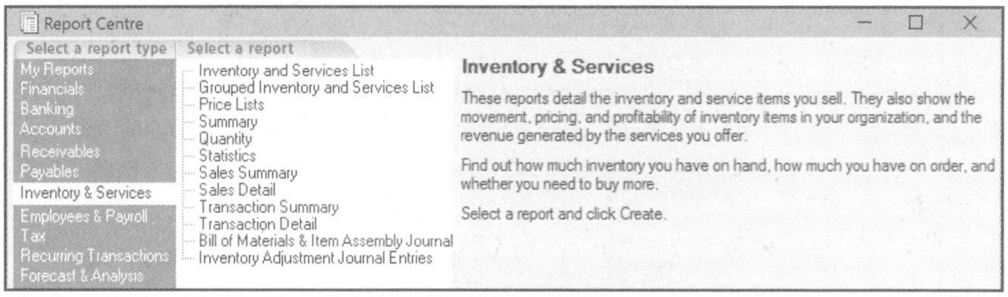

Displaying Inventory Lists

Click **Inventory And Services List**. **Click** **Modify This Report** to open the report options window:

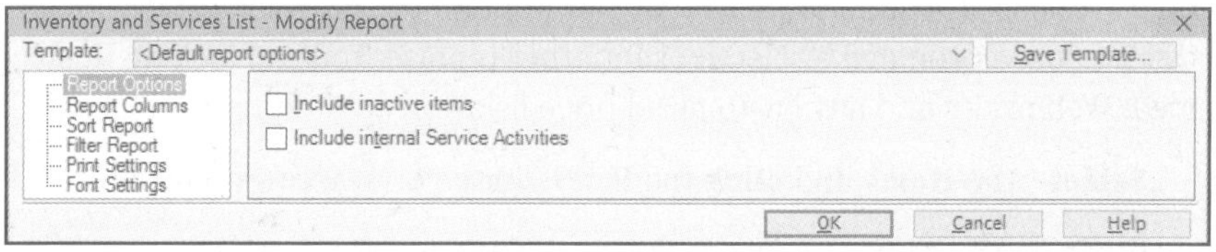

Or, you can choose the Reports menu and choose Lists, then click Inventory & Services for the report options.

The default report has the item number, description, type, quantity, total value and average cost. To select the fields for the report, choose Report Columns.

Click **OK** to produce the list. **Close** the **display** when you have finished.

Displaying Grouped Inventory Lists

Click **Grouped Inventory And Services List**. **Click** **Modify This Report** to open the report options window.

Click **Type** in the Group By field:

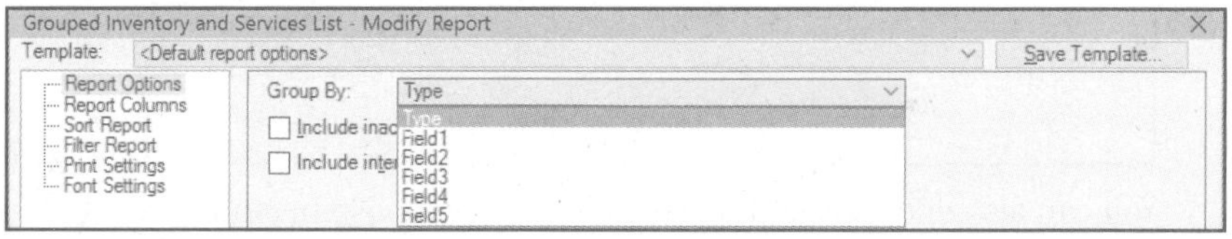

From this list, choose the way you want to sort the list. You can organize by Type (inventory and services are separated) or by any of the additional information fields you created for the ledger. To select the fields for the report, choose Report Columns.

Click **OK** to open the list. **Close** the **display** when you have finished.

NOTES
If you click the Report Centre icon in the Inventory & Services window, you will open the list of Inventory & Services reports with the first report selected and its sample displayed.

PRO VERSION
Item Assembly Journal Entries replaces Bill Of Materials & Item Assembly Journal Entries in the Select A Report Type list.

The Grouped Inventory and Services List and Forecast & Analysis reports are not available.

CLASSIC VIEW
Right-click the Inventory & Services icon. Click the Select a Report tool to open the Modify Report window.

PRO VERSION
The Pro version does not have the option to Include Internal Service Activities.

NOTES
You can drill down to the Inventory Transaction Detail Report from the Inventory List and from the Grouped Inventory List.

PRO VERSION
Grouped lists are not available in the Pro version.

NOTES
You cannot sort or filter the Price Lists Report. You can select or omit the Item and Description columns, but you cannot omit both in the same report.
There are no drill-down reports from Price Lists.

Displaying Inventory Price Lists

The different inventory prices — regular, preferred, Web and customized prices — are not available in the other inventory reports, but you can place all of these prices together on the Price Lists Report.

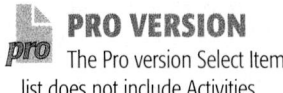

Click **Price Lists** from the Select A Report list.

Click **Modify This Report** to open the report options window:

PRO VERSION
The Pro version Select Items list does not include Activities.

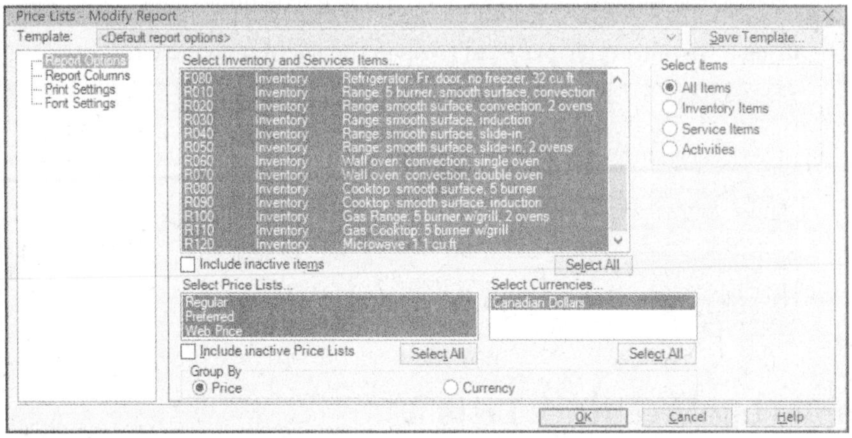

NOTES
If you have created other price lists or use additional currencies, they will be listed in the Modify Report screen and you can include them in the report.
If you use other currencies, you can also add the price lists in these currencies and then group your lists by currency or by price list.

You can also choose the Reports menu, then choose Inventory & Services and click Price Lists to display the report options.

You can choose the item or items that you want on the price list by selecting them from the list, just as you make selections for other reports. You can include Regular, Preferred, Web prices and any customized price lists you created.

Select the **items** and **click** the **Price Lists** you want to report on.

Click **OK** to open the price lists and **close** the **display** when you have finished.

Displaying Inventory Summary Reports

NOTES
You can customize Summary reports by selecting any of the columns usually included in the report. You can sort and filter by item or description.

The Inventory Summary Report provides detailed quantity and cost information for the inventory you have in stock.

Click **Summary** from the Select A Report list to open the sample report.

Click **Modify This Report** to open the report options window:

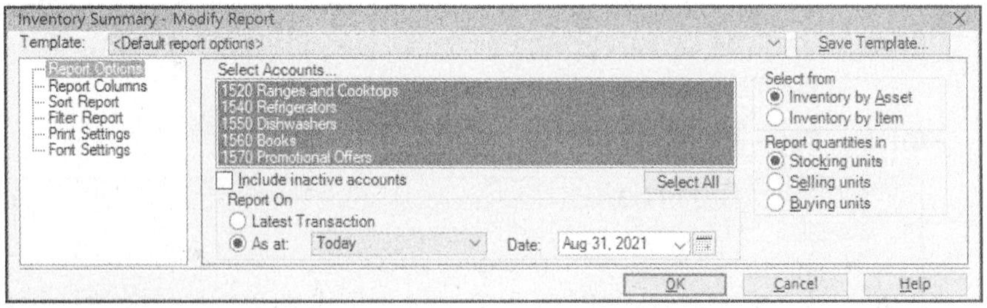

NOTES
Select All acts as a toggle switch. When all items are selected, clicking Select All will remove all selections. When none, one or a few, but not all, items are selected, clicking Select All will select all the entries on the list.

You can also choose the Reports menu, then choose Inventory & Services and click Summary to display the report options.

Selecting **Inventory By Asset** will provide information for all inventory items in the asset group(s) chosen. The **Inventory By Item** option will provide information for all the items selected. When you click Inventory By Item, the Select Accounts box lists all inventory items. Services are not included because there is no quantity or cost information for them.

Click a single asset or item to change selections or provide a report for that item only. To select multiple items, press and hold ctrl and then click the items you want in the report. To obtain information for all items, choose Select All.

> **NOTES**
> When you display the report with the Latest Transaction option, it includes the profit for each item – either the markup or margin, as selected in the Inventory Ledger Settings.

The **Summary Report** lists the quantity on hand, the unit cost of the inventory and the total value or cost of inventory on hand for the items requested. The total value of all inventory in the asset group is added when you select one asset group. You can create the Summary Report for the Latest Transaction Date or for another date that you enter in the **As At** Date field.

You can create the report with quantities in any of the units you use for the item if these are different, that is, the stocking, buying or selling units (refer to page 372).

> **NOTES**
> You can drill down to the Inventory Transaction Detail Report from the Inventory Summary or Quantity reports.

Choose the **options** you need for your report.

Press and **hold** ctrl and **click** the **items** or **assets** you want included.

Click **OK**. **Close** the **display** when you have finished.

Displaying Inventory Quantity Reports

The Inventory Quantity Report provides current information about the quantity on hand, the minimum stock levels and outstanding purchase and sales orders. The report also displays the order quantity needed to restore the minimum level when an item has fallen below the minimum level.

Click **Quantity** from the Select A Report list. **Click Modify This Report** to open the report options window:

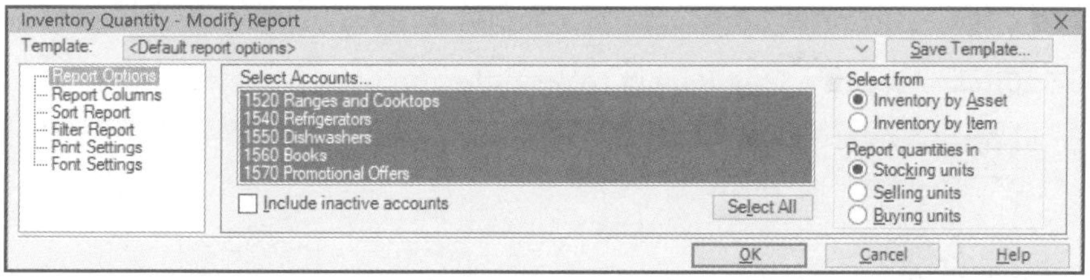

Or, choose the Reports menu, then choose Inventory & Services and click Quantity to display the report options.

> **NOTES**
> You can customize Quantity Reports by selecting any of the columns usually included in the report. You can sort and filter by most of the columns usually included in the report.

You can select the items for the report in the same way you did for the Inventory Summary Report. Selecting **Inventory By Asset** will provide information for all inventory items in the asset group(s) chosen. The **Inventory By Item** option will provide information for all the items selected. When you click Inventory By Item, the Select Accounts box lists all inventory items. Services are not included in the Quantity Report because there is no quantity or cost information for them.

Click a single asset or item to change selections or provide a report for that item only. To select multiple items, press and hold ctrl and then click the items you want in the report. To obtain information for all items, choose Select All.

You can prepare the report with quantities in any of the units you use for the item if they are different, that is, the stocking, buying or selling units (refer to page 372).

Choose the **options** you need for your report.

Press and **hold** ctrl and **click** the **names** of all the items or asset groups you want to include in the report.

Click **OK** and **close** the **display** when you have finished.

PRO VERSION
In the Report Centre list, click Item Assembly Journal Entries. Or, choose the Reports menu, then choose Journal Entries and click Item Assembly.

CLASSIC VIEW
Right-click the Bill Of Materials & Item Assembly icon. Click the Select A Report tool to open the Modify Report window.

Displaying the Item Assembly Journal

Click **Bill Of Materials & Item Assembly Journal Entries** to open the report sample and description.

Click **Modify This Report** to open the report options window:

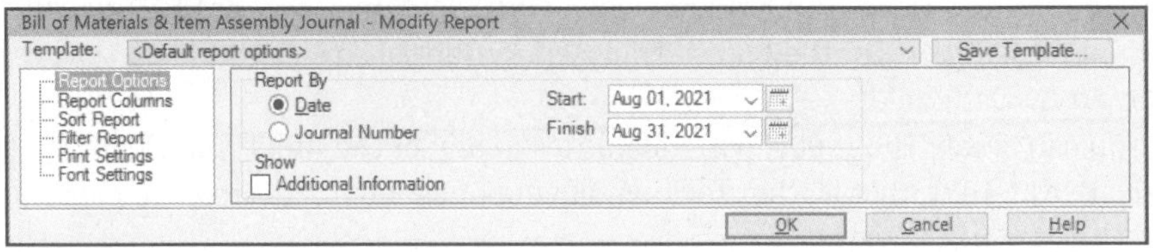

Or, choose the Reports menu, then choose Journal Entries and click Bill Of Materials & Item Assembly.

As usual, the earliest transaction date, session date and Report By Date options are provided by default. The sorting, filtering and column options are the same for all journal reports. There is no option to show corrections because these entries cannot be adjusted or reversed automatically.

Enter the **Start** and **Finish dates** you want for the report.

Click **OK**. **Close** the **display** when you have finished.

CLASSIC VIEW
Right-click the Inventory Adjustments icon. Click the Select A Report tool to open the Modify Report window.

NOTES
You can drill down to the General Ledger reports from the Item Assembly Journal and from the Adjustments Journal.

Displaying the Adjustments Journal

Click **Inventory Adjustment Journal Entries** to open the sample report.

Click **Modify This Report** to open the report options window:

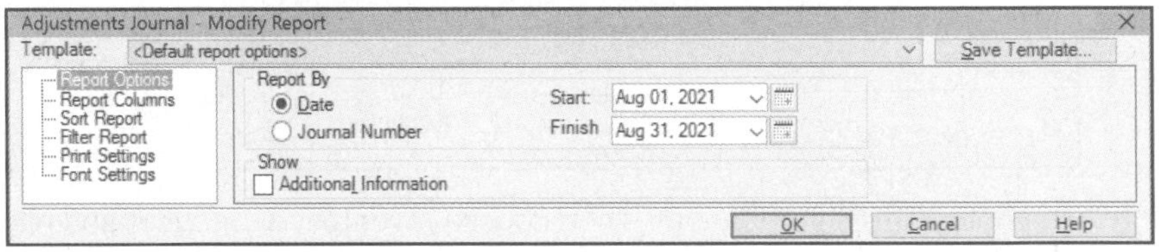

Or, you can choose the Reports menu, then choose Journal Entries and click Inventory Adjustments.

As usual, the earliest transaction date, session date and Report By Date options are provided by default. Showing corrections is not an option because these journal entries cannot be adjusted.

Enter the **Start** and **Finish dates** you want for the report.

Click **OK**. **Close** the **display** when you have finished.

Displaying Inventory Tracking Reports

Several reports provide information about the turnover of inventory products. These reports can let you know whether items are selling well and are profitable and how the sales are distributed over time and customers.

NOTES
For Inventory Statistics Reports, you can sort and filter by most of the columns usually included in the report.
You can customize Statistics Reports by selecting any of the columns usually included in the report.

Inventory Statistics Reports

Click **Statistics** from the Select A Report list. **Click** **Modify This Report** to open the report options window:

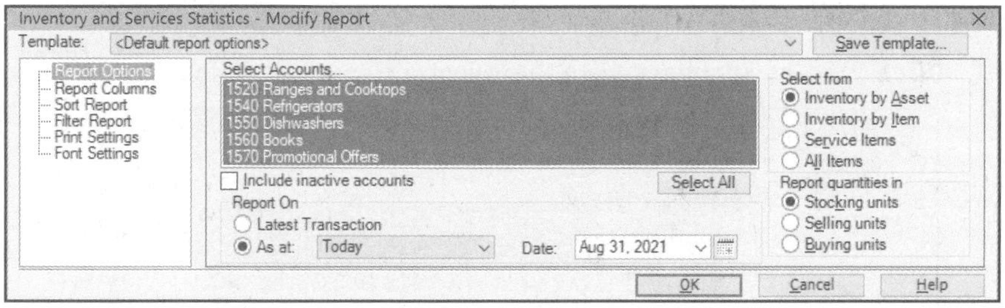

Or, choose the Reports menu, then choose Inventory & Services and click Statistics to display the report options.

The Statistics Report summarizes transactions for the year to date and the previous year, the same historical information that is contained in the Inventory Ledger record (refer to pages 374–375). For example, the report can let you know whether a large volume of sales resulted from a single sale for a large quantity or from a large number of smaller sales. Comparing the Statistics Report with the Statistics tab content in a ledger record for the same item will make the similarities apparent.

You can prepare the report for the session date (**Latest Transaction**) or for another date (**As At Date**). When you choose As At, the Date field is available. The report will include the statistics you request as at the date you enter.

The report has the **Number Of Transactions** (the number of separate sales invoices that included the inventory item), **Units Sold** (the total number of individual items of a kind that were sold in the period), the **Amount Sold** (the total revenue from all items sold) and the **Cost Of Goods Sold** (the total purchase cost of all the items that were sold). The average cost method is used to calculate the cost of goods sold for Kara's Kitchens. The cost method is selected as a ledger setting.

Press and hold ctrl and click one or more asset groups to include them in the report, or click Select All to include all asset groups in the report. Selecting an asset group will include all the inventory items in that group in the report. To select multiple assets or items, press ctrl and then click the items you want. The default selection — By Asset — will not include services in the report.

Click **Inventory By Item** to list individual inventory items. Select one or more items for the report, or click Select All to include all inventory items. Click **Service Items** to list individual services. Press ctrl and hold and click services to include them, or click Select All to include all services. Click **All Items** to include both individual inventory items and individual services in the report. Press ctrl and hold and click the items and services to include them in the report, or click Select All to include all items and services.

The list of items will expand according to your selection, and you can choose single or multiple items for inclusion. **Quantities** can be reported in any of the units on record — the units for stocking the inventory, for buying and for selling — if these are different.

Choose the **items** you want in the report.

Choose the **date** for the report (Latest Transaction or As At Date). **Enter** a **date** in the Date field if you chose the As At option.

Click **OK** to display the report. **Close** the **display** when you have finished.

NOTES
You can drill down to the Inventory Sales Detail Report from the Inventory Statistics Report.

NOTES
When you display the report with the Latest Transaction option, it includes the statistics for the previous year as well.

NOTES
You can also choose the FIFO (first-in, first-out) method of determining inventory costs. You make this choice in the Inventory Settings screen. This method is not available for the Pro version.

NOTES
Remember that Select All acts as a toggle switch – when all items are already selected, clicking Select All clears the selection. Clicking Select All when no items are selected, or when one or more items (but not all items) are selected, will select all items.

NOTES
When you click Modify This Report, the report options window always opens.

NOTES
You cannot sort or filter the Sales Report, but you can customize the report by selecting the columns you want to include.

NOTES
For the Inventory Sales Summary Report on Services, you must click Select From Service Items or choose All Items. Inventory By Item and Inventory By Asset – the default selection – include only inventory items.

NOTES
You can drill down to the Inventory Sales Detail Report from the Inventory Sales Summary Report. You can display the Customer Aged, Inventory Ledger and Journal Report. You can view Sales Invoices from the Inventory Sales Detail Report.

PRO VERSION
Item Assembly replaces Bill Of Materials & Item Assembly in the Pro version, and Adjustments replaces Adjustments and Transfers.

NOTES
You can drill down to the Transaction Detail Report from the Transaction Summary Report. You can display the Inventory Ledger and Journal Report from the Transaction Detail Report. You can also view invoices from the Detail Report.

Inventory Sales Reports

Click **Sales Summary** from the Select A Report list. **Click** **Modify This Report**:

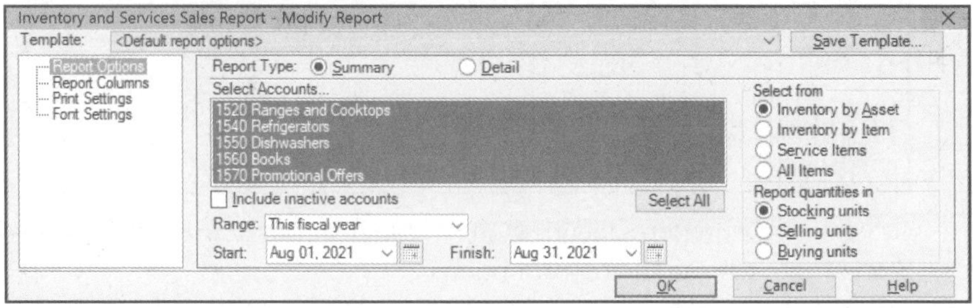

Or, choose the Reports menu, then choose Inventory & Services and click Sales.

The reports include the number of transactions (Summary option), the quantity of items sold, the revenue per item, the cost of goods sold and the profit for each item. Non-inventory sales are not included. The **Summary** option, selected by default, has the total for each detail for the selected inventory items organized by item. The **Detail** option provides the same information listed by individual journal entries, including the source document numbers and journal entry numbers. Click Detail to add these details.

As usual, you can choose to report on inventory items, services or both. To report only on all services, click **Service Items** and then Select All. Click **All Items** to include both inventory and services. The list of items will expand accordingly, and you can choose single or multiple items for inclusion. Select All at this stage will provide a report on all inventory and service items.

Again, **quantities** may be reported in stocking, buying or selling units.

Enter the **Start** and **Finish dates** you want for the report, or choose from the Range drop-down list.

Choose the **items** to include in the report.

Choose the **Summary** or **Detail** option.

Click **OK**. **Close** the **display** when you have finished.

Inventory Transaction Reports

The Transaction Report summarizes inventory activity according to the journal used to record the transaction.

Click **Transaction Summary**. **Click** **Modify This Report**:

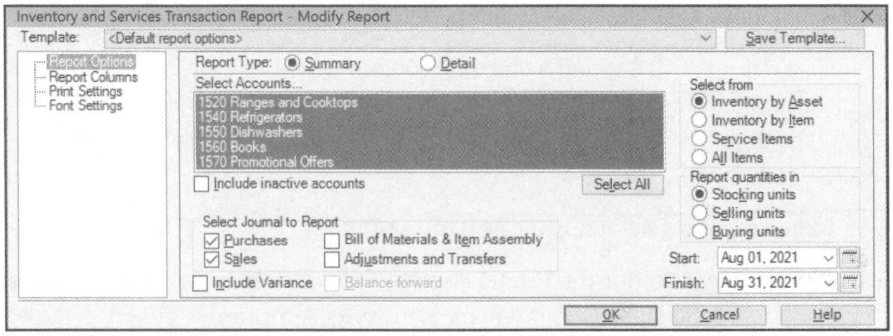

Or, choose the Reports menu, then choose Inventory & Services and click Transaction to display the report options.

The report includes details on the number of transactions (Summary option only), the **Quantity In** (increases to inventory from purchases, sales returns, recovery of lost items or assembled items) and **Out** (decreases in inventory from sales, purchase returns, losses and adjustments or assembly components used) and the **Amount In** and **Out** (total or cost price) for each item chosen in each of the selected journals.

The **Summary** option, the default, includes totals for the selected inventory items organized by item. The **Detail** option provides the same information listed by individual journal entries, including the source document numbers and journal entry numbers.

As in the Sales Report, you can prepare a report for one or more asset groups, inventory items or service items, or a combination of services and items (All Items). Click the appropriate entry in the Select From list to expand the selection list accordingly.

Quantities may be reported in stocking, buying or selling units. Variances can also be added to the report when they are used.

You can choose to add the Balance Forward and include opening balances or to Include Variance and add cost variances for each item.

Click **Detail** to include individual transaction details.

Enter the **Start** and **Finish dates** you want for the report. By default, the earliest transaction and session date appear.

Click the **journals** to include in the report.

Click **OK**. **Close** the **display** when you have finished.

Supplier Purchases Reports

The next two reports combine inventory information with supplier or customer details to let you know how purchases are spread among suppliers and how sales are divided among customers. The Supplier Purchases and Customer Sales reports also allow you to include information for non-inventory purchases or sales.

Click **Payables** in the Select A Report Type list.

Click **Supplier Purchases Summary**. **Click** **Modify This Report**:

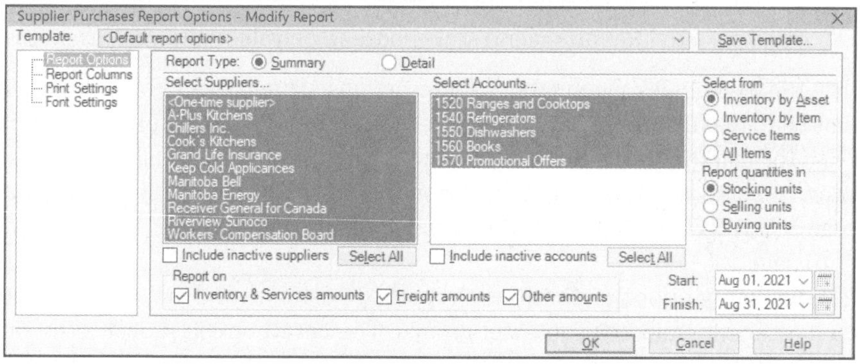

Or, choose the Reports menu and choose Payables and click Supplier Purchases.

The Supplier Purchases Report includes details on the number of transactions (Summary option only), the quantity purchased, the unit cost and the total cost of the purchase. Non-inventory purchases, such as telephone services, are listed as **Other**.

The **Summary** option organizes the report by supplier and includes totals for the selected categories and items or asset groups. The **Detail** option provides the same information by individual journal entries, including the source document numbers and journal entry numbers. Click Detail to choose the Detail option.

When other currencies are used, amounts for foreign suppliers may be displayed in either the home currency or the foreign currency.

The selection of inventory, services or asset groups is the same as for the other inventory reports. Reports can be prepared for either stocking, buying or selling units if these are different.

PRO VERSION

pro Choose Vendor Purchases Summary. This report is named the Vendor Purchases Report.

NOTES

You cannot sort or filter the Supplier Purchases Report, but you can select the columns you want in the report.

NOTES

You can drill down to the Inventory Purchases Detail Report from the Purchases Summary Report. You can look up invoices or drill down to the Supplier Aged and Purchases Journal Report from the Purchases Detail Report.

NOTES

To select multiple items, press and hold ctrl and then click the items or suppliers you want to add to the report.

> **NOTES**
> Inventory & Services Amounts will be automatically selected whenever you select an item in the Select Accounts list.

All items, categories and suppliers are selected initially.

Click a **supplier name** or **item** to begin a new selection.

Enter the **starting** and **ending dates** for the report in the Start and Finish fields.

All types of purchases are selected initially. Click a category — Inventory & Services, non-inventory (Other Amounts) and Freight Amounts — to remove the ✓ and deselect it for the selected supplier and item transactions. Click it again to select it.

Click **OK**. **Close** the **display** when you have finished.

Customer Sales Reports

> **NOTES**
> You cannot sort or filter the Customer Sales Report, but you can select the columns you want in the report.

The Customer Sales Report provides the same details as the Inventory Sales Report but organizes the details by customer as well as by item. Customer Sales reports also have the option to include non-inventory sales.

Click **Receivables** in the Select A Report Type list.

Click **Customer Sales Summary**. **Click Modify This Report**:

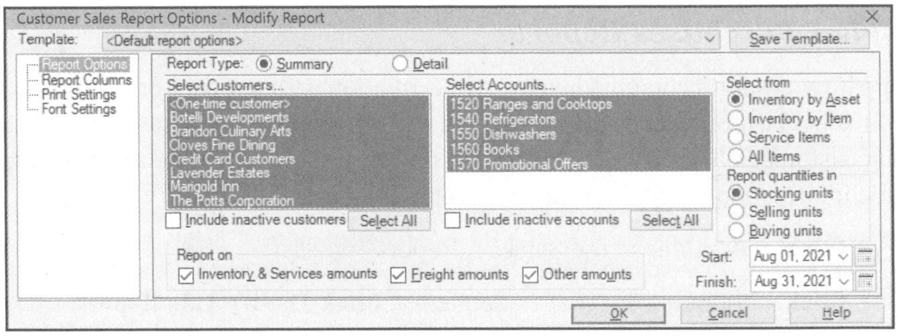

Or, choose the Reports menu and choose Receivables and click Customer Sales.

> **NOTES**
> If any item in the Select Accounts list is selected, Inventory & Services Amounts will be automatically selected.

> **NOTES**
> You can drill down to the Inventory Sales Detail Report from the Customer Sales Summary Report. You can drill down to the Customer Aged and Journal reports from the Detail Report and look up the sales invoice.

The report includes the number of transactions (Summary option only), the quantity of items sold, the total revenue per item, the cost of goods sold, the profit on the item's sales and the markup or margin. Non-inventory sales, such as sales allowances or non-inventory services, are listed as **Other Amounts**. All categories are selected initially. In Chapter 6, only the Customer list was included because there were no inventory items (refer to page 195).

The **Summary** option organizes the report by customer and includes totals for the selected categories and items or asset groups. The **Detail** option provides the same information listed by individual journal entries, including the source document numbers and journal entry numbers. Click Detail to choose the Detail option. Reports can be prepared for stocking, buying or selling units if these are different. All customers and items are selected initially.

Select **assets**, **inventory** or **services**, **customers**, **dates** and **categories** as you do for Supplier Purchases reports.

Click **OK**. **Close** the **display** when you have finished.

> **WARNING!**
> You must assign the correct account classes to expense accounts to generate the Gross Margin Income Statement. Cost of Goods Sold accounts must be correctly identified and separated from other types of expenses.

Gross Margin Income Statement

This financial report becomes relevant when a business sells inventory. The report shows the income after inventory costs have been deducted from revenue and before operating expenses are included. This report is available from the Financials report type list.

Click **Financials** in the Select A Report Type list.

Click the ⊞ beside **Income Statement** to expand the list.

Click **Gross Margin - Standard (under Income Statement)**.

Click **Modify This Report** to open the report options window:

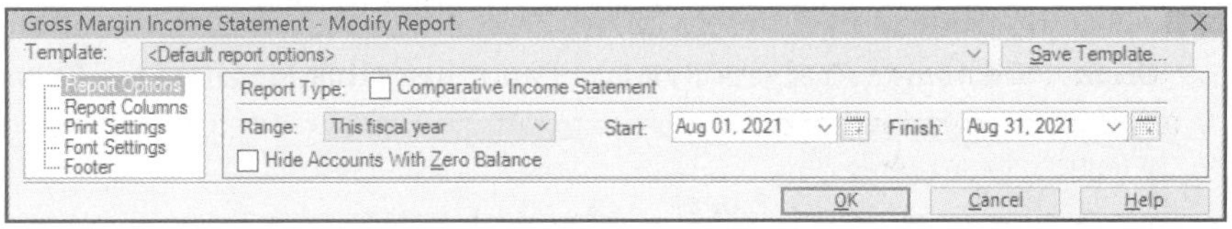

Or, choose the Reports menu, then choose Financials and click Gross Margin Income Statement to display the report options.

The report will include different income amounts: gross margin (revenue minus cost of goods sold, before taking into account the other operating expenses), income from operations (operating and payroll expenses are deducted from the gross margin) and net income (non-operating revenue and other expenses are entered).

The options for this Income Statement are the same as for regular Income Statements, including the option to generate a Comparative Income Statement.

Enter the **Start** and **Finish dates** you want for the report.

Click **OK**. **Close** the **display** when you have finished.

NOTES
Refer to page 60 for details on the Comparative Income Statement.

Displaying Forecast & Analysis Reports

This group of reports provides more detailed information about performance and trends.

Click **Forecast & Analysis** in the Select A Report Type list:

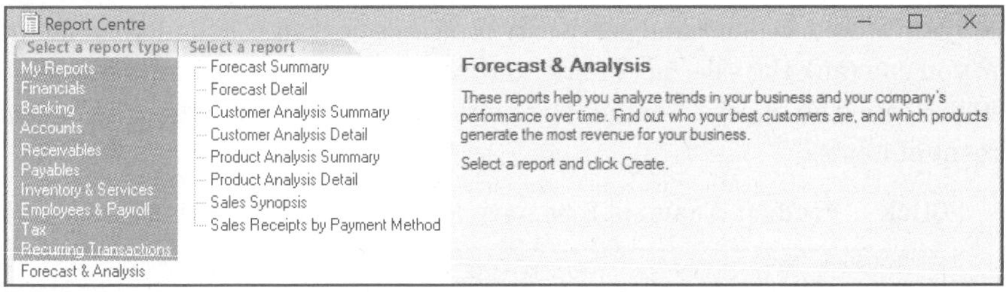

PRO VERSION
Forecast & Analysis Reports and Retail Reports (in the Reports menu) are not available in the Pro version.

Displaying the Forecast Report

The report will provide monthly forecasts for revenues and expenses based on the same month in the previous year. The Forecast Report requires data for more than one year, so you will be unable to create this report with the data for Kara's Kitchens.

Click **Forecast Summary** and then **click Modify This Report**:

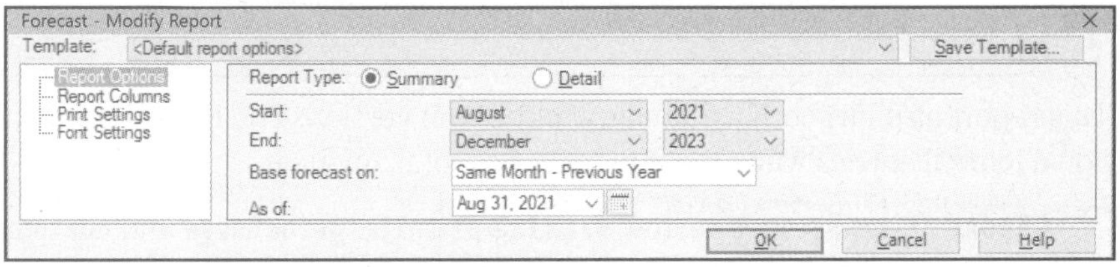

Choose the **months** for which you want the forecast and the date for the report.

Click **OK**. **Close** the **display** when you have finished.

> **NOTES**
> From the Home window Reports menu, you can choose Retail Reports (or the <industry type> Reports) and click either Customer Analysis – Top 20% By Profit, or Customer Analysis – Bottom 30% By Profit for the report options.
> The options screen will have the selections named in the menu report title (e.g., top 20%), but you can change the selections as you do in any report options window.

> **NOTES**
> You can drill down to the Detail Report from the Customer Analysis Summary Report. From the Detail Report, you can drill down to the Customer Sales Detail Report.

Displaying the Customer Analysis Report

From this report, you can observe the customer sales for the fiscal year to date to learn which customers account for the most sales. You can include the customers in the top or bottom x percent; rank them according to revenue, profit, quantity or return on investment (ROI); and you can select the items you want to report on.

Click **Customer Analysis Summary** and then **click Modify This Report**:

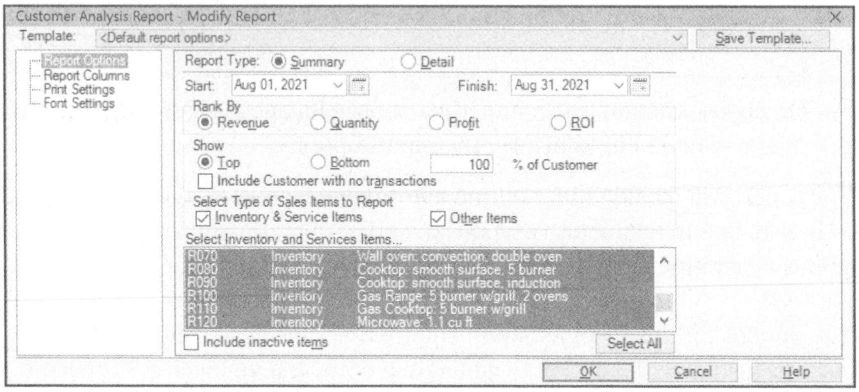

The Detail Report has individual journal entries while the Summary Report has total amounts.

Choose the **reporting period**, **ranking criteria**, **percentage** and **items**.

Click **OK**. **Close** the **display** when you have finished.

> **NOTES**
> From the Home window Reports menu, you can choose Retail Reports (or the <industry type> Reports) and click either Product Analysis – Top 20% Of Active Sales By ROI, or Product Analysis – Bottom 30% Of Sales Including Zero Sales By ROI for the report options.
> The options screen will have the selections named in the menu report title (e.g., top 30%), but you can change the selections as you do in any report options window.
> In the Product Analysis Report, ROI (return on investment) is measured as the profit divided by the average inventory value.

> **NOTES**
> You can drill down to the Detail Report from the Product Analysis Summary Report. From the Detail Report, you can drill down to the Inventory & Services Sales Detail Report.

Displaying the Product Analysis Report

The Product Analysis Report is similar to the Customer Analysis Report but organized primarily by product (items and services). You can select the customers to include. Again, you can rank the sales according to revenues, quantity sold, profit and return on investment. You can choose whether to report on the top x percent or the bottom x percent of items.

Click **Product Analysis Summary** and then **click Modify This Report**:

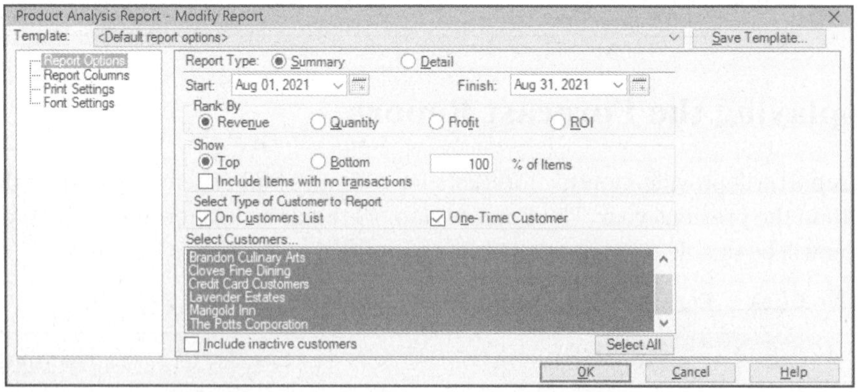

This report also has both a Summary and Detail version. The Detail Report has individual journal entries while the Summary has total amounts.

Choose the **reporting period**, **ranking criteria**, **percentage** and **customers**.

Click **OK**. **Close** the **display** when you have finished.

Displaying the Sales Synopsis Report

The Sales Synopsis Report summarizes sales and receipts. The report includes the items sold (quantity and number of transactions) and the gross sales per item.

Click **Sales Synopsis** and then **click** **Modify This Report**:

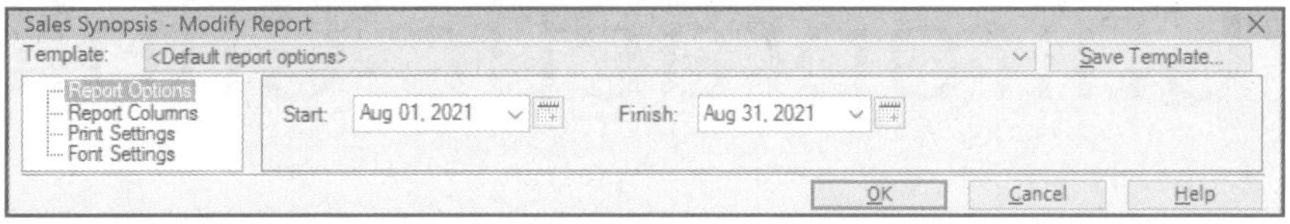

Choose the **reporting period**. Customize the report columns if you want to select details.

Click **OK**. **Close** the **display** when you have finished.

NOTES

From the Home window Reports menu, choose Retail Reports and click Daily Sales Summary for the report options window.

You can drill down to the Inventory & Services Transaction Report from the Sales Synopsis Report.

Displaying Sales Receipts by Payment Method Reports

The final Forecast & Analysis Report summarizes the sales and receipts according to the customer payment methods, that is, by cash, by credit card or on account (pay later).

Click **Sales Receipts by Payment Method** and then **click** **Modify This Report**:

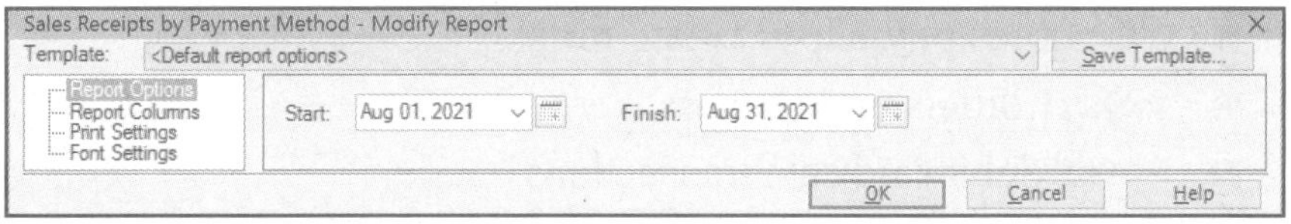

Choose the **reporting period**. Customize the report columns if you want to select details.

Click **OK**. **Close** the **display** when you have finished. **Close** the **Report Centre**.

NOTES

From the Home window Reports menu, choose Retail Reports and click Daily Sales Receipts for the report options window.

Printing Inventory Reports

Display the **report** you want to print.

Click the **Reports & Forms Settings tool** to check your printer settings.

Choose the **File menu** and **click** **Print** or **click** the **Print tool**. **Close** the **display** when finished.

REVIEW

The Student DVD with Data Files includes Review Questions and Supplementary Cases for this chapter.

CHAPTER ELEVEN

Andersson Chiropractic Clinic

OBJECTIVES

After completing this chapter, you should be able to

- ***enter*** receipts and payments with discounts
- ***track*** additional information for receipts, sales and purchases
- ***understand*** linked accounts for discounts
- ***place*** and ***fill*** purchase orders and quotes
- ***enter*** and ***fill*** sales quotes and orders
- ***convert*** sales and purchase quotes to orders
- ***fill*** quotes partially to create orders
- ***adjust*** orders and quotes
- ***enter*** debit card sale transactions
- ***make*** payments and deposits using multiple bank accounts and a line of credit
- ***enter*** deposits from customers and prepayments to vendors
- ***delete*** a stored transaction
- ***remove*** quotes

COMPANY INFORMATION

NOTES
Andersson Chiropractic Clinic
4500 Rae St.
Regina, SK S4S 3B4
Tel 1: (306) 577-1900
Tel 2: (306) 577-2199
Fax: (306) 577-1925

Company Profile

Andersson Chiropractic Clinic is a private clinic owned by Maria Andersson, who practises her profession in Regina, Saskatchewan. This is her second year in private practice after graduating with D.C. (Doctor of Chiropractic) and D.Ac. (Doctor of Acupuncture) degrees. She used some bank loans and her line of credit to consolidate her student loans and set up the clinic.

Andersson specializes in sports injuries and has some sports teams as clients. To treat patients, she uses chiropractic treatments and adjustments for back pain, and physiotherapy, massage, ultrasound, laser treatments, electrical stimulation and acupuncture for other joint and soft tissue injuries. Individual regular patients usually come two or three times per week, although some come daily. These patients settle their accounts bi-weekly. Sports teams have contracts and are billed monthly. Contract customers are offered a discount if they settle their accounts within 10 days. Cash, cheques and debit cards are accepted in payment.

A single assistant in the clinic divides her time between reception, administration and some basic treatments such as laser and ultrasound under the chiropractor's supervision. Andersson designates the precise area to be treated and the time and intensity settings for the equipment.

The office space that Andersson rents has a reception area and four treatment rooms with tables. The monthly rent includes heat but not hydro or telephone. One of the four treatment rooms doubles as Andersson's office and another room has the potential to accommodate a whirlpool. She is considering adding a whirlpool for hydrotherapy and deep water massage treatments because some sports injuries respond well to hydrotherapy.

For new sports team contracts, Andersson prepares sales quotes. When they accept a contract, they pay a deposit that is applied to the first month's payment.

Andersson has two bank accounts and a line of credit she uses to pay her bills. The limit on her line of credit is $50 000, and she has already borrowed $15 000 against it. A third bank account is used exclusively for debit card transactions.

Accounts for regular suppliers of treatment equipment, linens, laundry services, office maintenance and so on are set up. Some of these suppliers also offer discounts for early payments and some require Andersson to make prepayments with purchase orders.

No taxes are charged for medical treatments and supplies. Because GST is not charged to customers, the business is not eligible for a GST refund. Therefore tax amounts are not tracked — they are included with the expense or asset amounts. Andersson pays both PST and GST for other goods and services.

To convert her accounting records to Sage 50 on October 1, 2021, she used the following information:

- Chart of Accounts
- Trial Balance
- Supplier Information
- Patient/Customer Information
- Accounting Procedures

CHART OF POSTABLE ACCOUNTS

ANDERSSON CHIROPRACTIC CLINIC

ASSETS
1060 Bank: Regina Chequing
1080 Bank: Eastside Chequing
1100 Bank: Interac
1200 Accounts Receivable
1220 Prepaid Insurance
1240 Prepaid Subscriptions
1280 Purchase Prepayments
1300 Linen Supplies
1320 Office Supplies
1340 Other Supplies
1420 Computer Equipment
1430 Accum Deprec: Computers
1450 Treatment Equipment
1460 Accum Deprec: Equipment
1520 Office Furniture ▶
▶1530 Accum Deprec: Furniture
1550 Treatment Tables
1560 Accum Deprec: Tables
1580 Vehicle
1590 Accum Deprec: Vehicle

LIABILITIES
2100 Loans Payable
2200 Accounts Payable
2250 Prepaid Sales and Deposits
2300 Line of Credit Payable

EQUITY
3400 M.A. Capital
3450 M.A. Drawings
3600 Net Income ▶

▶REVENUE
4100 Revenue from Services
4150 Sales Discounts
4200 Interest Income

EXPENSE
5010 Bank Charges and Interac Fees
5030 Purchase Discounts
5050 Office Supplies Used
5060 Other Supplies Used
5080 Subscriptions and Books
5090 Insurance Expense
5100 Interest Expense
5110 Freight Expense
5120 Clinic Maintenance ▶
▶5140 Laundry Services
5150 Professional Dues
5180 Depreciation Expenses
5200 Hydro Expense
5240 Telephone Expense
5260 Rent
5300 Vehicle Expenses
5500 Wages Expense
5520 Payroll Services

NOTES: The Chart of Accounts includes only postable accounts and the Net Income or Current Earnings account.

TRIAL BALANCE

ANDERSSON CHIROPRACTIC CLINIC

September 30, 2021		Debits	Credits			Debits	Credits
1060	Bank: Regina Chequing	$47 730		▶ 3450	M.A. Drawings	$ 18 000	
1080	Bank: Eastside Chequing	29 900		4100	Revenue from Services		$114 000
1100	Bank: Interac	3 430		4150	Sales Discounts	140	
1200	Accounts Receivable	12 500		4200	Interest Income		160
1220	Prepaid Insurance	1 600		5010	Bank Charges and Interac Fees	390	
1240	Prepaid Subscriptions	480		5030	Purchase Discounts		210
1300	Linen Supplies	1 300		5050	Office Supplies Used	350	
1320	Office Supplies	270		5060	Other Supplies Used	1 130	
1340	Other Supplies	530		5080	Subscriptions and Books	2 400	
1420	Computer Equipment	4 200		5090	Insurance Expense	8 000	
1430	Accum Deprec: Computers		$ 1 050	5100	Interest Expense	2 500	
1450	Treatment Equipment	12 600		5110	Freight Expense	120	
1460	Accum Deprec: Equipment		2 100	5120	Clinic Maintenance	2 100	
1520	Office Furniture	9 600		5140	Laundry Services	1 800	
1530	Accum Deprec: Furniture		800	5150	Professional Dues	1 495	
1550	Treatment Tables	8 400		5180	Depreciation Expenses	10 850	
1560	Accum Deprec: Tables		1 400	5200	Hydro Expense	1 200	
1580	Vehicle	22 000		5240	Telephone Expense	1 100	
1590	Accum Deprec: Vehicle		5 500	5260	Rent	23 000	
2100	Loans Payable		45 000	5300	Vehicle Expenses	3 300	
2200	Accounts Payable		7 290	5500	Wages Expense	21 000	
2300	Line of Credit Payable		15 000	5520	Payroll Services	450	
3400	M.A. Capital		61 355 ▶			$253 865	$253 865

SUPPLIER INFORMATION

ANDERSSON CHIROPRACTIC CLINIC

Supplier Name (Contact)	Address	Phone No. Fax No.	E-mail Web Site	Terms
Canadian Chiropractic Association (O. Fisshal)	33 Backer Rd. Toronto, Ontario M4T 5B2	Tel 1: (416) 488-3713 Tel 2: (888) 488-3713	cca.ca	net 10
Cleanol and Laundry Services (Bessie Sweeps)	19 Duster Rd. Regina, Saskatchewan S4R 4L4	Tel: (306) 398-0908 Fax: (306) 398-8211	bsweeps@cls.com cls.com	net 30
Grasslands Fuel				net 1 (cheque)
Medical Linen Supplies (Oll Whyte)	500 Agar St. Saskatoon, Saskatchewan S7L 6B9	Tel: (306) 662-6192 Fax: (306) 662-4399	owhyte@medsupplies.com medsupplies.com	2/10, n/30
OnLine Books			onlinebooks.com	net 1 (cheque)
Prairie Power Corp. (M. Jouls)	48 Powers Bay Regina, Saskatchewan S4X 1N2	Tel: (306) 395-1125	prairiepower.ca	net 1 (cheque)
Pro Suites Inc. (Kendra Walls)	19 Tenant Cr. Regina, Saskatchewan S4N 2B1	Tel: (306) 396-6646 Fax: (306) 396-5397	walls@prosuites.com prosuites.com	net 1 (cheque) (first of month)
Sonartek Ltd. (T. Waver)	390 Retallack St. Regina, Saskatchewan S4R 3N3	Tel: (306) 579-7923 Fax: (306) 579-8003	twaver@sonartek.com sonartek.com	2/15, n/30
The Papery				net 15 (cheque)
Thera-Tables Inc. (Li Flatte)	60 Flatlands Cr. Saskatoon, Saskatchewan S7K 5B1	Tel: (306) 662-6486 Fax: (306) 662-7910	theratables.com	2/5, n/30
Western Communications (V. Du Parler)	99 Listener St. Regina, Saskatchewan S4R 5C9	Tel: (306) 395-5533	westcom.ca	net 1 (cheque)

OUTSTANDING SUPPLIER INVOICES

ANDERSSON CHIROPRACTIC CLINIC

Supplier Name	Terms	Date	Invoice No.	Amount	Total
Cleanol and Laundry Services	net 30	Sep. 14/21	CLS-2419	$90	
	net 30	Sep. 28/21	CLS-2683	90	
			Balance owing		$180
Medical Linen Supplies	2/10, n/30	Sep. 26/21	MLS-102		$690
Sonartek Ltd.	2/15, n/30	Sep. 22/21	SL-3456		$6 420
			Grand Total		$7 290

PATIENT INFORMATION

ANDERSSON CHIROPRACTIC CLINIC

Patient Name (Contact)	Address	Phone No. Fax No.	E-mail Web Site	Terms Credit Limit
Albert Blackfoot	16 Prairie Bay Regina, Saskatchewan S4N 6V3	Tel: (306) 582-1919	ablackfoot@shaw.ca	net 15 $500
Canadian Royals (K. Player)	1910 Buckingham St. Regina, Saskatchewan S4S 2P3	Tel: (306) 578-4567 Fax: (306) 578-7382	kplayer@canroyals.com canroyals.com	1/10, n/30 $5 000
Interplay Ballet School (S. Lightly)	2755 Flamenco St. Regina, Saskatchewan S4V 8C1	Tel: (306) 396-6190 Fax: (306) 396-8186	lightly@lighterthanair.com lighterthanair.com	1/10, n/30 $5 000
Roughrider Argos (B. Ball)	2935 Fowler St. Regina, Saskatchewan S4V 1N5	Tel: (306) 399-8000 Fax: (306) 399-8115	proball.com/ra	1/10, n/30 $5 000
Suzanne Lejeune	301 Pasqua St. Regina, Saskatchewan S4R 4M8	Tel: (306) 573-6296	slejeune@hotmail.com	net 15 $500

OUTSTANDING PATIENT INVOICES

ANDERSSON CHIROPRACTIC CLINIC

Patient Name	Terms	Date	Invoice No.	Amount	Total
Canadian Royals	1/10, n/30	Sep. 28/21	#638	$4 500	$4 500
Interplay Ballet School	1/10, n/30	Sep. 26/21	#632	$3 100	$3 100
Roughrider Argos	1/10, n/30	Sep. 29/21	#639	$4 900	$4 900
			Grand Total		$12 500

Accounting Procedures

Taxes

Medical services are not taxable, patients do not pay GST on the treatments and GST paid is not refundable. Andersson pays provincial tax at the rate of 6 percent and GST at 5 percent on normal purchases — medical equipment is not taxed. Therefore, no taxes have been set up in the data files, and no tax options are available in the journal tax fields. All prices are stated with taxes included, but taxes are not recorded separately — they are included with the expense or asset part of purchases.

Cash and Debit Card Sales

Andersson's individual patients frequently pay by Interac or debit card. Sales invoice amounts are deposited directly to the linked bank account. For this service, Andersson pays a small fee to the bank for each transaction, as well as a monthly rental fee for the terminal. These fees are deducted from the account periodically and are not deducted from deposits for individual transactions. Debit card transactions are summarized and recorded every two weeks.

NOTES
The terms Patient and Customer will be used interchangeably in this chapter. Sage 50 applies the label Patient for Customer for medical companies. For sports teams, we will use the term Customer unless the program displays the term Patient on the screen.

Payroll

Andersson's assistant is paid a monthly salary through arrangements with the bank. In lieu of a salary, Andersson draws $2 500 per month from her net income.

Discounts

Customers (sports teams) who have contracts with Andersson are offered a 1 percent discount if they pay their accounts in full within 10 days. Full payment is requested within 30 days. Individual patients are asked to pay their accounts every two weeks. Some suppliers also offer discounts for early payments.

All discount terms are set up in the customer and supplier records.

NOTES
All discounts are calculated on the full invoice amounts. For purchases, these amounts include taxes.

Deposits

When sports team managers sign new contracts for regular monthly billing for treating the team members, they pay a deposit to Andersson. Similarly, some suppliers ask for a deposit or prepayment when Andersson places a large order.

Revenue and Expense Accounts

The customer records for Andersson Chiropractic Clinic are set up with *Revenue from Services* as the default account. For suppliers, the account most often associated with purchases from a supplier has been entered as the default for that supplier.

Bank Accounts and Line of Credit

Andersson has two chequing accounts for deposits and payments. A third bank account is used for all Interac or debit card payments.

Andersson also uses her line of credit to make payments by cheque. At the end of each month, Andersson makes a payment for the interest owing on the line of credit used. When she has the funds, she also pays down the principal owing.

All cheque numbers are updated automatically when the correct account is selected.

NOTES
The line of credit is set up as a liability account (the money is owed to the bank), but the Bank class is applied so that the account can be selected in journals to write cheques and deposit receipts. The amount of credit available does not appear on the Balance Sheet or Trial Balance. It is usually added as a Note to the financial statements.

INSTRUCTIONS

1. **Record entries for the source documents** in Sage 50 using the Chart of Accounts, Supplier Information, Patient Information and Accounting Procedures for Andersson Chiropractic Clinic. The procedures for entering each new type of transaction in this application are outlined step by step in the Keystrokes section with the source documents.
2. **Print** the **reports** indicated on the following printing form after you have finished making your entries:

REPORTS

Accounts
- [ ] Chart of Accounts
- [ ] Account List
- [ ] General Journal Entries

Financials
- [x] Comparative Balance Sheet: amounts only for Oct. 1, 2021, and Nov. 30, 2021
- [x] Income Statement from Dec. 1, 2020, to Nov. 30, 2021
- [x] Comparative Trial Balance: amounts only for Nov. 30 and Dec. 1, 2021
- [x] All Journal Entries: Oct. 1 to Nov. 30
- [ ] General Ledger
- [x] Statement of Cash Flows from Oct. 1 to Nov. 30
- [x] Cash Flow Projection Detail Report for accounts 1060 and 1080 for 30 days

Taxes
- [ ] Tax

Banking
- [ ] Cheque Log Report

Payables
- [ ] Supplier List
- [x] Supplier Aged Detail for all suppliers
- [ ] Aged Overdue Payables
- [ ] Expenses Journal Entries
- [ ] Payments Journal Entries
- [x] Pending Supplier Orders as at Jan. 15, 2022

Receivables
- [ ] Patient List
- [x] Patient Aged Detail for all customers
- [ ] Aged Overdue Receivables
- [ ] Patient Statements
- [ ] Fees Journal Entries
- [ ] Receipts Journal Entries
- [x] Pending Patient Orders as at Jan. 15, 2022

Mailing Labels
- [ ] Labels

KEYSTROKES

Entering a Purchase Quote

On October 1, Andersson received two quotes for a treatment table that will be delivered later in the month. A quote usually provides a guaranteed price for some work or products. The offer is often limited to a stated time period. If the business chooses to accept the offer, the quote may be filled as a purchase for immediate delivery or converted to a purchase order for future delivery. When the goods are received, or the work is completed, the quote (or order) is filled and the purchase is completed. Supplier quotes are entered and filled in the Expenses or Purchases Journal.

✓ 1 **Purchase Quote #TT-44** **Dated October 1, 2021**

Delivery date October 10, 2021

From Thera-Tables Inc., $4 000 including taxes for custom-built adjustable height treatment table with drop ends. Terms: 2/5, n/30. Deposit of 10 percent required on accepting quote.

Open **SageData19\ANDERSSON\ANDERSSON** to access the data files for Andersson. **Enter Oct 7, 2021** as the session date.

Click **Payables** in the Modules pane list. Icons are added for quotes and orders.

NOTES

From the backup file, restore SageData19\ANDERSSON1.CAB or ANDERSSON1 to SageData19\ANDERSSON\ANDERSSON to open the data files for Andersson. Refer to Chapter 1, page 25, if you need assistance.

NOTES

The Payroll, Inventory and Project modules are not included in the Modules pane – they are hidden because these ledgers are not used and are not set up.

CLASSIC VIEW

Click the Expenses, Orders & Quotes icon 

to open the journal. Then choose Quote from the journal's Transaction drop-down list.

PRO VERSION

Vendor replaces the term Supplier. Purchase Quotes, Purchase Orders and Purchase Invoices are used as the Home window icon labels for tasks.

Click the Purchase Quotes icon to open the journal.

NOTES

For medical companies, Sage 50 replaces the term Purchases Journal with Expenses Journal.

Click the **Supplier Quotes icon**:

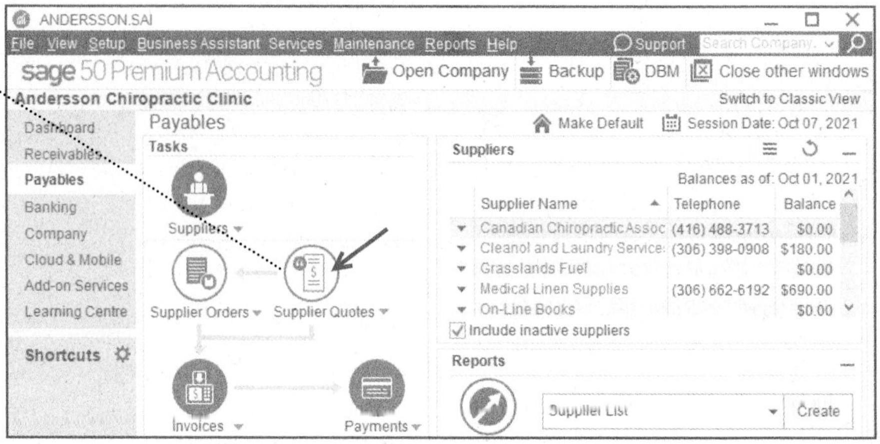

The Expenses Journal – Creating A Quote window opens:

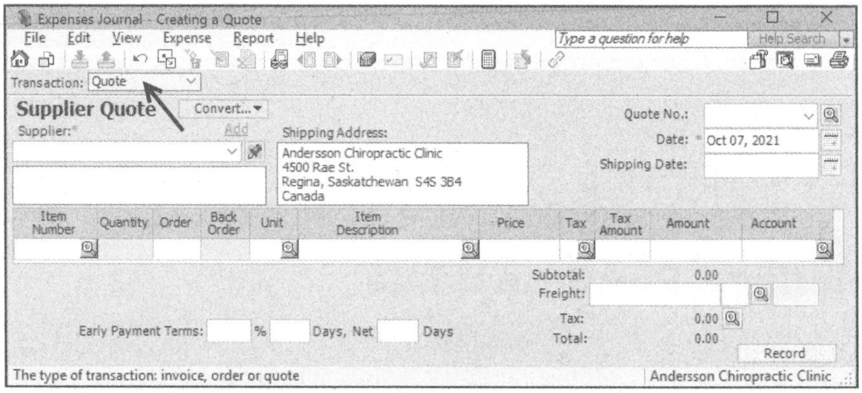

NOTES

Andersson's address is in the Shipping Address field for the quote.

NOTES

You must choose the supplier before entering the quote number because the supplier issues the quote number.

Quote is selected in the Transaction field.

Click the **Supplier field** and **select Thera-Tables Inc.**

Click the **Quote No.** field to advance the cursor and skip the address fields.

Type `TT-44`

Press *tab* **twice** to advance to the Date field.

Type `10-1-21`

Press *tab* **twice** to advance to the Shipping Date field.

PRO VERSION

The default tabbing order after the Vendor address fields is Date, Quote No. and Shipping Date. After entering the quote number, the cursor advances to the Shipping Date. Click the field you need.

Purchases Journal – Creating A Quote appears in the journal's title bar, and Purchase replaces Expense in the menu bar. The term Vendor replaces Supplier.

This is the date on which the order is to be received or the work is to be completed. Sometimes, instead of Shipping Date, we use the term Delivery Date for services or Starting Date for a contract because these terms are more appropriate for quotes and orders for services.

Type `10-10`

NOTES

You cannot access the Quantity field for quotes. This field and the Back Order field are dimmed.

The Item Number field refers to the code for inventory items. The Quantity (quantity received with this purchase) field will remain blank because this is not a purchase and no goods are received. However, you must enter the number of units that are ordered. You cannot leave the Order field blank. One table is being ordered.

NOTES

In a purchase order, the Back Order quantity field is filled in automatically with the order quantity. In a quote, this field remains blank.

Click the **Order field**. **Type** `1`

Press *tab* to advance to the Unit field that also applies to inventory.

Press *tab* to advance to the Item Description field.

Type `custom-built treatment table`

Press tab to advance to the Price field. This field refers to the unit price of the items.

Type 4000

Press tab to advance to the Tax field.

Because taxes are not used in this data set, we can skip the tax fields. The amount is entered automatically as the quantity on order times the unit price.

The account is also entered automatically from the supplier's ledger record, so the quote is complete:

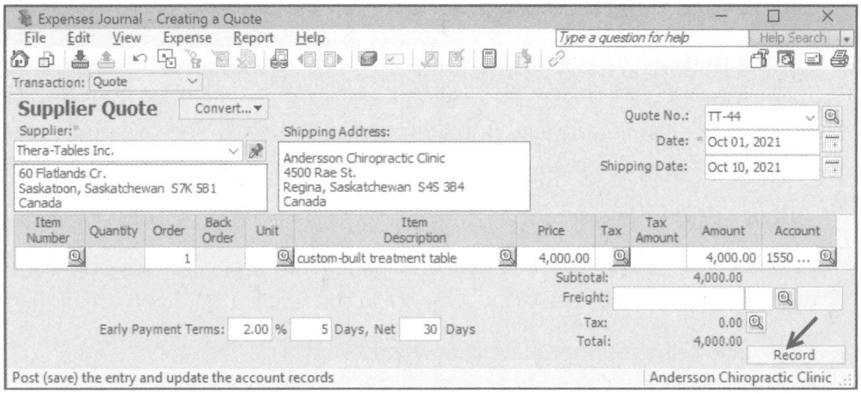

Check your **work** carefully and **make** any **corrections** necessary, just as you do for Purchases Journal entries.

If you try to display the journal entry, you will find that there is no journal entry associated with the quote. The Record button replaces Post for quotes (and orders). The related journal entry will be completed when the quote is filled and the purchase is completed. When you are sure that the entry is correct, you should record it.

Click the **Record button** Record or **choose** the **Expense menu** and **click** **Record** to save your transaction. **Click** **OK** to confirm successful recording. No journal entry number is included with the confirmation.

If you forgot to enter the quantity ordered, Sage 50 will warn you of this error:

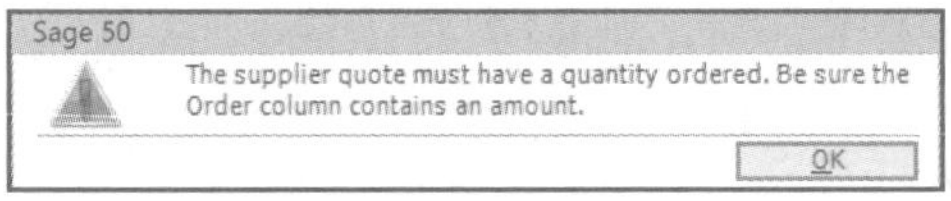

Click OK. Enter the quantity in the Order field and try again to record.

Enter the **second purchase quote** from a new supplier. Remember to add the account number and payment terms to the quote.

2

Purchase Quote #MT-511 **Dated October 1, 2021**

Delivery date October 20, 2021
From Medi-Tables (use Quick Add for the new supplier), $4 550 including all taxes for custom-built treatment table. Terms: net 20. Deposit of 20 percent required on accepting quote.

Placing a Purchase Order from a Quote

Sometimes purchase orders are entered without a quote and sometimes they are converted from a purchase quote. Entering a purchase order directly, without the quote, is the same as entering a purchase quote except that you choose Order as the type of transaction instead of Quote.

NOTES

If you want, you can customize the journal by removing the columns that are not required. Refer to page 163.

You can remove (do not show) the Item Number, Unit, Tax Code and Tax Amount fields because they are not needed.

Instead of entering the price, you can enter the total amount. Sage 50 will calculate and enter the unit price based on the order quantity and amount.

NOTES

Refer to page 116 if you need help correcting the entry.

NOTES

The Record button label replaces Post for quotes and orders because no journal entry is posted.

NOTES

Continue is not an option when you add a new supplier for a quote.

NOTES

We will use the terms purchase order and supplier order interchangeably, unless the term appears in the Sage 50 screen.

The purchase order to Thera-Tables Inc. is a quote converted to an order. The Expenses Journal should still be open with Quote selected as the Transaction type.

✓ 3

Purchase Order #TT-44 **Dated October 2, 2021**

Delivery date October 10, 2021
To Thera-Tables Inc., $4 000 including taxes for custom-built treatment table.
Terms: 2/5, n/30. Convert quote #TT-44 to purchase order #TT-44.

Click the **Quote No. field list arrow**:

NOTES
When you select Order (or Invoice) as the type of transaction, the Order No. (or Order/Quote No.) field will list both unfilled quotes and unfilled orders.

The drop-down list includes all unfilled purchase quotes. The two quotes entered above are listed.

Click **TT-44** to select it.

Press *tab* to select the quote and place it on-screen. Looking Up Quote TT-44 has replaced Creating A Quote in the title bar. All fields are dimmed.

You can change the quote to an order in different ways.

Click the **Convert list arrow** to display conversion options:

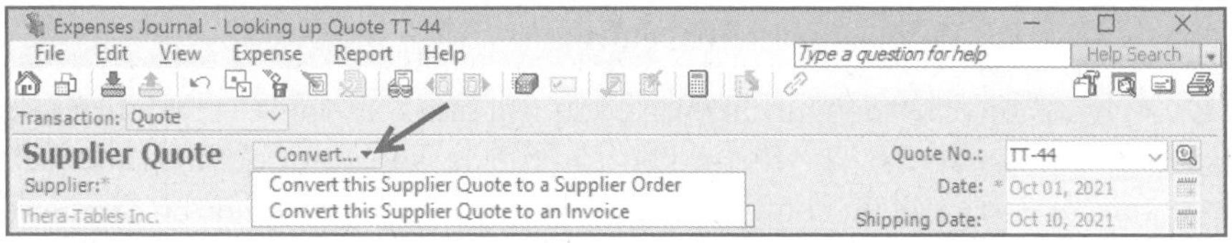

You can convert the quote to an order or directly to an invoice from this menu. Or,

Click the **Transaction list arrow** to display the transaction types:

PRO VERSION
Click Convert This Purchase Quote To A Purchase Order from the Convert drop-down list.

NOTES
The Project/Division module is hidden for Andersson because it is not needed, but when used, the term Partner will replace Division or Project for medical companies.

Click **Convert This Supplier Quote To A Supplier Order** from the Convert drop-down list, or

Click **Order** in the Transaction type drop-down list.

The quote screen changes to an order. Order No. replaces Quote No. as the field label:

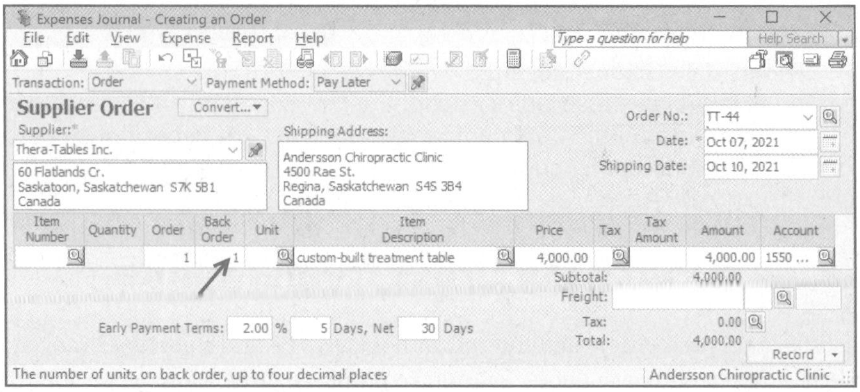

NOTES
The Record button replaces Post because the order does not generate a journal entry.

Order is now entered as the transaction type and Creating An Order replaces Looking Up Quote in the title bar. The Order quantity has been copied to the Back Order field.

All fields are no longer dimmed and are available for editing. However, if you change the quote number, you must confirm this is correct (read the margin Notes):

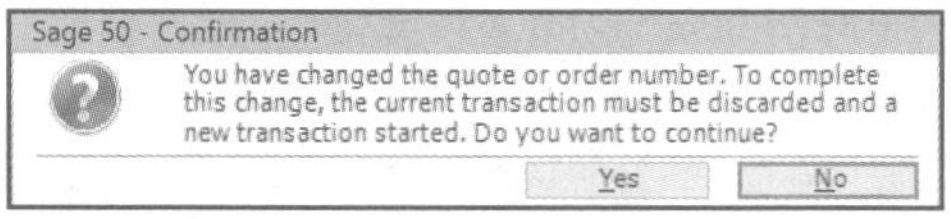

Click No to restore the original quote number.

The session date is entered on the revised form, so we need to change it.

Click the **Date field Calendar icon**. **Choose October 2**. **Press** *tab*.

Click the **Record button** Record.

The Record button now includes the option to print on its drop-down list because orders are generated within a company. You can select Print & Record as the default, just as you can choose the Print & Post option for cash purchases and sales.

The program displays the warning message:

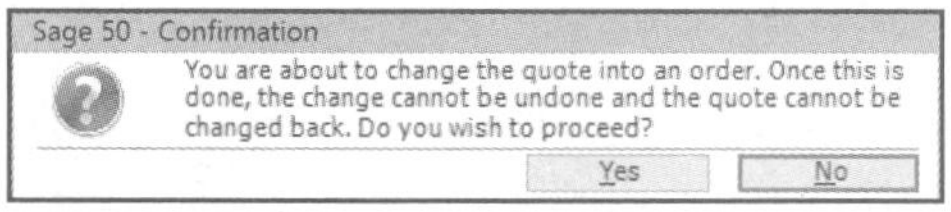

Since we want to convert the quote to an order, we can proceed. The order will replace the quote.

Click **Yes** and **OK** to confirm recording. No journal entry number appears in the confirmation message.

Purchase order numbers are updated automatically by the program, just like sales invoice and cheque numbers. (Alphanumeric numbers are not updated.) If the number for the quote that you are converting is larger than the next purchase order sequence number, a second warning will appear when you record the order because the number is out of sequence. Sage 50 will ask if you want to update your sequence starting number:

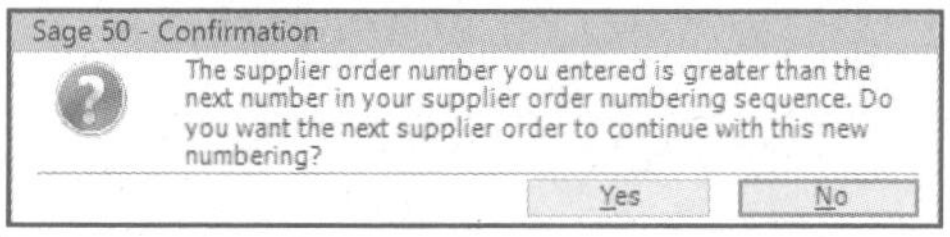

This does not apply to the alphanumeric number we used.

Click Yes if you want to reset the numbering sequence for future purchase orders. Click No to avoid resetting the automatic sequence to the higher number. When you choose No, the higher purchase order number will still be recorded, and later skipped, but the automatic counter will not be changed.

Close the **Supplier Order window**.

Making a Prepayment to a Supplier

Businesses frequently request a deposit — down payment or prepayment — when an order is placed, especially for customized orders. Deposits may be refundable or not. A deposit may be used to pay for materials that are ordered specifically for a project, it may ensure that the purchaser will follow through with the order or it may provide the supplier with some revenue if the order is cancelled and part of the deposit is not refundable.

Prepayments are made in the Payments Journal.

NOTES

To change the number of a purchase order to match the number sequence on preprinted forms, you should

- recall the quote
- choose the Adjust Quote tool (adjust purchase quotes in the same way as sales quotes – refer to page 417)
- change the quote number
- record the revised quote
- recall the newly adjusted quote
- convert the quote to an order by choosing Order from the Transaction drop-down list or by choosing Convert to an Order from the Convert drop-down list
- record the purchase order
- confirm the conversion
- check that the order sequence number is correct and update the next order number if necessary

NOTES

We will not continue the instruction to confirm successful posting or recording.

WARNING!

The order will be posted whether you choose Yes or No in the message about updating the order number.

NOTES

If you choose not to reset the number sequence, the higher order number will be skipped in the automatic numbering sequence when you reach it.

✓ 4

Payment Cheque #567 **Dated October 3, 2021**

To Thera-Tables Inc., $400 from Regina Chequing account as prepayment in acceptance of quote #TT-44 and to confirm order #TT-44.

PRO VERSION
Click the Enter Vendor Prepayments tool. Pay Purchase Invoices is entered as the type of transaction.

Click the **Payments icon** to open the Payments Journal.

Click the **Enter Supplier Prepayments tool** or **choose** the **Payment menu** and **click Enter Prepayments**.

This tool button/menu option acts as a switch that opens the fields for deposits:

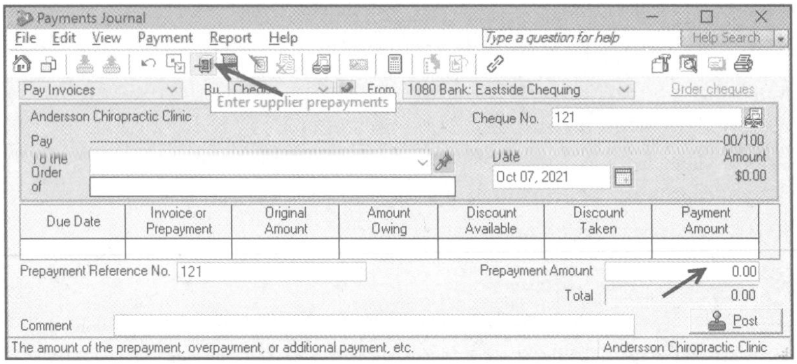

NOTES
You can change the Prepayment Reference Number and this will not affect the automatic cheque numbering sequence.

You can leave this tool selected so that the optional fields will always be available.

Two new fields are added to the journal: one for the **Prepayment Reference Number** and one for the **Amount**. The default reference number is the next cheque number in sequence for the selected bank account, and it is updated automatically by the program. The rest of the journal is the same as before, but the invoice payment lines are not used. If there are any outstanding invoices, they will be included in the journal.

When the payment is made by cheque, the **From** field has the list of bank accounts you can choose. The default bank account and cheque number for this payment are not correct. We must change them.

WARNING!
Two bank accounts and the line of credit are available for receipts and payments. Before posting a transaction, check carefully that you have selected the right account.

Click the **From field list arrow** to list the available bank accounts:

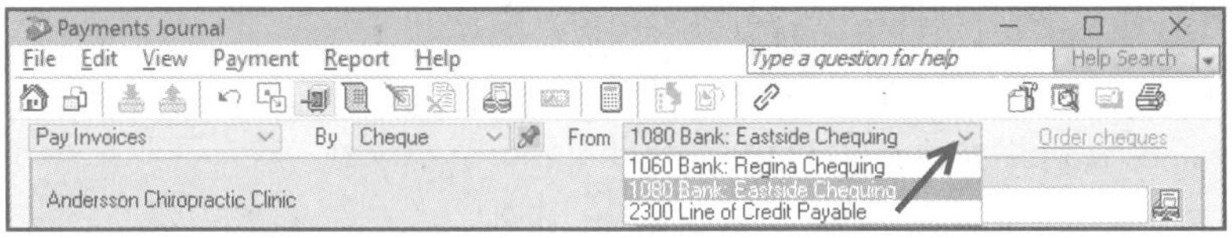

Click **Bank: Regina Chequing**. The cheque number changes.

When you choose a different bank account, the cheque and reference numbers are updated for the selected account. Each bank account has its own cheque number sequence, and these numbers are updated as you make payments from each account.

NOTES
Processing the prepayment in this way ensures that the prepayment will appear in the correct supplier account in the Payables Ledger. The manual approach, a General Journal entry that credits the bank account and debits Prepaid Expenses, an asset account, does not show this link with the supplier, the supplier's ledger must be updated separately.

This link provides another reason for using the Payables journals instead of the General Journal for supplier transactions.

Choose **Thera-Tables Inc.** as the supplier from the drop-down list.

Enter **October 3** as the date of the cheque.

Click the **Prepayment Amount field**.

Type `400`

Click the **Comment field**. Advancing the cursor updates the Total.

Type `Prepayment for order #TT-44`

If an outstanding invoice is paid with the same cheque, enter the invoice payment in the usual way in addition to the deposit amount.

The entry is now complete:

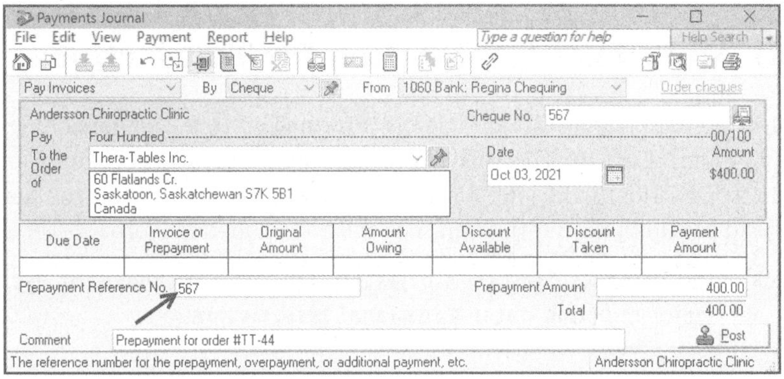

You are ready to review the journal entry.

Choose the **Report menu** and **click Display Payments Journal Entry**:

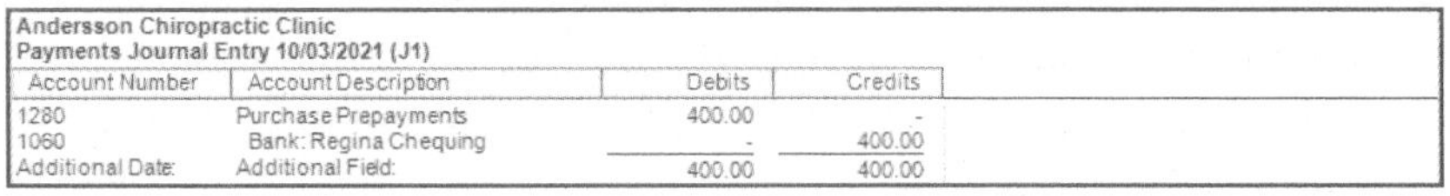

Andersson Chiropractic Clinic
Payments Journal Entry 10/03/2021 (J1)

Account Number	Account Description	Debits	Credits
1280	Purchase Prepayments	400.00	-
1060	Bank: Regina Chequing	-	400.00
Additional Date:	Additional Field:	400.00	400.00

As for other payments, the bank account is credited. However, the prepayment creates an asset until the order is filled, so *Purchase Prepayments*, the linked asset account, is debited — the supplier owes something to us. If there is no previous balance owing to the supplier, the prepayment creates a debit balance for the account. After the purchase, when you pay the supplier, the prepayment will be displayed in red under the heading "Prepayments" and you "pay" it by accepting the amount, just as you do to pay the invoice itself.

Close the **display** when you have finished and **make corrections** to the journal entry if necessary.

Click Post to save the transaction.

Click the Enter Supplier Prepayments tool again if you want to close the optional prepayment fields.

Entering Payments from a Line of Credit

Choose Sonartek from the Supplier list to prepare for the next payment.

✓ 5

Payment Cheque #103 **Dated October 3, 2021**

To Sonartek Ltd., $6 291.60 from the line of credit in payment of account including $128.40 discount for early payment. Reference invoice #SL-3456.

This payment is made from Andersson's line of credit. However, *Bank: Regina Chequing* is still selected as the bank account in the From field.

Click the **From list arrow** to select a different account:

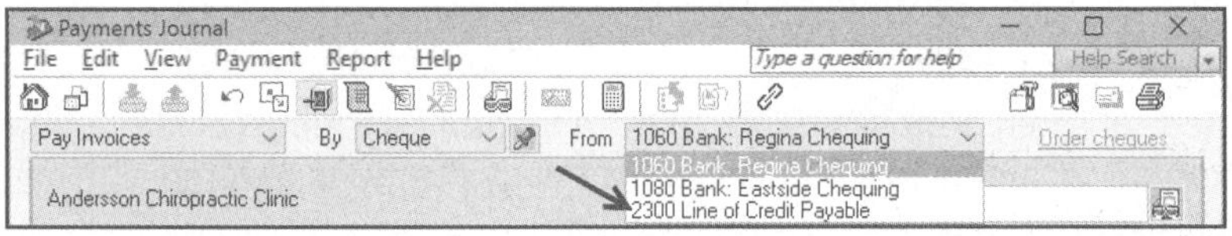

The line of credit is a liability account — it has a credit balance — but it operates like a bank account. By defining it as a Bank class account, it can be used to write cheques in the Payments Journal, as it would be in an ongoing business.

Choose Line of Credit Payable to select this account and to update the cheque number for the new account.

NOTES

You can also use the Prepayment Amount field if you are paying more than the full amount owing for an invoice. You cannot enter an amount in the Payment Amount field greater than the amount owing, but you can record this excess amount as a prepayment.

NOTES

The journal entry number (J1) has not increased because of the quotes and order.

NOTES

For corrections to deposits or prepayments after posting, use the Adjust tool or refer to Appendix C. They can also be reversed, just like receipts. (Refer to page 177.)

NOTES

The Credit Card account class is assigned to Bank: Interac, so it does not appear with the list of banks.

The Bank account class is available for all Balance Sheet accounts from the Options tab in the General Ledger. Account classes were introduced in Chapter 7, page 220.

> **NOTES**
> You can click the Invoice Or Prepayment field and press (tab) to accept the discount and payment amounts.

Enter the cheque **date**, the **discount** amount and the **payment amount**.

Entering Additional Information for Transactions

The tool bar in journals includes an **Additional Information tool** for adding information to a journal report. This tool allows tracking of one additional date and one other field for transactions in all journals. Andersson has chosen to enter the number of the invoice paid as additional information so it will be included in journal reports.

Click the **Enter Additional Information tool** or **choose** the **Payment menu** and **click Enter Additional Information**:

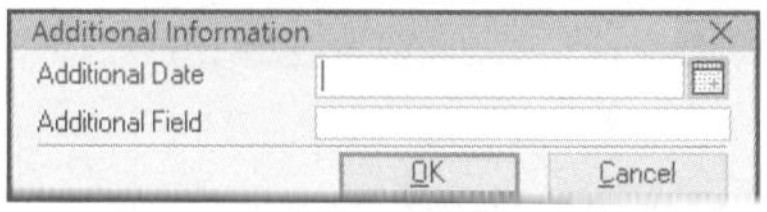

> **NOTES**
> You can name the additional fields in the Company Settings Names window.

You can enter one additional date for the transaction and additional text. Both will be available for journal reports when you show the Additional Information (page 450). You can rename these fields as part of the company setup (refer to pages 639–640).

Click the **Additional Field** text box.

Type `Ref: inv #SL-3456`

Click **OK** to return to the journal.

Adding the extra details does not change the appearance of the journal. You are ready to review the transaction before posting it.

Press (ctrl) + **J** to open the journal display:

Andersson Chiropractic Clinic
Payments Journal Entry 10/03/2021 (J2)

Account Number	Account Description	Debits	Credits
2200	Accounts Payable	6,420.00	-
2300	Line of Credit Payable	-	6,291.60
5030	Purchase Discounts	-	128.40
Additional Date:	Additional Field: Ref: inv #SL-3456	6,420.00	6,420.00

> **WARNING!**
> Because the additional information is optional, although it does appear in the journal display, the program does not warn if you forget to enter it. Therefore, you should make reviewing the journal entry routine practice.

One difference between this and earlier payment entries is the credit to a liability instead of an asset bank account for the payment. This increases the business liability — more money has been borrowed against the line of credit available.

In addition to the usual debit and credit details, the invoice number entered as additional information is included in the display so that you can check it as well.

> **NOTES**
> Details you enter in the Comment field are also added to the journal report, but the comment is not included in the journal display.

Close the **journal display**. **Check** your transaction **details** carefully.

Post the **payment** when you are certain the details are correct.

Enter the **next two transactions**. Remember to change bank accounts as needed.

6 **Cash Purchase #R-2021-10** **Dated October 3, 2021**

To Pro Suites Inc., cheque #121 for $2 300 from Eastside Chequing account to pay rent for October. Store the transaction as a monthly recurring entry.

7 **Payment Cheque #568** **Dated October 4, 2021**

To Medical Linen Supplies, $676.20 from Regina Chequing account in payment of account including $13.80 discount for early payment. Reference invoice #MLS-102.

Close the **Payments Journal**.

Click **Receivables** in the Modules pane. **Enter** the next **receipt** and then **close** the **journal**.

8

Receipt #58 **Dated October 4, 2021**

From Interplay Ballet, cheque #447 for $3 069 in payment of account including $31 discount for early payment. Reference invoice #632. Deposited to Eastside Chequing account. Add the invoice number as additional information.

NOTES

You can modify the tabbing order by placing the cheque number after the customer.

Entering a Sales (Patient) Quote

Sales quotes are like purchase quotes — your business offers a customer a guaranteed price for a limited time for merchandise or work to be completed. The customer may choose to accept or reject the offer.

Quotes are entered from the Patient Quotes icon in the Enhanced view Receivables window:

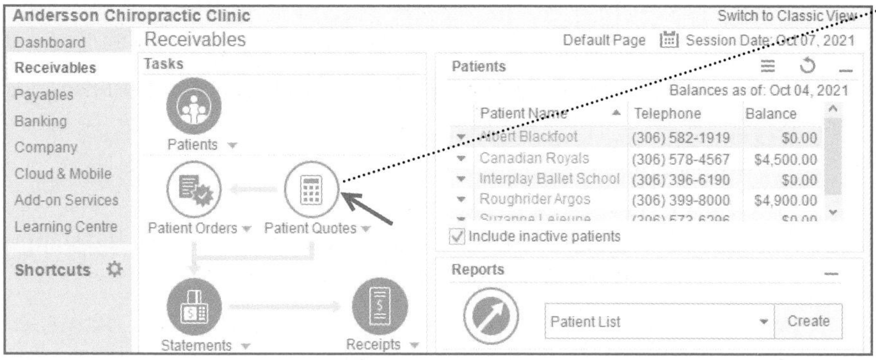

Separate icons are added for orders and quotes, just as they are for the suppliers.

PRO VERSION

Sales Quotes, Sales Orders and Sales Invoices will replace the icon labels Patient Quotes, Patient Orders and Statements. The term Customer replaces Patient.

Click the Sales Quotes icon to open the form you need.

✓ 9

Sales Quote #51 **Dated October 4, 2021**

Starting date October 15, 2021

To Giant Raptors (use Full Add for the new customer), a local basketball team, $3 500 per month for unlimited chiropractic services during the regular six-month training and playing season. Andersson will attend or be on call for all home games. If the team enters the playoffs, the contract may be extended for $1 200 per week. Terms: 1/10, n/30. A deposit of $2 000 will be required on acceptance of the contract. Enter 6 as the number ordered. Each month, the sales invoice for Giant Raptors will be entered as partially filling the order.

NOTES

For services such as those provided by Andersson, the term Shipping Date is not appropriate. In the source documents, we use Starting Date instead.

CLASSIC VIEW

Click the Fees, Orders & Quotes icon  to open the journal, and choose Quote from the journal's Transaction drop-down list.

Click the **Patient Quotes icon**  to open the Fees Journal.

The invoice screen changes to the form for a patient quote:

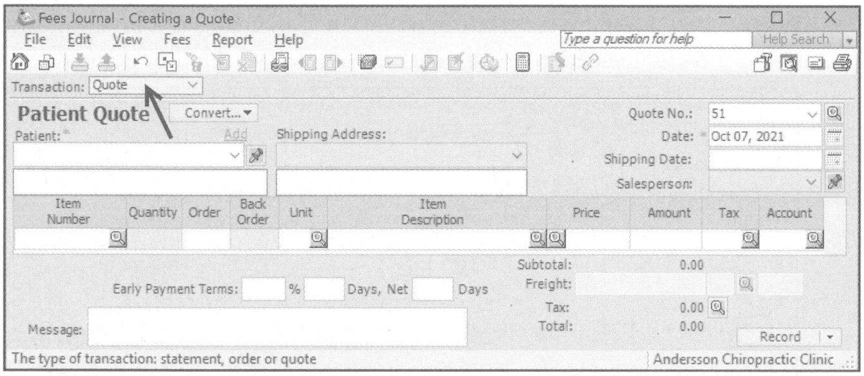

PRO VERSION

Sales Journal – Creating A Quote will appear in the journal's title bar instead of Fees Journal – Creating A Quote. Sales replaces Fees in the Menu bar.

NOTES

Statement replaces the term Invoice for a medical company. Fees Journal replaces Sales Journal.

The quote is completed in much the same way as the sales invoice. However, you must enter a quantity in the Order field, just as you did for purchase quotes and orders. The quote number is entered and updated automatically from the defaults for the Company Forms settings. As for purchase quotes, the Record button replaces Post.

WARNING!
You must choose Quote as the Transaction type before entering the customer. Otherwise, a blank quote screen will open.

Click the **Patient field**.

Type `Giant Raptors` **Click** the **Add link** above the Patient field to open the ledger directly.

If you type the new name and press *tab*, Continue will not be an option for the quote. You must create at least a partial ledger record.

Enter the following new **patient details**:

Patient Name (Contact)	Address	Phone No. Fax No.	E-mail Web Site	Revenue Account	Terms Credit Limit
Giant Raptors (Rex Saurus)	550 Tyrannus Dr. Regina, Saskatchewan S4R 5T1	Tel 1: (306) 398-8753 Tel 2: (306) 398-5338 Fax: (306) 398-5339	rex@raptors.com raptors.com	4100	1/10, n/30 (Pay Later) (change default terms) $5 000

Click Save and Close after entering all the customer details.

You will return to the quote screen with the account and payment terms added.

Drag through the **date** in the **Date field**.

Type `10 4 21`

Click the **Shipping Date field** to move the cursor because the shipping address and quote number are correct.

Type `10 15`

Click the **Order field**. You must enter an order quantity.

Instead of entering the quote as the monthly rate and filling it in the first month, we will enter it as a six-month contract with monthly unit prices. After each month of service, the quote will be partially filled with one month of service.

Type `6`

Click the **Item Description field**.

NOTES
Instead of entering the order quantity and price, you can enter the order quantity and amount – the unit price will be calculated and entered automatically.

Type `monthly fee for treatment`

Press *tab* to move to the Price field.

Type `3500`

Press *tab* to advance to the Amount field. The program enters the amount correctly as the quantity times the price.

Press *tab* to move to the Tax field. The Tax field is not used and the correct revenue account is already entered, so the quote is complete:

NOTES
You cannot enter additional information for quotes or orders. The tool is dimmed.

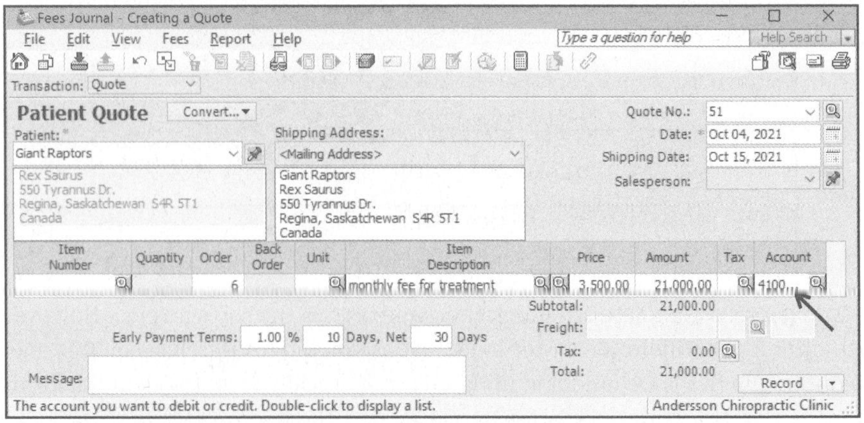

Check the **quote** carefully and **correct mistakes**, just as you do for sales invoices. Refer to page 163 for assistance if needed.

There is no journal entry to display. When a quote is filled by making a sale, the journal entry will be created.

Click **Record** [Record] to save the quote. No journal entry results from the quote.

Leave the **Fees Journal open** to adjust the quote.

Adjusting a Sales Quote

Sometimes a quote contains an error or must be changed if prices are renegotiated. You can adjust sales and purchase quotes and orders after recording them, just as you can adjust sales and purchase invoices after posting.

✓ 10

Memo #1 **Dated October 5, 2021**

After some negotiations with the Giant Raptors, Andersson agreed to reduce the contract price to $3 300 per month for the playing season. Playoff games will be billed at $1 100 per week. Adjust the sales quote to change the price.

The Fees Journal – Creating A Quote screen should still be open.

Click the **Quote No. field list arrow** to open the list of quotes on file.

Click **51** to select the quote you just entered.

Press *tab* to add the quote to the screen:

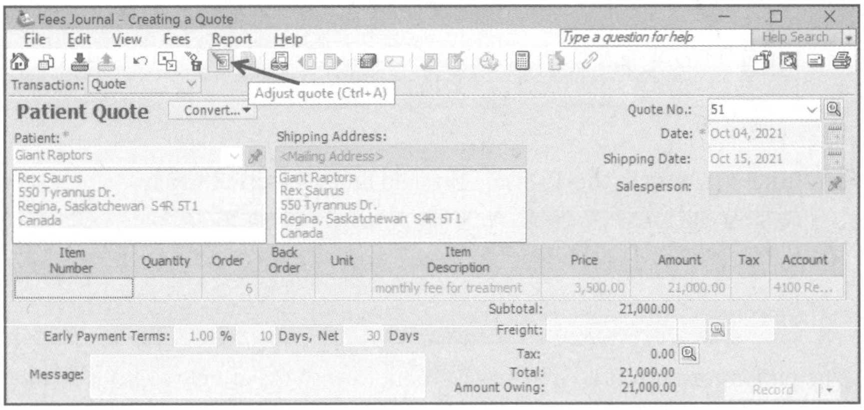

The List icon beside the Quote No. field opens the Search window for all quotes. By entering search criteria, it may be easier to find a quote on the resulting list.

At this stage, you cannot edit the quote. All fields are dimmed.

Click the **Adjust Quote tool** or **choose** the **Fees menu** and **click Adjust Quote** to open the fields for editing.

Adjusting Quote 51 replaces Looking Up Quote 51 in the title bar.

Click **3,500.00** in the Price field.

Type `3300` **Press** *tab* to update the subtotal and total amount to $19 800.

Drag through the **date in the Date field**.

Type `10-5` to enter the date for the revised quote.

Click the **Message field** and **type** `Revised quote`

NOTES

You can choose Print & Record or Record as the default action for the quote by selecting your preference from the Record button drop-down list. This allows you to create a customer copy immediately.

You can also preview quotes.

WARNING!

If Quote is not selected as the Transaction type, you will convert the quote to a sales order or fill the quote when you bring the quote on to the screen.

NOTES

To view orders and quotes, you do not need to use the lookup or search features we used to adjust purchase and sales invoices after posting. Orders and quotes are available directly from the Order/Quote No. field.

PRO VERSION

Choose the Sales Journal and click Adjust Quote or use the Adjust Quote tool.

NOTES

Pressing *ctrl* + A will open the quote fields for editing. In other journals, pressing *ctrl* + A opens the Adjust/Search window.

NOTES

All fields in a quote can be edited, except name and address details. To change the name, you must remove the quote and re-enter it for the correct customer. However, you cannot use the same quote number twice.

Check your **work** carefully.

Click Record to save the revised quote. Keep the journal open.

Converting a Sales Quote to a Sales Order

Sales quotes can be converted to orders just as purchase quotes can be converted to purchase orders.

✓ 11

Sales Order #51 **Dated October 5, 2021**

Starting date October 15, 2021
The Giant Raptors have accepted the modified sales quote #51. Convert the quote to a sales order. All terms and dates are unchanged from the revised quote for $3 300 per month.

NOTES
The Quote No. field list will include all unfilled quotes.

The Fees Journal should be open with Quote selected as the Transaction type.

Click the **Quote No.** field drop-down list.

Click **51**, the quote number we want, and **press** tab to recall the quote. All fields are dimmed or unavailable.

There are different ways to convert the quote to an order, as there were for supplier quotes.

PRO VERSION
Choose Convert This Sales Quote To A Sales Order from the Convert drop-down list or choose Order in the Transaction field.
The term Invoice will replace Statement in the Transaction list.

Click **Convert This Patient Quote To A Patient Order** from the Convert drop-down list.

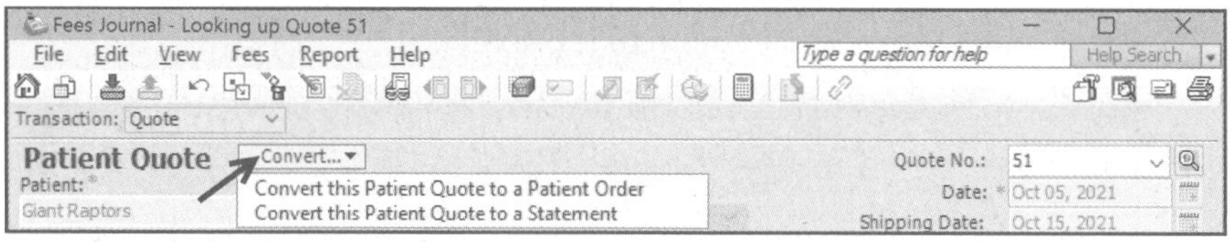

Or, you can

Click **Quote** in the Transaction field and then **click** **Order**:

The patient order replaces the revised quote with Creating An Order in the title bar:

PRO VERSION
Sales Journal – Creating An Order is displayed in the journal title bar.

NOTES
The Quote No. field is labelled Order No. as soon as you convert the quote.
The Order No. field list includes both quotes and unfilled orders.

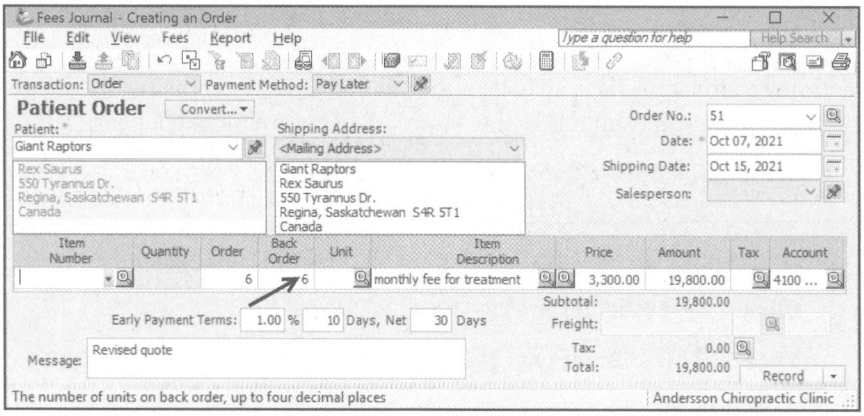

You can also first choose Order from the Transaction list, or click the Home window Patient Orders icon, then choose #51 from the Order No. drop-down list. Press tab to place the quote on-screen as an order.

All fields are now available for editing. The order quantity — 6 — has been added to the Back Order field.

Enter **Oct 5** as the order date to replace the session date.

Check all the **details** carefully because there is no journal entry to review.

All other details should be correct for the order because they have not changed. The order can be edited at this stage if needed. We will revise the comment.

Click the **Message field**. **Type** `Order based on revised quote`

Click **Record** [Record] to save the sales order. Sage 50 asks for confirmation:

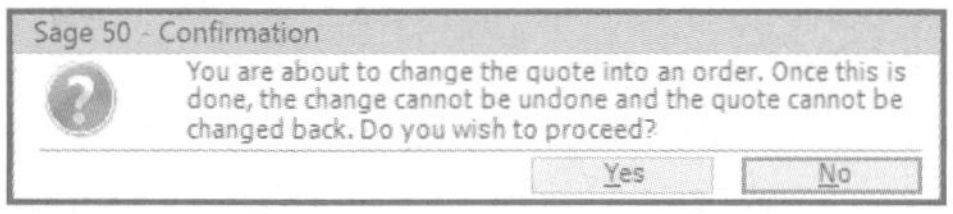

NOTES
You can make Print & Record the default action for the Record button by choosing this from the button's drop-down list, and you can preview the order.

Since we want to change the quote to an order, we should proceed.

Click **Yes**.

Close the **Fees Journal** so that you can enter the customer's deposit.

Entering a Sales Order

Sales orders are entered in the same way as sales quotes, except that you start with the Patient or Sales Order form instead of the Patient or Sales Quote form.

Click Receivables in the Modules pane and click the Patient Orders icon. Then choose the customer and complete the order details. The Order field cannot be left blank. Sales order numbers are usually generated by the customer, but they can also be entered and updated by the program, with the initial number entered in the Company Forms Settings window.

CLASSIC VIEW
Click the Fees, Orders & Quotes icon [Fees, Orders & Quotes] to open the journal, and choose Order from the journal's Transaction drop-down list.

Entering Customer Deposits

Andersson also requests deposits from new customers when they place orders. Deposits can be entered in the Receipts Journal in the same way as supplier prepayments are entered in the Payments Journal. The customer deposit tool opens fields for a reference number and an amount.

NOTES
We will enter the next customer deposit directly with the sales order (refer to page 427).

✓ 12

Receipt #59 **Dated October 6, 2021**

From the Giant Raptors, cheque #838 for $2 000 as deposit #14 to confirm sales order #51. Deposited to Regina Chequing account.

Click the **Receipts icon** [Receipts] to open the Receipts Journal.

Click the **Enter Patient Deposits tool** or **choose** the **Receipt menu** and **click** **Enter Deposits**.

PRO VERSION
Click the Enter Customer Deposits tool – Customer replaces the term Patient in the Pro version.

This tool button/menu option acts as a switch that opens the fields for deposits:

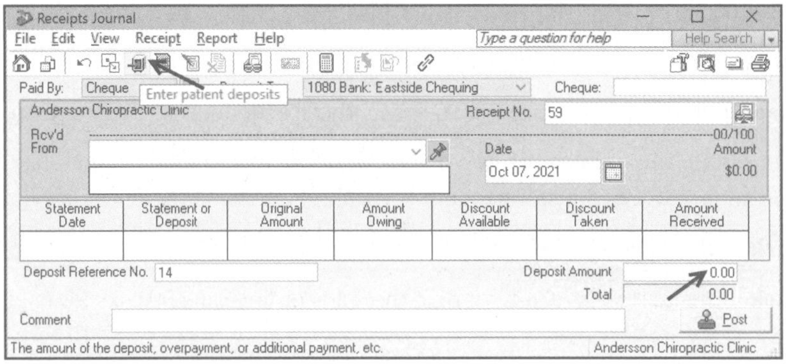

The two new fields added to the journal for the **Deposit Reference Number** and for the **Deposit Amount** serve the same purpose as they do for supplier prepayments. The reference number is the deposit number, and it is updated automatically by the program. The deposit number is different from and updated separately from the receipt number. Both are entered as Company Forms Settings. The invoice lines are not used for the deposit. Outstanding invoices, if there are any, will be included in the journal. If they are being paid with the same customer cheque, enter the receipt in the usual way in addition to the deposit amount.

The receipt number is updated and correct, but we need to change the bank account.

Choose **Giant Raptors** in the patient From drop-down list.

Click the **Cheque field**. **Type** `838`

Enter **October 6** as the date of the cheque.

Click the **Deposit To list arrow** to access the list of bank accounts:

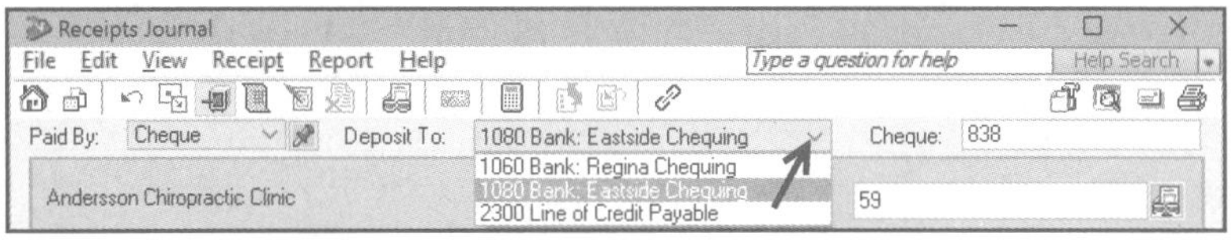

Just as we can pay from any of the accounts that we identify as Bank class accounts, we can deposit to any bank account, including the line of credit.

Choose **Bank: Regina Chequing** to change the account selection.

Click the **Deposit Amount field** at the bottom of the journal.

Type `2000` **Press** *tab*.

Click the **Enter Additional Information tool**, or **choose** the **Receipt menu** and **click** **Enter Additional Information**:

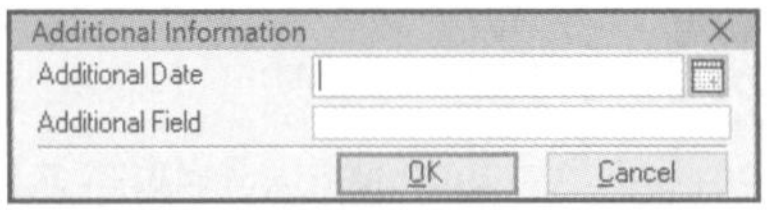

This data entry screen is the same for all journals.

Click the **Additional Field** text box. **Type** `Deposit for SO #51`

Click **OK** to return to the journal so you can review the transaction.

Choose the **Report menu** and **click** **Display Receipts Journal Entry**:

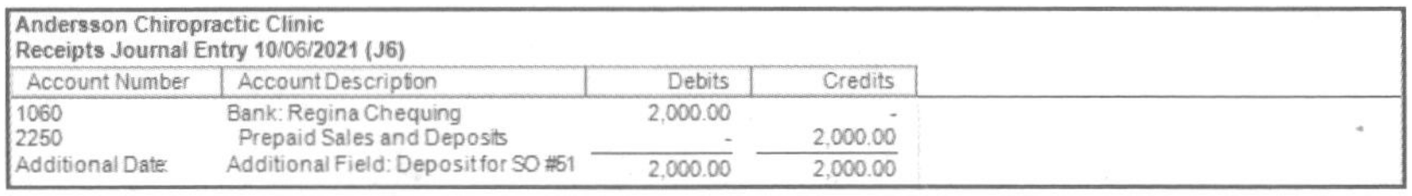

Andersson Chiropractic Clinic
Receipts Journal Entry 10/06/2021 (J6)

Account Number	Account Description	Debits	Credits
1060	Bank: Regina Chequing	2,000.00	-
2250	Prepaid Sales and Deposits	-	2,000.00
Additional Date:	Additional Field: Deposit for SO #51	2,000.00	2,000.00

NOTES

If you modified the tabbing order, pressing tab after selecting the customer will place the cursor in the Cheque field.

NOTES

The Credit Card account class is assigned to Bank: Interac, so it does not appear with the list of banks.

Line of Credit Payable has been defined as a Bank class account. Therefore, it appears on the list of bank accounts.

Cash class accounts will also appear on this list. We will use the Cash class in Chapter 15.

NOTES

If a customer overpays an invoice, you can enter the overpayment – the difference between the amount owing and the cheque amount – in the Deposit Amount field to create the required credit balance.

As for other receipts, the bank account is debited. The account credited is *Prepaid Sales and Deposits*, a liability account linked to the customer deposits field. If the customer has no previous outstanding balance, the deposit creates a credit entry for the account. Until the sale is completed, the deposit creates a liability — we owe the customer this amount until the order is filled. After the sale, when the customer pays the invoice, the deposit will be displayed in red under the heading "Deposits" and it is "paid" by accepting its amount, just as you enter receipts for the invoice itself.

Close the **display** when you have finished and **make corrections** to the journal entry if necessary.

Click Post to save the transaction.

Click the **Enter Patient Deposits tool** again if you want to close the deposit fields.

Close the **Receipts Journal** to return to the Receivables module window.

Change the **session date** to **October 14** and **make** a **backup**. **Enter** the **next two receipts** and then **close** the **journal**.

13 **Receipt #60** **Dated October 8, 2021**

From Roughrider Argos, cheque #1122 for $4 851 in payment of account including $49 discount for early payment. Reference sales invoice #639. Deposited to Eastside Chequing account.

14 **Receipt #61** **Dated October 8, 2021**

From Canadian Royals, cheque #3822 for $4 455 in payment of account including $45 discount for early payment. Reference sales invoice #638. Deposited to Regina Chequing account.

✓ 15 **Purchase Order #44 and Cheque #104** **Dated October 9, 2021**

Delivery date October 19, 2021
From Sonartek Ltd., $6 000 including taxes for ultrasound machine with multiple frequencies and interchangeable wands. Terms: 2/15, n/30.

Deposit of $1 500 paid with cheque #104 from Line of Credit Payable account to confirm order. (Use the Payments Journal to enter the deposit.)

Click **Payables** in the Modules pane list to open the Payables window.

Click the **Supplier Orders icon** Supplier Orders to open the Expenses Journal with Order selected as the Transaction type:

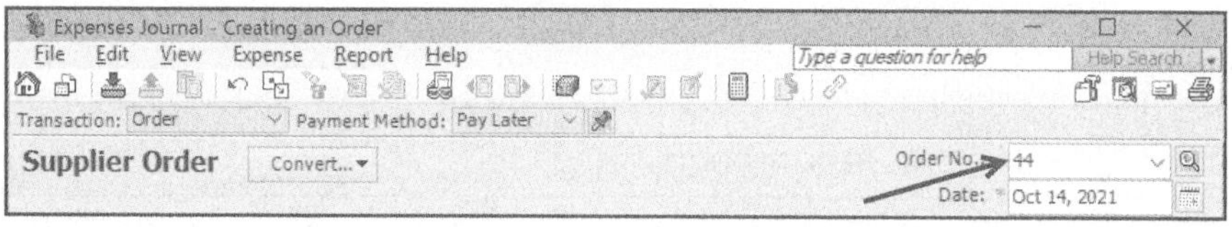

The Order No. is entered automatically (Forms Settings), and it will be incremented automatically because purchase orders are generated within your business.

Enter the **dates** and the **remaining order details**. **Record** the **order** and **close** the **Expenses Journal**.

Open the **Payments Journal** to **enter** the **prepayment** dated October 9.

Close the **Payments Journal**.

NOTES

Processing the deposit in this way ensures that the deposit will appear in the correct customer account in the Receivables Ledger. The manual approach, a General Journal entry that debits the bank account and credits Unearned Revenue, does not show this link with the customer directly – the customer's ledger is updated separately. This link gives us another reason for using the Receivables journals instead of the General Journal for customer transactions.

NOTES

Closing or hiding the deposit fields is not required.

NOTES

Remember to change the selected bank account when necessary.

Filling a Purchase Order

When an ordered item is received or work is completed you must complete a purchase invoice entry to record the transaction. Andersson will record the purchase order number in the Additional Field for the journal reports.

Again, there are different ways to turn the order into an invoice.

PRO VERSION
The Purchases Journal opens with Order as the Transaction type. Purchases Journal – Creating An Order appears in the journal's title bar.

Choose Invoice as the Transaction type or choose Convert This Purchase Order To A Purchase Invoice.

NOTES
After you choose the purchase order number, the order is not placed on-screen until you press tab or advance to the next field.

NOTES
On the Order form, the Order No. field list has all unfilled quotes and orders because you can convert and fill quotes.

On the Invoice form, this field label changes to Order/Quote No. and will also include all unfilled quotes and orders because both can be converted to invoices.

The form includes a tool to remove the order, that is, to cancel it.

✓ 16

Purchase Invoice #TT-4599 **Dated October 10, 2021**

From Thera-Tables Inc., to fill purchase order #TT-44 for $4 000 including taxes for custom-built treatment table. Terms: 2/5, n/30.

Click the **Supplier Orders icon** .

Choose **TT-44** from the Order No. field drop-down list. **Press** tab to recall the order. All fields are dimmed.

Choose **Convert This Supplier Order To An Invoice** from the Convert drop-down list. This is the only conversion option available now:

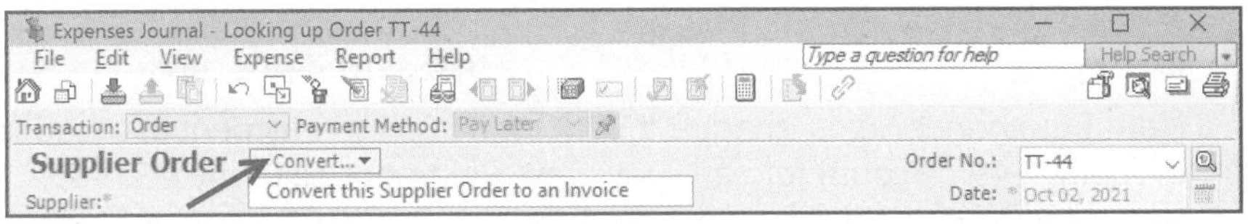

Instead, you can **click** the **Transaction drop-down list** and **choose Invoice**:

Or, choose Invoice from the Transaction list and then choose TT-44 from the Order/Quote No. drop-down list and press tab.

The purchase order details from October 2 will be entered on the invoice:

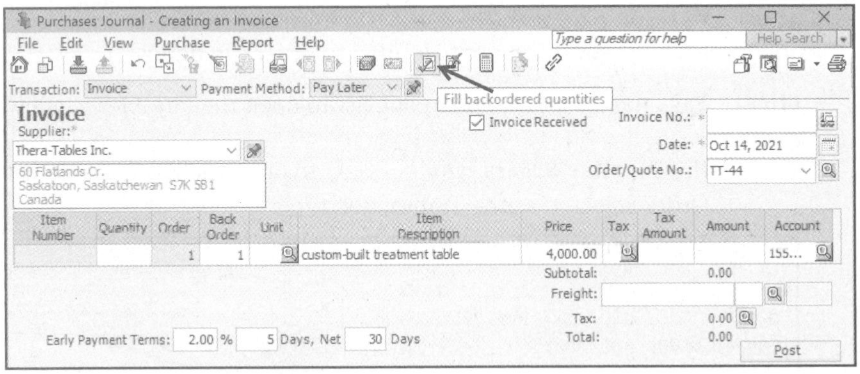

Pay Later, the supplier's default in the Payment Method field, is correct. Creating An Invoice now appears in the title bar. All fields are no longer dimmed and can be edited.

Click the **Invoice field**. **Type** `TT-4599`

Press tab **twice** to advance to the Date field.

Type `10-10`

The invoice is still incomplete because the quantity displays as backordered and the invoice amount is zero. We need to "fill" the order.

Click the **Fill Backordered Quantities tool** (refer to the previous screen) or **choose** the **Expense menu** and **click Fill Supplier Order**.

PRO VERSION
Choose the Purchase menu and click Fill Purchase Order.

The amount has been added to the invoice:

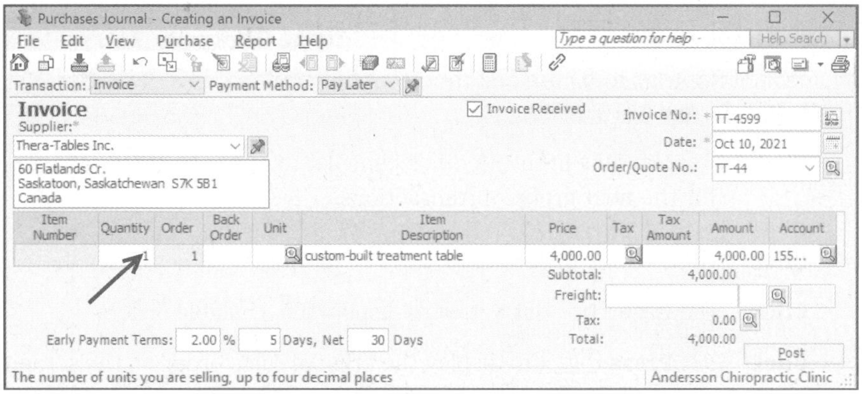

NOTES
If the order is partially filled, the backordered quantity will be reduced, as in the sales order on page 425.

The Back Order quantity has been added to the Quantity column to reflect the completion of the order. The prepayment made in the Payments Journal does not appear on the invoice and the full amount is invoiced.

Click the **Enter Additional Information tool** or **choose** the **Expense menu** and **click Enter Additional Information**.

PRO VERSION
Choose the Purchase menu and click Enter Additional Information.

Click the **Additional Field** text box.

Type `Ref: fill P.O. #TT-44`

Click **OK** to return to the journal.

Check the **entry** carefully to be sure that it is correct.

Choose the **Report menu** and **click Display Expenses Journal Entry**.

This is a normal journal entry with the order number as additional information. Prepayment amounts are not included.

Close the **display**. When the information is correct,

Click Post or **choose** the **Expense menu** and **click Post**. Sage 50 informs us that the filled order has been removed:

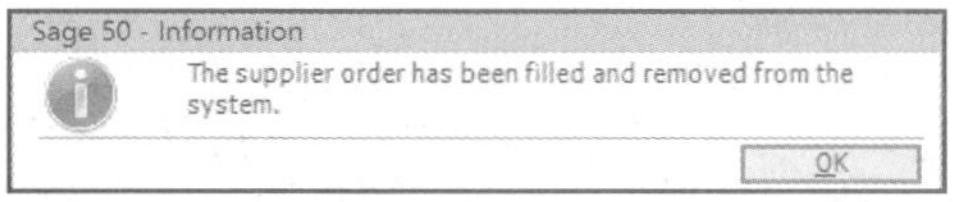

Filled orders and quotes are not saved, but their numbers cannot be used again.

Click **OK** to display a new Expenses Journal invoice form.

Close the **Expenses Journal**.

Filling a Purchase Quote

Filling a purchase quote is similar to filling an order. Choose Invoice, select the quote number and press *tab* to place the quote on-screen as an invoice. The Order quantity automatically moves to the Quantity column and the total Amount is added. You do not need to choose Fill Backordered Quantities for quotes. Again, you can record the quote number as an additional field for the journal.

NOTES
To fill a quote, you can start with the quote on-screen. Then choose Invoice from the Transaction drop-down list or Convert This Supplier/Purchase Quote To An Invoice from the Convert drop-down list. Refer to the screenshots on page 410.

Partially Filling a Sales Order

Filling a sales order is similar to filling a purchase order, and there are different ways to do this.

✓ 17

Sales Invoice #649 **Dated October 10, 2021**

To Giant Raptors, to fill the first month of the contract on sales order #51 for $3 300. Terms: 1/10, n/30.

PRO VERSION

Click the Sales Orders icon to open the Sales Journal. Choose Order #51 and press *tab*. Sales Journal – Looking Up Order 51 appears in the journal's title bar.

Choose Convert This Sales Order To A Sales Invoice from the Convert drop-down list or choose Invoice from the Transaction list.

Click **Receivables** in the Modules pane list to open the Receivables window for the next group of transactions.

Click the **Patient Orders icon** [Patient Orders] to open the Fees Journal.

Click the **Order No. list arrow** to display the available orders.

Click **51**. **Press** *tab* to display the original sales order on the screen — with all fields dimmed as usual.

Click **Convert This Patient Order To A Statement** from the Convert drop-down list. This is the only conversion option for orders:

NOTES

Only one conversion option is possible from the order screen, that is, changing the order to an invoice.

The list in the Order No. field will include both unfilled quotes and unfilled orders.

Or, **click** the **Transaction drop-down** list and **choose Statement**:

NOTES

Statement replaces Invoice for medical companies.

Or, choose the Statements icon from the Receivables module Home window. Then choose #51 from the Order/Quote field drop-down list and press *tab*.

Each of these three approaches will replace the order with an invoice:

NOTES

If you customized the columns for the Quote form, they will be restored for the Order. In the Premium version, Quote, Order and Invoice forms are customized separately.

PRO VERSION

If you customized the columns for the Quote form, the same changes will be applied on the Order and Invoice forms. You cannot customize them differently.

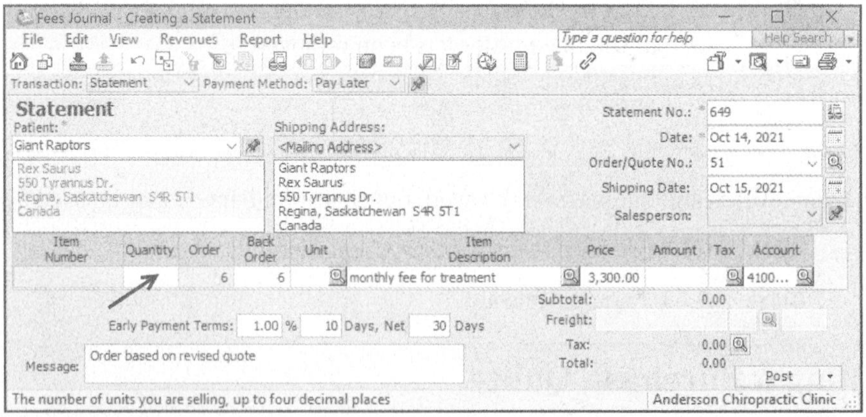

Sometimes only part of the order is received and the order is not completely filled at once, as in this case.

Pay Later, the customer's default, should be selected as the Payment Method for the Statement.

Enter **October 10** as the transaction date.

Click the **Quantity field**. Only one month is being billed at this time.

Type 1 **Press** tab to update the invoice:

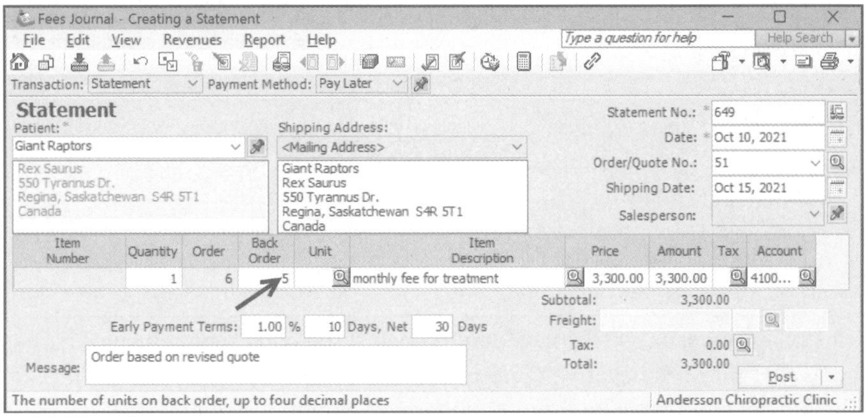

The Amount entered is the fee for one month of service, and the Back Order quantity is reduced to five. When the sixth and final month is completed, the order will be filled and removed.

To fill the sales order for all 6 months at the same time, you would choose to Fill Backordered Quantities, using the tool button or the Fees menu option.

Click the **Enter Additional Information tool** or **choose** the **Fees menu** and **click Enter Additional Information**.

Click the **Additional Field** text box. **Type** `Ref: S.O. #51`

Click **OK** to return to the journal. We should also modify the comment.

Click the **Message field**. **Type** `Invoice based on revised quote`

Review the **journal entry** and **check** your **work** carefully.

Choose the **Report menu** and **click Display Fees Journal Entry**.

Close the **display** to return to the invoice. **Make corrections** if necessary.

Click Post to record the invoice. The order is not filled, so you do not get the message that the order will be removed.

Close the **Fees Journal**.

Filling a Sales Quote

Filling a sales quote is similar to filling an order. Choose Statement (or Invoice), select the quote number and press tab to place the quote on-screen as an invoice. The order quantity automatically moves to the Quantity column and the total Amount is added. You do not need to choose Fill Backordered Quantities for quotes.

Entering Receipts on Accounts with Deposits

The next receipt pays the balance of an account for a customer who has made a deposit.

✓ 18

Receipt #62 **Dated October 13, 2021**

From the Giant Raptors, cheque #939 for $1 267 in full payment of account including $33 discount for early payment. Reference sales invoice #649 and deposit #14. Deposited to Eastside Chequing account.

Click the **Receipts icon** to open the Receipts Journal.

NOTES

You could also fill the invoice and then edit the number in the Quantity field from 6 to 1.

PRO VERSION

Choose the Sales menu and click Enter Additional Information.

NOTES

You can double-click the single word Order in the Message field and type Invoice to replace it.

NOTES

To fill the quote, you can start with the quote on-screen. Then choose Statement from the Transaction drop-down list or Convert This Patient Quote To A Statement from the Convert drop-down list. Refer to the screenshots on page 418.

NOTES

If necessary, drag the lower frame of the journal to include the deposit on the screen, or maximize the window.

Choose **Giant Raptors** from the customer drop-down list:

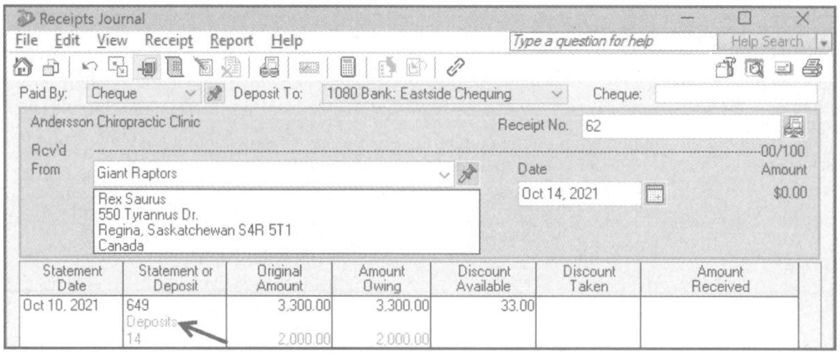

Customer deposits are displayed in red below the outstanding invoices. The colour indicates that they are negative invoices that reduce the balance owing. The invoice line has the full amount owing and the full discount amount available.

Enter **939** as the Cheque number and **enter** **Oct 13** in the Date field.

Click the **Discount Taken field** for invoice #649 to accept the discount.

Press tab to accept the Amount Received and add the Deposit amount.

Press tab to accept the Deposit amount and update the receipt.

Enter the **invoice** and **deposit numbers** as additional information.

The discount and deposit are subtracted from the full invoice amount so that the total amount now matches the cheque amount in the completed receipt:

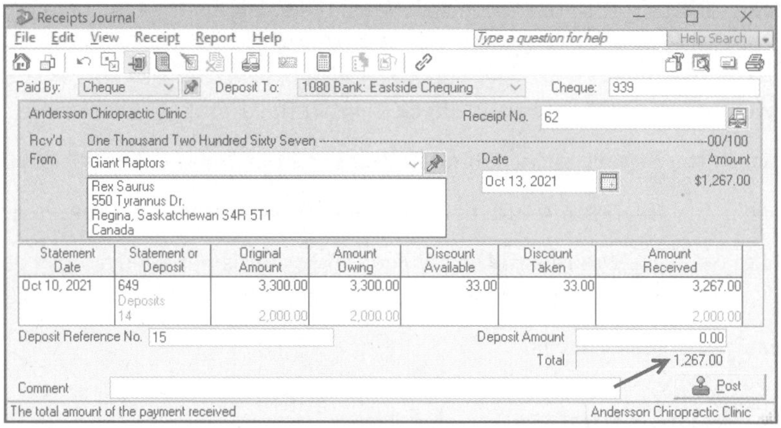

Choose the **Report menu** and **click** **Display Receipts Journal Entry**:

Andersson Chiropractic Clinic
Receipts Journal Entry 10/13/2021 (J12)

Account Number	Account Description	Debits	Credits
1080	Bank: Eastside Chequing	1,267.00	-
2250	Prepaid Sales and Deposits	2,000.00	-
4150	Sales Discounts	33.00	-
1200	Accounts Receivable	-	3,300.00
Additional Date:	Additional Field: Ref: inv #649 & d...	3,300.00	3,300.00

Accounts Receivable has been credited for the full invoice amount as in regular receipts. The *Sales Discounts* contra-revenue account has been debited to record the reduction to sales revenue. The *Prepaid Sales and Deposits* liability account has been debited for the full deposit amount to clear its credit balance, and the bank account is debited for the amount of the cheque.

The initial deposit creates a liability — the customer has paid us and we have not provided anything yet. When the order is filled, the liability is removed, so the *Accounts Receivable* balance debit is offset by the initial liability. When the customer pays the invoice for the balance owing, the initial credit entry must be removed from the record.

Close the **journal display window**. **Make corrections** if necessary. **Post** the **receipt** and then **close** the **Receipts Journal**.

Enter **sales quote #52** for a new customer.

19

Quote: 52
Date: Oct 13, 2021
Starting date: Oct 25, 2021
Customer: Veronica Kain
Veronica Kain School of Dance
35 Lady Slipper Rd.
Address: Regina, SK S3V 4H7
Phone No: (306) 376-3218

Andersson Chiropractic Clinic
betterbacks.com
4500 Rae St.
Regina, SK S4S 3B4
Tel 1: (306) 577-1900
Tel 2: (306) 577-2199 Fax: (306) 577-1925

QUOTE

Treatment description	Amount
Chiropractic services for the school year (Sep-Jun) Monthly contract rate $1 000 deposit when contract accepted Contract may be extended for summer months	2 500.00
TOTAL	2 500.00

Terms: 1/10, n/30
Signed: *Maria Andersson* **Customer Initials:** VK

Entering Deposits with Sales Orders

You can also enter customer deposits directly on the Patient Order form.

✓ 20 **Sales Order #52 and Deposit #15** **Dated October 14, 2021**

Starting date October 25, 2021
From Veronica Kain School of Dance, acceptance of quote #52. Convert the quote to a sales order leaving all terms and amounts unchanged. Received cheque #865 for $1 000 as deposit #15 to confirm sales order #52. Deposited to Eastside Chequing account.

The Fees Journal should still be open with Quote selected as the Transaction type.

Choose **52** from the Quote No. field list and **press** tab.

Choose **Order** as the Transaction type or **choose** **Convert This Patient Quote To A Patient Order** from the Convert list to convert the quote to an order.

Click the **Payment Method list arrow** for the payment options:

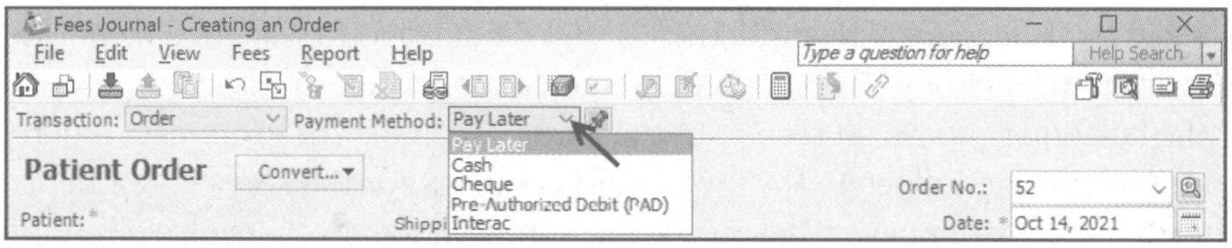

The same customer payment types are available here as in the Receipts Journal.

NOTES

Use Full Add for the new customer.

Email: vkain@dancestudio.ca
Revenue account: 4100
Credit limit: $4 000

Use the source document for the remaining customer details.

Change the default payment terms. Pay Later is correct as the default invoice payment method.

Enter 1 as the Order quantity.

PRO VERSION

Choose Order from the Transaction list in the Sales Journal, or choose Convert This Sales Quote To A Sales Order from the Convert drop-down list.

PRO VERSION

Sales Journal – Creating An Order will be the title for the journal.

NOTES
You cannot enter additional information for sales quotes and orders, even if the payment accompanies the order.

Click **Cheque** in the Payment Method list to open the extra payment fields:

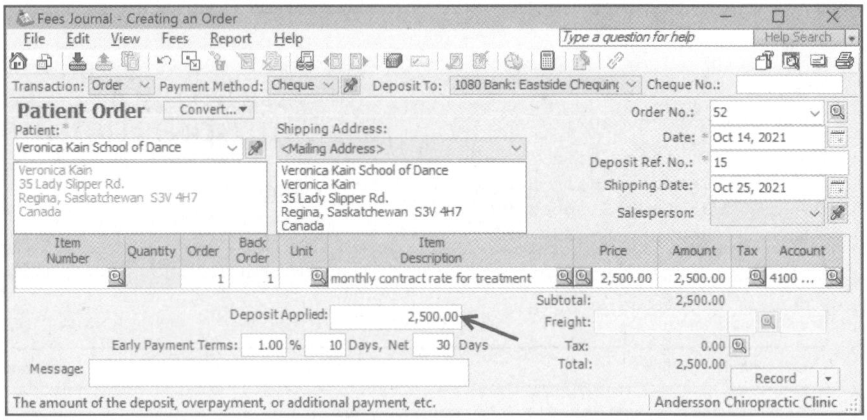

WARNING!
Although Sage 50 allows you to enter prepayments on the purchase orders by choosing from the Payment Method drop-down list, this method is not recommended because you will be unable to print the cheque. In addition, the cheque on the order will not be included in the Cheque Log Report, so the audit trail will be incomplete. Using the Payments Journal will always provide the correct reports and audit trail.

The default bank account is selected for the Deposit To field at the top of the order form. A Cheque No. field and a **Deposit Reference No.** field with the next deposit number have been added to the top of the form. A **Deposit Applied** amount field has been added to the bottom of the order form.

The session date and bank account are correct, so we can add the payment details.

Click the **Cheque No. field**.

Type 865

Double-click the **Deposit Applied field**. The full amount of the order ($2 500) is entered as the default amount and we need to change it.

Type 1000

Press *tab* to update and complete the form.

PRO VERSION
Choose the Report menu and click Display Sales Journal Entry.

Choose the **Report menu** and **click Display Fees Journal Entry**:

Andersson Chiropractic Clinic
Fees Journal Entry 10/14/2021 (J13)

Account Number	Account Description	Debits	Credits
1080	Bank: Eastside Chequing	1,000.00	-
2250	Prepaid Sales and Deposits	-	1,000.00
Additional Date:	Additional Field:	1,000.00	1,000.00

Except for the amounts and the bank account, this journal entry is identical to the journal entry for deposits entered in the Receipts Journal (page 420). The prepayment or deposit with the sales order creates a journal entry, although the sales order itself does not.

Close the **display** and **click** Record to save the transaction.

Click **Yes** to confirm that you are changing the quote to an order.

Entering Debit Card Sale Transactions

NOTES
Fees for debit cards can be lower than credit card fees because the amount is paid immediately. Debit card payments require the customer's bank balance to cover the amount before the payments are approved – no loan is involved.
For Andersson, we set up the debit card as a credit card with a 0.0% transaction fee.

Customers pay for purchases using cash, cheques, credit cards or debit cards. Debit and credit card purchases are similar for a store — the payment is deposited immediately to the linked bank account. The difference is that debit card transactions withdraw the money from the customer's bank account immediately while credit cards advance a loan that the customer repays on receipt of the credit card bill. The store pays a percentage discount or transaction fee to the credit card company for the service. For debit card transactions, the store pays a flat fee for each transaction. Both involve a setup fee and a monthly rental charge for the terminal that communicates electronically with the card-issuing company. Andersson uses the name Interac for all debit card transactions.

The Fees Journal should be open from the previous transaction. If it is not, open it by clicking the Statements icon. The session date is correct as the invoice date.

✓ 21

Debit Card Sales Summary Invoice #650 Dated October 14, 2021

To various one-time patients, $260 for initial assessments for new patients and $450 for follow-up treatment sessions. Total amount deposited in Interac bank account, $710. Store as a recurring bi-weekly transaction.

Choose **Statement** from the Transaction list.

Choose **One-Time Patient** from the Patient list and **press** tab.

For one-time customers, **Cash** is the default payment option — Pay Later is not an option for one-time customers. The Net Days field is removed to match the immediate payment option and the default bank account is selected. The terms for one-time customers offer no discount, so the discount fields are blank.

Click the **Payment Method list arrow** for the payment options:

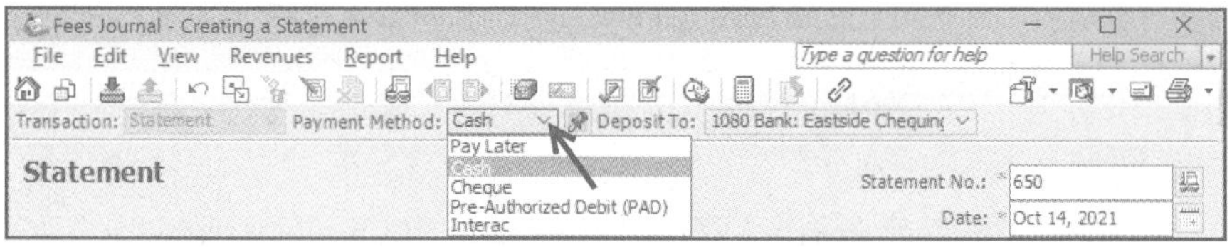

Click **Interac** as the method of payment to modify the invoice.

There is no Deposit To bank account field or Cheque Number field as there is when the payment is made by cheque. Interac is linked automatically to a dedicated bank account as part of the company file setup, just like credit cards. Interac Amount replaces Cash Amount as the label for the amount received.

Type `Debit Card Sales Summary` (in the Address field).

Complete the rest of the **invoice** in the same way as credit card or cash sales.

Click the **Item Description field** and **type** `initial assessments`

Click the **Amount field** and **type** `260`

The account is added automatically because we entered it as the default linked revenue account for the Receivables Ledger.

Click the **Item Description field** on the second line of the invoice.

Type `follow-up treatments`

Click the **Amount field** and **type** `450`

Press tab to complete the invoice:

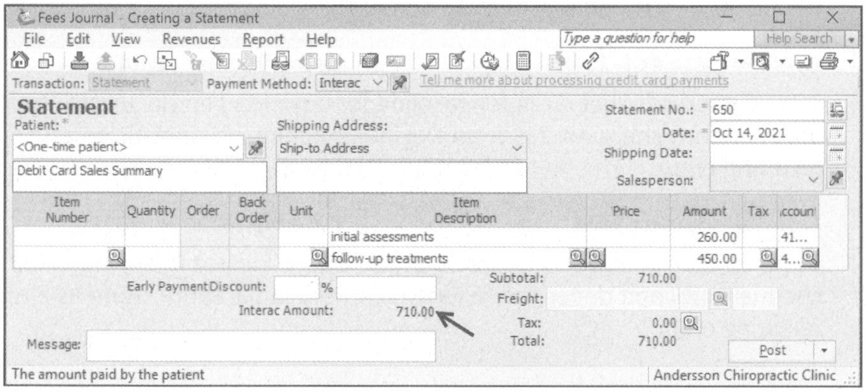

PRO VERSION
Choose Invoice from the Transaction list. Choose One-Time Customer from the Customer list.

NOTES
Although Pay Later is on the payment method drop-down list, you cannot select this method for one-time customers. Choosing it will generate an error message.

PRO VERSION
Sales Journal – Creating An Invoice appears in the journal's title bar.

PRO VERSION
pro Choose the Report menu and click Display Sales Journal Entry.

NOTES
The third-party provider that processes the Interac transactions does charge fees, but these would be entered at the time of account reconciliation when the statement is received and the account is reconciled.

If a message about credit card processing pops up, click Do Not Show Me Again and then close the message.

Choose the **Report menu** and **click Display Fees Journal Entry** to review the entry before posting:

Andersson Chiropractic Clinic
Fees Journal Entry 10/14/2021 (J14)

Account Number	Account Description	Debits	Credits
1100	Bank: Interac	710.00	-
4100	Revenue from Services	-	710.00
Additional Date:	Additional Field:	710.00	710.00

A new linked account is used for this transaction. The debit card account — *Bank: Interac* — replaces the usual bank account for other cash sales and *Accounts Receivable* for account sales. Unlike credit card sales, no additional fees are withheld.

Close the **display** to return to the Fees Journal input screen.

Make corrections if necessary, referring to page 163 for assistance.

We can store the entry and use it to enter the debit card summaries every second week. When you recall the transaction, you can edit the amounts. You will not need to save the changes and store the transaction again.

Click the **Store tool** to save the transaction for repeated entries.

Choose Biweekly as the frequency and **click OK** to save the stored entry.

Click Post.

Close the **Fees Journal**. **Click Payables** in the Modules pane list.

Enter the **next group of transactions**. **Change** the **session date** when needed and **make backups** when prompted.

22 **Payment Cheque #122** **Dated October 14, 2021**
To Cleanol and Laundry Services, $90 from Eastside Chequing account in payment of account. Reference invoice #CLS-2419.

NOTES
You may need to scroll down to include the line for the prepayment amount, or you can maximize the window.

23 **Payment Cheque #123** **Dated October 14, 2021**
To Thera-Tables Inc., $3 520 from Eastside Chequing account in full payment of account including $80 discount for early payment. Reference invoice #TT-4599 and cheque #567. Remember to "pay" the prepayment.

24 **Purchase Invoice #CLS-3926** **Dated October 14, 2021**
From Cleanol and Laundry Services, $120 for contracted twice-weekly laundry service. Terms: net 30. Store the transaction as a bi-weekly recurring entry.

SESSION DATE – OCTOBER 21, 2021

25 **Purchase Invoice #SL-4622** **Dated October 17, 2021**
From Sonartek Ltd., to fill purchase order #44, $6 000 including taxes for multi-frequency ultrasound machine. Terms: 2/15, n/30.

26 **Cash Purchase #GF-2641** **Dated October 18, 2021**
From Grasslands Fuel, $124 for gasoline for business vehicle. Invoice total $124 paid in full by cheque #569 from Regina Chequing account. Store as a bi-weekly recurring entry.

27 **Cash Sales Invoice #651** **Dated October 20, 2021**
To Albert Blackfoot, $315 for treatment sessions. Invoice total paid in full by cheque #426 and deposited to Eastside Chequing account. Store as a monthly recurring entry.

28 **Purchase Quote #SU-5532** **Dated October 21, 2021**

Starting date December 1, 2021
From Space Unlimited (use Quick Add), $2 250 per month for rent of office space for the next 12 months. (Enter 12 as the order quantity.) Rent does not include heat or hydro. Terms: security deposit of one month's rent required with postdated cheques for one year dated on the first of each month.

NOTES
Enter 12 in the Order column for the two rent quotes so that we can partially fill the quote.

29 **Purchase Quote #45** **Dated October 21, 2021**

Starting date December 1, 2021
From Pro Suites Inc., $2 350 per month for rent of office space for the next 12 months. (Enter 12 as the order quantity.) Rent includes heat and hydro. Rent payment is due on the first of each month with a series of postdated cheques.

Filling Sales Orders with Deposits

Change the **session date** to October 31 and **back up** your **data**.

When you advance the session date to October 31, you will open an Advisor message:

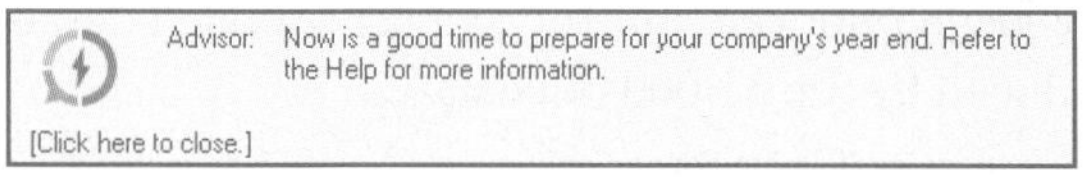

Click to close the message about year-end preparation.

✓ 30 **Sales Invoice #652** **Dated October 25, 2021**

To Veronica Kain School of Dance, to fill sales order #52, $2 500 for contracted services for one month. Terms: 1/10, n/30. Store as a recurring monthly entry.

Click the **Statements Icon** to open the **Fees Journal**. Statement should be selected as the Transaction type.

PRO VERSION
Click the Sales Invoices icon to open the Sales Journal. Invoice will be selected as the Transaction type.

Select **Sales Order #52** from the Order/Quote No. list and **press** tab to recall the order as a statement or invoice:

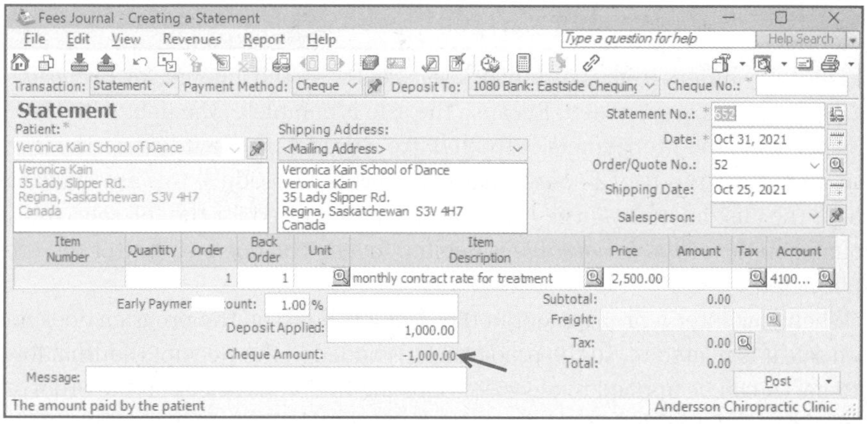

Or, click the Patient Orders icon to open the Order form of the journal. Choose #52 from the Order No. drop-down list and press tab to recall the order. Then choose Convert This Patient Order To A Statement from the Convert drop-down list, or choose Statement from the Transaction drop-down list to change the order to a statement.

NOTES
When the deposit for a sales order is entered as a receipt separately from the sales order, the deposit amount does not appear in the Sales Journal when you fill the order.

Information about the deposit is included on the invoice. Because the deposit was paid by cheque, this is also the default payment method for the invoice, and we need to change it.

Click the **Payment Method list arrow** and **choose Pay Later**.

In the modified form the Bank and Cheque Number fields have been removed.

PRO VERSION
Choose the Sales menu and click Fill Sales Order.

Click the **Fill Backordered Quantities tool** in the tool bar or **choose** the **Fees menu** and **click Fill Patient Order**.

With this step, you will update the amounts and fill the order:

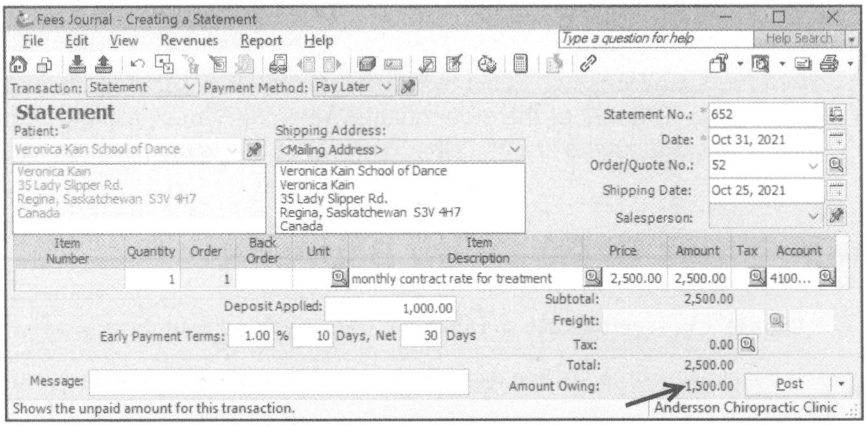

The Cheque Amount field has been removed, but the Deposit Applied details remain. The Amount Owing is reduced by the $1 000 deposit.

Enter **Oct 25** as the date for the sale.

PRO VERSION
Choose the Sales menu and click Enter Additional Information.

Click the **Enter Additional Information tool** or **choose** the **Fees menu** and **click Enter Additional Information**.

Type `Ref SO #52 & deposit #15` as the Additional Information.

Click **OK** to return to the journal.

Choose the **Report menu** and **click Display Fees Journal Entry**:

Andersson Chiropractic Clinic
Fees Journal Entry 10/25/2021 (J21)

Account Number	Account Description	Debits	Credits
1200	Accounts Receivable	1,500.00	-
2250	Prepaid Sales and Deposits	1,000.00	-
4100	Revenue from Services	-	2,500.00
Additional Date:	Additional Field: Ref: SO #52 & de...	2,500.00	2,500.00

NOTES
When the deposit for a sales order is entered as a receipt separately from the sales order, the journal entry for the sale that fills the order does not include the deposit amount.

The entry differs from the standard sales entry — the amount for *Prepaid Sales and Deposits* has been added. Because the sale is complete, the debt with the customer is removed and the prepayment is treated like a partial payment toward the invoice. Thus, *Prepaid Sales and Deposits* has been debited to reduce this account's balance to zero for the customer. *Revenue from Services* is credited for the full sales invoice amount, and *Accounts Receivable* is debited for the balance owing after the prepayment is subtracted.

When you enter a prepayment in the Receipts Journal, the program does not know which sale it is related to, so the prepayment is added in the Receipts Journal for that customer. It can be applied to any sale. Entering the prepayment on the order establishes a link to this sale.

Close the **display**. **Store** the **entry** as a monthly recurring transaction.

Click **Post** to save the invoice. **Click OK** to confirm the removal of the order.

Enter the **next group of transactions** up to Receipt #64. **Change modules** as needed, or **create shortcuts**.

31 **Sales Invoice #653** **Dated October 25, 2021**

To Interplay Ballet School, $2 500 for contracted services for one month. Terms: 1/10, n/30. Store transaction as a recurring monthly entry.

32 **Purchase Invoice #CLS-4723** **Dated October 28, 2021**

From Cleanol and Laundry Services, $120 for contracted laundry service. Terms: net 30. Recall stored transaction.

33

Sales Invoice: 654
Date: Oct 28, 2021

Customer: Debit card sales summary
Address:
Phone No:

Andersson Chiropractic Clinic
betterbacks.com
4500 Rae St.
Regina, SK S4S 3B4
Tel 1: (306) 577-1900
Tel 2: (306) 577-2199
Fax: (306) 577-1925

Treatment description	Amount
Initial assessments	130.00
Follow-up treatments	630.00

Terms: paid by Interac
Direct deposit to Interac account
Signed: *Maria Andersson* **Customer Initials:** **INVOICE TOTAL** 760.00

NOTES

Recall the stored transaction but do not store the changed transaction. When you post the transaction, you will be advised that the transaction has changed and the next due date will be updated. Click Yes to continue. Refer to page 187.

34 **Cash Purchase Invoice #WC-83825** **Dated October 28, 2021**

From Western Communications, $225 including taxes for one month of telephone and Internet service. Invoice total paid by cheque #124 from Eastside Chequing account. Store as a monthly recurring entry.

35 **Sales Invoice #655** **Dated October 28, 2021**

To Canadian Royals, $4 500 for contracted services for one month. Terms: 1/10, n/30. Store transaction as a recurring monthly entry.

36 **Sales Invoice #656** **Dated October 28, 2021**

To Roughrider Argos, $4 900 for contracted services for one month. Terms: 1/10, n/30. Store transaction as a recurring monthly entry.

37 **Receipt #63** **Dated October 29, 2021**

From Interplay Ballet School, cheque #501 for $2 475 in payment of account including $25 discount for early payment. Reference sales invoice #653. Deposited to Eastside Chequing account.

38

Payment Cheque #570 **Dated October 29, 2021**

To Cleanol and Laundry Services, $210 from Regina Chequing account in payment of account. Reference invoices #CLS-2683 and #CLS-3926.

39

Bank Debit Memo #477211 **Dated October 29, 2021**

From Eastside Trust, $2 700 for monthly payroll and $45 payroll service fee withdrawn from chequing account. Store payroll transaction as a monthly recurring entry. Use the General Journal for this payroll transaction.

Entering Receipts for Sales with Deposits on Orders

When a customer makes the final payment toward an invoice that had a deposit with the sales order, the journal entry is different from an entry with a separate deposit.

Open the **Receivables module window**.

✓ 40

Receipt #64 **Dated October 29, 2021**

From Veronica Kain School of Dance, cheque #878 for $1 475 in payment of account including $25 discount for early payment. Reference sales invoice #652 and deposit #15. Deposited to Eastside Chequing account.

Open the **Receipts Journal** and **select Veronica Kain School of Dance**:

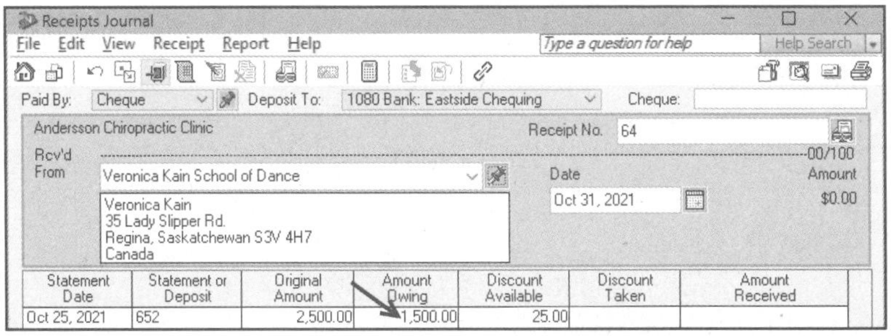

Because the prepayment was cleared at the time of the sale, it does not appear in the Receipts Journal. Instead, the Amount Owing has been reduced, so this is a standard receipt entry. The discount is based on the full invoice amount, or 1 percent of $2 500.

Enter the **remaining transaction details** to complete the entry. **Review** the **transaction** and then **post** it.

Enter the **remaining transactions** for the October 31 session date.

NOTES

Change modules as needed, or create and use shortcuts to enter transactions.

41

Purchase Quote #FS-644 **Dated October 29, 2021**

Starting date November 1, 2021

From Fresh Spaces (use Quick Add for the new supplier), $125 per week for daily laundry service. Terms: net 30.

42

PURCHASE QUOTE #46

Cleanol
and
Laundry Services

19 Duster Rd.
Regina, SK S4R 4L4
(306) 398-0908

Date: Oct 29, 2021
Starting date: Nov 1, 2021

For: Andersson Chiropractic Clinic
Address: 4500 Rae St.
Regina, SK S4S 3B4
Phone No: (306) 577-1900
Fax No: (306) 577-1925
Contact: Maria Andersson

Order description	Amount
Contract for daily laundry service bi-weekly rate including GST terms: net 30 days	210.00
Quote Total	210.00
Deposit	—
Total Amount	210.00

Authorization: Bessie Sweeps

43 **Purchase Order #46** **Dated October 29, 2021**

Starting date November 1, 2021
Convert quote #46 from Cleanol and Laundry Services to an order. The order confirms the price at $210 every two weeks for daily service. Terms: net 30.

44 **Memo #2** **Dated October 31, 2021**

Transfer $1 060 from the Regina Chequing account to pay down the line of credit. This amount includes $60 for one month of interest on the amount of credit used. Store as a monthly recurring entry. (Use the General Journal.)

Advance the **session date** to November 7. **Back up** your **data file**.

WARNING!
If Sage 50 warns that this purchase order number (#46) is greater than the next sequence number, choose Yes to continue with the new numbering sequence. Number 45 was used for the rent quote.

NOTES
To transfer the funds, you should debit the Line of Credit Payable and Interest Expense accounts and credit the Bank account.

Working from the Daily Business Manager

Sage 50 helps a business monitor its performance and cash flow by generating several of the reports covered in previous chapters. It also keeps track of recurring transactions, payments and receipts with the Daily Business Manager lists. These lists offer an additional method of internal control.

You should be in the Home window after changing the session date to November 7. You can enter many transactions directly from the Daily Business Manager.

You can open the Daily Business Manager from the Company window Daily Business Manager icon, the Business Assistant menu or the Daily Business Manager (DBM) tool, and you can also add a shortcut from the Company shortcuts list.

WARNING!
Back up your data file before entering transactions from the Daily Business Manager.

These alternatives are combined in the following screenshot:

Click the **DBM tool**  or click the **Daily Business Manager icon** in the Company module window or **choose** the **Business Assistant menu** and **click Daily Business Manager**:

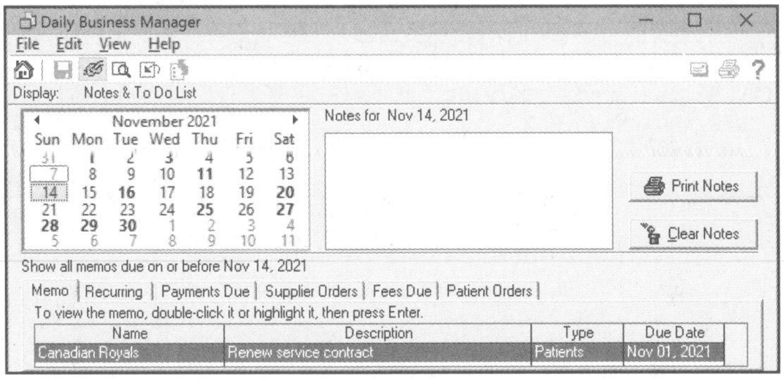

In any journal, you can access the Daily Business Manager from its tool icon  or from the View menu Daily Business Manager option.

You can show Daily Business Manager lists automatically each time you advance the session date, each time you start the program or both. Choose the Setup menu, then choose User Preferences and click View (refer to pages 82–83). Click At Startup and After Changing Session Date below Daily Business Manager to select these options. Menu and tool bar access to the lists are always available.

CLASSIC VIEW

Click the Daily Business Manager tool in the tool bar , or click the Daily Business Manager icon  in the My Business column.

PRO VERSION

The tab labels Purchase Orders, Sales Due and Sales Orders replace Supplier Orders, Fees Due and Patient Orders.

By default, Sage 50 chooses a date that is one week past the current session date for its Daily Business Manager. The date can be changed by clicking a new date on the calendar. Lists will be updated to reflect the change in date.

Each tab screen includes instructions for accessing journals or selecting an entry.

You can also type notes for a date directly into the Notes box. They will remain on-screen for that date until you choose Clear Notes. You can print these notes and clear them when they are no longer needed.

The Memo tab screen opens with a reminder to renew a customer contract. This memo was entered in the customer's ledger Memo tab screen with a due date and the option to display it in the Daily Business Manager.

✓ 45

Memo #3 **Dated November 1, 2021**

Review and update memos and enter the next transactions from the Daily Business Manager. The annual contract for Canadian Royals has been renewed.

Double-click **Canadian Royals** to open the memo in the customer's ledger:

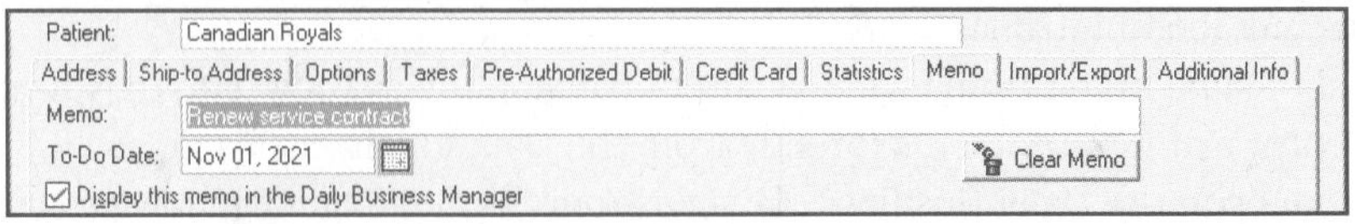

The customer's record opens at the Memo tab screen. You now have the option to edit the memo, remove it if it no longer applies (**Clear Memo**) or change the date that it will appear in the Daily Business Manager. We have checked the option to display the memo in the Daily Business Manager.

Change the **date** in the To-Do Date field to **Nov. 1, 2022**.

Click [Save and Close] in the ledger record to return to the Daily Business Manager. The memo has been removed from the list.

Payments Due

The first journal entry for November is a cheque issued for an outstanding invoice. To be certain that all outstanding invoices are paid in a timely fashion, we can enter payments from the Daily Business Manager.

✓ 46

Payment Cheque #571 **Dated November 1, 2021**

To Sonartek Ltd., $4 380 from Regina Chequing account in full payment of account including $120 discount for early payment. Reference purchase invoice #SL-4622 and cheque #104 (prepayment).

Click the **Payments Due tab**:

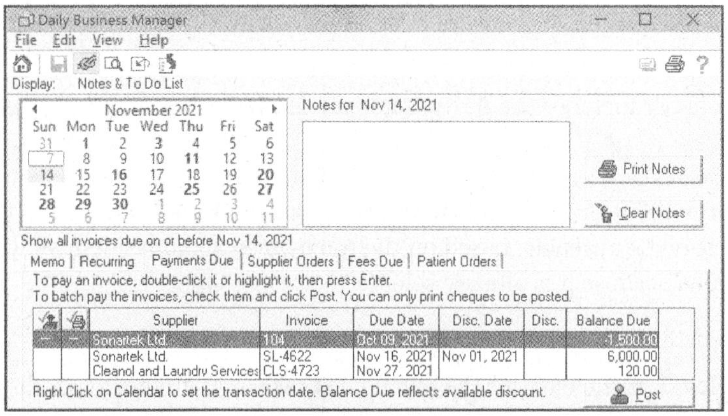

The list includes payments due and any applicable discounts. To add the payments due in a longer period, and to be sure that all discounts available will be included, you can select a later date on the calendar. You might use this list to plan a payment schedule. We want to take advantage of purchase discounts.

The list includes the Supplier name, Invoice number, payment Due Date, Discount Date, Discount availability and the Balance Due (owing). The Discount Date informs you when the discount period ends. You can pay the invoices directly from this screen when no changes are needed. You can also open the Payments Journal by double-clicking an invoice line or by clicking an invoice and pressing *enter*.

If you pay from the Daily Business Manager, the default bank account is used and the session date is the default, so the discount is no longer available. To change the cheque date, right-click the transaction date you want in the calendar.

Right-click Nov 1 on the calendar. The discount for Sonartek is now available.

In the calendar section, November 1 now has an open box framing it to indicate it will be the transaction posting date. The Disc. column now has a ✓ and the Balance Due for invoice #SL-4622 has been updated to include the discount:

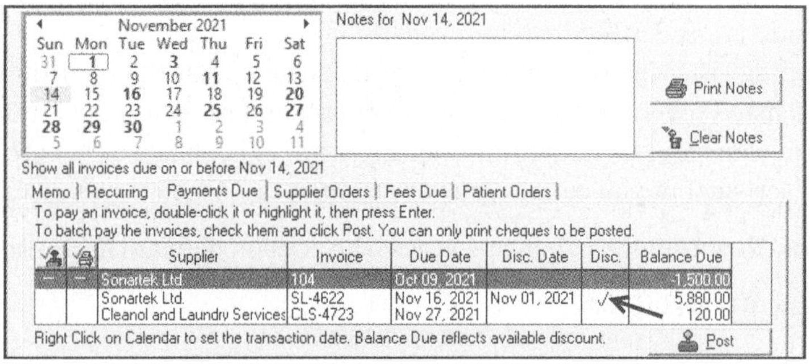

NOTES
After editing the due date for the memo in the ledger, its date is beyond the display period for the Daily Business Manager.

PRO VERSION
Vendor replaces Supplier as the column heading.

NOTES
No payments are due after November 27, so changing the calendar date will not change the display in this example.

NOTES
The prepayment to Sonartek is included on the Payments Due list because it can be selected and "Paid" with other invoices.

NOTES
Right-clicking selects the transaction or posting date, while left-clicking chooses the display period for listed transactions.

If we post from the Daily Business Manager now, the date and discount will be correct, but the bank account will not. The default amount and bank account (*Bank: Eastside Chequing*) will be entered when you pay from the Daily Business Manager, and you cannot change these fields. Therefore, we must open the journal to pay the invoice.

NOTES
You can double-click either the invoice or the prepayment to open the Payments Journal for the supplier.

Double-click the **entry for Sonartek** to open the Payments Journal:

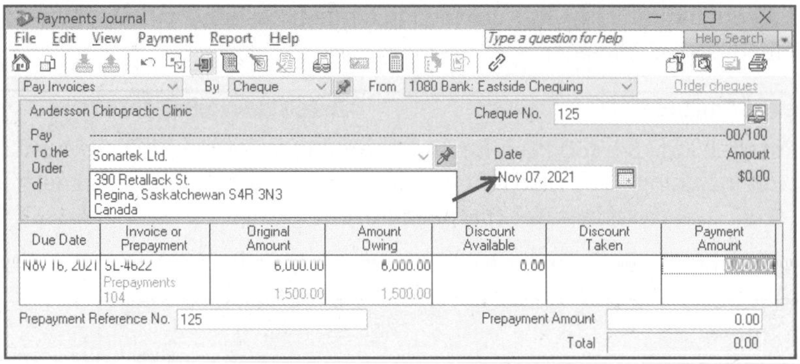

The journal tool bar includes the **Daily Business Manager tool**. All journals include this tool.

The session date is now entered again as the default, so the full amount owing is entered by default without the discount. We must change both the amount and the date. The discount will then be available, based on the full invoice amount. First we will delete the payment amount because it is already selected.

Press *del* to remove the amount.

Enter **Nov 1** as the date for the payment. **Press** *tab* to make the discount available.

Choose **Bank: Regina Chequing** in the From field to update the cheque number.

Click the **Discount Taken field** and then **click** the **Payment Amount field** for the invoice.

Click the **Payment Amount field** for the Prepayment, cheque #104.

Press *tab*. **Enter** the **Invoice** and **Prepayment numbers** as Additional Information to complete the payment. **Check** your **entry**.

Click Post to save the entry when you are certain it is correct.

Close the **Payments Journal** to return to the Daily Business Manager.

Both Sonartek Ltd. entries have been removed from the list.

Click the **Refresh tool** if the list is not updated immediately.

Recurring Transactions Due

The next transaction is a recurring cash purchase.

Another advantage to using the Daily Business Manager is that the recurring entries for all journals are listed together. You can open a journal and recall a stored transaction in a single step. You can also post and print sales invoices, individually or in batches, directly from this screen, but you cannot preview them.

Right-click **Nov 7** on the calendar to reset the session date as the posting date.

Click the **Recurring tab**:

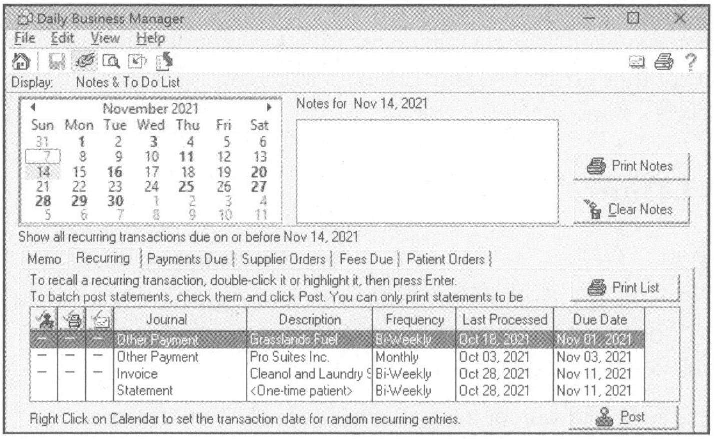

All recurring entries due on or before November 14 (the transaction display date marked on the calendar) should be listed, together with the Journal used for the original entry, the entry name (Description) and its recurring Frequency. The most recent posting date (Last Processed) and the Due Date are also included. The entries are listed according to the Due Date, with the earliest date at the top of the list. Columns for posting, printing and e-mailing that are blank (**without —**) indicate that these actions can be completed directly from the Daily Business Manager window.

✓ 47 **Cash Purchase Invoice #GF-3677** **Dated November 1, 2021**

From Grasslands Fuel, $124 for gasoline for business vehicle. Invoice total paid in full from Regina Chequing account by cheque #572. Recall stored entry.

The first recurring entry — the fuel purchase from Grasslands Fuel — is due Nov. 1. Recurring purchases require an invoice number as additional information, so we need to open the journal first. This payment does not use the default bank account selection.

Double-click **Grasslands Fuel**, the cash purchase entry, to open the journal with this transaction on-screen. (**Click** **30** in the November calendar if all the transactions are not listed.)

Bank: Regina Chequing is preselected as the bank account in the From field because we stored the transaction with this selection. This is another advantage to storing a transaction.

Enter **GF-3677** in the Invoice/Ref. field. If you are using the Make Other Payment approach, you should update the Comment as well.

Post the **transaction** when you are sure it is correct.

Close the **journal** to return to the Daily Business Manager. The Grasslands Fuel entry has been removed.

If necessary, click the Refresh tool to update the Daily Business Manager immediately.

✓ 48 **Cash Purchase #R-2021-11** **Dated November 3, 2021**

To Pro Suites Inc., cheque #125 for $2 300 from Eastside Chequing account to pay rent for November. Recall stored entry.

Double-click **Pro Suites**, the next cash purchase entry, to open the journal.

Enter **R-2021-11** in the Invoice/Ref. field. Copy this number to the Comment line as well if you are using the Make Other Payment method.

Post the **transaction** after making certain it is correct.

Close the **Payments Journal**.

NOTES

If you entered the purchases from Grasslands Fuel and Pro Suites in the Expenses/Purchases Journal, Invoice will be listed as the journal in the Daily Business Manager window and it will open instead of the Payments Journal. In this case, you should enter the transaction in the Expenses Journal.

Our examples used the Make Other Payment option in the Payments Journal.

NOTES

Advance the calendar date selection in the Daily Business Manager if the recurring transaction is not listed.

NOTES

You may need to scroll up in the transaction section of the Payments Journal to include the original entry. The transaction detail area of the journal may appear blank.

NOTES

Clicking anywhere in the Daily Business Manager window will also update the list, or you can click the Refresh tool.

The Recurring Transactions list has been updated again — the Pro Suites transaction has been removed. The remaining list items are not due this week, so we can proceed to another list in the Daily Business Manager.

We want to process some receipts next.

Fees (Sales) Due

✓ 49

Receipt #65 **Dated November 5, 2021**

From Canadian Royals, cheque #4011 for $4 455 in payment of account including $45 discount for early payment. Reference sales invoice #655. Deposited to Regina Chequing account.

PRO VERSION

Click the Sales Due tab. Customer, Invoice and Invoice Date replace Patient, Statement and Statement Date as the column headings.

Click the **Fees Due tab** for a list of Invoices due within the week:

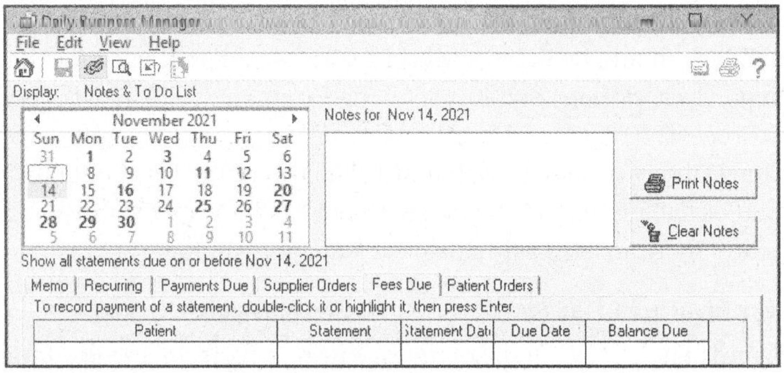

The Fees Due list is easy to use as well. It can be used to locate customers with outstanding debts. The display includes the Patient's name, Statement number and Date, payment Due Date and Balance Due (owing) on the due date without the discount. Invoices displayed can be matched against receipts on hand, and you can open the Receipts Journal directly from this window. No invoices are listed because they are not due in the next week. However, most of Andersson's customers take advantage of sales discounts, so we should look at sales due over a longer span than one week. Payments were received from Canadian Royals and Roughrider Argos. These payments are not due until late November, but the customers are paying early to take the discounts.

We cannot post receipts from the Daily Business Manager because customer cheque numbers should be added. We also need to change the bank account for the deposit when it is different from the default.

Click **30** (left-click) on the November calendar to include all sales invoices due on or before November 30:

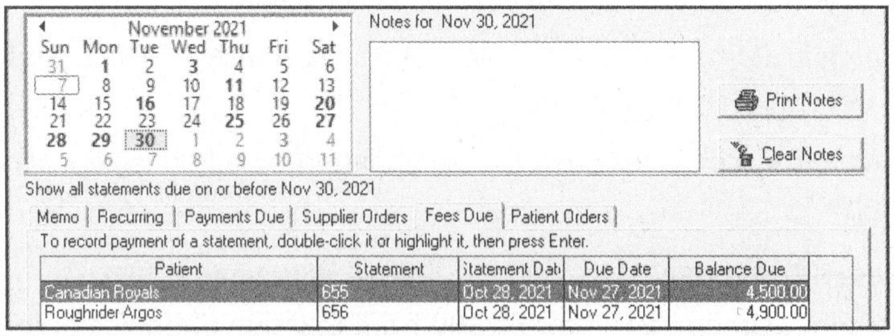

The invoices we need now appear on the list, so we can enter receipts for them.

To open the journal, you can double-click any part of the line for the entry you want or click the line and press *enter*.

Double-click the **Canadian Royals** (Statement #655) to open the Receipts Journal for the selected customer.

Press tab to accept the discount and amount for the first invoice. The amount should appear in the Total field and the upper cheque portion.

Choose **Bank: Regina Chequing** as the bank account in the Deposit To field.

Add the customer's **cheque number** (#4011) in the Cheque field.

Enter **Nov 5** as the date. **Add** the **invoice number** as additional information.

Display the **journal entry** to review your work. **Close** the **display** and **make corrections** if necessary.

Click Post to record the transaction.

Enter the next **receipt** from the Receipts Journal because it is already open.

50 **Receipt #66** **Dated November 7, 2021**

From Roughrider Argos, cheque #1636 for $4 851 in payment of account including $49 discount for early payment. Reference sales invoice #656. Deposited to Regina Chequing account.

Close the **Receipts Journal**. Both Sales Due entries have been removed. **Close** the **Daily Business Manager window** and **enter** the following **Purchase Order** and **Prepayment Cheque** for a new supplier:

51

PO#: 47
Date: Nov 7, 2021
Shipping date: Dec 28, 2021

Ordered from: Get Better Whirlpools
Address: 35 Eddy Circle
Saskatoon, SK S7K 6E3
Phone No: (306) 665-7210 or
(877) 699-1270
Fax No: (306) 663-6281
Contact: Ira Spinner

Andersson Chiropractic Clinic
betterbacks.com
4500 Rae St.
Regina, SK S4S 3B4
Tel 1: (306) 577-1900
Tel 2: (306) 577-2199 Fax: (306) 577-1925

PURCHASE ORDER

Order description	Amount
therapeutic whirlpool (Model WP-299X) including GST and PST terms: net 20 days	24 000.00
Deposit: $2 000 paid by cheque #573 (Regina Chequing Account)	
Order Total	24 000.00
Deposit	2 000.00
Balance Owing	22 000.00

Authorization: *Maria Andersson*

Patient (Sales) Orders Due

Two more Daily Business Manager lists are available: Supplier Orders and Patient Orders. To list outstanding items, click the corresponding tab. Lists for orders display unfilled orders due within the next week. You can access the journal windows for items

WARNING!
If the discount had expired by November 7, the session date, you would delete the default amount and change the date first, as we did for the payment entry. Then re-enter the discount taken and payment amount.

NOTES
If you return to the Daily Business Manager, the default date is correct for the receipt from Roughrider Argos, but you must change the bank account because the default account is incorrect. If you remain in the Receipts Journal, you must change the date.

NOTES
Use Full Add for the new supplier:
Web: gbw.com
Expense account: 1480 Whirlpool (create new account)
Use the source document for the remaining supplier details.

on these lists, just as you did for payments and fees due. We can enter the sale from order #51 on November 9 from the Daily Business Manager.

Advance the **session date** to November 14 and **back up** your data.

✓ 52

Sales Invoice #657 **Dated November 9, 2021**

To Giant Raptors, to fill one month of the contract in sales order #51 for $3 300. Terms: 1/10, n/30.

Open the **Daily Business Manager window**.

Click the **Patient Orders tab**:

PRO VERSION
Click the Sales Orders tab. Customer replaces Patient as the column heading.

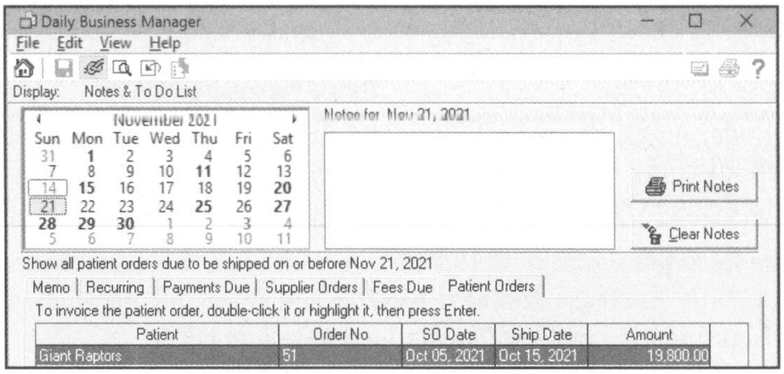

The list displays the Patient, Order Number, order date (SO Date), Shipping Date and Amount. Sales quotes are not displayed.

The order we want is listed. The Ship Date, Oct. 15, is the original one from the order because the order was not completely filled. You can turn the order into an invoice directly from the Daily Business Manager. As usual, double-clicking will open the transaction window we need — the invoice will open as an unfilled order.

Double-click **Giant Raptors** (Order #51).

The Fees Journal opens with the order converted to a statement or invoice. The backordered amount is 5. One month of the contract has already been completed.

Enter **Nov 9** in the Date field.

Click the **Quantity field** and **type** 1

Press *tab* to update the amount. The backordered amount changes to 4.

Check your **entry**, and when it is correct **click Post**.

Close the **Fees Journal** to return to the Daily Business Manager.

The order remains on the list because it has not been completely filled and because the initial shipping date precedes the session date. This date is still entered as the Ship Date.

Purchase Orders Due

The next transaction fills the order from Cleanol and Laundry Services.

✓ 53

Purchase Invoice #CLS-6543 **Dated November 11, 2021**

From Cleanol and Laundry Services, to fill purchase order #46, $210 for contracted daily laundry service. Terms: net 30. Store as a bi-weekly recurring entry. Remove the earlier stored entry then store the new one.

PRO VERSION
Click the Purchase Orders tab. Vendor replaces Supplier as the column heading.

Click the **Supplier Orders tab**:

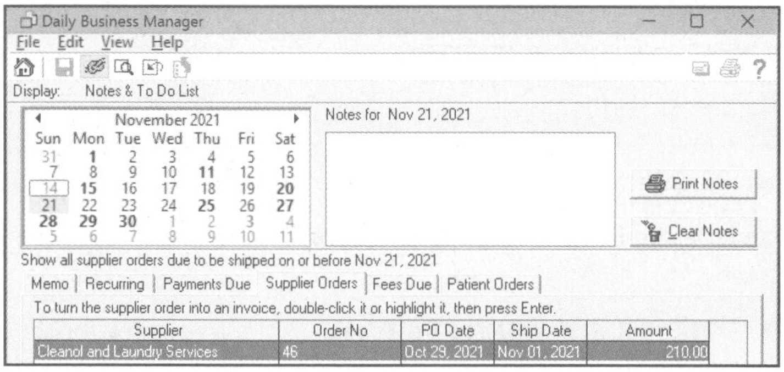

The list displays the supplier, order number, order date, shipping date and amount, making it easy to find orders that you need to track or follow up with the supplier.

We can turn the order from Cleanol and Laundry Services into an invoice from the Daily Business Manager — the journal opens with the invoice as an unfilled order.

Press *enter* to open the journal entry — Cleanol and Laundry Services is already selected.

Enter **CLS-6543** as the invoice number.

Enter **Nov 11** as the invoice date.

Click the **Fill Backordered Quantities tool**.

Enter the **order number** as Additional Information.

Do not post the **transaction** yet because we want to store it.

Removing Recurring Transactions

Sometimes a recurring transaction is no longer required, or it needs to be replaced. If you try to store the new purchase invoice from Cleanol and Laundry Services before removing the old entry, the program will not allow you to continue because the name duplicates the entry on file.

Click the **Store tool**. **Choose Bi-Weekly** as the frequency for the transaction and **click OK**.

You will be warned that the duplicate entry is not permitted. The name and frequency are already stored from a different source transaction:

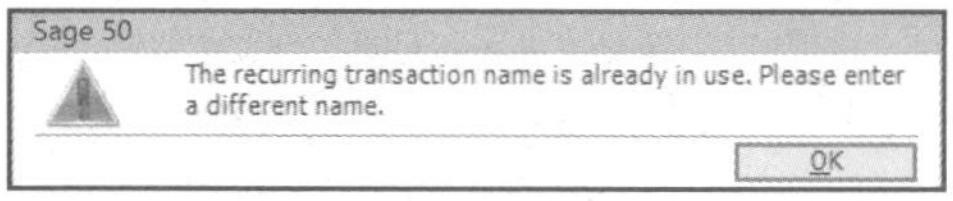

Click **OK** to return to the Store Recurring Transaction screen.

Click **Cancel** to return to the journal. We need to remove the old stored transaction first.

Click the **Recall tool** to open the Recall Recurring Transaction list:

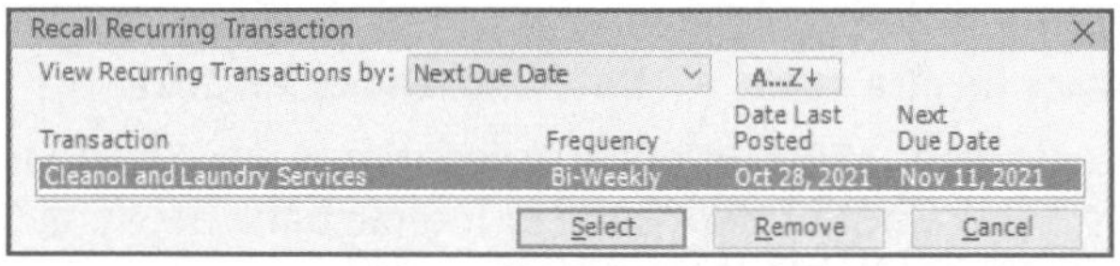

Cleanol and Laundry Services should be selected. If you entered the transactions for Pro Suites and Grasslands Fuel in the Purchases Journal instead of the Payments Journal, they will be listed in this window as well. The entry for Cleanol should still be selected because it is the next entry that is due. If it is not selected, click to select it.

NOTES
The order from Get Better Whirlpool is not listed because its delivery date is later than the Daily Business Manager display date.

NOTES
This is different from recalling a transaction, editing it and then storing it again. In that situation, you can replace the older version. In this situation, we have created a new journal entry first.

WARNING!
When we complete the entry in this way, we cause the next due date to advance, so the date in the Daily Business Manager and on the next Recall screen will be incorrect. You can edit the date in the journal.

Click **Remove** to open the confirmation warning:

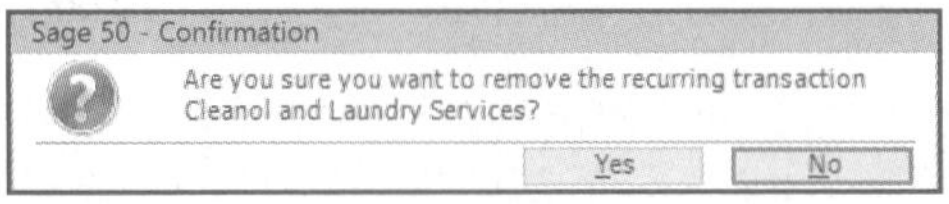

Click **Yes** to confirm the removal if you have selected the correct entry.

Click **Cancel** if the Recall Transaction window is still open. (Read the margin Notes.)

> **NOTES**
> If you have only one recurring transaction, the window closes after you remove it. If there are more transactions, the window stays open and you must click Cancel to close it.

Click the **Store tool**. **Choose Bi-Weekly** as the frequency for the revised recurring invoice.

Click **OK** and then **post** the **purchase transaction**.

Click **OK** to confirm that the filled order has been removed.

Close the **Expenses Journal** to return to the Daily Business Manager. The order is no longer listed.

54 **Debit Card Sales Summary Invoice #658** **Dated November 11, 2021**

To various one-time patients, $260 for initial assessments and $450 for follow-up treatment sessions. Total amount deposited in Interac bank account, $710. Enter the stored transaction from the Daily Business Manager.

Close the **Daily Business Manager**.

Enter the **next of group of transactions**, including the **recurring purchase from Cleanol and Laundry Services** on November 25.

55 **Cash Purchase Invoice #TP-1188** **Dated November 12, 2021**

From The Papery, $230 for paper supplies for treatment rooms and $50 for office supplies. Invoice total $280 paid in full from Eastside Chequing account by cheque #126.

SESSION DATE – NOVEMBER 21, 2021

56 **Receipt #67** **Dated November 18, 2021**

From the Giant Raptors, cheque #1334 for $3 267 in full payment of account including $33 discount for early payment. Reference sales invoice #657. Deposited to Eastside Chequing account.

57 **Purchase Order #48** **Dated November 19, 2021**

Starting date January 1, 2022
From HydraTub Care (use Full Add for new supplier), $200 per month including taxes for one-year service contract. The contract includes weekly maintenance of whirlpool and repairs. Parts required for repairs will be billed separately. Terms: net 20. You must enter 2022 as the year for the starting date.

> **NOTES**
> HydraTub Care
> 550 Splash St.
> Regina, SK S4T 7H5
> Tel: (306) 578-2996
> Terms: net 20 (Pay Later)
> Expense account: 5220
> (Create a new Group account: 5220 Whirlpool Maintenance)

> **WARNING!**
> You must enter the year as 2022 for order #48. If you do not, the program will enter Jan 1, 2021, and this date is not allowed.

SESSION DATE – NOVEMBER 28, 2021

> **NOTES**
> Close the year-end Advisor that opens when you advance the session date.

58 **Debit Card Sales Summary Invoice #659** **Dated November 25, 2021**

To various one-time customers, $260 for initial assessments and $630 for follow-up treatment sessions. Total amount deposited in Interac bank account, $890. Recall the stored transaction and edit the amounts.

59 **Purchase Invoice #CLS-8210** **Dated November 25, 2021**

From Cleanol and Laundry Services, $210 for contracted laundry service. Terms: net 30. Recall the stored transaction. Store it again. (Read the margin Notes.)

> **NOTES**
> If the next due date is incorrect, you can edit the date when you recall the entry. Store it again to reset the next due date.

Posting Directly from the Daily Business Manager

All the Daily Business Manager transactions so far have been posted after opening the journals. Cheques (payments) and recurring sales invoices can also be posted directly from the Daily Business Manager if you can accept the default information, that is, the bank account used.

Posting Sales Directly

Although you can post several sales invoices at the same time, you should open the journal and review each entry to verify it is correct. However, to demonstrate the method we will post one sale without opening the journal.

✓ 60 **Sales Invoice #660** **Dated November 25, 2021**

Post the recurring sale to Interplay Ballet School, $2 500 for contracted services for one month, directly from the Daily Business Manager. Terms: 1/10, n/30.

Open the **Daily Business Manager**. **Click** the **Recurring tab** if necessary.

If you need to print the invoices, click the Print column beside the invoice.

We will post the next recurring sale due on November 25 directly without opening the journal. The date will be entered from the recurring transaction information.

If you need to change the date, you can choose a posting date in the calendar. The calendar displays the week ending December 5. To choose another date in November, you must change the displayed month.
Click the left arrow at the top of the December calendar to access the November calendar.
Click (left-click) 28 to reset the dates and the entries listed. When you first return to the November calendar, November 1 is the session date and the recurring entries are removed.

Click the **Post column** (the first column) **beside** the sale for **Interplay Ballet** to add a ✓.

Click the **Post button** Post in the Daily Business Manager window.

Sage 50 asks if there is additional information to enter before posting:

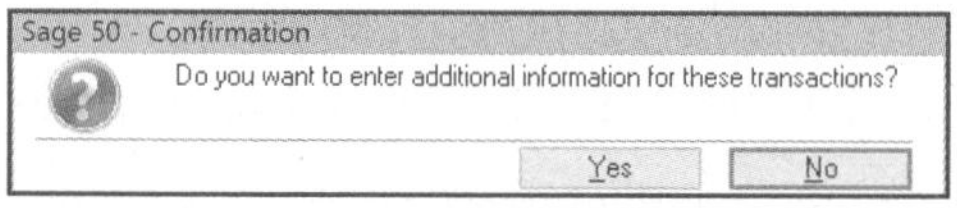

If you want to add details, click Yes to open the Additional Information screen. This screen will not open the journal itself for any other changes — this is the only change you can make. You cannot cancel to return and make other changes. We are not adding these details to the Sales Journal entry. We can continue.

Click **No**. A Sage 50 message names the invoices that are currently being processed and the confirmation:

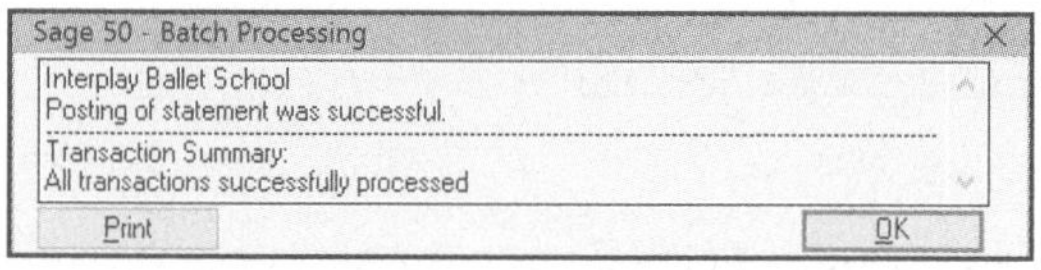

All the invoices that were processed will be listed.

Click **OK** to return to the list of recurring entries. The sale we posted has been removed.

NOTES
Only transactions in journals with print and e-mail options can be posted directly from the Daily Business Manager. The columns for these transactions will be blank so you can select an entry. In the Recurring tab screen on page 439, some entries have a dash (–) beside them signifying you cannot perform the action indicated by the column heading icon.

WARNING!
When you post directly from the Daily Business Manager, you cannot review the journal entry or make other changes.

Opening the journal entry before posting allows you to review the entry and correct errors, if there are any.

If you want to post directly from the Daily Business Manager, back up your data file first and check the posted journal entries to be sure they are correct.

After you click the Post button, you can make corrections only with adjusting entries.

NOTES
You can also right-click to set a posting date. In this case, if you have set the dates correctly, November 25 on the calendar (the posting date) should have an open box framing it and November 28 (the date for showing transactions) should appear in a solid, shaded and coloured box.

If the entry did not post successfully, Sage 50 will provide that information. Check the journal report for the transaction. If it is not included, open the Fees (Sales) Journal to enter the transaction.

Close the **Daily Business Manager**. **Enter** the next **four recurring transactions**. If you enter these from the Daily Business Manager, open the journals and review each journal entry to be certain they will be posted correctly.

NOTES
Advance the Daily Business Manager date to December 31 if necessary to include all recurring transactions.

NOTES
Check that the payment method for Sales Invoice #661 is Pay Later if you use the Daily Business Manager to recall the recurring entries.

61 **Sales Invoice #661** **Dated November 25, 2021**
To Veronica Kain School of Dance, $2 500 for contracted services for one month. Terms: 1/10, n/30. Recall the stored transaction.

62 **Sales Invoice #662** **Dated November 28, 2021**
To Canadian Royals, $4 500 for contracted services for one month. Terms: 1/10, n/30. Recall the stored transaction.

63 **Sales Invoice #663** **Dated November 28, 2021**
To Roughrider Argos, $4 900 for contracted services for one month. Terms: 1/10, n/30. Recall the stored transaction.

64 **Cash Purchase Invoice #WC-122022** **Dated November 28, 2021**
From Western Communications, $225 including taxes for telephone and Internet service. Invoice total paid from Eastside Chequing account by cheque #127. Recall the stored transaction.

Posting Payments Directly

The payment to Cleanol can be posted directly without opening the journal because it uses the default account. The cheque is posted on the session date.

WARNING!
Remember that when you pay from the Daily Business Manager, the default amount and bank account are selected. You cannot change them.
Opening the journal entry before posting allows you to review the entry and correct errors, if there are any.

✓ 65 **Payment Cheque #128** **Dated November 28, 2021**
To Cleanol and Laundry Services, $330 from Eastside Chequing account in payment of account. Reference invoices #CLS-4723 and CLS-6543.

Open the **Daily Business Manager** if necessary. **Click** the **Payments Due tab**.

Click the **Post column** beside **Inv #CLS-4723** and **CLS-6543 (Cleanol and Laundry Services)** to add two ✓s.

Click the **Post button** in the Daily Business Manager window.

You will be asked if you want to enter additional information for the cheque.

Click **Yes** to open the Additional Information window if you want to add the invoice numbers as a reference or **click No** to continue.

NOTES
Choosing to enter additional information will not open the journal, so you will not be able to make other changes.

After a brief period, Sage 50 will confirm the successful posting:

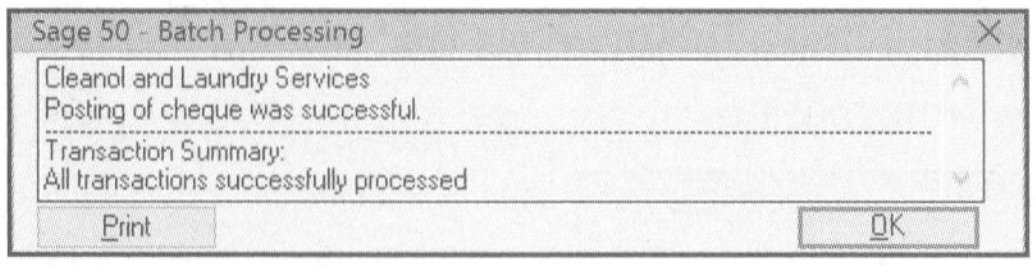

Click **OK**.

Click to close the Daily Business Manager and return to the Home window.

Advance the **session date** to November 30 and **back up** your data file.

Enter the **remaining transactions** for November 30, including memo #8.

66 **Receipt #68** **Dated November 29, 2021**

From Interplay Ballet, cheque #553 for $2 475 in payment of account including $25 discount for early payment. Reference invoice #660. Deposited to Eastside Chequing account.

67 **Bank Debit Memo #747721** **Dated November 29, 2021**

From Eastside Trust, $3 000 for monthly payroll and $45 payroll service fee withdrawn from chequing account 1080. Recall, edit and store the revised transaction because this will be the new monthly salary.

68 **Bank Debit Memo #120022** **Dated November 29, 2021**

From Regina Trust, $75 withdrawn from account for service charges.

69 **Memo #4** **Dated November 29, 2021**

Transfer $1 060 from the Regina Chequing account to pay down the line of credit. This amount includes $60 for one month of interest on the amount of credit used. Recall the stored transaction and change the date.

70 **Bank Debit Memo #747937** **Dated November 29, 2021**

From Eastside Trust, pre-authorized withdrawals from chequing account:
For bi-monthly loan repayment, $1 370 principal and $230 interest
For bank service charges and debit card fees, $108

71 **Cash Purchase Invoice #PPC-76511** **Dated November 30, 2021**

From Prairie Power Corp., $380 including taxes for two months of hydro service. Invoice total paid from Regina Chequing account by cheque #574.

72 **Memo #5** **Dated November 30, 2021**

From Manager: Record the adjusting entries for supplies used in the previous two months:

Office Supplies	$105
Paper and Other Supplies	260

73 **Memo #6** **Dated November 30, 2021**

From Manager: Record the accumulated depreciation for the two-month period for all fixed assets as follows:

Computer Equipment	$ 230
Treatment Equipment	420
Office Furniture	160
Treatment Tables	280
Vehicle	1 100

74 **Payment Cheque #129 & Memo #7** **Dated November 30, 2021**

To M. Andersson (use Quick Add), $5 000 from Eastside Chequing account for drawings to cover personal expenses.

75 **Memo #8** **Dated November 30, 2021**

From Manager: Close out the M.A. Drawings account by transferring the balance to M.A. Capital.

Partially Filling a Quote

Andersson has accepted the rent quote from Pro Suites Inc. and will fill the quote with an invoice paid by cheque for the first month's rent.

NOTES

Enter the drawings cheque in the Expenses (Purchases) Journal or as an Other Payment in the Payments Journal. You can add a memo number as the source if you want.

NOTES

To close the Drawings account, credit Drawings and debit Capital. You can find the amount in the Trial Balance, Balance Sheet or General Ledger.

✓ 76

Cash Purchase Invoice #R-2021-12 **Dated November 30, 2021**

From Pro Suites Inc., $2 350 for one month rent of office space. Fill quote #45 for one month and convert the remainder of the quote to an order. Invoice total paid from Regina Chequing account by cheque #575.

PRO VERSION
Click the Purchases icon or click the Create Purchase Invoice shortcut if you created shortcuts.

Click the **Invoices icon** in the Payables module window or **click** the **Create Invoice shortcut** if you added one to open the Expenses Journal.

Choose **quote #45** and **press** *tab* to place the quote on-screen as an invoice.

The entire quote for 12 months has been entered as the default for the invoice.

Click **12** in the Quantity field and **type** 1

Press *tab* to update the invoice and fill it for one month of rent.

Choose **Regina Chequing** as the account. Cheque is the default payment method.

Click **Post** to record the invoice and open another confirmation message:

WARNING!
If you click No, that is, you do not convert the unfilled part of the quote to an order, you will delete the balance, that is, remove the quote.

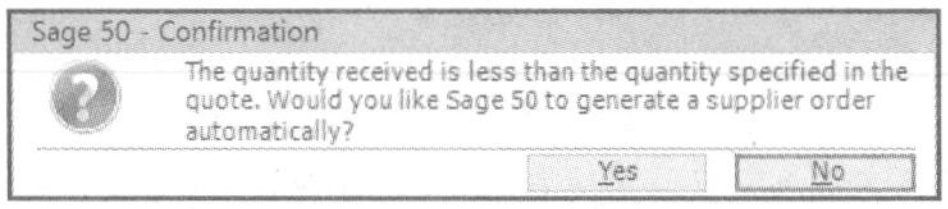

Sage advises you that the entire quote is not being filled and asks if you would like the program to convert the remainder of the quote to an order for 11 months of rent. This order can then be partially filled for one month at a time like any other order.

NOTES
If you open the Quote form now, the Quote number field no longer includes Quote #45. It was removed and converted to Order #45. The Order form will include #45 in the Order number field list.

Click **Yes** to continue and accept the conversion. Do not click No.

If you look up Order #45 now, the backordered quantity will be 11.

Removing Quotes and Orders

Quotes and orders that will not be filled should be removed so that they are not confused with active quotes and orders.

✓ 77

Memo #9 **Dated November 30, 2021**

From Manager: Three purchase quotes that are on file are no longer valid. Remove quote #MT-511 from Medi-Tables, quote #FS-644 from Fresh Spaces and quote #SU-5532 from Space Unlimited.
Remove the recurring transactions for Grasslands Fuel (cash purchase) and Albert Blackfoot (sale) because they will no longer be used.

Choose **Quote** from the Transaction list.

Choose **quote #MT-511** and **press** *tab* to place the quote on-screen.

WARNING!
If you click the Adjust tool, the Remove tool and option will not be available.

Click the **Remove tool** :

Or, **choose** the **Expense menu** and **click** **Remove Supplier Order Or Supplier Quote**. As usual, you must confirm this action:

NOTES
Instead of using the Remove tool, you can choose the Expense menu in the Expenses (Purchases) Journal and click Remove Supplier Order Or Supplier Quote, or the Fees menu in the Fees (Sales) Journal and click Remove Patient Order Or Patient Quote.

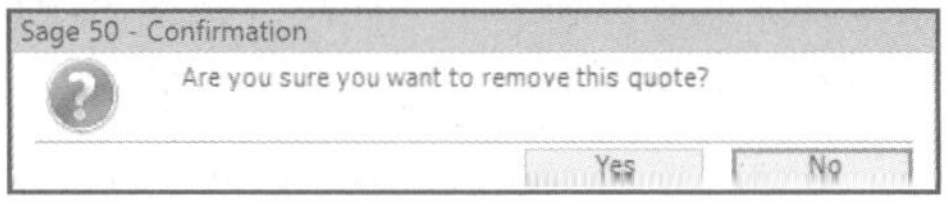

Click **Yes** to confirm.

To remove purchase orders, open the Expenses (Purchases) Journal. Choose Supplier Order from the Transaction list. Choose the order number and press tab to put the order on-screen. Click the Remove Supplier Order tool. Click Yes to confirm the deletion.

To remove sales quotes or sales orders, open the Fees (Sales) Journal. Choose Quote (or Patient Order) as the transaction and then select the Quote or Order No. from the list. Press tab to bring the quote or order onto the screen. Click the Remove Patient Quote Or Patient Order tool. Click Yes to confirm.

Remove the **other two quotes** and the recurring entries that are not needed.

Close the **journal** and then **enter Memo #10**.

78 **Memo #10** **Dated November 30, 2021**

From Manager: Print all financial reports. Back up the data files and start a new fiscal period on December 1, 2021.

NOTES
Refer to page 103 for assistance with starting a new fiscal period if needed.

Displaying Order Reports

Displaying Pending Supplier (Purchase) Orders

Any purchase orders that are not yet filled can be displayed in a report. You can also use this report to check for orders that are delayed or should be removed.

Open the **Report Centre**. **Click Payables** in the Select A Report list.

Click **Pending Supplier Orders Summary By Supplier**.

Click **Modify This Report** to open the report options window:

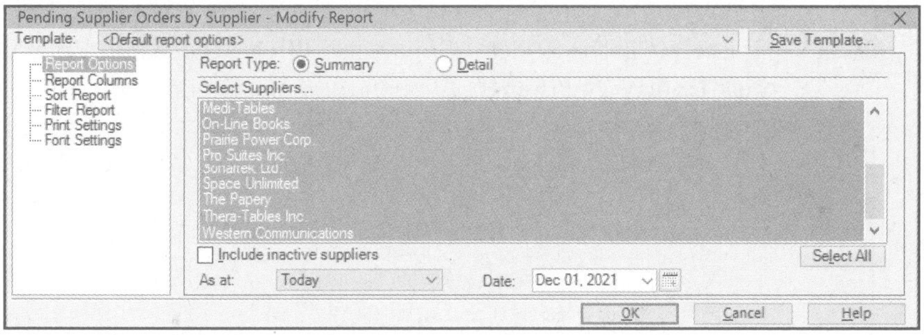

Press and **hold** ctrl and **click** the appropriate **names** in the Supplier list.

Enter **Dec. 31, 2021** as the date for the report. **Click OK** to view the report.

All orders due in the next month should be included in the report. The purchase order with HydraTub Care is not included because its starting date is January 1.

Double-click on any part of the order number line to display the order on-screen. At this stage you can convert and fill the order.

Click the **Modify Report tool** and **enter January 15, 2022** as the report date, or **type** this **date** in the Date field at the top of the report.

Display the **report** again to include all three outstanding orders. **Close** the **display** when you have finished.

Displaying Pending Patient (Sales) Orders

Any sales orders that are not yet filled can be displayed in the Pending Sales Orders Report. You can also use this report to check for orders that should be removed.

NOTES
The Home window Reports menu has an entry for Medical/Dental Reports. This replaces the entry for Service or Retail Reports used in previous chapters for those industry types.

PRO VERSION
Choose Pending Purchase Orders Summary By Vendor.

NOTES
From the Home window Reports menu, choose Payables and Pending Supplier Orders and click By Supplier to access the report options.

NOTES
The Pending Supplier/Patient Orders reports can be sorted and filtered by Order No., Order Date, Ship Date and Amount.

Quotes are not included in the report.

NOTES
From the Pending Orders reports, you can drill down to the Supplier/Patient Aged Report and to the order form.

If you drill down to the order, you can fill the order directly by choosing Invoice as the type of transaction and then filling the order as usual. Confirm your intention to change the order to an invoice.

PRO VERSION
The report is named Pending Sales Orders By Customers.

NOTES
You can also choose the Reports menu, then choose Receivables and Pending Patient Orders and click By Patient to view the report options.
Quotes are not included in the report.

Click **Receivables** in the Select A Report list.

Click **Pending Patient Orders Summary By Patient** to open the sample.

Click **Modify This Report** to open the report options window:

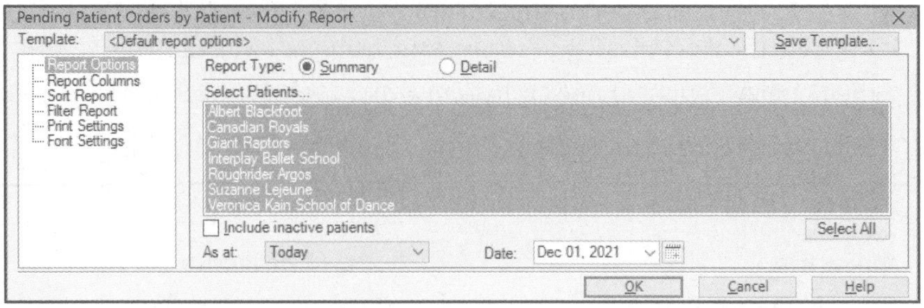

Press and **hold** ctrl and **click** the appropriate **names** in the Patient list.

Enter **Dec. 31, 2021** as the report date to display orders for the next month.

Click **OK** to view the report. One sales order is listed, the partially filled order for the Giant Raptors' contract. It still has the original Ship Date.

Double-click on any part of the order number line to display the order to an invoice and fill it.

Close the **display** when finished.

Displaying Additional Information in Journal Reports

When you choose to include additional fields in the journal entries, you can include these details in the journal reports.

NOTES
You can also choose the Reports menu, then choose Journal Entries and click All to open the report options.
Choose Previous Year as the period to report on. With this change, you will add October 1 and November 30 as the Start and Finish dates for the Journal Report.

Click **Financials** in the Select A Report list. **Click All Journal Entries** and **click Modify This Report** to open the report options window:

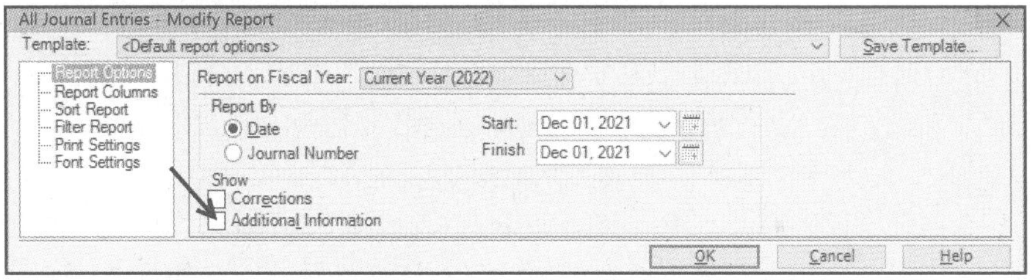

Click **Additional Information** to add a ✓. **Click Corrections**.

Enter the **Start** and **Finish dates** for the report. You must choose Previous year because dates before December 1 are not allowed.

Click **OK**.

Close the **display** when you have finished.

Close the **Report Centre**.

WARNING!
After you start a new fiscal year and change the Do Not Allow Transactions before date from October 1 to December 1, you cannot enter October and November 2021 dates. If you have not changed this earliest transaction date, these earlier dates will be allowed.

REVIEW

The Student DVD with Data Files includes Review Questions and Supplementary Cases for this chapter.

CHAPTER TWELVE

Maple Leaf Rags

OBJECTIVES

After completing this chapter, you should be able to

- ***make*** payments toward credit card accounts
- ***make*** GST, HST and PST remittances
- ***apply*** sales taxes to interprovincial sales
- ***enter*** sales and receipts for foreign customers
- ***enter*** purchases and payments for foreign suppliers
- ***access*** supplier or customer Web sites
- ***e-mail*** invoices to customers
- ***look up*** invoices after posting them
- ***track*** shipments to customers
- ***transfer*** funds between different currency bank accounts
- ***monitor*** business routines with checklists
- ***create*** an Accountant's Copy of data for year-end adjustments
- ***import*** Accountant's Copy journal entries

COMPANY INFORMATION

Company Profile

NOTES

Maple Leaf Rags Inc.
2642 Coldstream Avenue
Nanaimo, BC V9T 2X2
Tel 1: (250) 63M-USIC
Tel 2: (888) 63M-USIC
Fax: (250) 633-4888
Business No.: 128 488 632

Rag is a style of music set in ragtime. Many of Scott Joplin's tunes, including "Maple Leaf Rag," are examples of ragtime music.

Maple Leaf Rags Inc. is a privately held corporation operated by Jaz Bands. After a few years on the east coast, he missed the mountains and moved his small home office from Summerside, Prince Edward Island, to Nanaimo, British Columbia. Bands first considered starting his own business while studying fine arts at Concordia University and business administration at Queen's University. During these years he worked part time in local music stores, dealing with customers who were sometimes frustrated that they had to look in every department to find a variety of types of music by Canadians. With his knowledge and contacts in the music industry and after doing some careful business research, he was ready to establish Maple Leaf Rags Inc., a store specializing in Canadian recording artists. He also sells the book that he wrote and published — *A Guide to Canadian Music*.

NOTES
It was not possible to keep the exchange rates in this chapter current because they were changing so rapidly at the time of writing. The rates used were in effect at the time of writing this chapter.

Maple Leaf Rags Inc. sells music by Canadian artists over the Internet to individuals, both as CDs and as downloads of individual song titles. It also sells CDs to music stores throughout North America, usually to American stores that serve a large Canadian clientele. These stores rely on Bands as a convenient source of Canadian artists' recordings, including Indigenous and ethnic music produced by A.B. Original Sounds, Bands' recording company. Bands hopes to expand the business to other countries where pockets of Canadian populations can be found, such as countries with Canadian Armed Forces bases. His recent book has also been popular with these customers.

Bands is fortunate to be able to rely on the advice of his friend Dave Manga, who started his Outset Media boardgame business in a similar way to Maple Leaf Rags. His friend also shares information about suppliers who might be able to provide some of Bands' supplies.

Maple Leaf Rags has expanded rapidly, though Bands is still able to operate out of his own home because the demands for inventory storage space are small. He pays himself rent for use of his home office space.

Bands buys CDs from various recording studios. He buys CD masters from A.B. Original Sounds, and suppliers across Canada copy and package the CDs for his company at competitive prices. He has accounts set up for all his regular suppliers, many of whom offer discounts for early payments. Bands has also set up accounts for his wholesale customers with discounts for early payment.

At the end of each fiscal year, Bands creates a copy of the data files for the accountant, who checks the accuracy of the accounting records and adds the outstanding adjusting entries.

Bands converted his accounting records to Sage 50 after working carefully through a comprehensive Sage 50 textbook by Purbhoo. The following company information summarizes the conversion after the first nine months of the current fiscal period:

- Chart of Accounts
- Trial Balance
- Supplier Information
- Customer Information
- Accounting Procedures

CHART OF POSTABLE ACCOUNTS

MAPLE LEAF RAGS INC.

ASSETS
1020 Bank: Savings Account
1040 Bank: Chequing Account
1060 Bank: Visa
1080 Bank: MasterCard
1140 Bank: USD
1200 Accounts Receivable
1240 Purchase Prepayments
1280 Office Supplies
1300 CD Inventory
1340 Book Inventory
1380 Prepaid Expenses
1410 Computers
1420 Accum Deprec: Computers
1450 Furniture & Equipment
1480 Accum Deprec: Furn & Equip ▶

▶1500 Automobile
1520 Accum Deprec: Automobile

LIABILITIES
2100 Bank Loan
2180 Prepaid Sales and Deposits
2200 Accounts Payable
2250 Amex Payable
2260 Visa Payable
2460 PST Payable
2650 GST Charged on Sales
2660 HST Charged on Sales
2670 GST Paid on Purchases
2680 HST Paid on Purchases
2850 Long Term Loan ▶

▶EQUITY
3560 Common Stock
3600 Retained Earnings
3800 Current Earnings

REVENUE
4100 Revenue from Music Sales
4140 Revenue from Book Sales
4180 Sales Discounts
4200 Freight Revenue
4250 Interest Revenue
4280 Sales Tax Compensation
4300 Exchange Rate Differences

EXPENSE
5100 Advertising & Publicity
5150 Bank Charges & Card Fees ▶

▶5200 Depreciation Expense
5220 Freight & Shipping Expenses
5260 Purchase Discounts
5280 Interest Expense
5300 Internet & Web Site Expenses
5320 Storage Expense
5340 Cost of Books Sold
5360 Materials and Assembly Costs
5380 Cost of CDs Sold
5400 Office Rent
5500 Office Supplies Used
5520 Research Expenses
5560 Telephone Expenses
5580 Travel Expenses

NOTES: The Chart of Accounts includes only postable accounts and the Net Income or Current Earnings account.

TRIAL BALANCE

MAPLE LEAF RAGS INC.

June 30, 2021		Debits	Credits
1020	Bank: Savings Account	$ 76 675	
1040	Bank: Chequing Account	41 000	
1060	Bank: Visa	1 800	
1080	Bank: MasterCard	2 350	
1140	Bank: USD ($665 USD)	860	
1200	Accounts Receivable	71 680	
1280	Office Supplies	600	
1300	CD Inventory	180 350	
1340	Book Inventory	44 840	
1380	Prepaid Expenses	5 900	
1410	Computers	8 200	
1420	Accum Deprec: Computers		$ 1 100
1450	Furniture & Equipment	9 100	
1480	Accum Deprec: Furn & Equip		1 500
1500	Automobile	16 800	
1520	Accum Deprec: Automobile		9 800
2100	Bank Loan		12 000
2200	Accounts Payable		1 540
2250	Amex Payable		390
2260	Visa Payable		860
2460	PST Payable		450
2650	GST Charged on Sales		1 450
2660	HST Charged on Sales		3 634
2670	GST Paid on Purchases	800	
2680	HST Paid on Purchases	200	▶
▶ 2850	Long Term Loan		$ 60 000
3560	Common Stock		160 000
3600	Retained Earnings		29 261
4100	Revenue from Music Sales		389 000
4140	Revenue from Book Sales		61 000
4180	Sales Discounts	$ 6 840	
4200	Freight Revenue		5 460
4250	Interest Revenue		2 150
4280	Sales Tax Compensation		45
5100	Advertising & Publicity	18 800	
5150	Bank Charges & Card Fees	1 980	
5220	Freight & Shipping Expenses	4 810	
5260	Purchase Discounts		850
5280	Interest Expense	3 960	
5300	Internet & Web Site Expenses	2 540	
5340	Cost of Books Sold	32 400	
5360	Materials and Assembly Costs	1 800	
5380	Cost of CDs Sold	194 250	
5400	Office Rent	7 200	
5500	Office Supplies Used	800	
5520	Research Expenses	1 100	
5560	Telephone Expenses	905	
5580	Travel Expenses	1 950	
		$740 490	$740 490

SUPPLIER INFORMATION

MAPLE LEAF RAGS INC.

Supplier Name (Contact)	Address	Phone No. Fax No.	E-mail Web Site	Terms Tax ID
A.B. Original Sounds (Marie Raven)	380 Abbey Rd. Vancouver, BC V3P 5N6	Tel: (778) 882-6252 Fax: (778) 882-1100		1/10, n/30 (before tax) 129 646 733 RT0001
FedEx (DayLee Runner)	59 Effex Rd. Nanaimo, BC V9R 6X2	Tel: (800) 488-9000 Fax: (250) 488-1230	fedex.com	n/1
Grandeur Graphics (Kathy Grandeur)	26 Drawing Way Victoria, BC V8C 3D1	Tel: (250) 665-3998 Fax: (250) 665-3900	wedesignit.com	2/21, n/30 (before tax) 459 112 348 RT0001
Let 'm Know (Jabber Jaws Lowder)	599 Broadcast Rd. Nanaimo, BC V9S 7J8	Tel: (250) 604-6040 Fax: (250) 604-4660	wetellit.com	2/21, n/30 (before tax) 453 925 372 RT0001
Miles 'R on Us (N. Gins)	522 Drivers St. Saskatoon, SK S7F 5E3	Tel: (800) 592-5239 Fax: (306) 591-4929		n/1
Minister of Finance			gov.bc.ca/fin	n/1
Purolator (Speedy Carriere)	46 Shipping Mews Nanaimo, BC V9S 6S2	Tel: (800) 355-7447 Fax: (250) 355-7000	purolator.com	n/1
Receiver General for Canada	Summerside Tax Centre Summerside, PE C1N 6L2	Tel: (902) 821-8186	cra-arc.gc.ca	n/1
Western Tel (Manny Voyses)	45 Nexus Ave. Nanaimo, BC V9R 3D1	Tel: (250) 679-1011 Fax: (250) 679-1000	westerntel.ca	n/7
Wrap It (Able Boxer)	80 Cubit Rd. Richmond Hill, ON L5R 6B2	Tel: (905) 881-7739 Fax: (905) 881-7000		1/5, n/30 (before tax) 634 529 127 RT0001

OUTSTANDING SUPPLIER INVOICES

MAPLE LEAF RAGS INC.

Supplier Name	Terms	Date	Invoice No.	Amount	Tax	Total
Grandeur Graphics	2/21, n/30 (before tax)	6/28/21	GG-1304	$ 400	$ 20	$ 420
Let 'm Know	2/21, n/30 (before tax)	6/30/21	LK-692	$1 000	$120	$1 120
			Grand Total			$1 540

CUSTOMER INFORMATION

MAPLE LEAF RAGS INC.

Customer Name (Contact)	Address	Phone No. Fax No.	E-mail Web Site	Terms Credit Limit
Canadian Sounds (X. Pats)	46 Ontario St. Tampa, Florida 33607 USA	Tel: (813) 930-4589 Fax: (813) 930-7330	XPats@cansounds.com cansounds.com	3/30, n/60 (before tax) $20 000 USD
CDN Music (Michelle Strings)	230 Nightingale Pl. Vancouver, BC V4R 9K4	Tel: (778) 288-6189 Fax: (778) 288-6000	mstrings@upbeat.com cdn.music.ca	3/30, n/60 (before tax) $20 000
Entertainment House (Rob Blinde)	101 Booker St. Toronto, ON M4F 3J8	Tel: (647) 484-9123 Fax: (647) 488-8182	ent.house.com	3/30, n/60 (before tax) $150 000
It's All Canadian (Leaf Mapleston)	39 Federation Ave. Victoria, BC V8W 7T7	Tel: (250) 598-1123 Fax: (250) 598-1000	canstuff.com	3/30, n/60 (before tax) $20 000
Music Music Music (M. Porter)	10 Red Rock Canyon Sedona, Arizona 86336 USA	Tel: (520) 678-4523 Fax: (520) 678-4500	mporter@music3.com music3.com	3/30, n/60 (before tax) $10 000 USD
Total Music (Goode Sounds)	93 Waterside Rd. Fredericton, NB E3B 4F4	Tel: (506) 455-7746 Fax: (506) 455-7000	goode@totalmusic.com totalmusic.com	3/30, n/60 (before tax) $50 000
Treble & Bass (Bea Flatte)	399 Chord Blvd. Nanaimo, BC V9R 5T6	Tel: (250) 557-5438 Fax: (250) 557-5550	bflatte@t&b.com t&b.com	3/30, n/60 (before tax) $30 000
Web Store Customers				Prepaid by Credit Card

OUTSTANDING CUSTOMER INVOICES

MAPLE LEAF RAGS INC.

Customer Name	Terms	Date	Invoice No.	Amount	Tax	Total
CDN Music	3/30, n/60 (before tax)	6/25/21	591	$ 4 500	$ 225	$ 4 725
Entertainment House	3/30, n/60 (before tax)	1/4/21	233	$56 000	$7 280	$63 280
It's All Canadian	3/30, n/60 (before tax)	6/6/21	589	$ 3 500	$ 175	$ 3 675
			Grand Total			$71 680

Accounting Procedures

GST and HST

Maple Leaf Rags Inc. uses the regular method of calculating GST. The GST charged and collected from customers is recorded as a liability in *GST Charged on Sales*. Customers in Ontario pay HST at the rate of 13 percent instead of GST; and New Brunswick, Nova Scotia, Newfoundland and Labrador, and Prince Edward Island customers pay HST at 15 percent. These HST amounts are recorded in *HST Charged on Sales*. Customers in British Columbia pay GST at 5 percent and PST at 7 percent. In the remaining provinces and territories, customers pay 5 percent GST on all their purchases. Bands has set up both GST and HST as taxes with appropriate codes. GST (or HST) paid to suppliers is recorded in *GST Paid on Purchases* (or *HST Paid on Purchases*) as a decrease in tax liability. The balance owing is the difference between the GST plus HST charged and GST plus HST paid. Customers who buy books pay only GST at the rate of 5 percent on their purchases — books are exempt from PST and HST in all provinces.

NOTES

In 2013, British Columbia reverted to collecting and charging PST and GST separately.

Because Maple Leaf Rags is not registered for HST, it is not required to pay HST on purchases from suppliers in provinces that charge HST. For these purchases it pays GST, unless the goods or services are used or "consumed" in that province.

Cash Sales of Services

Cash transactions for Maple Leaf Rags are limited to credit card sales since most of its business is with wholesale customers who have accounts. Bands has merchant Visa and MasterCard arrangements with two financial institutions. Maple Leaf Rags pays a percentage of each sale directly to the credit card companies (the fee is withheld from the sale amount). To simplify the transaction entries, we provide summaries of these credit card sales as if they were to a single customer called Web Store Customers.

Bands uses a Visa gold card and an American Express card for some business purchases and pays annual user fees for these cards.

Discounts

Discounts are calculated automatically by the program when the discount terms are entered as part of the invoices. If the payments are made before the discount term has expired, the discount appears in the Payments and Receipts journals automatically. All discounts are calculated on before-tax amounts. Bands offers a 3 percent discount to wholesale customers to encourage them to pay their accounts on time. Customers who purchase from the Web store and pay by credit card do not receive discounts.

Some suppliers offer before-tax discounts to Maple Leaf Rags as well. These discount terms are set up in the supplier and customer records.

NOTES

The sales tax rules for discounts are complex and may vary from province to province. Rules for federal taxes may also be different from those for provincial taxes. Sage 50 calculates sales discounts as before or after tax but applies the same formula to GST and retail sales taxes. Adjusting General Journal entries may be required to adjust the amount of tax owing and calculate the tax remittance. We have omitted the tax adjustments for sales discounts.

PST

PST, also called Revenue Tax, is charged at the rate of 7 percent on the base price of goods in British Columbia. Wholesale customers do not pay PST on merchandise they buy for resale. Thus, when Bands sells directly to stores, he charges only GST; he does not charge PST to stores because they are not the final consumers of the product. Individual retail customers in British Columbia pay GST and PST on the purchase of CDs, but they pay only GST on books. Customers in other provinces pay GST at 5 percent or HST at the rate for their province. When Maple Leaf Rags makes the PST remittance, it reduces the amount of the remittance by 6.6 percent, the rate of sales tax compensation, when the PST collected amount is greater than $333.33 for the reporting period.

NOTES

Wholesale customers in HST provinces do pay HST on all purchases from Maple Leaf Rags except books.

Freight

Customers who order through the Internet pay a shipping rate of $5 for the first CD or book and $2 for each additional item. Wholesale customers pay the actual shipping costs. GST is charged on freight in British Columbia. Bands has accounts set up with three regular shippers so that he can track shipments online. Their Web site addresses are included in the shipping setup data.

NOTES
Prepayments to suppliers for purchase orders are entered in the Payments Journal (refer to page 411).

Sales Orders and Deposits

When a customer places a sales order, Bands requests a deposit as confirmation of the order. Deposits are entered on the Sales Order form (refer to page 427) or in the Receipts Journal (refer to page 419).

Foreign Customers and Suppliers

Customers outside Canada do not pay GST, HST or PST on goods imported from Canada. Therefore, sales outside the country do not have taxes applied to them. These customers also do not pay any taxes on their shipping charges.

Purchases from suppliers outside of Canada are subject to GST when the goods are used in Canada.

INSTRUCTIONS

NOTES
For Maple Leaf Rags' retail business type, the terms Customer and Supplier are used. Sales and Purchases are used as icon labels in journal names and in reports.

PRO VERSION
Vendors will replace Suppliers for icon, field and report names.

1. **Record entries for the source documents** in Sage 50 using the Chart of Accounts, Supplier Information, Customer Information and Accounting Procedures for Maple Leaf Rags. The procedures for entering each new type of transaction in this application are outlined step by step in the Keystrokes section with the source documents.

   Change module windows as needed, or create shortcuts for journals in other modules.

2. **Print** the **reports for the end of the fiscal period** suggested by the Sage 50 checklists after you have finished making your entries. Refer to the Monitoring Routine Activities section, pages 488–489. If you have started a new fiscal period, choose **Previous Year** to display the reports you need.

KEYSTROKES

Opening Data Files

PRO VERSION
Restore the backup file SageData19\MAPLE1.CAB or MAPLE1 to SageData19\MAPLE\MAPLE. Refer to Chapter 1, page 25, if you need assistance with restoring backup files.

Open **SageData19\MAPLE\MAPLE** to access the data files.

Enter **July 15, 2021** as the first session date for this application.

Click **OK** and then **click OK** again to bypass the session date warning.

Session dates are advanced semi-monthly for Maple Leaf Rags, and the backup frequency is set at half-month intervals. The Receivables Home window opens.

NOTES
Payroll, Inventory and Project are hidden from the Modules pane list because these ledgers are not set up.

Interprovincial Sales and Tracking Shipments

Businesses that ship goods to customers in other provinces usually have accounts set up with shipping companies so they can track shipments. First we enter the sale.

✓ 1

Visa Credit Card Sales Invoice #593 **Dated July 2/21**

To various Web Store Customers, for sales during previous three months:

CDs & downloads (BC customers)	$ 800 plus 5% GST and 7% PST
CDs & downloads (ON customers)	2 080 plus 13% HST
CDs & downloads (other HST customers)	700 plus 15% HST
CDs & downloads (GST customers)	900 plus 5% GST
Book sales	3 000 plus 5% GST
Shipping	680 plus 5% GST

(Shipped by Purolator #PCU773XT)
Invoice total $8 860.40. Paid by Visa.

Click the **Sales Invoices icon** to open the Sales Journal.

Choose **Web Store Customers** from the Customer list. Invoice is correct as the transaction type. Web Store purchases are usually paid by credit card.

Click the **Payment Method list arrow**:

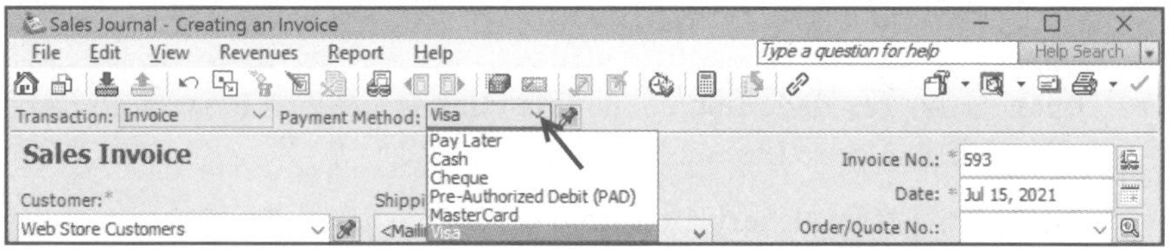

Internet customers have been set up without discounts, so the discount fields are blank. Two credit cards are accepted as methods of payment and Visa, the default entry, is correct for this sales summary.

Type `July 2` (as the transaction date).

Click the **Item Description field** and **type** `CDs & downloads - BC`

Click the **Amount field** and **type** `800`

Press *tab* to advance to the Tax field and **press** *enter* to list the tax codes:

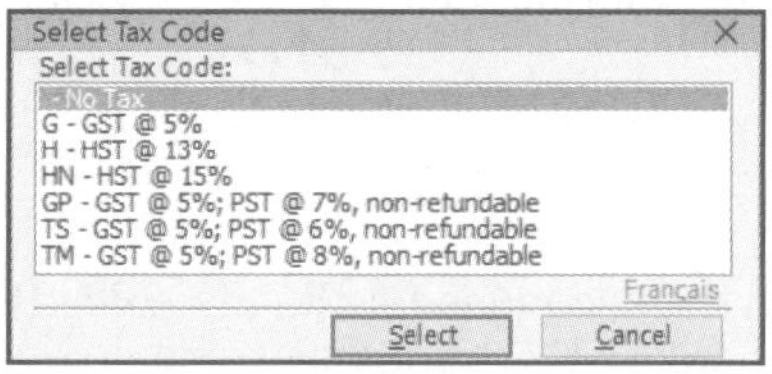

No default tax code has been entered for Internet sales because multiple codes are required. We have created tax codes to accommodate interprovincial sales to customers who pay HST (**code H**, or **HN** for eastern Canada customers) and to customers in other provinces who pay only GST (**code G**). For the first sale, to BC customers, the **code GP** is used (GST rate at 5 percent and PST rate at 7 percent).

Click **GP - GST @ 5%, PST @ 7%, non-refundable**.

Click **Select** to return to the sales invoice and advance to the Account field. Account 4100 is correctly entered as the default revenue account.

Click the **Item Description field** on the second invoice line.

Type `CDs & downloads - ON` **Enter 2080** in the Amount field. **Press** *tab*.

Customers in Ontario pay 13 percent HST, for which we created the tax code H.

Press *enter* or **click** the **List icon** to open the Tax Code list.

Double-click **H - HST @ 13%** to add the code and the account.

NOTES

The shipper has been added to this transaction for illustration purposes only.

NOTES

Usually the same tax code would apply for all invoice lines for a single customer and it can be entered from the customer's record.

NOTES

We have used the tax name PST for provincial sales tax. Three codes apply only to purchases – TS for Saskatchewan (GST @ 5%, PST @ 6%), Q for Quebec (GST @ 5%, QST @ 9.975%) and TM for Manitoba (GST @ 5%, PST @ 8%).

Goods and services purchased and consumed in a province are subject to the PST for that province. Goods shipped to other provinces are exempt from the PST, but not from HST or GST.

Click the **Item Description field** on the next invoice line.

Type `CDs & downloads - other HST provinces`

Click the **Amount field**. **Type** `700` **Press** *tab*.

> **NOTES**
> Remember that you can change the width of a column by dragging its border in the title line of the column. You can customize the journal by removing the Item and Unit columns.

The HST rate at 15 percent applies to sales to customers in the four eastern Canada provinces — code HN.

Press *enter* or **click** the **List icon** to open the Tax Code list.

Double-click **HN - HST @ 15%** to add the code and move to the Account field.

> **NOTES**
> You can also type the tax codes in the Tax field. For example, you can type G (or g) for GST @ 5%, or H (or h) for HST @ 13%.

Click the **Item Description field** on the next invoice line.

Type `CDs & downloads - other provinces - GST` in the **Item Description field** on the next invoice line.

Type `900` in the Amount field and **press** *tab*.

We now need to enter GST at 5 percent — this rate applies to the provinces that do not apply HST.

Open the **Tax Code list** and **double-click** **G - GST @ 5%** to add the code and advance to the Account field.

Click the **Item Description field** on the next line. **Type** `Book sales`

Click the **Amount field** and **type** `3000` **Press** *tab*.

Tax code G is also applied to the sale of books in all provinces.

Open the **Tax Code list** and **double-click** **G - GST @ 5%**.

The cursor advances to the Account field. Book sales are recorded in a separate revenue account, so we must change the default entry.

Type `4140`

There are two freight entry fields in the Sales Journal, below the subtotal amount:

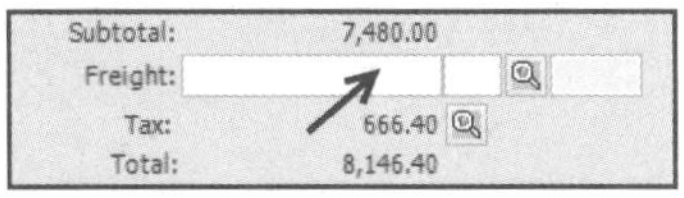

The first field is for the freight amount and the second is for the tax code. Because taxes are paid on freight you must enter a tax code if the customer pays freight. In British Columbia, only GST applies to freight.

Double-click the **first Freight field**. Close the Freight Tax Summary window if it opens.

Type `680` **Press** *tab* to advance to the tax code field for Freight.

Click the **List icon** to display the Tax Code list and **select Code G**.

The tax amount is calculated and added as soon as you enter the amount of freight charged and the tax code. This amount is added to the Tax total.

> **NOTES**
> The tracking number alone is usually sufficient for tracking the shipment.

We will now enter the shipping information so that the shipments can be traced if they are not delivered within the expected time. To track a shipment, you must have the tracking number for the package. To arrange for tracking shipments online, most businesses have an account with the shipper and a password to access the account. When an invoice for these shipments is received from the shipper, it will be entered as a purchase to record the expense to Maple Leaf Rags.

Shippers used regularly can be entered in the Company Settings under Shippers after activating the Track Shipments option:

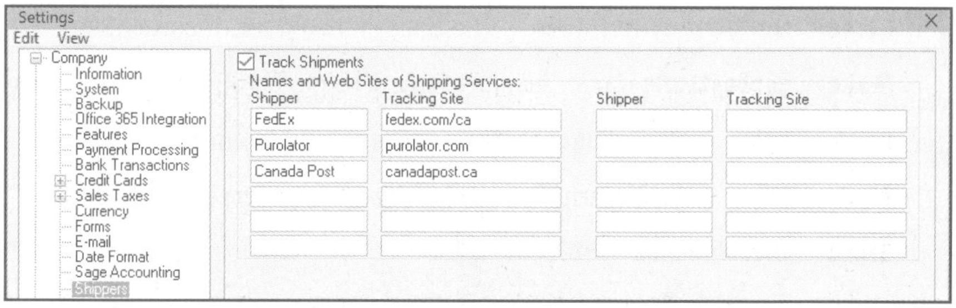

Click the **Track Shipments tool** or **choose** the **Sales menu** and **click** **Track Shipments** to open the shipping data entry window:

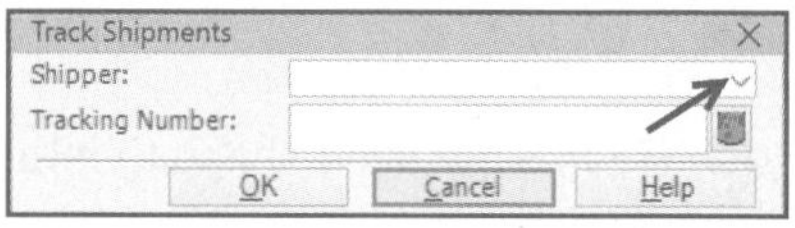

Click the **Shipper field list arrow** to open the list of shippers:

Click **Purolator**. **Press** tab to advance to the Tracking Number field.

Type PCU773XT **Click OK** to return to the completed invoice. Tracking details do not appear on the invoice form.

All taxes are combined on the invoice as a single entry in the Tax field below Freight. For the breakdown of individual taxes paid by the customer,

Click the **List icon** beside the Tax field to display the tax details:

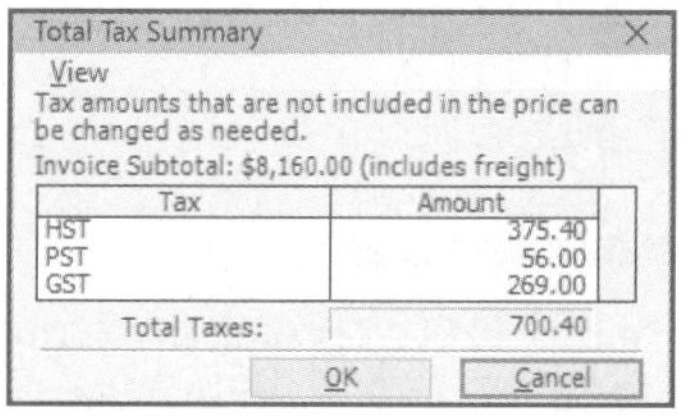

Individual amounts are listed for the three taxes applied to the sale. You can edit these tax amounts if they are incorrect.

Click **OK** to return to the Sales Journal so that you can review it.

Choose the **Report menu** and **click** **Display Sales Journal Entry**:

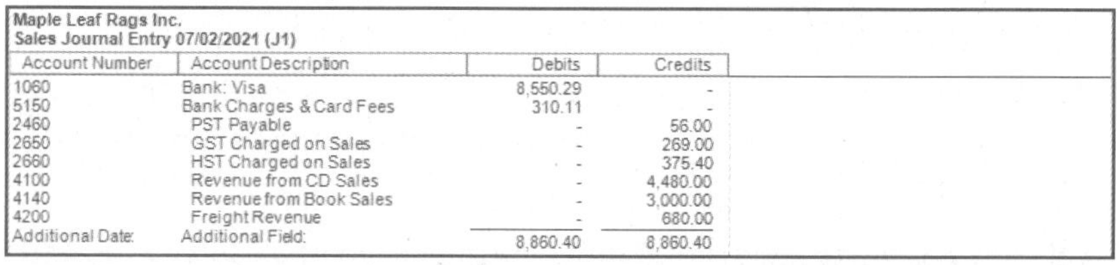
Maple Leaf Rags Inc.
Sales Journal Entry 07/02/2021 (J1)

Account Number	Account Description	Debits	Credits
1060	Bank: Visa	8,550.29	-
5150	Bank Charges & Card Fees	310.11	-
2460	PST Payable	-	56.00
2650	GST Charged on Sales	-	269.00
2660	HST Charged on Sales	-	375.40
4100	Revenue from CD Sales	-	4,480.00
4140	Revenue from Book Sales	-	3,000.00
4200	Freight Revenue	-	680.00
Additional Date:	Additional Field:	8,860.40	8,860.40

Several linked accounts are used for this transaction. The credit card account — *Bank: Visa* — is debited for the total invoice amount minus the transaction discount fees withheld by the credit card company. These fees are debited to the linked fees expense account — *Bank Charges & Card Fees*. Both the *GST* and *HST Charged on Sales* accounts are credited because they increase the tax liability to the Receiver General. PST collected from customers is credited to the *PST Payable* account to reflect

NOTES
You can access the settings for Shippers when the Sales Journal is open and enter additional shippers, but the check box for Track Shipments and the shippers already entered will be dimmed.

NOTES
Pressing ctrl + K will also open the Track Shipments screen from the journal.

NOTES
Tax amounts may be incorrect because rounded off amounts are added together. If tax is calculated for each line, the total may be different from the tax calculated on a single subtotal amount.

> **NOTES**
> When you close the Sales Journal, the Use The Same Customer Next Time tool is automatically turned off or deselected.
> You can also recall the stored Visa sale to enter the MasterCard sales summary. Change the method of payment and the amounts. You will not need to re-enter the descriptions, accounts and tax codes. Store this entry by adding MC to the description.

the increased liability to the Minister of Finance for British Columbia. Freight charged to customers is credited automatically to the linked *Freight Revenue* account.

Close the **display** to return to the Sales Journal input screen.

Make **corrections** if necessary, referring to page 163 for assistance.

Click **Store** and **choose** **Random** as the frequency.

Add **Visa** to the description to identify this recurring sale.

Click **OK** to return to the journal.

The next transaction is also a summary sale to Web Store Customers. We can choose to use the same customer next time so that the customer is selected automatically.

Click the **Use The Same Customer Next Time tool** beside the customer name.

The Use The Same Customer Next Time tool has changed shape to indicate it is selected. Clicking the tool again will turn off the selection.

Click Post. We will not repeat the reminder to click OK.

Create **shortcuts** to enter purchases, payments and General Journal transactions or **change** **modules** as needed.

Enter the second credit card **sale** and the Visa car rental **purchase**.

> **NOTES**
> Remember to select the correct credit card name.
> You do not need to enter shipping information for the remaining Web Store sales.

> **NOTES**
> If a message about credit card processing opens, you can click Do Not Show This Message Again and then close the message.

> **NOTES**
> Because the car rental is purchased and used in Saskatchewan, the Saskatchewan Provincial Sales Tax rate applies. Use tax code TS (GST plus Saskatchewan PST) – the default code for the supplier.

2

MasterCard Credit Card Sales Invoice #594 **Dated July 2/21**

To various Web Store Customers, for sales during previous three months:

CDs & downloads (BC customers)	$ 700	plus 5% GST and 7% PST
CDs & downloads (ON customers)	1 640	plus 13% HST
CDs & downloads (other HST customers)	740	plus 15% HST
CDs & downloads (GST customers)	920	plus 5% GST
Book sales	2 700	plus 5% GST
Shipping	630	plus 5% GST

Invoice total $7 950.70. Paid by MasterCard.

3

Visa Purchase Invoice #MR-1699 **Dated July 2/21**

To Miles ’R on Us, $520 plus 5% GST and 6% PST for two-week car rental while attending trade show in Saskatoon. Invoice total $577.20. Paid by Visa.

Entering Credit Card Bill Payments

Click **Payables** in the Modules pane to open this Home window, if necessary.

> **NOTES**
> If you changed modules for the previous transaction, the Payables window will be open. If you created and used the shortcut, you will need to change the module window.

✓ 4

Visa Payment: Cheque #761 **Dated July 2/21**

To Visa, $723.50 in payment of credit card account, including $609 for purchases charged from May 16 to June 15, $105 for annual renewal fee and $9.50 in interest charges on the unpaid balance from a previous statement.

Credit card payments are entered in the Payments Journal. You can access the bill payment window from the Pay Credit Card Bills shortcut with the Payments icon:

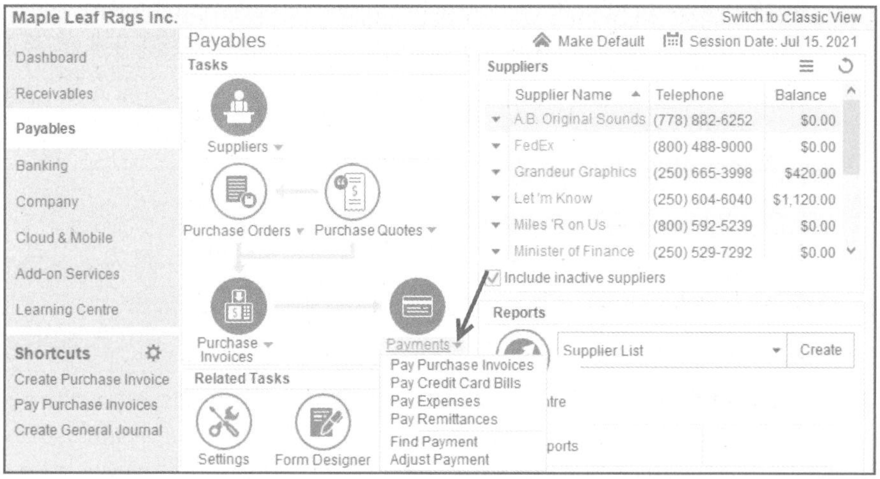

Click **Pay Credit Card Bills** in the Payments icon shortcuts list:

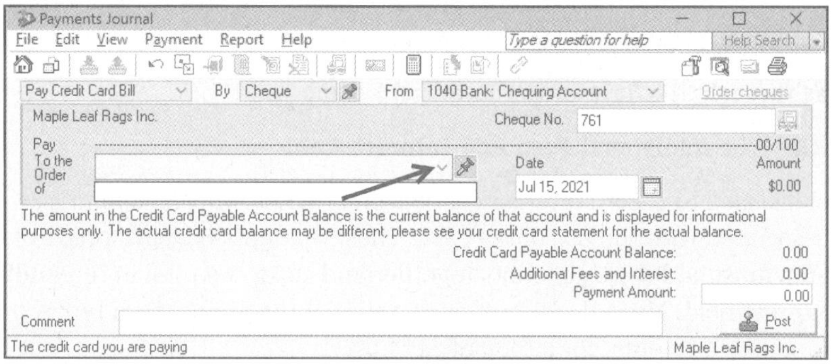

Pay Credit Card Bill is selected as the transaction type in the Pay field. The Pay list in the journal allows you to choose between paying suppliers, paying credit card bills, making cash purchases (other payments) and making payroll remittances. You have the same choices from the Pay field drop-down list as from the Home window.

To access the form you need, you can also click the Payments icon and select Pay Credit Card Bill from the transaction (Pay) drop-down list:

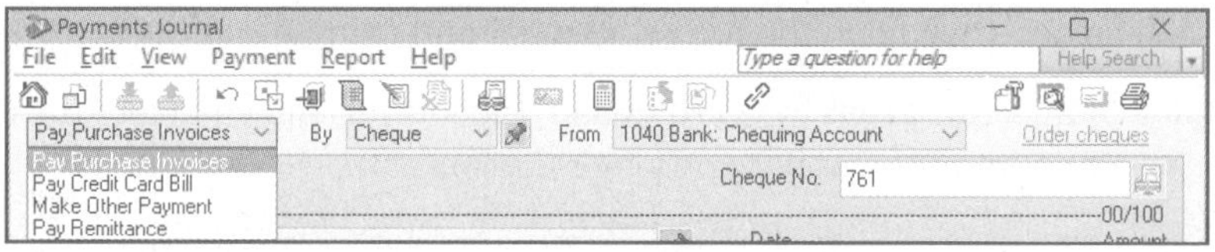

The **By** field (method of payment) has the same options as other journals — payment by cash, cheque or any of the credit cards set up. The **From** field allows you to select a bank account from which to pay because more than one bank account is defined as a Bank class account. The default payment is by cheque. The From list has three bank accounts. The bank account and the cheque number — the next one in the sequence for this account — are correct.

Click the **To The Order Of field list arrow** to access the list of credit cards Maple Leaf Rags has set up for purchases:

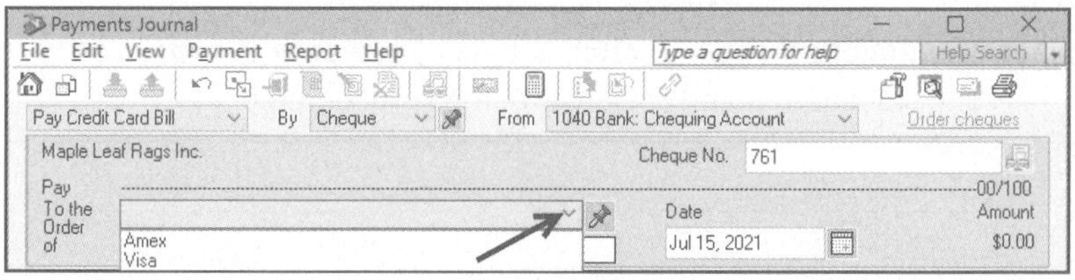

Credit card accounts are set up for Visa and Amex (American Express).

NOTES

All accounts defined as Bank class accounts are on the From list and available for deposits and cheques. Bank class is explained in Chapter 7.

Credit Card accounts are not designated as Bank class accounts in the data files for Maple Leaf Rags.

Bank: Savings Account is not used to write cheques, so cheque numbers are not entered for it.

NOTES
Credit card companies charge interest on cash advances and on statement balances that are unpaid by the due date.

NOTES
When a partial payment is made to a credit card bill, the payment is applied first to interest and additional fees before reducing the outstanding balance from current purchases.

Click **Visa** to update the journal with the Visa account information:

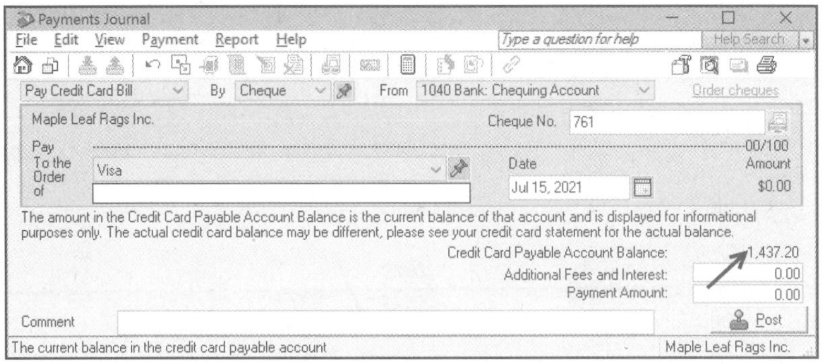

The Account Balance is the accumulation of all unpaid purchases to date according to the General Ledger *Visa Payable* account balance. This amount is not usually the same as the balance that appears on the credit card statement. Purchases after the statement date will not appear on the statement, and interest charges or renewal fees are not included in the General Ledger account balance. The on-screen information also directs you to use the statement for the amounts currently owing.

Drag through the **date in the Date field**. **Type** `Jul 2`

Click the **Additional Fees And Interest field**.

This field is used to record interest charges on previous unpaid amounts as well as other fees associated with the use of the card. These amounts usually appear on the statement. You must add these amounts together and enter the total in the Additional Fees And Interest field. Maple Leaf Rags owes $105 for the annual card renewal fee and $9.50 in accumulated interest for a total of $114.50.

Type `114.50` **Press** *tab* to advance to the Payment Amount field.

In the **Payment Amount** field you should enter the total amount of the cheque that is written in payment, including interest, fees and purchases. This will match the balance owing on the statement if the full amount is being paid, or some other amount if this is a partial payment. The remaining balance in the General Ledger *Visa Payable* account reflects current charges or purchases made after the statement date that will be included in the balance owing on the next statement and paid at that time.

Type `723.50` **Press** *tab* to update the journal and complete the cheque amount in the upper portion of the journal:

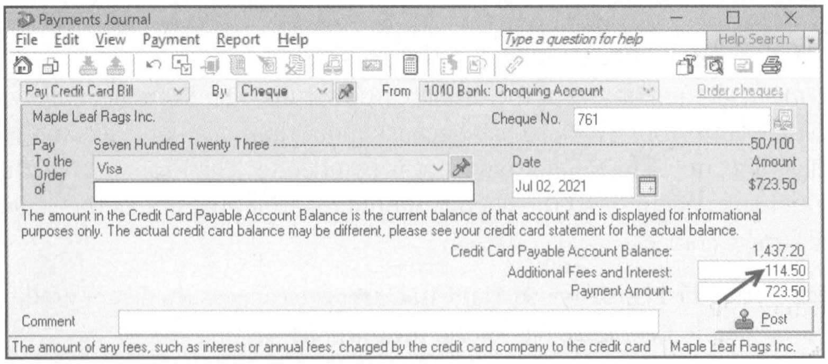

Choose the **Report menu** and **click Display Payments Journal Entry** to display the transaction and review it before proceeding:

Maple Leaf Rags Inc.
Payments Journal Entry 07/02/2021 (J4)

Account Number	Account Description	Debits	Credits
2260	Visa Payable	609.00	-
5150	Bank Charges & Card Fees	114.50	-
1040	Bank: Chequing Account	-	723.50
Additional Date:	Additional Field:	723.50	723.50

The linked Payables bank account is credited for the full amount of the payment. The payment amount is divided between the debit to *Visa Payable* to reduce the liability for prior purchases and the debit to *Bank Charges & Card Fees*, the linked expense account for additional credit card expenses.

Close the **display** when you have finished reviewing it to return to the Payments Journal.

Enter an appropriate **comment** in the Comment field.

Make **corrections** by reselecting from a drop-down list or by highlighting an incorrect entry and typing the correct amount. Press tab after changing an amount to update the totals.

Click Post. Sage 50 provides a message about using the cheque number as the source:

NOTES
This message appears only for credit card bill payments, and only for the first credit card bill payment.

Click **Yes** to continue processing the payment because the number is correct.

Close the **Payments Journal** to return to the Payables window.

NOTES
If you choose Visa in the journal after posting the payment, the balance will match the General Ledger account balance.

Accessing a Supplier's Web Site

Before making the GST remittance, we will search the Canada Revenue Agency Web site in case there are any recent tax changes that affect this business.

✓ 5

Memo #43 **Dated July 3/21**

From J. Bands: Access the Web site for the Canada Revenue Agency to learn whether any recent announcements about GST affect the business.

There are a number of ways to access a supplier record. Because the principles for finding records are the same in all ledgers, we will illustrate different methods.

PRO VERSION
Remember that the term Vendor will replace Supplier.

Click **Receiver General** in the Suppliers pane list in the Payables module window to open the record directly. **Close** the **ledger record**.

You can type text in the Home window Search field or use the Search tool.

Click the **Search field** on the right-hand side of the tool bar (beside Support) in the Home window.

Type `rec` and **press** enter:

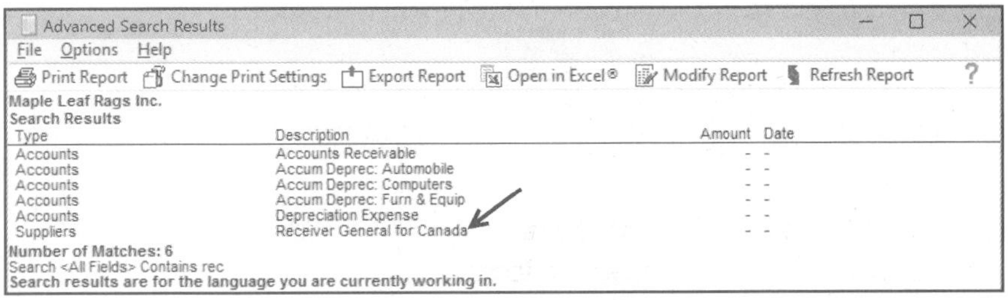

NOTES
The Search field is not case sensitive, so the results from the Search field entry will display all uses of the text you entered in the data file (both Rec and rec). The Search tool allows you to choose the search area, either records or transactions.

Several account names as well as the supplier record we want include this text.

Double-click the supplier **Receiver General for Canada** to open the record.

Close the **ledger record** and **Search window**.

PRO VERSION

The Advanced Search tab and option are not available in the Pro version.

The term Vendor replaces Supplier in all parts of the program.

NOTES

If the last window you had open was a Supplier Ledger, the initial search area will be Suppliers. It would be Payments if you last used the Payments Journal.

You can type a letter in the Search field to advance the list if you have many suppliers.

The Advanced Search feature allows you to define additional search parameters.

NOTES

If you click the Search tool after entering a transaction, you will open the search for a transaction screen. If you click the Search tool after viewing a ledger record, you will list the records for that module.

The Search field is not case sensitive.

NOTES

When you begin a search from another lookup or find location (Home window icon drop-down lists or journal windows), the Select A Record Or Transaction Type field will be dimmed – you will be able to search only for the type you started from.

NOTES

Choosing View Suppliers from the Suppliers icon list also opens the Suppliers window.

Click the **Search tool** :

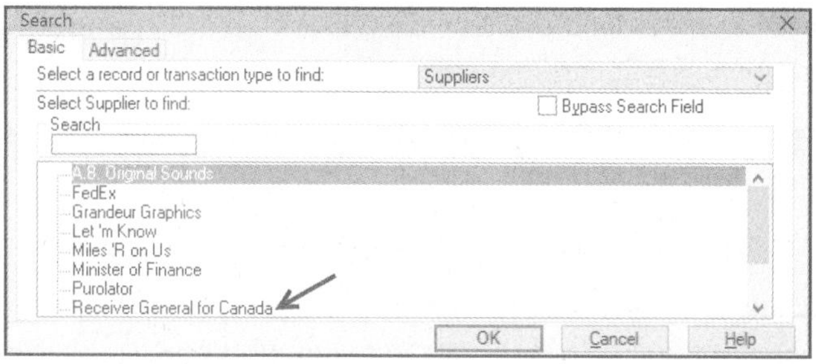

The Search window opens. The default list depends on your previous transaction. We opened a supplier record, so Suppliers is the starting point. When you start from the Home window Search tool, you can select the search area from the Select A Record Or Transaction Type To Find drop-down list in any Search window:

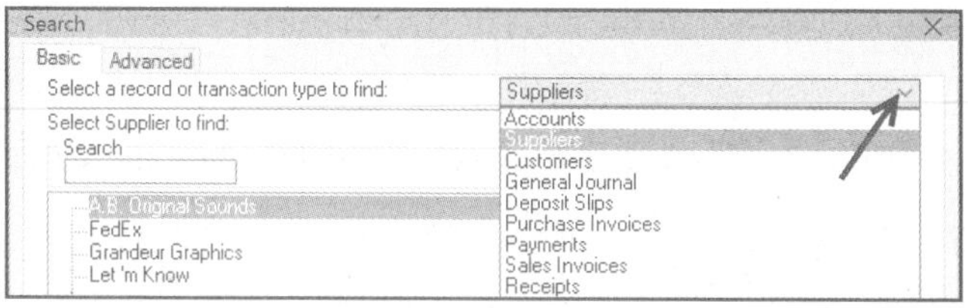

Clicking Suppliers will provide the list of suppliers. Click the Search field and type r to advance to that part of the list. Receiver General for Canada will be selected because it is the first record beginning with r.

Double-click **Receiver General** to open the record. **Close** the **ledger record**.

Another option is to start from the Suppliers icon shortcuts list.

Choose **Modify Supplier** from the Suppliers (Payables window) drop-down shortcuts list to open the Search window:

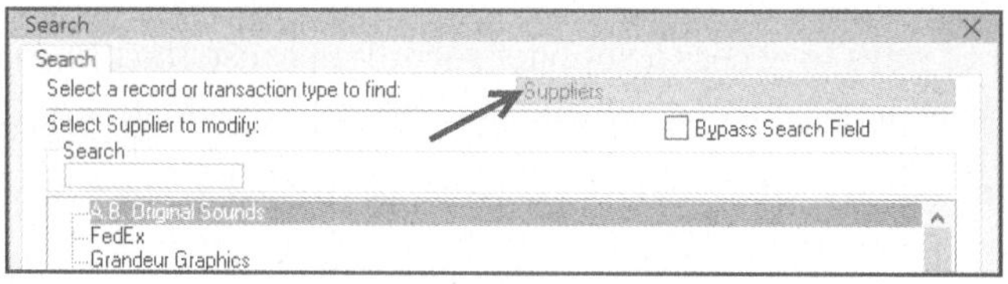

This Search screen looks the same, but **Supplier**, the entry for Select Record Or Transaction To Find, is dimmed. Select Supplier To Modify replaces Select Supplier To Find.

Double-click **Receiver General** to open the record. **Close** the **ledger record**.

You can also access the record from the Suppliers window.

Click the **Suppliers icon**  to open the Suppliers window:

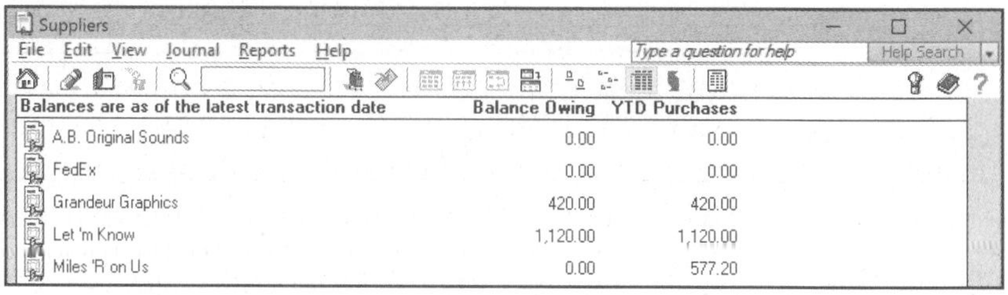

All suppliers are listed with their balances and total year-to-date purchases.

Start your **Internet connection**.

Double-click Receiver General for Canada to open the supplier's ledger:

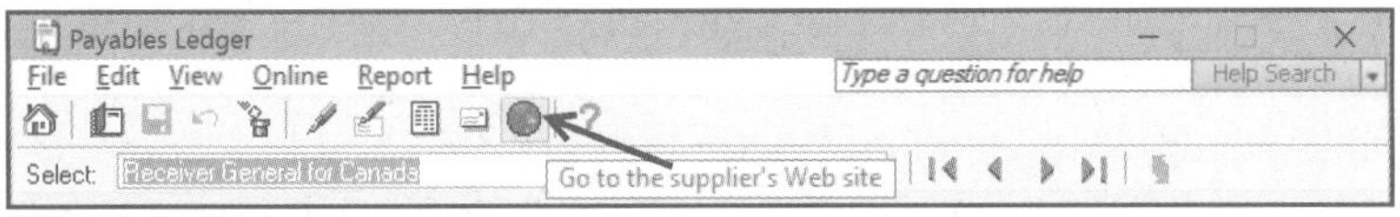

You can access the Web site directly from this Supplier Ledger page when the Web address has been included on the Address tab screen.

With most Internet connection setups you will access the Web site directly. Follow your usual procedure for starting your Internet connection because your setup may be different from ours.

Click the **Web tool** or **choose** the **Online menu** and **click Web Site**:

Canada Revenue Agency / Agence du revenu du Canada
CRA on Canada.ca
The Canada Revenue Agency's web content was successfully migrated to Canada.ca in July 2017. CRA is the theme lead for Taxes on Canada.ca. The majority of the CRA's content is found under the Taxes theme. The remaining content can be found on:
• CRA's institutional profile (for corporate information);
• Open Government (for proactive disclosure content); or
• One of our theme partner's pages (Benefits, Money and finances, Business and industry, or Jobs and the workplace).
Please visit the new Canada Revenue Agency section on Canada.ca.
L'ARC sur Canada.ca
La migration du contenu Web de l'Agence du revenu du Canada vers le site Canada.ca a été réalisée en juillet 2017. L'ARC est responsable du thème Impôts sur Canada.ca.
La majorité du contenu de l'ARC se trouve sous le thème Impôts. Le reste du contenu se trouve aux endroits suivants :
• Profil institutionnel de l'ARC (pour les renseignements d'entreprise);
• Gouvernement ouvert (contenu sur la divulgation proactive);
• Pages de l'un de nos partenaires de thème (prestations, argent et finances, entreprises et industrie, ou emplois et milieu de travail).
Veuillez visiter la nouvelle section de l'Agence du revenu du Canada sur Canada.ca.
Report a problem or mistake on this page
Share this page
Date modified: 2019-02-20

This action should open the Canada.ca home page for the Canada Revenue Agency.

Type `HST rates` in the Search field in the upper right-hand corner and **click** the **Search** icon.

Find some documents about tax rates in different provinces.

Close your **Internet browser** when you have found the information you need or when you have finished. You will return to the supplier's ledger.

Close the **Ledger window**. **Close** the **Suppliers window** if it is open.

Tax Remittances

Tax remittances are entered in the Purchases Journal as non-taxable purchase invoices with payment by cheque or as Other Payments in the Payments Journal. There are two parts to a GST/HST remittance — accounting for the GST (and HST) collected from customers and accounting for the GST (and HST) paid for purchases. The first is owed to the Receiver General while the second part — the input tax credit — is refunded or used to reduce the amount owing. Refer to Chapter 2 for further details. The GST/HST Report can be used to help prepare the return, but the ledger account balances for the date of the filing period should be used as a final check in case there are opening balance amounts that were not entered in the journals. For Maple Leaf Rags, the opening or historical balances are needed. These amounts were not entered through journal transactions, so we cannot use built-in tax reports.

NOTES
Web sites are continually updated, so your screens and sequence of steps may be different from the ones we provide.

NOTES
In 2016, HST rates changed in three Maritime provinces; the rates in PEI, New Brunswick and Newfoundland and Labrador all increased to 15%.

NOTES
The Pay Remittances shortcut for the Payments icon is used only to remit payroll taxes.

NOTES
Tax amounts that you enter on the Sales Taxes screen in the General Journal are included in the tax reports, but opening ledger balance amounts are not.

PST remittances also have two parts — accounting for the PST collected from customers and reducing the tax remitted by the sales tax compensation for filing the return on time.

The General Ledger balances you need are the GST, HST and PST amounts in the Trial Balance on page 453. You can also display or print the Trial Balance or Balance Sheet for June 30 to get the amounts for the following tax accounts:

- 2460 PST Payable
- 2650 GST Charged on Sales
- 2660 HST Charged on Sales
- 2670 GST Paid on Purchases
- 2680 HST Paid on Purchases

NOTES
Electronic filing of GST/HST returns is covered in Appendix K.

Display or **print** the **General Ledger Report** for the tax accounts for June 30, 2021. This report has the amounts you must enter. (Refer to page 61.)

Making GST Remittances

NOTES
If the Payments Journal is already open, choose Make Other Payment from the Pay transactions drop-down list.

CLASSIC VIEW
Click the Payments icon to open the journal and select Make Other Payment from the Pay drop-down list.

NOTES
No default account was entered for the Receiver General because four different accounts are required.

Choose **Pay Expenses** from the Payments icon shortcuts list.

✓ 6

Memo #44 **Dated July 5/21**

From J. Bands: Refer to June 30 General Ledger balances to remit GST and HST to the Receiver General. Issue cheque #762 for $4 084 from Chequing Account.

Choose **Receiver General for Canada** as the supplier.

Choose **July 5** from the pop-up calendar as the transaction date.

Click the **Account field List icon** to display the account list.

Choose **2650 GST Charged on Sales** to advance to the Description field.

Type `Debiting GST Charged on Sales`

Press *tab* to advance to the Amount field. **Type** `1450`

No Tax should be entered as the default tax code. If it is not, select the correct code from the Tax field list icon.

Click the **Account field List icon** on the next journal line.

Choose **2660 HST Charged on Sales** and advance to the Description field.

Type `Debiting HST Charged on Sales`

Press *tab* to advance to the Amount field. **Type** `3634`

Click the **Account field List icon** on the next journal line.

Choose **2670 GST Paid on Purchases**. In the Description field,

Type `Crediting GST Paid`

Press *tab* to advance to the Amount field.

Type `-800` (Use a **minus sign** or hyphen. The minus sign is necessary to enter a negative amount that credits the liability account.)

Click the **Account field List icon** on the next journal line.

Choose **2680 HST Paid on Purchases**. In the Description field,

Type `Crediting HST Paid` **Press** *tab*.

Type `-200` This entry also reduces the amount remitted.

Click the **Invoice/Ref. field**. **Type** `Memo 44` **Press** (tab).

Type `Memo 44, GST/HST remittance for June` in the Comment field to complete your entry:

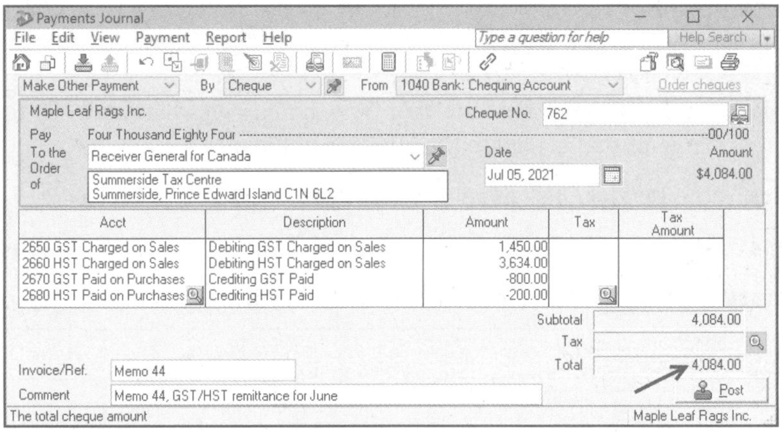

A review of the journal entry will help to clarify the transaction.

Choose the **Report menu** and **click Display Payments Journal Entry**:

Maple Leaf Rags Inc.
Payments Journal Entry 07/05/2021 (J5)

Account Number	Account Description	Debits	Credits
2650	GST Charged on Sales	1,450.00	-
2660	HST Charged on Sales	3,634.00	-
1040	Bank: Chequing Account	-	4,084.00
2670	GST Paid on Purchases	-	800.00
2680	HST Paid on Purchases	-	200.00
Additional Date:	Additional Field:	5,084.00	5,084.00

Normally, a positive amount will create a debit entry in the Payments Journal for an expense or an asset purchase and a credit to the bank account. *GST/HST Charged on Sales* are GST payable accounts with a credit balance. Therefore, entering a positive amount will reduce the GST payable balance by debiting the accounts, as we do when we pay suppliers. The negative entries or credits for the refundable *GST Paid on Purchases* and *HST Paid on Purchase*s will offset the debit balance in the ledger for these contra-liability accounts and will reduce the total amount that is paid to the Receiver General. The net cheque amount is credited to the bank account.

Close the **display** when finished. **Make corrections** if necessary.

Click [Post]. You are now ready to make the PST remittance.

NOTES
GST paid and HST paid are input tax credits that reduce the amount of the remittance.

Making PST Remittances

You should still be in the Payments Journal with Make Other Payment selected as the type of transaction.

✓ 7

Memo #45 **Dated July 5/21**

From J. Bands: Refer to the June 30 General Ledger balance to remit PST Payable to the Minister of Finance. Reduce the payment amount by the sales tax compensation of 6.6%. Issue cheque #763 for $420.30 from Chequing Account.

Choose **Minister of Finance** as the supplier. Accept the default bank account.

Accept **July 5** as the date and **accept** the default **account**, *2460 PST Payable*.

Click the **Description field**.

Type `Debiting for PST collected`

Press (tab) to move the cursor to the Amount field. **Type** `450`

NOTES

Click the Calculator tool to access the calculator if you need to calculate the sales tax compensation amount.

You are now ready to enter the revenue from sales tax compensation, 6.6 percent of the *PST Payable* amount.

Click the **Account field List icon** on the second journal line.

Choose **4280 Sales Tax Compensation**. The cursor advances to the Description field.

Type `Sales Tax Compensation` **Press** tab.

Type `-29.70` (Use a **minus sign**. The minus sign will reduce the total amount that is paid to the Minister of Finance.)

Click the **Invoice/Ref. number field. Type** `Memo 45` **Press** tab.

Type `Memo 45, PST remittance for June` in the Comment field.

Choose the **Report menu** and **click Display Payments Journal Entry**:

Maple Leaf Rags Inc.
Payments Journal Entry 07/05/2021 (J6)

Account Number	Account Description	Debits	Credits
2460	PST Payable	450.00	-
1040	Bank: Chequing Account	-	420.30
4280	Sales Tax Compensation	-	29.70
Additional Date:	Additional Field:	450.00	450.00

The full *PST Payable* amount is debited to reduce the entire liability. Credit entries to the bank account for the amount of the cheque and the *Sales Tax Compensation* revenue account for the amount of the tax reduction balance the transaction.

Close the **display** when you have finished. **Make corrections** if needed.

Click Post. **Close** the **Payments Journal**.

Entering Sales to Foreign Customers

Click **Receivables** in the Modules pane list to open the Receivables window.

Click the **Sales Invoices icon** to open the Sales Journal. Invoice and Pay Later, the default selections, are correct.

✓ 8

Sales Invoice #595 **Dated July 5/21**

To Canadian Sounds, $2 190 USD for CDs and $300 USD for books. Shipped by FedEx (#F19YTR563) for $140. Invoice total $2 630 USD. Terms: 3/30, n/60. The exchange rate is 1.315.

Choose **Canadian Sounds** from the Customer drop-down list and **press** tab:

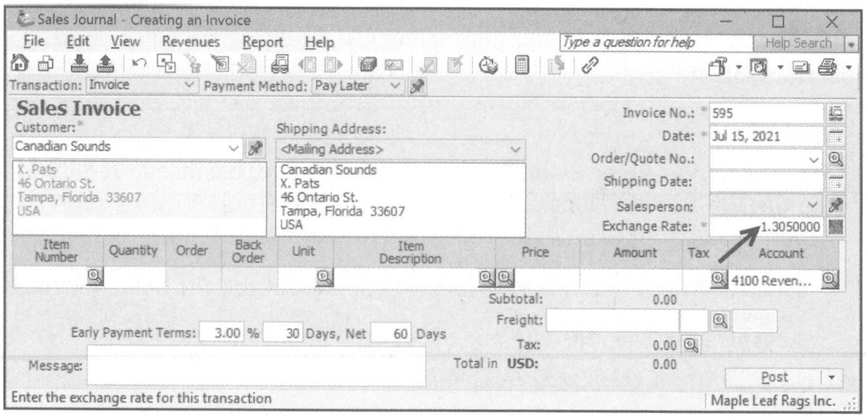

The invoice is modified for the foreign customer. A field for the exchange rate has been added, and the Total is expressed in USD (United States dollars) rather than in

Canadian dollars. An exchange rate button provides a list of exchange rates already entered for various dates. There is no rate for July 5.

Choose **July 5** from the Date field calendar.

The Exchange Rate screen opens because the exchange rate on record is more than one day old and no rate has been recorded for this date:

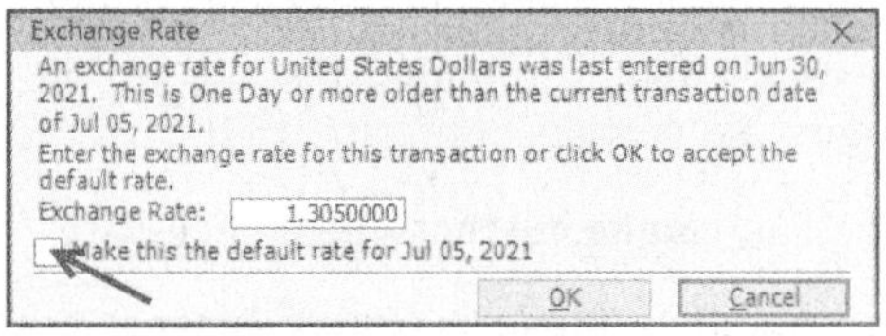

The Exchange Rate setting for the company file warns when the exchange rate on record is more than one day old so that an incorrect old rate is not accepted in error. The most recent exchange rate is entered and selected for editing. You can also edit the exchange rate directly in the journal screen, just as you enter information in other fields.

Type 1.315

Click **Make This The Default Rate For Jul 05, 2021**. **Press** enter or **click OK** to return to the Sales Journal.

Click the **Item Description field**. **Type** CDs

Click the **Amount field**. **Type** 2190 The default revenue account is correct.

Click the **Item Description field** on the next invoice line. **Type** books

Click the **Amount field**. **Type** 300

Click the **Account field List icon** and **select** account **4140**.

Exported goods are not taxable because they are "consumed" outside of Canada. The No Tax code (blank) is entered as the default and it is correct.

Double-click the **Freight field**. Close the Freight Tax Summary window.

Type 140 **Press** tab to update the amounts. Maple does not charge taxes on freight for exported goods.

Click the **Track Shipments tool** .

Choose **FedEx** as the shipper from the Shipped By list.

Press tab to advance to the Tracking Number field.

Type F19YTR563 **Click OK** to return to the completed journal entry:

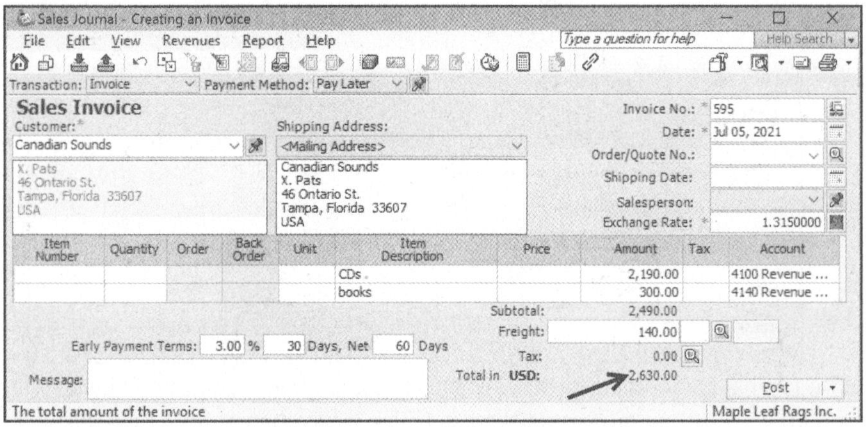

WARNING!
Always check that the date on the Exchange Rate screen matches the transaction date.

Choose the **Report menu** and **click Display Sales Journal Entry**:

Maple Leaf Rags Inc.
Sales Journal Entry 07/05/2021 (J7)

Account Number	Account Description	Foreign A...	Debits	Credits
1200	Accounts Receivable	US$2,630.00	3,458.45	-
4100	Revenue from CD Sales	US$2,190.00	-	2,879.85
4140	Revenue from Book Sales	US$300.00	-	394.50
4200	Freight Revenue	US$140.00	-	184.10
1 United States Dollars equals 1.3150000 Canadian Dollars			3,458.45	3,458.45

Although the journal itself looks the same as for regular invoices — with amounts in US dollars — the journal entry has both the Canadian amounts and the US amounts as well as the exchange rate applied to the transaction. Otherwise, the entry is the same as it would be for sales to Canadian customers. No new accounts are used.

Close the **display** when finished and **make corrections** if necessary.

Click Post to save the transaction. **Close** the **Sales Journal**.

Enter the **next three transactions**.

NOTES

You can use the Additional Field for the invoice number.

Use the default bank account 1040 for receipts from Canadian customers.

9

Receipt #125 **Dated July 5/21**

From It's All Canadian, cheque #884 for $3 570 in payment of account including $105 discount taken for early payment. Reference invoice #589.

NOTES

Wholesale customers who will be selling the product to their own customers do not pay PST.

Enter 1 as the order quantity for sales orders.

10

Sales Order #24 & Deposit #14 **Dated July 5/21**

Shipping date July 10/21

From Treble & Bass, $11 200 for CDs plus 5% GST. Enter one (1) as the order quantity. Shipping by Purolator for $120 plus GST. Invoice total $11 886. Terms: 3/30, n/60. Received cheque #911 for $2 000 as deposit #14 to confirm the order. Refer to page 427.

WARNING!

Remember to change the payment method to Pay Later for invoice #596. Cheque remains selected from the sales order. Refer to page 431. The balance owing is $9 886.

11

Sales Invoice #596 **Dated July 10/21**

To Treble & Bass, to fill sales order #24, $11 200 for CDs plus 5% GST. Shipped by Purolator (#PCU899XT) for $120 plus GST. Invoice total $11 886. Terms: 3/30, n/60. Enter the shipper so you can track the shipment.

Entering Foreign Customer Receipts

Click the **Receipts icon** Receipts to open the Receipts Journal.

✓ 12

Receipt #126 **Dated July 15/21**

From Canadian Sounds, cheque #2397 for $2 551.10 USD in payment of account less $78.90 discount for early payment. Reference invoice #595. The exchange rate for July 15 is 1.320.

Choose **Canadian Sounds** from the customer list:

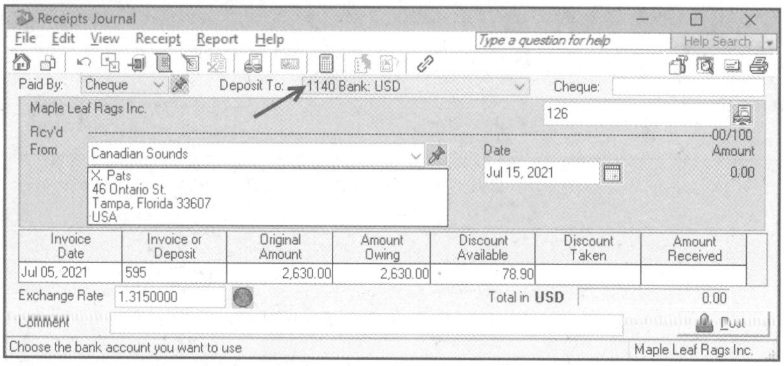

The journal is modified for the foreign customer. The outstanding invoice appears on the screen and the currency is marked as USD. An Exchange Rate field also becomes available with the most recent exchange rate entered.

Deposits from US customers are made to the USD bank account, and this bank is already entered because we chose a USD customer.

Click the **Cheque field**. **Type** `2397`

Click the **Calendar icon** .

Click **15** and **press** *tab* to open the Exchange Rate screen.

If the rate has not changed, you can accept it by clicking Make This The Default Rate For Jul 15, 2021 and clicking OK.

Again, because the last exchange rate we entered was for July 5, the rate is out of date, and we must enter a new one. The previous rate is highlighted.

Type `1.320`

Click **Make This The Default Rate For Jul 15, 2021**.

Click **OK** to return to the Receipts Journal. The cursor is on the calendar icon.

Click the **Discount Taken field**.

Press *tab* to accept the discount because the full invoice is being paid. The cursor advances to the Amount Received field.

Press *tab* to accept the amount and update the cheque portion of the form.

Click the **Enter Additional Information tool** .

Click the **Additional Field text box** to move the cursor.

Type `Ref: inv #595`

Click **OK** to return to the completed journal entry:

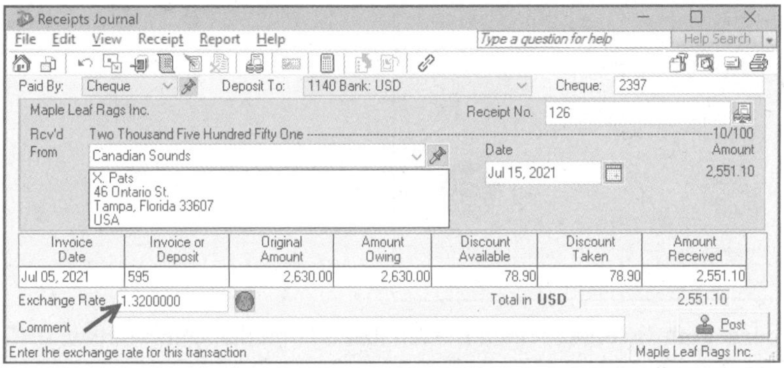

Choose the **Report menu** and **click Display Receipts Journal Entry** to review the entry:

Maple Leaf Rags Inc.
Receipts Journal Entry 07/15/2021 (J11)

Account Number	Account Description	Foreign A...	Debits	Credits
1140	Bank: USD	US$2,551.10	3,367.45	-
4180	Sales Discounts	US$78.90	104.15	-
1200	Accounts Receivable	US$2,630.00	-	3,458.45
4300	Exchange Rate Differences		-	13.15
1 United States Dollars equals 1.3200000 Canadian Dollars			3,471.60	3,471.60
Additional Date:	Additional Field: Ref inv #595			

In addition to the usual linked accounts for receipts, an entry for *Exchange Rate Differences* appears. Because the exchange rate was lower on the day of the sale, the date the revenue was recorded, than on the day of the receipt, there has been a credit to the account. Maple Leaf Rags has gained money on the delay in payment — more Canadian dollars are received for the same US dollar amount when the exchange rate is higher. When the rate decreases, there is a loss. As for foreign customer sales, the journal entry includes amounts in both currencies along with the exchange rate.

Close the **display** to return to the journal and **make corrections** if necessary.

NOTES

The Exchange Rate screen does not open until you "touch" the date field in some way. If the Exchange Rate screen does not open when you enter a date, you can type the exchange rate directly in the Exchange Rate field.

NOTES

The gain/loss situation is reversed for payments to foreign suppliers. When the rate increases, the purchased goods cost more and money is lost. A decrease in exchange rate creates a gain.

Click [Post] to save the transaction.

Close the **Receipts Journal** and **enter** the next **sales transaction**.

NOTES

The Exchange Rate screen does not open for the sale because we already entered a rate for July 15.

Remember to change the revenue account for books.

13

Sales Invoice #597 **Dated July 15/21**

To Music Music Music, $1 630 USD for CDs plus $450 USD for books. Shipped by FedEx (#F27CGB786) for $110. Invoice total $2 190 USD. Terms: 3/30, n/60. The exchange rate is 1.320.

Tracking Shipments and E-mailing Invoices

Lookup provides an exact copy of the posted invoice that you can store, print or e-mail if you have forgotten to do so before posting. This feature can be useful if a customer has an inquiry about a purchase or needs a copy of the invoice. Once a sales or purchase invoice is posted with details about the shipping company, you can look up the invoice to track the shipment to learn when delivery is expected. You can use the Find Invoice approach or the Search feature (read the margin Notes).

NOTES

You can also type Treble in the Search field and press enter.

The result will list the record for the customer and the sales invoice. Double-click the sales invoice entry to open the Lookup screen for this transaction.

The Next and Previous tools will not be available because this sales invoice is the only one that meets the criterion.

✓ 14

Memo #46 **Dated July 16/21**

From J. Bands: Treble & Bass called to inform you that they have not received their shipment of CDs. Look up invoice #596, e-mail a copy of the invoice to the customer and check the delivery status.

Advance the **session date** to **July 31**. **Back up** your data set.

Click the **Sales Invoices shortcuts list** and **choose Find Invoice**:

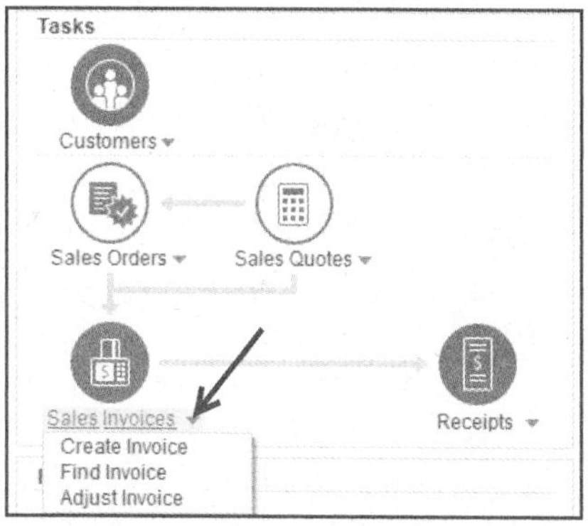

Choose Find Invoice to open the familiar Search dialogue window:

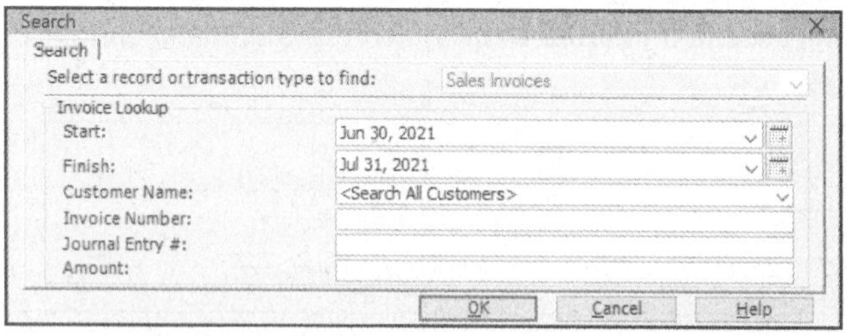

If the Sales Journal is open, you can click the **Look Up An Invoice tool** on the tool bar or beside the Invoice field, or choose the Sales menu and click Look Up Invoice to open this Search window.

The Search screen options for Look Up are like those for adjusting an invoice. You can search through all invoices for the fiscal year to date (or for the previous year if you have not cleared the transactions and lookup data) or enter a narrower range of dates; you can search through invoices for all customers or for a specific customer; or you can search for a specific invoice, journal entry number or amount. Your search strategy will depend on how much information you have before you begin the search and how many invoices there are altogether.

The default Start and Finish dates will include all transactions. You can change these dates to narrow the search, just as you would edit any other date fields, or you can choose dates from the drop-down list or calendar. We want to include all invoices in the search, so we can accept the default range of dates.

The Customer Name option allows you to Search All Customers, the default setting, or a specific customer's invoices. You can also look up the invoices for one-time customers.

To display the list of customers, click the Customer Name field or its drop-down list arrow and click the name you need to select a specific customer.

If you know the Invoice Number, Journal Entry number or the Amount, you can enter that detail in the related field and click OK.

In this case we will select from all invoices — the default to Search All Customers.

Click **OK** to display the list of invoices that meet the search conditions of date and customers:

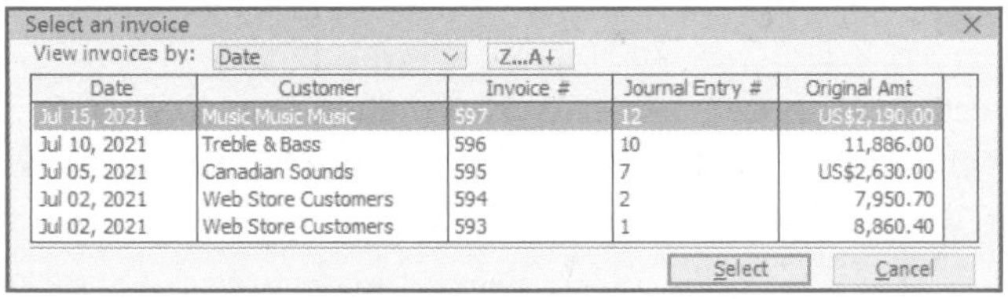

You can sort the list by order of posting date, customer, journal entry number, invoice number or amount. You can also reverse the order of the entries in the list by clicking the Z...A+ button.

Click **Treble & Bass, Invoice Number 596** for $11 886.00 to select it. Click anywhere on the line.

Click **Select** to display the requested invoice:

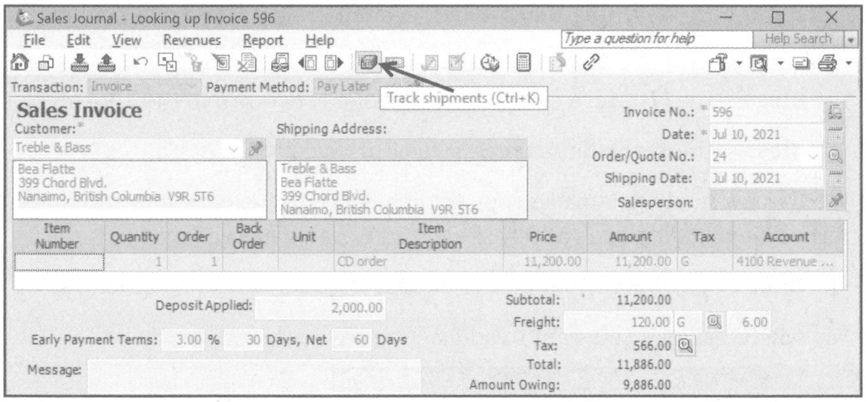

This is an exact copy of the original invoice, except that you cannot edit or post it — there is no Post button. All fields are dimmed, but several familiar tool options are available. You can store, preview, e-mail or print the invoice. Although you cannot adjust an invoice from the Lookup window directly, the Adjust Invoice tool is available. When you click the Adjust Invoice tool, the journal screen changes and the fields become available for editing and posting. You can use the Lookup method to locate the invoice you need to adjust. You can also reverse a transaction directly from the Lookup screen.

If you have selected the wrong invoice, or if you want to view other invoices, you can access them with any Lookup window as your starting point. If there are no invoices in one or both directions, the corresponding tools will be dimmed.

NOTES

If you search by Invoice or Journal Entry number or Amount, you must type an exact match for the invoice you want.

NOTES
If you entered other Search parameters, the Next and Previous tools will let you access all invoices that meet those criteria.

Click **Look Up Next Invoice** or **Look Up Previous Invoice**. Or, choose Previous or Next Invoice from the Sales menu to display other invoices. You can browse through the invoices in this way until you find the one you need. You should practise viewing other invoices by clicking the Look Up Next and Previous Invoice tools.

NOTES
Shippers' names are added with their Web addresses when you enter the Company Settings, making the direct Internet connection available (refer to page 459).

Click the **Track Shipments tool** or **choose** the **Sales menu** and **click Track Shipments** to obtain the shipping details for the sale.

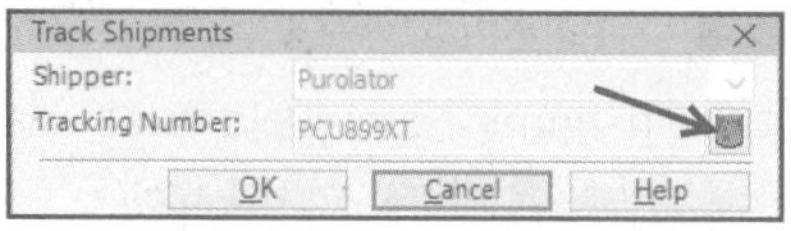

If you need to add or edit the shipping information, click Cancel to close the tracking details window. Click the Adjust Invoice tool in the journal. Make the necessary changes and post the invoice. Then click the Track Shipments tool.

WARNING!
Start your Internet connection before clicking the Track Shipments tool.

Click the Web icon to close the shipping details screen and continue:

If you have actually shipped an item and have entered the tracking number provided by the shipper, you can choose Yes and save the number for entering on the Web site tracking page. However, we do not have an actual tracking number or account with Purolator.

WARNING!
Web sites are continually updated, so your sequence of steps may be different from the ones we provide.

Click **No** to continue to the Internet connection.

Your screen at this stage will depend on your Internet setup — you may connect and access the Web site directly, or you may need to enter your account and password first.

Continue as you would for your **usual Internet connection**.

You will access the Web site for Purolator.

NOTES
You do not need an account to track shipments, but you do need the tracking number.

Enter the **Tracking Number** in the Track field, **click Track** and follow the instructions provided to continue tracking the shipment.

Close the **Web Site screen** when finished to return to the Lookup screen.

Close the **Track Shipments screen** by clicking OK or Cancel.

We are now ready to e-mail a copy of the invoice to the customer with information about the shipping date and carrier. (Read the Warning margin note.)

WARNING!
You must have a valid form file reference in the Reports & Forms Settings for E-mail (Invoice forms). If you have used different computers for your data file, the default form reference may be incorrect. If you get an error message about an invalid form, Click OK to open the Reports & Forms Settings. Choose the generic entry Invoices for both print and e-mail. Custom Form must be selected as the Print Using option.

Click the **E-mail tool** or **choose** the **File menu** and **click E-mail**.

You will be asked if you want to add a company logo:

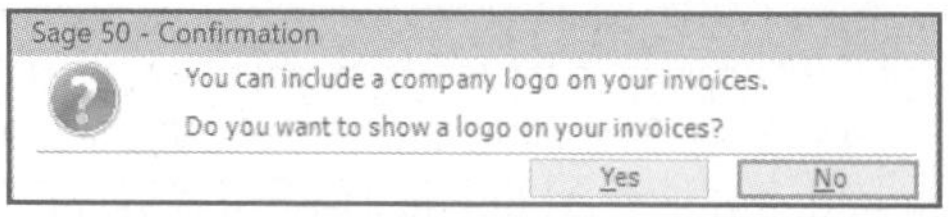

Choose No to continue:

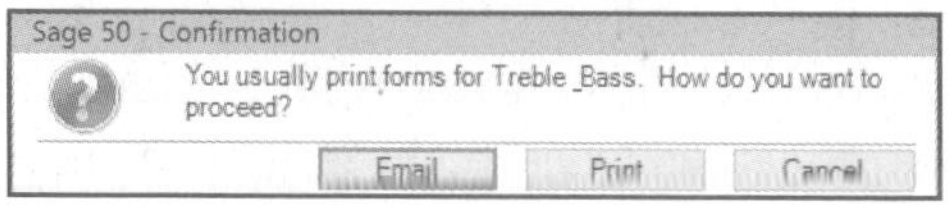

Since printing invoices is the default setting in the customer's ledger record, you are asked if you want to continue, just in case you clicked the wrong button.

Click **E-mail** to continue to the E-mail Information screen:

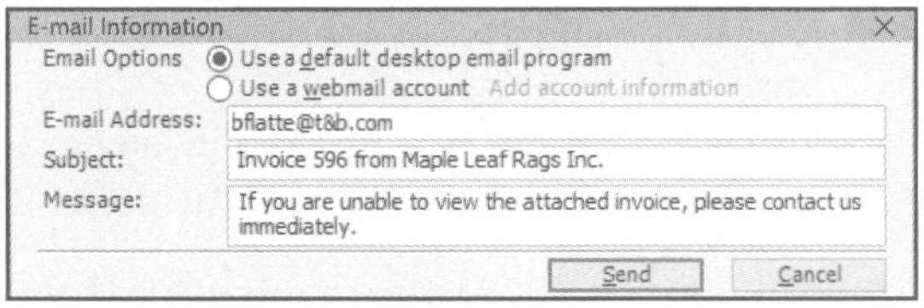

If the e-mail address is missing, you can enter it here. You should replace the address with your own e-mail address if you want to test the e-mail feature.

Type (Type your own e-mail address in this field, or that of a classmate.)

You can add a message in the Message field about the shipment tracking details to inform the customer of the expected delivery date.

Another screen asks whether you want to update the e-mail address in the ledger.

Click **Yes** to update the ledger record and proceed.

You must also enter your e-mail settings. For Webmail accounts you must add account information. Choose your e-mail provider from the drop-down list or select Other and enter the name. If the provider is recognized, you can choose to configure automatically after entering your e-mail address. Your setup will be saved with the data file and you will not need to repeat it.

Click **Send**. You will be asked for your e-mail password, if you have not saved it.

Type **your password** and **click OK** to return to the Sales Journal – Invoice Lookup window.

Close the **Lookup window** to return to the Receivables window.

Your e-mail program will have an e-mail message indicating the attached invoice document Invoice_596.PDF. The following screenshot is from Outlook:

If you have another e-mail program as your default, the single PDF invoice page may be included directly on-screen in your message along with the attached PDF document.

You can click Invoice_596.PDF and Preview File to preview the invoice:

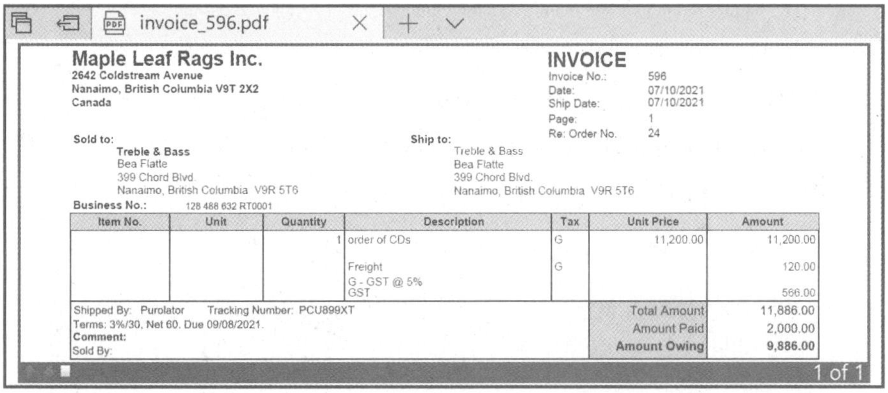

Double-clicking Invoice_596.PDF will open the attached invoice with Adobe Acrobat or Reader. The invoice has the date of the invoice as well as shipping and tracking details. You can print this email, or save a copy.

Close the **email** when finished and then close **the Fees (Sales) Journal**.

NOTES

Gmail, Yahoo and Outlook.com e-mail accounts can be configured automatically. If you are using another e-mail provider that is not recognized by Sage 50, you must configure the setup by entering your e-mail address and the SMTP server and SMTP port for your account.

NOTES

If a permission screen opens with the Yes and No buttons or Allow and Deny, you should click Yes or Allow.

Looking Up and Tracking Purchases

You can look up purchase invoices in the same way you look up sales invoices. You can look up purchase invoices from the Purchases Journal and from the Payments Journal.

Open the Purchases or Payments Journal, click Look Up An Invoice, decide whether you want to restrict the search dates or suppliers and click OK. Choose an invoice from the displayed list and click Select. If you know the invoice number, journal entry number or amount, you can enter it directly and click OK to display the requested invoice.

From the Payments Journal, choose Make Other Payment then click Look Up An Invoice to find cash invoices posted in the Payments Journal.

Once you look up a purchase invoice, you can track shipments and look up other invoices in the same way as you do for sales. You can also adjust the invoice. Tracking is not available for cash purchases entered as Other Payments in the Payments Journal.

Entering Purchases from Foreign Suppliers

Purchases from foreign suppliers are entered in much the same way as purchases from other suppliers. Once you choose a supplier who uses a different currency, the Purchases Journal changes to add the appropriate fields.

Click the **Create Purchase Invoice Shortcut** to open the Purchases Journal. Invoice and Pay Later are correctly selected.

NOTES
Use Full Add so you can enter the correct currency.
Design Anything
(contact Joy Pikchur)
900 Park St., Unit 5
Seattle, Washington 98195
USA
Tel: (800) 639-8710
Fax: (206) 755-8852
Currency: USD
Terms: net 30 (Pay Later)
Expense account: 5360
Tax code: G

WARNING!
You must choose Full Add for new foreign currency suppliers so that you can choose USD as the currency.

✓ 15

Purchase Invoice #DA-722 **Dated July 16/21**

From Design Anything (use Full Add for new US supplier), $3 200 plus 5% GST for designing and printing labels and CD case inserts for new CDs. Invoice total $3 360 USD. Terms: net 30. The exchange rate is 1.315.

Click the **Supplier field**. **Type** `Design Anything`

Entering a Foreign Supplier Record

Click the **Add link** above the Supplier field to open the Payables Ledger supplier input screen.

Type the supplier address details from the margin Notes.

Enter **July 16** as the date for the Supplier Since field.

Click the **Options tab**. The ledger has an additional field for currency.

Choose **5360 Materials and Assembly Costs** as the default expense account.

Click the **Currency list arrow**:

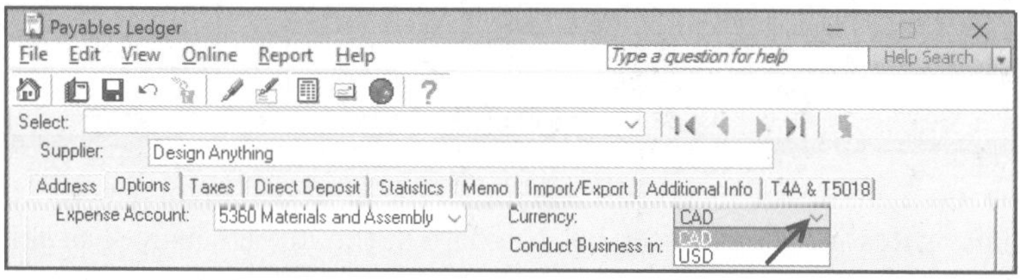

Choose **USD**. A Balance Owing In USD amount is added to the record.

Enter **net 30 days** as the payment terms. The default payment methods are correct.

Click the **Taxes tab** that has the default settings.

Click the **Tax Code list arrow** for the options:

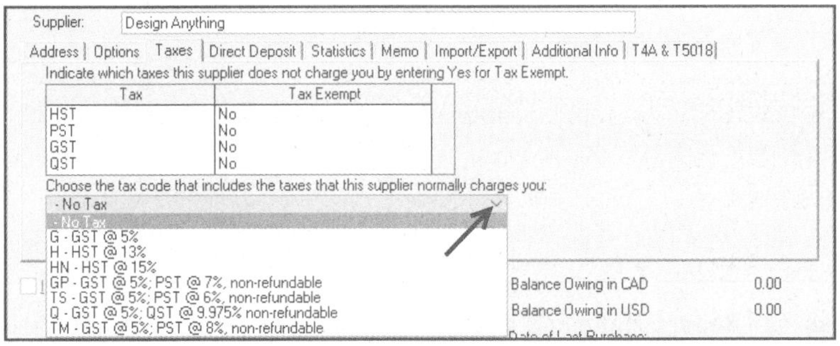

Maple Leaf Rags is not exempt from paying taxes on purchases from Design Anything, and that is the default selection. All tax codes will be available. Most purchases from US suppliers are subject to GST, so we should choose G - GST @ 5% as the default tax code. Maple pays GST on imported goods.

Click **Code G - GST @ 5%**.

Click Save and Close to return to the modified invoice:

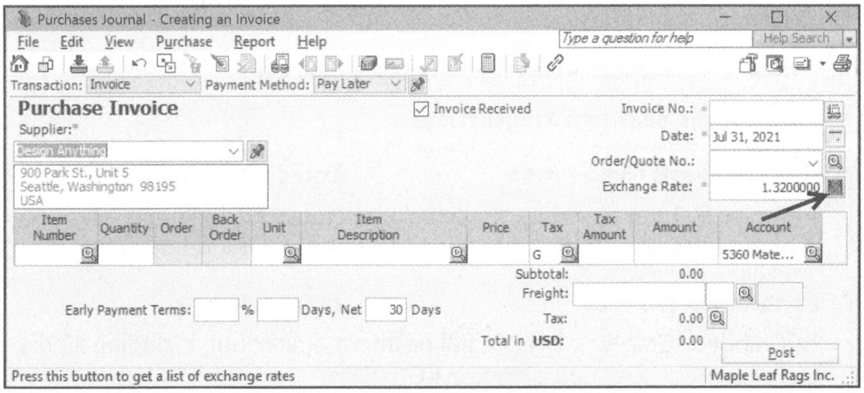

USD is now selected as the currency for the invoice and an Exchange Rate field has been added. The default terms, expense account and tax code are also on the invoice.

Enter the **Invoice number** and **Date**. **Do not press** (tab). If the Exchange Rate update screen opens, click Cancel.

Click the **Exchange Rate tool** beside the Exchange Rate field to open the list of rates we have already used so that we can choose from this list:

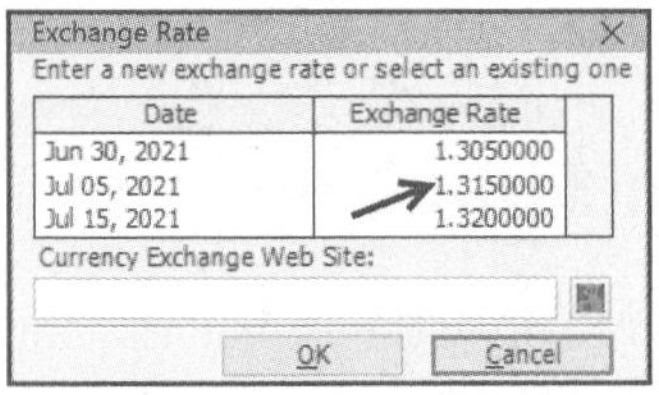

Click **1.315**, the rate for July 5. **Click OK** to return to the journal.

NOTES

The additional tax code, Q, is available for purchases in Quebec. Provincial taxes on purchases are added to the expense or asset part of the purchase, just like other PST paid amounts. Tax code Q is not in the Sales Journal tax list because no linked account was entered for taxes charged on sales.

WARNING!

Leave all Tax Exempt settings at No in case other tax codes are required for taxes on other purchases or on freight.

NOTES

GST or HST is paid directly to the Receiver General at the time the goods arrive in Canada. The foreign supplier does not collect these taxes.

To simplify the exercises, we omit this aspect of collecting taxes and instead include the GST on foreign purchases with the invoices.

Enter the **Amount** and **Description** to complete the invoice:

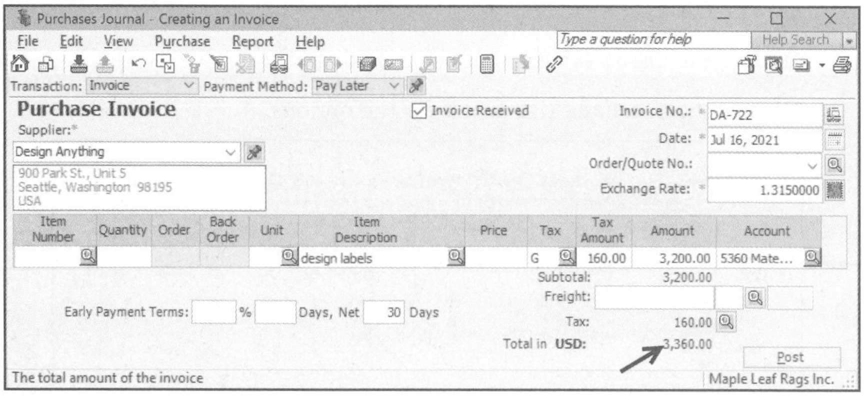

Choose the **Report menu** and **click Display Purchases Journal Entry** to review the entry:

Maple Leaf Rags Inc.
Purchases Journal Entry 07/16/2021 (J13)

Account Number	Account Description	Foreign A...	Debits	Credits
2670	GST Paid on Purchases	US$160.00	210.40	-
5360	Materials and Assembly Costs	US$3,200.00	4,208.00	-
2200	Accounts Payable	US$3,360.00	-	4,418.40
1 United States Dollars equals 1.3150000 Canadian Dollars			4,418.40	4,418.40

The only difference between this and other purchase entries is the addition of the USD currency amounts and exchange rate.

Close the **display** to return to the journal and **make corrections** if necessary.

Click Post. **Close** the **Purchases Journal**.

Enter the **next four transactions**.

16

Amex Payment: Cheque #764 **Dated July 16/21**

To Amex, $535 in payment of credit card account, including $290 for purchases charged from May 25 to June 25 and $245 for annual renewal fee.

17

Payment Cheque #765 **Dated July 18/21**

To Grandeur Graphics, $412 in full payment of account, including $8 discount for early payment. Reference invoice #GG-1304.

18

Payment Cheque #766 **Dated July 18/21**

To Let 'm Know, $1 100 in full payment of account, including $20 discount for early payment. Reference invoice #LK-692.

19

Receipt #127 **Dated July 20/21**

From CDN Music, cheque #28563 for $4 590 in payment of account including $135 discount taken for early payment. Reference invoice #591.

Entering Payments to Foreign Suppliers

Click the **Pay Purchase Invoices** shortcut to open the Payments Journal.

✓ 20

Payment Cheque #284 **Dated July 30/21**

To Design Anything, $3 360 USD in full payment of account. Reference invoice #DA-722. The exchange rate is 1.321.

Choose **Design Anything** from the Supplier list to modify the journal:

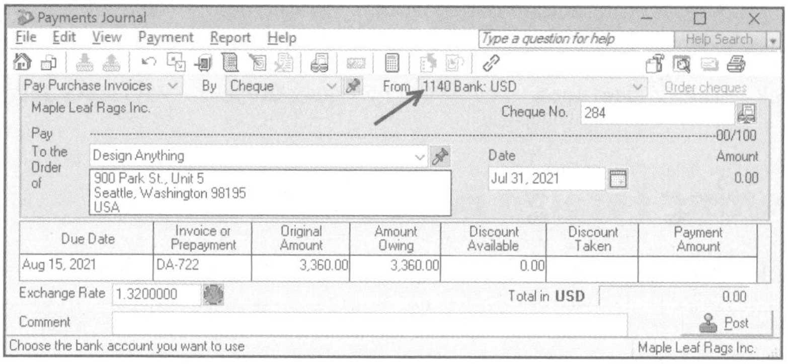

The outstanding invoice appears on the screen and the currency is marked as USD. An Exchange Rate field also becomes available.

Payments to US suppliers are made from the USD bank account. This bank and the next cheque number for it are entered.

Click the **Calendar icon** and **choose** **July 30** as the transaction date.

The Exchange Rate screen should open automatically — the rate is out of date.

Type 1.321 **Click** **Make This The Default Rate For Jul 30, 2021**.

Press *enter* to return to the journal. The cursor is on the calendar icon.

Click the **Payment Amount field**. There is no discount.

Press *tab* to accept the amount and complete the entry:

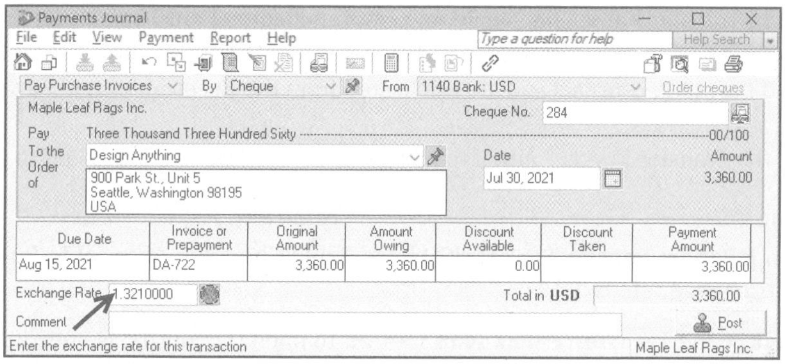

Press *ctrl* + **J** so you can review the journal entry:

Maple Leaf Rags Inc.
Payments Journal Entry 07/30/2021 (J18)

Account Number	Account Description	Foreign A...	Debits	Credits
2200	Accounts Payable	US$3,360.00	4,418.40	-
4300	Exchange Rate Differences		20.16	-
1140	Bank: USD	US$3,360.00	-	4,438.56
			4,438.56	4,438.56

1 United States Dollars equals 1.3210000 Canadian Dollars

Exchange Rate Differences has a debit entry because the exchange rate was lower on the day of the purchase (the date the purchase was recorded) than on the day of the payment. However, because this is a payment, Maple Leaf Rags has lost on the payment delay, as indicated by the debit entry for a revenue account — more Canadian dollars are needed to pay the same US dollar amount. As for other foreign currency transactions, amounts are given in both currencies and the exchange rate is included.

Close the **display** to return to the journal. **Make corrections** if necessary and **click** Post to display the advisor message:

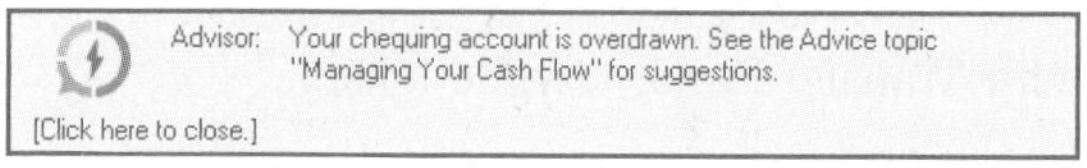

Advisor: Your chequing account is overdrawn. See the Advice topic "Managing Your Cash Flow" for suggestions.
[Click here to close.]

NOTES

The exchange rate we selected for July 16 from the list for June 30 was not entered as the most recent rate used because we did not save it as the default rate for July 16.

NOTES

If the Exchange Rate screen stays open after you click OK with the session date replacing the transaction date, you may enter an incorrect rate. Click Cancel to close the screen and select the correct exchange rate from the Exchange Rate select list.

Click the Exchange Rate tool beside the field to open the list of rates. You can also type the rate directly in the Exchange Rate field.

NOTES

The Accounts Payable amount is $4 418.40 CAD and the amount paid is $4 438.56. The difference ($20.16) is caused by the exchange rate change.

The advisor informs us that our chequing account is overdrawn. We will transfer funds to the USD account immediately to cover the cheque before the supplier has a chance to cash it.

Click the **Advisor icon** to close the message. **Close** the **Payments Journal**.

Transferring Foreign Funds

NOTES

Access to the Payments and Receipts journals from the Banking module allows all bank-related activities to be completed from this screen.

Account reconciliation and deposits are covered in Chapter 15.

Make Other Payment (Pay Expenses) is the default type of transaction from the Pay Bills icon.

Click **Banking** in the Modules pane list to open this module window:

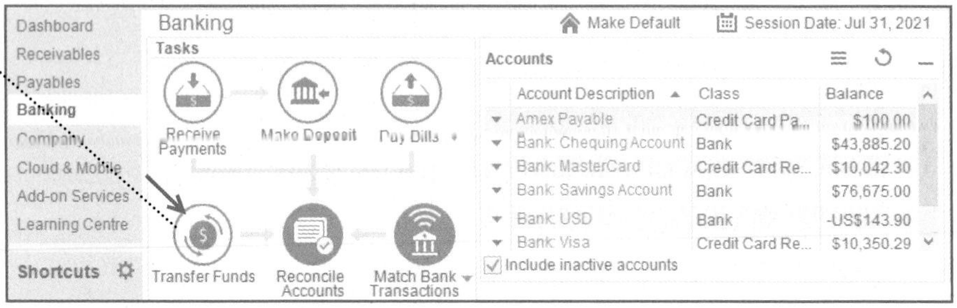

Clicking the **Refresh icon**  in the Accounts pane will update the account balances.

The Accounts pane list also informs us that *Bank: USD* is overdrawn — it has a negative balance amount. The Banking module window has no ledger icons, although it does allow direct access to the ledger records for all accounts involved in making or receiving payments (Cash, Bank and Credit Card class accounts). Four journal icons — Make Deposit, Transfer Funds, Reconcile Accounts and Match Bank Transactions — are for bank account transactions. The Receive Payments and Pay Bills icons open the Receipts and Payments journals and are duplicated from the Receivables and Payables modules.

We use the Transfer Funds Journal to move money from one bank account to another.

CLASSIC VIEW

The Transfer Funds Journal is not available in the Classic view, so you must use the General Journal instead.

✓ 21

Memo #47 **Dated July 30/21**

From J. Bands: Transfer $1 000 USD from Bank: Chequing Account to Bank: USD. The exchange rate is 1.321.

Click the **Transfer Funds icon**  to open the journal we need:

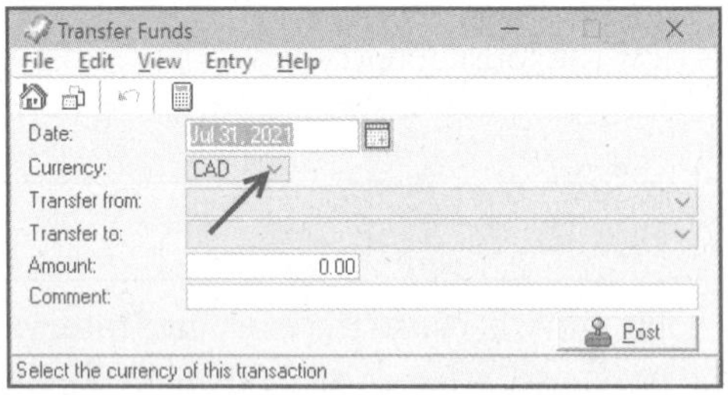

WARNING!

You must choose USD as the currency for the transfer of funds. The CAD bank account will be available for the foreign currency transaction. If you choose CAD as the currency, you cannot access the USD bank account.

Type `July 30` (as the Date).

Click the **Currency list arrow** for the currency options:

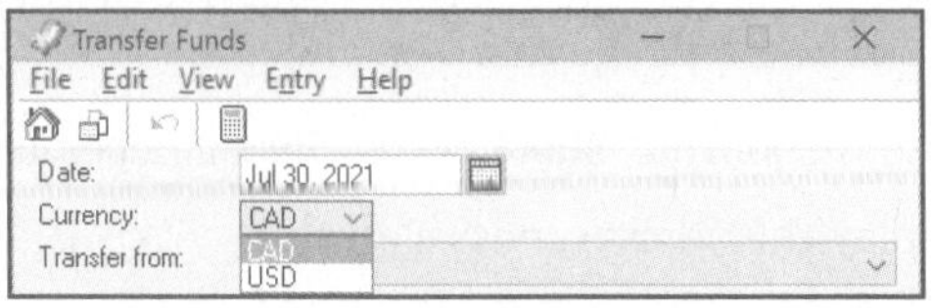

NOTES

The Exchange Rate window does not open because we have already entered a rate for July 30. You can still change the rate if needed by editing the amount in the Exchange Rate field.

Both currencies are available for Transfer Funds transactions.

Click **USD**. The exchange rate is entered correctly for this date.

Click the **Transfer From list arrow** for the list of available accounts:

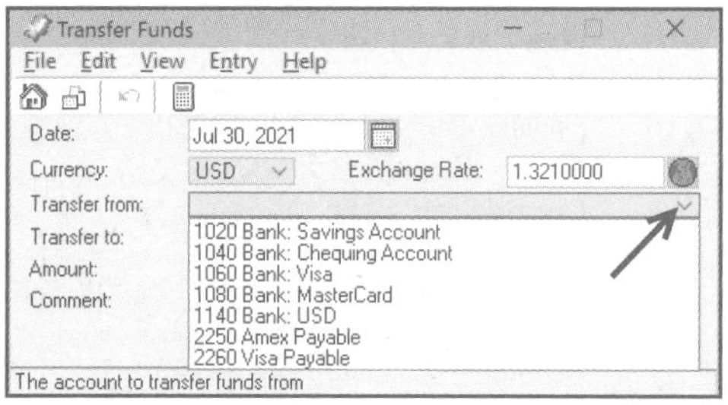

Choose **1040 Bank: Chequing Account** in the Account field. **Press** (tab).

Click the **Transfer To list arrow**; the same list of available accounts opens.

Choose **1140 Bank: USD** and **press** (tab) to advance to the Amount field.

Type `1000` **Press** (tab) to advance to the Comment field.

Type `Memo 47: Transfer funds to cover cheque`

Adding the comment will complete the entry:

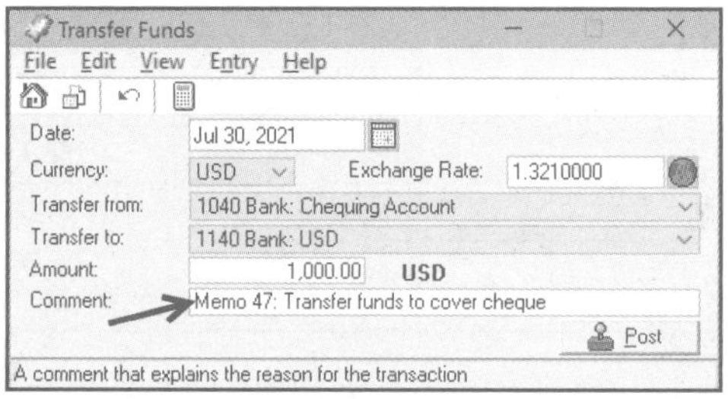

Check your transaction carefully. You cannot display the journal entry before posting. To make corrections after posting, adjust or reverse the transfer in the General Journal.

When you display the Journal Entries Report, the transfer is included as a typical debit and credit entry, with the amounts given in both currencies and the exchange rate that was applied, as for other foreign currency transactions.

Click (Post) to save the transaction.

Close the **Transfer Funds Journal**. The Banking Home window balances are updated.

Enter the **remaining transactions** up to memo #58 on September 30.

22 **Purchase Order #204 & Cheque #767** **Dated July 31/21**

Shipping date Aug. 15/21
To A.B. Original Sounds, $50 000 plus 5% GST for master copies of new CDs. Invoice total $52 500. Terms: 1/10, n/30. Use Materials and Assembly Costs account.
Paid $10 000 as prepayment with cheque #767.

23 **Purchase Order #205 & Cheque #768** **Dated July 31/21**

Shipping date Aug. 15/21
To Super Dupers (use Full Add for the new supplier), $15 000 to duplicate CDs and books plus 5% GST. Invoice total $15 750. Terms: 1/10, n/30.
Paid $4 000 as prepayment with cheque #768.

NOTES
All Bank, Cash and Credit Card class accounts that are used to make and receive payments are available in the Transfer Funds Journal.

NOTES
The funds transfer may also be entered in the General Journal. Both currencies are available for transactions. Again, you must choose the currency before selecting accounts.

WARNING!
Check your transaction carefully because you cannot display the journal entry before posting. You can adjust or reverse the transfers from the General Journal.

NOTES
Transfer Funds entries are included in General Journal Entry Reports. You can also adjust transfers from the General Journal.

NOTES
You can add a shortcut for Transfer Funds from the Banking Shortcuts list. View Accounts is also on the list of Banking module shortcuts.

NOTES
Enter 1 as the order quantity for purchase orders.

NOTES
Super Dupers
777 Copiers Ave.
Richmond Hill, ON L4T 6V2
Terms: 1/10, n/30 (Pay Later)
Calculate discount before tax
Tax code: G
Expense Account: 5360

24

Maple Leaf Rags

mapleleafrags.com

2642 Coldstream Ave.
Nanaimo, BC V9T 2X2
Tel 1: (250) 63M-USIC
Tel 2: (888) 63M-USIC Fax: (250) 633-4888

PURCHASE ORDER

PO#: 206
Date: July 31, 2021
Shipping date: Aug 15, 2021

Ordered from: Wrap It
Address: 80 Cubit Rd.
Richmond Hill, ON L5R 6B2
Phone No: (905) 881-7739
Fax No: (905) 881-7000
Contact: Able Boxer

Order description	Amount
Provide CD cases add labels and inserts terms: 1/5, n/30	6 300.00
Freight (Canada Post)	120.00
GST	321.00
HST	--
Order Total	6 741.00
Deposit	2 000.00
Balance Owing	4 741.00

Provided chq #769 for $2 000 as deposit

Approved by: *Jaz Bands*

NOTES
Change the default account to Prepaid Expenses for the invoice from Let 'm Know.

25 **Purchase Invoice #LK-2303** **Dated July 31/21**

From Let 'm Know, $1 500 plus 5% GST and 7% PST for series of ads to run for the next five months (prepaid expense). Invoice total $1 680. Terms: 2/20, n/30.

26 **Cash Purchase Invoice #WT-6632** **Dated July 31/21**

From Western Tel, $205 plus 5% GST and 7% PST for telephone services for two months. Invoice total $229.60. Terms: payment on receipt of invoice. Paid by cheque #770.

27 **Cash Purchase Invoice #PE-49006** **Dated July 31/21**

From Purolator, $1 400 plus 5% GST for shipping services used from May 25 to July 25. Invoice total $1 470. Terms: payment on receipt of invoice. Paid by cheque #771.

NOTES
Use Quick Add for the new supplier. Include gasoline costs with Travel Expenses. Use tax code G – GST @ 5%. The remaining provincial and federal taxes are not refundable and are already included in the price.

28 **Visa Purchase Invoice #PC-34992** **Dated July 31/21**

From Petro-Canada (use Quick Add), $120 plus 5% GST for gasoline for business use. Invoice total $126 paid by Visa.

SESSION DATE – AUGUST 15, 2021

29 **Visa Payment: Cheque #772** **Dated Aug. 2/21**

To Visa, $828.20 in payment of balance shown on Visa account statement for purchases before July 15, 2021.

30 **Receipt #128** **Dated Aug. 7/21**

From Music Music Music, cheque #8531 for $2 124.30 USD in payment of account less $65.70 discount for early payment. Reference invoice #597. The exchange rate for August 7 is 1.322. Deposit to Bank: USD account.

31 **Payment Cheque #773** **Dated Aug. 8/21**

To Let 'm Know, $1 650 in full payment of account, including $30 discount for early payment. Reference invoice #LK-2303.

32 **Receipt #129** **Dated Aug. 9/21**

From Treble & Bass, cheque #1144 for $9 546.40 in payment of account, including $339.60 discount taken for early payment. Reference invoice #596 and deposit #14. Deposit to Bank: Chequing Account.

33 **Sales Order #25** **Dated Aug. 9/21**

Shipping date Aug. 22/21

From Total Music, $28 000 plus HST for CDs and $9 000 for books plus 5% GST – items purchased by major music store chains. Shipping charges $200 plus GST. Invoice total $41 860. Terms: 3/30, n/60.

34

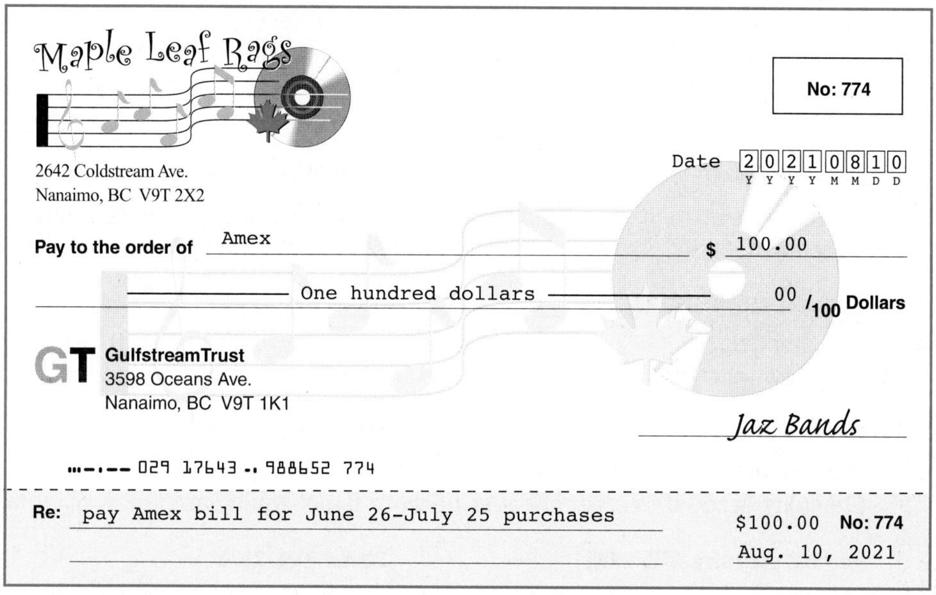

Maple Leaf Rags

No: 774

2642 Coldstream Ave.
Nanaimo, BC V9T 2X2

Date 20210810
Y Y Y Y M M D D

Pay to the order of Amex $ 100.00

One hundred dollars 00 /100 Dollars

GT GulfstreamTrust
3598 Oceans Ave.
Nanaimo, BC V9T 1K1

Jaz Bands

029 17643 .. 988652 774

Re: pay Amex bill for June 26-July 25 purchases $100.00 No: 774
Aug. 10, 2021

35 **Receipt #130** **Dated Aug. 11/21**

From Total Music, cheque #502 for $5 000 as down payment, deposit #15, to confirm sales order #25.

36 **Purchase Invoice #CA-7998** **Dated Aug. 12/21**

From Cars for All (use Quick Add for new supplier), $20 000 plus 5% GST and 7% PST for new automobile less $5 000 plus GST and PST as a trade-in allowance on old car. Invoice total $16 800. The entry to write off the old car will be made by the accountant at year-end.

37 **Purchase Invoice #ABO-8823** **Dated Aug. 12/21**

From A.B. Original Sounds, to fill purchase order #204, $50 000 plus 5% GST for CD masters. Invoice total $52 500. Terms: 1/10, n/30.

SESSION DATE – AUGUST 31, 2021

38 **Purchase Invoice #SD-9124** **Dated Aug. 18/21**

From Super Dupers, to fill purchase order #205, $15 000 to duplicate CDs and books plus 5% GST. Invoice total $15 750. Terms: 1/10, n/30.

NOTES

When you advance the session date to August 31, an Advisor message informs you that it is time to prepare for year-end. Read and then close the advice statement to proceed.

39 **Purchase Invoice #WI-3719** **Dated Aug. 18/21**

From Wrap It, to fill purchase order #206, $6 300 plus 5% GST to prepare CDs for sale. Shipped by Canada Post (#75 553 789 249) for $120 plus 5% GST. Invoice total $6 741. Terms: 1/5, n/30.

40 **Memo #48** **Dated Aug. 20/21**

From J. Bands: Owner invests $50 000 personal capital to finance production of new inventory. Amount deposited to Bank: Savings Account and credited to Common Stock.

41 **Sales Invoice #598** **Dated Aug. 21/21**

To Total Music, to fill sales order #25, $28 000 plus HST for CDs and $9 000 plus 5% GST for books. Shipping charges $200 plus GST. Invoice total $41 860. Terms: 3/30, n/60.

NOTES

Close the Advisor warnings about the overdrawn chequing account. The funds transfer in memo #49 will cover the cheques.

42 **Payment Cheque #775** **Dated Aug. 21/21**

To A.B. Original Sounds, $42 000 in full payment of account, including $500 discount for early payment. Reference invoice #ABO-8823 and prepayment by cheque #767.

43 **Payment Cheque #776** **Dated Aug. 23/21**

To Wrap It, $4 676.80 in full payment of account, including $64.20 discount for early payment. Reference invoice #WI-3719 and prepayment by cheque #769.

44 **Payment Cheque #777** **Dated Aug. 23/21**

To Super Dupers, $11 600 in full payment of account, with the $150 discount for early payment. Reference invoice #SD-9124 and prepayment by cheque #768.

45 **Memo #49** **Dated Aug. 23/21**

From J. Bands: Transfer $60 000 CAD from Bank: Savings Account to Bank: Chequing Account to cover cheques because the chequing account is overdrawn.

46 **Purchase Invoice #JH-0875** **Dated Aug. 25/21**

To J. Henry & Associates (use Quick Add), $1 500 plus $75 GST for legal fees to recover money owed by Entertainment House. Invoice total $1 575. Terms: net 30. Create new Group account 5240 Legal Fees.

47 **Visa Purchase Invoice #PC-49986** **Dated Aug. 28/21**

From Petro-Canada, $128 plus 5% GST for gasoline for business use. Invoice total $134.40 paid by Visa.

SESSION DATE – SEPTEMBER 15, 2021

NOTES

If you do not change the date for the purchase invoice adjustment, Sage 50 will warn you that the transaction date precedes the session date because the transaction was dated in a previous month. Click Yes to proceed because the original date was correct.

48 **Memo #50** **Dated Sep. 2/21**

When his Visa bill arrived, Bands realized that he had entered the purchase from Cars for All as a Pay Later invoice instead of a Visa payment. Adjust invoice #CA-7998 from Cars for All. Change the method of payment to Visa.

49 **Visa Payment: Cheque #778** **Dated Sep. 2/21**

To Visa, $16 926 in payment of account for purchases from July 16 to August 15, 2021.

50 **Sales Invoice #599** **Dated Sep. 5/21**

To Canadian Sounds, $4 500 USD for CDs and $750 for books. Shipped by FedEx (#F36FYT863) for $170. Invoice total $5 420 USD. Terms: 3/30, n/60. The exchange rate is 1.325.

51

Maple Leaf Rags
mapleleafrags.com

2642 Coldstream Ave.
Nanaimo, BC V9T 2X2
Tel 1: (250) 63M-USIC
Tel 2: (888) 63M-USIC Fax: (250) 633-4888
GST # 128 488 632

INVOICE

Sales Invoice: #600
Date: September 10, 2021

Customer: Music Music Music
Address: 10 Red Rock Canyon
Sedona, Arizona 86336 USA
Phone No: (520) 678-4523
Fax No:
Contact: M. Porter

Item description	Amount
150 CDs	1 500.00 USD
25 Books	750.00 USD
Freight	140.00 USD
GST	—
PST	—
HST	—
Invoice Total	2 390.00 USD

Shipped by: FedEx #F49XDT563

Payment: 3/30, n/60
Exchange rate for Sep 10 was 1.3205 – JB

Sold by: Jaz Bands

SESSION DATE – SEPTEMBER 29, 2021

52 **Receipt #131** **Dated Sep. 18/21**

From Total Music, cheque #574 for $35 774 in payment of account including $1 116 discount taken for early payment. Reference invoice #598 and deposit #15. Deposit to Bank: Chequing Account.

53 **Cash Purchase Invoice #WT-9810** **Dated Sep. 29/21**

From Western Tel, $245 plus 5% GST and 7% PST for telephone services for two months. Invoice total $274.40. Terms: payment on receipt of invoice. Paid by cheque #779.

54 **Cash Purchase Invoice #PE-62331** **Dated Sep. 29/21**

From Purolator, $1 200 plus 5% GST for shipping services. Invoice total $1 260. Terms: payment on receipt of invoice. Paid by cheque #780.

55 **MasterCard Credit Card Sales Invoice #601** **Dated Sep. 29/21**

To various Web Store Customers, for sales during previous three months:

CDs & downloads (BC customers	$1 740 plus 5% GST and 7% PST
CDs & downloads (ON customers)	1 900 plus 13% HST
CDs & downloads (other HST customers)	630 plus 15% HST
CDs & downloads (GST customers)	1 020 plus 5% GST
Book sales	2 800 plus 5% GST
Shipping	650 plus 5% GST

Invoice total $9 513.80. Paid by MasterCard.

NOTES

When you advance the session date to September 29, the Advisor message about the year-end adjustments required should open. Read and then close the advisory statement to proceed.

NOTES

If you recall the stored MC Web Store Customers sales summary, edit the amounts. Other parts of the invoice should be correct.

56 **Cash Purchase Invoice #FE-46678** **Dated Sep. 29/21**

From FedEx, $2 100 plus 5% GST for shipping services. Invoice total $2 205. Terms: payment on receipt of invoice. Paid by cheque #781.

57

Maple Leaf Rags
mapleleafrags.com

2642 Coldstream Ave.
Nanaimo, BC V9T 2X2
Tel 1: (250) 63M-USIC
Tel 2: (888) 63M-USIC Fax: (250) 633-4888
GST # 128 488 632

Sales Invoice: #602
Date: September 29, 2021

Customer: Web Store Customers
Address:

Phone No:
Fax No:
Contact:

INVOICE

Description	Amount
Sales summary for 3 months	
CDs & downloads - BC customers (add GST and PST)	1 800.00
CDs & downloads - Ontario customers (add 13% HST)	1 300.00
CDs & downloads - other HST customers (add 15% HST)	420.00
CDs & downloads - GST provinces (add 5% GST)	1 050.00
Books sold in all provinces (add 5% GST)	2 500.00

Shipped by: Purolator

Payment: Visa
Direct deposit to Visa bank account JB

Freight (add GST)	690.00
GST	302.00
PST	126.00
HST	232.00
Invoice Total	8 420.00

NOTES

If you recall the stored Visa Web Store Customers sales summary, edit the amounts. Other parts of the invoice should be correct.

SESSION DATE – SEPTEMBER 30, 2021

58 **Memo #51** **Dated Sep. 30/21**

From J. Bands: Refer to the Sep. 30 General Ledger balance to remit PST Payable to the Minister of Finance. Reduce the $352.80 payment by $23.28, the sales tax compensation of 6.6% of the balance owing. Issue cheque #782 for $329.52 from Bank: Chequing Account.

59 **Memo #52** **Dated Sep. 30/21**

From J. Bands: Prepare for closing the books by completing adjusting entries for prepaid expenses and supplies used.

Office Supplies	$ 280
Prepaid Internet Expenses (3 months)	165
Prepaid Rent (3 months of 6)	2 400
Prepaid Advertising (2 months of 5)	663

60 **Memo #53** **Dated Sep. 30/21**

From J. Bands: Complete an adjusting entry for goods sold during the quarter.

CDs	$46 500	(Debit Cost of CDs Sold and credit CD Inventory)
Books	$15 600	(Debit Cost of Books Sold and credit Book Inventory)

61 **Memo #54** **Dated Sep. 30/21**

From J. Bands: Complete an adjusting entry to transfer $77 308 in completed inventory. Transfer $68 508 to CD Inventory and $8 800 to Book Inventory. Debit the inventory asset accounts and credit Materials and Assembly Costs.

62 **Memo #55** **Dated Sep. 30/21**

From J. Bands: Received debit memo from Gulfstream Trust regarding pre-authorized withdrawals from Bank: Chequing Account for quarterly interest payments on loans. Complete adjusting entries for quarterly interest paid.

On bank loan	$ 200
On long term loan	1 100

63 **Memo #56** **Dated Sep. 30/21**

From J. Bands: The following transfers of funds were completed:
$10 000 from Bank: Chequing Account to Bank: Savings Account
$15 000 from Bank: Visa to Bank: Savings Account
$15 000 from Bank: MasterCard to Bank: Savings Account

64 **Memo #57** **Dated Sep. 30/21**

From J. Bands: Record Interest Revenue as follows:

Bank: Savings Account	$200
Bank: Chequing Account	10

Creating an Accountant's Copy

Many businesses rely on professional accountants to assist them with their accounting. The accountants will check the data entered by the business for errors and make corrections. They also may add the adjusting entries required at the end of a fiscal period to bring the books up to date and to prepare for filing tax returns. The business then begins the new year with a complete and accurate data file.

Sage 50 allows a data file to be saved as an Accountant's Copy. This backup data file can be restored and opened only in the Accountant Edition of Sage 50. The accountant makes journal entries in the file that can be added back to the original business data file. The business may continue with day-to-day journal entries and even start a new fiscal period while the accountant is preparing the additional entries.

✓ 65 **Memo #58** **Dated Sep. 30/21**

From J. Bands: Create an Accountant's Copy of the data files so the accountant can review the accounting entries and add the final adjustments for depreciation and the trade-in on the automobiles.

You can create an Accountant's Copy from the File menu or from the Company window Accountant's Tasks pane Accountant's Copy icon shortcuts.

Click **Company** in the Modules pane list to open that module window.

Choose the **File menu**, then **choose Accountant's Copy** and **click Create Accountant's Copy** or **choose Create Accountant's Copy** from the Accountant's Copy icon shortcuts drop-down list:

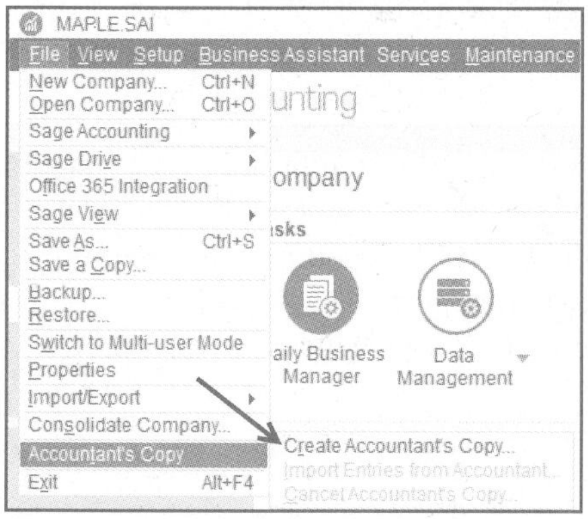

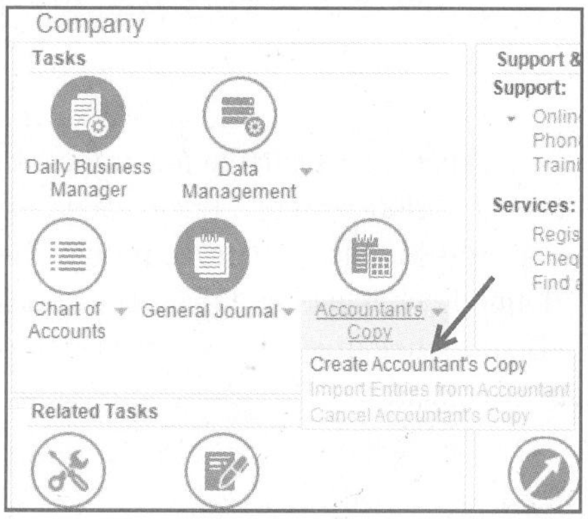

NOTES
Bands pays only interest on the loans. Both amounts are deducted from the Bank: Chequing Account.

NOTES
To use the Transfer Funds Journal for the transfer, you must enter the transfer for each account as a separate transaction. To complete the funds transfer entry as a single journal entry, you must use the General Journal.

PRO VERSION
The Pro version File menu does not have the options to Switch To Multi-User Mode or Consolidate Company.

NOTES
From the Company shortcuts list, you can add a shortcut to Create an Accountant's Copy.

After creating the Copy, you can add shortcuts to Import Entries From an Accountant's Copy and to Cancel the Accountant's Copy.

You will be asked to choose a location for the new backup file:

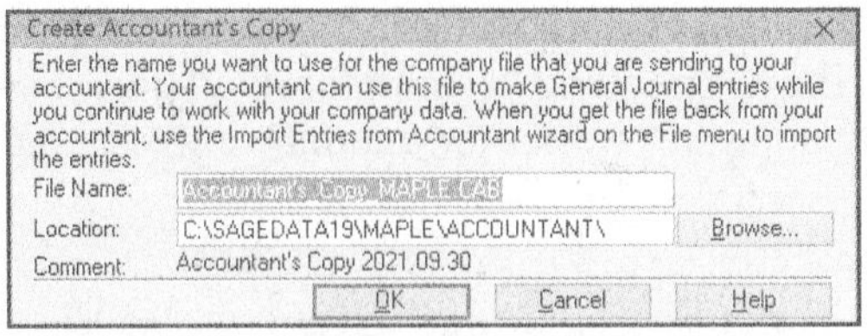

The default name for the file adds Accountant's_Copy_ to the original name so it will not be confused with your other backup files. The default location is a new folder inside your current data folder.

To choose a different folder, click Browse and choose the folder you want to use. Enter a different name for the file if you want.

Click **OK** to begin making the specialized backup.

When the copy is complete, Sage 50 provides a warning:

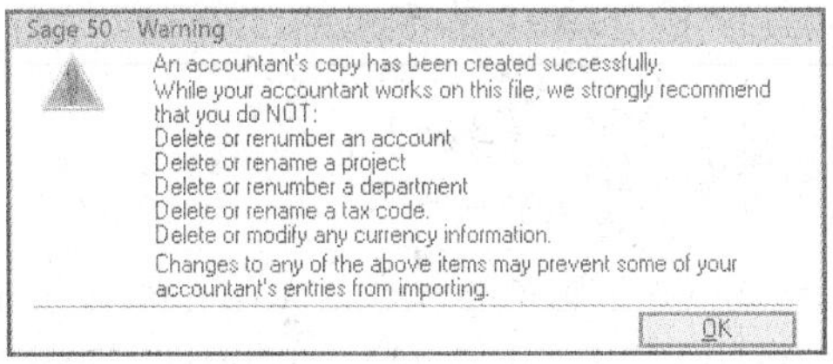

PRO VERSION
The warning message does not include the details about project and department.

Read this message carefully as it warns what changes you cannot make to your working file while the accountant is working with the Accountant's Copy of your file.

Click **OK** to return to your data file.

Monitoring Routine Activities

The end of September is the end of Bands' fiscal year. There are a number of steps to complete before beginning the new year. Sage 50 provides assistance with these steps in its checklists.

CLASSIC VIEW
Click , the Checklists tool, to open the Checklists window.

✓ 66

Memo #59 **Dated Sep. 30/21**

From J. Bands: Review the year-end checklists. Print all reports for the fiscal period ended. Back up the data files. Check data integrity. Advance the session date to October 1, the first day of the next fiscal period.

Choose the **Business Assistant menu** and **click Checklists**:

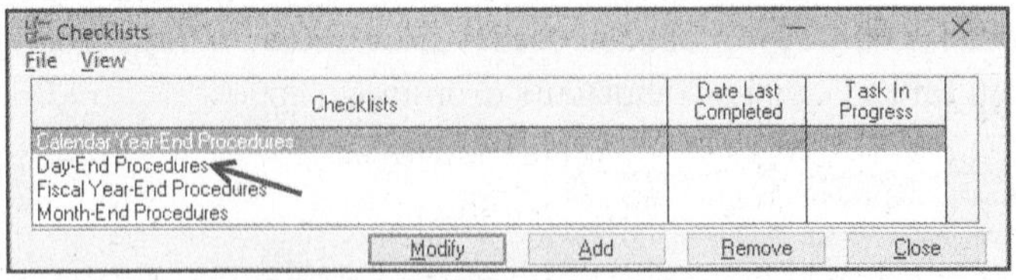

Checklists are available for different periods that are important for a business — end of a fiscal period, end of a business day, end of a month and end of a calendar year for payroll. You can also create your own checklists, add procedures to one of the predefined checklists and print the checklists for reference.

Before checking the fiscal year-end procedures, we will add a reminder to the daily tasks checklist.

Click **Day-End Procedures** and then **click Modify** to open the list:

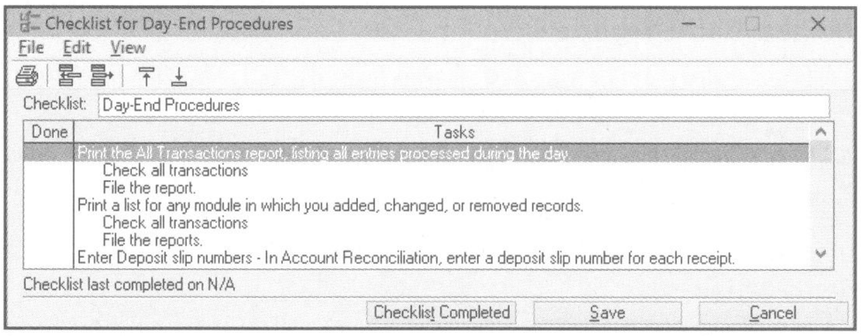

Each checklist can be customized for a company by using the tool buttons or the Edit menu options to insert tasks, delete them or rearrange them.

Click the **Insert Item tool** or **choose** the **Edit menu** and **click Insert** to add a blank line at the top of the task list.

Press *tab* to advance to the Tasks field.

Type `Check bank balances for possible overdrafts`

Click **Save** to return to the Checklists window.

Double-click **Fiscal Year-End Procedures** for the checklist we need:

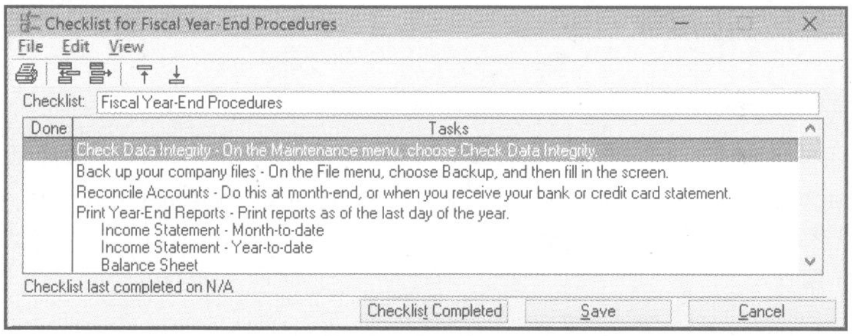

Maple Leaf Rags does not use the budgeting or account reconciliation features of the program, so we can remove these tasks from the checklist.

Scroll down and **click Print Budget Reports**.

Click the **Remove Item tool** or **choose** the **Edit menu** and **click Remove**.

Click **Yes** to confirm that you want to continue with the deletion.

Click the **Print tool** to print the checklist for reference.

Back up the **data files** and **print reports**. These are the most important elements on this list. There are no reports for Payroll, Inventory or Projects. You can remove these reports from the list if you want.

Click the **Done column** after completing a task — a ✓ will be added to the Done column.

Click Save if you want to leave the list and return later. A ✓ will appear in the Task In Progress column on the Checklists screen.

Complete all the **tasks** listed, except printing the reports for the modules that are not used. After finishing all the tasks,

Click **Checklist Completed**. The session date will be added to the Date Last Completed column on the Checklists screen.

Open the remaining checklists to learn which tasks to complete at the end of each month and at the end of a calendar year. Print these lists for reference.

NOTES
You cannot modify (edit) checklists in multi-user mode.

PRO VERSION
The Pro version does not include the View menu.

NOTES
You can use the tools or Edit menu options to move items up or down on the list.

NOTES
Reconciling accounts will be explained in Chapter 15, and budgeting is covered in Chapter 14.

NOTES
In Chapter 15, we describe how to clear data from company files.

NOTES
If you need to check or change your printer settings, you should print from the File menu.

NOTES
For partially completed lists, a ✓ is added to the Task In Progress column.

> **NOTES**
> Refer to page 103 for assistance with starting a new fiscal period.

Click **Close** to leave the Checklists window when you have finished.

Start the **new fiscal year** on October 1, 2021.

Displaying Exchange Rate Reports

> **NOTES**
> You can revalue amounts in the Balance Sheet for a different exchange rate. In the Trial Balance, you can display amounts in the home currency, in the foreign currency or in both. Journal Reports also have the option to include foreign amounts.

When a business has foreign currency transactions, Sage 50 will generate reports related to exchange rate gains and losses.

Open the **Report Centre** and **click Financials**:

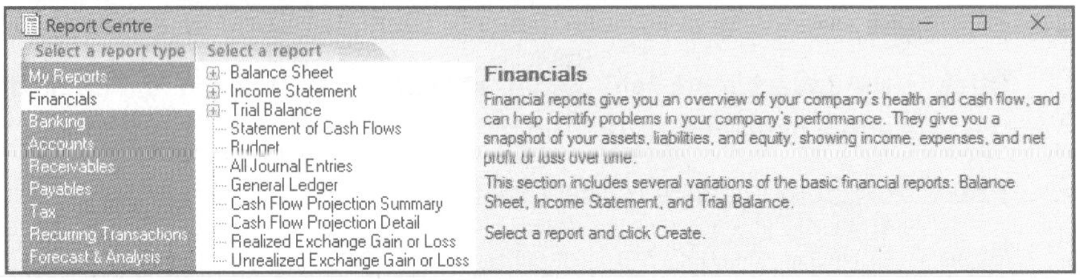

> **NOTES**
> From the Home window, choose the Reports menu, then choose Financials and click Realized Exchange Gain/Loss to access the report options.

Click **Realized Exchange Gain Or Loss**.

Click **Modify This Report** to open the report options window:

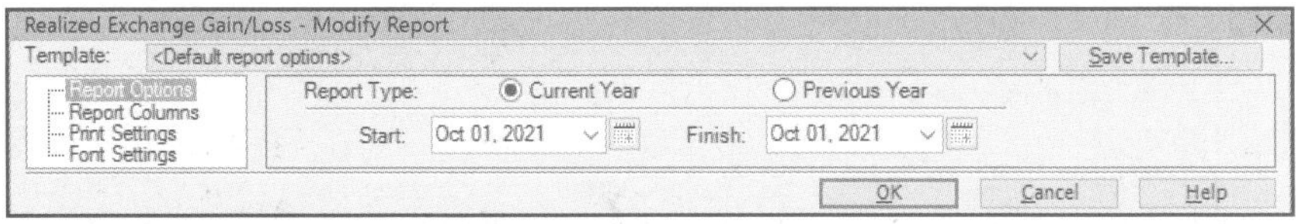

This first exchange rate report includes the gains or losses already realized or recorded because the payment has been made or received and the exchange rate differences are known.

> **NOTES**
> You cannot sort or filter the exchange rate reports. You can choose the columns for these reports.

Click **Previous Year** to generate reports for this application.

Enter the **dates** for the report (including the year) and **click OK**.

Close the **display** when finished.

To access the second exchange rate report,

> **NOTES**
> From the Home window, choose the Reports menu, then choose Financials and click Unrealized Exchange Gain/Loss to display the report options.

Click **Unrealized Exchange Gain Or Loss** in the Select A Report list.

Click **Modify This Report** to open the report options window:

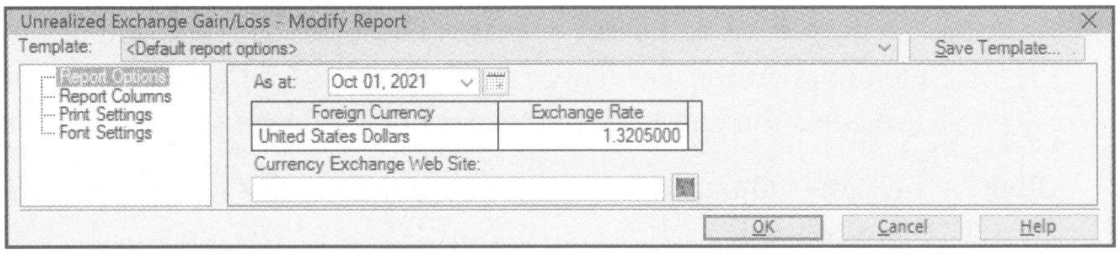

The second report includes the gains or losses that have not yet been realized or recorded — the payment has not been made but the exchange rate is known to have changed since the purchase or sale. When the payment is made or received, the actual gain may be different if the rate has changed again.

The report also revalues existing account balances and previous payments and receipts for the new exchange rate.

Enter the **date** for the report (including the year) and an **Exchange Rate** for that date. **Click OK**.

Close the **display** when finished. **Close** the **Report Centre**.

The Accountant Works with Your Data

When the accountant opens the file you sent, it will be restored in the same version of Sage 50 that you used — Pro, Premium and so on. Only the General Journal, the one used for adjusting entries, is available to the accountant. The following two screenshots represent your data file as it will open for the accountant using the special Accountant Edition version of Sage 50. The next two screens will not be available in your own program; we include them for reference only.

The accountant who opens your data file will have restrictions:

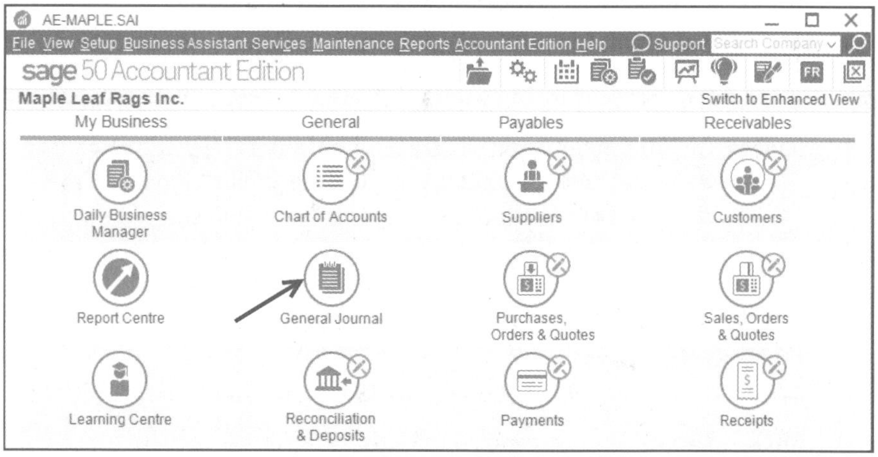

The **No Edit** symbol  appears with all the ledger and journal icons except for the General Journal. The accountant can view, but not change, the information in the other journals and ledgers.

After adding the required adjustments, the accountant exports the new journal entries to a text file. This option is available from the Accountant Edition menu by choosing Accountant's Copy and then Export Entries For Client:

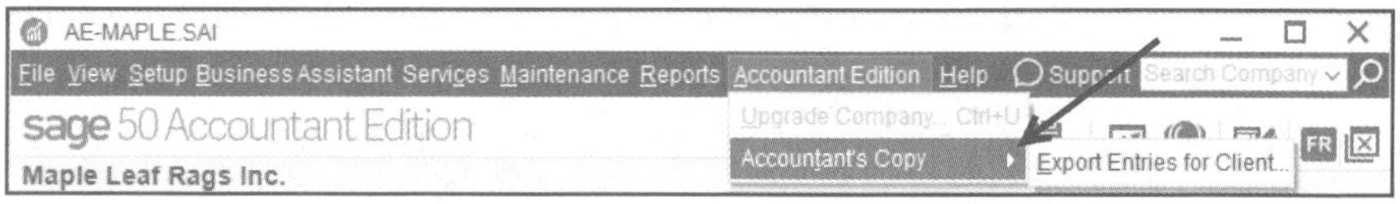

The exported text file of journal entries is sent back to you, the client.

Importing the Accountant's Journal Entries

Restore the data file **SageData19\ACCOUNTANT\AE-MAPLE1.CAB** for this step.

More menu options are available in the data file now:

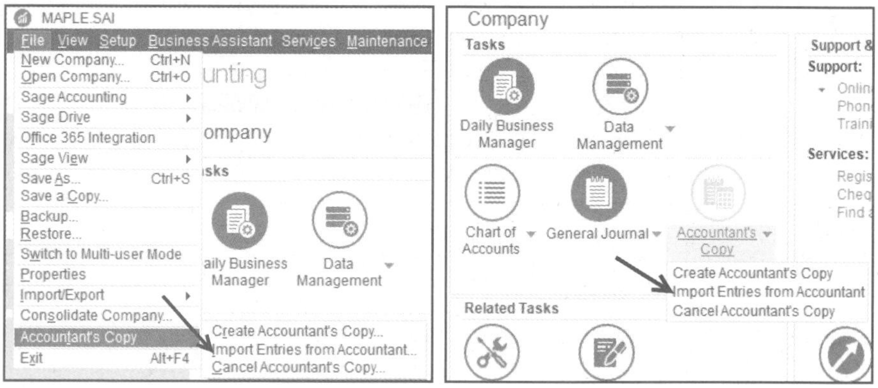

NOTES

The accountant works with a special version of the program – the Accountant Edition. This program must be used to restore the Accountant's Copy backup file you created.

The Accountant Edition allows full access to regular data files created in any version: Pro, Premium and Quantum. The Accountant's Copy data file restricts access to the General Journal in all versions but can access all accounts, including linked accounts not available in the other versions.

NOTES

On the Classic view Home window the restrictions are immediately apparent (the No Edit symbols).

NOTES

Year-end adjusting entries are typically General Journal entries.

WARNING!

Do not use your own Maple data file for this section.

You must use the special file we created for this part of the exercise because it matches the imported entries.

You must use the same file for creating the Accountant's Copy and importing the accountant's entries. You will not be able to import the accountant's entries to your own working file.

Both the File menu options and the shortcuts list for Accountant's Tasks in the Company module window have changed. Once you create an Accountant's Copy, the program stores the information that there is an outstanding Accountant's Copy for the file so you can import journal entries later. This option remains available until the entries have been imported. You cannot create another Accountant's Copy while there is one outstanding. If you discover an error after you create the Accountant's Copy, you can choose **Cancel Accountant's Copy** to cancel that version and then create a new Accountant's Copy. After cancelling, the option to create becomes available again.

When you receive the file from the accountant, you must import the journal entries created by the accountant to add them to your working file.

✓ 67

Memo #60 **Dated Oct. 1/21**

From J. Bands: Import the adjusting entries completed by the accountant.

Choose the **File menu**, then **choose Accountant's Copy** and **click Import Entries From Accountant**. Or, **choose Import Entries From Accountant** from the Accountant's Copy icon shortcuts list.

NOTES
The accountant cannot create new accounts in your data file, so we added the account 5600 Loss on Trade-in for the additional data file AE-MAPLE.

The Import Entries wizard begins:

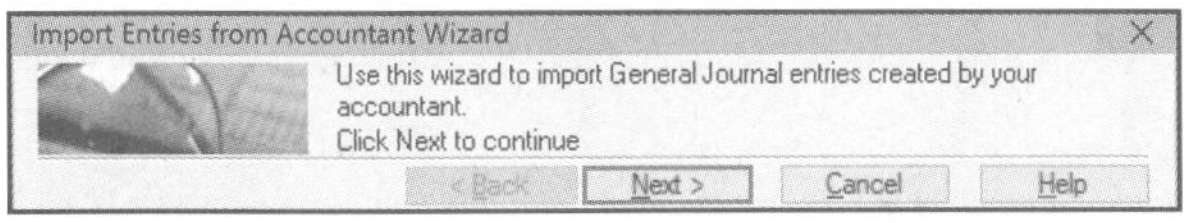

Click **Next**:

NOTES
The procedure for importing entries from the accountant is similar to importing other General Journal entries. Refer to Appendix J.

You are asked to make a backup before proceeding. Since the step of importing entries cannot be reversed, you should back up the data file first.

Click **Backup** and follow the backup wizard steps. **Click Next** to continue:

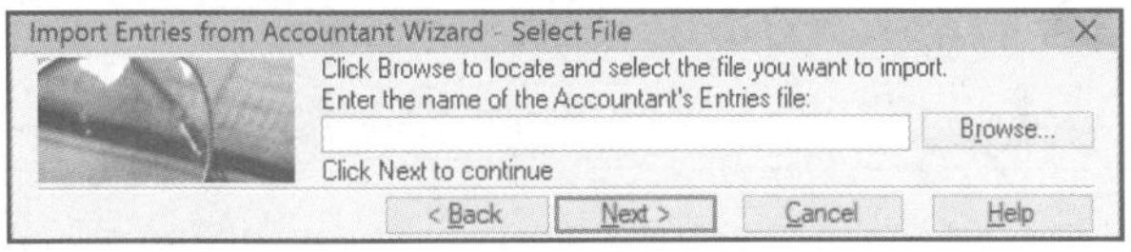

Now you must locate the file the accountant sent. We have added the file you need to the SageData19\ACCOUNTANT folder where the AE-MAPLE backup is stored.

Click **Browse**.

Locate **SageData19\ACCOUNTANT\Accountant's_Entries_AE-MAPLE.TXT** and **click** to select it.

Click **Open** to add the file name to the wizard screen and then **click Next**.

WARNING!
The file you need to import is Accountant's_Entries_AE-MAPLE.TXT. It is located in the SageData19\ACCOUNTANT folder.

If you try to import the journal entries to your own data file, or any file other than the one used to create the Accountant's Copy, you will get an error message:

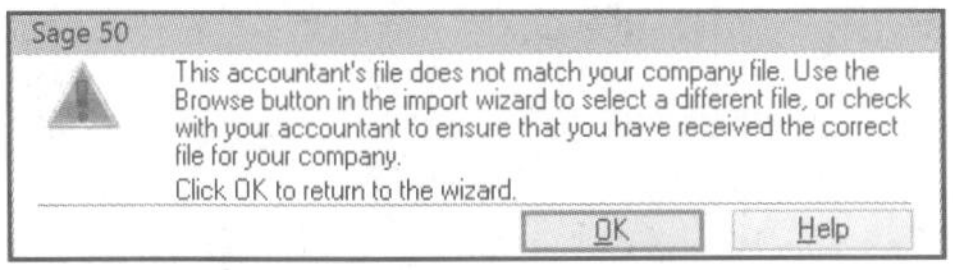

Click **OK** and **Cancel** to exit the import wizard. You must use the data file in the Accountant folder for this step.

If you are using the correct matching data file, Sage 50 will require confirmation:

Sage 50 - Confirmation
Transaction date on line 3 precedes the Fiscal Start date and will affect prior year reports. It will also affect the current year starting balances.
Do you wish to continue?
☐ Do not show this message again.
Yes | No

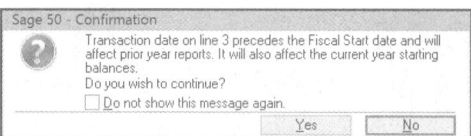

This warning appears because the entries are dated in the previous fiscal year. We want to accept the dates the accountant used because they are correct and the entries should be added to the financial reports for the previous year. We have already changed the settings for this file to allow transactions dated before October 1. Sage 50 still provides this warning whenever you are posting to a previous month. We need to allow all these entries and do not want the message to appear for each separate transaction.

Click **Do Not Show This Message Again**.

Click **Yes** to display the summary of entries added to your data file:

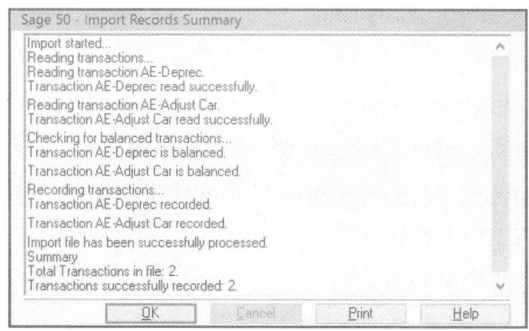

Sage 50 - Import Records Summary
Import started...
Reading transactions...
Reading transaction AE-Deprec.
Transaction AE-Deprec read successfully.
Reading transaction AE-Adjust Car.
Transaction AE-Adjust Car read successfully.
Checking for balanced transactions...
Transaction AE-Deprec is balanced.
Transaction AE-Adjust Car is balanced.
Recording transactions...
Transaction AE-Deprec recorded.
Transaction AE-Adjust Car recorded.
Import file has been successfully processed.
Summary
Total Transactions in file: 2.
Transactions successfully recorded: 2.
OK | Cancel | Print | Help

Click **OK**:

Import Entries from Accountant Wizard - Finish
Sage 50 has successfully imported your accountant's entries.
< Back | Finish | Cancel | Help

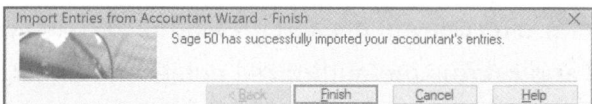

Click **Finish**. The process is now complete.

The General Journal Report for September 30 will include the accountant's entries:

Maple Leaf Rags Inc.
General Journal 06/30/2021 to 09/30/2021

		Account Number	Account Description	Debits	Credits
09/30/2021	J1***	AE-Deprec, Year-end depreciation adjustments			
		5200	Depreciation Expense depreciation on furniture & fixtures	1,520.00	-
		5200	Depreciation Expense depreciation on computers	3,900.00	-
		5200	Depreciation Expense depreciation on automobile	4,280.00	-
		1480	Accum Deprec: Furn & Equip	-	1,520.00
		1420	Accum Deprec: Computers	-	3,900.00
		1520	Accum Deprec: Automobile	-	4,280.00
09/30/2021	J2***	AE-Adjust Car, Adjustment for disposal of old car			
		1520	Accum Deprec: Automobile clear prior accum deprec amt	9,800.00	-
		1520	Accum Deprec: Automobile clear current year deprec amt	1,050.00	-
		5600	Loss on Trade-in	950.00	-
		1500	Automobile remove old car from asset (origi...	-	11,800.00

*** Imported accountant's entry

The journal entry numbers are marked *** with a note that they were created outside the regular file by the accountant.

REVIEW

The Student DVD with Data Files includes Review Questions and Supplementary Cases for this chapter, including a case with stock transactions that can be completed in the General Journal.

NOTES
If your system settings do not allow transactions in the previous year, you must first change this setting. Refer to page 106.

NOTES
For this report, we selected the journal options Previous Year and Include Only Entries Posted After Year End.

NOTES
The journal report has journal entry numbers 1 and 2. The AE-MAPLE file you are using has no other journal entries. It is provided only to demonstrate the step of importing the accountant's entries.

When you import entries to your working file, the journal entry numbers may be out of sequence if you have added transactions while the accountant was working with the file. The numbers will be the ones immediately following the last entry in the file you sent to the accountant.

CHAPTER THIRTEEN

SHADY CORNERS

OBJECTIVES

After completing this chapter, you should be able to

- ***enter*** transactions in all journals
- ***create*** new divisions
- ***change*** the Division Ledger name
- ***enter*** import duty on purchases from foreign suppliers
- ***allocate*** revenues and expenses in the General, Sales, Purchases, Payroll and Inventory journals
- ***make*** import duty remittances
- ***enter*** purchases with cost variances
- ***process*** credit card sales transactions
- ***set up*** records for direct payments and pre-authorized debits
- ***enter***, ***upload*** and ***review*** pre-authorized debits and direct deposits and payments
- ***display*** and ***print*** transactions with division details
- ***display*** and ***print*** division reports

COMPANY INFORMATION

Company Profile

NOTES
Shady Corners
599 Ivy Lane
Halifax, NS B3J 2N3
Tel 1: (902) 289-3904
Tel 2: (888) 289-3904
Fax: (902) 285-7532
Business No.: 230 192 825

Shady Corners, located in Halifax, Nova Scotia, owned and operated by Julie and Jules Jardin, is a brother-and-sister partnership. Both majored in science at university; Jules went on to complete a master's degree in landscape architecture while Julie earned a business degree.

The store carries a range of shade-tolerant plants and shrubs as well as a variety of high-end garden and patio furniture. Most of the plants are grown locally, many in the nursery Julie and Jules operate as a separate company. The modern-style, moulded plastic, teak and cast aluminum patio furniture pieces are imported from Denmark, while the hammocks and umbrellas are Canadian made.

Most customers are from the local Halifax region and buy for their city or nearby cottage properties. Delivery (shipping or freight) is charged on most orders. In addition, new development projects or office complexes place large orders for landscaping services, furniture and plants. Charges for services are based on hourly rates. Some homeowners complete their own work and pay only for the designs.

The business has six employees: planting and soil preparation are completed by two gardeners, designs are prepared by another employee and assistant or by Jules, a fifth employee works in and manages the store and the sixth delivers plants and furniture.

Preferred price list customers do not pay for delivery, and they receive discounted inventory prices. All account customers are entitled to a before-tax 2 percent discount if they settle their accounts within 15 days. After 30 days, interest charges accrue at the rate of 1.5 percent per month. Customer deposits from 20 to 25 percent of the total sale are required on all orders. Customers may pay by cheque, cash or credit card.

Some suppliers with whom Shady Corners has accounts require deposits to accompany purchase orders, and some suppliers offer after-tax purchase discounts for early payment. The store has a business credit card account with Visa.

The currency for all foreign transactions is the Danish krone (DKK). Because foreign prices for inventory are calculated from the exchange rate at the time of sale, foreign prices are not entered in the Inventory Ledger. There are currently no customers outside of Canada. Shady Corners pays import duties on the imported wood, plastic and metal furniture items.

Julie Jardin used the following to set up the accounting files in Sage 50:

- Chart of Accounts
- Post-Closing Trial Balance
- Supplier Information
- Customer Information
- Employee Information
- Employee Profiles and TD1 Information
- Inventory Information
- Division Information
- Accounting Procedures

PRO VERSION
The term Vendors will be used instead of Suppliers throughout the program.

CHART OF ACCOUNTS

SHADY CORNERS

ASSETS

Current Assets
1050 Bank: Chequing CAD
1060 Bank Account: DKK
1070 Bank: Visa and Interac
1080 Bank: MasterCard
1200 Accounts Receivable
1220 Purchase Prepayments
1230 Advances & Loans Receivable
1240 Plant Care Supplies
1260 Office Supplies

Inventory Assets
1340 Books
1360 Plants and Soil
1380 Shrubs
1400 Patio Furniture

Fixed Assets
1650 Cash Register & Computers
1670 Tools & Equipment ▶
▶1680 Store Fixtures
1700 Delivery Vehicles
1720 Store

LIABILITIES

Current Liabilities
2100 Bank Loan
2150 Prepaid Sales and Deposits
2200 Accounts Payable
2220 Import Duty Payable
2250 Credit Card Payable
2300 Vacation Payable
2310 EI Payable
2320 CPP Payable
2330 Income Tax Payable
2400 RRSP Payable
2410 Professional Dues Payable
2420 Union Dues Payable
2460 WCB Payable
2650 GST/HST Charged on Sales
2670 GST/HST Paid on Purchases
▶

▶Long Term Liabilities
2850 Mortgage Payable

EQUITY
3560 Jardins, Capital
3580 Jardins, Drawings
3600 Current Earnings

REVENUE
4020 Revenue from Store Sales
4040 Revenue from Services
4100 Revenue from Delivery
4150 Sales Discounts

EXPENSE

Operating Expenses
5060 Assembly Costs
5070 Cost of Goods Sold
5080 Variance Costs
5090 Cost of Services
5100 Freight Expense
5110 Inventory Losses ▶
▶5120 Exchange Rate Differences
5160 Credit Card Fees
5200 Advertising & Promotion
5230 Interest Expenses
5250 Truck Rentals
5260 Garden Supplies Used
5270 Purchase Discounts
5280 Repairs & Maintenance
5290 Utilities Expenses

Payroll Expenses
5450 Vacation Pay Expense
5460 Salaries
5470 General Wages
5480 Piece Rate Wage Expense
5490 Commissions and Bonuses
5500 Tuition Expense
5510 EI Expense
5520 CPP Expense
5530 WCB Expense

NOTES: The Chart of Accounts includes only postable accounts and the Net Income or Current Earnings account.

POST-CLOSING TRIAL BALANCE

SHADY CORNERS

May 31, 2021

		Debits	Credits
1050	Bank: Chequing CAD	$ 40 675.00	
1060	Bank Account: DKK (Dkr 20.040,00)	4 100.00	
1070	Bank: Visa and Interac	6 450.00	
1080	Bank: MasterCard	3 980.00	
1200	Accounts Receivable	4 140.00	
1240	Plant Care Supplies	3 980.00	
1260	Office Supplies	640.00	
1340	Books	500.00	
1360	Plants and Soil	1 648.00	
1380	Shrubs	1 370.00	
1400	Patio Furniture	22 465.00	
1650	Cash Register & Computers	10 800.00	
1670	Tools & Equipment	9 400.00	
1680	Store Fixtures	12 000.00	
1700	Delivery Vehicles	43 000.00	
1720	Store	230 000.00	
2100	Bank Loan		$ 40 000.00
2200	Accounts Payable		5 050.00
2220	Import Duty Payable		320.00
2250	Credit Card Payable		630.00
2300	Vacation Payable		2 588.40
2310	EI Payable		960.08
2320	CPP Payable		1 733.26
2330	Income Tax Payable		3 022.01
2400	RRSP Payable		550.00
2410	Professional Dues Payable		60.00
2420	Union Dues Payable		94.06
2460	WCB Payable		1 017.72
2650	GST/HST Charged on Sales		11 900.00
2670	GST/HST Paid on Purchases	$ 8 700.00	
2850	Mortgage Payable		160 000.00
3560	Jardins, Capital		183 922.47
3580	Jardins, Drawings	8 000.00	
		$411 848.00	$411 848.00

SUPPLIER INFORMATION

SHADY CORNERS

Supplier Name (Contact)	Address	Phone No. Fax No.	E-mail Web Site	Terms Tax ID
Bell Canada (I. Hurd)	1234 Listener Rd. Halifax, Nova Scotia B3R 2K8	Tel: (902) 310-2355	bell.ca	n/10
Canadian Agricultural Workers' Union (Membership Office)	Toronto, Ontario	Tel: (416) 699-2020		n/15
Capital Trust				n/1
Groen Fields (Arjen Groen)	RR #2 Truro, Nova Scotia B2N 5B1	Tel: (902) 454-6111 Fax: (902) 454-6900		n/60 186 522 330 RT0001
Home Energy (Serge Powers)	880 Gardenia Blvd. Halifax, Nova Scotia B3J 4B6	Tel: (902) 288-9988	home.energy.com	n/10 557 882 990 RT0001
Jorgensen Mobler (J. Jorgensen)	Gronladsvej 7640 7422 Harlev, Denmark	Tel: 011 45 7822 3402 Fax: 011 45 7822 9300	JMobler.dk	2/30, n/60
Mobler Dansk (Karl Nyberg)	Gronlandsdage 48 5000 Odense, Denmark	Tel: 011 45 2887 4334 Fax: 011 45 2887 8201	nyberg@moblerdansk.dk moblerdansk.dk	2/15, n/30
Office Plus	55 Industry Ave. Truro, Nova Scotia B2N 2L1	Tel: (902) 455-7231	officeplus.com	1/15, n/30
Professional Landscapers' Association (Membership Office)	Toronto, Ontario	Tel: (416) 783-4990		n/15
Receiver General for Canada	333 Laurier Ave. W. Ottawa, Ontario K1A 0L9	Tel: (613) 238-7125	cra-arc.gc.ca	n/1
Workers' Compensation Board				n/1

OUTSTANDING SUPPLIER INVOICES

SHADY CORNERS

Supplier Name	Terms	Date	Invoice No.	Amount CAD	Amount DKK
Groen Fields	net 60	May 27/21	GF-1142	$ 900	
Jorgensen Mobler	2/30, n/60	May 27/21	JM-842	$2 480	Dkr 12.100,00
Mobler Dansk	2/15, n/30	May 10/21	MD-724	$1 670	Dkr 8.160,00
			Grand Total	$5 050	

CUSTOMER INFORMATION

SHADY CORNERS

Customer Name (Contact)	Address	Phone No. Fax No.	E-mail Web Site	Terms Credit Limit
*Acadian Towers (Jardine LePlante)	88 Maple Ave. Halifax, Nova Scotia B3B 4B4	Tel: (902) 486-7298 Fax: (902) 486-6911	acadiantowers.ca	2/15, n/30 $15 000
*Eastrose Hotel (Janine Bouquet)	455 Rosehill Dr. Halifax, Nova Scotia B3T 1N2	Tel 1: (902) 277-8614 Tel 2: (888) 277-8614 Fax: (902) 277-2388	jbouquet@eastrose.com eastrose.com	2/15, n/30 $15 000
*Hopewell College (Holly Greene)	4500 Spruce Ave. Halifax, Nova Scotia B3F 7G9	Tel 1: (902) 782-5611 Tel 2: (902) 775-8014	h.greene@hopewell.edu hopewell.edu	2/15, n/30 $15 000
Rockcliff Manor (Aidel Weiss)	400 Rocky Ridge Rise Halifax, Nova Scotia B3B 5V8	Tel 1: (902) 972-7181 Tel 2: (902) 972-3939	aidel.weiss@gmail.com	2/15, n/30 $8 000

NOTES: Preferred price list customers are marked with an asterisk (*) beside their names. All discounts are after tax.

OUTSTANDING CUSTOMER INVOICES

SHADY CORNERS

Customer Name	Terms	Date	Invoice No.	Amount	Tax	Total
Acadian Towers	2/15, n/30	May 24/21	155	$1 200	$180	$1 380
Hopewell College	2/15, n/30	May 26/21	159	$1 500	$225	$1 725
Rockcliff Manor	2/15, n/30	May 29/21	163	$ 900	$135	$1 035
				Grand Total		$4 140

Employee Profiles and TD1 Information

General Information All employees are allowed 10 days per year for illness and five for personal reasons. All employees have their paycheques deposited directly into their bank accounts. Eligible tuition fees are partially reimbursed on successful completion of courses. All payroll remittances are due at the end of each month.

Three employees (Anthemum, Pine and Iola) receive a commission in addition to their regular pay, and three employees (Phlox, Aster and Fineum) receive a piece rate bonus based on the number of plantings they complete. Phlox, Aster and Fineum are union members and pay union dues; Anthemum and Pine pay professional association fees. The 6 percent vacation pay for hourly paid workers is retained.

Chris Anthemum is the senior landscape designer at Shady Corners. Her salary of $3 900 per month is supplemented by a commission of 2 percent of all revenue from services. She is paid at the end of each month and is allowed four weeks of vacation with pay. Anthemum is married with one eligible child under 12 and claims the basic, spousal and child (federal only) tax claim amounts. She has $200 deducted from each paycheque to invest in her RRSP and pays professional association dues.

Lou Pine is the assistant designer who helps Anthemum with all her design work and also manages the accounting records for the business. He is paid a monthly salary of $3 400 plus a commission of 1 percent of service revenue and is allowed three weeks of vacation with pay. He has only the basic tax claim amount because he is single and self-supporting. He invests $100 of each paycheque in his RRSP and also pays monthly professional association fees.

NOTES

Iola's commission is calculated at the rate of about 0.5 percent of sales revenue. We provide commission amounts for Iola in the source documents. This amount is included for the calculation of vacation pay because her commission is based on performance.

Salaried employees do not receive vacation pay on commissions because their vacation rate is 0 percent.

Glad Iola works in the store as the salesperson for an hourly rate of $22 (plus $33 per overtime hour and a commission on store sales). She is single and pays $50 from each paycheque toward the purchase of RRSP investments from her bi-weekly pay.

Rose Aster also invests in her RRSP through payroll deductions and pays union dues. She works as the gardener, planting shrubs and other plants for customers and assisting in the store for the hourly rate of $20 and $30 per overtime hour plus the piece rate bonus. As a recent graduate, she has tuition and provincial education amounts to increase her basic single tax claim amount and is reimbursed for her tuition at the rate of $100 per bi-weekly pay.

Dell Fineum also does gardening work and assists in the store for the hourly rate of $20 ($30 per overtime hour) plus the piece rate bonus for planting. He is single so has the basic claim amounts. Fineum has deductions for his RRSP and for his union dues from his bi-weekly pay.

Daisy Phlox is married, so she has the basic and spousal tax claim amounts. She does not invest in her RRSP through payroll but does have deductions for union dues from her bi-weekly salary of $1 650. Instead of vacation pay, Phlox takes three weeks of vacation each year. Her primary responsibility is delivery, but she also assists with gardening on job sites and is allowed the piece rate bonus for this work.

EMPLOYEE INFORMATION SHEET

SHADY CORNERS

	Chris Anthemum	Lou Pine	Glad Iola	Rose Aster	Dell Fineum	Daisy Phlox
Position	Designer	Asst Designer	Sales	Gardener	Gardener	Delivery
Social Insurance No.	618 524 664	821 887 114	398 577 619	572 351 559	404 535 601	464 375 286
Address	98 Arbutus Ave. Halifax, Nova Scotia B3J 2A5	44 Lilac Lane Halifax, Nova Scotia B3C 3E5	36 Locust Ave. Halifax, Nova Scotia B3V 4S3	8 Magnolia Cres. Halifax, Nova Scotia B3J 1Y7	18 Forsythia Cres. Halifax, Nova Scotia B3G 4K1	59 Cherry Rd. Halifax, Nova Scotia B3Z 3X3
Telephone	(902) 641-6773	(902) 648-1916	(902) 784-7195	(902) 738-5188	(902) 788-2826	(902) 645-6238
Date of Birth (mm-dd-yy)	05-28-84	08-08-86	05-21-88	02-03-89	08-19-90	09-28-77
Federal (Ontario) Tax Exemption TD1						
Basic Personal	$12 609 (8 481)	$12 609 (8 481)	$12 609 (8 481)	$12 609 (8 481)	$12 609 (8 481)	$12 609 (8 481)
Other Indexed	$14 839 (8 481)	-	-	-	-	$12 609 (8 481)
Other Non-indexed	-	-	-	$8 210 (9 810)	-	-
Total Exemptions	$27 448 (16 962)	$12 609 (8 481)	$12 609 (8 481)	$20 819 (18 291)	$12 609 (8 481)	$25 218 (16 962)

▶

EMPLOYEE INFORMATION SHEET CONTINUED

SHADY CORNERS

	Chris Anthemum	Lou Pine	Glad Iola	Rose Aster	Dell Fineum	Daisy Phlox
Employee Earnings						
Regular Wage Rate	–	–	$22.00	$20.00	$20.00	–
Overtime Wage Rate	–	–	$33.00	$30.00	$30.00	–
Regular Salary	$3 900/mo	$3 400/mo	–	–	–	$1 650/2 weeks
Pay Period	monthly	monthly	bi-weekly	bi-weekly	bi-weekly	bi-weekly
Hours per Period	150	150	75	75	75	75
Piece Rate	–	–	–	$0.50/shrub	$0.50/shrub	$0.50/shrub
Tuition	–	–	–	$100	–	–
Commission	2% (services)	1% (services)	based on sales	–	–	–
Vacation	4 weeks	3 weeks	6% retained	6% retained	6% retained	3 weeks
Vacation Pay Owed	–	–	$942.40	$818.50	$827.50	–
WCB Rate	4.93	4.93	2.48	4.93	4.93	6.72
Employee Deductions						
RRSP	$200	$100	$50	$50	$25	–
Professional Dues	$30	$30	–	–	–	–
Union Dues	–	–	–	0.78%	0.78%	1.2%
EI, CPP & Income Tax	Calculations built into Sage 50 program.					

INVENTORY INFORMATION

SHADY CORNERS

Code	Description	Unit	Min Qty	Selling Price Reg	(Pref)	Qty on Hand	Total (Cost)	Taxes Rate	Duty
Books: Total asset value $500 (Linked accounts: Asset 1340; Revenue 4020; COGS 5070; Variance 5080)									
BK01	Gardening in the Shade	book	10	$45	$38	20	$500	GST	n/a
Plants and Ground Covers: Total asset value $1 648 (Linked accounts: Asset 1360; Revenue 4020; COGS 5070; Variance 5080)									
PL01	Plant/ground cover: 5 litre	each	8	18	16	24	240	HST	n/a
PL02	Plant/ground cover: 10 litre	each	8	29	25	24	384	HST	n/a
PL03	Plant/ground cover starters	4-pack	8	8	6	40	160	HST	n/a
PL04	Plant: perennial specialty	each	6	49	42	16	400	HST	n/a
PL05	Plant: annual 10 cm	each	8	9	8	24	120	HST	n/a
PL06	Plant: annual 15 cm	each	6	16	13	24	216	HST	n/a
PS10	Topsoil: 50 litre bag	bag	20	6	4.50	32	128	HST	n/a
PS11	Topsoil: cubic metre	cu m	0	125	105	0	0	HST	n/a
Shrubs: Total asset value $1 370 (Linked accounts: Asset 1380; Revenue 4020; COGS 5070; Variance 5080)									
SH01	Shrubs: 50 cm	each	10	13	11	30	$180	HST	n/a
SH02	Shrubs: 1 metre	each	8	29	25	20	320	HST	n/a
SH03	Shrubs: 3 metre	each	6	55	48	10	320	HST	n/a
SH04	Shrubs: 1 metre specialty	each	6	89	80	10	550	HST	n/a
Patio & Garden Furniture: Total asset value $22 465 (Linked accounts: Asset 1400; Revenue 4020; COGS 5060; Variance 5070)									
FA01	Patio set: Cast Aluminum round table 1.5 m	7-pc set	1	1 340	1 090	2	$1 400	HST	8.0%
FA02	Patio set: Cast Aluminum rect. table 2 m	7-pc set	1	1 340	1 150	2	1 400	HST	8.0%
FA03	Patio table: Cast Aluminum round 2 m	each	1	795	690	4	1 600	HST	8.0%
FA04	Arm chair: Cast Aluminum	each	4	95	85	12	660	HST	8.0%
FA05	Ottoman: Cast Aluminum	each	2	55	50	5	125	HST	8.0%
FA06	End table: Cast Aluminum	each	2	105	95	5	300	HST	8.0%
FA07	Bench: Cast Aluminum	each	2	245	185	4	640	HST	8.0%

INVENTORY INFORMATION CONTINUED

SHADY CORNERS

Code	Description	Unit	Min Qty	Selling Price Reg	(Pref)	Qty on Hand	Total (Cost)	Taxes Rate	Duty
FP21	Patio table: Moulded Plastic 2 m	each	2	590	535	4	$ 1 240	HST	9.5%
FP22	Arm chair: Moulded Plastic	each	8	75	65	10	410	HST	9.5%
FP23	Folding chair: Moulded Plastic	each	12	55	48	10	300	HST	9.5%
FP24	Chaise longue: Moulded Plastic	each	3	165	140	4	360	HST	9.5%
FT31	Patio table: Teak round 1.5 m	each	2	925	750	2	1 040	HST	9.5%
FT32	Patio table: Teak rect. 2 m	each	2	1 180	950	2	1 160	HST	9.5%
FT33	Arm chair: Teak	each	8	725	615	8	3 040	HST	9.5%
FT34	Chaise longue: Teak	each	2	980	810	4	1 960	HST	9.5%
FT35	End table: Teak	each	2	245	210	5	700	HST	9.5%
FT36	Ottoman: Teak	each	4	105	95	4	220	HST	9.5%
FT37	Bench: Teak	each	2	1 125	980	4	2 320	HST	9.5%
FX41	Hammock w/stand	each	3	175	155	8	760	HST	n/a
FX42	Umbrella w/stand	each	6	225	200	10	1 100	HST	n/a
FX43	Cushion: deep seating chair	each	12	45	40	30	600	HST	n/a
FX44	Cushion: deep seating lounge	each	4	105	95	8	480	HST	n/a
FX45	Cushion: deep seating set	5-pc set	3	245	205	5	650	HST	n/a
Total Inventory Value							$25 983		
Services: (Linked Revenue account: 4040; COGS account: 5090)									
SC01	Consultation/Design	hour		110	90			HST	
SC02	Report	report		200	160			HST	
SC03	Planting & Soil Preparation	hour		50	40			HST	

Division Information

Shady Corners uses three divisions — one for store sales, one for planting work and one for design work. Pine will set up these divisions at the beginning of June and keep track of the percentage of time each employee works in each division. Because these times vary from one job to another, the percentage allocation is included with each source document. Allocation details for other expenses and revenues are also included with the source documents. Amounts for asset, liability and equity accounts are not allocated.

Accounting Procedures

Taxes: HST

NOTES

When PST only is charged – as for insurance – it is included with the expense or asset part of the journal entry because it is not refundable.

Shady Corners pays 15 percent HST on all goods and services that it buys, including the imported products, and charges HST on the sales and services it provides, except for books. It uses the regular method for remittance of the Harmonized Sales Tax. HST collected from customers is recorded as a liability in *GST/HST Charged on Sales*. HST paid to suppliers is recorded in *GST/HST Paid on Purchases* as a decrease in liability to the Canada Revenue Agency. The report is filed with the Receiver General for Canada by the last day of the month for the previous quarter, either including the balance owing or requesting a refund.

Some items, such as books, are exempt from HST and have only GST at the rate of 5 percent charged. A separate tax code has been created for this tax rate.

In Nova Scotia, PST is harmonized with GST. The provincial portion of HST is 10 percent.

NSF Cheques

When a bank returns a customer's cheque because there were insufficient funds in the customer's bank account to cover the cheque, the payment must be reversed. If the payment was processed through the Receipts Journal, the reversal should also be processed through the Receipts Journal (refer to page 177). If the sale was a cash sale to a one-time customer, the reversal must be processed through the Sales Journal. Create a customer record and process a credit (Pay Later) sale for the full amount of the NSF cheque without tax (taxes for the sale were recorded at the time of the original sale). Enter the amount as a **positive** amount in the Amount field and enter *Bank: Chequing CAD* in the Account field. On a separate invoice line, enter the amount of the handling charge for the NSF cheque in the Amount field with *Other Revenue* in the Account field. Again, the handling charge is non-taxable.

NOTES
The Sales Journal entry will credit Bank: Chequing CAD for the full amount of the sale including taxes and debit Accounts Receivable for the customer.

NOTES
If you created a customer record by using Quick Add or used an existing record (e.g., Cash Customers), you can adjust the sales invoice by changing the method of payment from Cheque to Pay Later. You cannot choose Pay Later as the payment method for one-time customers.

Returns

When customers return merchandise, they are charged a 20 percent handling charge unless the merchandise is defective. In the Sales Journal, enter the quantity returned with a **minus** sign at the regular sale price, add the tax code and enter *Sales Returns & Allowances* in the Account field. The amounts will automatically be negative because of the minus sign in the quantity field, so *Accounts Receivable* will be credited automatically as well. On a separate invoice line, enter the amount withheld — the handling charge — as a positive amount and credit *Other Revenue*. *Accounts Receivable* will be debited automatically for the amount of the handling charge.

If the original sale was a credit sale and the account is not yet paid, the return should also be entered as a credit sale so that *Accounts Receivable* will be credited. If the original sale was paid in cash or by credit card or the account has been paid, the return should be entered as a cash sale or credit card sale so that the appropriate bank account will be credited. (Refer to page 382.)

NOTES
If the refund is paid in cash, choose Cash as the payment method instead of Pay Later.

Reserved Inventory for Divisions

When customers sign a contract, the inventory items needed to complete the work are set aside or reserved by transferring them through the Item Assembly Journal to a designated account. (Refer to page 376.) In this way, these items cannot be sold to other customers because the inventory quantities available are already reduced. The minimum stock level for reserved inventory will be zero.

Cash, Credit and Debit Card, and Pre-Authorized Debit (PAD) Sales

Most types of businesses accept these different methods of payment. The program handles these transactions automatically through the Sales Journal when you choose the appropriate method of payment. For cash and debit and credit card sales, if this is not a regular customer, choose One-Time Customer from the Customer list, or type the new customer's name and choose Continue or Quick Add. For payments by cheque, a Cheque Number field opens. Shady Corners accepts Visa, MasterCard and Interac debit cards from customers for store sales. Instructions for setting up and processing credit card sales, pre-authorized credit card sales and pre-authorized debits are provided in this chapter (refer to pages 514–525).

The program will debit the related bank account instead of the *Accounts Receivable* control account and all other accounts will be appropriately debited or credited.

NOTES
We use the term Cash Sales and Purchases for cash and cheque transactions.

When you choose Continue, the name is added to the journal report without creating a customer record.

Cash Purchases and Direct Payments

Choose the supplier from the Supplier list or add the supplier using Quick Add and then choose the correct method of payment. Cash purchases may be entered in the

PRO VERSION
Remember that the term Vendors replaces the term Suppliers.

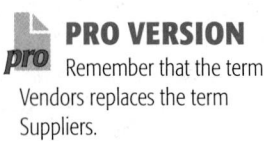

Payments Journal as Other Payments or in the Purchases Journal. For cheque payments, a Cheque Number field opens with the next cheque number entered. Complete the remainder of the cash transaction in the same way you would enter other transactions. Instructions for setting up direct payments are provided (refer to page 528).

The program will credit *Bank: Chequing CAD* instead of *Accounts Payable*, the control account. All other accounts for the transaction will be appropriately debited or credited.

NOTES
After completing the entry as usual in Sage 50, the payments are uploaded and the funds transferred through an account with a third-party supplier.

Electronic Funds Transfers (EFT)

Pre-authorized debits, direct payments and direct deposits use electronic transfers. Money is taken directly from the customer bank account and deposited to the business bank account, or taken from the business bank account and deposited to supplier and employee bank accounts. Shady Corners has an account set up with a third-party supplier to upload these bank account transfers from the program.

Freight Expense

When a business purchases inventory items, the cost of any freight that cannot be directly allocated to a specific item must be charged to *Freight Expense*. This amount will be regarded as an expense rather than charged to an inventory asset account.

NOTES
To preview, print or e-mail invoices, you must have the correct forms selected for invoices in the Reports & Forms Settings. You can access these settings from the journal tool bar.

Printing Invoices, Orders and Quotes

To print the invoices, purchase orders or sales quotes through the program, complete the journal transaction as you would otherwise. Before posting the transaction, preview the invoice. If the invoice is correct, you can print it from the preview window or directly from the invoice by choosing the File menu and then Print or by clicking the Print tool on the tool bar for the invoice form. Printing will begin immediately, so be sure you have the correct forms for your printer before you begin. If you and the customer or supplier have e-mail, click the E-mail tool to send the invoice or order.

Foreign Purchases

Shady Corners imports some inventory items from companies in Denmark. The currency for these transactions is the Danish krone (DKK) and the currency symbol is Dkr. Amounts in kroner are written as Dkr 10.500,50 (ten thousand, five hundred Danish kroner and fifty cents) — the period (.) separates the thousands and the comma (,) is the decimal point separator.

Shady Corners pays HST and import duties on these purchases. Duty rates are set up in the Inventory Ledger for the individual items and the amounts are calculated automatically by the program.

INSTRUCTIONS

NOTES
The transactions in this exercise provide a comprehensive practice set. If you want to use it only for review, you can complete the transactions without setting up divisions and entering allocations.

1. **Record entries** for the source documents for June 2021 in Sage 50 using the Chart of Accounts, Trial Balance and other information. The procedures for entering each new type of transaction are outlined step by step in the Keystrokes section with the source documents.
2. **Print** the **reports** indicated on the following printing form after you have finished making your entries:

REPORTS

Accounts
- [ ] Chart of Accounts
- [ ] Account List
- [ ] General Journal Entries

Financials
- [x] Comparative Balance Sheet: June 1 and June 30, difference in percentage
- [x] Income Statement from June 1 to June 30
- [x] Trial Balance date: June 30
- [x] All Journal Entries: June 1 to June 30 with division allocations, foreign amounts and corrections
- [x] General Ledger accounts: 1400 4020 4040 from June 1 to June 30
- [ ] Statement of Cash Flows
- [x] Cash Flow Projection Detail Report for account 1050 for 30 days
- [x] Gross Margin Income Statement from June 1 to June 30

Tax
- [x] Report on HST from June 1 to June 30

Banking
- [ ] Cheque Log Report

Payables
- [ ] Supplier List
- [ ] Supplier Aged
- [ ] Aged Overdue Payables
- [ ] Purchases Journal Entries
- [ ] Payments Journal Entries
- [ ] Supplier Purchases

Receivables
- [ ] Customer List
- [ ] Customer Aged
- [ ] Aged Overdue Receivables
- [ ] Sales Journal Entries
- [ ] Receipts Journal Entries
- [ ] Customer Sales
- [ ] Sales by Salesperson
- [ ] Customer Statements

Payroll
- [ ] Employee List
- [x] Employee Summary for all employees
- [ ] Deductions & Expenses
- [ ] Remittance
- [ ] Payroll Journal Entries
- [x] T4 Slips for all employees
- [ ] Record of Employment
- [x] Year End Review (PIER)

Inventory & Services
- [ ] Inventory & Services List
- [ ] Inventory Summary
- [ ] Inventory Quantity
- [ ] Inventory Statistics
- [x] Inventory Sales Summary for Plants and Soil from June 1 to June 30
- [x] Inventory Transaction Summary for Shrubs, all journals from June 1 to June 30
- [ ] Item Assembly Journal Entries
- [ ] Adjustment Journal Entries
- [ ] Inventory Price Lists

Division
- [ ] Division List
- [x] Division Income Summary: all divisions, all accounts from June 1 to June 30
- [ ] Division Allocation Report

Mailing Labels
- [ ] Labels

KEYSTROKES

Creating New Divisions

Sage 50 allows allocations for all accounts. Each account ledger record has a check box to allow allocations for the account (refer to page 93). If this box is checked, the allocation option is available for that account in any journal entry. If it is not checked, you cannot allocate an amount for that account. If you are unable to allocate an amount, check the ledger record for the account you are using to be sure that the option to **Allow Division Allocations** is selected. Shady Corners will allocate amounts for all revenue and expense accounts. This is the default setting for new income statement accounts. The option to allow allocations is already turned on for all these accounts in your data file.

Open **SageData19\SHADE\SHADE**. **Enter June 7, 2021** as the session date.

Click **OK** to enter the session date. The Receivables Home window appears.

Before entering any transactions with allocations, you should create the divisions as instructed in memo #1.

✓ 1 Based on memo #1 from Owner on June 1, create three new divisions: Store Sales, Planting and Design. All divisions begin June 1, 2021, and are active. Allocations will be made by percentage.

NOTES
If you are working with backups, you should restore SageData19\SHADE1.CAB or SHADE1 to SageData19\SHADE\SHADE.

PRO VERSION
The ledger record option is to Allow Project Allocations.

NOTES
For Shady Corners, the option to allow allocations is not selected in the ledger records for Balance Sheet accounts.

NOTES
We have used a straight text format for source documents in this chapter.

PRO VERSION
Click Projects in the Modules pane list. The ledger is named Projects instead of Divisions. We will change this name on page 506.
The term Vendor replaces Supplier throughout the program.

NOTES
For the Retail company type, Projects are named Divisions. For other industry types, the term Project, Fund, Job Site, Partner, Crops or Property will be applied. Refer to Appendix B in this text.

CLASSIC VIEW
In the Classic view, the Divisions module has its own column, labelled Division.

NOTES
You can also enter allocations in the Inventory Adjustments Journal, but the Divisions icon is not included in the Inventory module window.

PRO VERSION
Click the Projects icon. Until you change the name, Project and Project Ledger will be used as the headings in the Title bar for these screens instead of Division and Division Ledger.

NOTES
You can enter division names in French and English when you choose to use both languages.

Click **Divisions** in the Modules pane list to change the Home window:

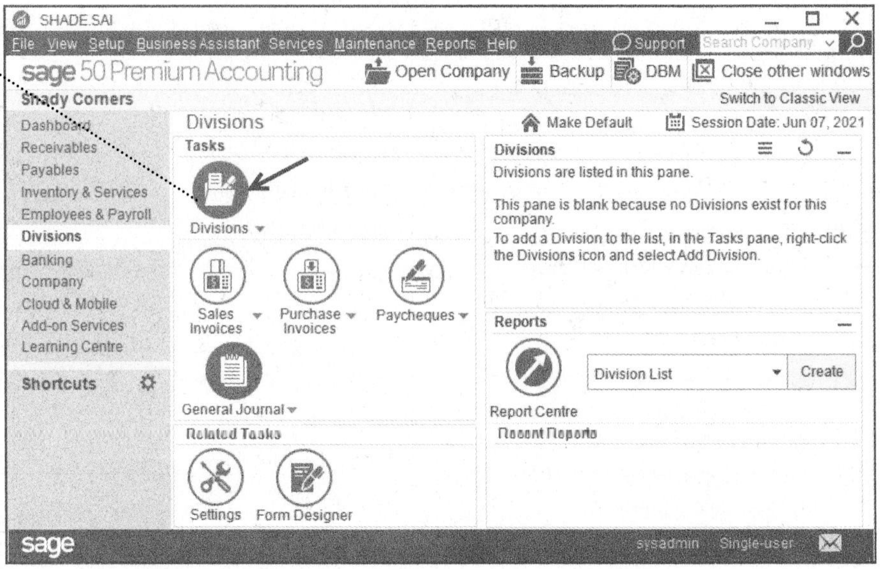

Click **Make Default** to keep this as the Home window.

The Divisions module window has access to the Division Ledger records, as well as to four journals that most often have allocated amounts. Divisions are created from the Divisions icon that opens the Division window. The Division window can also be accessed from the Company, Receivables, Payables and Employees & Payroll modules:

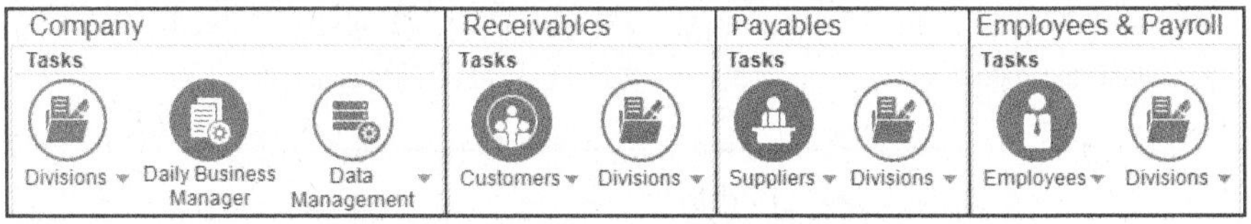

These four modules include the Divisions icon in the Tasks panes. These modules have journals that use allocations.

Click the **Divisions icon** to open the Division window:

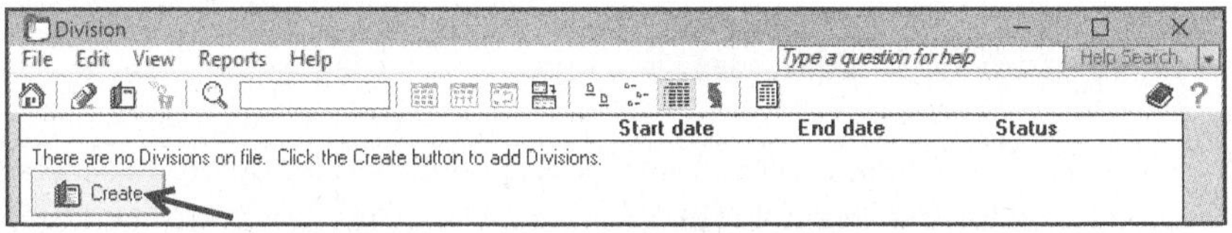

Click the **Create button** to open a new Division Ledger screen:

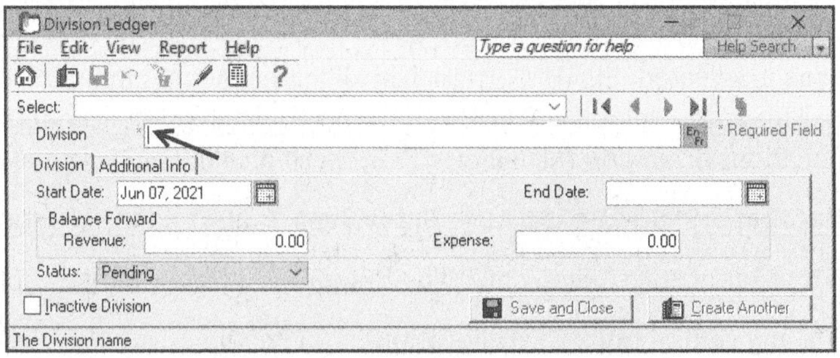

The cursor is in the Division name field, the only required field for the new record. You must enter the name of the first division.

Type `Store Sales` **Press** *tab* **twice** to skip the language button.

The cursor moves to the Start Date field. Enter the date on which you want to begin recording division information, June 1, 2021, to replace the default session date.

Type 6-01

You can enter an **Ending Date** for the division if this is appropriate. The ledger also has a **Balance Forward** field for **Revenue** and **Expense**. These fields can be used to enter historical information — the amount of revenue and expense generated by the division before the records were converted to Sage 50 or before the Division Ledger was used. The balances are zero for Shady Corners because a new fiscal period is beginning.

In the next field you must choose the Status for the division.

Click the **Status field** or its list arrow for the status options:

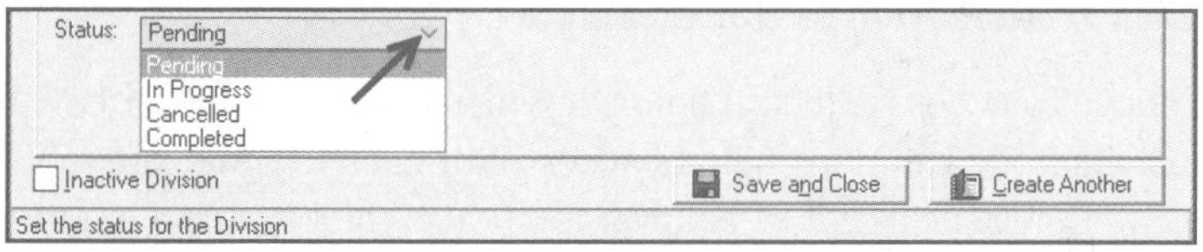

The division may be Pending (not yet started), In Progress or ongoing, Cancelled or Completed. All divisions at Shady Corners are In Progress or active.

Click **In Progress** from the Status drop-down list.

Click  to save the new division.

Create the **Planting** division and the **Design** division using the steps described above for Store Sales; **use June 1, 2021** as the starting date and **select In Progress** as the Status.

Click  to save the third division.

You will return to the Division window. Sage 50 has created a listing for each division, including the name, starting and ending dates and status.

Close the **Division window** to return to the module window. The **three** divisions are added to the Divisions pane in the module window.

Changing Division Settings

Click the **Settings icon**  to display the Settings window:

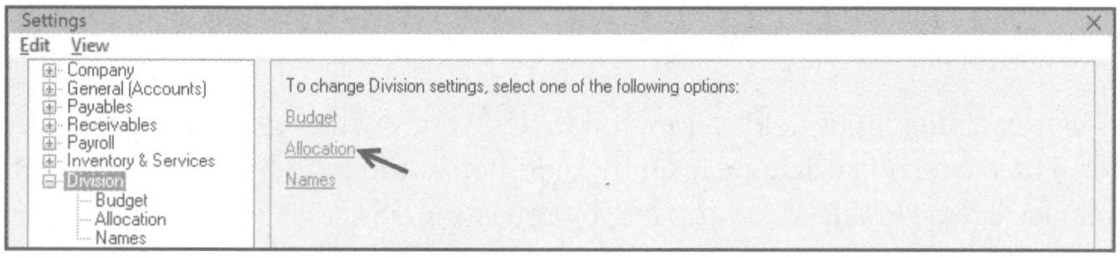

Or, choose the Setup menu, then choose Settings. If the Divisions module window is open, the Division Settings screen should open directly.

The Division Ledger has settings for budgeting, allocation and names. Budgeting is covered in Chapter 14. We need to view the settings for allocations.

Click **Allocation** either in the list under Division or in the list on the right:

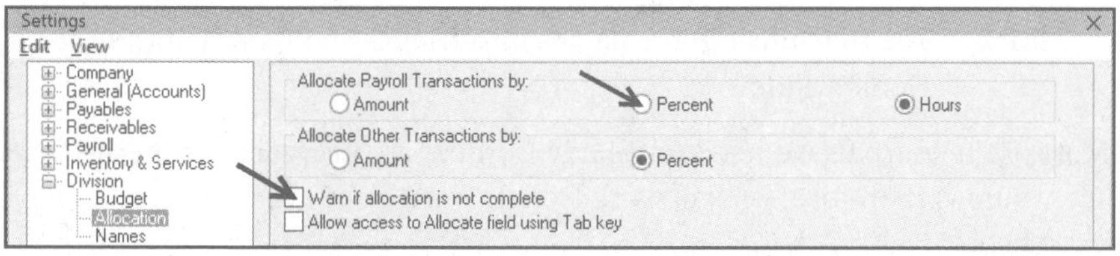

You can enter the allocation in different ways — by Amount, by Percent or by Hours (payroll only). The option to Allocate By Amount requires you to enter the exact dollar

NOTES
Project Ending Dates might be used for construction or other projects that have an expected or definite term.

NOTES
You can list divisions by icon in the Divisions window by choosing the View menu and icon.
You can re-sort the division icons if they are out of order by choosing the View menu and Re-Sort Icons.

CLASSIC VIEW
Right-click the Divisions icon and click the Settings tool . If the Divisions icon is not selected, choose Division from the Select Setup drop-down list and click Select.

PRO VERSION
Project will replace Division in the list of modules.

NOTES
You cannot change Division settings in multi-user mode.

amount for each division. Division work for payroll purposes is often recorded by time worked for the division, the default option for payroll allocations.

Sage 50 includes a warning for incomplete allocations. It is easy to miss an allocation because you must complete the allocation procedure even if 100 percent of the costs are allocated to a single division, and you must allocate each account line in the journals. You can choose to be warned if you try to post an entry that has not been fully allocated. If you are using divisions, you should always leave the warning turned on.

Click **Percent** as the method of allocating payroll amounts.

Click **Warn If Allocation Is Not Complete**.

You can also choose to access Allocate fields in journals with the tab key. Without this option, you must click the Divisions field to access it or click the Allocate tool to open the Allocation window. Using the tab key allows you to use the keyboard to enter the transaction and allocation. You can still click the field to move the cursor if you want.

NOTES
If you are not using the allocation feature, do not select the option to Allow Access To Allocate Field Using Tab Key so that the cursor will skip the unused Divisions column.

Click **Allow Access To Allocate Field Using Tab Key**.

Changing Division Names

In any version, you can change the name of the ledger to Project, Department, Profit Centre, Cost Centre or something that is more appropriate for a business. The new name will replace Division in all windows and reports. Division is an appropriate ledger name for Shady Corners.

PRO VERSION
pro These steps are included so that Pro version users will have the same names as the Premium version users.

Pro version users should change the name from Project to Division.

Click **Names** under the Division heading:

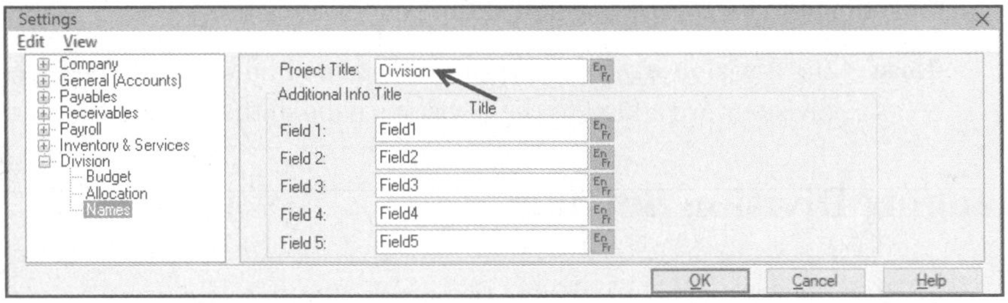

NOTES
We are not renaming Divisions as Departments because Sage 50 has a departmental accounting feature that is different from division allocation (refer to Chapter 19).

Double-click the Project Title field to select the default name. Type Division (or the name you want to use).

The remaining input fields allow you to add your own user-defined fields for the ledger. The new fields will appear on the Additional Info tab screen in the ledger record. The names can be changed at any time by repeating this step.

NOTES
Once the project is renamed by changing the Names setting, the new name will apply for all industry types. You must change the name on the Settings screen again if you want to use a different term.

Click **OK** to save the Division settings and display a confirmation message:

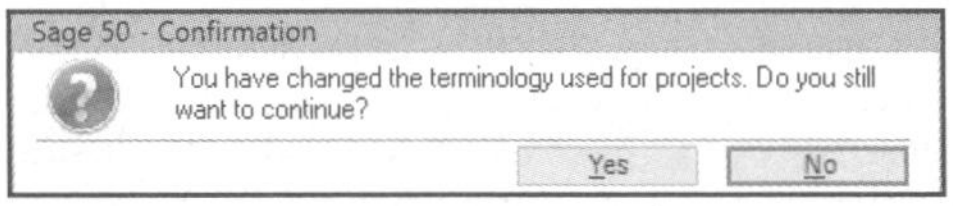

When you change the name, you must confirm that you want the name changed — all labels for the ledger icons, field names and report names will be changed.

Click **Yes** to confirm the changes in settings (and name) and return to the Home window.

Most of the journals we need for Shady Corners are accessible from the Divisions module window; therefore, we will work from here. We can create shortcuts for the other journals used.

Create **shortcuts** for **Pay Purchase Invoices** (Payables), **Create Receipt** (Receivables), **Transfer Funds** and **View Accounts** (Banking), **Item Assembly** and **Inventory Adjustments** (Inventory & Services) and **Payroll Cheque Run** (Employees & Payroll).

Entering Cost Allocations

Costs (or expenses) and revenues are allocated after the regular journal details are added but before the entry is posted. In a journal entry, whenever you use an account for which you have allowed division allocations in the General Ledger, the allocation option is available. For Shady Corners, all revenue and expense accounts allow division allocations.

Click the **Purchase Invoices icon** 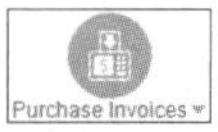

to open the Purchases Journal and prepare for entering the first transaction.

✓ 2 On June 1, received invoice #HE-4441 for store heat and hydro from Home Energy for $280 plus $42 HST for a total of $322. Terms: net 10 days. Charged 70% of the expenses to Store Sales, 20% to Planting and 10% to Design. The store is on an equal billing plan, so store this as a monthly recurring entry.

The journal has not changed with the setup of allocations, and we enter the purchase details the same way.

The first transaction does not involve the purchase of inventory items, so you will not use the inventory database to complete this transaction. Invoice is correct as the transaction type, and Pay Later is the correct payment method.

From the list of suppliers,

Click **Home Energy**.

Click the **Invoice No. field**. **Type** `HE-4441`

Type `jun 1` in the Date field to replace the default session date.

The tax code H and the account number 5290 should be added as the default. If they are not, you can add them or edit them as needed.

Enter a **description**.

Click the **Amount field** or press *tab* repeatedly to advance the cursor.

Type `280`

Press *tab* **twice** to enter the amount of the invoice and the tax amounts and advance to the Divisions column.

The journal still looks like a regular completed purchase transaction:

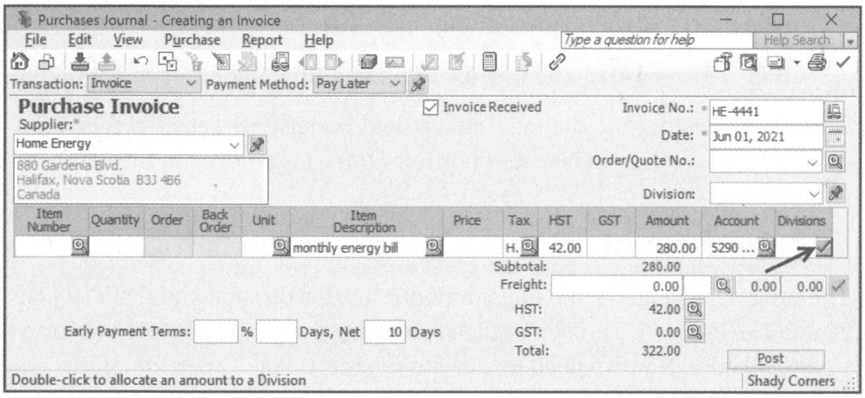

NOTES

All transactions can be completed from these shortcuts and journal windows. For example, other payments and payroll remittances are completed from the Payments Journal. Orders and Quotes are entered from the Sales Invoices or Purchase Invoices windows by selecting from the transactions drop-down list in the journal.

Alternatively, you can change module windows.

NOTES

You can allow allocations for Balance Sheet accounts, but we have not done so for Shady Corners.

To access the Division Allocation window, the cursor must be on an invoice line with an account that allows allocation. If the account does not allow allocation or if the cursor has advanced to an invoice line without an account or amount, the Allocate tool and menu option will be unavailable.

Click the invoice line for the amount you want to allocate to activate the Allocate option. Only accounts for which you have selected the option to Allow Division Allocations will activate the Allocate tool.

NOTES
You can also press *ctrl* + *shift* + A to open the Division Allocation window.

Click the **Allocate tool** in the tool bar or in the Divisions column, **double-click** the **Divisions column** beside the account, or **choose** the **Purchase menu** and **click Allocate**.

You will open the Division Allocation window for the Purchases Journal:

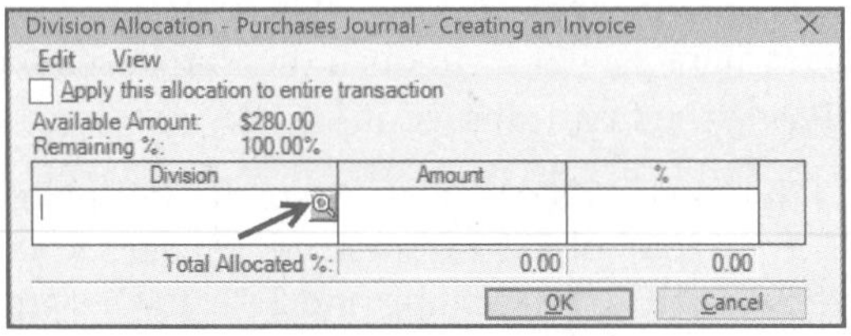

NOTES
When you change the ledger name, the new name you entered will appear in the screen and column headings in the allocation windows instead of Division.

The cursor is in the Division field. The full amount to be allocated, $280 (the base expense amount), is provided at the top for reference together with the proportion remaining to be allocated, 100.00%. Amounts can be allocated by percentage or by actual amount. This choice is made in the Division Settings window (refer to page 505). (Choose the Setup menu, click Settings and then click Division and Allocation.) The setting can be changed as needed. Shady Corners uses the Percentage allocation method as indicated in the Division Information.

NOTES
The refundable HST amount is not allocated because it is not part of the expense.

You must complete the allocation process even if 100 percent of the revenue or expense is assigned to a single division. You must complete the allocation process for each account or invoice line on your input form.

Click the **Division List icon** to display the Divisions in alphabetic order:

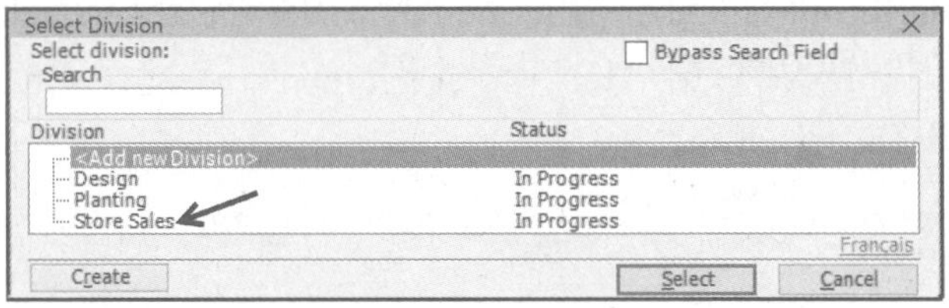

According to the source document information, the first division is Store Sales, which incurs 70 percent of the total energy expense. You can add a new division from the Select Division window.

Choose Add New Division or click the Create button to open the Division Ledger if you need to create a new division.

Click **Store Sales**, the first division used. **Click Select** to add it on the form.

The cursor advances to the Percentage field because we selected this method of allocation. By default the unallocated portion (100%) is entered in this field and selected for editing.

Type 70 **Press** *tab* to advance to the next line in the Division field.

The program calculates the dollar amount for this division automatically based on the percentage entered. The percentage remaining at the top of the input form has been updated to 30.00%. Now we need to allocate the remaining 30 percent of the expense amount to the other divisions.

Press *enter* to open the Select Division window.

Double-click **Planting** to add the division.

The cursor is in the Percentage field again, with 30.00 as the default because this was the unallocated percentage remaining.

Type 20 **Press** *tab* to enter it and update the unallocated amount to 10%.

Press *enter* to open the Select Division window.

Double-click **Design** to add the division with 10.00 as the default entry.

Press *tab* to accept this amount because it is correct and completes the allocation:

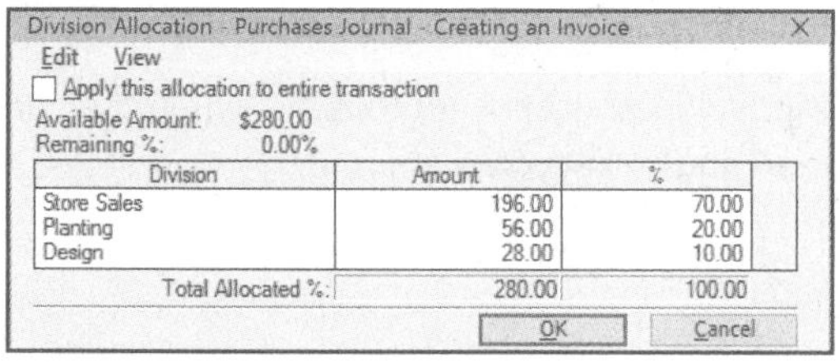

Click **OK** to return to the completed Purchases Journal entry:

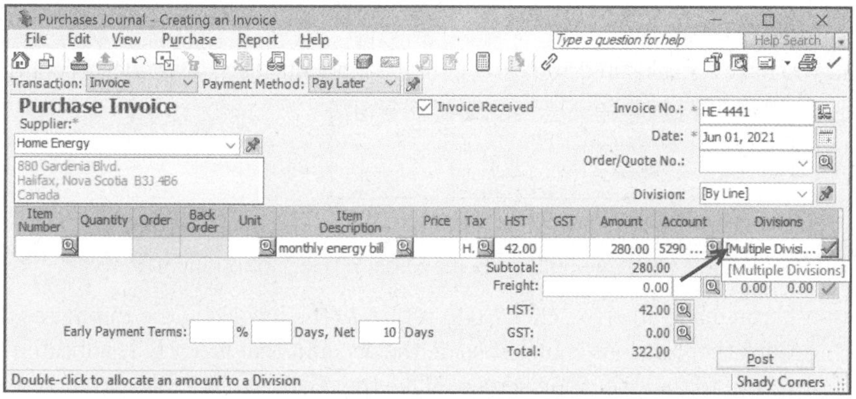

The journal appears unchanged, except for the entry in the Divisions column indicating that the amount has been allocated. Usually, the Division name is entered, but because more than one division was used, the entry is Multiple Divisions. The [By Line] entry in the Division field above the invoice lines also indicates that more than one division has been applied to the purchase.

Reviewing the Purchases Journal Allocation

Choose the **Report menu** and **click** **Display Purchases Journal Entry**:

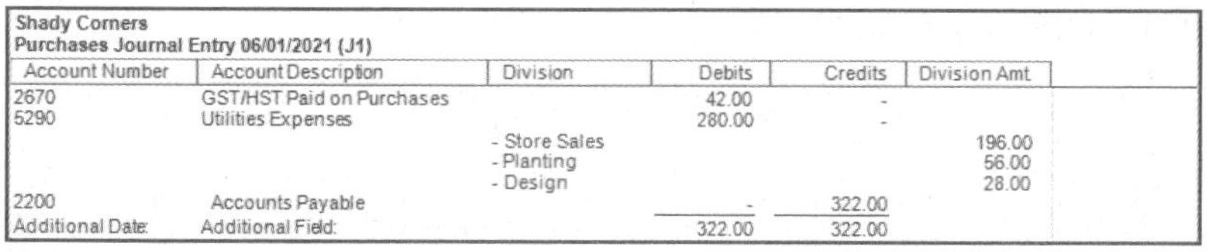

Shady Corners
Purchases Journal Entry 06/01/2021 (J1)

Account Number	Account Description	Division	Debits	Credits	Division Amt
2670	GST/HST Paid on Purchases		42.00	-	
5290	Utilities Expenses		280.00	-	
		- Store Sales			196.00
		- Planting			56.00
		- Design			28.00
2200	Accounts Payable		-	322.00	
Additional Date:	Additional Field:		322.00	322.00	

Sage 50 has automatically updated the *Accounts Payable* control account because the Payables and General ledgers are fully integrated. The utilities expense has been allocated to the three divisions according to the proportions we entered for them. Only the amount for the expense account *Utilities Expenses* is allocated because the other accounts are Balance Sheet accounts that are not set up to allow allocations.

Close the **display** to return to the Purchases Journal input screen.

NOTES

When PST is paid separately from GST, it will be included with the expense amount and fully allocated with it.

CORRECTING THE PURCHASES JOURNAL ENTRY ALLOCATION

Correct the Purchases Journal part of the entry as you would correct any other purchase invoice. Refer to page 116 if you need assistance.

If you have made an error in the allocation, **click** the **Allocate tool** to return to the Allocation window. **Click** the **line** for the amount being allocated to activate the Allocate tool if necessary. **Click** an **incorrect division** to highlight it. **Press** *enter* to access the Division list. **Click** the **correct division** and **click Select** to enter the change. **Click** an **incorrect percentage** and **type** the **correct information. Press** *tab* to save the correction. **Click OK** to return to the Journal window.

Click the **Store tool**. Accept the supplier **name** and **Monthly** as the frequency. **Click OK** to return to the journal.

When you store a transaction with allocations, allocation information is also stored.

To review or edit the allocation, click the Allocate tool when the cursor is on the relevant line or click the ✓ in the Divisions column.

Posting

When you are certain that you have entered all the information correctly,

Click Post to save the entry. **Click OK** to confirm posting.

If you have not allocated 100 percent of the amounts, Sage 50 requests confirmation:

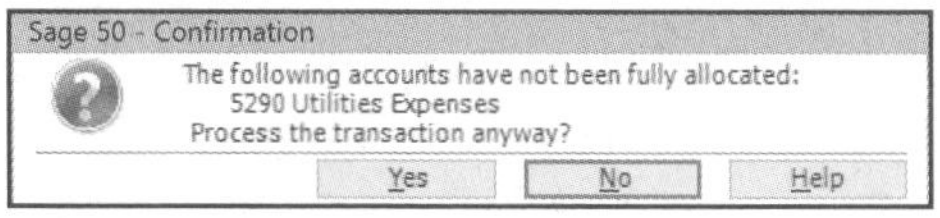

This message appears if you have not fully allocated a journal amount. If the warning option is not selected (page 505), you may post a transaction incorrectly.

If you made an error, click No to return to the invoice in the Purchases Journal. Click the Divisions column beside the account that is not fully allocated to return to the Allocation screen. Make the changes, click OK and then post.

If you do not want to allocate the full amount, or if the account was one for which you cannot access the allocation procedure, such as *Variance Costs* (refer to the screenshot on page 525), you should click Yes to continue.

Close the **Purchases Journal**. The Divisions list pane total expense amounts have been updated with amounts from this transaction. Click the list pane refresh tool if necessary to update division amounts.

If the option to allow allocations is not activated for the account in the ledger record, Sage 50 will block this action when you click the Allocation tool:

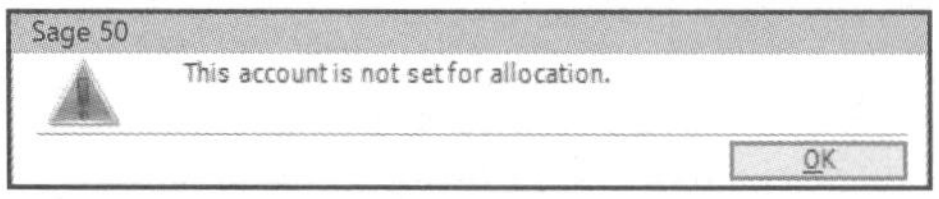

Open the ledger record for the account and click the Allow Division Allocations.

Enter the next **two payments** and the **receipt transaction**.

3 Sent cheque #581 for $900 to Groen Fields on June 1 to pay invoice #GF-1142 in full.

4 On June 2, sent cheque #375 for Dkr 8.160,00 to Mobler Dansk to pay invoice #MD-724. The exchange rate for June 2 was 0.201.

NOTES

You should click OK for the successful posting message each time you record or post a transaction. We will not repeat this instruction.

NOTES

Later in the chapter we will learn that cost variances are not allocated.

You may want to proceed with an incomplete allocation when part of the amount applies to none of the divisions or it applies to an earlier time period before division recording was started.

NOTES

Allocation is not available for invoice payments or receipts, so discount amounts are not allocated, but there is no warning about incomplete allocation.

NOTES

Note that the format for the Danish currency is Dkr 8.160,00 (for eight thousand, one hundred sixty kroner – the period [.] separates the thousands and the comma [,] indicates the decimal position).

5 Received cheque #4887 for $1 356 on June 2 from Acadian Towers. Receipt #420 was applied to invoice #155 with early payment discount of $24.

Entering Import Duties

Governments may apply import duties that raise the price of imported goods to encourage the local economy. Duty rates or tariffs vary for different kinds of items and for different countries. The duty is collected by the Canada Revenue Agency when the goods first enter Canada, before they are released to the buyer.

In Sage 50, before you can enter duty amounts with the purchase, you must change the Payables settings to charge and track import duties (refer to page 651). You must also indicate in the foreign supplier's record (Options tab screen) that duty is applied to purchases from that supplier (refer to page 664). In the Inventory Ledger records (Taxes tab screen), you can enter the duty applied as a percentage (refer to pages 682–683), or you can enter the rates in the Purchases Journal. For non-inventory purchases, you must enter the rate directly in the Purchases Journal.

The purchase invoice from Mobler Dansk has import duties applied.

✓ 6 Recorded invoice #MD-916 from Mobler Dansk on June 2/21. Terms: 2/15, net 30. The exchange rate on June 2 was 0.201. Total import duty charged was Dkr 1.447,60 (CAD $290.97). The freight expense was allocated entirely to Store Sales. Create new Group asset account for carpets: 1320 Carpeting.

items purchased			amount	duty rate
		Indoor/Outdoor Carpeting	Dkr 6.000,00	12.5%
4	FA04	Arm chair: Cast Aluminum	1.120,00	8%
2	FA01	Patio set: Cast Aluminum round table 1.5 m	7.600,00	8%
		Freight	1.200,00	
		HST Paid	2.388,00	
Invoice Total			Dkr 18.308,00	

Open the **Purchases Journal**. **Choose Mobler Dansk**. **Press** tab:

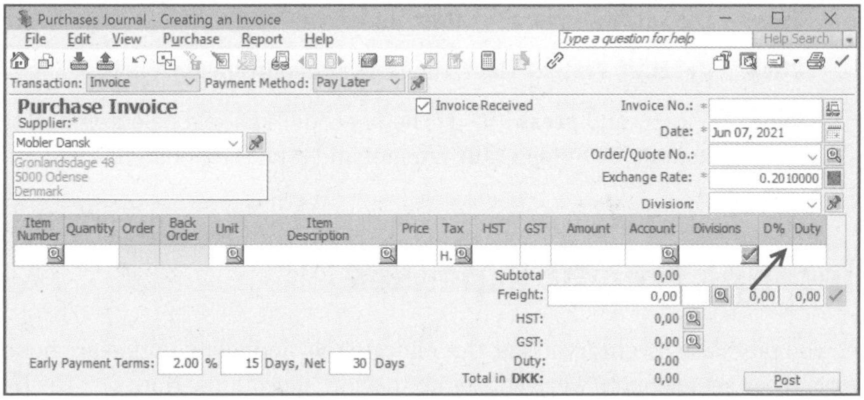

The company settings and the Supplier and Inventory Ledger records for Shady Corners are set up to apply duty. Refer to pages 651, 664 and 682.

In addition to the Exchange Rate field and the indication that Danish kroner (DKK) is the currency for this supplier, the duty fields are added because we selected a supplier for whom duty applies. The extra fields are used for the duty percentage and for the duty amount. Duty is charged on all items purchased from Mobler Dansk.

Click the **Invoice No. field** and **type** MD-916

Type Jun 2 in the Date field and **press** tab. The exchange rate is correct from the rate entered for the payment on this date.

NOTES

Edit the purchase amounts.

HST is charged on freight expenses.

Amounts for Balance Sheet accounts are not allocated so, except for the freight amount, there is no allocation for inventory purchases.

NOTES

If you need to update exchange rates in the Purchases Journal, the Exchange Rate screen may stay open after you click OK, with the session date replacing the transaction date. Click Cancel to close the screen and select the correct exchange rate from the Exchange Rate select list. Click the Exchange Rate tool beside the field to open the list.

Click **Cancel** to return to the journal if the Exchange Rate screen opens.

Click the **Item Description field**. **Type** `indoor/outdoor carpeting`

Click the **Amount field**. **Type** `6000` **Press** *tab*.

Type `1320` and **add** the new **account**. **Press** *tab* **twice**.

You will advance the cursor to the D% (duty rate) field where you should enter the rate that the government applies to this type of product.

WARNING!
Always verify that the rates and amounts are correct. If entering the duty rate as 12.5 does not provide the correct result, type 750 in the Duty field.

Type `12.5` **Press** *enter* to add the duty amount.

Double-click the **Item Number field** on the second line to open the Inventory Selection screen.

Double-click **FA04** to add this item to the invoice:

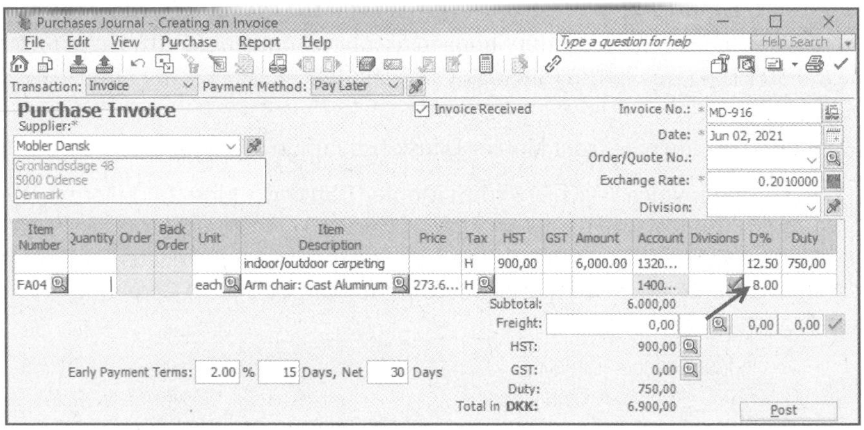

This time the duty rate is added automatically because the rate is recorded in the ledger record for the item. The Account field is dimmed (unavailable) for inventory items.

Type `4` to enter the quantity. **Type** `1120` as the Amount.

Enter the **second inventory item** in the same way.

Click the **first Freight field**, the freight amount field.

Type `1200` and **press** *tab*. The tax code H should be entered as the default. The freight tax amount and total are updated.

Allocating Freight Expenses

When you purchase inventory items, the Allocate tool and menu option are not available because the asset accounts were not set up to allow allocations. However, the freight expense for these purchases can be allocated.

The Freight field has an **Allocate button** ✓. Freight can be allocated separately from other amounts in the entry by using this tool:

NOTES
The Allocate button beside the Freight fields is the same as the main Allocate tool, but it applies only to the amount for freight.

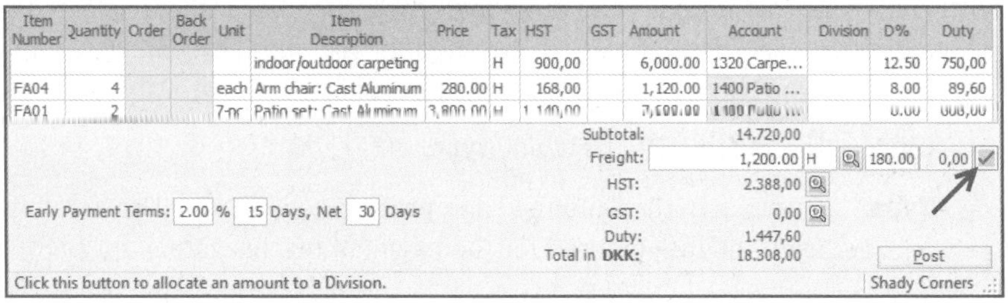

Click the **Allocate tool button** ☑ to the right of the Freight fields.

The Division Allocation screen opens. It is the same as the one we saw earlier. The Freight amount, Dkr 1.200,00, is entered as the amount to be allocated.

Choose **Store Sales** and **accept** the **amount** and percentage allocation.

Click **OK** to return to the journal. The journal has not changed in appearance.

Choose the **Report menu** and **click** **Display Purchases Journal Entry**:

Shady Corners
Purchases Journal Entry 06/02/2021 (J5)

Account Number	Account Description	Division	Foreign A...	Division Frgn Amt	Debits	Credits	Division Amt
1320	Carpeting		Dkr6.750,00		1,356.75	-	
1400	Patio Furniture		Dkr9.417,61		1,892.94	-	
2670	GST/HST Paid on Purchases		Dkr2.388,00		479.99	-	
5100	Freight Expense		Dkr1.200,00		241.20	-	
		- Store Sales		Dkr1.200,00			241.20
2200	Accounts Payable		Dkr18.308,00		-	3,679.91	
2220	Import Duty Payable		Dkr1.447,60		-	290.97	
1 Danish Kroners equals 0.2010000 Canadian Dollars					3,970.88	3,970.88	

Only the Freight Expense amount — the only Income Statement amount and the only amount allocated for the transaction — has a division allocation in the journal entry.

Close the **Journal Entry** to return to the journal.

To correct the freight expense allocation, click the Allocate button ☑ beside the field to open the Division Allocation screen and make the needed changes.

Click [Post] to save the entry.

If you have not allocated the freight amount, Sage 50 generates the warning on page 510 about incomplete allocations.

Enter the following **purchase transaction** from Jorgensen Mobler.

7 Recorded invoice #JM-876 from Jorgensen Mobler for furniture on June 2, 2021, at the exchange rate of 0.201. Terms: 2/30, net 60 days. Total import duty assessed was Dkr 695,40 (CAD $139.78). Freight was charged to Store Sales.

items purchased			amount	duty rate
4	FP21	Patio table: Moulded Plastic 2 m	Dkr 6.400,00	9.5%
2	FP24	Chaise longue: Moulded Plastic	920,00	9.5%
	Freight		800,00	
	HST Paid		1.218,00	
Invoice Total			Dkr 9.338,00	

Close the **Purchases Journal**. The next transaction is a credit card sale.

Allocating in the Sales Journal

✓ 8 Sale #166 to Efren Barrato was made on June 4/21. Barrato paid by Visa. 100% of revenue and expenses for inventory items and delivery was allocated to Store Sales, and the service item (SC03) was allocated to Planting. Create a new record for Barrato. Set up the data files to process credit card transactions before entering the sale.

items sold			amount	total
1	FT31	Patio table: Teak round 1.5 m	$ 925 each	$ 925.00
4	FT33	Arm chair: Teak	725 each	2 900.00
1	FT37	Bench: Teak	1 125 each	1 125.00
10	SH03	Shrubs: 3 metre	55 each	550.00
3	SC03	Planting & Soil Preparation	50 /hour	150.00
		Delivery		100.00
	Harmonized Sales Tax		15%	862.50
Total paid by Visa #4111 1111 1111 1111				$6 612.50

NOTES
The Import Duty Payable credit entry is matched by the total increase for the two asset accounts – the debit entries for Carpeting and Patio Furniture – over their purchase costs.

NOTES
You can allocate freight revenue amounts in the same way. Simply click the Allocate tool beside the Freight fields.

NOTES
Efren Barrato
(contact Efren Barrato)
35 Birchmount Rd.
Halifax, NS B3T 1G7
Terms: net 1
Payment method: Visa

NOTES
No discount applies to cash, credit card or debit card sales (Visa, MasterCard and Interac).

Amounts for revenue accounts in the Sales Journal are allocated in the same way as amounts for expense accounts in the Purchases Journal. Each revenue amount in the journal must be allocated completely, but you can assign the same allocation percentages to all accounts in the journal rather than repeating the allocation entry for each invoice line. We will demonstrate this method with the steps involved in the Visa sale to Barrato on June 4.

Because this is a credit card sale, we will first set up the data files to allow credit card processing. You cannot enter the credit card processing settings when the Sales Journal is open, so we must complete this step first.

If you do not have an Internet connection, you can skip this section and proceed to the Allocating the Revenue Amounts section (page 515). You will also skip the steps for processing the transaction after entering the sales details.

NOTES

The Sage Exchange program can be downloaded and installed from the Sage 50 link on the Company Credit Card Settings screen. You may need to temporarily disable your firewall program to run Sage Exchange and complete the installation, and you may need to install an update for Sage Exchange.

After the program is installed, clicking Processing Service will start the Sage Exchange program automatically.

Setting Up Credit Card Processing

If you do not want to process credit card transactions, do not complete the credit card setup section. Just enter the transaction in the usual way.

When credit card processing details are added to the Company Credit Card Settings, the credit card transaction can be processed directly. You must have a merchant account with the processing company. Sage 50 links with Sage Exchange, and all kinds of credit cards are processed through this single company. Merchants pay a fee for this service that is separate from the transaction fees charged by the credit card company. The advantage is that the transaction is processed directly as a bank transfer to the merchant.

You must have the Sage Exchange program installed and running on your computer to complete this next step. You can download this program from the Company Credit Card Settings screen.

NOTES

For illustration purposes, we will provide the steps to complete this process and the screens that would follow. If you do not want to complete this step, you should complete and post the transaction without entering the Paya account information.

Click the **Settings icon**, then click **Company**, **Credit Cards** and **Processing Service** to open the Settings screen you need:

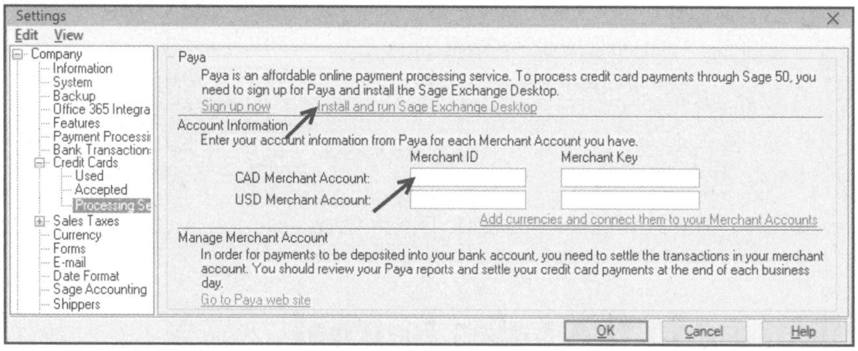

PRO VERSION

Credit card processing is available only for Canadian dollar credit cards.

Start your **Internet connection**.

Click the **Install And Run The Sage Exchange Desktop link** on the Settings screen. Follow the instructions to complete the installation.

You must add the Merchant ID number and Key (password) provided for this text by Paya to activate the feature.

NOTES

These merchant numbers are connected to a test account, courtesy of Paya. They will permit you to practise entering and authorizing credit card transactions.

Click the **Merchant ID field**. This is the number provided by Paya.

Type 651259884634

Press *tab* to advance to the Merchant Key field. This field holds the password for your account.

NOTES

The password sequence is letter, number, letter, number and so on.

Type B8B9O4S6E2K2 As you type, the characters are replaced by * or ●.

Click **OK** to close the Settings screen.

The Sage Exchange program will be running in the background. You are now ready to enter the sales transaction for Barrato.

> **WARNING!**
> If the Sage Exchange program does not start properly, your firewall may be blocking it. You may need to temporarily disable your firewall program to install Sage Exchange. You may also need to change the firewall settings to "allow" Sage Exchange. After this, you can start the program normally.

Allocating the Revenue Amounts

Click the **Sales Invoices icon** (Sales Invoices) to open the Sales Journal.

Type `Efren Barrato` in the Customer field. **Click Add** and **enter** the customer's **address** and **terms** — including **Visa** as the method of payment — to the ledger record. **Click Save And Close**.

Enter **Jun 4** as the invoice date. Visa is preselected now as the payment method.

Choose **FT31** from the inventory selection list as the first item for the sale. The cursor advances to the Quantity field.

Type 1 **Press** (tab) repeatedly to advance to the Divisions column.

Double-click the **Divisions column** or **click** ☑ in the Divisions column to open the Division Allocation window.

As long as the cursor is anywhere on the invoice line you are allocating the allocate function is available. Click the Allocate tool button in the tool bar or choose the Sales menu and click Allocate to open the Division Allocation screen.

> **NOTES**
> You can also press (ctrl) + (shift) + A to open the Division Allocation window whenever the cursor is on a line with an account that allows allocation.

Choose **Store Sales** for 100% of the revenue amount. **Press** (tab).

The allocation screen has a check box for the option Apply This Allocation To Entire Transaction:

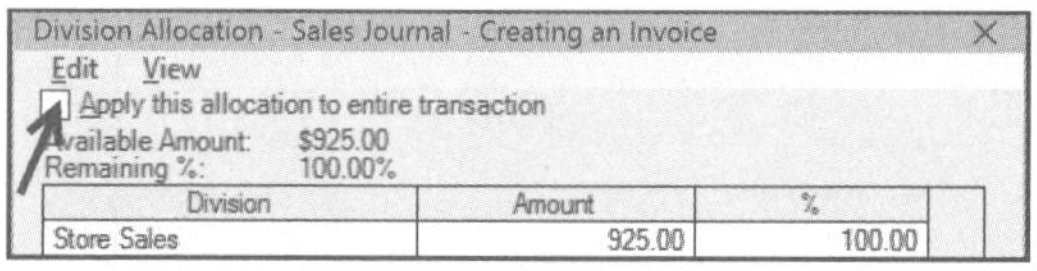

This option allows you to enter the allocation for one amount and have the program automatically apply the same percentages for all other amounts, including freight. Otherwise you need to repeat the allocation procedure for each account in the journal.

Click **Apply This Allocation To Entire Transaction** to open the message about this selection:

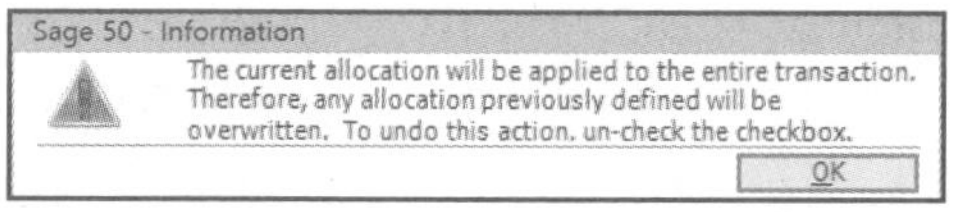

Read the **message** and then **click OK** to return to the allocation screen.

If you do not want to continue with this selection, click the check box again.

The Division Allocation screen has changed:

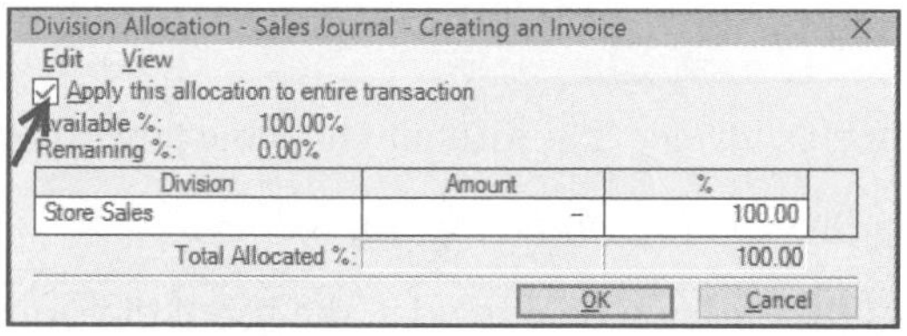

No amounts are entered now because the same percentages will be applied and the amounts will be different for each account.

Click **OK** to save the allocation and return to the journal.

Enter the **remaining inventory** and **service items** and the **delivery charge** for the sale.

The division name is added to the Divisions column for each line automatically as you complete the invoice:

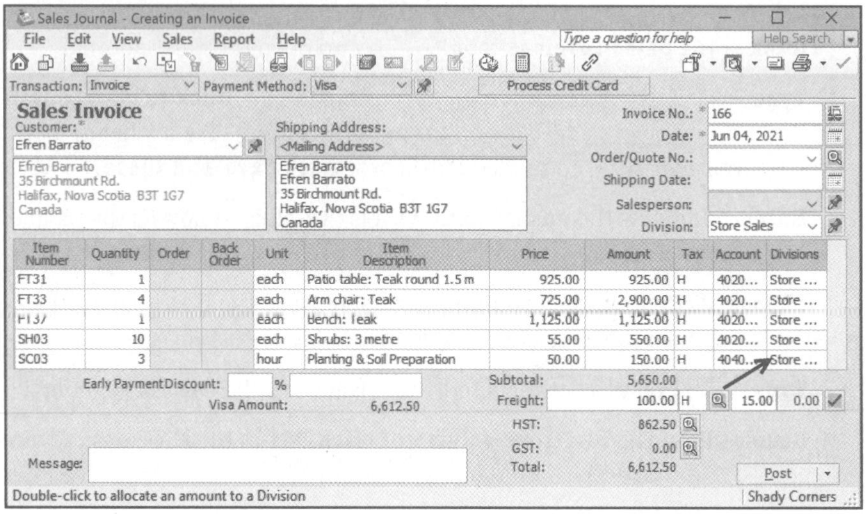

The invoice has been completely allocated, but the allocation is not correct, as you learn from reviewing the journal entry for the transaction.

Press ctrl + **J** to open the journal display:

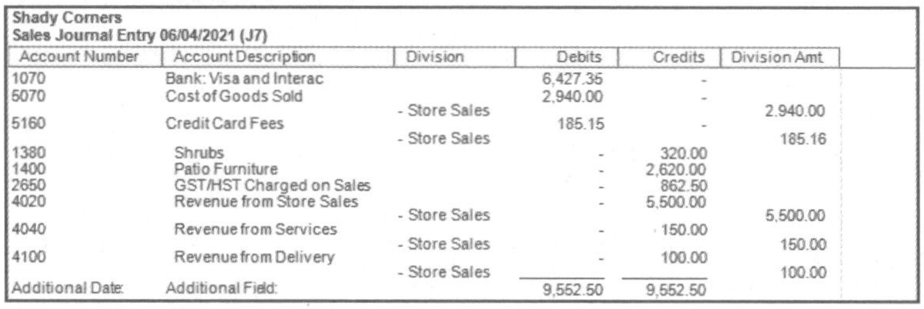

Shady Corners
Sales Journal Entry 06/04/2021 (J7)

Account Number	Account Description	Division	Debits	Credits	Division Amt
1070	Bank: Visa and Interac		6,427.35	-	
5070	Cost of Goods Sold		2,940.00	-	
		- Store Sales			2,940.00
5160	Credit Card Fees		185.15	-	
		- Store Sales			185.16
1380	Shrubs		-	320.00	
1400	Patio Furniture		-	2,620.00	
2650	GST/HST Charged on Sales		-	862.50	
4020	Revenue from Store Sales		-	5,500.00	
		- Store Sales			5,500.00
4040	Revenue from Services		-	150.00	
		- Store Sales			150.00
4100	Revenue from Delivery		-	100.00	
		- Store Sales			100.00
Additional Date:	Additional Field:		9,552.50	9,552.50	

All amounts, including delivery, are allocated to the Store Sales division. However, the service revenue should be allocated to the Planting division, so we must change it.

Close the displayed **report** to return to the journal.

Click anywhere on the line for **item SC03**.

Click the **Allocate tool**, **double-click Store Sales** in the Divisions column or **choose** the **Sales menu** and **click Allocate** to open the Allocation screen.

Click **Apply This Allocation To Entire Transaction** to remove the ✓.

Sage 50 displays a message about the effects of changing the allocation selection:

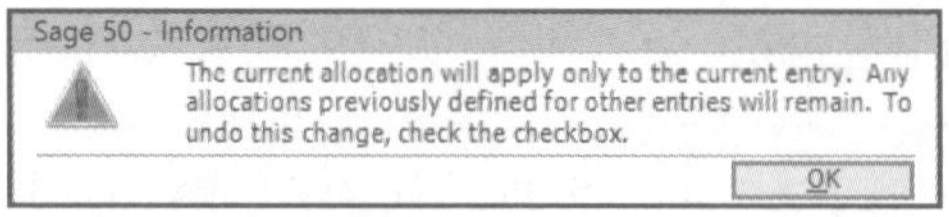

We can change the allocation for this invoice line without changing any other line.

Click **OK** to return to the Division Allocation screen.

Click the **List icon** in the Division field to open the list of divisions.

Double-click **Planting** to replace Store Sales on the Division Allocation screen.

Click **OK** to save the change. Planting has been entered in the journal.

NOTES

You can also press ctrl + shift + A for the selected item to open the Division Allocation screen.

NOTES

This message appears only for the first allocation you change. You can now change the allocation for additional amounts individually without displaying the message again and without affecting the remaining allocations.

Choose the **Report menu** and **click Display Sales Journal Entry**:

Shady Corners
Sales Journal Entry 06/04/2021 (J7)

Account Number	Account Description	Division	Debits	Credits	Division Amt
1070	Bank: Visa and Interac		6,427.35	-	
5070	Cost of Goods Sold		2,940.00	-	
		- Store Sales			2,940.00
5160	Credit Card Fees		185.15	-	
		- Store Sales			180.33
		- Planting			4.83
1380	Shrubs		-	320.00	
1400	Patio Furniture		-	2,620.00	
2650	GST/HST Charged on Sales		-	862.50	
4020	Revenue from Store Sales		-	5,500.00	
		- Store Sales			5,500.00
4040	Revenue from Services		-	150.00	
		- Planting			150.00
4100	Revenue from Delivery		-	100.00	
		- Store Sales			100.00
Additional Date:	Additional Field:		9,552.50	9,552.50	

The allocation is now correct. The allocation for *Credit Card Fees* is automatically split in the correct proportion. *Cost of Goods Sold* is also allocated correctly to Store Sales.

Close the **Journal Entry** to return to the journal.

The Division field in the journal (above the invoice lines) has By Line as the entry. SC03 has Planting in the invoice line Division field while the other lines still have Store Sales. You can now change allocations for other amounts individually if needed.

Processing a Credit Card Transaction

Once we are certain that the sales invoice is correct, we can process the credit card.

The Process Credit Card button beside the Visa Payment Method selection replaces the link Tell Me More About Processing Credit Card Payments — refer to page 183.

Start your **Internet connection** if you have not already done so.

Click the **Process Credit Card button** in the Sales Journal:

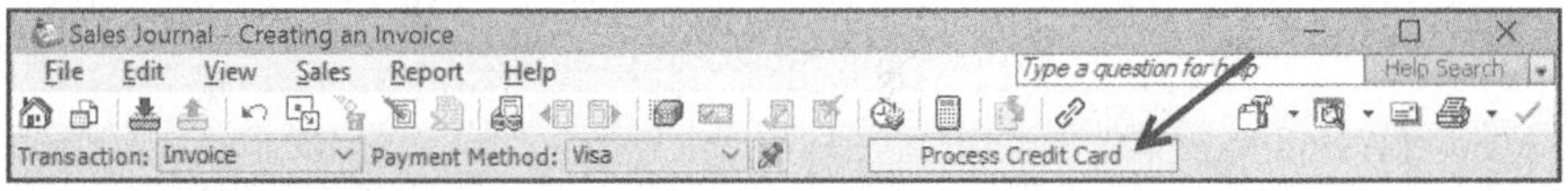

If Sage Exchange was not already running, clicking the Process Credit Card button will start the program, as long as your Internet connection is active.

The cardholder information screen opens:

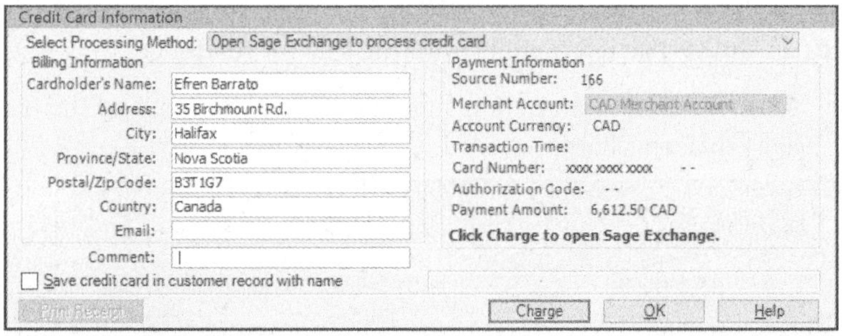

The first screen holds the customer information. If you select a customer for whom you have a complete ledger record, the address information will be added from the record. The entry from the Contact field will appear in the Name field. You must fill in the name and address fields to continue. You also have the option on this tab screen to Save A Credit Card in the customer's record. We will not choose this option for Barrato.

Enter the **cardholder's name** and **address** details if any information is missing or incorrect.

Card information may be processed/authorized manually or automatically. The default, to Open Sage Exchange To Process Credit Card, is selected and is correct for this transaction. If you have an account set up with Sage, you can complete the processing automatically. You should have the Sage Exchange program and your Internet connection running.

NOTES
If the Sage Exchange program does not start, check that your firewall is not blocking the program.

NOTES
If you did not complete the address fields in the customer's record, you must add the details here. Information from the Contact field in the ledger is entered in the Cardholder's Name field.

If you save the credit card in the customer's record, the details you entered here will be added to the Credit Card tab screen in the record. Refer to page 519.

PRO VERSION
Credit card processing is available only for Canadian dollar credit cards, so you will not have entries for CAD Merchant Account and Currency.

NOTES
The name on the credit card may be different from the customer account name, so you should verify that it is correct.

Click the **Charge button** in the lower right-hand side of the Payment Information pane to connect to the Sage Exchange Payment site (refer to the screenshot on the previous page):

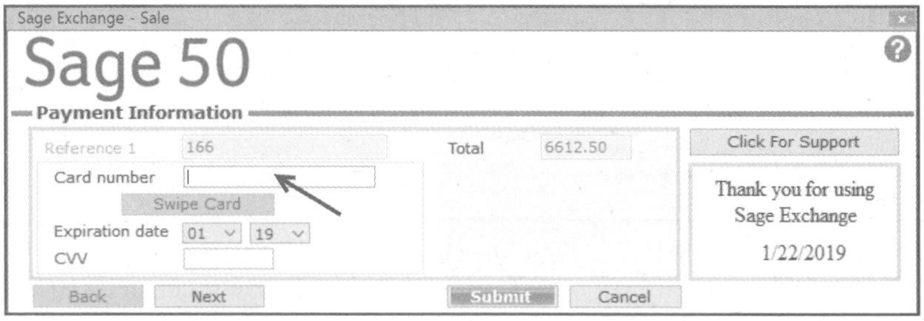

> **NOTES**
> The system date from your computer will be entered as the date below the Thank You message and as the starting point for the card expiry date.
> The lower left-hand corner will have a timer because the session/connection will time out after 15 minutes.

You are now connected to a secure site so that you can provide the credit card information. All Sage Exchange connections are timed — the connection will be broken after the time has elapsed. The cursor is in the Card Number field.

Type `4111 1111 1111 1111` the 16-digit credit card number.

Select the **month** and **year** for the Expiration Date from the drop-down lists. The date must be later than the current calendar date on your computer system — the card must not be expired.

> **NOTES**
> The only Visa number that will be accepted in the test account for processing is 4111111111111111 (4 followed by fifteen 1's).

Entering the CVV code (the code located on the back of the credit card) is optional.

Click **Next** to review the information and to add the customer's telephone number or e-mail address. Make corrections by clicking the Back button to return to previous screens.

Click **Submit** to begin the processing. If there is any delay, your screen may include the Processing message progress bar.

After the sale has been authorized, you will receive a confirmation with the authorization code:

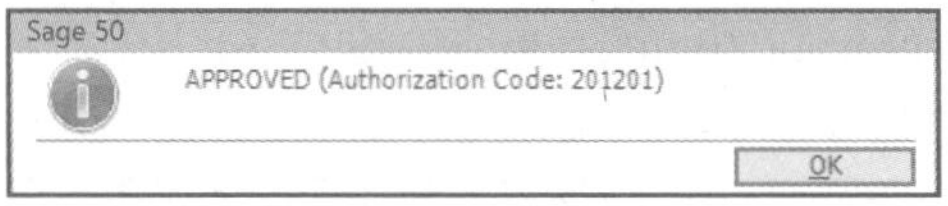

> **NOTES**
> If you omit any essential information, the program will warn you and prevent you from continuing until you provide the missing details.
> Separate authorization codes are generated for each transaction, so your code will be different from the one we have.

Record the **authorization** number with the sale for reference.

Click **OK** to open the transaction summary. The option to Void the transaction has replaced Charge:

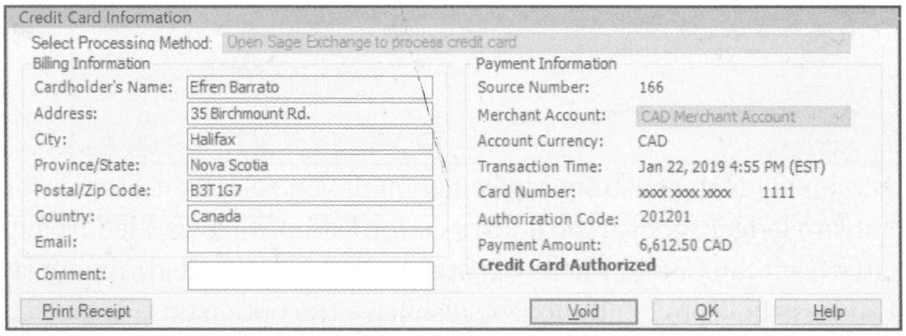

Click **OK** again to return to the Sales Journal.

> **NOTES**
> If you need to change credit card details after processing, you should reverse the sale. This step will void the sale and refund the credit card amount. Before posting, closing the journal will void the credit card amount automatically. The last four digits of the card number and an authorization code will be provided when you void the card payment.

The Sales Journal Credit Card button label has changed to **Credit Card Details**:

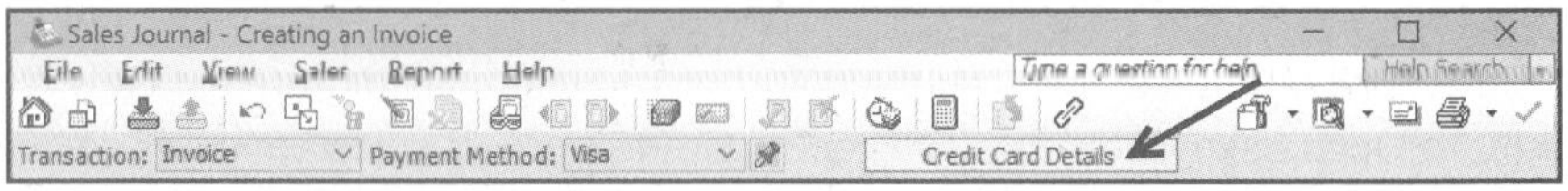

You can click the Credit Card Details button to review the details. The details screen includes the options to print a receipt and to void or cancel the Visa charge.

Click Post to save the entry. An Advisor message informs you that some inventory items have fallen below the reorder point. **Click** the **message** to continue.

If you change the method of payment after processing the credit card, you must confirm that the credit card payment will be voided:

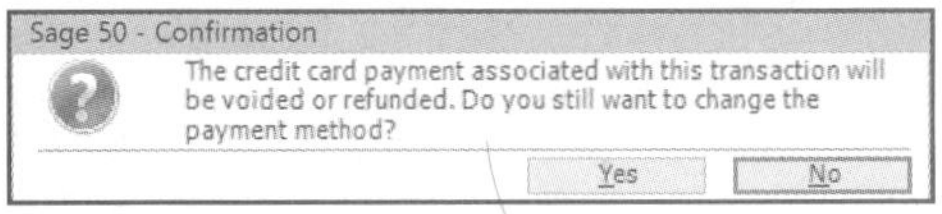

Or, if you do not post the transaction after processing the credit card, that is, you discard the transaction, you must also confirm that the payment will be voided:

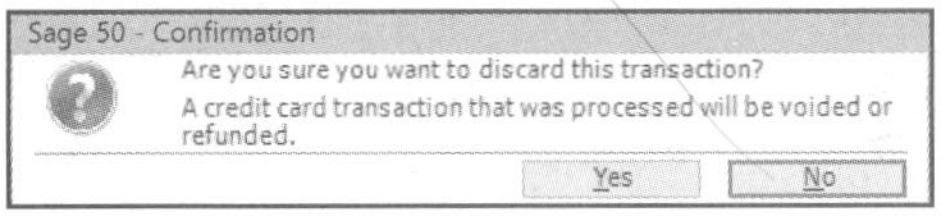

Click **Yes** to continue and void or reverse the charges.

Pre-Authorized Credit Card Processing with Sage Vault

If a customer has authorized automatic credit card payments, you can set these up in the customer's ledger record. This is similar to setting up pre-authorized payments from a bank account (refer to page 523).

We will process the next sales transaction for a new customer with Sage Vault.

✓ 9

Iola completed MasterCard sale #167 to Leanne McGill on June 4, 2021, and allocated 100% of revenue to Store Sales. McGill has authorized Shady Corners to withdraw the amounts automatically from her credit card. Create a new complete customer record and add her credit card details.

Complete the MasterCard sales transaction. The following items were sold:

items sold			amount	total
6	FT33	Arm chair: Teak	$725 each	$4 350.00
1	FT34	Chaise longue: Teak	980 each	980.00
		Delivery		100.00
	Harmonized Sales Tax		15%	814.50
Total paid by MasterCard #5499 7400 0000 0057				$6 244.50

Click the **Customer field** in the Sales Journal.

Type `Leanne McGill` **Click** the **Add link** to open the ledger.

Enter the **Address details**, **Payment Terms** and **Payment Method**.

Click the **Credit Card tab**:

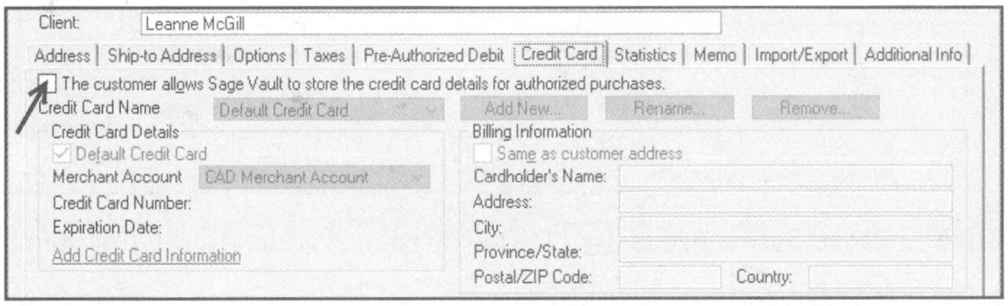

Click **The Customer Allows Sage Vault To Store The Credit Card Details....**

This will open the remaining fields for entering the credit card information.

Click **Same As Customer Address** under Billing Information to have the required address details added to these fields automatically.

NOTES
The low inventory advisor will open several times as you enter sales transactions because Shady Corners allows inventory to be oversold.

NOTES
Leanne McGill
10 Highland Rd.
Halifax, NS B3T 3R2
Terms: net 1
Payment method: MasterCard

PRO VERSION
Credit card processing is available only for Canadian dollar credit cards, so you will not see the CAD Merchant Account entry.

> **NOTES**
> If you chose to save the credit card information from a previous sale, this tab screen information will be completed automatically. Refer to page 517.
> The timer in the lower left-hand corners informs you how long your Internet connection will remain open and you have to complete the transaction.

Click the **Add Credit Card Information** link so we can add the card details:

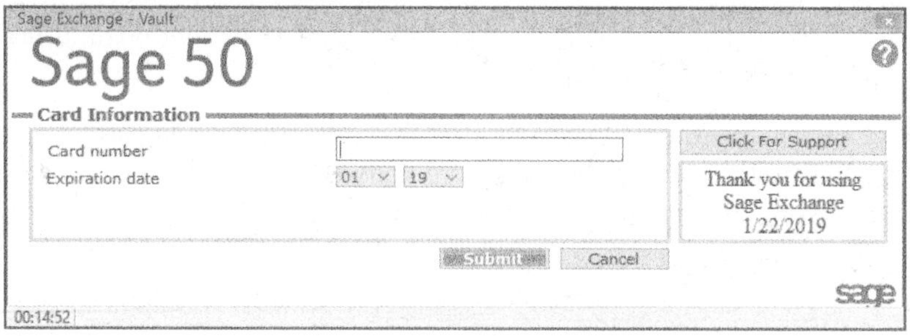

At this stage, you are connected to the Sage Exchange - Vault secure site. On this screen, you must add the card number and its expiry date.

> **NOTES**
> To process MasterCard sales automatically in our test account, enter 5499740000000057 as the credit card number.
> This is the only MasterCard number that will be accepted in the test account for processing.

Click the **Card Number field** and **type** 5499 7400 0000 0057

Choose **month** and **year** dates from the Expiration Date drop-down lists.

Click **Submit**. **Save** the **new record** to return to the Sales Journal.

Accept **MasterCard** as the Payment Method when prompted.

Enter **Jun 4** as the date for the sale.

Enter the first **inventory item** and **quantity**. **Press** *tab* to update the amount.

Entering Allocations from the Journal Division Field

Both the Sales Journal and the Purchases Journal have a Division field above the invoice lines with a drop-down list of divisions. By using this selection list, you can quickly apply the same division to all invoice lines and freight.

When you enter allocations with the methods we used earlier, this field has the entry [By Line] because we entered different or multiple allocations for one or more individual lines on the invoice, as in the Purchase Invoice on page 509. The Sales Invoice on page 516 has Store Sales as the entry in this field because, at that stage, we had allocated the entire transaction to that division.

When the entire transaction is allocated to one division, you can select the division from the Division field drop-down list. We will use this method for the sale to McGill.

Click the **Division field list arrow** to list all divisions available for selection:

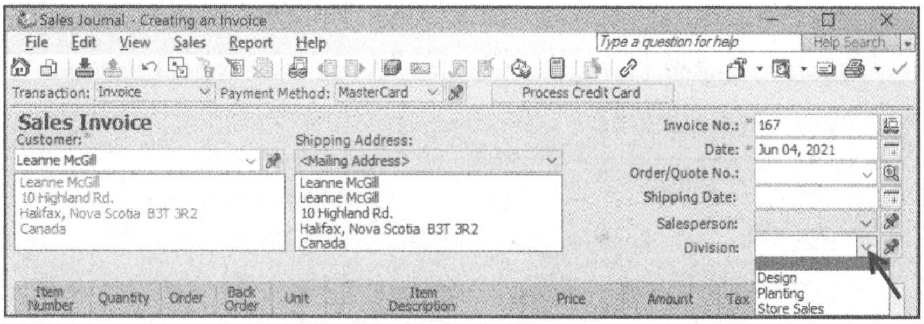

> **NOTES**
> You can use the journal's Division field list to allocate freight amounts as well. In the Purchases Journal for Inventory purchases, the allocation entry will apply only to freight.

Click **Store Sales**. **Press** *tab*. This division is added to the first invoice line.

Enter the **second item** and **quantity**. Store Sales is added automatically.

Enter the **delivery amount** to complete the transaction. Store Sales is added automatically for this charge as well.

When you open the Division Allocation window from either line on the invoice, a ✓ informs you that the same allocation applies to the entire transaction:

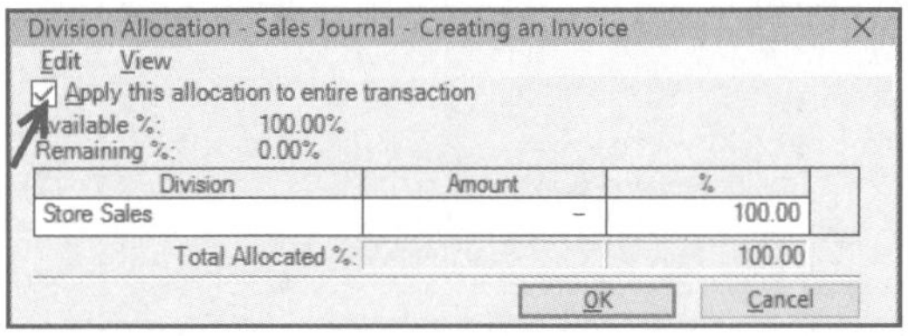

If you need to change the allocation for individual line amounts, you can do so from this window, as we did for the previous sale. Click OK to close this window.

Review your **journal entry** display and **make corrections** if necessary.

Click the **Process Credit Card button** in the Sales Journal. The Credit Card Information screen opens:

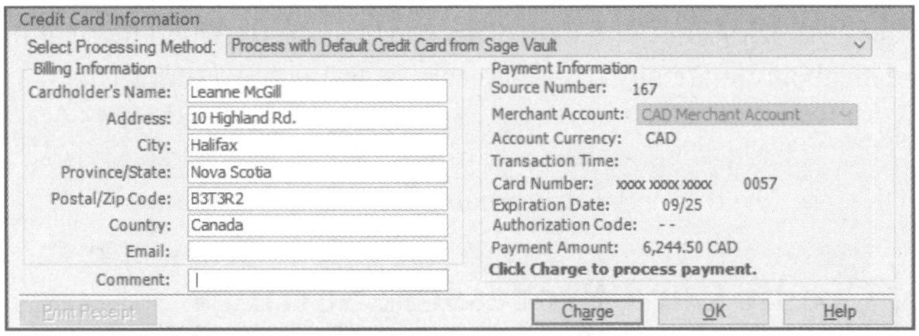

Once the ledger record has a customer's card information, the selection list changes. Processing with Sage Vault is now the default and it is correct for this transaction.

The first screen holds the customer information and includes the credit card number. If you select a customer for whom you have a complete record, the address information will be added from the record with the Contact field entry in the Name field. The name and address are required fields for credit card sales.

Click **Charge**. Sage 50 provides the authorization number for recording.

Click **OK**. **Click OK** again to return to the Sales Journal and **post** the **entry**.

Close the **Advisor message** about low inventory to continue and then **close** the **Sales Journal**.

The stock for item FT33 now is –2 — oversold by two units. This is the quantity in the updated Inventory List that opens from the Sales Journal Item Number field.

Processing Credit Card Transactions Manually

If you do not have a direct Internet connection, you can process the credit card transaction manually. This method may be used with charge slips or telephone orders. On the Credit Card Information screen,

Click the **Select Processing Method list arrow**:

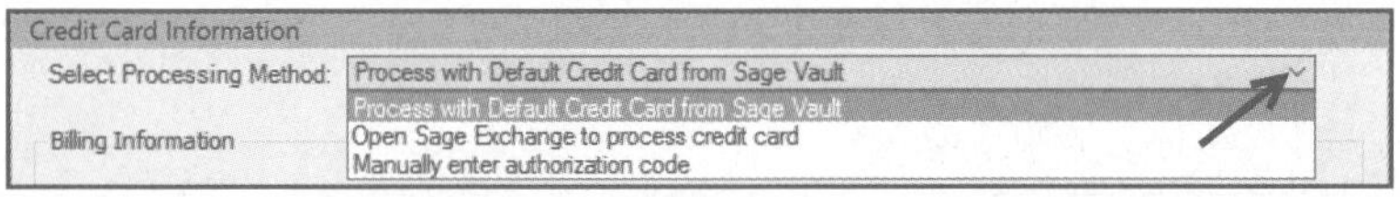

Once the ledger record has a customer's card information, the selection list includes Sage Vault and this is now the default. Otherwise, you will have only the option to Open Sage Exchange To Process Credit Card (as we did for the Visa sale to Barrato) or Manually Enter Authorization Code.

NOTES

You must process the MasterCard credit card sale if you have not removed the processing service account details. Use the card number provided in the source document.

PRO VERSION

pro Credit card processing is available only for Canadian dollar credit cards, so you will not have entries for CAD Merchant Account and Currency.

NOTES

The Advisor message about low inventory will appear several times. Shady Corners allows inventory levels to go below zero. You should close the message each time it appears.

If inventory levels have fallen below zero, they will trigger a cost variance entry when the item is purchased (refer to page 525).

NOTES

If you get a message that the credit card fees are not fully allocated, you must accept the incomplete allocation to continue.

NOTES

If you did not add the address details in the customer's record, you can enter them here – or use your own address for practice.

Select Manually Enter Authorization Code as the processing method from the drop-down list:

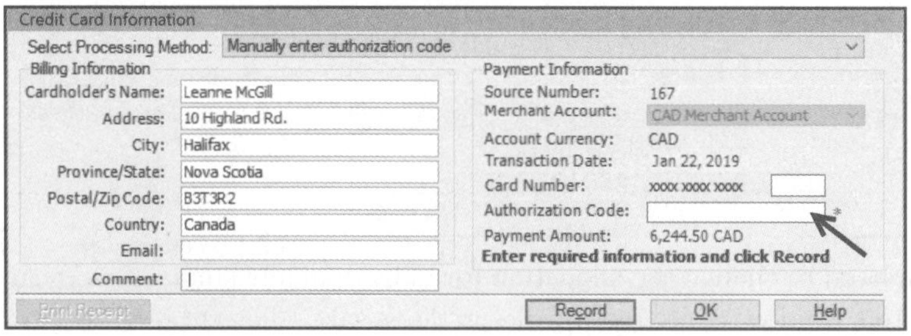

WARNING!

Both the card number and authorization code are required when you process the charge manually.

The Card Number field and the Authorization Code fields will become available.

Click the Card Number field. Enter the last four digits of the card number.

Type 1111 for Visa or 0057 for MasterCard.

Click the Authorization Code field. This code can be obtained by telephone or may be given automatically when the card is swiped on a terminal.

Type 488922

Click OK to return to the Sales Journal. Post the transaction.

Removing Credit Card Processing Settings

When entering a sale while you have account information in your credit card processing settings, you must process the transaction before you can post the sale. If you try to post the sale without the processing step, you will be blocked with this message:

NOTES

If you need to close the Sales Journal to change credit card processing information, you can store the transaction first and then recall it and enter the correct date. You can remove the stored transaction after recalling it.

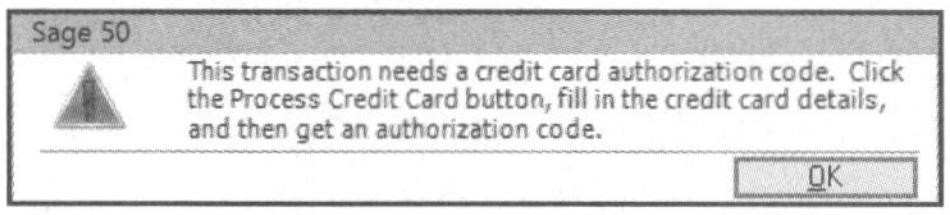

Click **OK**. **Close** the **Sales Journal**. You cannot access the merchant account settings while the journal is open.

You need to remove the credit card processing account information, unless you want to process all credit card sales and generate authorization codes.

Click the **Settings icon**, then click **Company**, **Credit Cards** and **Processing Service** to open the Settings screen you need:

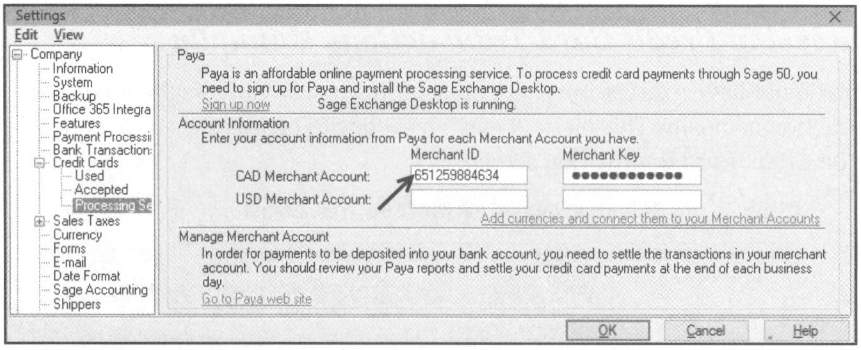

Double-click the **CAD Merchant ID number** and **press** *del*.

Double-click the **CAD Merchant Key password** and **press** *del*.

Click **OK** to save the changed settings.

Click **Yes** to confirm the changes you are making.

Pre-Authorized Payments and Deposits

Businesses may have bills paid directly from their bank accounts by allowing suppliers to make automatic withdrawals. Customers may also permit automatic withdrawals for bill payments, and many businesses arrange for paycheques to be deposited directly to employee bank accounts. For these transactions, funds are transferred electronically, directly from one bank account to another. Funds may be transferred between different banks and branches.

Third-party solution providers manage these electronic funds transfers (EFTs). Bambora is one of the providers whose services can be linked with features in Sage 50 for these transfers. We have a test account set up to illustrate the processes involved.

NOTES
The customer is still responsible for ensuring that the bank account has sufficient funds to pay the bill to avoid overdraft or NSF charges.

Pre-Authorized Debits (PAD)

When customers allow a business to withdraw funds directly to pay their accounts, usually for recurring bills, their method of payment is Pre-Authorized Debit. This arrangement removes concerns about lost cheques and overdue bills.

✓ 10

Received memo #2 from Owner: Two customers have authorized automatic debit payments. Set up the permission in the customer records and enter bank account details as follows:

customer	branch number	institution (bank) number	account number
Hopewell College	67320	001	6557777
Rockcliff Manor	78129	003	9928821

Setting Up Pre-Authorized Debits

Before entering a pre-authorized debit sale or receipt, the customer's ledger must be updated to authorize the transactions and to add the customer's bank account details.

Click **Receivables** in the Modules pane to switch to this window.

Click **Hopewell College** in the Customers List pane to open this record.

Click the **Pre-Authorized Debit tab** to access the screen we need:

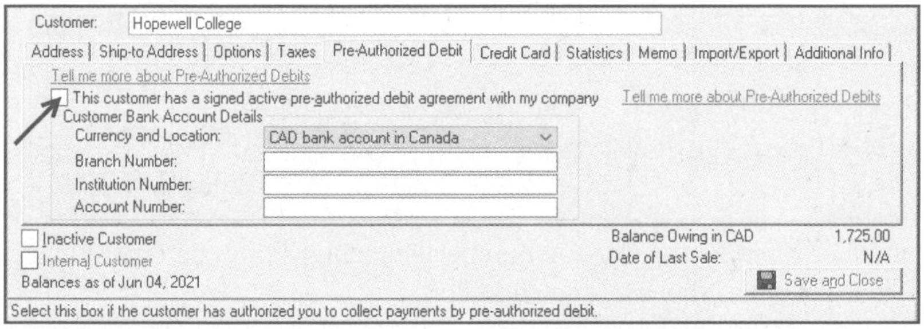

All the fields on this screen are required. The customer must complete and sign a form or agreement including the bank account details and authorizing the withdrawals. Often a blank void cheque accompanies the form to provide the information about the bank account. Withdrawals may be made in Canadian or US dollars from bank accounts in Canada or the United States. The **Currency And Location** drop-down list allows you to make this selection.

NOTES
As soon as you click the check box, a note is added to the tab screen to remind you that the data file does not have user passwords. Strong passwords are essential when bank details are included in your data files. For practice exercises, we have omitted passwords. Adding passwords is covered in Chapter 16.

Click **This Customer Has A Signed Active Pre-Authorized Debit Agreement With My Company** to add a ✓. The remaining bank information must now be entered before you can leave this tab screen.

Click the **Branch Number field**. **Type** 67320

NOTES

The bank account information is similar to that entered for employees who have paycheques deposited directly to their bank accounts (refer to page 337).

Each bank has a unique three-digit bank or institution number, with unique five-digit branch numbers for their different branch locations. The account number is unique for the account holder and varies in length from bank to bank.

Press tab to advance to the Institution (bank) Number field.

Type 001 **Press** tab to advance to the Account Number field.

Type 6557777

Click the **Select list arrow** and **click Rockcliff Manor** to open the ledger.

Sage 50 asks if you want to change the Payment Method default selections to Pre-Authorized Debit:

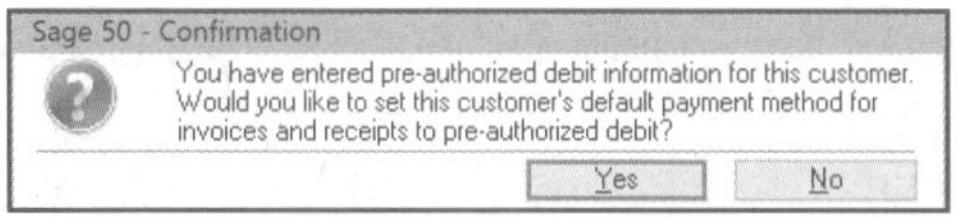

Click **Yes** to accept the change. **Click** the **Pre-Authorized Debit tab**.

Click the **authorized agreement check box** and **enter** the **bank account details** for Rockcliff Manor.

Click Save and Close. **Click Yes** to accept the change in payment method.

Entering Pre-Authorized Debits

Pre-authorized debit is available as a method of payment for both receipts and sales invoices from the Paid By/Method Of Payment drop-down lists, respectively. Receipts and sales are entered in the same way as regular receipts and sales. Only the method of payment selection differs.

✓ 11 Entered pre-authorized payment from Hopewell College on June 6 for $1 695 including $30 discount. Receipt #421 was applied to invoice #159. CP20 will be entered as the cheque number.

NOTES

The starting number for pre-authorized debits can be entered and edited on the Forms screen of Company Settings.

Open the **Receipts Journal**.

Choose **Hopewell College** as the customer.

Enter **Jun 6** as the transaction date. Pre-Authorized Debit is now selected as the default in the Paid By field, but you can change this selection.

Click the **Paid By list arrow** for the options:

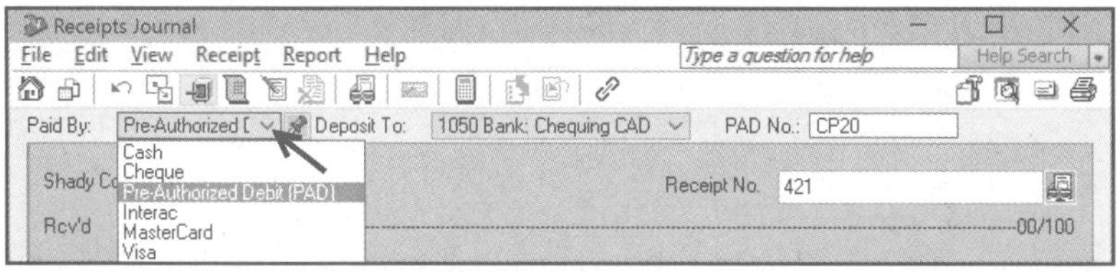

WARNING!

You must remove the customer's name from the journal before you can modify the ledger record.

PAD number replaces the Cheque number field and CP20 (customer payment #20) is entered in this field as the reference number.

If you have omitted any of the information in the customer's ledger record, either the authorization check box or the bank details, Sage 50 blocks the action when you select the Pre-Authorized Debit method of payment:

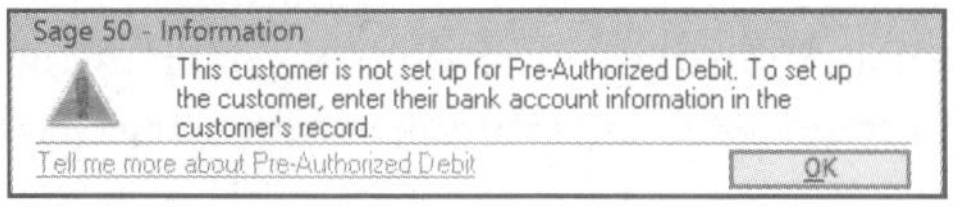

Click **OK**. Complete the ledger record before continuing.

Accept the **Discount** and **Amount** to complete the receipt.

Press ctrl + **J** to review the transaction.

It looks like a normal receipt — the bank account is debited for the amount received because EFT transactions transfer the money directly from the customer's account. *Sales Discounts* and *Accounts Receivable* are credited as usual.

Close the **journal entry** and **post** the receipt. Enter the next PAD receipt.

✓ 12 Entered pre-authorized payment (CP21) from Rockcliff Manor on June 6 for $1 017 including $18 discount. Receipt #422 was applied to invoice #163.

Close the **Receipts Journal**.

Click **Divisions** in the Modules pane so you can enter the next purchase.

NOTES
PAD reference numbers, CP20, CP21 and so on, are automatically updated.

Creating Cost Variances

If items are sold to a customer when the inventory stock is too low to fill the sale completely, the levels in inventory fall below zero and the outstanding items are backordered. The estimated cost of goods for the sale is based on the average cost for the items in stock at the time of the sale. When the items are received later the price may have changed, and the items that fill the rest of the customer's order will have a different cost price from the one recorded for the sale. The difference is the cost variance and is assigned to the linked variance account for the inventory item. The amount of the variance is added to the journal entry for the purchase. Thus two conditions are required for a variance to occur: the inventory is oversold and the cost has changed.

You do not have to do anything to record a cost variance other than allowing inventory levels to go below zero. The program makes the calculations automatically and assigns the amount to the linked variance account for the inventory item.

WARNING!
If you have not entered a cost variance linked account in the item's ledger record, you will be prompted to select one when a purchase creates a variance, but you cannot create a new account from this selection list.

If the company settings for inventory do not allow inventory levels to go below zero, you must reduce the quantity to continue with the sale as in Chapter 10.

Enter **purchase invoice #MD-1018** from Mobler Dansk.

✓ 13 Recorded purchase invoice #MD-1018 on June 6, 2021, from Mobler Dansk for teak patio furniture. Terms: 2/15, net 30. The exchange rate on June 6 was 0.205. Total import duty charged was Dkr 12.844,00 (CAD $2 633.02). The freight expense was allocated entirely to Store Sales.

items purchased			amount	duty rate
15	FT31	Patio table: Teak round 1.5 m	Dkr 40.500,00	9.5%
48	FT33	Arm chair: Teak	91.200,00	9.5%
5	FT35	End table: Teak	3.500,00	9.5%
		Freight	2.000,00	
		HST Paid	20.580,00	
Invoice Total			Dkr 157.780,00	

Display the **journal entry** with the variance amount included:

Shady Corners
Purchases Journal Entry 06/06/2021 (J11)

Account Number	Account Description	Division	Foreign Amount	Division Frgn Amt	Debits	Credits	Division Amt
1400	Patio Furniture		Dkr147.590,34		30,256.02	-	
2670	GST/HST Paid on Purchases		Dkr20.580,00		4,218.90	-	
5080	Variance Costs		Dkr453,66		93.00	-	
5100	Freight Expense		Dkr2.000,00		410.00	-	
		- Store Sales		Dkr2.000.00			410.00
2200	Accounts Payable		Dkr157.780,00		-	32,344.90	
2220	Import Duty Payable		Dkr12.844,00		-	2,633.02	
1 Danish Kroners equals 0.2050000 Canadian Dollars					34,977.92	34,977.92	

NOTES
If you have made corrections to journal entries, your variance cost amount may be different.

There was insufficient stock left for item FT33 on June 4 when sale #167 was recorded, so the average historic cost for six chairs, $2 280, was credited to *Cost of Goods Sold*. Only four chairs were in stock at the time of the sale, with an average cost of $380 per chair ($760 for two chairs). When the purchase of item FT33 was recorded, the total cost for 48 chairs was $18 696, or $779 for two chairs, plus duty at 9.5%, for a total of $853. The difference, $93, between the new cost and the cost in the sales transaction for the two out-of-stock chairs is the cost variance.

NOTES
The calculated price for the chairs includes the import duty at the rate of 9.5%.

The 48 chairs cost Dkr 91.200,00 plus 0.095% duty for a total cost of Dkr 99.864,00. This amount is multiplied by the exchange rate of 0.205 for a cost of CAD $20 472.12 ($426.50 per chair or $853 for two chairs.)

NOTES
Incomplete allocations for rounding errors that result from currency conversions or credit card fees must also be accepted.

When you post the transaction, Sage 50 requests confirmation:

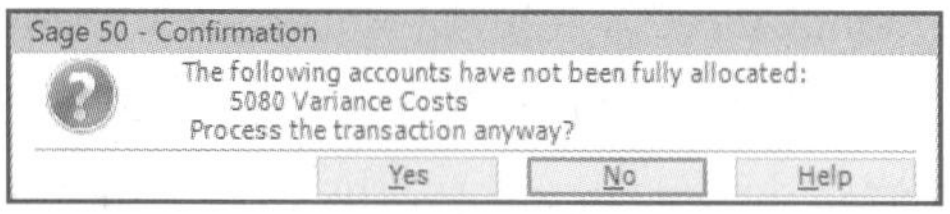

Variance costs cannot be allocated, so you must accept the incomplete allocation.

Click **Yes** to continue posting the purchase. Close the Purchases Journal.

Open the **Sales Journal** so you can enter the sale to Hopewell College.

Entering Sales with Pre-Authorized Debits

✓ 14

Sale #168 to Hopewell College was recorded by Iola on June 7. The preferred customer has pre-authorized debits and is entitled to free delivery and the 2% discount for immediate payment. All revenue was allocated to Store Sales.

items sold			amount
6	FT31	Patio table: Teak round 1.5 m	$750 each
30	FT33	Arm chair: Teak	615 each
10	FX42	Umbrella w/stand	200 each
30	FX43	Cushion: deep seating chair	40 each
		Harmonized Sales Tax	15%

$29 549.50 was uploaded to our bank account (reference number CP22).

NOTES
Preferred customers do not pay for delivery.
Although the Sales Discount amount is not allocated, Sage 50 does not warn about the incomplete allocation.

Choose **Hopewell College** as the customer for the sale.

Enter **Jun 7** as the transaction date.

Pre-Authorized Debit (PAD) is automatically selected from the ledger record and an updated PAD number, CP22, is entered.

Enter the **remaining details** for the sale, including the division allocations.

Review the **journal entry** — it looks like a regular sale paid by cash or cheque. The bank account is debited for the full amount (minus the 2 percent discount) instead of *Accounts Receivable*.

Close the **journal entry** and **post** the invoice.

Close the **Sales Journal**.

Uploading Pre-Authorized Debits

After the pre-authorized debit transactions are entered in Sage 50, they must be uploaded to the company that manages the transfer of funds. For our example, the author has a test account set up courtesy of Bambora.

✓ 15

Received memo #3 from Owner: Upload three pre-authorized customer receipts.

Click **Receivables** in the Modules pane. There are two methods you can use to upload pre-authorized transactions.

NOTES
The Banking module has an Upload Direct Payments icon. From its drop-down list you can upload pre-authorized debits, direct payments to suppliers and direct deposits for employees.

Click the **Upload Pre-Authorized Debits icon** in the Related Tasks pane:

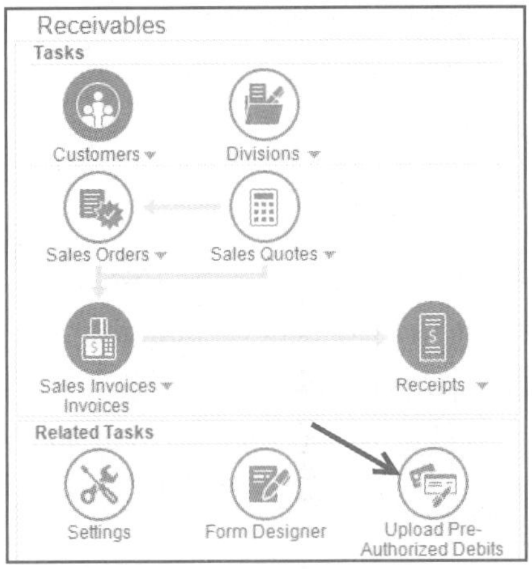

If you are not working in the Receivables module window, you can upload the transactions from the File menu in any Home window.

Choose the **File menu** and **Import/Export**, then **click Upload Direct Payments** and **Pre-Authorized Debits**:

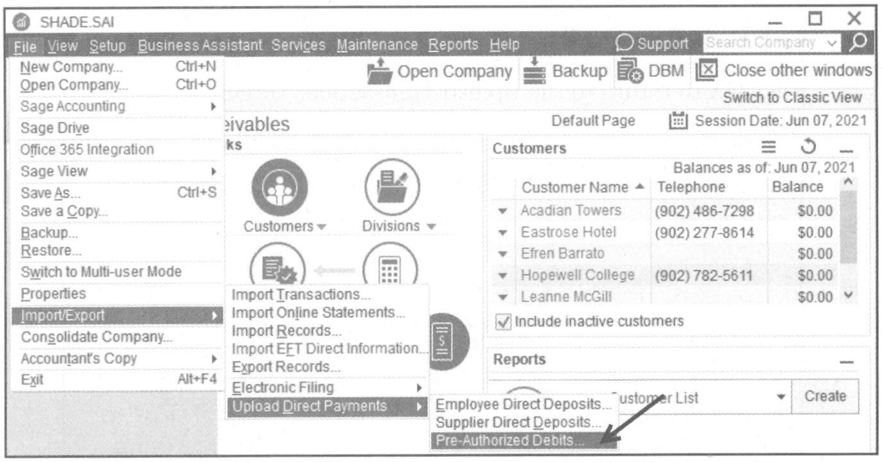

The Upload Transactions window opens, listing the pre-authorized debits entered:

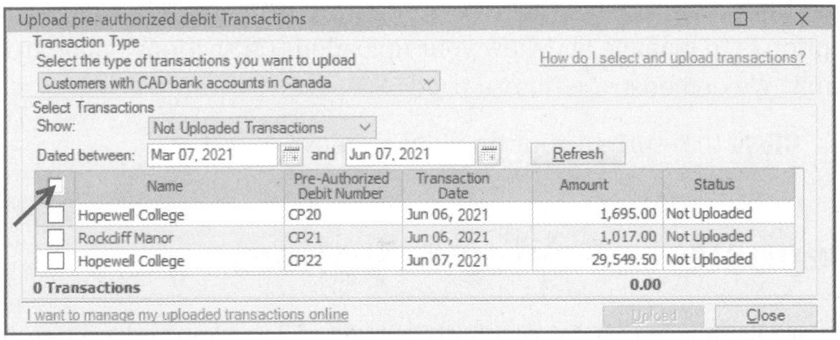

In this window, you can **Select Transactions** to display from the drop-down list for the **Show** field. The default setting is for **Not Uploaded Transactions**, and the receipts we entered are listed. You can also list only transactions already uploaded (refer to the next page) or all transactions — those uploaded and not yet uploaded.

Each transaction has a check box for selection.

You can select payments individually by clicking the box beside a transaction or select all of them by clicking the check box in the column heading (marked with the arrow in the previous screen).

Click the **column heading check box** to add checkmarks for all receipts. The Upload button is no longer dimmed.

PRO VERSION

The Pro version File menu does not have the options to Switch To Multi-User Mode or to Consolidate Company.

NOTES

You can view transactions for the previous three months.

NOTES

Because of the way this account is set up, you will not be able to follow through with uploading any direct payments.

To cancel the uploading process, click Close to return to the Upload Transactions screen and then click Close to return to your starting point.

Your journal entries will still be correct because the bank account was debited for these uploaded transactions.

Click the **Upload button** to open the authorization screen:

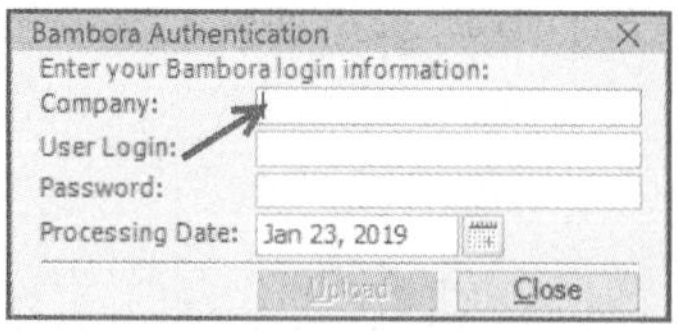

The screens we include for the rest of the process are for illustration purposes only. You will require a Bambora account or another direct payment account to continue.

Enter your Bambora Company name, User Login and Password. Choose the date you want these payments to be processed — the current calendar date and one day later are the defaults for the deposit, but before uploading you can change the processing date (refer to pages 535–536).

Click Upload to begin processing.

After the transfer is completed, Sage 50 informs us that the transactions have been uploaded successfully:

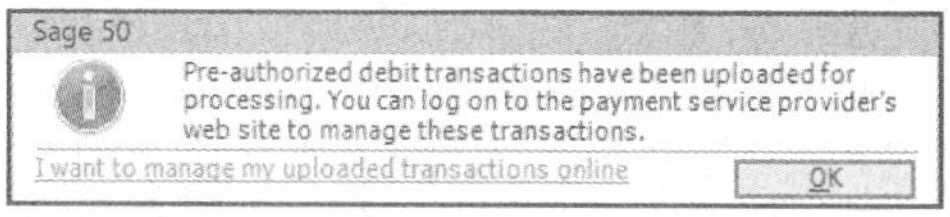

Click OK to return to the Upload Transactions screen.

Choose Uploaded Transactions from the Show field for Select Transactions:

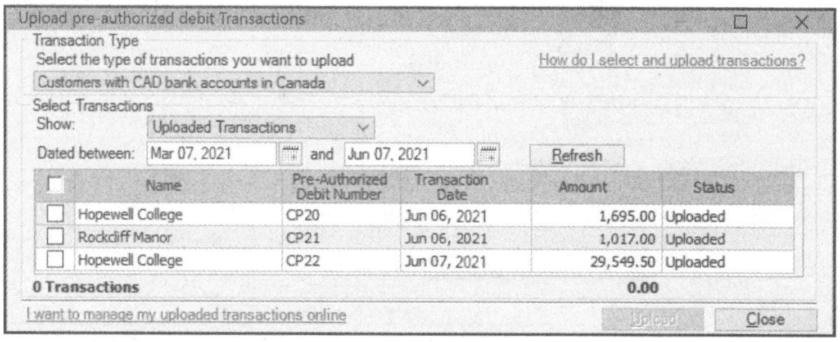

The status of the three receipts has changed to Uploaded. You can view these transactions and their status at any time.

Another option is to manage and view your uploaded transactions online from your Bambora account. We demonstrate this on page 535.

Click **Close** to return to your previous window.

Direct Deposits – Paying Suppliers

NOTES

The same chequing bank account is used for all Payables transactions, so we need to enter the same details for both supplier records. These suppliers will have customer records for Shady Corners authorizing the direct withdrawals.

Direct deposits are usually set up for regular bills such as insurance or utilities. The process for suppliers is similar to the one for customers. You need to modify the supplier record (authorize the withdrawal of funds from your bank account and enter your bank account details), choose Direct Deposit as the method of payment for the transactions, enter and post the transactions and upload the payments.

Memo # 4 requests that we modify two supplier records to set up direct deposits.

✓ 10 Memo #4 from Owner: Authorized direct payments and set up of bank account details for Capital Trust for insurance and Bell Canada for telephone services:

branch number	institution (bank) number	account number
38930	012	298899

Open the **Payables module window**.

Click **Capital Trust** in the Suppliers list pane to open the ledger.

Click the **Direct Deposit tab** to access the screen we need to edit:

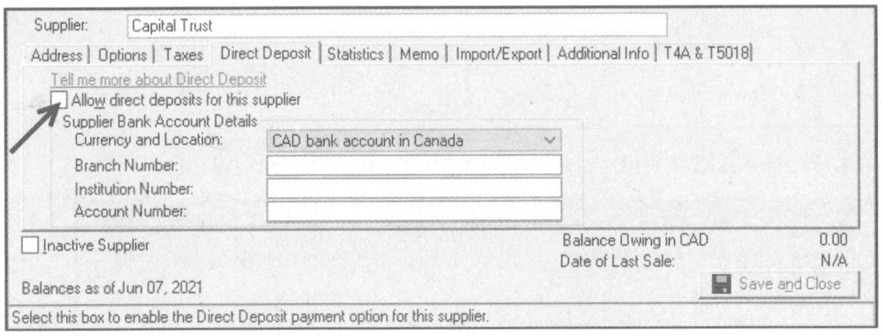

Click **Allow Direct Deposits For This Supplier**.

Enter the **Branch**, **Institution** and **Account numbers**. **Open** the record for **Bell Canada**.

Accept the **Payment Method change** to Direct Deposit.

Choose **Bell Canada** from the Select field list of suppliers and **make** the **same changes** for this supplier record. **Click** **Save And Close**.

You are now ready to enter the insurance bill for which we set up direct deposits.

✓ 17 Capital Trust notified us that the monthly insurance premium for $330 including PST for invoice #CT-36698 was withdrawn from our bank account on June 7 as direct deposit (number VP35). Create new Group expense account 5210 Insurance Expense. The expense was allocated as follows: Store Sales – 60%; Planting – 20%; Design – 20%. Store the payment as a monthly recurring entry.

Open the **Purchases Journal** (or the Payments Journal with Make Other Payment as the transaction type). **Choose** **Capital Trust** as the supplier.

Direct Deposit has been entered in the Payment Method field to modify the journal:

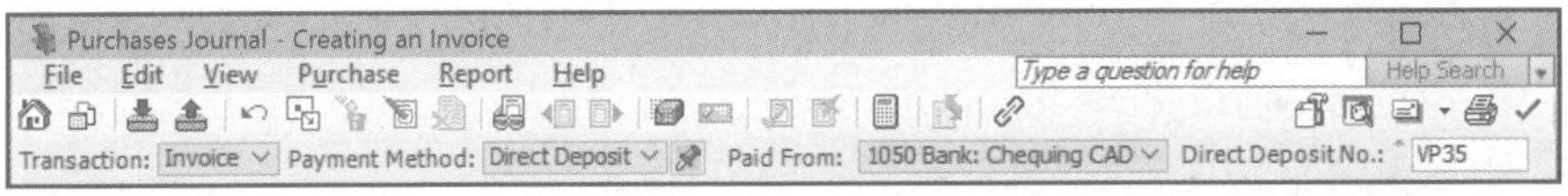

The bank account is entered in the Paid From field and the Cheque No. field label has been replaced by Direct Deposit No. with VP35 (vendor payment #35) entered as the reference.

Enter the **remaining invoice details**, including allocations, in the usual way.

The transaction you review looks like a regular cash or cheque purchase — the bank account has been credited for the total invoice amount.

Post the **entry**. **Enter** the next **direct deposit invoice** and **close** the **journal**.

18 Invoice #BC-64261 marked as PAID was received on June 7 from Bell Canada for $350 plus $52.50 HST for store telephones, staff mobile phones and Internet services. $402.50 was withdrawn from our chequing account (VP36). The expense was allocated to Store Sales – 40%, Planting – 20% and Design – 40%.

✓ 19 Memo #5 from Owner: Upload the two direct payments made to Capital Trust (VP35) and Bell Canada (VP36).

Choose the **File menu** and **Import/Export** in the Home window and then **click** **Upload Direct Payments** and **Supplier Direct Deposits**. Or,

NOTES
As soon as you click the Allow check box, Sage 50 will add a note to the ledger record recommending user passwords.

NOTES
The PST on insurance is not refundable and is included as part of the expense. HST is not charged on insurance.

NOTES
Until you choose a supplier for whom you have set up direct deposit, the Direct Deposit Number field does not open.

NOTES
Double-click the Allo column to open the Allocation screen.

NOTES
You can edit the starting reference number for direct payments on the Forms screen of Company Settings.

Click the **Upload Direct Deposit icon** in the Related Tasks pane of the Payables module window:

These two methods start the process of uploading the payments:

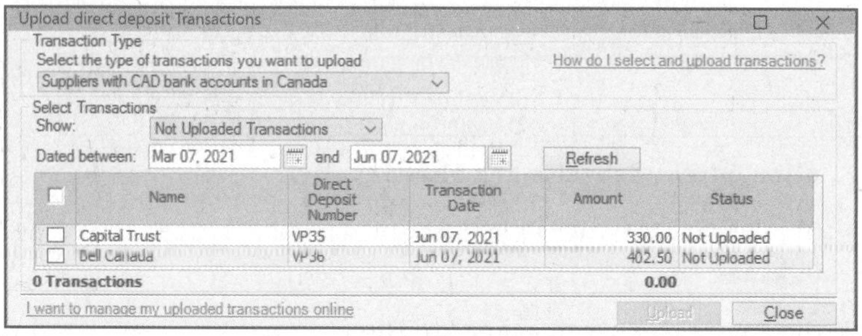

The two payment transactions are entered. As for receipts, we can show Not Uploaded Transactions (the default), Uploaded Transactions or All Transactions — both those uploaded and those not yet uploaded. The selection of payments is the same as for receipts. You can select all transactions or individual ones.

Click the **Select check box** in the column heading to choose both payments.

Click the **Upload button** to open the authorization window:

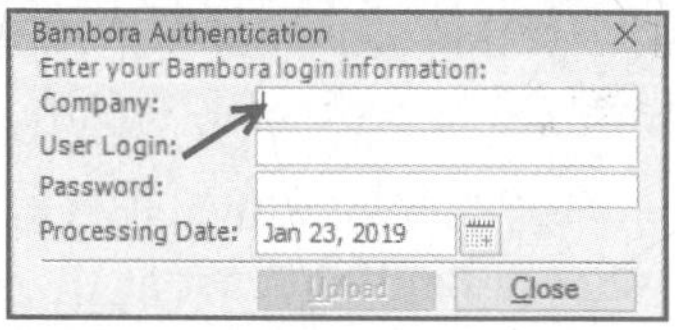

Enter your Bambora account Company name, User Login and Password and choose the date you want the payments to be processed. Click Upload.

After the uploading has been completed, you will receive a confirmation message:

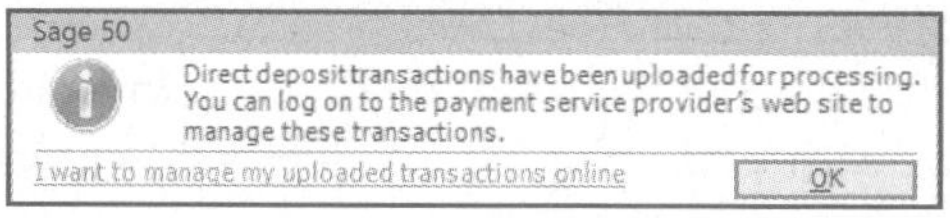

Sage 50
Direct deposit transactions have been uploaded for processing. You can log on to the payment service provider's web site to manage these transactions.
I want to manage my uploaded transactions online
OK

Click OK to return to the Upload Transactions window. Choose All Transactions from the Show drop-down list:

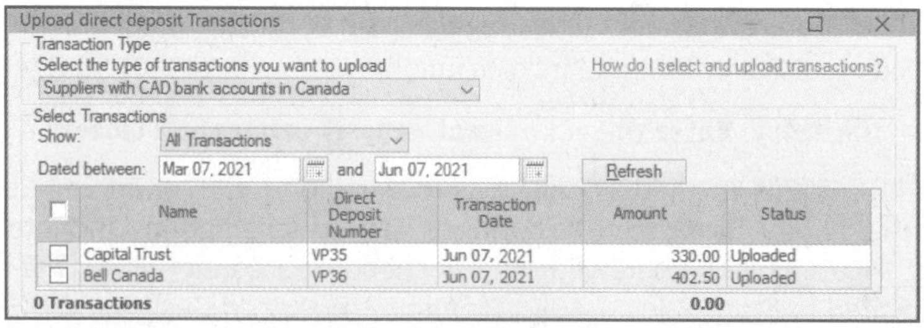

The change in status to Uploaded confirms that we uploaded both deposits.

Click **Close** to return to your previous window.

NOTES

Remember that unless you have a valid account with Bambora (or another provider), you cannot follow through with uploading the deposits.

To cancel the uploading process, click Close to return to the Upload Transactions screen and then click Close to return to your starting point.

NOTES

You can display transactions for the previous three months.

SESSION DATE – JUNE 14, 2021

20

Memo #6 from Owner. Created two new inventory records for summer garden specials, both including furniture, plants, one hour of consultation and one hour of planting service. A new Group asset account was used for the packages: 1420 Summer Garden Packages. The other linked accounts used were Revenue from Sales (account 4020) and Cost of Goods Sold (account 5070). Both items are taxed for HST. Import duty does not apply.

new item	description	min amt	regular (preferred) selling price/unit
SU01	Aluminum patio set/planting	0	$1 250 ($1 000) /pkg
SU02	Teak patio set/planting	0	$3 800 ($3 500) /pkg

21

Used Form ITA-1 dated June 8/21 to assemble four SU01 Aluminum patio set/planting packages using furniture and plants as follows:

components			unit cost	total
4	FA03	Table: Cast Aluminum round 2 m	$ 400 each	$1 600.00
16	FA04	Arm chair: Cast Aluminum	56.4456 each	903.13
4	FA06	End table: Cast Aluminum	60 each	240.00
8	SH01	Shrubs: 50 cm	6 each	48.00
4	BK01	Gardening in the Shade	25 each	100.00
Additional Costs (for services)				240.00

assembled items (package)			unit cost	total
4	SU01	Aluminum patio set/planting	$782.7825 each	$3 131.13

22

Used Form ITA-2 dated June 8/21 to assemble four SU02 Teak patio set/planting packages using furniture and plants as follows:

components			unit cost	total
4	FT31	Patio table: Teak round 1.5 m	$600.702 each	$ 2 402.81
16	FT33	Arm chair: Teak	426.5025 each	6 824.04
4	FT35	End table: Teak	148.566 each	594.26
8	SH04	Shrubs: 1 metre specialty	55 each	440.00
4	BK01	Gardening in the Shade	25 each	100.00
Additional Costs				240.00

assembled items (package)			unit cost	total
4	SU02	Teak patio set/planting	$2 650.2775 each	$10 601.11

23

Merchandise requested from Groen Fields was received on June 9 with invoice #GF-1299. Payment is due in 60 days.

items purchased			amount
20	PL01	Plant/ground cover: 5 litre	$ 200
20	PL02	Plant/ground cover: 10 litre	320
100	PL03	Plant/ground cover starters	4 000
30	PL04	Plant: perennial specialty	750
30	PL05	Plant: annual 10 cm	150
20	SH03	Shrubs: 3 metre	640
3	PS11	Topsoil: cubic metre	180
	HST Paid		936
Invoice Total			$7 176

24

Sale #169 to Marjorie Blackhorn was completed on June 10. Blackhorn paid for the consultation with Visa. 100% of revenue was allocated to Design.

items sold			amount	total
8	SC01	Consultation/Design	$110 /hour	$ 880
	HST Paid			132
Invoice total paid by Visa				$1 012

NOTES

Packages will not be oversold, so the variance account is not required.

NOTES

The services are included as additional costs. You cannot select service items with the inventory to create the package because no purchase costs are associated with the services. There is no allocation option for expense amounts in the Item Assembly Journal, but you do not get a message about incomplete allocations.

WARNING!

The unit costs change continually as new inventory is purchased at different prices.

Accept your default prices for assembly components and copy the total to the assembled items total. The totals for assembly components (including additional costs) and assembled items must be exactly the same.

NOTES

The plant starters have different buying and selling units. They are purchased in flats of ten 4-pack units and sold as individual 4-pack items.

NOTES

For cash, credit card or debit card sales, you can type the new customer name and choose Continue or choose One-Time Customer and use the Additional Field for the customer name. No discounts apply to these sales.

NOTES
Garden Crafts
(contact Jon Quill)
290 Daffodil Lane
Richmond Hill, ON L3T 1P1
Terms: net 30
Payment method: Pay Later
Tax code: H

25 Invoice #GC-6821 from Garden Crafts (use full add for new Canadian supplier) was received with the shipment of furniture on June 10. Terms for the new supplier are net 30. Allocate 100% of the freight expense to Store Sales.

items purchased			amount
10	FX42	Umbrella w/stand	$1 100
20	FX43	Cushion: deep seating chair	400
4	FX44	Cushion: deep seating lounge	240
4	FX45	Cushion: deep seating set	520
		Freight	100
		HST Paid	354
Invoice Total			$2 714

NOTES
The duty rate and Division columns are not included on purchase orders or quotes.
You may need to close and reopen the journal to have the Exchange Rate field added to the screen.

26 Recorded purchase order #140 from Mobler Dansk on June 10 at the exchange rate of 0.203. Terms: 2/15, n/30 days after delivery on June 13.

items purchased			amount
2	FA02	Patio set: Cast Aluminum rect. table 2 m	Dkr 7.200,00
4	FA03	Table: Cast Aluminum round 2 m	8.000,00
8	FA04	Arm chair: Cast Aluminum	2.240,00
4	FA06	End table: Cast Aluminum	1.200,00
		Freight	1.200,00
		HST	2.976,00
Invoice Total			Dkr 22.816,00

27 Recorded purchase order #141 from Jorgensen Mobler on June 10 at the exchange rate of 0.203. Terms: 2/30, n/60 days after delivery on June 13.

items purchased			amount
4	FT32	Patio table: Teak rect 2 m	Dkr 11.600,00
6	FT33	Arm chair: Teak	12.000,00
3	FT34	Chaise longue: Teak	7.350,00
		Freight	1.000,00
		HST Paid	4.792,50
Invoice Total			Dkr 36.742,50

NOTES
Remember to change the currency setting to DKK for the bank transfer.

28 Memo #7 from Owner, dated June 12, authorized bank transfer. Dkr 30.000,00 was taken from Bank: Visa and Interac account and deposited to Bank: DKK for upcoming payments. The exchange rate was 0.202.

29 Entered 0.202 as the exchange rate on June 12. Paid invoice #JM-842 from Jorgensen Mobler with cheque #376 for Dkr 11.858,00 including Dkr 242,00 discount for early payment.
Paid cheque #377 to Mobler Dansk for Dkr 17.941,84 including Dkr 366,16 discount for early payment for invoice #MD-916.

30 Violet Birch paid for her purchase on June 13 with her MasterCard, entered as cash sale #170. 100% of revenue from plant sales was allocated to Store Sales and 100% of consultation and report revenue was allocated to Design.

items sold			amount	total
30	PL03	Plant/ground cover starters	$ 8 each	$ 240.00
8	SC01	Consultation/Design	110 /hour	880.00
1	SC02	Report	200 /report	200.00
		HST Paid		198.00
Invoice total paid by MasterCard				$1 518.00

31 Sale #171 to Acadian Towers was completed on June 13. Terms for the sale were 2/15, n/30. 100% of revenue and expenses was allocated to Store Sales.

items sold			amount
1	FA01	Patio set: Cast Aluminum round table 1.5 m	$1 090 each
2	FA05	Ottoman: Cast Aluminum	50 each
2	FA06	End table: Cast Aluminum	95 each
2	FA07	Bench: Cast Aluminum	185 each
6	FX43	Cushion: deep seating chair	40 each
		Harmonized Sales Tax	15%

32 Received all items ordered from Mobler Dansk on purchase order #140 on June 13 with invoice #MD-1241 with payment terms of 2/15, net 30. Used the exchange rate of 0.203. Total import duty charged was Dkr 1.491,20 (CAD $302.72). The freight expense was allocated entirely to Store Sales.

items purchased			amount	duty rate
2	FA02	Patio set: Cast Aluminum rect. table 2 m	Dkr 7.200,00	8.0%
4	FA03	Table: Cast Aluminum round 2 m	8.000,00	8.0%
8	FA04	Arm chair: Cast Aluminum	2.240,00	8.0%
4	FA06	End table: Cast Aluminum	1.200,00	8.0%
	Freight		1.200,00	
	HST		2.976,00	
Invoice Total			Dkr 22.816,00	

33 On June 13, all items ordered from Jorgensen Mobler on purchase order #141 arrived. Invoice #JM-1088 confirmed payment terms of 2/30, net 60. Used the exchange rate of 0.203 for the invoice. Total import duty charged was Dkr 2.940,25 (CAD $596.97). The freight expense was allocated to Store Sales.

items purchased			amount	duty rate
4	FT32	Patio table: Teak rect 2 m	Dkr 11.600,00	9.5%
6	FT33	Arm chair: Teak	12.000,00	9.5%
3	FT34	Chaise longue: Teak	7.350,00	9.5%
	Freight		1.000,00	
	HST Paid		4.792,50	
Invoice Total			Dkr 36.742,50	

34 Sale #172 to Acadian Towers was completed on June 14. Terms for the sale were 2/15, n/30. 100% of revenue and expenses for inventory items was allocated to Store Sales; 100% of revenue from consultation was allocated to Design; and 100% of revenue from planting was allocated to Planting.

items sold			amount
4	PL01	Plant/ground cover: 5 litre	$ 16 each
4	PL02	Plant/ground cover: 10 litre	25 each
200	PL03	Plant/ground cover starters	6 /4-pack
10	PL04	Plant: perennial specialty	42 each
20	PL06	Plant: annual 15 cm	13 each
3	PS11	Topsoil: cubic metre	105 /cu m
5	SH01	Shrubs: 50 cm	11 each
5	SH02	Shrubs: 1 metre	25 each
24	SC01	Consultation/Design	90 /hour
20	SC03	Planting & Soil Preparation	40 /hour
		Harmonized Sales Tax	15%

✓ 35 Completed a payroll cheque run for the bi-weekly paid employees using Time Summary Sheet #51. The pay period starting and ending date were June 1/21 and June 14/21. Issue deposit slips #66 to #69.

NOTES
Credit card fees are not fully allocated because amounts are rounded off.

WARNING!
The exchange rate from the order will be the default and you will need to change it.

NOTES
If the duty fields are omitted when you convert the order, close and re-open the journal. They should now be included. You can add the rates manually if needed.

Variance costs will not be allocated.

NOTES
Choose 26 as the Pay Period Frequency for the cheque run.

EMPLOYEE TIME SUMMARY SHEET #51							**DATED JUNE 14/21**
Name of Employee	Regular Hours	Overtime Hours	No. of Plantings	Sick Days	Personal Days	Sales Commission	Allocations
Aster	75	0	100	1	–	–	90% Planting, 10% Store Sales
Fineum	75	2	120	–	1	–	80% Planting, 20% Store Sales
Iola	75	2	–	–	–	$106	100% Store Sales
Phlox	$1 650 Salary		40	–	–	–	10% Planting, 90% Store Sales

Allocating in the Payroll and Other Journals

NOTES
Instead of clicking the Division column ✓ beside an employee's name in the Payroll Run Journal, you can click the employee name and then click the Allocate tool bar button.

The same principles outlined above to allocate revenues and expenses also apply to the General Journal and Adjustments Journal, and the same Division Settings apply. Payroll allocations have their own setting: by amount, percentage or hours (refer to page 505). We chose percentage for Shady Corners.

Once you have entered the journal information for an account that allows allocation, the Allocate tool will be available. You can use it to enter the allocation information.

In the **Paycheques Journal**, click the Allocate tool to begin the allocation.

In the **Payroll Run Journal**, use the Divisions column for a selected employee. **Click** the **employee's name** and **double-click** the **Divisions column**.

In both Payroll journals, you can **choose** the **Paycheque/Payroll menu** and **click** **Allocate To Division** to begin the allocation for a single employee (after first selecting an employee in the Payroll Run Journal).

If the amounts for all employees should be allocated in the same proportions, you can apply the same allocation to the entire transaction by clicking **Apply This Allocation To Entire Transaction** as we did for sales.

To correct allocations, click to re-open the allocation screen.

NOTES
All the amounts for an employee will be allocated the same way.

In the Payroll journals, all payroll expenses for an employee are allocated by the same percentages (or amounts or hours). This includes the wage and vacation expenses as well as employer contributions such as EI, CPP and WCB. In the journal entry you review, all the payroll-related expenses are divided among the divisions according to the percentages you entered. They are provided under the Division column. You may have to scroll to include all the information.

Uploading Payroll Direct Deposits

All employees have direct deposit set up in their ledger records, so we can upload the payroll cheques for deposit to their accounts.

✓ 36 Memo #8 from Owner: Upload the payroll deposits.

Again, two methods are available for uploading payroll deposits.

Click the **Upload Direct Deposit icon** in the Related Tasks pane of the Employees & Payroll module window. Or,

Choose the **File menu** and **Import/Export** in the Home window and then **click** **Upload Direct Payments** and **Employee Direct Deposits**:

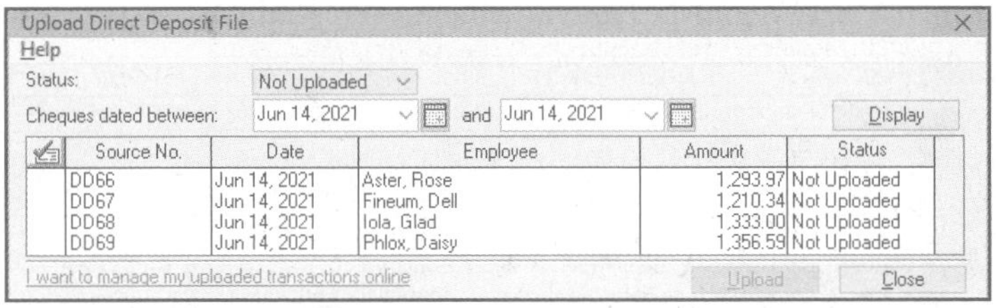

The four employees we paid are listed. **Not Uploaded** is entered as the Status selection with the range of our cheque dates. All deposits are not uploaded yet.

Click the **Select check box** in the column heading, to add ✓s for all employees.

Click the **Upload button** to open the authorization window.

Enter your Bambora account Company name, User Login and Password and choose the date you want the payments to be processed. Click Upload.

After the uploading has been completed, you will receive a confirmation message:

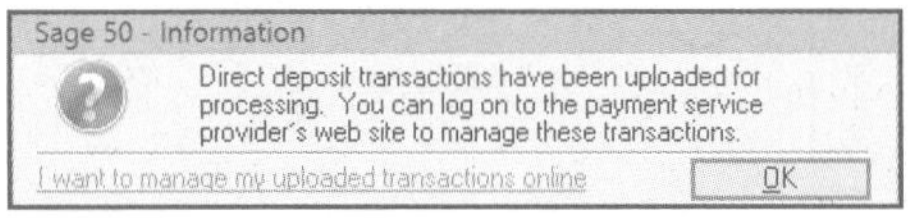

Click OK. Choose Uploaded from the drop-down list for Status. Click Display:

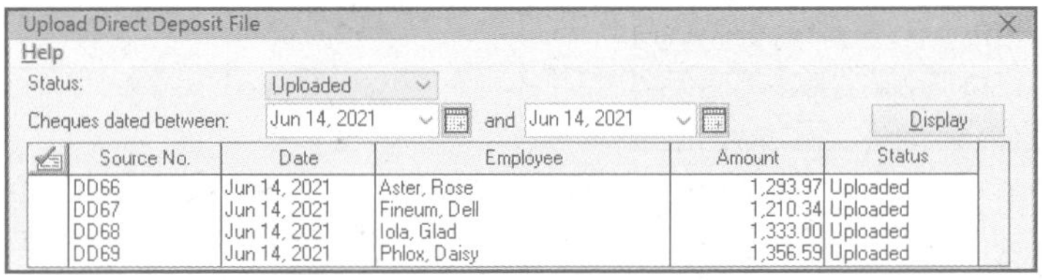

All transactions now have Uploaded as their status.

Click Close to finish your uploading session.

Reviewing the Uploaded Transactions

At any time you can review your uploaded transactions online.

To review your transactions, click **I Want To Manage My Uploaded Transactions Online** in any upload window. You will be connected to the Bambora login page. Enter your Bambora account Company name, User Login and Password. Click Processing and Employee Direct Deposit to list your employee transactions:

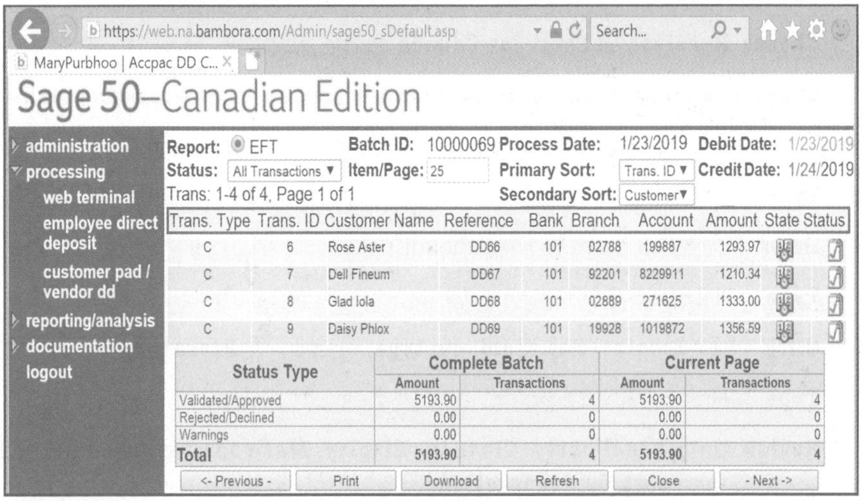

NOTES
The Upload button becomes available as soon as you select an employee.

NOTES
Our test account with Bambora will not permit you to follow through with uploading and reviewing transactions.

NOTES
Remember that unless you have a valid account with Bambora (or another provider), you cannot follow through with uploading the deposits.

To cancel the uploading process, click Close to return to the Upload Transactions screen and then click Close to return to your starting point.

NOTES
The Status drop-down list options are to list Uploaded deposits, Not Uploaded deposits or All deposits.

NOTES
Remember that your debits are the bank's credits and vice versa.

NOTES
The option to manage transactions online is available from all Upload Transactions windows as well as from the uploading confirmation message.

NOTES
Uploading a payment that you previously uploaded will generate the warning about the duplicate entry when you log into the account and view that item, even if you have deleted the original entry.

> **NOTES**
> There is a delay between the date of processing and the date that funds will be withdrawn. This allows time for corrections if necessary.

> **NOTES**
> Clicking a summary line such as eft3 for employee deposits or eft_CP_1 for customer pre-authorized debits will provide the details for all the items you uploaded in that single batch.

Click Customer PAD/Vendor DD and any line in the summary to provide details:

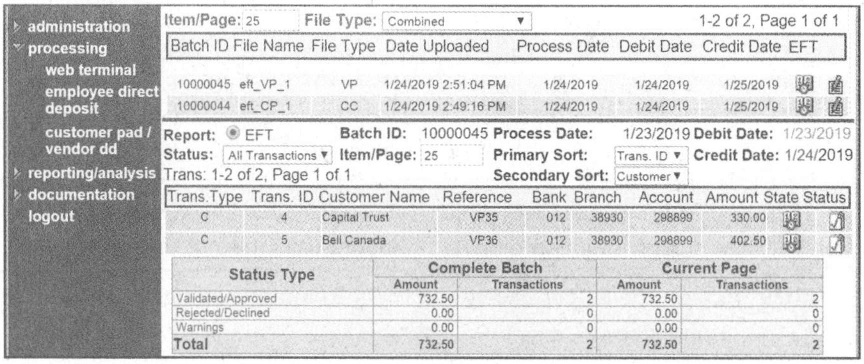

From your account, you can edit the transactions you have uploaded.

Click the Edit tool in a Summary line of the review page, that is, eft_CP_1, eft_VP_1 and so on, to open the options for editing:

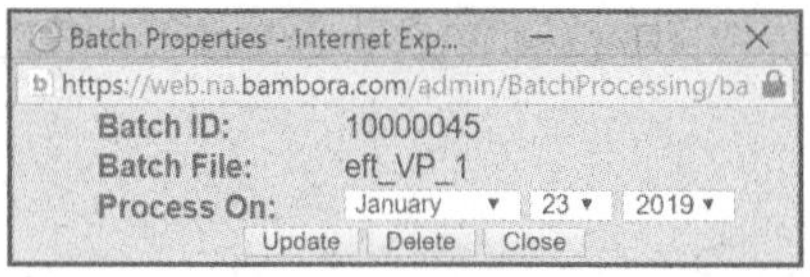

You can change the processing date or delete the batch of all items you uploaded at the same time. If you choose Delete, you will be asked to confirm your decision:

> **NOTES**
> You cannot delete individual receipts or payments that were part of an uploaded batch, or items that were already processed.

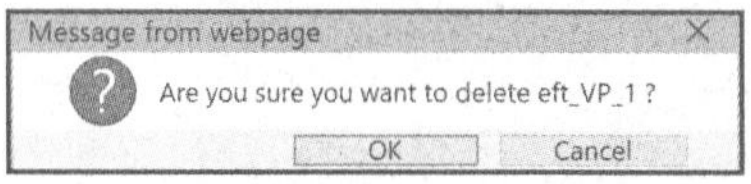

Click OK to continue. Click Logout when finished to end the session safely.

Making Import Duty Remittances

Paying the import duty owing on imported merchandise is like paying other taxes. Normally, duty must be paid before the package is released by Customs.

✓ 37

June 14 memo #9 from Owner requested payment to the Receiver General for import duty charged on purchases to date. Wrote cheque #582 for $4 283.36 to pay duty on invoices #MD-916, MD-1018, MD-1241, JM-876 and JM-1088.

> **NOTES**
> You can also enter the remittance in the Purchases Journal by choosing Cheque as the method of payment.

Open the **Payments Journal**. The cheque number, bank acounts and date are correct.

Choose **Make Other Payment**.

Choose **Receiver General for Canada** as the supplier.

Choose **2220 Import Duty Payable** as the account from the Selection list.

You should record the corresponding purchase invoice numbers in the journal as well.

Type `Duty re MD-916, MD-1018, MD-1241, JM-876 & JM-1088`

Press *tab* to move to the Amount field.

Type `4283.36`

Click the **Invoice/Ref. field** and **type** `Memo 9` **Press** *tab*.

Type `Memo 9, Import duty remittance`

Review the **journal entry**. **Close** the **display**. **Make corrections** if needed and then **post** the **transaction**.

Enter the remaining **transactions** for June.

38 Received sales order #24 on June 14 from Eastrose Hotel. The special order requires furniture and plants to be delivered and planted on June 21/21. The price for the order was $9 000 plus $1 350 HST. Eastrose Hotel provided cheque #9754 for $2 500 as a deposit (#81) for the contract. Terms for the balance of the payment are 2/15, n/30 on completion of work.

39 Recorded Sales Summary as sale #173 for one-time customers on June 14, 2021. The following allocations were applied: 100% of inventory and delivery revenue and expenses to Store Sales; 100% of report revenue to Design; 90% of revenue from SU01 and SU02 to Store Sales, 5% to Design and 5% to Planting.

items sold			amount	total
100	PL03	Plant/ground cover starters	$ 8 /4-pack	$ 800.00
10	PL05	Plant: annual 10 cm	9 each	90.00
10	PL06	Plant: annual 15 cm	16 each	160.00
20	PS10	Topsoil: 50 litre bag	6 /bag	120.00
2	SC02	Report	200 /report	400.00
2	SU01	Aluminum patio set/planting	1 250 /pkg	2 500.00
2	SU02	Teak patio set/planting	3 800 /pkg	7 600.00
5	BK01	Gardening in the Shade (GST @ 5%)	45 /book	225.00
	Delivery			400.00
	Goods and Services Tax		5%	11.25
	Harmonized Sales Tax		15%	1 810.50
Total cash deposited to chequing account				$14 116.75

SESSION DATE – JUNE 21, 2021

40 On June 16, invoice #JM-1134 from Jorgensen Mobler arrived with merchandise and payment terms of 2/30, net 60. The exchange rate was 0.201 on June 16. Total import duty charged was Dkr 1.786,00 (CAD $358.99). The freight expense was allocated to Store Sales.

items purchased			amount	duty rate
8	FP21	Patio table: Moulded Plastic 2 m	Dkr 12.800,00	9.5%
30	FP22	Arm chair: Moulded Plastic	6.000,00	9.5%
	Freight		1.200,00	
	HST Paid		3.000,00	
Invoice Total			Dkr 23.000,00	

41 Used Form ITA-3 dated June 16/21 to assemble eight plastic patio sets using furniture items on hand. Created new inventory item FP25 for assembled item.

new item	description	min amt	regular (preferred) selling price/unit
FP25	Patio set: Moulded Plastic	1	$820 (750) /5-pce set

linked accounts: Asset 1400; Revenue 4020; COGS 5070

assembly components			unit cost	total
8	FP21	Patio table: Moulded Plastic 2 m	$341.6144 each	$2 732.92
32	FP22	Arm chair: Moulded Plastic	43.2643 each	1 384.46

assembled item (5-pce set)			unit cost	total
8	FP25	Patio set: Moulded Plastic	$514.6725 /5-pce set	$4 112.38

42 On June 17, wrote cheque #583 to Trucks 4U (choose Quick Add) for $161 for truck rental needed for extra deliveries. Invoice #T4U-48221 amounted to $140 plus $21 HST. 90% of the expense was allocated to Store Sales and 10% to Planting.

NOTES
This is a non-inventory sales order. Credit Revenue from Store Sales.

NOTES
If the Divisions column is not included in the journal after recording the sales order, close and then re-open the journal. You can also use the Allocate tool in the Tool bar, but you must allocate each amount separately.

WARNING!
You must change the tax code for BK01 to G.

WARNING!
The unit costs change continually as new inventory is purchased at different prices or adjusting entries are made.

Accept your default prices for assembly components and copy the total to the assembled items total. The totals for assembly components (including additional costs) and assembled items must be exactly the same.

NOTES
No journal entry results from the assembly (ITA-3) because the same asset account is used for assembly components and the assembled item.

WARNING! You must change the tax code for BK01 to G.

43 Recorded Visa sale #174 for Holly Yew on June 17, 2021. The following allocations were applied: 100% of report revenue to Design; 100% of revenue from book to Store Sales.

items sold			amount	total
1	SC02	Report	$200 /report	$200.00
1	BK01	Gardening in the Shade (GST @ 5%)	45 each	45.00
		Goods and Services Tax	5%	2.25
		Harmonized Sales Tax	15%	30.00
Total amount paid by Visa				$ 277.25

44 Used Form RIF-1001 dated June 19/21 to reserve contract items for Eastrose Hotel. Free delivery included. All items entered at average cost prices. New inventory record was created for the contract using a new Group asset linked inventory account 1450 Reserved Inventory and existing accounts 4020 and 5070 for linked Revenue and COGS. HST is charged on the sale and duty does not apply.

new item	description	min amt	regular selling price
EH01	Eastrose Hotel Inventory	0	$9 000 /job

reserved (assembly) components			unit cost	total
100	PL03	Plant/ground cover starters	$ 4.00 /4-pack	$ 400.00
10	PL05	Plant: annual 10 cm	5.00 each	50.00
10	SH02	Shrubs: 1 metre	16.00 each	160.00
5	SH03	Shrubs: 3 metre	32.00 each	160.00
3	FX42	Umbrella w/stand	110.00 each	330.00
6	FP25	Patio set: Moulded Plastic	510.2925 /5-pce set	3 061.76
	Additional Costs			$1 000.00

job (assembled) item			unit cost	total
1	EH01	Eastrose Hotel Inventory	$5 161.76 each	$5 161.76

WARNING! Accept your default prices for assembly components and copy the total to the assembled items total. The totals for assembly components (including additional costs) and assembled items must be exactly the same.

45 June 19 memo #10 requested that sales order #24 from Eastrose Hotel be edited. Changed the order by entering EH01 as the item number. The quantity ordered (one), price ($9 000) and terms are unchanged.

NOTES Refer to page 417 for assistance with editing the sales order. Editing orders is like editing quotes. Choose Sales Order as the transaction type before choosing the order to adjust. Do not edit the prepayment amount.

46 Plant care supplies were purchased from Yardworks Inc. (choose Quick Add) on June 21 and paid for with cheque #584 for $241.50. Invoice #YI-484 provided the details of the sale: the cost of the supplies was $210 plus $31.50 HST.

47 Owner authorized bank transfer of Dkr 165.000,00 on memo #11, dated June 21, to cover cheques. Money was taken from Bank: Chequing account and deposited to Bank: DKK account. The exchange rate for the transfer was 0.202.

48 On June 21 paid invoice #MD-1018 from Mobler Dansk with cheque #378 for Dkr 154.624,40 including the discount of Dkr 3.155,60. Entered 0.202 as the exchange rate.

On the same day, also paid invoice #JM-876 from Jorgensen Mobler with cheque #379 for Dkr 9.151,24 including Dkr 186,76 discount.

SESSION DATE – JUNE 30, 2021

49 Sales order #24 for Eastrose Hotel was filled on June 22 as sale #175. Terms of sale were 2/15, n/30 with $7 850 as the balance owing. 20% of the revenue was allocated to Design, 25% to Planting and 55% to Store Sales.

items sold			amount
1	EH01	Eastrose Hotel Inventory	$9 000 /job
		Harmonized Sales Tax	15%

WARNING! When filling the sales order, change the method of payment to Pay Later.

50 Purchased new rototiller from Yardworks Inc. (use Quick Add) on June 22 for $600 plus $90 HST. Paid $690 for this purchase on invoice #YI-599 with cheque #585.

51 Efren Barrato returned a shrub because it died shortly after planting. The returned item was recorded on form #R-166 on June 22 using account 4130 Sales Returns & Allowances, a new Group revenue account. The returned item was written off according to memo #12. All amounts were allocated to Store Sales. With the Owner's permission, the refund was paid in cash. (Choose Cash as the payment method for the return. Refer to Accounting Procedures.)

items returned			amount	total
-1	SH03	Shrubs: 3 metre	$55 each	-$55.00
		Harmonized Sales Tax	15%	-8.25
Total cash paid to customer				-$63.25

52 On June 25, invoice #MD-1982 from Mobler Dansk arrived with merchandise and payment terms of 2/15, net 30. The exchange rate was 0.205 on June 25. Total import duty charged was Dkr 883,20 (CAD $181.06). The freight expense was allocated to Store Sales.

items purchased			amount	duty rate
2	FA01	Patio set: Cast Aluminum round table 1.5 m	Dkr 7.600,00	8.0%
8	FA04	Arm chair: Cast Aluminum	2.240,00	8.0%
4	FA06	End table: Cast Aluminum	1.200,00	8.0%
		Freight	1.000,00	
		HST Paid	1.806,00	
Invoice Total			Dkr 13.846,00	

53 Memo #13 from the Owner on June 27 requested that the HST owing be remitted as of May 31, 2021. Issued cheque #586 for $3 200 in full payment. (Use Trial Balance amounts on page 496.)

54 Complete a payroll cheque run for the bi-weekly paid employees using Time Summary Sheet #52. The pay period was June 15 to 28. The paycheque deposits (deposit slips #70 to #73) were dated June 28. Allocate the payroll expenses for employees as instructed below.

EMPLOYEE TIME SUMMARY SHEET #52 DATED JUNE 28/21

Name of Employee	Regular Hours	Overtime Hours	No. of Plantings	Sick Days	Personal Days	Sales Commission	Allocations
Aster	75	2	140	–	–	–	90% Planting, 10% Store Sales
Fineum	75	2	150	–	–	–	90% Planting, 10% Store Sales
Iola	75	4	–	–	–	$60	100% Store Sales
Phlox	$1 650 Salary		50	–	–	–	10% Planting, 90% Store Sales

55 Pre-authorized withdrawals from the chequing account were recorded on June 28. Debit memo #92564 from Capital Trust itemized the transaction details. The mortgage payment of $900 included an interest amount of $690 and the loan payment of $1 000 included $200 for interest. The remaining amounts for these withdrawals were principal. Bank charges of $65 were also on this memo. Create a new Group expense account: 5010 Bank Charges. All expense amounts were shared as follows: Store Sales 50%, Planting 10% and Design 40%.

NOTES

Remember to enter the quantity returned with a minus sign and to change the default revenue account.

Use the Inventory Adjustments Journal to write off the returned inventory.

NOTES

If you have difficulty accessing the Divisions column in the Payroll Run Journal, click an employee name and then click the Allocate tool button.

WARNING!

The unit costs change continually as new inventory is purchased at different prices.

Accept your default prices for assembly components and copy the total to the assembled items total. The totals for assembly components (including additional costs) and assembled items must be exactly the same.

56

SHADY CORNERS

ITEM ASSEMBLY COMPLETION FORM ITA-#4

Dated 06/28/21

Assembled items

			Unit cost		Total
3	SU01	Aluminum patio set/planting	848.3833/	pkg	2 545.15

Components used

3	FA03	Table: Cast Aluminum round 2 m	438.48	each	1 315.44
12	FA04	Arm chair: Cast Aluminum	61.69	each	740.28
3	FA06	End table: Cast Aluminum	66.1429	each	198.43
6	SH01	Shrubs: 50 cm	6.00	each	36.00
3	BK01	Gardening in the Shade	25.00/	book	75.00

Additional costs for services $180.00

WARNING!

You must change the tax code for BK01 to G.

You must also change the payment method to Pay Later.

57

SHADY CORNERS

Shady Corners
599 Ivy Lane, Halifax, NS B3J 2N3
Tel: (902) 289-3904 or (902) 289-3904 Fax: (902) 285-7532

Date of sale: June 28/21

To: Rockcliff Manor
400 Rocky Ridge Rise, Halifax, NS B3B 5V8

INVOICE 176

No.	Item		Price	Total	Division*
80	PL03	Plant/ground cover starters	8	640.00	1
10	SH01	Shrubs: 50 cm	13	130.00	1
10	SH03	Shrubs: 3 metre	55	550.00	1
2	FT37	Bench: Teak	1 125	2 250.00	1
2	FX41	Hammock w/stand	175	350.00	1
10	SC01	Consultation/Design	110	1 100.00	3
15	SC03	Planting & Soil Preparation	50	750.00	2
2	BK01	Gardening in the Shade (5% GST)	45	90.00	1
	GST 5%			4.50	
	HST 15%			865.50	

Division Code: 1 = Store Sales; 2 = Planting; 3 = Design

Terms: 2/15, net 30 days		**HST# 230 192 825**	
*** Internal use only**	**Salesperson:** Iola	**Total tax**	870.00
Total sale 6/28/210 G Iola			**6 730.00**

58 Recorded Sales Summary on June 28, 2021, as sale #177 for one-time customers. The following allocations were applied: 100% of inventory and delivery revenue and expenses to Store Sales; 100% of report and consultation revenue to Design; 90% of revenue from SU01 and SU02 to Store Sales, 5% to Design and 5% to Planting.

items sold		amount		total
20	PL02	Plant/ground cover: 10 litre	$ 29 each	$ 580.00
100	PL03	Plant/ground cover starters	8 /4-pack	800.00
10	SH03	Shrubs: 3 metre	55 each	550.00
2	FA02	Patio set: Cast Aluminum rect. table 2 m	1 340/ 7-pce set	2 680.00
2	FA07	Bench: Cast Aluminum	245 each	490.00
8	FP23	Folding chair: Moulded Plastic	55 each	440.00
5	SC01	Consultation/Design	110 /hour	550.00
1	SC02	Report	200 /report	200.00
1	SU01	Aluminum patio set/planting	1 250 /pkg	1 250.00
1	SU02	Teak patio set/planting	3 800 /pkg	3 800.00
5	BK01	Gardening in the Shade (GST @ 5%)	45 each	225.00
	Delivery			400.00
	Goods and Services Tax		5%	11.25
	Harmonized Sales Tax		15%	1 761.00
Total cash deposited to chequing account				$13 737.25

59

Shady Corners
599 Ivy Lane, Halifax, NS B3J 2N3
Tel: (902) 289-3904 or (902) 289-3904 Fax: (902) 285-7532

Date of sale: June 30/21

To: Luanne Bindweed
One-time customer

INVOICE 178

No.	Item		Price	Total	Division*
1	FT32	Patio table: Teak rect. 2 m	1 180	1 180.00	1
4	FT33	Arm chair: Teak	725	2 900.00	1
1	FT34	Chaise longue: Teak	980	980.00	1
1	FT35	End table: Teak	245	245.00	1
2	FT36	Ottoman: Teak	105	210.00	1
1	FX45	Cushion: deep seating set	245	245.00	1
5	SC01	Consulting/Design	110	550.00	3
1	SC02	Report	200	200.00	3
	Indoor/Outdoor Carpeting		300	300.00	1
	Delivery		100	100.00	1
	HST 15%			1 036.50	

Division Code: 1 = Store Sales; 2 = Planting; 3 = Design

Terms: Interac (8201 7827 4563 8900)	**HST#** 230 192 825	
* **Internal use only** **Salesperson:** Iola	**Total tax**	1 036.50
Total deposited to Visa account 6/30/21 G Iola		**7 946.50**

WARNING!
You must change the tax code for BK01 to G.

NOTES
Use revenue account 4020 and tax code H for the sale of Indoor/Outdoor Carpeting.

60

SHADY CORNERS

MEMO #14
Date 6/30/2021
From: Lou Pine
To: Owner

Paid import duty charged to Receiver General on all outstanding purchases (#MD-1982 and JM-1134).

Wrote cheque #587 for $540.05 to pay balance in full.

Lou Pine

NOTES
Use the Income Statement Revenue from Services amount to calculate the commissions.

61 Memo #15 from the Owner on June 30 authorized the payment of monthly salaries. Added 2 percent of service revenue for Anthemum and 1 percent of service revenue for Pine to deposit slips #74 and #75 as their sales commissions. Allocated 100% of Anthemum's and 80% of Pine's salary and commission to Design. The remaining 20% of Pine's amounts are to be allocated to Store Sales.

62 Memo #16 on June 30 required us to record inventory losses as follows:
 10 PL05 plants were not watered and died
 1 FP23 plastic folding chair had a leg broken during delivery
100% of the write-off was allocated to Store Sales.

WARNING!
Change the payment method to Cheque for the remittance to Capital Trust.

63 Memo #17 included a reminder to record payroll remittances for the pay period ending June 30. Entered Memo #17a, 17b, etc. as the reference. Cheques #588 to #592 were submitted in payment.
- Receiver General for Canada: EI, CPP and Income Tax
- Capital Trust: RRSP Payable
- Canadian Agricultural Workers' Union: Union Dues
- Workers' Compensation Board: WCB
- Professional Landscapers' Association: Professional Fees

NOTES
Allocation for new revenue and expense accounts should be the default setting.

64 Received credit memo #65925 from Capital Trust on June 30. $40 interest was deposited to chequing account. This entry required a new Group account 4200 Revenue from Interest. 50% of the interest revenue was allocated to Store Sales, 30% to Design and 20% to Planting.

NOTES
Account 5115 should be assigned to the Cost of Goods Sold class so that it will be included correctly in the Gross Margin Income Statement.

65 Memo #18 from Owner on June 30 reminded that adjusting entries were needed based on inventory counts. Allocated 90% of the plant and garden supplies to Store Sales and 10% to Planting. Allocated 100% of the carpets sold to Store Sales. Allocated 80% of the Office Supplies to Store Sales, 10% to Planting and 10% to Design.

supplies used	amount	new account required
Plant and garden supplies	$1 900	
Carpeting	200	5115 Carpeting Sold
Office supplies	130	5180 Supplies Used: Office

Displaying Division Reports

Division reports can be displayed from the Division window, from the Division module window Reports pane drop-down list, from the Home window Reports menu or from the Report Centre. We will continue to access reports from the Report Centre.

Click the **Report Centre icon** in the Home window.

Click **Division** to open the list of division reports:

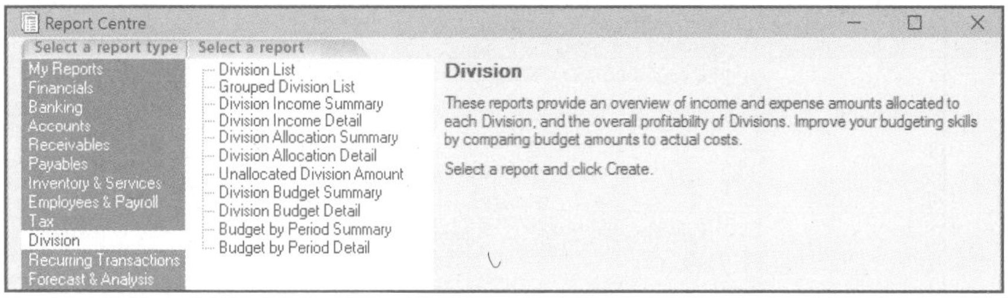

Displaying the Division List

Click **Division List**. **Click** **Modify This Report** to open the report options window:

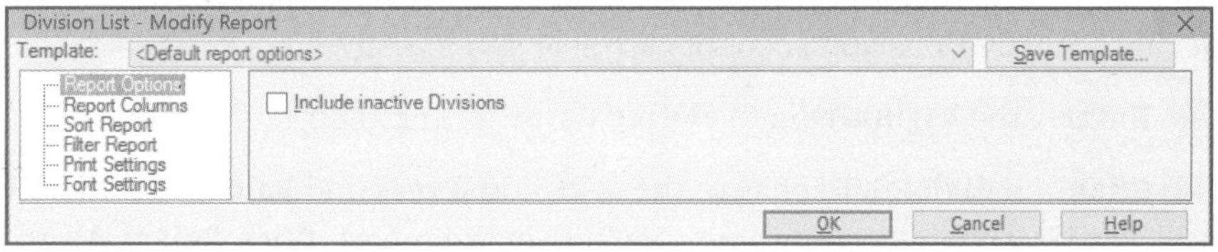

Or, choose the Reports menu, then choose Lists and click Division.

Click Report Columns to customize the fields included in the report.

Click **OK**. **Close** the **display** when you have finished viewing the report.

Displaying the Grouped Division List

Click **Grouped Division List**. **Click** **Modify This Report** to open the report options window.

Click the **Group By drop-down list arrow** for the ways you can organize the report:

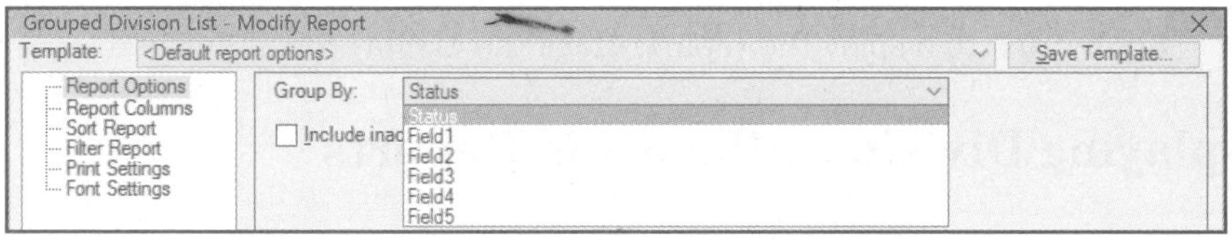

You can group the divisions by division status (e.g., pending, in progress and so on) or by any of the additional fields you added for the ledger.

Choose the **criterion** for grouping.

Click **OK**. **Close** the **display** when you have finished viewing the report.

PRO VERSION
Remember that if you have not changed the ledger name, Project will replace Division throughout the report menus and options.

NOTES
For other company types, Division may be replaced by a name that is appropriate for that type of company. The term will replace Division in all report titles and fields. Refer to Appendix B in this text.

PRO VERSION
The Pro version does not have Forecast & Analysis reports, Grouped Division Lists or the Unallocated Division Amount Report.

CLASSIC VIEW
Right-click the Divisions icon to select it. Click the Select A Report tool.

NOTES
You can display the Division Allocation Detail Report from the Division List.

> **NOTES**
> You can drill down to the Division Income Detail Report from the Division Income Summary Report. You can drill down to the Division Ledger, Journal Report, General Ledger, Customer or Supplier Aged or Employee Report or look up the transaction from the Division Income Detail Report.

Displaying Division Income Reports

The Division Income Report provides an Income Statement with revenue and expense amounts and net income for each division you select for the report.

Click **Division Income Summary**. **Click** **Modify This Report** to open the report options window:

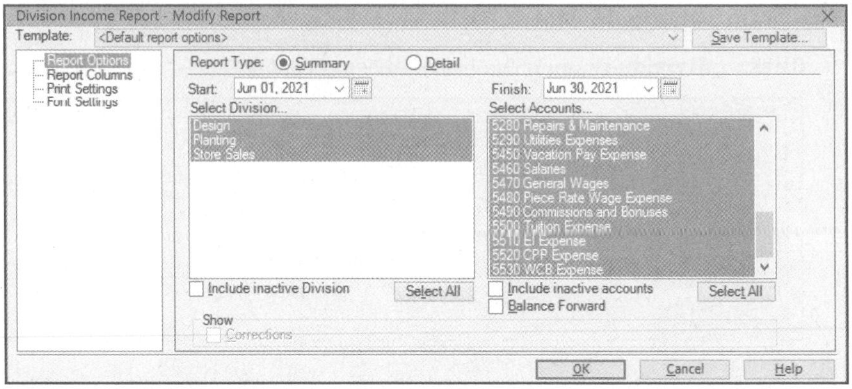

Or, choose the Reports menu, then choose Division and click Income to display the Options window.

You can sort and filter Division Income Detail reports by date, comment, source, journal number or amount per transaction. As usual, the fiscal start and session dates are the defaults. All divisions and accounts are selected initially.

Enter the **beginning** and **ending dates** for the report.

Click a **division** to change the selection. **Press** and **hold** *ctrl* and **click** the **divisions** you want to include in the report. **Click** **Select All** to include all divisions in the report. All are selected initially.

> **NOTES**
> Remember that Select All works as a toggle switch. When no or some items are selected, clicking will select all items. When all are selected, clicking will remove all selections.

Leave the **Summary** option, the one selected by default, if you want your report to provide summary information (i.e., totals) for each account selected for each division. The **Detail** option provides complete journal information for each account for each division selected, including the names of all customers, suppliers and employees, as well as the transaction's reference number, journal entry number and date. Both options provide a calculation for revenue minus expense.

Next you should select the revenue and expense accounts you want in the report.

Click an **account** to change the selection. **Press** and **hold** *ctrl* and **click** the **accounts** you want to include in the report or **click** **Select All** to include them all. All are selected initially.

Click **OK** to display the report. **Close** the **display** when finished.

> **NOTES**
> Drill-down reports from the Allocation Report are the same as the reports from the Division Income Report.

Displaying Division Allocation Reports

When you allow allocation for Balance Sheet accounts and enter allocation amounts for them, they are reported in the Division Allocation Report together with Income Statement accounts. The Division Income Report has only revenue and expense accounts.

Click **Division Allocation Summary**. **Click** **Modify This Report** to open the report options window:

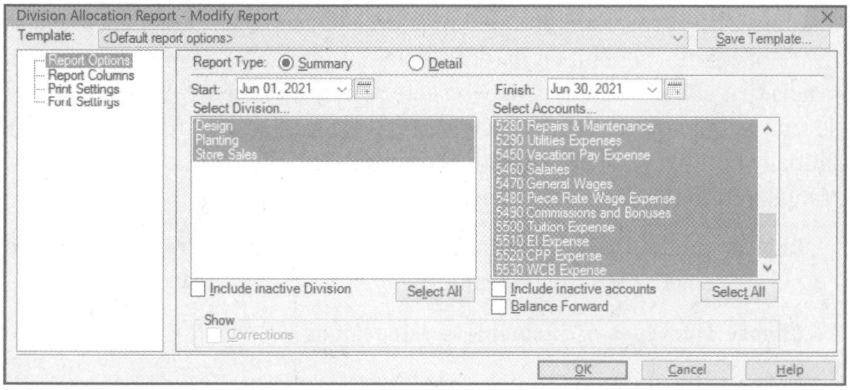

NOTES
You must allow allocations for the Balance Sheet accounts to include all the accounts in this report. Without this change, the Account list will include only the revenue and expense accounts.

From any Home window, choose the Reports menu, then choose Division and click Allocation to display the Division Allocation Report Options window.

The Division Allocation Report provides the breakdown of amounts for each division by account. It is similar to the Division Income Report, but the total revenue and expense and the net division income are replaced by a single total for all accounts for each division.

Although the report options look the same as for the Income Report, when you scroll up the list of accounts, all for which you have allowed allocation will be included, including the Balance Sheet accounts.

Enter the **Start** and **Finish dates** for the report.

Click a **division** to change the selection. **Press** and **hold** *ctrl* and **click** the **divisions** you want to include in the report or **click** **Select All**.

Like the Income Report, the Summary option has totals and the Detail option provides complete journal information for each account for each division.

After you have indicated which options you want, choose the accounts.

Press and **hold** *ctrl* and **click** the **accounts** you want or **click** **Select All**.

Click **OK** to display the report. **Close** the **display** when you have finished.

Displaying the Unallocated Division Amounts Report

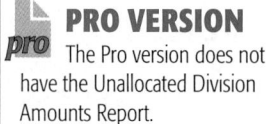

PRO VERSION
The Pro version does not have the Unallocated Division Amounts Report.

If you have any journal transactions with amounts that were not fully allocated, you can display all these transactions in the Unallocated Division Amounts Report. The incomplete allocation may have occurred because you did not add the allocation details or because the program did not allow you to enter them (such as for cost variance amounts).

Click **Unallocated Division Amount**. **Click** **Modify This Report** to open the report options window:

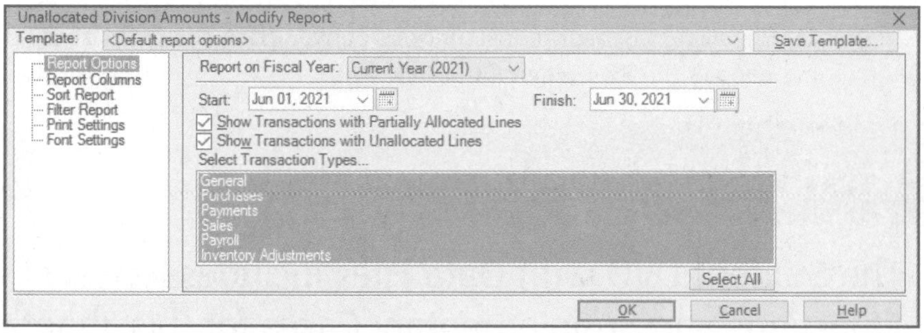

Or, choose the Reports menu, then choose Division and click Unallocated Amounts.

Amounts in the report are grouped by journal on separate detail lines that include the invoice or reference number, date, supplier or customer, account and amount. All journals that allow allocations may be selected for the report. You can choose to include transactions with amounts that were partially allocated, fully unallocated or both. Initially both types of incomplete allocations are selected for all journals with the dates ranging from the earliest transaction to the session date.

NOTES
Credit card expense amounts may be included with the partially allocated accounts. Variance amounts, exchange rate differences and some discount amounts will be included with the unallocated amounts.

Choose the **journals** you want included in the report. **Press** *ctrl* and **click** to select more than one journal.

Choose the **types of incomplete allocations** you want — partial or full.

Enter the **Start** and **Finish dates** for the report.

Click **OK** to display the report. **Close** the **display** when finished.

Adding Division Details to Journal Reports

When you have entered division information in a journal, you can include the allocation details in any journal report.

Click **Financials** in the Select A Report Type list.

Click **All Journal Entries**. **Click** **Modify This Report**:

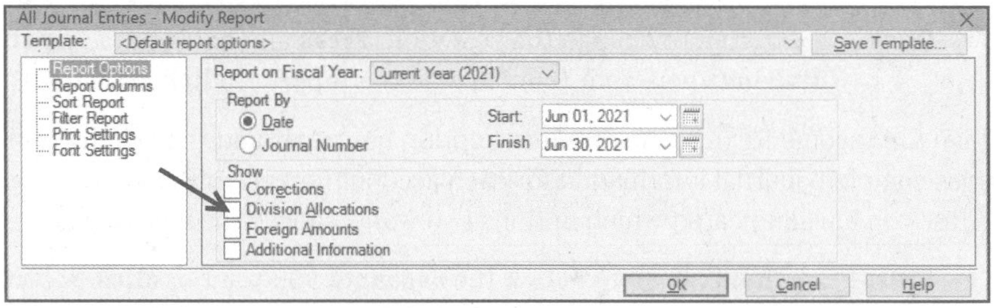

PRO VERSION
The Pro version does not include the Report On Fiscal Year field.

Or, choose the Reports menu, then choose Journal Entries and click All.

The Journal Report Options window includes a check box for Division Allocations under the Show heading. For a complete Journal Report, you should also show foreign amounts, corrections and additional information.

NOTES
If you include all the details in the Journal Report, you should print the report in landscape orientation.

Click **Division Allocations** to include division information in journal reports. By default, journal reports do not include division details.

Choose the **other details** that you want to include in the report and **click OK**.

Close the **display** when finished. **Close** the **Report Centre**.

Printing Division Reports

Display the **report** using the instructions above. **Click** the **Print tool** or **choose** the **File menu** and **click Print**.

REVIEW

The Student DVD with Data Files includes Review Questions and Supplementary Cases for this chapter.

CHAPTER FOURTEEN

PIANOS
KEYBOARDS
SYNTHESIZERS
AMPLIFIERS

OBJECTIVES

After completing this chapter, you should be able to

- ***turn on*** the budgeting feature in Sage 50
- ***determine*** and ***enter*** budgeting periods and amounts
- ***allocate*** budget amounts to revenue and expense accounts
- ***enter*** transactions involving Quebec Sales Tax
- ***display*** and ***print*** income statements with budget comparisons
- ***analyze*** budget reports
- ***print*** invoices in batches

COMPANY INFORMATION

Company Profile

NOTES
Sound, Inc.
2400 ch. Ste-Foy
Sainte-Foy, QC G1V 1T2
Tel: (418) 529-6391
Fax: (418) 529-7622
Business No.: 236 412 540

Sound, Inc., located in Sainte-Foy, near the downtown Québec area, is owned and operated by the Charale family. The small family-run business recently hired one employee, who will earn a commission on sales. She works in the store several days a week, but the Charales maintain the regular operation of the business. Renée Charale performs the accounting duties for the business. Occasionally, additional part-time help is needed and hired through a contract with an employment agency.

The store specializes in electronic instruments such as keyboards, pianos and synthesizers, and accessories for them such as amplifiers, headphones and software. Music and composition lessons are provided by the adult son and daughter, respectively. For these lessons and for customers who want to test the instruments before purchasing, the store space includes soundproof rooms.

Customers include music schools, bands and, of course, individuals from across the country. Delivery (shipping or freight) is charged on most orders. Preferred price list customers do not pay for delivery, and they receive discounted inventory prices. All account customers are entitled to a before-tax 2 percent discount if they settle their accounts within 10 days. After 30 days, interest charges accrue at the rate of 1.5 percent per month. Customer deposits from 20 to 25 percent of the total sale are required on all orders. Customers may pay by cheque, cash or credit card.

Some suppliers with whom Sound has accounts require deposits to accompany purchase orders, and some suppliers offer after-tax purchase discounts for early payments. The store has a business credit card account with American Express.

The currency for all foreign transactions, the purchases from Japan, is the Japanese yen (JPY ¥). Currently there are no foreign customers, so foreign prices are not entered in the Inventory Ledger. Sound, Inc. pays import duties on the imported goods. The appropriate duty rates are entered in the inventory ledger with the items.

Renée Charale used the following to set up the accounting files for Sound, Inc. in Sage 50 at the end of August 2021:

- Chart of Accounts
- Post-Closing Trial Balance
- Supplier Information
- Customer Information
- Employee Information
- Inventory Information
- Accounting Procedures

CHART OF ACCOUNTS

SOUND, INC.

ASSETS

Current Assets
1060 Chequing Bank Account
1070 Visa Bank Account
1080 MasterCard Bank Account
1090 Bank Account - Yen
1100 Investment Portfolio
1150 Purchase Prepayments
1200 Accounts Receivable
1220 Office Supplies
1240 Other Supplies
1260 Prepaid Insurance

Inventory Assets
1320 Keyboards
1340 Amplifiers
1360 Accessories

Fixed Assets
1440 Computer Equipment
1460 Equipment & Tools ▶
▶1480 Store Fixtures
1500 Store

LIABILITIES

Current Liabilities
2200 Accounts Payable
2220 Prepaid Sales and Deposits
2250 Credit Card Payable
2260 Import Duty Payable
2330 Income Tax Payable
2350 QPP Payable
2360 Quebec Income Tax Payable
2370 QHSF Payable
2380 CNESST Payable
2650 GST Charged on Sales
2670 GST Paid on Purchases
2800 QST Charged on Sales
2810 Refundable QST Paid ▶

Long Term Liabilities
2950 Mortgage Payable ▶

▶EQUITY

Owner's Equity
3500 Sound, Inc., Capital
3550 Drawings
3600 Current Earnings

REVENUE

4020 Revenue from Sales
4040 Revenue from Services
4060 Revenue from Delivery
4080 Sales Discounts
4100 Investment Revenue
4120 Interest Revenue

EXPENSE

Operating Expenses
5020 Advertising & Promotion
5030 Exchange Rate Differences
5040 Bank Charges
5050 Credit Card Fees
5080 Purchase Discounts ▶
▶5100 Supplies Used
5120 Hydro Expense
5140 Insurance Expense
5160 Interest Expense
5180 Telephone Expense
5300 Cost of Goods Sold
5310 Variance Costs
5320 Freight Expense
5330 Delivery Expense
5340 Damaged Inventory

Payroll Expenses
5410 Commissions
5420 CNESST Expense
5430 QPP Expense
5450 QHSF Expense
5460 Temp Agency Fees

NOTES: The Chart of Accounts includes only postable accounts and Current Earnings. QPP (Quebec Pension Plan) replaces CPP in Quebec. QHSF (Quebec Health Services Fund) is an employer-funded provincial health and services tax program.
Linked payable and expense accounts for EI, CPP and QPIP (Quebec Parental Insurance Plan) are also included because they are essential linked accounts, but they are not used in this example.

POST-CLOSING TRIAL BALANCE

SOUND, INC.

August 31, 2021

		Debits	Credits
1060	Chequing Bank Account	$ 81 790.50	
1070	Visa Bank Account	3 245.00	
1080	MasterCard Bank Account	1 855.00	
1090	Bank Account - Yen (¥558 400)	6 980.00	
1100	Investment Portfolio	90 000.00	
1200	Accounts Receivable	6 898.50	
1220	Office Supplies	610.00	
1240	Other Supplies	430.00	
1260	Prepaid Insurance	1 250.00	
1320	Keyboards	47 690.00	
1340	Amplifiers	10 580.00	
1360	Accessories	18 280.00 ▶	
▶ 1440	Computer Equipment	$ 7 500.00	
1460	Equipment & Tools	1 500.00	
1480	Store Fixtures	1 200.00	
1500	Store	250 000.00	
2200	Accounts Payable		$ 14 302.50
2250	Credit Card Payable		640.00
2260	Import Duty Payable		240.00
2650	GST Charged on Sales		1 680.00
2670	GST Paid on Purchases	980.00	
2800	QST Charged on Sales		1 926.00
2810	Refundable QST Paid	185.00	
2950	Mortgage Payable - Store		185 000.00
3500	Sound, Inc., Capital		327 185.50
		$530 974.00	$530 974.00

SUPPLIER INFORMATION

SOUND, INC.

Supplier Name (Contact)	Address	Phone No. Fax No.	E-mail Web Site	Terms Tax ID
Énergie Québec (Marie Nuclaire)	5010 avenue Atomique Sainte-Foy, QC G2B 6C9	Tel: (418) 782-6101	energie.quebec.ca	net 7
Hull Electronic Supplies (Perse Moquette)	40 rue de Chois Hull, QC J8K 2L7	Tel: (819) 288-4334 Fax: (819) 288-8201	moquette@HES.com HES.com	2/5, n/30 (after tax) 473 540 912 RT0001
Kenaki Keyboards (Sun Kenaki)	1 Chome-8-2 Misakicho Chiyoda, Tokyo 101-0061, Japan	Tel: 81 3-3293-9328	kenaki.keyboards.com	2/10, n/30 (after tax)
Minami Electronics (Mima Minaki)	Chuo ku, 2 Chome-9-4 Ginza, 104-0061, Tokyo, Japan	Tel: 81 3-4335-1111	minami.electronics.com	1/5, n/30 (after tax)
Ministre du Revenu du Québec	12 rue Saint-Louis Québec, QC G1R 5L3	Tel: (418) 652-6835		net 1
Papineau Delivery (Martin Camion)	56 Papineau Avenue Lévis, QC G6V 3B3	Tel: (581) 690-2810 Fax: (581) 691-7283	martin@papineau.com papineau.com	net 10 288 344 567 RT0001
Receiver General for Canada	Ottawa, Ontario	Tel: (800) 561-7761	cra-arc.gc.ca	net 1
Staples (Hélène Magazinier)	777 avenue de Bureau Sainte-Foy, QC G4K 1V5	Tel: (418) 759-3488 Fax: (418) 758-3910	staples.ca	net 15 128 634 771 RT0001
Telébec (Robert Bavardier)	84 rue Causerie Sainte-Foy, QV G3C 7S2	Tel: (418) 488-2355	telebec.ca	net 10

NOTES: All supplier discounts are calculated on after-tax amounts.

OUTSTANDING SUPPLIER INVOICES

SOUND, INC.

Supplier Name	Terms	Date	Invoice	Amount JPY	Amount CAD	Total (CAD)
Hull Electronic Supplies	2/5, n/30 (after tax)	August 31/21	HE-387		$6 837.00	$6 837.00
Kenaki Keyboards	2/10, n/30 (after tax)	August 29/21	KK-6165	¥632 000	$7 465.50	$7 465.50
					Grand Total	$14 302.50

CUSTOMER INFORMATION

SOUND, INC.

Customer Name (Contact)	Address	Phone No. Fax No.	E-mail Web Site	Terms Credit Limit
*Académie des Arts (Félice Harmonique)	Université Laval 400 rue des Arts Québec, QC G1V 0A6	Tel: (418) 788-3645 Fax: (418) 787-7114	feliceh@ulaval.com ulaval.ca	2/10, n/30 $25 000
Cash Customers				net 1
*Conservatoire Royale (Rose Timbre)	121 rue Musique Québec, QC G3K 4G5	Tel: (418) 499-7117 Fax: (418) 498-2889	conservatoireroyale.com	2/10, n/30 $20 000
*Helena's Academy (Helena Teutor)	250 Satchel Lane Edmonton, AB T7F 3B2	Tel: (780) 633-8201 Fax: (780) 633-8396	teutor@helenas.com helenas.com	2/10, n/30 $25 000
L'Église Ste Agathe (Pere Jacques)	10024 rue Notre Dame Sainte-Foy, QC G1B 6F4	Tel: (418) 466-2991 Fax: (418) 468-1826	pjacques@steagathe.ca steagathe.ca	2/10, n/30 $20 000
Les Scarabées (Jean-Paul Starr)	600 rue St. Mouton Sainte-Foy, QC G2K 7C9	Tel: (418) 729-8217 Fax: (418) 729-9283	jeanpaul.starr@istar.com	2/10, n/30 $15 000
Quatre Saisons (Francois Vallée)	344 rue Gaudie Sainte-Foy, QC G2K 7C9	Tel: (418) 621-6212		2/10, n/30 $10 000

NOTES: All customer discounts are calculated on amounts before tax. Customers pay 1.5% interest per month on accounts over 30 days. An asterisk (*) indicates preferred price list customer.

OUTSTANDING CUSTOMER INVOICES

SOUND, INC.

Customer Name	Terms	Date	Invoice	Amount	Tax	Total
Conservatoire Royale	2/10, n/30 (before tax)	August 24/21	468	$6 000	$898.50	$6 898.50

NOTES

Sound, Inc. makes employer contributions to the Quebec Health Services Fund equal to 2.5 percent of the total payroll amount for the provincial health care plan.

CNESST (La Commission de la Santé et de la Sécurité du Travail) is the workers' compensation agency in Quebec.

Employer and employee deductions for the Quebec Parental Insurance Plan are not required because Cléf-bas is not EI insurable.

Employee Profile and TD1 Information

Trevi Cléf-bas started working for the store on September 1, 2021. Using her music training and sales skills, she visits potential clients such as schools for consultations and suggests instruments that match their needs and modifications regarding soundproofing upgrades for the space available. She is paid a commission of 20 percent of her monthly sales and takes four weeks of vacation each year. Cléf-bas is single and self-supporting. Her tax claim amounts are $14 909 federal and $16 919 provincial for basic plus education (federal) and living alone (provincial) amounts. She works for the store part time and supplements her sales commission with her independent business as a performer.

Other employee details:

SIN:	566 811 014	Address:	45 rue College
Date of birth:	August 26, 1985		Sainte-Foy, QC G2G 4R5
CNESST (WCB) rate:	2.02	Tel:	(418) 639-9202
QHSF rate:	1.70% (entered in the Payroll Ledger Settings)		

QPP and Income Tax calculations are built into the program.

INVENTORY INFORMATION

SOUND, INC.

Code	Description	Unit	Min Qty	Selling Price (Reg)	Selling Price (Pref)	Qty on Hand	Total Cost	Duty Rate
Keyboards: Total asset value $47 690 (Linked accounts: Asset 1320; Revenue 4020; COGS 5300; Variance 5310)								
KB-01	Electronic Piano P-81	each	3	$ 810	$ 780	8	$3 320	6.0%
KB-02	Electronic Piano P-125	each	3	1 250	1 130	4	2 400	6.0%
KB-03	Electronic Piano P-259	each	2	2 590	2 240	4	4 880	6.0%
KB-04	Electronic Piano P-422	each	2	4 220	3 970	3	5 850	6.0%
KB-05	Keyboard K35	each	5	350	320	8	1 680	6.0%
KB-06	Keyboard K55	each	5	550	510	7	1 960	6.0%
KB-07	Electronic Organ	each	1	6 200	5 700	2	6 480	6.0%
KB-08	Synthesizer SY-16	each	3	1 670	1 560	5	4 950	6.0%
KB-09	Synthesizer SY-25	each	3	2 530	2 130	3	3 630	6.0%
KB-10	Synthesizer SY-40	each	2	4 000	3 680	3	6 060	6.0%
KB-11	Synthesizer SY-65	each	2	6 500	6 000	2	6 480	6.0%
Amplifiers: Total asset value $10 580 (Linked accounts: Asset 1340; Revenue 4020; COGS 5300; Variance 5310)								
AA-01	Amplifier JX-120	each	4	230	200	6	720	5.0%
AA-02	Amplifier JX-240	each	3	610	560	6	1 980	5.0%
AA-03	Amplifier JX-290	each	2	1 120	1 000	4	2 420	5.0%
AA-04	Amplifier JX-340	each	1	1 640	1 490	6	5 460	5.0%
Accessories: Total asset value $18 280 (Linked accounts: Asset 1360; Revenue 4020; COGS 5300; Variance 5310)								
AC-01	Sheet Music: miscellaneous	sheet	20	30	25	200	3 000	n/a
AC-02	Music Book: miscellaneous	book	10	90	80	50	3 000	n/a
AC-03	Piano Bench: padded	bench	3	140	120	5	420	9.5%
AC-04	Piano Stool: adjust/fold/lock	stool	3	165	150	8	720	9.5%
AC-05	Music Stand: keyboard	stand	4	110	95	10	600	9.5%
AC-06	Music Stand: folding	stand	4	65	55	20	700	8.0%
AC-07	Keyboard Travel Bag	bag	3	160	145	10	850	n/a
AC-08	Headphones: studio	set	4	180	165	6	570	n/a
AC-09	Headphones: closed	set	4	380	350	6	1 200	n/a
AC-10	Headphones: noise cancelling	set	3	420	380	6	1 320	n/a
AC-11	Headphones: 2-person shared	set	3	580	530	6	1 800	n/a
AC-12	Cables: miscellaneous 2 m	each	10	20	18	60	600	n/a
AC-13	Cables: miscellaneous 4 m	each	10	50	45	50	1 500	n/a
AC-14	DVD: Keyboard Techniques	4 DVD set	3	640	600	5	2 000	n/a
Total Inventory Value							$76 550	
Services (Linked accounts: Revenue 4040; COGS 5300)								
SL-01	Keyboard Lessons: half hour	30 min	n/a	80	75	n/a		
SL-02	Composition Lessons: half hour	30 min	n/a	90	80	n/a		

Accounting Procedures

The Goods and Services Tax (GST) and Quebec Sales Tax (QST)

Sound, Inc. uses the regular method for remittance of sales taxes. GST collected from customers is recorded as a liability in *GST Charged on Sales*. GST paid to suppliers is recorded in *GST Paid on Purchases* as a decrease in the liability collected provincially for remittance to the Canada Revenue Agency.

Provincial sales tax (Quebec Sales Tax, or QST) of 9.975 percent is applied to all cash and credit sales of goods and services in the province of Quebec. QST collected from customers is recorded as a liability in *QST Charged on Sales*. QST paid to suppliers, recorded in *Refundable QST Paid*, decreases the liability to Revenu Québec.

PRO VERSION
The term Vendor replaces Supplier throughout the program.

NOTES
In this chapter, insurance is the only item for which QST is not refundable. GST is not applied to insurance. The QST on all other purchases and services in this chapter is refundable and therefore is separated from expense or asset portions of purchases.

NOTES
Processing the deposit in this way ensures that the deposit will appear in the correct customer account in the Receivables Ledger. The manual approach, a General Journal entry that debits the bank account and credits Unearned Revenue, a liability account, does not link the prepayment to the customer – the customer's ledger is updated separately.

NOTES
Remember that if you want to preview or print invoices, you must select the correct printing form. Click the Change Print Forms tool in the Sales Journal to access the settings.

GST is administered provincially in Quebec, so Charale files returns for both GST and QST with the Ministère des Finances du Québec. Returns are remitted by the last day of the month for the previous quarter, either requesting a refund or remitting the balance — the difference between *QST Charged on Sales* and *Refundable QST Paid*.

Deposits on Custom Orders

When customers place an order, they may be asked for an advance of up to 20 percent of the price. The deposit may be entered in the Receipts Journal or on the Sales Order form. The Accounts Receivable Ledger for the selected customer will be credited for the advance and *Chequing Bank Account* will be debited. When the items have been delivered, fill the sales order to make a Sales Journal entry for the full amount of the contract, including relevant taxes. When the customer settles the account, accept both the invoice amount and the deposit (if you used the Receipts Journal) to indicate they are included and the full balance owing is paid. The balance in the Receipts Journal should then match the amount of the customer's cheque.

Partially filled quotes are automatically converted to orders for the backordered items by the Sage 50 program.

Freight Expenses

When a business purchases inventory items, the cost of freight that cannot be directly allocated to a specific item purchased must be charged to *Freight Expense*. This amount will be regarded as an expense and will not be part of the costs of any inventory asset account.

Printing Sales Invoices

If you want to print sales invoices through the program, complete the Sales Journal transaction as you would otherwise. Preview the transaction before posting it. Before printing, check that you have selected the correct printer and forms. Refer to page 164. To e-mail an invoice, click the E-mail tool.

Foreign Purchases and Import Duty

Goods imported from Japan are subject to GST and QST and to import duties at various rates. These taxes are collected at the time the goods are received. To simplify the transactions in Sage 50, we have set up the foreign supplier record so that the supplier collects GST and QST, just like suppliers in Canada.

Import duty is calculated automatically from the rates entered in the Inventory Ledger records. The amount is credited to the linked *Import Duty Payable* account instead of *Accounts Payable*, so the duty is not added to the balance owing to the supplier. The linked asset account is debited.

On receiving the merchandise, the business makes a payment to the Receiver General to pay the import duties on the purchase. Refer to page 536.

INSTRUCTIONS

1. **Open** the data files and set up the **budget** for Sound, Inc. on September 1, 2021, using Sage 50. Detailed keystroke instructions to assist you follow these instructions.
2. **Enter** the **source documents** for September 2021 in Sage 50 using all the company information provided.

3. **Print** the following **reports**:

- Balance Sheet as at September 30
- Journal Entries for all journals from September 1 to September 30
- Inventory Sales Detail Report for Amplifiers
- Inventory Quantity Report for all items to check reorder requirements
- Comparative Income Statement for September with Budget vs. Actual amounts

KEYSTROKES

Setting Up Budgets

It is important for a business to gauge its performance against some standards. These standards can be provided through comparisons with other companies that are in the same line of business or by comparing the same company over several time periods. It is common for a business to set goals for the future based on past performance. For example, there may be an expectation that profits will increase by 10 percent over the previous year or that expenses will be reduced because of the introduction of new cost-reduction methods. If a business waits until the end of the year to assess its progress toward its goals, it may be too late to make necessary corrections if things are not proceeding according to plan. Budgets offer a realistic financial plan for the future that can be used to assess performance.

Before creating and analyzing budget reports, you must turn on the option and enter the budget amounts for the relevant accounts.

NOTES
For instructions on displaying the Budget Report refer to page 558. Instructions for budget Income Statement reports begin on page 569.

Turning On the Budgeting Feature

Open **SageData19\SOUND\SOUND**. Do not advance the session date until you have finished the budget setup.

Click the **Settings icon** [Settings]. **Click General (Accounts)** to open the General Settings list:

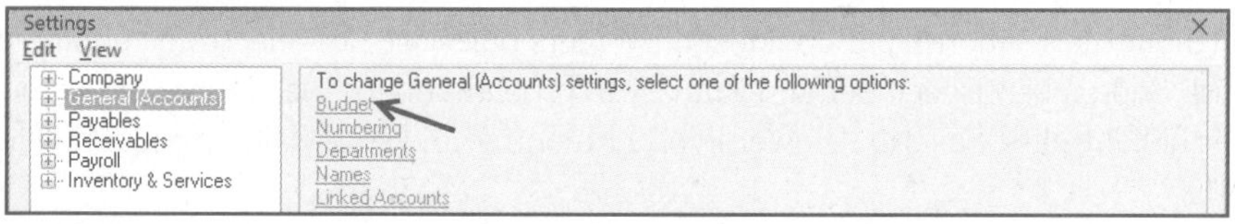

Click **Budget** to open the budgeting options:

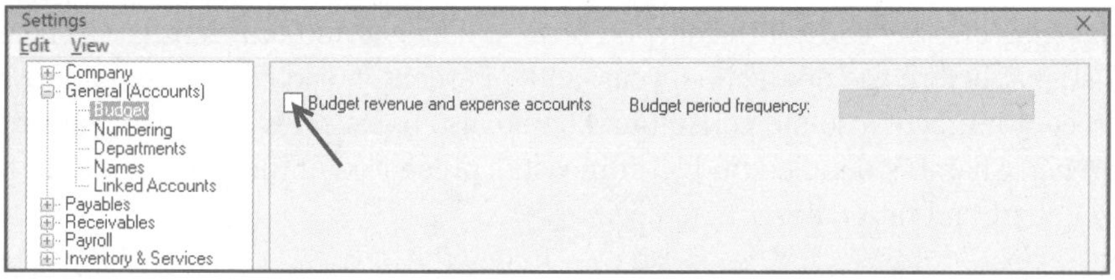

Click **Budget Revenue And Expense Accounts** to turn on the budget feature.

NOTES
If you are working from backups, restore the backup file SageData19\SOUND1.CAB or SOUND1 to SageData19\SOUND\SOUND.

PRO VERSION
Departments (for departmental accounting) are not available in the Pro version.

The first decision after choosing the budgeting feature involves a budget period. Whether a business chooses to budget amounts on a yearly, quarterly or monthly basis depends on the needs and nature of the business. Monthly budget reports will be appropriate if the business cycle of buying and selling is short, but not appropriate for long-term projects. The period chosen must provide meaningful feedback about performance. If the periods are too short, there may be insufficient information to judge performance; if the periods are too long, there may be no opportunity to correct problems because they will not be detected soon enough. Sound, Inc. will use monthly budget periods initially because the Charales want frequent progress reports.

Click the **Budget Period Frequency field** for the period options:

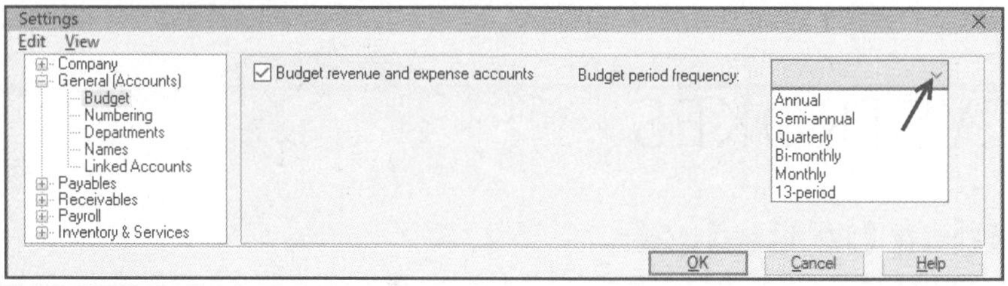

NOTES

You cannot activate the budget feature in multi-user mode, but you can add and change budget amounts.

Click **Monthly**.

Click **OK** to return to the Home window and save the settings.

Setting a Budget

The next step is to enter the budget amounts for all expense and revenue accounts.

Budgets can be determined in several different ways. The most common methods are zero-based and incremental budgeting. With the zero-based method, a forecast is made for each revenue and expense account based on expectations about specific planned activities and expenditures. Each budget item must be justified. More commonly, last year's budgets and income statements are used as the starting point and a specific percentage change is applied. Thus, a company might expect to improve its performance over last year by 10 percent, either by increasing sales or by decreasing expenses. Planned special events such as annual month-long sales, new customer drives, and peak or slow periods can be built into the changes in budgeted amounts from one period to the next. Whatever method is used, it is important that the budget be realistic.

Renée Charale examined previous income statements and business practices to learn where improvements could be made and to get a realistic forecast. The business has been growing by about 10 percent per year. The corresponding expenses, sales discounts, cost of goods sold and so on also increased by about the same amount. Sales are not divided evenly throughout the 12-month period. Most customers purchase new electronic equipment in August, September, December and January in preparation for the start of the school year and as holiday gifts. Sales are slower in other months, and store sales are planned for those months.

This pattern has led Charale to expect 20 percent of the year's sales to occur each September, at the start of the school year; 15 percent in December and January for holiday gifts and the start of the second term at colleges and universities; 10 percent in August, just before the new school year; and 5 percent in each of the remaining months. The recent hiring of a sound consultant should also boost sales over last year's results.

Renée Charale's detailed budget forecast is presented in the following item-by-item budget chart and rationale:

MONTHLY BUDGET FORECAST FOR 2021–2022

SOUND, INC.

Account	2021 Sep	2021 Oct-Nov	2021–2022 Dec-Jan	2022 Feb–Jun	2022 Jul	2022 Aug	2021–2022 Total for 12 months
REVENUE							
Revenue from Sales	$91 580	$22 895	$68 685	$22 895	$22 895	$45 790	$457 900
Revenue from Services	6 120	6 120	6 120	6 120	3 060	3 060	67 320
Revenue from Delivery	1 320	330	990	330	330	660	6 600
Sales Discount	–916	–229	–687	–229	–229	–458	–4 580
Investment Revenue	512	512	512	512	512	512	6 144
Interest Revenue	10	10	10	10	10	10	120
TOTAL REVENUE	$98 626	$29 638	$75 630	$29 638	$26 578	$49 574	$533 504
EXPENSES							
Advertising & Promotion	$ 920	$ 525	$ 800	$ 525	$ 525	$ 920	$ 7 640
Exchange Rate Differences	0	0	0	0	0	0	0
Bank Charges	70	70	70	70	70	70	840
Credit Card Fees	1 282	321	962	321	321	641	6 415
Purchase Discounts	–687	–172	–515	–172	–172	–343	–3 436
Supplies Used	150	130	140	130	130	140	1 610
Hydro Expense	310	335	380	365	380	380	4 325
Insurance Expense	435	435	435	435	435	435	5 220
Interest Expense	1 120	1 120	1 120	1 120	1 120	1 120	13 440
Telephone Expense	305	305	305	305	305	305	3 660
Cost of Goods Sold	45 790	11 448	34 343	11 448	11 448	22 895	228 955
Variance Costs	458	114	343	114	114	229	2 285
Freight Expense	916	229	687	229	229	458	4 580
Delivery Expense	916	229	687	229	229	458	4 580
Damaged Inventory	458	114	343	114	114	229	2 285
Commissions	4 575	1 145	3 430	1 145	1 145	2 290	22 885
CNESST Expense	114	29	86	29	29	57	575
QPP Expense	229	57	172	57	57	114	1 143
QHSF Expense	93	23	69	23	23	46	461
Temp Agency Fees	630	220	800	220	220	340	4 330
TOTAL EXPENSES	$58 084	$16 677	$44 657	$16 707	$16 722	$30 784	$311 793
NET INCOME	$40 542	$12 961	$30 973	$12 931	$ 9 856	$18 790	$221 711

BUDGET RATIONALE FOR 2021–2022

SOUND, INC.

Estimates used to create budget forecasts

Revenue from Sales: increase by 10% over previous year. September, 20% of annual sales; December and January, 15% each; August, 10%; all other months, 5% each

Revenue from Services: constant for 10 school year months; reduced in July and August to 50% of amount for other months

Revenue from Delivery: this has averaged around 1.5% of sales of merchandise; most account customers request delivery

Sales Discount: expect about 1% of sales on average; most sales are not discounted

Interest and Investment Revenue: constant monthly income; same as previous year

Advertising & Promotion: estimate; higher for peak sale months

Exchange Rate Differences: zero – these are expected to cancel each other over time

Bank Charges & Credit Card Fees: increase over last year for increased credit card usage

Purchase Discounts: average 1.5% of Cost of Goods Sold

Supplies Used: office and other supplies for maintaining store inventory; mostly constant; slightly higher in peak sale months

Insurance and Mortgage Interest: same amount each month; small decrease from previous year

Cost of Goods Sold: 50% of net sales (based on historical costs)

Variance Costs: estimated from price variations in previous year

BUDGET RATIONALE FOR 2021–2022 CONTINUED

SOUND, INC.

Estimates used to create budget forecasts

Freight Expense: average at about 2% of Cost of Goods Sold
Delivery Expense: 30% markup from Revenue from Delivery
Damaged Inventory: 1% of Cost of Goods Sold
Commissions: estimate, will pay 20% of direct contributions to sales
QPP, CNESST (WCB) and QHSF: straight percentage of commissions (QPP replaces CPP for Quebec)
Temp Agency Fees: estimated additional assistance needed for peak periods
Other Expenses: most are constant each month; no change over last year; Hydro Expense slightly higher in peak winter and summer periods
EI, CPP and QPIP: these do not apply; do not choose Budget This Account

Entering Budget Amounts in the General Ledger

NOTES

You can click the Chart of Accounts icon and then double-click the account to open its ledger record. Or create the View Accounts shortcut (Banking module) and use it to open the Accounts window.

Another option is to use the Search field in the Home window's tool bar. Type rev and press *enter*. Then double click Revenue from Sales in the Search list to open the Ledger Record.

Click **Company** in the Modules pane list to change windows.

Click the **Chart of Accounts shortcuts list arrow** and **click Modify Account** to open the Search window. Accounts is selected as the record type:

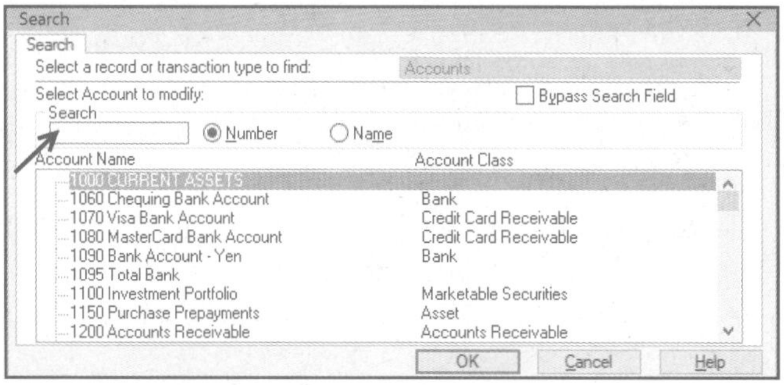

Click the **Search field**.

Type 4 to advance the cursor to the beginning of the 4000-level Revenue accounts.

Click **4020 Revenue from Sales** to highlight the first postable revenue account.

Click **OK** to open the Account Ledger window:

PRO VERSION

The Refresh tool is not available in the Pro version.

The term Project replaces Division.

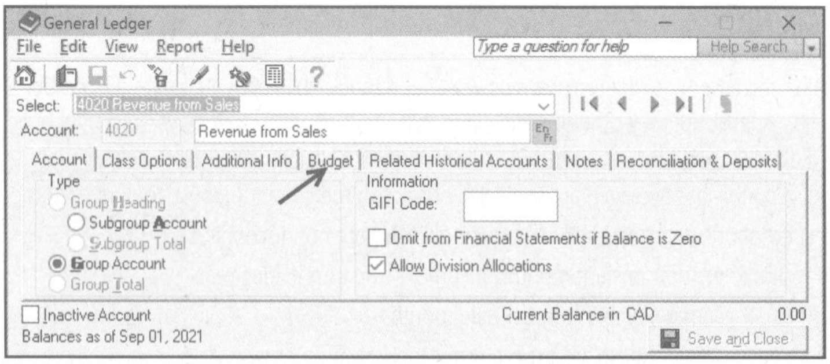

NOTES

Budgeting applies only to the postable revenue and expense accounts on the Income Statement. Budget reports are Income Statements.

Because we turned on the Budgeting feature in the General Settings window, the Budget tab has been added. This tab will be added only for Income Statement — revenue and expense — accounts.

Click the **Budget tab** to open the budget activation window:

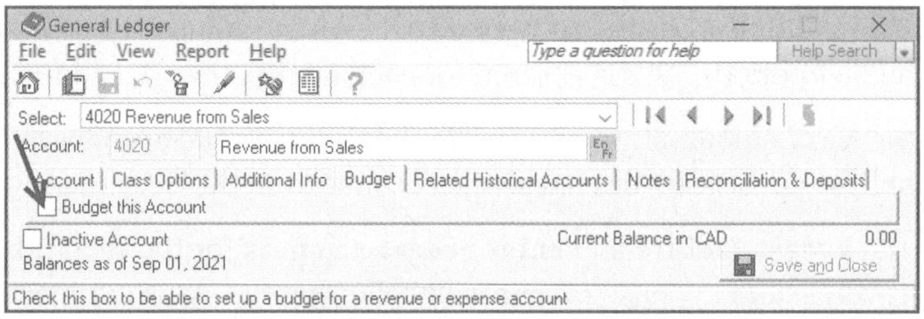

Click **Budget This Account** to open the Budget amount fields:

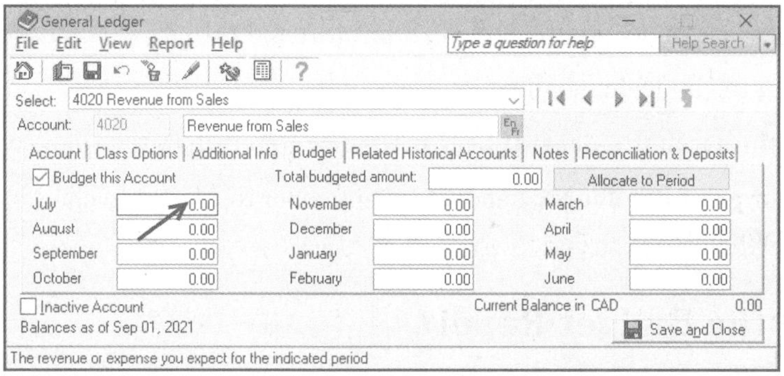

The budget periods displayed at this stage match the period frequency selected in the setup stage. Because we selected Monthly, a 12-month calendar is given, beginning with September, the first month of the fiscal year as entered in the Company Information window. If we had selected Quarterly, four input fields would be provided. You can enter the budget amounts for one period or for more, if the information is available. For Sound, Inc., we will enter the amounts determined earlier for each month.

You can change the budget frequency at any time in the General Settings Budget option window. The program will reallocate the previously budgeted amounts proportionately for the new periods after warning you that this will be done and giving you a chance to confirm that you want to proceed.

Refer to the chart on page 555 for budget amounts.

For each revenue and expense, you can add or omit budget amounts. Including budget details for all accounts will, of course, provide the most meaningful budget reports.

Click the **September field** to select the amount.

Type 91580 **Press** tab.

The cursor advances to the October field and highlights the entry for editing.

Enter the **amounts** for the **remaining 11 months** according to the budget forecast on page 555 by **typing** the **amount** and **pressing** tab to move to the next month.

You can use the **Copy** and **Paste** commands (Edit menu) to copy amounts from one field to another and save some data entry time.

The **Total Budgeted Amount** is updated continually as you enter amounts for each period. After entering all individual monthly amounts, use this Total Budgeted Amount to check your work. It should equal the total for 12 months in the chart on page 555.

When the budget amounts for each month are equal, you can use a shortcut to enter the amounts. For example, for *4100 Investment Revenue*, all amounts are equal.

Open the ledger for **4100 Investment Revenue**. **Click** **Budget This Account**.

NOTES

You can use keyboard shortcuts to copy budget amounts. Highlight the amount you need to copy and press ctrl + C. Then click the field you are copying to and press ctrl + V.

> **NOTES**
> Non-postable accounts, such as subtotals, headings and totals, do not have budget fields.
> Do not enter budget amounts for CPP Expense, QPIP Expense and EI Expense. These accounts are not used by Sound, Inc., but they are essential linked accounts for the Payroll Ledger.

Click the **Total Budgeted Amount field.**

Type 6144 **Click Allocate To Period** to divide the amount evenly among all budget periods (512 is entered for each month, that is, 6144/12).

Click the **Next button** to advance to the next revenue account in the budget tab screen, or choose the account from the Select list.

Turn on the **budget feature** and **enter budget amounts** for the **remaining** revenue and expense **accounts** by following the steps outlined above. Use the amounts determined for each account in the chart on page 555.

Remember to enter **negative** budget amounts for accounts that decrease the total in a group or section (e.g., *Sales Discount* and *Purchase Discounts*).

> **NOTES**
> Because we accessed the ledger record from the Modify Account shortcut Search window, we bypassed the Accounts window. Closing the ledger record therefore returns you directly to the Home window.

After entering the budget amounts for all accounts,

Close the **account's General Ledger window** to return to the Home window.

Display or **print** the **Budget Report** for September to August to check your amounts.

Displaying the Budget Report

You can check the budget amounts you entered for accounts from the Budget Report. Budget reports are available from the Financials report list in the Report Centre.

> **NOTES**
> You can also choose the Reports menu, then choose Financials and click Budget to open the report options screen.
> Only accounts that have the budgeting feature turned on will be included in the Select Accounts list.

Open the **Report Centre** and **click Financials** in the Select A Report Type list.

Click Budget and then **click Modify This Report** to open the report options window:

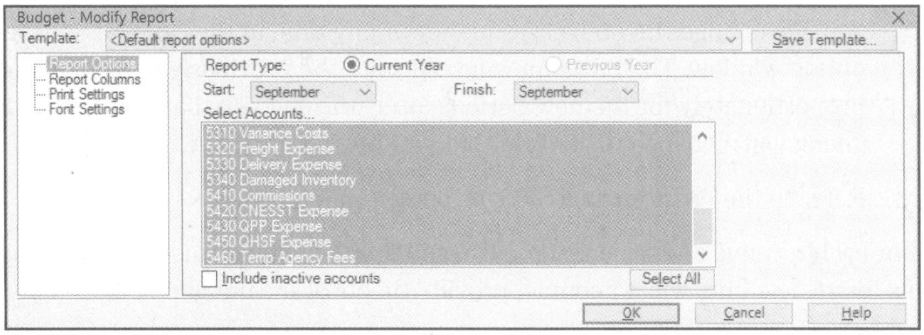

> **NOTES**
> From the Budget Report, you can drill down to the General Ledger for the account so you can edit the budget amounts if necessary.
> You can select report columns for the Budget Report, but you cannot sort or filter the report.

Select the **accounts** you want in the report. To check your entries at this stage, you should accept the default to **Select All** accounts.

Choose September and **August** in the Start and Finish fields and **click OK**. The report will include only the accounts for which you entered budget amounts.

Close the **display** when you have finished.

> **NOTES**
> For the next group of screens or to enter budget amounts for divisions, you must first view the module (Setup menu, User Preferences, View option; click the check box for Division).

Adding Budget Amounts to Divisions

If you are using division allocations, you can also enter budget amounts for each division. You must first turn on the budgeting feature and then choose a budget period or frequency. The following steps will illustrate this procedure.

> **PRO VERSION**
> Click Project instead of Division. The module label does not change when you select a different company type.

Click the Settings icon and click Division to open the Division Settings:

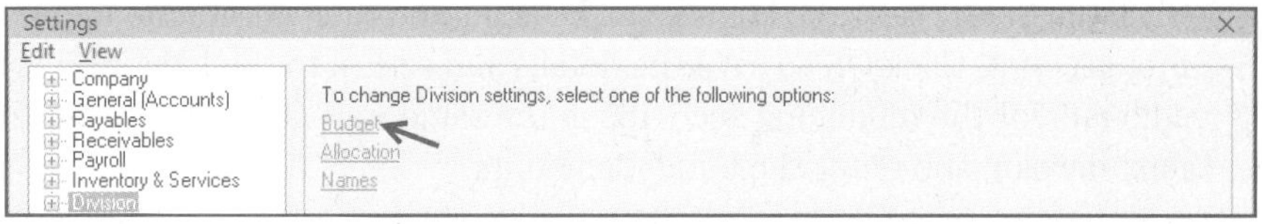

Click Budget to open the division budget activation screen with the familiar options:

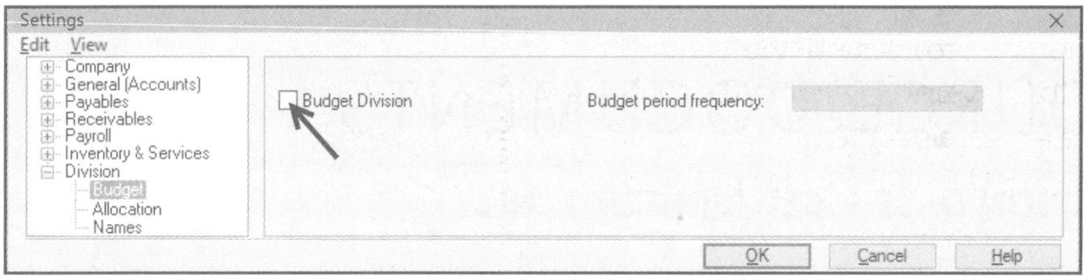

Click Budget Division. Choose a frequency from the Budget Period Frequency drop-down list, such as monthly or quarterly. Click OK to save the settings.

Click the Divisions icon to open the Division window. Create the divisions if you have not already done so. Open the Division Ledger. A Budget tab has been added. Click the Budget tab to open the budget activation window:

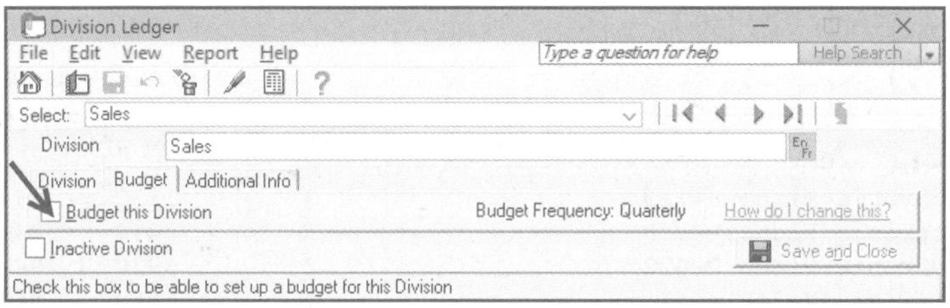

Click Budget This Division to open the budget amount fields. Quarterly periods have been selected for this illustration:

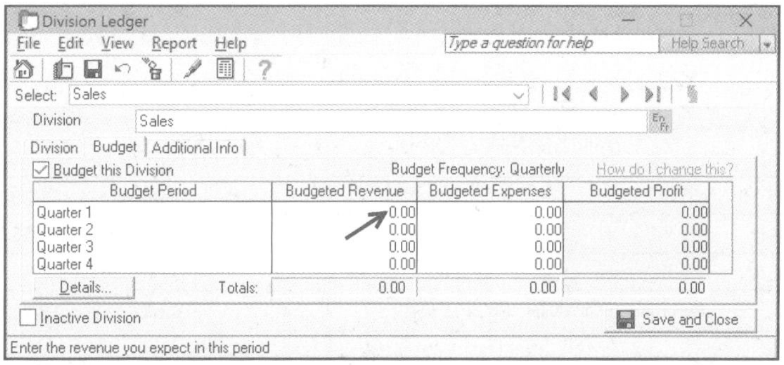

Enter the budgeted Revenue and Expense amounts for each period for this division. Click Details to enter division budget amounts for individual accounts:

PRO VERSION

The Pro version does not have the option to enter account details. You can enter only the total revenue and expense amounts for each budget period.

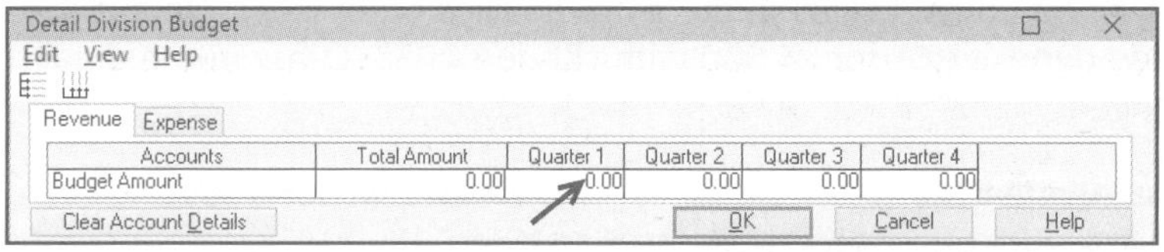

On the first line, enter the total revenue or expense amounts and the amounts for each period. The Select List icon will become available:

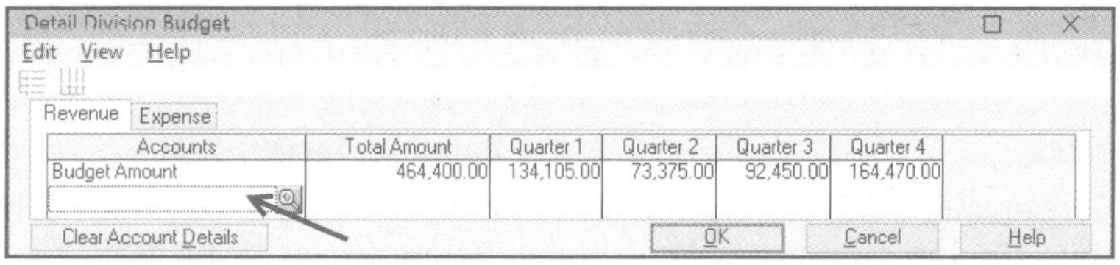

Click the Select list icon, choose the account and then enter amounts for the first account. Click OK to save the details and return to the ledger record. Enter amounts for the remaining accounts in the same way. Open the ledger for the next division and enter the budget amounts.

Close the ledger when you have finished and enter the allocations as usual in the journals. Division budget reports will be available.

NOTES
Create shortcuts for the journals from other modules, or change module windows as needed.

SOURCE DOCUMENTS

SESSION DATE – SEPTEMBER 7, 2021

1

2400 ch. Ste-Foy
Sainte-Foy, Quebec
G1V 1T2

SoundInc. PIANOS KEYBOARDS SYNTHESIZERS AMPLIFIERS

Telephone: (418) 529-6391
Fax: (418) 529-7622

Date: September 2/21
To be delivered: September 15/21
For: Helena's Academy
(Helena Teutor)
250 Satchel Lane
Edmonton, AB T7F 3B2

QUOTE #171

Description	Qty	Price	Total
KB-02 Electronic Piano P-125	3	1130	3390.00
KB-03 Electronic Piano P-259	1	2240	2240.00
KB-04 Electronic Piano P-422	2	3970	7940.00
AA-02 Amplifier JX-240	1	560	560.00
AC-03 Piano Bench: padded	4	120	480.00
AC-04 Piano stool: adjust/fold/lock	2	150	300.00
AC-10 Headphones: noise cancelling	4	380	1520.00
AC-11 Headphones: 2-person shared	2	530	1060.00
AC-12 Cables: miscellaneous 2 m	4	18	72.00

Sale Terms: 2/10, n/30	Delivery	100.00
GST # 236 412 540	GST 5.0%	883.10
QST # 3344992	QST 9.975%	N/A
Prices quoted will remain valid for 15 days	Total	18545.10

2 **Memo #1** **Dated September 2/21**
From Owner: Convert sales quote #171 to sales order #171. Helena's Academy provided deposit #61 for $3 500 with cheque #933. Other quote details are unchanged.

3 **Purchase Quote #224** **Dated September 2/21**
Policy start date September 5/21
From Quebecare Insurance Co. (use Quick Add), $5 220 for a one-year extension of business insurance policy. Terms: first two months' premium required as deposit on acceptance of quote. Balance is payable in 10 equal monthly payments. Enter 1 (one) as the quantity ordered and debit Prepaid Insurance.

4 **Receipt #43** **Dated September 2/21**
From Conservatoire Royale, cheque #8123 for $6 778.50 in payment of account, including $120 discount for early payment. Reference invoice #468.

5 **Purchase Order #224 & Cheque #426** **Dated September 2/21**

Convert purchase quote #224 from Quebecare Insurance Co., $5 220 for a one-year extension of business insurance policy, to a purchase order. Issue prepayment cheque #426 for $870 as deposit to confirm the order.

6 **Payment Cheque #427** **Dated September 3/21**

To Hull Electronics, $6 700.26 in payment of account, including $136.74 discount for early payment. Reference invoice #HE-387. Edit the cheque number.

7 **Purchase Invoice #QI-7711** **Dated September 3/21**

From Quebecare Insurance Co., to fill purchase order #224, $5 220 for a one-year extension of business insurance policy. The balance of the premium is due in 10 equal monthly payments.

8 **Purchase Invoice #KK-8577** **Dated September 4/21**

From Kenaki Keyboards (add new inventory item)

10	AC-15 Keyboard Stand: adjustable	¥ 90 000	8.0% duty
2	KB-02 Electronic Piano P-125	100 000	6.0% duty
6	KB-04 Electronic Piano P-422	960 000	6.0% duty
2	KB-07 Electronic Organ	580 000	6.0% duty
6	AC-03 Piano Bench: padded	48 000	9.5% duty
	Delivery	30 000	
	Goods and Services Tax	90 400	
	Quebec Sales Tax	180 349	
Invoice total		¥2 078 749	

Terms: 2/10, n/30. The exchange rate is 0.0119.

Duty ($1 310.90) ¥110 160

New inventory items

Number	**Description**	**Unit**	**Min**	**Prices Reg.**	**(Pref.)**
AC-15	Keyboard Stand: adjustable	stand	4	$240	($215)

Linked Accounts: Asset 1360 **Revenue** 4020 **Cost of Goods Sold** 5300 **Variance** 5310

Taxes: GST exempt No **QST exempt** No **Duty Rate** 8.0%

9 **Credit Card Purchase Invoice #A-1141** **Dated September 4/21**

From Antoine's Hardware Store (use Quick Add for the new supplier), $70.00 plus $3.50 GST and $6.98 QST for computer screen cleaning kit (office supplies). Purchase invoice total $80.48 paid in full by Amex credit card.

10 **Credit Card Purchase Invoice #PD-211** **Dated September 5/21**

From Papineau Delivery, $280.00 plus $14.00 GST and $27.93 QST for contracted delivery of merchandise. Purchase invoice total $321.93. Paid in full by Amex.

11 **Sales Invoice #471** **Dated September 6/21**

To Les Scarabées

2	KB-10	Synthesizer SY-40	$4 000.00	each
1	AA-04	Amplifier JX-340	1 640.00	
2	AC-07	Keyboard Travel Bag	160.00	each
2	AC-11	Headphones: 2-person shared	580.00	/set
4	AC-13	Cables: miscellaneous 4 m	50.00	each
	Delivery		100.00	
	Goods and Services Tax		5.0%	
	Quebec Sales Tax		9.975%	

Terms: 2/10, net 30.

12 **Memo #2** **Dated September 6/21**

From Owner: Pay import duties owing to the Receiver General. Issue cheque #428 for $1 550.90 in full payment of duty owing.

NOTES
Because it is non-refundable, the tax on insurance is included in the price. GST is not charged on insurance premiums.

NOTES
After editing the cheque number, you should accept the new numbering.

NOTES
Edit all inventory purchase prices as required by source document information.

NOTES
Duty rates are entered on the Taxes tab in the Inventory Ledger.

13

Payment Cheque #228 **Dated September 7/21**

To Kenaki Keyboards, ¥2 656 534 in payment of account including ¥54 215 discount for early payment. Reference invoices #KK-6165 and #KK-8577. The exchange rate is 0.01195.

14

Memo #3 **Dated September 7/21**

From Owner: Transfer ¥2 500 000 from Chequing Bank Account to Bank Account: Yen to avoid overdraft. The exchange rate is 0.01195.

SESSION DATE – SEPTEMBER 14, 2021

15

Memo #4 **Dated September 8/21**

From Owner: Adjust inventory for one KB-01 Electronic Piano P-81 damaged beyond repair. Charge to Damaged Inventory account.

16

Credit Card Purchase Invoice #QA-197 **Dated September 10/21**

From Quik-Ads (use Quick Add), $400.00 plus $20.00 GST and $39.90 QST for promotional cards and flyers to advertise new studio space and lessons. Purchase invoice total $459.90 paid in full by Amex credit card.

17

Cash Purchase Invoice #EQ-979784 **Dated September 13/21**

From Énergie Québec, $310.00 plus $15.50 GST and $30.92 QST for hydro service for one month. Purchase invoice total $356.42 paid in full by cheque #429.

NOTES

Allow the customer to exceed the credit limit.

18

Sales Invoice #472 **Dated September 13/21**

To L'Église Ste Agathe

2	KB-04	Electronic Piano P-422	$4 220.00	each
1	KB-07	Electronic Organ	6 200.00	
2	AA-04	Amplifier JX-340	1 640.00	each
3	AC-03	Piano Bench: padded	100.00	each
	Delivery		100.00	
	Goods and Services Tax		5.0%	
	Quebec Sales Tax		9.975%	

Terms: 2/10, net 30. Edit the selling price of AC03. The price was reduced because the bench legs were scratched.

19

Debit Card (Interac) Sales Invoice #473 **Dated September 14/21**

To Marie Broussard (use Continue)

1	KB-10	Synthesizer SY-40		$4 000.00
1	AC-03	Piano Bench: padded		140.00
	Goods and Services Tax		5.0%	207.00
	Quebec Sales Tax		9.975%	412.97
Invoice total paid by Interac				$4 759.97

NOTES

Credit Revenue from Delivery for the delivery to Broussard. You can use an invoice line or the Freight field.

20

Sales Invoice #474 **Dated September 14/21**

To Marie Broussard (use Quick Add), $50.00 plus $2.50 GST and $4.99 QST for delivery of sofa. Sales invoice total $57.49. Terms: net 10.

21

Receipt #44 **Dated September 14/21**

From Les Scarabées, cheque #367 for $12 901.75 in payment of account including $228.40 discount for early payment. Reference invoice #471.

22

Credit Card Purchase Invoice #QD-980 **Dated September 14/21**

From Quickie Delivery Service (use Quick Add), $100.00 plus $5.00 GST and $9.98 QST for delivery of keyboard to Marie Broussard. Purchase invoice total $114.98 paid in full by Amex. (Charge to Delivery Expense.)

SESSION DATE – SEPTEMBER 21, 2021

23

Sound Inc. — PIANOS, KEYBOARDS, SYNTHESIZERS, AMPLIFIERS

2400 ch. Ste-Foy
Sainte-Foy, Quebec
G1V 1T2

Telephone: (418) 529-6391
Fax: (418) 529-7622

Date: September 15/21
To: Helena's Academy
(Helena Teutor)
250 Satchel Lane
Edmonton, AB T7F 3B2

Invoice #475

Description	Qty	Price	Total
KB-02 Electronic Piano P-125	3	1130	3390.00
KB-03 Electronic Piano P-259	1	2240	2240.00
KB-04 Electronic Piano P-422	2	3970	7940.00
AA-02 Amplifier JX-240	1	560	560.00
AC-03 Piano Bench: padded	4	120	480.00
AC-04 Piano stool: adjust/fold/lock	2	150	300.00
AC-10 Headphones: noise cancelling	4	380	1520.00
AC-11 Headphones: 2-person shared	2	530	1060.00
AC-12 Cables: miscellaneous 2 m	4	18	72.00
Ref: quote/order #171 and deposit #61			
Less deposit			(3500.00)

Sale Terms: 2/10, n/30	**Delivery**	100.00
GST # 236 412 540	**GST 5.0%**	883.10
QST # 3344992	**QST 9.975%**	N/A
	Balance	15045.10

24 **Purchase Invoice #HE-7522** **Dated September 18/21**

From Hull Electronics

10	AC-08	Headphones: studio	$1 050.00
10	AC-10	Headphones: noise cancelling	2 400.00
6	AC-14	DVD: Keyboard Techniques	2 550.00
		Goods and Services Tax	300.00
		Quebec Sales Tax	598.50
Invoice total			$6 898.50

Terms: 2/5, n/30.

25 **Credit Card Bill #AM-09-21** **Dated September 19/21**

From American Express (Amex), $1 502.31 for new purchases as of the billing date, September 13, plus $40.50 monthly fee. Issued cheque #430 for $1 542.81 in total payment to avoid interest charges.

26 **Cash Purchase Invoice #T-82612** **Dated September 20/21**

From Telébec, $305.00 plus $15.25 GST and $30.42 QST for store and mobile telephone service. Purchase invoice total $350.67 paid in full by cheque #431.

27 **Receipt #45** **Dated September 21/21**

From L'Église Ste Agathe, cheque #1021 for $20 697.03 in payment of account including $366.40 discount for early payment. Reference invoice #472.

28 **Receipt #46** **Dated September 21/21**

From Helena's Academy, cheque #1108 for $14 691.86 in payment of account including $353.24 discount for early payment. Reference invoice #475 and deposit #61.

SESSION DATE – SEPTEMBER 30, 2021

29

SoundInc. PIANOS KEYBOARDS SYNTHESIZERS AMPLIFIERS

2400 ch. Ste-Foy
Sainte-Foy, Quebec
G1V 1T2

Telephone: (418) 529-6391
Fax: (418) 529-7622

Date: September 22/21
To be delivered: September 28/21
From: Académie des Arts
(Félice Harmonique)
400 rue des Arts
Québec, QC G1V 0A6

QUOTE#172

Description	Qty	Price	Total
KB-02 Electronic Piano P-125	1	1130	1130.00
KB-03 Electronic Piano P-259	3	2240	6720.00
KB-04 Electronic Piano P-422	3	3970	11910.00
KB-09 Synthesizer SY-25	1	2130	2130.00
AA-04 Amplifier JX-340	1	1490	1490.00
AC-03 Piano Bench: padded	2	120	240.00
AC-08 Headphones: studio	6	165	990.00
AC-11 Headphones: 2-person shared	1	530	530.00
AC-15 Keyboard Stand: adjustable	4	215	860.00
Telephone request for quote 9/22/21 RC			
Sale Terms: 2/10, n/30		Delivery	N/C
GST # 236 412 540		GST 5.0%	1300.00
QST # 3344992		QST 9.975%	2593.51
		Total	29893.51

30 **Purchase Invoice #ME-9611** **Dated September 22/21**

From Minami Electronics

3 AA-04 Amplifier JX-340		¥246 000	5.0% duty
Delivery		15 000	
Goods and Services Tax		13 050	
Quebec Sales Tax		26 035	
Invoice total		¥300 085	

Terms: 1/5, n/30. The exchange rate is 0.01185.
Duty ($145.76) ¥12 300

31 **Memo #5** **Dated September 23/21**

From Owner: Pay import duties owing to the Receiver General. Issue cheque #432 for $145.76 in full payment of duty owing.

32 **Memo #6** **Dated September 25/21**

From Owner: Adjust sales invoice #474. The invoice was entered with the old rate for delivery. She was actually charged the correct amount of $100 plus $5 GST and $9.98 QST. The invoice total was $114.98. Terms: net 10.

33 **Receipt #47** **Dated September 25/21**

From Marie Broussard, cheque #318 for $114.98 in payment of account. Reference invoice #474.

34 **Payment Cheque #229** **Dated September 25/21**

To Minami Electronics, ¥297 084 in payment of account including ¥3 001 discount for early payment. Reference invoice #ME-9611. The exchange rate is 0.01192.

35

2400 ch. Ste-Foy
Sainte-Foy, Quebec
G1V 1T2

PIANOS
KEYBOARDS
SYNTHESIZERS
AMPLIFIERS
Sound Inc.

Telephone:
(514) 529-6391
Fax:
(514) 529-7622

Date: September 28/21
To: Académie des Arts
(Félice Harmonique)
400 rue des Art
Québec, QC G1V 0A6

Invoice #476

Description	Qty	Price	Total
KB-02 Electronic Piano P-125	1	1130	1130.00
KB-03 Electronic Piano P-259	1	2240	2240.00
KB-04 Electronic Piano P-422	1	3970	3970.00
KB-09 Synthesizer SY-25	1	2130	2130.00
AA-04 Amplifier JX-340	1	1490	1490.00
AC-03 Piano Bench: padded	2	120	240.00
AC-08 Headphones: studio	4	165	660.00
AC-11 Headphones: 2-person shared	1	530	530.00
AC-15 Keyboard Stand: adjustable	2	215	430.00
Quote partially filled Balance of quote converted to order #172 Ref: sales quote #172 RC 7/28/21			
Sale Terms: 2/10, n/30		Delivery	N/C
GST # 236 412 540		GST 5.0%	641.00
QST # 3344992		QST 9.975%	1278.81
		Total	14739.81

NOTES
Choose Convert This Quote To An Invoice. The quote is automatically filled for the full order quantities. Enter 1 in the Quantity field for each item. When you post the sale, allow Sage 50 to generate the sales order automatically by clicking Yes. Refer to page 448.

36

Visa Sales Summary: Invoice #477 **Dated September 29/21**

To One-time customers

2	KB-01	Electronic Piano P-81	$ 810	each	$ 1 620.00
2	KB-06	Keyboard K55	550	each	1 100.00
1	KB-09	Synthesizer SY-25	2 530		2 530.00
4	AA-02	Amplifier JX-240	610	each	2 440.00
30	AC-01	Sheet Music: miscellaneous	30	/sheet	900.00
15	AC-02	Music Book: miscellaneous	90	/book	1 350.00
2	AC-04	Piano Stool: adjust/fold/lock	165	/stool	330.00
4	AC-06	Music Stand: folding	65	/stand	260.00
8	AC-08	Headphones: studio	180	/set	1 440.00
3	AC-12	Cables: miscellaneous 2 m	20	each	60.00
3	AC-14	DVD: Keyboard Techniques	640	/4 DVD set	1 920.00
4	AC-15	Keyboard Stand: adjustable	240	/stand	960.00
20	SL-01	Keyboard Lessons: half hour	80	/30 min	1 600.00
20	SL-02	Composition Lessons: half hour	90	/30 min	1 800.00
		Delivery total			600.00
		Goods and Services Tax	5.0%		945.50
		Quebec Sales Tax	9.975%		1 886.30
Invoice summary total paid by Visa					$21 741.80

37

Credit Card Purchase Invoice #PD-304 **Dated September 30/21**

From Papineau Delivery, $580.00 plus $29.00 GST and $57.86 QST for contracted delivery to customers. Purchase invoice total $666.86 paid in full by Amex.

38

Bank Debit Memo #643177 **Dated September 30/21**

From Bank of Montreal, $70 for bank service charges for one month and $1 700 for mortgage payment that included $1 120 interest and $580 principal.

39 **Memo #7** **Dated September 30/21**

From Owner: Make adjusting entries for September.

Office supplies used	$ 75
Other supplies used	50
Prepaid insurance expired	435

40 **Bank Credit Memo #46234** **Dated September 30/21**

From Bank of Montreal, $488 interest earned on investment securities and $10 interest on bank account. Both amounts were deposited to chequing account.

41 **MasterCard Sales Summary: Invoice #478** **Dated September 30/21**

To One-time customers

4	KB-01	Electronic Piano P-81	$ 810	each	$ 3 240.00
3	KB-05	Keyboard K35	350	each	1 050.00
3	KB-08	Synthesizer SY-16	1 670	each	5 010.00
4	AA-01	Amplifier JX-120	230	each	920.00
25	AC-01	Sheet Music: miscellaneous	30	/sheet	750.00
15	AC-02	Music Book: miscellaneous	90	/book	1 350.00
3	AC-05	Music Stand: keyboard	110	/stand	330.00
6	AC-09	Headphones: closed	380	/set	2 280.00
4	AC-12	Cables: miscellaneous 2 m	20	each	80.00
3	AC-14	DVD: Keyboard Techniques	640	/4 DVD set	1 920.00
4	AC-15	Keyboard Stand: adjustable	240	/stand	960.00
20	SL-01	Keyboard Lessons: half hour	80	/30 min	1 600.00
20	SL-02	Composition Lessons: half hour	90	/30 min	1 800.00
	Delivery				400.00
	Goods and Services Tax		5.0%		1 084.50
	Quebec Sales Tax		9.975%		2 163.58
Invoice summary total paid by MasterCard					$24 938.08

WARNING!
Do not "pay" or accept the prepayment amount for these post-dated cheques. This amount will cover the final two months of payment. If the prepayment is entered in the Payment Amount field, you must delete it.

42 **Memo #8** **Dated September 30/21**

From Owner: Issue cheque #433 for $435 – the premium for one month – to Quebecare Insurance Co. in partial payment of invoice #QI-7711. Repeat the entry three times to make the remaining payments for 2021 with postdated cheques. Issue cheques #434 to #436, dated October 31, November 30, and December 31.

43 **Memo #9** **Dated September 30/21**

From Owner: Trevi Cléf-bas earned $4 500 in commissions on her share of sales in September. Issue cheque #437 to pay her commissions.

Updating Budgets

Changing Budget Amounts

Budget amounts can be updated if needed based on feedback from earlier budget reports. They should not, of course, be changed without good reason.

If you discover that your budget forecasts are incorrect, you can update the amounts for each account individually by repeating the process described above for entering initial budget amounts. Or you can globally update all amounts by a fixed percentage. At the end of September, we are asked to update budget amounts by 10 percent.

✓ 44 **Memo #10** **Dated September 30/21**

From Owner: Increase all revenue budget amounts by 10%. New sales goals were set with higher revenue and no changes in costs.

Choose the **Maintenance menu** in the Home window and **click Update Budget Amounts** to open the Update Budget window:

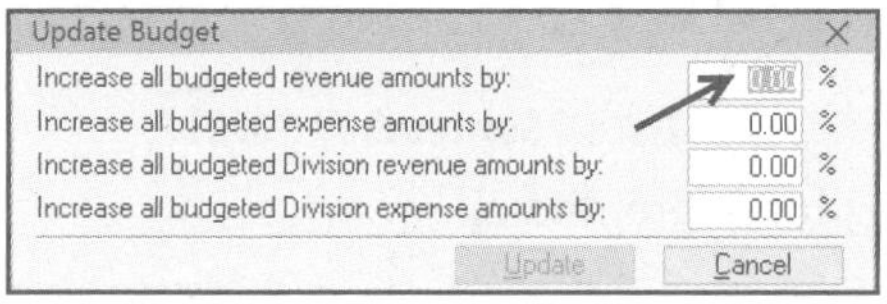

You can change the budgets for revenue and expense accounts separately. You can change division revenue and expense amounts by a different percentage. Use negative numbers to indicate a decrease in amounts and positive numbers for increases.

The entry for Increase All Budgeted Revenue Amounts By is selected.

Type 10 **Press** *tab* to advance to the field for expense amounts.

Click **Update** to apply the change.

The next screen asks you to confirm that you want to update the budget:

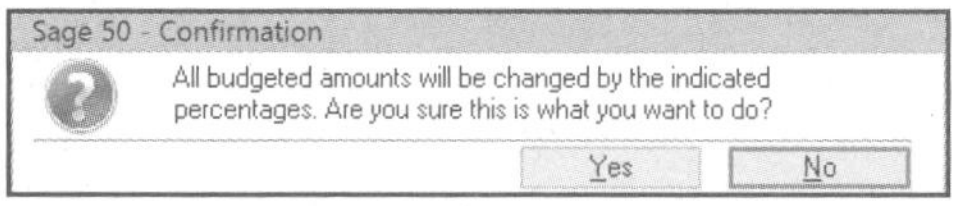

Click **Yes** to apply the changes and return to the Home window.

The account's budget information in the account ledger will have the changes applied. All budget amounts will be updated.

Changing Budget Frequencies

You can also change the budget frequency. This change is made in the General Ledger Settings screen.

For example, to change the period from monthly to quarterly,

> Choose the Setup menu, then click Settings. Click General (Accounts) and Budget. Then choose Quarterly from the Budget Period Frequency drop-down list and click OK.

NOTES

If you change the frequency from monthly to quarterly, the amount for each quarter will be the same. The budget amount you entered for Revenue from Sales will become $114 475 for each quarter – the total budget for the year, or 12 months, will be divided by 4 ($457 900/4).

When you have a quarterly budget with different amounts for each quarter and you change the frequency to monthly, each month will have the same budget amount — the total for the four quarters divided by 12. You must edit the amounts if they are incorrect.

For example, a quarterly budget of $1 000, $3 000, $2 000 and $6 000 for the four quarters becomes $1 000 each month if the frequency is changed to monthly ($12 000/12).

Before applying the new budget settings, Sage 50 generates a warning each time you change a budget frequency:

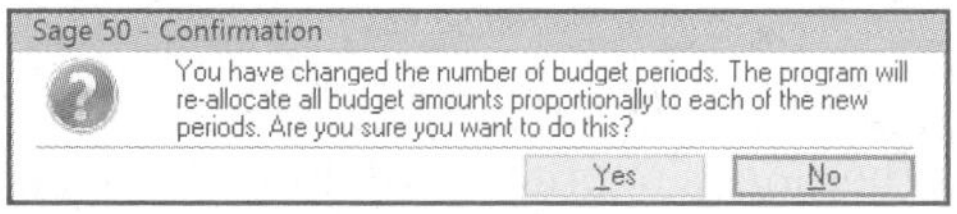

The statement warns that previous budget amounts will be reallocated evenly among the new number of periods. If you change a monthly budget to quarterly, each quarter will have the same budget amount. You can accept or cancel the change.

Printing in Batches

In addition to printing invoices, orders, quotes and cheques at the time of a transaction, you can print them in batches at the end of a period, such as the end of a business day.

Batch printing makes it easier to share printers. Any forms that can be printed individually can be printed in batches.

Memo #11 asks us to print all sales invoices.

✓ 45 **Memo #11** **Dated September 30/21**

From Owner: Print all sales invoices for September.

First you need to allow batch printing for the data file.

NOTES
To set up for printing in batches, you must work in single-user mode.

Choose the **Setup menu** and **click Settings**.

Click **Company** and then **click Forms** to open the Settings screen for Forms:

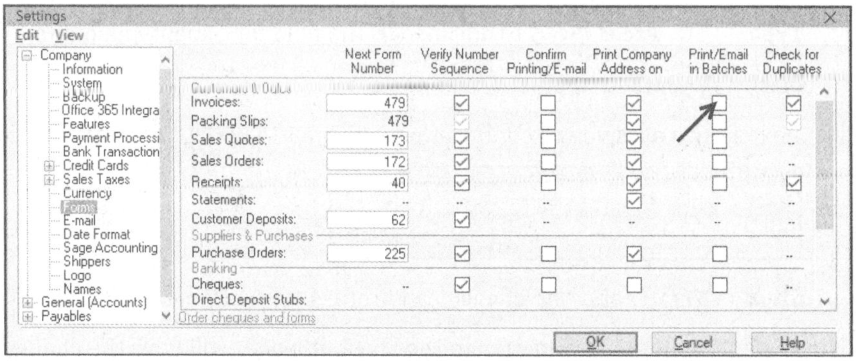

PRO VERSION
The Pro version does not have Packing Slips.

Click the **Print/Email In Batches check box for Invoices**, the first form listed.

Click the **check box for the other forms** that you want to prepare in batches.

Click **OK** to save the changes.

Now the Reports menu in the Home window has a Print Batches menu option.

Choose the **Reports menu** then **choose Batch Print/Email** and **click Sales Invoices** for the printing options:

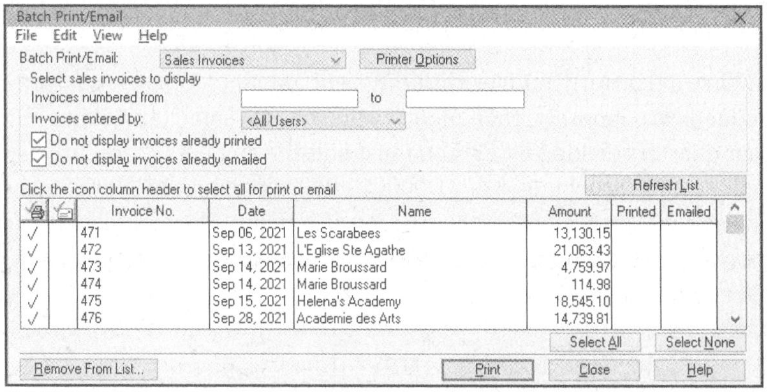

From this screen, you can choose other forms to print in batches. These are available from the **Batch Print/Email** drop-down list:

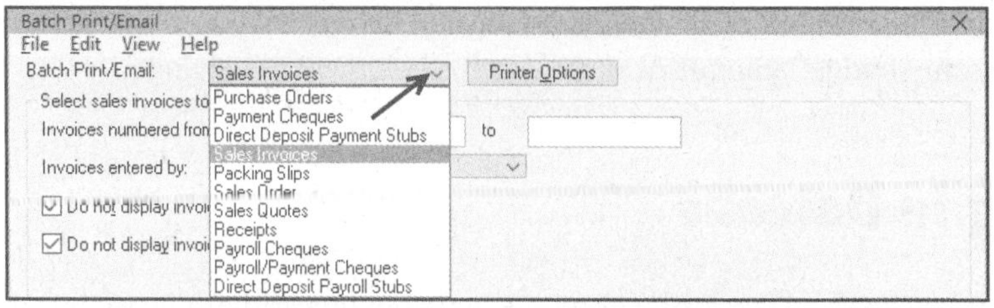

PRO VERSION
The Pro version does not have Packing Slips.

NOTES
The list will include all the forms for which you selected Print In Batches.

If some invoices have already been **Printed** or **E-mailed**, they will be have a ✓ in the corresponding column. You can remove them from the display by clicking the appropriate check boxes. You can choose a **range of Invoice Numbers** or a specific **User**. After making these selections, click **Display** to include only the requested invoices.

Initially, the ✓s in the Print column indicate all invoices are selected for printing. Clicking **Select None** will remove all the ✓s, and clicking **Select All** will select all listed invoices. You can also select invoices individually by clicking Select None and then clicking beside the invoices you want to print.

Choose the **invoices** you want to print so that only those invoices have a ✓.

Click **Print/Email**. Printing begins immediately, so be sure that you have loaded the forms you need (or use plain paper for practice).

Click **Close** or select another form from the Print Batch list to print other forms.

Printing in Batches from Journals

When you allow batch printing from the Forms Settings screen, you can print these forms in batches directly from the related journal.

All the journals that have a Print tool will have a **Batch Print/Email Invoice tool** added to the tool bar for this purpose, that is, the Sales, Purchases, Payments and Paycheques journals.

Budget Reports

Effective use of budget reports involves more than merely observing whether budgeted targets were met or not. Sometimes more information is gained when targets are not met, because the differences can lead to important questions:

- Were the targets realistic? What items were not on target and why?
- If performance exceeds the targets, how can we repeat the success?
- If performance did not meet the targets, were there factors that we failed to anticipate?
- Should we revise future budgets based on the new information?

The problem-solving cycle is set in motion. Even an Income Statement that is on target should be reviewed carefully. There may be room for improvement if the budget was a conservative estimate. Or you may want to include new information that will affect future performance and was unknown when the budget was drawn up.

Displaying Budget Income Statements

Reports used to analyze budget performance are Comparative Income Statements, comparing actual revenue and expense amounts with budgeted amounts.

Open the **Report Centre** and **click Financials**.

Click the ⊞ **beside Income Statement** to expand the list.

Click **Comparative 2 Period** and then **click Modify This Report**:

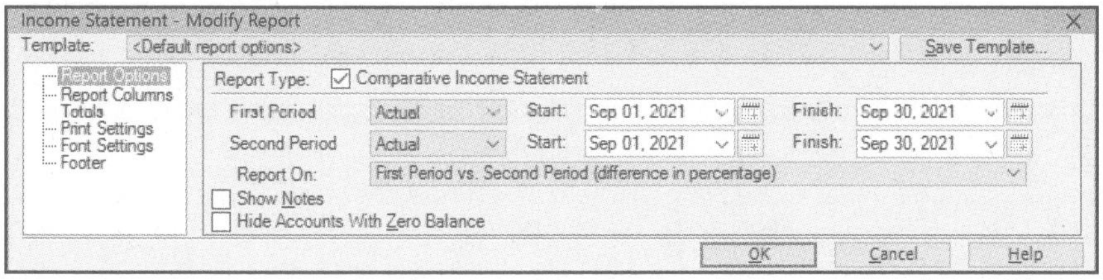

NOTES
Remember that you can customize invoices before printing them. Refer to Appendix F on the Student DVD.
You cannot preview the invoices from the Print Batches window.

NOTES
To print the invoices, you must choose Custom Form in the Reports & Forms settings on the Invoices screen. Choose Invoice in the Description field for invoices and e-mail.

NOTES
The Budget Report with budget amounts was described on page 558.

NOTES
You can also choose the Reports menu, then choose Financials and click Income Statement to display the Income Statement options. Click Comparative Income Statement as the Report Type.

> **NOTES**
> You can choose to display the budget amounts in either the first or the second period.
> In our example, we have the budget data in the second period.

Click **Actual** in the **Second Period field** to open the budget-related option:

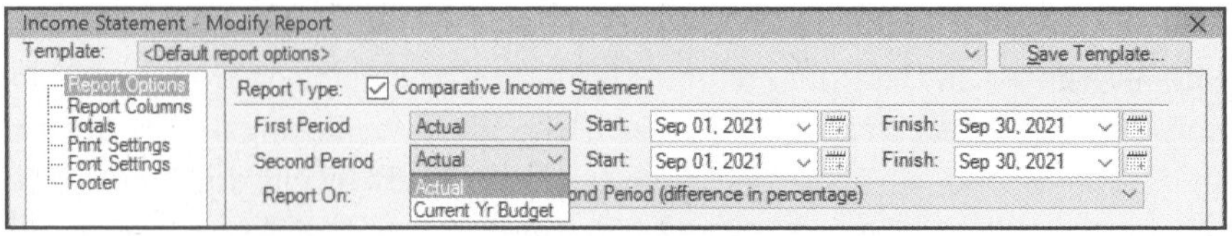

Click **Current Yr Budget** to change the option.

Budget Income Statements compare budgeted to actual amounts.

The **Report On** options are the same as the options for regular Comparative Income Statements, but now you can choose budgeted amounts for the Second Period. Three types of reports are available. The first type, **First** (actual) **Period Vs. Second** (budget) **Period (Amounts Only)**, lists the revenues and expenses actually obtained for the period indicated and the revenue and expense amounts that had been budgeted for the same period. The second type, **First** (actual) **Period Vs. Second** (budget) **Period (Difference In Percentage)**, gives these two amounts as well as the percentage that the actual amount is above or below the budgeted amount. The third option, **First** (actual) **Period Vs. Second** (budget) **Period (Difference In Amounts)**, provides budget and actual as base amounts, plus the difference between them as a dollar amount.

For the dollar difference and the percentage difference reports, a positive difference means that the budget was exceeded; a negative difference indicates the results came in under budget. Remember that for revenues, a positive difference (first period amounts are greater than second period amounts) means results were better than expected, but for expenses a positive difference means that results were poorer than expected (expenses were higher than budgeted). Cost of goods sold will increase directly with sales, so positive differences can mean either improved sales or higher costs, or both.

Click the type of comparative **budget report** you want to report on. **Close** the **display** when finished.

When you add budget details for divisions, you can also create **division budget reports**. Choose the Reports menu, then choose Division and click Budget. Choose the Report Type, dates and divisions and click OK.

Printing Budget Reports

Display the **report** you want to print. **Click** the **Print button** or **choose** the **File menu** in the report window and **click Print**.

Close the **displayed report** when you have finished. **Close** the **Report Centre**.

> **NOTES**
> Remember to check your printer selection before you print reports.

REVIEW

The Student DVD with Data Files includes Review Questions and Supplementary Cases for this chapter.

CHAPTER FIFTEEN

Tesses Tresses

OBJECTIVES

After completing this chapter, you should be able to

- ***prepare*** bank deposit slips
- ***print*** Transaction Reports for bank accounts
- ***compare*** bank statements with Transaction Reports
- ***turn on*** the account reconciliation feature
- ***create*** new linked accounts for reconciliation
- ***set up*** the account reconciliation information
- ***reconcile*** the bank account statement with the General Ledger
- ***reverse*** receipts for NSF cheques manually
- ***display*** and ***print*** account reconciliation reports
- ***clear*** paid invoices and ***remove*** accounts

COMPANY INFORMATION

Company Profile

NOTES
Tesses Tresses
55 Salon Rd.
Charlottetown, PE C1A 6D3
Tel: (902) 729-6211
Fax: (902) 728-4821
Business No.: 136 422 375

Tesses Tresses, a hair salon in Charlottetown, Prince Edward Island, is a family business owned by Tess Dubois, her husband, Ian, and her daughter, Felicia. All three had both professional and business management training to prepare them for running the salon. Together they provide a full range of hair care services to clients, most of whom return regularly. Unlike many salons where the price depends on the stylist and client, Tesses Tresses charges one price for each service regardless of client gender or stylist. It also sells a limited range of high-quality hair care products.

The salon building they own includes two apartments that are rented to students. These tenants provided postdated cheques for three months at the beginning of January.

Instead of hiring a maintenance, cleaning and laundry company to take care of the premises, the Dubois family shares this responsibility to reduce expenses. Cleaning is required almost continually to meet hygiene standards for health and safety.

The salon's regular suppliers provide inventory products, including those used in the salon for client services; office supplies; cleaning supplies for the salon; linens such as towels, capes and gowns; and hairdressing equipment. Supplier records are set up for all of these suppliers as well as for utility service companies and government agencies to which Tesses Tresses remits taxes. The salon pays HST on all purchases.

Although most clients are one-time clients who pay by cash and credit card, some repeat clients have accounts and are entitled to a 2 percent discount if they pay within five days. Net payment is due in 15 days. The cash clients do not receive a discount. A record called Cash Customers is set up for the weekly summaries of cash and credit card sales. Clients pay HST at 15 percent on merchandise they buy from the salon and on all services. The tax rates and codes are entered into client and inventory records, so the program automatically calculates taxes.

Tesses Tresses also provides hair styling services to local theatre companies, cutting and styling hair for cast members before performances, re-styling throughout the show for cast character changes and styling wigs. These evening commitments do not conflict with the usual daytime salon business hours. The theatre companies pay preferred prices at about 20 percent off regular prices in addition to the discount for early payment.

At the beginning of February, some unfilled purchase orders will provide the inventory for the additional sales anticipated for Valentine's Day.

The accounting records for Tesses Tresses were converted to Sage 50 at the beginning of January, and the transactions for January have been completed. The files are ready for January bank account transactions (deposits and account reconciliation) and February transactions. The current accounting records include the following:

- Chart of Accounts
- Trial Balance as at January 31, 2021
- Supplier Information
- Client Information
- Inventory Information
- Accounting Procedures

CHART OF ACCOUNTS

TESSES TRESSES

ASSETS

1030 Undeposited Cash and Cheques
1060 Bank: Chequing Account
1080 Bank: Credit Cards
1200 Accounts Receivable
1240 Prepaid Insurance
1260 Prepaid Subscriptions
1300 Towels and Capes
1320 Office Supplies
1340 Washroom & Cleaning Supplies
1360 Salon Supplies
1420 Hair Care Products ▶
▶1520 Computer and Cash Register
1540 Furniture and Fixtures
1560 Salon Equipment
1580 Salon and Building

LIABILITIES

2100 Bank Loan
2150 Credit Card Payable
2200 Accounts Payable
2750 HST Charged on Sales
2760 HST Paid on Purchases
2850 Mortgage Payable ▶

▶EQUITY

3100 TT Capital
3150 TT Drawings
3600 Net Income

REVENUE

4100 Revenue from Sales
4120 Revenue from Services
4140 Rental Income
4160 Sales Discounts
4220 Interest Revenue
4240 Other Revenue ▶

▶EXPENSE

5020 Advertising and Promotion
5040 Bank Charges
5060 Credit Card Fees
5080 Cost of Services
5180 Inventory Losses
5200 Cost of Goods Sold
5220 Purchase Discounts
5240 Insurance Expense
5260 Subscriptions Expense
5300 Supplies Used
5320 Utilities
5340 Interest Expense

NOTES: The Chart of Accounts includes only postable accounts and Net Income.

TRIAL BALANCE

TESSES TRESSES

January 31, 2021

		Debits	Credits
1030	Undeposited Cash and Cheques	$ 17 187.85	
1060	Bank: Chequing Account	34 117.66	
1080	Bank: Credit Cards	9 660.97	
1200	Accounts Receivable	29.90	
1240	Prepaid Insurance	750.00	
1260	Prepaid Subscriptions	270.00	
1300	Towels and Capes	530.00	
1320	Office Supplies	330.00	
1340	Washroom & Cleaning Supplies	365.00	
1360	Salon Supplies	807.00	
1420	Hair Care Products	2 435.00	
1520	Computer and Cash Register	4 200.00	
1540	Furniture and Fixtures	7 600.00	
1560	Salon Equipment	4 600.00	
1580	Salon and Building	220 000.00	
2100	Bank Loan		$ 23 510.00
2150	Credit Card Payable		80.50
2200	Accounts Payable		1 874.50 ▶
▶ 2750	HST Charged on Sales		$ 3 823.35
2760	HST Paid on Purchases	$ 856.05	
2850	Mortgage Payable		149 650.00
3100	TT Capital		104 799.00
4100	Revenue from Sales		5 618.00
4120	Revenue from Services		19 871.00
4140	Rental Income		1 070.00
4160	Sales Discounts	66.75	
5060	Credit Card Fees	373.53	
5200	Cost of Goods Sold	3 305.00	
5220	Purchase Discounts		103.36
5240	Insurance Expense	150.00	
5260	Subscriptions Expense	30.00	
5300	Supplies Used	1 140.00	
5320	Utilities	335.00	
5340	Interest Expense	1 260.00	
		$310 399.71	$310 399.71

SUPPLIER INFORMATION

TESSES TRESSES

Supplier Name (Contact)	Address	Phone No. Fax No.	E-mail Web Site	Terms Tax ID
Air Pro (Curly Locks)	390 Brows Lane Charlottetown, PE C1A 6M3	Tel: (902) 722-0217 Fax: (902) 723-8100	curly@airpro.com airpro.com	net 15 137 456 190 RT0001
All U Need	Maypoint Plaza #64 Charlottetown, PE C1E 1E2	Tel: (902) 728-4314	alluneed.com	net 1 382 732 162 RT0001
Atlantic Power Corp.	16 Lektrik Rd. Charlottetown, PE C1C 6G1	Tel: (902) 726-1615	apc.ca	net 1
Charlottetown City Treasurer	78 Fitzroy St. Charlottetown, PE C1A 1R5	Tel: (902) 725-9173	charlottetown.ca/fin	net 1
Eastern Tel (I.D. Caller)	36 Nassau St. Charlottetown, PE C1A 7V9	Tel: (902) 723-2355		net 1
Fine Brushes (Harry Bristle)	13 Ave. Costey Dorval, QC H9S 4C7	Tel: (514) 457-1826 Fax: (514) 457-1883	bristle@finebrushes.com finebrushes.com	net 20 188 462 451 RT0001
Lookin' Good (N. Vayne)	18 Vivanle Cr. Summerside, PE C1N 6C4	Tel: (902) 829-4763 Fax: (902) 829-7392	vayne@lookingood.com lookingood.com	net 10 192 721 215 RT0001
Pro-Line Inc. (Awl Fluff)	190 Rue Mutchmore Hull, QC J8Y 3S9	Tel: (819) 658-7227 Fax: (819) 658-7192	awl.fluff@proline.com proline.com	2/10, n/30 (after tax) 621 372 614 RT0001
Receiver General for Canada	Summerside Tax Centre	Tel: (902) 821-8186		net 1
Seaside Papers (Fyne Pulp)	40 Harbour View Dr. Charlottetown, PE C1A 7A8	Tel: (902) 720-1623 Fax: (902) 720-1639	pulp@seasidepapers.com seasidepapers.com	net 1 810 721 019 RT0001
Sharp Scissors (S. Cutter)	22 Bellevue Ave. Summerside, PE C1N 2C7	Tel: (902) 923-1995 Fax: (902) 923-1726	cutter@sharp.com sharp.com	net 10 138 221 106 RT0001
Zines Inc. (Buetee Tipps)	344 Lepage Ave. Summerside, PE C1N 3E6	Tel: (902) 553- 6291 Fax: (902) 553-7155	tipps@zines.com zines.com	net 10 205 602 303 RT0001

SUPPLIER INVOICES

TESSES TRESSES

Supplier Name	Terms	Date	Inv/Chq No.	Amount	Discount	Total
Fine Brushes	net 20	Dec. 20/20	FB-4321	$330.00		$330.00
		Jan. 9/21	CHQ 411	330.00		330.00
	net 20	Jan. 17/21	FB-6219	954.50		954.50
			Balance owing			$954.50
Pro-Line Inc.	2/10, n/30	Dec. 28/20	PL-1002	$ 945.00		$ 945.00
		Jan. 4/21	CHQ 410	926.10	$18.90	945.00
	2/10, n/30	Jan. 4/21	PL-1012	4 222.80		4 222.80
		Jan. 14/21	CHQ 413	4 138.34	84.46	4 222.80
Sharp Scissors	net 10	Jan. 24/21	SS-432	$920.00		$920.00
				Grand Total		$1 874.50

NOTES: Cash and Credit Card Purchases are not included in the chart of supplier invoices.

CLIENT INFORMATION

TESSES TRESSES

Client Name (Contact)	Address	Phone No. Fax No.	E-mail Web Site	Terms Credit Limit
Atta Schule (tenant)		Tel: (902) 724-2996	atta.schule@undergrad.upei.ca	first of month
Brioche Bridal Party (Bonnie Brioche)	75 Marital Way Charlottetown, PE C1E 4A2	Tel: (902) 723-1194 Fax: (902) 726-1921	brioche@weddingbells.com	2/5, n/15 $1 000
Cash Customers				cash/credit card
Conn Seted	14 Hi Brow St. Charlottetown, PE C1E 3X1	Tel: (902) 723-0099	conn.seted@aol.com	net 15 $1 000
Irma Vannitee	77 Makeover Cr. Charlottetown, PE C1B 1J5	Tel: (902) 726-7715	irma.van@skindeep.com	2/5, n/15 $1 000
*On Stage Theatre Company (Marvelle Stage)	100 Marquee Blvd. Charlottetown, PE C1A 2M1	Tel: (902) 727-8201 Fax: (902) 727-0663	marvelle@onstage.com onstage.com	2/5, n/15 $2 000
Proud Family	98 Proud St. Charlottetown, PE C1B 3C1	Tel: (902) 721-1113	theprouds@shaw.ca	net 15 $1 000
Stu Dents (tenant)		Tel: (902) 724-7103	stu.dents@undergrad.upei.ca	first of month
*Twilight Theatre (Ona Roll)	55 Footlights Dr. Charlottetown, PE C1B 6V2	Tel: (902) 728-4661 Fax: (902) 724-1556	ona.roll@twilight.com twilight.com	2/5, n/15 $2 000

NOTES: All client discounts are calculated on after-tax amounts.
* Indicates preferred customer.

CLIENT INVOICES

TESSES TRESSES

Client Name	Terms	Date	Inv/Chq No.	Amount	Discount	Total
Atta Schule	rent payment	Jan. 2/21	CHQ 415			$455.00
	rent payment	Feb. 1/21	CHQ 416 (postdated rent payment)			455.00
	rent payment	Mar. 1/21	CHQ 417 (postdated rent payment)			455.00

CLIENT INVOICES CONTINUED

TESSES TRESSES

Client Name	Terms	Date	Inv/Chq No.	Amount	Discount	Total
Brioche Bridal Party	2/5, n/15	Jan. 9/21	468	$143.75		$143.75
		Jan. 14/21	CHQ 206	140.87	$2.88	143.75
Conn Seted	net 15	Jan. 24/21	477	$59.80		$59.80
		Jan. 29/21	CHQ 238	$59.80		59.80
Irma Vannitee	2/5, n/15	Dec. 28/20	452	$120.00		$120.00
		Jan. 2/21	CHQ 464	117.60	$2.40	120.00
	2/5, n/15	Jan. 2/21	464	112.70		112.70
		Jan. 7/21	CHQ 918	110.45	2.25	112.70
	2/5, n/15	Jan. 7/21	467	159.85		159.85
		Jan. 17/21	CHQ CC-61	159.85		159.85
	2/5, n/15	Jan. 16/21	471	90.85		90.85
		Jan. 20/21	CHQ 74	89.03	1.82	90.85
	2/5, n/15	Jan. 27/21	478	29.90		29.90
			Balance owing			$29.90
On Stage Theatre Company	2/5, n/15	Dec. 29/20	455	$ 250.00		$ 250.00
		Jan. 3/21	CHQ 382	245.00	$ 5.00	250.00
	2/5, n/15	Jan. 20/21	474	1 205.20		1 205.20
		Jan. 24/21	CHQ 429	1 181.10	24.10	1 205.20
	2/5, n/15	Jan. 28/21	479	1 205.20		1 205.20
		Jan. 31/21	CHQ 498	1 181.10	24.10	1 205.20
Stu Dents	rent payment	Jan. 2/21	CHQ 161			$615.00
	rent payment	Feb. 1/21	CHQ 162 (postdated rent payment)			615.00
	rent payment	Mar. 1/21	CHQ 163 (postdated rent payment)			615.00
Twilight Theatre	2/5, n/15	Dec. 28/20	453	$210.00		$210.00
		Jan. 2/21	CHQ 5121	205.80	$4.20	210.00
				Grand Total		$29.90

INVENTORY ITEM INFORMATION

TESSES TRESSES

Item Code	Item Description	Unit	Min Qty	Selling Price Reg	(Pref)	Qty on Hand	Total (Cost)	Tax
Hair Products: Total asset value $2 435 (Asset account: 1420, Revenue account: 4100, Expense account: 5200)								
BRS1	Hair Brush: natural bristle	each	2	$32	(26)	17	$ 323.00	HST
BRS2	Hair Brush: styling	each	2	24	(20)	28	420.00	HST
CN1	Pro-Line Conditioner: 150 ml	bottle	3	34	(26)	7	126.00	HST
CN2	Pro-Line Hot Oil Treatment 75 ml	tube	3	35	(28)	24	456.00	HST
FRZ1	Pro-Line Defrizzer: cream 100 ml	jar	3	28	(22)	27	459.00	HST
GEL1	Pro-Line Spray Gel: shaper 150 ml	can	3	27	(22)	16	256.00	HST
SHM1	Pro-Line Shampoo: 225 ml	bottle	5	26	(21)	10	170.00	HST
SPR1	Pro-Line Hair Spray: gentle 150 ml	can	5	26	(21)	15	225.00	HST
							$2 435.00	
Salon Services (Revenue account: 4120, Expense account: 5080)								
SRV1	Colour	each		$ 55	($48)			HST
SRV2	Conditioning Treatment	each		24	(20)			HST
SRV3	Cut and Style	each		48	(42)			HST
SRV4	Highlights	each		110	(90)			HST
SRV5	Perm	each		88	(80)			HST
SRV6	Wash and Style	each		26	(21)			HST
SRV7	Wig Wash, Set and Style	each		32	(26)			HST

NOTES

In 2013, PEI modified its taxation rates and methods, adopting the HST at 14% to replace the separate 5 percent GST (on goods and services) and 9 percent PST on goods only. In 2016, PEI increased the HST rate from 14% to 15%.

Accounting Procedures

Taxes

HST at 15 percent is charged on all goods and services sold by the salon. Tesses Tresses remits the HST owing — *HST Charged on Sales* less *HST Paid on Purchases* — to the Receiver General by the last day of each month for the previous month.

Sales Summaries

Most salon sales are to one-time clients who do not have accounts. These sales are summarized weekly according to the payment method — by cash or by credit card — and entered for the client named Cash Customers. By choosing Cash Customers as the client for these sales, the default tax codes and terms should be correct.

Receipts and Bank Deposits

Cash and cheques received in payment are held for weekly deposits in the temporary bank clearing account, *Undeposited Cash and Cheques*. Therefore, Tesses Tresses uses this account as the default Receivables linked bank account for all receipts.

NSF Cheques

If a cheque is deposited from an account that does not have enough money to cover it, the bank returns it to the depositor as NSF (non-sufficient funds). To record the NSF cheque, enter a negative receipt in the Receipts Journal. Select *Bank: Chequing Account* as the Deposit To account. Turn on the option to Include Fully Paid Invoices and enter a negative payment amount. Enter the bank debit number as the receipt and add NSF to the original cheque number in the Cheque field. If a discount was taken for early payment, reverse this amount as well. Then enter a Sales Journal invoice for the amount of the service charge. Refer to pages 605 and A–23 if you need more help.

You must enter a negative receipt for these NSF cheques. You cannot reverse the receipt because different accounts are involved. The original receipt was deposited to *Undeposited Cash and Cheques*, but the NSF cheque credits the *Bank: Chequing Account* after the deposit was entered.

Cost of Supplies

Instead of buying separate salon supplies for regular client services, Tesses Tresses uses its inventory stock of shampoos, conditioners, gels and so on. Inventory Adjustment entries are completed to make these transfers at cost from the inventory asset account to the supplies account.

INSTRUCTIONS

1. **Enter** the **deposit slips** and **set up** and **complete** the **account reconciliation** for January using the Chart of Accounts, Trial Balance, Supplier, Client and Inventory information provided. Use the keystrokes with the source documents as a guide. The journal transactions for January have been completed for you.
2. **Enter** the **source documents** for February, including the account reconciliation.
3. **Print** the **reports** indicated on the following chart after completing your entries:

REPORTS

Accounts
- [ ] Chart of Accounts
- [ ] Account List
- [ ] General Journal Entries

Financials
- [x] Comparative Balance Sheet dates: Feb. 1 and Feb. 28 with difference in percentage
- [x] Income Statement from Jan. 1 to Feb. 28
- [x] Trial Balance date: Feb. 28
- [x] All Journal Entries: Feb. 1 to Feb. 28
- [x] General Ledger: for accounts 1060 and 1080 from Jan. 1 to Feb. 28
- [ ] Statement of Cash Flows
- [x] Cash Flow Projection Detail Report for account 1060 for 30 days
- [ ] Gross Margin Income Statement

Tax
- [ ] Tax

Banking
- [x] Account Reconciliation Summary Report: for 1060 and 1080 from Jan. 1 to Feb. 28
- [ ] Bank Transaction Report
- [ ] Reconciliation Transaction Report
- [x] Deposit Slip Detail Report for account 1060 from Jan. 1 to Feb. 28
- [x] Account Reconciliation Journal Entries: Jan. 1 to Feb. 28
- [x] Deposit Slip Journal Entries: Jan. 1 to Feb. 28
- [ ] Cheque Log Report

Payables
- [ ] Supplier List
- [ ] Supplier Aged
- [ ] Aged Overdue Payables
- [ ] Expenses Journal Entries
- [ ] Payments Journal Entries
- [ ] Supplier Expenses

Receivables
- [ ] Client List
- [ ] Client Aged
- [ ] Aged Overdue Receivables
- [ ] Revenues Journal Entries
- [ ] Receipts Journal Entries
- [ ] Client Revenues
- [ ] Client Statements

Inventory & Services
- [ ] Inventory & Services List
- [ ] Inventory Summary
- [ ] Inventory Quantity
- [x] Inventory Statistics: all items and all details
- [ ] Inventory Sales Summary
- [ ] Inventory Transaction Summary
- [ ] Item Assembly Journal Entries
- [ ] Adjustment Journal Entries
- [ ] Inventory Price Lists

KEYSTROKES

Entering Bank Deposit Slips

Previously, we recorded receipts directly as deposits to the linked bank accounts. In this chapter, we explain the procedure for recording receipts and deposits separately. The deposits for the cash and cheques received in January have not yet been recorded.

Open **SageData19\TESS\TESS**. **Accept January 31** as the session date.

Click **Banking** in the Modules pane list.

Deposits are made using the Make Deposit icon:

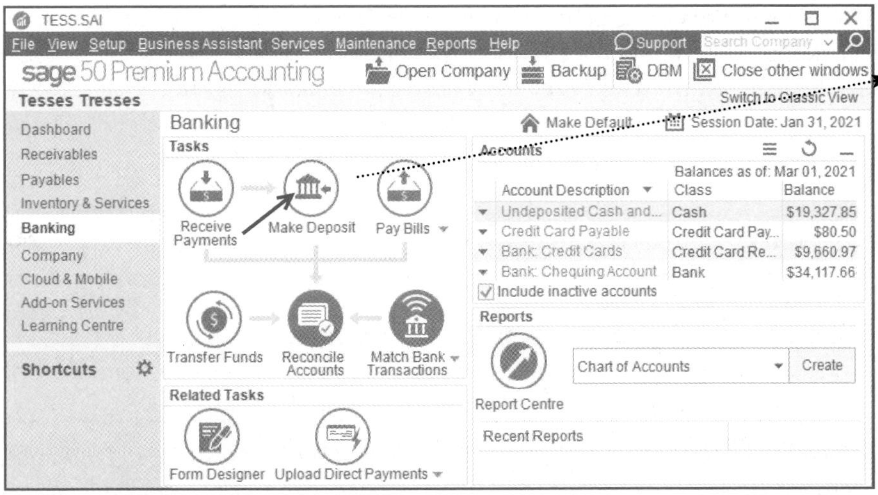

The account order was reversed in the previous screenshot by clicking ▲ beside the Account Description heading and changing it to ▼ to place undeposited amounts first.

The first memo requires us to record the deposits for January.

NOTES

If you are using backup files, restore SageData19\TESS1.CAB or TESS1 to SageData19\TESS\TESS.

NOTES

Home window ledger record balances for Tesses Tresses are calculated as at March 1, the latest transaction date (for the postdated rent cheques).

Remember that Make Other Payment is the default type of transaction from the Pay Bills icon in the Banking module window.

✓ 1 **Memo #7** **Dated Jan. 31/21**

Use the deposit information slips to prepare deposit slip #1. All amounts were deposited to Bank: Chequing Account.

✓ **DEPOSIT SLIP # 1** **JANUARY 7, 2021**

Date	Cheque #	Client	Amount
Jan 2	46	Irma Vannitee	$ 117.60
Jan 2	5121	Twilight Theatre	205.80
Jan 2	161	Stu Dents	615.00
Jan 2	415	Atta Schule	455.00
Jan 3	382	On Stage Theatre Company	245.00
Jan 7	918	Irma Vannitee	110.45
		Total Cheques	$1 748.85
		Cash	$2 626.60
		(Consisting of 5 × $5, 15 × $10, 30 × $20; 13 × $50; 12 × $100; Coin $1.60)	
		Total Deposit	$4 375.45

Click the **Make Deposit icon** to open the Reconciliation & Deposits Journal:

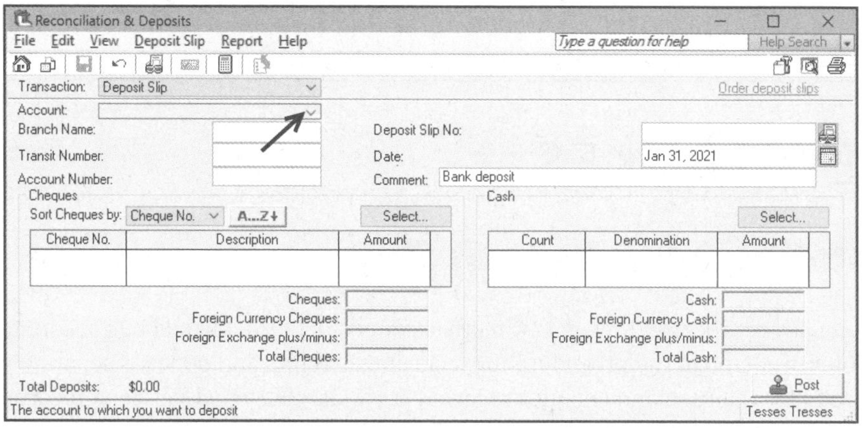

The journal is named Reconciliation & Deposits because both types of transactions are entered in this journal. You can choose from the **Transaction** drop-down list to change the type. Deposit Slip is selected in the Transaction field because we selected this Home window icon.

The deposit transaction has two parts: the Deposit To component that forms this main journal window and the Deposit From portion. All cash and cheques were debited to *Undeposited Cash and Cheques*, a Cash class **clearing account** that is the default account for all receipts. Now we need to transfer these receipts to the *Bank: Chequing Account* as deposits.

First, we choose the bank account receiving the deposit.

Click the **Account list arrow**:

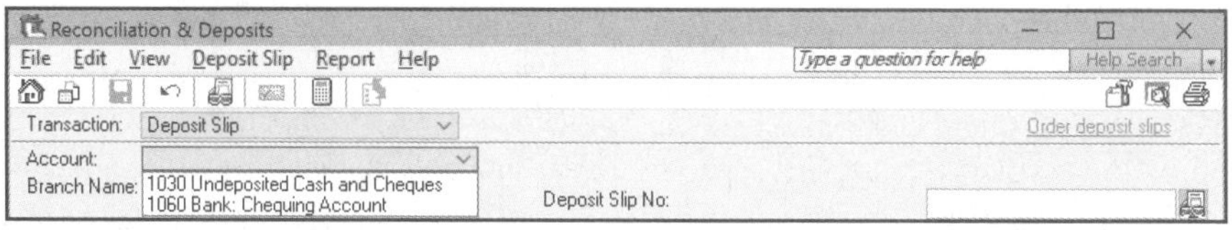

Two accounts are listed: *Undeposited Cash and Cheques* (the default linked Receivables Cash class account) and the Bank class *Bank: Chequing Account*. We must select *Bank: Chequing Account*, the account that is receiving the deposit.

Click **Bank: Chequing Account**.

WARNING!

You cannot adjust deposit slips or account reconciliation after posting, except with General Journal entries. Back up your data files before beginning the banking transactions.

PRO VERSION

The Pro version does not have the Save tool or the Refresh tool.

CLASSIC VIEW

Click the Reconciliation & Deposits icon in the General column to open the journal, and choose Deposit Slip from the Transaction drop-down list.

NOTES

Undeposited Cash and Cheques is set up as a Cash class account so that we can use it as the default linked principal bank account for the Receivables Ledger. You could also choose Bank as the class for this account. Both Bank and Cash class accounts can be selected as the default Receivables bank account.

The deposit slip number is entered and will be updated automatically, like the other form numbers in Sage 50.

Tesses Tresses makes weekly deposits to the bank account of all cash and cheques received during the week. We need to enter the date of the first deposit.

Enter **January 7, 2021** in the Date field for the first deposit.

Next, we must select the outstanding cheques and cash that will be deposited. The Deposit Slip has cheques on the left and cash on the right. There are separate **Select buttons** for these two types of currency. We will add the cheques first.

The Select button we need is in the centre of the journal, above the field for listing the cheques:

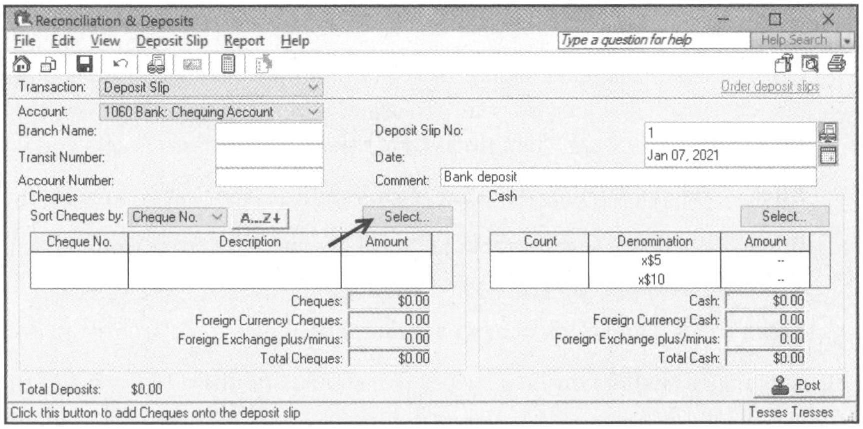

You can drag the column heading margins to change column sizes if all the information is not on-screen. Or you can maximize the journal.

Click the **Select button for Cheques** to open the list of outstanding cheques:

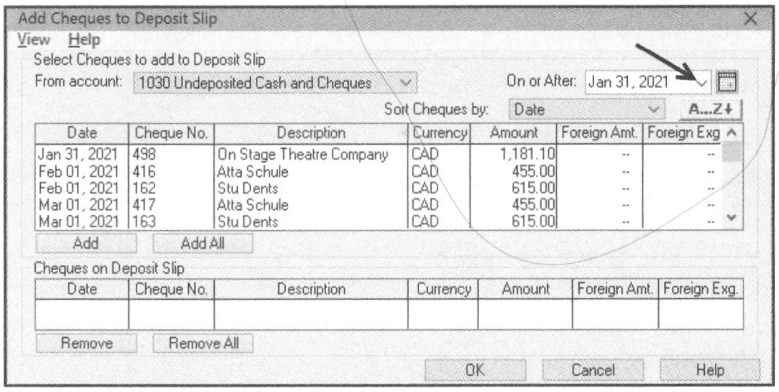

The first banking account, *Undeposited Cash and Cheques*, is selected as the default **From Account**, and this is the one we want. Cheques are listed by date in ascending order, but you can choose a different order from the **Sort Cheques By** drop-down list. Cheques may be sorted by any of the column headings for the list of cheques (cheque number, currency, amount, description, foreign amount or foreign exchange amount). You can click the **A...Z↓** button — changing it to **Z...A↓** — to sort in descending order.

The session date, January 31, is entered in the **On Or After date** field, so only the cheques for January 31 and the postdated rent cheques are listed. We need to deposit cheques that are dated on or after January 1, so this is the date we should enter. In this way, we will include all undeposited cheques.

Click the **On Or After field Calendar icon** and **click Jan 1** as the date.

NOTES
You do not need to type the year in the Reconciliation & Deposits Journal date fields. It will be added correctly by the program.

NOTES
When the bank account is set up for online reconciliation, the branch, transit and account numbers are required information in the ledger record and will be added to the Deposit Slip Journal. Online banking is illustrated in Appendix I on the Student DVD.

NOTES
Once the list is in descending order, the Sort order button label changes to **Z...A↓**. Clicking this button again restores the list to ascending order.

NOTES
You can also choose Jan 1 from the On Or After date field drop-down list. You can choose this date for all deposit slip transactions in this chapter if you want.

All the cheques received by the salon are now listed:

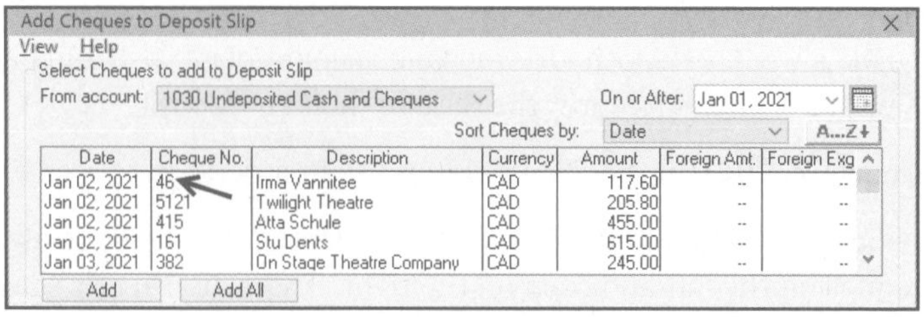

The next step is to select the cheques we want and add them to the deposit.

We should select the six cheques that are dated on or before January 7, cheques from Irma Vannitee, Twilight Theatre, Stu Dents, Atta Schule and On Stage Theatre Company.

Click to select a single cheque. To select multiple cheques, press and hold *ctrl* and click each cheque you want. To select several cheques in a row, click the first cheque you want, then press *shift* and click the last cheque you need.

Click **cheque number 46 from Irma Vannitee**, the first cheque on the list.

Click the **down scroll arrow** until cheque #918 from Vannitee is included on-screen.

Press *shift* and **click cheque number 918**.

All six cheques should now be selected. We should add them to the list of Cheques On Deposit Slip in the lower half of the form.

Click the **Add button** to place the selected six cheques in the Cheques On Deposit Slip section:

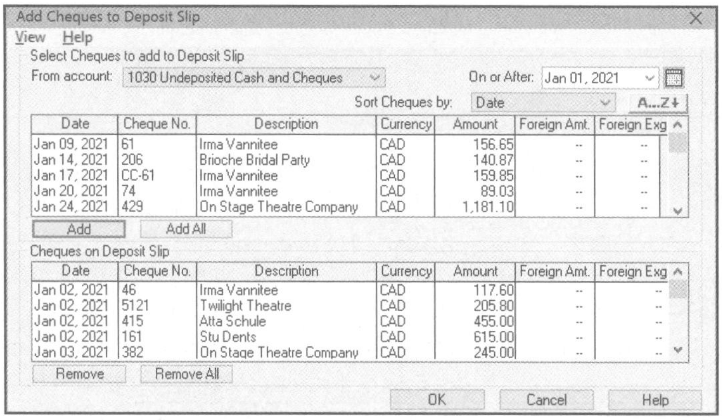

NOTES

You may prefer to select cheques one at a time when the ones you are depositing are not in sequence.

You can also add the cheques one at a time. Click a cheque and then click the Add button to move the cheque. Then click the next cheque and click Add. Repeat until all the cheques you want are in the Cheques On Deposit Slip list. If all cheques are deposited together, you can click Add All.

To **change a selection**, click a cheque in the Cheques On Deposit Slip list and click Remove. To start again, click Remove All to clear the list.

Click **OK** to return to the updated Reconciliation & Deposits Journal:

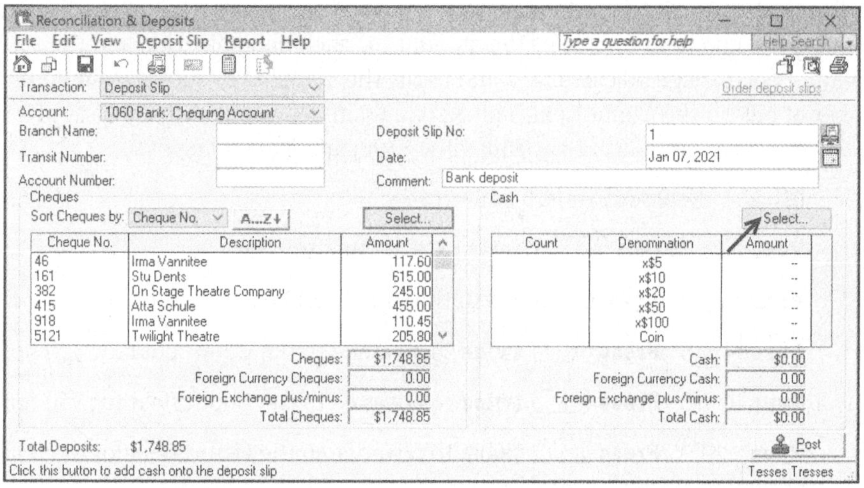

The selected six cheques are added and their total should match the amount on the Deposit Slip source document. If it does not, click the Select button again to correct the cheque selection. If a cheque amount is incorrect, close the journal without saving the changes and correct the original receipt transaction.

The next step is to add the cash portion of the deposit. Tesses Tresses has one cash sale summary amount to deposit, $2 626.60.

Click the **Select button for Cash** to open the deposit form for cash:

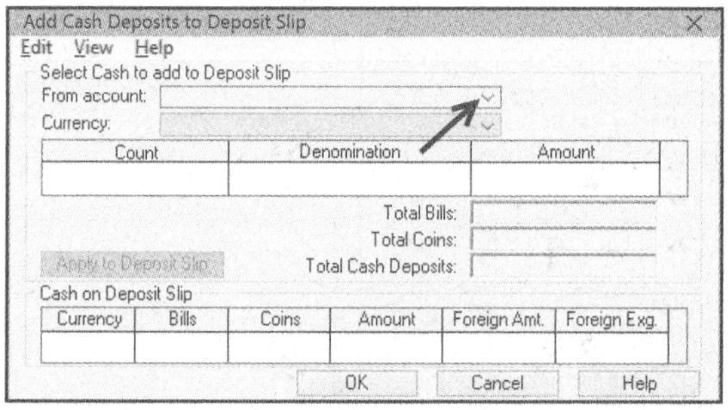

Cash receipts are not listed individually because they are usually combined in the store and held in the cash drawers or safe. When deposits are made, some cash is usually kept in the store to provide change for future clients. This balance may be transferred from *Undeposited Cash and Cheques* to a *Cash on Hand* account, recorded as a General Journal or Transfer Funds transaction. Similarly, the denominations of notes and coins that are received from clients may be different from the deposited ones. To simplify the exercise, we deposit the full amount of cash received each week.

No account is entered by default, so we first need to select the account that we are depositing from.

Choose **Undeposited Cash and Cheques** from the From Account drop-down list to modify the deposit form:

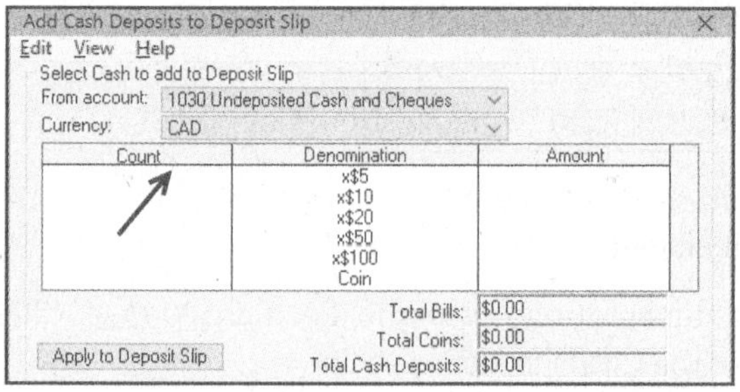

NOTES

The cheques on the deposit slip are sorted by cheque number. You can reverse the order (A...Z button) or sort the cheques by description or amount by making the selection from the Sort Cheques By drop-down list.

NOTES

If you are unable to finish the deposit slip entry now, you can save it at any time and complete it later.

NOTES

The procedure for depositing partial amounts of cash is the same as the one we describe in this chapter – only the amount will be different.

NOTES

After selecting the From Account, the currency is added – the denomination of the notes will be known and added to the deposit form. Tesses Tresses uses only Canadian currency.

The Cash Deposit form is completed in the same way as a deposit slip at the bank. You enter the number of notes or the amount for each denomination and the total amount of coins. Sage 50 calculates and totals the amounts as soon as you enter the number of bills in the Count field. The $2 626.60 in deposited cash consists of 5 × $5; 15 × $10; 30 × $20; 13 × $50; 12 × $100; and $1.60 in coins.

NOTES

Instead of pressing tab twice, you can press ↓ to move the cursor to the next Count line on the form.

Instead of entering the count for each denomination, you can enter the amount and Sage 50 will enter the corresponding count.

Click the **Count field beside** ×**$5**.

Type 5 **Press** tab to enter $25 as the Amount.

Press tab **again** to move to the Count field for $10 notes.

Type 15 **Press** tab **twice** to advance to the Count field for $20 notes.

Type 30 **Press** tab **twice** to advance to the Count field for $50 notes.

Type 13 **Press** tab **twice** to advance to the Count field for $100 notes.

Type 12 **Press** tab **twice** to advance to the Count field for coins.

The amount for coins is entered as a total amount in the Amount field. You cannot type in the Count field for Coin.

NOTES

If the coin amount is for a whole number, such as $6.00, you do not need to add the decimal and zeros. Instead, you can type 6, just as you do for amounts in other journals. To enter 1.60, you can type 1.6.

Press tab **again** to advance to the Amount field for coins.

Type 1.60 (You must enter the decimal for amounts less than one dollar.)

Press tab to update the total:

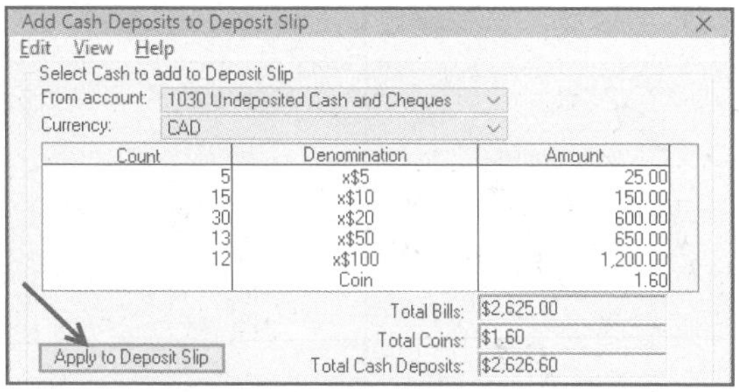

The total amounts for bills and coins remain separated, and the total for the cash deposit is calculated.

The next step is to apply the amount to the deposit slip.

Click the **Apply To Deposit Slip button** to update the form:

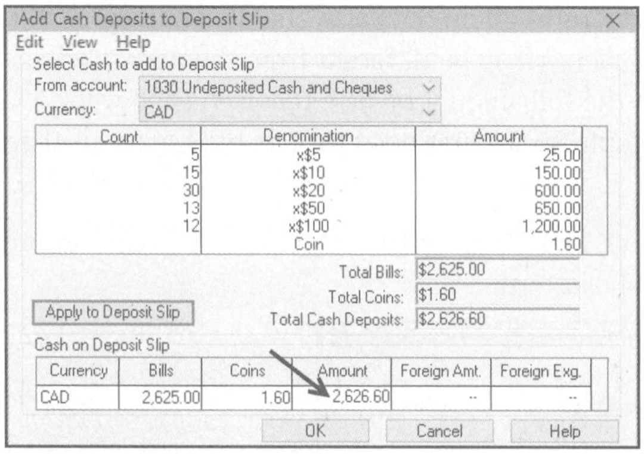

NOTES

Tesses Tresses does not have any foreign currency transactions.

The total cash deposit amount is added to the Cash On Deposit Slip section. The currency for the amount is also included.

To make changes, edit a number in the Count field and press tab. Click Apply To Deposit Slip to update the Cash On Deposit Slip.

Click **OK** to add this cash deposit information to the journal form:

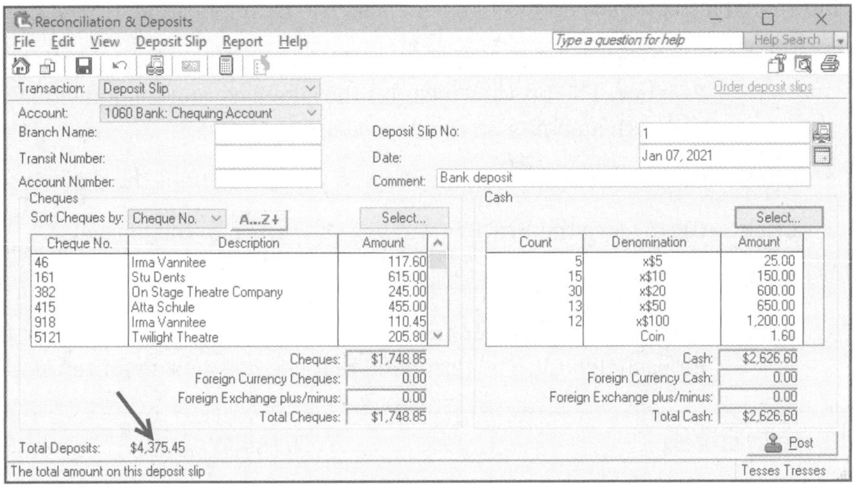

The form is complete. You can accept the default comment "Bank deposit" or change it. The comment will become part of the journal record.

Reviewing the Deposit Slip Entry

Before posting, we should review the journal entry created by the deposit.

Choose the **Report menu** and **click Display Deposit Slip Journal Entry**:

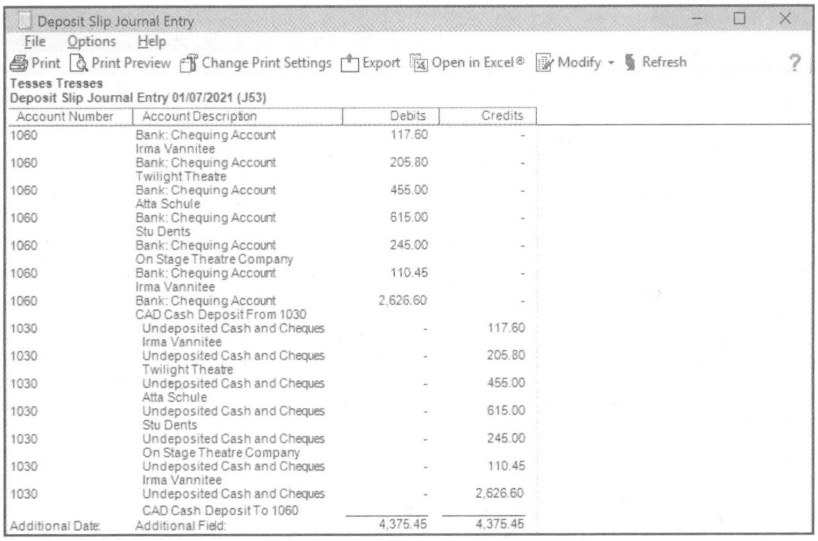
Deposit Slip Journal Entry

File Options Help

Print Print Preview Change Print Settings Export Open in Excel® Modify Refresh

Tesses Tresses
Deposit Slip Journal Entry 01/07/2021 (J53)

Account Number	Account Description	Debits	Credits
1060	Bank: Chequing Account Irma Vannitee	117.60	-
1060	Bank: Chequing Account Twilight Theatre	205.80	-
1060	Bank: Chequing Account Atta Schule	455.00	-
1060	Bank: Chequing Account Stu Dents	615.00	-
1060	Bank: Chequing Account On Stage Theatre Company	245.00	-
1060	Bank: Chequing Account Irma Vannitee	110.45	-
1060	Bank: Chequing Account CAD Cash Deposit From 1030	2,626.60	-
1030	Undeposited Cash and Cheques Irma Vannitee	-	117.60
1030	Undeposited Cash and Cheques Twilight Theatre	-	205.80
1030	Undeposited Cash and Cheques Atta Schule	-	455.00
1030	Undeposited Cash and Cheques Stu Dents	-	615.00
1030	Undeposited Cash and Cheques On Stage Theatre Company	-	245.00
1030	Undeposited Cash and Cheques Irma Vannitee	-	110.45
1030	Undeposited Cash and Cheques CAD Cash Deposit To 1060	-	2,626.60
Additional Date:	Additional Field:	4,375.45	4,375.45

In the journal entry, each cheque and cash amount is listed separately. The payer for each cheque is also included. Each deposit item is entered as a debit to *Bank: Chequing Account* and a credit to *Undeposited Cash and Cheques*. This detailed reporting makes it easier to find mistakes if any have been made.

Close the **Journal Entry Display** to return to the journal for corrections.

CORRECTING THE DEPOSIT SLIP JOURNAL ENTRY

To change the cheque part of the deposit, **click** the **Select button** for the **Cheque** part of the journal. To change a selection, **click** a **cheque** in the Cheques On Deposit Slip list and **click Remove**. To start again, **click Remove All** to clear the list. **Click Cancel** to close the Cheques Deposit form without saving changes.

If you need to make changes to the Cash part of the deposit, **click** the **Select button** on the **Cash** side of the Journal. **Click** the **incorrect amount** in the Count field and **type** the **correct amount. Press** tab to update the total. **Click Apply To Deposit Slip** to update the deposit amount that will be recorded. **Click Cancel** to close the Cash Deposit form without saving changes.

NOTES

The deposit slip entry is J53. Journal entry numbers 1 to 52 are accounted for in the transactions for January.

The order of cheques in the journal report matches the date of receipt (refer to pages 578 and 580). The default order in the Deposit Slip Journal is by cheque number.

WARNING!

You can look up deposit slips after posting them, but you cannot adjust them. You must make the correction with a General Journal entry. For example, you would reverse a deposit slip entry by debiting Undeposited Cash and Cheques and crediting Bank: Chequing Account. Then re-enter the individual cheques and cash amounts in the General Journal.

NOTES
If you get an error message about the form when you try to preview the deposit, click OK to open the Report & Form Settings. You must choose Deposit Slip in the Description field to preview the deposit slip, unless you are using your own customized forms.

You can also print the deposit slip from the journal's File menu, Print option.

NOTES
Click OK to confirm successful posting of transactions. We will not continue this reminder.

NOTES
For all deposits, choosing January 1 from the drop-down list in the On Or After field will include all cheques not yet deposited.

You should also preview and print the deposit slip before posting it.

Click the **Print Preview tool** or **choose** the **File menu** and **click Print Preview**. The preview includes the summary and the individual cheque and cash amounts on the deposit slip.

Click the **Print tool** in the Preview window to print the deposit slip.

Click **OK** to close the Preview window and return to the journal.

Click the **Post button** Post to save the transaction.

Enter the **remaining four deposits** for January. Remember to change the date for each deposit. The postdated rent cheques remain for future deposits.

DEPOSIT SLIP # 2 **JANUARY 14, 2021**

2

Date	Cheque #	Client	Amount
Jan 9	61	Irma Vannitee	$156.65
Jan 14	206	Brioche Bridal Party	140.87
		Total Cheques	$297.52
		Cash	$2 196.50
		(Consisting of 25 × $5; 24 × $10; 24 × $20; 11 × $50; 8 × $100; Coin $1.50)	
		Total Deposit	$2 494.02

DEPOSIT SLIP # 3 **JANUARY 21, 2021**

3

Date	Cheque #	Client	Amount
Jan 17	CC-61	Irma Vannitee	$159.85
Jan 20	74	Irma Vannitee	89.03
		Total Cheques	$248.88
		Cash	$2 535.75
		(Consisting of 25 × $5; 23 × $10; 24 × $20; 16 × $50; 9 × $100; Coin $.75)	
		Total Deposit	$2 784.63

DEPOSIT SLIP # 4 **JANUARY 28, 2021**

4

Date	Cheque #	Client	Amount
Jan 24	429	On Stage Theatre Company	$1 181.10
		Total Cheques	$1 181.10
		Cash	$2 248.25
		(Consisting of 27 × $5; 24 × $10; 21 × $20; 11 × $50; 9 × $100; Coin $3.25)	
		Total Deposit	$3 429.35

DEPOSIT SLIP # 5 **JANUARY 31, 2021**

5

Date	Cheque #	Client	Amount
Jan 29	238	Conn Seted	$ 59.80
Jan 31	498	On Stage Theatre Company	1 181.10
		Total Cheques	$1 240.90
		Cash	$2 863.50
		(Consisting of 12 × $5; 18 × $10; 21 × $20; 18 × $50; 13 × $100; Coin $3.50)	
		Total Deposit	$4 104.40

NOTES
At the end of January, the balance for Undeposited Cash and Cheques reflects the total of the four postdated rent cheques.

Close the **Reconciliation & Deposits Journal** and return to the Banking module window.

We are now ready to set up the bank accounts for reconciliation.

Account Reconciliation

For any bank account, the timing of monthly statements is usually not perfectly matched with the accounting entries of the corresponding transactions. Frequently some of the cheques written do not appear on the statement, and interest amounts earned on the account or bank charges are not yet recorded because they may be unknown until receipt of the statement. Thus the balance of the bank statement often does not match the General Ledger balance for the bank account on the same date. The process of identifying the differences to achieve a match is the process known as account reconciliation.

In Sage 50 you can apply account reconciliation to any Balance Sheet account for which you have regular statements, including credit card payable accounts. For each account you want to reconcile, you must complete the setup procedure.

✓ 6 **Memo #8** **Dated Jan. 31/21**

Set up account reconciliation for Bank: Chequing Account and Bank: Credit Cards.

Turning On the Account Reconciliation Feature

Before completing the reconciliation procedure, the General Ledger accounts that will be reconciled must be identified and modified. For the next stage, you will also need a report of all bank account transactions to compare with the bank statement. We will continue to work from the Banking module window to modify the account.

First, we will set up account reconciliation for *Bank: Chequing Account.*

Click **1060 Bank: Chequing Account** in the Banking module Home window Accounts list.

The ledger record for the bank account opens at the Account tab screen:

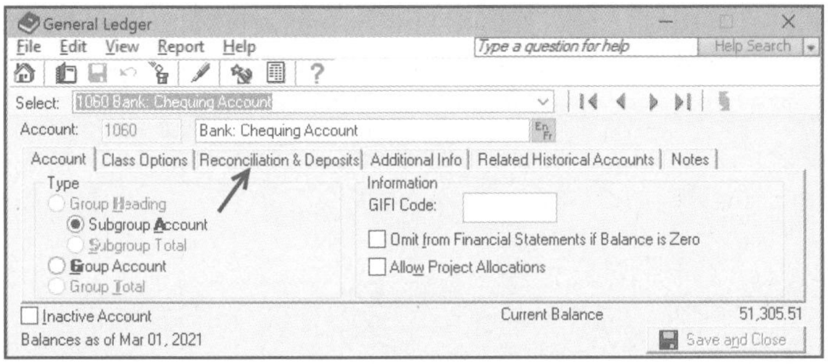

All postable Balance Sheet accounts have a Reconciliation & Deposits tab, but reconciliation is generally used for accounts with regular statements that summarize all transactions. Usually these are the bank accounts or credit card accounts.

Click the **Reconciliation & Deposits tab**:

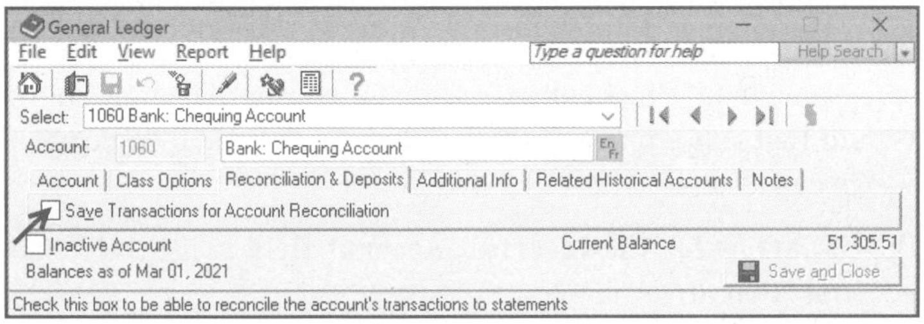

NOTES

Online bank reconciliation is explained in Appendix I on the Student DVD. The text enrichment Web site for this text is set up for online reconciliation so you can try this feature of the program.

Click **Save Transactions For Account Reconciliation** to add the Set Up button to the ledger window:

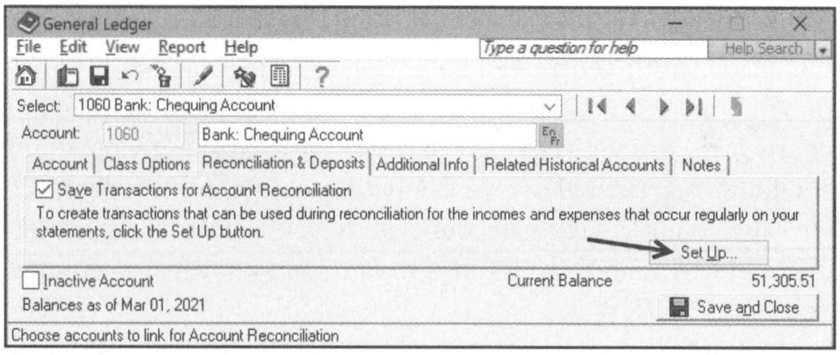

Naming and Linking Reconciliation Accounts

NOTES
You can save your work and exit at any time. Any changes you have made will be saved and you can continue from where you left off when you are ready.

NOTES
It is always preferable to correct journal entries before completing a reconciliation if you can find the error.

Most bank statements include monthly bank charges, loan or mortgage payments and interest on deposits. That is, there are usually some regular sources of income and expense. Normally the only source document for these bank account transactions is the bank statement. To use the account reconciliation feature in Sage 50, you should first create the accounts that link to these regular bank account transactions. In the January Bank Statement for Tesses Tresses on page 588, there is an interest deposit and a withdrawal for service charges. The salon already has accounts for both of these items.

The next step is to name bank statement–related transactions and identify the appropriate General Ledger accounts that link to these transactions. Tesses Tresses has income (interest received) from bank deposits and expenses associated with the bank account, such as bank charges or interest paid on bank loans. An additional account will be needed for adjustments — small discrepancies between the accounting entries and the bank statements, such as amounts entered incorrectly in journal transactions.

You can edit these names and accounts at any time, and you can add other sources of income or expense later if they are needed.

NOTES
You can enter these accounts at the time of reconciliation, but predefining them here will have them entered automatically in the journal (refer to page 596).

Click **Set Up** to display the Linked Accounts screen:

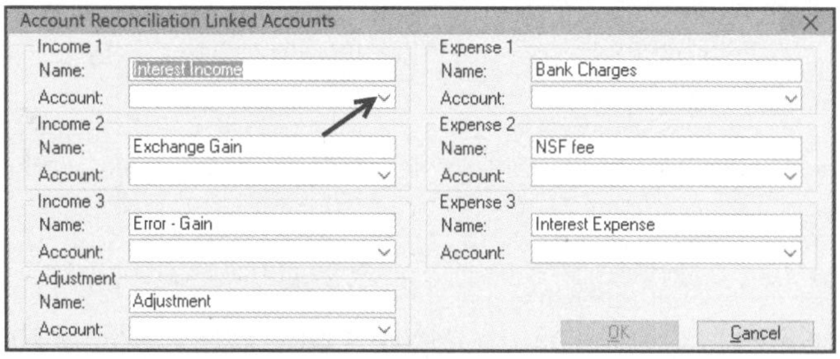

On this Account Reconciliation Linked Accounts form, you can identify up to three regular sources of income, three types of expenses and one adjustment account for each account you want to reconcile.

The name fields on this form cannot be left blank. You can leave the default names or enter "n/a" for "not applicable" if they are not needed.

The first Income Name field is highlighted, ready for editing. The only source of income for this account that is not recognized elsewhere is interest income. This name is already entered, so we can accept it.

NOTES
Although you can predefine only three income and expense accounts, you can add more income and expense transactions in the Account Reconciliation Journal and select other accounts for them.

Click the **list arrow for the Income 1 Account field** to list the revenue accounts that are available.

Click **4220 Interest Revenue**. **Press** tab to advance to the second Income field.

This field and the third Income field are not needed, so we will indicate that they are not applicable.

Type n/a

Press tab **twice** to skip the Account field and advance to the third Income field. **Type** n/a to indicate that it too is not applicable.

Leave the default name for adjustments unchanged.

Click the **Adjustment Account field list arrow**.

Either an expense or a revenue account can be used for adjustments. Tesses Tresses does not have an account for this purpose, so we will create a new expense account.

Type 5050 Reconciliation Adjustments

Press tab. **Click Add** to start the Add An Account wizard.

Accept the **remaining defaults** and **click Finish** to add the account to the Linked Accounts form. **Press** tab to advance the cursor.

NOTES
Typing the account number and name in the Account field for the new account will open the Add An Account wizard with this information already entered.

The Expense 1 Name field is highlighted. The salon has one automatic bank account–related expense, bank charges. NSF fee, the second expense, is also used but we do not expect this to be a regular expense. These names are already entered as the default, so we can accept them. Tesses Tresses uses the same account for both expenses.

Click the **Account field list arrow** for **Expense 1** to display the list of expense accounts.

Select **5040 Bank Charges** for this expense account.

Click the **Account field list arrow** for **Expense 2**.

Select **5040 Bank Charges** for this expense account.

Press tab to advance to the third Expense field.

Type n/a to indicate that it is not needed.

Check your **work** carefully. When you are certain that all the names and accounts are correct,

Click **OK** to save the new information. The Set Up button remains available because you can add and change linked accounts.

While the General Ledger is still open, we will set up the linked accounts for *Bank: Credit Cards*.

Click the **Next Account button** ▶ to open the ledger we need.

Click the **Reconciliation & Deposits tab** if necessary.

Click **Save Transactions For Account Reconciliation**.

Click **Set Up**.

Choose **4220** as the linked account for Interest Income.

Choose **5050** as the linked account for Adjustment. **Press** tab to advance to the Expense 1 Name field.

Type Card Fees **Press** tab.

Choose **5060** as the linked account for Card Fees.

Click **OK** to save the reconciliation accounts.

NOTES
You can enter "n/a" or leave the default names unchanged for the unused incomes and expenses.

Close the **Ledger window** to return to the Banking module window.

Reconciling the Bank Statement

Comparing the Bank Statement and Transactions Report

NOTES

The numbers in the Note column correspond to the explanation on pages 589–590.

1 Deposit recorded in December (outstanding prior transaction)

2 Deposit Slips: total amounts from deposit slips

3 Service charges

4 Interest received

5 Scheduled loan payments $2 100 (1 500 + 600)

✓ 7

Memo #9 **Dated Jan. 31/21**

Use the following bank statement to reconcile Bank: Chequing Account.

SAVERS TRUST

321 Queen St., Charlottetown, PE C1A 6D3 saverstrust.com

Tesses Tresses
55 Salon Road
Charlottetown, PE C1A 6D3

ACCOUNT STATEMENT
CHEQUING

Transit / Account No
02900 003 433 38-2

Statement period
Jan 1, 2021 to Jan 31, 2021

Date	Note #	Description	Deposits	Withdrawals	Balance
		Balance Fwd			37,238.00
2 Jan	1	Deposit	1,177.00		38,415.00
7 Jan		Cheque #410		926.10	37,488.90
7 Jan	2	Deposit	4,375.45		41,864.35
9 Jan		Cheque #411		330.00	41,534.35
14 Jan	2	Deposit	2,494.02		44,028.37
14 Jan		Cheque #412		241.50	43,786.87
14 Jan		Cheque #413		4,138.34	39,648.53
14 Jan		Transfer 0290 004 123 22-8	6,000.00		45,648.53
15 Jan		NSF Cheque #61		156.65	45,491.88
15 Jan	3	Service Charge – NSF cheque		40.00	45,451.88
17 Jan		Cheque #414		1,830.00	43,621.88
20 Jan		Cheque #415		143.75	43,478.13
21 Jan	2	Deposit	2,784.63		46,262.76
27 Jan		Cheque #416		431.00	45,831.76
27 Jan	5	Scheduled payment: loan		600.00	45,231.76
27 Jan	5	Scheduled payment: mortgage		1,500.00	43,731.76
28 Jan	2	Deposit	3,429.35		47,161.11
31 Jan	3	Service Charges		35.50	47,125.61
31 Jan	4	Interest	41.75		47,016.18
31 Jan		Closing balance			47,167.36

Total Deposits	# 7	$20,302.20
Total Withdrawals	# 12	$10,372.84

We need to compare this bank statement with the Bank Transaction Report provided by the program. Similar to the General Ledger Report, the Bank Account Transaction Report will include all transactions for the account.

Choose the **Reports menu**, then **choose Banking** and **click Bank Account Transactions Report**. The Modify Report window opens:

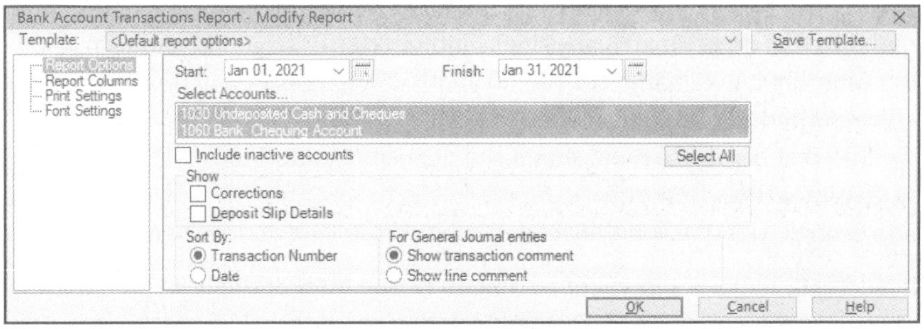

Only Bank and Cash class accounts are listed because the report is available only for bank accounts. The credit card bank account is not included because it is classified as a Credit Card Receivable account. In order to reconcile the credit card account, you can display or print the General Ledger Report for the period covering the bank statement.

For bank account reports, you can include corrections and deposit slip details or omit them. By default both items are omitted from the report. Since it is easier to work from a report that most closely matches the bank statement, you should omit corrections for this step. The deposit slip details do not appear on the bank statement, but they can be viewed or omitted in the Transactions Report. Because they can help us locate errors, we will include them at this stage. You may want to print the Transactions Report with and without deposit slip details to compare with the bank statement that has only the total deposit amounts.

You can report by date or transaction number and include transaction or line comments.

Click **1060 Bank: Chequing Account** to select the account.

The default report dates are correct. In an ongoing business, include the date of the oldest outstanding item from your previous bank statement up to the date of the most recent statement.

Click **Deposit Slip Details** to add the ✓. **Click** **OK** to view the report:

Bank Account Transactions Report

File Options Help

Print | Print Preview | Change Print Settings | Export | Open in Excel® | Modify | Refresh

Tesses Tresses
Bank Account Transactions Report 01/01/2021 to 01/31/2021
Sorted by: Transaction Number

Date	Comment	Source #	JE#	Debits	Credits	Balance
1060	**Bank: Chequing Account**					38,415.00 Dr
01/04/2021	Pro-Line Inc.	410	J14	-	926.10	37,488.90 Dr
01/09/2021	Fine Brushes	411	J17	-	330.00	37,158.90 Dr
01/10/2021	Atlantic Power Corp.: AP-57321...	412	J22	-	241.50	36,917.40 Dr
01/14/2021	Pro-Line Inc.	413	J24	-	4,138.34	32,779.06 Dr
01/14/2021	Memo 1, Transfer funds	FundsTran...	J25	6,000.00	-	38,779.06 Dr
01/14/2021	Receiver General for Canada: ...	414	J26	-	1,830.00	36,949.06 Dr
01/15/2021	Irma Vannitee	DM-61899	J27	-	156.65	36,792.41 Dr
01/18/2021	Eastern Tel: ET-4003, telephon...	415	J34	-	143.75	36,648.66 Dr
01/24/2021	Credit Card	416	J42	-	431.00	36,217.66 Dr
01/27/2021	Savers Trust - preauthorized wi...	DM-792218	J44	-	2,100.00	34,117.66 Dr
01/07/2021	Bank deposit	1	J53	117.60	-	34,235.26 Dr
01/07/2021	Bank deposit	1	J53	205.80	-	34,441.06 Dr
01/07/2021	Bank deposit	1	J53	455.00	-	34,896.06 Dr
01/07/2021	Bank deposit	1	J53	615.00	-	35,511.06 Dr
01/07/2021	Bank deposit	1	J53	245.00	-	35,756.06 Dr
01/07/2021	Bank deposit	1	J53	110.45	-	35,866.51 Dr
01/07/2021	Bank deposit	1	J53	2,626.60	-	38,493.11 Dr
01/14/2021	Bank deposit	2	J54	156.65	-	38,649.76 Dr
01/14/2021	Bank deposit	2	J54	140.87	-	38,790.63 Dr
01/14/2021	Bank deposit	2	J54	2,196.50	-	40,987.13 Dr
01/21/2021	Bank deposit	3	J55	159.85	-	41,146.98 Dr
01/21/2021	Bank deposit	3	J55	89.03	-	41,236.01 Dr
01/21/2021	Bank deposit	3	J55	2,535.75	-	43,771.76 Dr
01/28/2021	Bank deposit	4	J56	1,181.10	-	44,952.86 Dr
01/28/2021	Bank deposit	4	J56	2,248.25	-	47,201.11 Dr
01/31/2021	Bank deposit	5	J57	59.80	-	47,260.91 Dr
01/31/2021	Bank deposit	5	J57	1,181.10	-	48,442.01 Dr
01/31/2021	Bank deposit	5	J57	2,863.50	-	51,305.51 Dr
				23,187.85	10,297.34	

Print the **report** with and without deposit slip details so that you can compare it with the statement. **Close** the displayed **report** when finished.

Comparing the reports reveals the differences outlined below. The numbers with them correspond to the numbers in the margin Notes and the Note # column in the bank statement on page 588.

1 One deposit on January 2 appears on the bank statement and not in the Bank Transactions Report because the deposit was entered late in December.

PRO VERSION

pro The Bank Account Transactions Report is not available in the Pro version.

Use the General Ledger Report for account 1060 for this step. (Choose the Reports Menu, Financials and General Ledger.) Your report will have the deposit slip total amounts instead of details in the General Ledger Report.

NOTES

Printing the report with and without deposit slip details allows you to compare your entries with the bank statement and also to check your journal entries if the total amounts do not match.

Sorting by date will place the despoits in the correct order on the report.

NOTES

You can also compare the General Ledger Report with the bank statement, but you will not have the option to show individual deposit items on the deposit slips.

You can change the account class for Bank: Credit Cards to Bank. As a result of this change, you can print the Bank Account Transactions Report for it.

PRO VERSION

pro Remember that the General Ledger Report will have the deposit slip total amounts instead of details.

NOTES
These numbers correspond to the Note # column of the bank statement on page 588.
1 Deposit recorded in December
2 Deposit Slips: total amounts from deposit slips
3 Service charges
4 Interest received
5 Scheduled loan payments $2 100 (1 500 + 600)

2 Four deposits on the bank statement were multiple deposits entered on deposit slips and do not match any single entry in the Transactions Report.
3 Monthly bank charges of $35.50 and NSF charges of $40.00 have not been recorded in the Transactions Report.
4 Interest of $41.75 received on the deposit account does not appear in the Transactions Report.
5 A single General Journal entry combined the loan and mortgage payments.

In addition, deposit slip #5 for $4 104.40 — the total of the last three items in the report — is not listed on the bank statement, and the order of transactions is different. As a result of these differences, the total deposit and withdrawal amounts also differ.

All discrepancies must be accounted for in order to have the bank statement match the bank balance in the account's General Ledger or on the Balance Sheet.

Reconciling the Account

NOTES
Remember that you can save your work and exit at any time. Any changes you have made will be saved and you can continue from where you left off when you are ready.

NOTES
If you use online banking, you can download bank statement transactions and use the Match Bank Transactions icon and feature to match and clear transactions and reconcile the account. Refer to Appendix I on the Student DVD.

After entering the linked accounts, you can begin the reconciliation. The account reconciliation procedure in Sage 50 consists of the following steps:

1. Record the opening and ending balances from the bank statement for the account.
2. Add outstanding transactions from prior periods that were not resolved in the previous bank statement (only for the first reconciliation).
3. Identify all the deposits and withdrawals that have been processed by the bank.
4. Complete journal entries for any transactions for which the bank statement is the source document.

The result should be a match between the bank balances in the two statements. If the amounts do not match, the difference will be assigned to the linked Adjustment account. All these steps are completed in the Account Reconciliation Journal.

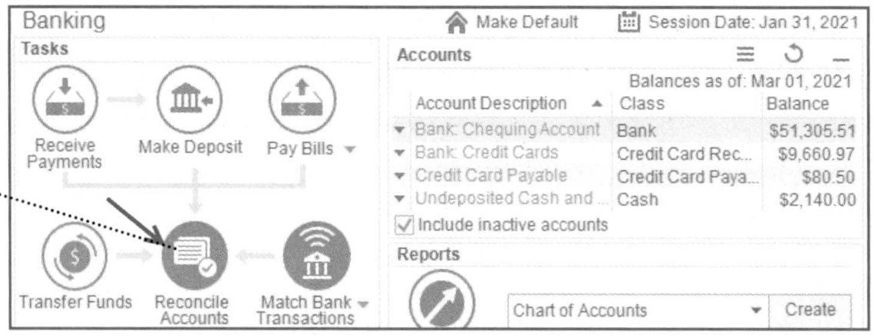

Account record balances in the Home window are displayed in ascending order at the latest transaction date, March 1, the date of the postdated rent cheques, as the Accounts pane informs us in the line above the accounts. The postdated cheques account for the *Undeposited Cash and Cheques* balance amount.

If you change User Preferences View Settings to view record balances as at the session date, the undeposited amount on January 31 will be zero:

CLASSIC VIEW
Click the Reconciliation & Deposits icon  to open the journal, and choose Account Reconciliation from the Transaction drop-down list if necessary.

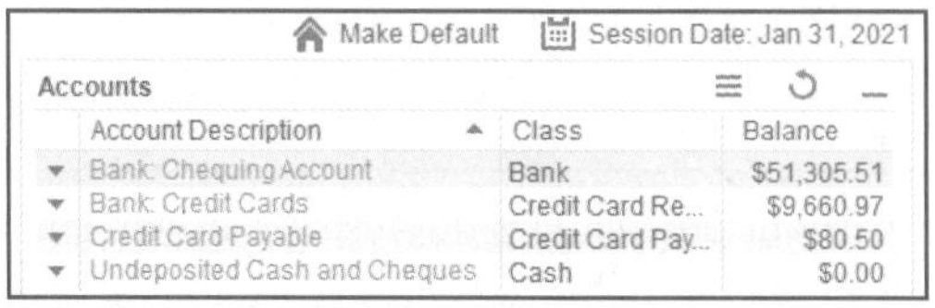

Make Default
Session Date: Jan 31, 2021
Accounts
Account Description
Class
Balance
Bank: Chequing Account
Bank
$51,305.51
Bank: Credit Cards
Credit Card Re...
$9,660.97
Credit Card Payable
Credit Card Pay...
$80.50
Undeposited Cash and Cheques
Cash
$0.00

NOTES
You can also start from the Accounts pane shortcuts list beside the bank account. Click the list arrow beside Bank: Chequing Account and choose Reconcile Account. The journal will open with the bank account already entered.

The additional information line (Balances As Of) above the accounts in the Accounts pane has been removed for this viewing option.

Click the **Reconcile Accounts icon**  to open the Reconciliation Journal:

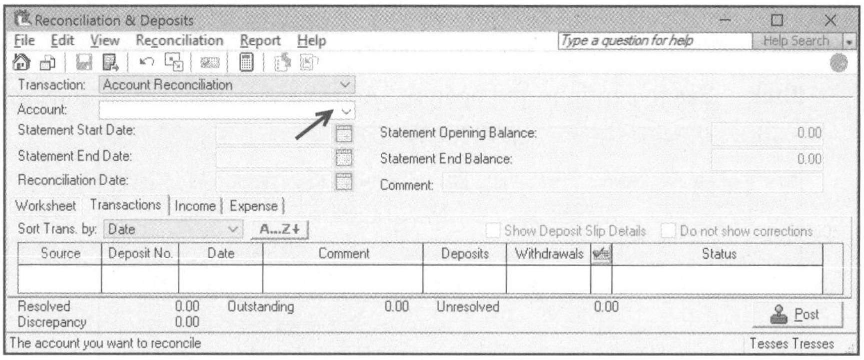

Click the **Account field list arrow**.

The list displays the bank and credit card accounts that we set up for account reconciliation. These are the only accounts available for reconciliation.

Select **1060 Bank: Chequing Account** to start the reconciliation:

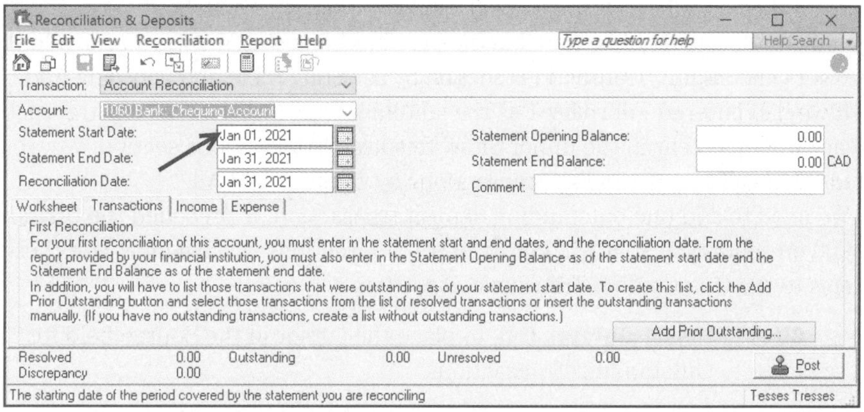

The account is added to the Account field. The first day of the month is entered as the Statement Start Date, and the session date is entered automatically in the Statement End Date field and the Reconciliation Date field. These dates will advance by one month — or the length of the reconciliation period of 31 days in this case — when you have finished reconciling the bank account for the current month. The dates for the first reconciliation are correct, so do not change them.

We need to add the opening and closing bank statement balances from page 588.

Click the **Statement Opening Balance field**.

Type 37238 **Press** tab to advance to the Statement End Balance field.

Type 47167.36 **Press** tab to advance to the Comment field.

Type January Bank Reconciliation

For the first reconciliation, we need to add one outstanding transaction from the previous period. A deposit of $1 177 appears on the bank statement but not in the ledger report. The deposit was made at the end of December, too late to be included in the December bank statement, so we need to add it now. Adding prior transactions in the Account Reconciliation Journal does not create a journal entry and does not affect the ledger balance. The step is necessary only to create a match between the bank statement and the current ledger.

Click **Add Prior Outstanding**. Sage 50 asks for confirmation:

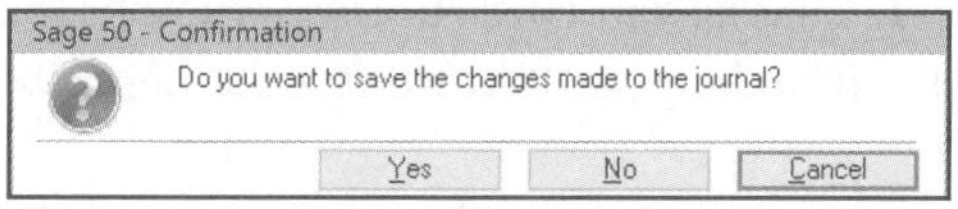

NOTES

There is no allocation option in the Account Reconciliation Journal but additional fields are available, as they are in the other journals.

NOTES

Read the instructions on the screen about the first reconciliation before proceeding. It advises that you must go through the step of adding prior transactions.

WARNING!
The first time you complete a reconciliation for any account, you must complete this step (click Add Prior Outstanding) even if there are no outstanding prior transactions. If there are no prior transactions to add, click OK from the Add Outstanding Transactions screen.

NOTES
The default date for showing resolved transactions is one month prior to the bank statement start date.

You must save the changes to the journal to continue. If you have not yet entered the account balances and dates, the Save Changes message will not open.

Click **Yes** to continue and open the Add Outstanding Transactions window:

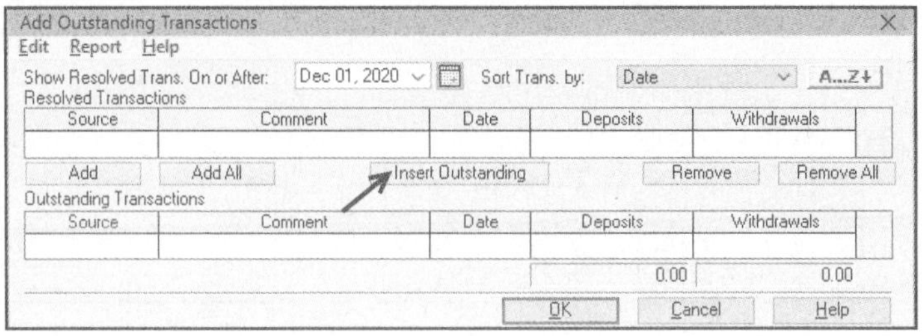

If there are no prior transactions that you need to insert, click OK at this stage to return to the journal.

If you have entered transactions in Sage 50 that precede the bank statement starting date, they will appear in the upper portion of the screen, in the Resolved Transactions section. If they have been resolved, you can leave them there. If, however, some of them were outstanding and not included in the previous bank statement, you can add them to the lower Outstanding Transactions section by selecting them and choosing Add.

If we had entered February 1 as the statement starting date, all the transactions for January would appear in the upper Show Resolved Transactions section. We would then include them all as outstanding transactions by clicking Add All.

We need to add one outstanding deposit transaction. It preceded the first entry in Sage 50 on January 1, so it will not be in the transactions list. We must add these types of items to the Outstanding Transactions section.

WARNING!
You cannot access the Outstanding Transactions input fields until you choose Insert Outstanding.

Click **Insert Outstanding** to place the cursor in the Source field for Outstanding Transactions.

Type `5117` to enter the client's cheque number as the Source.

Press *tab* to move to the Comment field. We will enter the client's name.

Type `Twilight Theatre` **Press** *tab* to move to the Date field.

December 31, 2020, is entered as the default date, the last date before our statement start date. This date is correct, so you do not need to change it. You can enter a different date if necessary.

NOTES
If all January transactions are already listed as Resolved Transactions, click Add All to place them in the lower Outstanding Transactions section. Then click Insert Outstanding to add a journal line for the December transaction. Additional prior transactions are inserted one at a time by clicking Insert Outstanding for each entry.

Press *tab* to move to the Deposits column.

Type `1177` **Press** *tab*.

If there are other outstanding prior transactions, enter them in the same way. For each additional outstanding transaction, you must click Insert Outstanding to move the cursor to the Source field on a new blank line for Outstanding Transactions.

If there are no prior transactions, click OK to return to the journal.

Click **OK** to return to the journal window.

NOTES
You can save your work at any time before posting and finish later from where you left off.

Marking Journal Entries as Cleared

You are now ready to begin processing individual journal entries to indicate whether they have been cleared in this bank statement. That is, you must indicate whether the bank has processed the items and the amounts have been withdrawn from or deposited to the account.

The journal window has been updated with outstanding transactions:

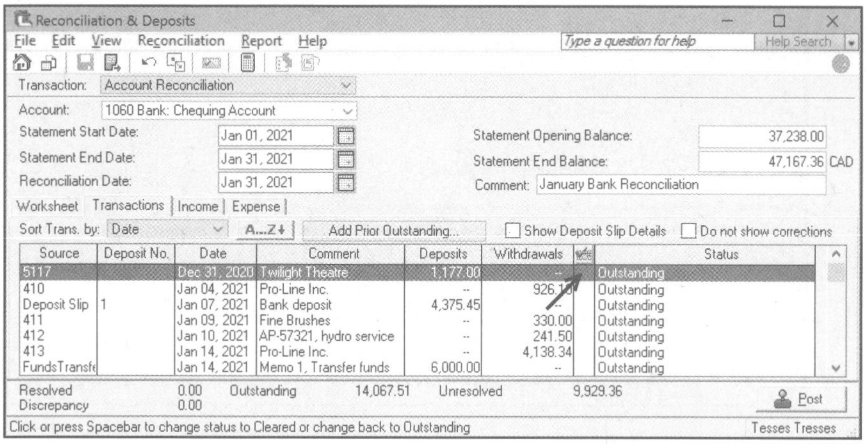

The Transactions tab is selected, and all January bank account transactions are now listed, including the one we just added. The bottom section of the screen contains a summary of the transactions. Our goal is to reduce the unresolved amount to zero with no discrepancy. At this stage, a discrepancy may indicate an incorrect account balance.

You can add or change the opening and end balances at this stage if necessary.

> **NOTES**
> Transactions are sorted by date in ascending order. You can also arrange them by source, comment, deposit amount, withdrawal amount, the order of entry (journal entry number) or deposit number. For any of these, you can choose ascending or descending order with the **A...Z** button. Choosing a different order may make it easier to find a specific transaction.

> **NOTES**
> The option to add prior transactions remains available until you post the reconciliation, so you can make further additions and corrections as needed.

Showing Corrections

You can hide correcting journal entries in the list of transactions by clicking **Do Not Show Corrections**. Removing incorrect and reversing entries can make the reconciliation easier by increasing the match with the statement. When you hide the corrections and then clear transactions, Sage 50 automatically applies the Reversed status to the original incorrect entry and the Adjustment status to the reversing entry created by Sage 50 (refer to page 595).

> **NOTES**
> Only the corrections made with the program's adjusting and reversing features will be hidden; manually reversed entries or corrections, like the NSF cheque on page 605, will not be hidden.

Group Deposits

Sometimes several cheques are deposited as a group, as they were on the weekly deposit slips. Each of these group deposits can now be cleared as a group. If you have not used the Deposit Slip Journal to record deposits, you can define a group deposit by entering the deposit slip number for each item in the Deposit No. field beside the Source. When you clear one item in the group, the others will be cleared at the same time.

You may want to drag the lower frame of the journal window or maximize the journal window to include more transactions on your screen at the same time.

You are now ready to mark the transactions that have been cleared, that is, the ones that appear on the bank statement.

Click the **Clear column** for **Cheque #5117** (click in the column), the first transaction on the list.

A checkmark appears in the Clear column, the Status has changed from Outstanding to Cleared and the Resolved Amount has increased to $1 177. As you clear each item, the Resolved and Unresolved amounts are updated.

Clear the **remaining journal entries** that appear on the bank statement on page 588 and scroll as necessary to display additional items.

Do not clear deposit slip #5 for $4 104.40.

> **NOTES**
> You can click the Clear column heading to clear all entries on the transactions list. Then you can click an individual ✓ to restore the Outstanding status if needed.

> **NOTES**
> Remember to clear the withdrawal on Jan. 27 for $2 100 to match the two bank statement entries for $600 and $1 500.

> **NOTES**
> The Outstanding Amount at the bottom of the journal is the amount for the outstanding deposit (deposit #5).

Your transactions list has been updated:

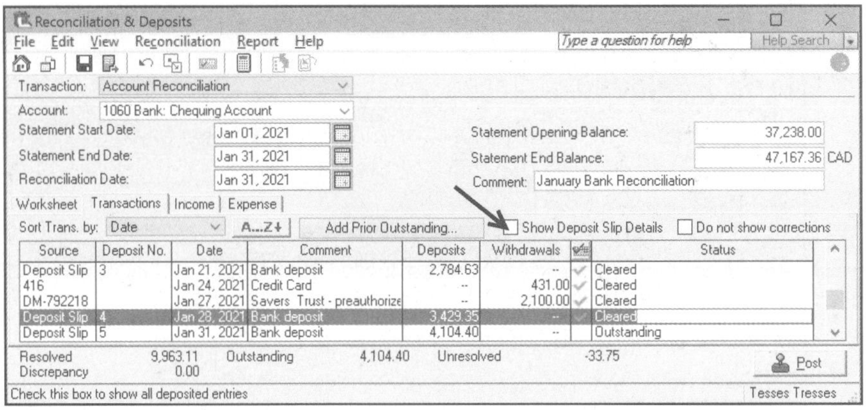

If you mark an item as Cleared by mistake, click the Clear column again to return the status to Outstanding.

After clearing all transactions from the bank statement, the unresolved amount should be –33.75. This is the net difference for the three unmatched bank statement items: the NSF charge, the service charge and the interest. Journal entries for these items will be added later (page 596).

The next section describes the procedure for clearing transactions that are different in some way, like NSF cheques. By marking their status correctly, you will have a more accurate picture of your business transactions. Cheque #61 for $156.65 from Irma Vannitee was returned as NSF and should be marked as such. This cheque was included on deposit slip #2 (refer to page 584).

Showing Deposit Slip Details

The NSF cheque we need to mark was part of a group deposit, so it does not appear individually on the Transactions list. First we need to include the details of the deposit slips. For this, we use the **Show Deposit Slip Details** option above the Transactions list (refer to the screenshot at the top of this page). Its check box is a toggle switch; you can hide the details when they are not required or include them if you need to change the status of a single item in the deposit group.

Click **Show Deposit Slip Details** to add a ✓.

> **NOTES**
> If you sort the transactions by Deposit Number, the deposit slip entries will appear together at the bottom of the list. If you sort by Source, they will appear together at the top of the list in our example because the deposit slip numbers (1 to 5) are smaller than all the cheque numbers.

All individual amounts on the deposit slips are now part of the transactions list, and all are marked as cleared because we cleared the entire deposit slip.

Press the **down scroll arrow** until the items for deposit slip #2 are included on your screen:

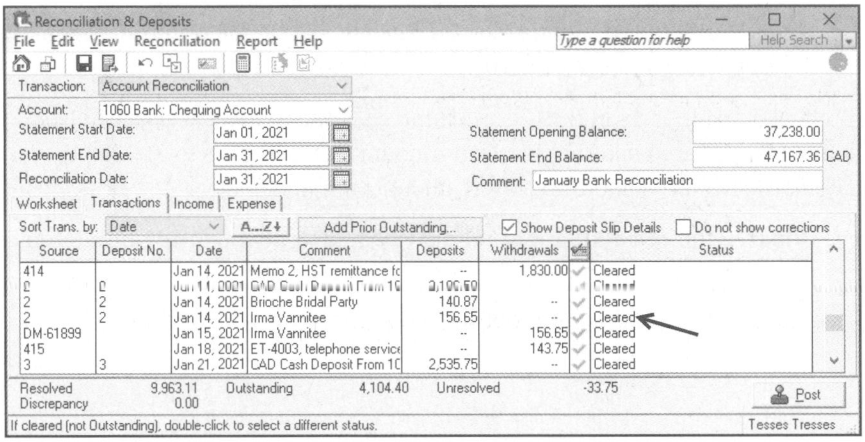

All three items on deposit slip #2, the two cheques and the cash amount, are marked as Cleared.

Marking NSF Cheques

For some items — for example, NSF cheques and their reversing entries — you should add further information because they have not cleared the account in the usual way.

To mark a cheque as NSF,

Click **Cleared** in the Status column for Irma Vannitee's cheque for $156.65 in deposit slip #2, the NSF cheque.

Press *enter* to display the alternatives for the Status of a journal entry:

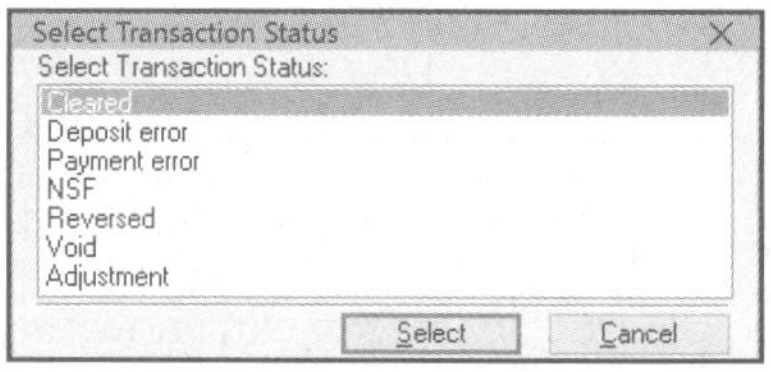

These status alternatives are explained in the Status Options chart that follows:

STATUS OPTIONS

Cleared	For deposits and cheques that have been processed correctly.
Deposit Error	For the adjusting journal entry that records the difference between the amount of a deposit that was recorded incorrectly and the bank statement amount for that deposit. Assign the Cleared status to the original entry for the deposit.
Payment Error	For the adjusting entry that records the difference between the amount of a cheque recorded incorrectly and the bank statement amount for that cheque. Assign the Cleared status to the original entry for the cheque.
NSF	For client cheques returned by the bank because there was not enough money in the client's account. Assign the Adjustment status to the adjusting entry that reverses the NSF cheque.
Reversed	For cheques that are cancelled by posting a reversing transaction entry to the bank account or the Sales or Purchases journals, that is, journal entries that are corrected. Assign the Adjustment status to the reversing entry that cancels the cheque.
Void	For cheques that are cancelled because of damage during printing. Assign the Adjustment status to the reversing entry that voids the cheque.
Adjustment	For the adjusting or reversing entries that are made to cancel NSF, void or reversed cheques. (Refer to the explanations for NSF, Void and Reversed above.)

Click **NSF** to highlight this alternative.

Click **Select** to enter it. The Cleared status changes to NSF for this item.

The final step is to change the status of the entry that reverses the payment or NSF cheque to Adjustment. The final certified cheque received in payment has been cleared normally, so its status as Cleared is already correct. Changing the status does not affect the resolved and unresolved amounts; the amounts are just cleared in different ways.

Double-click **Cleared in the Status column for Bank Debit Memo #61899**, the reversing entry (156.65 in the Withdrawals column).

Double-click **Adjustment** to select this as the status.

The unresolved, resolved and outstanding amounts have not changed.

NOTES

Void cheques are also used to set up automatic payments (direct deposit). Because these do not have amounts or journal entries associated with them, they will not appear in the Reconciliation Journal.

Your updated transactions list now has the revised status entries:

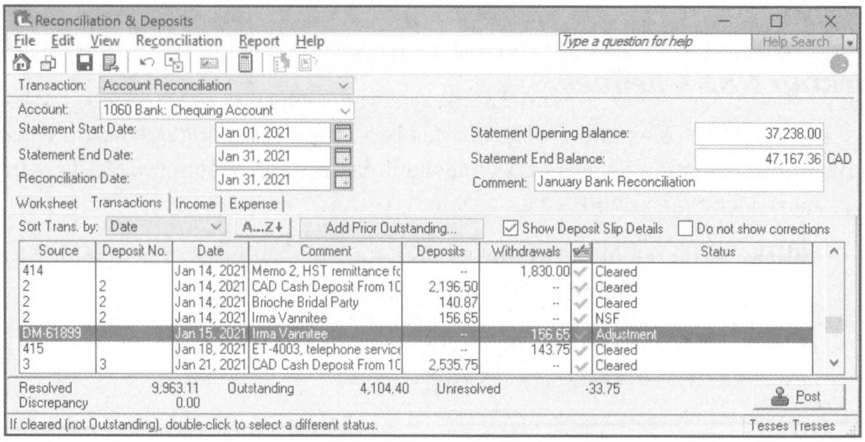

Click **Show Deposit Slip Details** to restore the summary version for deposits.

The status for deposit slip #2 has changed to Cleared again. You can show the details at any time again or, if you need to make corrections, by clicking the check box for it again.

The resolved, unresolved and outstanding amounts, the net of deposit and withdrawal amounts, are continually updated as you work through the reconciliation procedure. Your journal entry from the Report menu at this stage would have a credit to *Bank: Chequing Account* and a debit to the expense account *Reconciliation Adjustments* for $33.75, the unresolved amount at this stage — the net amount of interest and the two bank charges. The expense amount total is greater than the interest amount by $33.75. The journal entries for these items will reduce the unresolved amount to zero.

Adding Account Statement Journal Entries

Click the **Income tab**.

The Account Reconciliation Journal now includes journal entry fields:

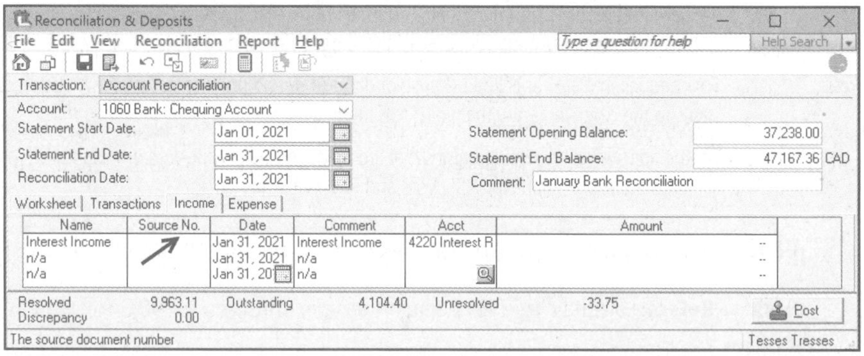

NOTES
You can drag the column heading margins if necessary to include all the input columns.

The entry for Interest Income — the income source we named earlier — is partially completed with the correct default entries for date, comment and account. You can change any of these entries by editing the contents or selecting a different account.

NOTES
You can select a different revenue account in the Reconciliation Journal for these predefined incomes if this is appropriate.

Click the **Source No. field** beside Interest Income to advance the cursor.

Type Bk-Stmt

Click the **Amount field**.

Type 41.75 **Press** *tab*. The unresolved amount — 75.50 — now matches the amount for the service fee plus the NSF charge.

You can edit these journal entries or transaction status entries at any time before posting. Choosing the **Save tool** will save the work you have completed so far, without posting, and still permit you to make changes later.

If there are other income categories, type the name, source, date, comment, account and amount on the second line. You can enter more than three sources of income on this form and you can choose any revenue account, although you can predefine only three linked accounts.

Click the **Expense tab** to open the input fields for expense transactions:

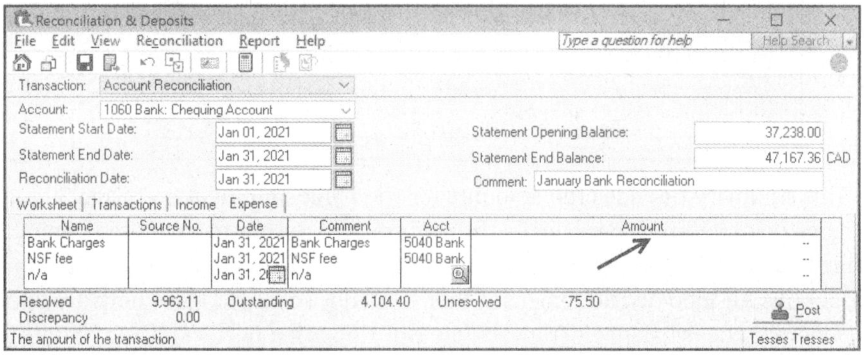

The expense transactions are also partially completed. We need to add the Source No. and the Amount. For the NSF fee, we need to change the date as well.

You can combine regular service charges with charges for other one-time or unusual services such as stopping a payment on a cheque or NSF fees. We have created a separate category for the NSF charge in order to track this expense. The bank statement contains the amounts for the expenses.

Click the **Source No. field**. Duplicate source document codes are allowed in this journal.

Type `Bk-Stmt`

Click the **Amount field**.

Type `35.50` **Press** tab to advance to the next journal line.

The unresolved amount is updated and matches the NSF charge. We can now enter the NSF service charges. You can use the same account for more than one journal entry, but you cannot choose the same expense or income category twice. The date for this charge was January 15, so we must also change the default date.

Click the **Source field**. We will enter the debit memo number as the source.

Type `DM61899` **Press** tab.

Type `Jan 15`

Click the **Amount field**. **Type** `40` **Press** tab to enter the amount.

If there are other expenses, enter the information in the same way. You can enter additional expenses and choose any expense account, although you can predefine only three linked accounts.

At this stage, your unresolved amount and discrepancy should be zero if everything is reconciled. We will look at the Worksheet — it summarizes the changes we made.

NOTES
Drag the column heading margins if necessary to include all the input columns.

NOTES
You can select a different expense account in the Reconciliation Journal for these predefined expenses if this is appropriate.

Click the **Worksheet tab**:

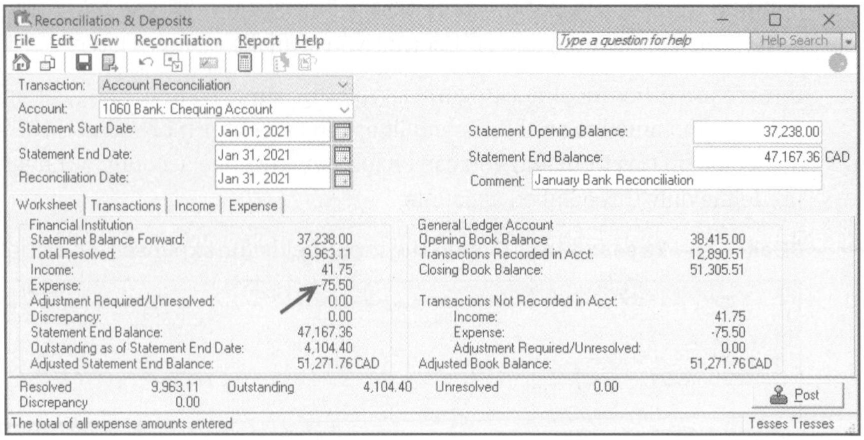

This summary provides the amounts for the bank statement and Sage 50 records that have been entered to reconcile the differences. Both lists have the opening and closing balances and net total transaction amounts. The Account Reconciliation Journal transactions for income and expenses that were not recorded elsewhere are added to the General Ledger balance (Transactions Not Recorded In Acct). Outstanding amounts that were in the General Ledger but not on the bank statement (Outstanding As Of Statement End Date) are added to the Bank Statement balance. The result is a match between the two adjusted balance amounts.

You should also review the Reconciliation Journal Entry before proceeding.

Press ctrl + **J**:

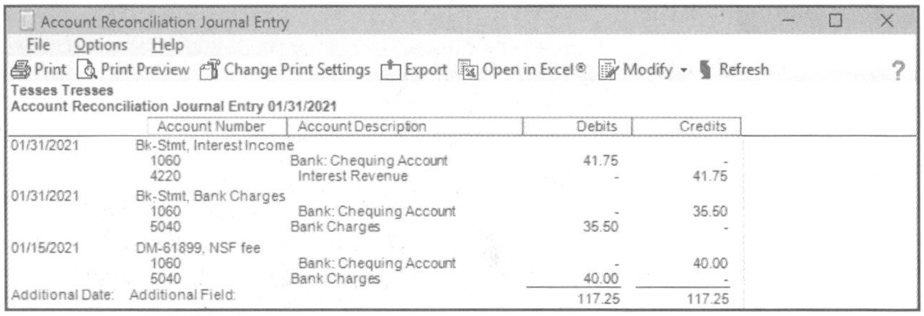

The income and expense journal entries are listed. In addition, an adjustment entry will be displayed if there is any unresolved amount.

Close the **Report window** when you have finished.

If the unreconciled amount is not zero, you should check your reconciliation journal entries to find whether you have made an error. Click each option and tab in the journal to review your work for the corresponding part of the reconciliation procedure. Make corrections if necessary. If you still have an unresolved amount, you can save the entry without posting and return later to try to determine whether you made a mistake or whether there was an error on the bank statement. You should also check your own original journal entries for possible errors as well.

Any discrepancy or unresolved amount will be posted as an adjustment to the *Reconciliation Adjustments* expense account created earlier. This account should be used only for small amounts not significant enough to warrant a separate journal entry, such as differences from payroll tax rates in this text.

Click the **Save button**. **Click** to close the journal without posting.

Back up the **data file**. **Open** the **Account Reconciliation Journal**, **select 1060 Bank: Chequing Account** and resume your work.

NOTES
The Opening Book Balance for the General Ledger Account includes the amount of the prior transaction we added.

WARNING!
You cannot adjust Account Reconciliation Journal entries, and correcting them after posting is quite difficult.

Do not post the Account Reconciliation Journal transaction until the unresolved amount is zero (or a small discrepancy that you can explain). You can click the Save button to save your work before posting, exit the journal and return later to find the error and make corrections.

NOTES
The program will warn you before posting an unresolved amount, allowing you to correct any mistakes before posting the journal entries.

NOTES
The confirmation message informs you that three journal entries were posted – the interest and expense transactions.

Click [Post]. You are ready to reconcile the next account.

✓ 8 **Memo #10** **Dated Jan. 31/21**

Use the following bank statement to reconcile Bank: Credit Cards. There is one outstanding item from the previous month: Sale #457 for $230 to Cash Sales was deposited on Dec. 31, 2020.

SAVERS TRUST

321 Queen St., Charlottetown, PE C1A 6D3 saverstrust.com

Tesses Tresses
55 Salon Road
Charlottetown, PE C1A 6D3

ACCOUNT STATEMENT
CREDIT CARD

Transit / Account No
02900 004 123 22-8

Statement period
Jan 1, 2021 to Jan 31, 2021

Date	Description	Deposits	Withdrawals	Balance
	Balance Fwd			1,970.00
2 Jan	Deposit	230.00		2,200.00
2 Jan	Deposit	2,682.12		4,882.12
9 Jan	Deposit	2,960.74		7,842.86
14 Jan	Transfer to 0290 003 433 38-2		6,000.00	1,842.86
16 Jan	Deposit	2,764.93		4,607.79
23 Jan	Deposit	2,742.55		7,350.34
30 Jan	Deposit	2,310.63		9,660.97
31 Jan	Service Charges		22.50	9,638.47
31 Jan	Interest	6.50		9,644.97
31 Jan	Closing balance			9,644.97

Total Deposits # 7 $13,697.47
Total Withdrawals # 2 $6,022.50

Choose **account 1080**.

Enter a **comment** and the **opening** and **closing bank statement balances**.

Enter the **prior outstanding transaction**.

Clear **transactions** to process the statement items.

Add **journal entries** for **service charges** and **interest**. **Review** your **work**, **make corrections** if necessary and then **post** the **transaction**.

Add **Shortcuts** for transactions in other modules, or change modules as needed.

Change the **session date** to **February 7** and then **enter** the **transactions for February** until the NSF cheque on Feb. 25.

9 **Payment Cheque #417** **Dated Feb. 2/21**

To Sharp Scissors, $920.00 in payment of account. Reference invoice #SS-432.

10 **Sales Invoice #482** **Dated Feb. 2/21**

To Irma Vannitee:

1	BRS1	Hair Brush: natural bristle	$32 each
1	CN2	Pro-Line Hot Oil Treatment 75 ml	35 each
1	SRV3	Cut and Style	48 each
1	SRV5	Perm	88 each
	HST		15%

Terms: 2/5, n/15.

NOTES

Refer to keystrokes beginning on page 590 to complete the reconciliation.

There are no deposit slips.

NOTES

HST applies to the purchase and sale of all merchandise sold and services offered by the salon.

NOTES

Ignore the message about late payments for Vannitee.

NOTES
All these inventory items are purchased in units of dozens. Therefore, the quantity 2 represents 24 units. Purchase orders were entered in January.

11

Purchase Invoice #PL-1988 **Dated Feb. 4/21**

From Pro-Line Inc., to fill purchase order #52:

2	CN1	Pro-Line Conditioner: 150 ml	$ 432.00
2	CN2	Pro-Line Hot Oil Treatment 75 ml	456.00
2	FRZ1	Pro-Line Defrizzer: cream 100 ml	408.00
2	GEL1	Pro-Line Spray Gel: shaper 150 ml	384.00
2	SHM1	Pro-Line Shampoo: 225 ml	408.00
2	SPR1	Pro-Line Hair Spray: gentle 150 ml	360.00
	HST	15%	367.20
	Invoice total		$2 815.20

Terms: 2/10, n/30.

12

Cash Purchase Invoice #CCT-21-2 **Dated Feb. 4/21**

From Charlottetown City Treasurer, $220 plus $33 HST for water and sewage treatment for three months. Purchase invoice total $253 paid by cheque #418. (Use the Utilities account and add the tax code.)

13

Sales Invoice #483 **Dated Feb. 4/21**

To Conn Seted:

1	FRZ1	Pro-Line Defrizzer: cream 100 ml	$28 /jar
1	GEL1	Pro-Line Spray Gel: shaper 150 ml	27 /can
1	SRV1	Colour	55 each
1	SRV3	Cut and Style	48 each
	HST		15%

Terms: net 15.

NOTES
Sales Invoice #484 provides services for four theatre performances for six cast members. Do not fill the order. Enter the numbers in the Quantity field. The remainder of the order will be filled later.

14

Sales Invoice #484 **Dated Feb. 5/21**

To Twilight Theatre to partially fill sales order #102:

6	SRV3	Cut and Style	$42 each
18	SRV6	Wash and Style	21 each
	HST		15%

Terms: 2/5, n/15.

15

Cash Purchase Invoice #CCT-299392 **Dated Feb. 6/21**

From Charlottetown City Treasurer, $4 800 for annual property tax assessment, payable in three equal instalments of $1 600. First instalment is due on receipt of invoice. Remaining two instalments are due May 6 and August 6. Issue cheques #419, 420 and 421 dated February 6, May 6 and August 6 in payment of account. Create new Group account 5380 Property Taxes. Store as a quarterly recurring entry and recall the entry for the two postdated payments.

NOTES
You will need to change the payment method for credit card sales when you choose Cash Customers. The default payment method is Cash.

16

Credit Card Sales Invoice #485 **Dated Feb. 6/21**

Sales Summary for credit card sales (to Cash Customers):

4	BRS1	Hair Brush: natural bristle	$ 32 each	$ 128.00
4	CN1	Pro-Line Conditioner: 150 ml	34 /bottle	136.00
3	FRZ1	Pro-Line Defrizzer: cream 100 ml	28 /jar	84.00
3	GEL1	Pro-Line Spray Gel: shaper 150 ml	27 /can	81.00
8	SHM1	Pro-Line Shampoo: 225 ml	26 /bottle	208.00
26	SRV3	Cut and Style	48 each	1 248.00
5	SRV4	Highlights	110 each	550.00
6	SRV6	Wash and Style	26 each	156.00
	HST		15%	388.65
	Invoice total paid by credit cards			$2 979.65

Deposited to credit card bank account.

17 **Credit Card Purchase Invoice #AUN-344** **Dated Feb. 7/21**

From All U Need department store, $300 plus $45 HST for 100 white hand towels for use in the salon. Purchase invoice total $345 paid in full by credit card. Change the default account.

18 **Cash Sales Invoice #486** **Dated Feb. 7/21**

Sales Summary for cash sales (to Cash Customers):

6	BRS2	Hair Brush: styling	$24 each	$ 144.00
4	CN2	Pro-Line Hot Oil Treatment 75 ml	35 /tube	140.00
5	GEL1	Pro-Line Spray Gel: shaper 150 ml	27 /can	135.00
5	SPR1	Pro-Line Hair Spray: gentle 150 ml	26 /can	130.00
4	SRV1	Colour	55 each	220.00
24	SRV3	Cut and Style	48 each	1 152.00
	HST		15%	288.15
Invoice total paid by cash				$2 209.15

Deposited to Undeposited Cash and Cheques.

19 **DEPOSIT SLIP # 6** **FEBRUARY 7, 2021**

Date	Cheque #	Client	Amount
Feb 1	416	Atta Schule	$ 455.00
Feb 1	162	Stu Dents	615.00
		Total Cheques	$1 070.00
		Cash	$2 209.15
		(Consisting of 17 × $5; 16 × $10; 18 × $20; 14 × $50; 9 × $100; Coin $4.15)	
		Total Deposit	$3 279.15

SESSION DATE – FEBRUARY 14, 2021

20 **Cash Purchase Invoice #AP-63322** **Dated Feb. 8/21**

From Atlantic Power Corp., $260 plus $39 HST for hydro services for one month. Purchase invoice total $299 paid by cheque #422.

21 **Sales Invoice #487** **Dated Feb. 9/21**

To Brioche Bridal Party to partially fill sales order #101:

3	SRV3	Cut and Style	$48 each
	HST		15%

Terms: 2/5, n/15.

22 **Sales Invoice #488** **Dated Feb. 9/21**

To Irma Vannitee:

1	SRV6	Wash and Style	$26
	HST		15%

Terms: 2/5, n/15. Store as a weekly recurring entry.

NOTES

Ignore the messages about late payments for Vannitee because her cheque is on hand.

23 **Purchase Invoice #Z-6775** **Dated Feb. 10/21**

From Zines Inc., $130 plus $19.50 HST to renew subscriptions for one year to hair and fashion magazines (Prepaid Subscriptions account). Purchase invoice total $149.50. Terms: net 10.

24 **Receipt #144** **Dated Feb. 10/21**

From Irma Vannitee, cheque #93 for $263.35 in payment of account. Reference sales invoices #478 and 482.

25

Purchase Order #55 **Dated Feb. 10/21**

Delivery date Feb. 22/21
From Air Pro, $300 for two bonnet-style hair dryers and $50 for two handheld hair dryers plus $52.50 HST. Purchase order total $402.50. Terms: net 15.

26

Purchase Invoice #FB-27731 **Dated Feb. 10/21**

From Fine Brushes, to fill purchase order #53 (to stock up for anticipated Valentine's purchases):

30	BRS1	Hair Brush: natural bristle	$ 570.00
20	BRS2	Hair Brush: styling	300.00
	HST	15%	130.50
	Invoice total		$1 000.50

Terms: net 20.

27

Payment Cheque #423 **Dated Feb. 10/21**

To Pro-Line Inc., $2 758.90 in full payment of account including $56.30 discount for early payment. Reference invoice #PL-1988.

28

Sales Invoice #489 **Dated Feb. 11/21**

To Proud Family:

2	BRS1	Hair Brush: natural bristle	$ 32 each
2	BRS2	Hair Brush: styling	24 each
2	SHM1	Pro-Line Shampoo: 225 ml	26 each
4	SRV3	Cut and Style	48 each
1	SRV4	Highlights	110 each
1	SRV5	Perm	88 each
	HST		15%

Terms: net 15.

29

Credit Card Sales Invoice #490 **Dated Feb. 13/21**

Sales Summary for credit card sales (to Cash Customers):

8	BRS1	Hair Brush: natural bristle	$ 32 each	$ 256.00
6	BRS2	Hair Brush: styling	24 each	144.00
5	CN1	Pro-Line Conditioner: 150 ml	34 /bottle	170.00
8	SHM1	Pro-Line Shampoo: 225 ml	26 /bottle	208.00
30	SRV3	Cut and Style	48 each	1 440.00
7	SRV4	Highlights	110 each	770.00
3	SRV5	Perm	88 each	264.00
4	SRV6	Wash and Style	26 each	104.00
	HST		15%	503.40
	Invoice total paid by credit cards			$3 859.40

Deposited to credit card bank account.

30

Cash Sales Invoice #491 **Dated Feb. 14/21**

Sales Summary for cash sales (to Cash Customers):

6	BRS2	Hair Brush: styling	$ 24 each	$ 144.00
3	FRZ1	Pro-Line Defrizzer: cream 100 ml	28 /jar	84.00
8	GEL1	Pro-Line Spray Gel: shaper 150 ml	27 /can	216.00
7	SPR1	Pro-Line Hair Spray: gentle 150 ml	26 /can	182.00
6	SRV1	Colour	55 each	330.00
24	SRV3	Cut and Style	48 each	1 152.00
2	SRV4	Highlights	110 each	220.00
	HST		15%	349.20
	Invoice total paid by cash			$2 677.20

Deposited to Undeposited Cash and Cheques.

31 **Purchase Invoice #SS-555** **Dated Feb. 14/21**

From Sharp Scissors, to fill purchase order #54, $600 plus $90 HST for professional high-grade stainless steel stylist scissors. Purchase invoice total $690. Terms: net 10.

32 **DEPOSIT SLIP # 7** **FEBRUARY 14, 2021**

Date	Cheque #	Client	Amount
Feb 10	93	Irma Vannitee	$263.35
		Total Cheques	$263.35
		Cash	$2 677.20
		(Consisting of 23 × $5; 27 × $10; 27 × $20; 17 × $50; 9 × $100; Coin $2.20)	
		Total Deposit	$2 940.55

33 **Memo #11** **Dated Feb. 14/21**

From Owners: Transfer $12 000 from credit card account to chequing account.

SESSION DATE – FEBRUARY 21, 2021

34 **Sales Invoice #492** **Dated Feb. 16/21**

To Irma Vannitee:

1	SRV6	Wash and Style	$26 each
	HST		15%

Terms: 2/5, n/15. Recall stored transaction.

35 **Memo #12** **Dated Feb. 17/21**

From Owners: Pay HST owing to the Receiver General for the period ending January 31, 2021. Issue cheque #424 in payment.

NOTES

You can use the Tax Report for HST for January to obtain the HST amounts for the remittance, or you can refer to the General Ledger Report for the two HST accounts.

36 **Cash Purchase Invoice #ET-4588** **Dated Feb. 17/21**

From Eastern Tel, $130 plus $19.50 HST for telephone service. Purchase invoice total $149.50 paid in full by cheque #425.

37 **Sales Quote #103** **Dated Feb. 19/21**

First performance date Mar. 1/21

To On Stage Theatre Company (for 12 theatre performances for three cast members) at preferred customer prices:

3	SRV3	Cut and Style	$42 each
36	SRV6	Wash and Style	21 each
9	SRV7	Wig Wash, Set and Style	26 each
	HST		15%

Terms: 2/5, n/15.

38 **Receipt #145** **Dated Feb. 19/21**

From Conn Seted, cheque #269 for $181.70 in payment of account. Reference invoice #483.

39 **Receipt #146** **Dated Feb. 19/21**

From Twilight Theatre, cheque #5635 for $724.50 in payment of account. Reference invoice #484.

40 **Credit Card Purchase Invoice #SP-399** **Dated Feb. 20/21**

From Seaside Papers, $200 plus $30 HST for office supplies for salon. Purchase invoice total $230 paid in full by credit card.

41

Receipt #147 **Dated Feb. 20/21**

From Brioche Bridal Party, cheque #986 for $165.60 in payment of account. Reference invoice #487.

42

Credit Card Sales Invoice #493 **Dated Feb. 20/21**

Sales Summary for credit card sales (to Cash Customers):

3	BRS1	Hair Brush: natural bristle	$32 each	$ 96.00
2	CN2	Pro-Line Hot Oil Treatment 75 ml	35 /tube	70.00
2	FRZ1	Pro-Line Defrizzer: cream 100 ml	28 /jar	56.00
7	SPR1	Pro-Line Hair Spray: gentle 150 ml	26 /can	182.00
6	SRV1	Colour	55 each	330.00
26	SRV3	Cut and Style	48 each	1 248.00
	HST		15%	297.30
	Invoice total paid by credit cards			$2 279.30

Deposited to credit card bank account.

43

Cash Sales Invoice #494 **Dated Feb. 21/21**

Sales Summary for cash sales (to Cash Customers):

5	BRS2	Hair Brush: styling	$24 each	$ 120.00
8	CN1	Pro-Line Conditioner: 150 ml	34 /bottle	272.00
6	GEL1	Pro-Line Spray Gel: shaper 150 ml	27 /can	162.00
4	SHM1	Pro-Line Shampoo: 225 ml	26 /bottle	104.00
3	SRV1	Colour	55 each	165.00
21	SRV3	Cut and Style	48 each	1 008.00
10	SRV6	Wash and Style	26 each	260.00
	HST		15%	313.65
	Invoice total paid by cash			$2 404.65

Deposited to Undeposited Cash and Cheques.

44

DEPOSIT SLIP #8 Date: Feb 21, 2021

Tesses Tresses
55 Salon Rd.
Charlottetown PE C1A 6D3

Account No: 02900 3433382

Cheques

269	Conn Seted	181.70
5635	Twilight Theatre	724.50
986	Brioche Bridal Party	165.60

Amount

18	× 5	90	00
33	× 10	330	00
34	× 20	680	00
14	× 50	700	00
6	× 100	600	00
	coin	4	65
Total cash		2404	65
Total cheque		1071	80
Subtotal		3476	45
Cash received			
Net Deposit		3476	45

Signature *Tess Dubois*

02/21/21 PW

45 **Credit Card Purchase Invoice #AUN-478** **Dated Feb. 21/21**

From All U Need department store, $90 plus $13.50 HST for cleaning supplies. Purchase invoice total $103.50 paid in full by credit card.

46 **Purchase Order #56** **Dated Feb. 21/21**

Shipping date Mar. 3/21
From Lookin' Good, $400 plus $60 HST for 25 polyester and nylon water-resistant monogrammed capes for salon client use. Unit price is $16. Purchase invoice total $460. Terms: net 10.

47 **Payment Cheque #426** **Dated Feb. 21/21**

To Sharp Scissors, $690 in payment of account. Reference invoice #SS-555.

SESSION DATE – FEBRUARY 28, 2021

48 **Purchase Invoice #AP-7111** **Dated Feb. 23/21**

From Air Pro, to fill purchase order #55, $350 plus $52.50 HST for two bonnet-style hair dryers and two handheld hair dryers. Purchase invoice total $402.50. Terms: net 15.

49 **Sales Invoice #495** **Dated Feb. 23/21**

To Irma Vannitee:

1	SRV6	Wash and Style	$26 each
	HST		15%

Terms: 2/5, n/15. Recall stored transaction.

50 **Sales Invoice #496** **Dated Feb. 23/21**

To Brioche Bridal Party to fill remainder of sales order #101:

5	SRV6	Wash and Style	$26 each
	HST		15%

Terms: 2/5, n/15.

51 **Credit Card Bill Payment #2-21** **Dated Feb. 24/21**

From credit card company, $425.50 for purchases made before Feb. 11 and $24 for card fees. Total payment due to avoid interest penalty $449.50. Issued cheque #427 for $449.50 in full payment.

NOTES
You will be warned about using the next cheque number for the credit card payment.

Reversing NSF Cheques on Deposit Slips

In previous chapters, we reversed NSF cheques with the Reverse Receipt shortcut tool in the Adjusting receipt window of the Receipts Journal. In these cases, *Bank: Chequing Account* was the linked principal bank account for the Receivables module, so the cheque was recorded (deposited) directly to this account. The reversing procedure would select this same account. For Tesses Tresses, *Undeposited Cash and Cheques* is the principal linked bank account for deposits. The NSF cheque, however, is withdrawn from *Bank: Chequing Account* — until we deposit the cheque in the bank its validity is unknown. For this situation, we need to enter a negative receipt for the paid invoice that credits *Bank: Chequing Account*. The following steps describe the procedure for reversing the cheque from Brioche Bridal Party.

52 ✓ **Bank Debit Memo #983321** **Dated Feb. 25/21**

From Savers Trust Co., cheque #986 from Brioche Bridal Party was returned because of insufficient funds. The cheque amount, $165.60, was withdrawn from the chequing account.

WARNING!
Do not reverse the receipt to record this NSF cheque.

Open the **Receipts Journal**.

Choose **Brioche Bridal Party** as the client.

Choose **1060 Bank: Chequing Account** from the drop-down list in the Deposit To field.

Click the **Cheque field** so we can enter the client cheque number.

Type NSF-986

Click the **Receipt No. field**. We will enter the bank debit number here.

Type DM-983321 **Enter February 25** as the date for the transaction.

Click the **Include Fully Paid Invoices/Deposits tool** or **choose** the **Receipt menu** and **click Include Fully Paid Invoices/Deposits**.

The two paid invoices (#468 and #487) are added to the form with the unpaid invoice. Invoice #487 was paid with the NSF cheque, so we need to select it.

Click **487** in the Invoice Or Deposit column.

Press tab until the cursor is in the Amount Received column for the line. We need to enter the full amount of the cheque as a negative number.

Type -165.60 **Press** tab to enter the amount.

The discount for the unpaid invoice is now selected and we need to remove it.

Press del to complete the entry.

Review the **journal entry**.

Accounts Receivable has been debited to restore the amount owing, and *Bank: Chequing Account* is credited to reverse the previous deposit. Verify that the discount for the unpaid invoice is not included.

Close the **journal display** and then **post** the **receipt**.

Click the **Include Fully Paid Invoices/Deposits tool**.

Choose **Brioche Bridal Party** again.

The invoice amount owing has been fully restored. When the payment is received, you will enter it in the usual way.

Close the **Receipts Journal** and **continue** with the **remaining transactions**.

WARNING!
Remember to delete the selected discounts and amounts for any other invoices.

NOTES
If a discount has been included with the payment, you will need to reverse it as well. Enter the amount of the discount as a negative amount in the Discount Taken field and press tab. The cheque amount may automatically be entered as the Amount Received, with the minus sign added. If it is not, enter it as a negative amount.

You should review the entry carefully before posting and then check the Receipts Journal again for the customer to ensure that the invoice has been fully restored.

53 **Memo #13** **Dated Feb. 25/21**

Prepare sales invoice #497 for $30 to charge Brioche Bridal Party for the NSF fee. Credit Other Revenue. Terms: net 15. (Do not charge tax or allow discount.)

NOTES
For Brioche, you may get an advisory message about the client often paying late.

54 **Receipt #148** **Dated Feb. 27/21**

From Brioche Bridal Party, certified cheque #RBC7333 for $195.60 in payment of account. Reference invoices #487 and #497 and bank debit memo #983321.

55 **Sales Invoice #498** **Dated Feb. 27/21**

To Twilight Theatre to fill the remainder of sales order #102 (for four nights of theatre performances for four cast members) at preferred customer prices.

4	SRV3	Cut and Style	$42 each
16	SRV6	Wash and Style	21 each
4	SRV7	Wig Wash, Set and Style	26 each
	HST		15%

Terms: 2/5, n/15.

56 **Credit Card Sales Invoice #499** **Dated Feb. 27/21**

Sales Summary for credit card sales (to Cash Customers):

6	BRS2	Hair Brush: styling	$24 each	$ 144.00
4	CN1	Pro-Line Conditioner: 150 ml	34 /bottle	136.00
6	FRZ1	Pro-Line Defrizzer: cream 100 ml	28 /jar	168.00
8	SPR1	Pro-Line Hair Spray: gentle 150 ml	26 /can	208.00
3	SRV1	Colour	55 each	165.00
26	SRV3	Cut and Style	48 each	1 248.00
2	SRV5	Perm	88 each	176.00
2	SRV6	Wash and Style	26 each	52.00
	HST		15%	344.55
	Invoice total paid by credit cards			$2 641.55

Deposited to credit card bank account.

57 **Cash Sales Invoice #500** **Dated Feb. 28/21**

Valentine's Day sales did not meet expectations, so all hair brushes were sold at discounted prices. Edit the selling price for BRS1 and BRS2.

Sales Summary for cash sales (to Cash Customers):

20	BRS1	Hair Brush: natural bristle	$22 each	$ 440.00
10	BRS2	Hair Brush: styling	16 each	160.00
28	SRV3	Cut and Style	48 each	1 344.00
4	SRV6	Wash and Style	26 each	104.00
	HST		15%	307.20
	Invoice total paid by cash			$2 355.20

Deposited to Undeposited Cash and Cheques.

58

DEPOSIT SLIP #9 Date: Feb 28, 2021

Tesses Tresses
55 Salon Rd.
Charlottetown PE C1A 6D3

Account No: 02900 3433382

Cheques

RBC7333 Brioche Bridal Party 195.60

		Amount	
16	× 5	80	00
19	× 10	190	00
14	× 20	280	00
18	× 50	900	00
9	× 100	900	00
	coin	5	20
Total cash		2355	20
Total cheque		195	60
Subtotal		2550	80
Cash received			
Net Deposit		2550	80

Signature *Tess Dubois*

02/28/21 PW

59 **Bank Debit Memo #100121** **Dated Feb. 28/21**

From Savers Trust Co. pre-authorized withdrawals for Mortgage: $1 500 ($1 140 interest & $360 principal) and for Loan: $600 ($105 interest & $495 principal).

60

Memo #14 **Dated Feb. 28/21**

Convert sales quote #103 for On Stage Theatre Company to a sales order. All amounts, the service (shipping) date and the terms are unchanged.

61

Memo #15 **Dated Feb. 28/21**

Enter the adjustments for expired prepaid expenses and supplies used:
Prepaid Insurance expired: $150
Prepaid Subscriptions expired: $40
Office Supplies used: $60
Salon Supplies used: $585
Washroom & Cleaning Supplies used: $75

NOTES

Use the Inventory Adjustments Journal to transfer the inventory to the supplies account. Enter **negative** quantities and change the default Inventory Losses account to Salon Supplies for all items. Refer to Accounting Procedures, page 576.

62

Memo #16 **Dated Feb. 28/21**

The following items were transferred from inventory at cost for salon use:

8	CN1	Pro-Line Conditioner: 150 ml
6	CN2	Pro-Line Hot Oil Treatment 75 ml
8	GEL1	Pro-Line Spray Gel: shaper 150 ml
11	SHM1	Pro-Line Shampoo: 225 ml
9	SPR1	Pro-Line Hair Spray: gentle 150 ml

63

Memo #17 **Dated Feb. 28/21**

Use the following statement to reconcile the Bank: Chequing Account for February.

NOTES

Enter Feb. 28 as the Statement and Reconciliation dates to replace March 3 (31 days after the previous reconciliation).

NOTES

After the first reconciliation, you do not need to add linked accounts or prior transactions. Enter the statement ending balance and then mark journal entries as cleared (keystrokes on page 592) to complete the reconciliation.

There are four deposit slips for group deposits.

The loan and mortgage payments were entered together: $1 500 + $600 = $2 100.

Remember to change the status of the NSF cheque from Brioche Bridal Party for $165.60 (in deposit slip #8) to NSF and the status of its reversing entry to Adjustment.

At the end of February, a cheque for $449.50 and one deposit for $2 550.80 are outstanding.

SAVERS TRUST

321 Queen St., Charlottetown, PE C1A 6D3 saverstrust.com

Tesses Tresses
55 Salon Road
Charlottetown, PE C1A 6D3

ACCOUNT STATEMENT
CHEQUING

Transit / Account No
02900 003 433 38-2

Statement period
Feb 1, 2021 to Feb 28, 2021

Date	Deposit #	Description	Deposits	Withdrawals	Balance
		Balance Fwd			47,167.36
1 Feb	5	Deposit	4,104.40		51,271.76
5 Feb		Cheque #417		920.00	50,351.76
5 Feb		Cheque #418		253.00	50,098.76
7 Feb	6	Deposit	3,279.15		53,377.91
8 Feb		Cheque #419		1,600.00	51,777.91
10 Feb		Cheque #422		299.00	51,478.91
14 Feb	7	Deposit	2,940.55		54,419.46
16 Feb		Cheque #423		2,758.90	51,660.56
18 Feb		Transfer funds from 004 123 22-8	12,000.00		63,660.56
19 Feb		Cheque #425		149.50	63,511.06
21 Feb	8	Deposit	3,476.45		66,987.51
21 Feb		Cheque #424		2,967.30	64,020.21
25 Feb		NSF Cheque #986		165.60	63,854.61
25 Feb		Service Charge - NSF cheque		40.00	63,814.61
26 Feb		Cheque #426		690.00	63,124.61
28 Feb		Scheduled loan payment		600.00	62,524.61
28 Feb		Scheduled mortgage payment		1,500.00	61,024.61
28 Feb		Service Charges - chequing acct		35.50	60,989.11
28 Feb		Interest	44.25		61,033.36
28 Feb		Closing balance			61,033.36

Total Deposits	# 6	$25,844.80
Total Withdrawals	# 13	$11,978.80

64 **Memo #18** **Dated Feb. 28/21**

Use the following statement to reconcile the Bank: Credit Cards Account.

SAVERS TRUST

321 Queen St., Charlottetown, PE C1A 6D3 saverstrust.com

Tesses Tresses
55 Salon Road
Charlottetown, PE C1A 6D3

ACCOUNT STATEMENT
CREDIT CARD

Transit / Account No
02900 004 123 22-8

Statement period
Feb 1, 2021 to Feb 28, 2021

Date	Deposit # Description	Deposits	Withdrawals	Balance
	Balance Fwd			9,644.97
6 Feb	Deposit	2,899.20		12,544.17
13 Feb	Deposit	3,755.20		16,299.37
18 Feb	Transfer funds to 003 433 38-2		12,000.00	4,299.37
20 Feb	Deposit	2,217.76		6,517.13
28 Feb	Service charges		22.50	6,494.63
28 Feb	Interest	5.25		6,499.88
28 Feb	Closing balance			6,499.88

Total Deposits # 4 $8,877.41
Total Withdrawals # 2 $12,022.50

NOTES
Enter Feb. 28 as the Statement and Reconciliation dates. There is one outstanding deposit at the end of February.

Displaying Banking Reports

Click the **Report Centre icon** in the Home window.

Click **Banking** to open the list of banking reports in the Report Centre:

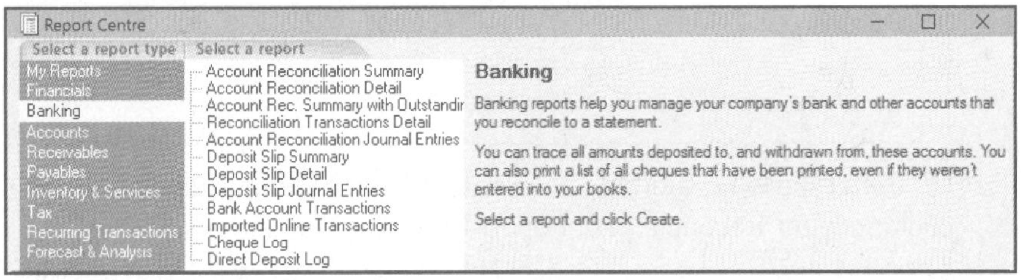

Account Reconciliation Journal

Click **Account Reconciliation Journal Entries**. **Click Modify This Report**:

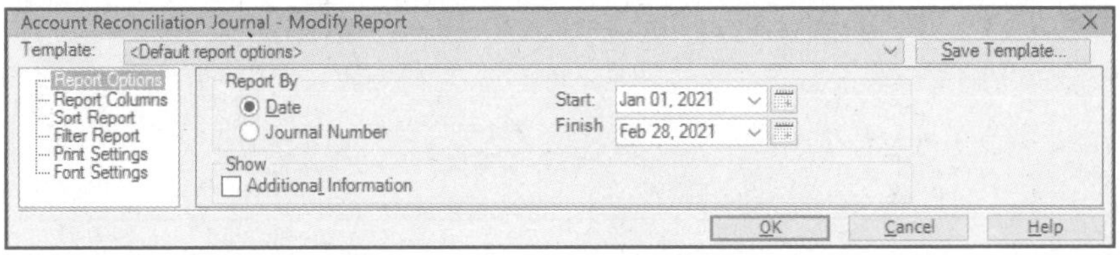

Or, choose the Reports menu, then choose Journal Entries and click Account Reconciliation to open the report options screen.

The journal can be prepared by selecting journal entry numbers or dates. By default, the report uses posting dates. The usual journal report customizing, sorting and filtering options are available. There is no option to show corrections.

NOTES
The Reports pane list in the Banking module window has Account and Banking reports.

PRO VERSION
The Pro version does not have the Bank Account Transactions Report.

NOTES
The Cheque Log Report was covered in Chapter 5. Refer to page 151.
For the Bank Account Transactions Report, refer to pages 588–589.
The Direct Deposit Log is similar to the Cheque Log, but it reports on payroll direct deposits.

NOTES
The report options window will open each time as soon as you click Modify This Report.

CLASSIC VIEW
Right-click the Reconciliation & Deposits icon to select the journal. Click the Select A Report tool to open the report options.

Enter the **Start** and **Finish** dates or journal numbers for the report.

Click **OK**. **Close** the **display** when you have finished.

Deposit Slip Journal

CLASSIC VIEW
With no icons selected, click the Select A Report tool to open the report list. Choose Deposit Slip Journal.

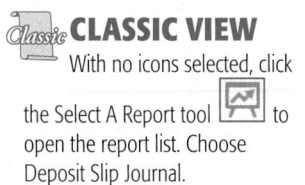

Click **Deposit Slip Journal Entries** and **click Modify This Report**:

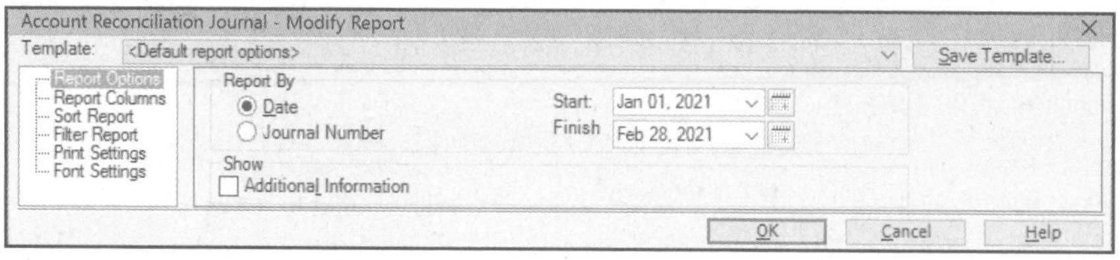

Or, from the Home window, choose the Reports menu, then choose Journal Entries and click Deposit Slip to open the report options screen.

The journal can be prepared by selecting journal entry numbers or dates. By default, the report uses posting dates. The usual journal report customizing, sorting and filtering options are available. There is no option to show corrections.

Enter the **Start** and **Finish** dates or journal numbers for the report.

Click **OK**. **Close** the **display** when you have finished.

Account Reconciliation Report

NOTES
You can display Journal reports, Supplier or Client Aged or Employee reports (if applicable) and look up invoices from the Account Reconciliation Detail Report.
The Reconciliation Report cannot be customized except by choosing columns.

Click **Account Reconciliation Summary** to display the report sample and **click Modify This Report** for the report options:

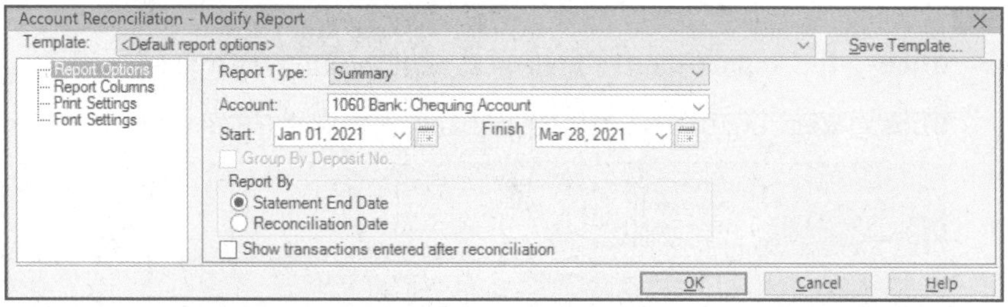

Or, from the Home window, choose the Reports menu, then choose Banking and click Account Reconciliation Report to display the options.

Accept **1060** as the bank account or choose another account from the drop-down list for the Account field.

Enter the **Start** and **Finish** dates. The default Finish date is one month past the latest reconciliation or bank statement date.

Click the **Report Type list arrow**:

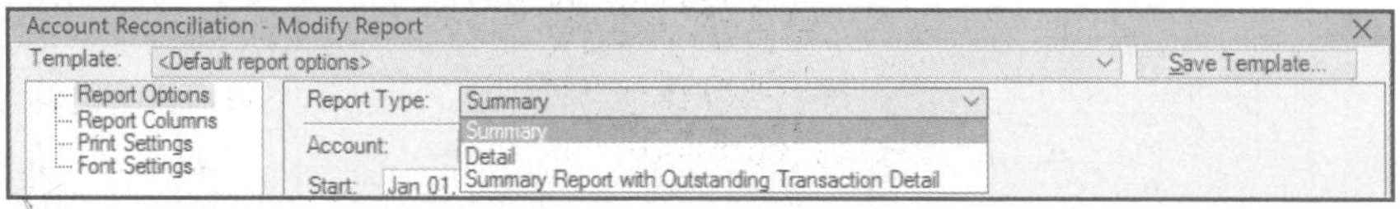

The Report Type drop-down list has three options. The **Summary** Report provides totals for deposits, withdrawals, income and expense categories for the bank statements and the General Ledger account, and outstanding amounts that will reconcile the two balances. Unresolved amounts and discrepancies are also reported, if there are any. The **Detail Report** lists all journal entries with their status, such as Cleared, NSF and so on. You can group the Detail Report by Deposit Number. Choose **Summary Report With**

Outstanding Transaction Detail to include only the total outstanding amounts and the adjusted bank and General Ledger balances. You can **report by** either the bank **Statement End Date** or the **Reconciliation Date** recorded in the journal for the report.

Choose the **report type** and **date (Report By) options**.

Click **OK**. **Close** the **displayed report** when you have finished.

Reconciliation Transaction Report

Click **Reconciliation Transactions Detail** and **click Modify This Report** to open the report options window:

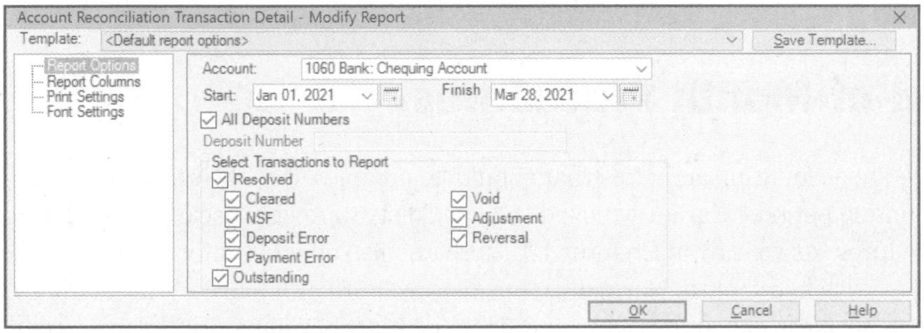

Or, from the Home window, choose the Reports menu, then choose Banking and click Account Reconciliation Transaction Report.

This detail report will list all the transactions with their reconciliation status for the selected bank account for all the status types you chose.

Choose the **account** for the report from the drop-down list.

Enter **Start** and **Finish** dates for the report.

Choose the **Status categories** to include in your reports. By default, all are included, so clicking a category will remove the ✓ from the check box and omit this category from your report.

Click **OK**. **Close** the **displayed report** when you have finished.

> **NOTES**
> You can drill down to Supplier or Client Aged or Employee reports (if applicable) and look up invoices from the Reconciliation Transaction Detail Report.

> **NOTES**
> You can customize the Reconciliation Transaction and Deposit Slip reports by selecting the columns to include, but you cannot sort or filter the reports.
> You cannot drill down to other reports from the Deposit Slip Report.

Deposit Slip Report

Click **Deposit Slip Summary** and **click Modify This Report**.

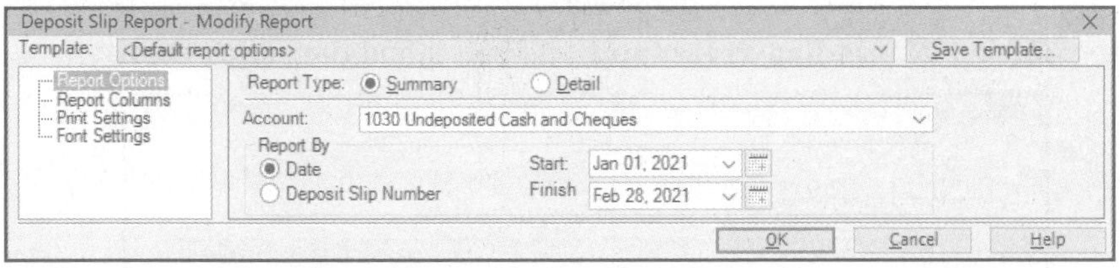

Or, from the Home window, choose the Reports menu, then choose Banking and click Deposit Slip Report to display the options.

The Deposit Slip **Summary Report** has the total amounts for cash and cheques on each deposit slip, while the **Detail Report** lists all cheque, bill and coin amounts separately for each deposit.

Choose the **account** for the report from the drop-down list.

You can display the report for a range of dates or deposit slip numbers.

Choose the **Summary** option to provide a list of totals for cash and cheques for each deposit slip. Choose **Detail** to include the individual items on each deposit slip and totals.

Enter **Start** and **Finish** dates for the report.

Click **OK**. **Close** the **displayed report** and the **Report Centre** when finished.

NOTES
Remember to check your printer selection before you begin printing.

Printing Banking Reports

Display the **report** you want to print. **Click** the **Print tool** or **choose** the **File menu** and **click Print** to print the report. **Close** the **Report window** when finished.

End-of-Month Procedures

There are accounting activities that should be completed at the end of regular accounting periods. Earlier we used the checklists to review fiscal year-end accounting procedures. As we saw in Chapter 12, there are also checklists for the end of each business day and month. Normally a business will print all journal transactions at the end of each business day. Statements and financial reports will be printed at the end of each month, and all reports should be printed at the end of the fiscal period. T4s should be printed at the end of the calendar year.

Periodically, a business will clear old information from its accounting files. In the manual system, it might store the details in archives or with a secured offsite backup storage provider to keep the current files manageable. Computerized systems should be similarly maintained by making backups of the data files and then clearing information that is not required. These periodic procedures include clearing data and reports for prior periods, removing paid invoices from client and supplier records and removing suppliers and clients who no longer do business with the company. Checklists in Sage 50 can assist with these routine procedures.

WARNING!
Before clearing any data, back up the data files and print all relevant available reports: journals; supplier and client detail reports; inventory tracking reports; and the other reports listed in the month-end checklist.

You may want to create a separate copy of the data file to practise clearing data. Use the File menu Save As command, enter a different file name and work with the new file that opens.

✓ 65

Memo #19 **Dated Feb. 28/21**

Back up the data files. Clear journal entries and paid transactions that are no longer needed using January 31 as the date for clearing. Do not clear data for February.

Choose the **Business Assistant menu** in the Home window and **click** **Checklists**. Several lists are available (refer to page 488).

CLASSIC VIEW
You can click the Checklists tool button.

Click **Month-End Procedures** to select it and then **click Modify**:

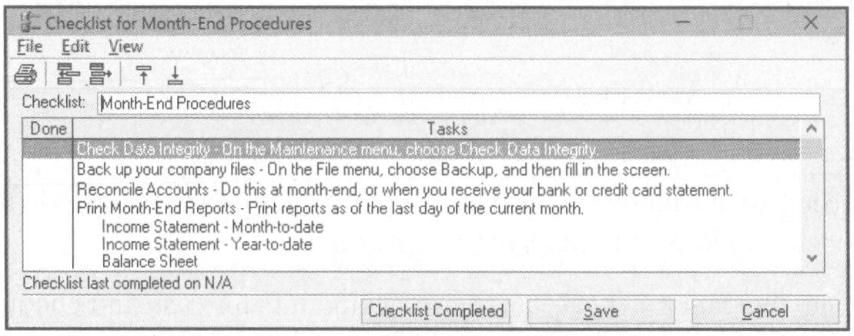

You will open the list of routines that should be completed at the end of a month.

Read the task list. You have already completed some tasks on this list.

Click the **Done column** beside the two tasks that are completed — **Back Up** and **Reconcile Accounts**. We will complete the remaining tasks before marking them.

NOTES
Remember that you can print the task list for reference. Choose the File menu and click Print, click the Print tool or press ctrl + P to print the task list.

Click the **Home window** if part of it is visible or point to the Sage 50 button on the task bar and click the Home window pop-up.

Choose the **Maintenance menu** and **click Check Data Integrity**.

If you do not get the message "Data OK," make a note of any data inconsistencies and return to your most recent backup copy of the file.

Click **OK** to close the Integrity Summary window.

Click the **Done column** beside **Check Data Integrity**.

Click **Save** to return to the main checklists window. A ✓ appears in the Task In Progress column beside Month-End Procedures.

Click **Close** to leave the Checklist window and return to the Home window.

NOTES
You can switch back and forth between the Home window and the Checklist window by clicking the corresponding Sage 50 pop-up on the task bar.

Clearing Paid Supplier and Client Transactions

Choose the **Maintenance menu**, then **choose Clear Data** and **Clear Paid Transactions** and **click Clear Paid Supplier Transactions** to open the list of suppliers:

PRO VERSION
You will choose Clear Paid Vendor Transactions. The term Vendor replaces Supplier.

NOTES
You cannot clear data when you are working in multi-user mode.

You can clear invoices for one or more suppliers at the same time. Unpaid invoices are always retained.

Enter **Jan 31** as the latest date for which you want to remove invoices.

Click **Select All**. (To select individual suppliers, **press** *ctrl* and **click** their **names**.) We also have stored lookup details that we no longer need.

Click **Clear Lookup Data For All Paid Transactions**.

Click **OK**. Sage 50 warns about the consequences of removing these details:

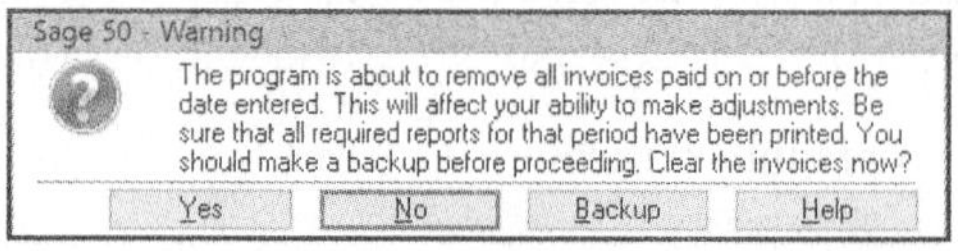

WARNING!
The step of clearing transactions cannot be reversed!

If you have selected correctly and are ready to proceed,

Click **Yes**. When you choose to clear lookup data another warning opens:

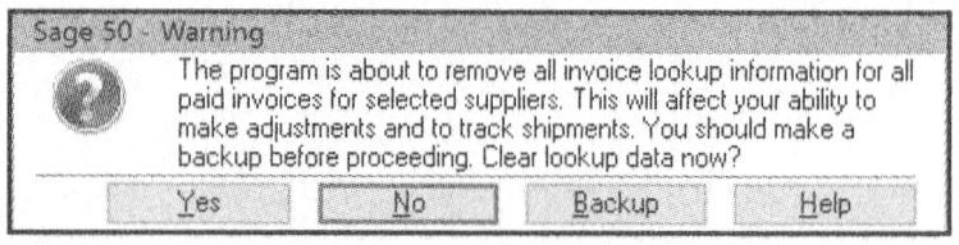

Click **Yes** if you are certain that you should continue.

You can clear client transactions in the same way.

Choose the **Maintenance menu**, then **choose Clear Data** and **Clear Paid Transactions** and **click Clear Paid Client Transactions**.

NOTES
After clearing data, display the relevant reports to verify that the information has been cleared. You will be unable to look up and adjust posted invoices if you have removed lookup details for cleared paid transactions.

PRO VERSION
You will choose Clear Paid Customer Transactions. The term Customer replaces Client.

The list of clients and clearing options opens:

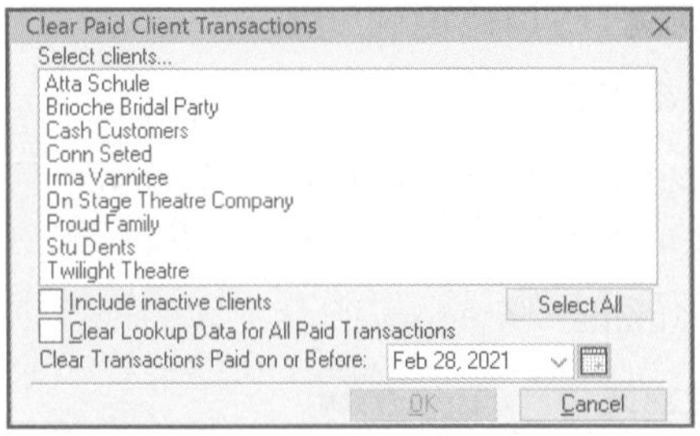

Enter **Jan 31** as the last date for which you want to remove invoices.

Clearing client invoices is similar to clearing supplier invoices.

We will keep all transactions for February. We can clear the invoices and lookup data for Cash Customers and Atta Schule because these are not needed. You can clear paid invoices for all clients by clicking Select All.

Click **Atta Schule**. **Press** ctrl and **click** **Cash Customers**.

Click **Clear Lookup Data For All Paid Transactions**. **Click** **OK**.

The next warning is the same as the one we saw for removing supplier invoices. If you are ready, you should proceed.

Click **Yes**. Again, the additional warning for lookup data is provided. If you are certain that you want to continue,

Click **Yes** to remove the lookup data and return to the Home window.

Clearing Tax Reports

You should clear tax reports after filing the tax returns for the period covered by the return so that the next report will include only the current reporting period.

Choose the **Maintenance menu**, then **choose** **Clear Data** and **click** **Clear Tax Report** to display the options:

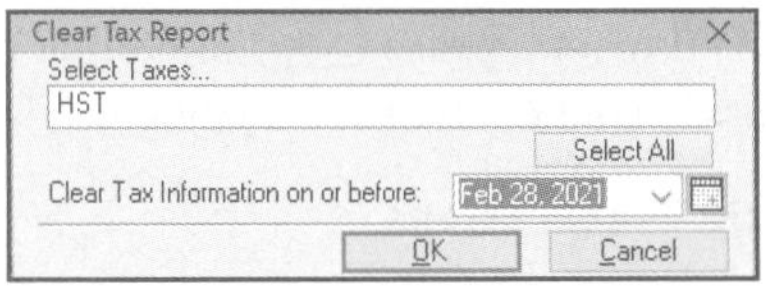

Select the tax or taxes for which you want to clear the reports or click Select All. Then enter the date. Entries on and before the date you enter will be removed.

Click **OK**. Sage 50 provides the familiar warning:

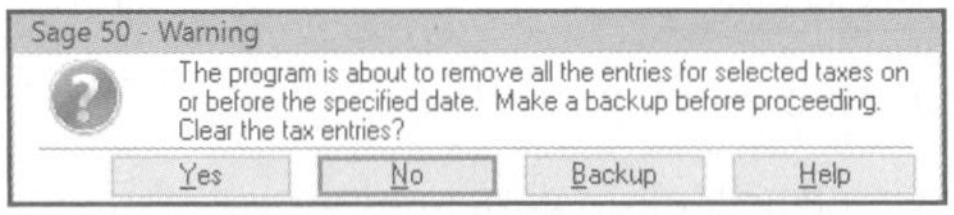

We do not want to remove any tax data because we have not submitted the returns for February.

Click **No** to cancel and return to the Home window.

NOTES
When you use online banking to reconcile accounts, you can also clear imported bank transactions using the Match Bank Transactions feature. These methods are covered in Appendix I on the Student DVD.

Clearing Account Reconciliation Data

Choose the **Maintenance menu**, then **choose** **Clear Data** and **Clear Account Rec.** and **click** **Clear Account Rec. Data** to display the options:

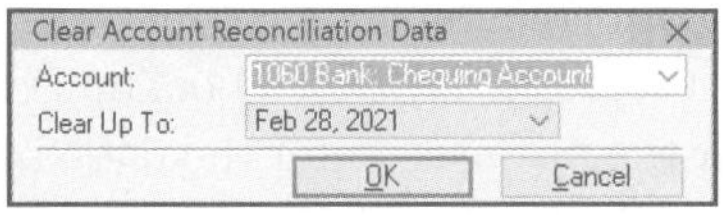

Select the account for which you want to remove the data. Then enter the date. Entries on and before the date you enter will be removed.

We do not want to remove the data at this time. If you choose to continue, Sage 50 will present the familiar warning before any information is removed.

Click **Cancel** to return to the Home window.

NOTES
You can clear account reconciliation data for only one account at a time, and you must select the Clear Up To date from the drop-down list in that field.

Clearing Inventory Tracking Data

Choose the **Maintenance menu**, then **choose** **Clear Data** and **click** **Clear Inventory Tracking Data** to display the clearing date dialogue box:

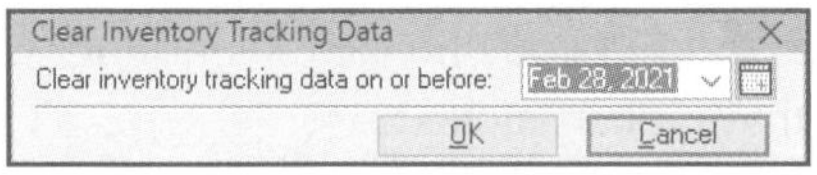

Enter **Jan 31** as the date. Entries on and before January 31 will be removed.

Click **OK**. Again, the warning is displayed before any data is removed.

If you are certain that you want to proceed,

Click **Yes** to delete the requested information and return to the Home window.

Clearing Lookup Data

You can clear invoice lookup data for both purchase and sales invoices together in a single step or you can clear purchase and sales invoices in separate steps. You can also clear lookup data for remittances from this menu.

Choose the **Maintenance menu**, then **choose** **Clear Data** and **Clear Lookup Data** and **click** **Clear Supplier Invoice & Client Invoice Lookup Data** to display the clearing options:

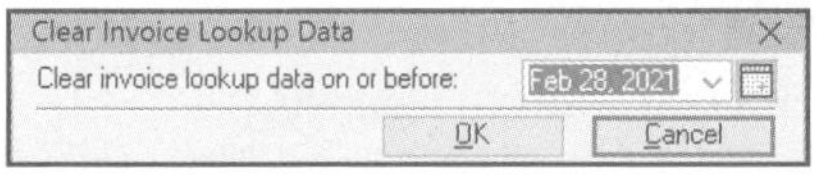

Enter **Jan 31** as the date. Entries on and before January 31 will be removed.

Click **OK**.

Once again, Sage 50 warns you before removing any data. If you are certain that you want to proceed,

Click **Yes** to continue.

If you cleared the lookup data with the paid transactions, you will receive the message stating that there is no invoice data to clear. Click OK to continue.

The requested information is deleted and you will return to the Home window.

To clear only purchase invoice data, choose the Maintenance menu, Clear Data and Clear Invoice Lookup Data and click Clear Supplier Invoice Lookup Data. Choose suppliers for which you want to clear the invoices, enter the date and click OK to display the warning. Click Yes to continue with clearing the data.

PRO VERSION
You will choose Clear Purchase Invoice Lookup Data to clear data for purchase invoices.
You will choose Clear Sales Invoice Lookup Data to clear data for sales invoices.

NOTES
If you choose to clear invoice lookup data for purchases or sales separately, you can choose to clear the data for one or more suppliers (or clients) or for all of them.

To remove only sales invoice data, choose the Maintenance menu, Clear Data and Clear Invoice Lookup Data and click Clear Client Invoice Lookup Data. Select clients for which you want to clear the invoices, enter the date and click OK. Click Yes to continue with clearing the data.

Clearing Deposit Slip Lookup Data

Choose the **Maintenance menu**, **Clear Data** and **Clear Lookup Data**. **Click Clear Lookup Data For Deposit Slips** to display the options:

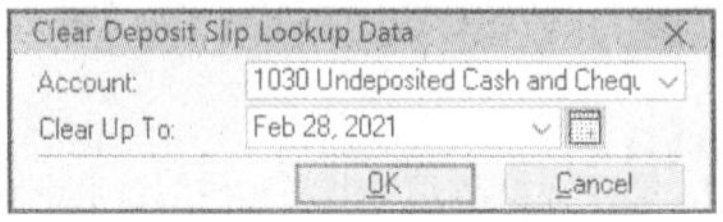

Select the account for which you want to remove the data. Then enter the date. Entries on and before the date you enter will be removed.

We do not want to remove the data at this time. If you choose to continue, you will receive the familiar warning before any information is removed.

Click **Cancel** to return to the Home window.

Clearing Lookup Data for Other Payments

Lookup data for other payments are cleared separately from Purchases Journal invoices.

Choose the **Maintenance menu**, **Clear Data** and **Clear Lookup Data**. **Click Clear Lookup Data For Other Payments** to display the list of suppliers and the clearing options:

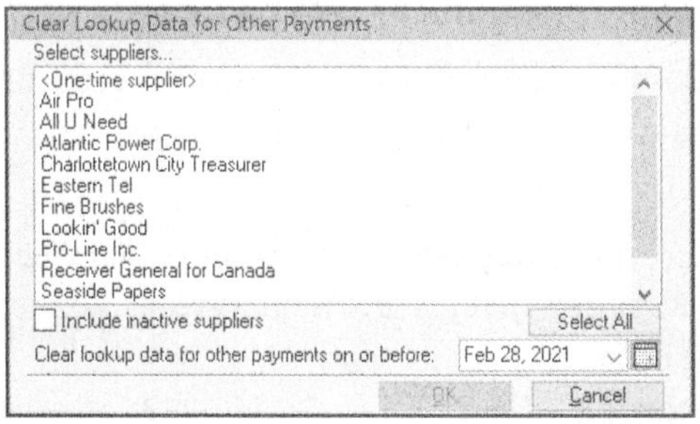

Enter **Jan 31** as the date for the data you want to remove.

Choose the **suppliers**. **Click Select All** to select all suppliers.

Click **OK**. Sage 50 will require confirmation before removing data. To proceed,

Click **Yes**.

> **NOTES**
> If you cleared the lookup data when you cleared the paid transactions, you will get the message stating that there is no lookup data to clear.

The requested information is deleted, and you will return to the Home window.

From the Maintenance menu, Clear Data option, you can also clear lookup data for remittances, notes that you create in the Daily Business Manager, financial history and direct deposits. For each one, you can enter a date after which all data will be retained. You will be warned before any information is removed.

Automatically Clearing Data

You can also choose to clear data automatically when you start a new fiscal period.

Choose the **Maintenance menu**, then **choose Clear Data** and **click Automatically Clear Data** to view your options:

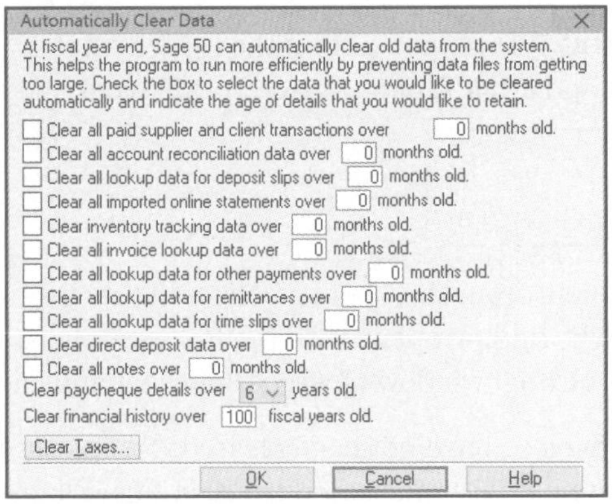

From this screen you can choose what data to clear and how many months of each type of data should be kept when the clearing occurs at the end of the fiscal period.

Click **Cancel** to return to the Home window.

Automatically Clearing Tax Data

Tax information can also be cleared automatically, but it has separate settings.

Choose the **Maintenance menu**, then **choose Clear Data** and **click Automatically Clear Data**. **Click** the **Clear Taxes button**:

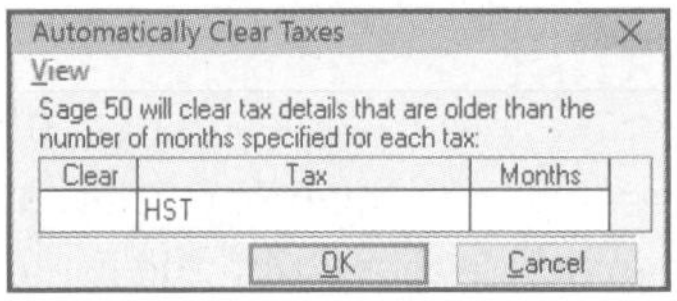

On this screen you can choose what taxes to clear. Data older than the number of months you enter will be removed when the clearing occurs at the end of the fiscal period.

Click the **Clear column** beside the tax to select it and then **enter** the number of **months**. The default is to keep the tax details for 12 months.

Click **Cancel** to return to the Automatically Clear Data screen and **click Cancel** again to return to the Home window.

Removing Supplier and Client Records

Sometimes you know that you will not be doing business with a client or supplier again. Removing their records reduces the length of the lists to scroll through for journal entries and saves on mailing costs. Suppliers are removed from the Suppliers window. Clients are removed from the Clients window. We will remove the client (tenant) Stu Dents because he will be moving out of his apartment after March, the date of his final cheque. First we must clear the paid transactions for this client.

Choose the **Maintenance menu**, then **choose Clear Data** and **Clear Paid Transactions** and **click Clear Paid Client Transactions**.

Click **Stu Dents** on the client list. **Enter February 28, 2021** as the date. **Click OK**. When the warning is provided,

Click **Yes** to confirm. **Click Yes** to confirm removing lookup data if asked.

Click **Receivables** in the Modules pane list.

Click **Stu Dents** in the Home window Clients list to open the ledger record.

NOTES
Financial history can be stored for 100 years in the Premium version and 7 years in the Pro version.

PRO VERSION
The default entry for Clear Financial History Over is 6 Years.

NOTES
Refer to page 105 for the query about clearing old data. The periods you choose here will determine how much data will be cleared.

NOTES
When you click the Clear column for a tax, the default number of months, 12, is entered and you can change it.

NOTES
An alternative to removing records is to mark clients or suppliers as Inactive and not include them in reports. Inactive clients and suppliers are also not included in the drop-down lists in journals.

The record will be saved and you can restore it to active status at any time.

NOTES
In the ledger window, you can also press ctrl + R to remove the record.

NOTES
There are postdated rent cheques for Stu Dents, so not all the paid transactions were cleared when February 28 was selected as the date.

Click the **Remove The Current Client tool** in the ledger window, or **choose** the **File menu** and **click Remove**. Sage 50 will block the action:

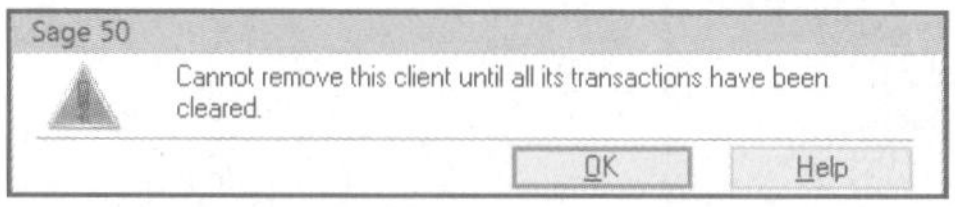
Sage 50
Cannot remove this client until all its transactions have been cleared.
OK
Help

You can also choose Remove Client from the Clients icon shortcuts list in the Receivables window. The Search window opens with the Remove Client option selected. Click Stu Dents in the Search window to select the client and click OK.

We selected a client for whom all invoices have not been cleared. The program will not permit you to remove a client or supplier with uncleared transactions. Clients with unpaid transactions can never be removed.

Click **OK** to return to the Receivables module window. Clear the details using March 1 as the date and then remove the client's record. If all transactions are cleared, you will get the familiar warning.

Check that you have selected the client you want before continuing.

Click **Yes** if you have selected correctly.

Click Yes to confirm if you get the message about removing lookup data. If you get the message stating that there is no lookup data, click OK to continue.

Completing the Month-End Checklist

We will now return to the month-end checklist by marking the remaining tasks as done. The tasks relating to budgeting do not apply, so we can delete them from the list and customize the list for Tesses Tresses.

Choose the **Business Assistant menu** and **click Checklists**.

Double-click **Month-End Procedures** to open this list.

You can customize any checklist. Click on the list where you want to add a task, choose the Edit menu and click Insert. Then type the task description.

NOTES
Click the Insert tool to add a task or delete task items from the list to further customize your checklist.
Refer to pages 488–489 for more information on removing or adding tasks in checklists.

NOTES
Instead of removing checklist items – because you may need them later – you can mark them as Done so you can complete the checklists.

Scroll down the **list** to the budget-related tasks.

Click **Check Your Budget** to select this line.

Click the **Remove Item tool** or **choose** the **Edit menu** and **click Remove**.

Click **Yes** to confirm and select the next task. Remove it and the following one relating to budgets.

Click the **Done column** for the remaining tasks.

Click **Checklist Completed** to return to the opening Checklist window. The session date appears as the Date Last Completed beside Month-End Procedures. **Click Close** to return to the Home window.

REVIEW

The Student DVD with Data Files includes Review Questions and Supplementary Cases for this chapter.

CHAPTER SIXTEEN

VELOCITY

OBJECTIVES

After completing this chapter, you should be able to

- ***plan*** and ***design*** an accounting system for a small business
- ***prepare*** procedures for converting from a manual system
- ***understand*** the objectives of a computerized system
- ***create*** company files
- ***set up*** company accounts, ledgers and records
- ***enter*** settings for foreign currency transactions
- ***prepare*** files for foreign currency transactions and importing goods
- ***identify*** preferred customers for reduced prices
- ***enter*** preferred customer prices and import duty rates for inventory
- ***enter*** Inventory Ledger settings and records
- ***finish*** entering the accounting history for all modules
- ***insert*** new accounts, suppliers, customers and employees as required
- ***add*** users, ***create*** passwords and ***enter*** access rights
- ***export*** reports
- ***use*** spreadsheets for analyzing, planning and decision making
- ***enter*** end-of-accounting-period adjustments
- ***perform*** end-of-accounting-period closing routines
- ***create***, ***analyze*** and ***interpret*** comparative reports

INTRODUCTION

NOTES

If you change the province, remember that rules for the application of the Harmonized Sales Tax (HST), provincial sales taxes and payroll may vary from one province to another, and amounts in the source documents will change.

This application provides a complete accounting cycle for a merchandising business. It is a comprehensive application covering a three-month fiscal period. You will use Sage 50 to convert a manual accounting system to a computerized accounting system and then enter transactions. The routines in this application are common to many small businesses, so they should be useful. The information in this chapter reflects the business realities in Ontario in April 2019.

You may substitute information relevant to other provinces or the latest payroll and tax regulations wherever it is appropriate to do so.

NOTES
Because of the length of the application, group work is encouraged in setting up error-free company files and completing the transactions.

NOTES
VeloCity Inc.
27 Gearing Avenue
Niagara on the Lake
ON L0S 1J0
Tel 1: (905) 468-8356 (velo)
Tel 2: (888) 468-8356 (velo)
Fax: (905) 468-9100
Business No.: 335 677 829

NOTES
In this chapter, the terms Vendors and Suppliers will be used interchangeably, as will the terms Purchases and Expenses, and the terms Sales and Revenues.

NOTES
Foreign customers pay HST when they rent bicycles in Ontario because the services are "consumed" in Canada and not exported.

Because of the length of the setup, instructions for working with the source documents are presented with those documents on page 692.

COMPANY INFORMATION

Company Profile

VeloCity, in Niagara on the Lake, Ontario, sells a small range of bicycles and accessories. Steve Ryder, the owner, a regular participant in bicycle races and competitions, opened the shop in the popular tourist region because of the proximity to trails along the Niagara River and Peninsula. The flat terrain makes this area popular with casual bikers.

All the bicycles are high-quality, light-weight, 27-gear cycles with Shimano gears and derailleurs. The extras, such as the carriage and third-wheel attachments, have attracted touring families with young children, and the annual sell-off of all rental bikes appeals to budget-conscious residents and visitors.

Three employees assist with the work in the store that includes selling and servicing the bicycles, while Ryder spends more time promoting the rental services of the business with theatre and tourism businesses throughout the province.

Several suppliers offer discounts to the store for early payment, including two suppliers in the United States. Accounts are also set up for other supplies and services that are provided locally. The store uses a credit card for some of these purchases.

Most customers are situated in the Niagara region, but Ryder has contracts with some travel companies in New York State to include bicycle rentals with their tour packages. Prices in US dollars are entered in the ledger records so that all prices will be entered automatically in the correct amount and currency when the customer is selected. With the Canadian dollar valued below the US dollar, US dollar prices are currently about 25 percent below Canadian dollar prices.

All account customers are given discounts for early payment, and some preferred customers receive additional discounts. Individual customers usually pay by cash, debit or credit card and do not receive any discounts. Delivery is provided at a small charge and includes assembly and a brief demonstration on bicycle care.

All items and services sold by the store are set up as inventory so that sales can be monitored. HST is charged on all sales and services, except to foreign customers. The store pays HST on all taxable purchases, including inventory purchased for resale. The exception is books, for which the store pays 5 percent GST on purchases and customers pay 5 percent at the time of sale.

The owner decided to use Sage 50 for record keeping after a consultant prepared the report on pages 621 and 622. Ryder found an application in an older Sage 50 textbook by Purbhoo. It appeared similar in complexity and structure to VeloCity and even included complete instructions for creating the data files. Before converting the books for the store, he asked his assistant to work through this application for practice. After completing this exercise, she printed all the relevant business guide information and prepared the following reports to assist with the conversion on May 1, 2021:

- Income Statement
- Business Information
- Chart of Accounts
- Balance Sheet
- Post-Closing Trial Balance
- Supplier Information
- Customer Information
- Employee Information
- Inventory Information
- Accounting Procedures

MANAGER'S REPORT ON SAGE 50

PREPARED FOR VELOCITY

1. Sage 50 allows a business to process all source documents in a secure and timely fashion. It can prepare both single-period and comparative accounting reports for planning, decision making and controlling operations within the business.
2. The software eliminates some of the time-consuming manual clerical functions. It can prepare invoices, cheques and statements; store and recall repeating transactions; and it can perform all the necessary mathematical calculations. Being freed from these chores, the accountant can assume a much higher level of responsibility, for example, analyzing reports and making business decisions.
3. Sage 50 can easily export reports to spreadsheets for further analysis, or link with the Internet, with other software programs and with suppliers and customers for interactive data exchange. When combined with the account reconciliation and budgeting features, these reports permit the owner to analyze past trends and to make better predictions about the future behaviour of the business.
4. As the business grows, the manager can divide work more meaningfully among new accounting personnel. Since Sage 50 provides subsidiary ledgers that are linked to control accounts in the General Ledger, it automatically coordinates accounting work performed by different users. Customizable window backgrounds can even accommodate mood changes of the different users.
5. Sage 50 allows the owner to exercise business controls in a number of areas:

IN GENERAL

- Access to confidential accounting records and editing capability can be restricted to authorized personnel by using passwords.
- Mechanical errors can be virtually eliminated, since journal transactions with unequal debits and credits cannot be posted. Customer, supplier, employee, inventory and project names appear in full on the journal entry input forms, making errors less likely.
- The ability to customize and preview forms, store recurring entries and look up posted invoices makes it possible to avoid errors in repeated information and to double check invoices in response to customer and supplier inquiries.
- General, Sales, Receipts, Purchases, Payments and Payroll journal entries can be easily adjusted or reversed if they were entered incorrectly. The software automatically creates and posts the reversing entries.
- Sage 50 provides an audit trail for all journals.
- Bank account, customer, supplier and inventory records can be set up to calculate many foreign currency transactions automatically, including import duties. Payments may be transmitted electronically and securely.
- Daily Business Manager lists and checklists provide reminders of upcoming discounts, recurring entries and routine tasks.
- Business advice, management reports and built-in warnings all provide helpful information for running the business.
- Sage 50 provides a directory of customers, suppliers and employees that you can link to Microsoft Office, and can create mailing labels.

GENERAL LEDGER

- Sage 50 provides a directory of accounts used by the business, including all linked accounts for the other ledgers.
- The information in these accounts can be used to prepare and analyze financial reports, such as the Balance Sheet and Income Statement.

RECEIVABLES LEDGER

- Credit limit entries for each customer should reduce the losses from non-payment of accounts. Customers with poor payment histories can have their credit limits reduced or their credit purchase privileges removed.
- Customers can be linked to price lists so that they automatically receive differential prices.
- Sales quotes and order entries result in automatic Sales Journal entries when the quotes or orders are filled.
- Tax codes, accounts, payment terms and payment methods, including pre-authorized bank or credit card payments, can be added to the customer record and automatically entered for sales when the customer is selected.
- Accounts receivable can be aged, and each customer's payment behaviour can be analyzed to calculate the likelihood of bad debts.

PAYABLES LEDGER

- The information from the review of transactions with suppliers and from the accounts payable aged analysis can be combined with detailed cash flow reports to establish payment schedules and predict short-term cash needs.
- The GST/HST remittance or refund is calculated automatically because of the linked GST/HST accounts in the Payables and Receivables ledgers. Canada Revenue Agency tax remittance reports can be prepared and then submitted electronically.
- Sage 50 purchase quotes and order entries result in automatic Purchases Journal entries when quotes or orders are filled.
- The usual invoice details for a supplier can be entered in the supplier record so that they are entered automatically for purchases when the supplier is selected. These details include tax code, payment terms, expense account, payment method and pre-authorized direct deposits.

PAYROLL LEDGER

- Sage 50 maintains employee records with both personal and payment information for personnel files.
- Paycheques for several employees can be processed as a single payroll run entry with direct payroll deposit.
- Once records are set up, the program automatically withholds employee deductions, including income tax, CPP (Canada Pension Plan) and EI (Employment Insurance), and is therefore less prone to error. Sage provides updated tax tables with new releases every six months.
- Payroll reports are available for compulsory and optional payroll expenses and benefits, employee contributions and entitlements.

▶

Manager's Report on Sage 50 — Page 2

PAYROLL LEDGER CONTINUED

- Different kinds of income can be linked to different expense accounts. In addition, the wages for different employees can be linked to different expense accounts, again permitting better tracking of payroll expenses.
- Sage 50 automatically links payroll with control accounts in the General Ledger. Remittance amounts are tracked and linked with the corresponding payroll authorities for monthly or quarterly remittance. Government reports in Sage 50 can be prepared and then submitted electronically.

INVENTORY LEDGER

- The software provides an inventory summary or database of all inventory and service items that can be tracked.
- Inventory reports flag items that need to be reordered, and the reports can be used to make purchase decisions.
- Import duty rates and different prices in home and foreign currencies can be set up in the ledger so they appear automatically in the journals. Additional price lists can be added.
- Inventory codes can be matched to the supplier and customer item codes so that orders can be exported and imported.
- The software calculates inventory variance costs when the items sold are out of stock and later purchased at different prices.
- Sage 50 automatically updates inventory records for multiple locations when inventory is purchased, sold, transferred, lost, recovered or returned. It warns when you try to oversell inventory.
- Different units for stocking, selling and buying items can be saved for inventory items so that prices are automatically entered correctly for both sales and purchases. Reports can be prepared for any of the units on record.
- Inventory tracking reports can monitor sales and purchase activity on individual inventory items to assess profitability and determine which ones are selling well and which are not. These reports can be used to determine optimum inventory buying patterns to reduce storage costs.
- Inventory costs can be tracked using either the FIFO (first-in, first-out) or the average cost methods.

6. In summation, Sage 50 provides an integrated management accounting information system with extensive built-in controls.

INCOME STATEMENT

VELOCITY

February 1 to April 30, 2021

Revenue			
4000	GENERAL REVENUE		
4020	Revenue from Sales	$69 520.00	
4040	Revenue from Services	28 430.00	
4060	Sales Discounts	−965.00	
4100	Net Sales		$96 985.00
4120	Exchange Rate Differences		−12.00
4150	Interest Revenue		980.00
4200	Freight Revenue		245.00
4390	TOTAL GENERAL REVENUE		$98 198.00
TOTAL REVENUE			$98 198.00
Expense			
5000	OPERATING EXPENSES		
5010	Advertising and Promotion		$ 830.00
5020	Bank Charges		169.00
5030	Credit Card Fees		870.00
5040	Damaged Inventory	$ 210.00	
5050	Cost of Goods Sold: Accessories	4 535.00	
5060	Cost of Goods Sold: Bicycles	11 710.00	
5070	Cost of Goods Sold: Books	4 300.00	
5080	Cost Variance	64.00	
5090	Freight Expense	432.00	
5100	Purchase Discounts	−620.00	
5110	Purchases Returns & Allowances	−425.00	
5120	Net Cost of Goods Sold		20 206.00
5130	Depreciation: Computer Equipment	910.00	
5140	Depreciation: Furniture & Fixtures	80.00	
5150	Depreciation: Service Tools	120.00	

5160	Depreciation: Van	$ 190.00	
5170	Depreciation: Retail Premises	2 740.00	
5180	Net Depreciation		$ 4 040.00
5190	Delivery Expense		63.00
5200	Hydro Expense		828.00
5210	Insurance Expense		1 800.00
5220	Interest on Loan		1 240.00
5230	Interest on Mortgage		5 200.00
5240	Maintenance of Premises		1 055.00
5250	Supplies Used		265.00
5260	Property Taxes		2 700.00
5270	Uncollectable Accounts Expense		500.00
5280	Telephone Expense		795.00
5285	Van Maintenance & Operating Expense		1 638.00
5290	TOTAL OPERATING EXPENSES		$42 199.00
5295	PAYROLL EXPENSES		
5300	Wages (including Vacation paid)		10 303.00
5320	Salaries		23 400.00
5330	Commissions & Bonuses		360.00
5410	EI Expense		790.00
5420	CPP Expense		1 548.00
5430	WSIB Expense		403.00
5440	EHT Expense		332.00
5450	Gp Insurance Expense		306.00
5460	Employee Benefits		930.00
5490	TOTAL PAYROLL EXPENSES		$38 372.00
TOTAL EXPENSE			$80 571.00
NET INCOME			$17 627.00

BUSINESS INFORMATION

VELOCITY

USER PREFERENCES: Options
Use Accounting Terms
Automatically save changes to records
Calculate record balances by session date
Automatically refresh balances

View Daily Business Manager and Checklists off
Show Company name, Advice, Session date at startup, and Paid stamps

Pop-Ups Your own preferences

Transaction Confirmation Turned on

COMPANY SETTINGS: Information

Address	27 Gearing Avenue Niagara on the Lake, ON L0S 1J0
Tel 1	(905) 468-8356 (VELO)
Tel 2	(888) 468-8356 (VELO)
Fax	(905) 468-9100
Industry	Retail

Business No. 335 677 829 RT0001
Fiscal Start May 1, 2021
Earliest Transaction May 1, 2021
Fiscal End July 31, 2021

System Warn if accounts not balanced
No transactions before May 1, 2021

Backup Semi-monthly; Display reminder
Scheduled, automatic backup off

Features All used

Forms Settings (Next Number)
Sales Invoices No. 2210
Sales Quotes No. 56
Sales Orders No. 248
Receipts No. 812
Customer Deposits No. 21
Purchase Orders No. 38
Employee Direct Deposits No. 25
Check for duplicates
Print/Email in batches

Date Format MM dd yyyy and Long Dates

Logo SageData19\LOGOS\VELO.BMP

Names Additional Field Ref. Number

Credit Card Information
Used: Visa
Payable 2250 Expense 5030

Accepted:	Visa	Interac
Fee	2.5%	0%
Asset	1120	1120
Expense	5030	5030

Sales Taxes

Tax	ID on forms	Track: Purch	Sales
HST	335 677 829	2670	2650
GST	335 677 829	2670	2650

	Exempt?	Taxable?	Report?
HST	No	No	Yes
GST	No	No	Yes

Tax Codes
H: HST, taxable, 13%, not included, refundable
G: GST, taxable, 5%, not included, refundable
IN: HST, taxable, 13%, included, refundable

Foreign Currency
USD United States Dollars
Tracking Account 4120
Exchange Rate on 05/01/21 1.315

GENERAL SETTINGS No changes

PAYABLES SETTINGS
Address Niagara on the Lake, Ontario, Canada

Options: Aging periods 15, 30, 60 days
Discounts before tax Yes

Import Duty
Track import duty
Linked account 2220

RECEIVABLES SETTINGS
Address Niagara on the Lake, Ontario, Canada

Options: Aging periods 10, 30, 60 days
Interest charges Compound; 1.5% after 1 day overdue (monthly rate)
Statements include invoices for 31 days
Use tax code H for new customers

Discount: Payment terms 2/10, n/30
Discounts before tax No
Line Discounts Not used

Comments
On Sales Invoice Interest @ 1.5% per month charged on accounts over 30 days.

PAYROLL SETTINGS
Names: Income and Deduction
Income 1 Salary
Income 2 Commission
Income 3 No. Clients
Income 4 Bonus
Income 5 Tuition
Income 6 Travel Exp
Deduction 1 VRSP
Deduction 2 Savings Plan
Deduction 3 Garnishee

Names: Additional Payroll
Field 1 Emergency Contact
Field 2 Contact Number
User Expense 1 Gp Insurance
Entitlement 1 Vacation
Entitlement 2 Sick Leave
Entitlement 3 PersonalDays

Incomes

Income	Type	Taxable	Vac. Pay
Regular	Hourly rate	Yes	Yes
Overtime 1	Hourly rate	Yes	Yes
Salary	Income	Yes	No
Bonus	Income	Yes	No
Commission	Income	Yes	No
No. Clients	Piece Rate	Yes	Yes
Tuition	Income	Yes	No
Travel Exp	Reimburse	No	No

Deductions all deductions are by amount
VRSP Before tax, after other deductions
Savings Plan After tax and other deductions
Garnishee After tax and other deductions

Taxes
EI factor 1.4
WSIB rate 1.29
EHT factor 0.98

Entitlements

Name	Track %	Max Days	Clear
Vacation	8.0%	25	No
Sick Leave	5.0%	15	No
PersonalDays	2.5%	5	No

Remittance

Payroll Liability	Remittance Supplier
EI, CPP, Income Tax	Receiver General
WSIB	Workplace Safety & Insurance Board
EHT	Minister of Finance
VRSP	Manulife Financial
Gp Insurance	Welland Insurance
Savings Plan	Escarpment Investments
Garnishee	Receiver General

End of next remitting period: May 1

Job Categories
Sales: employees are salespersons
All employees are in Sales category

INVENTORY SETTINGS
Profit evaluation by markup
Sort inventory by number
Foreign prices from inventory records
Allow inventory levels to go below zero

ACCOUNT CLASS SETTINGS
Bank
1060 Bank: Niagara Trust Chequing (CAD)
Next cheque no. 1101
Next deposit no. 18
1080 Bank: Niagara Trust Savings (CAD)
1140 Bank: USD Chequing (USD)
Next cheque no. 346
Cash
1030 Undeposited Cash and Cheques
Credit Card Receivable
1120 Bank: Visa and Interac
Credit Card Payable
2250 Credit Card Payable
Operating Expense Class
All postable expense accounts except COGS subgroup (accounts 5040–5110)

LINKED ACCOUNTS FOR LEDGERS
Refer to pages 650–655, 660–661, 663

CHART OF ACCOUNTS

VELOCITY

ASSETS

1000 CURRENT ASSETS [H]
1010 Test Balance Account
1030 Undeposited Cash and Cheques [A]
1060 Bank: Niagara Trust Chequing [A]
1080 Bank: Niagara Trust Savings [A]
1120 Bank: Visa and Interac [A]
1140 Bank: USD Chequing [A]
1150 Net Bank [S]
1200 Accounts Receivable [A]
1210 Allowance for Doubtful Accounts [A]
1220 Advances & Loans Receivable [A]
1230 Interest Receivable [A]
1240 Net Receivables [S]
1250 Purchase Prepayments
1260 Prepaid Advertising
1270 Prepaid Insurance
1280 Office Supplies
1290 Bicycle Repair Parts
1300 Rental Bicycles
1400 TOTAL CURRENT ASSETS [T]

1500 INVENTORY ASSETS [H]
1520 Accessories
1540 Bicycles
1560 Books
1580 TOTAL INVENTORY ASSETS [T]

1600 CENTRE & EQUIPMENT [H]
1610 Computer Equipment [A]
1620 Accum Deprec: Computer Equipment [A]
1630 Net Computer Equipment [S]
1640 Furniture & Fixtures [A]
1650 Accum Deprec: Furniture & Fixtures [A]
1660 Net Furniture & Fixtures [S]
1670 Service Equipment & Tools [A]
1680 Accum Deprec: Service Tools [A]
1690 Net Service Tools [S]
1700 Van [A]
1710 Accum Deprec: Van [A]
1720 Net Van [S]
1730 Retail Premises [A]
1740 Accum Deprec: Retail Premises [A]
1750 Net Retail Premises [S]
1890 TOTAL CENTRE & EQUIPMENT [T] ▶

▶LIABILITIES

2000 CURRENT LIABILITIES [H]
2100 Bank Loan
2200 Accounts Payable
2210 Prepaid Sales and Deposits
2220 Import Duty Payable
2250 Credit Card Payable
2280 Accrued Wages
2300 Vacation Payable
2310 EI Payable [A]
2320 CPP Payable [A]
2330 Income Tax Payable [A]
2350 Receiver General Payable [S]
2380 EHT Payable
2400 VRSP Payable
2410 Savings Plan Payable
2420 Group Insurance Payable
2430 Garnisheed Wages Payable
2460 WSIB Payable
2500 Business Income Tax Payable
2650 GST/HST Charged on Sales [A]
2670 GST/HST Paid on Purchases [A]
2750 GST/HST Owing (Refund) [S]
2790 TOTAL CURRENT LIABILITIES [T]

2800 LONG TERM LIABILITIES [H]
2820 Mortgage Payable
2890 TOTAL LONG TERM LIABILITIES [T]

EQUITY

3000 OWNER'S EQUITY [H]
3560 S. Ryder, Capital
3600 Current Earnings [X]
3690 TOTAL OWNER'S EQUITY [T]

REVENUE

4000 GENERAL REVENUE [H]
4020 Revenue from Sales [A]
4040 Revenue from Services [A]
4060 Sales Discounts [A]
4100 Net Sales [S]
4120 Exchange Rate Differences
4150 Interest Revenue
4200 Freight Revenue
4390 TOTAL GENERAL REVENUE [T] ▶

▶EXPENSE

5000 OPERATING EXPENSES [H]
5010 Advertising and Promotion
5020 Bank Charges
5030 Credit Card Fees
5040 Damaged Inventory [A]
5045 Item Assembly Costs [A]
5050 Cost of Goods Sold: Accessories [A]
5060 Cost of Goods Sold: Bicycles [A]
5070 Cost of Goods Sold: Books [A]
5075 Cost of Services [A]
5080 Cost Variance [A]
5090 Freight Expense [A]
5100 Purchase Discounts [A]
5110 Purchases Returns & Allowances [A]
5120 Net Cost of Goods Sold [S]
5130 Depreciation: Computer Equipment [A]
5140 Depreciation: Furniture & Fixtures [A]
5150 Depreciation: Service Tools [A]
5160 Depreciation: Van [A]
5170 Depreciation: Retail Premises [A]
5180 Net Depreciation [S]
5190 Delivery Expense
5200 Hydro Expense
5210 Insurance Expense
5220 Interest on Loan
5230 Interest on Mortgage
5240 Maintenance of Premises
5250 Supplies Used
5260 Property Taxes
5270 Uncollectable Accounts Expense
5280 Telephone Expense
5285 Van Maintenance & Operating Expense
5290 TOTAL OPERATING EXPENSES [T]

5295 PAYROLL EXPENSES [H]
5300 Wages
5320 Salaries
5330 Commissions & Bonuses
5350 Travel Expenses
5410 EI Expense
5420 CPP Expense
5430 WSIB Expense
5440 EHT Expense
5450 Gp Insurance Expense
5460 Employee Benefits
5490 TOTAL PAYROLL EXPENSES [T]

NOTES: The Chart of Accounts includes all accounts and Current Earnings. Group account types are not marked. Other account types are marked as follows: [H] Heading, [A] subgroup Account, [S] Subgroup total, [T] Total, [X] Current Earnings.

BALANCE SHEET

VELOCITY

April 30, 2021

Assets

1000	CURRENT ASSETS		
1060	Bank: Niagara Trust Chequing	$ 52 744.00	
1080	Bank: Niagara Trust Savings	118 110.00	
1120	Bank: Visa and Interac	5 925.00	
1140	Bank: USD (7 220 USD)	9 500.00	
1150	Net Bank		$186 279.00
1200	Accounts Receivable	17 110.00	
1210	Allowance for Doubtful Accounts	−800.00	
1220	Advances & Loans Receivable	100.00	
1230	Interest Receivable	420.00	
1240	Net Receivables		16 830.00
1260	Prepaid Advertising		480.00
1270	Prepaid Insurance		4 800.00
1280	Office Supplies		300.00
1290	Bicycle Repair Parts		1 150.00
1300	Rental Bicycles		7 520.00
1400	TOTAL CURRENT ASSETS		$217 359.00
1500	INVENTORY ASSETS		
1520	Accessories	6 540.00	
1540	Bicycles	40 840.00	
1560	Books	5 000.00	
1580	TOTAL INVENTORY ASSETS		$ 52 380.00
1600	CENTRE & EQUIPMENT		
1610	Computer Equipment	7 000.00	
1620	Accum Deprec: Computer Equip	−3 000.00	
1630	Net Computer Equipment		4 000.00
1640	Furniture & Fixtures	2 000.00	
1650	Accum Deprec: Furn & Fixtures	−400.00	
1660	Net Furniture & Fixtures		1 600.00
1670	Service Equipment & Tools	3 000.00	
1680	Accum Deprec: Service Tools	−900.00	
1690	Net Service Tools		2 100.00
1700	Van	30 000.00	
1710	Accum Deprec: Van	−5 000.00	
1720	Net Van		25 000.00
1730	Retail Premises	200 000.00	
1740	Accum Deprec: Retail Premises	−5 000.00	
1750	Net Retail Premises		195 000.00
1890	TOTAL CENTRE & EQUIPMENT		$227 700.00
	TOTAL ASSETS		$497 439.00 ▶

Liabilities

▶ 2000	CURRENT LIABILITIES		
2100	Bank Loan		$ 50 000.00
2200	Accounts Payable		12 699.08
2250	Credit Card Payable		220.00
2280	Accrued Wages		760.00
2300	Vacation Payable		706.00
2310	EI Payable	$ 557.79	
2320	CPP Payable	1 168.48	
2330	Income Tax Payable	1 610.65	
2350	Receiver General Payable		3 336.92
2380	EHT Payable		331.00
2400	VRSP Payable		350.00
2410	Savings Plan Payable		350.00
2420	Group Insurance Payable		102.00
2430	Garnisheed Wages Payable		200.00
2460	WSIB Payable		403.00
2500	Business Income Tax Payable		3 600.00
2650	GST/HST Charged on Sales	6 860.00	
2670	GST/HST Paid on Purchases	−2 990.00	
2750	GST/HST Owing (Refund)		3 870.00
2790	TOTAL CURRENT LIABILITIES		$ 76 928.00
2800	LONG TERM LIABILITIES		
2820	Mortgage Payable		180 000.00
2890	TOTAL LONG TERM LIABILITIES		$180 000.00
	TOTAL LIABILITIES		$256 928.00

Equity

3000	OWNER'S EQUITY	
3560	S. Ryder, Capital	$222 884.00
3600	Current Earnings	17 627.00
3690	TOTAL OWNER'S EQUITY	$240 511.00
	TOTAL EQUITY	$240 511.00
	LIABILITIES AND EQUITY	$497 439.00

POST-CLOSING TRIAL BALANCE

VELOCITY

April 30, 2021

		Debits	Credits
1060	Bank: Niagara Trust Chequing	$ 52 744.00	
1080	Bank: Niagara Trust Savings	118 110.00	
1120	Bank: Visa and Interac	5 925.00	
1140	Bank: USD Chequing (7 220 USD)	9 500.00	
1200	Accounts Receivable	17 110.00	
1210	Allowance for Doubtful Accounts		$ 800.00
1220	Advances & Loans Receivable	100.00	
1230	Interest Receivable	420.00	
1260	Prepaid Advertising	480.00	
1270	Prepaid Insurance	4 800.00	
1280	Office Supplies	300.00	
1295	Bicycle Repair Parts	1 150.00	
1300	Rental Bicycles	7 520.00	
1520	Accessories	6 540.00	
1540	Bicycles	40 840.00	
1560	Books	5 000.00	
1610	Computer Equipment	7 000.00	
1620	Accum Deprec: Computer Equipment		3 000.00
1640	Furniture & Fixtures	2 000.00	
1650	Accum Deprec: Furniture & Fixtures		400.00
1670	Service Equipment & Tools	3 000.00	
1680	Accum Deprec: Service Tools		900.00
1700	Van	30 000.00	▶
▶ 1710	Accum Deprec: Van		$ 5 000.00
1730	Retail Premises	$200 000.00	
1740	Accum Deprec: Retail Premises		5 000.00
2100	Bank Loan		50 000.00
2200	Accounts Payable		12 699.08
2250	Credit Card Payable		220.00
2280	Accrued Wages		760.00
2300	Vacation Payable		706.00
2310	EI Payable		557.79
2320	CPP Payable		1 168.48
2330	Income Tax Payable		1 610.65
2380	EHT Payable		331.00
2400	VRSP Payable		350.00
2410	Savings Plan Payable		350.00
2420	Group Insurance Payable		102.00
2430	Garnisheed Wages Payable		200.00
2460	WSIB Payable		403.00
2500	Business Income Tax Payable		3 600.00
2650	GST/HST Charged on Sales		6 860.00
2670	GST/HST Paid on Purchases	2 990.00	
2820	Mortgage Payable		180 000.00
3560	S. Ryder, Capital		240 511.00
		$515 529.00	$515 529.00

SUPPLIER INFORMATION

VELOCITY

Supplier Name (Contact)	Address	Phone No. Fax No.	E-mail Web Site	Terms Pay Method	Expense Acct Tax Code
Complete Cycler Inc. (Strate Spokes) (USD supplier)	1500 Redmond Rd. Suite 100, Woodinville, Washington 98072 USA	Tel: (425) 628-9163 Fax: (425) 629-7164	sspokes@cycler.com cycler.com	2/10, n/30 (before tax) Pay Later	H
Energy Source (Manny Watts)	91 Power Rd. Niagara Falls, ON L2H 2L9	Tel: (905) 463-2664	watts@energysource.ca energysource.ca	net 1 Cheque	5200 G
Escarpment Investments (P. Cuniary)	122 King St. W. Hamilton, ON L8P 4V2	Tel: (905) 462-3338 Fax: (905) 461-2116	pc@escarp.invest.ca escarp.invest.ca	net 1	2410 no tax (exempt)
Lakeshore Sunoco (Mick Annick)	101 Lakeshore Rd. Niagara on the Lake, ON L0S 1J0	Tel: (905) 622-6181	mick@goodforcars.com goodforcars.com	net 1 Visa	5285 IN
Manulife Financial	PO Box 344, Stn A, Toronto, ON M2W 1S1			net 1	no tax (exempt)
Minister of Finance (N.O. Money)	631 Queenston Rd. Hamilton, ON L8K 6R5	Tel: (905) 462-5555	gov.on.ca/fin	net 1	no tax (exempt)
Niagara Bell (Noel Coller)	100 Parkway Ave. Niagara Falls, ON L2E 2K5	Tel: (905) 525-2355	bell.ca	net 1 Cheque	5280 H
Pro Cycles Inc. (C. Glider)	7 Trackway Dr. Waterloo, ON N2G 4S5	Tel: (519) 588-3846 Fax: (519) 588-7126	glider@procycles.com procycles.com	1/15, n/30 (before tax) Pay Later	H
Receiver General for Canada		Tel: (800) 561-7761	cra-arc.gc.ca	net 1	no tax (exempt)
Welland Insurance (Feulle Cuvver)	718 Montgomery Dr. Welland, ON L3B 3H5	Tel: (905) 588-1773 Fax: (905) 588-1624	fc@welland.insur.ca welland.insur.ca	net 1	no tax (not exempt)

▶

SUPPLIER INFORMATION CONTINUED

Supplier Name (Contact)	Address	Phone No. Fax No.	E-mail Web Site	Terms Pay Method	Expense Acct Tax Code
Wheel Deals (Onna Roller) (USD supplier)	4900 Tubular Circle El Cerrito, California 94533 USA	Tel 1: (510) 525-4327 Tel 2: (800) 567-9152 Fax: (510) 526-1135	onna@wheeldeals.com wheeldeals.com	2/10, n/30 (before tax) Pay Later	H
Workplace Safety & Insurance Board (I.M. Hurt)	PO Box 2099 Oshawa, ON L1J 4C5	Tel: (800) 525-9100 Fax: (905) 523-1824	wsib.on.ca	net 1	2460 no tax (exempt)

OUTSTANDING SUPPLIER INVOICES

VELOCITY

Supplier Name	Terms	Date	Inv/Chq No.	Amount	Rate	Tax	Total
Complete Cycler Inc.	2/10, n/30 (before tax)	Apr. 28/21	CC-918	$3 600 USD	@1.31	$468 USD	$5 329.08 CAD
		Apr. 28/21	Chq 344	2 000 USD	@1.31		2 000.00 USD
							$2 709.08 CAD
Pro Cycles Inc.	1/15, n/30 (before tax)	Apr. 20/21	PC-618	$8 000		$1 040	$9 040.00
		Apr. 21/21	Chq 1096	3 000			3 000.00
			Balance Owing				$ 6 040.00
Wheel Deals	2/10, n/30 (before tax)	Apr. 20/21	WD-391	$2 660 USD		$345.80 USD	$ 3 950.00 CAD
				Grand Total			$12 699.08 CAD

CUSTOMER INFORMATION

VELOCITY

Customer Name (Contact)	Address	Phone No. Fax No.	E-mail Web Site	Terms Tax Code	Credit Limit
*Americas Vinelands Tours (B. Bacchus)	75 Graperie Ave. Buffalo, New York 14202 USA	Tel: (716) 367-7346 Fax: (716) 367-8258	bbacchus@avt.com avt.com Currency: USD	2/10, n/30 no tax	$15 000 ($15 000 USD)
*Backstage Tours (G. O. Rideout)	13 Wellspring Dr. Stratford, ON N5A 3B8	Tel: (519) 526-3344 Fax: (519) 525-1166	rideout@backstagetours.ca backstagetours.ca	2/10, n/30 H	$15 000
Festival Tours (Bea Player)	62 Ibsen Court Niagara Falls, New York 14301 USA	Tel: (716) 399-1489 Fax: (716) 399-2735 Currency: USD	bplayer@festivaltours.com festivaltours.com	2/10, n/30 no tax	$15 000 ($15 000 USD)
*Niagara Rapids Inn (Eddy Currents)	339 Picton St. Niagara on the Lake, ON L0S 1J0	Tel 1: (905) 468-3000 Tel 2: (905) 468-3198 Fax: (905) 468-3477	currents@niagararapids.ca niagararapids.ca	2/10, n/30 H	$15 000
*Park 'N Ride Tours (G. O. Carless)	4900 Airport Rd. Toronto, ON M9P 7F2	Tel 1: (416) 622-9250 Tel 2: (416) 622-9238 Fax: (416) 622-9729	carless@parknride.ca parknride.ca	2/10, n/30 H	$15 000
Shavian B & B (G. B. Shaw)	93 Workout Rd. Niagara on the Lake, ON L0S 1J0	Tel: (905) 468-1800 Fax: (905) 468-1278	gbshaw@shavianBB.com shavianBB.com	2/10, n/30 H	$15 000
Cash and Interac Customers	Terms: net 1	Tax code: H	Choose Cash as the default payment method.		
Visa Sales (for Visa customers)	Terms: net 1	Tax code: H	Choose Visa as the default payment method.		

NOTES: Preferred price list customers are marked with an asterisk (*). The ship-to address is the same as the mailing address for all customers. All customers have Pay Later as the default payment method unless otherwise indicated in the list above.

OUTSTANDING CUSTOMER INVOICES

VELOCITY

Customer Name	Terms	Date	Inv/Chq No.	Amount	Total
Backstage Tours	2/10, n/30 (after tax)	Apr. 30/21	2199	$9 040	
		Apr. 30/21	Chq 488	2 100	
			Balance Owing		$6 940
Niagara Rapids Inn	2/10, n/30 (after tax)	Apr. 26/21	2194	$5 650	$5 650
Shavian B & B	2/10, n/30 (after tax)	Apr. 23/21	2191	$4 520	$4 520
				Grand Total	$17 110

EMPLOYEE INFORMATION SHEET

VELOCITY

Employee	Dunlop Mercier (Male)	Pedal Schwinn (Female)	Shimana Gearie (Female)
Position	Full-time Service/Sales	Full-time Sales/Tour Guide	Full-time Sales/Accounting
Address	55 Trailview Rd. Niagara on the Lake, ON L0S 1J0	2 Fallsview Dr. Niagara Falls, ON L2J 4F8	300 Vineland Rd. Niagara on the Lake, ON L0S 1J0
Telephone	(905) 468-1817	(905) 489-4412	(905) 468-5778
Social Insurance No.	532 548 625	783 455 611	488 655 333
Date of Birth (mm-dd-yy)	09/19/88	03/15/85	05/24/88
Date of Hire (mm-dd-yy)	01/06/17	02/15/15	08/25/18
Federal (Ontario) Tax Exemption - TD1			
Basic Personal	$12 609 (10 582)	$12 609 (10 582)	$12 609 (10 582)
Other Indexed	–	–	$19 749 (13 972)
Other Non-Indexed	$2 100 (2 100)	–	$4 210 (4 210)
Total Exemptions	$14 709 (12 682)	$12 609 (10 582)	$36 568 (28 764)
Additional Federal Tax	–	$50.00	–
Employee Taxes			
Historical Income Tax	$1 668.29	$3 022.96	$1 224.36
Historical EI	$232.97	$308.32	$284.78
Historical CPP	$547.31	$761.00	$760.39
Deduct EI; EI Factor	Yes; 1.4	Yes; 1.4	Yes; 1.4
Deduct CPP	Yes	Yes	Yes
Employee Income			
Loans: Historical Amount	$100.00	(use) ✓	(use) ✓
Benefits per Period	$16.00	$35.00	$35.00
Benefits: Historical Amount	$128.00	$140.00	$140.00
Vacation Pay Owed	$706.00	(do not use)	(do not use)
Vacation Paid	$386.00	(do not use)	(do not use)
Regular Wage Rate (Hours per Period)	$18.00/hr (80 hours)	(do not use)	(do not use)
Regular Wages: Historical Amount	$11 520.00	(do not use)	(do not use)
Overtime 1 Wage Rate	$27.00/hr	(do not use)	(do not use)
Overtime 1 Wages: Historical Amount	$486.00	(do not use)	(do not use)
Salary (Hours per Period)	(do not use)	$4 100.00 (150 hours)	$3 700.00 (150 hours)
Salary: Historical Amount	(do not use)	$16 400.00	$14 800.00
Commission	(do not use)	(do not use)	(use) ✓ 2% (service revenue)
Commissions: Historical Amount	(do not use)	(do not use)	$348.00
No. Clients (piece rate)	$10	$10	$10
Bonus:	(use) ✓	(use) ✓	(use) ✓

▶

EMPLOYEE INFORMATION CONTINUED			
Employee	**Dunlop Mercier**	**Pedal Schwinn**	**Shimana Gearie**
Employee Income continued			
Tuition: Per Period	$110	(use) ✓	$310
Tuition: Historical Amount	–	–	$1 240
Travel Exp.: Historical Amount	(use) ✓	$120.00	(use) ✓
Pay Periods	26	12	12
Vacation Rate	6% retained	0%, not retained	0%, not retained
Record Wage Expenses in	Linked Accounts	Linked Accounts	Linked Accounts
Deductions			
VRSP (Historical Amount)	$50.00 ($450.00)	$100.00 ($400.00)	$100.00 ($400.00)
Savings Plan (Historical Amount)	$50.00 ($450.00)	$100.00 ($400.00)	$100.00 ($400.00)
Garnishee (Historical Amount)	(do not use)	$200.00 ($800.00)	(do not use)
WSIB and Other Expenses			
WSIB Rate	1.29	1.29	1.02
Group Insurance (Historical Amount)	$16.00 ($128.00)	$35.00 ($140.00)	$35.00 ($140.00)
Entitlements: Rate, Maximum Days, Clear? (Historical Amount)			
Vacation	–	8%, 25 days, No (15)	8%, 25 days, No (15)
Sick Leave	5%, 15 days, No (12)	5%, 15 days, No (10)	5%, 15 days, No (8)
Personal Days	2.5%, 5 days, No (4)	2.5%, 5 days, No (2)	2.5%, 5 days, No (3)
Direct Deposit			
Yes/No	Yes	Yes	Yes
Branch, Institution, Account No.	89008, 102, 2998187	94008, 102, 3829110	89008, 102, 2309982
Percent	100%	100%	100%
Additional Information			
Emergency Contact & Number	Adrian Ingles (905) 548-0301	Alex Schwinn (905) 688-2973	Martha Gearie (905) 458-5778
T4 and RL-1 Reporting			
EI Insurable Earnings	$12 392.00	$16 400.00	$15 148.00
Pensionable Earnings	$12 520.00	$16 540.00	$16 528.00
Withheld	$3 348.57	$5 692.28	$3 069.53
Net Pay	$9 143.43	$10 827.72	$13 318.47

Employee Profiles and TD1 Information

All Employees VeloCity pays group insurance premiums for all employees. They also are reimbursed for tuition fees when they successfully complete a university or college course. These two benefits are taxable. In addition, when they use their personal vehicles for company business, they are reimbursed for car expenses.

All employees work full time and are entitled to three weeks' vacation, 10 days' sick leave and five days of personal leave per year. All three employees have sick leave and personal days that they can carry forward from the previous year. The two salaried employees take three weeks' vacation as paid time, and the hourly employee receives 6 percent of his wages as vacation pay when he takes his vacation.

Starting in May, as an incentive to provide excellent customer service, all employees will receive a quarterly bonus of $10 for every completed satisfied-customer survey.

Dunlop Mercier is responsible for shipping, receiving, delivery and assembly for customers. He also does all the repair work in the store. As a single male, he uses the basic claim amount plus his tuition fees. Every two weeks his pay, at the rate of $18 per hour, is deposited to his account. For the hours beyond 40 hours in a week, he receives an overtime rate of $27 per hour. He is owed four months of vacation pay. He contributes to the investment savings plan through payroll deductions. He still owes $100 from a loan of $200 for which he will pay back $50 in each of the next two pay periods.

NOTES
Wages may be garnisheed by any creditor, but the most common one is the Receiver General to pay back taxes owing.

Pedal Schwinn is the store manager for VeloCity, and she assists with store sales. Her monthly salary of $4 100 is deposited directly into her bank account. Schwinn is married with one child, but uses the basic single claim amount because her husband is also employed and he uses the federal child tax claim amount. Her payroll deductions include additional federal income tax for other income, wages garnisheed to pay for prior taxes owing and regular contributions to her Registered Retirement Savings Plan and an investment savings plan.

Shimana Gearie does the accounting and manages the Payables, Receivables and Payroll in addition to sales in the store. Although she is single, she supports her infirm mother so she has the spousal equivalent claim and a caregiver amount in addition to the basic single claim and tuition amounts. A commission of 2 percent of revenue from services supplements her monthly salary of $3 700, which is deposited directly into her bank account. She has VRSP and investment savings plan contributions withheld from her paycheques.

INVENTORY INFORMATION

VELOCITY

Code	Description	Min Stock	CAD Prices Reg	CAD Prices (Pref)	USD Prices Reg	USD Prices (Pref)	Stock/Sell Unit	Buying Unit	Relationship	Qty on Hand	Total (Cost)
Accessories: Total asset value $6 540 (Linked Accounts: Asset 1520, Revenue 4020, COGS 5050, Variance 5080) Charge HST											
AC010	Bicycle Pump: standing model	5	$ 50	($ 45)	$ 37	($ 33)	unit	box	4/box	10	$ 300
AC020	Bicycle Pump: hand-held mini	5	80	(70)	60	(54)	unit	box	10/box	10	500
AC030	Helmet	15	120	(105)	90	(80)	helmet	carton	10/carton	40	2 400
AC040	Light: halogen	10	25	(22)	18	(16)	unit	box	10/box	20	200
AC050	Light: rear reflector	20	15	(12)	11	(10)	unit	box	10/box	30	210
AC060	Lock: kryptonite tube	10	70	(65)	52	(47)	lock	box	5/box	15	600
AC070	Pannier: front wicker clip-on	3	80	(75)	60	(54)	basket		same	6	300
AC080	Pannier: rear mesh	3	60	(55)	44	(40)	basket		same	10	380
AC090	Trailer: 2-child closed	1	620	(570)	445	(400)	unit		same	4	1 200
AC100	Trailer: third-wheel rider	1	260	(235)	190	(170)	unit		same	3	450
Books: Total asset value $5 000 (Linked Accounts: Asset 1560, Revenue 4020, COGS 5070, Variance 5080) HST exempt, charge GST only											
BK010	Books: Complete Bicycle Guide	10	40	(35)	30	(27)	book		same	110	2 200
BK020	Books: Endless Trails	10	40	(35)	30	(27)	book		same	140	2 800
Bicycles: Total asset value $40 840 (Linked Accounts: Asset 1540, Revenue 4020, COGS 5060, Variance 5080) Charge HST											
CY010	Bicycle: Commuter Steel frame CX10	3	640	(590)	475	(430)	bike		same	12	3 720
CY020	Bicycle: Commuter Alum frame CX90	3	960	(850)	715	(645)	bike		same	12	6 480
CY030	Bicycle: Racer Ultra lite RX480	1	3 100	(2 800)	2 300	(2 070)	bike		same	4	6 200
CY040	Bicycle: Trail Alum frame TX560	4	1 220	(1 090)	900	(810)	bike		same	16	9 920
CY050	Bicycle: Mountain Alum frame MX14	2	1 850	(1 650)	1 380	(1 240)	bike		same	6	5 580
CY060	Bicycle: Mountain Carbon frame MX34	1	2 950	(2 600)	2 175	(1 960)	bike		same	2	3 440
CY070	Bicycle: Youth YX660	4	460	(420)	340	(305)	bike		same	16	3 520
CY090	Stationary Converter	2	870	(800)	655	(590)	unit		same	6	1 980

NOTES: No duty is charged on these items imported from the United States. The duty rate is 0%.
Stocking and selling units are the same for all items.
Buying units and the relationship to stocking units are entered in the Relationship column only when these are different from the stocking/selling units.
"Same" is entered in the relationship column when the same unit is used for all measures.

▶ **INVENTORY INFORMATION CONTINUED**

Code	Description	CAD Prices Reg	(Pref)	USD Prices (Reg)		Unit	Taxes
Services (Linked Accounts: Revenue 4040, Expense 5075)							
S010	Boxing for shipping	$ 75	($70)	$57	($50)	job	HST (not exempt)
S020	Maintenance: annual contract	110	(100)	82	(75)	year	HST (not exempt)
S030	Maintenance: complete tune-up	70	(65)	53	(48)	job	HST (not exempt)
S040	Rental: 1 hour	10	(9)	7	(6)	hour	HST (not exempt)
S050	Rental: 1 day	30	(25)	22	(20)	day	HST (not exempt)
S060	Repairs	45	(40)	33	(30)	hour	HST (not exempt)

Accounting Procedures

Harmonized Sales Taxes: HST, GST and PST

HST at the rate of 13 percent is applied to all goods and services offered by VeloCity, except books. The Harmonized Sales Tax includes the provincial sales tax of 8 percent. Goods that are exempt for PST, such as books, have a different tax code applied (code G – GST @ 5%).

VeloCity uses the regular method for remittance of the Harmonized Sales Tax. HST and GST collected from customers are recorded as liabilities in *GST/HST Charged on Sales*. HST and GST paid to suppliers are recorded in *GST/HST Paid on Purchases* as a decrease in liability to the Canada Revenue Agency (CRA). These two postable accounts are added together in the subgroup total account *GST/HST Owing (Refund)* because a single return is remitted for both taxes. The balance of HST and GST to be remitted or the request for a refund is sent to the Receiver General for Canada by the last day of the current month for the previous month.

Tax calculations will be correct only for customers and suppliers for whom the tax exempt option was set as No. The GST and HST reports available from the Reports menu will include transactions completed in the Sales, Purchases and General journals, but the opening historical balances will not be included. Therefore, the amounts in the tax reports may differ from the balances in the General Ledger accounts. You should use the General Ledger accounts to verify the balance owing (or refund due) and make adjustments to the report manually as necessary.

After the report is filed, clear the HST and GST reports up to the last day of the previous month. Always back up your files before clearing the tax details.

NOTES

Because VeloCity also sells books that are exempt for HST but not GST, GST/HST is added to account names.

PRO VERSION

pro The term Vendors replaces Suppliers throughout the program.

NOTES

To clear the tax report, choose the Maintenance menu, then Clear Data. Click Clear Tax Report and select HST and GST.

The Employer Health Tax (EHT)

The Employer Health Tax (EHT) is paid by employers in Ontario to provide Ontario Health Insurance Plan (OHIP) coverage for all eligible Ontario residents. The EHT is based on the total annual remuneration paid to employees. Employers whose total payroll is less than $200 000 pay EHT at the rate of 0.98 percent. The EHT rate increases with total payroll to a maximum of 1.95 percent for payroll amounts of $400 000 and more. In this application, EHT will be remitted quarterly. *EHT Payable* is set up as a liability owing to the supplier, Minister of Finance. The Remittance Payments Journal will provide the balance owing to the Minister of Finance when the liability is linked to this supplier.

Aging of Accounts

VeloCity uses aging periods that reflect the payment terms it provides to customers and receives from suppliers. For customers, this will be 10, 30 and 60 days, and for suppliers,

15, 30 and 60 days. Interest at 1.5 percent per month is charged on customer accounts that are not paid within 30 days. Regular customer statements have the interest amounts, and invoices are then prepared to add the interest to the amount owing in the ledger record.

Discounts

NOTES
Daily Business Manager lists are helpful for making sure that you take advantage of available discounts.

VeloCity offers a 2 percent discount to regular account customers if they settle their accounts within 10 days. Full payment is requested within 30 days. These payment terms are set up as defaults. When the receipt is entered and the discount is still available, the program provides the amount of the discount and the net amount owing. No discounts are given on cash or credit card sales. Customer discounts are calculated on after-tax amounts.

Some customers receive preferred customer prices that are approximately 10 percent below the regular prices. These customers are identified in the ledger records and the preferred prices are set up in the Inventory Ledger records.

Some suppliers also offer discounts for early settlement of accounts. Again, when the terms are entered for the supplier and payment is made before the discount period expires, the program displays the discount as available and automatically calculates a net balance owing. Payment terms vary from supplier to supplier. Supplier discounts may be calculated on before-tax amounts or after-tax amounts.

Freight

When a business purchases inventory items, the cost of any freight that cannot be directly allocated to a specific item must be charged to *Freight Expense* — a general expense that is not charged to the costs of any inventory asset account. Customers also pay for delivery. HST is charged on freight for both sales and purchases (tax code H).

Bank Deposits

Deposit slips are prepared weekly when cash and cheques are received. Receipts are debited to *Undeposited Cash and Cheques* and transferred weekly to *Bank: Niagara Trust Chequing*.

NOTES
Although import duties are not charged on the items imported by VeloCity from the United States, we explain the procedure for setting up import duties and set the rates at zero so that no tax will be charged.

Imported Inventory

Some inventory items are imported from the United States. The bank accounts, supplier records and inventory records are modified to accommodate the foreign currency transactions and import duties automatically.

Purchase Returns and Allowances

A business will sometimes return inventory items to suppliers because of damage, poor quality or shipment of the wrong items. Usually a business receives a credit note from a supplier for the return. The return of inventory is entered in the Purchases Journal as an inventory purchase:

- Select the item in the Item field and enter the quantity returned as a **negative** amount in the Quantity field. The program will automatically calculate a negative amount as a default in the Amount field. You cannot change the account number.
- Accept the default amount and enter other items returned to the supplier.
- Enter the appropriate tax code for each item returned.

The program will create a negative invoice to reduce the balance owing to the supplier and will reduce the applicable inventory asset accounts, the freight accounts, *GST/HST Paid on Purchases* and the quantity of items in the Inventory Ledger database.

Purchase allowances for damaged merchandise that is not returned are entered as non-inventory negative purchase invoices. Enter the amount of the allowance as a **negative** amount in the Amount field and choose taxes included as the tax code. Enter *Purchases Returns & Allowances* in the Account field.

Sales Returns and Allowances

Sometimes customers will return inventory items. Usually, a business issues a credit note for the return. The return is entered in the Sales Journal as a negative inventory sale, choosing the same customer and payment method as in the original sale:

- Select the appropriate item in the Item field.
- Enter the quantity returned with a **negative** number in the Quantity field.
- The price of the item appears as a positive number in the Price field, and the Amount field is calculated automatically as a negative amount.
- Enter the tax code for the sale and the account number for *Sales Returns & Allowances*.

The program will create a negative invoice to reduce the balance owing by the customer and to reduce *Cost of Goods Sold* and *GST/HST Charged on Sales*. The applicable inventory asset accounts and the quantity of items in the Inventory Ledger database will be increased.

Sales allowances are entered as non-inventory negative sales invoices with taxes included, creating a debit entry for *Sales Returns & Allowances* and a credit for *Accounts Receivable*. If the allowance is paid by cheque, enter the allowance in the Payments Journal as an Other Payment paid by cheque.

NSF Cheques

If a cheque is deposited from an account that does not have enough money to cover it, the bank returns it to the depositor as NSF (non-sufficient funds). If the cheque was in payment for a cash sale, you must process the NSF cheque through the Sales Journal because there was no Receipts Journal entry. Create a customer record if necessary and enter a positive amount for the amount of the cheque. Choose *Bank: Niagara Trust Chequing* as the account. Choose Pay Later as the method of payment. If the customer is expected to pay the bank charges, enter these on the second invoice line as a positive amount and select the appropriate revenue account.

If the NSF cheque in payment of an invoice was deposited to a different account than the one used in the Receipts Journal, create a negative receipt to reverse the cheque. Choose Include Fully Paid Invoices. Click the invoice line that this cheque was applied to. Enter the discount taken as a negative amount. Enter the Payment Amount as a negative amount. Choose the correct bank account from the Deposit To field. Refer to page 605 and Appendix C.

Adjustments for Bad Debt

Most businesses set up an allowance for doubtful accounts or bad debts, knowing that some customers will fail to pay. The amount entered for this will be a reasonable guess at how much of the *Accounts Receivable* amount will never be collected. When the allowance is set up, a bad debts or uncollectable accounts expense account is debited and the allowance is credited (effectively reducing the net receivables balance). When a business is certain that a customer will not pay its account, the debt should be written off by crediting *Accounts Receivable* and debiting *Allowance for Doubtful Accounts*. When taxes apply, an extra step is required. Part of the original sales invoice was entered as a credit (increase) to *GST/HST Charged on Sales*. By entering the full amount and the code IN for taxes included, the GST/HST payable amount will automatically be correctly reduced.

NOTES
Purchases Returns & Allowances is a contra-expense account with a credit balance. The return creates a credit entry that will reduce total expenses.

NOTES
The sales tax rules for credits, allowances and discounts are complex. They may be different for provincial and federal taxes and they may differ from one province to another. Adjusting General Journal entries may be required to adjust the amount of tax owing and calculate the tax remittance. We have chosen to leave out the tax component for transactions of this type. Refer to Chapter 2 for more information about sales taxes.

NOTES
Sales Returns & Allowances is a contra-revenue account with a debit balance. The sales return creates a debit entry that will reduce total revenue and Accounts Receivable.

NOTES
The Sales Journal entry for the NSF cheque will credit the bank account and debit Accounts Receivable for the allowance.

NOTES
Allowance for Doubtful Accounts is a contra-asset account that normally has a credit balance. Therefore, a debit entry from the negative amount will reduce this credit balance, reducing both the allowance and the Accounts Receivable balances.

In Sage 50, record the write-off of the debt in the Sales Journal:

- Select the customer whose debt will not be paid.
- Enter a source document number to identify the transaction (e.g., memo).
- Enter a **negative** amount for the total unpaid invoice in the Amount field.
- Enter *Allowance for Doubtful Accounts* in the Account field.
- Enter the tax code **IN** (taxes included).

Enter NSF charges, if any, on the next invoice line:

- Enter a **negative** amount for the total NSF charge in the Amount field.
- Enter *Allowance for Doubtful Accounts* in the Account field.
- Enter the tax code **No tax**.

Review the transaction. *Accounts Receivable* is credited (reduced) by the full amount of the invoice to remove the balance owing by this customer. *Allowance for Doubtful Accounts* has been debited (reduced) by the amount of the invoice minus taxes. *GST/HST Charged on Sales* has been debited for the tax portion of the invoice to reduce the tax liability.

After recording the write-off, "pay" both the original invoice and the write-off in the Receipts Journal. The balance will be zero and there will be no journal entry. This step removes the items from the Receipts Journal for the customer so that you can clear the paid transactions and later remove the customer's record.

Manually you would complete the entry as follows:

1. Set up the Allowance for Doubtful Account (bad debts).

Date	Particulars	Debit	Credit
04/01	5270 Uncollectable Accounts Expense	1 000.00	
	1210 Allowance for Doubtful Accounts		1 000.00

2. Customer G. Bell declares bankruptcy. Write off outstanding balance, $226, including HST.

Date	Particulars	Debit	Credit
04/30	1210 Allowance for Doubtful Accounts	200.00	
	2650 GST/HST Charged on Sales	26.00	
	1200 Accounts Receivable, G. Bell		226.00

Occasionally, a bad debt is recovered after it has been written off. When this occurs, the above procedure is reversed and the GST/HST liability must also be restored. The recovery is entered as a non-inventory sale in the Sales Journal as follows:

- Select the customer and enter the date and source document number.
- Type a comment such as "Debt recovered" in the Item Description field.
- Enter a **positive** amount for the total invoice amount in the Amount field.
- Enter the tax code **IN** (taxes included).
- Enter *Allowance for Doubtful Accounts* in the Account field.

NOTES
You would also follow these steps when only part of the bad debt amount is recovered.

Review the transaction — *Accounts Receivable* has been debited for the full amount of the invoice. *Allowance for Doubtful Accounts* has been credited for the amount of the invoice minus taxes. *GST/HST Charged on Sales* has been credited for the tax portion of the invoice to restore the tax liability.

As the final step, record the customer's payment in the Receipts Journal as you would record any other customer payment.

Remittances

For all remittances, the next payment is due in May for the pay period ending April 30. Because May 1 is the earliest transaction date, we cannot enter a date before this. Therefore, May 1 will be the first end of remitting period date for all remittances.

The Receiver General for Canada:
- Monthly EI, CPP and income tax deductions withheld from employees must be paid by the 15th of each month for the previous month.
- Monthly GST/HST owing or requests for refunds must be filed by the end of each month for the previous month.
- Business income tax is paid in quarterly instalments, based on income in the previous year.
- Garnisheed wages are submitted by the 15th of each month for the previous month. A separate cheque is issued for this remittance.

The Minister of Finance:
- Quarterly Employer Health Tax (EHT) deductions must be paid by the 15th of May, July, October and January for the previous quarter.

The Workplace Safety and Insurance Board:
- Quarterly Workplace Safety and Insurance Board (WSIB) assessment for employees must be paid by the 15th of the month for the previous quarter.

Escarpment Investments:
- Monthly investment (Savings Plan) deductions withheld from employees must be paid by the 15th of the month for the previous month.

Welland Insurance:
- Group insurance contributions paid by the employer must be paid by the 15th of the month for the previous month.

Manulife Financial:
- Monthly Registered Retirement Savings Plan (VRSP) deductions withheld from employees must be paid by the 15th of the month for the previous month.

NOTES
In practice, a business would make these four federal tax remittances to different federal offices. Separate supplier accounts would be needed for each remittance. For this application, one supplier account and address has been used for the Receiver General to reduce the length of the supplier list.

INSTRUCTIONS FOR SETUP

Set up the **company accounts** in Sage 50 using the Business Information, Chart of Accounts, Balance Sheet, Income Statement, Post-Closing Trial Balance and Supplier, Customer, Employee and Inventory Information provided above for April 30, 2021. Instructions to assist you in setting up the company accounts follow. The setup of the Inventory Ledger is given in detail. Abbreviated instructions are included for the remaining steps. Refer to the Love It Again (Chapter 4), Air Care Services (Chapter 7) and Northern Lights (Chapter 9) applications if you need more detailed explanations for other ledgers. Page references for the coverage of these topics in earlier chapters are included in this chapter.

KEYSTROKES FOR SETUP

Creating Company Files

We will create the company files from scratch. Once we create the files and define the defaults, we will add the accounts; define linked accounts for all ledgers; set up additional features; create supplier, customer, employee and inventory records; and add historical data.

NOTES
Refer to page 208 for detailed instructions on creating company files.

NOTES
Save your work and update your backup file frequently as you complete the setup.

NOTES
You cannot complete the company setup in multi-user mode. Many of the settings options are dimmed and unavailable when you are working in multi-user mode.

NOTES
Add your own name to the company name to personalize your data files.

NOTES
Because we selected Ontario as the province, some defaults will be added to the data file. WCB will be renamed WSIB.

NOTES
If you later change the province, you may have to change some settings linked to the province selection.

NOTES
The default date format for new companies is determined by your own computer system settings and is provided below the date fields. Day, month or year may be first.

NOTES
You can select another folder by clicking Browse to open the folder path screen and then clicking the folder you want to use. Click OK to return to the File Name screen.

If the folder you want does not yet exist, click the folder into which you want to place the new folder and click OK. Type VELOCITY at the end of the path in the Location field.

Start the **Sage 50 program**. The Select Company window should be open.

Click **Create A New Company**.

Click **OK** to open the Setup wizard welcome screen.

Click **Next** to open the Company Name and Address screen. The cursor is in the Name field.

Type `VeloCity` (and your own name) **Press** *tab* to advance to the Street 1 address field.

Type `27 Gearing Ave.` **Press** *tab*. **Press** *tab* again.

Type `Niagara on the Lake` **Press** *tab*.

Type `o` to enter the province code (ON) and province (Ontario).

Click the **Postal Code field**.

Type `l0s1j0` **Press** *tab*.

Type `Canada` **Press** *tab*.

Type `9054688356` **Press** *tab* to enter the first phone number.

Type `8884688356` **Press** *tab* to enter the second phone number.

Type `9054689100` to enter the fax number.

Click **Next** to open the company Dates window.

The cursor is in the Fiscal Year Start field, the date on which the business begins its fiscal year. VeloCity closes its books quarterly and is beginning a new quarter in May. To be certain that you have the correct year, type the date in text style using four digits for the year. Until we change the date format, it is displayed in the short form.

Enter the **fiscal dates** as follows:

- Fiscal Start: May 1, 2021
- Earliest Transaction Date: May 1, 2021
- Fiscal End: July 31, 2021

Remember that you can edit the company information and fiscal dates later from the Setup menu, Settings option (choose Company and Information).

Click **Next**.

Click **Let Me Build The List Of Accounts Myself...**. **Click** **Next**.

Click **Yes** to confirm your selection and continue to the industry type list.

Choose **Retail** as the Industry for the business. **Click** **Next**.

Type `VELOCITY` to replace the default entry for the file name.

Drag through **Tess** in the folder name field (or the folder you last worked with).

Type `VELOCITY`

If you are using an alternative location for your company files, substitute the appropriate path, folder or drive in the example.

Click Browse to locate the folder you want or type the complete path in the File Location field (e.g., type C:\SageData19\VELOCITY).

Click **Next**.

Click **Yes** to confirm that you are creating a new folder.

Click **Finish** to save the information. **Be patient**, and wait for Sage 50 to finish creating the data files.

Click **Close** to close the Setup wizard screen.

Click **Show This Window On Startup** in the Welcome/Getting Started window and **click Close** to close the Welcome window.

The Home window has the name VELOCITY in the title bar and non-accounting term labels for the modules in the Modules pane list. The program will automatically set up defaults based on the information you have just entered.

NOTES
The Welcome/Getting Started screen may be open in the background, behind the Home window. Click its button on the task bar or click the Sage 50 icon on the task bar and then click the Welcome/Getting Started pop-up window to bring it to the front. You can then close it.
The Shortcuts pane initially has a shortcut for the Getting Started window.

Preparing the System

The next step involves changing the defaults. Change the defaults to suit your own work environment, such as selecting your printer or choosing forms for cheques, invoices or statements. The keystroke instructions are given for computer-generated cheques, invoices and statements. Refer to the Business Information Chart on page 623 for the company default settings.

NOTES
Use the Backup feature frequently while setting up your files and each time you finish your work session to update your backup copy.
You may finish your session at any time while completing the setup. Simply open the data file, accept the session date and continue from where you left off.

Changing the User Preference Settings

You should make the following changes to the User Preferences from the Setup menu. Refer to Chapter 4, page 81, for assistance if necessary.

Choose the **Setup menu** and **click User Preferences** to open the Options.

Click **Use Accounting Terms** and **Automatically Save Changes To Supplier...**.

You can show Home window ledger record balances by the session date or the latest transaction date, and automatically recalculate these balances or refresh them manually when you want. Make the selections you prefer for your own use.

Click **View**.

Click **After Changing Session Date** for **Daily Business Manager** and for **Checklists** to turn off these features and remove the ✓s.

Click **Show Change Session Date At Startup** to select this option.

Hiding the Division module and Time & Billing is optional. You can finish the history without this step because they have no linked accounts.

Click Division in the Pages column and Time & Billing in the Features column if you choose to hide them.

Transaction Confirmation should be selected by default.

Click **Pop-ups** and **choose** the **messages** you want to display and hide.

Click **OK** to save the settings and return to the Home window.

After changing these settings, modules have accounting term names. The user preference settings can be modified at any time by repeating these steps.

CLASSIC VIEW
Division and Time & Billing are both included in the Module column.

WARNING!
Do not skip any ledger icon windows before completing the setup.

CLASSIC VIEW

You can right-click any Home window icon and then click the Settings tool.

When the Settings window opens, click Company and then click Information.

If you select a journal, you will open the Linked Accounts window for the ledger. If you click a ledger icon, you will open the Settings window for the ledger.

The Classic View has no icon that will open the Company Settings directly from the Settings tool.

Changing Company Defaults

Correcting Company Information

The first steps in setting up the company data files apply to the Company module. We will work from that window.

Click OK at any time to save the settings and close the Settings window. To continue later, you can use the Settings icon to access Settings.

Click **Company** in the Modules pane list to change the Home window.

Click the **Settings icon**, or **choose** the **Setup menu** and **click Settings**.

Click **Information**.

Click the **Business No. field**. **Type** 335 677 829 RT0001

Changing System Settings

Click **System**. Use the following System settings:

- Use Cheque No. As The Source Code For Cash Purchases And Sales
- Do Not Allow Transactions Dated Before May 1, 2021
- Allow Transactions In The Future (Beyond The Session Date)
- Warn If Transactions Are More Than 7 Days In The Future
- Warn If Accounts Are Not Balanced When Entering A New Month

Changing Backup Settings

Click **Backup**. Use the following Backup settings:

- Semi-monthly Backup Frequency
- Display A Backup Reminder When Closing This Company

Click **Automatically Back Up This File** to **remove** the ✓. We do not want to schedule automatic backups for instructional files.

Changing Features Settings

NOTES

If you chose to hide the Division module, Division will not appear in the Features Settings window.

VeloCity uses all features of the program except Divisions — orders, quotes and language options should be selected. Division and Packing Slips may be left unselected.

Click **Features**.

Click **each feature** to change its setting.

Changing Default Settings for Forms

NOTES

Credit Cards, Sales Taxes and Currency settings require linked accounts, so we will add them after creating accounts.

Click **Forms** to display the defaults.

Use the Forms options to set up the automatic numbering and printing of all cheques and invoices. They apply only to numerical invoices.

Typing the next number from the source documents allows automatic numbering to take over from the manual system. Using automatic numbering reduces the risk of typing and recording an incorrect invoice or cheque number even when you are not printing cheques and invoices through the program. For VeloCity, the next invoice is #2210.

Click **1** in the **Invoices Next Form Number field**. **Type** 2210

Click the **Sales Quotes Next Form Number field**. **Type** 56

Click the **Sales Orders Next Form Number field**. **Type** 248

Click the **Receipts Next Form Number field**. **Type** 812

Click the **Customer Deposits Next Form Number field**. **Type** 21

Click the **Purchase Orders Next Form Number field**. **Type** 38

Click the **Employee Direct Deposit Stubs Next Form Number field**.

Type 25 (Scroll down to access this field.)

Leave selected the option to verify number sequences for all forms so that the program will warn you if you skip or duplicate a number.

Click a check box to add other features or to turn off an option once it is selected. The ✓ in the appropriate boxes indicates a feature is being used.

The option to Confirm Printing/E-mail will warn you to print before posting a transaction. When printing invoices, statements or cheques you should include the company address, unless it is already printed on your forms.

If you print or e-mail invoices and cheques through the computer, you should turn on the option to Confirm Printing/E-mail.

We want to allow batch printing, that is, printing several forms at once after posting instead of one at a time while entering a transaction. We should also check for duplicate numbers. This control is not selected by default.

Click the **Print/Email In Batches check box** for each form to add a ✓ to each box.

Click the **Check For Duplicates check box** for Invoices and Receipts.

Changing Date Format Settings

Click **Date Format**.

We want to use the long date form for all dates on the screen to verify that we are entering dates correctly. For the reports, you may use either the long or short form. MM (month) should be the first entry in the Short Date Format field.

Choose **MM dd yyyy** from the Short Date drop-down list.

Click **Long Dates** as the setting for On The Screen, Use.

Adding the Company Logo

Click **Logo**. **Click Browse**. **Click This PC** in the folders and links pane on the left-hand side.

Double-click **C:**. Then **double-click SageData19** to open this folder.

Double-click the **LOGOS folder**.

Double-click **VELO.BMP** or **VELO** to enter this file name. The picture and file name should be added to the Logo Settings screen.

Changing Default Names

VeloCity uses the additional information fields in journals. You can label these fields. However, you must use the same names for all journals. We will therefore enter a generic label for the Additional Information field.

NOTES

Many invoices include the alpha or letter portion of the invoice number on the preprinted invoice form. You could then enter the next number from the numeric portion in the Invoices Number field. Alphanumeric invoice numbers, such as VC-399, cannot be increased automatically by the computer.

NOTES

If you hide Time & Billing, the next number for time slips will not be included on the Forms screen. You can leave the field blank if you are not hiding the feature.

WARNING!

Check that the short date format begins with month (MM) so that your dates will match the ones we use for source documents.

Click **Names**:

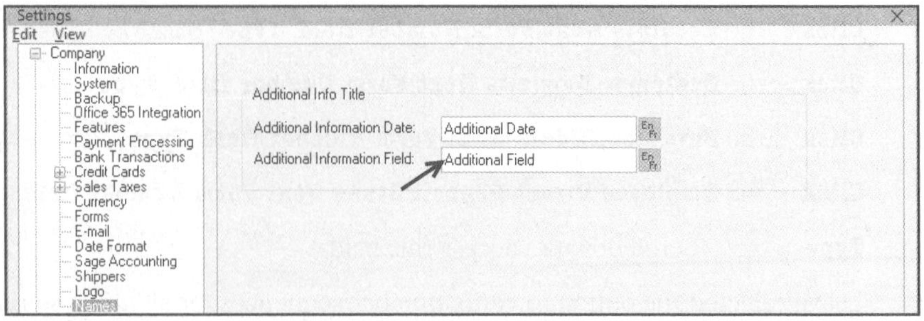

Drag through **Additional Field** and **type** `Ref. Number`

Click **OK** to save the new information and return to the Home window.

Many of the other settings require linked accounts. Therefore, we will create all the General Ledger accounts before entering the remaining settings.

Preparing the General Ledger

The next stage in setting up an accounting system involves preparing the General Ledger for operation. All accounting reports and records have been gathered. The following stages remain:

1. creating new accounts and adding opening balances
2. printing reports to check the accuracy of your records

NOTES
Remember that you can finish your session at any time. To continue, just open the file, accept the session date and start again from where you left off.

Creating New Accounts

The next step is to create the accounts, including the non-postable accounts. Remember to enter the correct type of account. For postable accounts, you should also indicate whether you want to omit accounts with zero balances from financial statements. You need to refer to the company Chart of Accounts on page 624 to complete this step. While creating the accounts, keep the Accounts window open in the background for reference.

Current Earnings is the only predefined account, and you do not need to edit it.

Refer to The Format of Financial Statements (page 86) for a review of these topics, if needed. Refer to the instructions in the Love It Again application, pages 89–96, if you need help with creating accounts. You can use the Accounts window or the Setup Guide.

NOTES
Maximizing the Accounts window allows you to have the list of accounts as well as the new ones you are creating on-screen at the same time.
The Accounts window must be closed if you are using the Setup Guide to create accounts.

NOTES
You can press ctrl + N to open a New Account ledger window and create a new account.
Or, you can use the Setup Guide to create new accounts.

Click the **Chart of Accounts icon** [Chart of Accounts] to open the Accounts window.

Click [maximize] to maximize the Accounts window.

If the accounts are not displayed by name or by type, you should change the view. Click the Display By Type tool or choose the View menu and click Type.

Click the **Create tool** in the Accounts window tool bar or **choose** the **File menu** and **click Create**.

Drag the ledger window to a screen position that makes the list of accounts in the Accounts window and the ledger windows visible to monitor your progress.

Type the **account number**. **Press** tab and **type** the **account name**.

Click the correct **account type**. Remember subgroup accounts (A) must be followed by a subgroup total (S).

Click **Omit From Financial Statements If Balance Is Zero** to select this option.

Allow Division Allocations will be selected by default for all postable revenue and expense accounts, so you do not need to change this option, even if you use divisions.

You will enter the account balances in the next stage.

When all the information is correct, you must save your account.

Click [Create Another] to save the new account and advance to a blank ledger account window.

Create the **other accounts** by repeating these procedures.

Close the **General Ledger window** when you have entered all the accounts on page 624, or when you want to end your session.

After entering all the accounts, you should check for mistakes in account number, name, type and order.

Click [Check tool] or **choose** the **File menu** and **click Check The Validity Of Accounts** to check for errors in account sequence such as missing subgroup totals, headings or totals. The first error will be reported.

Correct the **error** and **check** the **validity** again. Repeat this step until the accounts are in logical order.

Display or **print** your updated **Chart of Accounts** at this stage to check for accuracy of account names and numbers. **Choose** the **Reports menu** and **click Display Chart of Accounts**. Compare the report with the chart on page 624 and make corrections as needed.

Entering Historical Account Balances

The opening historical balances for VeloCity can be found in the Post-Closing Trial Balance dated April 30, 2021 (page 626). All Income Statement accounts have zero balances because the books were closed at the end of the first quarter. Headings, totals and subgroup totals (i.e., the non-postable accounts) do not have balances. Remember to put any forced balance amounts into the *Test Balance Account*.

Open the account information window for **1060 Bank: Niagara Trust Chequing**, the first account requiring a balance.

Click the **Opening Balance field**. **Type** the **balance**.

Correct the **information** if necessary by repeating the above steps.

Click the **Next button** [▶] to advance to the next ledger account window.

Enter **negative numbers for accounts that decrease the total** in a group or section (e.g., *Allowance for Doubtful Accounts*, *Accum Deprec*, *GST/HST Paid on Purchases*). These account balances are indicated with a minus sign (–) in the Balance Sheet on page 625.

Repeat these **procedures** to **enter** the **balances** for the remaining accounts in the Post-Closing Trial Balance on page 626. The *Test Balance Account* should have a zero balance.

Close the **Ledger window**.

After entering all account balances, you should display the Trial Balance to check them against the amounts on page 626. You can do this from the Accounts window.

Choose the **Reports menu** and **click Trial Balance**. **Click** the **Print tool**.

NOTES
If you use the Setup Guide to create accounts, you can accept the default settings for omitting zero balances and allowing allocations.

NOTES
We will change the account class for expense accounts when we change the class for other accounts that are used as linked accounts.

WARNING!
It is important to have the accounts in logical order at this stage. You will be unable to display some reports when the accounts are not in logical order, so you will not be able to check some of your work. You cannot finish the history if accounts are not in logical order.

NOTES
If you want to use the Retained Earnings linked account to enter account balance discrepancies, you must delay entering account balances until after you enter General Linked Accounts (refer to pages 227–228).

NOTES
For account 1140 Bank: USD Chequing, enter $9 500, the balance in Canadian dollars. The USD balance will be added after we set up currencies.

Close the **display** when finished. Leave the Accounts window open.

Check all **accounts** and **amounts** and **make corrections** if necessary.

Defining Account Classes

> **NOTES**
> The foreign currency and cheque numbers will be added later (page 648) – we need to add the foreign currency to the company settings before we can choose it in the bank account's Ledger Record.

Defining bank accounts involves changing the account class to Bank, choosing the currency for the accounts and adding the next cheque and deposit numbers. If you use online banking, you must also enter the bank name, account numbers and Web site. We must also change the class for *Undeposited Cash and Cheques* to either Bank or Cash to use it as the linked account for receipts. Cash is the appropriate selection. Remember that the bank account class changes must be saved before we can enter the next cheque numbers. Changes are saved automatically when we open the next ledger record.

In addition, we must define the account class for the credit card asset and the credit card payable accounts and change the account class for expense accounts. We will make all these changes before continuing the setup.

> **NOTES**
> Refer to the chart on page 623 for bank information and to page 219 for a review of Bank class accounts.

> **NOTES**
> We must define 1030 Undeposited Cash and Cheques as a Bank or Cash class account in order to enter it as the linked bank account for Receivables. Cash is the most appropriate selection.
> Both Bank and Cash class accounts are available in the Deposit To field for cash sales and receipts.

Double-click **1030 Undeposited Cash and Cheques** to open the ledger.

Click the **Class Options tab**.

Choose **Cash** from the drop-down list of account classes.

Click the **Next Account button** to open the ledger for account **1060**.

Choose **Bank** from the list of account classes.

Click the **Next Deposit Number field**. **Type** 18

Click the **Next Account button**.

Choose **Bank** as the account class for *1080 Bank: Niagara Trust Savings.*

Click **Chequing** (Account Type field). **Click** **Savings** from the list.

Click the **Next Account button** to **open** the ledger for **1120 Bank: Visa and Interac**.

Choose **Credit Card Receivable** as the account class.

Click the **Next Account button** to **open** the ledger for **1140 Bank: USD Chequing**.

Choose **Bank** as the account class.

Click the **Select account list arrow**.

> **NOTES**
> To open the ledger for Credit Card Payable, you can click the Next Account button repeatedly or choose the account from the Select Account list arrow.

Click **2250 Credit Card Payable** to open its ledger screen at the Class Options tab screen.

Choose **Credit Card Payable** as the account class. Credit Card Receivable is not available as a class option for the liability account.

Click the **Select account list arrow** again and **choose 5010 Advertising and Promotion**.

> **NOTES**
> Leave the account class for all accounts from 5040 to 5110 unchanged (set to Cost of Goods Sold class) so that you can create Gross Margin Income Statements.
> If you used the Setup Guide, you must change the class for COGS accounts but not for other expense accounts.

Select **Operating Expense** or **Expense** as the account class.

Click . **Select** the **Operating Expense** or **Expense** class for all postable expense accounts except the cost of goods subgroup accounts (#5040–5110).

Close the **General Ledger window** and the **Accounts window**.

Additional Company Default Settings

Adding a Foreign Currency

VeloCity purchases some inventory items from suppliers in the United States and must set up the company files to allow transactions in USD, United States dollars. We will set up the foreign currency now because we need this information for bank account and supplier and customer settings.

Click the **Settings icon** and **Company**.

Click **Currency** under Company to open the Currency Information window:

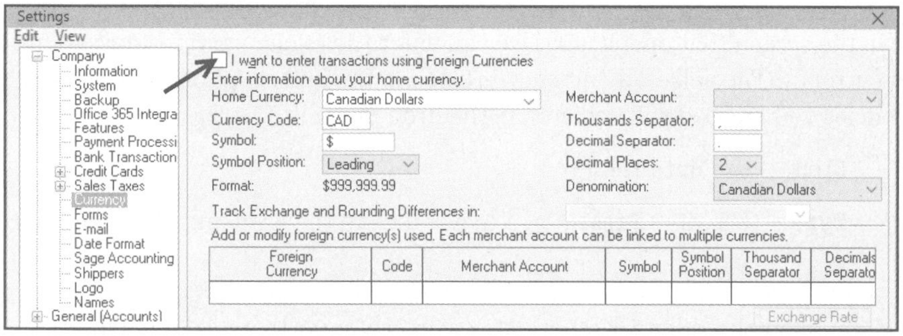

Canadian Dollars is the default in the Home Currency field, and its code, symbol, format and so on are added. You enter the other currencies in the columns in the lower half of the screen, but first you must turn on the option to use other currencies.

Click **I Want To Enter Transactions Using Foreign Currencies**.

Exchange rates vary from day to day and even within the day. When purchases and payments are made at different times, they are subject to different exchange rates — as we demonstrated in the Maple Leaf Rags application (Chapter 12).

Exchange rate differences may result in a gain — when the rate drops before a payment is made or when the rate increases before a payment is received from a customer — or a loss — when the rate increases before a payment is made or when the rate drops before a customer makes a payment. These differences are tracked in the linked account designated on this screen. Rounding differences may also result in gains and losses because the amounts are recorded with two decimal places and exchange rates usually have several significant digits. The account for these differences may be an expense account or a revenue account. VeloCity uses a revenue account.

Click the **list arrow** for **Track Exchange And Rounding Differences In**.

Both revenue and expense accounts are available for linking.

Click **4120 Exchange Rate Differences** to enter the linked account.

The next step is to identify the foreign currency or currencies.

Click the **Foreign Currency field**. **Type** U

Click the **List icon** for the field to open the list of currencies:

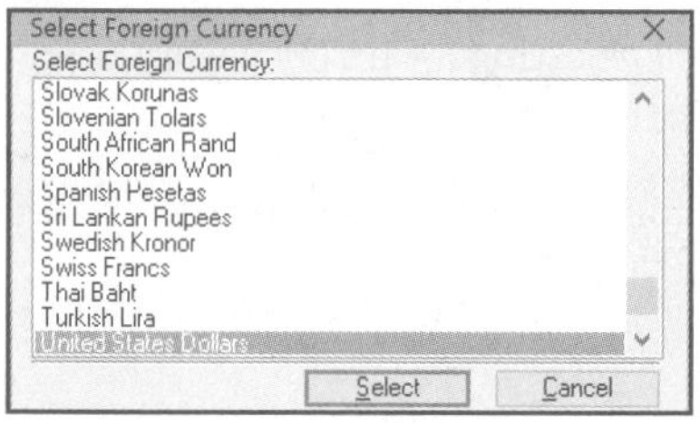

NOTES
Remember that you can finish your session at any time. To continue, just open the file, accept the session date and start again from where you left off.

PRO VERSION
The Merchant Account field is not included.

NOTES
After allowing transactions in a foreign currency, you can change the column sizes by dragging the heading margins so that all headings are visible.

PRO VERSION
The Pro version of Sage 50 allows only two currencies – the home currency plus one foreign currency.

After you click Allow Transactions In A Foreign Currency, the screen expands with the fields you need to add the currency. Choose the account for tracking exchange rate differences. Then select United States Dollars from the Foreign Currency field drop-down list. Click the Exchange Rate button and enter the date and exchange rate in the Date and Exchange Rate columns.

NOTES
You can add a new account at this stage if necessary. Type the new account number and press *tab*. Click Add to start the Add An Account wizard.

NOTES
The Premium version of Sage 50 accepts more than one foreign currency.

The list of currencies opens and United States Dollars should be selected.

Scroll down if necessary, and **double-click United States Dollars** to add it to the Currency Information screen. The currency code, symbol and format are added for the selected currency. Accept the defaults.

Click the **Exchange Rate button**:

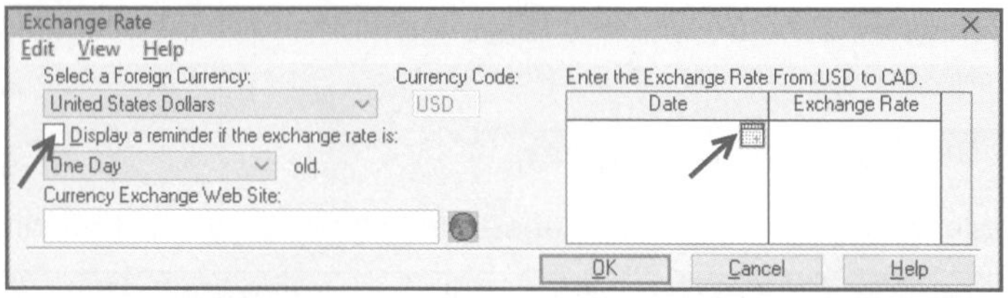

On the screen that opens next, we can enter the exchange rates for various dates for each currency. The selected currency is listed in the Select A Foreign Currency field. All currencies you created will be listed in the drop-down list for this field.

Click the **Date field**.

Type `05 01` **Press** tab to advance to the Exchange Rate field.

Type `1.315`

If you know the rates for other dates, you can enter them as well. Otherwise, you can enter current rates in the journals, as we did in the previous chapters. These rates will be added to the list on this screen and the list will be available in journals.

To ensure that you do not use an old exchange rate that is no longer accurate, you should turn on the reminder that warns if the rate is out of date. A one-day period for updating should be sufficient.

Click **Display A Reminder If The Exchange Rate Is**.

Accept **One Day Old** as the time interval.

Now every time the transaction date is one day past the date of the rate previously used, the program will warn you and give you an opportunity to change the rate. If the rate has not changed, you can accept the old rate.

Click **OK** to return to the Currency Settings screen.

NOTES
If you have a Web site that you use for exchange rate information, you can enter it here as well. Then, with your Internet connection active, click the Web tool to access the Web site directly and obtain current rates. The Web tool appears on the Exchange Rate list screen that you access by clicking the Exchange Rate tool beside the Exchange Rate field in the journals.

Setting Up Credit Cards

VeloCity accepts Visa credit card payments from customers as well as debit cards (Interac). The store also uses a Visa card to pay for some purchases. Setting up credit cards includes naming them, identifying the linked accounts and entering fees associated with the cards.

Click **Credit Cards** for the next step. You will be asked for confirmation:

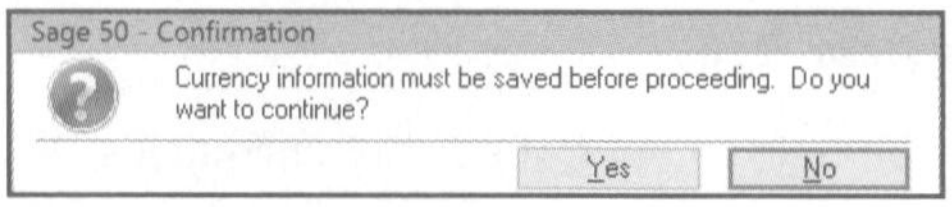

Click **Yes** to save the updated currency settings. Currencies are used with other settings, so they must first be saved.

Click **Used** to open the Credit Card Information screen for the cards that the business uses.

Click the **Credit Card Name field**.

Type `Visa` **Press** tab to move to the Payable Account field.

NOTES
Refer to the Business Information Chart on page 623 for credit card details. To review credit card setup, refer to page 222 for additional information.

Press (enter) for the list of available accounts.

Double-click **2250** to add the account and move to the Expense Account field.

Press (enter) to open the account list.

Double-click **5030**.

Click **Accepted** under Credit Cards to open the Credit Card Information screen for the cards that the business accepts from customers.

Click the **Credit Card Name field**.

Type `Visa` **Press** (tab) to advance to the Currency field.

Click the **List icon** for the Currency field to open the list of currencies:

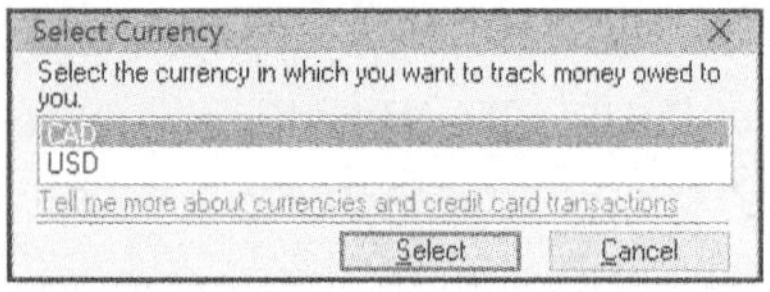

Sage 50 Premium version accepts credit cards in a foreign currency, but they must have separate linked accounts. The Home currency is correctly selected.

Click **Select** to return to the Cards Accepted screen. **Press** (tab). The cursor advances to the Asset Account field.

Press (enter) to list the accounts available for linking.

Double-click **1120** to choose and add the credit card bank account. **Press** (tab).

Type `2.5` to enter the discount fee. **Press** (tab).

Press (enter) to list the accounts available for linking as the Expense Account.

Double-click **5030** to choose and enter the account.

Enter **Interac** as the name, **1120** as the Asset account, **0** as the %, and **5030** as the Expense Account to set up the debit card.

Click **Processing Services only if you want to set up this service**:

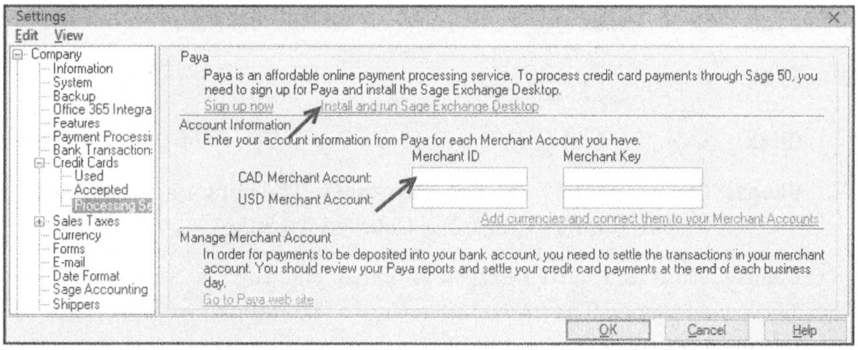

If you want to use the **credit card processing** service feature, you can use the merchant ID and key provided in Chapter 13 (read the margin Notes).

Click the Merchant ID field and enter your number. Press Tab. Type your Merchant Key in this field.

Setting Up Sales Taxes

VeloCity charges and pays GST on books and HST on all other purchases. We will set up codes for these two taxes. We want to generate reports on both taxes.

WARNING!
You must choose a Credit Card Payable or Bank class account as the Payable Account for cards used.
Although accounts in other classes appear on the Select Account list, selecting them will generate an error message when you try to save the entries.

PRO VERSION
The Pro version does not allow credit cards in foreign currencies. You will not have the currency list screen or the column to select the currency.

NOTES
You must choose a Credit Card Receivable or Bank class account as the Asset Account for cards accepted.

NOTES
You can enter these account details for processing credit cards:
Merchant ID: 651259884634
Merchant Key: B8B9O4S6E2K2
Remember that when you set up for processing credit cards, you must follow through with the processing for all Visa sales. And you must enter 4111111111111111 as the Visa number and leave your Internet connection on.
For Interac (debit card) sales, process the card transaction manually (refer to page 521).
If you already installed Sage Exchange, this screen will inform you that Sage Exchange Desktop is running.

NOTES
Refer to the Business Information Chart on page 623 for sales tax information. Refer to page 224 for a review of sales taxes.

Both taxes are linked to the GST/HST accounts because a single remittance to the Receiver General for Canada is made for both taxes; only the rates are different.

Click **Sales Taxes** under Company. There are settings for tax names and codes.

Click **Taxes** to access the Taxes information screen:

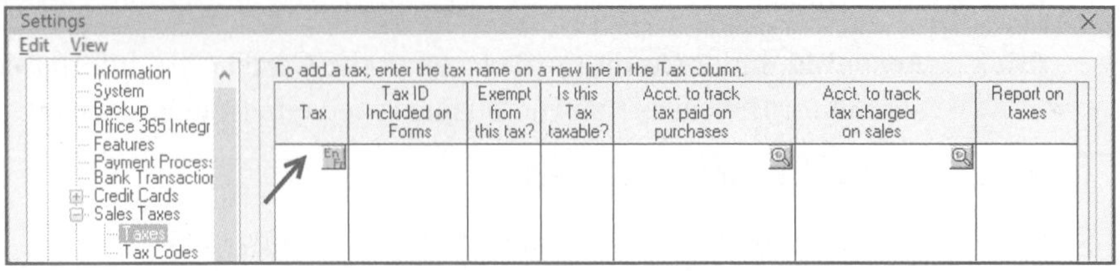

Press tab to advance to the Tax field on the Taxes screen where you should enter the name of the tax. We will enter the HST first.

Type HST **Press** tab to advance to the Tax ID field where we enter the business number.

Type 335 677 829 **Press** tab to advance to the **Exempt From This Tax?** column.

VeloCity is not tax exempt for HST, so the default, No, is correct. HST is also not taxable in Ontario (no other tax is charged on HST).

NOTES

PST is still charged separately on insurance in Ontario. Because this tax is not refundable, you do not need to track it or create a tax code for it. It will be included directly in the expense or asset component of the purchase.

Click , the **List icon for Acct. To Track Tax Paid On Purchases**.

Choose **2670 GST/HST Paid on Purchases**. The cursor advances to the field for the Account To Track Tax Charged On Sales.

Choose **2650 GST/HST Charged on Sales** from the List icon list of accounts. The cursor advances to the Report On Taxes field.

Click **No** to change the default entry to Yes.

Press tab so you can enter the information for GST.

VeloCity is not exempt from GST. The ID number and linked accounts are the same as for HST. GST is not taxable, and the tax is refundable.

Type GST **Press** tab to advance to the Tax ID field.

Type 335 677 829

Click , the **List icon for Acct. To Track Tax Paid On Purchases**.

Choose **2670 GST/HST Paid on Purchases**. The cursor advances to the field for the Account To Track Tax Charged On Sales.

Choose **2650 GST/HST Charged on Sales** from the List icon list of accounts. The cursor advances to the Report On Taxes field.

Click **No** in the Report On Taxes column to change the entry to Yes.

Entering Tax Codes

Click **Tax Codes** to open the next information screen:

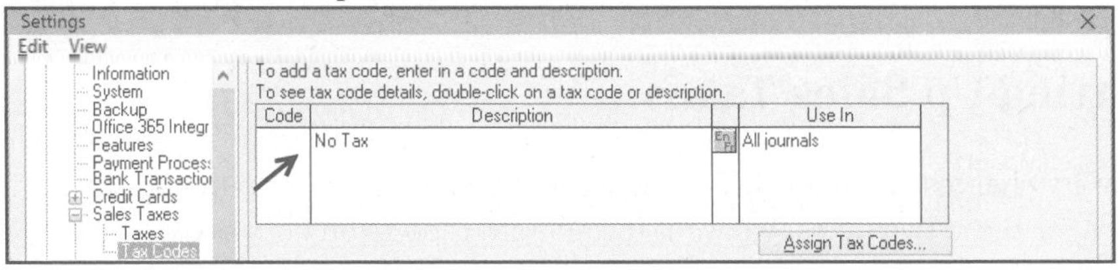

A single code, No Tax, is created as a default.

We need to create tax codes for sales and purchases when HST is charged and when only GST applies. There are also purchases with HST included, so we need a code for this situation as well (e.g., gasoline is priced with all taxes included).

Click the **Code column** below the blank on the first line.

Type H **Press** *tab* to move to the Description field.

Press *enter* or **double-click** to open the Tax Code Details screen:

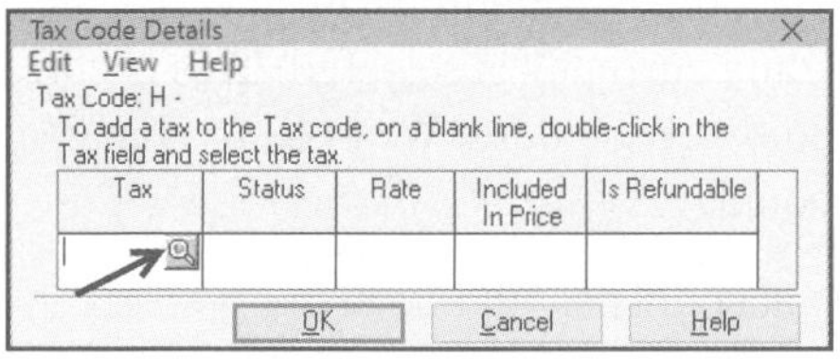

Click the **Tax field List icon** to open the list of taxes entered.

Both taxes from the Taxes screen appear on the list.

Click **Select** because HST is already selected. You will return to the Tax Code Details.

Defaults are entered for the remaining fields. The **Status** is **Taxable** and the tax is **not included** — these are correct — tax is calculated, charged and not included in the price.

Click the **Rate field**. **Type** 13

Click **No** in the Is Refundable column to change the entry to Yes.

Click **OK** to return to the Tax Codes screen for additional codes.

The description "HST @ 13%" appears beside the code H and the tax is used in all journals. You can edit the description if you want. If the tax were not refundable, non-refundable would be added to the description automatically. We are ready to enter the second code, to apply only GST.

Press *tab* until you advance to the next line in the Code column.

Type G **Press** *tab* to move to the Description field.

Press *enter* to open the Tax Code Details screen.

Click the **Tax field List icon**.

Select **GST**. Taxable and not included are the correct selections.

Type 5 in the **Rate field**.

Click **No** in the Is Refundable column to change the entry to Yes.

Click **OK** to return to the Tax Codes screen. The description "GST @ 5%" has been added.

Press *tab* until you advance to the next line in the Code column, below G.

Type IN **Press** *tab* to move to the Description field.

Press *enter* or **double-click** to open the Tax Code Details screen.

Enter **HST** as the tax, and **13%** as the rate. Taxable as the status is correct.

Click **No** in the Included In Price column to change the entry to Yes.

NOTES

If you need to remove a tax code detail line, click the line to be removed, choose the Edit menu and click Remove Line.

Click **No** in the Is Refundable column to change the entry to Yes.

Click **OK** to return to the Tax Codes screen. The description "HST @ 13%, included" appears beside the code IN. **Click OK** to close the Settings.

Updating Bank Account Settings

Adding Currency to a Bank Account

NOTES
We added the next deposit number for the chequing account when we changed the account class.

We need to complete more steps for bank accounts — identify the currency and enter the next cheque number. By default, the home currency is selected. This is correct for the main chequing account and for the credit card account. We need to change the currency setting for the USD chequing account.

Click the **Search tool**. The accounts should be listed.

Double-click **1140 Bank: USD Chequing**.

Click the **Class Options tab** — we already entered Bank as the account class.

Click the **Currency list arrow**:

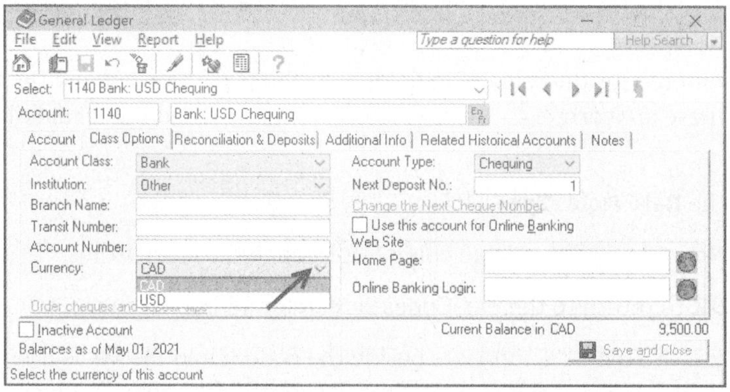

Once we identify an account as a bank account and allow foreign currency transactions, we identify the currency for the account on the Class Options tab screen.

NOTES
You cannot change the currency in the Setup Guide, although you can enter the foreign currency amount after adding the currency in the ledger record.

Click **USD**. Zero now appears as the balance amount for the USD currency.

Click **Change The Next Cheque Number**. You will not be allowed to continue:

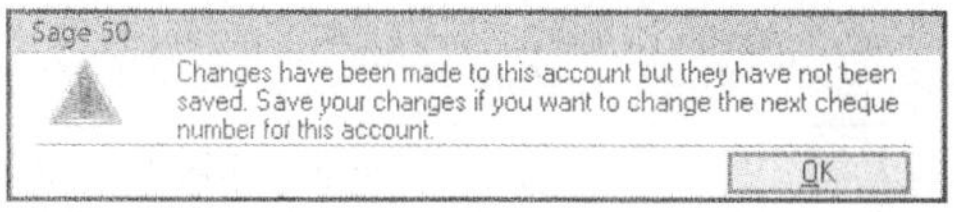

Click **OK** to return to the ledger window; we must first save the changes.

Click the **Save tool** or **choose** the **File menu** and **click Save**:

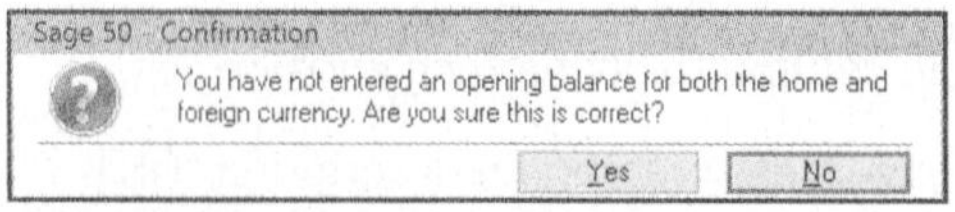

Because we have entered the balance only in the home currency, we are now asked to confirm that this is correct. It is not.

Click **No** to return to the ledger window so we can add the USD balance.

Click the **Account tab** to return to the Opening Balance fields. A second field has been added for the balance in USD.

Click the **Opening Balance In USD field**. **Type** 7220

Click the **Save tool**.

You should now be able to add the next cheque number in the sequence.

Click the **Class Options tab**.

Click **Change The Next Cheque Number** to open the cheque Form settings:

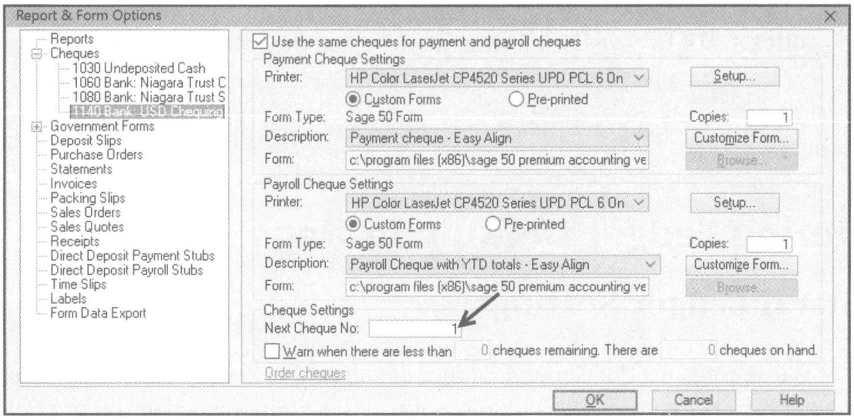

The USD bank account we started from is selected, so the cheque number field for it is available.

Click the **Next Cheque No. field**. **Type** `346`

Click **1060 Bank: Niagara Trust Chequing** in the left panel under Cheques.

Click the **Next Cheque No. field**. **Type** `1101`

We will make additional printer setting changes before proceeding, while the Reports & Forms window is open.

Changing Other Printer Settings

Reports and forms settings apply only to the data file that you are using. They must be set for each data file separately, and the settings are saved with each file.

Click Reports or click the form for which you want to enter settings.

Choose the printer you will be using for reports. Change the margins if necessary. Choose fonts and type sizes for the report from the lists. Click Setup to choose other options for your printer, such as paper size, two-sided printing and so on.

Click OK to save your settings and return to the previous Printer setting screen.

Each type of form — cheques, invoices and so on — has its own setup.

Click **Invoices** to open the settings for printing invoices.

Check that the **file locations** for the forms are correct or dimmed.

For all **E-mail** and **Printed Forms**, choosing a generic (not user-defined) form in the Description field should automatically provide the correct form file locations — the Forms folder in your Sage 50 Premium Accounting Version 2019 program folder.

As you did for reports, select the printer and set the margins, font and type size to match the forms you are using. Preprinted forms were included as part of the program installation and are located in the Forms folder in the main Sage 50 program folder. You should Print Subtotals In Invoices.

To preview invoices you must select **Custom Forms**.

If you want to customize the invoice form choose Custom Forms and click **Customize Form**.

WARNING!
The entries in the Form fields should be valid locations. The Form field references should be the Forms folder in your Sage 50 Premium Accounting Version 2019 program folder.

NOTES
You can change other printer settings at this stage if you want, or you can change them at any time as needed.

NOTES
From the Home window, choose the Setup menu and click Reports & Forms. The printer setting options for reports are given. More information about changing printer settings is available in Appendix E on the Student DVD.

NOTES
Refer to Appendix F on the Student DVD if you want to customize printed invoices.

To print labels, click Labels and enter the size of the labels and the number that are placed across the page.

To set the printer options for cheques or other forms, click the form you want and make the necessary changes.

Click **OK** to save the information when all the settings are correct. You can change printer settings at any time.

Close the **Ledger window** to continue entering the settings.

CLASSIC VIEW

You can access the Linked Accounts screens for any ledger directly. Right-click a journal icon to select it for the ledger you want and then click the Settings tool.

For example, to access General Linked Accounts, right-click the General Journal or the Reconciliation & Deposits icon, General Journal or Reconciliation & Deposits.

Click the Settings tool. The General Linked Accounts screen opens. If no icon is selected, click General in the Select drop-down list.

Follow the same steps for other ledgers. Start with the Sales or Receipts icon to open the linked accounts screen for the Receivables Ledger, and so on.

Entering Ledger Default Settings

General Ledger Settings

Most of the settings for the General Ledger are already correct. VeloCity is not setting up budgets or departments yet, and it does not use the additional ledger record fields. Using and showing numbers for accounts and four-digit account numbers, the default settings, are also correct for VeloCity. We need to add linked accounts.

Choose the **Setup menu** and **click Settings** to continue entering the settings.

Defining Linked Accounts

Linked accounts are General Ledger accounts that are affected by entries in other journals. For example, recording an inventory purchase will update the Inventory Ledger, several General Ledger accounts and the balance owing to the supplier. Refer to page 227 for a review of linked accounts. Refer to page 88 for a review of the *Current Earnings* account. Linked accounts are also needed for other features.

NOTES

Refer to page 227 to review General Linked Accounts.

Identifying General Linked Accounts

The *Current Earnings* capital account records the changes in net income resulting from sales and expenses. At the end of the fiscal period, the net income (the balance from *Current Earnings*) is transferred to the Retained Earnings capital account (*S. Ryder, Capital* is the Retained Earnings account for VeloCity) and income and expense accounts are reset to zero to prepare for the new fiscal period.

Click **General (Accounts)**.

Click **Linked Accounts under General (Accounts)**.

NOTES

You can create new accounts from any Linked Accounts screen by typing a new account number in the Account field and pressing tab to start the Add An Account wizard.

The General Ledger has two linked accounts. Both must be capital accounts.

GENERAL LINKED ACCOUNTS	
Retained Earnings	3560 S. Ryder, Capital
Current Earnings	3600 Current Earnings

Type the **account number** or **select** the **account** from the drop-down list.

Payables Ledger Settings

NOTES

Refer to page 228 if you want to review Payables settings.

PRO VERSION

Remember that the term Vendors will replace Suppliers.

Click **Payables** and then **click Address**.

Enter **Niagara on the Lake**, **Ontario** and **Canada** as the default city, province and country for suppliers.

Click **Options**.

You should change the intervals for the aging of accounts. Some suppliers offer discounts for payment within 5, 10 or 15 days. Discounts from one-time suppliers are calculated on before-tax amounts.

Set the **aging** intervals at **15**, **30** and **60** days.

Click **Calculate Discounts Before Tax For One-Time Suppliers**.

Setting Up Import Duties

Goods imported from another country may be subject to tariffs or import duties, so you should know how to set up this feature. We will set up the program to charge duty but set the rate at zero so that no duty will be applied on purchases. You must activate the Duty option before creating supplier records so that you can indicate in the supplier records those suppliers that supply goods on which duty is charged. Without these two steps, the duty fields in the Purchases Journal will be unavailable.

Click **Duty** to access the settings we need:

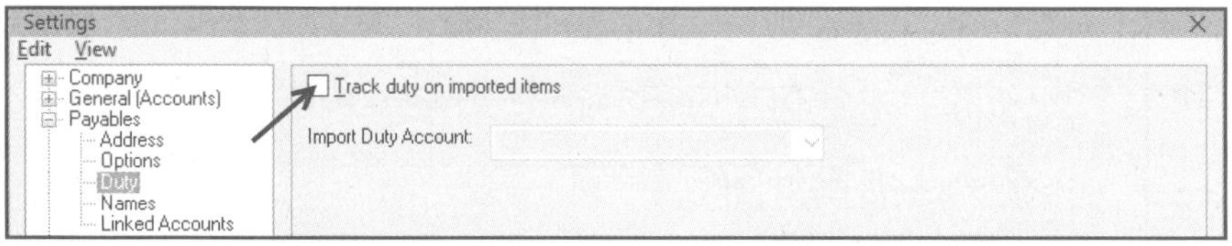

Click **Track Duty On Imported Items** to use the feature and open the linked Account field.

A Payables Account is linked to import duties for the liability to the Receiver General.

Click **2220 Import Duty Payable** from the Import Duty Account drop-down list.

Changing Payables Terminology

Sage 50 chooses a set of terms that is appropriate for the type of business. These terms can be modified by the user on the Names Settings screen. For the companies in this text, we have accepted the default terms Sage 50 applies for the industry. To change them,

Click **Names** to open the settings:

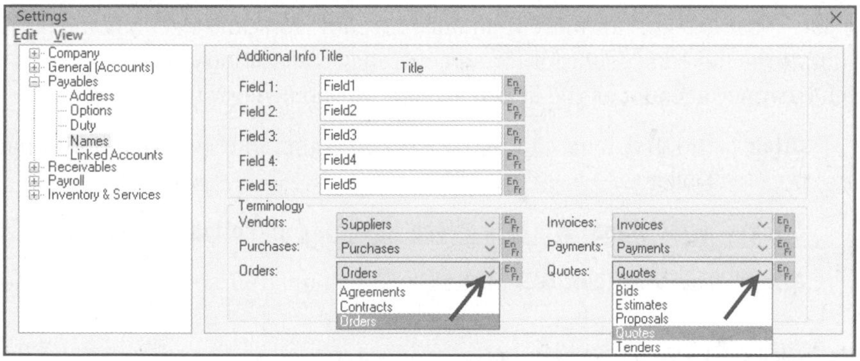

The upper part of the screen has five fields for the additional information you can add to the ledger records. You can rename these fields if you want to use them.

The lower part of the screen has drop-down lists of terms for the various icons in the module. The names you select here will appear throughout the program as the names for icons, fields and reports. The drop-down lists for Orders and Quotes provide the options for naming these. For the terms you can choose for Vendors, Purchases and Invoices, refer to Chapter 7, page 229.

WARNING!
Sage 50 will not allow you to remove an account while it is being used as a linked account. When you try to remove an account, click OK in the Warning window to return to the Accounts window. First, turn the linking function off by deleting the account in the Linked Accounts window. Then delete the account balance, save the changes and, finally, remove the account in the Accounts window. You cannot remove an account if it has a balance or if journal entries have been posted to it.

NOTES
At the time of writing this text, the inventory in this chapter was not subject to duties. However, trade agreements are regularly reviewed and can be changed.

PRO VERSION
The Terminology part of the Names Settings screen is not included in the Pro version because you cannot change the terms used.

NOTES
You can change the terminology used for Vendors, Purchases, Invoices, Orders and Quotes from the Names Settings screen if you want.

NOTES
Refer to Appendix B, page A–16, for a list of the terms used for different types of industry.

To change the terms, click the term you want to change and choose a different term from the drop-down list.

Identifying the Payables Linked Accounts

VeloCity uses *Bank: Niagara Trust Chequing* as its principal linked bank account for all home currency cheque transactions in the subsidiary Payables and Payroll ledgers.

PAYABLES	
Bank Account to Use for Canadian Dollars	1060 Bank: Niagara Trust Chequing
Bank Account to Use for United States Dollars	1140 Bank: USD Chequing
Accounts Payable	2200 Accounts Payable
Freight Expense	5090 Freight Expense
Early Payment Purchase Discount	5100 Purchase Discounts
Prepayments and Prepaid Orders	1250 Purchase Prepayments

To enter the Payables Ledger linked accounts,

Click **Linked Accounts** to display the Linked Accounts window:

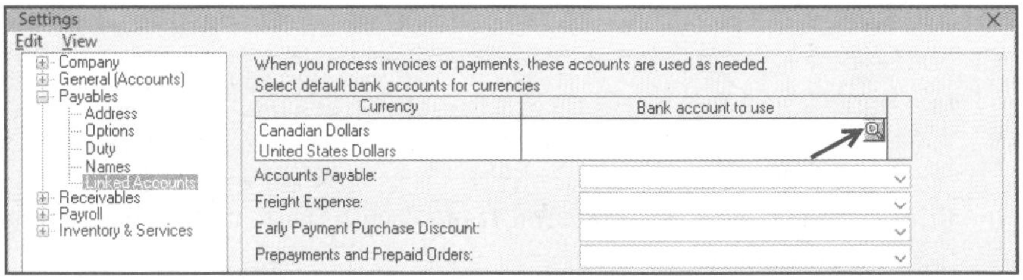

We need to identify the default General Ledger bank accounts used for payments to suppliers. Cash transactions in the Payments Journal will be posted to the bank account you select in the journal window. Bank and Cash class accounts are available in the journals, and the principal linked account defined here will be selected as the default.

You can list the accounts available for linking by clicking the drop-down list arrow for any linked account field. Only Bank and Cash class accounts may be used in the bank fields. That is why we needed to classify the bank accounts first.

VeloCity uses two bank accounts for payments. The chequing account is the principal bank account for Canadian currency transactions, and the USD chequing account is used for transactions in United States dollars.

You can choose a separate linked account for each currency, or you may use the Canadian dollar account for more than one currency. You can select a home currency account as the linked account for foreign currency transactions, but you cannot select a foreign currency account as the linked account for home currency transactions.

Click the **List icon** in the Bank Account To Use column for Canadian Dollars.

Click **1060 Bank: Niagara Trust Chequing** and **click Select**.

Click the **List icon** in the Bank Account To Use column for United States Dollars.

Click **1140 Bank: USD Chequing** and **click Select**.

Enter the **remaining linked accounts** from the chart above. **Type** the **account number** or **select** the **account** from the drop-down list.

Check the linked accounts carefully. To delete a linked account, click it to highlight it in the Linked Accounts window and press *del*. You must complete this step of deleting the linked account before you can remove the account in the General Ledger from the Accounts window.

CLASSIC VIEW

To add the Payables Ledger linked accounts from the Home window, right-click the Purchases or the Payments Journal icon in the Home window to select it.

Click the Settings tool. Or, choose the Setup menu, then choose Settings, Payables and Linked Accounts.

NOTES

The Linked Accounts screen for VeloCity is different from the one on page 230 for Air Care Services, which uses only one currency.

WARNING!

You cannot change the currency for an account when it is used as a linked account. You can choose a home currency account as the linked account to use with a foreign currency. If you had not yet changed the currency for 1140 Bank: USD Chequing, you could still choose it as the linked account. However, you would then be unable to change the currency to USD.

NOTES

The remaining Payables linked accounts were introduced in Chapter 7. Refer to page 230 if you need to review these accounts.

Receivables Ledger Settings

Click **Receivables** and then **click Address**.

Enter **Niagara on the Lake**, **Ontario** and **Canada** as the default address.

Click **Options**.

NOTES
Refer to page 231 if you need to review Receivables Ledger settings.

VeloCity prints the salesperson's name on all customer forms for the customer's reference in case a follow-up is required. Most customers (and inventory items) use the tax code H, so we will use this as the default for new customers. The default tax code will be preselected when we enter the customer records.

VeloCity charges 1.5 percent interest per month on accounts after 30 days (one day overdue), includes paid invoices on customer statements for 31 days (an appropriate period for the monthly statements) and uses payment terms to set aging intervals.

Enter **10**, **30** and **60** days as the **aging** periods.

Click **Interest Charges** to add a ✓ and turn on the calculation.

Click **Compound** to enter the way interest is calculated.

Press *tab* to advance to the % field for Interest Charges.

Type 1.5 **Press** *tab*. **Choose Monthly Interest Rate**. **Press** *tab*. **Type** 1

Click the **Tax Code For New Customers field** for the list of tax codes.

Click **H - HST @ 13%**.

Click **Print Salesperson On Invoices, Orders And Quotes**.

Entering Discount Settings

VeloCity offers its account customers a 2 percent after-tax discount for 10 days; full payment is due in 30 days. VeloCity does not use the line discount feature.

Click **Discount** to open the next Receivables settings screen.

Click the **% field** of the **Early Payment Terms** section.

Type 2 **Press** *tab*.

Type 10 **Press** *tab*.

Type 30

Click **Calculate Line Discounts On Invoices ...** to turn off the feature. Sage 50 advises that this action will remove the related columns from the Sales Journal:

PRO VERSION
Line Discounts are not available in the Pro version.

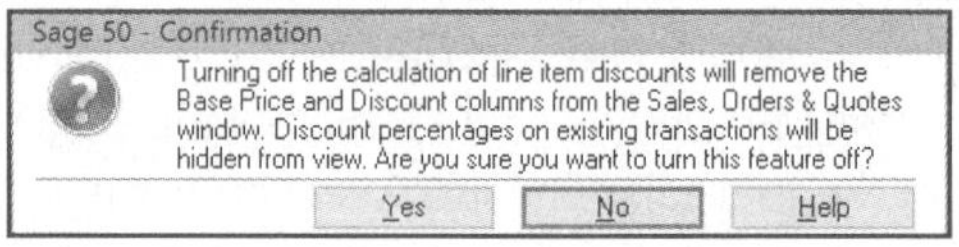

Click **Yes** to confirm your selection.

Changing Default Comments

Click **Comments** under Receivables. **Press** *tab*.

You may add a comment or notice to all your invoices and quotes and to order confirmations. You could use this feature to include payment terms, a company motto or notice of an upcoming sale. Remember that you can change the default message any time you want. You can also edit it for a particular sale or quote when you are completing the invoice. The cursor is in the Sales Invoices field.

Type `Interest @ 1.5% per month on accounts over 30 days.`

Repeat this procedure to enter comments for the other forms.

Changing Receivables Terminology

Click **Names** under Receivables:

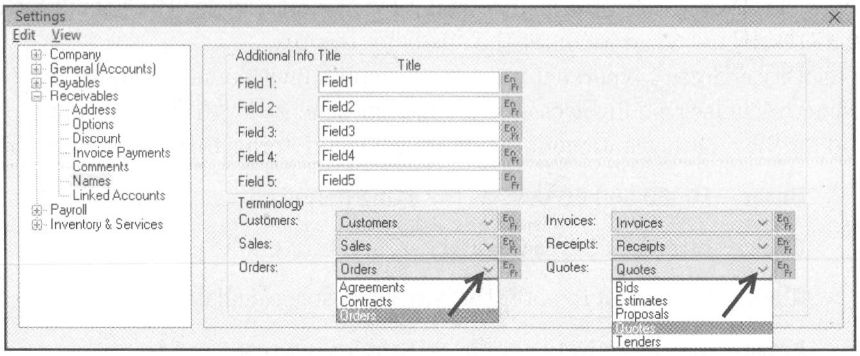

This screen has the same structure as the one for Payables additional information field names and ledger terminology.

The drop-down lists of terms for Orders and Quotes provide the options. The names you select here will appear throughout the program as the names for icons, fields and reports. For the terms you can choose for Customers, Sales and Invoices, refer to Chapter 7, page 233.

To change the terms, click the term you want to change and choose a different one from the drop-down list.

Defining the Receivables Linked Accounts

The Receivables Ledger linked accounts parallel those for the Payables Ledger.

Click **Linked Accounts** under Receivables:

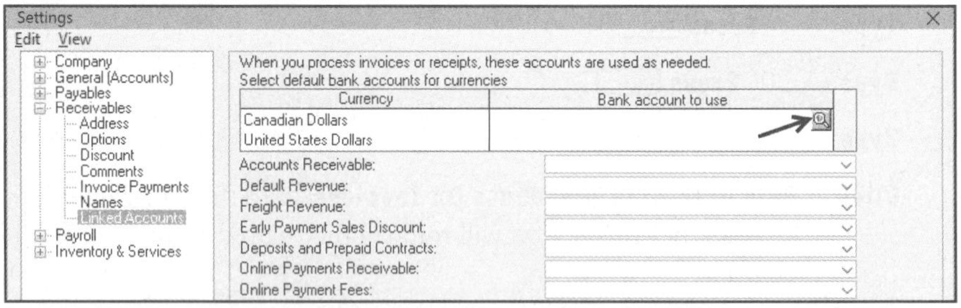

We need to identify the default General Ledger bank account used to receive payments from customers. Cash transactions in the Sales and Receipts journals will be posted to the bank account you select in the journals. The linked account will be the default, but any Bank or Cash class account may be selected in the journals.

VeloCity has several bank accounts. Cheques and cash receipts are held in the *Undeposited Cash and Cheques* clearing account and then deposited weekly to the *Bank: Niagara Trust Chequing* account. Therefore, the default Canadian bank account for receipts is *Undeposited Cash and Cheques*. *Bank: USD Chequing* is the default account for foreign currency customer transactions. Although most linked accounts may be used only once, one Canadian dollar bank account can be linked to the Payables, Receivables and Payroll ledgers and all currencies.

The following accounts are required as linked accounts for the Receivables Ledger:

PRO VERSION
The Terminology part of the Names Settings screen is not included in the Pro version because you cannot change the terms used.

NOTES
You can change the terminology used for Customers, Invoices, Sales, Orders and Quotes from the Names Settings screen if you want.

CLASSIC VIEW
To add the Receivables Ledger linked accounts from the Home window, right-click the Sales, Orders & Quotes or the Receipts Journal icon in the Home window to select it.

Click the Settings tool. Or, choose the Setup menu, then choose Settings, Receivables and Linked Accounts.

NOTES
The Linked Accounts screen has changed because of the second currency. You can compare it with the one on page 234 for Air Care Services.

NOTES
Any home currency Cash or Bank class account may also be linked to foreign currency receipts.

RECEIVABLES LINKED ACCOUNTS

Bank Account to Use for Canadian Dollars	1030 Undeposited Cash and Cheques
Bank Account to Use for United States Dollars	1140 Bank: USD Chequing
Accounts Receivable	1200 Accounts Receivable
Default Revenue	do not use – leave blank
Freight Revenue	4200 Freight Revenue
Early Payment Sales Discount	4060 Sales Discounts
Deposits and Prepaid Orders	2210 Prepaid Sales and Deposits

NOTES
The linked Revenue account from the Inventory Ledger record will replace the Receivables Ledger Default Revenue account as the default for sale.

Click the **List icon** in the Bank Account To Use column for Canadian Dollars.

Click **1030 Undeposited Cash and Cheques** and **click Select**.

Click the **List icon** in the Bank Account To Use column for United States Dollars.

Click **1140 Bank: USD Chequing** and **click Select**.

Enter the **remaining linked accounts** from the chart on this page. **Type** the **account number** or **select** the **account** from the drop-down list.

NOTES
The remaining linked accounts were introduced in Chapter 7. Refer to page 234 if you need to review these accounts.

Payroll Ledger Settings

At this stage, we will change the settings for Payroll Names, Income, Deductions, Taxes and Entitlements. After creating supplier and employee records, we can change the Remittance and Job Category settings.

NOTES
Refer to pages 320–326 to review payroll settings if necessary.

Entering Payroll Names

Because the names we use will appear on the remaining payroll settings screens, we will define them first.

Click **Payroll** and then **click Names** in the list of Payroll options.

Click **Incomes & Deductions** to access the first group of payroll names.

Many of the standard income types are mandatory and cannot be changed. These fields are on a shaded background. Some of the other default names are also correct, so you do not need to redefine them. You can leave Income 1 and Income 2, labelled "Salary" and "Commission," unchanged because VeloCity has two salaried employees and pays a sales commission to one employee. There is allowance for 20 different kinds of income in addition to the compulsory fields and 20 different payroll deductions. Each income and deduction label may have up to 12 characters.

VeloCity uses the additional income fields for bonuses, piece rate pay and taxable benefits (tuition fee payments) so that these incomes can be identified by name on the paycheque. The piece rate pay is based on the number of completed satisfied-client surveys. Travel expenses repaid directly to employees are also entered as income, but they are reimbursements and will not be taxed.

VeloCity also has three payroll deductions at this time: VRSP — the Registered Retirement Savings Plan; Savings Plan — an investment plan; and Garnishee — the wages that are withheld and submitted to the Receiver General for prior years' taxes.

NOTES
Reimbursements are added to net pay (the amount of the paycheque) but are not included when calculating taxes.

Click **Income 3 in the Name Column** to highlight the contents.

Type `No. Clients` **Press** tab to advance to the Income 4 field.

Type `Bonus` **Press** tab to advance to the Income 5 field.

NOTES
If clicking does not highlight the field contents, drag through an entry to select it. Double-clicking may open the language labels screen.

NOTES
You can also enter travel expenses as a user-defined expense and issue separate cheques to the employee for them. In Chapter 9 we included tuition with the generic Benefits.

NOTES
You can press ⬇ to access the next Deduction Name field instead of pressing tab.

NOTES
You can add names for additional incomes and deductions later if you need to.

Type `Tuition` **Press** tab to advance to the Income 6 field.

Type `Travel Exp.` **Press** tab to advance to the Income 7 field.

Press del to remove the entry. **Press** tab to select the next field.

Delete the **remaining Income names** until they are all removed.

Press tab after deleting Income 20 to select Deduction 1 in the Deductions column.

Press tab again if necessary to select Deduction 1 in the Name column.

Type `VRSP` **Press** tab to advance to the second deduction Name field.

Type `Savings Plan` **Press** tab to highlight the next field.

Type `Garnishee` **Press** tab to highlight the next field.

Press del. VeloCity does not have other payroll deductions.

Press tab to select the next field. **Delete** the **remaining deductions**.

Entering Additional Payroll Names

VeloCity keeps an emergency contact name and phone number for each employee as additional information in the personnel files. We will name these extra fields for the Payroll Ledger.

On this same screen, we name the additional payroll expenses for VeloCity and the entitlements for employees. VeloCity has group insurance as a user-defined expense and offers sick leave and personal leave days for all employees as well as vacation days for salaried employees.

We will briefly review income, benefits and user-defined expenses.

Group insurance (Gp Insurance) is classified as a benefit for employees because the premiums are paid to a third party rather than to the employee. The employer's expense for the benefit is entered as a user-defined expense. Tuition is classified as an income because it is paid to the employee through regular paycheques. The employer's expense for this benefit is recorded in the expense account linked to the income, just like wage expenses. Reimbursements may also be entered as income or as user-defined expenses, depending on how the payment is made. If we entered travel expenses as a user-defined expense, we would create linked payable and expense accounts and then issue a separate cheque to the employee to provide the reimbursement. If we repay the expense on the payroll cheque, we define it as an income (with a linked expense account) — reimbursement — that is not taxable.

The Prov. Tax field is used for Quebec payroll taxes. Since we will not choose Quebec as the employees' province of taxation or enter linked accounts for them, the program will automatically skip the related payroll fields. WSIB is entered as the name for WCB (Workers' Compensation Board) because we selected Ontario as the business province. The field has a drop-down list of alternative names for WCB and other taxes you may use as an employer expense.

NOTES
HST is one alternative on the WCB drop-down list because some employee benefits are taxable. In that case, you could enter WSIB as a user-defined expense.

NOTES
On the Additional Payroll screen, you need to press tab twice to skip the Fr/Eng language button. If you are not using both languages (Company Settings, Features), press tab once to move to the next field. On the Incomes & Deductions screen, the language button is automatically skipped when you press tab.

Click **Additional Payroll**.

Double-click **Field1**. **Type** `Emergency Contact`

Press tab **twice** to highlight the next field. (Read margin Notes.)

Type `Contact Number`

Delete the **names for fields 3 to 5**.

Drag through **User Exp 1**, the Expense 1 field, to highlight the contents.

Type `Gp Insurance`

Delete the **remaining expenses**.

Drag through **Days 1**, the Entitlement 1 field, to highlight the contents.

Type `Vacation` **Press** *tab* **twice** to highlight the next entitlement name.

Type `Sick Leave` **Press** *tab* **twice** to highlight the next name.

Type `PersonalDays`

Delete the **remaining entitlement names**.

NOTES
You can use up to 12 characters for User-Defined Expense and Entitlement names including spaces – that is why we omitted the space for the Personal Days entitlement name.
You can use the language button to enter labels in the second language.

Entering Settings for Incomes

Click **Incomes** under Payroll.

This screen designates the types of income and the taxes that apply. By deleting the names we do not need this list becomes easier to work with. As we did for Northern Lights (Chapter 9), we can modify this screen by hiding the columns that apply to Quebec so that only the columns we need are on-screen at the same time.

NOTES
If necessary, scroll to the right to include the column margin you need.

Point to the **right column heading margin for Calc. Tax (Que.)**.

When the pointer changes to a two-sided arrow, **drag** the **margin to the left** until the column is hidden.

Remove the **column for Calc. QHSF** and **Calc. QPIP** in the same way.

NOTES
When you close and re-open the Payroll Settings screen, the hidden and resized columns will be restored.
QPIP (Quebec Parental Insurance Plan) provides parental leave benefits to EI-insurable employees. Both employers and employees pay into the plan.

For each type of income, you must indicate what taxes are applied and whether vacation pay is calculated on the income. Most of the information is correct. Regular and overtime hours are paid on an hourly basis, while salary and commissions are paid at designated income amounts per period. All taxes apply to these types of income at VeloCity, so these default settings are correct. Vacation pay and EI, however, are not calculated on all incomes, so some of these checkmarks should be removed. In addition, we should designate the type of income for the income names that we created and the taxes that apply to them. First, we should choose the type of income because that will change the defaults that are applied.

By default, all new incomes are assigned to the Income type. This assignment is correct for Bonus, the extra annual holiday payment. The tuition fee payment is a taxable benefit paid directly to the employee, so it is also classified as an Income. The generic Benefits field in journals is used for items that the employer pays directly to a third party on behalf of the employee. The monetary value of the premiums would be added as a benefit to the employee's gross wages to determine taxes and then subtracted again to determine the net pay. The employee does not receive the actual dollar amount. If a benefit is added to net pay, it should be classified as an Income. Therefore, in this example tuition is an Income.

NOTES
Tuition is defined as a type of income because it is paid directly to the employee. It is not a reimbursement because it is taxable.
Using the generic Benefits requires a linked expense account and payable account (paid to the third party, as for Northern Lights in Chapter 9) while Income type and Reimbursements require only linked expense accounts (paid directly to the employee on the paycheque).

Travel Expenses are **Reimbursements** and No. Clients is the name for the **Piece Rate** basis of paying bonuses. **Differential Rates** apply to different hourly rates paid at different times and are not used by VeloCity.

Click **No. Clients** to place the cursor on the correct line.

Press *tab* to move to the Type column. A List icon is added.

Click the **List icon** to list the different income types.

Click **Piece Rate** to select this type for No. Clients.

Click **Select** to add the Type to the Settings screen. **Press** *tab* to advance to the Unit of Measure field — the entry here has changed to Item.

The amount paid to employees is based on the number of completed surveys. The Insurable Hours checkmark was removed when we changed the type.

Type Survey

Click **Travel Exp** to select this income line. **Press** tab.

Click the **List icon**. **Double-click Reimbursement** to enter this income type. All taxes are removed because this type of payment is not taxable.

Many changes are made automatically when we select the income type, but we need to make more modifications. Insurable Hours, the number of work hours, is used to determine eligibility for Employment Insurance benefits. Regular, overtime and salary paid hours are counted, but commissions, bonuses and tuition are not; no time can be accurately attached to them, so they are not counted. EI is not calculated on benefits, so we also need to remove the Calc. EI ✓ for Tuition.

Click **Commission** to select this income line.

Press tab **repeatedly** until the cursor is in the **Calc. Ins. Hours field**.

Click to remove the ✓, or **press** the **space bar**.

Press ↓ **twice** to place the cursor in the **Calc. Ins. Hours field for Bonus**.

Click to remove the ✓, or **press** the **space bar**.

Press ↓ **again** to place the cursor in the **Calc. Ins. Hours field for Tuition**.

Click to remove the ✓, or **press** the **space bar**.

Press ← to place the cursor in the **Calc. EI field for Tuition**.

Click to remove the ✓, or **press** the **space bar**.

We still need to modify the entries for vacation pay. In Ontario, vacation pay is calculated on all performance-based wages. This includes the regular wages, overtime wages and piece rate pay. We need to remove the remaining ✓s. All ✓s for Travel Exp have been removed. Salaried workers receive paid time off rather than a percentage of their wages as vacation pay. We do not need to remove the ✓ for Overtime 2. If it is used later, vacation pay will be calculated on it as well. VRSP is deducted by amount, so the Calc. column for it does not apply.

Click **Salary** in the Income column.

Press tab **repeatedly** until the cursor is in the **Calc. Vac. column**.

Click to remove the ✓, or **press** the **space bar**.

Remove the ✓ for **Calc. Vac.** for **Salary**, **Commission**, **Bonus** and **Tuition**.

We do not need to change the settings for Quebec taxes or tracking of tips — they do not apply to Ontario employees — so the setup for Income Settings is complete:

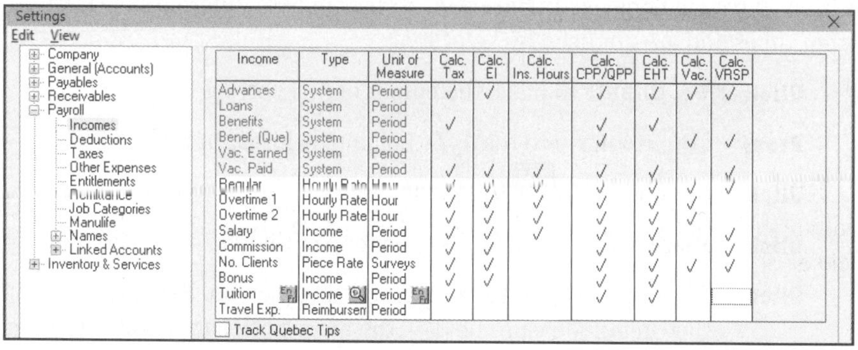

Income	Type	Unit of Measure	Calc. Tax	Calc. EI	Calc. Ins. Hours	Calc. CPP/QPP	Calc. EHT	Calc. Vac.	Calc. VRSP
Advances	System	Period	✓	✓		✓	✓	✓	✓
Loans	System	Period							
Benefits	System	Period	✓			✓	✓		
Benef. (Que)	System	Period				✓		✓	✓
Vac. Earned	System	Period							
Vac. Paid	System	Period	✓	✓	✓	✓	✓		✓
Regular	Hourly Rate	Hour	✓	✓	✓	✓	✓	✓	✓
Overtime 1	Hourly Rate	Hour	✓	✓	✓	✓	✓	✓	
Overtime 2	Hourly Rate	Hour	✓	✓	✓	✓	✓	✓	
Salary	Income	Period	✓	✓	✓	✓	✓		✓
Commission	Income	Period	✓	✓		✓	✓		✓
No. Clients	Piece Rate	Surveys	✓	✓		✓	✓	✓	✓
Bonus	Income	Period	✓	✓		✓	✓		
Tuition	Income	Period	✓			✓	✓		
Travel Exp.	Reimbursem	Period							

NOTES

A full-time employee for whom commission is the only source of income and who is eligible for EI benefits may have a regular number of hours attached to the pay period and entered in the ledger.

Commissions paid to hourly wage employees should have vacation pay applied to this amount because it is performance-based pay.

NOTES

If VRSP were calculated as a percentage of gross pay, you would remove the ✓ for Bonus and Tuition in the Calc. VRSP column and add one for Commission. The VRSP settings will not apply when we deduct by amount.

Sage 50 does not allow you to add ✓s for Overtime for VRSP.

NOTES

Vacation pay is calculated on all wages. This calculation includes the piece rate pay – number of client evaluations – because it is a performance-based wage or income. Bonuses are not based on measurable performance; therefore, vacation pay is not applied to these amounts or to the other benefits.

The regulations governing vacation pay are set provincially.

The Calc. Vac. ✓ for Salary will have no effect because we will enter 0.0 percent as the vacation pay rate in the Ledger Records.

Entering Tax Settings for Deductions

Click **Deductions** under Payroll:

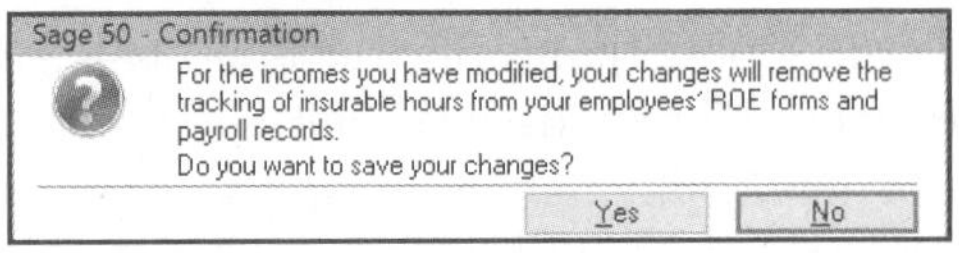

Click **Yes** when prompted to save the settings and confirm that ROE information connected to the deleted incomes will not be tracked.

NOTES
You can modify the Tax Settings screen for deductions as we modified the one for incomes so that only the columns we need are on-screen. You can remove the Deduct After Tax (Que.), QHSF and QPIP columns.

Only the deduction names you entered earlier appear on this screen. You can calculate deductions as a percentage of the gross pay or as a fixed amount. Some deductions, like union dues, are usually calculated as a percentage of income. The Amount settings are correct for VeloCity.

All deductions are set by default to be calculated by amount after all taxes (Deduct After Tax is checked). For Savings Plan and Garnishee, this is correct — they are subtracted from income after income tax and other payroll taxes have been deducted. However, VRSP contributions qualify as tax deductions and will be subtracted from gross income before income tax is calculated, but not before EI, CPP and so on, so you must change its setting.

NOTES
Garnisheed wages for family support may be exempt for taxes when the family receiving them must claim the amount as taxable income.

Click the **Deduct After Tax column** for VRSP to remove the ✓ and change the setting to Before Tax.

The remaining settings are correct. VRSP is deducted after the other payroll taxes and vacation pay because these deductions are based on gross wages.

Defining Default Tax Rates

Click **Taxes** under Payroll.

WARNING!
If you later change the province in the Company Information screen, the name entered for WCB does not change. You must enter the correction manually on the Additional Payroll names screen.

This group of fields refers to the rate at which employer tax obligations are calculated. The factor for Employment Insurance (**EI Factor**) is correct at 1.4 — the employer's contribution is set at 1.4 times the employee's contribution. In the next field, you can set the employer's rate for **WSIB** (Workplace Safety and Insurance Board) premiums. On this screen, you will enter 1.29, the rate that applies to the majority of employees. You can modify rates for individual employees in the ledger records.

The next field, **EHT Factor**, is the percentage of payroll costs that the employer contributes to the provincial health plan. The rate is based on the total payroll costs per year; the percentage for VeloCity is 0.98 because the total payroll is less than $200 000.

The **QHSF Factor** (Quebec Health Services Fund) applies only to Quebec employees, so we do not need to enter a rate for it. QHSF is similar to EHT.

NOTES
WSIB is the name for WCB in Ontario.
QHSF was used for Sound, Inc. (Chapter 14).

Click the **WSIB Rate field**. **Type** `1.29`

Press *tab* to advance to the EHT Factor field.

Type `.98`

Defining Other Expenses

Click **Other Expenses** under Payroll.

On this screen, you must indicate whether expenses are calculated by percentage or by amount. The default selection — Amount — is correct for Gp Insurance, the single expense.

NOTES
Entitlements may also be given directly as a number of days without tracking hours by entering only the number of days in the Maximum Days field.

NOTES
When the number of days accrued reaches the maximum, the Days Earned entries on the paycheques Entitlements tab screen will be zero.

NOTES
Refer to page 326 to review payroll linked accounts if necessary.

WARNING!
Sage 50 will not allow you to remove an account while it is being used as a linked account. When you try to remove an account, click OK in the Warning window to return to the Accounts window. First, turn the linking function off by deleting the account in the Linked Accounts window. Then delete the account balance, save the changes and, finally, remove the account in the Accounts window. You cannot remove an account if it has a balance or if journal entries have been posted to it.

Defining Entitlements

Click **Entitlements** under Payroll.

On this screen you should enter the rules for entitlements that apply to all or most employees. These will be added to new employee records as defaults.

Entitlements are usually linked to the number of hours worked. Employees at VeloCity are not entitled to take vacation time until they have worked for a certain period of time or to take paid sick leave immediately after being hired. The **Track Using % Hours Worked** determines how quickly entitlements accumulate. For example, 5 percent of hours worked yields about one day per month or 12 days of leave per year. VeloCity has **Maximums** for the number of days per year that an employee can take or accumulate. And finally, the days unused are not **cleared at the end of a year**. The number of days carried forward is still limited by the Maximum number of days available. The calculations are based on an eight-hour day as the default.

VeloCity gives salaried workers three weeks of vacation (8 percent) and allows a maximum of 25 days. Sick leave at 10 days per year is earned at the rate of 5 percent to a maximum of 15 days. Personal leave days (five days) accrue at the rate of 2.5 percent for a maximum of five days per year. VeloCity allows two of the three weeks of vacation time and five of the ten days of sick leave to be carried over to the next year; that is, they are not cleared at the end of the year. Personal leave days cannot be carried forward — the maximum is the same as the yearly allotment.

Click the **Track Using % Hours Worked field for Vacation**.

Type 8 **Press** tab to advance to the Maximum Days field.

Type 25 **Press** tab.

Click the **Track Using % Hours Worked field for Sick Leave**.

Type 5 **Press** tab to advance to the Maximum Days field.

Type 15 **Press** tab.

Click the **Track Using % Hours Worked field for PersonalDays**.

Type 2.5 **Press** tab to advance to the Maximum Days field.

Type 5 **Press** tab.

Entering Payroll Linked Accounts

The following linked accounts are used by VeloCity for the Payroll Ledger for incomes and deductions:

PAYROLL LINKED ACCOUNTS

INCOMES

Principal Bank	1060 Bank: Niagara Trust Chequing		
Vac. Owed	2300 Vacation Payable	Advances & Loans	1220 Advances & Loans Receivable

Income

Vac. Earned	5300 Wages	Commission	5330 Commissions & Bonuses
Regular	5300 Wages	No. Clients	5330 Commissions & Bonuses
Overtime 1	5300 Wages	Bonus	5330 Commissions & Bonuses
Overtime 2	Not used	Tuition	5460 Employee Benefits
Salary	5320 Salaries	Travel Exp.	5350 Travel Expenses

DEDUCTIONS	Linked Account	Payment Adjustment Account
VRSP	2400 VRSP Payable	1060 Bank: Niagara Trust Chequing
Savings Plan	2410 Savings Plan Payable	1060 Bank: Niagara Trust Chequing
Garnishee	2430 Garnisheed Wages Payable	1060 Bank: Niagara Trust Chequing

There are many linked accounts for payroll. Each type of income, tax, deduction and expense that is used must be linked to a General Ledger account. The payroll journals use only linked accounts — you cannot enter accounts in the journals themselves.

Click **Linked Accounts** under Payroll, then **click** **Incomes**.

The names here are the ones you entered in the Names windows. If you deleted a name, it will not appear here.

The linked accounts for all types of income appear together on this first screen. You must identify a wage account for each type of employee payment used by the company, even if the same account is used for all of them. Once the Payroll bank account is identified as the same one used for Payables, the program will apply a single sequence of cheque numbers for all cheques prepared from the Payables and Payroll journals.

Type the **account number** or **select** the **account** from the drop-down list.

Choose **1060 Bank: Niagara Trust Chequing** for the Principal Bank field.

Press *tab* to advance to the next linked account field.

Choose **2300 Vacation Payable** for the Vac. Owed field.

Choose **1220 Advances & Loans Receivable** for the Advances & Loans field.

Choose **5300 Wages** for Regular and Overtime 1 and for Vacation Earned.

Choose **5320 Salaries** for Salaries.

Choose **5330 Commissions & Bonuses** for Commission, No. Clients and Bonus.

Choose **5460 Employee Benefits** for Tuition.

Choose **5350 Travel Expenses** for Travel Exp.

Click **Deductions** so you can enter the next set of Payroll linked accounts.

Enter the **linked payable** and **payroll adjustment accounts** for **VRSP**, **Savings Plan** and **Garnishee** from the chart on the previous page.

The following linked accounts are used for taxes and user-defined expenses:

PAYROLL LINKED ACCOUNTS CONTINUED

TAXES	Payables	Expenses	Payment Adjustment
EI	2310 EI Payable	5410 EI Expense	5410 EI Expense
CPP	2320 CPP Payable	5420 CPP Expense	5420 CPP Expense
Tax	2330 Income Tax Payable		1060 Bank: Niagara Trust Chequing
WSIB	2460 WSIB Payable	5430 WSIB Expense	5430 WSIB Expense
EHT	2380 EHT Payable	5440 EHT Expense	5440 EHT Expense
Not used	Tax (Que.), QPP, QHSF, QPIP	**Not used** QPP, QHSF, QPIP	**Not used** Tax (Que.), QPP, QHSF, QPIP

USER-DEFINED EXPENSES

	Payables	Expenses	Payment Adjustment
Gp Insurance	2420 Group Insurance Payable	5450 Gp Insurance Expense	5450 Gp Insurance Expense

Click **Taxes** for the next set of Payroll linked accounts.

Enter the **linked payables**, **expenses** and **payment adjustment accounts** for **EI**, **CPP**, **Tax**, **WSIB** and **EHT** from the chart above.

Click **User-Defined Expenses** for the final Payroll linked accounts.

Enter the **linked payable**, **expense** and **payment adjustment accounts** for **Gp Insurance** from the chart above.

Check the **linked** payroll **accounts** against the charts on page 660 and this page.

CLASSIC VIEW

To add payroll linked accounts, you can right-click the Paycheques or the Payroll Cheque Run Journal icon in the Home window to select it. Click the Settings tool . Or, choose the Setup menu, and then choose Settings, Payroll and Linked Accounts.

If no Home window icon is selected, you can use the Settings tool's Select Setup drop-down list, choose Payroll and click Select.

NOTES

The deleted income and deduction names do not appear on the screens for linked accounts.

NOTES

You can add accounts from the Linked Accounts windows. Type a new number, press *enter* and choose to add the account.

NOTES

If you can use an account for more than one link, the account will be available in the drop-down list. Otherwise, once an account is selected as a linked account, it is removed from the list.

PRO VERSION
The Price List, Locations and Categories options are not available in the Pro version.
The FIFO method of costing is also not available in the Pro version. Therefore, in this section of the book, we use the Average Cost method.

Inventory & Services Ledger Settings

Click **Inventory & Services** for the ledger options:

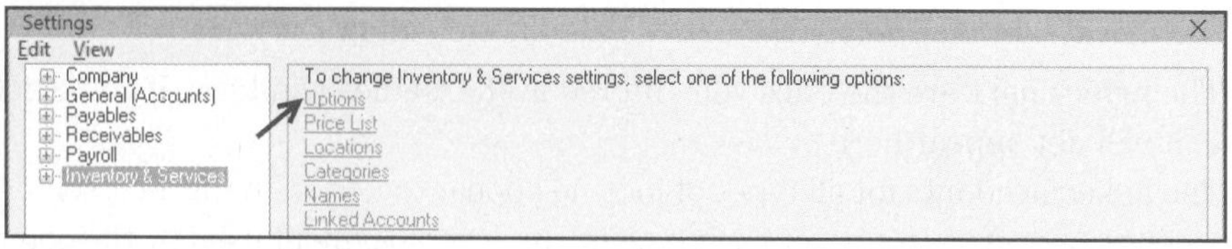

Click **Options**:

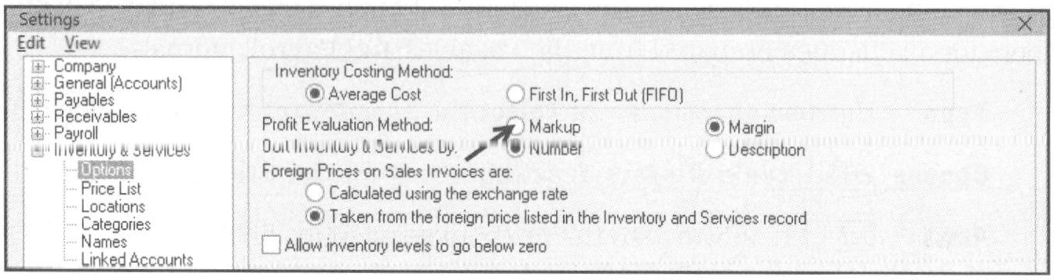

NOTES
Categories are used to group similar inventory items.

Inventory costs may be calculated in two ways. In the average cost method, costs are continually updated as you buy and sell at different prices. With the FIFO method, costs are tracked with the items and do not change for any one item — its historic purchase price remains as the cost price at the time of sale. VeloCity uses average costs.

Profits may be calculated on the basis of margin or markup. You can change the setting at any time, so you can prepare reports using both evaluation methods. The formulas for profit evaluation by margin and markup are as follows:

Margin = (Selling Price – Cost Price) x 100%/Selling Price

Markup = (Selling Price – Cost Price) x 100%/Cost Price

VeloCity uses the markup method of evaluating the profit on inventory sales, so we need to change the default setting.

NOTES
The list of items in the Item Description field in the Sales and Purchases journals is always sorted by description. The Item Number field list in these journals is always sorted by number.
The choice you make on the Inventory Settings screen affects the selection lists in the Item Assembly and Adjustments journals, in the Inventory & Services window and in the Inventory & Services module window.

Click **Markup** to change the calculation method.

If you choose to sort Inventory Ledger items by description, the product name field will appear before the product number in the Inventory Ledger input forms, and inventory selection lists will be sorted alphabetically by name (read the margin Notes). When item numbers are not used, sorting by description will make it easier to find the item you want.

Because we added a foreign currency, the option to take foreign prices for sales from the Inventory Ledger or from the exchange rate is added. The default setting to use the foreign price in the Inventory Ledger Record is correct for VeloCity. With this option, you can switch pricing methods for individual items. If you choose the exchange rate method, you cannot choose different methods for different items.

The final option is to Allow Inventory Levels To Go Below Zero. VeloCity will choose this option to permit customer sales for inventory that is backordered.

Click **Allow Inventory Levels To Go Below Zero** to select the option.

NOTES
Price lists are used in Chapter 18 to update prices. You can change one price relative to another for all items in a single step. Inventory locations are also covered in Chapter 18.

In the Premium version, you can create additional price lists and modify price lists from this settings screen. You can also set up the locations for inventory if you have more than one place where inventory is stored or sold.

Inventory Linked Accounts

VeloCity currently uses both linked accounts for inventory, the one for inventory adjustments or damaged merchandise and the one for additional item assembly costs. The linked accounts for the Inventory Ledger are in the following chart:

INVENTORY	
Item Assembly Costs	5045 Item Assembly Costs
Adjustment Write-off	5040 Damaged Inventory

Click **Linked Accounts** under Inventory & Services:

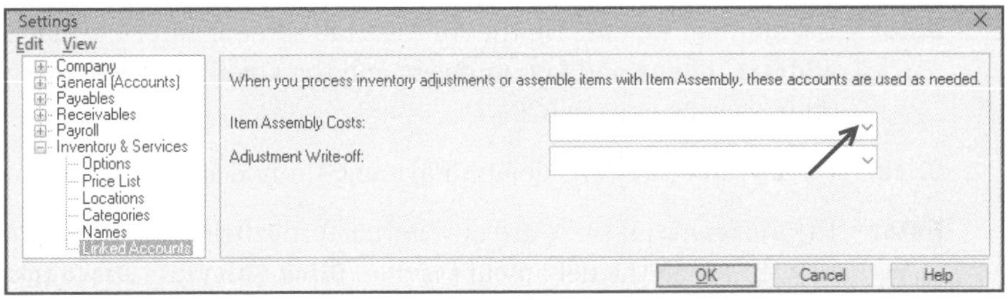

Type the **account number** or **select** the **account** from the drop-down list.

Choose **Item Assembly Costs** as the Item Assembly Costs linked account.

Press tab. **Choose** **5040 Damaged Inventory** as the Adjustment Write-off linked account.

Settings options for the Division module will be hidden if you chose to hide the module (User Preferences, View settings). Time and Billing, introduced in Chapter 18, has no settings options.

Click **OK** to save the new settings.

You will get several confirmation messages. Because we deleted some payroll names, we are being warned that any accounts linked to these deleted fields will also be removed. The next message refers to the additional payroll names, and we are again being warned that their linked accounts will be removed. Refer to Chapter 9, page 329.

A second group of warnings relates to required account class changes for linked accounts. Refer to Chapter 7, pages 234–235.

Read **each message carefully** and **click Yes** in response to return to the Home window.

Preparing the Subsidiary Ledgers

We have now completed the General Ledger setup, including

1. organizing all accounting reports and records
2. creating new accounts
3. identifying linked accounts for all ledgers
4. activating additional features and entering their linked accounts

The remaining steps involve setting up the records in the subsidiary ledgers:

5. inserting supplier, customer, employee and inventory information
6. entering historical startup information
7. printing reports to check the accuracy of your records

Preparing Payables Ledger Records

Use VeloCity's Supplier Information on pages 626–627 to create the supplier records and add the outstanding historical invoices. If any information is missing for a supplier, leave that field blank. The first supplier, Complete Cycler Inc., is a foreign currency supplier.

CLASSIC VIEW
To add inventory linked accounts, you can right-click the Item Assembly or the Inventory Adjustments Journal icon in the Home window to select it. Click the Settings tool. Or, choose the Setup menu, and then choose Settings, Inventory & Services and Linked Accounts.

NOTES
To access the Division module options, refer to page 505.

NOTES
If you clicked OK to save the Settings and close the window earlier, the corresponding messages for your work up to that point would be displayed and will not be displayed again now.

WARNING!
Check your work carefully. Although you can change the designated linked accounts at any time, journal entries will be posted incorrectly if you do not have the correct linked accounts.

NOTES
For a review of the Payables Ledger setup, refer to page 235.

PRO VERSION
Remember that the term Vendors will replace Suppliers.
Click Vendors in the Modules pane to change modules.

Click **Payables** in the Modules pane list.

Click the **Suppliers icon** 

to open the Suppliers window.

Click the **Create Button** 

or **choose** the **File menu** and **click Create** or **press** ctrl + **N**. The cursor is in the Supplier field.

Enter the supplier's **name**. On the Address tab screen, enter the **contact**, **address**, **phone** and **fax** numbers, and the **e-mail** and **Web site** addresses from page 626.

Click the **Options tab**. The default Payment Method selections are correct.

Enter the **discounts**, if there are any, in the Terms fields, and the number of days in which the net amount is due. **Click Calculate Discounts Before Tax** if the discounts are before tax. Otherwise, leave the box unchecked.

WARNING!
You cannot change the currency for a supplier or customer after entering historical invoices, so you must select the currency first. Otherwise, you must pay the invoices, clear paid transactions, remove the supplier and then re-create the supplier record from scratch.
After you enter historical invoices for a foreign supplier or customer, you cannot change the currency setting for the company, even if you delete the supplier.
You cannot access the duty fields in the Purchases Journal unless Charge Duty On Items Purchased is checked in the supplier's ledger.

Identifying Foreign Suppliers

Foreign suppliers are also identified on the Options tab screen.

Click the **Currency field list arrow**:

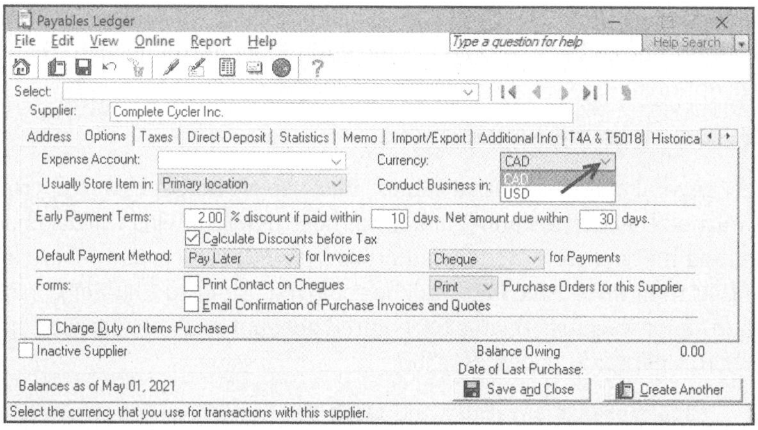

Click **USD**.

Click **Charge Duty On Items Purchased**.

You must activate this duty setting to make the duty fields in the Purchases Journal available for this supplier.

You can print the contact on cheques if this is appropriate for the supplier.

Enter the **default expense account** for the supplier if there is one.

Do not enter a default expense account for inventory suppliers — the linked asset account from the Inventory Ledger record is selected automatically by the program.

We will enter tax codes for all suppliers and customers later using the Assign Tax Codes feature in the Company Sales Tax Codes Settings (page 677). It is not necessary to change Tax Exempt entries. Leaving the setting at No will make all tax codes available. As long as the tax code in the journal is correct, taxes will be calculated correctly.

You do not need to enter details on the Statistics, Memo or Import/Export tab screens.

The Balance Owing will be entered automatically by the program once you have entered historical invoices.

NOTES
Leaving the code as No Tax and leaving the exempt status set at No will permit you to charge taxes if needed.
If taxes are not calculated correctly for a supplier or customer, check that the ledger entries for Tax Exempt are set to No.

NOTES
Year-to-date purchases and payments are not recorded because this is a new fiscal period.

Correct any **errors** by returning to the field with the mistake, highlighting the errors and entering the correct information.

Entering Historical Supplier Transactions

The chart on page 627 provides the information for this stage. Complete Cycler Inc. has an outstanding balance, so we must enter the historical transactions.

Click the **Historical Transactions tab**. **Click Save Now**. **Click Invoices**:

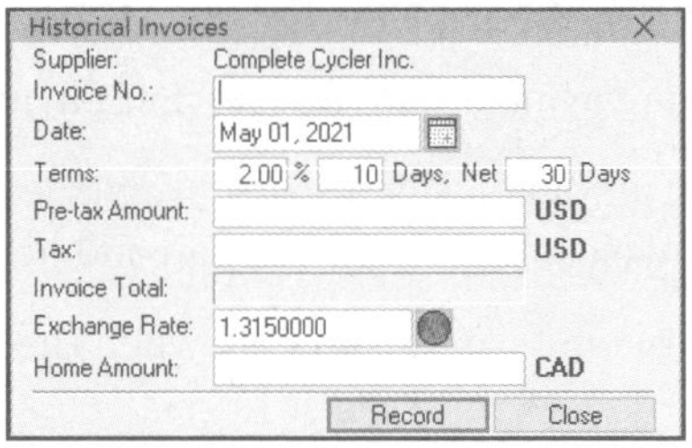

The Historical Invoices input screen for foreign suppliers has additional fields for the second currency information.

You can edit the payment terms for individual invoices if needed.

Enter **CC-918** as the **Invoice Number** and **Apr 28** as the invoice **Date**.

Press *tab*. The Exchange Rate screen opens.

Enter **1.31** as the exchange rate and **click Make This The Default Rate For April 28**. **Click OK**.

Click the **Pre-Tax Amount field for USD**.

Type 3600 **Press** *tab* to advance to the Tax amount field for USD.

Type 468 **Press** *tab*.

In the Home Amount field, $5 329.08 should be entered correctly automatically.

Click **Record**.

Repeat these steps to **enter other invoices** for this supplier, if there are any.

When you have recorded all outstanding invoices for a supplier,

Click **Close** to return to the Historical Transactions tab screen.

The invoices you entered have been added to the Balance fields for both currencies.

To enter the historical invoice for **Wheel Deals**, click Cancel if the exchange rate screen opens to close it without entering a new rate. Enter **$2 660** and **$345.80** as the **USD** pretax and tax amounts, and then enter **$3 950** as the **Home Amount**. Press *tab* and allow the program to recalculate the exchange rate. Do not save the revised exchange rate when prompted.

Historical invoices for home currency suppliers are recorded in the same way, except for the entry of the exchange rate. We will enter historical payments next.

Historical Payments

Click **Payments** on the Historical Transactions tab screen:

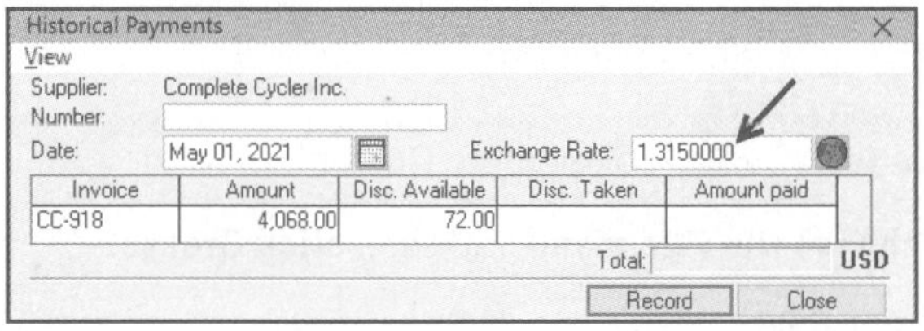

NOTES

You can refer to page 240 to review entering historical supplier invoices and payments if necessary.

NOTES

Because discounts from Complete Cycler Inc. are calculated before taxes, there are separate fields for pretax and tax invoice amounts.

WARNING!

If you save an incorrect invoice amount, you must pay the invoice, clear paid invoices for the supplier (Home window, Maintenance menu), reset the payments for the year to zero (supplier's ledger, Statistics tab) and re-enter the outstanding invoices. Refer to page 251.

Historical payments for foreign suppliers have one additional field, the one for the exchange rate. You must enter an exchange rate for these payments — there is no field for the home currency amount.

Click the **Number field**.

Type 344 (the **cheque number** for the first payment).

Press *tab* and **enter April 28** as the payment date for the first payment.

The exchange rate, 1.31, should be entered automatically because we made it the default rate for April 28 when we entered the invoice. If it is not, you can add it.

WARNING!
Remember not to include any discounts taken in the historical payments. If you do include them, the Payables Ledger will not be balanced and you will be unable to finish the history.
By clicking the Amount field directly, you can avoid including the discount.

Skip the **Discount fields** because discounts are taken only when the early payment is a full payment.

Click the **Amount Paid column** (on the line for the invoice being paid).

Type 2000 for the **payment amount**.

Press *tab* to advance to the next invoice if there is one. **Delete** any **amounts** or **discounts** that are not included in the payment.

Click **Record** to save the information and to display an updated statement for this supplier.

Repeat these steps to **enter other payments** to this supplier, if there are any.

NOTES
The Statistics tab screen has the summary amounts in both Canadian and US dollars.
The historical invoices and payments will be entered on the Statistics tab screen as Last Year's Purchases and Payments because we are starting a new fiscal period on May 1.

When you have recorded all outstanding payments for a supplier,

Click **Close** to return to the Payables Ledger for the supplier. The payment you have just entered has reduced the Balance amount.

Click the **Create tool** to display a new blank Payables Ledger screen.

Click the **Address tab**.

Repeat these procedures to **enter** the **remaining suppliers** and their **historical transactions** from pages 626–627.

If there are no historical invoices and payments,

Click **Create Another** to save the record and open a blank Payables Ledger window. **Click** the **Address tab**.

Display or **print** the **Supplier List** and the **Supplier Aged Detail Report**, including terms, historical differences and foreign amounts. Compare these reports with the information on pages 626–627 to check the accuracy of your work.

Preparing Receivables Ledger Records

NOTES
For a review of the Receivables Ledger setup, refer to page 242.

Use VeloCity's Customer Information on pages 627–628 to create the customer records and add the outstanding historical invoices. Revenue accounts are added from the inventory records, so they are not needed in the customers' records. If any information is missing for a customer, leave that field blank.

Click **Receivables** in the Modules pane list.

Click the **Customers icon** to open the Customers window.

Click Create or **choose** the **File menu** and then **click Create**.

The cursor is in the Customer field.

Enter the customer's **name**. On the Address tab screen, enter the **contact**, **address**, **phone** and **fax numbers**, and the **e-mail** and **Web site addresses** from the chart on page 627.

You can edit the default payment terms for individual customers or for individual historical invoices if necessary.

The Mailing Address is already selected as the default ship-to address, so the same address will apply to both fields on invoices, orders and quotes. No changes are needed.

Click the **Options tab**.

Most entries on the Options tab screen are correct. Terms are entered from the default Receivables settings. Customer statements should be printed. Americas Vinelands Tours and Festival Tours are USD customers. All other customers are Canadian and use the home currency (CAD).

NOTES
The preferred customers are
- Americas Vinelands Tours
- Backstage Tours
- Niagara Rapids Inn
- Park 'N Ride Tours

Choose **USD** from the Currency list for Americas Vinelands Tours (and for Festival Tours).

Choose **Preferred** from the Price List field list for **Americas Vinelands Tours** and for other preferred customers (the ones marked with an asterisk * in the customer information chart on page 627) to change the price list for these customers.

WARNING!
Do not forget to remove the discount terms for cash and credit card customer sales. Changing the ledger records will make the sales invoice terms correct automatically.

Change the payment **terms** to **net 1** for **Cash and Interac** and **Visa Sales customers** and **payment methods** as **Cash** and **Visa**, respectively.

The default code H is entered as the default tax code for all customers. We will change the codes for the USD customers from the Assign Tax Codes option.

Click the **Statistics tab**.

Enter the **credit limit**. Enter both CAD and USD limits for USD customers.

This is the amount that the customer can purchase on account before payments are required. If the customer goes beyond the credit limit, the program will issue a warning before posting an invoice.

The balance owing will be included automatically once you have provided the outstanding invoice information. If the customer has outstanding transactions, proceed to the next section on historical information. Otherwise,

Click Create Another to save the information and advance to the next new Receivables Ledger input screen.

Click the **Address tab**.

Entering Historical Customer Information

NOTES
You can refer to page 245 to review entering historical customer invoices and payments if necessary.

The chart on page 628 provides the information you need to complete this stage.

Enter the customer's **name**, **address**, **options**, **taxes** and **credit limit**.

Click the **Historical Transactions tab**. **Click Save Now**.

Click **Invoices**.

WARNING!
If you save an incorrect invoice amount, you must pay the incorrect invoice, clear paid transactions for the customer, then re-enter the customer's outstanding invoices. Refer to page 251.

Enter the **invoice number**, **date** and **amount** for the first invoice. The default terms should be correct.

Press *tab* to advance to the next field after entering each piece of information.

When all the information is entered correctly, you must save the customer invoice.

Click **Record** to save the information and to display another blank invoice for this customer.

Repeat these procedures to **enter** the **remaining invoices** for the customer, if there are any.

When you have recorded all outstanding invoices for a customer,

Click **Close** to return to the Historical Transactions window for the customer.

The invoices you entered have been added to the Balance field. Continue by entering payments received from this customer, if there are any, or proceed to enter the next customer.

Click **Payments** on the Historical Transactions tab screen.

Click the **Number field**.

Enter the **cheque number** for the first payment.

WARNING!
Remember not to include any discounts taken in the historical payments. If you include them, the Receivables Ledger will not be balanced and you will be unable to finish the history.

Press *tab* and **enter** the **payment date** for the first payment. Again, discounts apply only to full payments made before the due dates, so you should skip the Discount fields.

Click the **Amount Paid column** (on the line for the invoice being paid).

Enter the **payment amount**.

Press *tab* to advance to the next amount if other invoices are being paid. **Delete** any **amounts** or **discounts** that are not included in the payment.

Click **Record** to save the information and to display the updated balance for this customer.

Repeat these procedures if there are **other payments** from the customer.

When you have recorded all outstanding receipts from a customer,

Click **Close** to return to the Receivables Ledger window for the customer.

The payment you entered has updated the customer's Balance field amount.

Click the **Create tool** to open a new Receivables Ledger input screen.

Click the **Address tab** to prepare for entering other customers. After entering all customer records and historical data,

Click Save and Close (or ☒) after adding the last customer. **Close** the **Customers window** to return to the Home window.

Display or **print** the **Customer List** and the **Customer Aged Detail Report**, including terms and historical differences. Compare these reports with the information on pages 627–628 to check your work.

Preparing Payroll Ledger Records

Use the VeloCity Employee Information Sheet, Employee Profiles and Additional Payroll Information on pages 628–630 to create the employee records and add historical information.

We will enter the information for VeloCity employee Dunlop Mercier.

NOTES
For a review of the Payroll Ledger setup, refer to pages 329–339.

Click **Employees & Payroll** in the Modules pane list.

Click the **Employees icon** in the Home window.

Click Create or **choose** the **File menu** and **click Create**.

Entering Personal Details for Employees

The Payroll Ledger new employee information form will open at the Personal information tab screen so you can begin to enter the employee record.

The Payroll Ledger has a large number of tabs for the different kinds of payroll information. The cursor is in the Employee field. By entering the surname first, your employee lists will be in correct alphabetic order.

Type `Mercier, Dunlop` **Press** tab.

Type `55 Trailview Rd.` to enter the Street address.

The default city and province, those for the store, are correct.

Click the **Postal Code field**. **Type** `l0s1j0` **Press** tab.

The program corrects the postal code format and advances to the Phone 1 field.

Type `9054681817`

The default **Language Preference** is correctly set as English.

Click the **SIN (Social Insurance Number) field**. You must use a valid SIN. The program has corrected the telephone number format.

Type `532548625` **Press** tab.

NOTES

Social Insurance Number is not a required field until you are filing CRA reports. If you enter it, you must enter a valid number.

Birth Date is a required field – it is used to determine CPP eligibility and requirements.

The cursor advances to the Birth Date field. Enter the month, day and year using any accepted date format. Birth Date is a required field and it must be correct because it is linked to CPP calculations.

Type `9-18-88` **Press** tab **twice** to advance to the Gender field.

Choose **Male** from the drop-down list.

Press tab to advance to the Hire Date field. This is the date the employee began working for VeloCity.

Type `1-6-17`

The default entry for **Job Status** — Full time — is correct for all employees.

The next two fields will be used when the employee leaves the job — the date of termination and the reason for leaving that you can select from the drop-down list. The final option designates employees as active or inactive. All employees at VeloCity are active, so the default selection is correct.

NOTES

Refer to page 299 for more information about employee terminations.

We have not yet created job categories to identify salespersons, so we will assign employees to them later. The program will automatically enter the Date Last Paid.

Entering Employee Tax Information

Click the **Taxes tab** to advance to the next set of employee details.

NOTES

Refer to page 331 to review entering employee tax details.

This screen allows you to enter income tax–related information for an employee, including the historical amounts for the year to date. Tax Table is a required field.

Click the **Tax Table list arrow** for the list of provinces and territories.

Click **Ontario**, the province of taxation for VeloCity employees.

Press tab to advance to the **Federal Basic Personal Amount field**.

Type `12609` **Press** tab.

Type 10582 to enter the Provincial Basic Personal Amount.

Click the **Federal Non-indexed Amount field** and **type** 2100

Press tab and **type** 2100 to add the Provincial Non-Indexed Amount.

Gearie is the only employee with additional indexed claim amounts. Schwinn is the only employee who chooses to have additional taxes withheld.

For **Gearie**, entering the **three federal and provincial claim amounts** from page 628 in their respective fields will provide the correct total, indexed and non-indexed amounts.

For **Schwinn**, click the **Additional Fed. Tax** field and type **50**.

WARNING!
Enter employee historical payroll details carefully. You will be unable to edit these fields after finishing the history or after making Payroll Journal entries for the employee.
They must also be correct because they are used to create T4s for tax reporting.

If an employee is insurable by EI, you must leave the box for **Deduct EI** checked. The default EI contribution factor, 1.4, for VeloCity is correct. We entered it in the Payroll Taxes Settings window (page 659).

All employees at VeloCity make CPP contributions and pay income tax, so leave these check boxes selected. We will enter the historical income tax amounts next.

Click the **Historical Amount field** for **Income Tax**.

Type 1668.29 **Press** tab to advance to the EI Premiums Historical Amount field.

Type 232.97 to enter the amount of EI paid to date. **Press** tab to move to the CPP Contributions Historical Amount field.

Type 547.31

NOTES
The program skips the Quebec tax fields because no linked accounts were entered for them.

Entering Income Amounts for Employees

We defined all the types of income for VeloCity in the Names, Incomes & Deductions setup (page 655). All employees use the following types of income, although not all will have regular amounts and not all will be used on all paycheques:

- No. Clients
- Bonus
- Tuition
- Travel Exp.

NOTES
Refer to page 333 if you need to review entering employee income details.
The checkmarks for Advances, Loans, Benefits and Vacation Owed and Vacation Paid cannot be removed.

In addition, all employees used Loans and Benefits and Mercier uses Vacation (Vac.) Owed, Vacation (Vac.) Paid, Regular and Overtime 1.

For Gearie and Schwinn, Salary is also used, and for Gearie, Commission is used. Because Quebec is not selected as the province of taxation, Benefits (Que) is not preselected.

All the details you need to complete the Income tab chart are on pages 628–629.

NOTES
The chart on pages 628–629 has the incomes that are used by an employee with a ✓ or an amount in the employee's column.

Click the **Income tab**.

On the Income chart you can indicate the types of income that each employee receives (the **Use** column), the usual rate of pay for that type of income (**Amount Per Unit**), the usual number of hours worked (**Hours Per Period**), the usual number of pieces for a piece rate pay base (**Pieces Per Period**) and the amounts received this year before the earliest transaction date or the date used for the first paycheque (**Historical Amount**). The **Year-To-Date (YTD) Amount** is added automatically by the program based on the historical amounts you enter and the paycheques entered in the program.

Checkmarks must be entered in the Use column for all fields that are needed in the Payroll journals, even if they will not be used on all paycheques.

NOTES
Checkmarks are added by default for all incomes, deductions and expenses that have linked accounts.

Click **Regular** in the Income column to select the line.

Press tab to advance to the Amount Per Unit field where we need to enter the regular hourly wage rate.

Type 18 **Press** tab to advance the Hours Per Period field.

The usual number of work hours in the bi-weekly pay period is 80. You can change the default amount in the Payroll journals. Salaried workers normally work 150 hours each month.

Type 80 **Press** tab to advance to the Historical Amount field.

Historical income and deduction amounts for the year to date are necessary so that taxes and deductions can be calculated correctly and T4 statements will be accurate.

Type 11520 **Press** tab.

The amount is entered automatically in the YTD column and the cursor advances to the Use column for Overtime 1.

Press tab so you can enter the overtime hourly rate.

Type 27

Press tab **twice** to advance to the Historical Amount field. There is no regular number of overtime hours.

Type 486

The next three income types do not apply to Mercier, so they should not be checked. The next income that applies is No. Clients, the piece rate method of pay. There is no historical amount, but we need to enter the rate or amount per unit (survey). The remaining incomes (No. Clients, Bonus and Travel Exp.) are correctly checked. There is no fixed amount per unit or period and there are no historical amounts.

Pressing the space bar in the Use column will also add a ✓ or remove one if it is there. Pressing ↓ will move you to the next line in the same column.

Click the **Use column beside Salary** to remove the ✓.

Click the **Use column beside Commission** to remove the ✓.

Click **No. Clients** in the Income column to select the line. **Press** tab.

Type 10 to enter the amount received for each completed survey.

Click **Tuition** in the Income column to select the line. **Press** tab.

Type 110 to enter the amount per paycheque.There is no historical amount.

If employees have received vacation pay, enter this amount in the **Vac. Paid** field. Vacation pay not yet received is entered in the **Vac. Owed** field. Any loans (or advances) paid to the employees and not yet repaid are recorded in the **Loans** or (**Advances**) **Historical Amount** field. There is no record of advance or loan amounts recovered.

We need to add the historical loans, benefits and vacation amounts for Mercier. Mercier has $100 in loans not yet repaid, and he has not received all the vacation pay he has earned this year.

Scroll **to the top** of the list so that the information for Loans is available.

Click the **Historical Amount column beside Loans**.

Type 100

Press tab to move to the Amount Per Unit column for Benefits. The group insurance premiums paid by the employer are employee benefits.

WARNING!
Do not click the Use column beside Regular or No. Clients for Mercier as that will remove these checkmarks.

NOTES
If you added a linked account for Overtime 2, it will have a ✓ in the Use column and you should remove it for all employees.

WARNING!
The totals for all employees for advances paid, loans paid and vacation pay owing must match the corresponding General Ledger account balances before you can finish entering the history.

NOTES
Remember that commissions must be calculated manually and entered in the Payroll journals. The Commission field in the Payroll Ledger allows only a fixed amount, not a percentage of sales, as the entry.

NOTES
Employees may be paid yearly (1), semi-annually (2), monthly for 10 months (10), monthly (12), every four weeks (13), every two weeks for a 10-month year (22), twice a month (24), every two weeks (26) or weekly (52).

NOTES
When you select a specific account, all payroll income expenses for that employee will be linked to the same account – the one you identify in this field. If you want to use different accounts for different wage expenses, you must use the linked accounts.

NOTES
Refer to page 335 to review entering employee deductions.

NOTES
For one-time changes, you can edit deduction amounts in the Payroll journals on the Deductions tab screen.
The Use column in the ledger record must be checked for the field to become available in the journal.

Type 16 **Press** tab to move to the Historical Amount for Benefits.

Type 128 **Press** tab to advance to the Historical Amount for Vac. Owed.

Type 706 **Press** tab to advance to the Historical Vac. Paid Amount.

Type 386

For **Schwinn**, click the Use column for Regular, Overtime 1 and Commission to remove the ✓. Enter the monthly salary and press tab. Enter 150 as the number of hours worked in the pay period. Press tab and enter the historical amount. For No. Clients, enter 10 as the amount per unit. For Travel Exp., enter 120 as the historical amount. You cannot remove the ✓ for Vac. Owed and Vac. Paid, even if they are not used.

For **Gearie**, repeat these steps but leave Commission checked and enter the historical amount. For Tuition, enter the per period and historical amounts.

Pay Periods Per Year, another required field, refers to the number of times the employee is paid, or the pay cycle. Mercier is paid every two weeks, so 26 times per year.

Click the **list arrow** beside the field for **Pay Periods Per Year**.

Click **26**.

Retaining Vacation pay is normal for full-time hourly paid employees. Part-time and casual workers often receive their vacation pay with each paycheque because their work schedule is irregular. For these employees, you will turn off the option to retain vacation because they receive their vacation pay with each paycheque (refer to page 277). If the employee is salaried and does not receive vacation pay, the option should also be turned off. For Mercier, or any employee who receives vacation pay, leave the option to Retain Vacation checked and type the vacation pay rate in the % field.

Double-click the **% field beside Vacation Rate**. **Type** 6

For **Schwinn** and **Gearie**, click Retain Vacation to remove the ✓.

Employee wages may all be linked to their individual and different linked expense accounts or to one single account. Wage expenses for all VeloCity employees are linked to the default accounts on page 660.

Entering Default Payroll Deduction Amounts

Click the **Deductions tab** to open the screen for payroll deductions.

On this screen you can indicate which deductions apply to the employee, the amount normally deducted and the historical amount — the amount deducted to date this year. All deductions are selected in the Use column. These are the deductions you entered previously (page 656).

By entering deduction amounts here, they will be included automatically on the Payroll Journal input forms. Otherwise, you must enter them manually in the journal for each pay period. Since all three employees participate in the VRSP and savings plans, you can enter the information here so that the deductions are made automatically. You should make permanent changes by editing the employee ledger record.

If you choose to calculate deductions as a percentage of gross pay in the Payroll Settings, the Percentage Per Pay Period fields will be available.

Click **VRSP** in the Deduction column to select the line.

Press tab. You should enter the amount that is withheld in each pay period.

Type 50 **Press** tab to advance the cursor to the Historical Amount field.

Type 450 **Press** tab to advance the cursor to the Use column for Savings Plan.

Press tab. Enter the amount that is to be withheld in each pay period.

Type 50 **Press** tab to advance the cursor to the Historical Amount field.

Type 450 **Press** tab to update the YTD Amount and advance to the Use column for Garnishee.

Click the **Use column for Garnishee** to remove the ✓. Mercier does not have wages withheld.

For **Schwinn**, enter 200 as the Amount and 800 as the YTD amount for Garnishee.

The remaining deductions are not used by VeloCity. Their names were deleted (page 656), so only the three we named appear in the ledger.

Entering WSIB and Other Expenses

Click the **WSIB & Other Expenses tab**.

The user-defined expenses we created in the Additional Payroll Names screen (page 656) and the default WSIB rate (page 659) are entered on this screen.

In Ontario, WSIB (Workplace Safety and Insurance Board) is the name for the Workers' Compensation Board, so the tab is labelled WSIB. In other provinces, the tab label will be WCB & Other Expenses or the name selected on the Additional Payroll Names screen.

The default WSIB rate is entered from our setup information, but you can enter a different rate for an individual employee in this field. The rate is correct for Mercier.

For **Gearie**, enter 1.02 as the WSIB rate.

Other user-defined expenses are also added on this screen. VeloCity has only group insurance as a user-defined expense.

Click the **Gp Insurance Amt. Per Period**. Enter the amount that the employer contributes in each pay period.

Type 16 **Press** tab to advance to the Historical Amount field.

Type 128

The remaining expense fields are not used by VeloCity at this time.

Entering Employee Entitlements

We entered the default rates and amounts for entitlements as Payroll Settings (page 660), but they can be modified in the ledger records for individual employees.

We must also enter the historical information for entitlements. This historical number will include any days carried forward from the previous periods. The number of days accrued cannot be greater than the maximum number of days defined for the entitlement for an employee. The number of Net Days Accrued, the amount unused and available for carrying forward, is updated automatically from the historical information and current payroll journal entries. Entitlements information is included in the chart on page 629.

Click the **Entitlements tab**.

NOTES
Refer to page 336 to review entering WSIB (WCB) details.

NOTES
The name WSIB in Ontario emphasizes safety rather than compensation for accidents. WSIB (or WCB) pays workers when they have been injured on the job and are unable to work.

NOTES
Refer to page 337 if you need to review entering employee entitlements.

You cannot enter information directly in the Net Days Accrued fields on the Entitlements tab screen.

Mercier receives vacation pay instead of paid time off, so the vacation entitlements details should be removed. The defaults for sick leave and personal days are correct.

Click **8.00** in the **Track Using % Hours Worked field for Vacation**.

Press del to remove the entry.

Press tab to advance to the Maximum Days field.

Press del to remove the entry.

Click the **Historical Days field for Sick Leave**.

Type 12

Press ↓ to advance to the Historical Days field for PersonalDays. The number of days is added to the Net Days Accrued.

Type 4 **Press** tab to enter the amount.

For **Gearie** and **Schwinn**, the default entries for tracking and maximum days are correct, but you must enter the Historical Days for each entitlement.

NOTES
If employees take days before the sufficient number of hours worked have been accrued, the program will warn you. Then you can allow the entry for entitlements or not. This entry is similar to allowing customers to exceed their credit limits.

Entering Direct Deposit Information

Click the **Direct Deposit tab**.

All three employees have elected to have their paycheques deposited directly to their bank accounts. On this screen we need to enter the bank account details. For each employee who has elected the direct deposit option, you must turn on the selection in the Direct Deposit Paycheques For This Employee check box. Then you must add the five-digit **Branch** or Transit **Number**, the three-digit **Bank Number**, the bank **Account Number** and finally the amount that is deposited, or the percentage of the cheque. Direct deposit information is included in the chart on page 629.

Click the **Direct Deposit Paycheques For This Employee check box** to add a ✓.

Click the **Branch No. field**.

Type 89008 **Press** tab to advance to the Institution No. field.

Type 102 **Press** tab to advance to the Account No. field.

Type 2998187 **Press** tab **twice** to advance to the Percentage field.

Type 100

The **Memo** tab will not be used at this time. You could enter a note with a reminder date to appear in the Daily Business Manager, for example, a reminder to issue vacation paycheques on a specific date or to recover advances.

NOTES
Refer to page 337 if you need to review entering direct deposit details.

NOTES
All banks in Canada are assigned a three-digit bank number, and each branch has a unique five-digit transit number. Account numbers may range from five to twelve digits.

NOTES
The paycheque deposit may be split among multiple bank accounts by entering different percentages for the accounts, but the total must be 100%.
To delete bank account details, click the Direct Deposit check box, change the deposit status to Inactive and then delete the bank information.

Entering Additional Information

VeloCity has chosen to enter the name and phone number of the person to be contacted in case of an emergency involving the employee at work. We added the names for these fields in the Payroll Settings (page 656).

Click the **Additional Info tab** to access the fields we added for the ledger when we entered Names.

NOTES
Refer to page 338 to review entering additional information details for employees.

You can indicate whether you want to display any of the additional information when the employee is selected in a transaction. We do not need to display the contact information in the Payroll Journal. Refer to the chart on page 629 for contact details.

Click the **Emergency Contact field**.

Type Adrian Ingles

Press tab **twice** to move to the Contact Number field.

Type (905) 548-0301

NOTES
Additional information for other ledgers may also be displayed or hidden in journal transactions.

WARNING!
The Contact Number field is not predefined as a telephone number, so its format will not be corrected automatically by the program.

Entering T4 and RL-1 Reporting Amounts

The next information screen allows you to enter the year-to-date EI insurable and pensionable earnings. By adding the historical amounts, the T4 slips prepared for income taxes at the end of the year and the Record of Employment termination reports will also be correct.

Because there are yearly maximum amounts for CPP and EI contributions, these historical details are also needed. Totals for optional deductions are also retained in the employee record. The amounts you need are in the chart on page 629.

NOTES
Refer to page 339 if you need to review entering T4 and RL-1 reporting details.

Click the **T4 and RL-1 Reporting tab** to open the next screen we need.

In the **Historical EI Ins. Earnings** field, you should enter the total earned income received to date that is EI insurable. The program will update this total every time you make payroll entries until the maximum salary on which EI is calculated has been reached. At that time, no further EI premiums will be deducted.

Pensionable Earnings are also tracked by the program. This amount determines the total income that is eligible for the Canada Pension Plan; CPP deductions will stop automatically when the maximum has been reached. The Pension Adjustment amount is used when the employee has a workplace pension program that will affect the allowable contributions for personal registered pension plans and will be linked with the Canada Pension Plan. Workplace pension income is reduced when the employee also has income from the Canada Pension Plan. Since VeloCity has no company pension plan, the Pension Adjustment amount is zero.

NOTES
The EI Insurable amount is the total of gross wages, including overtime wages and vacation pay, but not benefits.

Pensionable earnings include these same incomes plus benefits.

The T4 Employee Code applies to a small number of job types that have special income tax rules.

Click the **Historical Amounts field for EI Ins. Earnings**.

Type 12392

Click the **Historical Amounts field for Pensionable Earnings**.

Type 12520

Correct any employee information **errors** by returning to the field with the error. **Highlight** the **error** and **enter** the **correct information**. **Click each tab** in turn so that you can check all the information.

When all the information is entered correctly, you must save the employee record.

Click Create Another to save the record and open a new blank employee information form.

Click the **Personal tab** so that you can enter address information.

Repeat these procedures to **enter** other employee **records**.

Click Save and Close after entering the last record to save the record and close the Payroll Ledger.

NOTES
We will not use the remaining tax information fields for VeloCity. VeloCity does not have a company pension plan with regular payroll deductions, so there is no plan registration number. The Pension Adjustment amount is used when an employee contributes to a company pension plan and these payments reduce the amount the employee can contribute to a private registered pension plan. Income from company pension plans may also be reduced when CPP is collected at retirement.

CPP contribution rates are set federally.

NOTES

You can print these reports from the Reports menu in the Employees window.

Display or **print** the **Employee List** and the **Employee Summary Report**.
Compare them with pages 628–630 to check the accuracy of your work.

Close the **Employees window** to return to the Home window.

Entering Job Categories

NOTES

Refer to page 341 if you want to review the setup for job categories.

Now that we have entered all the employees, we can set up job categories and indicate which employees are in each category.

Click the **Settings icon**. Then **click Payroll** and **Job Categories**.

On the Job Categories screen, you enter the category names and indicate whether the employees in each category submit time slips and whether they are salespersons.

Categories may be active or inactive. We need a new category called Sales.

If you do not create categories, the employees in the default selection <None> are salespersons so they can still be selected in the Sales Journal.

Click the **Job Category field below <None>**.

Type `Sales` **Press** *tab* to add checkmarks to the next two columns and set the status to Active.

Click **Assign Job Categories** to change the screen.

The Sales category is selected and the screen is updated with employee names. Initially, all are Employees Not In This Job Category.

You can add employee names to the category by choosing an employee and clicking **Select** or by choosing **Select All**. Once employees are in a category (the column on the right), you can remove them. Select an employee and click **Remove** or click **Remove All** to move all names at the same time.

Click **Select All** to place all employees in the Sales category. **Click OK**.

Setting Up Payroll Remittances

NOTES

Refer to page 340 if you want to review payroll remittance setup.

Because we have entered all payroll settings and all suppliers, we can set up the payroll remittances information. This process has three steps: linking the suppliers to the taxes or deductions they receive, entering remittance frequency and entering the pay period end date for the next remittance. Refer to the chart on page 623 and the Accounting Procedures on page 635.

Click **Remittance** under **Payroll**.

All the payroll items that are linked to liability (remittance) accounts are listed: taxes, deductions and user-defined expenses. For each liability, we can select a supplier and enter the payment frequency and due date for the next payment.

NOTES

All payroll remittances are made monthly except those for EHT to the Minister of Finance and WSIB to the Workplace Safety and Insurance Board. These two remittances are made quarterly.

The end of the next remitting period for all suppliers is May 1.

Click the **List icon** in the Remittance Supplier column on the line for EI.

Click **Receiver General for Canada** in the list of suppliers that opens.

Click **Select** or **press** *enter* to return to the Remittance Settings screen with the cursor in the Remitting Frequency field for EI.

Choose **Monthly** from the Frequency drop-down list. **Press** *tab*.

Type `May 1`

Enter the remaining **Remittance Suppliers**, **Frequencies** and dates for the **End Of Next Remitting Period**. Refer to the chart on page 623.

For **EHT** and **WSIB**, select the **Quarterly Remitting Frequency**.

Assigning Sales Tax Codes

Instead of entering tax codes in the individual ledger records, we can assign them in groups with the Assign Tax Codes feature. You can use this feature to enter initial tax code settings, as we do here for suppliers, or to update tax codes, as we do here for clients.

Click **Company**, **Sales Taxes** and **Tax Codes** to open the Settings window:

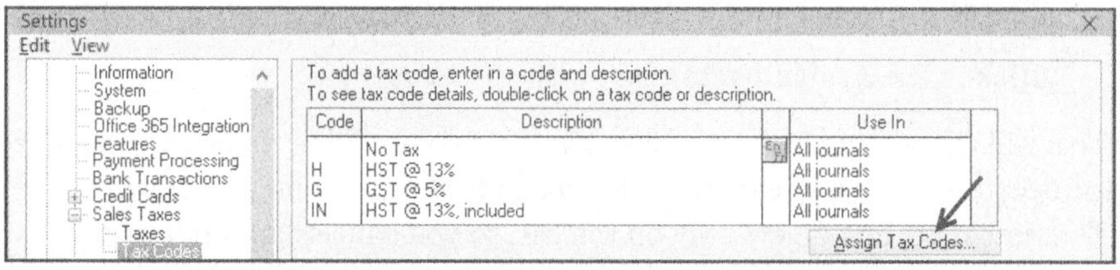

Click the **Assign Tax Codes** button below the list of codes:

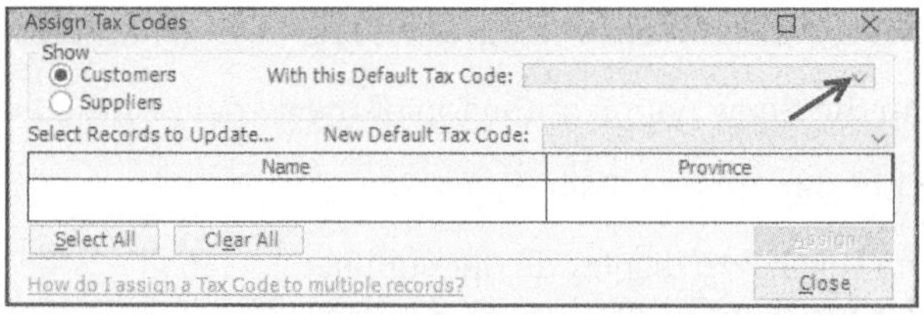

You can assign codes for suppliers and for customers. Customers are selected initially. None are listed because no tax code is selected. All customers were assigned the tax code H as part of the setup for the Receivables Ledger. As a result, showing all customers With This Default Tax Code (code H) will include all customers.

Choose **H – HST @ 13%** from the With This Default Tax Code drop-down list:

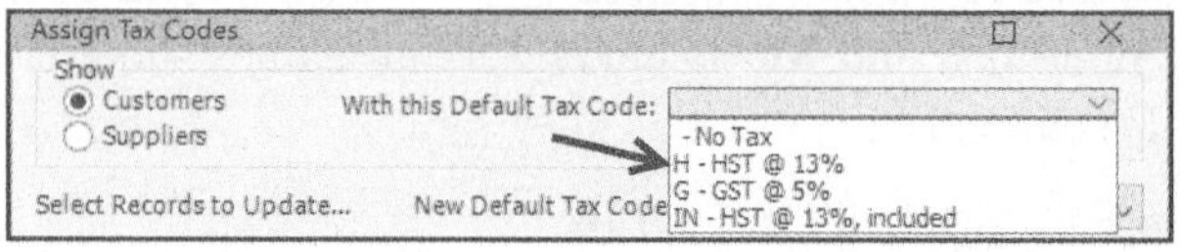

This will include all customers in the selection list:

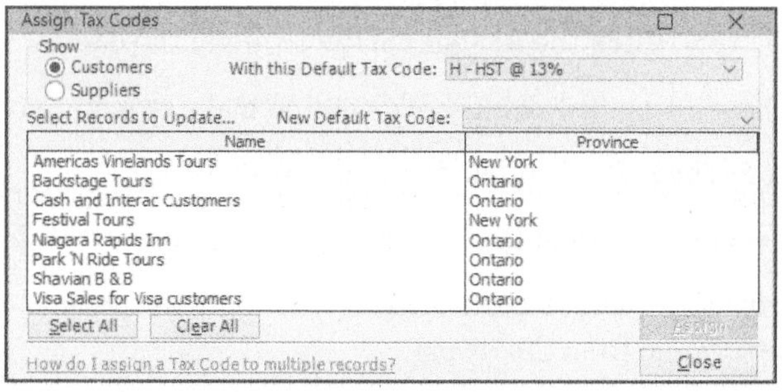

The next step is to select the customers that require a different tax code.

You can select one customer, more than one customer or all customers (by clicking Select All). We need to select the two USD customers.

Click **Americas Vinelands Tours**.

Press and **hold** ctrl and then **click Festival Tours**. Both names are now highlighted and we are ready to choose a new default code for them.

NOTES
You can also access the Assign Tax Codes screens from the Home window Maintenance menu.

NOTES
If you already entered No Tax for the USD customers, they will not appear on this list.

> **NOTES**
> Remember that you can still choose a different tax code in the journal. We left this option open by indicating that suppliers and clients are not Tax Exempt for HST and GST.

Click the **New Default Tax Code list arrow**:

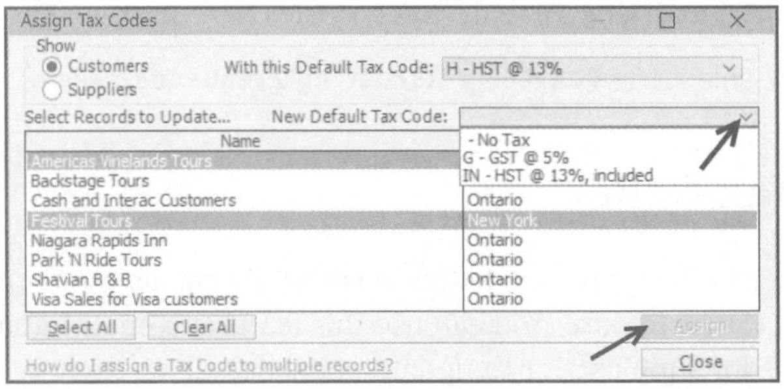

Our options are to change from code H to one of the codes not already applied. We can choose from No Tax, G and IN. USD customers do not pay taxes on exported goods.

Choose **No Tax** from the drop-down list. The Assign button becomes available.

Click the **Assign button** below the list of names.

> **WARNING!**
> You must click the Assign button before the changes are applied.

This will change the code for these two customers. Their names are removed from the list because they no longer have the tax code H — the one we chose.

The remaining customers stay on the list, so you can assign other tax codes if necessary. Tax code H is correct for the other customers, so we can continue by applying supplier tax codes. We have not entered any supplier tax codes yet, so the default entry will be No Tax. This is correct for the government agencies and payroll authorities.

Click **Suppliers** in the Show option at the top of the screen.

Click the **With This Default Tax Code list arrow**.

Select **No Tax** from this list to display all our suppliers:

> **NOTES**
> If you already entered tax codes for the suppliers, your list of suppliers at this stage will be different.

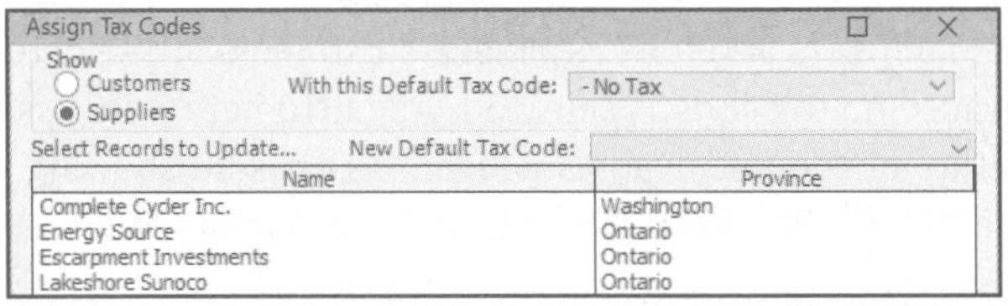

Click **Complete Cycler Inc. Press** and **hold** ctrl and then **click Niagara Bell**, **Pro Cycles Inc.** and **Wheel Deals**. All four names should remain highlighted (selected).

Click the **New Default Tax Code list arrow**.

We are changing from the code No Tax, so this is not on the drop-down list.

Click **H - HST @ 13%**. **Click** the **Assign button** to apply the code.

The four names are removed from the display. We need to make two more changes.

Click **Lakeshore Sunoco**, which requires the IN tax code.

Click the **New Default Tax Code list arrow**.

Click **IN - HST @ 13%, included**. **Click Assign** to apply the code and remove the supplier's name from the display.

Click **Energy Source**. **Select G - GST @ 5%** as the new default tax code and **click Assign**.

The remaining suppliers are government agencies and payroll authorities for which the default No Tax code is correct.

Click **Close** to save all the changes and return to the Tax Codes Settings.

Click **OK** to save all the new settings and return to the Home window.

Preparing Inventory Ledger Records

Use the VeloCity Inventory Information and chart on page 630 to record details about the inventory items on hand.

The next set of keystrokes will enter the information for VeloCity's first inventory item, Bicycle Pump: standing model.

Click **Inventory & Services** in the Modules pane list.

Click the **Inventory & Services icon** Inventory & Services. Again, with no inventory items on file, the window is empty.

Click Create or **choose** the **File menu** and **click** **Create**:

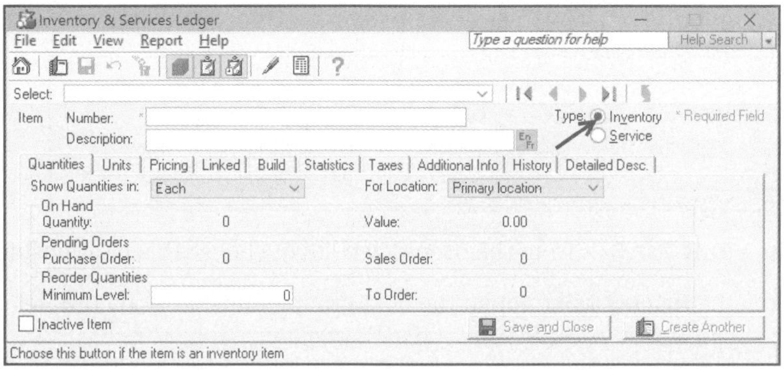

The Type is set correctly for this item as Inventory rather than Service.

The cursor is in the Item Number field. Use this field for the item's code or number. When you sort inventory by description, the two item fields will be reversed — the Description field will appear first. Item Number is a required field.

Type AC010 **Press** tab to advance to the Item Description field, the field for the name of the inventory item.

Type Bicycle Pump: standing model

The Show Quantities In field allows you to select the units displayed in the ledger. If you have entered different units for stocking, selling and buying, these will be available from the drop-down list. The Quantity On Hand and Value fields are updated by the program, as are the Purchase Orders and Sales Orders Pending.

Click the **Minimum Level field**. Here you should enter the minimum stock level or reorder point for this inventory item.

Type 5

Click the **Units tab** to advance to the next information screen:

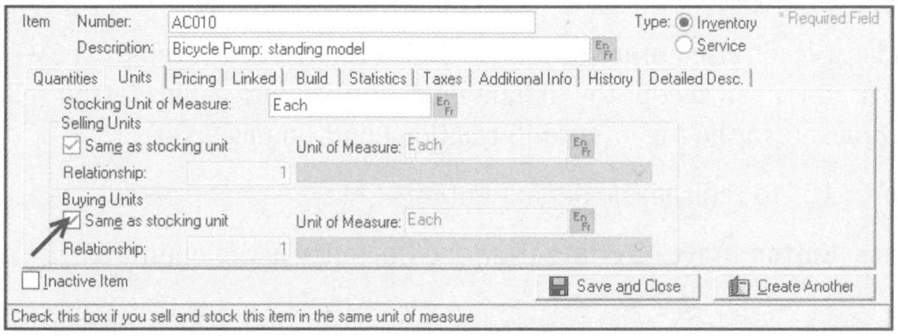

You can enter different units for items when the units for buying, stocking and selling differ. VeloCity uses the same units for stocking and selling but some buying units are different. For example, if items are purchased in dozens and stocked individually, the

PRO VERSION

There isn't a Build tab in the Pro version, and only two show icons will be included in the tool bar. The Show Activities tool applies only to Premium features, and the Refresh tool is used with the multi-user option in Premium.

NOTES

If you hide the Inventory icon window (Setup menu, User Preferences, View), you will open this Inventory Ledger immediately when you click the Inventory & Services icon.

NOTES

The Item Description is not a required field, even when you sort by description.

WARNING!

Enter inventory details very carefully. You cannot remove an inventory record or change the Type if there is a quantity on hand. You must edit the History fields to reduce the quantity and value to zero and save the changes. Then remove the item and re-enter all the details correctly.

Changing the Type requires an additional step. Close the ledger to save the changes in the history (with zero quantity). When you open the ledger again, you can edit the Type.

relationship is 12 to 1. The Stocking Unit for bicycle pumps must be changed — they are purchased in boxes of four pumps and stocked and sold individually (unit).

Double-click the default entry **Each** for the Stocking Unit Of Measure.

Type unit

Click **Same As Stocking Unit** in the **Buying Units section** to remove the ✓ and open the relationship fields. Here you should indicate how many stocking units are in each buying unit.

WARNING!
You must enter the unit relationship information before entering the history for inventory so that purchase prices and average costs will be calculated correctly.

Press tab to advance to the Unit Of Measure field.

Type box **Press** tab **twice** to advance to the Relationship field.

Type 4 **Press** tab. **Click** the **list arrow** beside the Relationship number field:

NOTES
The relationship may be units per box or boxes per unit. VeloCity purchases boxes that include four items. Therefore, the correct relationship is unit per box.

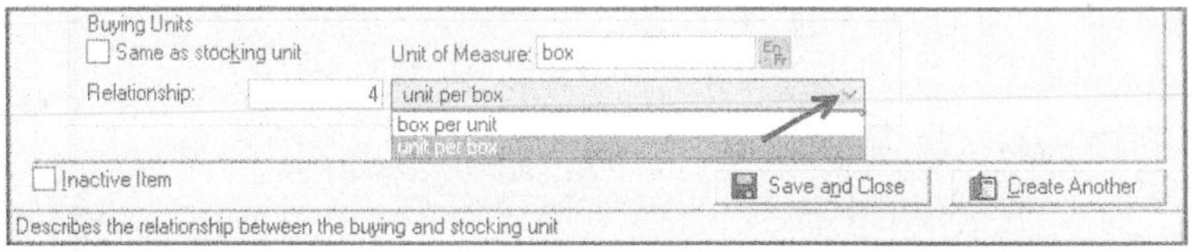

Click **Unit Per Box** from the drop-down list to choose this relationship.

Click the **Pricing tab** to open the next group of inventory record fields:

NOTES
By working from the Inventory Ledger Settings, Price Lists screen, you can create new price lists and enter and update all prices from one screen. In Chapter 18, we update inventory prices using this approach.

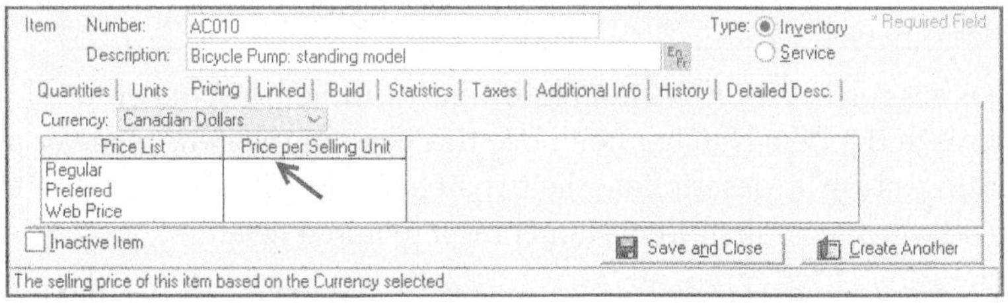

The Currency field and foreign price fields are available only if you indicated that inventory prices should be taken from the Inventory Ledger record and not calculated using the exchange rate. The pricing option appears on the Inventory Settings screen only after you enter foreign currency information for the company. Therefore, you must add and save currency information first. Taking prices from the ledger record is the default setting.

On the Pricing tab screen, you can enter regular, preferred and Web prices in the currencies that you have set up. If you created additional price lists, their names will also appear on this screen. The home currency (Canadian Dollars) is selected first.

NOTES
Refer to page 662 for the Inventory Ledger Settings screen. You cannot change these settings while the Inventory Ledger is open, that is, while you are entering an inventory item.

Click the **Regular Price Per Selling Unit field**. Here you should enter the selling price for this inventory item.

Type 50 **Press** tab to advance to the Preferred Selling Price field.

The regular price is also entered as the default Preferred and Web Price. We do not have Web sales, so we can accept the default entry for Web prices. Preferred selling prices are in brackets in the Inventory Information chart on page 630.

PRO VERSION
You cannot create additional price lists or update them globally in the Pro version.

Type 45 to replace the default entry.

Choose **United States Dollars** from the Currency list to open USD price fields:

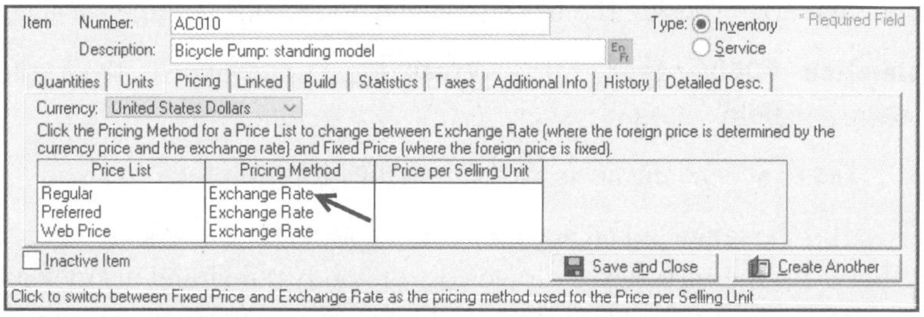

The pricing method is entered separately for each price. You can choose either Exchange Rate or Fixed Price for Regular, Preferred and Web prices.

Click **Exchange Rate** beside Regular to change the entry to Fixed Price.

Press tab to advance to the Regular Price Per Selling Unit field.

Type 37 **Press** tab to advance to the Pricing Method field.

Click **Exchange Rate** to change the entry to Fixed Price.

Press tab to advance to the Preferred Price Per Selling Unit field.

Type 33 **Press** tab.

Click the **Linked tab** to open the linked accounts screen for the item:

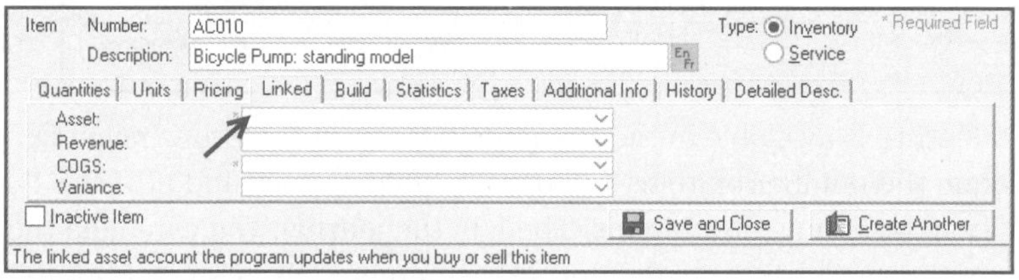

Click the **Asset field list arrow**.

Here you must enter the **asset** account associated with the sale or purchase of this inventory item. All accessories in the Inventory chart on page 630 use account *1520*. All bicycles use *1540*, and the books use *1560* as the asset account. All available asset accounts are in the displayed list. Asset account is a required field.

Enter the account by clicking the list arrow and choosing from the drop-down account list, or

Type 1520 **Press** tab.

The program asks you to confirm the account class change for account *1520*:

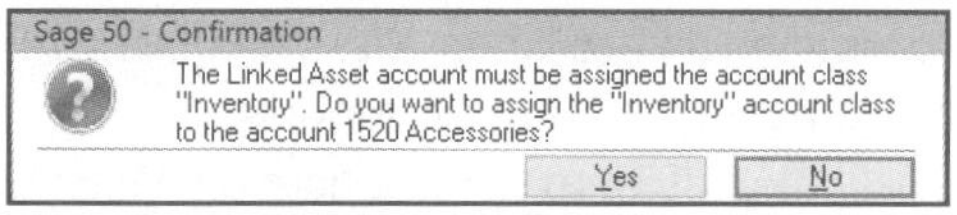

Click **Yes** — you must accept the change in account class.

The cursor advances to the **Revenue** field. Here you must enter the revenue account that will be credited with the sale of this inventory item.

Again, you can display the list of revenue accounts by clicking the list arrow. Or,

Type 4020 **Press** tab.

The cursor advances to the **COGS** field. Here you must enter the expense account to be debited with the sale of this inventory item, normally the *Cost of Goods Sold* account. VeloCity keeps track of each inventory category separately and has different expense accounts for each category. The appropriate expense account is updated automatically when an inventory item is sold. The COGS account is another required field.

NOTES

The ledger option to change the way foreign prices are calculated is available only when you selected Foreign Prices Are Taken From The Foreign Price Listed In The Inventory And Services Record as your Inventory Setting (page 662).

NOTES

Revenue accounts are not required fields for inventory items. Entering them in the ledger will add them automatically in the journal when the item is bought or sold.

Variance accounts are not required accounts, but they are needed when a purchase triggers a variance.

NOTES

If you add a new account at this stage, you can include an Opening Balance using the Add An Account wizard. Because the history is not finished, the Opening Balance field is added to the wizard.

NOTES

If you created the expense accounts in the General Ledger and you did not change the account class, you will not get the message about account class changes for 5050 and 5070 because Cost of Goods Sold is the default account class. However, if all expense accounts are defined as Cost of Goods Sold accounts, you cannot produce an accurate Gross Margin Income Statement.

PRO VERSION

The Build tab screen is not included in the Pro version. Click the Statistics tab as the next step.

NOTES

Building an item from a bill of materials is covered in Chapter 18.

Click the list arrow beside the field to display the available expense accounts.

Double-click **5050** or **type** 5050 **Press** tab to advance to the Variance field.

Click **Yes** to accept the account class change if prompted.

Sage 50 uses the **Variance** linked account when you restock oversold items. If there is a difference between the historical average cost of goods remaining in stock and the actual cost when the new merchandise is received, the price difference is charged to the variance expense account at the time of the purchase (refer to page 525). If you have not indicated a variance account, the program will ask you to identify one when you are entering the purchase that has a variance.

Type 5080 or **click** the **list arrow** and **choose** the **account**.

Click the **Build tab**.

Click **Yes** to accept the account class change and access the Build screen:

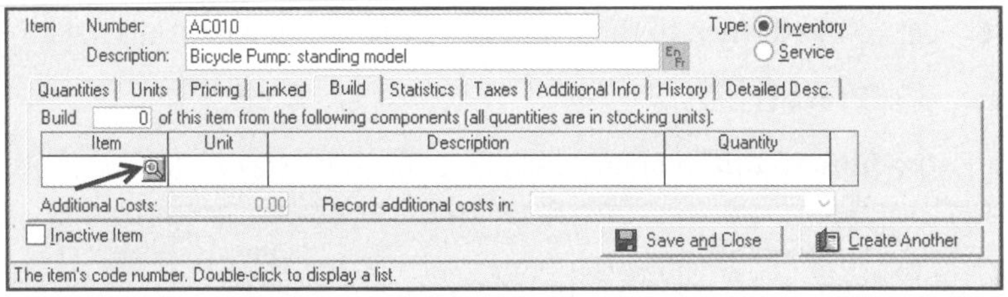

The Build feature is available in the Premium but not in the Pro version. On this screen you define the number of items you usually build at once and how this quantity is made or built from other inventory items. Then, in the journal, you can build the item by choosing it from the available list and entering the number of units you want to build at that time. This screen holds the components portion of the Item Assembly Journal.

Click the **Statistics tab** to open the next tab information screen:

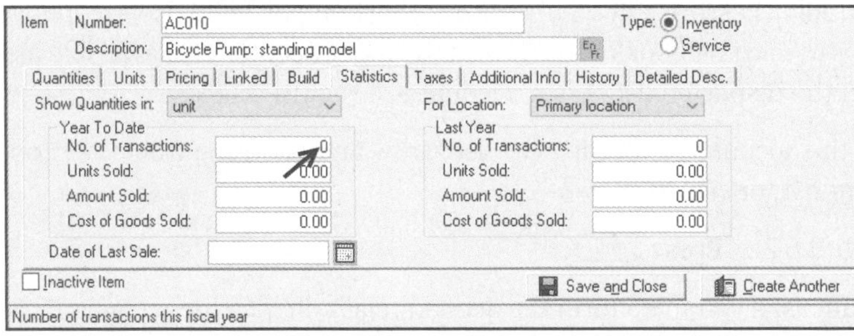

On this screen, you can enter historical information about the sale of the product. It would then be added to the inventory tracking information for reports.

The first activity field, the Date Of Last Sale, refers to the last date on which the item was sold. The next two sections contain information for the Year To Date and the previous year. Since VeloCity has not kept this information, you can skip these fields. Refer to page 374 in the Flabuless Fitness application (Chapter 10) for a more detailed description of these historical Statistics fields.

Click the **Taxes tab** to input the sales taxes relating to the inventory item:

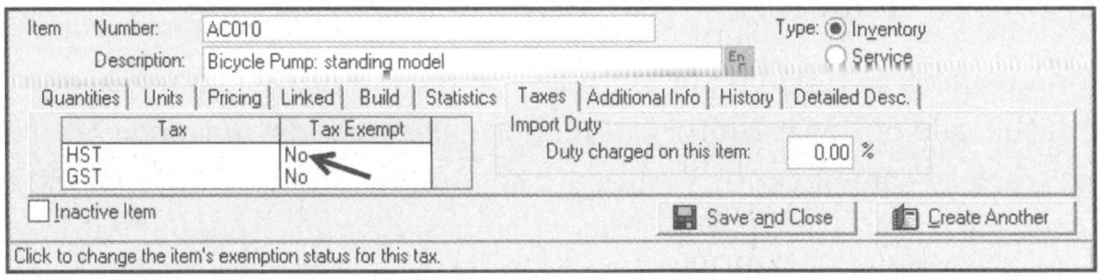

You can indicate whether the item is taxable for all the taxes you set up, GST and HST in this case. HST is charged on sales of all inventory items except for books, so the default entry No for **Tax Exempt** is correct for bicycle pumps.

The exemption settings in the ledger record do not control the tax code entered in the Sales Journal. They prevent a tax from being applied.

For **Books: Complete Bicycle Guide** and **Books: Endless Trails**, items BK010 and BK020, **click No** beside **HST** for Tax Exempt to change the entry to Yes.

Duty is also entered on this screen. You must activate the duty tracking option (page 651) before the duty rate field becomes available. Since no duty is charged on the imported inventory, you can leave the duty rate at 0%.

We have not added fields to the ledger record as we did for Payroll, so we can skip the **Additional Info** screen.

The next step is to add the opening historical balances for the inventory items.

Click the **History tab**:

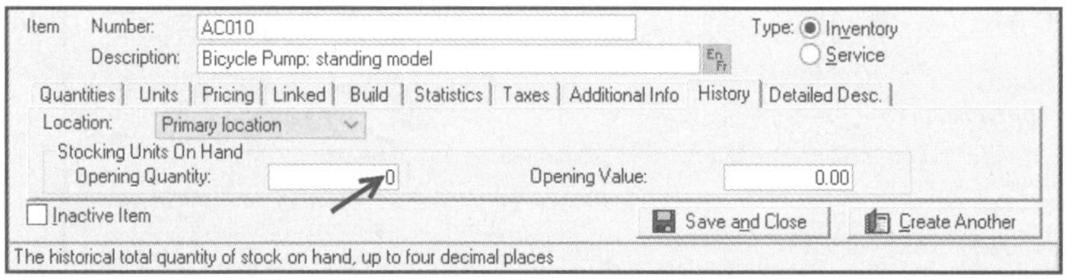

This screen has information about the starting quantities for the item at the time of conversion to Sage 50. The opening quantities and values are added to the Quantity On Hand and Value on the Quantities tab screen (page 679). History is entered in stocking unit quantities (the same as selling units for VeloCity).

Click the **Opening Quantity field** to enter the opening level of inventory — the actual number of items available for sale.

Type 10 **Press** (tab).

The cursor advances to the **Opening Value** field, where you should enter the actual total cost of the inventory on hand.

Type 300

Click the **Detailed Desc. tab**:

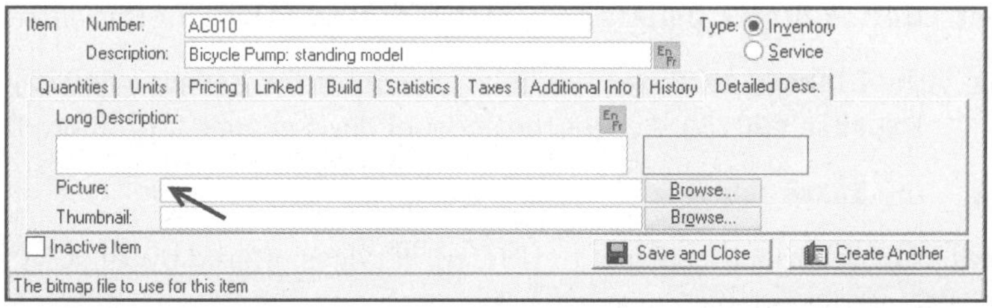

The final tab screen allows you to enter further descriptive information. This optional information provides a detailed description of the inventory item (up to 500 characters) as well as a picture in image file format.

Type the detailed item description in the Long Description text box.

Click **Browse** beside Picture. **Click This PC**. **Double-click C:**, **SageData19**, **LOGOS** and **PUMP.BMP** or **PUMP** to add the file name and picture.

Correct any **errors** by returning to the field with the mistake. **Highlight** the **error** and **enter** the **correct information**. **Click** the different **tabs** to review all the information you entered.

NOTES

To include the duty fields in the Purchases Journal, you must activate tracking of duty information and indicate in the supplier record (Options tab screen) that duty is charged on purchases from the supplier. Rates entered in the Inventory Ledger records will appear automatically in the Purchases Journal for those items. Duty rates can also be entered in the journal if you have not entered them in the ledger records.

NOTES

When you set up multiple locations, you can enter the quantity and value for items at each location. The Primary location is the default. In Chapter 18, we add Ryder's Routes as a second location for VeloCity.

PRO VERSION

The Pro version does not have a Location field.

WARNING!

Enter inventory history details carefully. To change historical quantities, you must delete the history entries, save the item, then remove the item and re-enter it. Otherwise the cost information in journal entries will be incorrect.

The total opening value amounts for all items in an asset group must match the General Ledger asset account balance before you can finish the history.

NOTES

A picture file for the Bicycle Pump: standing model has been added to the SageData19\LOGOS folder with your other data files. We have not provided picture files for the remaining inventory items.

NOTES

Pictures using either .BMP or .JPG formats can be displayed on-screen for inventory items.

NOTES
An entry for each item is added to the Home window Inventory Item list pane as you create and save it.

Click the **Quantities tab** to prepare for entering the next item. The quantity information (historical information) has been added.

Click Create Another to save the record and advance to a new input screen after you have added all the information.

Repeat these procedures to **enter** the **other** inventory **records** on page 630.

Entering Inventory Services

The final items on the inventory chart (page 631) are services that VeloCity provides. Entering services is similar to entering inventory, but there are fewer details.

You should have a blank Inventory & Services Ledger window open at the Quantities tab screen.

PRO VERSION
The Time & Billing tab screen is used to set up Time & Billing, a feature that is not available in the Pro version. The Activity setting and Internal Service Activity also apply to the Time & Billing feature, so they do not appear on the Pro version screen.

Click **Service** in the upper-right section of the screen to change the Type:

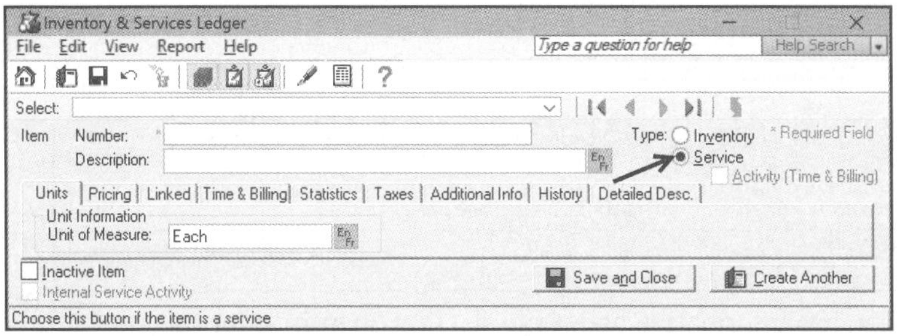

Some item details do not apply, so there are fewer tabs and fields for services. The Unit Of Measure and Selling Price have the same meaning for services as they do for inventory items. Because service items are not kept in stock or purchased, only the selling unit is applicable, there is no minimum quantity and the History fields are removed. Only expense and revenue accounts are linked for services, and even these are not required. The other two linked account fields do not apply and are removed for services. Remember to use *Revenue from Services* and *Cost of Services* as the linked accounts for inventory services.

Item Number is the only required field for service items.

Enter the **Item Number** and **Description** and the **Unit Of Measure**.

Click the **Pricing tab** and add **Regular** and **Preferred prices** in Canadian dollars. Select Canadian Dollars as the currency if necessary.

NOTES
Enter USD prices because some US customers will use these services in Canada and will pay taxes.

Select **United States Dollars** and **enter** the **fixed prices** for this currency.

Click the **Linked tab**. **Enter** the linked accounts for **Revenue (4040)** and **Expense (5075)**. Accept the account class change if prompted.

NOTES
Linked accounts for services are not required. However, adding them to the ledger record will have them entered into the journal automatically.

Click the **Taxes tab**.

Most services in Ontario are subject to HST. All services offered by VeloCity are not exempt from HST, so the default is correct at No.

Click Create Another.

Click the **Units tab**. **Repeat** these procedures to **enter other service records**.

Click Save and Close after entering the last service record.

Close the **Inventory & Services window** to return to the Home window.

Display or **print** the **Inventory List**, **Summary**, **Quantity** and **Price Lists** reports. Compare them with the information on pages 630–631 to check them for accuracy.

Finishing the History

The last stage in setting up the accounting system involves finishing the history for each ledger. Although most transactions can be completed when the history is not finished, there are some restrictions — you will be unable to calculate payroll taxes automatically or start a new fiscal period.

Before proceeding, you should check the data integrity (Home window, Maintenance menu) to learn whether there are any out-of-balance ledgers that will prevent you from proceeding. Correct these errors and then make a backup copy of the files.

You may also want to create a complete working copy of the not-finished files.

Making a Backup of the Company Files

Choose the **File menu** and **click Backup**; **click** the **Backup tool** or **click** the **Data Management icon** (Company module window) to start the Backup wizard.

Click **Browse** and **choose** the **data folder you want** for the not-finished backup of the data file.

Double-click the **File name field** in the Backup wizard screen.

Type NF-VELO

Click **OK** to create a backup copy of all the files for VeloCity.

The "NF" designates files as not finished to distinguish them from the ones you will work with to enter journal transactions. You will return to your working copy of the file so you can finish the history.

Changing the History Status of Ledgers to Finished

Refer to page 97 and page 251, respectively, for assistance with finishing the history and correcting history errors.

Choose the **History menu** and **click Finish Entering History**.

If your amounts, account types and linked accounts are correct, you will be warned that this step is not reversible and advised to back up the file first.

Click **Proceed** when there are no errors and you have backed up your files.

If you have made errors, you will not get the warning message. Instead Sage 50 will generate a list of errors.

Click **Print** so that you can refer to the list for making corrections.

Click **OK** to return to the Home window. **Make** the **corrections**, **replace** your **backup** file and then **try again** to finish the history.

Click **Proceed**.

The VeloCity files are now ready for you to enter transactions. The ledger icons in all module windows now appear without the open history icons. All the ledgers are ready for transactions.

Congratulations on reaching this stage! This is a good time to take a break.

Finish your **session**. This will give you an opportunity to read the next section and the instructions before starting the source document transactions.

WARNING!

Before you finish entering the history, make a backup copy of the VeloCity company files. This is necessary if you find that you need to correct some of the historical information later. Remember, once you finish entering the history, you cannot add information for any period before the earliest transaction date.

NOTES

To make a new folder, type NF-VELO in the path for the location to replace Backup.

You can also click Make New Folder in the Browse window and type NF-VELO when the New Folder name appears. Click OK to return to the Backup wizard.

To make a complete working copy backup, choose Save A Copy from the File menu to start the save procedure. Your current working copy will remain open when you have finished.

NOTES

If modules are hidden and then later unhidden, they will appear with the open history symbol, as we saw when we added the Payroll Ledger for Northern Lights in Chapter 9. When you later view these modules and choose the History menu, open or unfinished modules will be listed individually so you can set them as finished one at a time.

Project and Time & Billing do not have the not-finished (open history) symbols.

Entering Users and Security Passwords

WARNING!
Before adding passwords for practice, make a backup of your data file without passwords. You can restore this file to continue working if you forget your password or lock yourself out of the data file.

We strongly advise you not to set passwords for working copy data files used for tutorial purposes.

Sage 50 allows you to set up passwords for different users. The password for the system administrator (sysadmin) controls access to the system or program. Passwords for other users control viewing and editing privileges for different ledgers, journals, reports and messages. If different employees work with different accounting records, they should have different passwords.

Restricting access by setting passwords is different from hiding ledgers using the Setup menu, User Preferences, View screen. Since the View preferences are unrestricted user settings, these hidden ledgers can be restored at any time by another user. Ledgers hidden by restricted access passwords can be accessed and restored only by opening the files with the system administrator (**sysadmin**) password and changing access rights.

Users and passwords are entered from the Setup menu in the Home window.

NOTES
Passwords have not been added to any data files for this text.

Choose the **Setup menu** and **click Set Up Users** to display the control window:

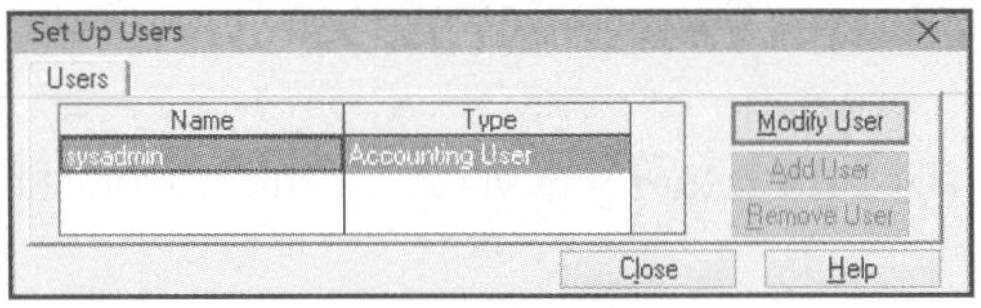

NOTES
You must work in single-user mode to set up passwords and users.

This Set Up Users window lists all users currently set up in the data files. Initially, the only user is sysadmin (system administrator). The highest level of access comes with the sysadmin password that allows the user to enter, use or modify any part of the data files, including creating users and setting passwords. The sysadmin password must be set before any other passwords can be set, so this user is selected initially. You can set up passwords for additional users to allow them access to different parts of the program. Begin by adding a password for sysadmin. You cannot change the sysadmin user name.

WARNING!
If you have forgotten your password, you will be unable to open the files. For this reason, you should

- keep the code in a safe place
- choose a code that is unique to you but easy for you to remember
- keep a backup copy of the unprotected files in a safe place

Click **Modify User** to open the Modify User password entry screen:

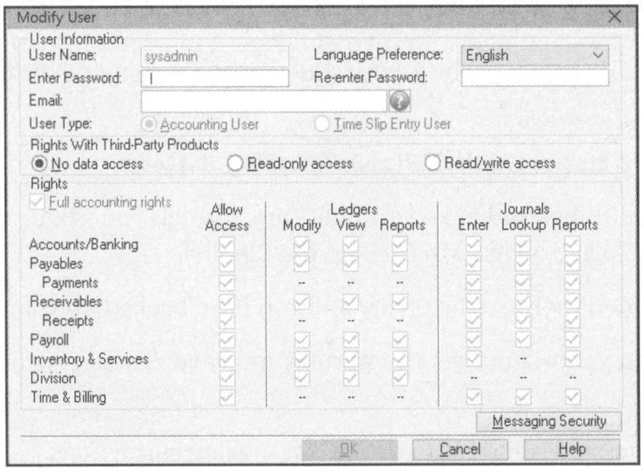

PRO VERSION
The Pro version does not have the Time & Billing feature, so the User Type options are omitted. All users are accounting users.

You cannot modify access privileges (or name) for the sysadmin because someone (the system administrator) must have full access to the data. All the Accounting Rights options are dimmed. The cursor is in the Enter Password field.

If you want **e-mail messages** from Sage, in addition to receiving them in the Messages centre, enter your e-mail address in the E-mail field.

You can use up to seven letters and/or numbers as the code. Passwords are case sensitive — that is, ABC is different than Abc. If you enter a password with an upper case (capital) letter, you must use an upper case letter each time.

NOTES
Passwords must be different for each person to achieve their purpose of restricting access.

Type the **word** or **code** that you want as your password. For practice, choose a simple password such as your first name or your initials.

Press *tab* to advance to the next field, Re-enter Password.

For security reasons, the password is never revealed on the screen — an asterisk (*) or some other symbol will replace each letter or number that you type. As an added precaution, Sage 50 requires you to enter the code twice in exactly the same way.

Type the **password** or **code** again and **press** *tab*.

If the two password entries do not match, Sage 50 generates an error message when you try to save the user information.

Click OK and re-enter the password code twice. Go back to the Enter Password field and type in the code. Then enter the same password in the Re-enter Password field.

NOTES

Access to third-party products is required to link the accounting data with the Microsoft Office Word and Excel documents (refer to Appendix L on the Student DVD).

Access to **third-party products** can also be limited — the read/write access option provides the fullest level of access. No access — the highest security level — is selected by default. This is the only access setting you can modify for the sysadmin.

Click the **Messaging Security** button to open the list of different types of Sage communications:

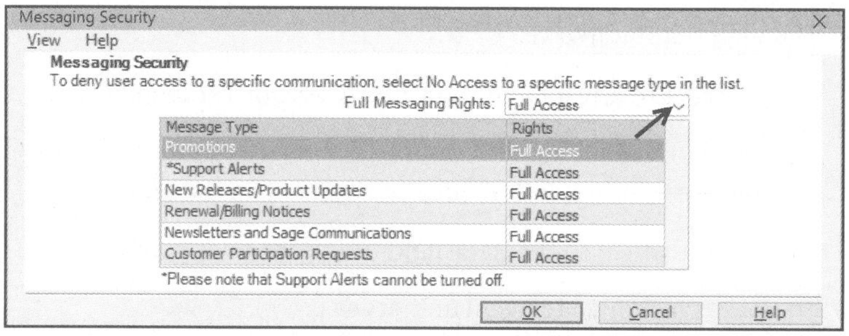

NOTES

After choosing rights for Full Messaging Rights, you can choose access rights for each message separately. When you change the rights for an individual type of message, the Full Messaging Rights entry changes to Custom Access.

The drop-down list beside Full Messaging Rights allows full access or no access for each user. Support messages are always displayed. Click OK to return to the Add User screen. By default, the system administrator has full access to all types of messages.

Click **OK**. You will return to the Modify User screen. **Click OK** again to return to the Set Up Users screen.

If you have allowed read and write access to third-party products, and the password you entered is weak, the program will recommend selecting a more secure password.

For practice, you can click No to continue with the easy password.

The **Add User** button is now available. You can now enter additional users.

If you return to the Home window now, there will be one password for the data files, the one for sysadmin.

NOTES

Weak passwords are ones that may be easy to guess. Strong passwords combine upper and lower case letters and numbers without using real words or simple number patterns. Using a simple password will generate a warning recommending a strong password.

Click **Add User** to open the new user setup screen:

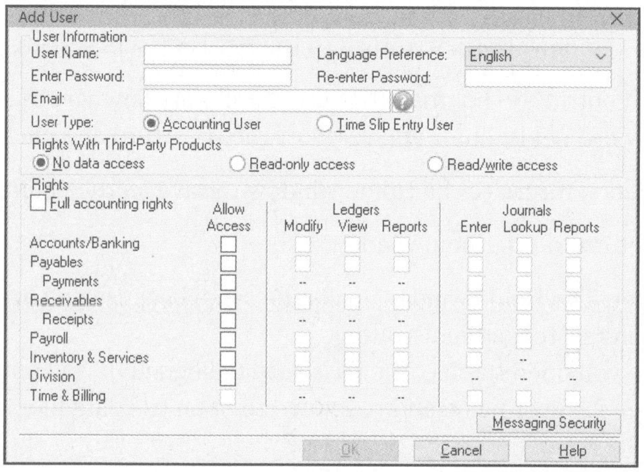

PRO VERSION

The option to set up an Accounting Entry User or a Time Slip Entry User is not available in the Pro version. The Time & Billing module is also not listed because this is a Premium feature.

If you get a message about updating to multi-user Premium or Quantum versions, click Do Not Show This Message Again (unless you want to upgrade).

Adding Other Users

NOTES
You cannot add users until you have saved a password for sysadmin.

NOTES
Even with full accounting rights, other users cannot change their own rights. Only the sysadmin can add users, and modify rights and change passwords for other users.

After you have added a password for the system administrator (sysadmin), you can set up additional users with unique passwords.

Each user can be allowed access to all parts of the program (full accounting rights) or access to only some of the ledgers and journals. Access to ledgers, journals and reports can be controlled separately. The Add User window should be open.

To give a user full access, click Full Accounting Rights below the Password and Third Party Rights sections. For each ledger and journal, you can allow the following: no access (no ✓ for Allow Access); modifying (editing) rights that include viewing; viewing rights only; or access to ledger reports. For journals, you can allow no access, enter rights (enter and look up transactions), lookup only or access to journal reports. Rights for each ledger and journal can be controlled separately, and each user may have different access rights. Each user must have a unique name and password.

Initially, the Add User options are given for an Accounting User for access to the ledgers and journals, but you can also restrict a user to accessing only the Time Slips. Refer to Appendix G for setting up time slip users.

The cursor should be in the User Name field.

Type the **name** of the first user.

Press tab **twice** to advance to the Enter Password screen.

Type the **word** or **code** that you want as your restricted usage password. You can use up to seven letters and/or numbers as the code.

Press tab to advance to the next field, Re-enter Password.

Type the **password** or **code** again and **press** tab.

Again, for security purposes, to be sure you entered the password that you intended, you must enter the same code twice. The E-mail address is optional — adding it will have product information sent to the user. The next step is defining the user's access rights.

To allow access, click the check boxes beside the ledger name in the appropriate columns. For example, to allow viewing access only for the General Ledger, click the Allow Access check box beside Accounts/Banking. The program adds ✓s for all columns beside Accounts/Banking. Click Modify and Reports to remove those ✓s. To allow no access, leave the Allow Access check box in the first column empty.

Similarly, you can restrict access to third-party information (such as Microsoft Office documents) and messages for each user. Passwords do not serve their purpose if the user cannot view reports in Sage 50 but can access and modify those reports in another program.

Click **OK** to save the new user and return to the Set Up Users screen.

If the two password entries do not match, Sage 50 will not allow you to continue. Return to the password fields; enter and re-enter the password and click OK.

After entering all the users, return to the Home window to save all the changes.

Click **Close** to return to the Home window.

Nothing has changed yet. The Home window looks the same because you are using the program as the sysadmin (system administrator).

However, the next time you open the file, the password dialogue box will appear, and you will be required to enter the user name and password to open the data file:

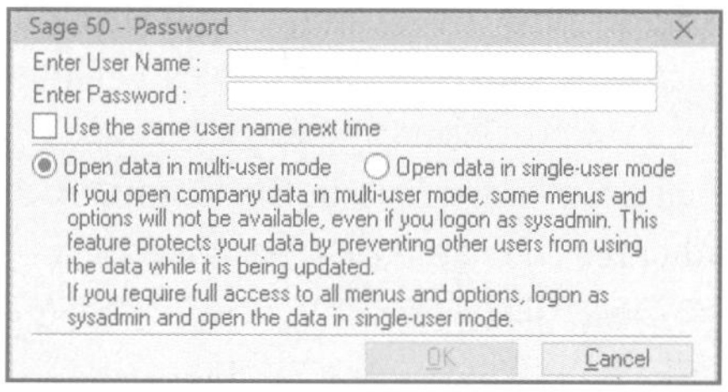

Type the **user name**, either sysadmin or another user name. **Press** *tab*.

Type the **password** or **code** for this user.

Choose the **Single-User** or **Multi-User Mode** for accessing the file. **Click OK**.

If you enter an incorrect code, nothing happens — the Password dialogue box remains open. If you enter the sysadmin user name and password, you will have full access to all parts of the program, including the security settings. If you have set passwords, you must enter the program using the sysadmin user name and password in order to change the security settings and user passwords. Other users can change their own passwords at any time; they cannot access the passwords for other users.

If you enter as a user other than the sysadmin and do not have full accounting rights, you will have restrictions in the Home window, like the one below. The following Classic view Home window illustrates restrictions for a user and the access rights allocated to that user:

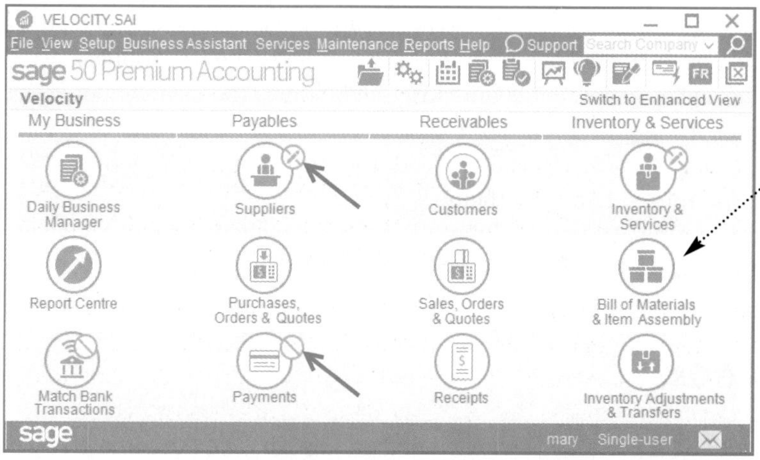

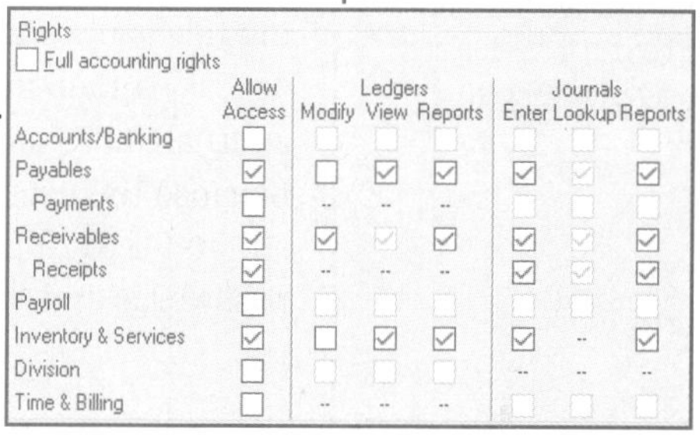

The user above can input normal sales journal entries and inventory entries, accept payments from customers and enter purchases. He/she cannot write cheques to suppliers, pay employees, reconcile accounts, make deposits or make General Journal entries.

The user does not have access to the General Ledger or journals, the Payroll Ledger or journals or to the Division Ledger — their icons are missing (no ✓ appears for these ledgers in the Allow Access settings of the Rights pane). Only the Customers Ledger in this example can be modified.

The **No Edit** symbol  on the Suppliers and Inventory & Services ledger icons means that these ledgers can be viewed but not edited (✓ for View, but not for Modify in the Rights pane). If you open these ledgers, all fields will be dimmed.

The **No Entry** symbol  on the Payments Journal indicates no access is permitted (the user cannot write cheques — there is no ✓ for Allow Access in the Rights pane). The Receivables (Customers & Sales) and Inventory journals are not restricted — no extra icon appears with them (✓ for Enter, Lookup and Reports in the Rights pane).

When access to reports is restricted for any journal or ledger (no ✓ for Reports in the Rights pane), those report menu options will be dimmed.

PRO VERSION

The Pro version is a single-user program. The Password screen does not have the option to open in single- or multi-user mode. You will need to enter your user name and password (and, if appropriate, the option to use the same user name next time).

STUDENT VERSION

The Student Premium version is also a single-user program. If you try to open a Student version file in multi-user mode, you will get an error message.

NOTES

Changing passwords is covered in Appendix G on the Student DVD.

CLASSIC VIEW

The Classic view Home window demonstrates all access rights on a single screen.

PRO VERSION

The Pro version does not have a Time & Billing entry, and the labels for the inventory journals will be Item Assembly and Inventory Adjustments.

> **NOTES**
> Restricted menu options are directly related to the user's access rights.
> The same set of access right restrictions is applied as in the previous illustration.

Several main menu options are also restricted. Only the system administrator can access the Set Up Users menu option after passwords are set. All users can change their own passwords.

The following composite screenshot of all drop-down lists in the Company and Payables windows in the Enhanced view indicates the same restrictions:

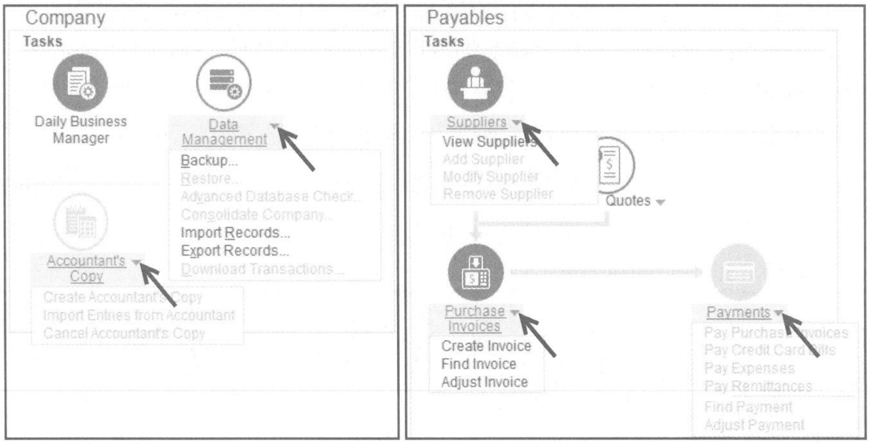

> **NOTES**
> Although users can change their own passwords, the sysadmin retains final control. He/she can still reset all passwords and remove users when necessary.

> **NOTES**
> We did not include the Receivables module icons and drop-down lists because they have no restrictions in this setup and are, therefore, unchanged.

The Home window icons do not have symbols added. Instead, the drop-down shortcuts lists have dimmed entries for the restricted tasks. In the Payables module, the user can view the supplier records but not change them — only the View shortcut is available. The user's access to the Purchases Journal is unrestricted — all menu options are still available (not dimmed). Access to the Payments Journal is completely denied — the user cannot write cheques, and all menu options are dimmed. The Receivables module is unchanged because access to it is unrestricted. Modules the user cannot access — Banking and Payroll — are removed from the Modules pane list. The General Journal and Chart of Accounts icons are also removed from the Company window because the user is not permitted to access them.

Refer to Appendix G on the Student DVD for information on changing and removing passwords and using the wizard to create time slip entry and accounting users.

Exporting Reports

> **NOTES**
> Integration with Microsoft Office software is described further in Appendix L on the Student DVD.

Sage 50 allows you to export reports to a specified drive and path. The files created by the program may then be used by spreadsheet or word processing programs. Exporting files will allow you to perform additional calculations and interpret data for reporting purposes. This process of integrating Sage 50 files with other software is an important step in making the accounting process meaningful.

The next set of keystrokes will export the opening Balance Sheet for VeloCity to a spreadsheet.

> **NOTES**
> Depending on your previous export selection, your default format and folder may be different from ours.
> LOGOS may be entered in the Save In field if you did not change folder selections after adding the picture file.

Display the **Balance Sheet** or the report you want to export.

Click the **Export Report tool** or **choose** the **File menu** and **click Export**:

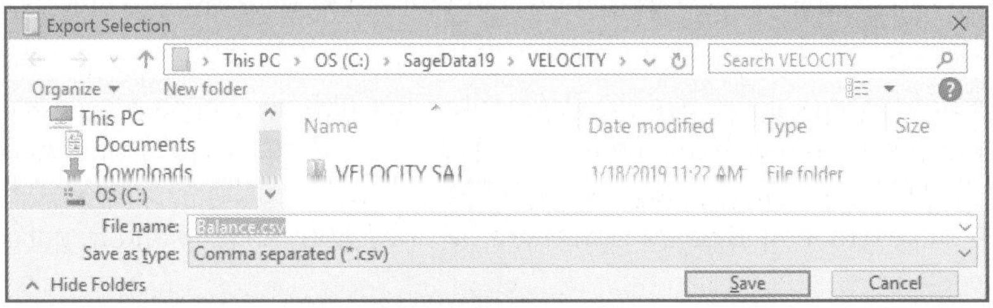

> **NOTES**
> By default your working folder is selected, or the folder you opened most recently.

Click the **Save As Type list arrow** for the list of file types you can create:

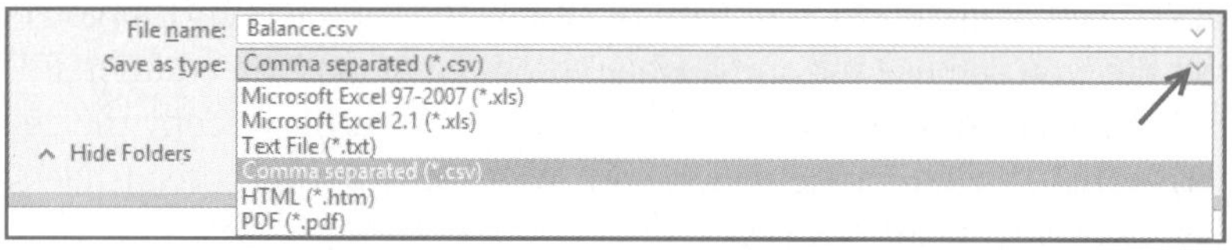

File formats available for export purposes include HTML for Web pages, Text for a word processing format file, Microsoft Excel Versions 97–2007 and 2.1, Comma Separated and PDF.

Click **Microsoft Excel 97-2007** as the type for the Balance Sheet in the Save As Type field. Use the field list arrow to display the file type options if needed.

Choose the **location** for your exported file.

Click **Open** if you changed the default folder.

Accept the default **file name**, or **type** the **name** you want for your file in the File Name field. The program assigns an extension to the file name so that Microsoft Excel will recognize the new file as an Excel file.

Click **Save**. You will return to your displayed report.

To create a text file, click Text File. To generate a file that you can view with Acrobat Reader, but not modify, click PDF.

Any Sage 50 report that you have displayed can be opened directly as a Microsoft Excel spreadsheet. Formulas for totals and so on are retained and you can then use the spreadsheet file immediately.

Display the **Sage 50 report** you want to use in Excel.

Click the **Open In Excel tool** or **choose** the **File menu** and **click** **Open In Microsoft Excel** to open the file name window:

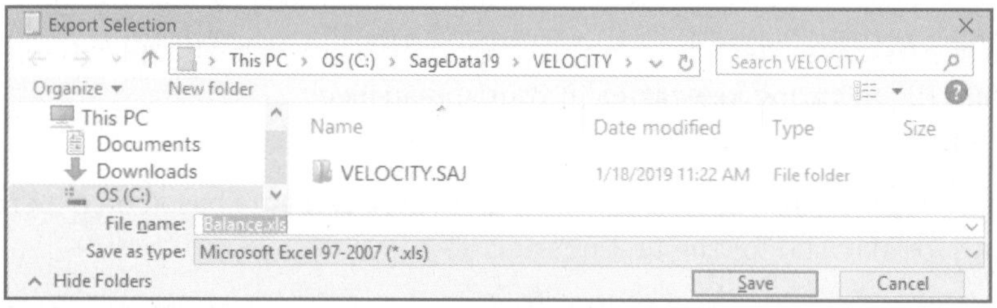

Choose a **location** for your spreadsheet data file.

Click **Save** to open the spreadsheet. Your Sage 50 data file will remain open.

Close the **Excel file** when finished. You can now work with a report that you have exported.

Using Your Data Files and Reports with Other Software

Finish the session using Sage 50. Start the program you want to use with the exported file. Open the file you exported.

Some spreadsheet programs can open and convert a file that was saved in the format of a different program. For example, Microsoft Excel can open (or save) text files or Comma Separated Files. Simply choose the alternative file type in your Open File (or Save File) window. Click OK. Your exported file should replace the blank document screen.

Once you have exported a financial statement as a text file, you can include it in a written report prepared with any word processing program. You can then use the features of the word processing software to enhance the appearance of the statement

NOTES
The bank statements for this text were created by exporting the General Ledger reports as .CSV files to a spreadsheet, modifying the data and then copying the results to a desktop publishing program file.

NOTES
The .XLS format files retain the formulas from the Sage 50 reports while the .CSV files do not.

NOTES
The Open In Excel feature saves the Excel file before opening it, so you can return to it later.

NOTES
When you open an Excel file, be sure that the selected file type also matches the format of your exported file (e.g., .TXT for a text file, or .XLS for Excel).

Refer to the built-in help or program manuals if necessary for assistance with the third-party program.

NOTES
Comma Separated (*.CSV) format files opened in Excel and resaved as *.XLS files provide the best format and view for working with the files in Excel if you need to modify the file or add formulas.
A .XLS exported file will include formulas.

using format styles that are consistent with the remainder of the report. If you exported a spreadsheet file, you can use the spreadsheet program to perform additional calculations. Then you can save the modified report as a text file or copy the cells you want to incorporate in a word processing report. We used exported spreadsheets to create the bank statements for this text.

When working with a spreadsheet program, you can use the calculation capabilities of the spreadsheet program to make comparisons between statements from different financial periods. You might also want to use the charting or graphing features to prepare presentation materials.

Exporting reports offers advantages over re-creating the statements — you save the time of retyping, and you ensure greater accuracy by avoiding errors while retyping.

SOURCE DOCUMENT INSTRUCTIONS

Instructions for May

1. **Enter** the **transactions** for May using all the information provided.
2. **Print** the following **reports**:
   a. Journal Entries (All Journals) for May, including foreign amounts, corrections and additional transaction details
   b. Customer Aged Detail Report for all customers for May
   c. General Ledger account reports for
      - Bank: Niagara Trust Chequing
      - Revenue from Sales
      - Sales Returns and Allowances
   d. Supplier Purchases Summary for Wheel Deals, all items, for May
3. **Export** the **Balance Sheet** as at May 31, 2021, to a spreadsheet application. **Calculate** the following **key ratios** in your spreadsheet:
   a. current ratio b. quick ratio
4. **Set up** a **budget** for use in June and July and **enter amounts** based on expenses and revenues for May and for the first quarter.

Instructions for June

1. **Enter** the **transactions** for June using all the information provided.
2. **Print** the following **reports**:
   a. Journal Entries (All Journals) for June, including foreign amounts, corrections and additional transaction details
   b. Supplier Aged Detail Report for all suppliers for June
   c. Employee Summary Report for all employees for the pay period ending June 30, 2021
   d. Inventory Sales Summary Report (observe and report items that have not sold well over the two-month period)
   e. Customer Sales Summary (all customers, items and categories) for June
3. **Export** the **Comparative Balance Sheet** for May 31 and June 30, 2021, to a spreadsheet application to use for three-month comparisons at the end of July.
4. **Compare** June's **performance against** May's budget **forecast**.

NOTES
The Premium version allows you to create Multi-Period Income Statements and Balance Sheets. Refer to Chapter 18, page 783.

Instructions for July

1. **Enter** the **transactions** for July using all the information provided.
2. **Print** the following **reports**:
   a. Journal Entries (All Journals) for July, including foreign amounts, corrections and additional transaction details
   b. Trial Balance, Balance Sheet and Income Statement on July 31
   c. Inventory Statistics Report for Bicycles (All Journals) for July
   d. Bank Transaction Report for all bank accounts from May 1 to July 31
3. **Export** the **Balance Sheet** and **Income Statement** to a spreadsheet application. Combine the Balance Sheet with the comparative one for May and June. **Compare** first- and second-quarter figures, item by item, to assess the performance of VeloCity. You may want to use multi-period reports for this comparison.
4. **Make** a **backup copy** of your data files. **Advance** the **session date** to August 1, 2021, to start a new fiscal period.
5. **Print** the **Trial Balance**, **Balance Sheet** and **Income Statement** for August 1. **Compare** the end of July and the first of August **statements** and note the changes that result from Sage 50 closing the books for the new fiscal period.

PRO VERSION
Print the General Ledger Report for the bank accounts instead of the Bank Transaction Report.

WARNING!
Chapter 16, Case 8, in Appendix D on the Student DVD has the data you need to complete the bank account reconciliation for VeloCity. You must use your data files for July 31 to complete the reconciliation, so be sure to make a backup copy before you advance the session date to the new fiscal year.

SOURCE DOCUMENTS

SESSION DATE – MAY 15, 2021

1 **Memo #5-1** **Dated May 1, 2021**
Reverse the Accrued Wages adjustment from previous quarter. (Debit Accrued Wages and credit Wages expense account.)

2 **Receipt #812** **Dated May 1, 2021**
From Shavian B & B, cheque #147 for $4 429.60 in payment of account including $90.40 discount for early payment. Reference invoice #2191.

NOTES
Remember that receipts are deposited to Undeposited Cash and Cheques. This should be the default account.

3 **Payment Cheque #1101** **Dated May 2, 2021**
To Pro Cycles Inc., $5 960 in payment of account including $80 discount for early payment. Reference invoice #PC-618.

4 **Purchase Order #38** **Dated May 2, 2021**
Shipping date May 25, 2021
From Wheel Deals

25	CY020	Bicycle: Commuter Alum frame CX90	$10 200.00 USD
4	CY070	Bicycle: Youth YX660	680.00 USD
3	AC100	Trailer: third-wheel rider	360.00 USD
		Freight	200.00 USD
		HST	1 487.20 USD
		Total	$12 927.20 USD

Terms: 2/10, n/30. The exchange rate is 1.320.

NOTES
Edit the default purchase cost entered in the Amount field for all inventory purchases as required.

5 **Receipt #813** **Dated May 2, 2021**
From Niagara Rapids Inn, cheque #73 for $5 537 in payment of account including $113 discount for early payment. Reference invoice #2194.

NOTES
Fallsview Riverside Resort
Contact: T. Player
190 Water St.
Niagara Falls, ON L8C 2V8
Tel: (905) 466-5576
Fax: (905) 466-7284
E-mail: tplayer@frr.ca
Web: frr.ca
Terms: 2/10, n/30; Pay Later
Credit limit: $15 000
Tax code: H

6

Sales Order #248 **Dated May 2, 2021**

Delivery date May 6, 2021
To Fallsview Riverside Resort (use Full Add for new customer)

1	AC010	Bicycle Pump: standing model	$ 50/ unit
2	AC020	Bicycle Pump: hand-held mini	80/ unit
10	AC030	Helmet	120/ helmet
9	AC040	Light: halogen	25/ unit
18	AC050	Light: rear reflector	15/ unit
9	AC060	Lock: kryptonite tube	70/ lock
2	AC070	Pannier: front wicker clip-on	80/ basket
2	AC080	Pannier: rear mesh	60/ basket
1	AC090	Trailer: 2-child closed	620/ unit
1	AC100	Trailer: third-wheel rider	260/ unit
1	CY010	Bicycle: Commuter Steel frame CX10	640/ bike
4	CY020	Bicycle: Commuter Alum frame CX90	960/ bike
4	CY040	Bicycle: Trail Alum frame TX560	1 220/ bike
2	CY090	Stationary Converter	870/ unit
	Freight	(tax code H)	50
	HST		13%

Terms: 2/10, n/30.
Received cheque #496 for $3 000 as down payment (deposit #21) to confirm sales order.

7

Payment Cheque #346 **Dated May 5, 2021**

To Wheel Deals, $3 005.80 USD in payment of account. Reference invoice #WD-391. The exchange rate is 1.319.

8

Memo #5-2 **Dated May 5, 2021**

Re Damaged Inventory: Two (2) wicker panniers, item AC070, were crushed and damaged beyond repair. Adjust the inventory to recognize the loss.

NOTES
Remember to change the payment method to Pay Later for the sales invoice that fills the order.

If you want, you can enter Gearie as the salesperson for all sales.

9

Sales Invoice #2210 **Dated May 5, 2021**

To Fallsview Riverside Resort, to fill sales order #248

1	AC010	Bicycle Pump: standing model	$ 50/ unit
2	AC020	Bicycle Pump: hand-held mini	80/ unit
10	AC030	Helmet	120/ helmet
9	AC040	Light: halogen	25/ unit
18	AC050	Light: rear reflector	15/ unit
9	AC060	Lock: kryptonite tube	70/ lock
2	AC070	Pannier: front wicker clip-on	80/ basket
2	AC080	Pannier: rear mesh	60/ basket
1	AC090	Trailer: 2-child closed	620/ unit
1	AC100	Trailer: third-wheel rider	260/ unit
1	CY010	Bicycle: Commuter Steel frame CX10	640/ bike
4	CY020	Bicycle: Commuter Alum frame CX90	960/ bike
4	CY040	Bicycle: Trail Alum frame TX560	1 220/ bike
2	CY090	Stationary Converter	870/ unit
	Freight	(tax code H)	50
	HST		13%

Terms: 2/10, n/30.

NOTES
Niagara Courier
Contact: Dawn Spokesman
28 Torstar St. N.
Niagara Falls, ON L2E 5T8
Tel: (905) 577-1800
E-mail: spokesman@niagaracourier.ca
Web: niagaracourier.ca
Terms: net 10; Visa payments
Tax code: H
Expense account: 1260

10

Credit Card Purchase Invoice #NC-114 **Dated May 6, 2021**

From Niagara Courier (use Full Add for new vendor), $500 plus $65 HST for prepaid advertisement to run over the next 12 weeks. Purchase invoice total $565 paid in full by Visa.

11

Payment Cheque #347 **Dated May 6, 2021**

To Complete Cycler Inc., $1 996 USD in payment of account including $72 discount for early payment. Reference invoice #CC-918. The exchange rate is 1.316.

12

Memo #5-3 **Dated May 7, 2021**

From Visa, received monthly credit card statement for $340 including $220 for purchases up to and including May 3 and $120 annual renewal fee. Submitted cheque #1102 for $340 in full payment of the balance owing.

13

Deposit Slip #18 **Dated May 7, 2021**

Prepare deposit slip for all receipts for May 1 to May 7 to deposit the funds to Bank: Niagara Trust Chequing from Undeposited Cash and Cheques. The total deposit for the three cheques is $12 966.60.

14

Receipt #814 **Dated May 9, 2021**

From Backstage Tours, cheque #523 for $6 759.20 in payment of account including $180.80 discount for early payment. Reference invoice #2199.

15

Credit Card Purchase Invoice #PS-1149 **Dated May 10, 2021**

From Paper & Stuff (use Full Add for new vendor), $150 plus $19.50 HST for stationery and other office supplies for store. Purchase invoice total $169.50 paid in full by Visa.

16

Credit Card Purchase Invoice #LS-612 **Dated May 14, 2021**

From Lakeshore Sunoco, $92 including HST for gasoline purchase for delivery vehicle. (Use tax code IN.) Purchase invoice total paid in full by Visa.

17

Employee Time Summary Sheet #14 **Dated May 14, 2021**

For the Pay Period from April 24 to May 7, 2021
Dunlop Mercier worked 80 regular hours and 2 hours of overtime in the period. Enter May 1 and May 7 as the pay period start date and end dates. Recover $50 loan. Issue payroll deposit slip #DD25.

18

Deposit Slip #19 **Dated May 14, 2021**

Prepare deposit slip for all receipts for May 8 to May 14 to deposit the funds. One cheque for $6 759.20 is being deposited.

19

Memo #5-4 **Dated May 14, 2021**

Payroll Remittances: Use May 1 as the End of Remitting Period date to make the following payroll remittances in the Payments Journal. Read the margin Warning.

a) Record payment for EI, CPP and Income Tax Payable up to May 1 to the Receiver General for Canada. Issue cheque #1103 in full payment.
b) Record payment for Garnisheed Wages Payable up to May 1 to the Receiver General for Canada. Issue cheque #1104 in full payment.
c) Record payment for EHT Payable up to May 1 to the Minister of Finance. Issue cheque #1105 in full payment.
d) Record payment for VRSP Payable up to May 1 to Manulife Financial. Issue cheque #1106 in full payment.
e) Record payment for Savings Plan Payable up to May 1 to Escarpment Investments. Issue cheque #1107 in full payment.
f) Record payment for Group Insurance Payable up to May 1 to Welland Insurance. Issue cheque #1108 in full payment.
g) Record payment for WSIB Payable up to May 1 to Workplace Safety and Insurance Board. Issue cheque #1109 in full payment.

WARNING!

You will need to change the bank account for the payment to Visa. The USD bank account may remain selected after the US dollar payment.

NOTES

All deposits are made to Bank: Niagara Trust Chequing from Undeposited Cash and Cheques.

NOTES

Paper & Stuff
Contact: Clip Papers
26 Pulp Ave.
Niagara on the Lake, ON
L0S 1J0
Terms: net 30; Visa payments
Tax code: H
Expense account: 1280

NOTES

You cannot enter a date prior to May 1 for the Paycheque Journal though the pay period began earlier. There is an Accrued Wages amount for the last week of April.

NOTES

Enter Memo #5-4A, Memo #5-4B and so on in the Reference Number and Comment fields for the payroll remittances.

WARNING!

When you remit the payroll taxes to the Receiver General, the Pay Period date for Garnisheed Wages is updated to June 1 at the same time. You must change the date back to May 1 when making this remittance before paying the amounts to avoid including the amounts from the May 14 paycheque. Choose Yes to save the new dates when prompted.

Sage 50 groups the remittances to suppliers. To avoid this, you would need to create a separate supplier account for each remittance.

20 **Memo #5-5** **Dated May 14, 2021**

Record payment for GST and HST for the period ending April 30 to the Receiver General for Canada. Issue cheque #1110 in full payment.

21 **Cash Purchase Invoice #ES-64329** **Dated May 15, 2021**

From Energy Source, $130 plus $6.50 GST paid for hydro service. Purchase invoice total $136.50. Terms: payment on receipt. Issue cheque #1111 in full payment.

22 **Receipt #815** **Dated May 15, 2021**

From Fallsview Riverside Resort, cheque #595 for $13 439.35 in payment of account including $335.50 discount for early payment. Reference invoice #2210 and deposit #21.

23 **Purchase Order #39** **Dated May 15, 2021**

Shipping date May 20, 2021
From Complete Cycler Inc.

1	AC020	Bicycle Pump: hand-held mini	$ 380.00 USD
7	AC030	Helmet	3 220.00 USD
5	AC040	Light: halogen	380.00 USD
5	AC050	Light: rear reflector	270.00 USD
10	AC060	Lock: kryptonite tube	1 520.00 USD
	Freight		100.00 USD
	HST		763.10 USD
	Invoice total		$6 633.10 USD

Terms: 2/10, n/30. The exchange rate is 1.322.

24 **Purchase Order #40** **Dated May 15, 2021**

Shipping date June 1, 2021
From Wheel Deals

4	AC090	Trailer: 2-child closed	$ 920.00 USD
4	AC100	Trailer: third-wheel rider	460.00 USD
20	CY020	Bicycle: Commuter Alum frame CX90	8 200.00 USD
	Freight		120.00 USD
	HST		1 261.00 USD
	Invoice total		$10 961.00 USD

Terms: 2/10, n/30. The exchange rate is 1.322.

SESSION DATE – MAY 31, 2021

25 **Cash Purchase Invoice #NB-59113** **Dated May 19, 2021**

From Niagara Bell, $80 plus $10.40 HST paid for phone service. Purchase invoice total $90.40. Terms: payment on receipt. Issue cheque #1112 in full payment.

26 **Purchase Invoice #CC-2014** **Dated May 20, 2021**

From Complete Cycler Inc., to fill purchase order #39

1	AC020	Bicycle Pump: hand-held mini	$ 380.00 USD
7	AC030	Helmet	3 220.00 USD
5	AC040	Light: halogen	380.00 USD
5	AC050	Light: rear reflector	270.00 USD
10	AC060	Lock: kryptonite tube	1 520.00 USD
	Freight		100.00 USD
	HST		763.10 USD
	Invoice total		$6 633.10 USD

Terms: 2/10, n/30. The exchange rate is 1.324.

27

Credit Card Sales Invoice #2211 **Dated May 20, 2021**

To Visa Sales (sales summary)

5	AC020	Bicycle Pump: hand-held mini	$ 80/ unit	$ 400.00
10	AC030	Helmet	120/ helmet	1 200.00
8	AC040	Light: halogen	25/ unit	200.00
8	AC050	Light: rear reflector	15/ unit	120.00
8	AC060	Lock: kryptonite tube	70/ lock	560.00
4	AC080	Pannier: rear mesh	60/ basket	240.00
1	AC090	Trailer: 2-child closed	620/ unit	620.00
1	AC100	Trailer: third-wheel rider	260/ unit	260.00
20	BK010	Books: Complete Bicycle Guide (code G)	40/ book	800.00
20	BK020	Books: Endless Trails (code G)	40/ book	800.00
1	CY030	Bicycle: Racer Ultra lite RX480	3 100/ bike	3 100.00
3	CY040	Bicycle: Trail Alum frame TX560	1 220/ bike	3 660.00
1	CY060	Bicycle: Mountain Carbon frame MX34	2 950/ bike	2 950.00
2	CY090	Stationary Converter	870/ unit	1 740.00
4	S010	Boxing for shipping	75/ job	300.00
4	S020	Maintenance: annual contract	110/ year	440.00
8	S030	Maintenance: complete tune-up	70/ job	560.00
20	S040	Rental: 1 hour	10/ hour	200.00
18	S050	Rental: 1 day	30/ day	540.00
14	S060	Repairs	45/ hour	630.00
	GST		5%	80.00
	HST		13%	2 303.60
	Total paid by Visa			$21 703.60

28

Deposit Slip #20 **Dated May 21, 2021**

Prepare deposit slip for all receipts for May 15 to May 21 to deposit the funds. The total deposit for the single cheque is $13 439.35.

29

Cash Purchase Invoice #N-2021-1 **Dated May 23, 2021**

From Niagara Area Treasurer (use Full Add), $900 in full payment of first instalment of quarterly property tax assessment. Terms: EOM. Issued cheque #1113 in full payment. Store as a monthly recurring entry. Recall the stored transaction to issue cheques #1114 and #1115 as postdated cheques for the next two instalments, dated June 23 and July 23.

30

Sales Invoice #2212 **Dated May 23, 2021**

To Park 'N Ride Tours (preferred customer)

1	AC010	Bicycle Pump: standing model	$ 45/ unit
2	AC020	Bicycle Pump: hand-held mini	70/ unit
10	AC030	Helmet	105/ helmet
6	AC040	Light: halogen	22/ unit
6	AC050	Light: rear reflector	12/ unit
6	AC060	Lock: kryptonite tube	65/ lock
2	AC070	Pannier: front wicker clip-on	75/ basket
1	AC100	Trailer: third-wheel rider	235/ unit
10	BK020	Books: Endless Trails (code G)	35/ book
2	CY020	Bicycle: Commuter Alum frame CX90	850/ bike
2	CY040	Bicycle: Trail Alum frame TX560	1 090/ bike
2	CY070	Bicycle: Youth YX660	420/ bike
6	S020	Maintenance: annual contract	100/ year
	GST		5%
	HST		13%

Terms: 2/10, n/30.

WARNING!

You must change the tax code for books (items BK010 and BK020) to G so that taxes will be correctly applied for these items.

NOTES

Niagara Area Treasurer
Contact: Budd Jett
53 Price St.
Niagara Falls, ON L2K 2Z3
Tel: (905) 461-0063
Web: NAT.ca
Terms: net 1; Pay by Cheque
Tax code: no tax (exempt)
Expense account: 5260

Use N-2021-2 and N-2021-3 as the invoice numbers for the postdated payments for property taxes.

NOTES

Remember to change the tax code for books to G.

31 **Purchase Invoice #WD-364** **Dated May 26, 2021**

From Wheel Deals, to fill purchase order #38

25	CY020	Bicycle: Commuter Alum frame CX90	$10 200.00 USD
4	CY070	Bicycle: Youth YX660	680.00 USD
3	AC100	Trailer: third-wheel rider	360.00 USD
	Freight		200.00 USD
	HST		1 487.20 USD
	Total		$12 927.20 USD

Terms: 2/10, n/30. The exchange rate is 1.325.

32 **Employee Time Summary Sheet #15** **Dated May 28, 2021**

For the Pay Period from May 8 to May 21, 2021
Dunlop Mercier worked 80 regular hours and 4 hours of overtime. Recover $50 loan. Issue payroll deposit slip #DD26.

NOTES
Remember to change the tax code for books to G.

33 **Sales Invoice #2213** **Dated May 28, 2021**

To Backstage Tours (preferred customer)

20	AC030	Helmet	$105/ helmet
10	BK020	Books: Endless Trails (code G)	35/ book
10	S040	Rental: 1 hour	9/ hour
20	S050	Rental: 1 day	25/ day
	GST		5%
	HST		13%

Terms: 2/10, n/30.

NOTES
Use the same payment terms for the return as for the sale so that the discount will be correctly reduced for the returned item.

34 **Sales Return 2213-R** **Dated May 29, 2021**

Backstage Tours returned one damaged helmet (AC030) priced at $105 plus 13% HST. Total sales return amount $118.65 credited to account. Create new Subgroup account 4070 Returns and Allowances. Terms: 2/10, n/30. Delete or change the comment.

Create an Adjustments Journal entry to write off the damaged helmet.

NOTES
Use the General Journal for the transfer of funds, or create two separate entries in the Transfers Journal.

35 **Memo #5-6** **Dated May 29, 2021**

Transfer $24 000 USD to USD Chequing account: transfer $19 000 from Visa and Interac account and $5 000 from Savings account. The exchange rate is 1.327.

36 **Payment Cheques #348 and 349** **Dated May 29, 2021**

To Complete Cycler Inc., $6 515.70 USD in payment of account including $117.40 discount for early payment. Reference invoice #CC-2014.

To Wheel Deals, $12 698.40 USD in payment of account including $228.80 discount for early payment. Reference invoice #WD-364.

The exchange rate for both payments is 1.327.

NOTES
Pedlar Maintenance Co.
Contact: Moe Pedlar
890 Braker St.
Niagara on the Lake, ON
L0S 1J0
Tel: (905) 468-2331
Terms: net 1; Pay by Cheque
Tax code: H
Expense account: 5240

37 **Cash Purchase Invoice #PMC-55** **Dated May 29, 2021**

From Pedlar Maintenance Co. (use Full Add), $300 plus $39 HST paid for cleaning and maintenance of premises. Terms: payment on receipt. Issue cheque #1116 for $339 in full payment. The company bills monthly for its services, so store the entry as a monthly recurring transaction. You will need to change the bank account if you use the Payments Journal for this entry.

38 **Bank Debit Memo #91431** **Dated May 31, 2021**

From Niagara Trust, authorized withdrawals were made from the chequing account on our behalf for the following:

Bank service charges: $55
Mortgage payment: $1 480 interest and $220 principal reduction
Bank loan payment: $420 interest and $480 principal reduction

39 **Credit Card Purchase Invoice #LS-6533** **Dated May 31, 2021**

From Lakeshore Sunoco, $69 including HST for gasoline (tax code IN) and $80 plus $10.40 HST for oil change (tax code H). Purchase invoice total $159.40 charged to Visa account.

40 **Memo #5-7** **Dated May 31, 2021**

Prepare the May payroll for the two salaried employees, Pedal Schwinn and Shimana Gearie. Add 2 percent of revenue from services for May as a commission to Gearie's salary. Issue payroll deposit slips #DD27 and #DD28.

SESSION DATE – JUNE 15, 2021

41 **Receipt #816** **Dated June 1, 2021**

From Backstage Tours, cheque #623 for $3 222.78 in payment of account including $65.77 discount for early payment. Reference sales invoice #2213 and 2213-R.

42 **Purchase Invoice #WD-1804** **Dated June 1, 2021**

From Wheel Deals, to fill purchase order #40

From Wheel Deals

4	AC090	Trailer: 2-child closed	$ 920.00 USD
4	AC100	Trailer: third-wheel rider	460.00 USD
20	CY020	Bicycle: Commuter Alum frame CX90	8 200.00 USD
		Freight	120.00 USD
		HST	1 261.00 USD
		Invoice total	$10 961.00 USD

Terms: 2/10, n/30. The exchange rate is 1.328.

43 **Sales Invoice #2214** **Dated June 1, 2021**

To Festival Tours (monthly recurring sale)

40	S040	Rental: 1 hour	$ 7/ hour	USD
20	S050	Rental: 1 day	22/ day	USD
		HST	13%	

Terms: 2/10, n/30. The exchange rate is 1.328.

44 **Cash Purchase Invoice #WI-6921** **Dated June 2, 2021**

From Welland Insurance, $2 592 (including PST) for six months of insurance coverage. Invoice total $2 592. Issued cheque #1117 in payment.

45 **Sales Invoice #2215** **Dated June 2, 2021**

To Americas Vinelands Tours (USD preferred customer, no delivery charge)

2	AC020	Bicycle Pump: hand-held mini	$ 54/ unit	USD
20	AC030	Helmet	80/ helmet	USD
6	AC040	Light: halogen	16/ unit	USD
6	AC050	Light: rear reflector	10/ unit	USD
6	AC060	Lock: kryptonite tube	47/ lock	USD
20	BK010	Books: Complete Bicycle Guide	27/ book	USD
20	BK020	Books: Endless Trails	27/ book	USD
8	CY010	Bicycle: Commuter Steel frame CX10	430/ bike	USD

Terms: 2/10, n/30 and free delivery. The exchange rate is 1.329.

46 **Receipt #817** **Dated June 5, 2021**

From Americas Vinelands Tours, cheque #198 for $6 532.68 USD in payment of account, including $133.32 discount for early payment. Reference invoice #2215. The exchange rate is 1.3292.

NOTES
Enter the two items purchased from Lakeshore Sunoco on separate lines because you need different tax codes for them.

NOTES
You must calculate the amount of the commission manually and then enter the amount in the journal.

NOTES
Using the same payment terms for the return as for the sale ensured that the discount would be correctly reduced for the returned item.

NOTES
Because the services for Festival Tours were provided in Canada, HST is charged. Change the tax code to H.

NOTES
PST is charged on insurance in Ontario. PST paid is not refundable, so there is no need to track it or record it separately. It will be included with the amount for Prepaid Insurance.

NOTES
Taxes are not charged on exported goods or on freight for foreign customers.

47 **Deposit Slip #21** **Dated June 5, 2021**

Prepare deposit slip for all receipts for May 29 to June 5 to deposit the funds. The total deposit for the single cheque is $3 222.78.

48 **Receipt #818** **Dated June 7, 2021**

From Festival Tours, cheque #1257 for $797.33 USD in payment of account, including $16.27 early payment discount. Reference invoice #2214. The exchange rate is 1.3295.

49 **Credit Card Purchase Invoice #LS-6914** **Dated June 8, 2021**

From Lakeshore Sunoco, $69 including HST for gasoline. Purchase invoice total $69 charged to Visa account.

50 **Memo #6-1** **Dated June 9, 2021**

From Visa, received monthly credit card statement for $985.90 for purchases up to and including June 3. Prepare cheque #1118 for $985.90 to pay the Visa bill.

51 **Credit Card Sales Invoice #2216** **Dated June 9, 2021**

To Visa Sales (sales summary)

1	AC010	Bicycle Pump: standing model	$ 50/ unit	$ 50.00
8	AC030	Helmet	120/ helmet	960.00
8	AC040	Light: halogen	25/ unit	200.00
8	AC050	Light: rear reflector	15/ unit	120.00
8	AC060	Lock: kryptonite tube	70/ lock	560.00
2	AC090	Trailer: 2-child closed	620/ unit	1 240.00
12	BK010	Books: Complete Bicycle Guide (code G)	40/ book	480.00
24	BK020	Books: Endless Trails (code G)	40/ book	960.00
5	CY020	Bicycle: Commuter Alum frame CX90	960/ bike	4 800.00
2	CY050	Bicycle: Mountain Alum frame MX14	1 850/ bike	3 700.00
1	CY070	Bicycle: Youth YX660	460/ bike	460.00
6	S010	Boxing for shipping	75/ job	450.00
12	S020	Maintenance: annual contract	110/ year	1 320.00
20	S040	Rental: 1 hour	10/ hour	200.00
20	S050	Rental: 1 day	30/ day	600.00
20	S060	Repairs	45/ hour	900.00
	GST		5%	72.00
	HST		13%	2 022.80
	Total paid by Visa			$19 094.80

NOTES

Remember to change the tax code for books to G.

52 **Payment Cheque #350** **Dated June 9, 2021**

To Wheel Deals, $10 767 USD in payment of account including $194 early payment discount. Reference invoice #WD-1804. The exchange rate is 1.3288.

53 **Sales Order #249** **Dated June 12, 2021**

Delivery Date: June 14, 2021

From Shavian B & B

16	AC030	Helmet	$120/ helmet
10	AC040	Light: halogen	25/ unit
10	AC050	Light: rear reflector	15/ unit
10	AC060	Lock: kryptonite tube	70/ lock
1	AC090	Trailer: 2-child closed	620/ unit
1	AC100	Trailer: third-wheel rider	260/ unit
7	CY020	Bicycle: Commuter Alum frame CX90	960/ bike
3	CY070	Bicycle: Youth YX660	460/ bike
10	S020	Maintenance: annual contract	110/ year
	HST		13%

Terms: 2/10, n/30.

54

Purchase Invoice #PC-1031 **Dated June 12, 2021**

From Pro Cycles Inc.

2	AC010	Bicycle Pump: standing model	$ 240.00
1	AC020	Bicycle Pump: hand-held mini	500.00
6	AC030	Helmet	3 600.00
5	AC040	Light: halogen	500.00
5	AC050	Light: rear reflector	350.00
5	AC060	Lock: kryptonite tube	1 000.00
10	AC070	Pannier: front wicker clip-on	500.00
10	AC080	Pannier: rear mesh	380.00
		Freight	140.00
		HST	937.30
		Invoice total	$8 147.30

Terms: 1/15, n/30.

55

Employee Time Summary Sheet #16 **Dated June 12, 2021**

For the Pay Period from May 22 to June 5, 2021
Dunlop Mercier worked 80 regular hours in the period (no overtime). He will receive $200 as a loan and have $50 recovered from each of the next four paycheques. Issue payroll deposit slip #DD29.

56

Receipt #819 **Dated June 13, 2021**

From Shavian B & B, cheque #284 for $2 000 as down payment (deposit #22) in acceptance of sales order #249.

57

Memo #6-2 **Dated June 14, 2021**

Record payment for GST and HST for the period ending May 31 to the Receiver General for Canada. Issue cheque #1119 in full payment. Clear the tax reports up to May 31.

58

Memo #6-3 **Dated June 14, 2021**

Payroll Remittances: Make the following remittances for the period ending May 31. Choose Pay Remittance for payroll remittances.

a) Record payment for EI, CPP and Income Tax Payable for May to the Receiver General for Canada. Issue cheque #1120 in full payment.
b) Record payment for Garnisheed Wages Payable for May to the Receiver General for Canada. Issue cheque #1121 in full payment.
c) Record payment for VRSP Payable for May to Manulife Financial. Issue cheque #1122 in full payment.
d) Record payment for Savings Plan Payable for May to Escarpment Investments. Issue cheque #1123 in full payment.
e) Record payment for Group Insurance Payable for May to Welland Insurance. Issue cheque #1124 in full payment.

NOTES
Enter Memo #6-3A, Memo #6-3B and so on in the Reference Number and Comment fields for payroll remittances.

WARNING!
Remember to reset the Pay Period date to June 1 for the second remittance to the Receiver General to avoid including the amounts from the June 12 paycheque.

59

Purchase Invoice #WD-3047 **Dated June 15, 2021**

From Wheel Deals

3	AC090	Trailer: 2-child closed	$ 690.00 USD
3	AC100	Trailer: third-wheel rider	345.00 USD
4	CY030	Bicycle: Racer Ultra lite RX480	4 700.00 USD
4	CY060	Bicycle: Mountain Carbon frame MX34	5 200.00 USD
4	CY090	Stationary Converter	1 000.00 USD
		Freight	200.00 USD
		HST	1 577.55 USD
		Invoice total	$13 712.55 USD

Terms: 2/10, n/30. The exchange rate is 1.330.

60 **Sales Invoice #2217** **Dated June 15, 2021**

To Shavian B & B, to fill sales order #249

16	AC030	Helmet	$120/ helmet
10	AC040	Light: halogen	25/ unit
10	AC050	Light: rear reflector	15/ unit
10	AC060	Lock: kryptonite tube	70/ lock
1	AC090	Trailer: 2-child closed	620/ unit
1	AC100	Trailer: third-wheel rider	260/ unit
7	CY020	Bicycle: Commuter Alum frame CX90	960/ bike
3	CY070	Bicycle: Youth YX660	460/ bike
10	S020	Maintenance: annual contract	110/ year
	HST		13%

Terms: 2/10, n/30.

61 **Memo #6-4** **Dated June 15, 2021**

Old rental bicycles will be sold and replaced with new ones. Create new inventory item: CY200 Used Bicycles with a selling price of $200 each. Enter an Inventory Adjustment to add 20 Used Bicycles (CY200) from Rental Bicycles asset account. The unit cost is $375. (Enter 20 as a positive quantity to increase the inventory. Change the default account to 1300.)

Enter an Inventory Adjustment to move 20 Bicycles (CY020) from inventory to Rental Bicycles asset account. Accept the default unit cost. (Enter a negative quantity to decrease the inventory. Change the default account to 1300.)

NOTES

New inventory:
Item: CY200 Used Bicycles
The CAD and USD selling price for all customers will be $200 and the minimum quantity is 0.

Linked accounts used:
Asset:1540 Bicycles
Revenue: 4020 Revenue from Sales
Expense: 5060 Cost of Goods Sold: Bicycles
The Variance account is not used.

SESSION DATE – JUNE 30, 2021

62 **Memo #6-5** **Dated June 16, 2021**

Transfer $16 000 USD to Bank: USD Chequing to cover cheque to Wheel Deals. Transfer $12 000 USD from 1120 Bank: Visa and Interac Account and $4 000 USD from 1080 Bank: Niagara Trust Savings. The exchange rate is 1.331.

63 **Payment Cheque #351** **Dated June 16, 2021**

To Wheel Deals, $13 469.85 USD in payment of account including $242.70 discount for early payment. Reference invoice #WD-3047. The exchange rate is 1.331.

64 **Cash Purchase Invoice #NB-71222** **Dated June 18, 2021**

From Niagara Bell, $95 plus $12.35 HST paid for phone service. Purchase invoice total $107.35. Terms: payment on receipt of invoice. Issue cheque #1125 in full payment.

65 **Payment Cheque #1126** **Dated June 18, 2021**

To Pro Cycles Inc., $8 075.20 in payment of account including $72.10 discount for early payment. Reference invoice #PC-1031.

66 **Deposit Slip #22** **Dated June 19, 2021**

Prepare deposit slip for the single cheque for $2 000 for June 13 to June 19.

67 **Cash Purchase Invoice #ES-79123** **Dated June 20, 2021**

From Energy Source, $160 plus $8 GST paid for hydro service. Purchase invoice total $168. Terms: payment on receipt. Issue cheque #1127 in full payment.

68 **Credit Card Purchase Invoice #M-1034** **Dated June 21, 2021**

From Mountview Delivery (use Quick Add for the new supplier), $80 plus $10.40 HST paid for delivery services. Invoice total $90.40. Full amount paid by Visa. Enter tax code H for the purchase.

69

Sales Invoice #2218 **Dated June 22, 2021**

To Candide's B & B (use Full Add for new customer)

2	AC020	Bicycle Pump: hand-held mini	$ 80/ unit
2	AC090	Trailer: 2-child closed	620/ unit
1	AC100	Trailer: third-wheel rider	260/ unit
20	BK020	Books: Endless Trails (code G)	40/ book
40	S050	Rental: 1 day	30/ day
	GST		5%
	HST		13%

Terms: 2/10, n/30.

70

Receipt #820 **Dated June 24, 2021**

From Shavian B & B, cheque #391 for $12 506.94 in payment of account with $296.06 discount for early payment. Reference invoice #2217 and deposit #22.

71

Receipt #821 **Dated June 26, 2021**

From Candide's B & B, cheque #532 for $3 990.36 in payment of account including $81.44 discount for early payment. Reference invoice #2218.

72

Memo #6-6 **Dated June 26, 2021**

Add Charitable Donations as a payroll deduction. Since VeloCity will match employee donations, a user-defined expense is also needed.

Create new Group accounts:
- 2440 Charitable Donations - Employee
- 2450 Charitable Donations - Employer
- 5470 Charitable Donations Expense

Add Donations as new name (Setup, Settings, Payroll, Names):
- for Deduction 4 on Names, Incomes & Deductions screen
- for User-Defined Expense 2 on Names, Additional Payroll screen

Deduction Settings (Payroll, Deductions):
- Deduct Donations by Amount After Tax, EI, CPP, EHT and Vacation Pay

Add new payroll linked accounts (under Payroll Settings):
- 2440 for Employee Donations (Linked Accounts, Deductions)
- 2450 for Employer Donations (Linked Accounts, User-Defined Expenses, Payables)
- 5470 for Employer Donations (Linked Accounts, User-Defined Expenses, for Expenses and for Payment Adjustment)

Enter amounts in Payroll Ledger for Deductions and WSIB & Other Expenses:
- Gearie: Check Use for the deduction; enter $20 as the deduction and the expense amount per period
- Schwinn: Check Use for the deduction; enter $25 as the deduction and the expense amount per period

73

Employee Time Summary Sheet #17 **Dated June 26, 2021**

For the Pay Period from June 6 to June 19, 2021

Dunlop Mercier worked 80 regular hours in the period and 2 hours of overtime. Recover $50 loan and issue payroll deposit slip #DD30.

74

Deposit Slip #23 **Dated June 26, 2021**

Prepare deposit slip for all receipts for June 20 to June 26 to deposit the funds. The total deposit for two cheques is $16 497.30.

75

Cash Purchase Invoice #PMC-68 **Dated June 29, 2021**

From Pedlar Maintenance Co., $330 plus $42.90 HST paid for maintenance. Terms: payment on receipt. Issue cheque #1128 for $372.90 in payment. Recall the stored transaction. Edit the amount and store the changed entry.

NOTES

Remember to change the tax code for books to G.

NOTES

Candide's B & B
Contact: Candide Shaw
190 Playtime Circle
Niagara on the Lake, ON
L0S 1J0
Tel: (905) 468-5576
Terms: 2/10, n/30; Pay Later
Credit limit: $15 000
Tax code: H

NOTES

To add deductions, refer to
- page 655 for names
- page 659 for payroll deductions settings
- page 660 for linked accounts
- page 672 for entering the employee deduction
- page 673 for WSIB & other expense amounts

76	**Debit Card Sales Invoice #2219**			**Dated June 29, 2021**	
	To Bruno Scinto (Cash and Interac customer)				
	1	AC010	Bicycle Pump: standing model	$ 50/ unit	$ 50.00
	2	AC030	Helmet	120/ helmet	240.00
	2	AC040	Light: halogen	25/ unit	50.00
	2	AC050	Light: rear reflector	15/ unit	30.00
	2	AC060	Lock: kryptonite tube	70/ lock	140.00
	2	CY030	Bicycle: Racer Ultra lite RX480	3 100/ bike	6 200.00
	2	S020	Maintenance: annual contract	110/ year	220.00
		HST		13%	900.90
		Invoice total paid in full			$7 830.90

Debit card #5919 7599 7543 7777. Amount deposited to Visa and Interac account.

77 **Credit Card Purchase Invoice #LS-7823** **Dated June 30, 2021**

From Lakeshore Sunoco, $115 including HST for gasoline and $80 plus $10.40 HST for tire repairs. Purchase invoice total $205.40 paid in full by Visa. (Remember to change the tax code for the tire repairs.)

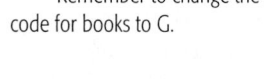

NOTES

Remember to change the tax code for books to G.

78 **Credit Card Sales Invoice #2220** **Dated June 30, 2021**

To Visa Sales (sales summary)

2	AC010	Bicycle Pump: standing model	$ 50/ unit	$ 100.00
2	AC030	Helmet	120/ helmet	240.00
2	AC040	Light: halogen	25/ unit	50.00
4	AC050	Light: rear reflector	15/ unit	60.00
20	AC060	Lock: kryptonite tube	70/ lock	1 400.00
8	AC080	Pannier: rear mesh	60/ basket	480.00
8	BK010	Books: Complete Bicycle Guide (code G)	40/ book	320.00
40	BK020	Books: Endless Trails (code G)	40/ book	1 600.00
2	CY030	Bicycle: Racer Ultra lite RX480	3 100/ bike	6 200.00
1	CY060	Bicycle: Mountain Carbon frame MX34	2 950/ bike	2 950.00
2	CY090	Stationary Converter	870/ unit	1 740.00
30	S040	Rental: 1 hour	10/ hour	300.00
40	S060	Repairs	45/ hour	1 800.00
	GST		5%	96.00
	HST		13%	1 991.60
	Total paid by Visa			$19 327.60

NOTES

Wellness in Print
Contact: Slim Writer
29 Editorial Circle
Hamilton, ON L6G 2S6
Tel: (905) 488-1000
Terms: net 30: Pay Later
Tax code: G

79 **Purchase Invoice #WP-4489** **Dated June 30, 2021**

From Wellness in Print (use Full Add for new supplier)

150	BK010	Books: Complete Bicycle Guide	$3 000.00
200	BK020	Books: Endless Trails	4 000.00
	GST		350.00
	Purchase invoice total		$7 350.00

Terms: net 30 days.

80 **Bank Debit Memo #96241** **Dated June 30, 2021**

From Niagara Trust, authorized withdrawals were made from the chequing account on our behalf for the following:

Bank service charges: $85
Mortgage payment: $1 470 interest and $230 principal reduction
Bank loan payment: $400 interest and $500 principal reduction

81 **Memo #6-7** **Dated June 30, 2021**

Prepare the June payroll salaries for Pedal Schwinn and Shimana Gearie. Add 2 percent of service revenue for June as a commission to Gearie's salary. Issue payroll deposit slips #DD31 and #DD32.

82 **Memo #6-8** **Dated June 30, 2021**
Prepare invoice #2221 to charge Park 'N Ride Tours $30.48 interest – 1.5% of the overdue amount. Terms: net 15.

SESSION DATE – JULY 15, 2021

83 **Sales Invoice #2222** **Dated July 1, 2021**
To Festival Tours, recall stored entry

40	S040	Rental: 1 hour	$ 7/ hour	USD
20	S050	Rental: 1 day	22/ day	USD
	HST		13%	

Terms: 2/10, n/30. The exchange rate is 1.339.

84 **Employee Time Summary Sheet #18** **Dated July 9, 2021**
For the Pay Period from June 20 to July 3, 2021
Dunlop Mercier worked 80 regular hours in the period (no overtime) and took one day of sick leave. Recover $50 loan and issue payroll deposit slip #DD33.

85 **Receipt #822** **Dated July 9, 2021**
From Park 'N Ride Tours, cheque #1431 for $8 911.40 in payment of account. Reference invoices #2212 and #2221.

86 **Memo #7-1** **Dated July 9, 2021**
From Visa, received monthly credit card statement for $364.80 for purchases made before July 3, 2021. Submitted cheque #1129 for $364.80 in full payment of the balance owing.

87 **Deposit Slip #24** **Dated July 9, 2021**
Prepare deposit slip for the single cheque for $8 911.40 being deposited.

88 **Memo #7-2** **Dated July 14, 2021**
Record payment for GST and HST for the period ending June 30 to the Receiver General for Canada. Issue cheque #1130 in full payment. Remember to clear the tax report up to June 30 after making the remittance.

89 **Memo #7-3** **Dated July 14, 2021**
Create a new supplier record for Canadian Cancer Society. Choose the new supplier in the Payroll Remittance Settings screen for both Donations entries. Include employee and employer contributions in the remittance.

Payroll Remittances: Make the following payroll remittances for the pay period ending June 30 in the Payments Journal.

a) Record payment for EI, CPP and Income Tax Payable for June to the Receiver General for Canada. Issue cheque #1131 in full payment.
b) Record payment for Garnisheed Wages Payable for June to the Receiver General for Canada. Issue cheque #1132 in full payment.
c) Record payment for VRSP Payable for June to Manulife Financial. Issue cheque #1133 in full payment.
d) Record payment for Savings Plan Payable for June to Escarpment Investments. Issue cheque #1134 in full payment.
e) Record payment for Group Insurance Payable for June to Welland Insurance. Issue cheque #1135 in full payment.
f) Record payment for Charitable Donations Payable for June to Canadian Cancer Society. Issue cheque #1136 in full payment.

NOTES
Remember that if you want to preview the customer statement, you must choose Custom Form, Sage 50 Form and Statements in the Reports and Forms settings on the screen for Statements. Refer to page 165.

NOTES
Enter Memo #7-3A, Memo #7-3B and so on in the Reference Number and Comment fields for the payroll remittances.

WARNING!
Remember to reset the Pay Period date to July 1 for the second remittance to the Receiver General to avoid including the amounts from the July 9 paycheque.

NOTES
You cannot create the new supplier from the Pay Remittance form in the Payments Journal – you must close the Remittance Journal.

Refer to page 676 for setting up payroll remittances.

NOTES
Remember to change the tax code for books to G.

90

Credit Card Sales Invoice #2223 **Dated July 14, 2021**

To Visa Sales (sales summary)

5	AC020	Bicycle Pump: hand-held mini	$ 80/ unit	$ 400.00
14	AC030	Helmet	120/ helmet	1 680.00
21	AC040	Light: halogen	25/ unit	525.00
36	AC050	Light: rear reflector	15/ unit	540.00
4	AC060	Lock: kryptonite tube	70/ lock	280.00
3	AC080	Pannier: rear mesh	60/ basket	180.00
2	AC100	Trailer: third-wheel rider	260/ unit	520.00
18	BK010	Books: Complete Bicycle Guide (code G)	40/ book	720.00
35	BK020	Books: Endless Trails (code G)	40/ book	1 400.00
2	CY020	Bicycle: Commuter Alum frame CX90	960/ bike	1 920.00
6	CY040	Bicycle: Trail Alum frame TX560	1 220/ bike	7 320.00
2	CY070	Bicycle: Youth YX660	460/ bike	920.00
2	CY090	Stationary Converter	870/ unit	1 740.00
20	CY200	Used Bicycle	200/ bike	4 000.00
30	S020	Maintenance: annual contract	110/ year	3 300.00
	GST		5%	106.00
	HST		13%	3 032.25
	Total paid by Visa			$28 583.25

91

Receipt #823 **Dated July 15, 2021**

From Festival Tours, cheque #638 for $813.60 USD in payment of account. Reference invoice #2222. The exchange rate is 1.3391.

92

Memo #7-4 **Dated July 15, 2021**

Transfer $30 000 from the Visa bank account to the savings account.
Transfer $20 000 from the Visa bank account to the CAD chequing account.

SESSION DATE – JULY 31, 2021

93

Memo #7-5 **Dated July 18, 2021**

Pay $8 000 to the Receiver General for Canada for quarterly business income tax instalment. Issue cheque #1137. Create new Group account 5550 Business Income Tax Expense. (Hint: Remember Business Income Tax Payable.)

94

Memo #7-6 **Dated July 18, 2021**

Create appropriate new Heading and Total accounts around the new Group account 5550 to restore the logical order of accounts.

95

Cash Purchase Invoice #NB-86344 **Dated July 18, 2021**

From Niagara Bell, $120 plus $15.60 HST paid for monthly phone service. Purchase invoice total $135.60. Terms: payment on receipt of invoice. Issue cheque #1138 in full payment.

96

Cash Purchase Invoice #ES-89886 **Dated July 18, 2021**

From Energy Source, $150 plus $7.50 GST paid for hydro service. Purchase invoice total $157.50. Terms: payment on receipt. Issue cheque #1139 in full payment.

97

Sales Invoice #2224 **Dated July 19, 2021**

To Fallsview Riverside Resort

4	CY020	Bicycle: Commuter Alum frame CX90	$960/ bike
30	S040	Rental: 1 hour	10/ hour
30	S050	Rental: 1 day	30/ day
	HST		13%

Terms: 2/10, n/30.

98 **Cash Sales Invoice #2225** **Dated July 19, 2021**

To Jim Ratter (choose one-time customer or Continue)

1	AC030	Helmet	$120/ helmet	$120.00
1	AC070	Pannier: front wicker clip-on	80/ basket	80.00
		HST	13%	26.00
		Invoice total paid in full with cheque #16.		$226.00

99 **Deposit Slip #25** **Dated July 23, 2021**

Prepare deposit slip for single cheque totalling $226 to deposit funds.

100 **Employee Time Summary Sheet #19** **Dated July 23, 2021**

For the Pay Period from July 4 to July 17, 2021
Dunlop Mercier worked 80 regular hours in the period (no overtime) and took 1 day of sick leave. Recover $50 loan and issue payroll deposit slip #DD34.

101 **Memo #7-7** **Dated July 25, 2021**

Issue a cheque to Dunlop Mercier for vacation pay. Dunlop wants to pay for his vacation. Record 40 hours for this payment. Enter July 18 and July 24 as the Start and End dates. Issue cheque #1140. (Read the margin Warning.)

102 **Credit Card Sales Invoice #2226** **Dated July 25, 2021**

To Visa Sales (sales summary)

3	AC010	Bicycle Pump: standing model	$ 50/ unit	$ 150.00
14	AC030	Helmet	120/ helmet	1 680.00
12	AC040	Light: halogen	25/ unit	300.00
16	AC050	Light: rear reflector	15/ unit	240.00
8	AC060	Lock: kryptonite tube	70/ lock	560.00
2	AC070	Pannier: front wicker clip-on	80/ basket	160.00
3	AC090	Trailer: 2-child closed	620/ unit	1 860.00
1	AC100	Trailer: third-wheel rider	260/ unit	260.00
18	BK010	Books: Complete Bicycle Guide (code G)	40/ book	720.00
25	BK020	Books: Endless Trails (code G)	40/ book	1 000.00
3	CY010	Bicycle: Commuter Steel frame CX10	640/ bike	1 920.00
6	CY020	Bicycle: Commuter Alum frame CX90	960/ bike	5 760.00
6	CY070	Bicycle: Youth YX660	460/ bike	2 760.00
20	S020	Maintenance: annual contract	110/ year	2 200.00
12	S030	Maintenance: complete tune-up	70/ job	840.00
12	S060	Repairs	45/ hour	540.00
		GST	5%	86.00
		HST	13%	2 499.90
		Total paid by Visa		$23 535.90

103 **Memo #7-8** **Dated July 25, 2021**

Received Bank Debit Memo #99142 from Niagara Trust. Cheque #16 from Jim Ratter for $226.00 was returned as NSF. Prepare sales invoice #2227 to charge Ratter for the sales amount and add $50 in service charges for the cost of processing the cheque. Create new Group account 4220 Other Revenue. Change the tax code to No Tax. Terms: net 30. (Read the margin Notes.)

104 **Purchase Order #41** **Dated July 25, 2021**

Shipping date August 10, 2021
From Wheel Deals

10	AC070	Pannier: front wicker clip-on	$380.00 USD
10	AC080	Pannier: rear mesh	290.00 USD
		HST	87.10 USD
		Invoice total	$757.10 USD

Terms: 2/10, n/30. The exchange rate is 1.3395.

WARNING!

Remember to remove all wage and benefit amounts, deductions, user-defined expense amounts and entitlements for the vacation paycheque. Refer to page 277.

NOTES

Remember to change the tax code for books to G.

NOTES

You cannot reverse Ratter's NSF cheque or enter a negative receipt for it because it was a cash sale. You cannot adjust the invoice by changing the method of payment because there is no record for One-Time Customers or when you choose Continue.

Entering the bank account in the sales invoice for the amount of the NSF cheque will reverse the bank deposit and restore the accounts receivable.

Use Quick Add to create a new partial record for Jim Ratter. For the Ratter invoice, credit Niagara Trust Chequing account for $226, credit Other Revenue for $50, debit Accounts Receivable for $276. Refer to Accounting Procedures, page 633.

105

Purchase Order #42 **Dated July 25, 2021**

Shipping date August 10, 2021
From Pro Cycles Inc.

6	CY010	Bicycle: Commuter Steel frame CX10	$ 1 860.00
10	CY020	Bicycle: Commuter Alum frame CX90	5 400.00
4	CY030	Bicycle: Racer Ultra lite RX480	6 200.00
4	CY040	Bicycle: Trail Alum frame TX560	2 480.00
3	CY050	Bicycle: Mountain Alum frame MX14	2 790.00
4	CY060	Bicycle: Mountain Carbon frame MX34	6 880.00
6	CY070	Bicycle: Youth YX660	1 320.00
4	CY090	Stationary Converter	1 320.00
	Freight		200.00
	HST		3 698.50
	Invoice total		$32 148.50

Terms: 2/10, n/30. Edit the payment terms for this order.
Paid $5 000 deposit with cheque #1141.

106

Purchase Order #43 **Dated July 25, 2021**

Shipping date August 10, 2021
From Complete Cycler Inc.

2	AC010	Bicycle Pump: standing model	$ 190.00 USD
1	AC020	Bicycle Pump: hand-held mini	380.00 USD
5	AC030	Helmet	2 300.00 USD
5	AC040	Light: halogen	400.00 USD
5	AC050	Light: rear reflector	280.00 USD
8	AC060	Lock: kryptonite tube	1 200.00 USD
	Freight		120.00 USD
	HST		633.10 USD
	Invoice total		$5 503.10 USD

Terms: 2/10, n/30. The exchange rate is 1.3395.

NOTES

Use tax code IN for $226, the sale portion of the bad debt. Use No Tax as the code for the $50 handling charge. Remember to "pay" the account. Refer to Accounting Procedures, pages 633–634.

107

Memo #7-9 **Dated July 27, 2021**

Write off Jim Ratter's account because attempts to contact him were unsuccessful. The outstanding amount is considered a bad debt. Improved customer screening for payment by cheque will be implemented for new customers. (Read the margin Notes.)

108

Credit Card Purchase Invoice #LS-9855 **Dated July 27, 2021**

From Lakeshore Sunoco, $98 including HST paid for gasoline. Purchase invoice total $98 paid in full by Visa.

109

Cash Purchase Invoice #PMC-89 **Dated July 29, 2021**

From Pedlar Maintenance Co., $330 plus $42.90 HST paid for cleaning and maintenance of premises. Terms: payment on receipt. Issue cheque #1142 for $372.90 in full payment. Recall stored transaction.

110

Bank Credit Memo #7642 **Dated July 31, 2021**

From Niagara Trust, semi-annual interest was deposited to bank accounts. $25 was deposited to chequing account and $845 to the savings account. Interest deposit includes the General Ledger Interest Receivable account balance $420.

111

Memo #7-10 **Dated July 31, 2021**

Prepare the payroll for Pedal Schwinn and Shimana Gearie, the salaried employees. Gearie took one day of personal leave. Add 2 percent of service revenue for July as a commission to Gearie's salary. Issue payroll deposit slips #DD35 and #DD36.

112 **Memo #7-11** **Dated July 31, 2021**

Prepare separate cheques to pay all employees for completed surveys and quarterly bonuses. Withhold 10 percent income tax. (Read the margin Notes.)

Gearie $300 bonus, 20 completed client surveys, $50 income tax
Schwinn $250 bonus, 28 completed client surveys, $53 income tax
Mercier $250 bonus, 26 completed client surveys, $51 income tax

Issue cheques #1143, #1144 and #1145.

113 **Memo #7-12** **Dated July 31, 2021**

Increase the allowance for doubtful accounts by $500 (credit entry) in preparation for the next fiscal period. (Refer to the Accounting Procedures on pages 633–634.)

114 **Bank Debit Memo #143661** **Dated July 31, 2021**

From Niagara Trust, authorized withdrawals were made from the chequing account on our behalf for the following:

Bank service charges: $75
Mortgage payment: $1 450 interest and $250 principal reduction
Bank loan payment: $380 interest and $520 principal reduction

115 **Memo #7-13** **Dated July 31, 2021**

Increase the salaries and wages for all employees to begin with their next paycheques in July. Gearie and Shimana will receive an additional $200 per month. Mercier will be paid $20 per hour for his regular hours and $30 per hour for his overtime hours.

116 **Memo #7-14** **Dated July 31, 2021**

Prepare quarterly adjusting entries for depreciation on fixed assets using the following amounts:

Computer equipment	$ 550
Furniture & fixtures	80
Service tools	120
Retail premises	2 450
Van	1 875

117 **Memo #7-15** **Dated July 31, 2021**

Prepare adjusting entries for the following:

Office supplies used	$ 190
Bicycle repair parts used	200
Prepaid insurance expired	2 016
Prepaid advertising expired	680
Payroll liabilities accrued for Mercier	720

Create a new Group expense account 5255 Repair Parts Used.

NOTES

Use the Paycheques Journal to enter the piece rate pay and bonuses.

- Enter the piece rate pay and bonus amounts.
- On the Income tab screen, remove all hours, wage, salary and benefit amounts.
- Do not remove the Vacation Earned amount for Mercier.
- On the remaining tab screens, remove entitlement hours and deduction and user-defined expense amounts.
- Click the Taxes tab.
- Click the Enter Taxes Manually tool so that you can edit the income tax amounts.
- Enter the income tax amount. Do not change the EI or CPP amounts.
- Click Enter Taxes Automatically after creating the bonus cheques.

R E V I E W

The Student DVD with Data Files includes Review Questions and Supplementary Cases for this chapter that encourage group work and report analysis. The DVD also includes bank reconciliation and online banking for this chapter.

CHAPTER SEVENTEEN

Stratford Country Inn

OBJECTIVES

After completing this chapter, you should be able to

- ***plan*** and ***design*** an accounting system for a small business
- ***prepare*** a conversion procedure from manual records
- ***understand*** the objectives of a computerized accounting system
- ***create*** company files
- ***set up*** company accounts
- ***assign*** appropriate account numbers and account classes
- ***choose*** and ***enter*** appropriate settings for all ledgers
- ***create*** supplier, guest, employee and inventory records
- ***enter*** historical data and account balances in all ledgers
- ***finish*** entering historical data to prepare for journal entries
- ***enter*** accounting transactions from realistic source documents

COMPANY INFORMATION

Company Profile

NOTES
Stratford Country Inn
100 Festival Rd.
Stratford, ON
N5A 3G2
Tel 1: (519) 222-6066
Tel 2: (888) 272-6000
Fax: (519) 272-7960
Business No.: 767 698 327 RT0001

NOTES
For the accommodation business, the terms Guest and Supplier replace Customer and Vendor.

Stratford Country Inn is situated in Ontario just outside the Stratford city limits, close to Stratford Festival Theatres. The Inn has room for approximately 50 guests, with additional cots available for families who want to share rooms with their children. In addition to the theatre, which attracts most of the guests, the Inn has facilities for rowing and canoeing on the small lake area near the Thames River, and a forested area nearby is used for lovely summer walks or cross-country skiing in winter. Boxed lunches are available for picnics on the waterfront before theatre events or for afternoons in the park, and fixed price dinners are offered in the dining room. Many guests stay for several days at a time.

For an additional cost, a private consultant will pamper the guests with aromatherapy sessions. The consultant pays the Inn for use of her studio.

Guests come from near and far, and even a few American theatre groups have become regular visitors. The Inn prepares invoices and accepts payment in US dollars for US accounts. For groups and clubs, the Inn bills the entire group as a single client. Most individual guests pay by Visa or MasterCard. All guests pay HST on the services provided by the Inn and GST on the historic books. Regular guests, clubs, groups or agencies that reserve blocks of theatre tickets and accommodation have credit accounts. Groups place a deposit to confirm their accommodation. For groups that are offered preferred rates, no deposits are required. In the event of overbooking, guests who cannot be placed at the Inn are put up at a nearby bed and breakfast at the Inn's expense.

The grounds of the Inn include conference rooms for discussions and debates about theatre performances and related topics. Buses take guests to the theatre and return them to the Inn on a scheduled basis. Meals can be included for those who want an all-inclusive package. The Inn's dining room caters to its full accommodation guests as well as non-resident guests.

The owner, manager and desk attendant look after the front office. The owner also provides tours of the main theatre district that include backstage access. Five additional staff members cater to the other needs of the guests.

Accounts payable have been set up for food supplies, a maintenance contract (a cleaning crew vacuums the Inn), maintenance and repairs (electrical and carpentry work), linen supplies for kitchen and guest rooms and laundry services for towels and bedding.

By June 30, the Inn was ready to convert its accounting records to Sage 50 and had gathered the following reports to make the conversion:

- Chart of Accounts
- Post-Closing Trial Balance
- Supplier Information
- Guest Information
- Employee Information and Profiles
- Inventory and Services Information

PRO VERSION
The terms Customer and Vendor will replace the terms Guest and Supplier.

CHART OF ACCOUNTS

STRATFORD COUNTRY INN

ASSETS
Bank: Stratford Trust CAD Chequing
Bank: Stratford Trust USD Chequing
Bank: Credit Card
Accounts Receivable
Advances and Loans Receivable
Purchase Prepayments
Prepaid Advertising
Prepaid Insurance
Food Inventory
Linens & Towels
Blankets & Bedding
Supplies: Computer
Supplies: Office
Supplies: Dining Room
Supplies: Washroom
Books
Computer Equipment
Accum Deprec: Computers
Furniture & Fixtures ▶
▶Accum Deprec: Furn & Fix
Vehicle
Accum Deprec: Vehicle
Country Inn & Dining Room
Accum Deprec: Inn & Dining Room
Grounds & Property

LIABILITIES
Bank Loan
Accounts Payable
Prepaid Sales and Deposits
Credit Card Payable
Vacation Payable
EI Payable
CPP Payable
Income Tax Payable
EHT Payable
Group Insurance Payable
Tuition Fees Payable
WSIB Payable
GST Charged on Sales ▶
▶GST Paid on Purchases
HST Charged on Services
HST Paid on Purchases
Mortgage Payable

EQUITY
E. Prospero, Capital
Current Earnings

REVENUE
Revenue from Books
Revenue from Inn
Revenue from Dining Room
Revenue from Tours
Rental Fees
Other Revenue
Exchange Rate Differences

EXPENSE
Advertising & Promotion
Bank Charges and Card Fees
Cost of Books Sold
Cost of Services ▶
▶COGS: Food
Depreciation: Computers
Depreciation: Furn & Fix
Depreciation: Vehicle
Depreciation: Inn & Dining Room
Purchase Discounts
Interest Expense: Loan
Interest Expense: Mortgage
Hydro Expenses
Maintenance & Repairs
Overflow Accommodation
Telephone Expense
Vehicle Expenses
Wages: Management
Wages: General
Wages: Dining Room
EI Expense
CPP Expense
WSIB Expense
EHT Expense
Tuition Fees Expense

NOTES: Use appropriate account numbers and add subgroup totals, headings and totals to organize your Chart of Accounts as necessary. Remember to add a test balance account for the setup.

POST-CLOSING TRIAL BALANCE

STRATFORD COUNTRY INN

June 30, 2021	Debits	Credits		Debits	Credits
Bank: Stratford Trust CAD Chequing	$47 703		▶ Accum Deprec: Vehicle		$ 10 000
Bank: Stratford Trust USD Chequing (2 300 USD)	3 000		Country Inn & Dining Room	$400 000	
Bank: Credit Card	12 000		Accum Deprec: Inn & Dining Room		20 000
Accounts Receivable (deposit)		$ 1 000	Grounds & Property	200 000	
Advances and Loans Receivable	250		Bank Loan		25 000
Prepaid Advertising	50		Accounts Payable		8 068
Prepaid Insurance	400		Credit Card Payable		395
Food Inventory	1 650		Vacation Payable		5 725
Linens & Towels	2 000		EI Payable		3 127
Blankets & Bedding	3 000		CPP Payable		6 694
Supplies: Computer	400		Income Tax Payable		8 778
Supplies: Office	500		EHT Payable		577
Supplies: Dining Room	800		Group Insurance Payable		330
Supplies: Washroom	250		WSIB Payable		1 631
Books	4 000		GST Charged on Sales		310
Computer Equipment	4 000		GST Paid on Purchases	200	
Accum Deprec: Computers		1 200	HST Charged on Services		5 970
Furniture & Fixtures	38 000		HST Paid on Purchases	3 700	
Accum Deprec: Furn & Fix		4 200	Mortgage Payable		300 000
Vehicle	50 000 ▶		E. Prospero, Capital		368 898
				$771 903	$771 903

SUPPLIER INFORMATION

STRATFORD COUNTRY INN

Supplier Name (Contact)	Address	Phone No. Fax No.	E-mail Web Site	Terms Tax ID
Avon Maintenance Services (Ken Sparkles)	66 Kleen Rd. Stratford, Ontario N5A 3C3	Tel: (519) 272-4611 Fax: (519) 272-4813	avonservices.com	net 30 631 393 469 RT0001
Bard's Linen & Towels (Jason Bard)	21 Venice St. Stratford, Ontario N5A 4L2	Tel: (519) 271-2273 Fax: (519) 271-9333	bard@bards.com bards.com	2/10, n/30 after tax 763 271 673 RT0001
Bell Canada (Bea Heard)	30 Whisper Rd. Stratford, Ontario N5A 4N3	Tel: (519) 273-2355	bheard@bell.ca bell.ca	net 1 634 345 375 RT0001
Minister of Finance				net 1
Perth County Hydro (Wynd Mills)	66 Power Rd. Stratford, Ontario N5A 4P4	Tel: (519) 272-6121	perthenergy.com	net 1 721 431 211 RT0001
Receiver General for Canada				net 1
Stratford Service Centre (A.L.L. Ledfree)	33 MacBeth Ave. Stratford, Ontario N5A 4T2	Tel: (519) 271-6679 Fax: (519) 276-8822	ledfree@ssc.com ssc.com	net 1 634 214 217 RT0001
Tavistock Laundry Services (Martin Tavistock)	19 Merchant Rd. Stratford, Ontario N5A 4C3	Tel: (519) 271-7479 Fax: (519) 271-7888	tavistock.com	net 30 639 271 345 RT0001
Tempest Food Wholesalers (Vita Minns)	35 Henry Aved Stratford, Ontario N5A 3N6	Tel: (519) 272-4464 Fax: (519) 272-4600	vita@tempest.com tempest.com	net 30 673 421 939 RT0001
Travellers' Life				
Workplace Safety & Insurance Board				
Zephyr Advertising Agency (Tom DeZiner)	32 Portia Blvd. Stratford, Ontario N5A 4T8	Tel: (519) 271-6066 Fax: (519) 271-6067	tom@westwinds.com westwinds.com	net 1 391 213 915 RT0001

LIST OF REMITTANCE SUPPLIERS

STRATFORD COUNTRY INN

Remittance Supplier	Payroll Remittance	Frequency	Next Pay Period Ending Date
Receiver General for Canada	EI, CPP and Income Tax	Quarterly	Jul 1
Workplace Safety & Insurance Board	WSIB	Quarterly	Jul 1
Minister of Finance	EHT	Quarterly	Jul 1
Travellers' Life	Group Insurance	Quarterly	Jul 1

OUTSTANDING SUPPLIER INVOICES

STRATFORD COUNTRY INN

Supplier Name	Terms	Date	Inv/Chq No.	Amount	Total
Avon Maintenance Services	net 30	June 7/21	AM-68	$565	
	net 30	June 14/21	AM-85	565	
	net 30	June 21/21	AM-101	565	
	net 30	June 28/21	AM-127	565	
			Balance owing		$2 260
Tavistock Laundry Services	net 30	June 8/21	TL-693	$904	
	net 30	June 22/21	TL-742	904	
			Balance owing		$1 808
Tempest Food Wholesalers	net 30	June 23/21	TF-113	$2 000	
	net 30	June 30/21	TF-183	2 000	
			Balance owing		$4 000
			Grand Total		$8 068

GUEST INFORMATION

STRATFORD COUNTRY INN

Guest Name (Contact)	Address	Phone No. Fax No.	E-mail Web Site	Terms Credit Limit
Festival Club of Rosedale (Jane Birken)	3 Rosedale Valley Rd. Toronto, Ontario M5G 3T4	Tel: (416) 482-6343	janebir@conundrum.com	net 5 $10 000
Hamlet Holiday Agency (Ron Doleman)	60 Tibault Ave. Stratford, Ontario N5A 3K3	Tel 1: (519) 272-6461 Tel 2: (800) 777-7777	rdoleman@hamlet.com hamlet.com	net 5 $10 000
* Metro Arts Appreciation Group (R. Downey)	4400 Yonge St. North York, Ontario M6L 3T4	Tel: (416) 923-8142	RDowney@artnet.com artnet.com	net 5 $10 000
* NY Friends of Shakespeare (J. Monte)	33 16th Ave. Buffalo, NY 13002	Tel 1: (716) 755-4992 Tel 2: (888) 755-5000	monte@aol.com	net 5 $10 000 (USD)
Waterloo University Literary Club (T. Fornello)	88 College Rd. Waterloo, Ontario N2A 3F6	Tel: (519) 431-6343	fornello4@uwo.ca	net 5 $10 000

NOTES: * indicates preferred price list guest

OUTSTANDING GUEST INVOICES

STRATFORD COUNTRY INN

Guest Name	Terms	Date	Inv/Chq No.	Total
Hamlet Holiday Agency	net 30	June 30/21	Deposit #40 (Chq 317; enter a negative invoice)	$1 000

EMPLOYEE INFORMATION SHEET

STRATFORD COUNTRY INN

	Owen Othello	Clara Claudius	Mary MacBeth	Hedy Horatio	Juliet Jones	Shelley Shylock	Bud Romeo
Position	Manager Male, full time	Clerk Female, full time	Cook Female, full time	Waiter Female, full time	Concierge Female, full time	Waiter Female, full time	Service Male, full time
Social Insurance No.	691 113 724	873 863 211	284 682 556	294 654 421	177 162 930	891 263 634	254 685 829
Address	38 Falstaff St. Stratford, ON N5A 3T3	147 King Henry St. Mary's, ON N4X 1B2	3 Bard Cr. Stratford, ON N5A 6Z8	17 Elizabeth St. Stratford, ON N5A 4Z1	5 Capella Cres. Stratford, ON N5A 5M1	29 Avon St. Stratford, ON N5A 5N5	42 Hosteller St. New Hamburg, ON N0B 2G0
Telephone	(519) 272-2191	(519) 373-6495	(519) 277-1338	(519) 278-5343	(519) 273-9122	(519) 273-5335	(519) 381-3738
Date of Birth (mm-dd-yy)	6-29-81	4-21-74	8-3-79	12-3-86	1-25-80	3-12-90	5-27-79
Date of Hire (mm-dd-yy)	3-1-12	5-2-05	6-1-15	6-1-17	1-1-16	1-1-19	12-16-14
Federal (Ontario) Tax Exemption - TD1							
Basic Personal	$12 609 (10 582)	$12 609 (10 582)	$12 609 (10 582)	$12 609 (10 582)	$12 609 (10 582)	$12 609 (10 582)	$12 609 (10 582)
Other Indexed	–	–	$14 839 (8 985)	–	$27 243 (19 138)	–	$12 609 (8 985)
Other Non-indexed	$4 900 (4 900)	–	–	$3 840 (3 840)	–	$8 540 (8 540)	–
Total Exemptions	$17 509 (15 482)	$12 609 (10 582)	$27 448 (19 567)	$16 449 (14 422)	$39 852 (29 720)	$21 149 (19 122)	$25 218 (19 567)
Additional Federal Tax	–	–	–	$50	–	$50	–
Employee Taxes							
Historical Income Tax	$4 594.20	$2 642.94	$3 132.22	$2 678.00	$1 437.67	$1 521.88	$1 550.12
Historical EI	$451.20	$360.96	$478.01	$321.62	$446.29	$189.54	$358.54
Historical CPP	$1 294.44	$863.76	$1 172.08	$818.09	$1 088.36	$599.87	$857.35
Employee Income							
Loans: Historical	–	–	–	$100.00	–	–	$150.00
Benefits: Historical	$4 400.00	–	–	$3 240.00	–	$7 540.00	–
Vacation Pay Owed	–	–	$1 525.18	$1 026.48	$1 424.28	$604.80	$1 144.26
Regular Wage Rate	–	–	$26.00/hr	$18.00/hr	$24.00/hr	$16.00/hr	$20.00/hr
No. Hours per Period	160	160	80	80	80	80	80
Wages: Historical	–	–	$24 960.00	$16 640.00	$22 880.00	$10 080.00	$18 720.00
Overtime 1 Wage Rate	–	–	$39.00/hr	$27.00/hr	$36.00/hr	$24.00/hr	$30.00/hr
Overtime 1: Historical	–	–	$468.00	$468.00	$858.00	$168.00	$351.00
Regular Salary	$4 400/mo.	$3 600/mo.	–	–	–	–	–
Salary: Historical	$24 000.00	$19 200.00	–	–	–	–	–
Commission	1% (Revenue from Inn)		–	–	–	–	–
Pay Periods	12	12	26	26	26	26	26
Vacation Rate	4 weeks	4 weeks	6% retained	6% retained	6% retained	6% retained	6% retained
Wage Account	Management	General	Dining Room	Dining Room	General	Dining Room	General
Deductions							
Group Insurance	$30.00	$60.00	$30.00	$15.00	$30.00	$15.00	$30.00
Insurance: Historical	$180.00	$360.00	$390.00	$195.00	$390.00	$195.00	$390.00
WSIB and User-Defined Expenses							
WSIB Rate	2.55	2.55	1.70	1.70	2.55	1.70	2.55
Tuition: Historical	$4 400.00	–	–	$3 240.00	–	$7 540.00	–
Entitlements (Rate, Maximum Days, Clear, Days Accrued)							
Vacation	8%, 30, No, 20	8%, 30, No, 20	–	–	–	–	–
Sick Leave	5%, 15, No, 9	5%, 15, No, 7	5%, 15, No, 8	5%, 15, No, 9	5%, 15, No, 10	5%, 15, No, 3	5%, 15, No, 8
T4 and RL-1 Reporting							
EI Insurable Earnings	$24 000.00	$19 200.00	$25 428.00	$17 208.00	$23 738.00	$10 248.00	$19 071.00
Pensionable Earnings	$28 400.00	$19 200.00	$25 428.00	$20 348.00	$23 738.00	$17 788.00	$19 071.00
Withheld	$6 519.84	$4 227.66	$5 172.31	$4 012.71	$3 362.32	$2 506.29	$3 156.01
Net Pay	$17 480.16	$14 972.34	$20 255.69	$13 195.29	$20 375.68	$7 741.71	$16 064.99

Payroll Information

General Payroll Information E. Prospero, the owner, has arranged group insurance for his employees, and all employees have elected to join the plan. As entitlements, all staff may take 10 days' sick leave per year, and the vacation allowances are quite generous for the industry — four weeks of paid vacation for salaried staff after three years of service and 6 percent for all hourly paid employees. As an additional benefit, employees are reimbursed for their tuition fees on completion of eligible courses. Salaried employees are paid monthly, and hourly employees are paid every two weeks. All employees work full time, are eligible for EI and pay CPP and income tax; the EI factor is 1.4. The Inn pays 0.98 percent of payroll for EHT, the provincial health tax. WSIB rates vary for different types of work performed by the employees of the Inn. All wage and salary amounts were increased on July 1 to reflect the provincial minimum wage increase.

Wage expenses for the manager, the dining room staff and the remaining general employees are tracked separately in three different payroll expense accounts.

NOTES

Enter entitlements as Payroll Settings and edit records for each employee as needed.

Tuition is a user-defined payroll expense and taxable benefit. The benefits for Othello, Horatio and Shylock have already been paid, so only historical amounts are entered.

Remember that WSIB is the name for WCB in Ontario.

Employee Profiles and TD1 Information

E. Prospero owns the Inn and oversees all activities. Together with family members, he fills in where needed. He does not collect a salary and is not recorded as an employee.

Owen Othello is the salaried manager for the Inn. He welcomes guests, instructs other employees and discusses issues, problems and plans with the owner. He is single and studies part time in an MBA program. One night a week he commutes to Toronto. A tuition claim for $4 900 increases his basic tax claim. Othello is the salesperson for all sales, and beginning in July he will receive a commission of 1 percent of the revenue from the Inn.

Clara Claudius has been with the Inn the longest and works as the desk attendant. Although her primary job is reservations clerk, she also performs the accounting for the Inn. She too is salaried. Because her husband is also fully employed, she uses the basic single tax claim amounts plus the federal claim for her dependent child.

Mary MacBeth works as the cook in the dining room. As a single parent with three dependent children, she claims the spousal equivalent for tax purposes for one child and the federal child credit for the other two. She is paid at an hourly rate of $26 per hour for the first 40 hours each week and $39 per hour after that.

Hedy Horatio divides her time between waiting tables and helping the cook for her pay at the rate of $18 per hour plus $27 per hour for overtime hours. She studies part time at Conestoga College in the chef training program. The $3 840 tuition fee supplements her basic single tax claim.

Juliet Jones deals with requests from guests, working as the concierge and arranging for room service. She lives with and cares for her father and therefore has the eligible dependent claim plus a caregiver claim. She also has the age deduction transferred from her father ($7 494 federal and $5 166 provincial) to supplement her basic single tax claim. Her hourly wage rate is $24 for the first 40 hours each week and $36 for additional hours.

Shelley Shylock waits tables in the dining room at the Inn. During the summer and festival months, she works full time for the Inn at the rate of $16 per hour and $24 for hours beyond the first 40 each week. She is a full-time student at the University of Waterloo and works part time until summer. The tuition fee at $8 540 supplements her tax claim amounts.

NOTES

The claim amounts subject to indexing do not include tuition amounts. The amount subject to indexing is used by the program to update claim amounts when a new tax table is introduced, based on the government indexing rate.

NOTES

All hourly paid employees also receive gratuities from the guests.

Bud Romeo takes care of room service requests and also handles the baggage for the guests. He is married with two dependent children, so he has the spousal claim amount in addition to the basic single amount and federal child claim. He too is paid hourly at the rate of $20 per hour and $30 per hour for the time beyond 40 hours per week.

INVENTORY AND SERVICES INFORMATION

STRATFORD COUNTRY INN

Description	Min Stock	CAD Prices Reg (Pref)	USD Prices Reg (Pref)	Unit	Qty on Hand	Total (Cost)	Taxes
Books: Total asset value $4 000 (Linked Accounts: Books, Revenue from Books, Cost of Books Sold)							
Two Stratfords: England and Ontario	5	$80 ($70)	$65 ($55)	each	20	$1 000	G
Annotated Plays of Shakespeare	5	80 (70)	65 (55)	each	40	2 000	G
History of Stratford Country Inn	5	50 (45)	40 (35)	each	40	1 000	G
Services: Rooms (Linked Accounts: Revenue from Rooms, Cost of Services)							
Single Room		$150 ($130)	$120 ($105)	room/night			H
Double Room		200 (175)	160 (145)	room/night			H
Services: Meals (Linked Accounts: Revenue from Dining Room, Cost of Services)							
Boxed Lunch		$30 ($25)	$23 ($18)	meal			H
Dinner - Prix Fixe		$70 ($65)	56 (48)	meal			H
Services: Tours (Linked Accounts: Revenue from Tours, Cost of Services)							
Guided Tour		$500 ($450)	$400 (350)	tour			H

INSTRUCTIONS

1. Use all the information presented in this application to set up the company accounts for Stratford Country Inn in Sage 50 using the following steps:
   a. Create company files in a new data folder for storing the company records.
   b. Enter the company information. Start a new fiscal period on July 1, 2021, and finish the period on September 30, 2021. Choose Accommodation as the industry.
   c. Enter names and printer information.
   d. Prepare the settings by changing the default settings as necessary.
   e. Organize the Balance Sheet and Income Statement accounts.
   f. Create accounts to correspond to your Balance Sheet and Income Statement. Add appropriate account numbers and types.
   g. Set up currency information for the USD transactions. The exchange rate on June 30 is 1.312.
   h. Change the account class for bank and credit card accounts and set up the cheque sequence.
   i. Enter linked accounts for the ledgers and credit cards. The fee for the credit card accepted from guests is 2.75 percent.
   j. Enter sales tax information and create tax codes for GST @ 5%, refundable, and HST @ 13%, refundable. Reports should be available for both taxes.
   k. Enter guest, supplier, employee and inventory information. The tax code for all suppliers and guests is H, except for the payroll remittance suppliers and for Tempest Food Wholesalers, which supplies tax exempt foods. Choose appropriate payment methods.
   l. Enter historical balances in all ledgers.

WARNING! Save your work and make backups frequently.

WARNING! Remember to use a Test Balance account or the Retained Earnings account to check the Trial Balance before finishing the history for the General Ledger. Print the appropriate reports to check your work as you enter the company data.

NOTES Guests from the United States pay taxes on their Ontario purchases because the services and goods are consumed in Ontario.

PRO VERSION Remember that the terms Vendors and Customers will replace Suppliers and Guests.

m. Create two Job Categories: Sales (employees in this category are salespersons) and Other (employees in this category are not salespersons). Assign Othello to Sales and all other employees to the Other category.
n. Set up Payroll Remittances. Add the supplier and remittance frequency and enter July 1, 2021, as the end date of the next remitting period.
o. Back up your files.
p. Finish entering the history for all ledgers and finish your session.

2. Using the information provided, enter the source documents for July using Sage 50.

3. After you have completed your entries, print the following reports:
a. Journal Entries (All Journals) from July 1 to July 31, 2021
b. Supplier Aged Detail Report for all suppliers on July 31, 2021
c. Guest Aged Detail Report for all guests on July 31, 2021
d. Employee Summary (all employees) for the pay period ending July 31, 2021
e. Income Statement for the period ending July 31, 2021

SOURCE DOCUMENTS

Create new accounts or supplier and guest records as needed for the source documents that follow. Change session dates as needed.

☐ 1

Telephone: (519) 271-BARD (2273)
Fax: (519) 271-9333

Bard's Linen & Towels

Website: bards.com
E-mail: bard@bards.com

Invoice: BLT-64

Date: July 1, 2021

Sold to: Stratford Country Inn
100 Festival Rd.
Stratford, ON
N5A 3G2

STOCK NO.	QTY.	DESCRIPTION	PRICE	AMOUNT
1601	20	Satin Sheets	35.00	700.00
1801	100	Bath Towels	10.00	1000.00
2802	100	Face Cloths	3.00	300.00

CUSTOMER COPY	Terms on Account: 2/10, N/30			GROSS	2000.00
Method of payment:	On Account	C.O.D.	Credit Card		
HST #763 271 673	✓			HST 13%	260.00
				TOTAL	2260.00

☐ 2

AVON Maintenance Services
66 Kleen Rd., Stratford, ON N5A 3C3
Telephone (519) 272-4611
Fax: (519) 272-4813
avonservices.com

Invoice:	AM-148
Date:	July 1, 2021
Sold to:	Stratford Country Inn 100 Festival Rd. Stratford, ON N5A 3G2
Phone:	(519) 222-6066

Code	Service Description	Price
KX-55	Vacuum Premises Floor Polishing Washroom Cleaning Maintenance and Repairs Recurring monthly billing	2200.00

Signature: E Prospon	**Terms:** Net 30 days	**HST**	286.00
	HST #631 393 469	**Amount owing**	2486.00

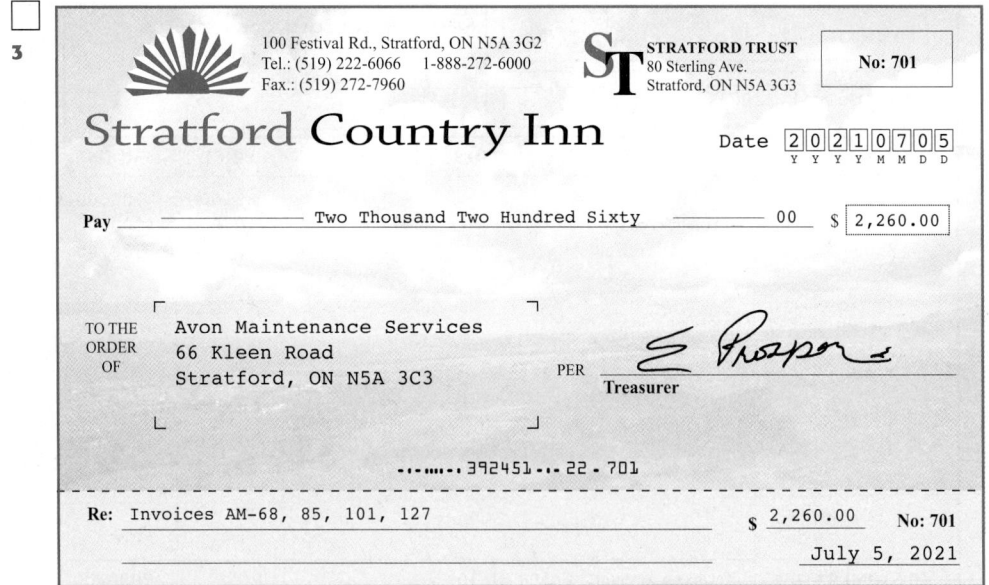

☐ 3

100 Festival Rd., Stratford, ON N5A 3G2
Tel.: (519) 222-6066 1-888-272-6000
Fax.: (519) 272-7960

ST STRATFORD TRUST
80 Sterling Ave.
Stratford, ON N5A 3G3

No: 701

Stratford Country Inn

Date 2 0 2 1 0 7 0 5
Y Y Y Y M M D D

Pay Two Thousand Two Hundred Sixty 00 $ 2,260.00

TO THE ORDER OF
Avon Maintenance Services
66 Kleen Road
Stratford, ON N5A 3C3

PER E Prospon
Treasurer

⑈⑈392451⑈⑈22⑈701

Re: Invoices AM-68, 85, 101, 127 $ 2,260.00 **No: 701**

July 5, 2021

4

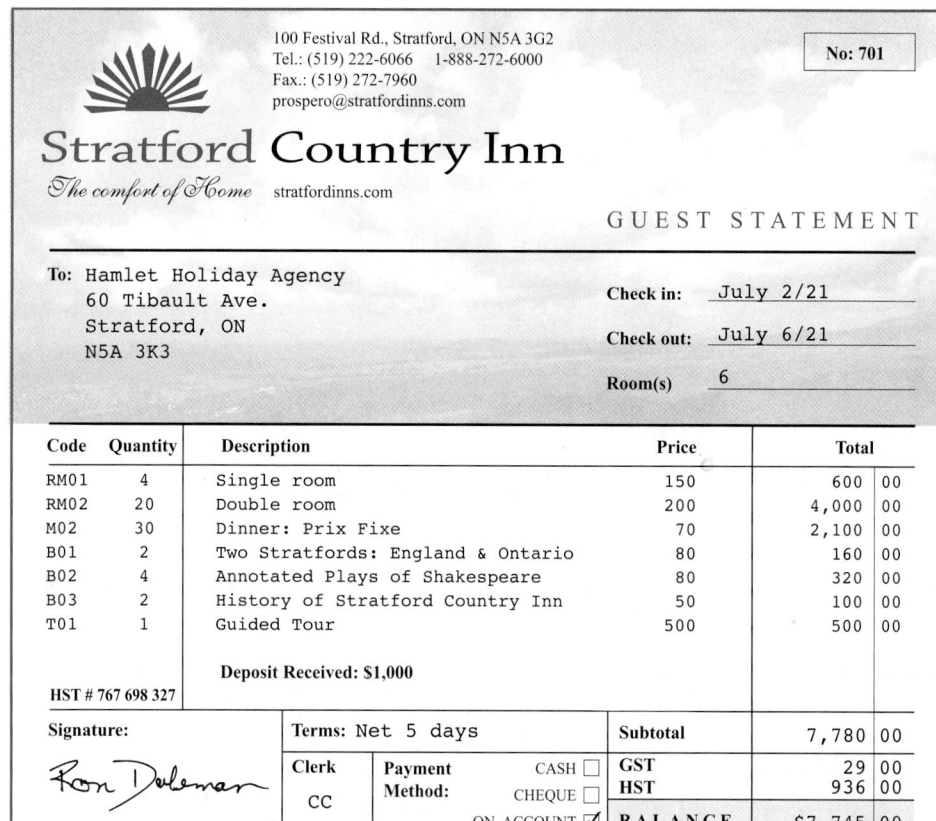

100 Festival Rd., Stratford, ON N5A 3G2
Tel.: (519) 222-6066 1-888-272-6000
Fax.: (519) 272-7960
prospero@stratfordinns.com

No: 701

Stratford Country Inn
The comfort of Home stratfordinns.com

GUEST STATEMENT

To: Hamlet Holiday Agency
60 Tibault Ave.
Stratford, ON
N5A 3K3

Check in: July 2/21
Check out: July 6/21
Room(s) 6

Code	Quantity	Description	Price	Total	
RM01	4	Single room	150	600	00
RM02	20	Double room	200	4,000	00
M02	30	Dinner: Prix Fixe	70	2,100	00
B01	2	Two Stratfords: England & Ontario	80	160	00
B02	4	Annotated Plays of Shakespeare	80	320	00
B03	2	History of Stratford Country Inn	50	100	00
T01	1	Guided Tour	500	500	00
		Deposit Received: $1,000			
HST # 767 698 327					

Signature: Ron Doleman

Terms: Net 5 days

Clerk CC

Payment Method: CASH ☐ CHEQUE ☐ ON ACCOUNT ☑

Subtotal	7,780	00
GST	29	00
HST	936	00
BALANCE	$7,745	00

5

Waterloo University Literary Club
88 College Rd.
Waterloo, ON N2A 3F6

No: 413

Date 20210706 (YYYYMMDD)

Pay to the order of Stratford Country Inn $ 1,000.00

One Thousand 00/100 **Dollars**

Waterloo Trust
550 King St.
Waterloo, ON N2A 3F8

T. Fornello
Chair

⑈—⑆—— 60431 ⑆ 105 ⑆ 413

Re: Deposit #41 – booking rooms in Inn
Receipt #55 $1,000.00

No: 413
July 6, 2021

WARNING!
You must change the tax code for books to G on all sales invoices so that taxes will be correctly applied for these items.

NOTES
Invoice balance amounts are shown net of deposit amounts.

6

100 Festival Rd., Stratford, ON N5A 3G2
Tel.: (519) 222-6066 1-888-272-6000
Fax.: (519) 272-7960

STRATFORD TRUST
80 Sterling Ave.
Stratford, ON N5A 3G3

No: 702

Stratford Country Inn

Date 2 0 2 1 0 7 0 7
Y Y Y Y M M D D

Pay One Thousand Eight Hundred Eight 00 $ 1,808.00

TO THE ORDER OF
Tavistock Laundry Services
19 Merchant Road
Stratford, ON N5A 4C3

PER E Prospero
Treasurer

⑈⑆392451⑈22⑈702

Re: Invoices TL-693, 742 $ 1,808.00 **No: 702**

July 7, 2021

7

100 Festival Rd., Stratford, ON N5A 3G2
Tel.: (519) 222-6066 1-888-272-6000
Fax.: (519) 272-7960
prospero@stratfordinns.com

Stratford Country Inn

The comfort of Home stratfordinns.com

VISA

SALES SUMMARY STATEMENT

No: 702

July 7, 2021

Code	Quantity	Description	Price	Total	
RM01	8	Single room	150	1,200	00
RM02	25	Double room	200	5,000	00
M01	6	Boxed Lunch	30	180	00
M02	10	Dinner: Prix Fixe	70	700	00
B01	2	Two Stratfords: England & Ontario	80	160	00
B02	4	Annotated Plays of Shakespeare	80	320	00
B03	4	History of Stratford Country Inn	50	200	00
T01	2	Guided Tour	500	1,000	00

HST # 767 698 327	**Subtotal**	8,760	00
Approved: E Prospero	**Goods & Services Tax**	34	00
	Harmonized Sales Tax	1,050	40
	VISA Receipts	$9,844	40

8

Sold to: Stratford Country Inn
100 Festival Road
Stratford, ON
N5A 3G2

Billing Date: July 8, 2021
Invoice No: TF-284
Customer No.: 3423
Customer Copy

TEMPEST Food Wholesalers
35 Henry Avenue
Stratford, ON N5A 3N6

Telephone: (519) 272-4464
Fax: (519) 272-4600
Website: www.tempest.com

Date	Description	Charges	Payments	Amount
July 8/21	Fish and Meats	1000.00		1000.00
	Fresh Fruits	200.00		200.00
	Fresh Vegetables	200.00		200.00
	Dry Goods	200.00		200.00
	Dairy Products	200.00		200.00
	Baking Goods	200.00		200.00
	Recurring bi-weekly billing			
Terms: Net 30 days			Subtotal	2000.00
HST #673 421 939				
Signature: E Prospero			HST 13%	exempt
Overdue accounts are subject to 16% interest per year			Owing	2000.00

9

Invoice No: TL-798
Date: July 8, 2021
Customer: Stratford Country Inn
100 Festival Rd.
Stratford, ON
N5A 3G2

Phone: (519) 222-6066

TAVISTOCK LAUNDRY Services
19 Merchant Rd.
Stratford, ON
N5A 4C3
Phone: (519) 271-7479
Fax: (519) 271-7888
tavistock.com

HST #639 271 345

Code	Description	Price	Amount
C-11	10 Loads Sheets	40.00	400.00
C-14	5 Loads Pillow Covers	20.00	100.00
C-20	15 Loads Towels	20.00	300.00
	Recurring bi-weekly billing		
Overdue accounts are subject to a 2% interest penalty per month		Sub-total	800.00
Terms: Net 30 days		HST	104.00
Signature: E Prospero		Total	904.00

10

100 Festival Rd., Stratford, ON N5A 3G2
Tel.: (519) 222-6066 1-888-272-6000
Fax.: (519) 272-7960

Stratford Country Inn

ST STRATFORD TRUST
80 Sterling Ave.
Stratford, ON N5A 3G3

No: 703

Date 2 0 2 1 0 7 0 9
Y Y Y Y M M D D

Pay Four Thousand 00 $ 4,000.00

TO THE ORDER OF
Tempest Food Wholesalers
35 Henry Avenue
Stratford, ON N5A 3N6

PER E Prospero
Treasurer

392451 22 703

Re: Invoices TF-113, 183 $ 4,000.00 **No: 703**
July 9, 2021

11

Hamlet Holiday Agency
60 Tibault Ave.,
STRATFORD, ON N5A 3K3

SB Scotia Bank
44 Welland Ave.
STRATFORD, ON N5A 3F6

No: 349

Date 2 0 2 1 0 7 1 0
Y Y Y Y M M D D

Pay Seven thousand, seven hundred & forty-five 00 $ 7,745.00

TO THE ORDER OF
Stratford Country Inn
100 Festival Road
Stratford, ON N5A 3G2

PER Ron Doleman
Treasurer

64299 168 349

Re: Invoice #701 & Cheque #317 **No: 349**
Receipt #56 $7,745.00 July 10, 2021

☐ 12

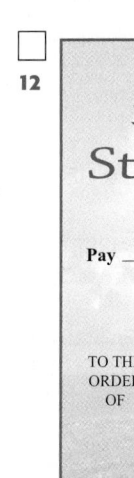

100 Festival Rd., Stratford, ON N5A 3G2
Tel.: (519) 222-6066 1-888-272-6000
Fax.: (519) 272-7960

Stratford Country Inn

STRATFORD TRUST
80 Sterling Ave.
Stratford, ON N5A 3G3

No: 704

Date 2 0 2 1 0 7 1 0
Y Y Y Y M M D D

Pay ——— Two Thousand Two Hundred Fourteen ——— 80 $ 2,214.80

TO THE ORDER OF
Bard's Linen & Towels
21 Venice Street
Stratford, ON N5A 4L2

PER E Prosper
Treasurer

⑈⑆⑈ 392451 ⑈⑆ 22 ⑈ 704

Re: Invoice BLT-64, Discount taken $45.20 $ 2,214.80 No: 704
July 10, 2021

☐ 13

STRATFORD SERVICE CENTRE
33 MacBeth Ave.
Stratford, ON N5A 4T2
Tel: (519) 271-6679
Fax: (519) 276-8822
ssc.com

Date: July 11, 2021 **Invoice:** 1143

Customer: Stratford Country Inn
100 Festival Rd.
Stratford, ON
N5A 3G2

Phone: (519) 222-6066

HST #634 214 217

Code	Description	Price	Amount
M-114	Lube, Oil and Filter	40.00	40.00
XF-1	Fuel	120.00	120.00
		Sub-total	160.00

APPROVAL	CUSTOMER COPY				
	Cash	VISA	On Account	HST	20.80
EP		✓		Owing	180.80

☐ 14

100 Festival Rd., Stratford, ON N5A 3G2
Tel.: (519) 222-6066 1-888-272-6000
Fax.: (519) 272-7960

Stratford Country Inn

ST STRATFORD TRUST
80 Sterling Ave.
Stratford, ON N5A 3G3

No: 705

Date 2 0 2 1 0 7 1 2
Y Y Y Y M M D D

Pay —— Two Thousand Three Hundred Eighty —— 00 $ 2,380.00

TO THE ORDER OF
Receiver General for Canada
PO Box 20002, Stn A
Sudbury, ON P3A 5C3

PER
Treasurer

⑈392451⑈22⑆705

Re: HST and GST Remittance for June 30, 2021 $ 2,380.00 **No: 705**
July 12, 2021

☐ 15

100 Festival Rd., Stratford, ON N5A 3G2
Tel.: (519) 222-6066 1-888-272-6000
Fax.: (519) 272-7960

Stratford Country Inn

ST STRATFORD TRUST
80 Sterling Ave.
Stratford, ON N5A 3G3

No: 706

Date 2 0 2 1 0 7 1 2
Y Y Y Y M M D D

Pay — Eighteen Thousand Five Hundred Ninety-nine —— 00 $ 18,599.00

TO THE ORDER OF
Receiver General for Canada
PO Box 20002, Stn A
Sudbury, ON P3A 5C3

PER
Treasurer

⑈392451⑈22⑆706

Re: EI, CPP and Income - 2021 quarterly tax remittances $ 18,599.00 **No: 706**
July 12, 2021

16

100 Festival Rd., Stratford, ON N5A 3G2
Tel.: (519) 222-6066 1-888-272-6000
Fax.: (519) 272-7960
prospero@stratfordinns.com

No: 703

Stratford Country Inn
The comfort of Home stratfordinns.com

GUEST STATEMENT

To: Waterloo University
Literary Club
88 College Rd.
Waterloo, ON
N2A 3F6

Check in: July 9/21
Check out: July 13/21
Room(s) 8

Code	Quantity	Description Transaction	Price	Total	
RM01	16	Single room	150	2,400	00
RM02	24	Double room	200	4,800	00
M01	7	Boxed Lunch	30	210	00
M02	16	Dinner: Prix Fixe	70	1,120	00
B01	1	Two Stratfords: England & Ontario	80	80	00
B02	2	Annotated Plays of Shakespeare	80	160	00
B03	1	History of Stratford Country Inn	50	50	00
T01	1	Guided Tour	500	500	00
		Deposit Received: $1,000			
HST # 767 698 327					

Signature: T. Fornelle

Terms: Net 5 days

Clerk: CC

Payment Method: CASH ☐ CHEQUE ☐ ON ACCOUNT ☑

Subtotal	9,320	00
GST	14	50
HST	1,173	90
BALANCE	$9,508	40

17

100 Festival Rd., Stratford, ON N5A 3G2
Tel.: (519) 222-6066 1-888-272-6000
Fax.: (519) 272-7960
prospero@stratfordinns.com

VISA

No: 704

SALES SUMMARY STATEMENT

July 14, 2021

Stratford Country Inn
The comfort of Home stratfordinns.com

Code	Quantity	Description	Price	Total	
RM01	7	Single room	150	1,050	00
RM02	12	Double room	200	2,400	00
M01	10	Boxed Lunch	30	300	00
M02	40	Meals	70	2,800	00
B01	2	Two Stratfords: England & Ontario	80	160	00
B02	3	Annotated Plays of Shakespeare	80	240	00
B03	3	History of Stratford Country Inn	50	150	00
T01	1	Guided Tour	500	500	00

HST # 767 698 327

Approved: E Prospero

Subtotal	7,600	00
Goods & Services Tax	27	50
Harmonized Sales Tax	916	50
VISA Receipts	$8,544	00

18

100 Festival Rd., Stratford, ON N5A 3G2
Tel.: (519) 222-6066 1-888-272-6000
Fax.: (519) 272-7960
prospero@stratford.com

ET27

Stratford Country Inn

The comfort of Home stratfordinns.com

EMPLOYEE TIME SUMMARY SHEET

Pay period: July 1 - July 14, 2021 **Paycheque date:** July 14, 2021

Name of Employee	Regular hours	Overtime hours	Sick days
Horatio, Hedy	80	0	0
Jones, Juliet	80	0	1
MacBeth, Mary	80	2	0
Romeo, Bud	80	2	0
Shylock, Shelley	80	2	0

Memo: Issue cheques #707 to #711
Recover $100 loan from Horatio and Romeo

19

VELOCITY

27 Gearing Ave., Niagara on the Lake, ON L0S 1J0
Telephone (888) 468-VELO
Fax: (905) 468-9100
VeloCity.com

quote

Quote No. 60
Date: July 15, 2021
Sold to: Stratford Country Inn
100 Festival Rd.
Stratford, ON
N5A 3G2
Phone: (519) 222-6066

Code	Service Description	Price
CY-020	3 Bicycles: @ $850 each Commuter Alum frame CX90 Suitable for moderately-heavy urban rental use Delivery scheduled for August 1, 2021 Quote accepted and converted to order #60	2550.00

Signature: E. [illegible]

Terms: 2/10, net 30

HST #335 677 829

HST	331.50
Amount owing	2881.50

20

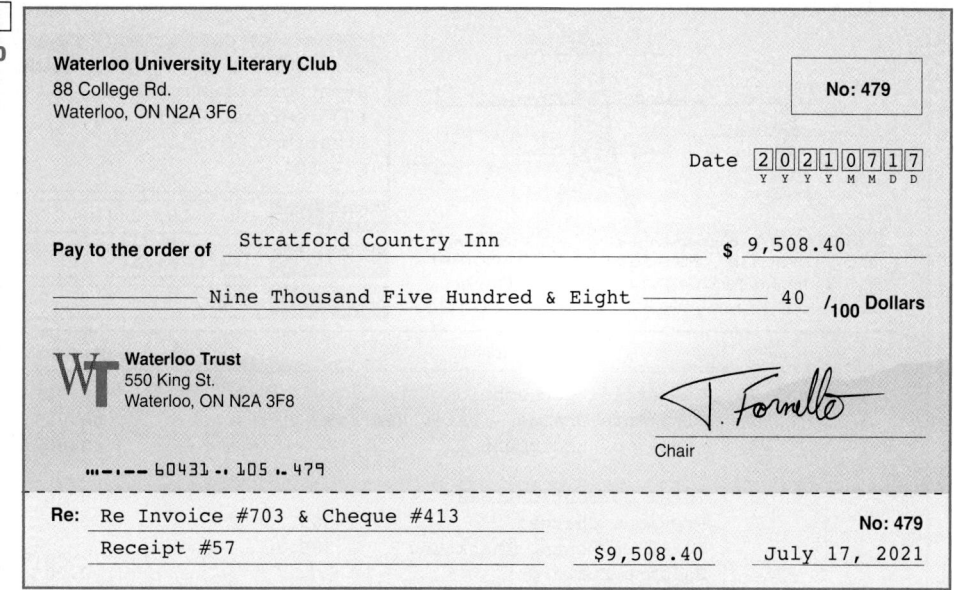

Waterloo University Literary Club
88 College Rd.
Waterloo, ON N2A 3F6

No: 479

Date 20210717
YYYYMMDD

Pay to the order of Stratford Country Inn $ 9,508.40

Nine Thousand Five Hundred & Eight 40 /100 **Dollars**

Waterloo Trust
550 King St.
Waterloo, ON N2A 3F8

Chair

⑈⑆ 60431 ⑆ 105 ⑈ 479

Re: Re Invoice #703 & Cheque #413
Receipt #57 $9,508.40

No: 479
July 17, 2021

21

100 Festival Rd., Stratford, ON N5A 3G2
Tel.: (519) 222-6066 1-888-272-6000
Fax.: (519) 272-7960

STRATFORD TRUST
80 Sterling Ave.
Stratford, ON N5A 3G3

No: 712

Stratford Country Inn

Date 20210718
YYYYMMDD

Pay Two Thousand Five Hundred Ninety-two 00 $ 2,592.00

TO THE ORDER OF
Hartford Insurance Group
88 Careful Way
Stratford, ON N3Y 7P7

PER
Treasurer

⑈⑆ 392451 ⑆ 22 ⑈ 712

Re: Renewal of Insurance policy for 1 year
$2,592 including PST.
$ 2,592.00

No: 712
July 18, 2021

☐ **22**

PERTH COUNTY HYDRO
66 Power Rd., Stratford, Ontario N5A 4P4
perthenergy.com

Customer Care: 272-6121

CUSTOMER NAME / SERVICE ADDRESS
Stratford Country Inn
100 Festival Road
Stratford, ON
N5A 3G2

Date:	July 18, 2021
Account No:	3921 462 513
Invoice No:	37232

Months	Reading	Description		Net Amount
1	86527	Commercial Consumption		300.00
1		Flat Rate Charge — Water Heaters		60.00
1		Rental of Equipment		40.00
		Total Current Charges		400.00
		Previous Charges	385.20	
		Total Payments, Thank You	385.20	
		Balance Forward		0.00
		Adjustments		0.00

Paid in Full with cheque #713 for $420 07/19/21 E Prosper

Average Daily KWh Consumption		HST #721 431 211	Due Date	GST 5%	20.00
Same Period Last Year	This Bill	After due date, a 1.5% monthly late payment interest charge will apply.	July 25/21		
269	258		Pay This Amount	TOTAL	420.00

☐ **23**

Bell

30 Whisper Rd.
Stratford, ON
N5A 4N3

bell.ca

Account Inquiries: 273-BELL (2355)

Account Number
519-222-6066

Account Address
Stratford Country Inn
100 Festival Rd.
Stratford, ON
N5A 3G2

July 19, 2021

ACCOUNT SUMMARY

Current Charges	
Monthly Services (June 12 to July 12)	240.00
Equipment Rentals	50.00
Chargeable Messages	30.00
HST 634 345 375	41.60
Total Current Charges	361.60
Previous Charges	
Amount of Last Bill	323.00
Payment Received June 19 — Thank You	323.00
Adjustments	0.00
Balance Forward	0.00

Paid in Full – chq #714 – 07/19/21 E Prosper

Invoice: BC-66431	PLEASE PAY THIS AMOUNT UPON RECEIPT ⟹	$361.60

24

100 Festival Rd., Stratford, ON N5A 3G2
Tel.: (519) 222-6066 1-888-272-6000
Fax.: (519) 272-7960
prospero@stratfordinns.com

No: 705

Stratford Country Inn

The comfort of Home stratfordinns.com

GUEST STATEMENT

To: NY Friends of Shakespeare
33 16th Ave.
Buffalo, NY
13002

Check in: July 17/21
Check out: July 20/21
Room(s) 9

Code	Quantity	Description	Price	Total	
RM01	6	Single room	105	630	00
RM02	21	Double room	145	3,045	00
M01	20	Boxed Lunch	18	360	00
M02	16	Dinner: Prix Fixe	48	768	00
B01	2	Two Stratfords: England & Ontario	55	110	00
B03	4	History of Stratford Country Inn	35	140	00
T01	1	Guided Tour	350	350	00
		**Preferred customer - no deposit required			
HST # 767 698 327		Exchange rate: 1.321 CAD			

Signature: J.Monte

Terms: Net 5 days

Clerk CC

Payment Method: CASH ☐ CHEQUE ☐ ON ACCOUNT ☑

Subtotal	5,403	00
GST	12	50
HST	669	89
BALANCE	USD $6,085	39

25

Festival Club of Rosedale
3 Rosedale Valley Rd.
Toronto, Ontario
M5G 3T4

No: 61

Date 20210720
Y Y Y Y M M D D

Pay to the order of Stratford Country Inn $ 1,000.00

One Thousand 00 /100 Dollars

Royal Bank
56 Bloor St.
Toronto, ON M5N 3G7

Jane Birker
Chairperson

⑈--- 34298 ⑆021⑆ 061

Re: Deposit #42 – booking rooms in Inn

No: 61

$1,000.00 July 20, 2021

26

ST **STRATFORD TRUST**
80 Sterling Ave.
Stratford, ON N5A 3G3

VISA

Statement Period M D Y		Account Number	Account Enquiries	Daily Interest Rate	Annual Interest Rate
From	06/15/21	4512 6221 1384 6201	1-800-272-VISA	.05068%	18.5%
To	07/15/21				

Trans. Date	Post Date	Particulars	Amount	Bus. Exp.
06/13	06/16	Stratford Service Centre, Stratford, ON	85.00	EP
06/18	06/21	Office Supplies Unlimited, Stratford, ON	88.00	EP
06/25	06/27	Stratford Service Centre, Stratford, ON	133.00	EP
06/28	06/30	Bullrich Dept. Store #32, Stratford, ON	113.00	EP
06/28	06/30	Bullrich Dept. Store #32, Stratford, ON	-24.00	EP
07/11	07/13	Stratford Service Centre, Stratford, ON	180.80	EP
06/20	06/20	Payment — Thank You	-422.00	EP

Balance $575.80 paid in Full by cheque # 715 E Prospero July 21/21

Credit Limit	Opening Balance	Total Credits	Total Debits	Your New Balance
8500.00	422.00	446.00	599.80	575.80

Available Credit	Payment Due Date Month Day Year	Overlimit or Past Due	Current Due	Minimum Payment	Payment Amount
7924.20	07/24/21		57.00	57.00	575.80

27

100 Festival Rd., Stratford, ON N5A 3G2
Tel.: (519) 222-6066 1-888-272-6000
Fax.: (519) 272-7960
prospero@stratfordinns.com

Stratford Country Inn
The comfort of Home stratfordinns.com

VISA

No: 706

SALES SUMMARY STATEMENT

July 21, 2021

Code	Quantity	Description	Price	Total	
RM01	4	Single room	150	600	00
RM02	18	Double room	200	3,600	00
M01	8	Boxed Lunch	30	240	00
M02	22	Meals	70	1,540	00
B01	2	Two Stratfords: England & Ontario	80	160	00
B02	5	Annotated Plays of Shakespeare	80	400	00
B03	3	History of Stratford Country Inn	50	150	00
T01	1	Guided Tour	500	500	00
HST # 767 698 327			Subtotal	7,190	00
Approved: *E Prospero*			Goods and Services Tax	35	50
			Harmonized Sales Tax	842	40
			VISA Receipts	$8,067	90

28

Sold to: Stratford Country Inn
100 Festival Rd.
Stratford, ON
N5A 3G2

Billing Date: July 22, 2021
Invoice No: TF-344
Customer No.: 3423
Customer Copy

TEMPEST Food Wholesalers
35 Henry Ave.
Stratford, ON N5A 3N6

Telephone: (519) 272-4464
Fax: (519) 272-4600
Website: tempest.com

Date	Description	Charges	Payments	Amount
July 22/21	Fish and Meats	1000.00		1000.00
	Fresh Fruits	200.00		200.00
	Fresh Vegetables	200.00		200.00
	Dry Goods	200.00		200.00
	Dairy Products	200.00		200.00
	Baking Goods	200.00		200.00
	Recurring bi-weekly billing			

Terms: Net 30 days	Subtotal	2000.00
HST #673 421 939		
Signature: E Prospor	HST 13%	exempt
Overdue accounts are subject to 16% interest per year	Owing	2000.00

29

Invoice No: TL-841
Date: July 22, 2021
Customer: Stratford Country Inn
100 Festival Rd.
Stratford, ON
N5A 3G2

Phone: (519) 222-6066

TAVISTOCK LAUNDRY Services
19 Merchant Rd.
Stratford, ON
N5A 4C3
Phone: (519) 271-7479
Fax: (519) 271-7888
tavistock.com

HST #639 271 345

Code	Description	Price	Amount
C-11	10 Loads Sheets *	45.00	450.00
C-14	5 Loads Pillow Covers	20.00	100.00
C-20	15 Loads Towels	20.00	300.00
	Recurring bi-weekly billing * new prices		

Overdue accounts are subject to a 2% interest penalty per month	Sub-total	850.00
Terms: Net 30 days	HST	110.50
Signature: E Prospor	Total	960.50

30

Zephyr Advertising Agency
32 Portia Blvd.
Stratford, ON
N5A 4T2

Telephone (519) 271-6066
Fax (519) 271-6067
westwinds.com
orders: contact tom@westwinds.com

Stratford Country Inn
100 Festival Rd.
Stratford, ON
N5A 3G2

ZA - 6998

Date	Description	Charges	Amount
July 23, 2021	Brochures & Flyers	300.00	300.00
	Paid in full cheque # 716 July 23/21 E Prosper		
		HST	39.00
HST # 391 213 915	Terms: Cash on Receipt	Total	339.00

31

NY Friends of Shakespeare
33 16th Ave.
Buffalo, NY 13002

No: 181

Date 2 0 2 1 0 7 2 4
Y Y Y Y M M D D

Pay to the order of Stratford Country Inn $ 6,085.39 (USD)

Six thousand, eighty-five 39 /100 Dollars

CB Chase Bank
4 12th Ave.
Buffalo, NY 13002

J.Monte

93937 - 301 - 181

Re: Re Invoice #705; Receipt #59
U.S. Currency. Currency Exchange 1.322 Cdn. $6,085.39(USD)

No: 181
July 24, 2021

☐ 32

STRATFORD SERVICE CENTRE
33 MacBeth Ave.
Stratford, ON N5A 4T2
Tel: (519) 271-6679
Fax: (519) 276-8822
ssc.com

Date: July 25, 2021 **Invoice:** 1207

Customer: Stratford Country Inn
100 Festival Rd.
Stratford, ON
N5A 3G2

Phone: (519) 222-6066

HST #634 214 217

Code	Description	Price	Amount
R-69	Transmission–overhaul	500.00	500.00
XF-1	Fuel	100.00	100.00
		Sub-total	600.00

APPROVAL	CUSTOMER COPY				
	Cash	VISA	On Account	HST	78.00
EP		✓		Owing	678.00

☐ 33

100 Festival Rd., Stratford, ON N5A 3G2
Tel.: (519) 222-6066 1-888-272-6000
Fax.: (519) 272-7960
prospero@stratfordinns.com

No: 707

Stratford Country Inn

The comfort of Home stratfordinns.com

GUEST STATEMENT

To: Metro Arts Appreciation Group
4400 Yonge St.
North York, ON
M6L 3T4

Check in: July 23/21
Check out: July 26/21
Room(s) 10

Code	Quantity	Description	Price	Total	
RM01	6	Single room	130	780	00
RM02	24	Double room	175	4,200	00
M01	10	Boxed Lunch	25	250	00
M02	16	Meals	65	1,040	00
B01	1	Two Stratfords: England & Ontario	70	70	00
B02	4	Annotated Plays of Shakespeare	70	280	00
B03	1	History of Stratford Country Inn	45	45	00
T01	1	Guided Tour	450	450	00
		**Preferred Customer - no deposit required			
HST # 767 698 327					

Signature:	Terms: Net 5 days		Subtotal	7,115	00
R. Downey	Clerk: CC	Payment Method: CASH ☐ CHEQUE ☐ ON ACCOUNT ☑	GST	19	75
			HST	873	60
			BALANCE	$8,008	35

34

100 Festival Rd., Stratford, ON N5A 3G2
Tel.: (519) 222-6066 1-888-272-6000
Fax.: (519) 272-7960
prospero@stratford.com

ET28

Stratford Country Inn

The comfort of Home stratfordinns.com

EMPLOYEE TIME SUMMARY SHEET

Pay period: July 15 - July 28, 2021 **Paycheque date:** July 28, 2021

Name of Employee	Regular hours	Overtime hours	Sick days
Horatio, Hedy	80	2	0
Jones, Juliet	76	4	0
MacBeth, Mary	80	0	0
Romeo, Bud	80	0	1
Shylock, Shelley	80	2	0

Memo: Issue cheques #717 to #721
Recover $50 loan from Romeo

35

100 Festival Rd., Stratford, ON N5A 3G2
Tel.: (519) 222-6066 1-888-272-6000
Fax.: (519) 272-7960
prospero@stratfordinns.com

Stratford Country Inn

The comfort of Home stratfordinns.com

VISA

No: 708

SALES SUMMARY STATEMENT

July 28, 2021

Code	Quantity	Description	Price	Total	
RM01	7	Single room	150	1,050	00
RM02	14	Double room	200	2,800	00
M01	35	Boxed Lunch	30	1,050	00
M02	20	Dinner: Prix Fixe	70	1,400	00
B01	3	Two Stratfords: England & Ontario	80	240	00
B02	5	Annotated Plays of Shakespeare	80	400	00
B03	6	History of Stratford Country Inn	50	300	00
T01	2	Guided Tour	500	1,000	00
HST # 767 698 327			Subtotal	8,240	00
Approved: E Prospero			Goods and Services Tax	47	00
			Harmonized Sales Tax	949	00
			VISA Receipts	$9,236	00

36

100 Festival Rd., Stratford, ON N5A 3G2
Tel.: (519) 222-6066 1-888-272-6000
Fax.: (519) 272-7960
prospero@stratfordinns.com

No: 709

Stratford Country Inn

The comfort of Home stratfordinns.com

GUEST STATEMENT

To: Festival Club of Rosedale
3 Rosedale Valley Rd.
Toronto, ON
M5G 3T4

Check in: July 26/21
Check out: July 30/21
Room(s) 8

Code	Quantity	Description	Price	Total	
RM01	8	Single room	150	1,200	00
RM02	24	Double room	200	4,800	00
M01	28	Boxed Lunch	30	840	00
M02	28	Meals	70	1,960	00
B01	1	Two Stratfords: England & Ontario	80	80	00
B02	2	Annotated Plays of Shakespeare	80	160	00
B03	2	History of Stratford Country Inn	50	100	00
T01	1	Guided Tour	500	500	00
		Deposit Received: $1,000			
HST # 767 698 327					

Signature: Jane Birker

Terms:
Clerk: CC
Payment Method: CASH ☐ CHEQUE ☐ ON ACCOUNT ☑

Subtotal	9,640	00
GST	17	00
HST	1,209	00
BALANCE	$9,866	00

37

Hamlet Holiday Agency
60 Tibault Ave.
STRATFORD, ON N5A 3K3

SB **Scotia Bank**
44 Welland Ave.
STRATFORD, ON N5A 3F6

No: 393

Date 2 0 2 1 0 7 3 1
Y Y Y Y M M D D

Pay One thousand 00 $ 1,000.00

TO THE ORDER OF
Stratford Country Inn
100 Festival Rd.
Stratford, ON N5A 3G2

PER Ron Doleman

⑈—⑆—— 64299 ⑉ 168 ⑉ 393

Re: Deposit #43 – booking rooms in Inn

No: 393

$1,000.00 July 31, 2021

38

100 Festival Rd., Stratford, ON N5A 3G2
Tel.: (519) 222-6066 1-888-272-6000
Fax.: (519) 272-7960
prospero@stratfordinns.com

Stratford Country Inn
The comfort of Home stratfordinns.com

MEMO #31

From: the owner's desk
To: Clara Claudius
July 31, 2021

1. Transfer $40,000 from Credit Card Bank account to CAD Chequing account.
2. Transfer $6,000 USD from USD Chequing account to CAD Chequing account. The exchange rate is 1.323.

39

100 Festival Rd., Stratford, ON N5A 3G2
Tel.: (519) 222-6066 1-888-272-6000
Fax.: (519) 272-7960
prospero@stratfordinns.com

Stratford Country Inn
The comfort of Home stratfordinns.com

MEMO #32

From: the owner's desk
To: Clara Claudius
July 31, 2021

1. Pay salaried employees Clara Claudius and Owen Othello. Add sales commission (1% Revenue from Inn) to Othello's salary. Issue cheques #722 and #723.
2. Pay quarterly balances owing as at July 1:
   a) To Minister of Finance (EHT), cheque #724
   b) Workplace Safety and Insurance Board (WSIB), cheque #725
   c) Travellers' Life (Group Insurance), cheque #726
3. Prepare adjusting entries for the following:
   a) Write off $216 of Prepaid Insurance
   b) Write off $50 of Prepaid Advertising
   c) Depreciation on Country Inn & Dining Room $600
      Depreciation on Computers $200
      Depreciation on Furniture & Fixtures $600
      Depreciation on Vehicles $800
   d) Food Inventory on hand $1 395

REVIEW

The Student DVD with Data Files includes a comprehensive supplementary case for this chapter and bank reconciliation.

Part 3
Advanced Premium Features

CHAPTER EIGHTEEN

Ryder's Routes

OBJECTIVES

After completing this chapter, you should be able to

- ***set up*** inventory service activities for time and billing
- ***update*** prices from Inventory Settings
- ***enter*** employee time slips
- ***import*** time slip activities to prepare employee paycheques
- ***import*** time slip activities to prepare customer invoices
- ***display*** and ***print*** time and billing reports
- ***set up*** additional currencies
- ***build*** new inventory from Inventory Ledger record details
- ***set up*** multiple inventory locations
- ***add*** inventory locations to journal entries
- ***transfer*** inventory between locations
- ***understand*** related accounts for multiple fiscal periods
- ***display*** and ***print*** multi-period financial reports

COMPANY INFORMATION

Time and Billing Profile

Ryder's Routes, under the management of Steve Ryder and VeloCity, provides bicycle tour guide services in Canada and internationally to travel companies wanting to add cycling to their group package tours. Tour guides will also service the guests' bicycles while on tour. Guests may rent bicycles for their trips or ship their own bicycles. To accommodate this new service, Ryder will use the Time & Billing module to create customer invoices and pay employees. After modifying the service records to price the services according to the time taken to complete the work and adding the new services, the company can track the work performed by each employee for each customer.

PRO VERSION
You will be unable to complete this chapter if you are using the Pro version.
You can download and install the Student Premium version program to complete Chapters 18 and 19. You must uninstall your Pro version before you can install the Student version. Refer to Appendix A.

Additionally, Ryder has contracted with new suppliers and customers in Europe. No duty is charged on imported exercise equipment.

In August, Ryder's Routes began providing guided tours in addition to the existing services for the bicycles it sells. Services are billed in three ways: at an hourly rate, at a flat rate regardless of the time required to complete the work and at no charge for repairs to bicycles under warranty. All tour and service work will be managed from Ryder's Routes, a new store near the VeloCity showroom. Ryder's Routes will also sell bicycle accessories. Other inventory can be transferred to Ryder's Routes as needed. Separate inventory locations will be set up for the two stores so that Ryder can track the inventory at each location.

Ryder hired two new employees: Yvonne Leader will serve as tour guide and Moishe Alee will work as the primary sales associate in the new store.

The company's fiscal period will be reduced to one month and cash sales summaries will be entered at the end of the month to reduce the number of source documents.

NOTES
Sales and services provided by Ryder's Routes in Canada will have HST added. Tour guide services that are provided outside of Canada (in Europe or the United States) will not be taxable. The location of this service, not the home country of the customer, determines the taxability.

KEYSTROKES

Modifying Company Information

Changing Fiscal Dates

Open **SageData19\RYDER\RYDER** to access the data files for this chapter and **accept August 1, 2021** as the session date.

Click **Company** in the Modules pane list to open the Company window.

Enter the **adjustment** for accrued wages and then **change** the **fiscal dates**.

NOTES
If you are working from the backup files, restore SageData19\RYDER1.CAB or RYDER1 to SageData19\RYDER\RYDER.

NOTES
The wage expense credit entry that reverses the accrued payroll ensures that the correct amount from this pay period will be assigned to the previous fiscal period, adhering to the principle of recording expenses in the period in which they were incurred.

1

Memo #8-1 **Dated August 1, 2021**

Prepare an adjusting entry to reverse the year-end adjustment for $720 for accrued payroll. (Debit Accrued Wages and credit Wages.)

✓ 2

Memo #8-2 **Dated August 1, 2021**

Change the company fiscal dates. The new fiscal end is August 31, 2021. Change the company name to VeloCity - Ryder's Routes

Click the **Settings icon** 

, then **click Information**, or **choose** the **Setup menu** and **click Settings**, **Company** and **Information**:

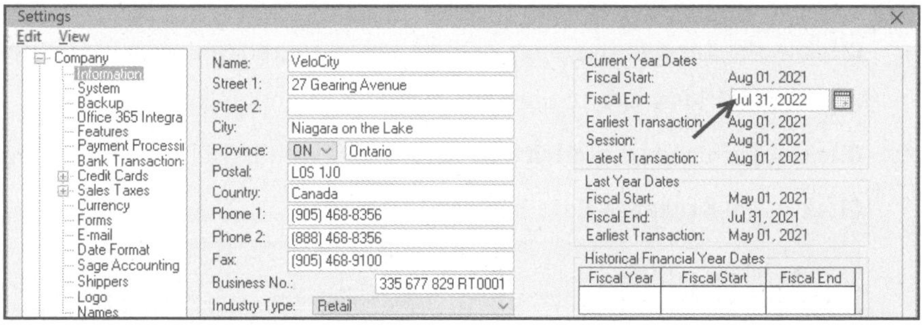

Most fiscal dates cannot be changed. Only the fiscal end can be edited. After starting a new fiscal period, the fiscal end is updated to one year past the new fiscal start because this period is most commonly used. Ryder's Routes, however, will use a one-month fiscal period to allow for more frequent performance review.

Drag through Jul 31, 2022 in the Fiscal End field.

Type 08-31-2021

Drag through VeloCity in the Name field.

Type `VeloCity - Ryder's Routes`

Leave the Settings window open so you can add the currency.

Adding a Foreign Currency

The Premium version of Sage 50 allows more than one foreign currency. Setting up additional currencies is similar to adding the first one. We will add the euro as the second foreign currency because a new supplier in Germany will provide some inventory items and European tours have been negotiated.

✓ 3

Memo #8-3 **Dated August 1, 2021**

Add the euro as a foreign currency to prepare for transactions with customers and suppliers in Europe. The linked account for exchange rate differences is 4120 and the exchange rate on August 1 is 1.52.
Change the account number for 1150 Net Bank to 1190 to accommodate the new bank account for foreign currency transactions.
Create a new Subgroup account, 1150 Bank: Euro Chequing. 1150 is a Bank class account and the next cheque number is 101.
Add 1150, the new bank account, as the linked account for Payables and Receivables bank transactions in euros.

Click **Currency** to open the Currency Settings window:

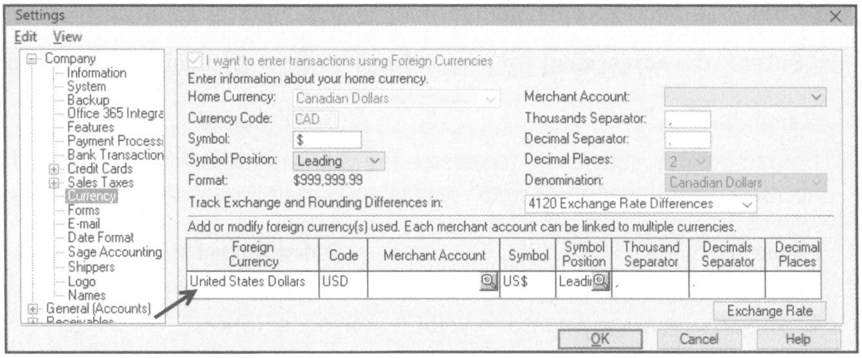

The currency added previously and its linked account for exchange rate differences are entered. You can select a different linked account, but you must use the same linked account for all currencies.

Click the **Foreign Currency column** below United States Dollars. **Click** the **List icon** to open the currency selection list.

Click **Euro** and then **click Select**. The codes and symbols for euro are added.

Click the **Exchange Rate button**:

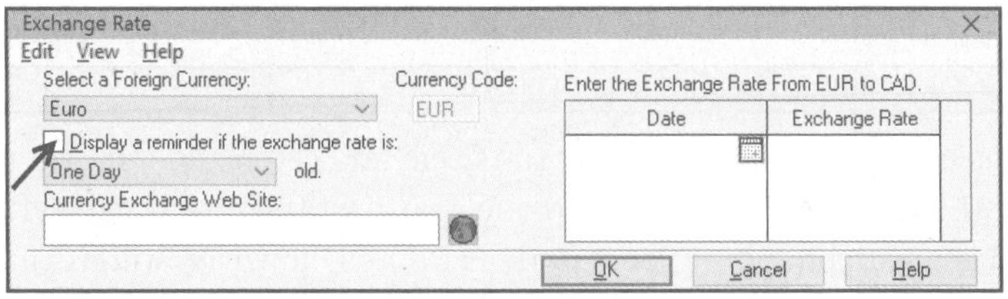

Euro is selected as the currency because the cursor was on this line in the previous screen. All other currencies you entered will be available from the Select A Foreign Currency drop-down list. You can add exchange rates for any of them.

Click the **Date column**. **Type** `Aug 1`

NOTES

If you choose United States Dollars from the Select A Foreign Currency list, you will open a screen with all the dates and exchange rates you have already saved as default rates.

Press tab to move to the Exchange Rate column. **Type** 1.52

Click **Display A Reminder If The Exchange Rate Is**.

The ✓ is added and we will accept the default **One Day** as our reminder period.

Click **OK** to return to the Settings. **Click OK** to return to the Home window.

> **NOTES**
> If you continue directly to the next Settings screen (for Linked Accounts) from the currency settings, you will be prompted to save the currency settings. Click OK to save the settings and continue.

Adding a Foreign Bank Account

Before using the currency in transactions, we need to create a new Bank class account for euro transactions.

Click the **Chart of Accounts icon** to open the Accounts window.

Double-click 1150 Net Bank. Click 1150, the account number. **Type** 1190 to change the account number.

Click the **Create tool** to open a new ledger window and **add** the new account **1150 Bank: Euro Chequing**.

Click **Subgroup Account** to change the Type if necessary.

Click the **Class Options tab. Choose Bank** from the Account Class drop-down list.

Click the **Currency list arrow** to access the options:

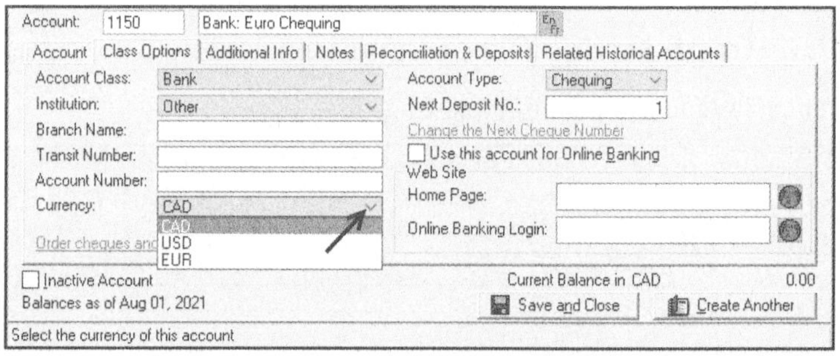

Click **EUR. Click** the **Save tool** before adding the cheque number.

Click **Change The Next Cheque Number** to open the Reports & Forms settings.

Click the **Next Cheque No. field** near the bottom of the form.

Type 101 **Click OK** to save the number and return to the ledger window.

Close the **Ledger window** and then **close** the **Accounts windows**.

> **NOTES**
> You can change the account number for Net Bank because it is not a postable account.
> You can click the Create tool in the Accounts window or in any ledger account window to open a new account ledger record window.

> **NOTES**
> Refer to page 648 for a review of setting up a bank account for a foreign currency.

Adding Linked Bank Accounts

We need to identify the new account as the linked account for euro transactions.

Click the **Settings icon**. Then **choose Payables** and **Linked Accounts**:

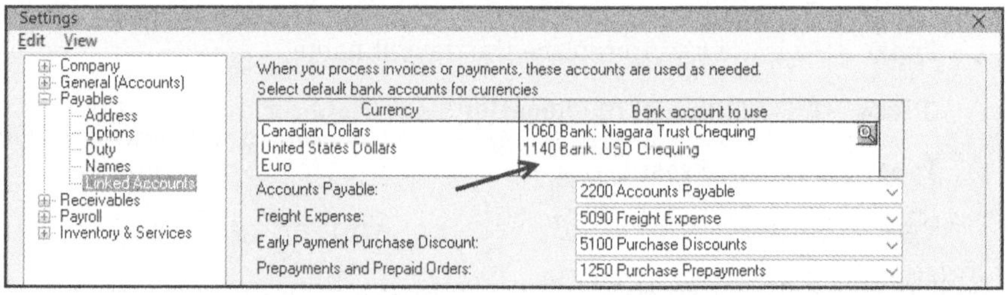

> **NOTES**
> You can create the new account at this stage too. But you must remember to choose Subgroup as the account type and Bank as the class. Once you select the Bank class, you can choose the currency.

NOTES
Undeposited Cash and Cheques is defined as a Canadian Cash account, so it is included with the linked account selection list for euros. You cannot use the USD chequing account for euro transactions – it is not on the list of available accounts.

Click the **Bank Account To Use column** beside Euro.

Click the **List icon**. Only the Canadian and euro cash or bank accounts can be selected as the linked euro currency bank account.

Double-click **1150**. **Press** tab.

Click **Receivables** and **Linked Accounts**.

Click the **Bank Account To Use column** beside Euro.

Type `1150` **Press** tab. Leave the Settings window open.

Entering Inventory Locations

Before leaving the Settings window, we will add the two stores as the locations for the business and for inventory. Items can be purchased for and sold from either store. Adjustments can also be made for the separate locations. The number of items in each store can, therefore, be monitored. If needed, items can be transferred from one location to another.

✓ 4

Memo #8-4 **Dated August 1, 2021**

Set up inventory locations for the two stores: VeloCity and Ryder. The VeloCity store is the primary location for inventory and the Ryder store is the secondary location for accessories and tour guide services.

NOTES
Click the button beside modules to collapse the expanded lists.

Click **Inventory & Services** in the Settings modules list.

Click **Locations** in the Inventory settings list:

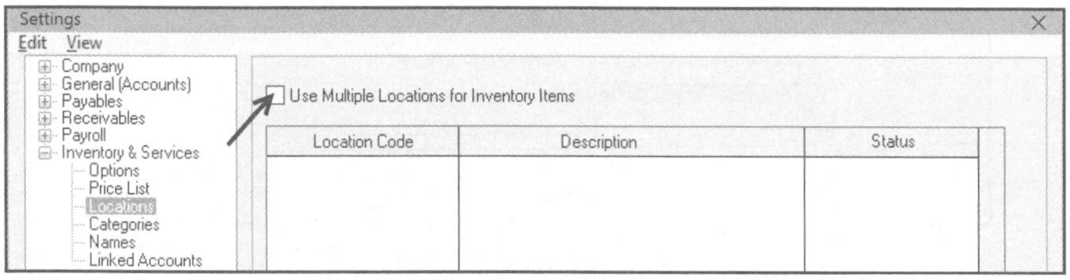

Click **Use Multiple Locations For Inventory Items** to activate the option:

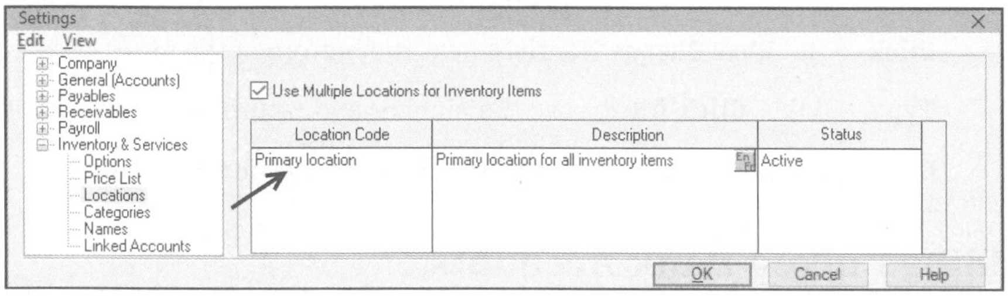

The Code, Description and Status fields are now available; we can enter the two stores. We will accept the default description for the first location.

Press tab **twice** to select Primary Location.

Type `VeloCity` to replace the default name.

Click the next line of the **Location Code field** for the next store.

Type `Ryder` **Press** tab.

Type `Ryder Store for tours and accessories`

Both locations are active, so the Status settings are correct.

Click **OK** to return to the Home window.

Click **Inventory & Services** in the Modules pane list.

Click **AC010 Bicycle Pump: standing model** in the Home window Inventory Item list.

The Quantities tab screen includes a For Location field.

Click the **For Location field list arrow**:

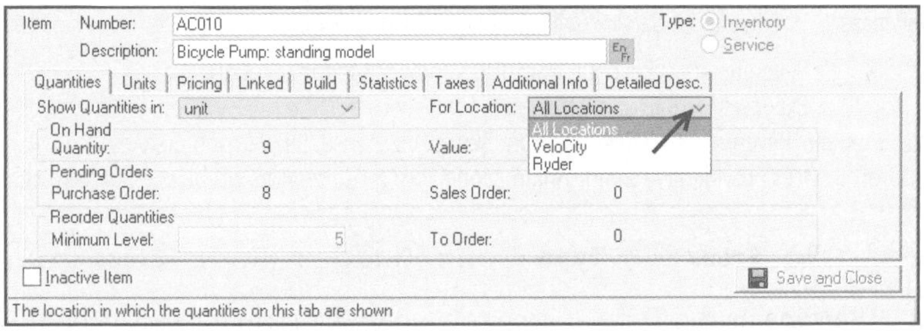

The two locations you entered are on the drop-down list.

Choose **VeloCity** from the For Location drop-down list to display the quantity at that store. **Choose** **Ryder** from the For Location drop-down list.

Initially, all the stock is at the primary location, the VeloCity store. The quantity at the VeloCity store is the same as the quantity for the All Locations selection. The quantity at the Ryder store is zero, including the minimum level entry.

Close the **Ledger window** to return to the Inventory & Services module window.

> **NOTES**
> You can set separate minimum levels for each location. When you select a location, the Minimum Level field becomes available for that location. When All Locations is selected, the field is dimmed.

Time and Billing

Many businesses that provide services use time as the basis for billing customers. Law firms, consulting businesses and service businesses that complete maintenance and repair work are just a few examples. In addition, these businesses may keep track of how much time each employee spends on a particular job and then compare this with the standard number of hours expected for that type of work. Some jobs can be billed at a flat rate and some, such as warranty repairs or work performed for other departments of the same company, may be provided at no charge. In each of these cases, it is still important to know how much time was spent on the job. Businesses might also want to track non-billable and non-payroll times, such as for lunch breaks, when an employee is at a customer site.

The Time & Billing module in Sage 50 tracks these kinds of activities by integrating the Payroll, Inventory and Sales ledgers.

Setting Up Time and Billing Activities

Before recording the services provided by employees to customers, that is, filling in time slips, we must modify the service records to apply time and billing. First we will create the new services. We will work from the Inventory module. It should still be open.

Choose **Add Inventory & Service** from the Inventory & Services icon drop-down shortcuts list to open a new record for inventory.

NOTES

Prices for tour guide services are group rates based on groups of 10 to 15 cyclists. Smaller and private groups may be served, but the rates will be the same. USD and euro prices will be added later.

✓ 5

Memo #8-5 **Dated August 1, 2021**

Create the new records described in the chart below to add services and include Time & Billing information:

Item	Description	Selling Price Reg	(Pref)	Unit	Related to Time?	Billable?	Billing Basis	Rate	Payroll
S070	Tour Guide: Hour	$150	($120)	Hour	Yes	billable	billable time	per hour	Regular
S080	Tour Guide: Day	640	(560)	Day (8 hours)	Yes	billable	billable time	per day	Regular
S100	Warranty Repairs	0	(0)	Service Call	No	non-billable			Regular

Linked accounts for tours: Revenue: 4050 Revenue from Tours (new Subgroup account)
Expense: 5075 Cost of Services

Linked accounts for repairs: Revenue: 4040 Revenue from Services; Expense: 5075 Cost of Services

Taxes: Charge HST on services provided in Canada. International tour guide services will be exempt from HST.

Type `S070` **Press** (tab). **Type** `Tour Guide: Hour` **Press** (tab).

Click **Service** as the Type of item to modify the form for service items:

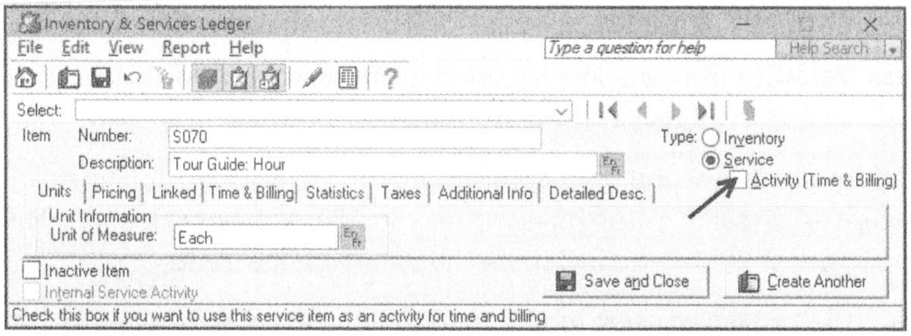

The Units tab window opens, and Activity is available as an option under Service.

Click **Activity (Time & Billing)** to add a ✓.

This selection will open the fields related to time and billing on the Time & Billing tab. The Units information is now dimmed and the Required Field indicator (*) is added back to the screen. We will enter units on the Time & Billing tab screen, as instructed by the message that appears on the Units tab screen. The Internal Service Activity option becomes available because this also applies to the Time & Billing module. We will enter the other item information first.

NOTES

Businesses often track the number of hours of service provided internally to other departments in the company as a way of monitoring internal efficiency or tracking departmental costs. They may monitor the time even if there is no charge for the service to the other department.

NOTES

The linked Revenue account is a required field for Activities, although it is not required for regular inventory or service items.

Click the **Pricing tab** to open the Canadian dollar (home currency) price list.

Click the **Regular Price Per Selling Unit field**.

Type `150` **Press** (tab) to advance to the Preferred Selling Price field.

Type `120`

Click the **Linked tab**.

Click the **Revenue account field**. We will add the new account.

Type `4050 Revenue from Tours` **Press** (tab) and **click Add** to start the Add An Account wizard with the name and number added.

WARNING!

If you do not change the account type to Subgroup Account, the accounts will not be in logical order, and you will be unable to display some reports.

You can make the correction later from the General Ledger to restore the logical account order.

Click **Next three times** to accept the defaults to access the **Subgroup And Group Accounts** screen.

Click **Yes** because this account is a Subgroup account.

Accept the **remaining defaults** to finish creating the account.

Click the **Expense field** and **type** `5075`

Click the **Time & Billing tab** to access the next group of fields to be set up:

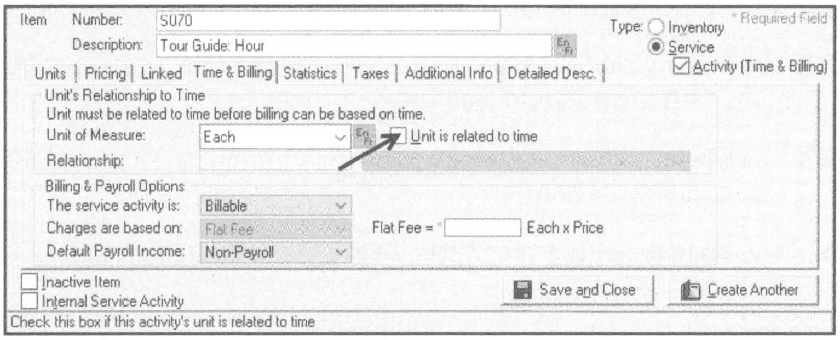

This screen has all the details that relate to the Time & Billing module. We must define the unit that the price is based on, indicate whether the unit is based on time and then add the relationship between the time and the unit of measure. Each is not recognized as a unit related to time, so the check box is empty.

Click the **list arrow beside Each** in the Unit Of Measure field.

Click **Hour**.

This Unit is automatically recognized as related to time, and the Relationship fields are now dimmed because we have already indicated a time unit. The next three fields define the **Billing & Payroll Options**:

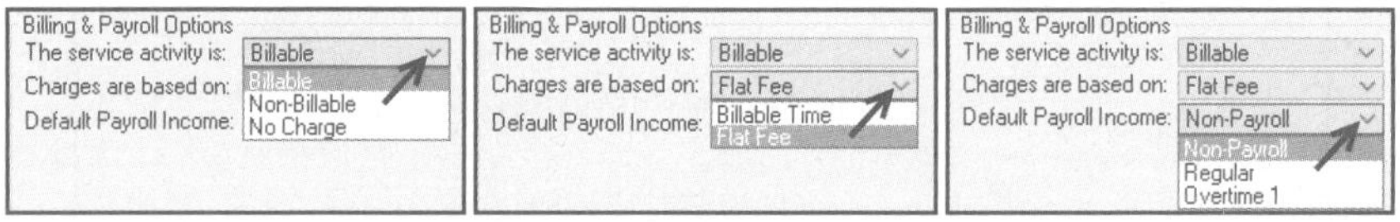

Billable is selected as the default for the service activity, and this is correct. Instead, an activity may be Non-Billable or there may be No Charge for the activity. Charges can be based on a Flat Fee or on Billable Time. Tour guide work is based on billable time.

The next option allows the time worked on the activity to be applied to an employee's paycheque. You can choose whether the time should be charged to the default payroll income account or to overtime. The non-payroll option may be selected if the work is completed by salaried employees. All services offered by Ryder's Routes are provided by the regular employees at the regular hourly wage rate.

Click **Flat Fee** in the Charges Are Based On field or its list arrow.

Click **Billable Time** to change the entry.

Click **Non-Payroll** in the Default Payroll Income field or its list arrow.

Click **Regular** to complete the Time & Billing tab screen:

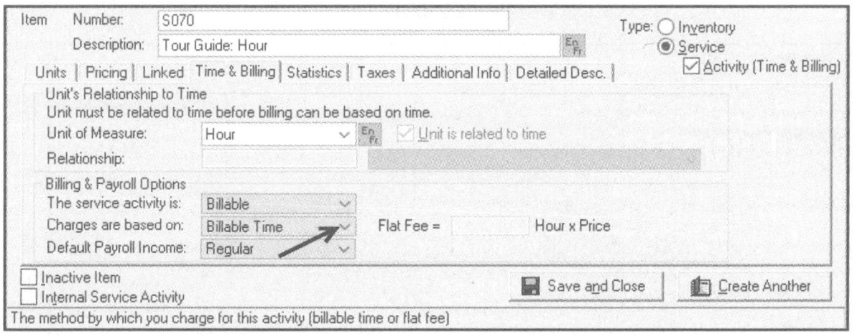

Click the **Taxes tab**. You can accept the defaults. HST is charged, so the service is not tax exempt for HST.

Click 

to save the record.

You are now ready to enter the next service. Service and Activity (Time & Billing) remain selected from the previous entry and are correct.

NOTES

A service activity may be non-payroll if salaried workers or managers complete the activity, because these individuals are not paid on the basis of hours worked.

Employee lunch hours on customer premises may also be tracked as non-payroll activities.

NOTES

In Ontario, most services are taxable for HST.

> **NOTES**
> Day is not automatically recognized as a unit of time. Hours and minutes are the only default time units in the program.

Type S080 as the Number and Tour Guide: Day as the Description.

Click the **Pricing tab** and **type** 640 as the Regular Price Per Selling Unit and 560 as the Preferred Price.

Click the **Linked tab** and **enter 4050** as the Revenue account and **5075** as the Expense account.

Click the **Time & Billing tab**. **Enter Day** as the Unit Of Measure.

This service requires additional information to indicate how many hours, or units of time, are in the day. The service will still be billed at an hourly rate, but Ryder's Routes charges a lower rate when a longer time period is purchased. Day as the unit is not automatically recognized as a unit related to time.

Click **Unit Is Related To Time** to add a ✓ and open the Relationship fields.

Each day is based on eight billable hours of activity, so the relationship should be entered as eight hours per day. The Relationship field is a required field when the unit is not Hour or Minute and you indicate that it is related to time.

Click the **first Relationship field**. **Type** 8

Click the **list arrow beside the second Relationship field**:

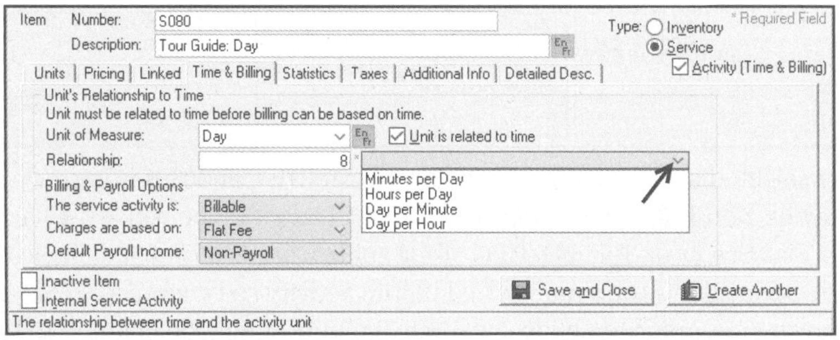

From the drop-down list, you can choose a relationship based on the number of hours or minutes per unit, or the number of units per hour or minute.

Click **Hours Per Day**.

The next option is correct — the activity is Billable. However, it is charged on the basis of time, not at a flat rate. We need to change the entry for Charges Are Based On.

Click **Flat Fee** in the Charges Are Based On field or its list arrow.

Click **Billable Time** and then **choose Regular** as the Default Payroll Income category to complete the record:

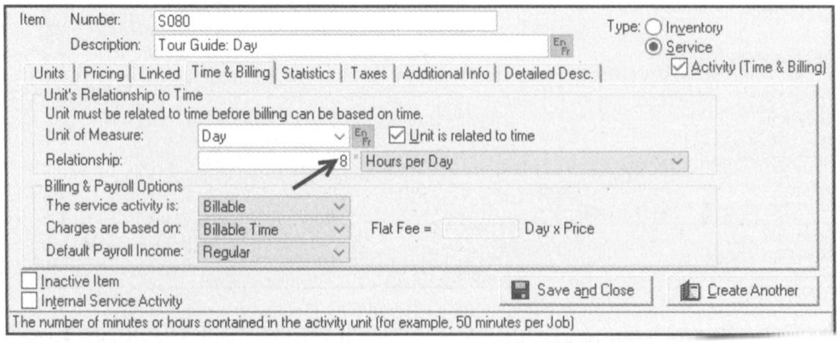

Click  to save the record.

The final service is provided at no charge to customers, but it is entered as an inventory item so that the time spent on warranty repairs can be monitored. The price will be entered as zero.

Type S100 as the Number and Warranty Repairs as the Description.

Click the **Pricing tab**. Do not enter any prices for the warranty service so that the prices will remain at zero.

Click the **Linked tab** and **enter 4040** as the Revenue account and **5075** as the Expense account.

Click the **Time & Billing tab**. **Enter Service Call** as the Unit Of Measure.

The service call for warranty work is not related to time because there is no charge for this service. We must indicate that the work is not billable. In addition, employees are paid at their usual wage rate for completing warranty work, even though the customer does not pay, so we must change the payroll category.

Click the **list arrow beside Billable**. **Click Non-Billable** to change the entry.

Choose Regular as the Default Payroll Income category to complete the record:

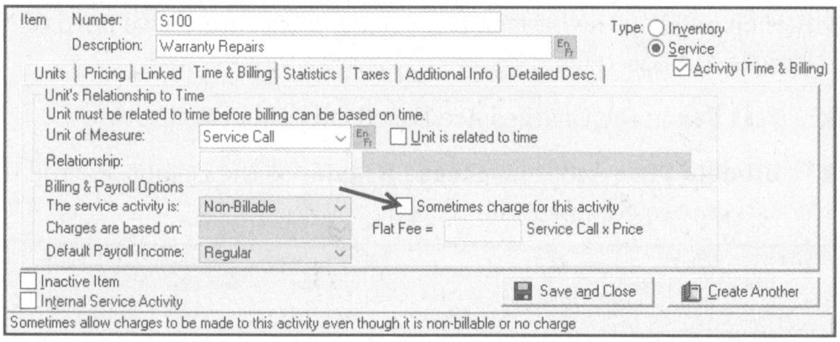

Another option for services that are normally not billed is to **sometimes charge**. When you choose the No Charge or Non-Billable options, this category becomes available. The pricing options are the same as for billable activities. You can relate the unit to time and enter the number of hours or minutes per unit, or enter a flat fee for the exceptional price. Prices are taken from Price fields on the Pricing tab screen.

Click 

to save the record and return to the Inventory & Services module window.

Adding Time and Billing Information to Services

You are now ready to edit the remaining service records to apply time and billing.

✓ 6 **Memo #8-6** **Dated August 1, 2021**

Edit the remaining service inventory records to add Time & Billing information. Then change the Canadian dollar prices and add foreign currency prices for services.

Item	Unit	Related to Time?	Relationship	Billable?	Billing Basis	Payroll
S010	box	yes	30 minutes/box	billable	billable time	Regular
S030	tune-up	no		billable	flat rate: 1 tune-up × price	Regular
S060	hour	yes		billable	billable time	Regular

Scroll down the Inventory Item list in the Inventory & Services module window.

Click **S010 Boxing for shipping** in the Home window list of items and services to open the record.

Click the **Time & Billing tab** to open the Time & Billing screen.

NOTES

Sales of annual service contracts and rentals are not entered as service activities – there is no service time associated with them.

All the fields are dimmed because we still need to mark the service as an activity for time and billing.

Click **Activity (Time & Billing)** to open the extra fields.

Type `box` as the Unit Of Measure.

Again, as a unit, box is not automatically related to time.

Click **Unit Is Related To Time** to add a ✓ and open the Relationship fields.

Each boxing job is based on 30 minutes of billable time, so the relationship is 30 minutes per box. This is the average time required to box one bicycle.

Click the **first Relationship field**. **Type** `30`

Click the **list arrow beside the second Relationship field**.

Click **Minutes Per Box**.

The activity is charged on the basis of time, not at a flat rate, so we need to change the entry for Charges Are Based On.

Click **Flat Fee** in the Charges Are Based On field or its list arrow.

Click **Billable Time** and then **choose Regular** as the Default Payroll Income category to complete the record:

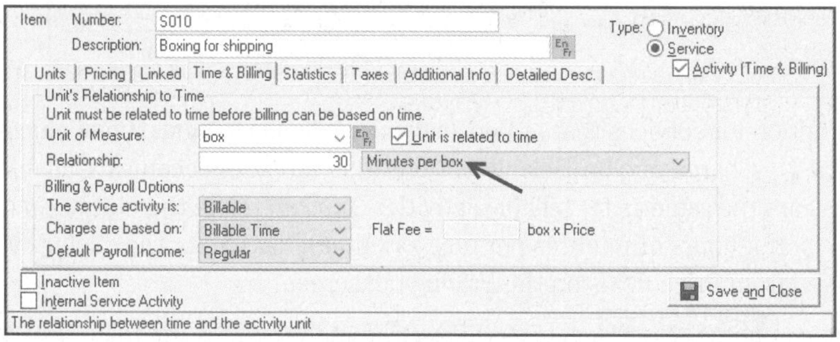

Click the **Next Item tool** **twice** to open the record for S030 Maintenance: complete tune-up.

Click **Activity (Time & Billing)** to change the item type.

Type `tune-up` as the Unit Of Measure.

The service is priced at a flat rate, so the unit is not related to time. Tune-up is not recognized as a unit of time, so the ✓ is not added. Billable is also the correct choice, but we need to enter the rate. By default, charges are based on a flat fee when the unit is not related to time, and the entry Flat Fee is dimmed. Flat Fee = ___ tune-up × Price is entered as the field label. This means that we must enter a number, not a price. The price will be calculated as the number of completed tune-ups multiplied by the price that is taken from the Pricing tab fields.

The flat rate for this service is one times the price; each tune-up is priced at $70 ($65 for preferred customers).

Click the **field beside Flat Fee =**.

Type `1`

Choose **Regular** as the Default Payroll Income category to update the Time & Billing screen:

NOTES

When the relationship entry is 30 minutes per unit with the ledger price based on units, the charge in the Time Slip, which is based on the number of hours, would be for two boxes when you enter one hour.

Alternatively, you could enter 2 in the Relationship field and select "2 box per hour."

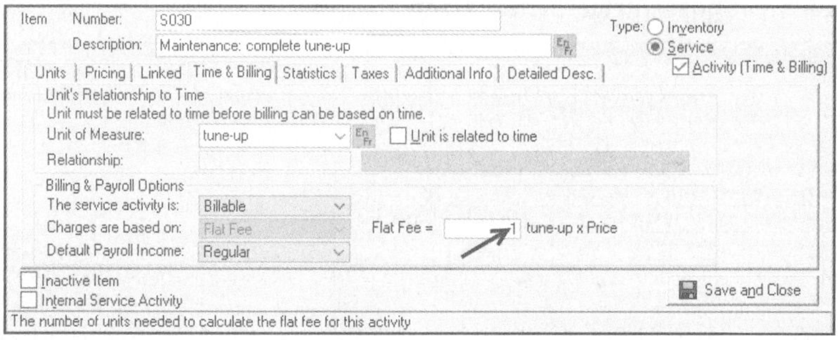

Click the **Next Item tool** (three times) to open the record for **S060 Repairs**.

Click **Activity (Time & Billing)**.

Again, because Hour is the unit, it is automatically related to time and most of the default details are correct.

Choose **Regular** as the Default Payroll Income category.

Click Save and Close to save the record and return to the Inventory & Services module window.

We will now edit the prices for these services using the Update Price Lists feature in the Inventory Settings window. You should still be in the Inventory Home window.

Updating Service Activity Prices

The Premium version allows you to define additional price lists and to update all prices from one screen. This feature is available as one of the settings for the Inventory Ledger. You can change individual item prices from this location or, if prices are raised by a fixed amount or percentage for one or more items or services, you can make the price changes globally. You can also set the prices in one list relative to the prices in another list by indicating the increase or decrease. All activity prices that require updating are listed in the following chart (the remaining prices are unchanged):

Item	Canadian Prices		USD Prices			Euro Prices		
	Reg	(Pref)	Reg	(Pref)		Reg	(Pref)	
S010	$ 80	($ 70)	$60	($ 52)	fixed price	€52	(€48)	fixed price
S060	50	(40)	35	(33)	fixed price	N/A	N/A	
S070	150	(120)	120	(110)	fixed price	100	(90)	fixed price
S080	640	(560)	480	(440)	fixed price	440	(410)	fixed price

Click the **Settings icon**. **Click Price List** to open the Price List Settings:

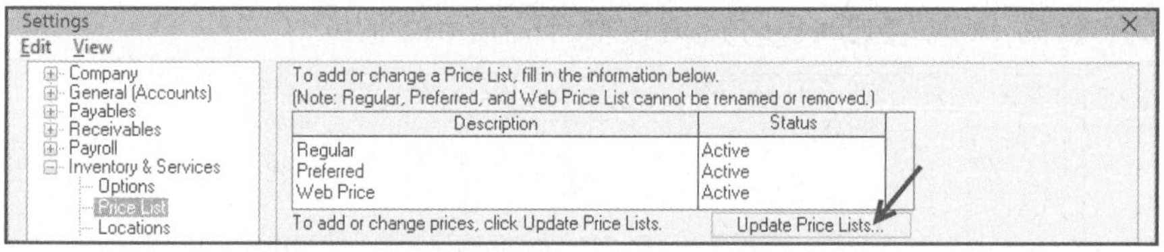

On this screen, you can define new price lists. You cannot remove or modify the three predefined price list names. If you want to create a new price list, you can type the new price list name below Web Price in the Description column and click Update Price Lists to open the item list. We need to update Regular and Preferred prices.

NOTES
The Flat Fee rate is a required field when the Flat Fee method of pricing is selected. The screenshot at the top of page 745 has an asterisk * beside this field.

NOTES
The remaining services (rentals and annual service contract) cannot be related to a specific amount of employee time, so they are not marked as activities.

NOTES
Price increases and decreases may be entered as amounts or percentages relative to the reference price.

NOTES
Foreign currency prices are not needed for services provided only in Canada to Canadian customers. The remaining services do not apply to customers in Europe.

Click the **Update Price Lists button**:

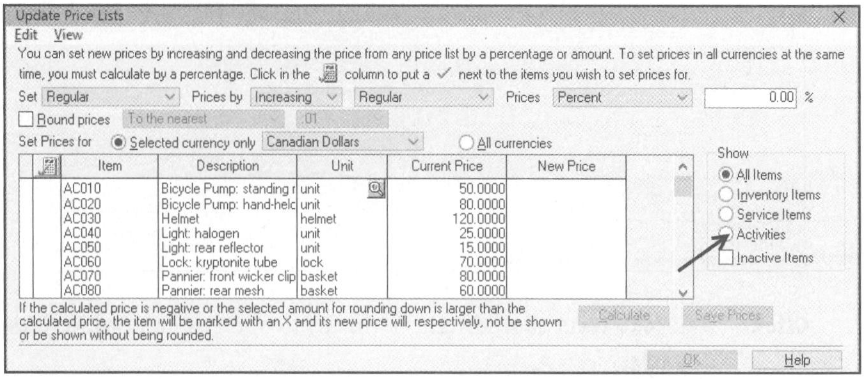

The inventory list opens with all items and services listed in Canadian regular prices. You can display All Items, Inventory Items only, Service Items only or Activities only.

You can select the items whose prices you want to update globally. You can set the prices in one list relative to another list by increasing or decreasing the reference prices by a fixed percentage or amount. Then you can round off the prices to the nearest unit — ranging from 0.0001 dollar to 1 000 dollars. You can make the price changes for one currency or for all currencies at the same time. You can also enter or edit individual prices in the new price column, so you can use this list to enter price changes manually for several inventory items on a single screen, without opening each ledger record separately.

You can Round Prices if you want to work with even amounts. Choose the direction for rounding off the price — up to the nearest, down to the nearest or to the nearest unit. Choose the nearest unit you want to round to from the drop-down list.

We will work from the smaller list of Activities. When you are changing a large number of prices, it is more efficient to work from the Update Price List screen.

Click **Activities** under Show on the right-hand side of the screen:

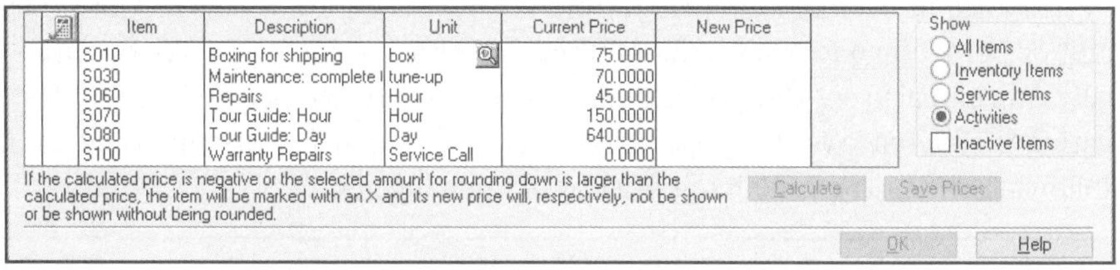

Item Description Unit Current Price New Price
S010 Boxing for shipping box 75.0000
S030 Maintenance: complete tune-up 70.0000
S060 Repairs Hour 45.0000
S070 Tour Guide: Hour Hour 150.0000
S080 Tour Guide: Day Day 640.0000
S100 Warranty Repairs Service Call 0.0000
Show
All Items
Inventory Items
Service Items
Activities
Inactive Items
If the calculated price is negative or the selected amount for rounding down is larger than the calculated price, the item will be marked with an X and its new price will, respectively, not be shown or be shown without being rounded.
Calculate
Save Prices
OK
Help

The list now has the Canadian dollar Regular prices for all activities. We will edit these first. We will change the prices directly by entering the revised price in the New Price column. The prices for S010 and S060 have changed.

Click **S010** and **press** *tab* until the cursor is in the New Price column.

Type 80

Press ↓ **twice** to place the cursor in the New Price column for activity S060.

Type 50 **Press** *tab* to update the price list:

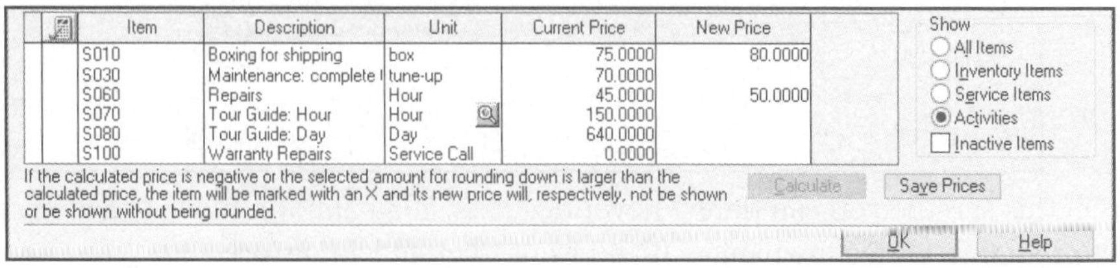

Now we will update USD regular prices. Canadian preferred prices are not changing.

NOTES

You can also access the Update Price Lists screens from the Home window Maintenance menu.

NOTES

If you have different units for stocking and selling, you can select the unit as well. The Unit field has a List icon. Selling unit prices are listed initially.

Click an item to select it. Then click the List icon that opens beside the entry in the Unit column for the different units you can choose.

NOTES

You can select individual items by clicking the Select column beside an item. Click the column for the next item you want to change, and so on. Pressing the space bar when the cursor is in the Select column will also add the checkmark and select an item.

Then apply the change rules you want to only the selected items. For example, you could select items S010 and S060 and then apply the rule to increase these prices by a fixed amount of $5. We apply change rules to edit prices on page 775

Click **Canadian Dollars** in the Selected Currency Only field:

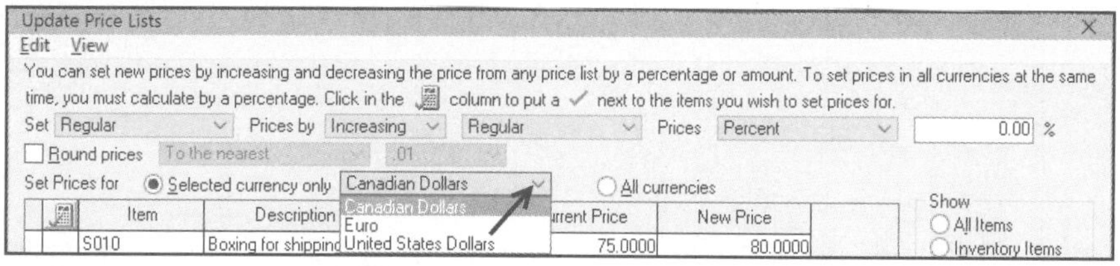

Select **United States Dollars**. Sage 50 requests confirmation with a warning:

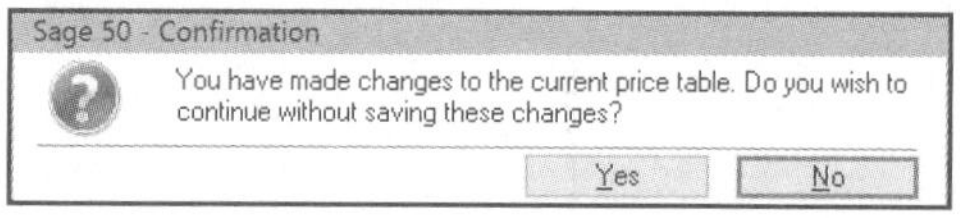

We do not want to continue without saving the new Canadian dollar prices.

Click **No** to return to the Canadian Dollars price list. **Click Save Prices**. The new prices move to the Current Price column:

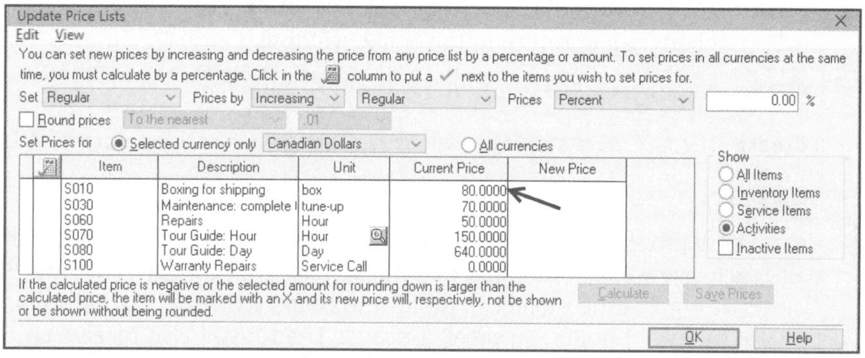

Click **Canadian Dollars** again in the Selected Currency Only field and **select United States Dollars** to view the prices in United States Dollars:

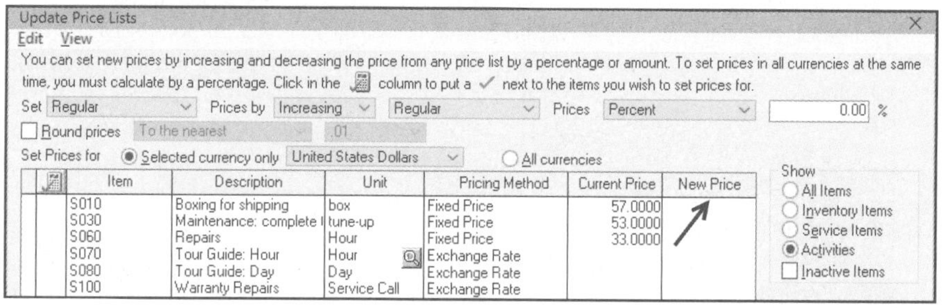

We need to change the prices for S010 and S060, as we did for Canadian Dollar prices, and we need to add prices for the new service activities.

Click **S010** and **press** *tab* until the cursor is in the New Price column.

Type 60

Press ⇩ **twice** to place the cursor in the New Price column for activity S060.

Type 35

Click **Exchange Rate** for item S070 to change the entry to Fixed Rate.

Press *tab* to advance to the New Price column. **Type** 120

Click **Exchange Rate** for item S080 to change the entry to Fixed Rate.

Press *tab* to advance to the New Price column. **Type** 480

Click **Save Prices**. The new prices move to the Current Price column.

We can now update the Preferred USD prices.

WARNING!

You must save the new prices by clicking Save Prices. If you click OK first, or choose another price list, Sage 50 will request confirmation that you want to continue without saving.

NOTES

The price for Warranty Repairs is zero, so you do not need to enter any price changes for this service.

Click **Regular** in the Set field to open the drop-down list:

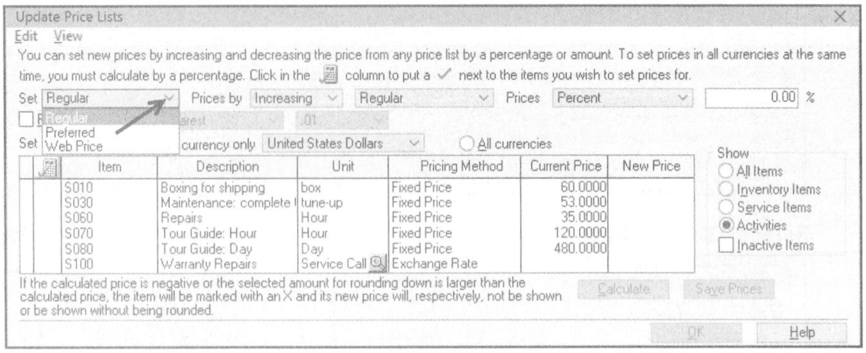

> **NOTES**
> To enter the euro prices, first save the US prices, then select Euro as the currency and Regular as the price list. Enter the prices on page 749. Click Save Prices. Select Preferred as the price list and enter the preferred prices from page 749. Click Save Prices.

Click **Preferred**. **Enter** the **preferred prices** for United States dollars. **Enter** the **regular** and **preferred prices** for euros from the chart on page 749. Remember to **click Save Prices** after each set. Read the margin Notes.

Click **OK** to return to the Settings window. **Click OK** again to save all the changes and return to the Home window.

Click **Employees & Payroll** in the Modules pane list.

Create the **two new employee records**. **Change** the **session date to August 14**.

7

Memo #8-7 **Dated August 1, 2021**

Create new employee records for Yvonne Leader and Moishe Alee. Leader will work exclusively as a tour guide (activities), billing on the basis of time. She is classed as a part-time worker (paid for the hours worked), but her minimum pay will be for 20 hours per week. Because Leader will also receive customer tips that she tracks on her own, she will pay additional taxes each pay period. Alee will be paid a monthly salary as a full-time sales assistant in the new store.

> **NOTES**
> Refer to pages 329–339 if you need assistance with entering the new employees. There is no historical information for the new employees.
> Leader and Alee will not receive the group insurance benefit or the piece rate pay (No. Clients) or Bonus initially. Those benefits will apply after they finish the probationary work period. They also have no additional deductions at this time for VRSP, Savings Plan, Donations or Garnishee.

	Leader, Yvonne (Female)	Alee, Moishe (Male)
Address	499 Itinerant Dr. Mt. Hope, ON L0R 1W0	551 Spoker Dr. St. Catharines, ON L2V 8H3
Telephone	(905) 418-7192	(905) 688-9101
SIN	420 011 009	128 663 887
Date of Birth	06-23-88	08-31-90
Date of Hire	08-01-21	08-01-21
Job Category	Sales	Sales
Tax Table	Ontario	Ontario
Basic Indexed: Fed (Prov)	$12 609 ($10 582)	$12 609 ($10 582)
Additional Federal Tax	$50 per week	
Regular Wage	$24/hour	N/A
# hours	20 hours (part time) (min hours in paycheque)	150 hours (full time)
Overtime Wage	$36/hour	N/A
Salary	N/A	$3 480/month
Do not use	Salary, Commission	Regular, Overtime, Commission
Pay Period	Weekly (52 per year)	Monthly (12 per year)
Vacation	6% Retained	3 weeks (0%, not retained)
Record Wage Expenses in	Payroll linked accounts	Payroll linked accounts
WSIB Rate	1.29	1.29
Vacation	delete entry	8%, 25 days max
Sick Leave	5%, 15 days max	5%, 15 days max
Personal Days	2.5%, 5 days max	2.5%, 5 days max
Direct Deposit	100% of paycheque to branch #89008 institution #102 account #341002	100% of paycheque to branch #67752 institution #102 account #198823

Preparing Time Slips

After setting up the service records to mark the activities and enter billing information, you can track the amount of time that each employee works for each customer at each activity by completing time slips.

Time slips for employees like the following one for Mercier may be entered from the Employees & Payroll module window or from the Receivables module window:

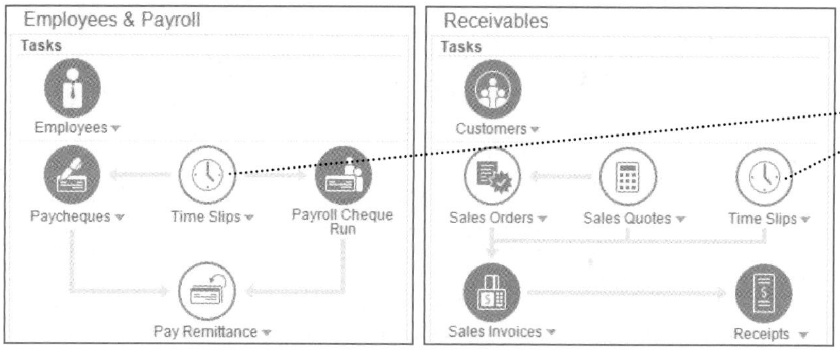

NOTES

From the Time Slips icon shortcuts drop-down lists, you can create, find and adjust time slips. From the Employees Time Slips icon, you can also pay employees. From the Receivables module Time Slips icon, you can also create invoices.

You can add a shortcut for Create A Time Slip.

NOTES

The * indicates that preferred customer prices apply.

✓ 8 **TIME SLIP #1** **DATED AUGUST 7, 2021**

For Dunlop Mercier

Customer	Item	Actual Time	Billable Time	Billable Amount	Taxable	Payroll Time
Cathedral Tours	S010	3 hours	2.5 (5 boxes)	€260.00	yes	3 hours
Niagara Rapids Inn*	S060	4 hours	3.5 hours	$140.00	yes	4 hours
Niagara Rapids Inn*	S030	2 hours	2 hours	$65.00	yes	2 hours
Niagara Rapids Inn*	S100	4 hours	–	–	yes	4 hours
Festival Tours	S100	2 hours	–	–	yes	2 hours

Click the **Time Slips icon** in the Receivables module Tasks pane or in the Employees & Payroll module Tasks pane:

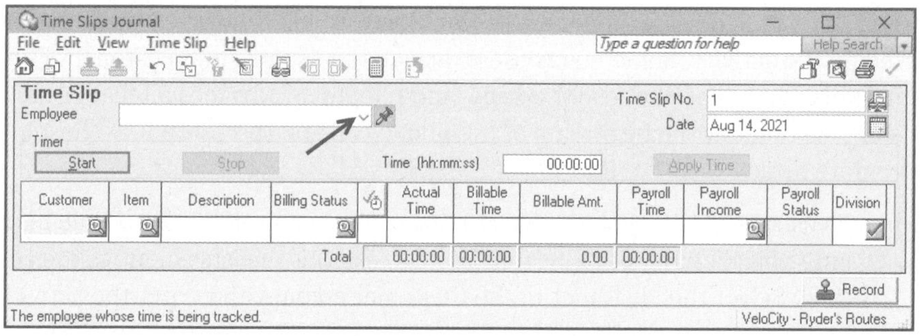

CLASSIC VIEW

Click the Time Slips icon  in the Time & Billing column.

The Time Slips Journal opens. All the tool icons in this window are the same as those found in other journals. Also, as in other journals, employees can be selected from a drop-down list and List icons are available for many of the fields.

Many features in other journals are also available for time slips. You can access these options from the tool buttons as you do in other journals or from the Time Slip menu. For example,

- Click the Store tool  and enter a name and frequency to store the time slip as a recurring transaction.
- Click the Look Up Time Slip tool  to look up a time slip just as you look up purchases or sales invoices.
- Click the Adjust Time Slip tool  to adjust a time slip after recording. You cannot adjust a time slip for selecting the wrong employee.

> **NOTES**
> Remember that you can maximize the window, scroll to include additional information or change the width of the columns by dragging.

The Time Slip number is updated automatically by Sage 50. Its starting number is taken from the Forms Settings, just like the next number for other forms. If the Time & Billing module is not hidden, the Next Number field for Time Slips is included in the Forms Settings screen. The number is correct.

The first time slip is for Mercier. His first job was completed for Cathedral Tours, a new regular-price customer in Europe. Use Full Add for the new customer.

> **NOTES**
> Use Full Add for the new customer in Europe so that you can add the currency:
> New regular-price customer:
> Cathedral Tours
> 550 Kirchestrasse
> 1020 Vienna, Austria
> Tel: 01 316 521
> Currency: Euro
> Terms: 2/10, n/30; Pay Later
> Tax Code: No tax
> Credit Limit: $10 000 CAD (€6 000)

Click the **Employee list arrow** and **choose Dunlop Mercier**.

Enter **August 7** in the Date field for the Time Slip.

Click the **Customer field** and **type** `Cathedral Tours` **Press** *tab*.

Add the **complete record** details for the new customer.

Click the **Item field List icon** to open the Select Activity list:

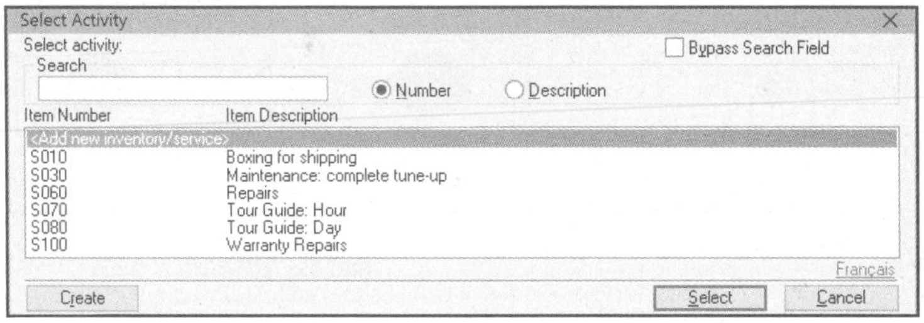

All services for which you selected Activity as the type of Service and added time and billing details will be on this list. Other services and inventory will not be included.

Double-click **S010 Boxing for shipping** to add it to the journal.

The Item and Description fields are the usual ones for inventory and service transactions. The next field, **Billing Status**, is completed from the Time & Billing tab details in the ledger record. Usually the defaults are correct, but you can change them if needed. The Billing Status field has a List icon and a selection list. Activities may be Billable, Non-Billable or provided at No Charge.

> **NOTES**
> If there is no checkmark in the Stopwatch column, clicking will add it. Clicking will also remove the checkmark once it is there.

If an activity is billable, you can use the **Timer** in this window to track the time worked on the activity. Some businesses track all time spent for a customer. For example, if a customer phones for advice, and telephone advice is a billable activity, you can start the timer at the beginning of the phone call and then stop it at the end to have an accurate measure of the duration of the call.

To use the timer, click the **Start** button. The counter will keep time in seconds until you click the **Stop** button. You can use this measurement as the actual time. Select the customer in the Customer column and enter the activity.

To apply the time to a customer, ensure the **Stopwatch column** has a ✓ and then click the **Apply Time** button. The stopwatch time will be entered in the Actual, Billable and Payroll Time columns.

> **NOTES**
> The best way to learn the formats for entering times is to enter different numbers and observe how Sage 50 records them in the journal.

Time is entered as the number of hours, minutes and seconds (hhmmss). You can also enter the times as decimal amounts, such as 2.75 for two hours and 45 minutes. The simplest way to explain the format for entering time is with a few examples. The following chart summarizes the examples and outlines some of the rules:

EXAMPLES OF TIME ENTRIES IN THE TIME SLIPS JOURNAL

Entering This Number	Records This Time	Displays in Journal as
1 or 01 or 100 or 10000	Records 1 hour	01:00:00
001 or 0001 or 000100	Records 1 minute	00:01:00
00001 or 000001	Records 1 second	00:00:01
130 or 0130 or 013000	Records 1.5 hours (1 hour and 30 minutes)	01:30:00
0110 or 110 or 11000	Records 1 hour and 10 minutes	01:10:00
1030 or 103000	Records 10 hours and 30 minutes	10:30:00
11515 or 011515	Records 1 hour, 15 minutes and 15 seconds	01:15:15
995959	Records 99 hours, 59 minutes and 59 seconds	99:59:59

RULES FOR TIME ENTRIES IN THE TIME SLIPS JOURNAL

- You can enter up to six digits (hhmmss). A one- or two-digit number is always interpreted as the number of hours (zero minutes, zero seconds). The remaining missing digits are always assumed to be zero.
- For a three-digit entry, the first number represents hours and the next two represent the minutes.
- For a four-digit number, the first two numbers represent hours and the next two represent minutes.
- For a five-digit number, the first number represents the number of hours, the next two, minutes, and the final two, seconds.
- For a six-digit entry, the first two numbers represent hours, the next two, minutes, and the last two, seconds.
- You can omit seconds and minutes if they are zero. Leading zeros are not needed for hours.
- The times allowed on a line for one activity range from the shortest time of 1 second, entered as 000001 or 00001, to the longest, 99 hours, 59 minutes and 59 seconds, entered as 995959.

NOTES

Decimals are not used for the display of the time entries. The format for the displayed time is hours, minutes and seconds (hh:mm:ss), even when you enter the time with decimals.

There are three columns for time: the **Actual Time** spent at the activity, the **Billable Time** or amount of time that the customer pays for, and the **Payroll Time** or hours the employee is paid for. Sometimes the customer is billed for fewer hours than the job actually required. For example, if an estimate has been given and the work is much more complex than anticipated, a business will usually not bill the customer for the full amount in the interest of good customer relations. At other times, the customer may be charged for more time than the activity requires. For example, a job may have a minimum time component, such as one hour of labour. Most companies will want to keep track of all times so that they can revise their prices to reflect their true costs.

Mercier spent 3 hours packing the five boxes (actual time); the customer will pay for 2.5 hours of work (billable time for five boxes); and Mercier will be paid for 3 hours of work for this job (payroll time).

NOTES

An employee may be paid for the actual number of hours, the billable number of hours or some other time agreed on between the employee and the employer. For example, the pay may be limited to a maximum number of hours for a specific job to encourage efficient work habits.

Click the **Actual Time field.**

Type 3 **Press** tab to update the time slip:

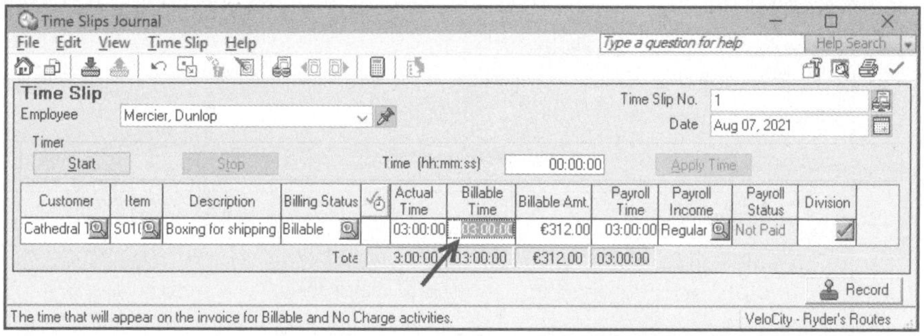

The program enters 03:00:00, the actual time, as the billable time and the payroll time. The price (**Billable Amt.**) is the billable time multiplied by the price from the ledger — €52 per box (half-hour). The currency is added for foreign currency amounts.

For this customer, five bicycles were packed for shipping. Recall that we entered 30 minutes as the usual time (or 0.5 hours) for the job. The hourly rate was determined as the Selling Price divided by the usual number of hours, that is, €52 (for 30 minutes) divided by 0.5, or €104 per hour. Thus the amount for 2.5 hours is 2.5 × €104, or €260.

The **Payroll Status** is Not Paid. You can edit the billable time, the billable amount, the payroll time and payroll income category for individual activities. We need to change the billable time to 2.5 hours, 2 hours and 30 minutes. The billable time is already selected.

Type 230 or 2.5 **Press** tab to update the billable amount to €260.

Click the **Customer list icon** and **select Niagara Rapids Inn** for the second activity.

Click the **Item list icon** and **select S060 Repairs**.

Click the **Actual Time column**.

Type 4 **Press** tab. **Type** 330 to update the Billable Time and Amount.

NOTES

Remember that a single digit represents the number of hours.

The currency of the customer is used for prices on time slips.

Repair service work is billed at a straight hourly rate, so the amount is the billable time multiplied by the hourly rate for the preferred customer.

Click the **Customer list icon** on the next line. **Select Niagara Rapids Inn** again.

Click the **Item list icon** and **select S030 Maintenance: complete tune-up**.

Click the **Actual Time column**. **Type** 2 **Press** tab.

This time the flat rate of $65 is entered for the preferred price customer and you cannot edit the billable time. However, you can edit the billable amount.

Click the **Customer list icon** and **select Niagara Rapids Inn** for the fourth activity.

Click the **Item list icon** and **select S100 Warranty Repairs**.

Click the **Actual Time column**.

Type 4 **Press** tab. No amount is entered because the activity is non-billable, but the hours are added to the employee's payroll time.

Click the **Customer list icon** and **select Festival Tours**.

Click the **Item list icon** and **select S100 Warranty Repairs**.

Click the **Actual Time column**.

Type 2 **Press** tab to complete the entry:

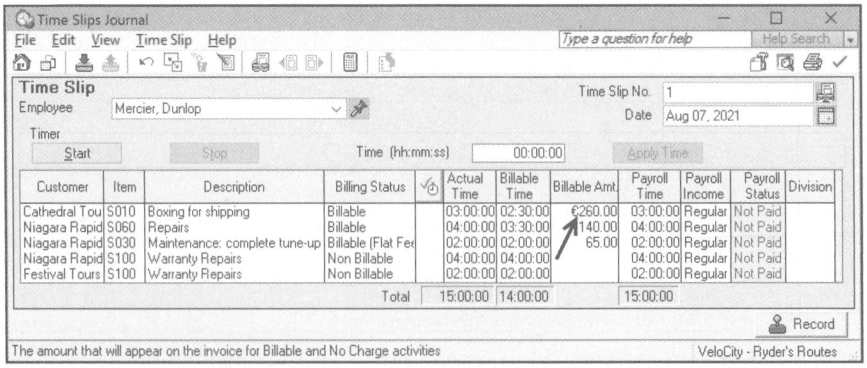

WARNING!

There is no journal entry to review the time slip, so check it carefully.

You can adjust the time slip if you find an error after you record it.

You cannot reverse time slips automatically. If you selected the wrong employee, edit the time slip by deleting all time entries. The program will remove the time slip from the system.

Check the **time slip** carefully before recording and **correct mistakes**.

You can also allocate time slip details to divisions — on the basis of either percent or time (from the Division settings, as on page 505) and on the basis of actual, billable or payroll time (from the Allocate Based On drop-down list in the next screen).

Click the Division column for the activity line to open the Allocation screen:

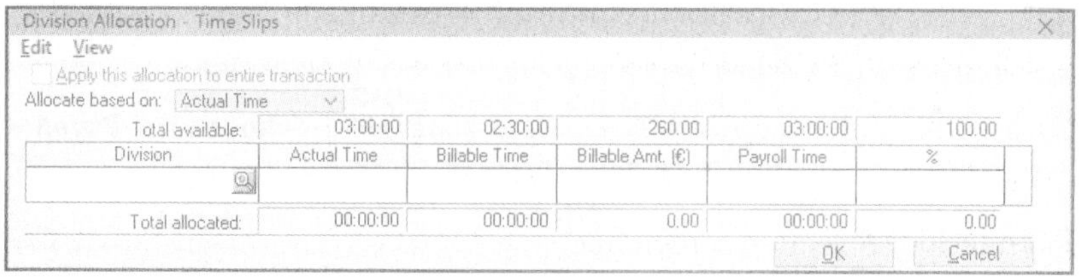

Choose the basis of allocation and division. Enter the time or percentage allocated to the division for that activity. Click OK to return to the journal when finished.

Click the **Record button** Record to save the entry.

Complete **Time Slip #2** and then **close** the **Time Slips Journal**.

> **NOTES**
> You can allocate on the basis of actual, billable or employee time, or on a percentage basis. You can choose separately for each activity or apply the same allocation to the entire time slip.

> **NOTES**
> The successful recording confirmation message does not include a journal entry number.

☐ 9

TIME SLIP #2 **DATED AUGUST 7, 2021**

For Yvonne Leader

Customer	Item	Actual Time	Billable Time	Billable Amount	Taxable	Payroll Time
Cathedral Tours	S080	13 hours	12 hours	€660.00	no	13 hours
Cathedral Tours	S070	3 hours	2 hours	€200.00	no	3 hours
Festival Tours	S080	8 hours	8 hours	USD $480.00	yes	8 hours
Niagara Rapids Inn*	S070	4 hours	3.5 hours	$420.00	yes	4 hours

> **NOTES**
> Service items S070 and S080 are not taxed when they are provided outside of Canada. They are deemed to be part of the tour. Services provided in Canada are taxable.
> The * indicates that preferred customer prices apply.

Add a **shortcut** for the **Time Slips Journal**. **Choose** **Create Time Slip** under the Time & Billing heading.

Paying Employees from Time Slips

After filling in the time slips, we use them to prepare paycheques.

✓ 10

Employee Time Summary Sheet #20 **Dated August 7, 2021**

For the Pay Period ending August 7, 2021

Use time slips to prepare the paycheque for Yvonne Leader for one week. Issue deposit slip #37. Pay Dunlop Mercier for 80 regular hours in the two-week period plus 2 hours of overtime. Recover $50 loaned and issue deposit slip #38.

> **NOTES**
> You cannot enter a date prior to August 1. Mercier is currently owed for two weeks of work.

Open the **Payroll Journal**.

Choose **Leader** from the Employee list and **press** tab to enter her information.

Enter **August 1** as the Period Start Date and **August 7** as the Cheque Date and the Period End Date to update the paycheque:

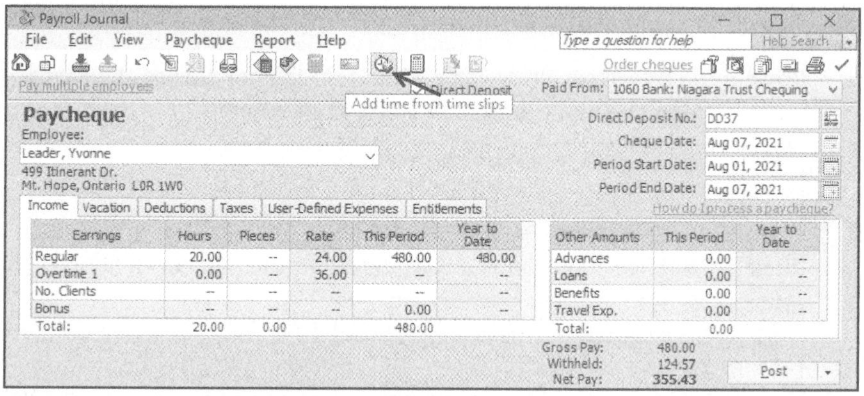

> **NOTES**
> You can also add time slips information in the Payroll Cheque Run Journal by selecting the employees and clicking the Add Time tool button or by choosing Add Time From Time Slips from the Payroll menu. The option to increase the number of hours to those in the ledger record must be applied the same way – to all employees or to none of them.

When activities are set up in the Inventory and Services Ledger and time slips are entered for employees, Sage 50 tracks the hours worked so you can use the summary of these time slips to prepare paycheques.

NOTES
The Time Slip tool remains unavailable until you select an employee.

We will use this method to prepare the paycheque for the new employee, Yvonne Leader, because these activities are her primary responsibility. We are using the Payroll Journal to demonstrate the Sage 50 options for processing time slips.

Click the **Add Time From Time Slips tool** or **choose** the **Paycheque menu** and **click Add Time From Time Slips**.

The Payroll Hour Selection screen opens:

When you choose Pay Employee From Time Slip from the Employees & Payroll module Time Slips icon, a Search window opens. After you select the employee, the Payroll Hour Selection screen opens with the Payroll Journal in the background.

You should enter the dates for the time slips that apply to this pay period. Leader has worked for one week; therefore, you should include the time slips up to August 7.

These dates are entered as the defaults because we already entered August 7 as the period ending date and August 1 is the date Leader was hired.

Click **OK** to return to the journal.

The number of hours is updated and the journal entry is completed:

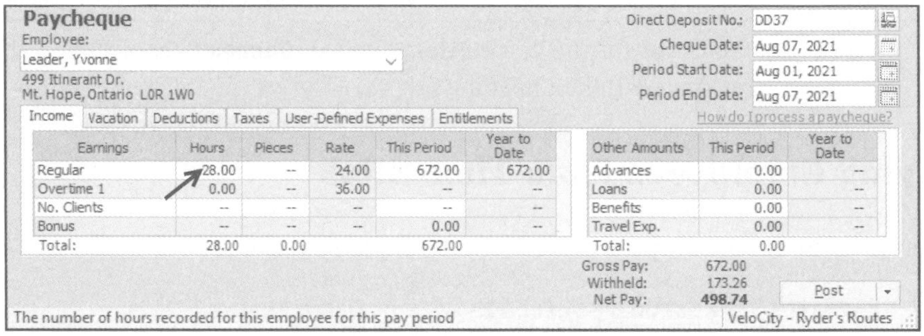

You can edit the number of hours as usual if necessary, and you can add advances or other deductions if they are appropriate.

Review the **journal entry** and, when you are certain it is correct,

Click **Post** to save the transaction. **Click Yes** to continue.

Choose **Mercier** from the Employee list and press *tab*.

Enter **August 1** as the Pay Period Start Date and **August 7** as the Pay Period End and Cheque Dates.

August 1 is the earliest transaction date allowed in the system settings.

Click the **Add Time From Time Slips tool** or **choose** the **Paycheque menu** and **click Add Time From Time Slips**:

WARNING!
You must complete the step of adding time from the time slips. If you do not, the payroll status for these activities will remain as Not Paid and the employee could be incorrectly paid a second time for the same work.

You must also complete this step before adding overtime hours.

Click **OK**. Sage 50 presents a warning about the number of hours:

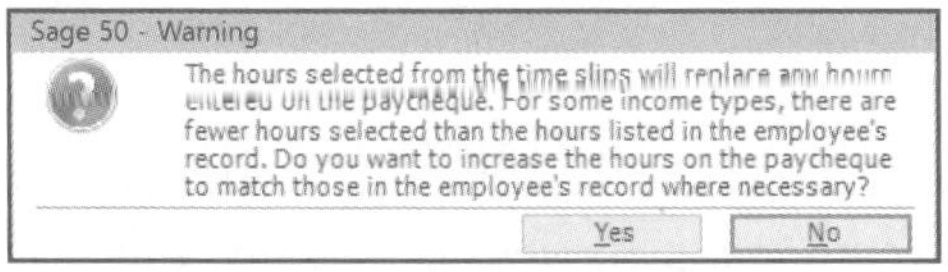

For Mercier, the hours worked exceed the hours on his time slip for the various customer jobs because he also performs other duties at the store. You have the option of

accepting the time slip information or increasing the hours to match the default in the employee records. For Mercier, the Payroll Ledger entry is the correct one.

Click **Yes** to increase the number of hours and return to the journal. The number of Regular hours remains unchanged at 80 hours.

Click the **Overtime 1 field**. **Type** 2 to add the overtime hours.

Click the **Loans field** and **accept** the **default** $50 remaining to be repaid.

Review the **journal entry** and make corrections if necessary.

Click **Post**. **Click** **Yes** to continue and save the transaction.

Close the **Payroll Journal**.

The program will update the Payroll Hours Selection dates for the next paycheque and the Payroll Status on these Time Slips.

Open the **Time Slips Journal** from the shortcut or from the icon.

Click the **Look Up Time Slips tool**.

Type 2 in the Time Slip Number field. **Click** **OK** to open Leader's time slip.

The time slip information has Paid in the Payroll Status column for each job completed by this employee, indicating that the employee has been paid for the work on this time sheet. You cannot use this time slip information for payroll again.

Click the **Look Up Time Slips tool** and **type** 1 in the Time Slip Number field. **Click** **OK** to review Mercier's time slip.

His payroll status is also marked as Paid because we added time from the time slips, even though the hours were not used to determine his pay.

Close the **Time Slips Journal**.

Preparing Sales Invoices from Time Slips

When sales invoices are prepared for mailing to customers, the service activities completed for this customer from time slips for all employees can be added directly to the invoices without re-entering each activity.

Click **Receivables** in the Modules pane list, if necessary.

Click the **Sales Invoices icon** to open the Sales Journal.

✓ 11

Sales Invoice #2228 **Dated August 7, 2021**

To Cathedral Tours: Complete sales invoice for €1 120 plus HST from time slip activities. Include all activities to date. Enter H as the tax code for S010. Sales invoice total €1 153.80. Terms: 2/10, n/30. The exchange rate is 1.525.

Choose **Cathedral Tours** as the customer. Invoice and Pay Later are correct.

Enter **August 7, 2021** as the invoice date and **1.525** as the **exchange rate**.

Time slip activities may be entered using the tool icon or the Sales menu option:

NOTES
When you add time slip hours in the Payroll Run Journal, you must do so for all selected employees. You cannot choose individual employees for this. You get the confirmation message about number of hours being increased, but again, it will apply to all employees.

NOTES
When you use the time slip number to look up the time slip, the Previous and Next tools will not be available.
You can Search All Employees in the Search lookup window and click OK to list all the time slips and then select one, as we did in other journals. This approach will make the Next and Previous tools available.

NOTES
From the Receivables module Time Slips icon shortcuts list, you can choose Create Invoice From Time Slip. After choosing the customer from the Select Customer screen, the Service Activities Selection screen on page 760 opens for that customer.

NOTES
If necessary, scroll or change the column width to include all the columns.

NOTES
Selecting non-billable activities will include Warranty Repair hours on the selection list. Non-billable activities are not added to the sales invoice.

Click the **Add Time Slip Activities tool** or **choose** the **Sales menu** and **click Add Time Slip Activities** to open the activities list for this customer:

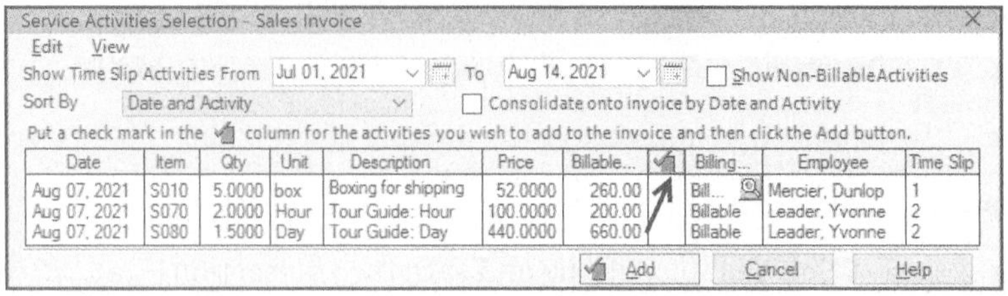

Services provided to the customer by all employees will be listed, and you can also include Non-Billable Activities by clicking its check box. You may need to scroll to include information in all columns. You can Sort the list By Date And Activity, the default, By Employee And Activity or By Activity. You can also Consolidate the list By Date And Activity, combining the amounts for each activity recorded for the same date. You can select all the activities for the invoice or omit some if they are incomplete or come after the billing date. All activities should be included on the invoice for Cathedral Tours.

NOTES
Clicking , the Add Activity column heading, will select all the activities in the list. Then you can click any activity to deselect it if you need to.

Enter **Aug 1 2021** and **Aug 7 2021** as the date range in the Show Time Slip Activities From and To date fields.

Click the **Add Activity column** for the first activity, S010. Only activities with a ✓ in this column are added to the sales invoice.

Click the **Add Activity column** for the remaining activities.

Click the **Add button** Add to return to the Sales Journal.

The activities are now added to the journal.

WARNING!
Enter tax codes on sales invoices for foreign customers carefully. Refer to the Time Slip if necessary.

Taxes are charged on the boxing service for Canadian customers on European tours because the work was completed in Canada, so we need to change this tax code entry.

Double-click the **blank Tax code field for item S010**, and **choose H** as the code to complete the entry:

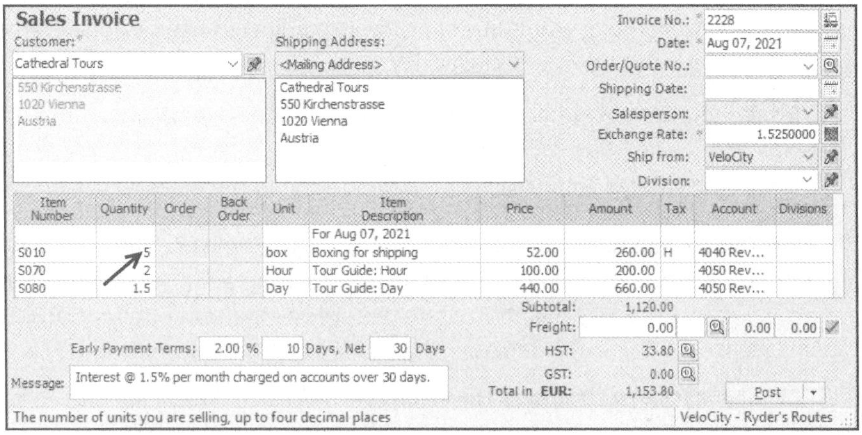

NOTES
You can edit the amount billed to the customer in the Sales Journal by changing the Amount or the Price. You can also choose a different account number for the sales.

The Quantity refers to the units in the ledger — for S010, the customer pays for five completed units or boxes at one-half hour each. On the time sheet, we entered 230 (or 2.5) as the billable time. The 12 hours of tour guide service are entered as 1.5 days, the unit in the ledger. You can add other regular services or inventory to the sales invoice if they were sold to the same customer; you do not need to create a separate invoice for them.

You should review the journal entry before posting it.

NOTES
If the information in the time slip was incorrect, close the Sales Journal without posting the invoice and adjust the time slip. Then re-enter the sales invoice.

Choose the **Report menu** and **click Display Sales Journal Entry**:

VeloCity - Ryder's Routes
Sales Journal Entry 08/07/2021 (J4)

Account Number	Account Description	Foreign A...	Debits	Credits
1200	Accounts Receivable	€1,153.80	1,759.55	-
2650	GST/HST Charged on Sales	€33.80	-	51.55
4040	Revenue from Services	€260.00	-	396.50
4050	Revenue from Tours	€860.00	-	1,311.50
1 Euro equals 1.5250000 Canadian Dollars			1,759.55	1,759.55

The journal entry is like other sales journal entries.

Close the **report** after viewing it and **make corrections** if necessary.

To correct the activities, click the Add Time Slip Activities tool to return to the Service Activities Selection list. Previously selected activities have Invoiced in the Billing Status column.

Clicking the Add Activity column will add the ✓ and restore the status to Billable so you can select a different group of activities.

Click Post to save the journal entry.

Enter the next **four transactions**.

NOTES
If you look up the time slip now, the billing status will have changed to Invoiced.

NOTES
Selecting non-billable activities will add Warranty Repairs to the selection lists for Niagara Rapids Inn and Festival Tours. However, this service will not be added to the invoice.

12 **Sales Invoice #2229** **Dated August 7, 2021**

To Niagara Rapids Inn: Complete sales invoice for $625 plus HST from time slip activities. Include all activities to date. Sales invoice total $706.25. Terms: 2/10, n/30.

13 **Sales Invoice #2230** **Dated August 7, 2021**

To Festival Tours: Complete sales invoice for $480 USD from time slip activities. Include all activities to date. No tax is charged for tours in the United States. Sales invoice total $480 USD. Terms: 2/10, n/30. The exchange rate is 1.329.

NOTES
Click the Exchange Rate tool or type in the new rate for the sale to Festival Tours. The option to change the rate will not open automatically.

14 **Receipt #825** **Dated August 7, 2021**

From Fallsview Riverside Resort, cheque #1628 for $5 695.20 in full payment of account. Reference sales invoice #2224.

15 **Memo #8-8** **Dated August 7, 2021**

From Visa, received monthly credit card statement for $98 for purchases made before August 1, 2021. Submitted cheque #1146 for $98 in full payment.

Building New Inventory

Instead of assembling inventory using the Item Assembly method, you can set up the inventory assembly components in the ledger record and then use this information to build an item using the Bill of Materials method. We will create the new inventory Promotional Safety Package, including the items or materials that make up the package.

✓ 16 **Memo #8-9** **Dated August 7, 2021**

Create a new inventory record for a Promotional Safety Package that bundles several popular accessories. Create new Group asset linked account: 1510 Promotions.

Item: AP100 Promotional Safety Package
Unit: package
Minimum: 0
Linked accounts: Asset 1510 Promotions; Revenue 4020; COGS 5050

Currency	**CAD**	**USD**	**Euro**
Regular Selling Price	$375	$280	€260
Preferred Selling Price	$350	$255	€240

NOTES
The unbundled selling price for the Promotional Safety Package items would be $405.

Tax exempt: No

Build Components: use 1 of each AC020 Bicycle Pump: hand-held mini
AC030 Helmet
AC040 Light: halogen
AC060 Lock: kryptonite tube
AC070 Pannier: front wicker clip-on
and 2 of AC050 Light: rear reflector

Choose **Inventory & Services** from the Modules pane list.

Choose **Add Inventory & Service** from the Inventory & Services icon shortcuts list to open the Inventory Ledger for new Service Activity items. The cursor is in the Item Number field.

Type AP100 **Press** tab.

Type Promotional Safety Package

Click **Inventory** as the Type to modify the form for the inventory item.

The Units tab screen is displayed. All units are the same for this package.

Double-click **Each** and **type** package

Click the **Quantities tab**. The Minimum level is correct at 0.

Click the **Pricing tab** to access the price fields.

On the Pricing tab screen, you can enter regular and preferred prices in all the currencies that you have set up. Canadian prices are given initially.

Click the **Regular Price Per Selling Unit field**.

Type 375 **Press** tab to advance to the Preferred Price field.

Type 350

Choose **United States Dollars** from the Currency list.

Foreign prices for Ryder's Routes are fixed, so we need to change the default setting. Clicking the entry will change the setting.

Click **Exchange Rate** beside Regular to change the setting to Fixed Price.

Press tab to advance to the Regular Selling Price for United States Dollars.

Type 280 **Press** tab to advance to the Preferred Pricing Method.

Click **Exchange Rate** to change the setting to Fixed Price. **Press** tab.

Type 255

Choose **Euro** from the currency list.

Click **Exchange Rate** beside Regular to change the setting to Fixed Price.

Press tab to advance to the Regular Price for Euro.

Type 260 **Press** tab to advance to the Preferred Pricing Method.

Click **Exchange Rate** to change the setting. **Press** tab. **Type** 240

Click the **Linked tab** to open the Linked Accounts screen.

Click the **Asset field**.

Type 1510 Promotions **Press** tab. We need to add the account.

Click **Add** and **press** tab to open the Add Account wizard.

Accept the remaining **defaults** for the account and **click Yes** to change the account class.

Press *tab* to advance to the Revenue account field.

Type 4020 **Press** *tab* to advance to the COGS account field.

Type 5050

The variance linked account is not needed — the package will not be oversold.

Click the **Taxes tab** to open the list of sales taxes relating to the inventory.

The default entry No for Tax Exempt is correct — HST is charged on the sale of this item. Duty is not charged on this item because it is not purchased.

Click the **Build tab** to access the information screen we need for entering the assembly or building components for inventory items:

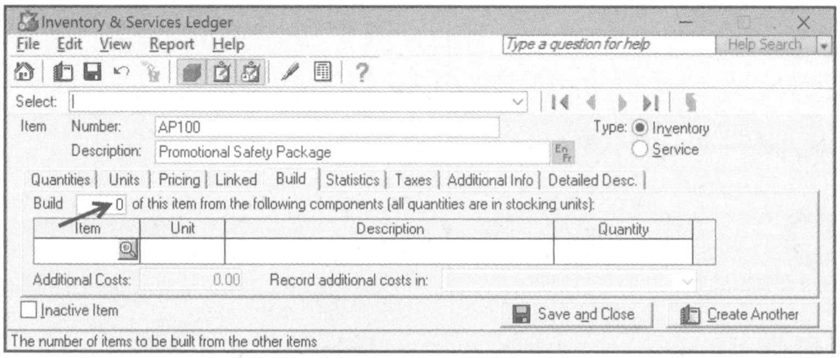

On this screen, we enter the relationship between the new inventory and its components — that is, how many new items we are building and how many of each input item this number of units requires. This is very similar to the Item Assembly Journal, except that we are only defining the building process at this stage. The actual building or assembly still takes place in the journal. One package is created from this set of accessories — we are defining the rules for building one package.

Click the **Build field** to enter the default number of packages being assembled from this set of components.

Type 1 **Press** *tab* to advance to the Item (number) field.

Click the **List icon** and **select AC020 Bicycle Pump: hand-held mini** to enter the first item.

The cursor advances to the Quantity field after entering the unit and description. Here you need to enter the number of pumps included in each Promotional Safety Package. We are defining the unit relationship between the assembled item and its components. One component item is used to make the package.

Type 1 **Press** *tab* to advance to the second Item line.

Enter the **next four components** and **enter 1** as the quantity for each. For **A050**, **enter 2** as the quantity.

The **Additional Costs** and its linked account field (**Record Additional Costs In**) became available once we entered the number of units to build. These fields have the same meaning as they do in the Item Assembly Journal. However, in the Bill of Materials method, costs are entered in the ledger record and separate assembly linked accounts can be defined for each item. There are no additional costs associated with creating the package, so we should leave these fields blank.

Click the **Quantities tab**.

NOTES

You can mark the new inventory as exempt for GST, but you do not need to do so.

NOTES

This screen is similar to the upper Components section of the Item Assembly Journal (page 378), but you cannot enter unit costs for the components.

NOTES

In the Pro version, there is one linked Item Assembly Costs account for the ledger, and it is entered on the Inventory Linked Accounts screen. This linked account is used for all Build From Item Assembly transactions in both Pro and Premium versions.

In the Premium version, you can enter a different linked account for additional costs for each item you build. These different linked accounts will be used for Build From Bill Of Materials transactions.

The quantity on hand remains at zero until we build the item in the journal. Quantities for the component items also remain unchanged.

NOTES
Built items may also be purchased if this is appropriate. They are available for selection in the Purchases Journal.

Correct any **errors** by returning to the field with the mistake. **Highlight** the **error** and **enter** the **correct information**. **Click** the different **tabs** to check all the information that you entered.

Click  to save the record.

Building an Inventory Item in the Journal

The quantity of Promotional Safety Packages is still zero. In order to create stock of the package for sale, we must build the item in the Bill Of Materials & Item Assembly Journal:

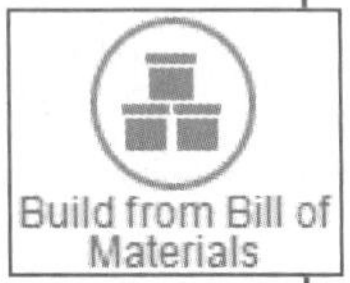

CLASSIC VIEW
Click the Bill Of Materials & Item Assembly icon  to open the journal. Choose Build From Bill Of Materials from the Build drop-down transactions list if necessary.

✓ 17

Memo #8-10 **Dated August 7, 2021**

Build five (5) packages of the new item Promotional Safety Package (AP100).

Click the **Build From Bill Of Materials icon** to open the journal:

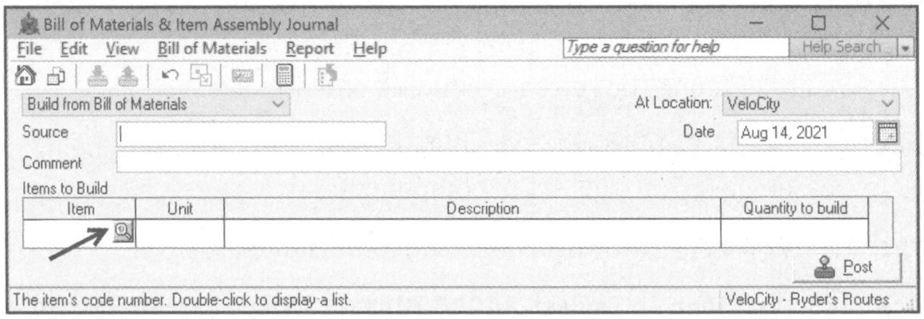

NOTES
Remember that you can choose Build From Item Assembly or Build From Bill Of Materials from the transactions drop-down list once the journal is open (refer to page 377).

In the Premium version, you can assemble new inventory items either by using the Item Assembly method that we used in previous applications or the Bill of Materials method that follows.

The journal resembles the lower half of the Build From Item Assembly Journal screen, the Assembled Items section, but without components and costs (refer to page 377). Information for the upper half of the Item Assembly screen — for components and costs — is located in the ledger record. The default location is VeloCity.

NOTES
The additional costs and the components information are taken from the ledger record – the Build tab screen details. Item cost, as usual, is the average cost for each component because we selected this method for the company file (refer to page 662).

Click the **Source field**.

Type `Memo 8-10` **Press** *tab* to advance to the Date field.

Type `8-7` **Press** *tab* **twice** to advance to the Comment field.

Type `Create promotional packages` **Press** *tab*. The cursor moves to the Item field.

Click the **List icon** to open the selection list:

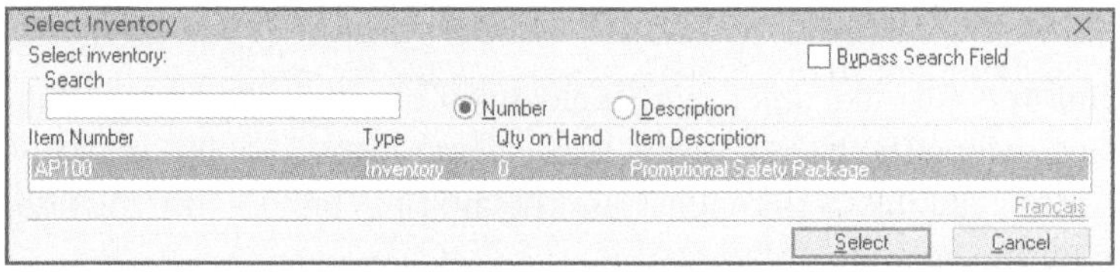

All items for which you have added build information will be listed on this screen. Because we have entered these details only for the Promotional Safety Package, it is the only one listed. You cannot create a new item from this Select screen.

Double-click **AP100** to add it to the journal.

The unit and description are added for the package and the default quantity is 1. These details are taken from the ledger record. The quantity is selected, so we can change it. We are creating five packages.

Type 5 to complete the journal entry:

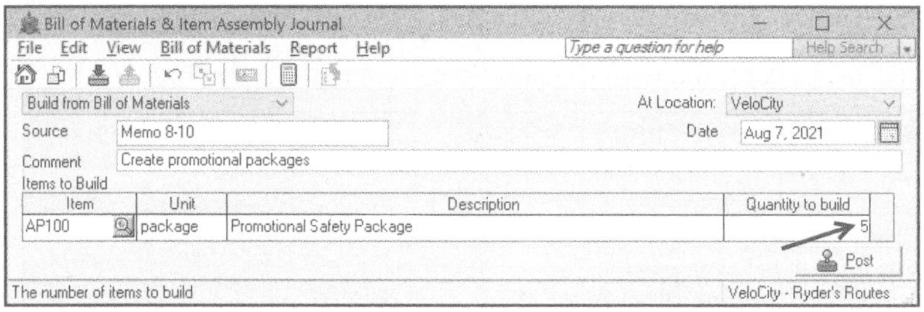

If you have other items to build, you can continue by choosing the items and entering quantities for each of them.

Review your **work** before posting the transaction.

Choose the **Report menu** and **click Display Bill Of Materials & Item Assembly Journal** to display the journal transaction:

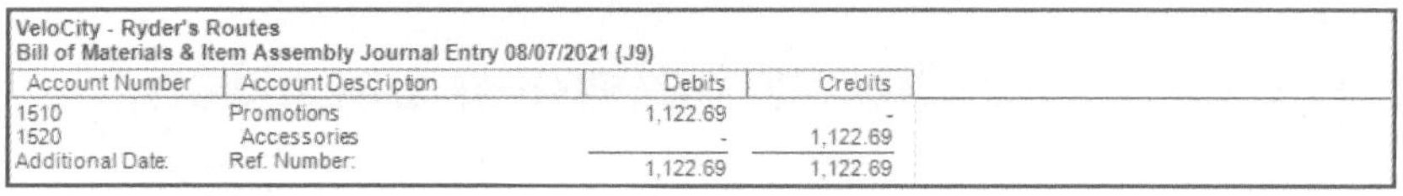

VeloCity - Ryder's Routes
Bill of Materials & Item Assembly Journal Entry 08/07/2021 (J9)
Account Number
Account Description
Debits
Credits
1510
Promotions
1,122.69
-
1520
Accessories
-
1,122.69
Additional Date:
Ref. Number:
1,122.69
1,122.69

The asset account balances have been updated by the transaction, just as they are in an Item Assembly transaction. Compare this journal entry with the one on page 379. The inventory quantities are also updated from the transaction — the quantity of packages increases and the quantities for the component accessory items decrease. Additional costs, if any, would be credited to the linked cost account for the package and debited to the assembled item asset account.

Close the **journal display** and **make corrections** if necessary.

If there is not enough inventory of any item in stock to complete the build, Sage 50 will ask you to reduce the quantity to build:

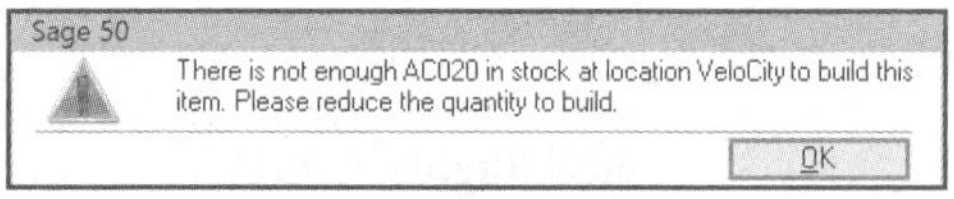

Click OK and reduce the number of units you are building.

Click Post to save the entry. **Close** the **advisor** about low inventory.

Click the Item List icon — the number of promotional packages has been changed to five. Click Cancel to close this screen without making a selection.

You can now sell the package just like any other inventory item.

NOTES

You cannot change the unit cost using the Build method. The Cost fields are not available in the journal or in the ledger record.

The default quantity is taken from the ledger record's Build tab screen, where we entered the rule for building one item at a time.

NOTES

When you link the same asset account to the assembled item and its components, you will get the message that no journal entry results from the transaction. However, all inventory quantities are updated by the transaction.

NOTES

The insufficient quantity note refers only to the first item in the entry. If other items also have insufficient quantities, they will be mentioned in subsequent messages.

NOTES

Quantities do not change till you have posted the transaction.

Multiple Levels of Build

You can use a built item just like any other single inventory item. The process is the same when you are selling the item or using it as a component to build other inventory. We created an additional built item to illustrate the multiple build — we include the next two screenshots for information only.

Nested building components are common in construction work. When you use a built item as a component for a second-stage build, you select it on the Build tab screen just like other inventory. When you are building the new second-stage item in the Bill of Materials Journal, the built component may be out of stock. In this case, Sage 50 offers to build the missing item when you try to post the entry:

You can now automatically build the primary item, the built component, as part of the same journal transaction.

Click Yes to continue with the additional build:

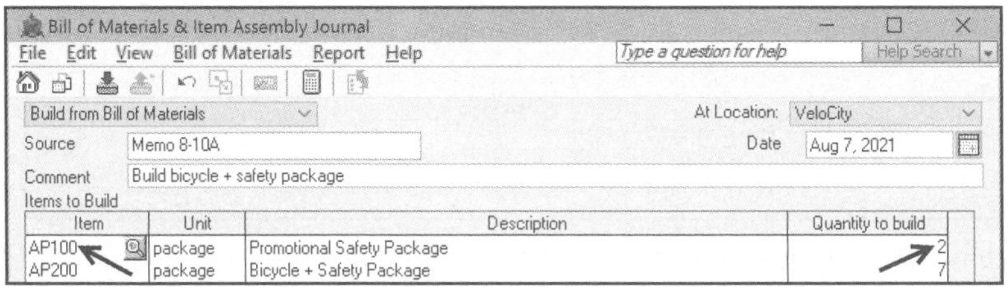

Sage 50 will add the out-of-stock built item to the journal as the first item to build. The number of units built will be those required to complete the secondary build.

Close the **Journal**.

NOTES

If there are further layers of building nested in a transaction, Sage 50 will offer to build the necessary components at each stage in the same way to complete the initial transaction.

The multiple build option lets you build the final items and allow Sage 50 to complete the intermediate builds.

Transferring Inventory between Locations

Items can be transferred from one location where the stock is available or stored to another. In Sage 50, the option to transfer items is available in the Inventory Adjustments & Transfers Journal, accessed from the Transfer Inventory icon:

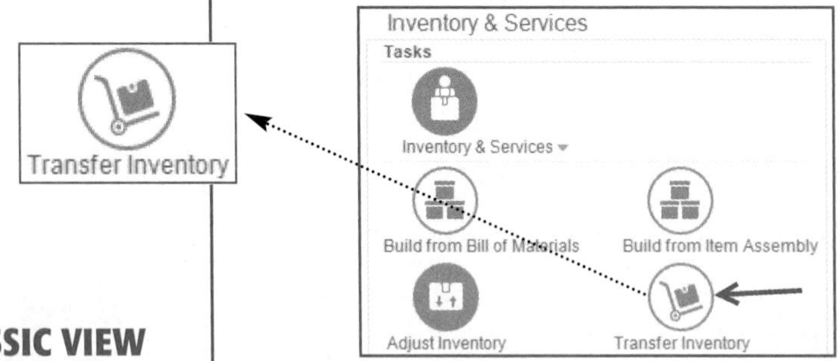

NOTES

Transfers may also be made when the item a customer wants is not located at the store the customer is visiting.

✓ 18	**Memo #8-11**	**Dated August 7, 2021**

The Ryder store is preparing for its official opening. Transfer the following inventory items from the VeloCity store to the Ryder store:

5	AP100 Promotional Safety Package
10	AC030 Helmet
10	AC040 Light: halogen
20	BK010 Books: Complete Bicycle Guide
20	BK020 Books: Endless Trails

CLASSIC VIEW

Click the Inventory Adjustments & Transfers icon

to open the journal. Choose Transfer Between Locations from the drop-down transactions list if necessary.

Click the **Transfer Inventory icon** to open the journal with Transfer Between Locations, the type of transaction we need, already selected:

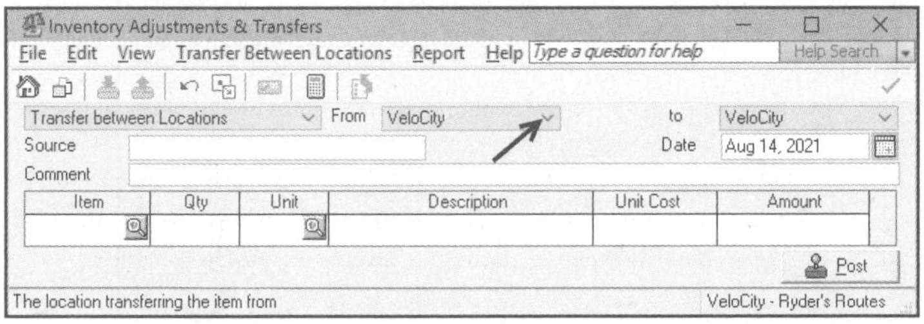

This is the same journal we used for other inventory adjustments in previous chapters, but now there is no field for account numbers. When multiple locations are used, transfers between locations are made in this journal. You can select the type of transaction from the transactions drop-down list:

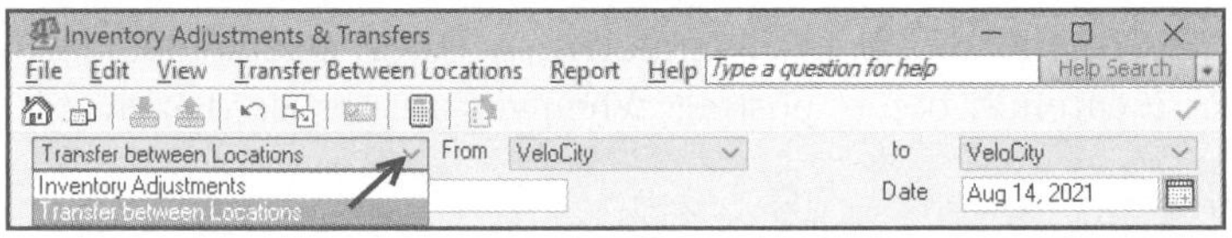

We need to indicate the direction of the transfer, in this case from the VeloCity store to the Ryder store. VeloCity is the default location for both fields because it is the primary location. This is correct as the From location.

Click the **From** drop-down list arrow — both locations are listed.

Click the **To** drop-down list arrow:

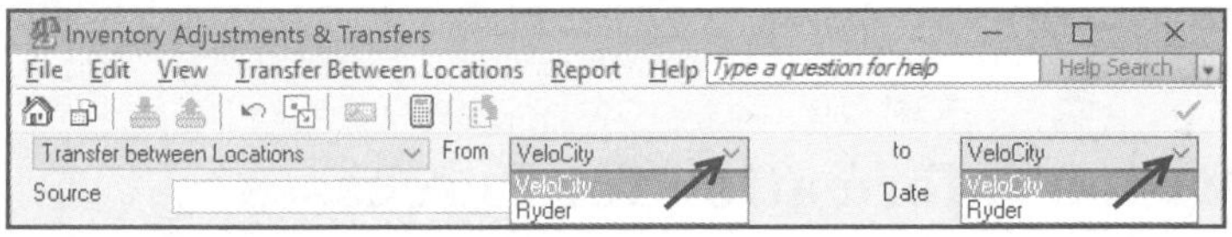

Both locations are available in both lists. You can make transfers to and from either location.

Click **Ryder** to add the second location for the To field.

As for other types of transactions, we need to enter the date, the source and a comment. Then we will enter the items that are being moved.

Click the **Source field**.

Type `Memo 8-11` **Press** *tab* to move to the Date field.

Enter **August 7** as the date of the inventory move.

Click the **Comment field**.

Type `Move inventory to Ryder store`

Press *tab* to advance to the Item code field. A list of items is available, as it is for inventory fields in other journals.

You can access the inventory list by pressing *enter* in the Item field, clicking the List icon or double-clicking the field.

Click the **List icon** and **select AP100**, the first item on the transfer list.

Press *tab* to move to the Qty (quantity) field.

Type 5

NOTES

Both locations are listed in the From and the To location drop-down lists because items may be transferred from either location to the other.

NOTES
Accept your own default cost prices for items transferred.

NOTES
You can store the transfer just like any other transaction. If you need to make a correction later, you can recall the entry to use as a reference for making changes.

NOTES
The successful recording message for the transfer does not include a journal entry number.

Enter the **remaining items** in the same way to complete the entry:

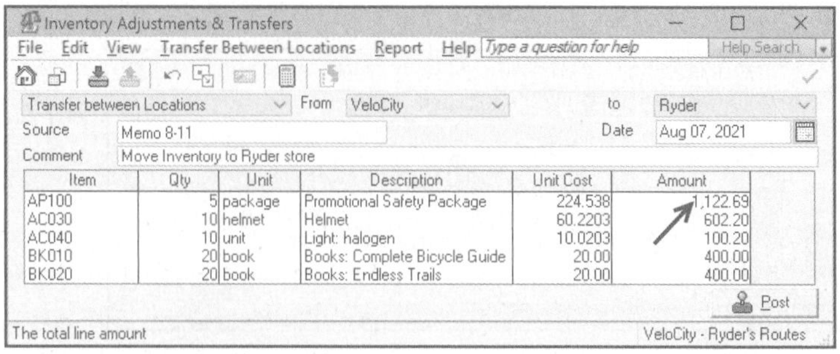

When you record (post) the transfer, the inventory at the two locations will be updated — the quantity at the VeloCity store is reduced and the quantity at the Ryder store is increased. You can verify that the changes have been made by accessing the ledger records for the items and choosing the locations on the Quantity tab screen. However, no journal entry results from this transaction and you cannot look up or adjust the entry, so check it carefully before posting. When you are certain that the transaction is correct, you must save it.

Click Post to save the entry. **Close** the **journal** to return to the Inventory Home window.

CORRECTING THE INVENTORY TRANSFER AFTER POSTING

To correct the transfer after posting, **repeat** the original **transfer** but **reverse** the **direction** of the **transfer** of goods – enter the original From location in the To location field and the original To location in the From location field. Refer to Appendix C, page A–27.

Adding Location Information for Purchases

Now that we have multiple locations for inventory, we must indicate which location the inventory is taken from or sent to when we make purchases, sales and adjustments. By choosing the correct location, we can accurately keep track of the quantity on hand at each store.

The purchase order from Complete Cycler Inc. was delivered to the Ryder store.

✓ 19

Purchase Invoice #CC-3775 **Dated August 10, 2021**

From Complete Cycler Inc. to fill purchase order #43
All items shipped to Ryder store location

2	AC010	Bicycle Pump: standing model	$ 190.00 USD
1	AC020	Bicycle Pump: hand-held mini	380.00 USD
5	AC030	Helmet	2 300.00 USD
5	AC040	Light: halogen	400.00 USD
5	AC050	Light: rear reflector	280.00 USD
18	AC060	Lock: kryptonite tube	2 700.00 USD
		Freight	120.00 USD
		HST	828.10 USD
		Invoice total	$7 198.10 USD

Terms: 2/10, n/30. The exchange rate is 1.325.

WARNING!
You will need to edit the purchase order date before you can fill it. The order quantity for item AC060 has been increased from 8 to 18 and the location has changed.

Open the **Purchases Journal** (click the Create Purchase Invoice shortcut).

Choose PO #43 in the Order No. field and **press** tab.

The order is placed on-screen as an invoice:

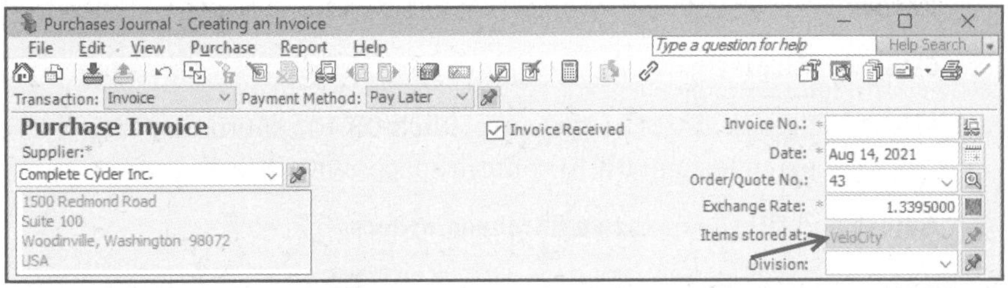

When the order was entered, locations were not set up, so the location field (**Items Stored At**) is dimmed and unavailable. VeloCity, the primary location, is entered, and this is not correct. We need to edit the order to change the location before filling it. We must also change the quantity ordered for item AC060.

Choose **Order** from the Transaction drop-down list to restore the purchase order. **Click Yes** to confirm that you are discarding the invoice.

Choose **PO #43** in the Order No. field list. **Press** tab to place the order on the screen. The fields are still dimmed and cannot be edited.

Click the **Adjust Purchase Order tool**, or **choose** the **Purchase menu** and **click Adjust Purchase Order** or **press** ctrl + **A**.

Click the **Items Stored At drop-down list arrow**:

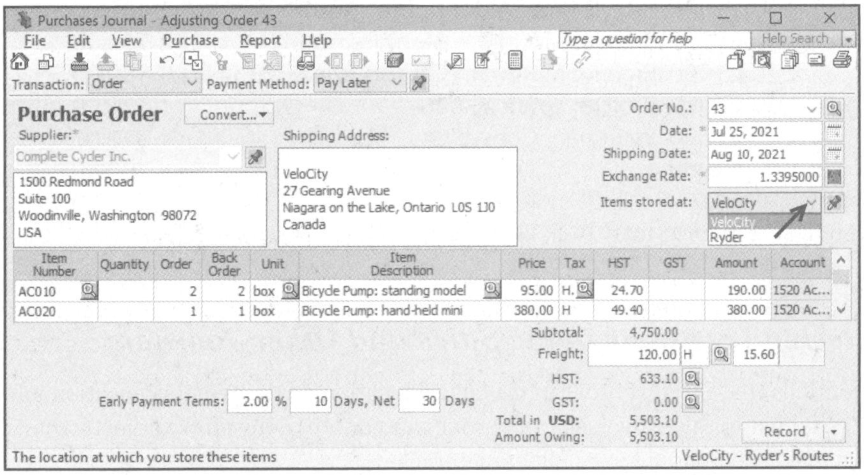

Click **Ryder**. **Enter Aug 10 21** as the order date. If you do not change the date, Sage 50 will warn you because we do not allow dates before August 1:

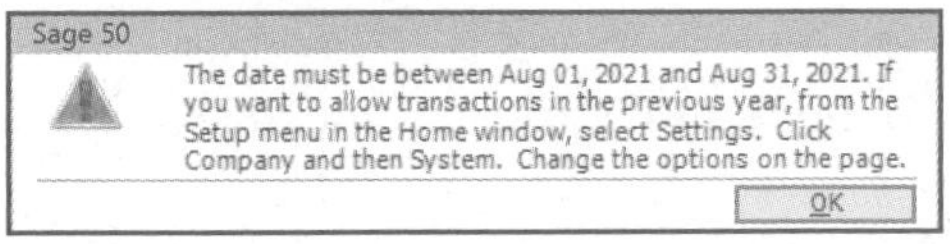

Enter **1.325** as the exchange rate when prompted to change the rate.

Click **8**, the order quantity for AC060 and **type** 18 **Press** tab. We can now fill the order.

Choose **Invoice** from the Transaction drop-down list or **choose Convert This Purchase Order To A Purchase Invoice** from the Convert drop-down list.

Click **Yes** to confirm that you are changing the order to an invoice.

Click the **Fill Backordered Quantities tool**, or **choose** the **Purchase menu** and **click Fill Backordered Quantities**. **Add CC-3775** as the invoice number and **Aug 10** as the invoice date to complete the transaction.

WARNING!

You must change the date for the purchase order. The original purchase order was placed on July 25. You cannot continue with this date because it precedes August 1, the start of the fiscal period and the date in the Do Not Allow Transactions Dated Before (Company, System Settings) field.

NOTES

If the Exchange Rate screen opens again, click Cancel because we already entered the date for August 10.

When you convert the order to an invoice, check the date – it may have reset to the session date.

NOTES
Location details are not included in the journal entry, but the inventory records will be correctly updated.

Review your **journal entry**. Location details are not added to the journal entry.

Close the **display** when finished and make corrections if necessary.

Click Post to save the entry. **Click OK** to confirm that the order has been filled and **OK** to confirm successful posting.

Adjust and **fill** the next **two purchase orders.**

NOTES
Add Ryder as the location. Enter August 10 as the Order Date to adjust purchase order #41. Fill the order and add WD-4558 as the invoice number.

20

Purchase Invoice #WD-4558 **Dated August 10, 2021**

From Wheel Deals to fill purchase order #41
All items shipped to Ryder store location

10	AC070	Pannier: front wicker clip-on	$380.00 USD
10	AC080	Pannier: rear mesh	290.00 USD
		HST	87.10 USD
		Invoice total	$757.10 USD

Terms: 2/10, n/30. The exchange rate is 1.325.

NOTES
Because you are not adjusting the order, you can leave the original order date unchanged.
Change the payment method to Pay Later.

21

Purchase Invoice #PC-3877 **Dated August 10, 2021**

From Pro Cycles Inc. to fill purchase order #42 for VeloCity store

6	CY010	Bicycle: Commuter Steel frame CX10	$ 1 860.00
10	CY020	Bicycle: Commuter Alum frame CX90	5 400.00
4	CY030	Bicycle: Racer Ultra lite RX480	6 200.00
4	CY040	Bicycle: Trail Alum frame TX560	2 480.00
3	CY050	Bicycle: Mountain Alum frame MX14	2 790.00
4	CY060	Bicycle: Mountain Carbon frame MX34	6 880.00
6	CY070	Bicycle: Youth YX660	1 320.00
4	CY090	Stationary Converter	1 320.00
		Freight	200.00
		HST	3 698.50
		Invoice total	$32 148.50

Terms: 2/10, n/30.

Entering Locations in the Sales and Other Journals

NOTES
Location information may also be entered on the Options tab screens in supplier ledger records (Usually Store Item In field) and customer ledger records (Usually Ship Item From field).

All journals that use inventory items have a location field. Inventory location information can be added to sales invoices (and orders and quotes), inventory adjustments, item assemblies and building from bill of materials.

✓ 22

Sales Invoice #2231 **Dated August 10, 2021**

To Candide's B & B (from VeloCity store)

8	AC030	Helmet	$120/ helmet
4	AC060	Lock: kryptonite tube	70/ lock
4	CY020	Bicycle: Commuter Alum frame CX90	960/ bike
		HST	13%

Terms: 2/10, n/30.

Open the **Sales Journal** and **click** the **Ship From list arrow**:

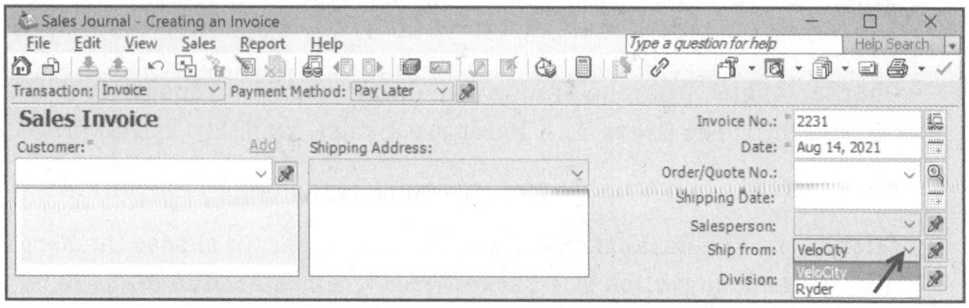

Choose VeloCity. **Enter** the remaining details for **Sales invoice #2231**. **Review** and then **post** the **entry**. **Close** the **Sales Journal**.

The location selection is also available in the Inventory Adjustments and Bill Of Materials & Item Assembly journals from the At Location drop-down list:

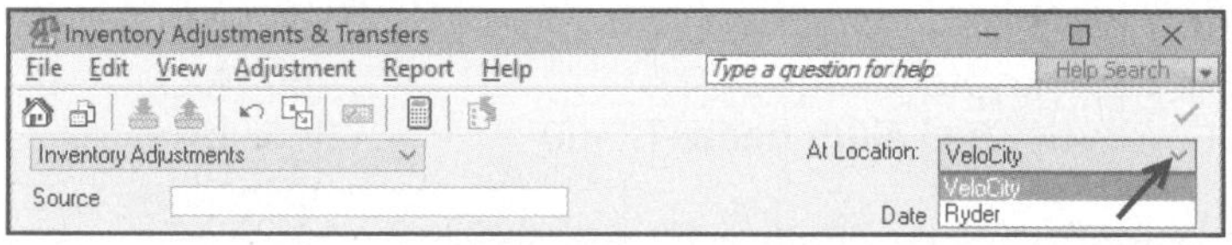

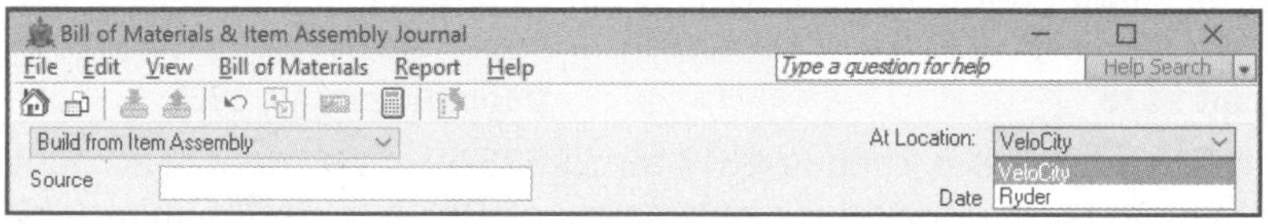

If the location you chose does not have any stock of an item needed to complete the build or assembly, Sage 50 provides an error about the insufficient inventory:

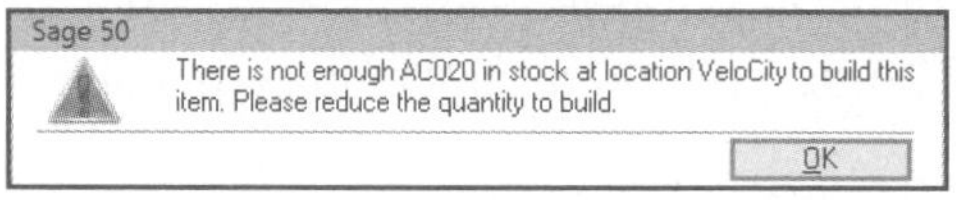

Click OK. In this case, you must first transfer or purchase the required item.

Enter the **remaining transactions** for August up to Memo #8-18.

23 **Memo #8-12** **Dated August 14, 2021**

Remittances: Use the August 1 balances to make the following remittances in the Payments Journal. (Read margin Notes and Warning.)

a) Record payment for GST and HST for July to the Receiver General for Canada. Issue cheque #1147 in payment.
b) Record payment for Garnisheed Wages Payable for July to the Receiver General for Canada. Issue cheque #1148 in full payment.
c) Record payment for EI, CPP and Income Tax Payable for July to the Receiver General for Canada. Issue cheque #1149 in full payment.
d) Record payment for EHT Payable for July for the quarter to the Minister of Finance. Issue cheque #1150 in payment.
e) Record payment for VRSP Payable for July to Manulife Financial. Issue cheque #1151 in payment.
f) Record payment for Savings Plan Payable for July to Escarpment Investments. Issue cheque #1152 in payment.
g) Record payment for Group Insurance Payable for July to Welland Insurance. Issue cheque #1153 in payment.
h) Record payment for Charitable Donations Payable for July to Canadian Cancer Society (employer and employee contributions). Issue cheque #1154 in payment.
i) Record payment for WSIB Payable for the quarter to the Workplace Safety & Insurance Board. Issue cheque #1155 in payment.

24 **Purchase Invoice #ABS-7597** **Dated August 14, 2021**

From ABS International (use Full Add for new foreign supplier)

10 CY040 Bicycle: Trail Alum frame TX560	€3 800.00
Freight	100.00
HST	507.00
Purchase invoice total	€4 407.00

The duty rate for these items is 0%.
Terms: net 30. The exchange rate is 1.522.
Change the default amounts.
All items shipped to the VeloCity store.

NOTES
Choose Previous Year in the report options window to make the July 31 balances available for sales tax amounts.
Choose Pay Remittance to remit payroll taxes and deductions.
Clear the GST and HST reports for July 31.

WARNING!
Remember to reset the Pay Period date to August 1 for the second remittance to the Receiver General to avoid including the amounts from the August 7 paycheque.

NOTES
Use Full Add for the new supplier because you need to add currency information.
ABS International
Contact: Derek Rad
Schumacher Str. 96
55123 Mainz, Germany
Tel: (49-6131) 468 913
Fax: (49-6131) 468 248
Currency: Euro
Terms: net 30; Pay Later
Tax code: H

SESSION DATE – AUGUST 31, 2021

25

Sales Order #250 & Deposit #23 **Dated August 16, 2021**

Delivery date August 24, 2021 (from VeloCity store).
From Park 'N Ride Tours. Special volume discounts will apply.

20	AC030	Helmet	$100/ helmet
10	AC060	Lock: kryptonite tube	60/ lock
10	CY040	Bicycle: Trail Alum frame TX560	900/ bike
	HST		13%

Terms: 2/10, n/30. Change all prices for this order.
Deposit cheque #438 for $5 000 received with order.

26

Receipt #826 **Dated August 18, 2021**

From Candide's B & B, cheque #614 for $5 625.59 in payment of account including $114.81 discount for early payment. Reference sales invoice #2231.

27

Cash Purchase Invoice #NB-00124 **Dated August 20, 2021**

From Niagara Bell, $220 plus HST for one month of phone service for two stores. Purchase invoice total $248.60. Terms: cash on receipt of invoice. Issue cheque #1156 in full payment.

28

Deposit Slip #26 **Dated August 21, 2021**

Prepare deposit slip for $16 320.79 for cheques received in previous two weeks.

29

Cash Purchase Invoice #ES-93215 **Dated August 21, 2021**

From Energy Source, $320 plus GST for hydro service for two stores. Purchase invoice total $336. Terms: cash on receipt of invoice. Issue cheque #1157 in full payment.

30

Memo #8-13 **Dated August 21, 2021**

Transfer 10 helmets (item A030) and 30 kryptonite tube locks (item AC060) from Ryder to the VeloCity store.
Build five AP100 Promotional Safety Packages at the Ryder store location.

31

TIME SLIP #3 **DATED AUGUST 21, 2021**

For Dunlop Mercier

Customer	Item	Actual Time	Billable Time	Billable Amount	Taxable	Payroll Time
Cathedral Tours	S010	8 hours	8 (16 boxes)	€832.00	yes	8 hours
Gallery Tours*	S010	4 hours	4 (8 boxes)	€384.00	yes	4 hours
Park 'N Ride Tours	S100	2 hours	2 hours	–	N/A	2 hours
Backstage Tours*	S030	1.5 hours	N/A	$65.00	yes	1.5 hours
Backstage Tours*	S060	4 hours	4 hours	$160.00	yes	4 hours
Americas Vinelands Tours*	S080	8.5 hours	8 hours	USD $440.00	yes	8.5 hours

32

TIME SLIP #4 **DATED AUGUST 21, 2021**

For Yvonne Leader

Customer	Item	Actual Time	Billable Time	Billable Amount	Taxable	Payroll Time
Backstage Tours*	S070	4 hours	4 hours	$480.00	yes	4 hours
Backstage Tours*	S080	9 hours	8 hours	$560.00	yes	9 hours
Gallery Tours*	S070	3.5 hours	3 hours	€270.00	no	3.5 hours
Gallery Tours*	S080	26 hours	24 hours	€1 230.00	no	26 hours
Cathedral Tours	S070	6 hours	6 hours	€600.00	no	6 hours
Cathedral Tours	S080	17 hours	16 hours	€880.00	no	17 hours

NOTES
The * indicates preferred customer prices apply.

NOTES
Use Full Add for the new customer in Europe so you can add the currency and price list:
New preferred price customer:
Gallery Tours
21 Via Della Mosca
50122 Florence, Italy
Tel: 055 282 691
Currency: Euro
Terms: 2/10, n/30; Pay Later
Tax Code: No tax
Credit Limit: $10 000 CAD
(€6 000)

NOTES
You cannot change the billable time for S030 because a flat rate is charged, the equivalent of one hour.

33 **Employee Time Summary Sheet #21** **Dated August 21, 2021**

For the Pay Period from August 8 to August 21, 2021
Edit the employee record for Yvonne Leader. Leader will be paid every two weeks (26 pay periods per year) and her minimum number of hours will be 40. If her contract hours from time slips are less than 40 hours, she will be paid for 40 hours. Change the Additional Federal Tax amount to $100.
Use time slips to prepare the bi-weekly paycheque for Yvonne Leader for the actual number of hours worked. Issue deposit slip #39.

Dunlop Mercier worked 80 regular hours in the period and 4 hours of overtime. Issue deposit slip #40 in payment. (Add time from time slips but choose Yes to use regular hours when prompted.)

34 **Sales Invoice #2232** **Dated August 21, 2021**

To Cathedral Tours: Complete sales invoice for €2 312 plus HST from time slip activities. Include all activities to date. Enter H as the tax code for item S010. Sales invoice total €2 420.16. Terms: 2/10, n/30. The exchange rate is 1.515.

35 **Sales Invoice #2233** **Dated August 21, 2021**

To Backstage Tours: Complete sales invoice for $1 265 plus HST from time slip activities. Include all activities to date. Sales invoice total $1 429.45. Terms: 2/10, n/30.

36 **Sales Invoice #2234** **Dated August 21, 2021**

To Gallery Tours: Complete sales invoice for €1 884 plus HST from time slip activities. Enter H as the tax code for item S010. Include all activities to date. Sales invoice total €1 933.92. Terms: 2/10, n/30. The exchange rate is 1.515.

37 **Sales Invoice #2235** **Dated August 21, 2021**

To Americas Vinelands Tours: Complete sales invoice for $440 USD plus HST from time slip activities. Change the tax code for S080 to H. Include all activities to date. Sales invoice total $497.20 USD. Terms: 2/10, n/30. The exchange rate is 1.331.

38 **Credit Card Purchase Invoice #LS-12331** **Dated August 24, 2021**

From Lakeshore Sunoco, $125 including HST paid for gasoline and $380 plus HST for vehicle repairs. Purchase invoice total $554.40 paid in full by Visa. Use tax code IN for the gasoline purchase and tax code H for the repairs.

39 **Sales Invoice #2236** **Dated August 28, 2021**

To Park 'N Ride Tours, to fill sales order #250 (VeloCity store)

20	AC030	Helmet	$100/ helmet
10	AC060	Lock: kryptonite tube	60/ lock
10	CY040	Bicycle: Trail Alum frame TX560	900/ bike
	HST		13%

Terms: 2/10, n/30. Remember to change the payment method to Pay Later.

40 **TIME SLIP #5** **DATED AUGUST 31, 2021**

For Dunlop Mercier

Customer	Item	Actual Time	Billable Time	Billable Amount	Taxable	Payroll Time
Shavian B & B	S010	2 hours	2 (4 boxes)	$320.00	yes	2 hours
Shavian B & B	S100	3 hours	–	–	yes	3 hours
Niagara Rapids Inn*	S030	2 hours	2 hours	$65.00	yes	2 hours
Niagara Rapids Inn*	S060	4 hours	4 hours	$160.00	yes	4 hours
Americas Vinelands Tours*	S010	2 hours	2 (4 boxes)	USD $208.00	yes	2 hours
Americas Vinelands Tours*	S060	4 hours	4 hours	USD $132.00	yes	4 hours

NOTES
Pay Periods and Hours are entered on the Income tab and Additional Federal Tax on the Taxes tab of the Employee Ledger record.
Add Overtime hours after adding time slip hours. They will be changed back to zero if you enter them first.

NOTES
Enter tax codes for foreign customers carefully.

NOTES
The tour for Americas Vinelands Tours is taxable because it is provided in Canada for the US customer.

NOTES
Do not forget to change the payment method for invoice #2236.

41

TIME SLIP #6 **DATED AUGUST 31, 2021**

For Yvonne Leader

Customer	Item	Actual Time	Billable Time	Billable Amount	Taxable	Payroll Time
Backstage Tours*	S070	5 hours	4.5 hours	$540.00	yes	5 hours
Backstage Tours*	S080	15 hours	16 hours	$1 120.00	yes	15 hours
Festival Tours	S070	4 hours	3 hours	USD $360.00	yes	4 hours
Festival Tours	S080	12 hours	12 hours	USD $720.00	yes	12 hours
Americas Vinelands Tours*	S070	2.5 hours	2 hours	USD $220.00	yes	2.5 hours
Americas Vinelands Tours*	S080	8 hours	8 hours	USD $440.00	yes	8 hours

42

Sales Invoice #2237 **Dated August 31, 2021**

To Shavian B & B: Complete sales invoice for $320 plus HST from time slip activities. Include all activities to date. Sales invoice total $361.60. Terms: 2/10, n/30.

43

Sales Invoice #2238 **Dated August 31, 2021**

To Niagara Rapids Inn: Complete sales invoice for $225 plus HST from time slip activities. Include all activities to date. Sales invoice total $254.25. Terms: 2/10, n/30.

44

Sales Invoice #2239 **Dated August 31, 2021**

To Americas Vinelands Tours: Prepare sales invoice for $1 000 USD plus HST from time slip activities for all activities to date. All activities are taxable (tax code H). Sales invoice total $1 130.00 USD. Terms: 2/10, n/30. The exchange rate is 1.330.

45

Sales Invoice #2240 **Dated August 31, 2021**

To Backstage Tours: Sales invoice for $1 660 plus HST from time slip activities for all activities to date. Sales invoice total $1 875.80. Terms: 2/10, n/30.

46

Credit Card Sales Invoice #2241 **Dated August 31, 2021**

To Visa Sales (sales summary). Sold from VeloCity store.

12	AC040	Light: halogen	$ 25/ unit	$ 300.00
12	AC060	Lock: kryptonite tube	70/ lock	840.00
2	AC100	Trailer: third-wheel rider	260/ unit	520.00
18	BK010	Books: Complete Bicycle Guide (code G)	40/ book	720.00
25	BK020	Books: Endless Trails (code G)	40/ book	1 000.00
6	CY020	Bicycle: Commuter Alum frame CX90	960/ bike	5 760.00
2	CY030	Bicycle: Racer Ultra lite RX480	3 100/ bike	6 200.00
2	CY050	Bicycle: Mountain Alum frame MX14	1 850/ bike	3 700.00
1	CY060	Bicycle: Mountain Carbon frame MX34	2 950/ bike	2 950.00
6	CY070	Bicycle: Youth YX660	460/ bike	2 760.00
2	CY090	Stationary Converter	870/ unit	1 740.00
10	S020	Maintenance: annual contract	110/ year	1 100.00
	GST		5%	86.00
	HST		13%	3 363.10
	Total paid by Visa			$31 039.10

NOTES

Remember to change the tax code for books to G.

47

Bank Debit Memo #120092 **Dated August 31, 2021**

From Niagara Trust, authorized withdrawals were made from the chequing account on our behalf for the following:

Bank service charges	$ 55
Mortgage interest payment	1 450
Mortgage principal reduction	250
Bank loan interest payment	380
Bank loan principal reduction	520

48 **Debit Card Sales Invoice #2242** **Dated August 31, 2021**

To Interac customers (sales summary). Sold from Ryder store.

10	AP100	Promotional Safety Packages	$375/ unit	$3 750.00
10	AC030	Helmet	$120/ helmet	1 200.00
6	S030	Maintenance: complete tune-up	70/ job	420.00
6	S060	Repairs	50/ hour	300.00
14	BK020	Books: Endless Trails (code G)	40/ book	560.00
	GST		5%	28.00
	HST		13%	737.10
	Total paid by Interac			$6 995.10

49 **Memo #8-14** **Dated August 31, 2021**

Prepare the payroll for Pedal Schwinn, Shimana Gearie and Moishe Alee, the salaried employees. Add 2 percent of service revenue for August as a commission to Gearie's salary. Issue deposit slips #41, #42 and #43.

50 **Memo #8-15** **Dated August 31, 2021**

Interest earned but not yet received for bank accounts for August is $180.

51 **Memo #8-16** **Dated August 31, 2021**

Prepare month-end adjusting entries for depreciation on fixed assets using the following amounts:

Computer equipment	$180
Furniture & fixtures	25
Service tools	40
Van	625
Retail premises	810

52 **Memo #8-17** **Dated August 31, 2021**

Prepare end-of-period adjusting entries for the following:

Office supplies used	$ 100
Repair parts used	90
Prepaid insurance expired	672
Prepaid advertising expired	100
Payroll liabilities accrued	1 540

> **WARNING!**
> This is the first sale from the Ryder store, so you must change the default location.

> **NOTES**
> Remember to change the tax code for books to G.

Updating Inventory Prices

At the end of the month, inventory prices will be adjusted. Rather than changing each record for regular and preferred prices in both Canadian and US dollars, we will use the Update Price List method that we used earlier to edit the activity prices. This method is more efficient when many prices must be changed or when they are changed by a fixed amount or percentage. In this case, we are changing all prices by fixed percentages. The Update Price Lists feature also allows us to round off the prices automatically.

✓ 53 **Memo #8-18** **Dated August 31, 2021**

With two stores open and increased expenses, the prices for all inventory items will be raised. All regular Canadian prices will increase by 10 percent and all US regular prices will increase by 5 percent. All new preferred prices (Canadian and US) will be 15 percent lower than the new regular prices. All prices are rounded up to the nearest five-dollar amount.

Click the **Settings icon** [Settings].

Click **Inventory & Services** and then **click** **Price List**.

NOTES
The euro prices are not changing.

NOTES
If the prices in all currencies are changing in the same way, you can update them all at the same time by choosing All Currencies.

NOTES
Prices may be set relative to any of the price lists in the same currency for the data set, including the ones you created, as well as relative to the cost price.
You cannot globally set the price list in one currency relative to prices in a different currency.

Click **Update Price Lists**. **Click** **Inventory Items** to list only the items we need. Prices for services are not changing.

Click the **select item column heading** to select all items:

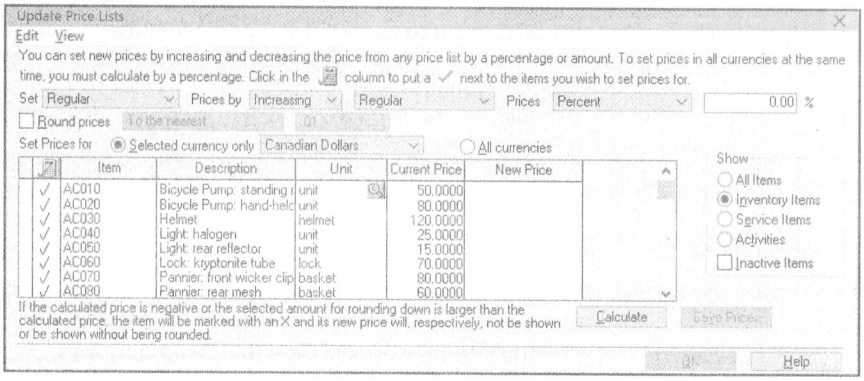

The upper part of the screen has the rules for the change. We can change any price list by increasing or decreasing the prices from another price list by a percentage or a fixed amount. These options are available from the respective drop-down lists:

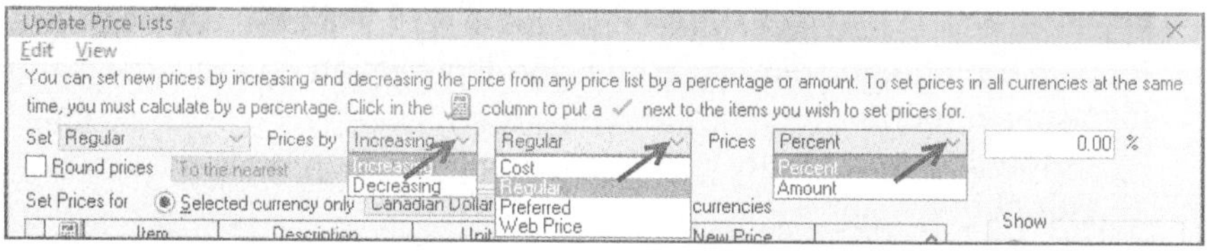

We are increasing Canadian Regular prices by a fixed percentage, so these entries are already correct. We are rounding the new prices up to the nearest five-dollar amount. First, we need to enter the percentage of the increase.

Click **0.00 in the % field**. **Type** 10

Press tab to move to the check box for rounding.

Click the **Round Prices check box** to add a ✓ and open the field we need.

Again, we have some options. You can round up, round down or round to the nearest amount. We want to round up to the nearest five-dollar amount. To The Nearest and one cent (.01) are the default entries. The units range from one ten-thousandth of a dollar (.0001) to one thousand dollars (1 000.00). These two selections are made from their respective drop-down lists:

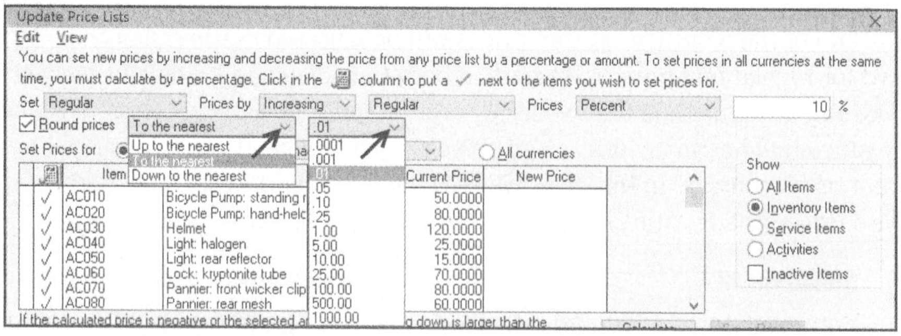

Click **To The Nearest** to open the rounding options list and **choose Up To The Nearest**.

Click **.01** to open the selection list and **choose 5.00** (five dollars) as the amount to complete the selection of options:

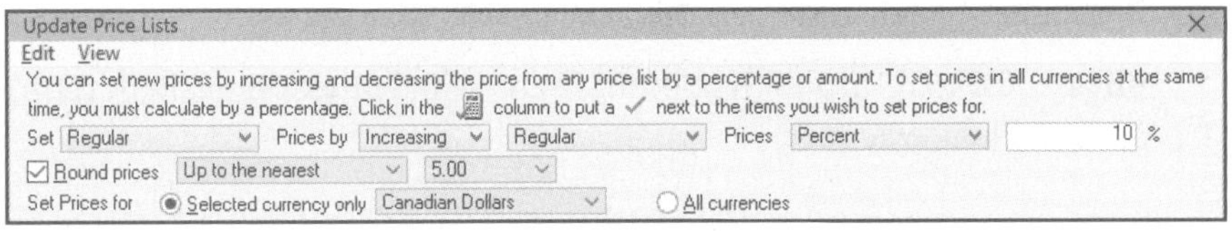

We do not want to increase prices for books or for AP100, the new promotion item, so we will deselect them. In this way, the change rules will not apply to these items.

Click the Select column for AP100 to remove the ✓. **Press** ⬇

Click to remove the ✓ for BK010. **Press** ⬇ and **click** to remove the ✓ for BK020.

Click **Calculate** to update the prices and add them to the New Price column.

Click **Save Prices** to transfer the new prices to the Current Price column.

We will set the preferred prices relative to the new regular prices, decreasing them by 15 percent and rounding up to the nearest $5.00. We need to change the selected price list, the direction of the change and the percentage.

Click **Regular** in the Set field:

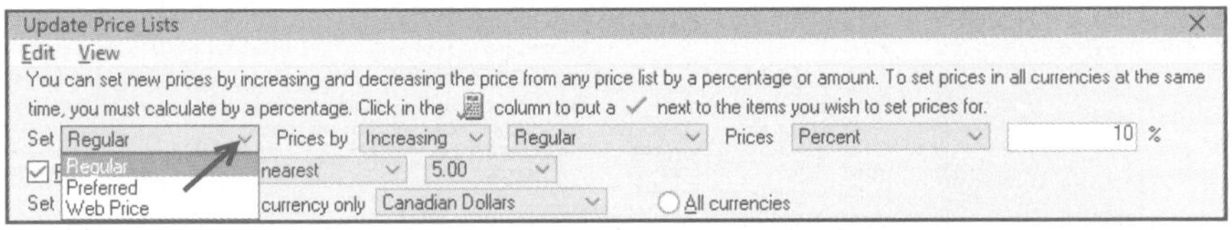

Choose **Preferred**. **Click** **Increasing** in the Prices By field and **choose** **Decreasing**. Regular is correct as the reference price list.

Click **10** in the % field and **type** 15

The three items for which prices will not change – AP100, BK010 and BK020 — will remain selected. The remaining options are correct, so your selections are completed:

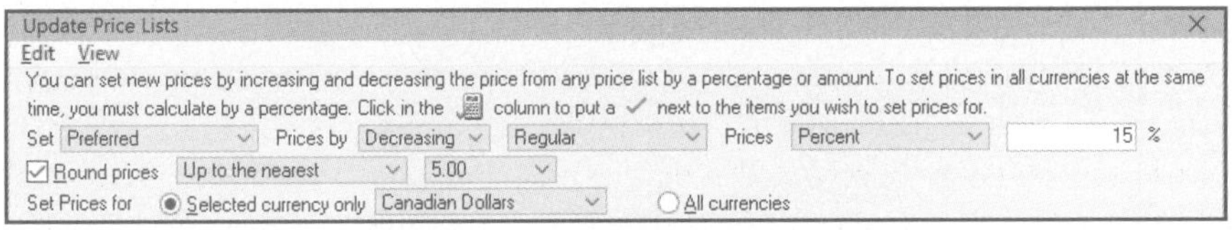

Click **Calculate** to update the prices and add them to the New Price column.

Click **Save Prices** to transfer the new prices to the Current Price column.

You can now change the prices for US dollars.

Click **Canadian Dollars** in the Selected Currency Only field:

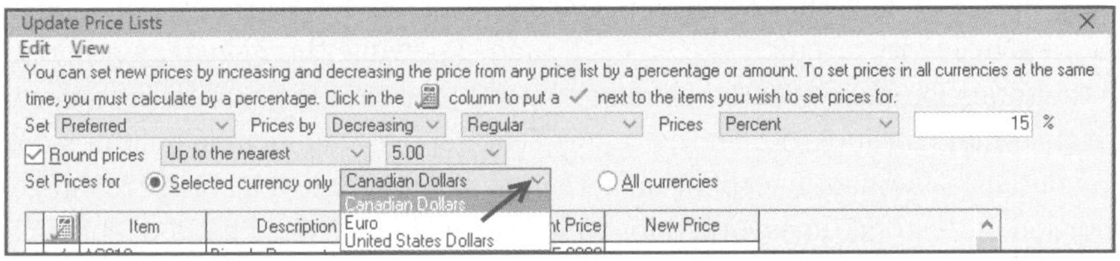

Choose **United States Dollars**.

Now apply the changes to the US dollar prices. First, increase the regular prices by 5 percent and round up to the nearest $5.00. Change the preferred prices by decreasing the regular prices by 15 percent and rounding up to the nearest $5.00 amount. The prices for AP100, BK010 and BK020 will not be changed. These items will remain excluded until you close the window.

NOTES

After you click Calculate, the New Price column remains empty for the three items we deselected.

NOTES

You could also calculate new prices for the AP100 and the book items and then change the prices after calculating but before saving.

Until you save the new prices, you can edit individual amounts.

NOTES

You could update the euro prices in the same way, by selecting euro as the currency. You can also update the prices for all currencies at the same time when the same updating rule applies to them all. You can, of course, adjust individual prices after.

Remember to **calculate** and then **save each price set**.

Click **OK** to return to the Settings screen and **click OK** again to return to the Home window.

Displaying Time and Billing Reports

The various Time and Billing reports provide different ways of organizing the same information. You can view the reports by customer, by employee or by activity.

Customer Time and Billing Report

NOTES

Sorting and filtering are not available for Time and Billing reports, but you can choose the columns to include in the report.

Click the **Report Centre icon** in the Home window. **Click Time & Billing**. **Click** the ⊞ beside **Billing**, **Payroll** and **Purchases** to expand the list of available reports:

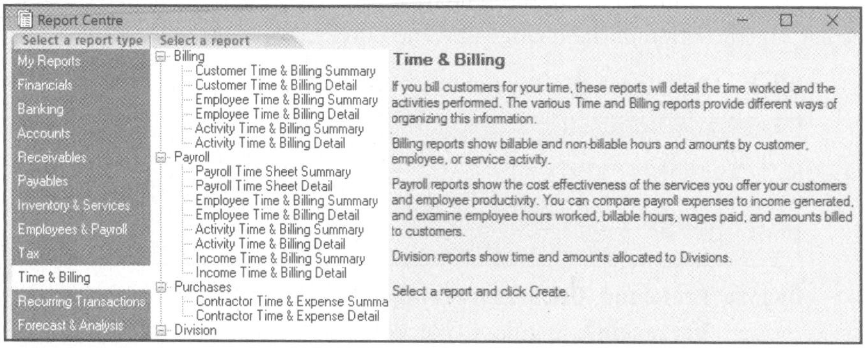

NOTES

Contractor Time & Billing reports (under Purchases) and Division reports do not apply to Ryder's Routes.

Click **Customer Time & Billing Summary** under **Billing**. **Click Modify This Report** to open the report options window:

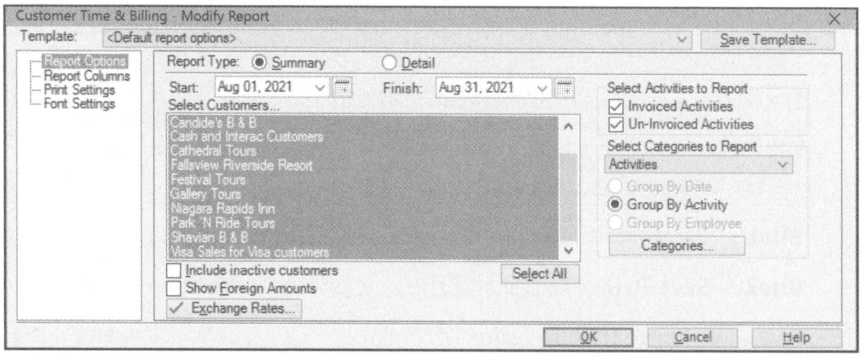

NOTES

From the Home window, choose the Reports menu, then choose Time & Billing. Click Billing and click Time By Customer to open the report options.

NOTES

Time and Billing reports can include a large amount of information. A good way to understand these reports is to prepare a very complete report. For example, select the Detail Report, choose all employees, click all Details and Activities and choose Activities and Customers as the categories for the report. Then choose all service activities from the next list. Print the report. Click the Modify tool or choose Modify Report from the Options menu in the report. Compare this report with the Summary Report for the same details and categories.

Time and Billing reports by customer provide the time and billed amounts organized by customer. Summary and Detail reports are available. **Detail** reports include a report line for each activity or employee on each time slip, while the **Summary** reports have only the totals for each selected category (activity or employee). You can select one or more customers for inclusion in the report. The reports will include columns for several billing details — actual time spent on activities, billable time, billable percentage (the proportion of the total time worked for which the customer was charged), billable amounts and invoiced amounts. In addition, if you changed the prices for any of the service activities in the Sales Journal, the report will include these changes as amounts written down or up. In the report, the invoiced amounts will then be different from the billable amounts. The effective billable percentage provides the relation between the invoiced amount and the billable amount. The non-billable time, no-charge time and amounts written down or up as percentages of the billable amounts are not in the default report, but you can add them by customizing the report columns. Some of the default columns may also be removed, and the report details can be grouped by date, by activity or by employee.

You can include **invoiced activities** (bills have been sent) or **uninvoiced activities** (bills have not been created and sent) or both.

The next decision for the report relates to the **categories** you want to include. You can report on the time spent according to the **activities** performed for the customer or according to the **employee** who completed the work or both. In all cases, the categories are included for each customer you selected.

Enter **Start** and **Finish dates** for the report.

Choose the **customers** for the report. **Press** and **hold** ctrl and **click** the **customer names** to begin a new selection. **Click Select All** to include (or remove) all customers.

Choose the **invoicing details** for the report. **Click** a **detail** to remove a ✓ or to add it.

Click the **Select Categories To Report list arrow** to select activities or employees or both.

Click the **Categories button** to open the secondary selection list.

If you choose Activities as the category, you will list the activities:

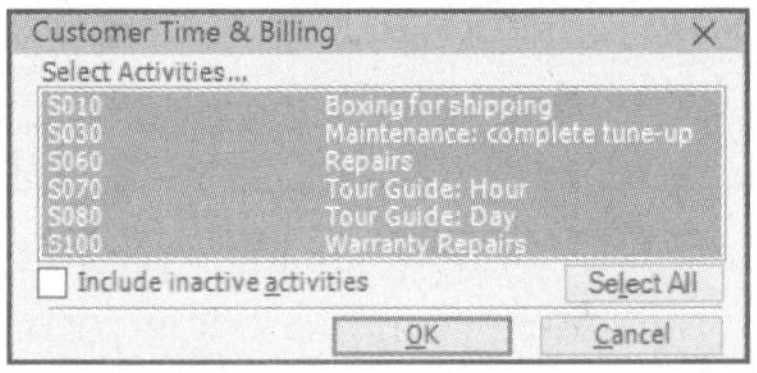

If you choose Employees as the category, you must select from the Employee list. If you choose both Activities and Employees, you must choose from lists for both.

Initially, all activities are selected, and clicking will change the selection. The Select All button acts like a toggle switch. To begin a new selection of activities,

Click **Select All** to clear all selections.

Press and **hold** ctrl and **click** the **activities** you want in the report to begin a new selection. **Click Select All** to include (or remove) all activities.

Click **OK** to return to the report options screen.

Click **OK** to generate the report.

The report has the amount of time worked for each customer according to the activity, employee or both, depending on the category you selected.

Close the **report** when you have finished.

Employee and Activity Time and Billing Reports

The other two Time and Billing reports are similar to the Time by Customer Report, except that they organize the amounts by employee or by activity. The first options screen for the **Employee Time & Billing Report** (Summary or Detail) will include the Employee list, and the second selection screen will list the customers, the activities or both, depending on the category you choose. The Time by Employee Report has the time and billed amounts for each employee for each customer, each activity or both, depending on the categories you choose.

NOTES
The service activities for Festival Tours have not been invoiced.

NOTES
From the Exchange Rates button you can access a window that allows you to enter current exchange rates for foreign customer amounts in the report.

NOTES
When you select two categories, you can group the report details by either one.

NOTES
Remember that Select All acts as a toggle switch. Initially, all items (or customers) are selected. Clicking Select All will clear the selection. If no items or a few items are selected, clicking Select All will include all items.

Similarly, the first options screen for the **Activity Time & Billing Report** (Summary or Detail) will include the Activity list, and the second selection screen will list the customers, the employees or both, depending on the categories you choose. The Time by Activity Report has the time and the billed amounts for each activity for each customer or by each employee or both, depending on the categories you choose.

Other report options are the same as they are for the Time by Customer Report, and both reports are available as a Summary or a Detail report.

Payroll Time Sheet Reports

The Time Sheet Report provides a summary of the hours of each income category that is on the time sheets. The number of hours of non-payroll, regular payroll and overtime for each employee can be included.

NOTES
From the Home window, choose the Reports menu, then choose Time & Billing. Click Payroll and click Time Sheet to access the report options.

Click **Payroll Time Sheet Summary** under **Payroll**. **Click** **Modify This Report** to open the report options window:

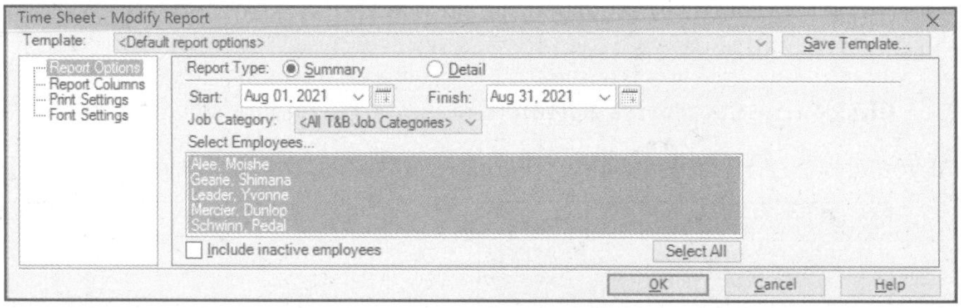

The **Summary Report** will provide the total number of hours in each payroll category (Non-payroll, Regular and Overtime 1 — the payroll category in the ledger record for the activity) for each employee selected for each time period during the report interval. The **Detail Report** will provide the number of hours in each payroll category for each time sheet.

You can customize the report by selecting columns for the payroll category. Non-payroll, Regular and Overtime 1 columns may be included or omitted.

Enter **Start** and **Finish dates** for the report.

If you created job categories, you can choose from the Job Category drop-down list either one category or all categories for the report.

NOTES
VeloCity and Ryder's Routes have only Sales as the job category and all employees are in it.

Choose the **employees** for the report. **Press** and **hold** ctrl and **click** the **employee names** to begin a new selection. **Click** **Select All** to include (or remove) all employees.

Click **OK** to display the report.

Close the **report** when you have finished.

Employee Time and Billing Payroll Reports

NOTES
From the Home window, choose the Reports menu, then choose Time & Billing. Click Payroll and click Time By Employee to access the report options.

The remaining Payroll Time reports provide information about the cost effectiveness of the service activities by comparing the labour costs with the income generated — the amount billed to the customer. Employee productivity is also measured by examining the actual hours, billable hours, payroll hours, wages paid and invoiced amounts

Click **Employee Time & Billing Summary** under **Payroll**.

Click **Modify This Report** to open the report options window:

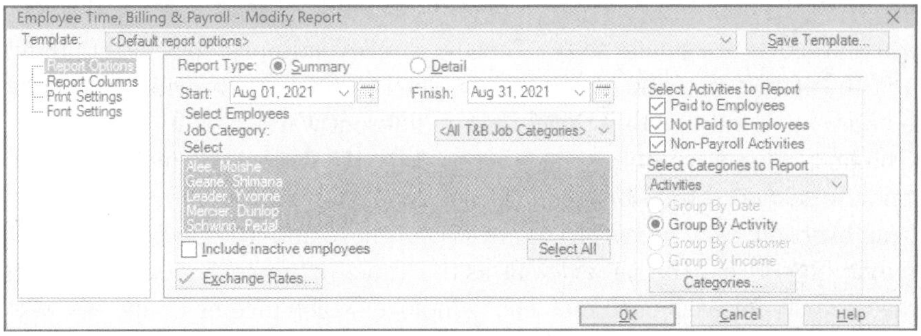

Summary and Detail reports are available. The **Detail Report** includes a report line for each time sheet entry, while the **Summary Report** includes only the totals for each selected category. You can select one or more employees for inclusion in the report. The reports will include several time and billing **details** — actual time spent on activities, payroll time, billable time, billable amounts, the actual payroll expense and the productivity ratio (the billable amount compared to the payroll expense) can be included. The effective productivity ratio percentage is the relation between the invoiced amount and the payroll expense amount. Payroll percentage (payroll time as a proportion of actual time) and billable percentage (the proportion of the total time worked for which the customer was charged) can be added to the report when you customize the report by selecting these time and billing details (report columns). The default report columns may be included or removed.

The report can include **activities** for which you have **paid** the employees, activities that have **not yet been paid**, activities that are **non-payroll** or all three payroll details.

The next decision for the report relates to the **categories** you want to include. You can report on the time spent according to the **activity** performed by the employee, according to the **customer** for whom the work was completed, according to the **income** (that is, regular, non-payroll or overtime) or any two of these three categories. In all cases, the categories are given for each employee you selected.

When you choose two categories for the report, you can group report details by one of them — select from date, activity, customer or income.

Enter **Start** and **Finish dates** for the report.

Choose the **employees** for the report. **Press** and **hold** *ctrl* and **click** the **employee names** to begin a new selection. **Click** **Select All** to include (or remove) all employees.

Choose the **payroll status details**. **Click** a **detail** to add or remove a ✓.

Choose the **categories** for the report from the Select Categories To Report drop-down list.

Click the **Categories button** to open the secondary selection list.

If you select the Activities category, you will list all services defined as activities in the ledger.

Choose the **activities** for the report. **Press** and **hold** *ctrl* and **click** the **activity names** to begin a new selection. **Click** **Select All** to include (or remove) activities.

Click **OK** to return to the report options screen.

Click **OK** to open the report. By default the report will print in landscape orientation (sideways on the page) so that all details can fit on a line.

Close the **report** when you have finished.

NOTES

If you select Customers or Income as the category, you will open selection lists for each category. If you selected two categories, you can choose from selection lists for both categories.

NOTES

The August 31 report for Ryder informs us that both employees have been partially paid for their time sheet entries – the August 31 time sheet has not yet been added to their paycheques. The same report for August 21 lists all time sheet activities as paid.

NOTES

If you created job categories, you can choose from the Job Category drop-down list either one category or all categories for the report.

Activity and Income Time and Billing Payroll Reports

These two reports are similar to the Time by Employee Report except that they organize amounts by activity or by income category. The three reports provide essentially the same information but organize the details in different ways.

The first options screen for the **Time by Activity Report** will include the Activity list, and the second selection screen will list the customers, employees, incomes (regular, overtime or non-payroll) or any two of these options that you select. The Time by Activity Report has the same details as the Time by Employee Report but lists them for each activity for each customer, each employee, each income or any two of these options.

Similarly, the first options screen for the **Time by Income Report** will provide the income list, and the second selection screen will list the customers, employees, activities or any two of these three options. The Time by Income Report has the same details as the Time by Employee Report but lists them for each activity for each customer, each employee, each activity or any two of these options.

Other report options are the same as they are for the Time by Employee Report, and both reports are available as a Summary or a Detail Report.

Multiple Fiscal Periods and Reports

After you have accumulated two fiscal periods of financial data, you can produce historical reports for these additional periods. Data for the current and previous years are always available, unless you have cleared the information.

NOTES
Financial reports for August:
- Income Statement
- Balance Sheet
- Trial Balance
- Supplier and Customer Aged reports
- Employee Summary Report
- Inventory Summary and Inventory Quantity Detail reports, including location

✓ 54

Memo #8-19 **Dated August 31, 2021**

Back up the data files and print all financial reports for the August fiscal period.
Start a new fiscal year. Do not clear old data.
Change the fiscal end to September 30, 2021.

Prepare a **list** of inventory items that should be ordered for each location.

Choose the **Maintenance menu** and **click Start New Year** to begin a new fiscal year.

Choose **Yes** when asked if you want to Back Up Your Data Files Before Beginning The New Fiscal Year and follow the backup instructions.

Choose **No** when asked if you want to clear the old data.

The Update Locking Date screen opens.

Enter **09/01/21** as the new date. **Click OK** to update the earliest transaction.

Choose the **Setup menu**, then **click Settings**, **Company** and **Information**:

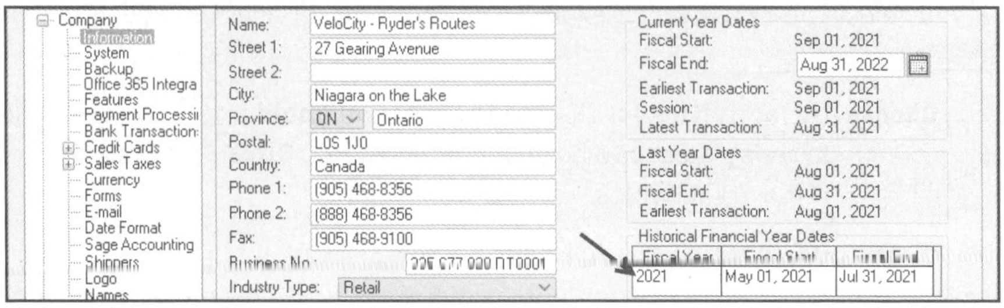

The first fiscal period, May 1 to July 31, 2021, is now listed in the section for Historical Financial Year Dates.

NOTES
The Pro version stores up to seven years of historical financial data; the Premium version stores up to 99 years of data.

Drag through Aug 31, 2022, the Fiscal End date.

Type 09-30-21 **Click OK** to save the date and return to the Home window.

Multi-Period Financial Reports

Multiple-period reports are available for the Balance Sheet, Income Statement and Trial Balance. All are accessed from the Financials list of reports.

Click the **Report Centre icon**.

Click **Financials** to expand this list of reports.

Click the ⊞ beside **Balance Sheet**, **Income Statement** and **Trial Balance** to expand the Select A Report list. **Click Multi-Period** under **Balance Sheet**:

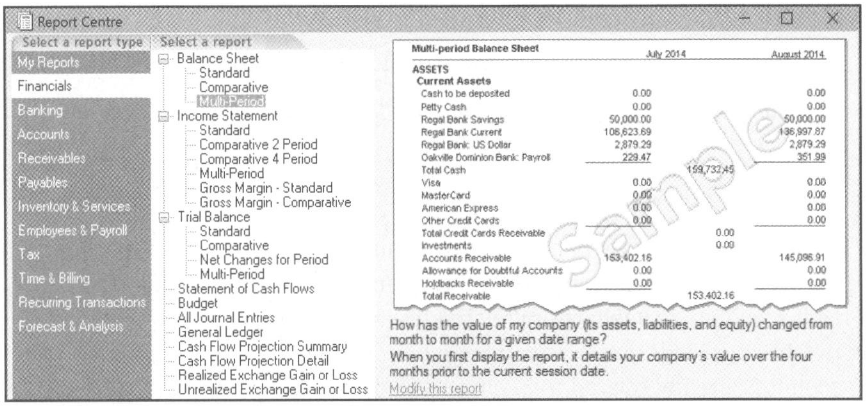

Click **Modify This Report** to open the report options window:

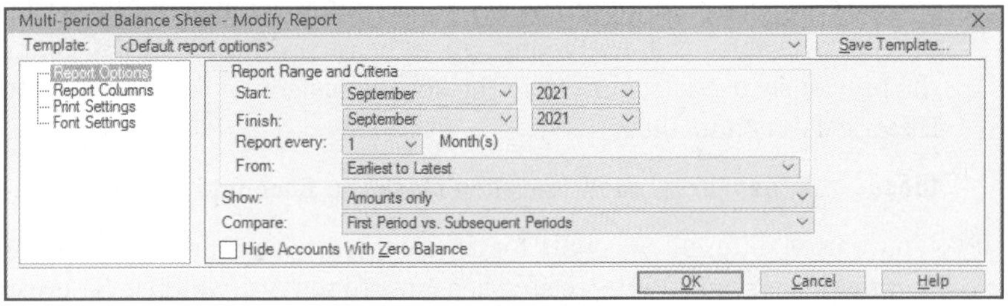

From the Home window, choose the Reports menu, then choose Financials and Multi-Period Reports and click Balance Sheet to access the report options.

The regular financial reports available in comparative form compare two fiscal periods or dates. Reports for the previous fiscal period are also available in regular reports. The multi-period reports include more than two periods and can even include multiple fiscal periods before the previous one.

For VeloCity and Ryder's Routes, monthly data can be viewed in a single report for May, the first month for which we entered data in Sage 50, to August.

There are several options for displaying the report. You can have the balances for each month for any interval ranging from one to twelve months. The report can be ordered from the earliest period to the latest, or from latest to earliest. You can include Amounts Only, Difference In Percentage or Difference In Amounts, just as you do for regular comparative reports. And you can compare the first period with each subsequent period, or you can compare each period with subsequent periods.

After choosing the options for the report,

Click **OK** to open the report.

NOTES
From the Home window, choose the Reports menu, Financials, Multi-Period Reports, and click Balance Sheet, Income Statement or Trial Balance.

NOTES
Dates before the previous fiscal period that are eligible for the report will be those in the Historical Financial Year Dates section of the Company Information screen on page 782.

Close the **report** when you have finished.

The **Income Statement** and **Trial Balance** are available for the same periods as the Balance Sheet. They have the same report options. To generate these reports,

Click **Multi-Period** under **Income Statement** (or **Trial Balance**) and then **click Modify This Report**.

Choose the **report options** and **click OK**.

Close the **report** when you have finished. **Close** the **Report Centre**.

Related Historical Accounts

Because we have advanced to the next (third) fiscal period, we can create the list of related accounts. You can access and edit the related historical accounts in the General Ledger record for the account in the Related Historical Accounts tab screen.

Click the **Chart of Accounts icon** in the Company module window.

Double-click an **account** to open its General Ledger record.

Click the **Related Historical Accounts tab** to list the accounts used in previous periods.

If an account currently being used has a different name and number than the account used for the same purpose in a previous period, you can link them.

Each account has itself as the related historical account if it has been used for more than two fiscal periods. Each account can be related to only one account. Therefore, if the account is already related to itself, you cannot select it again.

Open the record for the (old) previously used account. Delete the account listed as the related account in the Related Historical Accounts tab. This will make the account available again for linking. Open the record for the new account. Choose the previously used account from the account selection list in the Related Historical Accounts tab.

Close the **Ledger window** and then **close** the **Accounts window**.

If you have used different accounts for the same purpose over the periods and you have related them, you can add the related accounts to the Account List. To create the report of related account numbers,

Choose the **Reports menu**, then **choose Lists** and **click Accounts**.

Click **Include Related Historical Accounts** and then **click OK**.

The report will list all General Ledger accounts with the current information and the accounts that were used for those same purposes in previous fiscal periods — the information that is stored in the General Ledger Related Historical Accounts tab fields.

Close the **report** when you have finished.

Close the **Home window** to exit the Sage 50 program.

REVIEW

The Student DVD with Data Files includes Review Questions and Supplementary Cases for this chapter.

CHAPTER NINETEEN

Able & Associates

OBJECTIVES

After completing this chapter, you should be able to

- ***activate*** departmental accounting
- ***create*** departments
- ***add*** departments to accounts, vendors and clients
- ***add*** departments in journal entries
- ***apply*** line discounts in sales journal entries
- ***display*** and ***print*** department reports

COMPANY INFORMATION

Company Profile

NOTES
Able & Associates Inc.
88 Practice Blvd.
Huntsville, ON P1H 1T2
Tel: (705) 463-2145
Fax: (705) 465-1110
Business No.: 167 344 571

Able & Associates Inc. is a partnership of two chartered accountants, Count and Memor Able. They began their practice in Huntsville, Ontario, two years ago, shortly after receiving their C.P.A. designations. They each invested capital to start up the office. By relying extensively on electronic communications, remote access to client computers and frequent phone calls, they are able to serve clients throughout a large geographic area. Only occasional on-site meetings are required, and local clients often come to their office. Most of their revenue comes from auditing and preparing regular financial statements and income tax returns for small business clients. They share office space and office expenses, including a full-time office assistant. Count works in the office full time, but Memor is there only three days a week, spending the other two days working in a small family business. Thus, they allocate their joint expenses using a 60/40 percent division.

Most of the clients have contracts with Able & Associates and pay fees on a monthly basis. These clients are entitled to a discount of 2 percent of their fees if they pay within 10 days of the invoice date. Full payment is requested within 30 days. One-time clients do not receive discounts. Some regular vendors also offer discounts for early payment.

On March 31, at the end of the fiscal period, they decided to use the departmental accounting feature in Sage 50 to track their financial performance. Payroll taxes were remitted at year-end. To prepare for allocating opening account balances to departments, all opening account balances were transferred to

NOTES
For this professional service business, the terms Client and Vendor are used.

unallocated accounts in the corresponding financial statement section. The following business information was used to set up the accounts:

- Chart of Accounts
- Post-Closing Trial Balance and Statement of Opening Account Balances
- Vendor Information
- Client Information
- Employee Information
- Accounting Procedures

CHART OF POSTABLE ACCOUNTS

ABLE & ASSOCIATES INC.

ASSETS
10800 Bank: Chequing
11000 Investments
11200 Prepaid Association Dues
11400 Prepaid Subscriptions
11600 Prepaid Insurance
12000 Accounts Receivable
13400 Office Supplies
14400 Office Equipment
14800 Office Furniture
15000 Library

LIABILITIES
21000 Bank Loan
22000 Accounts Payable
22500 Visa Payable
23000 EI Payable
23100 CPP Payable
23200 Income Tax Payable
24200 WSIB Payable
26500 HST Charged on Services
26700 HST Paid on Purchases

EQUITY
34500 Invested Capital: C. Able
34800 Invested Capital: M. Able
35500 Retained Earnings
36000 Current Earnings

REVENUE
41000 Revenue from Services
41500 Revenue from Interest
41800 Other Revenue
42000 Sales Discounts

EXPENSE
51200 Association Dues
51300 Bank and Card Fees
51400 Interest Expense
51500 Insurance Expense
51600 Publicity and Promotion
51800 Purchase Discounts
52000 Subscriptions
52200 Telephone Expense
52400 Rent
54000 Salaries
54100 EI Expense
54200 CPP Expense
54300 WSIB Expense

NOTES: The Chart of Accounts includes only postable accounts and the Current Earnings account. Able & Associates uses five-digit account numbers for the General Ledger accounts.

POST-CLOSING TRIAL BALANCE

ABLE & ASSOCIATES INC.

April 1, 2021	Debits	Credits
10800 Bank: Chequing	$ 21 300	
11000 Investments	44 000	
11200 Prepaid Association Dues	2 800	
11400 Prepaid Subscriptions	1 500	
11600 Prepaid Insurance	4 500	
12000 Accounts Receivable	2 260	
13400 Office Supplies	1 800	
14400 Office Equipment	12 000	
14800 Office Furniture	8 000	
15000 Library	4 800	
21000 Bank Loan		$ 15 000
22000 Accounts Payable		2 260
22500 Visa Payable		1 400
26500 HST Charged on Services		2 200
26700 HST Paid on Purchases	$ 1 640	
34500 Invested Capital: C. Able		33 000
34800 Invested Capital: M. Able		22 000
35500 Retained Earnings		28 740
	$104 600	$104 600

STATEMENT OF ACCOUNT OPENING BALANCES

ABLE & ASSOCIATES INC.

April 1, 2021	Debits	Credits
19500 Unassigned Assets	$102 960	
29500 Unassigned Liabilities		$ 19 220
39500 Unassigned Capital		83 740
	$102 960	$102 960

NOTES: The true account balances for the regular postable accounts are in the Trial Balance. The three unassigned accounts in the Statement of Opening Balances are temporary holding accounts. The temporary balance in these accounts is the sum of all balances for that section of the Balance Sheet (which temporarily have zero balances). These balances will be transferred back to the regular accounts to set up the departmental opening balances.

VENDOR INFORMATION

ABLE & ASSOCIATES INC.

Vendor Name (Contact)	Address	Phone No. Fax No.	E-mail Web Site	Terms Payment Method
Bell Canada (Yap Long)	500 Central Line Huntsville, Ontario P1F 2C2	Tel: (705) 466-2355	yap.l@bell.ca bell.ca	net 1 Cheque
Muskoka Maintenance (M. Handimann)	72 Spoiler St. Huntsville, Ontario P1P 2B8	Tel: (705) 469-0808 Fax: (705) 469-6222	handimann@yahoo.com	2/10, n/30 Pay Later
Northlands Office Mgt. (Hi Bilding)	59 Condor St. Huntsville, Ontario P1D 4F4	Tel: (705) 283-9210 Fax: (705) 283-2310	bilding@northlands.com	net 1 Cheque
Office Plus (B. Laser)	4 Paper Corners Huntsville, Ontario P1E 1G1	Tel: (705) 466-3335	officeplus.ca	1/15, n/30 Pay Later
Receiver General for Canada	Sudbury Tax Services Office PO Box 20004 Sudbury, ON P3A 6B4	Tel 1: (800) 561-7761 Tel 2: (800) 959-2221	cra-arc.gc.ca	net 1 Cheque

OUTSTANDING VENDOR INVOICES

ABLE & ASSOCIATES INC.

Vendor Name	Terms	Date	Invoice No.	Amount	Total
Office Plus	1/15, n/30	Mar. 21/21	OP-2339	$2 260	$2 260

CLIENT INFORMATION

ABLE & ASSOCIATES INC.

Client Name (Contact)	Address	Phone No. Fax No.	E-mail Web Site	Terms Credit Limit
Adrienne Aesthetics (Adrienne Kosh)	65 Bytown Ave. Ottawa, Ontario K2C 4R1	Tel 1: (613) 722-9876 Tel 2: (613) 722-8701 Fax: (613) 722-8000	a.kosh@adrienneaesthetics.com adrienneaesthetics.com	2/10, n/30 $10 000
Dorfmann Design (Desiree Dorfmann)	199 Artistic Way, Unit 500 Hamilton, Ontario L8T 3B7	Tel: (905) 642-2348 Fax: (905) 642-9100	dd@dorfmann.com dorfmann.com	2/10, n/30 $10 000
Gorgeous Gifts (Gitte Gurlosi)	600 First St. Huntsville, Ontario P1L 2W4	Tel: (705) 462-1203 Fax: (705) 462-3394	gg@ggifts.com ggifts.com	2/10, n/30 $10 000
Truman Tires (Tyrone Truman)	600 Westminster St. London, Ontario N6P 3B1	Tel: (519) 729-3733 Fax: (519) 729-7301	tt@trumantires.com trumantires.com	2/10, n/30 $10 000

NOTES: The default invoice payment method is Pay Later for all clients.

OUTSTANDING CLIENT INVOICES

ABLE & ASSOCIATES INC.

Client Name	Terms	Date	Invoice No.	Amount	Total
Adrienne Aesthetics	2/10, n/30	Mar. 25/21	843	$2 260	$2 260

EMPLOYEE INFORMATION SHEET

ABLE & ASSOCIATES INC.

Tryin, Reelie (Office Assistant)

Social Insurance No.	429 535 644	Total Federal (Ontario) Tax Exemption - TD1 $12 609 (10 582)	
Address	200 Water St. #301 Huntsville, Ontario P1H 2L8	Employee Income (Reg. hours) Salary	 $3 800 /month (150 hours)
Telephone	(705) 446-2190		
Date of Birth (mm-dd-yy)	04-04-87	WSIB Rate	0.89
EI, CPP & Income Tax	Calculations are built into the Sage 50 program.		

Accounting Procedures

Taxes (HST)

Able & Associates Inc. is a professional service business using the regular method of calculating HST. HST, at the rate of 13 percent, is charged on all services and paid on purchases. The difference between the HST charged and HST paid is remitted to the Receiver General for Canada quarterly.

NOTES
Able & Associates Inc. pays GST at the rate of 5 percent on subscriptions to professional journals and other books purchased for the business.

Departments

Able & Associates has two departments, one for each partner. The division of most assets is 60 percent and 40 percent, to be consistent with their initial investments in the partnership and their time in the office.

Discounts for Early Payments

Able & Associates offers discounts to regular clients if they pay their accounts within 10 days. Full payment is expected in 30 days. No discounts are allowed on partial payments. Additional discounts are applied occasionally for clients in special circumstances. These are entered as line discounts for the sales.

Some vendors with whom Able & Associates has accounts set up also offer discounts for early payments.

INSTRUCTIONS

1. **Set up two departments** for Able & Associates.
2. **Record entries for the source documents** in Sage 50. Transactions indicated with a ✓ in the completion box beside the source document have step-by-step keystroke instructions.
3. **Print** the following **reports** after you have finished making your entries. Instructions for departmental reports begin on page 804.
   a. Comparative Balance Sheet with Departments for April 1 and April 30
   b. Income Statement with Departments for April 1 to April 30
   c. Departmental Income Statement
   d. Journal Report for April 1 to April 30 for all journals

KEYSTROKES

Departmental Accounting

Most companies are divided into departments, such as sales, marketing, service, finance, human resources and manufacturing. And most companies want to track the costs and performance of these departments separately. The departmental accounting feature in Sage 50 permits more detailed company reporting and analysis.

Unlike projects that work only through journal entries, departments are connected to all ledgers and journals. Departments can be associated with individual accounts, vendors and clients, and you can choose departments for accounts in journal entries.

Each account may be used exclusively by one department or by more than one department. For example, automotive parts in a car dealership will be used by the service department but not by the human resources or sales departments. Other accounts, such as a bank account, may be connected to all departments. Similarly, individual vendors, such as a car-parts vendor, may be linked to a specific department while others, such as utility providers, are linked to all departments. Clients, too, may be connected to specific departments. When you set up these connections, the departmental links are added to journal entries automatically, and you can generate detailed reports with departmental information.

Departmental account balances are generated when you add departmental information to journal entries, but they cannot be added as opening account balances in the ledgers. Therefore, ideally, you will add departmental information when you create company files so that you can have departmental information for all accounts. You can also choose to use departments only for Income Statement accounts and start using departments at the beginning of a fiscal period when these accounts have zero balances.

WARNING!
You cannot remove departments once you add them and use them, so you should back up data files before adding departments.

Setting Up Departments

Open **SageData19\ABLE\ABLE**. **Enter** **April 30, 2021** as the session date.

The history for the company files is not finished. Some linked accounts are missing and the ledgers are not balanced. (Read the margin Notes.)

NOTES
If you are working from backups, you should restore SageData19\ABLE1.CAB or ABLE1 to SageData19\ABLE\ABLE.

NOTES
This exercise has few source documents, so we use a single session date for all transactions.

Creating Departments

Before using departmental accounting, you must activate the feature and create the departments. The feature is not turned on by default, and you can add departments to an existing Sage 50 data file.

WARNING!
Do not attempt to finish the history yet. Essential linked accounts are missing.

✓ 1	**Memo #1**	**Dated April 1/21**
	Create two departments for Able & Associates: 1001: C. Able and 2001: M. Able	

Click the **Settings icon** (Settings) and **General (Accounts)** and **Departments**:

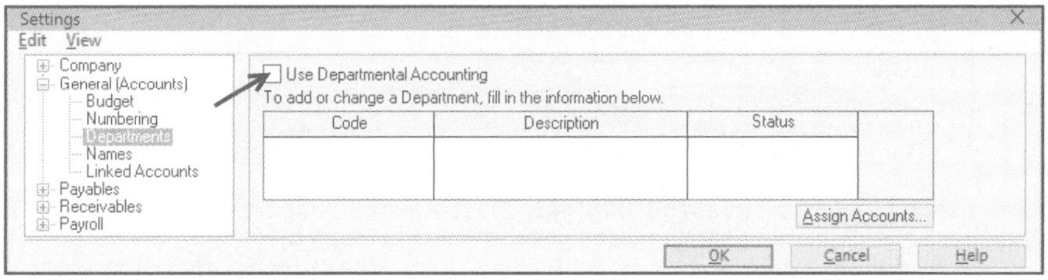

NOTES
The history for the data set must remain unfinished for now. Accounts Receivable and Accounts Payable accounts are needed in journal entries (to add opening department balances – refer to page 792), so they have not yet been defined as linked accounts. In addition, Accounts Receivable and Accounts Payable begin with zero balances. As a result, these opening balances do not match the totals of the historical client and vendor invoices.

Click **Use Departmental Accounting**. Sage 50 warns you about this step:

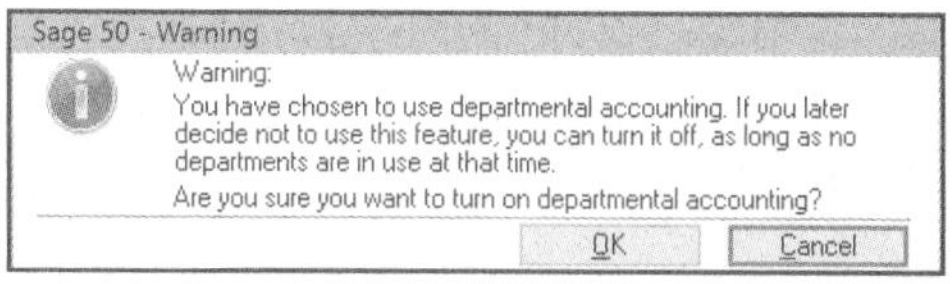

Adding departments is not a reversible step, unless the departments have not yet been used.

Click Cancel if you are not working with a separate copy of the data file. Make a backup first.

Click **OK** to return to the Departments Settings screen.

For each department you want, you must assign a four-digit code and a name.

Click the **Code field**.

Type `1001` **Press** *tab* to advance to the Description field. The Status is automatically set as Active.

Type `C. Able`

Unused departments can have their status changed to Inactive by clicking Active.

Click the **Code field** on the next line. **Type** `2001`

Press *tab* to advance to the Description field. **Type** `M. Able`

Click the **Assign Accounts button** to open the next screen:

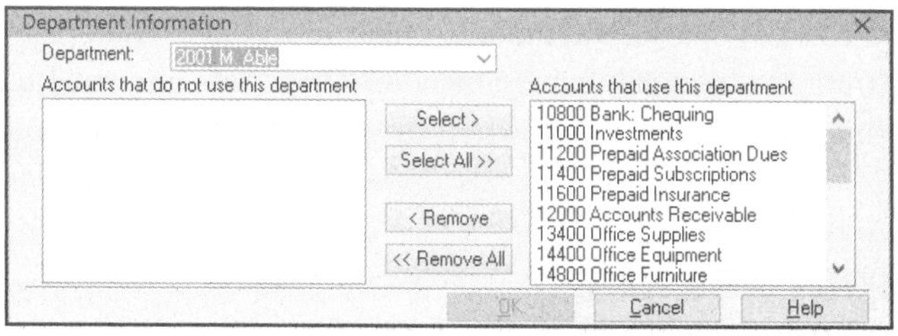

From this screen, you can indicate which accounts use the departments. The cursor was on M. Able in the previous screen, so this department is selected. You can select departments from the drop-down list in the Department field.

Initially, all accounts use all departments. From this window, you can select accounts that are to be removed for a department.

The two investment accounts are separated according to the partner, so we should assign each one only to its correct department. That is, we can remove *34500 Invested Capital: C. Able* for M. Able and remove *34800 Invested Capital: M. Able* for C. Able. We are working with the M. Able department first.

Scroll down the list of Accounts That Use This Department.

Click **34500 Invested Capital: C. Able** to select the account.

Click **Remove**. The account moves to the list of Accounts That Do Not Use This Department on the left-hand side of the screen.

Click the **Department list arrow** and **choose 1001 C. Able**:

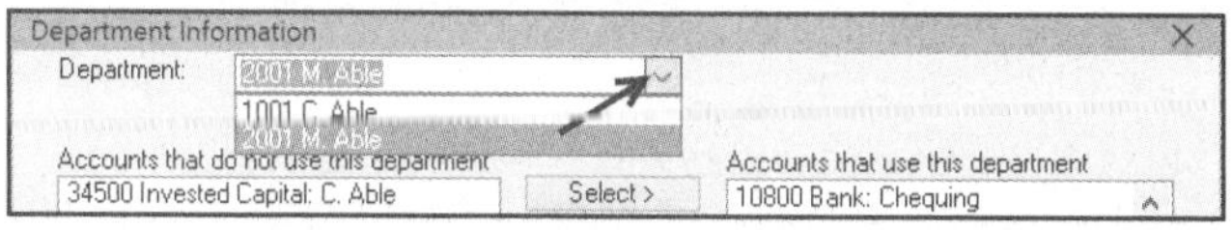

Click **34800 Invested Capital: M. Able** to select the account. **Click Remove**.

To move an account back to the "Use" list, click it again and then click Select.

WARNING!
The Department Code must be a four-digit number. No letters or other characters are allowed.

NOTES
Able & Associates uses five-digit account numbers. This selection is made from the Settings screen for General (Accounts) as a Numbering option (refer to page 81).

Click an account that you want to change and then press and hold *ctrl*. Click each account you want until all the accounts you want are included.

Click the Remove button to shift the selected accounts to the "Do Not Use" column.

Click Remove All to shift all the accounts to the "Do Not Use" column.

If only a few accounts use a department, it is easier to place them all on the "Do Not Use" side and then move the few to the "Use" side.

Reverse this procedure to move an account from the "Do Not Use" to the "Use" side. Click the account on the "Do Not Use" side and then click the Select button.

Click **OK** to return to the Settings window. **Click** **OK** to return to the Home window.

Adding Departments to Accounts

Instead of adding department information to accounts from the Department Information window, you can add departments in the account ledger record directly.

✓ 2

Memo #2 **Dated April 1/21**

Assign accounts to departments. Invested Capital accounts are used by the department named in the account. All other accounts are used by both departments.

NOTES
You can also create a View Accounts shortcut (Banking Module) that will open the Accounts window. Double-click the account you need.

Click **Company** in the Modules Pane list. **Click** the **Chart of Accounts icon**.

Double-click **34500 Invested Capital: C. Able** in the list of accounts to open the General Ledger.

A new tab, Departments, has been added to the ledger record.

Click the **Departments tab** to open the new screen:

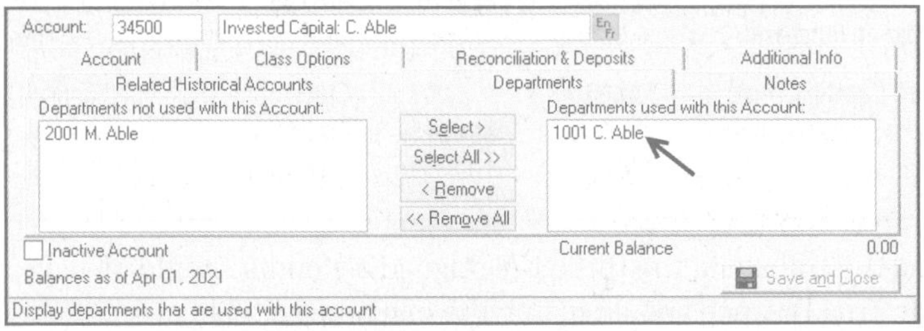

Department 2001 M. Able is located on the left-hand side under **Departments Not Used With This Account** because we moved it earlier on the Settings screen. The **Departments Used With This Account** column has 1001 C. Able in it.

On this screen, you can designate the departments that the account uses. You can modify these selections at any time. This screen is the same as the one for Department Information, except that now we are selecting the department instead of the account. However, in the General Ledger, you change the information for only one account at a time.

Click a department to select it or press *ctrl* and click more than one department if you want to select additional departments. Clicking Select will add the department to the account. Clicking Remove will remove a selected department from the account and place it on the "Not Used" side. Remove All and Select All will move all departments at once to the other side.

Close the **Ledger window**. **Close** the **Accounts window**.

Adding Opening Departmental Balances

NOTES

An alternative method would be to enter all opening account balances as usual and then make General Journal entries to divide the principal account amount between the two department accounts. Using this method, you would credit 10800 and debit 10800 - 1001 and 10800 - 2001.

In this case, you must still start with the history unfinished and before entering the linked accounts for Accounts Receivable and Accounts Payable so that you can access these accounts in the journal (refer to page 794).

NOTES

Remember to reverse the usual liability entries for HST Paid on Purchases because this contra-liability account normally has a debit balance.

When you create a new company data file and add General Ledger accounts, you must enter the opening account balances as well, but you cannot split these balances among the departments. However, when you are entering transactions and have set up departments, you can choose a department from any Account field that allows you to select an account. We will use this approach to enter the opening departmental balances for all accounts. Initially we placed the total for all Balance Sheet accounts in the "unassigned" placeholder accounts for each section. When we transfer these amounts back to their appropriate accounts through General Journal entries, we can also assign departments.

✓ 3

Memo #3 **Dated April 1/21**

Assign departmental opening account balances by transferring the unassigned balances from the chart below. Add linked accounts and then finish the history.

Account		Department Amounts 1001: C. Able	2001: M. Able	Source
10800	Bank: Chequing	$ 12 780	$ 8 520	Debit from Unassigned Assets
11000	Investments	26 500	17 500	Debit from Unassigned Assets
11200	Prepaid Association Dues	1 400	1 400	Debit from Unassigned Assets
11400	Prepaid Subscriptions	900	600	Debit from Unassigned Assets
11600	Prepaid Insurance	2 700	1 800	Debit from Unassigned Assets
12000	Accounts Receivable	2 260		Debit from Unassigned Assets
13400	Office Supplies	1 080	720	Debit from Unassigned Assets
14400	Office Equipment	7 200	4 800	Debit from Unassigned Assets
14800	Office Furniture	4 000	4 000	Debit from Unassigned Assets
15000	Library	2 400	2 400	Debit from Unassigned Assets
21000	Bank Loan	9 000	6 000	Credit from Unassigned Liabilities
22000	Accounts Payable	1 356	904	Credit from Unassigned Liabilities
22500	Visa Payable	840	560	Credit from Unassigned Liabilities
26500	HST Charged on Services	1 320	880	Credit from Unassigned Liabilities
26700	HST Paid on Purchases	984	656	Debit from Unassigned Liabilities
34500	Invested Capital: C. Able	33 000		Credit from Unassigned Capital
34800	Invested Capital: M. Able		22 000	Credit from Unassigned Capital
35500	Retained Earnings	17 244	11 496	Credit from Unassigned Capital

After entering the transfers, the three Unassigned accounts should all have zero balances and your Trial Balance should match the one on page 786.

Click the **General Journal icon** General Journal.

Type `Memo 3A` as the Source, and **enter April 1** as the date.

Click the **Comment field** and **type** `Transfer opening asset account balances to departments`

Click the **Account field List icon**. The modified Select Account list opens.

Each account has a ⊞ icon added to indicate additional information is available. When you click the ⊞, all departments used by that account will be listed, so you can select a department for the transaction.

Click the ⊞ **icon** beside **10800 Bank: Chequing**:

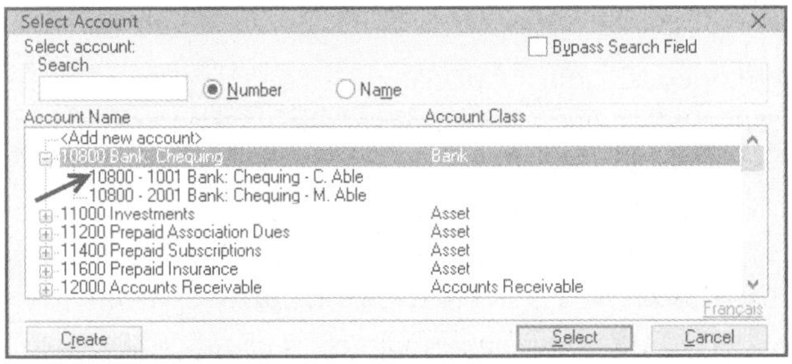

The modified list now has the departments connected with the account.

Bank: Chequing has both departments available for a journal transaction. If you click the ⊞ beside *34500 Invested Capital: C. Able*, you can select only the one department that we assigned to it.

Click **10800 - 1001 Bank: Chequing - C. Able**.

Click **Select** to return to the journal with the cursor in the Debits field.

Type 12780 to enter the portion of the asset for this department.

Click the **Account field List icon** again. **Click** ⊞ beside **10800**.

Double-click **10800 - 2001 Bank: Chequing - M. Able**. The cursor advances to the Credits field.

Type −8520 (add a minus sign to the amount). **Press** tab. The amount moves to the Debits column because we typed the minus sign.

Click the **Account field** and **type** 19500

Press tab to enter the total balance for the asset as a credit entry.

Accounts with departments all use the same format: account number, space, hyphen, space, department number. We can use this format to enter account numbers directly in a journal without using the Select Account list. You can omit the spaces when typing these numbers; Sage 50 will add them.

Click the **Account field** on the next blank line.

Type 11000-1001

Press tab to enter the account and advance to the Debits field.

Type 26500

Click the **Account field** and **type** 11000-2001

Press tab and **type** −17500 to move the amount to the Debits field.

Click the **Account field** and **type** 19500 **Press** tab to enter the credit amount. **Press** tab again to update the totals.

At this stage, your journal entry should look like the one below:

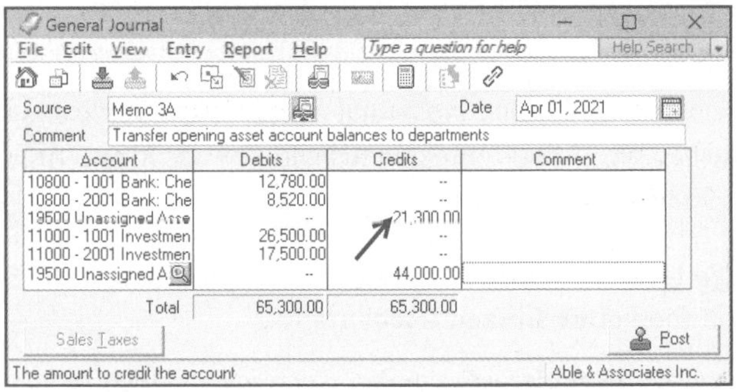

NOTES

You can enter all the debit asset accounts first and then enter a single total for 19500 Unassigned Assets. We have chosen to transfer the balances for one account at a time so we can check our work more easily. For each transfer, the amount from 19500 Unassigned Assets should match the amount for the General Ledger account in the Trial Balance on page 786.

NOTES

Typing the account number may be faster because the Select Account list appears without the department subaccounts expanded. You must click ⊞ each time.

Before continuing, we will review the partially completed journal entry.

Press *ctrl* **+ J** to open the journal display:

Able & Associates Inc.
General Journal Entry 04/01/2021 (J1)

Account Number	Account Description	Debits	Credits
10800 - 1001	Bank: Chequing - C. Able	12,780.00	-
10800 - 2001	Bank: Chequing - M. Able	8,520.00	-
19500	Unassigned Assets	-	21,300.00
11000 - 1001	Investments - C. Able	26,500.00	-
11000 - 2001	Investments - M. Able	17,500.00	-
19500	Unassigned Assets	-	44,000.00
Additional Date:	Additional Field:	65,300.00	65,300.00

The journal entry is different from the usual one in one significant way — we were able to divide the balance in each asset account between the two departments. These separate amounts can be added to the standard financial reports and will enable us to produce separate reports for each department.

Close the **journal display**.

Enter the **remaining asset account balance transfers** from memo #3 on page 792.

Review the **journal entry** again to verify that the total debits and credits match the initial account balance for *Unassigned Assets*.

Post the **journal entry** after entering all the asset account balances.

Enter the **liability account balance transfers** from memo #3 on page 792 as the second journal entry.

NOTES
Do not enter sales tax information when prompted for the HST accounts (click Yes to confirm that you do not want to add sales tax details).

Review the **transaction**, **make corrections** and then **post** it:

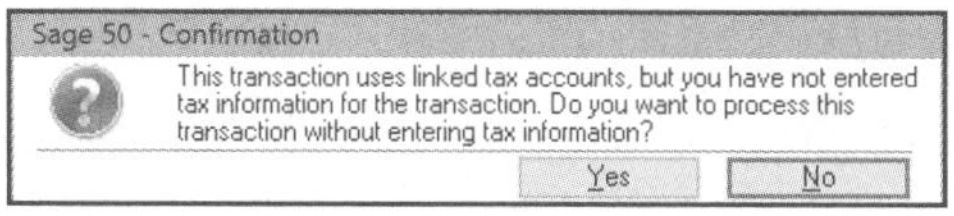

Sage 50 warns that you are using linked tax accounts without entering sales tax details. In this case you should continue because we are not entering sales or expenses.

Click **Yes** to process the transaction as entered.

Enter the **capital account balance transfers** from memo #3 on page 792 as the third journal entry.

NOTES
Remember you can adjust General Journal entries after posting. Refer to page 47.

Review the **transaction** and then **post** it when the amounts are correct.

Close the **General Journal** to return to the Company module window.

Compare your **Trial Balance** with the one on page 786 and make corrections if needed.

WARNING!
If you try to finish the history now, you will get the error message that the essential linked accounts are missing.

If you entered the amounts correctly, the account balances for *Accounts Receivable* and *Accounts Payable* should match the historical invoice balances. However, before we can finish the history, we must add the missing essential linked accounts.

Finishing the History

Because we needed to access *Accounts Receivable* and *Accounts Payable* as postable accounts in the General Journal, we did not enter them as linked accounts. To finish the history, you must add these essential linked accounts.

Click the **Settings icon** Settings. **Click Payables** in the left panel of the Settings window and then **click Linked Accounts**.

Enter **22000 Accounts Payable** as the linked account for Accounts Payable.

Enter **22000 Accounts Payable** as the linked account for Prepayments and Prepaid Orders.

Click **Receivables** in the left panel of the Settings window and then **click Linked Accounts**.

Enter **12000 Accounts Receivable** as the linked account for Accounts Receivable.

Enter **12000 Accounts Receivable** as the linked account for Deposits and Prepaid Orders.

Click **OK** to save the settings.

Choose the **History menu** and **click Finish Entering History**.

Click **Backup** and continue to back up the not-finished file. **Click OK** when the backup is complete.

Click **Proceed** to finish the history.

NOTES
Prepayments and deposits are not used, but linked accounts for them are required. Therefore, we can use Accounts Payable and Accounts Receivable.

WARNING!
Make a backup copy of the not-finished file so you can correct opening balance amounts later if necessary.

Adding Departments to Client Records

If some clients or vendors deal with only one department, you can add this information to the ledger record. C. Able has Adrienne Aesthetics as an exclusive client, and Dorfmann Design deals only with M. Able.

✓ 4

Memo #4 **Dated April 1/21**

Clients: Assign C. Able to Adrienne Aesthetics and M. Able to Dorfmann Design. The remaining clients are associated with both departments.

Click **Receivables** in the Modules pane list. **Click Adrienne Aesthetics** in the Clients List pane to open the record at the Address tab screen.

A Department field has been added to the Address tab screen.

Click the **Department list arrow** for the drop-down list of departments:

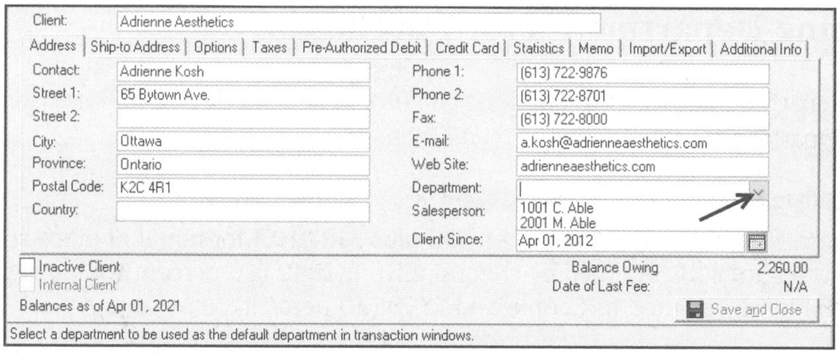

Click **1001 C. Able** to select the department.

Next we need to select the departmental revenue account as the client's default.

Click the **Options tab** so you can change the default revenue account.

Click the **Revenue Account field list arrow** for the expanded account list:

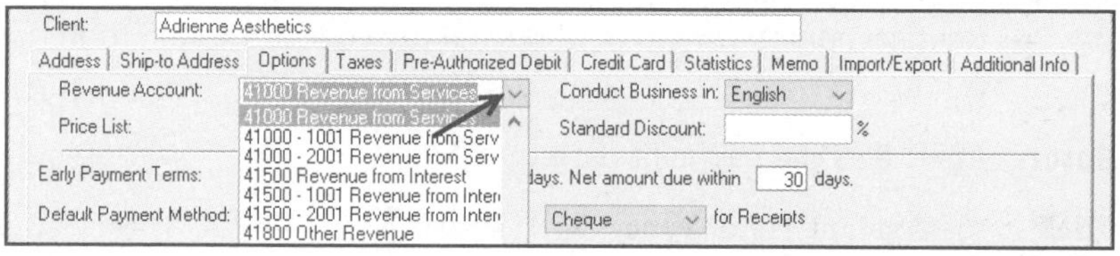

NOTES
If a client or vendor is used by more than one department, you should not add a department to the record.

NOTES
Another field is added to the ledger record – the Standard Discount field. Entering a rate in this field will add it to the Sales Journal automatically as the line discount rate (refer to page 799). You can still change the line discount rate in the journal.

Each account has three numbers associated with it — one for the main account and one for each department. By selecting the departmental account in the ledger record, department information will be added as the default when you sell to this client.

Choose **41000 - 1001 Revenue from Services - C. Able** from the Account list.

Click the **Next Client tool** to open the record for Dorfmann Design.

Choose **41000 - 2001 Revenue from Services - M. Able** from the Revenue Account list.

Click the **Address tab** and **enter 2001 M. Able** in the Department field.

Click Save and Close.

The remaining clients work with both departments, so we cannot add one department exclusively for them.

Adding Departments to Vendor Records

If a vendor is connected exclusively with one department, you can add the department to the vendor record, just as you do for clients. At this time, all vendors are used by both departments, so we will not add departments to the records.

If you want to add departments to vendor records, open the Payables module window and then open the vendor record. The Department field has been added to the Address tab screen.

Click the Department field list arrow and click the department you want.

On the Options tab screen, choose the departmental account as the default for expenses.

Repeat this procedure for other vendors. Close the last vendor record.

Adding Departments to Journal Transactions

Entering Departments for Purchases

Adding departmental details to purchases involves selecting the appropriate General Ledger departmental subaccount instead of the main one.

NOTES
You can also enter this purchase in the Payments Journal as an Other Payment. Enter the amounts and choose the departmental accounts in the same way as described here.

✓ 5

Cheque Purchase Invoice #NO-2021-4 **Dated April 3/21**

From Northlands Office Mgt., $1 400 plus $182 HST for rental of office suite. Invoice total $1 582 paid by cheque #3011. $840 (60 percent) of the expense should be assigned to C. Able and $560 (40 percent) to M. Able.

Before proceeding, you should create shortcuts for the journals in other modules.

Create **shortcuts** to Create and Pay Vendor Invoice, to Create Paycheques and to Create General Journal Entries.

Click the **Create Vendor Invoices shortcut** to open the journal.

Choose **Northlands Office Mgt.** as the vendor. **Press** tab. The default general Rent account, payment method and tax code are added from the vendor's record.

Enter **April 3** as the payment date.

Click the **Amount field**. **Type** 840 **Press** tab.

Click the **List icon** beside *Rent* in the Account field to open the Select Account screen.

Click the icon beside **52400 Rent**:

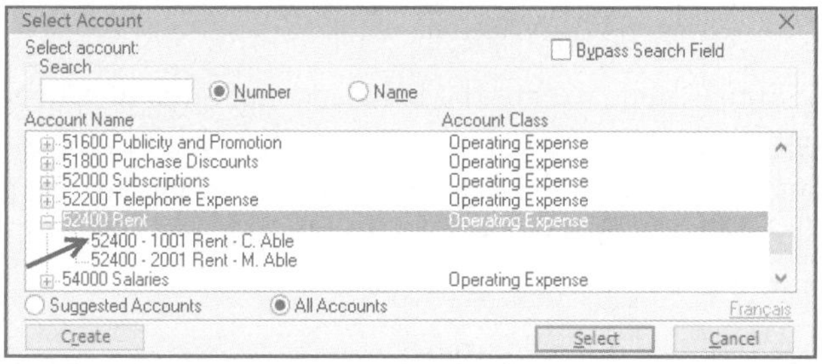

Department subaccounts are added, just as they were in the General Journal.

Click **52400 - 1001 Rent - C. Able**. **Press** *enter* to add the account for C. Able's share.

Click the **Amount field** on the second journal line. **Type** 560

Press *tab*. **Click** the **Account field List icon**.

Choose **52400 - 2001 Rent - M. Able**. **Press** *enter* to add the account for M. Able's share.

Enter **line Descriptions** and **Source** information to complete the entry.

Choose the **Report menu** and **click** **Display Payments Journal entry**:

Able & Associates Inc.
Expenses Journal Entry 04/03/2021 (J4)

Account Number	Account Description	Debits	Credits
26700	HST Paid on Purchases	182.00	-
52400 - 1001	Rent - C. Able	840.00	-
52400 - 2001	Rent - M. Able	560.00	-
10800	Bank: Chequing	-	1,582.00
Additional Date:	Additional Field:	1,582.00	1,582.00

The rental expense amount has been shared between the two departments, but the other amounts have not. Because no single department is linked to the vendor, and the other accounts for the transaction are not accessible, they remain unallocated.

Close the **journal display** to return to the journal.

Click the **Paid From bank account list arrow**:

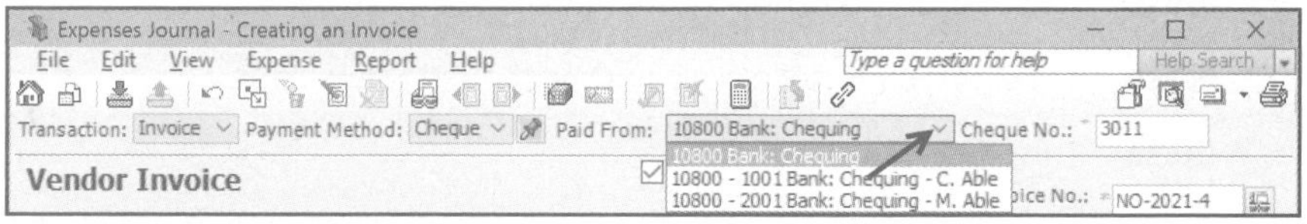

You can change the default bank account for this payment, but you can choose only one account for the single cheque. A complete allocation requires access to both bank department subaccounts. Therefore, you cannot allocate the bank amount.

Make **corrections** if necessary. **Post** the **transaction** and **close** the **journal**.

NOTES

You can create separate bank accounts that link to the different departments.

You could also make separate payment journal entries for each department amount. This will allow you to choose the associated departmental bank account number, but not the department for tax accounts.

Entering Departments for Receipts

✓ 6

Receipt #48 **Dated April 4/21**

From Adrienne Aesthetics, cheque #3101 for $2 214.80, including $45.20 discount in full payment of invoice #843. Assign all amounts to C. Able.

Restore the **Receivables module** as the Home window if necessary.

Click the **Receipts Journal icon** to open the journal.

Choose **Adrienne Aesthetics**. **Press** tab to add the outstanding invoice.

Enter **Apr 4 20** as the date and **enter 3101** as the client's cheque number.

Accept the **discount taken** and **amount received**.

Press ctrl + **J** to review the transaction.

NOTES

If a client works with more than one department, you will be unable to allocate the amounts for the receipt.

All amounts are allocated to C. Able except the bank account amount. The accounts are allocated because we set up a unique department link for the client in the ledger record. The allocated amounts are those for the default linked accounts for the journal. In this case, we can also allocate the bank amount — because only one department is involved, we can select the account.

Close the **display** to return to the journal.

Click the **Deposit To bank account list arrow**:

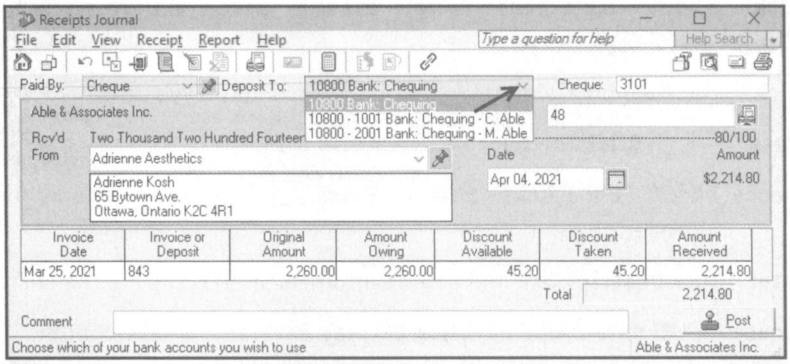

Click **10800 - 1001 Bank: Chequing - C. Able** to update the journal entry.

Press ctrl + **J** to review the transaction:

Able & Associates Inc.
Receipts Journal Entry 04/04/2021 (J5)

Account Number	Account Description	Debits	Credits
10800 - 1001	Bank: Chequing - C. Able	2,214.80	-
42000 - 1001	Sales Discounts - C. Able	45.20	-
12000 - 1001	Accounts Receivable - C. Able	-	2,260.00
Additional Date:	Additional Field:	2,260.00	2,260.00

The entry is now completely allocated and it is correct. All amounts, including the discount, are attributed to C. Able's department.

Close the **display** to return to the journal.

Make **corrections** if necessary and **post** the **transaction**.

Close the **Receipts Journal**.

Entering Departments for Sales with Line Discounts

Click the **Client Invoices icon** Client Invoices to open the Fees Journal.

✓ 7

Sales Invoice #851 **Dated April 4/21**

To Adrienne Aesthetics, $5 800 plus HST for auditing financial statements and $900 plus HST for monthly accounting fee. Invoice total $7 243.30. Terms: 2/10, n/30. Additional 5 percent discount applies to the fee for auditing, by special arrangement with client. Adrienne Aesthetics is C. Able's client.

Choose **Adrienne Aesthetics**. **Press** tab to add the client's record details.

Enter **April 4** as the date. This time the default revenue account is correct:

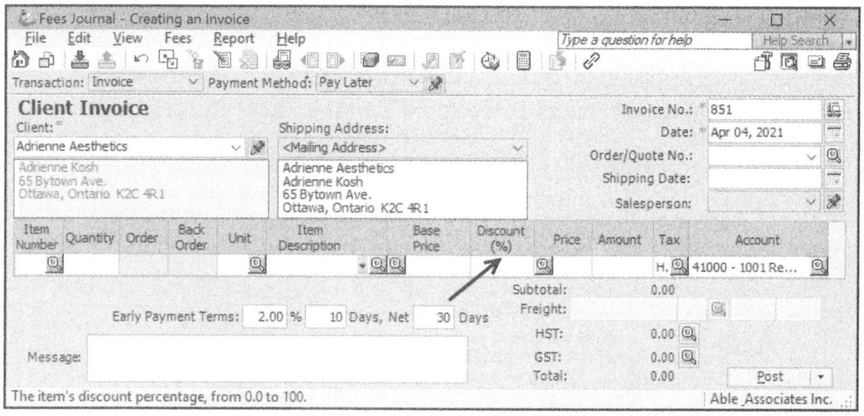

The department subaccount is taken from the record because a single department is linked to the client and we added the department subaccount as the default revenue account.

Two columns — **Base Price** and **Discount %** — have been added to the journal. These fields allow us to add discounts that apply only to a single invoice line, so you can enter different discount rates for each invoice line. Able & Associates offers some clients additional discounts. For the auditing services, a 5 percent discount applies.

Entering Line Discounts

Click the **Item Description field**.

Type `prepare audited financial statements`

Press *tab* to advance to the Base Price field.

Type `5800`

Press *tab* to advance to the Discount % field.

Type `5`

Press *tab* to apply the amount of the discount — $290.00.

The new discounted unit price, $5 510, has been added to the Price field, but the Amount field is still blank. To enter the amount automatically, you must enter the quantity for the line.

Click the **Quantity field**. **Type** `1` **Press** *tab* to update the line.

The discounted amount, $5 510, is now entered as the amount.

Press *ctrl* **+ J** to review the transaction as we have entered it so far:

Able & Associates Inc.
Fees Journal Entry 04/04/2021 (J6)

Account Number	Account Description	Debits	Credits
12000 - 1001	Accounts Receivable - C. Able	6,226.30	-
26500 - 1001	HST Charged on Services - C. Able	-	716.30
41000 - 1001	Revenue from Services - C. Able	-	5,510.00
Additional Date:	Additional Field:	6,226.30	6,226.30

Again, all amounts are allocated correctly because we have linked a single account and department to the record. The discount is taken directly to reduce revenue; it is not linked to the sales discount account used for early payments.

Close the **display** to return to the journal and complete the entry.

Click the **Item Description field**. **Type** `monthly fee`

Click the **Amount field**. No discount applies to this service.

Type 900

Press tab **twice** to add the tax code and advance to the Account field. The default account should be entered automatically.

Review the **entry**, **make corrections** and then **post** the **transaction**.

Close the **Sales Journal**.

If the client is eligible for line discounts on a regular basis, you can add that information directly to the ledger record on the Options tab screen in the Standard Discount field:

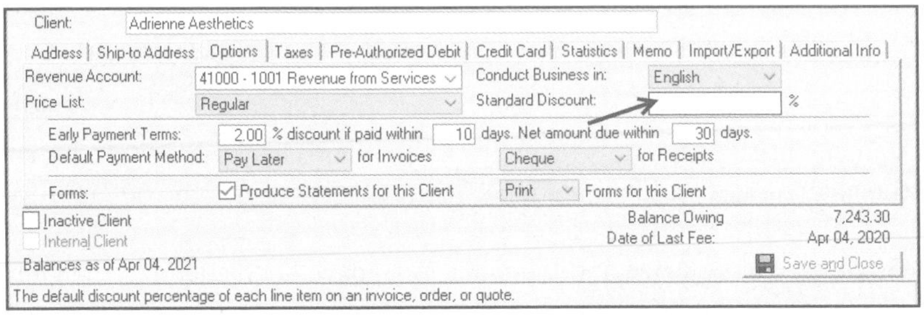

Continue with the **transactions** up to the payroll entry on April 30.

NOTES

You will be unable to allocate the payment to Office Plus because more than one department is involved and you cannot select accounts for payments. As for the cash purchase, you can choose only one bank account, so this amount also remains unallocated.

8 **Payment Cheque #3012** **Dated April 5/21**

To Office Plus, $2 237.40, including $22.60 discount in full payment of invoice #OP-2339. (You cannot assign these amounts – read the margin Notes.)

NOTES

For the sale to Truman Tires, enter 600 as the amount for account 41000 - 1001, and on the second line enter 400 as the amount for account 41000 - 2001. The amounts for Bank: Chequing, Sales Discounts and HST will remain unallocated.

Remember to change the payment method.

9 **Cash Sales Invoice #852** **Dated April 10/21**

To Truman Tires, $1 000 plus $130 HST for monthly fee for accounting assistance. Assign $600 (60%) of the fee to C. Able and $400 (40%) to M. Able. Received cheque #2900 for $1 107.40 in full payment, including 2% discount for early payment. (Read the margin Notes.)

10 **Sales Invoice #853** **Dated April 14/21**

To Dorfmann Design, $5 000 plus HST for preparing special financial reports for potential investors and $700 plus HST for monthly accounting fee. Invoice total $5 876 (with discount). Terms: 2/10, n/30. Additional 10 percent discount applies to the fee for preparing financial reports. Assign 100% of all amounts to M. Able.

11 **Sales Invoice #854** **Dated April 20/21**

To Gorgeous Gifts, $3 000 plus $390 HST for assistance with response to Canada Revenue Agency audit and $500 plus $65 HST for monthly accounting fee. Invoice total $3 955. Terms: 2/10, n/30. Assign $1 800 plus $300 (60%) of revenue amounts to C. Able and $1 200 and $200 (40%) to M. Able.

12 **Cash Purchase Invoice #BC-233008** **Dated April 22/21**

From Bell Canada, $400 plus $52 HST for monthly telephone and Internet service for one multi-line office telephone, two mobile phones and networked Internet service. Invoice total $452 paid by cheque #3013. Assign $240 (60%) of expense amount to C. Able and $160 (40%) to M. Able.

NOTES

For the purchase from Office Plus, enter 1800 as the amount for account 14800 - 1001, and on the second line enter 1200 as the amount for account 14800 - 2001. The amounts for Accounts Payable and HST will remain unallocated.

13 **Purchase Invoice #OP-5102** **Dated April 25/21**

From Office Plus, $3 000 plus $390 HST for new boardroom table and chairs (Office Furniture account). Invoice total $3 390. Terms: 1/15, n/30. Assign $1 800 (60%) of the asset account amount to C. Able and $1 200 (40%) to M. Able. (Read the margin Notes.)

14 **Cash Sales Invoice #855** **Dated April 28/21**

To various one-time clients, $6 000 plus $780 HST for personal income tax preparation. Total cash received, $6 780, deposited to bank account. Assign $3 600 (60%) of revenue amount to C. Able and $2 400 (40%) to M. Able.

15 **Memo #5** **Dated April 28/21**

Remit the HST owing to the Receiver General as at March 31. Issue cheque #3014 for $560 in payment. Assign $1 320 for HST Charged on Services and $984 for HST Paid (60% of HST amounts) to C. Able and $880 for HST Charged on Services and $656 for HST Paid (40%) to M. Able.

Entering Departments for Payroll Transactions

Payroll amounts are allocated to departments differently than amounts in other journals. If an employee works only with one department, you can add the department to the employee's ledger record.

✓ 16 **Memo #6** **Dated April 30/21**

Prepare payroll for Tryin, office assistant. Issue cheque #3015. Assign 60% of all amounts to C. Able and 40% to M. Able.

Click the **Create Paycheque shortcut** to open the journal.

Choose **Tryin, Reelie**. **Press** tab to add the employee's default record details.

All Payroll Journal accounts are linked accounts, so you cannot choose the department subaccounts to enter allocations. Instead, you can open the Department Allocation screens from the Paycheque menu:

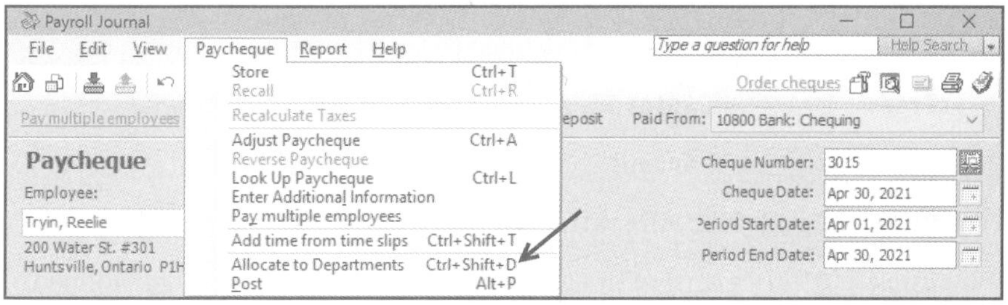

You can also use the Departments tool:

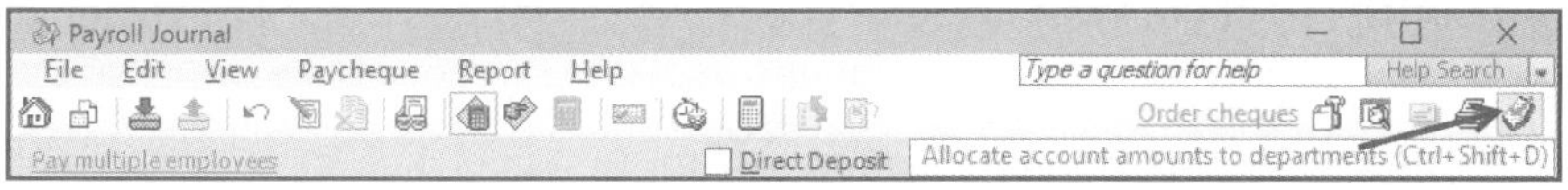

Choose the **Paycheque menu** and **click** **Allocate To Departments**, or

Click the **Allocate Account Amounts To Departments tool**.

Both methods will open the Allocation screen:

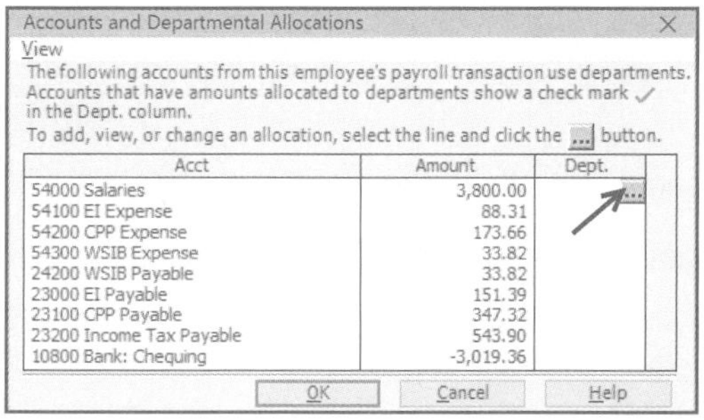

NOTES

The Payroll Run Journal has the same departmental allocation options – the tool button and the Payroll menu. Select an employee and then click the tool button or choose from the Payroll menu to begin. The amounts for the selected employee will open. Allocations are made separately for each employee – you cannot complete the allocations for all employees in a single step.

You can allocate the individual journal amounts for each employee differently.

All accounts used in the journal entry are listed, and you can allocate one or more of them, or all, in the same way, or you can use different percentages or amounts.

Click the **Department Detail button** (in the Dept. column) for Salaries:

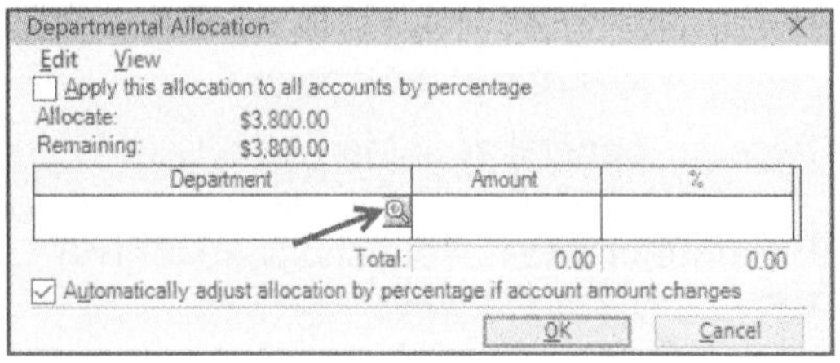

This screen is similar to the one we use to enter division allocations (refer to page 508). You can select one or more departments for each journal entry amount, and each of these amounts can be allocated differently. Or, you can apply the same allocation to all accounts, just as we did for divisions in Chapter 13 (pages 515–517). Payroll amounts for the Ables are allocated by percentage, but you can allocate by amount if you prefer. You do not need to allocate the entire amount for an account. We want the same breakdown to apply to all amounts.

Click the **Department List icon** to open the selection list for departments:

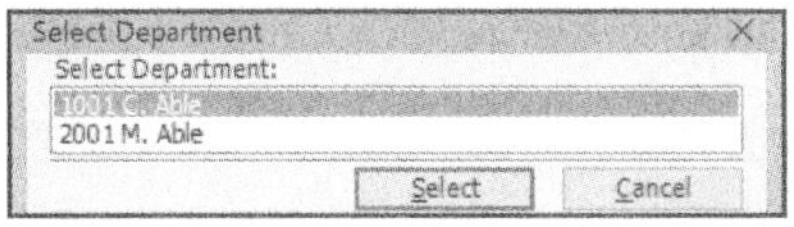

Click **1001 C. Able**. **Click Select** to add the department.

Press tab to advance to the % (percentage) field.

Type 60 **Press** tab to advance to the Department field again.

Press enter and **enter M. Able** for the rest of the allocation.

Press tab and **accept** the **default entry** — 40 percent.

Click **Apply This Allocation To All Accounts By Percentage**.

Click **OK** to return to the account list screen. A ✓ has been added to each account in the Dept. column.

Click **10800 Bank: Chequing** to select the account line. The Detail button now appears on this line.

Click the **Dept. Detail button** for this account:

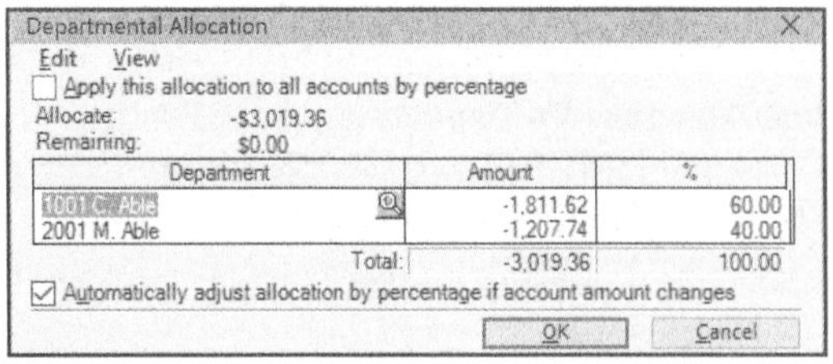

The same 60–40 allocation is applied. But in this window, you have the option to change the allocation for the single account without affecting the others.

Click **OK** to accept the amounts already entered (or Cancel).

Click **OK** again to return to the journal and review the entry.

Press *ctrl* + **J** to view the journal entry:

Able & Associates Inc.
Payroll Journal Entry 04/30/2021 (J15)

Account Number	Account Description	Debits	Credits
54000 - 1001	Salaries - C. Able	2,280.00	-
54000 - 2001	Salaries - M. Able	1,520.00	-
54100 - 1001	EI Expense - C. Able	52.99	-
54100 - 2001	EI Expense - M. Able	35.32	-
54200 - 1001	CPP Expense - C. Able	104.20	-
54200 - 2001	CPP Expense - M. Able	69.46	-
54300 - 1001	WSIB Expense - C. Able	20.29	-
54300 - 2001	WSIB Expense - M. Able	13.53	-
10800 - 1001	Bank: Chequing - C. Able	-	1,811.62
10800 - 2001	Bank: Chequing - M. Able	-	1,207.74
23000 - 1001	EI Payable - C. Able	-	90.83
23000 - 2001	EI Payable - M. Able	-	60.56
23100 - 1001	CPP Payable - C. Able	-	208.39
23100 - 2001	CPP Payable - M. Able	-	138.93
23200 - 1001	Income Tax Payable - C. Able	-	326.34
23200 - 2001	Income Tax Payable - M. Able	-	217.56
24200 - 1001	WSIB Payable - C. Able	-	20.29
24200 - 2001	WSIB Payable - M. Able	-	13.53
Additional Date:	Additional Field:	4,095.79	4,095.79

All amounts are automatically applied in the 60–40 ratio for the two departments.

Close the **display** to return to the journal.

Make **corrections** if necessary and **post** the **transaction**.

Close the **Paycheques Journal**.

Enter the final **two General Journal entries** with allocations for all accounts.

17

Memo #7 **Dated April 30/21**

The following transactions appeared on the monthly bank statement for the Bank: Chequing account. Assign 60% of all amounts to C. Able and 40% to M. Able.

	Amounts for C. Able	Amounts for M. Able
Bank charges $60	$ 36	$ 24
Bank loan principal $300	180	120
Bank loan interest $200	120	80
Interest from investments $180	108	72
Bank net withdrawal $320	228	152

18

Memo #8 **Dated April 30/21**

Enter the adjustments for supplies used and prepaid expenses expired in April. Assign all amounts as indicated in the following summary. Create new Group Expense account 52600 Supplies Used.

	Amounts for C. Able	Amounts for M. Able
Office Supplies $100	$ 60	$ 40
Prepaid Insurance $500	300	200
Prepaid Association Dues $400	200	200
Prepaid Subscriptions $250	150	100

NOTES

If you credit (or debit) the bank account for each charge (or deposit) amount separately, you will not enter the final net withdrawal amounts.

Handling Unallocated Amounts

We saw that the amounts for some accounts in the journals were not allocated. Most of the affected accounts are Balance Sheet accounts, so many users prefer to apply departmental accounting only to Income Statement accounts to avoid these incomplete entries. Unallocated amounts can also leave Departmental Balance Sheets out of balance since some amounts will not be included. For example, in a purchase of assets, the asset account was allocated but the HST account was not.

To prepare complete Departmental reports without unallocated amounts, you can enter General Journal adjusting entries to transfer the balances from the main account to the correct departmental subaccount. Clearly this could be a time-consuming exercise, as you would have to first determine all the appropriate amounts. Furthermore, the linked *Accounts Receivable* and *Accounts Payable* accounts are not accessible as postable accounts, so you would still be unable to allocate these amounts. For this exercise, we will not enter the adjustments for unallocated amounts.

NOTES

In the Accountant Edition of Sage 50, all accounts are available for posting. Your accountant would be able to make these adjustments for you by working with an Accountant's Copy of your data file. Refer to Chapter 12.

Departmental Reports

Many of the standard Sage 50 reports can have department information added to them. In addition, the primary financial statements — the Balance Sheet, Income Statement and Trial Balance — are available as departmental reports. As before, we will work from the Report Centre.

Click the **Report Centre icon** 

in the Home window.

Click **Financials** to open the list of financial reports.

Click the ⊞ **beside Balance Sheet** to expand this list.

Click the ⊞ **beside Income Statement** to expand this list.

Click the ⊞ **beside Trial Balance** to expand this list:

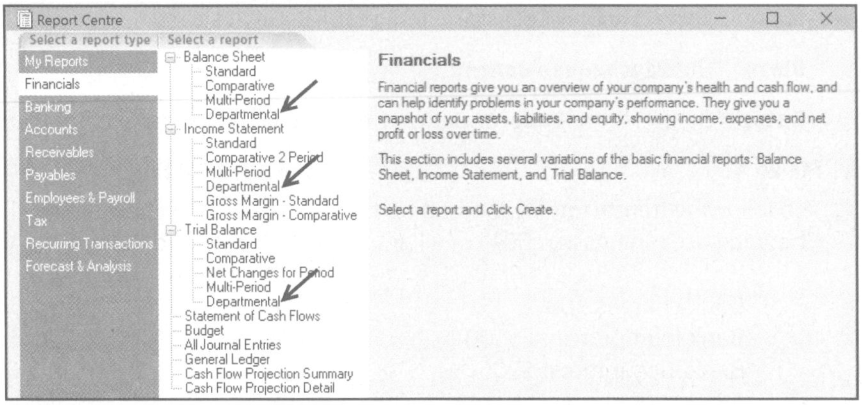

You can prepare a Departmental version of each of these reports.

Displaying Departmental Balance Sheets

NOTES
Including unallocated amounts – those not assigned to departments – and totals will provide balanced reports.

If you want Balance Sheet information for each department, you should prepare the Departmental Balance Sheet.

Click **Departmental** under **Balance Sheet**. **Click** **Modify This Report** to open the report options window:

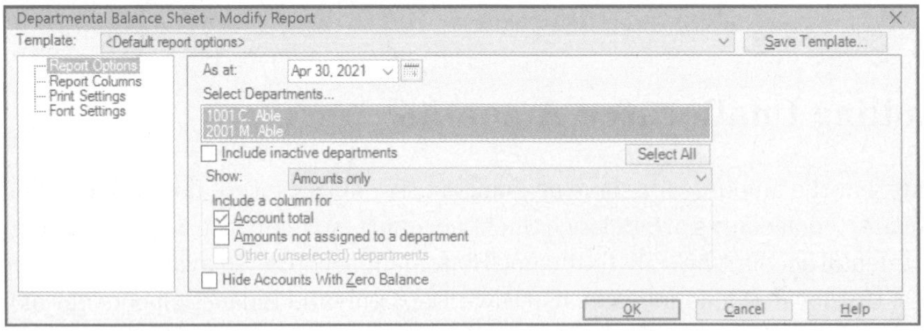

From the Home window, choose the Reports menu, then choose Financials and Departmental Reports and click Balance Sheet to open the report options.

You can report on one or more departments or all departments. The departmental amounts are in separate columns with headings, so you have a complete Balance Sheet for each department you selected. Remember that the sum of Balance Sheet amounts for each department may not equal the amount for the total Balance Sheet if some amounts were not allocated. Including Amounts Not Assigned To A Department will fill in these missing amounts.

Reports can include **Amounts** only or each amount as a **Percentage Of The Total**. You can also add **extra columns** for the total amount for each account, for amounts that are not assigned to any department and for the total amount for other departments not included in the report.

Choose the **departments** you want to include.

Choose the **Amounts Only** or **Percentage Of Total** option.

Choose the **additional columns** you want.

Enter the **date** for the report and **click OK**.

Close the **display** when you have finished.

Departmental Income Statement and Trial Balance Reports

Departmental Income Statements and Departmental Trial Balances are also available. The Departmental Income Statement is probably the most frequently used of these reports.

For both reports, select the departments to include in the report and choose whether you want to include amounts that are not assigned to a department. You can include amounts only or add the percentage of the total amount in your reports. The Trial Balance will also include adjustment amounts that are required to balance the debit and credit amounts. In other respects, these reports are like the standard non-departmental reports.

Adding Departments to Other Reports

Many other reports allow departmental details to be added after you set up and use departments. **Journal reports** automatically include the department number with the account numbers if you have added that information to the journal transaction.

The **Balance Sheet**, **Income Statement**, **Trial Balance** and **General Ledger** all have a **Show Departments** check box added. Division reports also have this option.

Access the **report options** in the usual way from the Report Centre or from the Reports menu.

The Standard Balance Sheet Report Options window, for example, has the Show Departments option added:

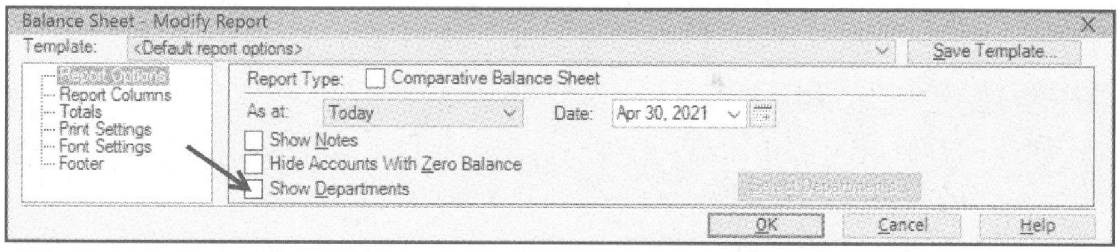

Click **Show Departments** to have the details added to the report.

Click the **Select Departments button** to open the department list:

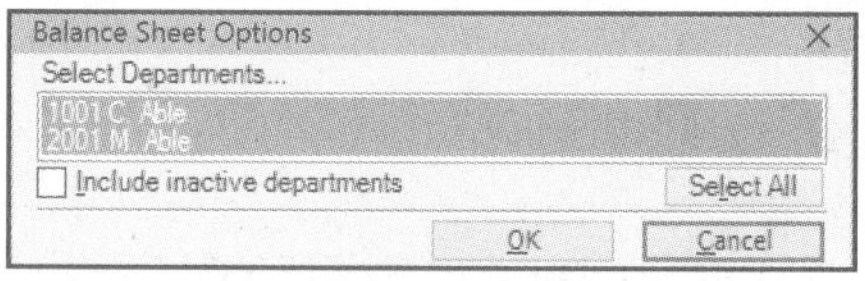

Select the **departments** you want to add to the report.

Click **OK** to return to the initial Balance Sheet Options window.

NOTES

Clicking Show Departments will make the Select Departments button available.

Choose other **report options** in the usual way and **click OK** to open the report.

Close the **display** when you have finished.

Department information can also be added to client and vendor reports. The Vendor Aged and Aged Overdue reports and the Pending Purchase Order Report allow you to group the vendors by department for the report. The Client Aged and Aged Overdue reports and the Pending Sales Order Report have the same option for grouping clients by department.

The Client Aged Report - Modify Report screen has this option:

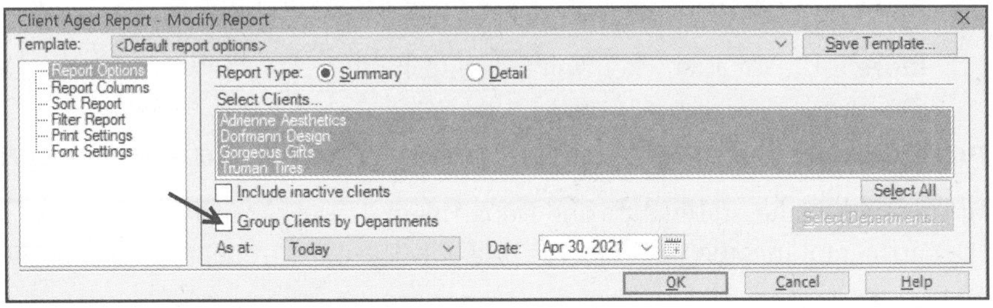

Click **Group Clients By Departments** to select the option.

Click the **Select Departments button** to open the department list.

Select the **departments** you want to add to the report.

You can include or omit clients that do not have an assigned department.

Click **OK** to return to the Client Aged Report options screen.

Choose other **report options** in the usual way.

Click **OK** to open the report.

The sale to Gorgeous Gifts will be listed in the report under the heading No Departments, Adrienne Aesthetics will be listed under C. Able and Dorfmann Design will be under M. Able.

Close the **display** when you have finished.

Close the **Report Centre** if it is open.

Congratulations on finishing the entire book!

PS... The Appendices on the Student DVD provide many advanced topics used in many businesses.

R E V I E W

The Student DVD with Data Files includes Review Questions and Supplementary Cases for this chapter.

Part 4

Appendices

APPENDIX A

Downloading, Installing and Activating the Student Version of Sage 50

Downloading the Sage 50 Student Program

STUDENT VERSION
The Student version is a single-user program.

NOTES
Your Internet screens will depend on the version of Windows and the Internet browser you are using. In addition, Web sites are updated regularly – always read and follow the instructions provided for you.

We used Windows 10 and Google Chrome for the screens in this Appendix.

WARNING!
If you have previously installed Sage 50, or an earlier Sage 50 Accounting Student version, you must uninstall that program before you can install the 2019 Sage 50 program. Use the Control Panel, Programs – Uninstall A Program function to uninstall the program properly.

Refer to Using This Book, page xii, for more information about different versions and the limitations of the Student version.

NOTES
You should complete your program registration before downloading the program. In this way, you will have the activation codes when you reach that stage (refer to page A–9).

NOTES
Sage Business Cloud Accounting and Sage 300 are other Sage programs that have a student version.

Farther down on this same Web page, you will find links for Support and Help as well as Training and Certification.

Most steps for installing the program are the same for all versions. The boxed notes on pages A–3 – A–4 outline the procedures for the retail Premium and Pro versions, including CD installation, registration and Payroll activation.

The Sage 50 Premium Student version is available only as a download.

Start your **computer** and open your **Internet browser** window.

Type `sage.com/ca/about-us/education` in the Web address field. **Press** *enter*:

Click **each step** to expand it (refer to page A–4) and read all instructions.

INSTALLING SAGE 50 RETAIL VERSION

If you have an active licence for Sage 50, you can install the 2019 program by **downloading** the **update** for your current installation. You can install this new release only from the latest release, so you must first update your current program (choose Check For Updates under the Help menu in the Home window). Your registration and activation information will be taken from your current installation. The 2019 program will be installed in a folder separate from the 2018 program.

INSTALLING SAGE 50 FROM THE PROGRAM CD

Insert the **Sage 50 program CD** in the CD/DVD drive. The Installation screen should open immediately. If it does not, in the **Windows Search field**, **type setup.EXE**. **Click** the entry that matches the program on your Sage 50 disk in the CD drive. On the **desktop** screen, **right-click** the **Start menu icon** and **choose Run**. **Type D:\Setup\setup.EXE** or **click Browse** to locate the program. Then **click This PC** or Computer and **double-click** the **Sage 50 CD**, **double-click** the **Setup** folder and **double-click setup** (or **setup.EXE**).

INSTALLING FROM A NEW DOWNLOAD

Download the **Sage 50** program from the Sage Web site <sage.com/ca/sage-50-accounting/>. **Click Buy Now** or **Start My Free Trial**. **Enter** the **Requested Information** and then **submit** your request. **Select** the **Sage 50 version** you want. **Choose Save File** when prompted and then choose to **Run** the program if you get an additional security message. **Click** the icon for the Download Manager that was placed on your desktop.

You can **choose** the **location** for the program files that will be extracted. **Accept** the **default location** or **choose** another **location**. Make a note of the location for later. **Click Save** to start the Sage Download Manager.

When you are ready to install the program, find the file you downloaded in the location you selected. **Double-click** the **program** icon or the **Sage folder** and **program** icon (or filename **SA_20190cp1.EXE**) to begin the installation. You will be asked to enter the location for the installer control files. **Accept** the **default location** or **click Browse** and **choose** another **location**.

Click Next. You will open the Sage 50 Installation screen on page A–6. **Click Install Sage 50** and follow the steps on the following pages until the registration screen opens, advising that you have XX days remaining (until the trial version expires).

REGISTERING AND ACTIVATING SAGE 50

Until you register and activate the program, you will be allowed to use the program for a limited number of days. The key code for each copy of the program is unique and applies only to that serial number.

Have your product serial number ready for the registration. You can **register online** or **by telephone**. The telephone number is provided. To register online, start your Internet connection. **Click** the **Register Online link** on the registration information screen. Follow the instructions provided. **Print** a copy of the **codes screen** for reference.

When you register **by telephone**, you will **provide** the **serial number** from your online purchase, program package or CD and **receive** an **account ID number**, a **key code number** and a **payroll ID number**. These numbers will be linked to the serial number you provided and cannot be used for a different copy of the program.

If you chose **Remind Me Later**, **open any data file**, **choose** the **Help menu** and **click Enter Key Code**. This reminder message will appear each time you start the program until you complete the activation.

To **retrieve** the **key code online**, the default selection, start your Internet connection and **click OK**. You will be connected to the Sage 50 Web site and the account ID and serial number will be uploaded from your program to create a key code. The **key code** will be **added** to your program **automatically**.

If you have already registered and have the activation codes, **click Activate Now**. **Enter** your **Company Name** and the **account ID** provided by Sage for the program you have registered. To **enter** the code on this screen **manually**, **click Use This Key Code** to open the Key Code fields. **Enter** the **Key Code** provided by Sage for this program. Enter all names and numbers exactly as they are given to you, including spaces and punctuation. The key code is not case sensitive. If you make a mistake, the program will warn you and you can re-enter the details.

Click OK. When you have completed the registration, Sage 50 will confirm that activation was successful. **Click OK** to continue to the Sage 50 Welcome/Select Company screen (refer to page A–9).

NOTES
From the Computer window, you can right-click D: and click Open Autoplay and Run Launch.EXE to start the auto-run feature and open the Installation options screen.

WARNING!
Do not remove the program CD before clicking Exit on the opening Sage 50 Installation screen (refer to the screenshot on page A–6).

NOTES
When you download the retail version, only the latest release will be available and it will be later than release 2019.0, the one we used for this text.

NOTES
The default installation destination folder will be Sage 50 Premium Accounting 2019 or Sage 50 Pro Accounting 2019.

STUDENT VERSION
The serial number for all copies of the Student version is 242P1U2-1000020.

NOTES
The letters o and i are not used in serial numbers, key codes or Payroll IDs.

NOTES
If you have not activated the program yet, you can do so from the Help menu. Choose Enter Key Code from the Help menu to open the You Have XX Days Remaining screen.

NOTES
If you have an existing account with Sage, registration may be completed automatically. You must still activate the program.

WARNING!
Do not install program updates when prompted if you are using this text. If you install program updates, you may use a later version than the one we use and your payroll amounts may be different from the ones we provide. Payroll tables are updated every six months and the Release number is linked to payroll tax table dates. After updating, you will no longer be able to open these data files with Release 2019.0.

WARNING!
This Web page has links for downloading several Sage 50 programs. Make sure that you choose 2019.0 in Step 3, the Download step.

NOTES
The arrows on this screenshot point to key parts of this Web page that you will need.

In Step 1, the documentation provides the system requirements for the Sage 50 program.

REGISTERING AND ACTIVATING SAGE 50 CONTINUED

Click Open Sample Company. **Click OK** to continue to the Session Date window. **Click OK** to accept the default session date. The session date is explained in Chapter 3 when you need to enter transactions.

With an open Internet connection, you can now view a short video to learn more or access this video later from the Help menu. These are some of the options on the Getting Started screen. **Click Close** to close the Getting Started window. For now, you can close any information screens about Sage services that pop up.

UNLOCKING SAGE 50 PAYROLL

You should unlock and activate the Payroll module before proceeding.

Choose the **Help menu** and **click Unlock Payroll**. An information screen about payroll services for Sage 50 opens, advising that you need a payroll ID and subscription to the Sage 50 Payroll Plan – a fee-based service – to use the payroll features in the program. To learn more about the payroll plan or to subscribe, **click Tell Me More**.

Click Enter Payroll ID. You must enter the account payroll ID numbers provided for your program registration.

The default selection is to **retrieve** the **payroll ID online**. Be sure that your Internet connection is open. **Click** the **Account ID field** and **type** your **account number**. **Click OK**. The **payroll ID** will be **downloaded directly** to your program.

If you have the number already, you can enter it **manually**. **Click Use This Payroll ID** to make this selection. **Click** the **Payroll ID field** and **type** the **number** provided, exactly as it is given to you. The code is not case sensitive. **Click OK**.

When Sage 50 confirms that payroll activation was successful, **click OK** to continue.

After you have activated your program and unlocked payroll, you can retrieve these codes automatically by selecting the online options if you need to reinstall the program.

The expanded instructions are combined here:

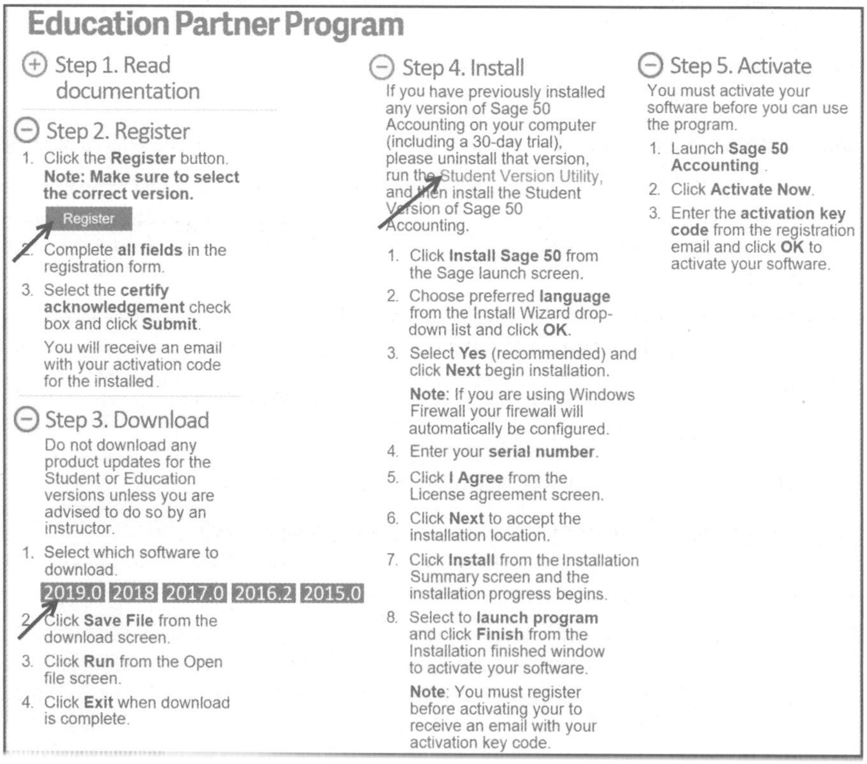
Education Partner Program

Step 1. Read documentation

Step 2. Register
1. Click the **Register** button. **Note: Make sure to select the correct version.**
Register
2. Complete **all fields** in the registration form.
3. Select the **certify acknowledgement** check box and click **Submit**.
You will receive an email with your activation code for the installed.

Step 3. Download
Do not download any product updates for the Student or Education versions unless you are advised to do so by an instructor.
1. Select which software to download.
2019.0 | 2018 | 2017.0 | 2016.2 | 2015.0
2. Click **Save File** from the download screen.
3. Click **Run** from the Open file screen.
4. Click **Exit** when download is complete.

Step 4. Install
If you have previously installed any version of Sage 50 Accounting on your computer (including a 30-day trial), please uninstall that version, run the Student Version Utility, and then install the Student Version of Sage 50 Accounting.
1. Click **Install Sage 50** from the Sage launch screen.
2. Choose preferred **language** from the Install Wizard drop-down list and click **OK**.
3. Select **Yes** (recommended) and click **Next** begin installation.
Note: If you are using Windows Firewall your firewall will automatically be configured.
4. Enter your **serial number**.
5. Click **I Agree** from the License agreement screen.
6. Click **Next** to accept the installation location.
7. Click **Install** from the Installation Summary screen and the installation progress begins.
8. Select to **launch program** and click **Finish** from the Installation finished window to activate your software.
Note: You must register before activating your to receive an email with your activation key code.

Step 5. Activate
You must activate your software before you can use the program.
1. Launch **Sage 50 Accounting**.
2. Click **Activate Now**.
3. Enter the **activation key code** from the registration email and click **OK** to activate your software.

By registering first, you will have the key code you need to activate the program after you finish the installation.

Registering the Student Version

Click **Register** in **Step 2 number 1**.

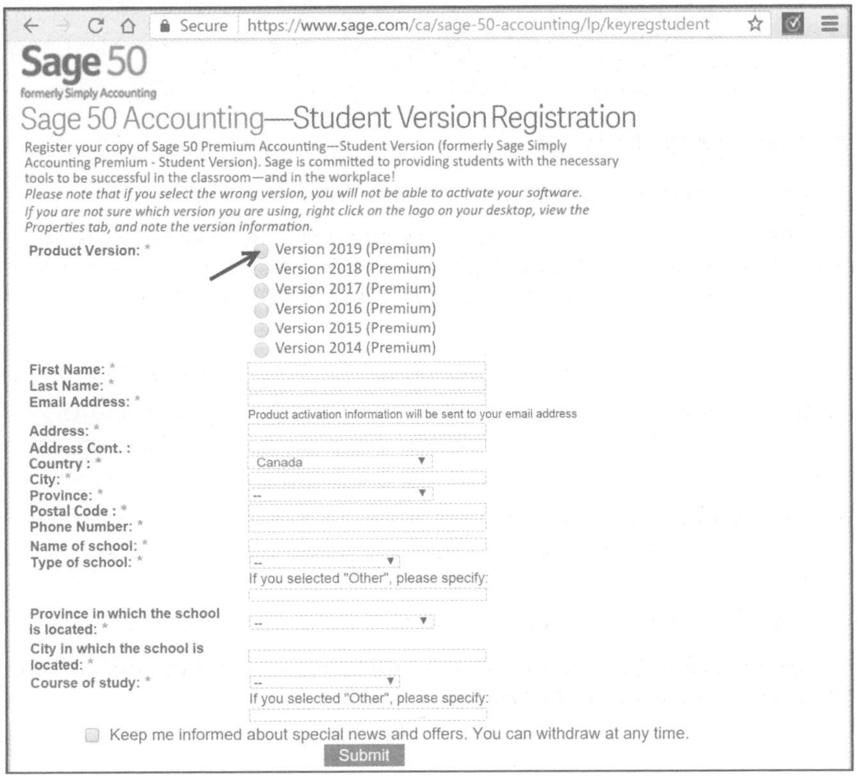

All fields are **required** for your registration. First you should choose the version you are registering. Several versions of Sage 50 are registered from this page, so you must choose the right one.

Click **Version 2019 (Premium)**.

Enter **your own first and last name** and **e-mail address** in the appropriate fields.

Enter your **address** (**street**, **country**, **city**, **province** and **postal code**) and **phone number**.

Enter the name of **your school**, and select the **type of school** and **province** from the drop-down lists.

Enter the **city** your school is located in and **select** the **course of study** from the drop-down list.

Click **Submit** when you have finished.

Sage 50 provides a message confirming the successful registration:

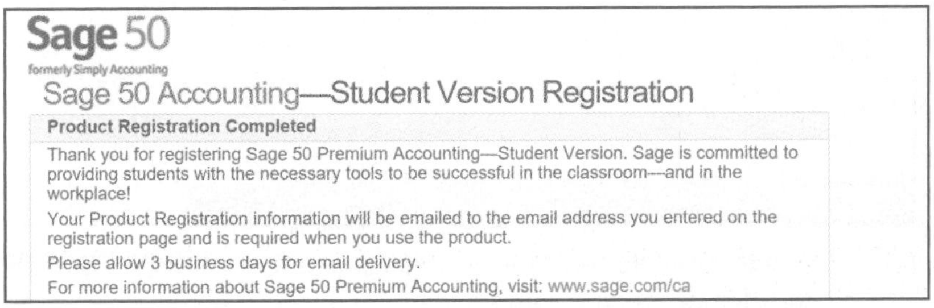

WARNING!
Several versions of the student Sage 50 programs can be activated from this site, so be sure to select Version 2019 (Premium).

> **NOTES**
> You may get various warnings about security when you download and install programs from the Internet. The warnings you have will depend on the download and security settings on your computer. You must allow these programs to download, and to run and make changes to your device.

> **NOTES**
> Your options for opening and saving downloaded files will depend on your own computer settings. Desktop or the Downloads folder are the most common default locations.

You should receive an e-mail shortly with your activation code (although the registration message asks you to allow 3 business days). You will return to the instruction page.

Click **2019.0** in **Step 3: Download, number 1** on the Sage Education Partner Program home page (on page A–4). This link will use the Download Manager as in the following steps.

If you get a security warning asking for permission, you should allow the program (the Download Manager) to make changes to your computer.

If you are asked, you can choose a location for the downloaded program. Otherwise, your default location will be used, usually the Desktop or the Downloads folder.

Make a note of the location you selected in case you need to reinstall the program. In this way, you will not need to download the program again.

While the program is downloading, you may have a progress bar or a progress wheel like the one in the lower left-hand corner of the Google Chrome screen with Windows 10:

After the program has finished downloading, an icon has been placed on the desktop or in the folder you selected:

If you are viewing the folder contents in detail or list view, the program name will be **SA_20190CP1_Edu** — or **SA_20190CP1_Edu.EXE** if you show file extensions, as we do.

If you have any other programs running, close them before installing Sage 50.

Installing Sage 50

> **STUDENT VERSION**
> It may take several minutes for all the program files to be extracted from the SA_20190CP1_Edu.EXE file before the installation screens start.

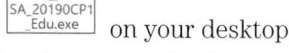

Double-click the **Sage 50 program installation icon**  on your desktop, or  in the lower left-hand corner of the Web page, or the program name SA_20190CP1_Edu.EXE (or SA_2019CP1_Edu) in the folder you used to save the program.

The next screen allows you to choose the location for the installer files:

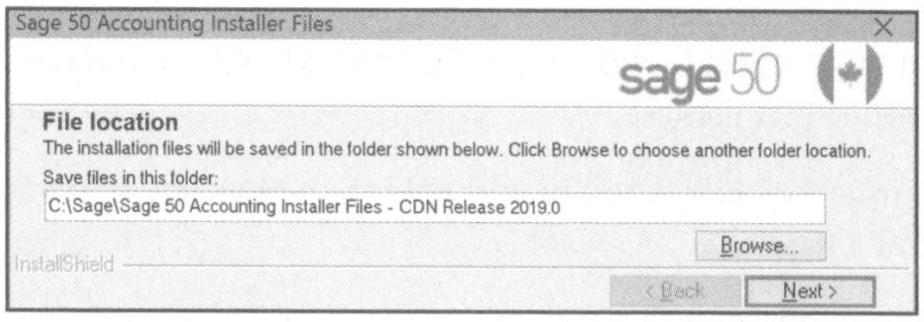

Accept the **default** location and then **click Next** to open the Installation options:

Click **Install Sage 50**. Wait for the Select A Language To Use With This Installation screen to appear:

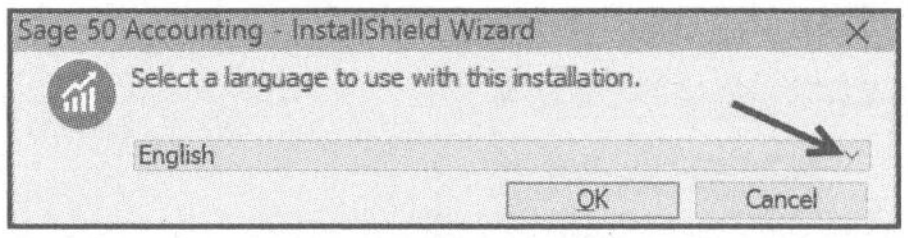

Choose your **language preference** from the drop-down list and **click OK**.

The next screen relates to the firewall you are using:

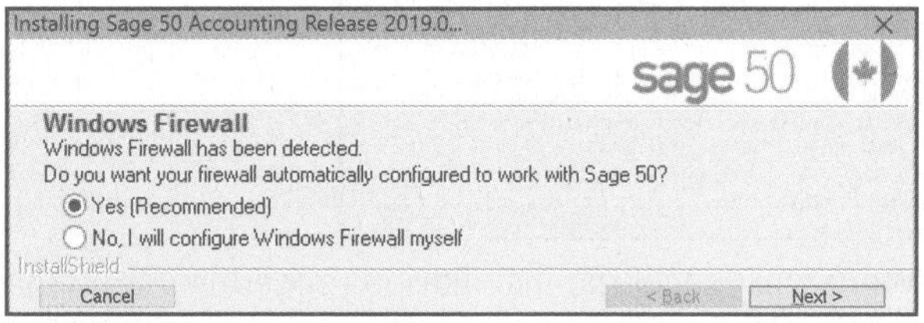

If you use the Windows Firewall, you should allow the firewall settings to be updated automatically.

Click **Next** to continue.

If you click No, or if Windows is not your default firewall, your screen will list all the programs for which you must modify the firewall settings. We include all these programs on the following screenshot:

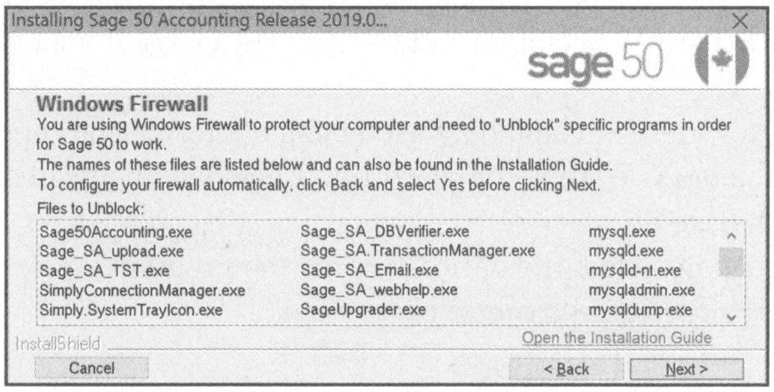

You can make a list of these programs now or view them in the Help information when you search for Firewall.

You are now ready to begin installing the program:

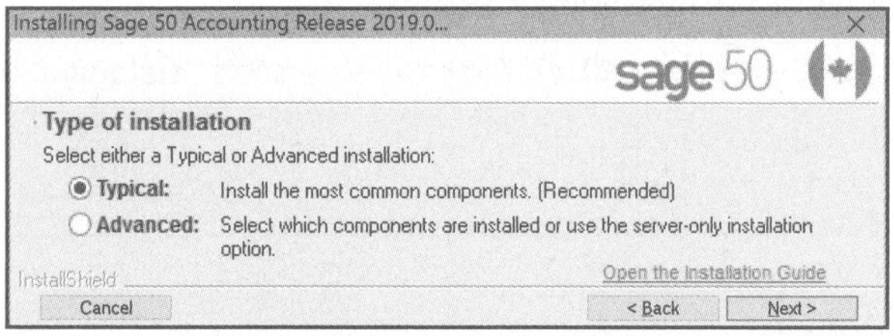

The default option, **Typical**, will provide all the basic components you need. You should choose the Advanced option only if you want to customize the installation selection or omit some features. Leave the default selection unchanged.

Click **Next**. The next step requires you to enter the serial number:

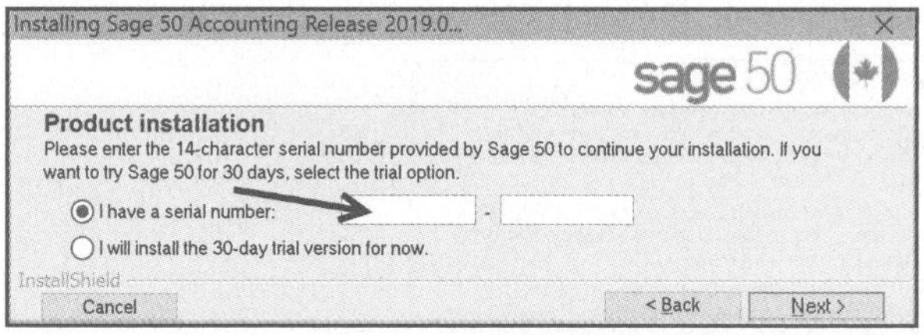

The cursor is in the Serial Number field, ready for you to enter the number.

Type `242P1U2-1000020` when you are prompted to enter the serial number. (This serial number applies to all copies of the Student version.)

WARNING!

You must configure your firewall program to allow access to all the programs listed on this screenshot.

NOTES

Sage 50 may not start properly, or may fail to open a Sage 50 data file, if the firewall is blocking any of these programs. You may also need to start the Connection Manager program. The programs listed are those required for Windows 10.

A complete list of the programs your firewall must not block is also available from the Help menu when you enter Firewall in the Help menu Search field (refer to Chapter 1, page 17).

NOTES

Each copy of the retail version has a unique serial number and the serial number reflects the program version you are installing. The Student version is not available as a trial version.

NOTES
The retail Premium version will have Installing Sage 50 Premium Accounting Release 2019.0 in the title bar after you enter the unique serial number.

PRO VERSION
The title bar will have Installing Sage 50 Pro Accounting Release 2019.0 in the title bar after you enter the unique serial number.

NOTES
For older or 32-bit Windows programs, the Sage program will be placed in the Program Files folder.

Click **Next** to advance to the licence agreement:

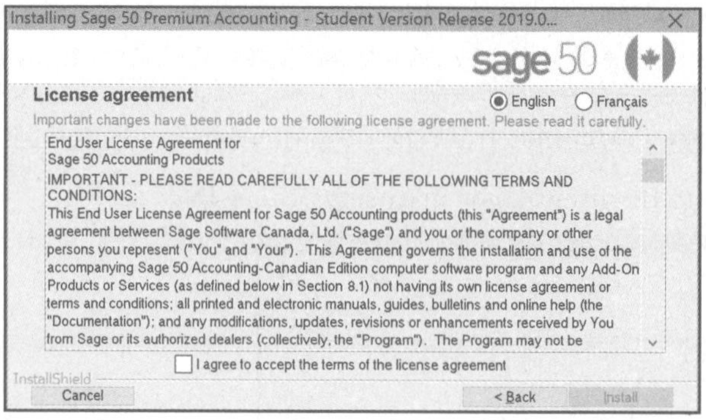

Not accepting the agreement will cancel the installation procedure. You must accept the agreement to install the program.

Read the **agreement** and **click I Agree**. Then **click Install** to continue.

By default, the program and all components will be included as follows:

- **Sage 50 Program**: the program that you will need to perform the accounting transactions for your company (installed to C:\Program Files (X86)\Sage\Sage 50 Premium Accounting Version 2019).
- **Sample Data**: complete records for a sample company — Universal Construction.
- **Templates**: predefined charts of accounts and settings for a large number of business types.
- **Customizable Forms**: a variety of commonly used business forms and reports.
- **Microsoft Office Documents**: a variety of Microsoft Office documents designed for integrated use with Sage 50.

After the program has been installed, the option to start the program is selected:

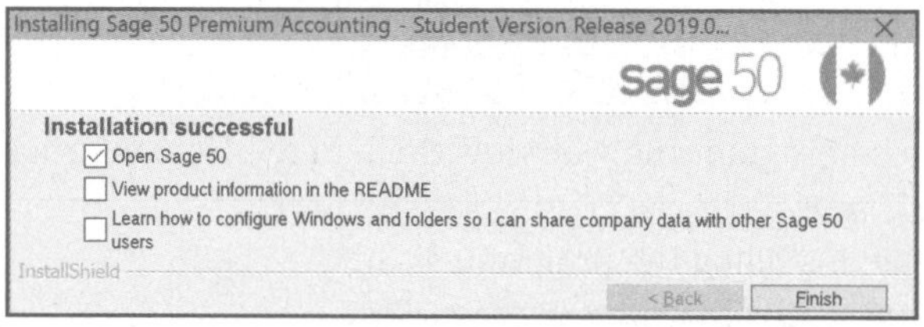

Click **Finish** to close this screen. **Click Exit** to close the initial installation screen.

The installation process has placed a shortcut on your desktop 

. This icon is used to start the Sage 50 program.

Activating the Student Version

At this point, the Welcome page will open to allow you to continue with the activation. You must activate the Student version before you can use it — there is no trial period:

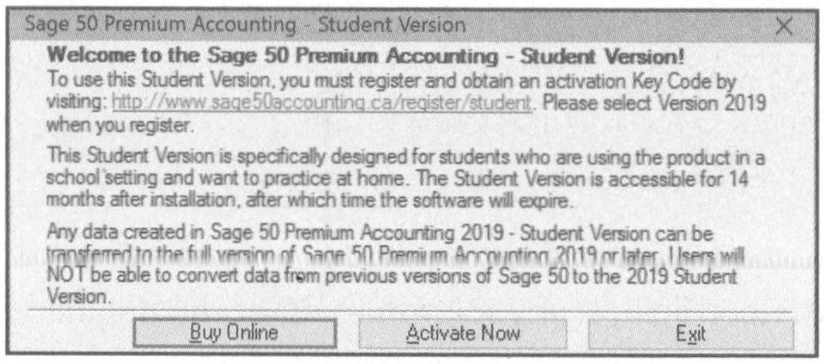

If you have not yet received the e-mail from Sage with the serial number and key code, wait for them. When they arrive, keep these numbers for reference.

If you did not complete the Registration step earlier (page A–5), click the underlined link on the Activation Welcome screen to open the screen on page A–5, enter the required information, submit the form, click Exit and wait for your e-mail from Sage. After you receive the codes, double-click the Sage 50 Premium icon on your desktop to open the Welcome screen again.

Write down the **23-character key code** from your e-mail message — you will enter this on the Activation screen. The name and serial number you provided are also included.

You can copy and paste the information from your e-mail into the activation fields.

Click the **Activate Now button** to open the Student Version Activation screen:

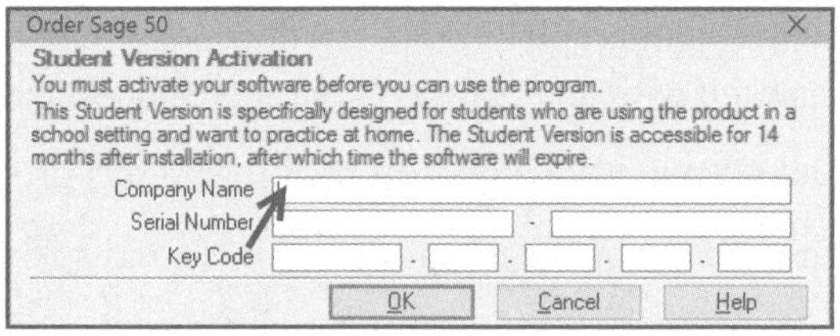

Type **your name** in the Company Name field. **Press** tab to advance to the Serial Number field.

Type 242P1U2-1000020 (This is the serial number for all copies of the Student version program.)

Press tab to advance to the **first Key Code field**.

Type the **23-character key code** from the e-mail message you received.

Click **OK**. Your Sage 50 Welcome screen opens:

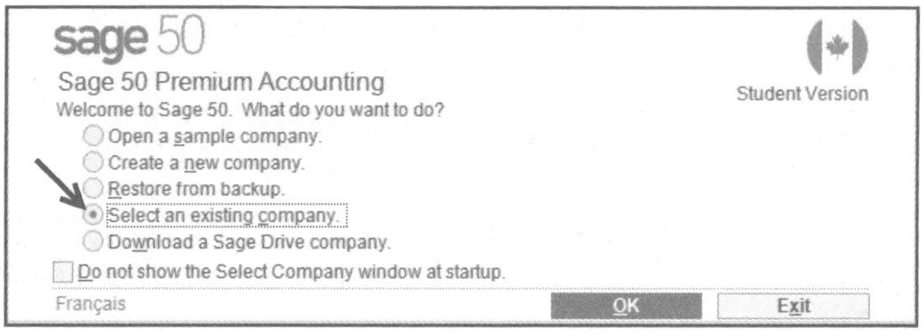

You can now use the program for 14 months.

If you do not activate the program immediately, the activation screen will open each time you start the Sage 50 program; you will be unable to open a data file.

Student Version Expired Error Message

When you try to activate the Student version, Sage may generate a message that the Student version or the data has expired and you can no longer use it.

If you have not used the program for 14 months, the "expired" message may be triggered by registry file information from a previous installation. If you get this message, you may have previously installed a version of the Sage 50 program. You must uninstall that program before you can install the current Sage 50 program.

Click **Exit** to close this window and **uninstall** the **Student 2019 version** and any other version of Sage 50 you have installed.

Open **Windows Settings – Apps**. **Click** the **Sage 50 Accounting Program** and **Uninstall** to uninstall the program properly.

NOTES

The activation message warns that you can use the program for only 14 months and you will not be able to open data from previous versions of Sage 50.

You do not need a payroll account or ID to use the Student version. Payroll is already unlocked or activated.

STUDENT VERSION

The Student version must be registered and activated before you can use the program. You can use the link in Step 2: Register on the Web site <sage.com/ca/about-us/education> to obtain the key code you will need to activate the Student version. Refer to page A–4.

NOTES

Instructions for starting Sage 50 are included in Chapter 1 of this text, beginning on page 8.

The retail versions can be used before activation (trial period). The message with the number of days remaining before activation is required will open each time you start the program until you have activated the program. The Student version will open with the Welcome/Activation screen on the previous page and you cannot continue before activating the program.

NOTES

The data files for this text were created with the retail versions and do not expire.

WARNING!
You must uninstall Sage 50 before you run the CleanUp program. And you must run the CleanUp utility program before starting the new installation.

If you have already uninstalled all other Sage 50 programs and you still get this message when you try to activate the 2019 Student version, you will need to uninstall the 2019 Student version program. Click the **Student Version Utility** link to download StudentVerCleanUp.ZIP. Double-click the StudentVerCleanUp folder to open it, and then double-click StudentVerCleanUp.EXE to run the program and clear your registry information.

Uninstall the **Sage 50 2019 Student version program**.

Start your **Internet connection** and **open** your **Web browser** if necessary.

Type `na.sage.com/ca/about-us/education` in the Web address field. **Press** enter.

Click **Step 4: Install** and then **click** the **Student Version Utility program link** in the introductory paragraph of Step 4 to download this program to your desktop (marked with an arrow in the screenshot on page A–4).

Double-click the **desktop icon StudentVerCleanUp.EXE** to run this program.

Click **OK** when the confirmation that the program has finished displays.

NOTES
You will not need to download the Sage 50 program again, and you can use your original activation key code. The original downloaded program will not be removed by this procedure, so you can reinstall from it.

You should now be able to install and activate Sage 50 Release 2019.0 by following the instructions on page A–6.

Online Help for Students

Students needing help with the program should work with their instructor. Additional help for students is available online on the Sage 50 Student Forum.

Open your **Internet browser**.

Type `sagecity.com/support_communities/sage_students` in the address bar and **press** enter:

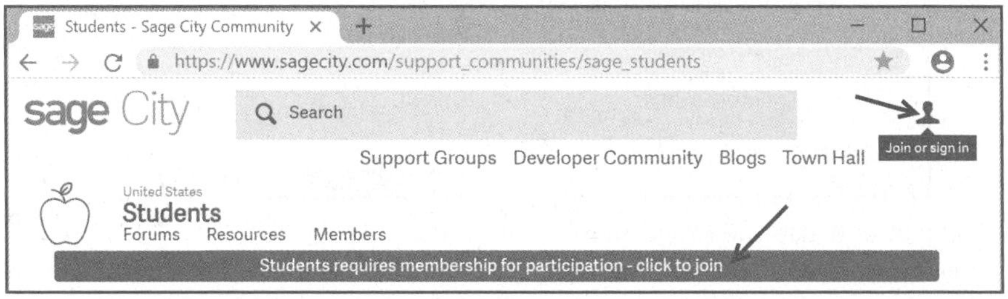

NOTES
Remember that Web pages are frequently updated.

From this page you can access student forums and a variety of resources, including learning videos, open the knowledge base for a variety of Sage programs, send an email to Sage and download the Sage 50 program.

If you are already a member, click the avatar and then click Join Or Sign In on the pop-up menu. Enter your user name and password.

If you are not yet a member, you must join and then sign in.

Click **Students Requires Membership For Participation - Click To Join**. Or,

Click the **avatar** and **Join Or Sign In** on the previous page.

NOTES
Clicking Join Or Sign In (the avatar pop-up) on this SageCity home page will open the Sign In page. Enter your user name and password to participate in discussions or ask questions. Click Join Here below the Password field to become a member of the forum.

These steps will open the Sign In page:

Join or sign in
Enter your email address to sign in or to create an account with Sage ID.
Email Address
Join or sign in
Curious about our new login process? Read more here

Enter your **email address** and password and **click Join Or Sign In**.

If the email address is not recognized as an existing member name, the registration process will begin, asking for a display name and then additional profile details.

Enter the **remaining information** as instructed until you have completed the registration.

Click the **New button**:

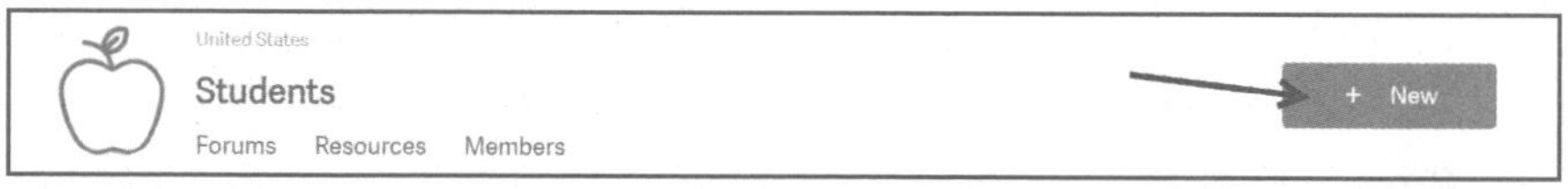

This will open the drop-down list of topics:

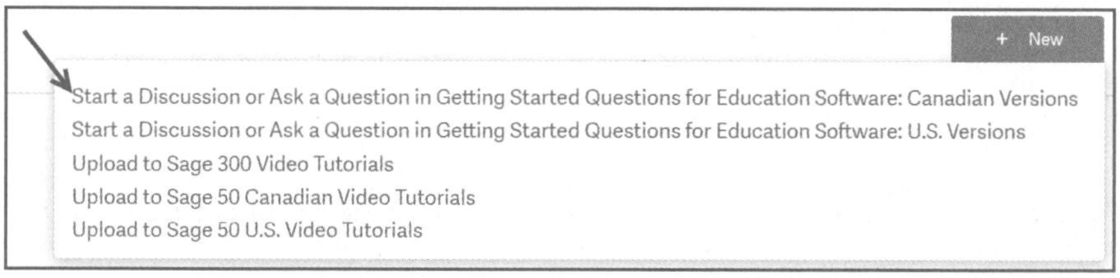

Click **Start A Discussion Or Ask A Question In Getting Started Questions for Education Software: Canadian Versions** or another topic you want to participate in:

You can now enter your question or start a new discussion on the topic you selected.

Choose **Question** or **Discussion** to indicate which you are entering.

Type your **question** in the Subject text box.

Provide **additional information** in the Description text box and choose the Category that applies from the drop-down list.

Click **Post** to submit your question.

NOTES

Your name and e-mail address will not be displayed for other members; only your user name will appear on the screen.

Your question and responses to it will appear on the forum page for Sage 50 Canadian Edition with your user name, or you can choose to be notified. Your Notification icon will indicate that you have a reply.

You can also reply to discussions posted by other members.

The Resources and Forums tab also offer assistance for students. Although, you can access these without joining SageCity, some aspects within the sites require membership.

Click **Resources** to open the list of additional resources:

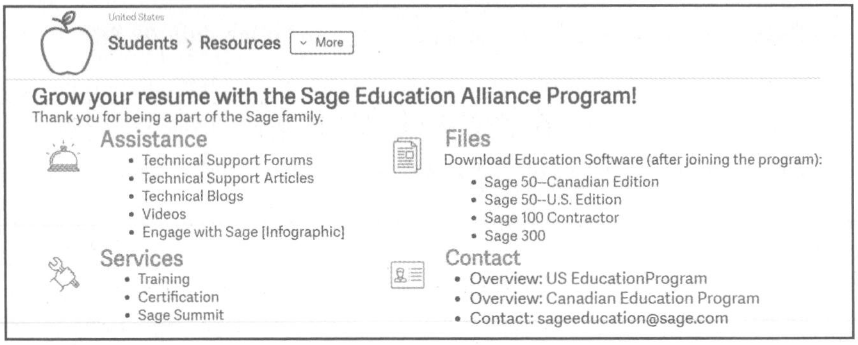

Click **Forums**:

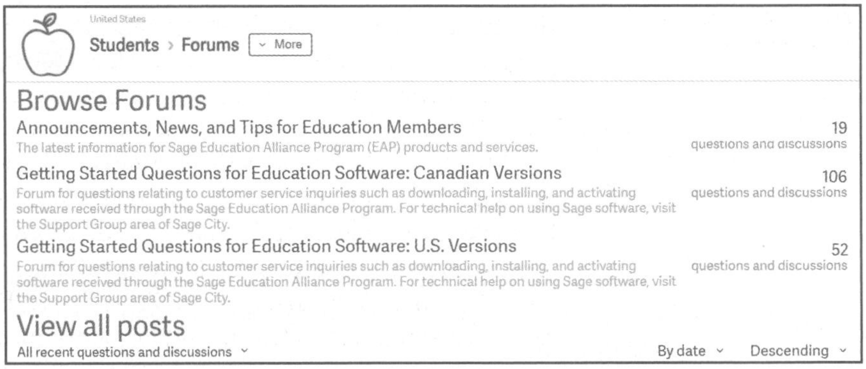

This site has questions and answers previously posted. You can view these discussions, but you must sign in to participate in a discussion.

Click the **avatar** and **click Sign Out** to end your session:

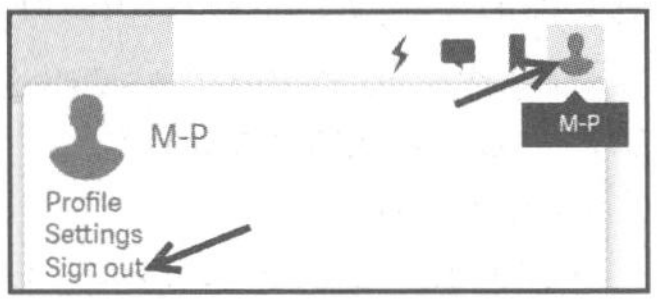

APPENDIX B

Shortcuts & Terminology

KEYBOARD SHORTCUTS

Using the Keyboard Instead of a Mouse

All Windows software applications are designed to be used with a mouse, trackpad or touch screen. However, there may be times when you prefer to use keyboard commands. And, if the mouse itself is inoperative, the keyboard alternatives may prevent you from losing data. A few basic principles will help you understand how they work. Some commands are common to more than one Windows software program. For example, ctrl + **C** (press and hold the Control key while you press C) is the copy command and ctrl + **V** is the paste command. Any selected text or image will be copied or pasted when you use these commands.

Pressing alt accesses the first menu bar item. Then press the arrow keys, ↑ and ↓, to move up and down through the pull-down menu choices of a highlighted menu item, or ← and → to go back and forth to other menu items. Some menu choices have direct keyboard alternatives or shortcuts. For example, alt + **F** (press and hold alt while you press F) accesses the File pull-down menu. Then pressing B (the underlined letter for Backup) will give you the dialogue box for backing up a file. In the backup window, you can press alt + **C** (the underlined character on the Cancel button) to close the backup window and cancel the procedure. Some tool buttons and menu choices in Sage 50 have a direct keyboard command. When available, these direct keystrokes are given with the tool button name or to the right of a menu choice. For example, alt + f4 is the shortcut for closing the active window or exiting from the Sage 50 program when the Home window is the active window.

To cancel a menu display, press esc.

To choose or open a highlighted or selected button, press enter.

When input fields are displayed in a Sage 50 window, press tab to move to the next field or shift and tab together to return to the previous field. The tab key is used frequently in this workbook as a quick way to accept input, advance the cursor to the next field and highlight field contents to prepare for editing. Using the mouse while you input information requires you to remove your hands from the keyboard, while the tab key does not.

A summary of keyboard shortcuts used in Sage 50 is included on page A–14. Additional shortcuts using more than two keys, such as ctrl + shift + **A** in a journal window for Allocate, are also available. They are displayed in pull-down menus or with the tools for those commands.

NOTES
The illustration in Chapter 1, page 13, shows several keyboard alternative commands in the pull-down Entry menu.

NOTES
Pressing alt + P, the underlined character on the Post button in journal windows, will post or record the transaction.

NOTES
The same shortcuts in Sage 50 may have different functions, depending on the window you start from.

NOTES
pro
The shortcuts in the Pro version may not work the same way.

SUMMARY OF BASIC KEYBOARD SHORTCUTS

Shortcut	Resulting Action
ctrl + A	**Adjust**, begin the Adjust a Posted Entry function.
ctrl + B	Bring the **Home window** to the front.
ctrl + C	**Copy** the selected text.
ctrl + E	Look up the **previously posted invoice** (from a journal lookup window).
ctrl + F	**Search**, begin the search function, except in a journal window.
ctrl + J	**Display** the **journal entry** report.
ctrl + K	**Track shipment** from a previously posted invoice lookup screen.
ctrl + L	Look up a **previously posted transaction** (from the journal window).
ctrl + N	Look up the **next posted invoice** (from a journal lookup window).
ctrl + N	Open a **new record** window (from a ledger icon or ledger record window).
ctrl + P	**Print**, open the print dialogue box when the option to print is available.
ctrl + R	**Recall** a stored journal entry (from a journal window when an entry is stored).
ctrl + R	**Remove** the account record or remove the quote or order (from a ledger, quote or order window).
ctrl + S	Access the **Save As** function from the Home window (Home window, File menu) to save the data file under a new name. Keep the new file open.
ctrl + S	**Save** changes to a record; keep the ledger window open (from any ledger window).
ctrl + T	**Store** the current journal entry (open the Store dialogue box).
ctrl + V	**Paste** the selected text at the cursor position.
ctrl + X	**Cut** (delete) the selected text.
ctrl + Z	**Undo** the most recent change.
alt + C	**Create another** record; save the record you are creating and open a new record form to create another new record.
alt + N	**Save and close**; save the new record and close the ledger.
alt + P	**Post** the journal entry or record the order or quote.
alt + f4	**Close** the active window (if it has a close button). Close the program if the Home window is active.
alt + **the underlined character on a button**	**Select** the button's action. An alternative to clicking the button and/or pressing enter.
alt	Access the first item on the **menu bar**.
tab	Advance the cursor to the **next field**.
shift + tab	Move the cursor to the **previous field**.
Click	**Move** the cursor to this position or **select** an item or entry.
shift + Click	**Select all** the items between the first item clicked and the last one.
ctrl + Click	**Select** this item **in addition** to ones previously selected.
enter	**Choose** the selected item or action.
Double-click	**Select** an entire word or field contents. In fields with lists, open the selection list.
→	**Move right** to the next icon to select it or to the next character in text.
←	**Move left** to the next icon to select it or to the next character in text.
↓	**Move down** to the next icon or entry in a list to select it.
↑	**Move up** to the previous icon or entry in a list to select it.

ACCOUNTING VS. NON-ACCOUNTING TERMS

We have used accounting terms in this workbook because they are familiar to students of accounting and because we needed to provide a consistent language for the book. The most frequently used non-accounting terms are included here for reference and comparison, in case you want to leave the non-accounting terms selected (Home window, Setup menu, User Preferences, Options screen — refer to page 81).

The chart shows the terms used for the Pro version and for the Premium version when the Other Industry type is selected. For other industries in the Premium version, the terms in the chart on page A–16 — Terminology Used for Different Types of Industries — will replace the Non-accounting Terms for Payables and Receivables. For example, the terms Providers and Expenses or Supporters and Revenues may be used. The term Suppliers generally replaces Vendors.

SUMMARY OF EQUIVALENT TERMS

MAJOR TERMS	ACCOUNTING TERMS	NON-ACCOUNTING TERMS
	Journal Entries	Transaction Details
	Payables	Vendors & Purchases
	Receivables	Customers & Sales
	Post	Process

DETAILED LIST: LOCATION	ACCOUNTING TERMS	NON-ACCOUNTING TERMS
Setup menu – Settings screen	Payables	Vendors & Purchases
	Receivables	Customers & Sales
Setup menu, User Preferences, View screen – Modules/Pages	Payables (Classic View)	Vendors & Purchases
	Receivables (Classic View)	Customers & Sales
Graphs menu	Payables	Unpaid Purchases
	Receivables	Unpaid Sales
Reports menu and Report Centre – Financials	General Ledger	Transactions by Account
Report Centre – Financials	All Journal Entries	All Transactions
Reports menu and Report Centre	Payables	Vendors & Purchases
	Receivables	Customers & Sales
Reports menu	Journal Entries	Transaction Details
Reports menu – Management Reports	Payables	Vendors & Purchases
	Receivables	Customers & Sales
All Icon window menus	Journal	Transactions
Accounts ledger window	General Ledger	Chart of Accounts Records
Vendors ledger window	Payables Ledger	Vendor Records
Customers ledger window	Receivables Ledger	Customer Records
All journals (button and menu)	Post	Process

INDUSTRY TYPES AND TERMS

In the Premium version, the terms and labels change when you select different types of industries (Setup menu, Settings, Company, Information screen — refer to pages 76–78). The chart on the following page summarizes the terms you will see when you apply different industry types. You can change the default industry terminology on the Settings, Names screens for the Payables and Receivables modules.

TERMINOLOGY USED FOR DIFFERENT TYPES OF INDUSTRIES

INDUSTRY	**TERMS OR LABELS USED IN RECEIVABLES LEDGER**				
	Customers	**Sales Invoices**	**Sales Quotes**	**Sales Orders**	**Sales Journal – Invoice**
Pro Version (all)	Customers	Sales Invoices	Sales Quotes	Sales Orders	Sales Journal – Invoice
Premium Version					
Accommodation	Guests	Charges	Sales Quotes	Sales Orders	Sales Journal – Charge
Agriculture	Customers	Customer Invoices	Customer Quotes	Customer Orders	Revenues Journal – Invoice
Construction/ Contractor	Customers	Bills	Estimates	Contracts	Sales Journal – Bill
Educational Service	Clients	Statements	Client Quotes	Client Orders	Fees Journal – Statement
Entertainment	Customers	Sales Invoices	Sales Quotes	Sales Orders	Sales Journal – Invoice
Food & Beverage	Guests	Charges	Sales Quotes	Sales Orders	Sales Journal – Charge
Manufacturing/ Industrial	Customers	Sales Invoices	Sales Quotes	Sales Orders	Sales Journal – Invoice
Medical/Dental	Patients	Statements	Patient Quotes	Patient Orders	Fees Journal – Statement
Non-Profit	Supporters	Statements	Supporter Quotes	Supporter Orders	Revenues Journal – Statement
Other	Customers	Sales Invoices	Sales Quotes	Sales Orders	Sales Journal – Invoice
Personal Service	Clients	Client Invoices	Client Quotes	Client Orders	Revenues Journal – Invoice
Professional Service	Clients	Client Invoices	Client Quotes	Client Orders	Fees Journal – Invoice
Real Estate/Property	Clients	Statements	Client Quotes	Client Orders	Revenues Journal – Statement
Retail	Customers	Sales Invoices	Sales Quotes	Sales Orders	Sales Journal – Invoice
Service	Clients	Client Invoices	Client Quotes	Client Orders	Revenues Journal – Invoice
Transportation	Customers	Sales Invoices	Sales Quotes	Sales Orders	Sales Journal – Invoice

INDUSTRY	**TERMS OR LABELS USED IN PAYABLES LEDGER**				
	Vendors	**Purchase Invoices**	**Purchase Quotes**	**Purchase Orders**	**Purchases Journal – Purchase Invoice**
Pro Version (all)	Vendors	Purchase Invoices	Purchase Quotes	Purchase Orders	Purchases Journal – Invoice
Premium Version					
Accommodation	Suppliers	Invoices	Purchase Quotes	Purchase Orders	Purchases Journal – Invoice
Agriculture	Suppliers	Purchase Invoices	Purchase Quotes	Purchase Orders	Purchases Journal – Invoice
Construction/ Contractor	Suppliers	Invoices	Quotes	Orders	Purchases Journal – Invoice
Educational Service	Suppliers	Invoices	Purchase Quotes	Purchase Orders	Purchases Journal – Invoice
Entertainment	Suppliers	Supplier Invoices	Supplier Quotes	Supplier Orders	Expenses Journal – Invoice
Food & Beverage	Suppliers	Invoices	Purchase Quotes	Purchase Orders	Purchases Journal – Invoice
Manufacturing/ Industrial	Suppliers	Purchase Invoices	Purchase Quotes	Purchase Orders	Purchases Journal – Invoice
Medical/Dental	Suppliers	Invoices	Supplier Quotes	Supplier Orders	Expenses Journal – Invoice
Non-Profit	Providers	Invoices	Provider Quotes	Provider Orders	Expenses Journal – Invoice
Other	Vendors	Purchase Invoices	Purchase Quotes	Purchase Orders	Purchases Journal – Invoice
Personal Service	Suppliers	Supplier Invoices	Supplier Quotes	Supplier Orders	Expenses Journal – Invoice
Professional Service	Vendors	Vendor Invoices	Vendor Quotes	Vendor Orders	Expenses Journal – Invoice
Real Estate/Property	Suppliers	Invoices	Supplier Quotes	Supplier Orders	Expenses Journal – Invoice
Retail	Suppliers	Purchase Invoices	Purchase Quotes	Purchase Orders	Purchases Journal – Invoice
Service	Suppliers	Supplier Invoices	Supplier Quotes	Supplier Orders	Expenses Journal – Invoice
Transportation	Vendors	Purchase Invoices	Purchase Quotes	Purchase Orders	Purchases Journal – Invoice

Terms for Project Project (for Other, Service, Personal Service, Professional Service, Transportation and all industries in Pro version), Division (for Accommodation, Education, Entertainment, Food, Manufacturing and Retail), Crops (for Agriculture), Job Site (for Construction), Partner (for Medical), Fund (for Non-Profit), Property (for Real Estate)

APPENDIX C

Correcting Errors after Posting

We all make mistakes. This appendix outlines briefly the procedures you need to follow for those rare occasions when you have posted a journal entry incorrectly and you need to reverse it manually. In most cases, you can use the Adjust Journal Entry or Reverse Entry procedures to make corrections.

Obviously, you should try to detect errors before posting. Reviewing journal entries should become routine practice. The software also has built-in safeguards that help you avoid mistakes. For example, outstanding invoices cannot be overpaid, and employee wages and payroll deductions are calculated automatically. Furthermore, names of accounts, customers, vendors, employees and inventory items appear in full, so that you can check your journal information easily.

Before making a reversing entry, consider the consequences of not correcting the error. For example, misspelled customer names may not be desirable, but they will not influence the financial statements. After making the correction in the ledger, the newly printed statement will be correct (the journal will retain both spellings). Sometimes, however, the mistake is more serious. If amounts or accounts are wrong, financial statements will be incorrect. Payroll tax deduction amounts will be incorrect if a wage amount or linked account is incorrect. GST/HST and PST remittances may be incorrect as a result of incorrect tax codes or sales or purchase amounts. Discounts will be incorrectly calculated if an invoice or payment date is incorrect. Some errors also originate from outside sources. For example, purchase items may be incorrectly priced by the vendor.

NOTES

Adjusting entry procedures are provided on the following pages:

page 47 – General Journal
page 129 – Purchases
page 131 – Other Payments
page 139 – Payments
page 184 – Sales
page 275 – Paycheque
page 295 – Payroll Run Entry

Reversing entry procedures are explained on

page 49 – General Journal
page 141 – Purchases
pages 177 and 605 – Receipts
page 277 – Paycheques
page 251 – Historical Invoices

For audit purposes, prepare a memo explaining the error and the correction procedure. A complete reversing entry is often the simplest way to make the correction for a straightforward audit trail. With the one-step reversing entry feature from the Adjust Entry or Lookup window in Sage 50, the reversing entry is made automatically. This feature is available for General Journal entries, paycheques, sales, purchases, receipts and most payments. Choose Adjust Invoice from the pull-down menu under the corresponding transaction menu, or click the Adjust Invoice tool in the journal. Then make the corrections if possible, or choose Reverse Entry from the pull-down menu under the corresponding transaction menu or click the Reverse tool. Under all circumstances, you should follow generally accepted accounting principles. Sage 50 will create the reversing entry automatically. Reports will include the correct entries after you post the adjusted journal entry. Including the original and reversing entries in reports is optional.

However, this feature is not available for all journals. And when the journal entry deposit account for a receipt is not the bank account (because the deposit was made later), you need to reverse a receipt manually to record an NSF cheque (refer to page 605).

In this appendix we will illustrate the procedure for reversing entries in all journals. Reversing entries in all journals have several common elements. In each case, you should use an appropriate source number that identifies the entry as reversing (e.g., add ADJ or REV to the original source number). You should use the original posting date and terms, and add a comment. Make the reversing entry as illustrated on the following pages. Display the journal entry, review it carefully and, when you are certain it is correct, post it. Next, you must enter the correct version of the transaction as a new journal entry with an appropriate identifying source number (e.g., add COR to the original source number).

Reversing entries are presented for each journal. The screenshots have only the transaction portion because the remaining parts of the journal screen do not change. The original and reversing entry screens and their corresponding journal displays are included. Explanatory notes appear beside each set of entries.

GENERAL JOURNAL

Use the same accounts and amounts in the reversing entry as in the original entry.

Accounts that were debited originally should be credited, and accounts that were credited originally should be debited.

Click the Sales Taxes button if you used this screen. Choose the tax code and, if necessary, enter the Amount Subject To Tax with a minus sign.

Repeat the allocation using the original percentages.

The General Journal display basically looks the same as the journal input form.

You can use the Adjust Entry or Reverse Entry features instead (page 47 and page 49).

GENERAL JOURNAL: Original Entry

Account	Debits	Credits	Comment	Allo
1360 Supplies	170.00	--	paint & stencils	
2670 GST Paid on Purchases	8.50	--	GST @ 5%	
2100 A/P - Badlands Hardware	--	178.50	terms: net 20	
Total	178.50	178.50		

Reversing Entry

Account	Debits	Credits	Comment	Allo
2100 A/P - Badlands Hardware	178.50	--	reversing A/P amount	
1360 Supplies	--	170.00	reversing supplies amount	
2670 GST Paid on Purchases	--	8.50	reversing GST amount	
Total	178.50	178.50		

PURCHASES JOURNAL

The only change you must make is that positive amounts in the original entry become negative amounts in the reversing entry (place a minus sign before the amount in the Amount field).

Similarly, negative amounts, such as for GST/HST Paid in GST/HST remittances, must be changed to positive amounts (remove the minus sign).

If freight was charged, enter the amount of freight with a minus sign.

Use the same accounts and amounts in the reversing entry as in the original entry. Tax amounts change automatically.

Repeat the allocation with the original percentages.

You can use the Adjust Invoice and Reverse Invoice options instead (page 129 and page 141). Reversing a paid invoice will generate a credit note.

Remember to "pay" the incorrect and reversing invoices to remove them from the Payments Journal and later clear them.

PURCHASES JOURNAL (NON-INVENTORY): Original Entry

Item Number	Quantity	Order	Back Order	Unit	Item Description	Price	Tax	HST	Amount	Account	Divisions
					office repairs		H	30.00	200.00	5280 Repairs...	[Multiple Divisions]

Subtotal: 200.00
Freight:
Early Payment Terms: 1.00 % 15 Days, Net 30 Days
HST: 30.00
Total: 230.00

Purchases Journal Entry 06/07/2021 (J19)

Account Number	Account Description	Division	Debits	Credits	Division Amt
2670	HST Paid on Purchases		30.00	-	
5280	Repairs & Maintenance		200.00	-	
		- Store Sales			160.00
		- Design			40.00
2200	Accounts Payable		-	230.00	
Additional Date:	Additional Field:		230.00	230.00	

Reversing Entry

Item Number	Quantity	Order	Back Order	Unit	Item Description	Price	Tax	HST	Amount	Account	Divisions
					reversing repairs		H	-30.00	-200.00	5280 Repairs...	[Multiple Divisions]

Subtotal: -200.00
Freight:
Early Payment Terms: 1.00 % 15 Days, Net 30 Days
HST: -30.00
Total: -230.00

Purchases Journal Entry 06/07/2021 (J20)

Account Number	Account Description	Division	Debits	Credits	Division Amt
2200	Accounts Payable		230.00	-	
2670	HST Paid on Purchases		-	30.00	
5280	Repairs & Maintenance		-	200.00	
		- Store Sales			-160.00
		- Design			-40.00
Additional Date:	Additional Field:		230.00	230.00	

PAYMENTS JOURNAL – OTHER PAYMENTS: Original Entry

Acct	Description	Amount	Tax	HST	Allo
5290 Utilities	telephone services	210.00	H	31.50	√

Subtotal	210.00
Tax	31.50
Total	241.50

Payments Journal Entry 06/07/2021 (J21)

Account Number	Account Description	Division	Debits	Credits	Division Amt
2670	HST Paid on Purchases		31.50	-	
5290	Utilities Expenses		210.00	-	
		- Store Sales			126.00
		- Design			63.00
		- Planting			21.00
1050	Bank: Chequing CAD		-	241.50	
Additional Date:	Additional Field:		241.50	241.50	

Reversing Entry

Acct	Description	Amount	Tax	HST	Allo
5290 Utilities	reversing telephone entry	-210.00	H	-31.50	√

Subtotal	-210.00
Tax	-31.50
Total	-241.50

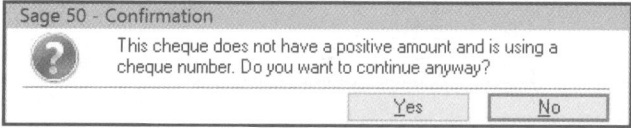

Payments Journal Entry 06/07/2021 (J22)

Account Number	Account Description	Division	Debits	Credits	Division Amt
1050	Bank: Chequing CAD		241.50	-	
2670	HST Paid on Purchases		-	31.50	
5290	Utilities Expenses		-	210.00	
		- Store Sales			-126.00
		- Design			-63.00
		- Planting			-21.00
Additional Date:	Additional Field:		241.50	241.50	

Sage 50 - Confirmation

This cheque does not have a positive amount and is using a cheque number. Do you want to continue anyway?

Yes No

PAYROLL REMITTANCES: Original Entry

Remitting Frequency: Monthly End of Remitting Period: Jun 01, 2021

Remittance	Amount Owing	Payment Adjustment Account	Payment Adjustment	Payment Amount
RRSP	550.00	2400 RRSP Payable		550.00
			Total	550.00

Payments Journal Entry

		Account Number	Account Description	Debits	Credits
06/01/2021	(J23)	Memo 6, Capital Trust : RRSP remittance			
		2400	RRSP Payable	550.00	-
		2200	Accounts Payable	-	550.00
06/14/2021	(J24)	584, Capital Trust : RRSP remittance			
		2200	Accounts Payable	550.00	-
		1050	Bank: Chequing CAD	-	550.00
Additional Date:	Additional Field:			1,100.00	1,100.00

Reversing Entry

Remitting Frequency: Monthly End of Remitting Period: Jun 01, 2021

Remittance	Amount Owing	Payment Adjustment Account	Payment Adjustment	Payment Amount
RRSP	0.00	2400 RRSP Payable		-550.00
			Total	-550.00

OTHER PAYMENTS

The only change you must make is that positive amounts in the original entry become negative amounts in the reversing entry (place a minus sign before the amount in the Amount field).

Similarly, negative amounts, such as for GST/HST Paid in GST/HST remittances, must be changed to positive amounts (remove the minus sign).

Use the same accounts and amounts in the reversing entry as in the original entry. Tax amounts change automatically.

Repeat the allocation with the original percentages.

You can use the Adjust Invoice and Reverse Invoice options instead (page 131).

If Sage 50 generates a message about using the next cheque number with a negative amount, click No and enter a memo number or other reference in the Cheque Number field.

PAYROLL REMITTANCES

Payroll remittances are reversed in the same way as other payments. Enter the same cheque date and End Of Remitting Period date as you did for the original transaction, and then enter the original amounts with a minus sign added.

Enter a memo number or other reference in the Cheque Number field to avoid using a cheque number for a negative amount.

You can also adjust and reverse these payments automatically. Open the Remittance Journal and search for the remittance you want. From the Adjust window, you can make changes or use the Reverse tool to reverse the entry completely.

PAYMENTS

Click [icon], the Include Fully Paid Invoices tool button.

The change you must make is that positive amounts in the original entry become negative amounts in the reversing entry.

If a discount was taken, click the Discount Taken field on the invoice line for the payment being reversed. Type the discount amount with a minus sign. Press *tab* to enter the payment amount. The minus sign will be added.

If no discount was taken, click the Payment Amount field on the invoice line for the payment being reversed. Type a minus sign and the amount.

Click No if Sage 50 provides the warning about posting a negative cheque amount and enter another reference number instead. This will restore the original balance owing for the invoice.

You can also use the Adjust Payment tool or the Reverse Payment feature (page 139 and page 177).

If you have already cleared the paid invoice, prepare a new Purchases Journal entry for the amount of the payment (non-taxable) to restore the balance owing. Enter a positive amount for the amount of the cheque and the Bank account in the Account field (to avoid entering the expense twice). On the next line, enter the discount amount (positive) with the Purchase Discounts account in the Account field. This will debit the Bank and Purchase Discounts accounts and credit Accounts Payable.

CREDIT CARD PAYMENTS

Enter the same amounts as in the original entry.

Add a minus sign to the Additional Fees And Interest amount and to the Payment Amount in the reversing entry.

Enter a memo number or other reference in the Cheque Number field to avoid using a cheque number for a negative amount.

Payments Journal Entry

		Account Number	Account Description	Debits	Credits
06/01/2021	(J25)	Memo 6A, Capital Trust : Reversing RRSP remittance			
		2200	Accounts Payable	550.00	-
		2400	RRSP Payable	-	550.00
06/14/2021	(J26)	584R, Capital Trust : Reversing RRSP remittance			
		1050	Bank: Chequing CAD	550.00	-
		2200	Accounts Payable	-	550.00
Additional Date:	Additional Field:			1,100.00	1,100.00

PAYMENTS: Original Entry

Due Date	Invoice or Prepayment	Original Amount	Amount Owing	Discount Available	Discount Taken	Payment Amount
Jul 31, 2021	GF-7880	460.00	460.00	9.20	9.20	450.80
					Total	450.80

Payments Journal Entry 06/07/2021 (J30)

Account Number	Account Description	Debits	Credits
2200	Accounts Payable	460.00	-
1050	Bank: Chequing CAD	-	450.80
5270	Purchase Discounts	-	9.20
Additional Date:	Additional Field:	460.00	460.00

Reversing Entry

Due Date	Invoice or Prepayment	Original Amount	Amount Owing	Discount Available	Discount Taken	Payment Amount
Jul 26, 2021	GF-1142	900.00	0.00	0.00		
Jul 31, 2021	GF-7880	460.00	0.00	0.00	-9.20	-450.80
					Total	-450.80

Payments Journal Entry 06/08/2021 (J31)

Account Number	Account Description	Debits	Credits
1050	Bank: Chequing CAD	450.80	-
5270	Purchase Discounts	9.20	-
2200	Accounts Payable	-	460.00
Additional Date:	Additional Field:	460.00	460.00

CREDIT CARD PAYMENTS: Original Entry

Credit Card Payable Account Balance:	630.00
Additional Fees and Interest:	60.00
Payment Amount:	460.00

Payments Journal Entry 06/05/2021 (J32)

Account Number	Account Description	Debits	Credits
2250	Credit Card Payable	400.00	-
5160	Credit Card Fees	60.00	-
1050	Bank: Chequing CAD	-	460.00
Additional Date:	Additional Field:	460.00	460.00

Reversing Entry

Credit Card Payable Account Balance:	230.00
Additional Fees and Interest:	-60.00
Payment Amount:	-460.00

Payments Journal Entry 06/06/2021 (J33)

Account Number	Account Description	Debits	Credits
1050	Bank: Chequing CAD	460.00	-
2250	Credit Card Payable	-	400.00
5160	Credit Card Fees	-	60.00
Additional Date:	Additional Field:	460.00	460.00

INVENTORY PURCHASES: Original Entry

Item Number	Quantity	Order	Back Order	Unit	Item Description	Price	Tax	HST	Amount	Account	Divisions
PL06	20			each	Plant: annual 15 cm	9.00	H	27.00	180.00	1360 Plants...	
PS10	20			bag	Topsoil: 50 litre bag	4.00	H	12.00	80.00	1360 Plants...	

Subtotal: 260.00
Freight: 50.00 H 7.50
Early Payment Terms: % Days, Net 60 Days HST: 46.50
Total: 356.50

Purchases Journal Entry 06/10/2021 (J34)

Account Number	Account Description	Division	Debits	Credits	Division Amt
1360	Plants and Soil		260.00	-	
2670	HST Paid on Purchases		46.50	-	
5100	Freight Expense		50.00	-	
		- Planting			50.00
2200	Accounts Payable		-	356.50	
Additional Date:	Additional Field:		356.50	356.50	

Reversing Entry

Item Number	Quantity	Order	Back Order	Unit	Item Description	Price	Tax	HST	Amount	Account	Divisions
PL06	-20			each	Plant: annual 15 cm	9.00	H	-27.00	-180.00	1360 Plants...	
PS10	-20			bag	Topsoil: 50 litre bag	4.00	H	-12.00	-80.00	1360 Plants...	

Subtotal: -260.00
Freight: -50.00 H -7.50
Early Payment Terms: % Days, Net 60 Days HST: -46.50
Total: -356.50

Purchases Journal Entry 06/11/2021 (J35)

Account Number	Account Description	Division	Debits	Credits	Division Amt
2200	Accounts Payable		356.50	-	
1360	Plants and Soil		-	260.00	
2670	HST Paid on Purchases		-	46.50	
5100	Freight Expense		-	50.00	
		- Planting			-50.00
Additional Date:	Additional Field:		356.50	356.50	

SALES JOURNAL (INVENTORY AND NON-INVENTORY): Original Entry

Item Number	Quantity	Order	Back Order	Unit	Item Description	Price	Amount	Tax	Account	Divisions
FA06	2			each	End table: Cast Aluminum	95.00	190.00	H	4020 Revenue...	Store Sales
FA07	2			each	Bench: Cast Aluminum	185.00	370.00	H	4020 Revenue...	Store Sales
					custom design work		400.00	H	4040 Revenue...	Design

Subtotal: 960.00
Freight: 100.00 H 15.00
Early Payment Terms: 2.00 % 15 Days, Net 30 Days HST: 159.00
Total: 1,219.00

Sales Journal Entry 06/06/2021 (J36)

Account Number	Account Description	Division	Debits	Credits	Division Amt
1200	Accounts Receivable		1,219.00	-	
5070	Cost of Goods Sold		440.00	-	
		- Store Sales			440.00
1400	Patio Furniture		-	440.00	
2650	HST Charged on Sales		-	159.00	
4020	Revenue from Store Sales		-	560.00	
		- Store Sales			560.00
4040	Revenue from Services		-	400.00	
		- Design			400.00
4100	Revenue from Delivery		-	100.00	
		- Store Sales			100.00
Additional Date:	Additional Field:		1,659.00	1,659.00	

INVENTORY PURCHASES

Change positive quantities in the original entry to negative ones in the reversing entry (place a minus sign before the quantity in the Quantity field).

Similarly, change negative quantities, such as for returns, to positive ones (remove the minus sign).

Add a minus sign to the freight amount if freight is charged.

Use the same accounts and amounts in the reversing entry as in the original entry. Tax amounts are corrected automatically.

Repeat the allocation using the original percentages.

You can use the Adjust Invoice and Reverse Invoice options instead (page 129 and page 141).

Remember to "pay" the incorrect and reversing invoices to remove them from the Payments Journal and later clear them.

SALES JOURNAL

For inventory sales, change positive quantities in the original entry to negative ones in the reversing entry (place a minus sign before the quantity in the Quantity field). Similarly, change negative quantities, such as for returns, to positive ones (remove the minus sign).

For non-inventory sales, change positive amounts in the original entry to negative amounts in the reversing entry (place a minus sign before the amount in the Amount column).

Add a minus sign to the freight amount if freight is charged. Add the salesperson.

Use the same accounts and amounts in the reversing entry as in the original entry, and the same method of payment.

Repeat the allocation using the original percentages.

You can use the Adjust Invoice and Reverse Invoice options instead (page 184). Reversing a paid invoice will generate a credit note.

Remember to "pay" the incorrect and reversing invoices to remove them from the Receipts Journal and later clear them.

Reversing Entry

Item Number	Quantity	Order	Back Order	Unit	Item Description	Price	Amount	Tax	Account	Divisions
FA06	-2			each	End table: Cast Aluminum	95.00	-190.00	H	4020 Revenue...	Store Sales
FA07	-2			each	Bench: Cast Aluminum	185.00	-370.00	H	4020 Revenue...	Store Sales
					reverse design charge		-400.00	H	4040 Revenue...	Design

Subtotal: -960.00
Freight: -100.00 H -15.00
Early Payment Terms: 2.00 % 15 Days, Net 30 Days
HST: -159.00
Total: -1,219.00

Sales Journal Entry 06/08/2021 (J37)

Account Number	Account Description	Division	Debits	Credits	Division Amt
1400	Patio Furniture		440.00	-	
2650	HST Charged on Sales		159.00	-	
4020	Revenue from Store Sales		560.00	-	
		- Store Sales			-560.00
4040	Revenue from Services		400.00	-	
		- Design			-400.00
4100	Revenue from Delivery		100.00	-	
		- Store Sales			-100.00
1200	Accounts Receivable		-	1,219.00	
5070	Cost of Goods Sold		-	440.00	
		- Store Sales			-440.00
Additional Date:	Additional Field:		1,659.00	1,659.00	

NOTES

The Cost of Goods Sold amounts may have changed if you are using the average cost method and other transactions with different prices have taken place since the original sale. You cannot edit these amounts in the Sales Journal.

DEPOSITS or PREPAYMENTS: Original Entry

Invoice Date	Invoice or Deposit	Original Amount	Amount Owing	Discount Available	Discount Taken	Amount Received
Jun 09, 2021	170	2,438.00	2,438.00	42.40		

Deposit Reference No. 81
Deposit Amount 1,200.00
Total 1,200.00

DEPOSITS

You cannot enter a negative amount in the Deposit field, so you must "pay" the deposit.

Click the Amount Received field for the Deposit line and press *tab*. Deposit amounts are included in red type under the heading Deposits.

Receipts Journal Entry 06/10/2021 (J38)

Account Number	Account Description	Debits	Credits
1050	Bank: Chequing CAD	1,200.00	-
2150	Prepaid Sales and Deposits	-	1,200.00
Additional Date:	Additional Field:	1,200.00	1,200.00

Reversing Entry

Invoice Date	Invoice or Deposit	Original Amount	Amount Owing	Discount Available	Discount Taken	Amount Received
Jun 09, 2021	170	2,438.00	2,438.00	42.40		
	Deposits 81	1,200.00	1,200.00			1,200.00

Deposit Reference No. 81-REV
Deposit Amount 0.00
Total -1,200.00

Receipts Journal Entry 06/12/2021 (J39)

Account Number	Account Description	Debits	Credits
2150	Prepaid Sales and Deposits	1,200.00	-
1050	Bank: Chequing CAD	-	1,200.00
Additional Date:	Additional Field:	1,200.00	1,200.00

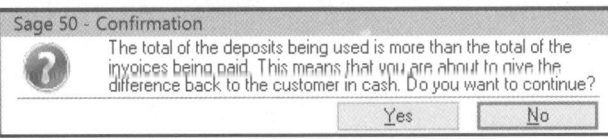

Sage 50 - Confirmation

The total of the deposits being used is more than the total of the invoices being paid. This means that you are about to give the difference back to the customer in cash. Do you want to continue?

Yes No

NOTES

When you post the transaction, you will be asked to confirm that you want to make the payment to the customer — you are returning the deposit. Click Yes to continue.

RECEIPTS WITH DEPOSITS: Original Entry

Invoice Date	Invoice or Deposit	Original Amount	Amount Owing	Discount Available	Discount Taken	Amount Received
Jun 09, 2021	170	2,438.00	2,438.00	42.40	42.40	2,395.60
	Deposits 82	1,100.00	1,100.00			1,100.00

Deposit Reference No. 83 Deposit Amount 0.00
Total 1,295.60

Receipts Journal Entry 06/11/2021 (J42)

Account Number	Account Description	Debits	Credits
1050	Bank: Chequing CAD	1,295.60	-
2150	Prepaid Sales and Deposits	1,100.00	-
4150	Sales Discounts	42.40	-
1200	Accounts Receivable	-	2,438.00
Additional Date:	Additional Field:	2,438.00	2,438.00

Reversing Entry

Invoice Date	Invoice or Deposit	Original Amount	Amount Owing	Discount Available	Discount Taken	Amount Received
Jun 09, 2021	170	2,438.00	0.00	0.00	-42.40	-2,395.60
	Deposits 82	1,100.00	0.00			-1,100.00

Deposit Reference No. 82-REV Deposit Amount 0.00
Total -1,295.60

Receipts Journal Entry 06/11/2021 (J43)

Account Number	Account Description	Debits	Credits
1200	Accounts Receivable	2,438.00	-
1050	Bank: Chequing CAD	-	1,295.60
2150	Prepaid Sales and Deposits	-	1,100.00
4150	Sales Discounts	-	42.40
Additional Date:	Additional Field:	2,438.00	2,438.00

PAYROLL JOURNAL: Original Income Tab Entry

Income | Vacation | Deductions | Taxes | User-Defined Expenses | Entitlements How do I process a paycheque?

Earnings	Hours	Pieces	Rate	This Period	Year to Date
Regular	75.00	--	20.00	1,500.00	19,000.00
Overtime 1	4.00	--	30.00	120.00	780.00
Plantings	--	200.00	0.50	100.00	685.00
Bonus	--	--	--	100.00	100.00
Tuition	--	--	--	100.00	700.00
Total:	79.00	200.00		1,920.00	

Other Amounts	This Period	Year to Date
Advances	0.00	--
Loans	100.00	100.00
Benefits	50.00	50.00
Total:	150.00	

Gross Pay: 1,970.00
Withheld: 551.32
Net Pay: **1,468.68** Post

Reversing Income Tab Amounts

Income | Vacation | Deductions | Taxes | User-Defined Expenses | Entitlements How do I process a paycheque?

Earnings	Hours	Pieces	Rate	This Period	Year to Date
Regular	-75.00	--	20.00	-1,500.00	17,500.00
Overtime 1	-4.00	--	30.00	-120.00	660.00
Plantings	--	-200.00	0.50	-100.00	585.00
Bonus	--	--	--	-100.00	--
Tuition	--	--	--	-100.00	1,000.00
Total:	-79.00	-200.00		-1,920.00	

Other Amounts	This Period	Year to Date
Advances	0.00	--
Loans	-100.00	--
Benefits	-50.00	--
Total:	-150.00	

Gross Pay: -1,970.00
Withheld: -551.32
Net Pay: **-1,468.68** Post

RECEIPTS

Click [Include Fully Paid Invoices tool icon], the Include Fully Paid Invoices tool.

Change positive amounts in the original entry to negative amounts in the reversing entry.

If a discount was taken, click the Discount Taken field on the invoice line for the receipt being reversed. Type the discount amount with a minus sign. Press *tab* to enter the payment amount. The minus sign will be added. Type a minus sign and enter the amount for the deposit.

If no discount was taken, click the Amount Received field on the invoice line for the receipt being reversed. Type a minus sign with the invoice receipt amount and with the deposit amount.

This will restore the original balance owing for the invoice, including the deposit.

You can use the Adjust Receipt and Reverse Receipt options instead (page 177).

If an NSF cheque uses a different bank account from the deposit entry, you must reverse the receipt manually. Choose the Bank account in the Deposit To field (page 605).

If you have already cleared the invoice, make a new Sales Journal entry for the payment amount (non-taxable) to restore the balance owing. Enter both the cheque and discount amounts as positive amounts and enter the Bank and Sales Discounts accounts instead of Revenue. To restore a deposit amount, enter the amount of the invoice minus the deposit amount.

PAYROLL JOURNAL

Redo the original incorrect entry but DO NOT POST IT!

Then, click the Enter Taxes Manually tool to open all the tax amount fields for editing and to stop them from changing when you enter the other negative amounts.

Type a minus sign in front of the number of hours (regular and overtime) or in front of salary, commission and bonus amounts and piece rate quantity. Press *tab* to update gross pay and vacation pay earned. ▶

PAYROLL JOURNAL CONTINUED

▶For the Advances and Loans fields, change the sign for the amount. Advances and loans should have a minus sign in the reversing entry and advances and loans recovered should be positive amounts.

Add a minus sign to the Benefits amount.

If vacation pay was paid out, add a minus sign to the amount paid in the Vacation Paid Amount field and to the EI Insurable Hours for this amount.

Click the Deductions tab and edit each deduction amount by typing a minus sign in front of it.

Click the Taxes tab. Check the amounts for CPP, EI and Tax with the original journal entry because these amounts may be incorrect (the employee may have reached the maximum contribution since the original entry or may have entered a different tax bracket). Change the amounts to match the original entry if necessary. The Employee Detail Report will provide the amounts entered for each paycheque.

Click the User-Defined Expenses tab. Change the original positive amounts to negative amounts by adding a minus sign.

Click the Entitlements tab. Add a minus sign to the number of hours worked. You cannot enter a negative number for Days Taken and earned. Add the number of days taken to the Days Earned amount. Add the number of days earned to the Days Taken amount.

Repeat the allocation with the original percentages and post.

Remember to click the Calculate Taxes Automatically button before you make the correct payroll entry.

The year-to-date balances will be restored.

Enter a memo number or other reference in the Cheque or Deposit Number field to avoid using a cheque number for a negative amount. ▶

Original Payroll Vacation Tab Entry

Income | Vacation | Deductions | Taxes | User-Defined Expenses | Entitlements — How do I process a paycheque?

Type	This Period Hours	This Period Amount	Year to Date Hours	Year to Date Amount
Balance Forward (as of Jan 01, 2021)	--	--	--	--
Vacation Earned	--	103.20	--	1,027.90
Vacation Paid *	0.00	0.00	--	--
Vacation Owed	--	--	--	1,027.90

* These hours are recorded as EI Insurable Hours

Reversing Vacation Tab Amounts

Income | Vacation | Deductions | Taxes | User-Defined Expenses | Entitlements — How do I process a paycheque?

Type	This Period Hours	This Period Amount	Year to Date Hours	Year to Date Amount
Balance Forward (as of Jan 01, 2021)	--	--	--	--
Vacation Earned	--	-103.20	--	924.70
Vacation Paid *	0.00	0.00	--	--
Vacation Owed	--	--	--	924.70

* These hours are recorded as EI Insurable Hours

Original Entries for Deductions and Taxes Tabs

Income Vacation Deductions Taxes User-Defined Expenses Entitlements

Deduction	This Period	Year to Date
RRSP	25.00	300.00
Union Dues	15.37	161.61
Total:	40.37	

Income Vacation Deductions Taxes User-Defined Expenses Entitlements

Tax	This Period	Year to Date
CPP	90.85	838.82
EI	34.22	386.63
Tax	385.88	3,604.30
Total:	510.95	

Reversing Amounts for Deductions and Taxes Tabs

Income Vacation Deductions Taxes User-Defined Expenses Entitlements

Deduction	This Period	Year to Date
RRSP	-25.00	275.00
Union Dues	-15.37	146.24
Total:	-40.37	

Income Vacation Deductions Taxes User-Defined Expenses Entitlements

Tax	This Period	Year to Date
CPP	-90.85	747.97
EI	-34.22	352.41
Tax	-385.88	3,218.42
Total:	-510.95	

Original Entries for User-Defined Expenses and Entitlements Tabs

Income Vacation Deductions Taxes User-Defined Expenses Entitlements

Employer-paid payroll expenses

Expense	This Period	Year to Date
Medical Prem	50.00	550.00
Total:	50.00	

Income Vacation Deductions Taxes User-Defined Expenses Entitlements

Hours worked this period: 75.00

Entitlement	Days Earned	Days Taken	Net Days Accrued
Vacation	0.00	0.00	0.00
Sick Days	0.50	1.00	6.50
PersonalDays	0.25	1.00	3.25

Reversing Amounts for User-Defined Expenses and Entitlements Tabs

Income Vacation Deductions Taxes User-Defined Expenses Entitlements

Employer-paid payroll expenses

Expense	This Period	Year to Date
Medical Prem	-50.00	500.00
Total:	-50.00	

Income Vacation Deductions Taxes User-Defined Expenses Entitlements

Hours worked this period: -75.00

Entitlement	Days Earned	Days Taken	Net Days Accrued
Vacation	0.00	0.00	0.00
Sick Days	1.00	0.50	7.00
PersonalDays	1.00	0.25	4.00

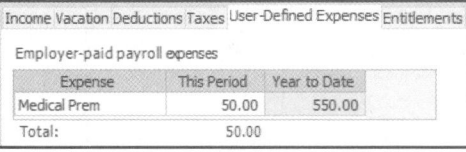

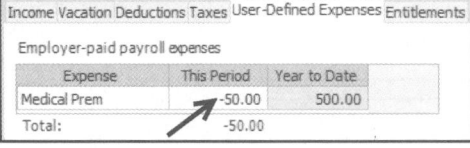

Original Payroll Journal Entry

Payroll Journal Entry 06/14/2021 (J44)

Account Number	Account Description	Debits	Credits
1230	Advances & Loans Receivable	100.00	-
5450	Vacation Pay Expense	103.20	-
5470	General Wages	1,620.00	-
5480	Piece Rate Wage Expense	100.00	-
5490	Commissions and Bonuses	100.00	-
5500	Tuition Expense	100.00	-
5510	EI Expense	47.91	-
5520	CPP Expense	90.85	-
5530	WCB Expense	97.13	-
5550	Medical Expense	50.00	-
1050	Bank: Chequing CAD	-	1,468.68
2300	Vacation Payable	-	103.20
2310	EI Payable	-	82.13
2320	CPP Payable	-	181.70
2330	Income Tax Payable	-	385.88
2400	RRSP Payable	-	25.00
2420	Union Dues Payable	-	15.37
2450	Medical Payable	-	50.00
2460	WCB Payable	-	97.13
Additional Date:	Additional Field:	2,409.09	2,409.09

Reversing Payroll Journal Entry

Payroll Journal Entry 06/14/2021 (J45)

Account Number	Account Description	Debits	Credits
1050	Bank: Chequing CAD	1,468.68	-
2300	Vacation Payable	103.20	-
2310	EI Payable	82.13	-
2320	CPP Payable	181.70	-
2330	Income Tax Payable	385.88	-
2400	RRSP Payable	25.00	-
2420	Union Dues Payable	15.37	-
2450	Medical Payable	50.00	-
2460	WCB Payable	97.13	-
1230	Advances & Loans Receivable	-	100.00
5450	Vacation Pay Expense	-	103.20
5470	General Wages	-	1,620.00
5480	Piece Rate Wage Expense	-	100.00
5490	Commissions and Bonuses	-	100.00
5500	Tuition Expense	-	100.00
5510	EI Expense	-	47.91
5520	CPP Expense	-	90.85
5530	WCB Expense	-	97.13
5550	Medical Expense	-	50.00
Additional Date:	Additional Field:	2,409.09	2,409.09

Sage 50 - Confirmation

This direct deposit stub does not have a positive amount and is using a direct deposit stub number. Do you want to continue anyway?

Yes No

PAYROLL JOURNAL CONTINUED

▶When you enter a negative number of hours or salary amount and press tab, vacation pay will be automatically calculated as a negative amount, but the tax amounts will not change because you have chosen Enter Taxes Manually.

Before posting the reversing entry, always check it carefully against the original one to ensure that all amounts were correctly reversed.

You can use the Adjust Cheque option or Reverse Cheque instead to reverse and correct the Paycheque or Payroll Run journal entry (page 275 and page 295). Using the reverse cheque approach is safer, because payroll transactions are complex.

NOTES

When you are reversing a payroll entry, you must confirm that you are using a cheque or direct deposit number for a negative amount.

Click No. Enter a memo number or other reference in the Cheque or Deposit Number field instead.

ITEM ASSEMBLY JOURNAL

Re-enter the assembly as you did originally.

Type a minus sign in front of each quantity in the Qty field in both the Assembly Components and Assembled Items sections.

Also type a minus sign in front of the amount for Additional Costs.

If you know the original unit costs and they have changed, you can enter the cost amounts from the original item assembly in the reversing entry.

ITEM ASSEMBLY JOURNAL: Original Entry

Assembly Components

Item	Qty	Unit	Description	Unit Cost	Amount
SH01	20	each	Shrubs: 50 cm	6.00	120.00
PL06	20	each	Plant: annual 15 cm	9.00	180.00
				Additional Costs	200.00
				Total	500.00

Assembled Items

Item	Qty	Unit	Description	Unit Cost	Amount
S100	10	Each	Planting Special	50.00	500.00
				Total	500.00

Bill of Materials & Item Assembly Journal Entry 06/13/2021 (J46)

Account Number	Account Description	Debits	Credits
1510	Promotions	500.00	-
1360	Plants and Soil	-	180.00
1380	Shrubs	-	120.00
5060	Assembly Costs	-	200.00
Additional Date:	Additional Field:	500.00	500.00

Reversing Entry

Assembly Components

Item	Qty	Unit	Description	Unit Cost	Amount
SH01	-20	each	Shrubs: 50 cm	6.00	-120.00
PL06	-20	each	Plant: annual 15 cm	9.00	-180.00
				Additional Costs	-200.00
				Total	-500.00

Assembled Items

Item	Qty	Unit	Description	Unit Cost	Amount
S100	-10	Each	Planting Special	50.00	-500.00
				Total	-500.00

Bill of Materials & Item Assembly Journal Entry 06/14/2021 (J47)

Account Number	Account Description	Debits	Credits
1360	Plants and Soil	180.00	-
1380	Shrubs	120.00	-
5060	Assembly Costs	200.00	-
1510	Promotions	-	500.00
Additional Date:	Additional Field:	500.00	500.00

ADJUSTMENTS JOURNAL

Change the sign for the quantity in the Qty field (positive to negative or negative to positive).

If you know the original unit costs and they have changed, you can enter the cost amounts from the original adjustments entry in the reversing entry.

Repeat the allocation using the original percentages.

ADJUSTMENTS JOURNAL: Original Entry

Item	Qty	Unit	Description	Unit Cost	Amount	Acct	Allo
PL01	-12	each	Plant/ground cover: 5 l	10.00	-120.00	5110 Inventory Losses	✓
				Total	-120.00		

Inventory Adjustments Journal Entry 06/11/2021 (J48)

Account Number	Account Description	Division	Debits	Credits	Division Amt
5110	Inventory Losses		120.00	-	
		- Planting			120.00
1360	Plants and Soil		-	120.00	
Additional Date:	Additional Field:		120.00	120.00	

Reversing Entry

Item	Qty	Unit	Description	Unit Cost	Amount	Acct	Allo
PL01	12	each	Plant/ground cover: 5 l	10.00	120.00	5110 Inventory Losses	√
				Total	120.00		

Inventory Adjustments Journal Entry 06/11/2021 (J51)					
Account Number	Account Description	Division	Debits	Credits	Division Amt
1360	Plants and Soil		120.00	-	
5110	Inventory Losses		-	120.00	
		- Planting			-120.00
Additional Date:	Additional Field:		120.00	120.00	

NOTES

In this example the positive amount is associated with the recovery of losses.

TRANSFER FUNDS JOURNAL: Original Entry

Currency:	DKK — Exchange Rate: 0.2000000
Transfer from:	1050 Bank: Chequing CAD
Transfer to:	1060 Bank Account: DKK
Amount:	10,000.00 DKK
Comment:	Transfer funds to cover payments

Reversing Entry

Currency:	DKK — Exchange Rate: 0.2000000
Transfer from:	1060 Bank Account: DKK
Transfer to:	1050 Bank: Chequing CAD
Amount:	10,000.00 DKK
Comment:	Reversing funds transfer

General Journal 06/14/2021 to 06/14/2021					
	Account Number	Account Description	Debits	Credits	Foreign A...
06/14/2021 J52	FundsTransfer, Transfer funds to cover payments				
	1060	Bank Account: DKK	2,000.00	-	Dkr10.000,00
	1050	Bank: Chequing CAD	-	2,000.00	Dkr10.000,00
1 Danish Kroners equals 0.2000000 Canadian Dollars					
06/14/2021 J53	FundsTransfer, Reversing funds transfer				
	1050	Bank: Chequing CAD	2,000.00	-	Dkr10.000,00
	1060	Bank Account: DKK	-	2,000.00	Dkr10.000,00
1 Danish Kroners equals 0.2000000 Canadian Dollars			4,000.00	4,000.00	

TRANSFER FUNDS JOURNAL

The easiest way to reverse the transfer is to enter the same amounts but switch the bank accounts. Enter the original Transfer From account in the Transfer To field. Enter the original Transfer To account in the Transfer From field.

There is no journal entry to review. The reversal will be part of the General Journal Report. Our screenshot has the two related General Journal Report entries.

For foreign currency transfers, use the same exchange rate for both the original and the reversing transfer.

You can also use the Adjust Entry or Reverse Entry procedure for the transfer in the General Journal. When you look up transactions, the transfer entry is included. You can select it and then adjust it or reverse it like any other General Journal transaction (page 47 and page 49).

TRANSFER INVENTORY JOURNAL: Original Entry

Transfer between Locations — From: VeloCity — to: Ryder

Source: Memo 22 — Date: Aug 14, 2021

Comment: Transfer inventory to create extra packages

Item	Qty	Unit	Description	Unit Cost	Amount
AC010	5	unit	Bicycle Pump: standing model	30.00	150.00
BK010	20	book	Books: Complete Bicycle Guide	20.00	400.00

Reversing Entry

Transfer between Locations — From: Ryder — to: VeloCity

Source: Memo 23 — Date: Aug 14, 2021

Comment: Reverse inventory transfer

Item	Qty	Unit	Description	Unit Cost	Amount
AC010	5	unit	Bicycle Pump: standing model	30.00	150.00
BK010	20	book	Books: Complete Bicycle Guide	20.00	400.00

TRANSFER INVENTORY JOURNAL

You cannot enter a negative quantity in the Transfer Inventory Journal.

Enter the transaction in the same way as the original one with one change – switch the locations for the From and To fields. Enter the original From location in the To field and the original To location in the From field.

No journal entry results from this transaction. However, the inventory ledger records will be updated for both locations.

If costs have changed, you can enter the costs from the original transfer entry if you know them.

BILL OF MATERIALS JOURNAL

Change the sign for the quantity in the Quantity To Build field (positive to negative or negative to positive).

Notice that the journal entries are the same as those for the Item Assembly Journal transactions on page A–26.

Costs may have changed since you entered the original transaction when you are using the average cost of goods method. You cannot change the unit costs in the Bill of Materials method.

BILL OF MATERIALS JOURNAL: Original Entry

Items to Build

Item	Unit	Description	Quantity to build
AP100	package	Promotional Safety Package with Bike	3

Bill of Materials & Item Assembly Journal Entry 08/14/2021 (J13)

Account Number	Account Description	Debits	Credits
1510	Promotions	2,051.45	-
1520	Accessories	-	671.45
1540	Bicycles	-	930.00
5045	Item Assembly Costs	-	450.00
Additional Date:	Ref. Number:	2,051.45	2,051.45

Reversing Entry

Items to Build

Item	Unit	Description	Quantity to build
AP100	package	Promotional Safety Package with Bike	-3

Bill of Materials & Item Assembly Journal Entry 08/14/2021 (J14)

Account Number	Account Description	Debits	Credits
1520	Accessories	671.45	-
1540	Bicycles	930.00	-
5045	Item Assembly Costs	450.00	-
1510	Promotions	-	2,051.45
Additional Date:	Ref. Number:	2,051.45	2,051.45

INDEX

Pages A–29 – A–202 on the Student DVD

Appendix D, A–29 – A–76
Appendix E, A–77 – A–90
Appendix F, A–91 – A–100
Appendix G, A–101 – A–114
Appendix H, A–115 – A–142
Appendix I, A–143 – A–152
Appendix J, A–153 – A–164
Appendix K, A–165 – A–180
Appendix L, A–181 – A–190
Appendix M, A–191 – A–202

A

Pages A-29 – A-202 on the Student DVD

Appendix D, A-29 – A-76
Appendix E, A-77 – A-90
Appendix F, A-91 – A-100
Appendix G, A-101 – A-114
Appendix H, A-115 – A-142
Appendix I, A-143 – A-152
Appendix J, A-153 – A-164
Appendix K, A-165 – A-180
Appendix L, A-181 – A-190
Appendix M, A-191 – A-202

Pages A-29 – A-202 on the Student DVD

Appendix D, A-29 – A-76
Appendix E, A-77 – A-90
Appendix F, A-91 – A-100
Appendix G, A-101 – A-114
Appendix H, A-115 – A-142
Appendix I, A-143 – A-152
Appendix J, A-153 – A-164
Appendix K, A-165 – A-180
Appendix L, A-181 – A-190
Appendix M, A-191 – A-202

Pages A–29 – A–202 on the Student DVD

Appendix D, A–29 – A–76
Appendix E, A–77 – A–90
Appendix F, A–91 – A–100
Appendix G, A–101 – A–114
Appendix H, A–115 – A–142
Appendix I, A–143 – A–152
Appendix J, A–153 – A–164
Appendix K, A–165 – A–180
Appendix L, A–181 – A–190
Appendix M, A–191 – A–202

H

I

Pages A-29 – A-202 on the Student DVD

Pages A–29 – A–202 on the Student DVD

Appendix D, A–29 – A–76
Appendix E, A–77 – A–90
Appendix F, A–91 – A–100
Appendix G, A–101 – A–114
Appendix H, A–115 – A–142
Appendix I, A–143 – A–152
Appendix J, A–153 – A–164
Appendix K, A–165 – A–180
Appendix L, A–181 – A–190
Appendix M, A–191 – A–202

Pages A-29 – A-202 on the Student DVD

Appendix D, A-29 – A-76
Appendix E, A-77 – A-90
Appendix F, A-91 – A-100
Appendix G, A-101 – A-114
Appendix H, A-115 – A-142
Appendix I, A-143 – A-152
Appendix J, A-153 – A-164
Appendix K, A-165 – A-180
Appendix L, A-181 – A-190
Appendix M, A-191 – A-202

Pages A-29 – A-202 on the Student DVD

Appendix D, A-29 – A-76
Appendix E, A-77 – A-90
Appendix F, A-91 – A-100
Appendix G, A-101 – A-114
Appendix H, A-115 – A-142
Appendix I, A-143 – A-152
Appendix J, A-153 – A-164
Appendix K, A-165 – A-180
Appendix L, A-181 – A-190
Appendix M, A-191 – A-202

T

Pages A–29 – A–202 on the Student DVD

"AS IS" LICENSE AGREEMENT AND LIMITED WARRANTY